Federal Land Series

Federal Land Series

A CALENDAR OF ARCHIVAL MATERIALS ON THE LAND PATENTS ISSUED BY THE UNITED STATES GOVERNMENT, WITH SUBJECT, TRACT, AND NAME INDEXES

Volume 4 • Part 1

Volume 4 • Part 2

GRANTS IN THE VIRGINIA MILITARY DISTRICT OF OHIO

Clifford Neal Smith

CLEARFIELD

Reprinted, Two Parts in One,
with permission
of the estate of the author
for
Clearfield Company by
Genealogical Publishing Co.
Baltimore, Maryland
1999, 2003, 2007

Volume IV ISBN-13: 978-0-8063-4908-4
Volume IV ISBN-10: 0-8063-4908-5
Set ISBN-13: 978-0-8063-4904-6
Set ISBN-10: 0-8063-4904-2

Made in the United States of America

Federal Land Series

A CALENDAR OF ARCHIVAL MATERIALS ON THE LAND PATENTS ISSUED BY THE UNITED STATES GOVERNMENT, WITH SUBJECT, TRACT, AND NAME INDEXES

Volume 4 • Part 1

GRANTS IN THE VIRGINIA MILITARY DISTRICT OF OHIO

Clifford Neal Smith

Contents

Introduction

This fourth volume of the *Federal Land Series* is a work in two parts, each separately bound, that summarizes and indexes the land grants in the Virginia Military District of Ohio made to Virginia veterans of the American Revolution. Although the land grants covered in this volume were not strictly federal in origin, their inclusion in this Series is considered important to genealogists and other researchers; for, despite having been granted by a state of the Union, they were made under an obligation to veterans of the American Revolution that was as much the federal government's as it was of the Commonwealth of Virginia.

The archival materials pertaining to the early settlement of the Virginia Military District of Ohio have not heretofore been indexed systematically, despite the fact that population movement into south-central Ohio in the first decades of the nineteenth century is of major significance to genealogical researchers. Seen demographically, the diversion of Virginia-born migrants into Ohio represents a northward deflection from their expected westward expansion pattern, which would most directly have been via Kentucky to Missouri, Kansas, and westward. In south-central Ohio the

Virginians encountered numerous land-hungry Pennsylvanians and other northerners, so that the population mix in the District probably represents the first large-scale merging of tobacco-growing farmers, typical of Virginia, with the small, diversified freeholders of Pennsylvania and the northern states. Genealogically seen, the District represents the merging of Virginians, ethnically English and mainly Episcopalian and Methodist in persuasion, with the more varied Presbyterian, Lutheran, Reformed, and Dunkard groups from Pennsylvania, ethnically Scotch-Irish and German.

During the Revolutionary War period, eight of the original thirteen colonies promised their soldiers land for military service.[1] These eight colonies, understandably, were those having vacant lands available. The amount of land promised for military service varied from colony to colony; Virginia and North Carolina were the most generous, because of their claims to territories reaching as far westward as the Mississippi River and, in Virginia's case, as far northward as Lake Superior. The Commonwealth of Virginia promised its soldiers and sailors the following amounts of land:

Rank/Rate	*Acreage*
Major General	15,000
Brigadier General	10,000
Colonel	6,667
Lieutenant Colonel	6,000
Major	5,667
Captain	4,000
Subaltern	2,667
Noncommissioned Officer*	400
Noncommissioned Officer**	200
Every Soldier or Seaman*	200
Every Soldier or Seaman**	100

*Individuals enlisting for, and serving to the end, of the war.

**Individuals enlisting for, and serving three years.

After the Revolution, the newly-founded federal government had the clear task of organizing the western territories, setting off new states, and supervising the expansion of population. A particular problem was the quieting of ancient territorial claims of certain of the former colonies. Even before the end of the Revolution, the Legislature of the Commonwealth of Virginia[2] had declared its willingness to yield all right, title, and claim to western lands to the Congress of the United States, with the provision that, if lands in Kentucky[3] reserved for Virginia veterans should prove insufficient, additional lands north of the Ohio River would be set aside to meet Virginia's obligation to its veterans. The United States Congress agreed to the cession, on the condition above mentioned, by its Act of 13 September 1783. As it turned out, the Kentucky lands set aside to satisfy veterans' claims under Virginia law proved to be quite insufficient, so that the larger part of the claims had to be located in the Virginia Military District of Ohio. As of 31 October 1831, near the end of the distribution period, grants of land could be summarized as follows:[4]

	Kentucky	*Ohio*	*Total*
To Continental Line Veterans	*(In thousands of acres)*[5]		
Located and patented by 1831	800	3183	
Located but not yet patented	-	50	
Quantity remaining unsatisfied	-	127	
Additional appropriated, 1830	-	50	
	800	3410	4210
To State Line and Navy Veterans			
Located and patented by 1831	1200[6]	-	1200
Additional appropriated, 1830	-	-	260
Resolution Warrants[7]			
Issued to 1822	-	-	187
	2000	3410	5857

Assuming that all the acreages appropriated in 1830 for the State Line and Navy and 100,000 acres of the land under resolution warrants were eventually located in Ohio, one arrives at the conclusion that about 64 percent of Virginia's obligation to its veterans were satisfied by the land grants in the Virginia Military District of Ohio.

The records of the land grants made to Virginia veterans are to be found dispersed in a surprising number of archives and governmental offices:

Kentucky land grants	Kentucky Land Office Frankfort, Kentucky
	Archives Division Virginia State Library Richmond, Virginia
Ohio land grants	University of Illinois Library Illinois Historical Survey Collection Champaign, Illinois
	Auditor of State State Land Office Columbus, Ohio

Smaller remnants are to be found in the Henry E. Huntington Library, San Marino, California; in the Western Reserve Historical Society, Manuscript Collections, Cleveland, Ohio; and in the National Archives, Washington, D.C. If one were to include the papers of private individuals associated with these land grants, such as those of Duncan McArthur and Nathaniel Massie, the list of archival collections would be even larger.

Land grants made by Virginia in Kentucky have been listed in Jillson's well-known work, first published in 1925.[8] Kentucky grants began shortly after the end of the Revolution and, by 4 August 1788,

Edmund Randolph of the Virginia Legislature was able to report to the United States Congress that

> ". . . we do not yet possess any formal documents upon which we can positively assert that there is a deficiency of good land on the southeast side [Kentucky] of the Ohio [River]. But we are thoroughly persuaded, from the number of acres for which warrants have already issued, that a deficiency, great indeed, does exist. . . ."[9]

When the first grants were made in Ohio is not entirely clear, but it seems probable that they did not occur until some time after 1792.[10]

For grants made in the Virginia Military District of Ohio, the largest corpus, and certainly the most valuable, of the source materials is to be found in the Illinois Historical Survey Collection in the University of Illinois Library, a total of 10,000 items.[11] This fourth volume of the *Federal Land Series* is based on the entries in only one ledger (number 6) thereof, described as follows:

> "6. Ohio Manuscripts. Original Records of the Virginia Military District. Number 6 (Colonel R. C. Anderson). Leather-bound volume, 10½" x 15". Backbone stamped 'Record Book.' List of persons making entries in the Virginia Military District arranged numerically (by survey number). Entries 102-15763 (volume continues into Allen Latham's administration). [Contains survey number, name of original proprietor, acreage, county, township. Right-hand pages contain unidentified names, presumably of purchasers, lessees, persons with preemption claims thereto.]"

The entries in this ledger have been compared with those in a "smooth copy" ledger, now in the National Archives, prepared for Samuel Kendrick, a surveyor. Kendrick's ledger bears the following prefatory statement:

> "I hereby certify that this volume was purchased from Albert Douglass, administrator of the estate of Samuel Kendrick in accordance with the Act of March 3, 1899 (30 *Stat*. 1099). [Signed] Chas. Brush, Recorder, General Land Office. 1899/819510. [Gives survey number, acreage, page and book (of survey description), original proprietor, watercourse, county, and warrant number.]"

Numerous discrepancies between the original ledger in Illinois and the National Archives "smooth copy" are noted in the *Federal Land Series* summaries.

Two further registers (notebooks 9 and 10) in the Illinois Historical Survey Collection have been used to identify the original warrantees. These notebooks are described as follows:

> "9. Ohio Manuscripts. Original Records of the Virginia Military District. Number 9. Leather-bound notebook, 4½" x 7½". Stamped 'A. Latham.' Contents names of persons [warrantees] 1-3115, with number of acres granted, to whom transferred, etc.
>
> 10. Ohio Manuscripts. Original Records of the Virginia Military District. Number 10. Leather-bound notebook, 4½" x 7½". Stamped 'A. Latham.' (both [notebooks] fall in Col. R. C. Anderson's administration). List of persons [warrantees] 1840-1939, 3116-6729."

These notebooks are very early (probably prepared before 1800), poorly written at best, but apparently the ones which Richard Clough Anderson, first administrator of the Virginia Land Office, used in his everyday work. Many names therein vary from the list of veterans published in Gwathmey.[12]

The National Archives, Map Division, has a series of 25 maps showing entry (survey) numbers and names.[13] Unfortunately, these valuable plats are faded beyond possibility of photocopying. The Ohio State Land Office has a number of survey books, listed in the appendix to this Introduction, as does the Western Reserve Historical Society, Manuscript Collections. The Illinois Historical Survey also has a large number of surveys,[14] so that it seems likely that, among the three collections, researchers needing detailed information on individual surveys should be able to find the information they seek. In the descriptive list of the Virginia Military District records held by the Ohio State Land Office is the following notation: ". . . Even today, it is difficult to find the county and township where a particular survey is located. The State Land Office is the ONLY source of Surveys and Entries. . . ." With the publication of this volume of the *Federal Land Series*, the note is no longer factual, as nearly every survey has now been located by county and township in this volume.

Entry Format

Entries to be found in volume 4 of the *Federal Land Series* have been compiled from several source documents. No one of the original registers contains all of the data herein, and discrepancies between source documents are frequent. Entries are presented in the following format:

```
 1            2          3              4             5
  S-0102      740a       C:163          X-0340        UNIO:ALLE
                                                      CHAM:RUSH
6 → a.  W-2349 Captain Henry Whiting
7 → b.  Henry Whiting
8 → c.  Rhoda Askew;  Thomas Dunn, 1833
```

1. *Survey Number*. This is the key by which references to a land tract were made in all the records. The researcher will note large gaps between survey numbers; no explanation of these gaps is to be found in any of the extant registers, and the method by which survey numbers were originally assigned is unknown. Survey numbers appearing in the registers seem to be the only ones which actually resulted in land patents, however, so that missing numbers seem not to be of importance. The consecutive listing of survey numbers, with its gaps, is taken from Register 6 (called Source A in textual footnotes) and has been compared with the Kendrick "smooth copy" in the National Archives (called Source B in the footnotes). Notebooks 9 and 10 are called Source C in these footnotes.

2. *Acreage in the Grant or Parcel.* Separate parcels to the same patentee frequently bear the same survey number, and the description of each parcel will normally be found within the same survey book.

3. *Survey Book and Page Number Citation.* The description of the land surveyed was entered in one of several survey books, denominated by letters of the alphabet, and can be found on the page indicated: For example, C:163 means Survey Book C, page 163. Since the land grants were not in the rectangular system typical of federal grants, but in the ancient English metes-and-bounds system customary in Virginia, researchers must refer to the survey books if they wish to know the shape of the grants. These shapes were often most irregular and exceedingly complicated to describe in words.

4. *Watercourse.* In order to conserve space (and to facilitate computer indexing) the names of watercourses have been reduced to numerical coding preceded by an *X*. The first three numbers of the coding designate the stream name; the last (or fourth) digit designates the branch thereof. For example, X-0340 breaks down to mean: 034 = Darby's Creek, 0 = no branch listed. The complete watercourse coding is set forth in the *Index to Watercourses* at the back of this volume. As a practical matter, genealogical researchers may find watercourse designations of slight significance, excepting that during the period before the organization of counties and townships the watercourse may have been the only descriptive locational device. Likewise, it may be that the earliest residents settled along navigable watercourses, in the absence of roads, and that early commercial and social relationships among them can be posited from a knowledge of the watercourses near which they lived. This writer suggests that, having

located the place of settlement of an ancestor of interest, genealogical researchers should refer to the *Index to Watercourses* to determine who the ancestor's contemporary neighbors might have been. In this manner eventual familial relationships can probably be determined.

5. *County and Township.* It will be seen that many grants extended beyond county and township limits, a phenomenon rare in the rectangular federal system of land division. The name of the county, reduced to the first four letters thereof, appears first, followed by the name of the township, similarly abbreviated. For example: UNIO:ALLE means Union County, Allen Township; CHAM:RUSH means Champaign County, Rush Township. Researchers should remember that these designations are the *original* historical ones. No doubt, county and township lines have been redefined in later years, so that Ohio maps of the 1810-1830 period should be compared with the modern ones to determine the exact location of grants. Here, again, the researcher should refer to the special *Index by County and Township* in the back of this volume for insight into relationships among early settlers, as determined by propinquity. The code used for county (cty) and township (twp) designations is as follows:

ADAM	Adams Cty
ALLE	Allen Twp
ANDE	Anderson Twp
BATA	Batavia Twp
BEAV	Beaver Creek Twp
BENT	Benton Twp
BOAK	Boake's Creek Twp
BOWL	Bowling Green Twp
BROW	Brown Cty & Twp
BRUS	Brush Creek Twp
BUCK	Buckskin Twp
BYRD	Byrd Twp
CAES	Caesar's Creek Twp
CAMP	Camp Creek Twp
CANA	Canaan Twp
CHAM	Champaign Cty
CHES	Chester Twp
CLAI	Claiborne Twp
CLAR	Clark Cty & Twp
CLAY	Clay Twp
CLER	Clermont Cty
CLIN	Clinton Cty
CONC	Concord Twp
DARB	Darby Twp

DEER	Deer Creek Twp
DELA	Delaware Cty
DODS	Dodson Twp
DOVE	Dover Twp
DUDL	Dudley Twp
EAGL	Eagle Twp
FAIR	Fairfield Twp
FAYE	Fayette Cty
FRAN	Franklin Cty & Twp
GOSH	Goshen Twp
GREE	Green Cty & Twp
HALE	Hale Twp
HAMI	Hamilton Cty & Twp
HARD	Hardin Cty
HARM	Harmony Twp
HIGH	Highland Cty
HUNT	Huntington Twp
JACK	Jackson Twp
JEFF	Jefferson Twp
JERO	Jerome Twp
LAKE	Lake Twp
LEES	Leesburg Twp
LEWI	Lewis & Clark Twp
LIBE	Liberty Twp
LOGA	Logan Twp
MADI	Madison Cty & Twp
MARI	Marion Cty & Twp
MEIG	Meigs Twp
MIAM	Miami Twp
MIFF	Mifflin Twp
MILL	Mill Creek Twp
MONR	Monroe Twp
MORG	Morgan Twp
MUHL	Muhlenberg Twp
NEWM	New Market Twp
NEWT	Newton Twp
NILE	Nile Twp
NORW	Norwich Twp
OHIO	Ohio Twp
PAIN	Paint Twp
PARI	Paris Twp
PAXT	Paxton Twp
PEBB	Pebble Twp
PEEP	Pee Pee Twp
PERR	Perry Twp
PICK	Pickaway Cty
PIKE	Pike Cty & Twp
PLEA	Pleasant Twp
PRAI	Prairie Twp
RANG	Range Twp
RICH	Richland Twp
ROSS	Ross Cty & Twp
RUSH	Rush Twp
SALE	Salem Twp
SCIO	Scioto Cty & Twp
SCOT	Scott Twp
SILV	Silver Creek Twp
SPRI	Sprig Twp
STER	Sterling Twp
STOK	Stokes Twp
STON	Stonelick Twp
SUGA	Sugar Creek Twp
SUMM	Summerford Twp
SUNF	Sunfish Twp
TATE	Tate Twp
TAYL	Taylor Creek Twp
THOM	Thompson Twp
TIFF	Tiffin Twp
TWIN	Twin Twp
UNIO	Union Cty & Twp
VERN	Vernon Twp
WARR	Warren Cty
WASH	Washington Twp
WAYN	Wayne Twp
WHIT	White Oak Twp
WILL	Williamsburg Twp
WINC	Winchester Twp
XENI	Xenia Twp
YORK	York Twp
ZANE	Zane Twp

6. *Warrant Number and Warrantee.* Since all the land grants were made for service with Virginia military units in the American Revolution (with a few warrants perhaps including prior service in immediately preceding Indian skirmishes), the first step in the land-granting process was the presentation of a valid military bounty-land warrant. The warrant numbers appear in both Register 6 and in the Kendrick "smooth copy." The names of the corresponding warrantees and their assignees have been taken from Registers 9 and 10 of the Illinois Historical Survey collection. As mentioned above, Registers 9 and 10 are poorly written and partly illegible. The spelling of names is often primitive and not in agreement with other extant lists of veterans. Indeed, it is clear that Registers 9 and 10 were not always consistent as to who was the original warrantee and who was his assignee or heir. It is hoped that in the second part of volume 4 of this Series space will allow a comparison of these names and possible resolution of the numerous orthographic discrepancies which are known to exist.

7. *Patentee.* The patentee was the person to whom the land grant was actually made by the Virginia Land Office. Very frequently, this was not the war veteran, and occasionally the warrant itself may have been made out in the name of the patentee. For example, Duncan McArthur was the recipient (patentee) of numerous land grants in which he is also shown as the warrantee; he simply bought up the rights to the warrants from veterans or their heirs and assignees and had the warrants made out in his own name.

8. *Unidentified Names.* The right-hand pages of Register 6 contain lists of names corresponding to most survey numbers. It is thought that these are the names of actual settlers on the land,

purchasers or lessees of portions thereof, possibly squatters or persons having preemptive rights by reason of having settled on the land before it was granted to the patentee. Wherever a date appears in Register 6 it is reproduced herein, even though its significance can only be conjectured. It seems likely that most patentees did not themselves take up residence on their grants, and that they authorized the Virginia Land Office to sell, lease, or rent land, either in entirety or in parcels, to actual settlers. Thus, despite the difficulty of determining the business relationships between patentees and these unidentified persons, it is obvious that the latter are of significance to researchers. Probably, the only way to determine the nature of these relationships is to study the corresponding survey records and deeds recorded in the county seats. No doubt, reference to early federal censuses for the county and township, and to tax records, would shed additional light.

Notes

1. Only Connecticut, Delaware, New Hampshire, and New Jersey made no such promises to their servicemen. Massachusetts did so only in 1801, however.

2. By its Act of 2 January 1781.

3. "Upon the waters of Cumberland river, and between the Green river and Tennessee river." U.S. Congress, House of Representatives (First Congress, First Session), communicated 31 July 1789, *American State Papers, Series: Public Lands* (Washington,

D.C.: Gales & Seaton, 1832), volume 1, p. 5.

4. Statement submitted to the U.S. House of Representatives by Allen Latham, Surveyor of the Virginia Military District of Ohio. *Ibid.*, volume 6, p. 366.

5. All figures have been rounded off to the nearest thousand acres.

6. Latham estimated between 1.0 and 1.2 million acres.

7. Normally granted by the Virginia Legislature for special and outstanding services, usually by civilians, during the Revolution. Latham gave no breakdown by state.

8. Willard R. Jillson, *The Kentucky Land Grants: A Systematic Index to All of the Land Grants Recorded in the State Land Office in Frankfort, Kentucky, 1782-1924.* Filson Club Publications No. 33 (1925; reprinted Baltimore: Genealogical Publishing Co., 1972). See also Jillson's *Old Kentucky Entries and Deeds: A Complete Index of All the Earliest Land Entries, Military Warrants, Deeds and Wills of the Commonwealth of Kentucky.* Filson Club Publication No. 34 (1926; reprinted Baltimore: Genealogical Publishing Co., 1972).

9. Letter, dated 4 August 1789, reported in *American State Papers, op. cit.*, volume 1, p. 6.

10. All the land grants made in Kentucky to Virginia veterans appear to have been made before 1798, when Kentucky became a state. After that date, it appears that few locations were made within Kentucky. Jillson reports in the Introduction to his *Old Kentucky Entries and Deeds . . ., op. cit.*, as follows:

> ". . . The military warrants . . . comprise a group of medium size totaling 4,744, and extend from 1782 to 1793. The Military entries . . . comprise the smallest group of all, with only 1,567 names extending in the period from 1784 to 1797. All of the . . . enumerated records are found in the Kentucky Land Office at Frankfort, Kentucky."

11. Entry 61-2301 in the *National Union Catalog of Manuscript Collections* describes this corpus of records as follows:

> "Anderson, Richard Clough, 1750–1826. Virginia Military District [of Ohio] survey records, 1784–ca. 1852; ca. 10,000 items. University of Illinois, Illinois Historical Survey Collection."

12. John H. Gwathmey, *Historical Register of Virginians in the Revolution: Soldiers, Sailors, Marines, 1775-1783* (1938; reprinted Baltimore: Genealogical Publishing Co., 1973).

13. General Services Administration. National Archives and Records Service. The National Archives. *List of Cartographic Records of the General Land Office*. Special List No. 19 (Washington, D.C.: mimeographed, 1964), page 72, number 22.

14. The loose material in the Illinois Historical Survey collection is contained in 169 folders and has been inventoried in a typescript of 536 pages.

SUMMARIES OF LAND GRANT ENTRIES

S-0102 740a C:163 X-0340 UNIO:ALLE CHAM:RUSH
a. W-2349 Captain Henry Whiting
b. Henry Whiting
c. Rhoda Askew; Thomas Dunn, 1833

S-0142 1000a B:402 X-0732 CLAR:HARM
a. W-2418 Lieutenant Thomas Sears
b. Thomas Sears
c. D. McArthur; S. M. Wheeler, 1838

S-0143 1000a A:454 X-0136 ADAM:WAYN
a. W-0610 Captain John Winston
b. John Winston
c. None

S-0158 1200a D:103 X-0345 UNIO:ALLE
a. W-0351 Lieutenant Colonel Charles Simms
b. Charles Simms
c. W. P. Darst, 1840

S-0160* 212a C:170 X-0340 CHAM:RUSH
a. W-0196 Lieutenant James Mabon
b. James Mabon
c. None
*Source B says "not patented."

S-0220 1251a C:165 X-0480 UNIO:CLAI
a. W-2347 Lieutenant Richard Claiborne
b. Richard Claiborne
c. None

S-0220 416a C:165 X-0480 UNIO:CLAI
a. W-2347 Lieutenant Richard Claiborne
b. Richard Claiborne
c. None

S-0235 1200a B:272 X-0570 ROSS:SCIO
a. W-0815 Brigadier General Charles Scott
b. Charles Scott
c. Elizabeth Troutner; Charles Crozier

S-0239 1000a B:265 X-0840 ROSS:HUNT X-1140 PIKE*:--
a. W-0397 Captain Drury Ragsdale
b. Drury Ragsdale
c. None
*Not mentioned in Source B.

S-0258 500a D:147 X-1005 MARI:BOWL
a. W-0135 Lieutenant George Washington
b. George Washington
c. None

S-0258 500a D:147 X-1005 MARI:BOWL
a. W-0135 Lieutenant George Washington
b. George Washington
c. None

S-0261 765a A:245 X-0800 CLER:OHIO
a. W-0145 Captain William Fowler
b. William Fowler
c. W. Dun, exec.; S. Medary, 1829; James Taylor; John Hill, 1831; R. Dunkain, 1836

S-0274 666a C:46 X-0800 CLER:OHIO CLER:MONR
a. W-0108 Lieutenant John Green
b. William Green, heir
c. W. Arthur; James Taylor, 1823; Hugh Ferguson; Calvin A. Warren, 1834; T. Manning; R. Dunkan, 1836; James Whiting; Lieutenant Hugh Ferguson

S-0281 2000a A:368 X-0130 ADAM:WINC HIGH:CONC
a. W-1734 Lieutenant Colonel Richard Taylor
b. Richard Taylor
c. Peter Muhlenburg; Lieutenant Lyne Starling, 1828

S-0287 1000a D:48 X-1005 FRAN:NORW
a. W-0183 Thomas Bentley
b. Thomas Bentley
c. William Hay; Lieutenant Lyne Starling, 1828

S-0366 2000a B:186 X-0176 BROW:LEWI CLER:TATE CLER:FRAN
a. W-2025 Major James Knox
b. James Knox
c. Benjamin Latman? [Tatman?]; Abner Brett, 1824; Henry O'Neal; Lieutenant Stephen B. Cleveland, 1831 (Clermont County); Joseph Poe, Junior; E. Shaw, 1826?; John Gray

S-0386 1000a A:222 X-0800 BROW:UNIO
a. W-0738* Doctor Mace Clements
b. Mace Clements
c. Ignatius Mitchel; N. H. Masterson, 1826; M. E. Masterson; John S. Bearley, 1840; J. Brown, 1801
*Act of 12 May 1794? 28 *Stat.* 76?

S-0387 1200a A:484 X-0660 GREE:XENI
a. W-0192 Lieutenant Colonel John Jameson
b. John Jameson
c. None

S-0388 1400a A:223 X-0800 CLER:WASH
a. W-0937 Colonel John Nevill
b. Colonel John Nevill
c. John G. Gilfillan

S-0389 1000a A:484 X-0660 GREE:XENI
a. W-2261 Lieutenant Henry Bell
b. Henry Bell
c. Reuben Haines; J. O'Bannon, 1801; R. D. Forsman, 1832; B. C. Taber; G. Galloway, 1831; G. Clement, 1838; Lieutenant P. Gatch, 1803; William McFarland, 1805

S-0390 1000a C:114 X-0660 GREE:XENI
a. W-1396 Captain John Stokes
b. John Stokes
c. D. Gibbons, 1806; W. Maxwell, 1806; M. Wynans, 1828; Lieutenant J. O'Bannon, 1801; J. Wheeler, 1805

S-0391 1000a A:223 X-0800 CLER:WASH*
a. W-2183 Major Peter B. Brewen? [Brewer?]; George F. Norton [assignee?]
b. Richard C[lough] Anderson
c. John Payne; James McKinney; H. Irvin; O. C. Massie; Holley Roper, 1824; Lieutenant J. M. Kincaid, 1826; Z. Hunt, 1827; Demus & Fabus, steammill; H. Buchanan, 1833; A. Stark, 1832; Thomas Taylor; Elias Fee, 1831; John Fletcher; J. Gilfillan, 1835; M. F. H. Vaitch? [Veitch], 1835; William Keyes; John H. Taylor, 1839; J. Middleswart, 1839; W. S. Bank; W. Redman; T. Redman; A. C. Medary, 1842.
*Source B notation: "Moscow."

S-0392 1000a A:393 X-0840 ROSS:PAIN
a. W-2629 Captain Simon Morgan
b. Simon Morgan
c. W. M. Latta, 1801

S-0395 1667a B:238 X-0800 X-0660 HAMI:ANDE
a. W-2497 Bennett Tompkins
b. Bennett Tompkins
c. William McFarland, 1805; Lieutenant T. Smith, 1806

S-0396 1000a A:224 X-0800 BROW:HUNT
a. W-0069 Captain Philip Slaughter
b. Philip Slaughter
c. Nathan Ellis, heirs; William Grimes, 1826; Michael McDaniel; N. H. Masterson, 1826; D. McKinney, heirs; W. Shepherd, 1832; W. A. M. Wood; P. L. Wilson, 1841

S-0397 1000a C:242 X-0800 BROW:PLEA BROW:LEWI
a. W-1693 Captain Robert Higgins
b. Robert Higgins
c. T. L. Haines; Robert? Higgins; J. J. Higgins, 1827; J. Cochran, 1827; D. G. Devore, 1842

S-0398 1000a A:305 X-0134 BROW:EAGL
a. W-0673 Colonel Abraham Buford
b. Abraham Buford
c. None

S-0399 1333a A:485 X-0660 WARR:WAYN
a. W-0046 Colonel -- Read; also Clement Read, heir to Colonel -- Read
b. Clement Read
c. Gabriel Crane; Francis Dunlavy, 1832

S-0400 563a A:225 X-0800 BROW:PLEA
a. W-0200 Lieutenant Ballard Smith
b. Ballard Smith
c. None

S-0401 667a A:519 X-0800 ADAM:SPRI
a. W-2545 Captain Nathaniel Fox
b. Nathaniel Fox
c. P. Lee, 1801; A. Ellison, 1806; J. Brown, 1806; H. Brush, 1808; J. Martin; T. Keiken? 1806; Wills & Yates; R. N. Carder, 1841

S-0403 1000a A:225 X-0800 CLER:OHIO*
a. W-0135 Lieutenant George Washington
b. George Washington
c. Isaac Vorehuse? [Vorhees?]; W. Dillon, 1838; Sarah Gray, 1839; John W. Alfred; Ebenezer Worby; John Hull, 1841
*Source B notation: "Palentine."

S-0404 3000a A:370 X-0841 ROSS:CONC*
a. W-2553 Major James Lucas
b. James Lucas
c. Leroy Swormstead?; Robert Stewart; John Shepherd; J. D. Wiley, 1835; J. Dunlap, 1805
*Source B notation: "Frankfurt."

S-0407 2333a A:385 X-0841 ROSS:CONC*
a. W-2553 Major James Lucas
b. James Lucas
c. John Gottard?; George Newberry, 1831
* Source B notation: "Frankfurt."

S-0408 2000a A:385 X-0841 ROSS:CONC
a. W-0586 Doctor Edward Duff
b. Edward Duff
c. None

S-0410 1000a A:283 X-0660 HAMI:ANDE
a. W-1007 Lieutenant John Crittendon
b. John Crittendon
c. None

S-0414 1000a A:385 X-0841 ROSS:CONC
a. W-1967 Captain Henry Fauntleroy, heirs of
b. Henry Fauntleroy, heir
c. Joseph Bowdle; Charles Crozier, 1824; William Blade; Moses McLelland; Andrew Gibson? [Gipson]; Dickenson? Bent?; T. Arrohead; John Tarlton, 1827; S. & F. Edwards, 1833; R. Davison, 1801; J. Hunt, 1806; R. Hill, 1806; D. Hitchcock, 1807

S-0415 1000a A:226 X-0800 CLER:MONR*
a. W-0199 Captain Lawrence Butler
b. Lawrence Butler
c. J. Cunningham; J. D. Morris, 1824; William Wainwright, 1826; Henry Ludlam; J. Reily? 1823; W. B. & E. Sherwin; E. Salt, 1823; Alexander Oliver; Elias Fei, 1831; Isaac N. Morris, 1834; C? A. Warren, 1834; John Hill, 1831; William Lytle
*Source B notation: "Point Pleasant."

S-0416 667a A:386 X-0841 ROSS:CONC
a. W-0050 Peterfield Archer
b. Peter F. Archer
c. Mrs. John Savory

S-0417 1000a A:485 X-0660 GREE:SUGA
a. W-2311 Captain Churchill Jones
b. Churchill Jones
c. None

S-0418 1000a B:239 X-0800 BROW:UNIO*
a. W-0014 Samuel Oldham, heir to Captain C. Oldham
b. James Poage
c. Ann Poage; Archibald Liggett, 1826; William Trimble, heirs of; William Hewitt, 1834; J. Poage, Junior?; Elizabeth Poage; Andrew W. Poage; George Poage; Griffin W. Jones? [Jonas?] 1831; J. Moone? [Moore?]; Wilson & Middleton, 1842; S. Swain; J. S. Beasley, 1842; J. Thornhill
*Source B notation: "Ripley."

S-0419 1200a B:476 X-0340 UNIO:DARB
a. W-0712 Doctor William Brown; James Gallaway [assignee?]
b. William Brown
c. None

S-0420 1000a B:13 X-1000 FRAN:FRAN
a. W-0216 Doctor John Knight
b. John Knight
c. None

S-0421 1167a B:175 X-0660 WARR:WAYN
a. W-2374 Lieutenant George Holland
b. George Holland
c. William Faulkner; George King, 1831; J. Ferguson, 1803; R. Means, 1805; H. Bracken, 1806; Alexander Hamilton, 1806; H. Reeder, 1806

S-0422 1000a B:14 X-1000 FRAN:FRAN
a. W-0153 Captain John Overton
b. John Overton
c. Joseph Breckenridge; E. Backus? 1832; J. & J. Miner; Jeremiah Miner, 1840

S-0423 667a A:519 X-0800 ADAM:SPRI
a. W-2383 Lieutenant Archelaus Perkins
b. Archelaus Perkins
c. John Rodgers; Ab[ner?] Lafferty, 1826

S-0424 1000a B:61 X-1000 FRAN:FRAN
a. W-0853 Captain Robert Beall
b. Robert Beall
c. William Miller; C. Thomas, 1832

S-0426 1000a B:51 X-1000 FRAN:JACK
a. W-2655 William Lawson, heir to C. Lawson
b. William Lawson
c. John Kile; Bob Brotherton, 1826; Lyne Starling, 1833

S-0427 750a A:276 X-0660 HAMI:ANDE*
a. W-2367 Captain John Anderson
b. John Anderson
c. None
*Source B notation: "By Newtown."

S-0428 1667a A:458 X-0840 ROSS:BUCK* FAYE:--**
a. W-2367 Captain John Anderson
b. John Anderson
c. None
*Source B notation: "Opposite Greenfield."
**Not mentioned in Source B.

S-0429 1000a A:485 X-0660 GREE:XENI
a. W-1821 Lieutenant John Heth; George Scott [assignee?]
b. George Scott
c. Henry Chapman; R. D. Forsman, 1831; N. & R. Gregg, 1801; George Clark, 1803; Thomas Stone, 1805; William McFarland, 1805; William Stillas, 1806; William Hillas, 1806; George Galloway, 1809; S? & M. Witham, 1806; J. Kerr, 1801

S-0430 1000a A:284 X-0665 CLER:UNIO* CLER:MIAM
a. W-0903 Captain Robert Powell
b. Robert Powell
c. D. McClelland; Bryant & Barber, 1823
*Source B notation: "By Milford."

S-0431 1667a A:289 X-0130 ADAM:TIFF ADAM:MEIG
a. W-0128 Epaphroditus Rudder; J. T. Griffin [assignee?]
b. John T. Griffin
c. Sol[omon] Shoemaker; Wes[ley] Lee, 1826; Thomas Thurman, Senior?; A. Ellison, 1824; C. Thompson; H. Thompson, 1828; Catharine Thompson

S-0432 1000a A;486 X-0665 GREE:SUGA GREE:XENI
a. W-1474 Captain Francis Muir; Allen Latham & William McKnight [assignees?]
b. Francis Muir [also Muire]
c. W. Kelley; T? [F?] Heath, 1823; A. McConnel?; W. H. Good, 1824; R[obert?] Davidson, 1801; Mathew Taylor, 1803; James? [Joseph?] Taylor, 1805

S-0434 400a B:139 X-1303 BROW:EAGL BROW:WASH
a. W-1509 Robert Mush, 200a
W-1514 Edmund Absalam; Samuel Jones & C. Carrington [assignees?] 200a
b. Mayo Carrington
c. George Shultz, 1824; W. Baldwin, 1801? [1807?]; J[ames] Fleming; John Machir?; George Clark, 1808; Mathew Kincaid, 1831

S-0435 180a B:394 X-0660 GREE:MIAM
a. W-1435 Read Hutt; John Kat [assignee]
b. Samuel Finley
c. None

S-0435 400a B:395 X-0740 GREE:MIAM GREE:XENI
a. W-1450 Major Samuel Finley
b. Samuel Finley
c. None

S-0436 1000a A:227 X-0800 ADAM:GREE
a. W-0743 Ensign Edward Williams
b. Mayo Carrington
c. Alexander Hamilton, 1806; John Heath; Jonathan? Smith, 1806; William Raynolds, 1807; S. Smith; J. P. Smith, 1841

S-0437 1000a A:222 X-0800 CLER:OHIO
a. W-0077 Captain John Dandridge
b. John Danddridge
c. None

S-0438 1000a B:118 X-0660 GREE:MIAM GREE:XENI
a. W-0131 Lieutenant Francis Whiting
b. Francis Whiting
c. R. Boggess; George Townsley, 1829; Arthur Beattie; W. McLaughlin, 1834

S-0439 1667a A:382 X-1000 ROSS:UNIO
a. W-0761 Lieutenant Benjamin Lawson
b. Benjamin Lawson
c. A. Dunlap? & Company; William Sterrit; David Ross, heirs of (negro); John Kenshaw; David McQuey; John Tarlton, 1827; James Morgan, 1829; W? [M?] Pardon? [Purdom?]

S-0440 718a A:425 X-1000 ROSS:UNIO
a. W-0043 Archibald Blair, heir to Captain -- Blair
b. Archibald Blair
c. None

S-0441 1000a A:425 X-1000 ROSS:UNIO
a. W-1850 Doctor Robert Rose
b. Robert Rose
c. P. Mincer, Senior; William Bussard, 1840; J. Richart; A. McCoy, 1842

S-0443 1000a A:425 X-1000 ROSS:UNIO PICK*
a. W-2223 Captain Patrick Carnes
b. Patrick Carnes
c. J. Evans, 1805
*Mentioned in Source B only.

S-0445 460a A:421 X-1000 X-0800 PICK:WAYN
a. W-0174 Captain William White
b. William White
c. W. Stanard; John Evans, 1806; Jacob Engle, 1831

S-0446 1000a A:426 X-1000 PICK:WAYN
a. W-1186 Captain Whitehead Coleman
b. Whitehead Coleman
c. M. & W. Snow; W. Y? Emmitt, 1831; David Sisk, 1841; heirs of C. Nichols; Robert Campbell, 1841; W. McNemar; E. Everts, 1842

S-0447 73a C:304 X-0360 PICK:PERR
a. W-2274 Doctor Basil Middleton; John Campbell [assignee?]
b. John Campbell
c. The above entry marked out: 850a, plus following names: Robert J. Beard; Elias Langham, 1806; T. Jones, 1801.

S-0449 1000a A:426 X-1000 PICK:WAYN*
a. W-2509 Captain John Jordan
b. John Jordan
c. James Moore; William Longworth, 1832; Unknown; John Dalby, 1836; W. Oliphant, heirs of; S? S? Francis? [Frame?]; J. Caldwell; W. P. Darst & P. N. White, 1840; J. & P. Dalby; R. C. Dalby; William Renick; L. Oliphant; T? J. B. Mills, 1841; Hall & Walker; W. Renick, Junior, 1842
*Source B notation: "Westfall & Montgomery."

S-0450 2667a B:204 X-1000 PICK:WAYN PICK:JACK
a. W-0825 John Jolliffe, heir to Lieutenant John Jolliffe
b. John Jolliffe
c. E. Sittler? [Littler?] 1805; J. Hedges, 1826; George Glaze; William McDowell, 1806; George Renix, 1806

S-0451 1000a A:426 X-1000 PICK:WAYN
a. W-0194 James Galt, heir to Doctor P. Galt
b. James Galt, heir
c. A. Dukes; J. Hedges, 1826; D. McArthur; T. J. McArthur, 1828

S-0452 440a A:426 X-1000 PICK:WAYN
a. W-1938 Jeremiah Walker, 100a
W-1909 Phillip Langfelt, 100a
W-1787 Elijah Osburn, 200a
W-1962 John Depriest, 200a; Richard Edmonton [assignee]
b. Clement Biddle
c. None

S-0453 1000a A:223 X-0800 SCIO:NILE
a. W-1868 James Culvertson*
b. James Culbertson*
c. C. & G. Mathews; James R. Walker, 1834; James wright, 1805; G. Brown, 1806
*So spelled.

S-0455 1000a A:222 X-0800 SCIO:NILE
a. W-0771 Lieutenant Peter Higgins
b. Alex[ander] Parker [assignee?]
c. William Robinson; T. Morgan, 1824

S-0456 190a D:62 X-1000 PICK:WAYN
a. W-2377 Doctor John Trezevant; John Tench, Wallace & Thomas J. McArthur [assignees]
b. John Tench
c. N. Kenedy, 1803; S. F. Randolph; N. Wills, 1805; L? [S?] Sullivant, 1805; James Kerr, 1806; J. Taylor, 1806

S-0456 210a D:62 X-1000 PICK:WAYN
a. W-2377 Doctor John Trezevant; John Tench, Wallace & Thomas J. McArthur [assignees]
b. John Tench
c. None

S-0457 1000a B:40 X-1000 PICK:WAYN
a. W-0200 Lieutenant Ballard Smith
b. Ballard Smith
c. None

S-0459 1000a A:226 X-0800 ADAM:MONR
a. W-2311 Captain Churchill Jones
b. Churchill Jones
c. William Rowland; David Bradford, 1823; John P. Neal, 1805; Candace? Gatch, 1806

S-0460 1000a A:227 X-1150 ADAM:SPRI
a. W-2272 Captain Callohill Minnis
b. Callohill Minnis
c. Henry Gutridge; George Bryan, 1826; John Brown, 1801; Moses Wright, 1808; T. Patton, 1803

S-0462 1333a B:3 X-0360 MADI:PLEA
a. W-0305 Captain Thomas Bell
b. Thomas Bell
c. Heirs of L? Lane; S. N. Kerr, 1840; S. Anderson, 1842

S-0463 1333a B:5 X-0360 FAYE:MADI* PICK:MONR
a. W-0044 Captain Thomas Overton
b. Thomas Overton
c. Samuel Adams; *illegible*, 1827; J. Hall; W. McFarland, 1805; H. Bricken, 1806; W. Winship, 1806; C. W. Stewart, 1807
*Source B notation: "Yanktown."

S-0464 2922a B:4 X-0360 PICK:DARB* MADI:PLEA
a. W-2317 & W-0101 Colonel George Baylor
b. George Baylor
c. R. Denton; S. Moore, 1826; E. Pritchard; T. Bond, 1823; Strain & Howell; R. Douglass; John Riddle, 1831; heirs of C. Tanner; John Moore, 1835; W. Baylor; Moses Wright, 1805
*Source B notation: "Mt. Sterling."

S-0465 1000a B:295 X-1000 PICK:JACK PICK:SCIO
a. W-0217 Doctor John Knight
b. John Knight
c. None

S-0467 1000a B:5 X-0360 PICK:MONR PICK:PERR
a. W-0630 Lieutenant Jacob Brown
b. Jacob Brown
c. S. Kelly; P. H. Baker, 1828; John Timmons; Henry Rudy, 1833; J. & H. Johnson, 1801; Jonathan? Taylor, 1803

S-0468 700a B:124 X-0420 BROW:BYRD BROW:JACK
a. W-0025 Major William Croghan
b. William Croghan
c. Charles McManis; C. Snideher, 1825

S-0469 1000a B:14 X-1000 FRAN:JACK
a. W-0088 Captain Strothers Jones
b. Strothers Jones
c. J. Badger; A. J. McDowell, 1824; William Badger; R. Brotherton, 1827; heirs of John Ball; Clark Higgins, 1834; Saul Clark; Jeremiah McLem? 1831; J. H. Ball; E. Bachus, 1836; J. McDonald; heirs of Ira? Delano; W. Conrad, 1835; S. Jones; J. L? Taylor, 1836; Lyne Sterling [*also* Starling]; N. Briggs, 1838; Patton, Thompson, & Hackley; James Pumsey? [Penrey?] 1809; William Miller, 1841

S-0470 2000a B:4 X-0360 FAYE:MADI* PICK:MONR PICK:PERR
a. W-0827 Captain John Holcomb; Richard James [assignee?]
b. Richard James
c. William Fulton; W. Loofborough, 1826; Margaret Gaskell; James Scott; Caleb Gaskell; Caleb Everston; heirs of John Kerr; A. Douglas, 1838; J. Mortimor; J? G? Grau, 1836; C. Taylor; N. G? Jones, 1836; Nathan Loofborrow; George Clark, 1801; John Kerr, 1803; Moses Wright, 1805; J. Vandolah, 1806
*Source B notation: "Waterloo."

S-0471 1000a B:4 X-0360 PICK:MONR MADI:PLEA FAYE:MADI
a. W-1852 Captain John Stith; Doctor James Currie [assignee?]
b. James Currie
c. David Currie; Adley? Gregory, 1828; J. Y. Green, 1831; Henry Hollar; R. Douglas, 1833; heirs of J. Gordon; Battail Harrison, 1833; J. Currie; Delumur Kinnear, 1833 (Pickaway County); W. Loofborough, 1837; Samuel Loofborough, 1835

S-0472 1000a B:5 X-0360 PICK:MONR PICK:PERR
a. W-2309 Captain John H. Fitzgerald
b. John H. Fitzgerald
c. None

S-0473 1200a A:411 X-1000 PIKE:PEEP
a. W-2199 Captain William Johnson
b. William Johnson
c. George Clark, 1801; Gideon Coover? [Conner?] 1803; J. Woodbridge, 1807

S-0475 1000a A:235 X-0800 SCIO:NILE SCIO:WASH
a. W-0619 Captain Larkin Smith
b. Larkin Smith
c. William McLain; J. Noel & C. Overton, 1834; William McClaren; William Roby, 1829; D. McArthur; heirs of J. Perry; R. Hamilton, 1842

S-0476* 1000a A:461 X-0841 ROSS:CONC
a. W-0456 Captain Lieutenant William F. Gaines; Henry Gaines [assignee?]
b. Henry Gaines
c. J. Porter, 1803; J. McDougal, 1805; J. Mallow; T. H. Luckett, 1842
*Source B notation: "Not patented."

S-0478 1200a B:26 X-1000 FRAN:JACK
a. W-0289 Doctor Cornelius Baldwin
b. Cornelius Baldwin
c. William Mooberry? 1829

S-0479 1000a B:219 X-0340 LOGA:ZANE
a. W-0214 Doctor David Holmes; David Duncan [assignee?]
b. David Duncan
c. L? [S?] Sullivant; L. Starling, 1826; D. Duncan

S-0480 1360a A:401 X-1000 ROSS:SCIO
a. W-1174 Major Thomas Massey*
b. Thomas Massie
c. N. Johnson, 1801; J. & H. Johnson, 1803; George Clark, 1806
*So spelled, Source C.

S-0484 1000a A:410 X-1000 PIKE:JACK
a. W-0023 Captain Thomas H. Drew; John T. Griffin [assignee?]
b. John T. Griffin
c. None

S-0485 1000a A:424 X-1000 ROSS:FRAN
a. W-2133 Captain Nathaniel Burwell
b. Nathaniel Burwell
c. None

S-0486 1000a A:423 X-1000 SCIO:WASH
a. W-2601 Captain Nathaniel Terry
b. Nathaniel Terry
c. Heirs of G. Graves; Samuel Coil, 1840; G. Calvert; W. V. Peck, 1842; L. Moss; J. M. Merrill, 1842; Waller? [Wallis?] & Coles, 1842

S-0488 1000a A:424 X-1000 ROSS:FRAN
PIKE* --
a. W-0844 Thomas Holloby, 400a
W-1472 William Green, 200a
W-1562 George Salmon, 400a; *all three warrants to* Pickering & Hodgden [assignees?]
b. -- Pickering & -- Hodgden
c. None
*Not mentioned in Source B.

S-0489 910a A:410 X-1000 ROSS:FRAN
a. W-1792 Lieutenant Colonel Edward Carrington
b. Edward Carrington
c. J. Heath; D. Cassett, 1803

S-0490 200a A:412 X-1000 PIKE:PEEP*
a. W-1651 John Burk
b. John Burk
c. J. Kerr, 1801; J. Wright, 1805; George Clark, 1806
*Source B notation: "By Waverly."

S-0490 200a A:412 X-1000 PIKE:PEEP*
a. W-2322 Jean Babtiste** (with Bradford Cott)***
b. Jean Babtist**
c. J. May, 1805; Heirs of A. Barnes; Charles McCollister, 1841
*Source B notation: "By Waverly."
**So spelled.
***This might read "with Captain Bradford" (*see, for example,* S-0490 Francis Barbee, *below*).

S-0490 100a A:412 X-1000 PIKE:PEEP
a. W-0292 Daniel Bedinger
b. Daniel Bedinger
c. None*
*Source B (at bottom of page) shows D. Bryney, 1806.

S-0490 200a A:412 X-1000 PIKE:PEEP
a. W-1210 Francis Barbee (with Captain -- Bradford)
b. Francis Barber*
c. None
*Source B shows Barbee.

S-0490 200a A:412 X-1000 PIKE:PEEP
a. W-2155 Henry Bradford (with? Captain -- Bradford)
b. Henry Bradford
c. C. Cisna? [Cesna?]; Arthur Chinowith, 1829

S-0490 100a A:412 X-1000 PIKE:PEEP
a. W-2382 Presley Cockrel
b. Presley Cockrel*
c. None
*Source B shows Crockett.

S-0491 450a B:10 X-0800 ADAM:GREE
a. W-0815 Brigadier General Charles Scott
b. Charles Scott
c. S. Shannon; T. Huston, 1840; R. Kerr; L. Cole, 1841

S-0491 615a B:11 X-0800 ADAM:GREE
a. W-0815 Brigadier General Charles Scott
b. Charles Scott
c. None

S-0491 490a B:11 X-0800 ADAM:GREE
a. W-0815 Brigadier General Charles Scott
b. Charles Scott
c. None

S-0491 445a B:11 X-0800 ADAM:GREE
a. W-0815 Brigadier General Charles Scott
b. Charles Scott
c. None

S-0492 215a A:411 X-1000 PIKE:PEEP
a. W-2260 Major Richard Call
b. Richard Call
c. None

S-0493 1000a A:264 X-0663 CLER:BATA
CLER:OHIO
a. W-0207 Robert Gibins, heir to Major E. Dickinson
b. Robert Gibbon*, heir
c. W. C. Bowden; M. F. H. Vetch [*also* Veitch]; R. McFarland, 1836; Mary Brunaugh [*also* Brunaw]; H. Butler; T. J. Buchannon, 1840; S. McLaughlin; J. Smith; W. Dillon, 1840
*So spelled; Source B notation: "Amelia."

S-0494 1400a A:411 X-1000 PIKE:PEEP
a. W-1912 Doctor Thomas Christie
b. Thomas Christie
c. D. McNeil; J. Dennie, 1806

S-0495 500a C:271 X-0360 CLAR:PLEA
a. W-1451 Lieutenant Charles Jones
b. Charles Jones
c. William Tomlinson, 1831; D. Hitchcock, 1807

S-0496 1000a A:227 X-1150 ADAM:SPRI
a. W-2667 James Tompkins, heir to Daniel Tompkins; Bird Hendricks [assignee?]
b. Byrd Hendricks
c. None

S-0500 50a B:323 X-0665 HAMI:ANDE
a. W-2507 Colonel Holt Richerson
b. Holt Richerson*
c. None
*Source B spells Richardson.

S-0500 1150a B:251 X-0665 HAMI:ANDE*
a. W-2507 Colonel Holt Richerson
b. Holt Richerson**
c. J. Miller; R. W. Dawson? 1825; T. Canneal? [Carneal?]
*Source B notation: "Newtown."
**Source B spells Richardson.

S-0501 200a B:37 X-0340 PICK:JACK
a. W-2748 Tilman Walton
b. Tilman Walton
c. None

S-0501 200a B:37 X-0345 PICK:JACK
a. W-2506 Larkin Self
b. Larkin Self
c. J. Hall, 1803; William McFarland, 1805; G. Brown, 1805; M. Wright, 1805; J. Kerr, 1806

S-0501 100a B:37 X-0345 PICK:JACK
a. W-2146 Daniel Donnakin
b. Daniel Donnakin
c. J. Craiger, 1801; William Elliott, 1803; H. Shirley, 1805

S-0501 200a B:37 X-0340 PICK:JACK
a. W-2662 Phillip Webber; Edward Dowse [assignee?]
b. Philip Webber
c. None

S-0501 200a B:37 X-0345 PICK:JACK
a. W-1248 George Chisholm
b. George Chisholm
c. G. Craiger, 1801; J. Craiger, 1805; J. Kerr, 1807

S-0501 100a B:37 X-0340 PICK:JACK
a. W-0017 William Ray
b. William Ray
c. None

S-0502 700a* A:451 X-0663 CLER:MIAM
a. W-0083 Joseph Davis; Captain Thomas Overton, assignee
b. Thomas Overton
c. None
*Source A notation: "88-3/14 acres with[hel]d."

S-0503 300a F:246 X-1000 ROSS:SCIO
a. W-0903 Captain Robert Powell
b. Arthur Watts*
c. J. Tarlton, 1827
*Source B says grantee is Robert Powell for 865 acres; mentions Chillicothe [Land Office] books.

S-0506 2000a A:269 X-0663 CLER:BATA CLER:OHIO
a. W-1198 John Catlett, heir to John? B. Catlett
b. John Cutlett? [Cullett?]* heir
c. J. Smith; Z. Dooley, 1835; Jane Smith; A. McKibben; A. Miley, 1839
*Source B lists as John Catlet.

S-0507 1000a A:400 X-0840 ROSS:PAXT
a. W-1734 Lieutenant Colonel Richard Taylor
b. Richard Taylor
c. J. Stewart, 1801

S-0508 900a A:235 X-0800 X-1000 SCIO:WASH*
a. W-1892 Captain Alexander Parker
b. Alexander Parker
c. C. Thorn, heirs; William Roby, 1829; S? W. Stillwell; R. Craine, 1838
*Source B notation: "Alexandria."

S-0508 400a A:240 X-0800 CLER:FRAN
a. W-1892 Captain Alexander Parker
b. Alexander Parker
c. R. Reddick; P. Emery, 1825

S-0509 1000a D:184 X-1000 ROSS:SCIO
a. W-1387 Captain Ferdinand Oneal
b. Ferdinand ONeal
c. William Lamb; William Waddle, 1831; Cox & Eckart; J. Sill, 1842
*Source B notation: "Pat[ented] to John Watts."

S-0510 31a C:9 X-0436 ADAM:--*
a. W-2402 Lieutenant Jordan Harris
b. Jordan Harris
c. None
*Source B does not give township; marginal notation says "Brush Creek."

S-0511 1000a A:454 X-0663 CLER:BATA
a. W-0299 Colonel James Wood; Robert Baylor [assignee]
b. Robert Baylor
c. Daniel Kirgaw? [Kirgan?]; E. Frazier, 1839; Z. Ferguson; A. Halick, 1839; P. Machirte? 1805; G. West heirs; John Hull, 1841

S-0512 1000a B:36 X-0340 PICK:JACK
a. W-0002 Lieutenant Willis Wilson
b. Willis Wilson
c. W. Basket; S. Corn? 1827; J. Craigen? [Craiger?]; S. F. Randolph, 1805; A. Wilson; J. Barnes, 1805

S-0513 800a D:358 X-0340 PICK:MUHL
a. W-0001 James Askew*
b. -- Ball, -- Dabney, & -- Hoomes**
c. C. Wallace; D. Ross, 1801
*Warrant number must be in error, as James Askew was entitled only to 100a therewith.
**Source B spells Holmes.

S-0514 1000a A:264 X-0800 CLER:OHIO
a. W-2452 Colonel William Davies*
b. Colonel William Davis*
c. John Snyder; James Snyder, 1832
*So spelled.

S-0515 1200a B:6 X-0340 PICK:MUHL*
a. W-0289 Doctor Cornelius Baldwin
b. Cornelius Baldwin
c. D. C. Noble, heirs; George Botkin, 1836
*Source B notation: "Darbyville."

S-0516 2000a B:81 X-0840 GREE:ROSS
a. W-2263* Lieutenant Colonel William Washington
b. William Washington
c. John L. Ireland; N. Peyton; C. Wallace, 1809; D. Sutton; C. A. Stewart, 1808; H. Moss, 1806; W. Sterrett, 1806
*Source A mistakenly states W-2663.

S-0516 170a B:252 X-0840 ROSS:PAXT
a. W-2263 Lieutenant Colonel William Washington
b. William Washington
c. None

S-0517 1340a B:36 X-0340 PICK:JACK
a. W-0291 Captain Henry Bedinger
b. Henry Bedinger
c. None

S-0518 912a A:393 X-0840 ROSS:TWIN
a. W-2638 John McAdams, heir to Joseph? McAdams; Benjamin Grimes [assignee?]
b. Benjamin Grimes
c. J. Pancake, heirs; H? Fullerton, 1841

S-0519 1000a A:310 X-0790 CLER:MIAM CLER:GOSH
a. W-0023 Captain Thomas H. Drew; John T. Griffin [assignee?]
b. John T. Griffin
c. S. Anderson; W. Wainwright, 1824; Timothy Buzett; C. Zugg; John Randel, 1837; J. McLaughlin; M. F. H. Veitch, 1835; J. Pickens, 1839

S-0520 1000a A:331 X-0660 WARR:HAMI
a. W-2499 Lieutenant William McGuire
b. William McGuire
c. None

S-0523 1750a B:250 X-1170 CLIN:UNIO
a. W-2483 Captain Daniel Duval
b. Daniel Duval
c. M. G. Wallace, 1805; T. Babb, Senior; F. Casta [*also* Casto] 1842

S-0524 1000a A:310 X-0790 CLER:GOSH
a. W-2260 Major Richard Call
b. Richard Call
c. George Mathews; Z. Chapman, 1836

S-0525* 240a? -- -- BROW:HUNT
a. --
b. Mace Clements
c. J. Brown; W. Dun, 1808; J. Taylor, 1806
*Not listed in Source A.

S-0526 856a B:482 X-0663 CLER:BATA CLER:STON
a. W-1450 Major Samuel Finley
b. Samuel Finley
c. David Duckwall

S-0526 144a B:482 X-0663 CLER:BATA CLER:STON
a. W-1450 Major Samuel Finley
b. Samuel Finley
c. None

S-0527 1500a A:393 X-0840 ROSS:TWIN
a. W-0101 Colonel George Baylor
b. George Baylor
c. None

S-0528 1667a A:331 X-0660 WARR:WAYN WARR:WASH
a. W-2252 Lieutenant John Harris
b. John Harris
c. None

S-0529 1200a A:399 X-0840 ROSS:SCIO
a. W-0035 Lieutenant Colonel Richard C[lough] Anderson
b. Mayo Carrington
c. None

S-0530 1000a B:30 X-1000 FRAN:FRAN
a. W-2515 Lieutenant John Trabue
b. John Trabue
c. L. Starling, 1809; N. Kennedy, 1801

S-0532 1000a A:409 X-0840 ROSS:PAXT
a. W-2700 Doctor? Miles King
b. Miles King
c. None

S-0534 2667a B:7 X-0340 PICK:DARB PICK:MUHL
a. W-0587 Captain John Blackwell
b. John Blackwell
c. None

S-0534 200a A:231 X-0800 HAMI:ANDE
a. W-0906 John Halfpenny
b. John Halfpenny
c. George Clark, 1801; J. Bennett*; G. W. Jones, 1826*; John Hill*; N. W. Lawrence, 1825*; J. Mathews*; P. Skinner, 1826?*
*Written in Source B margin and could pertain to any grant within this survey.

S-0535 100a A:231 X-0800 HAMI:ANDE
a. W-0960 John Demsey
b. John Denny*
c. J. Zane, 1801; J. Donaldson, 1803; D. McArthur, 1806; W. McFarland, 1803; J. McDougall, 1805; W. Casto, 1806
*Source B says Dempsey.

S-0535 100a A:232 X-0800 HAMI:ANDE
a. W-0932 William Casell
b. William Casell
c. J. Smith, 1801; J. Russel? [Rassel?] 1803; S. French, 1805; W. McFarland, 1805; J. Taylor, 1806; J. Thomas, 1806

S-0535 100a A:232 X-0800 HAMI:ANDE
a. W-0934 John Mead
b. John Mead
c. E. Rector, 1801; Massie & Cossett, 1803; W. McFarland, 1805; J. Taylor, 1806; W. Raynolds, 1807; W. Ellison, 1805

S-0535 100a A:232 X-0800 HAMI:ANDE
a. W-0962 Robert Blair
b. Robert Blair
c. J. Smith, 1801; W. McFarland, 1803; J. S. Wills, 1805; R. Blair, 1806; William Raynolds, 1807

S-0535 100a A:232 X-0800 HAMI: --
a. W-0971 Benjamin Gray*
b. Benjamin Grey*
c. N. Ellis, 1801; D. Riddle, 1803; W. Campbell, 1805; William Raynolds; W. Lytle, 1807
*So spelled.

S-0535 100a A:232 X-0800 HAMI: --
a. W-0972 David Lahaw*
b. David Lahan*
c. W. Murfin, 1801; J. Darlington, 1803; W. G. Wilson, 1805; E. Dewitt, 1806; W. McFarland, 1806; J. Taylor; A. Ellison, 1808
*So spelled; Source B shows Lahaw.

S-0535 100a A:233 X-0800 HAMI:ANDE
a. W-0987 James Giles
b. James Giles
c. Bradwell & Day, 1801; S. Reeve, 1803; E. Dewitt? [Demitt?] 1805; J. Taylor, 1806; S. Reeves

S-0535 100a A:233 X-0800 HAMI:ANDE
a. W-0916 John Green
b. John Green
c. J. Brown, 1801; G. Brown, 1808; J. McFarland, 1803; J. Buffington, 1805; J. Bradwell, 1805; J. Taylor, 1806; W. McFarland, 1805

S-0536 667a A:273 X-0660 HAMI:ANDE
a. W-0602 John Steel
b. John Steel
c. None

S-0538 1200a A:393 X-0840 ROSS:TWIN
a. W-0192 Lieutenant Colonel John Jameson*
b. John Jemison*
c. Hugh Finley, heirs; John Sommerville, 1837
*So spelled.

S-0539 1000a A:428 X-1000 ROSS:UNIO
a. W-2309 Captain John H. Fitzgerald
b. John H. Fitzgerald
c. None

S-0540 200a B:276 X-0840 MADI:STOK
a. W-2018 Joel Grissett*
b. Joel Grissel*
c. J. Gardner, Junior, heir; W. Barlow, 1806; J. Denny
*So spelled.

S-0540 200a B:276 X-0840 MADI:STOK
a. W-2152 Miles Jennins*; Joshua Stevens [assignee?]
b. Miles Jennings*
c. T. Scott, 1801; W. Barlow, 1803; J. Fields, 1805; J. Evans, 1805
*So spelled.

S-0540* 100a B:276 X-0840 MADI:STOK
a. W-2632 John Redwood
b. John Redwood
c. George Simson? [Sinson?] 1831; J. Singan? 1835; S. Drew, 1801; W. Barlow, 1803?; H. Bracken, 1805
*Source B notation: "Not patented."

S-0540 100a B:276 X-0840 MADI:STOK
a. W-1178 Zachariah Jones
b. Zachariah Jones
c. W. Barlow, 1805; W. Snell, 1801?; J. Zachariah; W. McFarland, 1806

S-0540* 100a B:276 X-0840 MADI:STOK
a. W-2749 John Boman*
b. John Bowman*
c. A. Franklin, 1801; S. Fennimore? [Fennimen?] 1805; Patrick Donnelly, 1806; George Sinson, 1831
*Source B notation: "Not patented."

S-0540 100a B:276 X-0840 MADI:STOK
a. W-2750 Joshua Stephens* heir to John Stevens*
b. Heirs of Joshua Stevens**
c. T. Bond, 1823; S. Stull? [Steell?] 1801; J. Taylor, 1803; J. Fields, 1805
*So spelled.
**Source B says Stevenson.

S-0541 1500a A:407 X-0840 ROSS:PAIN HIGH:PAIN
a. W-1850 Doctor Robert Rose
b. Robert Rose
c. J. Davis, 1807

S-0542 1000a B:272 X-1000 ROSS:UNIO
a. W-0685 Lieutenant Obadiah Smith
b. Obadiah Smith
c. None

S-0543 778a A:243 X-0800 ADAM:GREE
a. W-0602 John Steel
b. John Steel
c. None

S-0544 1000a B:30 X-1000 FRAN:NORW
a. W-1849 Major John Belfield
b. John Belfield
c. Augustine Neile; John Lynch, 1834; Miskel? Sanders; S. G. Renick, 1840; Sarah Sanders; J. Smith, 1801; J. Strawn, 1805; M? [W?] Reeder, 1806; J. Hill, 1806; L. Sullivant, 1807

S-0545 500a B:439 X-0340 LOGA:ZANE UNIO: --
a. W-2418 Lieutenant Thomas Sears
b. Thomas Sears
c. None

S-0546 770a B:29 X-1000 PICK:JACK
a. W-0057 Captain Robert Porterfield
b. Robert Porterfield
c. George Davis; Samuel Kinnear, 1831; Joseph Hull, heirs; William McArthur, 1830

S-0547 2000a B:31 X-1000 FRAN:NORW
a. W-2236 Captain John Nelson
b. John Nelson
c. Joseph? Black & William Black; Robert Elliot, 1826; H. McCracken, 1827; A. Fulviler?; William O. Kinson; G. Blank, 1827; Jonas Snyder; David Smiley; C. Higgins, 1835; J. Nelson; J. L. Taylor, 1836; Peter Strickland; B. Boyd, 1837; G. Jefferies, 1837

S-0548 2200a A:486 X-0660 GREE:XENI
a. W-1606 John Woodford, heir to General -- Woodford
b. John Woodford
c. None

S-0549 1000a B:28 X-1000 PICK:JACK
a. W-0652 Lieutenant David Meriwether
b. David Meriwether*
c. George Davis; Samuel Kinnear, 1831
*Source B spells Merriweather.

S-0550 2000a A:433 X-0660 CLIN:UNIO CLIN:GREE CLIN:RICH CLIN:WAYN
a. W-0856 Captain George Rice; -- Anderson & -- Carrington [assignees?]
b. Robert Anderson & Mayo Carrington
c. Coleman Botts; Jonathan Harris; A. E. Strickle, 1838; P. Wycle? [Wyele?]; Amelia Cripfield? & Mary Cripfield?; Levi Gustin, 1836; George Fallis, 1840; James Stitt; D. C. Herrman? [Henman?] 1840; John Tammons, 1841; J. Wood, 1842

S-0550 2000a A:433 X-0660 CLIN:UNIO CLIN:GREE CLIN:RICH CLIN:WAYN
a. W-0856 Captain George Rice; -- Anderson & -- Carrington [assignees?]
b. R. C. Anderson & Mayo Carrington
c. None

S-0551 500a A:413 X-0800 ADAM:SPRI
a. W-1670 Phillip Barbour, heir to James Robertson; Albert Gallatin [assignee?]
b. Albert Gallatin
c. None

S-0552 600a A:331 X-0660 HAMI:ANDE
a. W-0903 Captain Robert Powell
b. Robert Powell
c. S. F. Randolph; William Smith, 1826; Francis Martin, executors; John Phares, 1832

S-0553 1000a B:330 X-0360 MADI:UNIO MADI:DEER
a. W-2270 Lieutenant Stephen Southall
b. Stephen Southall
c. None

S-0554 2000a A:351 X-0426 BROW:BYRD
a. W-0707 Captain Nathaniel Fox
b. Nathaniel Fox
c. Iratis? Holland; Ph. Rice, 1826; S. Hatfield; George Edwards, 1842

S-0555 1000a A:386 X-0841 ROSS:CONC
a. W-0050 Peterfield Archer
b. Peter F. Archer
c. None

S-0556 872a B:143 X-0660 GREE:ROSS
a. W-1912 Doctor Thomas Christie
b. Thomas Christie
c. None

S-0557 1000a B:27 X-1000 PICK:SCIO
a. W-0002 Lieutenant Willis Wilson
b. Willis Wilson
c. Amasa Delano; J. Olds & P. Loutz, 1826

S-0558 1000a A:131 X-0660 GREE:ROSS
a. W-0096 Captain Baylor Hill
b. Baylor Hill
c. None

S-0559 880a* C:100 X-0660 GREE:ROSS
a. W-0630 Lieutenant Jacob Brown
b. Jacob Brown
c. None
*Source B says 888a.

S-0560 1000a A:423 X-0130 ADAM:SCOT
a. W-0070 Lieutenant Francis Smith
b. Francis Smith
c. J. Campbell; S? [L?] Cole, 1842

S-0561 1000a B:41 X-0270 CLER:TATE
BROW: --*
a. W-2349 Captain Henry Whiting
b. Henry Whiting
c. J. Musgrove; M. Mullen, 1842
*Source B does not show Brown County or township.

S-0562 2000a A:399 X-0840 ROSS:SCIO
a. W-2240 Francis Coleman, heir to Captain R. Coleman
b. Francis Coleman
c. John Haines; R. Long, 1827

S-0563 2000a A:332 X-0180 WARR:WAYN
a. W-0072 Major William Lewis; John T. Griffin [assignee]
b. John T. Griffin
c. S. Minton; W. Sinnard, 1825

S-0564 535a B:508 X-0270 CLER:WILL
CLER:TATE
a. W-0727 Lieutenant Robert Dandridge
b. Robert Dandridge
c. J. Watkins; Z. Chapman, 1828; William Johnson; E. Stebbins

S-0564 465a B:508 X-0270 CLER:WILL
CLER:TATE
a. W-0727 Lieutenant Robert Dandridge
b. Robert Dandridge
c. None

S-0565 760a B:184 X-0180 WARR:WAYN
a. W-2610 Lieutenant John Foster
b. John H. Foster
c. None

S-0566 1000a B:41 X-0270 BROW:CLAR
CLER:TATE
a. W-0088 Captain Strother Jones
b. Strother Jones
c. T. & J. Gibson; William Shepherd, 1827

S-0567 967a A:332 X-0180 CLIN:CHES*
WARR:WAYN?
a. W-0823 Thomas Richards, 200a
W-1571 William Haley, 233a
W-1393 Robert Brayson, 200a
W-1662 John Gressel, 100a
W-1555 William Morgan, 233a; *all to* Clement Biddle [assignee?]
b. Clement Biddle
c. S. Bates; J. Brown; Noah Haines, 1825
*Source B notation: "By Harveysburg."

S-0569 1000a A:332 X-0180 CLIN:CHES
WARR:WAYN
a. W-0043 Archibald Blair, heir to Captain -- Blair
b. Archibald Blair, heir
c. Jesse Lewis; Ebed Stowel, 1839

S-0570 1000a A:395 X-0180 CLIN:CHES
a. W-2367 Captain John Anderson
b. John Anderson
c. S. Millhouse; A. E. Strickle, 1840

S-0571 767a A:333 X-0180 GREE: --*
CLIN:CHES
a. W-1670 Phillip Barbour, heir to John Robertson; Albert Gallatin [assignee?]
b. Albert Gallatin
c. None
*Source B states "Sugar Cr[eek] & Caesars Cr[eek]."

S-0572 600a D:110 X-0270 CLER:WILL
CLER:TATE
a. W-0745 Peter Casey, heir to Benjamin Casey
b. Peter Casey
c. John Trees

S-0573 200a B:41 X-0270 BROW:CLAR
a. W-2561 Jacob Goldwin?; J. Ellis, assignee
b. Jacob Goulden
c. Unknown

S-0573 200a B:41 X-0270 BROW:CLAR
a. W-1616 Anthony Mullens
b. Anthony Mullens
c. None

S-0573 200a B:42 X-0270 BROW:CLAR
a. W-2680 Edmond Clark; assignee John Lawler; General? -- Clark
b. George R. Clark
c. Unknown; William Neil, 1832

S-0573 200a B:42 X-0270 BROW:CLAR
a. W-1974 Edmund Terrall*
b. Edmund Terrell*
c. -- Neil & -- Leming? [Seming?]; Unknown; William Neil & John Brooks, 1832
*Source B spells Terrill.

S-0573 200a B:42 X-0270 BROW:CLAR
a. W-2484 William Tomlin
b. William Tomlin*
c. William Niel**
*Source B notation: "Patented to him 1799."
**So spelled.

S-0574 1000a A:356 X-0180 GREE:SUGA
GREE:CAES
a. W-0013 William Pugh, heir
b. James Poage
c. None

S-0575 1000a A:333 X-0180 CLIN:CHES
WARR:WAYN
a. W-0673 Colonel Abraham Buford
b. Alexander Buford
c. H. Craus; J. Egbert, 1841

S-0575* 82a -- -- PICK: --
a. --
b. John Fowler
c. --
*Shown in Source B only.

S-0577 1300a A:487 X-0660 GREE:XENI GREE:BEAV
a. W-1892 Captain Alexander Parker
b. Alexander Parker
c. None

S-0578 910a A:333 X-0180 WARR:WAYN
a. W-2637 Lieutenant John Eustes*
b. John Eustace*
c. None
*So spelled.

S-0579 1000a B:187 X-0660 GREE:SUGA GREE:BEAV
a. W-0201 Captain Robert Yancy; Wilson C. Pemberton [assignee?]
b. Wilson C. Pemberton
c. None

S-0581 967a A:374 X-0663 CLER:TATE*
a. W-0794 Lieutenant Phillip Clayton
b. Philip Clayton
c. William White; S. G. Clark, 1834; J. Higby, Junior; J. D. Morris, 1835; John Justus; R. McFarland, 1836
*Source B notation: "By Bantam."

S-0582 400a C:23 X-0340 PICK:DARB
a. W-0303 Captain Robert White
b. Robert White
c. M. & S. Hodge; J. D. Lutz, 1838

S-0583 1000a A:333 X-0180 WARR:WAYN CLIN:CHES
a. W-2246 Lieutenant Isaac Webb
b. Isaac Webb
c. Unknown; James A. Scott, 1831

S-0584 1000a B:67 X-0130 HIGH:CONC
a. W-0588 Captain John Gillison
b. John Gillison
c. None

S-0585 1000a A:452 X-0663 CLER:BATA CLER:WILL
a. W-2321 Captain William Parsons
b. William Parsons
c. T. Hopkins; D. Kidd; J. Duckwall, 1826; J. Cochran, heirs

S-0586 1000a A:282 X-0663 CLER:BATA
a. W-1887 Captain Joseph Scott, Junior
b. Joseph Scott, Junior
c. None

S-0587 1000a A:334 X-0660 WARR:WASH
a. W-0012 Joseph Holmes, heir to Lieutenant T? [F?] Holmes; Clement Biddle [assignee?]
b. Clement Biddle
c. Samuel Harper; John Kitchen, 1831; J. Gaunt; S. Rogers; William Watson; E. Stowell, 1840

S-0588 1000a B:40 X-0420 BROW:BYRD
a. W-0069 Captain Philip Slaughter
b. Philip Slaughter
c. J. H. Lockhart; J. H. Johnston, 1842

S-0589 500a B:448 X-0841 ROSS:UNIO ROSS:CONC
a. W-1734 Lieutenant Colonel Richard Taylor
b. Richard Taylor
c. None

S-0590 1000a A:267 X-0660 CLER:MIAM
a. W-0126 Captain John Pryor; John T. Griffin [assignee?]
b. John T. Griffin
c. W. Salter; L. Lane, 1826; D. Linegar? [Sinegar?]

S-0591 1000a B:20 X-0420 ADAM:TIFF ADAM:LIBE
a. W-1347 Lieutenant David Allen; Ambrose Bohanan* [assignee?]
b. Ambrose Bohannon*
c. Arthur McFarland; John Patterson, 1823
*So spelled.

S-0592 1100a A:400 X-0840 ROSS:SCIO
a. W-2372 Samuel Cochran, 200a
W-2371 Zachariah Lewis, 200a
W-2346 John Haley, 200a
W-2344 Nichlas Shores? [Shires?] 200a
W-2343 Hensley Grubbs, 200a
W-2337 W. Anderson, 100a; *all to* William Reynolds [assignee?]
b. William Reynolds
c. Samuel T. Patton; R. Stewart, 1831

S-0593 667a A:267 X-0663 CLER:BATA CLER:WILL*
a. W-0727 Lieutenant Robert Dandridge
b. Robert Dandridge
c. William Jackson; Z. Chapman, 1835; J. G. Smith, 1827
*Source B entry is crossed out.

S-0594 230a C:152 X-1140 PIKE:SUNF
a. W-0290 Captain Abraham Shepherd
b. Abraham Shepherd
c. W. Statham; H. Hempstead; John Machir, heirs; John Anderson, 1833; -- Rees & -- Myre; T. B. Anderson, 1831; Joseph Penniston, 1836

S-0595 100a B:472 X-0420 ADAM:TIFF
a. W-0303 Captain Robert White
b. Robert White
c. L? [S?] Hoge; Thomas Huston, 1838

S-0597 667a A:279 X-0660 CLER:MIAM
a. W-0651 Representative of Lieutenant John White
b. John White
c. A. Magrew? [Megrew?]; Henry Reest, 1824; A. McGuire, Junior; Shed Lane, 1826; H. Rush; R. Tweed, 1826; A. Megrew, heirs; Jona[than?] Megrew, 1830

S-0598 1000a A:487 X-0660 GREE:SUGA WARR:WAYN
a. W-0342 Lieutenant Albert Russell
b. Albert Russell
c. Daniel Jones; William Sinnard, 1831; S. Rogers, 1836

S-0599 1333a A:462 X-0841 ROSS:CONC ROSS:DEER
a. W-0744 Ensign Joseph Vanmeter
b. Joseph Vanmeter*
c. John Shepherd, 1824; T. Arrohead? 1827; Simon Taylor
*Source B spells Vanmetre.

S-0601 1000a B:118 X-0340 FRAN:PLEA
a. W-0744 Ensign Joseph Vanmetre
b. Oliver Towles*
c. None
*Source B spells Towls.

S-0602 1000a A:461 X-0841 ROSS: --* FAYE:WAYN
a. W-2330 John Depriest; assignees D. Shepherd, William Hendrick, 100a
W-2325 John Depriest; assignees W. Bowman, William Hendrick, 200a
W-2333 Elias Hubbard; William Hendrick [assignee?] 100a
W-2306 Thomas Stape, William Hendrick [assignee?] 200a
W-2054 Samuel Griffin; assignees Thomas Becker? William Hendrick, 100a
W-2334 Beverly Spence; William Hendrick [assignee?] 100a
W-2412 John Depriest; assignee T. Graves; William Hendrick, 100a
b. Richard Archer
c. None
*Source B does not mention Ross County.

S-0603 990a B:184 X-0740 GREE:XENI
a. W-0242 Captain George Gray
b. George Gray
c. None

S-0604 1000a A:461 X-0841 ROSS:CONC FAYE: --*
a. W-2443 Captain William Pierce
b. William Pierce
c. T. Arrohood? [Arrohead?] 1827
*Source B does not mention Fayette County.

S-0605 666a B:309 X-0740 GREE:XENI
a. W-1868 James Culvertson*
b. James Culbertson*
c. None
*So spelled.

S-0605* 800a B:309 X-0740 GREE:XENI
a. W-1868 James Culvertson**
b. James Culbertson**
c. None
**See also* S-616.
**So spelled.

S-0606 450a C:323 X-0360 ROSS:UNIO ROSS:DEER
a. W-0057 Captain Robert Porterfield
b. Robert Porterfield
c. None

S-0607 1000a A:462 X-0841 FAYE:WAYN FAYE:MADI
a. W-2381 Lieutenant Robert Quarles
b. Robert Quarles
c. None

S-0608 1000a A:254 X-0800 HAMI:ANDE
a. W-0301 Captain Abraham Hite
b. Captain Abraham Hite
c. None

S-0609 1000a A:255 X-0260 HAMI:ANDE
a. W-1386 Major Joseph Eggleston
b. Joseph Eggleston
c. None

S-0610 600a C:44 X-0660 GREE:MIAM*
a. W-0194 James Galt
b. James Galt
c. None
*Source B notation: "By Clifton."

S-0611 1000a B:119 X-0660 GREE:MIAM
a. W-0811 Captain Robert Randolph
b. Robert Randolph
c. None

S-0612 1000a A:520 X-0663 BROW:PERR*
a. W-0207 Robert Gibins** heir of Major E. Dickinson
b. Heir of Robert Gibbons**
c. None
*Source B notation: "Cedarville."
**So spelled.

S-0613 1000a A:520 X-0663 BROW:PERR*
a. W-0073 Captain Samuel Hogg; Colonel Edward Carrington [assignee?]
b. Edward Carrington
c. David Johnson, 1823; Joel Carless? [Canless?] 1826; Daniel Fox; A. White; D. G. Devore, 1842
*Source B notation: "Fayetteville."

S-0614 444a A:424 X-1000 SCIO:UNIO
a. W-2411 Lieutenant John Linton
b. John Linton
c. None

S-0615 1000a B:119 X-0660 CLAR:GREE GREE:ROSS*
a. W-2547 Lieutenant William Fitzhugh
b. William Fitzhugh
c. None
*Not listed in Source A.

S-0616* 500a B:309 X-0740 GREE:XENI
a. W-1868 James Culvertson**
b. James Culbertson**
c. None
*See also S-605.
**So spelled.

S-0618 2000a A:263 X-0260 HAMI:ANDE
a. W-0638 Captain Robert Morrow
b. Robert Morrow
c. H. Abbot; William Orr, 1826; S. Crosby; G. W. Jones, 1827; Robert? Hutchinson; Samuel Phares, 1830

S-0619 1000a A:533 X-0660 CLIN:WASH
a. W-0152 Captain Lieutenant Thomas Dix
b. Thomas Dix
c. None

S-0620 1333a A:256 X-0260 HAMI:ANDE
a. W-0209 Colonel Theodorick Bland
b. Colonel Theodorick Bland
c. John Maddox; William Orr, 1826

S-0621 890a B:523 X-0340 PICK:DARB PICK:MUHL
a. W-1451 Lieutenant Charles Jones
b. Charles Jones
c. James Kepler; W. P. Darst & P. N. White, 1840; J. Older, 1842

S-0622 1333a B:186 X-0806 BROW:LEWI
a. W-2025 Major James Knox
b. James Knox
c. Samuel Hannah; D. G. Devore, 1839; J. S. Beasley, 1841

S-0623 300a B:62 X-0360 ROSS:UNIO
a. W-2518 Lieutenant James Brodus
b. James Brodus
c. None

S-0624 515a B:251 X-0660 HAMI:ANDE
a. W-2120 Captain Anthony Singleton
b. Anthony Singleton
c. None

S-0625 1000a A:531 X-0660 CLIN:UNIO
a. W-0125 Captain Lieutenant Thomas Fenn
b. Thomas Fenn
c. None

S-0626 1150a B:275 X-1130 FAYE:CONC
a. W-2256 Captain William Barrett
b. William Barrett
c. Adam Cayler; A. Latham, 1825; B. Latham

S-0627 1000a B:54 X-1000 ROSS:UNIO*
a. W-0345 Captain Arthur Lind; John Fowler [assignee]
b. John Fowler
c. None
*Source B notation: "Andersonville."

S-0628 1000a A:463 X-0841 FAYE:MADI
a. W-2117 Captain John B. Johnson
b. John B. Johnson
c. None

S-0630* 1110a A:444 X-0800 BROW:LEWI
a. W-0347 Major David Stephenson
b. David Stephenson
c. Thomas Brade? [Brude?]; Joshua Inskeep, 1838
*See also S-1058.

S-0631 500a A:310 X-0660 CLER:MIAM WARR: --*
a. W-2425 Stephen Petters, heir to John Petters; William Hendrick [assignee?]
b. Joseph Carrington
c. W. Simonton; Samuel Paxton, 1840; John Seirs; John Bills, 1831
*Source B does not mention Warren County.

S-0633 1000a A:461 X-0841 FAYE:WAYN
a. W-0115 Major William Moseley*
b. William Mosley*
c. None
*So spelled.

S-0634 1000a A:387 X-0841 ROSS:CONC ROSS:TWIN
a. W-0194 James Galt
b. James Galt
c. James Maxfield; J. Tarlton; H. White; Robert? Stewart, 1830

S-0635 1000a A:388 X-0841 ROSS:TWIN
a. W-2631 Captain James Grey*
b. James Gray*
c. Joseph? [James?] Wright; William Piley, 1823; George Denney; L? [S?] Lewis, 1824

S-0636 1000a A:399 X-0841 ROSS:CONC ROSS:TWIN
a. W-2637 Lieutenant John Eustes*
b. John Eustace*
c. None
*So spelled.

S-0637 1000a A:255 X-0260 HAMI:ANDE CLER:UNIO
a. W-0132 Major William Taylor
b. Major William Taylor
c. John Jolly; S. Lane, 1827; Shadrack Lane; Robert McFarland; W. Porter; W. Hulick, 1837; Reynolds & Ward; G. V. Witham, 1839; John Tuttle

S-0638 667a A:507 X-0840 FAYE:WAYN ROSS: --*
a. W-1677 Lieutenant William Winston; John Harvie [assignee?]
b. John Harvie**
c. William Knox; James Woods, 1830; J. Vandervender; S. Sollars, 1840; John Sample; James H. Jones, 1841
*Source B does not give township.
**Source B spells Harvey.

S-0639 667a B:149 X-0663 CLER:WILL
a. W-0414 Lieutenant William Robertson
b. William Robertson
c. None

S-0640 666a A:277 X-0800 BROW:HUNT ADAM: --*
a. W-0323 Lieutenant Robert Green
b. Robert Green
c. Allen Butt, 1826; Robert Greers? [Green?]; M. Weaver; J. S. Davis, 1828; James Lowden, 1830
*Source B does not give township.

S-0641 1400a A:351 X-0420 BROW:BYRD ADAM: --*
a. W-0688 Lieutenant Colonel Samuel Hopkins
b. Samuel Hopkins
c. Jonas Sergeant; M. Thomb, 1823
*Source B does not mention Adams County.

S-0642 1049a A:387 X-0841 ROSS:CONC
a. W-2273 Captain Thomas Buckner
b. Thomas Buckner
c. None

S-0644 1000a D:249 X-1005 HARD:HALE
a. W-0139 Lieutenent Markes Vandewall
b. James Taylor
c. None

S-0646 1300a A:242 X-0800 CLER:MONR CLER:OHIO
a. W-1892 Captain Alexander Parker
b. Alexander Parker
c. J. Bettle; W. Wainwright, 1826; William Lytle; John Lakin? [Sakin?] 1825; R. M. Michael; John Duckwall, 1826; H. Brainam; S. G. Clark, 1835

S-0647 1000a A:459 X-0840 HIGH:MADI
a. W-1936 Captain Reuben Taylor
b. John Watts
c. A. Vurlgamore?; T. M. Sanders, 1826; A. Murray, heirs; J? Coffee, Junior, 1842

S-0648 1500a A:459 X-0840 HIGH:MADI FAYE:WAYN
a. W-0905 Lieutenant Colonel Burges* Ball
b. Burgess* Ball
c. William Cochran; Joseph? [James?] Jones; George Douglas; John L. Taylor, 1831 (Fayette County)
*So spelled.

S-0650 950a A:459 X-0840 HIGH:MADI
a. W-2272 Captain Callohill Minnis
b. Callohill Minnis
c. R. Means; J. A. Trimble, 1824; John Hogsett? [Hoglett?] 1836

S-0651 1000a A:399 X-0420 ADAM:SPRI ADAM:LIBE
a. W-2038 William Case; William Holliday [assignee?] 200a
W-2043 Benjamin McDonald; William Holliday [assignee?] 200a
W-2042 John Lowe; William Holliday [assignee?] 200a
W-2040 Benjamin Wyne; William Holliday [assignee?] 200a
W-2276 James Murray; William Holliday [assignee] 200a
b. William Holliday
c. None

S-0653 1000a A:457 X-0840 ROSS:BUCK ROSS:PAIN
a. W-2321 Captain William Parsons
b. William Parsons
c. None

S-0654 1000a B:435 X-1000 PICK:SCIO
a. W-2012 Major General Charles Scott; Stephen T. Mason [Assignee?] 600a?
W-0715 William Perry; Stephen T. Mason [assignee?] 100a
W-0767 Michael Smith; Stephen T. Mason [assignee?] 200a
W-1738 David Hull; Stephen T. Mason [assignee?] 100a
b. Stephen T. Mason
c. Richard Douglas, 1831; John Diffenbaugh, 1837

S-0657 1000a A:507 X-0840 ROSS:PAIN
a. W-0052 Lieutenant Matthew Clay
b. Matthew Clay
c. Walter Dun; Peter Douglas, 1836

S-0658 2000a A:508 X-0840 FAYE:WAYN
a. W-1619 Doctor George Munroe*
b. George Monroe*
c. John Buck, Senior; Samuel Buck, 1825; James M. Broom; R. Douglas, 1826; Peter Douglas, 1829; George Monroe; -- Phelps & -- Woods, 1828; James Wood, 1830
*So spelled.

S-0659 2222a A:234 X-0800 CLER:WASH*
a. W-0020 Brigadier General Daniel Morgan
b. General Daniel Morgan
c. Martha Gwinn and/or David [Gwinn]; R. McFarland, 1837; J. G. Gilfillin; Hy Mains; John Fletcher
*Source B notation: "Neville."

S-0660 1500a A:501 X-0840 FAYE:WAYN
a. W-2279 Colonel Christian Febiger
b. Christian Febiger
c. Chrisley Miller; Nathaniel Jones; James Wood; William Miller; J. Sellers, 1829; Gerham Anderson; Robert Burnett, 1838

S-0661 1000a A:465 X-0840 FAYE:WAYN FAYE:GREE
a. W-0456 Captain Lieutenant William F. Gaines; Henry Gaines [assignee?]
b. Henry Gaines
c. John Clousen? [Clouser?]; J. Melliken, 1823; Thomas Hewitt; Hump[hrey?] Fullerton, 1825; Joseph? [James?] Y. Green, 1831

S-0663 5000a A:465 X-0840 FAYE:UNIO FAYE:WAYN FAYE:GREE
a. W-0104 Major General Baron -- Steuben
b. Major General -- Steuben
c. Agnes Hathaway; W. Loofboro, 1823; John McFarland; Nancy Hathaway; R. Waddle, 1827; J. McKay; James Woods, 1828

S-0664 800a A:413 X-1120 BROW:FRAN BROW:PLEA
a. W-0021* --
b. John Crawford, heir
c. John Hall; Allen Butt & J. Woods, 1826; G. Poage; S. King, 1827; S. Robinson; -- Hill & -- Slayton? 1829; John Hall, heirs; James Wood, 1832; William Masterson; W. Hewitt, 1833; N. H. Robinson; R. McKnight, 1837; Samuel King; John Abbot, 1831
*This warrant not listed in Source C.

S-0666 1000a A:225 X-0660 HAMI:ANDE CLER:UNIO
a. W-0638 Captain Robert Morrow
b. Robert Morrow
c. None

S-0668 1000a B:191 X-0340 PICK:JACK
a. W-0846 Captain Presley Thornton
b. Presley Thornton
c. None

S-0669 600a A:507 X-0840 FAYE:WAYN
a. W-1471 Thomas Aubany; Daniel Clark [assignee?] 200a
W-1160 Patrick Carney; N. Johnson; Daniel Clark [assignee?] 200a
W-1626 Matthew Ogden; N. Johnson; Daniel Clark [assignee?] 200a
b. Daniel Clark
c. None

S-0669 400a A:510 X-0840 ROSS:BUCK FAYE: --*
a. W-1035 Thomas Wood; James Dougherty [assignee?]
b. James Doherty
c. None
*Source B does not mention Fayette County and township.

S-0670* 1000a A:508 X-0840 FAYE:WAYN
a. W-1425 John Knight; David Nisbett [assignee?] 100a
W-1337 Joseph Clayton; David Nisbett [assignee?] 200a
W-1231 Georg Geig? [Grig?]**; David Nisbett [assignee?] 200a
W-1326 John Berro?; David Nisbett [assignee?] 200a
W-1319 Richard Skinner; David Nisbett [assignee?] 100a
W-0710 Cole Robinson, heir to William Robinson; David Nisbett [assignee?] 200a
b. David Nesbitt***
c. None
*Source B notation: "Not patented."
**W-1231 was also issued to Andrew Cypress; Cadwallader Wallace [assignee?] for 200a.
***So spelled.

S-0671 300a D:107 X-0420 ADAM:SPRI ADAM:LIBE
a. W-0941 William Hicks; William Holliday [assignee?] 100a
W-0976 Solomon Bishop; William Holliday [assignee?] 100a
W-1867 William Jais? [Inis?]; William Holliday [assignee?] 100a
b. William Holliday
c. None

S-0671 600a B:466 X-0420 ADAM:LIBE
a. W-0931 Absalom Brown; William Hickman, Junior [assignee?] 100a
W-0974 Joseph Murdock; William Hickman [assignee?] 100a
W-0955 William Dollar? [Dallas?]; William Hickman, Junior [assignee?] 100a
W-0824 Thomas Rycroft; William Hickman, Junior [assignee?] 100a
W-0909 Joshua Buckley; William Hickman, Junior [assignee?] 200a
b. William Hickman
c. John Machir; -- Hickman & -- Holliday; J. L? [S?] Francis, 1827

S-0672 100a B:525 X-0420 ADAM:SPRI
a. W-2664 George Maples
b. George Maples
c. John Machir; William Bell

S-0673 667a B:188 X-0840 FAYE:WAYN
a. W-2381 Lieutenant Robert Quarles
b. Robert Quarles
c. None

S-0674 662a A:268 X-0663 CLER:UNIO
a. W-0052 Lieutenant Matthew Clay
b. Matthew Clay
c. Samuel Eveart; D. Hawkins, 1824; Thomas Hawkins; Samuel Vail, 1825; J. & N? Maguire; John Maguire

S-0675* 1000a B:400 X-1000 DELA:THOM**
a. W-0172 Lieutenant Colonel Jonathan Clark
b. Johnathan*** Clark
c. G. C. Knight; Isaac Meed
*This survey entered out of sequence on page 113 of Source A.
**Source B notation: "By Middletown."
***So spelled.

S-0676 667a A:451 X-0663 CLER:UNIO
a. W-2291 Lieutenant Samuel Seldon
b. Samuel Seldon
c. John O'Bannon; John Day, 1824; John O'Bannon, heirs; E. Day, 1826; W. F. H. Veitch, 1835

S-0678 1000a A:458 X-0840 ROSS:BUCK
a. W-1849 Major John Belfield
b. John Belfield
c. T. Adams; A. Cochran, 1842

S-0680 1000a A:466 X-0840 FAYE:UNIO
a. W-1438 James Coleman; Clement Biddle [assignee?] 400a
W-1544 Robert Owl; Clement Biddle [assignee?] 200a
W-0395 Joseph Locke; Clement Biddle [assignee?] 100a
W-0625 John Ross; Clement Biddle [assignee?] 200a
W-0328 Edward Clarke; Clement Biddle [assignee?] 100a
b. Clement Biddle
c. James Kellar; W. Loofboro, 1827; John Thomas, heirs; Charles Arthur, 1832; Perry Coen?; J. Cord; E. Huston

S-0681 1667a A:442 X-0665 CLER:STON
a. W-2305 Lieutenant John Linton
b. John Linton
c. G. W. McCormick; D. C. Richardson; J. Noe; A. Hill, 1835

S-0683* 1000a A:466 X-0840 FAYE:UNIO
a. W-0397 Captain Drury Ragsdale
b. Drury Ragsdale
c. John Ross; D. McLain & W. Loofboro, 1827; John McMinnis, heirs; J. Hinton, 1832; James Wallace, heirs; Norman F. Jones, 1834; Mag. Smith; John L. Taylor, 1831; John Rankin, 1830
*Source B notation: "Not patented."

S-0684 1494a A:452 X-1004 X-0130 ADAM:SCOT
a. W-0818 Lieutenant J. William Ludeman
b. William Ludiman*
c. Peter Machir; Joseph Riggs, 1823
*So spelled.

S-0688 1000a B:20 X-0663 CLIN:CLAR CLIN:JEFF
a. W-2323 Captain Colin Cocke? [Cooke?]
b. Colen Cocke*
c. None
*Source B spells Coke.

S-0690 4300a B:241 X-0363 ROSS:UNIO ROSS:CONC ROSS:DEER
a. W-1893 Doctor William McMeehin*
b. William McMeeken*
c. None
*So spelled.

S-0693 1000a B:189 X-0840 FAYE:UNIO FAYE:CONC
a. W-0811 Captain Robert Randolph
b. Robert Randolph
c. None

S-0695 1000a A:467 X-0840 ROSS:BUCK
a. W-1450 Major Samuel Finley
b. Samuel Finley
c. None

S-0698 1000a A:433 X-0660 CLIN:RICH
a. W-0172 Lieutenant Colonel Jonathan Clark
b. Jonathan Clark
c. Philip Grandin; B. Hinkson, 1823

S-0699 1000a A:534 X-0660 CLIN:UNIO CLIN:VERN CLIN:WASH
a. W-0105 Doctor John Roberts
b. John Roberts
c. Ez. Garrison; E. O? McGregor; Eli McGregor; Josiah Biggs; Thomas Osburn; Joseph W. Hackney, 1841; William Bloom

S-0700 4000a A:296 X-0424 BROW:BYRD* BROW:JACK BROW:FRAN
a. W-0599 Captain Thomas Fox
b. Thomas Fox
c. Ab. Shepherd; William Shepherd; Adam Sellman; D. Barney, 1826; John Baird, 1833; Job Leroy; W. Hewit, 1835; James Baird; R. W. Clark, 1836 (Clermont County); Eli Collins; John S. Beasley, 1839
*Source B notation: "Russelville."

S-0701 700a A:486 X-0660 GREE:BEAV GREE:XENI
a. W-2025 Major James Knox
b. James Knox
c. None

S-0705 667a D:497 X-0663 CLER:WILL
a. W-2121 Lieutenant William Whitaker
b. William Whitaker
c. None

S-0706 200a A:443 X-0660 HAMI:ANDE
a. W-2049 James Figgins
b. James Figgins*
c. None
*Source B spells Feagins.

S-0706 200a A:443 X-0660 HAMI:ANDE CLER: --*
a. W-2300 John McDowell
b. John McDowell
c. None
*Source B does not mention Clermont County.

S-0706 95a A:443 X-0660 HAMI:ANDE CLER: --
a. W-2297 James Peyton
b. James Peyton
c. None

S-0706 100a A:443 X-0660 HAMI:ANDE CLER: --*
a. W-2296 Robert Brown
b. Robert Brown
c. None
*Source B does not mention Clermont County.

S-0706* 200a A:443 X-0660 HAMI:ANDE CLER:--**
a. W-2048 Jacob Fear
b. Jacob Fear
c. Cyrus Broadwell; Lewis Broadwell, 1842
*Source B notation: "Not patented."
**Source B does not mentioned Clermont County.

S-0706 200a A:443 X-0660 HAMI:ANDE
a. W-2294 John Brown
b. John Brown
c. None

S-0707* 1380a B:47 X-0840 HIGH:FAIR CLIN:GREE
a. W-0785 John Barnett** heir to W. Bernard
b. John Bernard
c. James Fisher; James Smith, 1830
*Source B notation: "Not patented."
**So spelled.

S-0710 1000a A:310 X-0790 CLER:GOSH
a. W-2256 Captain William Barrett
b. William Barrett
c. J. Williams, 1839

S-0711 1000a A:530 X-0660 CLIN:GREE
a. W-2443 Captain William Pierce
b. William Pierce
c. None

S-0712 850a B:190 X-1300 BROW:PLEA
a. W-0649 Captain Lawrence Trent
b. Lawrence Trent
c. Z. Riley; A. Wood, 1829; M. Levi; D. Johnson, 1839; D. G. Devore, 1841

S-0713 667a B:157 X-0840 MADI:STOK FAYE: --*
a. W-2642 Captain Francis Cowherd
b. Francis Cowherd**
c. None
*Source B does not mention Fayette County.
**Source B lists James Cowherd.

S-0714 1525a A:452 X-0570 CLER:WASH
a. W-2576 Captain Cadwallader Jones
b. Cadwallader Jones
c. James Holmes; F. Sapp, 1823; D. Duff; A. C. Medary, 1842

S-0715 450a B:156 X-0570 CLER:WASH
a. W-2433 Lewis Starke, assignee of B. Starke, W. Starke
b. Lewis Starke
c. P. Casat; T. Rush, 1836

S-0717 1000a B:13 X-1000 FRAN:FRAN
a. W-0216 Doctor John Knight
b. John Knight
c. William Harrison, heirs; Jacob Grub, 1826; Jonas Smith; Peter Sells, 1826; Unknown; John Macey, 1827; Nicholas Demerast [*also* Demarest]; Elijah Bachus, 1833; William McMullen; A. Brotherlin [*also* Brotherton]; L Sullivant, 1832

S-0720 1000a A:311 X-0790 CLER:MIAM
a. W-1476 Captain Leroy Edwards
b. Leroy Edwards
c. S. Hutchins; F. Motsinger, 1829

S-0721 1000a A:460 X-0840 HIGH:MADI
a. W-1386 Major Joseph Eggleston
b. Joseph Eggleston
c. Guzzie Mathew

S-0722 1200a A:243 X-0800 CLER:OHIO
a. W-0347 Major David Stephenson
b. David Stephenson
c. None

S-0723 655a C:511 X-0570 CLER:WASH
a. W-0064 Thomas Bowne
b. Thomas Bowne
c. J. Abrams; D. W. Shotwell, 1823; John Graham; John Duckwall; W. Dun; M. Mullen, 1842

S-0724 1000a B:10 X-0130 ADAM:JEFF
a. W-1296 Timothy Peyton, heir to V. Peyton
b. Timothy Peyton
c. T. James & Company; Thomas Huston, 1837

S-0725 1000a B:420 X-0570 CLER:WASH
a. W-0681 Captain Lieutenant William Brownlee
b. William Brownlee
c. Elizabeth McKinley; William Curry, 1831

S-0727 1000a A:435 X-0660 CLIN:RICH
a. W-1756 Richard Murry; Clement Biddle [assignee?] 100a
W-1370 John Proctor; William Richardson & George Richardson [assignees?] 200a*
W-1891 Thomas Hoodd; Clement Biddle [assignee?] 400a
W-1789 James Prichard; Clement Biddle [assignee?] 200a
W-1906 John Morris; Clement Biddle [assignee?] 100a
b. Clement Biddle
c. D. Reed & S. Beck**; Samuel Buck** 1831
*See also S-0768, where this warrant is apparently used a second time!
**So spelled.

S-0728 1000a A:283 X-0570 CLER:FRAN CLER:WASH
a. W-0649 Captain Lawrence Trent
b. Captain Lawrence Trent
c. J. S. Woodmansee; T. Rush, 1836

S-0729 1200a E:295 X-0840 CLIN:RICH*
a. W-2377 Doctor John Trezevant; John Tench, Wallace McArthur, & Thomas J. McArthur [assignees?]
b. William Anderson, *et al***
c. William Rhonemous [Heironimus?]; -- Tench, heirs; Josephus Reed & Cyrus [Reed]; -- Rhonemus & -- Read, 1827; T. J. McArthur; William P. Hunnicut, 1830; C. P? Gallagher, 1834; John Cole, 1837; S. McCane, 1836; S. McCune; Edwin Wiley, 1838; William David; G. Fallis, 1840; William Cue; Patrick Douglas, 1831; John? Palmer; John Reed, 1831
*Source B notation: "Claysville."
**Source B says John Tench.

S-0730 1000a A:434 X-0660 CLIN:RICH
a. W-2235 Lieutenant Nathaniel Anderson
b. Nathaniel Anderson
c. None

S-0732 1000a A:434 X-0660 CLIN:RICH
a. W-1199 Captain William Lindsay
b. William Lindsay
c. Robert Stark; Cyrus Reed, 1824; R. B. Stark; A. Grantham, 1837; A. E. Strickle, 1837

S-0733 1275a B:65 X-0130 HIGH:CONC
a. W-1912 Doctor Thomas Christie
b. Thomas Christie
c. H. Massie; G. W. Barriere, 1826

S-0735 1000a B:426 X-0570 CLER:FRAN CLER:WASH
a. W-1383 Lieutenant Robert Kirk
b. Robert Kirk
c. R. W. Smith

S-0736 1000a A:444 X-0660 CLIN:RICH
a. W-0132 Major William Taylor
b. William Taylor
c. None

S-0737 667a A:331 X-0660 WARR:WASH
a. W-0701 Lieutenant Luke Cannon
b. Luke Cannon
c. None

S-0738 1333a A:464 X-0840 FAYE:WAYN
a. W-0783 Major William Cunningham; John T. Griffin [assignee?]
b. John T. Griffin
c. Mark Morris, 1824; J. King, 1827

S-0739 1000a A:464 X-0840 FAYE:WAYN
a. W-0785 John Barnett* heir to W. Bernard
b. John Bernard* heir
c. Ab. Collins; James? Jameson, 1826; J. Culber?; N. Torbert? 1827; James Barker
*So spelled.

S-0741 1667a B:275 X-0840 HIGH:LIBE HIGH:UNIO
a. W-2647 William Worsham, heir to J. W[orsham]
b. William Worsham
c. W. Maxley; J. Jones, 1824

S-0743 1000a A:436 X-0660 CLIN:RICH
a. W-0814 David Walker, heir to Captain -- Walker
b. David Walker
c. William Walker; John Coulter, 1825; J. Douglas; A. E. Strickle, 1838; D. Padgett; P. S? [L?] Wilson, 1840

S-0746 667a B:170 X-0420 BROW:BYRD
a. W-2669 Lieutenant Daniel Ball
b. Daniel Ball
c. J. Hardesty; J. Meharry, 1829

S-0747 800a A:534 X-0660 CLIN:UNIO
a. W-0105 Doctor John Roberts
b. John Roberts
c. -- Anderson & -- Carrington; M. Howard, 1826; Thomas Osburn; J. W. Hackney, 1841

S-0748* 1400a -- -- --
a. --
b. John Hart
c. None
*Entry stricken out of Source B; does not appear in Source A.

S-0749 1000a A:436 X-0660 CLIN:RICH
a. W-0012 Joseph Holmes, heir to Lieutenant T? [F?] Holmes; Clement Biddle [assignee?]
b. Edward Dowse
c. Albert Gallatin; Isaac Shepherd; Jehu Reed, 1835; A. E. Strickle, 1836; J. Darbyshire, *et al*

S-0750* 100a B:136 X-1300 HIGH:CLAY BROW:WASH
a. W-0898 James Anderson
b. James Anderson
c. W. Barlow; F. Bingaman, 1823; J. Hotsefeller? [*also* Hutsenpellar] 1825; G. W. Barriere, 1832; Unknown; W. Vance, 1835; James Taylor; J. Hogsett, 1836 (Highland County)
*Source B notation: "Not patented."

S-0750 200a B:136 X-1300 HIGH:CLAY BROW:WASH BROW:PIKE
a. W-0888 John Williams
b. John Williams*
c. None
*Source B notation: "Patented [to] Jasper Shotwell, 25 Aug 1801."

S-0750 400a B:136 X-1300 HIGH:CLAY BROW:GREE
a. W-0887 John Williams
b. John Williams
c. None

S-0750* 200a -- -- BROW:GREE
a. --
b. Thomas French*
c. Jonathan Benjamin; George Benjamin, 1826; David Johnson, 1823
*Mentioned in Source B only, which also says: "Patented [to] Fred Bingaman."

S-0750 100a B:136 X-1300 HIGH:CLAY BROW:GREE
a. W-0886 John Farrell
b. John Farwell*
c. F. Bingaman, 1828
*Source B notation: "Patented Fassel? [Farrel?] 2 Jul 1813; delivered [to] General Taylor."

S-0753 200a B:268 X-0840 HIGH:UNIO
a. W-2404 John Weaver
b. John Weaver
c. None

S-0753 200a B:274 X-0840 HIGH:UNIO
a. W-2165 Robert Wallerson*
b. Robert Watterson*
c. D. Smith, 1829
*So spelled.

S-0753 200a B:274 X-0840 HIGH:UNIO
a. W-2361 Thomas Wotten
b. Thomas Wotten*
c. Thomas Walton; Dorsey Fenner, 1831
*Source B may read Wooten; says "not patented."

S-0753 100a B:274 X-0840 HIGH:UNIO
a. W-2134 Peter Waterfield
b. Peter Waterfield
c. None

S-0755 1000a B:21 X-0340 PICK:MONR
a. W-0242 Captain George Gray
b. George Gray
c. None

S-0756 900a A:311 X-0420 X-0950 BROW:UNIO
a. W-2402 Lieutenant Jordan Harris
b. Jordan Harris
c. Elias Lane; G. W. King, 1826

S-0757 1200a A:467 X-0840 FAYE:UNIO*
a. W-2417 Colonel Benjamin Temple
b. Benjamin Temple
c. None
*Source B notation: "Washington."

S-0758 1000a A:437 X-0840 CLIN:RICH
a. W-2133 Captain Nathaniel Burwell
b. Nathaniel Burwell
c. Jesse Hadley, 1835; Jacob Hawes; George Fallis, 1840

S-0760 1000a B:174 X-0660 GREE:SUGA GREE:XENI
a. W-0145 Captain William Fowler
b. William Fowler
c. None

S-0761 1333a A:283 X-0570 CLER:TATE CLER:FRAN CLER:WASH
a. W-1273 John Burton, heir to H. Burton
b. John Burton
c. B. Parish; W. Pollard, 1839

S-0762 1000a A:284 X-0570 CLER:TATE
a. W-0614 Captain Henry Moss
b. Captain Henry Moss
c. James Machir; John Bogges [*also* Boggs] 1824; S. Tarr; D. Hawkins? [Hankins?] 1823; James Daugherty

S-0763 1400a A:444 X-0660 CLIN:RICH
a. W-0018 Colonel Presley Nevill
b. Presley Nevill*
c. None
*Source B spells Neville.

S-0764 1000a B:197 X-0666 CLIN:MARI WARR:SALE CLER:WAYN BROW: --*
a. W-0297 Colonel James Wood; Andrew Epple [assignee?]
b. Andrew Epple
c. James Taylor
*Source B does not mention Brown County; but does mention "Woodville."

S-0765 1333a A:274 X-0570 CLER:WASH CLER:MONR
a. W-0315 Lieutenant Lipscomb Norvell
b. Lipscomb Norvell
c. E. Boring?; E. Salt, 1824; H. Carter; J. Salt & George T. Cotton; J. Taylor; F. Everhart? 1824

S-0766 1400a A:445 X-0660 CLIN:RICH
a. W-0018 Colonel Presley Nevill
b. Presley Nevill*
c. Obadiah Floyd; J. B. Leamons [*also* Semans] 1826; John Herter; William Mellikan; John Watts; Samuel Winston, 1826; Warren Sabin, 1831; William Hallam; C. B. Harlan, 1831; E. H. Bradbury, 1831; John Reed; Levi Gustin, 1834; Thomas Stitt; M? M? [W? W?] Hale, 1837; William P. Hunnicut; A. E. Stricklen? 1837; J. Miller & W. Williamson; A. E. Strickle, 1838; J. Darbyshire, 1839; J. Fyfe, 1842
*Source B spells Neville.

S-0767 1400a B:22 X-0340 PICK:MONR
a. W-0937 Colonel John Nevill
b. John Nevill*
c. None
*Source B spells Neville.

S-0768 1000a A:272 X-0570 CLER:TATE
a. W-0433 Jesse New; William & George Richardson [assignees?] 100a
W-1370 John Proctor; William & George Richardson [assignees?] 200a*
W-1392 Richard Cooper; William & George Richardson [assignees?] 233a
W-1760 Jesse Hughes; William & George Richardson [assignees?] 100a
W-1766 William Atkinson; William & George Richardson [assignees?] 200a
W-1858 John Biswell; David Anderson [assignee?] 400a
b. William Richardson & George Richardson
c. None
**See also* S-0727, where this warrant is used a second time. Note, likewise, that total acreage of the warrants exceeds the amount needed for this survey, possibly W-1370 or W-1392 belongs elsewhere.

S-0770 1000a A:355 X-0180 CLIN:CHES WARR: --*
a. W-2381 Lieutenant Robert Quarles
b. Robert Quarles
c. James Brown; J. Fife, 1832; James Fyfe; A. Hill, 1839; Thomas Gaddis, Junior; Allison Hill, 1839; A. E. Strickle, 1841
*Source B does not list Warren County.

S-0771 800a A:334 X-0180 WARR:WAYN WARR:WASH
a. W-1764 John Brett; Doctor James Currie [assignee?] 200a
W-1755 Luke Bullen; Doctor James Currie [assignee?] 400a
W-1802 John Hayles; Doctor James Currie [assignee?] 200a
b. James Currie
c. None

S-0772 700a C:22 X-0640 CLIN:WAYN FAYE: --*
a. W-0243 Lieutenant William Gray
b. William Gray*
c. None
*Source B does not mention Fayette County.
**Source B spells Grey.

S-0773 800a C:361 X-0080 BROW:HUNT ADAM: --
a. W-2648 Lieutenant Zachariah Tatum
b. Zachariah Tatum
c. None

S-0774 1000a A:334 X-0180 WARR:WAYN
a. W-0560 Captain Peter Garland
b. Peter Garland
c. None

S-0775* 1059a B:537 X-0750 LOGA:BOAK UNIO:--**
a. W-1249 Captain Thomas Chilton, heir
b. Thomas Chilton, heir
c. Robert Means; John Liggett, 1834
**See also* S-6155.
**Source B does not mention Union County.

S-0777 1000a A:421 X-0180 CLIN:CHES
a. W-0115 Major William Moseley
b. William Mosley*
c. Ralph Myres; S? [L?] Wilson, 1826; Arza Gaze; J. B. Posey, 1835
*Source B spells Moseley.

S-0778 1000a A:391 X-1000 ROSS:UNIO
a. W-0051 Captain Joseph Scott, Senior
b. Joseph Scott
c. None

S-0779 2000a A:387 X-0841 ROSS:CONC
a. W-0083 [Surgeon] Joseph Davis; Captain Thomas Overton, assignee
b. Thomas Overton
c. None

S-0780 400a A:386 X-000* ROSS:CONC
a. W-0350 Captain Samuel K. Bradford
b. Samuel K. Bradford
c. None
*Source A does not give watercourse.

S-0783 1000a A:241 X-1120 BROW:UNIO BROW:PLEA
a. W-0057 Captain Robert Porterfield
b. Robert Porterfield
c. None

S-0784 1000a B:151 X-0660 GREE:ROSS
a. W-1967 Heir of Captain Henry Fauntleroy
b. Henry Fauntleroy
c. None

S-0785 1000a B:256 X-0190 PIKE:CAMP
a. W-0241 Captain Thomas Barbee
b. Thomas Barbee
c. Peter Spurck, 1833; John Glaze; Samuel Reid, 1833; Caleb Pyles; Legrand Byington, 1839; A. Glaze, heirs; James Wallace, 1841

S-0786 1000a B:151 X-0660 GREE:ROSS
a. W-2433 Lewis Starke, assignee of B. Starke [&] W. Starke
b. Lewis Starke
c. Francis Spencer; David Davis, 1840

S-0787 1400a A:390 X-1000 ROSS:UNIO
a. W-0753 Major John Willis; Clement Biddle [assignee?]
b. Clement Biddle
c. None

S-0788* 1000a E:288 X-0841 ROSS:CONC
a. W-2377 Doctor John Trezevant; John Tench, Wallace McArthur & Thomas J. McArthur [assignees?]
b. Cadwallader Wallace**
c. None
**See also* S-12354.
**Source B says John Tench.

S-0789 1000a A:437 X-0660 CLIN:GREE
a. W-2120 Captain Anthony Singleton
b. Anthony Singleton
c. None

S-0790 1667a A:279 X-1120 BROW:UNIO BROW:PLEA
a. W-0652 Lieutenant David Merriwether
b. David Merriwether
c. Hugh Lemon; C. Snedeker, 1825; George Shultz, 1824; John M. Kirkpatrick, 1831

S-0791 660a A:487 X-0660 WARR:WAYN
a. W-0630 Lieutenant Jacob Brown
b. Jacob Brown
c. None

S-0792 801a C:39 X-0360 ROSS:CONC
a. W-1890 Lieutenant David Walker; Colonel Joseph Jones [assignee?]
b. Joseph Jones
c. August M. Marshall; James S. Swearingen, 1825

S-0793 1000a A:514 X-1170 CLIN:VERN
a. W-1774 Cornet William B. Harrison
b. William B. Harrison
c. None

S-0795 1000a A:391 X-1000 ROSS:UNIO
a. W-2577 Captain Cadwallader Jones
b. Cadwallader Jones
c. None

S-0796 1000a B:61 X-1300 BROW:PLEA BROW:CLAR BROW:SCOT
a. W-2444 Lieutenant Charles Scott
b. Charles Scott, Junior
c. None

S-0798 5333a A:417 X-0130 X-0420 ADAM:LIBE
a. W-0076 Major Thomas Hill
b. Thomas Hill
c. Thomas Holmes; Andrew Ellison, 1826; R. Anderson; S. W. Lafferty for A. Latham, 1840; L. Cole, 1842

S-0799 1200a A:352 X-0420 BROW:BYRD ADAM: --*
a. W-2360 Colonel Charles Harrison
b. Charles Harrison
c. Jonas Sergeant; Hugh Mahary? [Mehary?] 1823
*Source B does not mention Adams County.

S-0800 200a B:273 X-0133 HIGH:BRUS PIKE: --*
a. W-1895 Samuel Jones; David Anderson [assignee?]
b. John Reed
c. J. Machir; Jacob Barger & John Barger, 1824
*Source B does not mention Pike County.

S-0800 200a B:273 X-0133 HIGH: --* PIKE:PERR
a. W-1048 Bryan Gowran; William Richardson [assignee?]
b. William Richardson
c. None
*Source B does not mention Highland County.

S-0800 400a B:273 X-0133 PIKE:PERR
a. W-0890 Anthony Headen; Joseph Richardson [assignee?] 200a
W-1030 William Edmondson; Joseph Richardson [assignee?] 200a
b. Joseph Richardson
c. Unknown; Enoch McChord, 1836

S-0800 200a B:273 X-0133 PIKE:PERR
a. W-1058 James Reynolds; Charles McGinnes [assignee?]
b. Charles McGinnis
c. None

S-0801 490a C:133 X-1001 ROSS:UNIO ROSS:CONC
a. W-1391 Captain Nathaniel Pendleton
b. [Matthew*] Pendleton
c. None
*According to Source B.

S-0802 1000a A:463 X-0840 FAYE:GREE FAYE:CONC
a. W-0056 Captain John Peyton
b. John Peyton
c. Robert Duncan; H. Y. Phelps, 1831

S-0803 1000a C:36 X-0110 UNIO:LEES
a. W-1332 Lieutenant James De la Plane; William Semple [assignee?]
b. William Semple
c. Moses Wright; Benjamin Temple; John R. Parish, 1823; Unknown; S. G. Strong, 1836; Samuel Jameson, 1831

S-0804 1500a A:389 X-0841 ROSS:CONC
a. W-1792 Lieutenant Colonel Edward Carrington
b. Edward Carrington
c. None

S-0805 666a C:52 X-0660 CLAR:GREE CLAR:MADI
a. W-0108? William Green, heir to Lieutenant John Green
b. William Green
c. None

S-0807 1000a A:389 X-0841 ROSS:CONC
a. W-0560 Captain Peter Garland
b. Peter Garland
c. None

S-0808 2000a A:446 X-0660 CLIN:WAYN
a. W-2560 Major Everard Meade
b. Everard Meade
c. Cyrus Reed, Junior; Josephus Reed, 1838; Lewis Vimont; A. E. Strickle, 1837; J. Hadley, Junior, 1840

S-0810 2000a A:464 X-0840 FAYE:UNIO FAYE:WAYN
a. W-0104 Major General Baron -- Steuben
b. Major General -- Steuben
c. James Epex; W. Loofboro, 1827

S-0811 1033a A:447 X-0660 CLIN:RICH CLIN:WAYN
a. W-1252 Joshua Clifton; Edward Dowse [assignee?] 233a
W-1717 Presley Sanders; Edward Dowse [assignee?] 200a
W-1063 James Sweall? [Sewall?]; Edward Dowse [assignee?] 200a
W-2437 Lewis Ford; Zachariah Forrest & Edward Dowse [assignees?] 200a
W-2436 Lewis Ford; Lewis Brandon & Edward Dowse [assignees?] 200a
b. Edward Dowse
c. Andrew Ellison; Jeremiah? Hadley, 1834; H. Higby; A. E. Strickle, 1838; H. Nelson; R. B. Harlan, 1837; -- Browning & -- Stearnes; J. Morris, 1836; S. Kincaid; G. Foos, 1839; W. Oliver; A. Hallam; G. Fallis, 1840

S-0815 1000a A:389 X-0841 ROSS:CONC ROSS:DEER
a. W-0651 Representative of Lieutenant John White
b. John White, heir
c. None

S-0816 810a B:207 X-0660 GREE:ROSS
a. W-2443 Captain William Pierce
b. William Pierce
c. John Haywood; John Andrews, 1837

S-0817* 1000a C:225 X-0180 GREE:CAES GREE:SILV GREE:ROSS
a. W-0206 Captain Samuel Eddens
b. Samuel Eddins**
c. W. Browder; S. W. McCracken, 1823; James Browder; W. Beacham, 1834
*See also S-8380.
**Source B spells Eddings.

S-0818 1000a A:437 X-0660 CLIN:RICH
a. W-2641 Colonel Thomas Gaskins
b. Thomas Gaskins
c. None

S-0820 1050a B:141 X-1301 HIGH:SALE HIGH:CLAY BROW: --*
a. W-1693 Captain Robert Higgins
b. Robert Higgins
c. None
*Source B does not mention Brown County.

S-0822* 1000a -- -- --
a. --
b. David Stephenson
c. --
*Entry crossed out in Source B and does not appear in Source A.

S-0824 726a A:459 X-0840 FAYE:WAYN
a. W-1889 Captain Peter Jones; Colonel Joseph Jones [assignee?]
b. Joseph Jones
c. None

S-0825 1000a B:45 X-0660 WARR:HAMI
a. W-2328 Lieutenant Thomas Martin
b. Thomas Martin
c. Robert Patton; Joel A. Stokes? 1823

S-0827 200a C:276 X-1000 PICK:WAYN
a. W-0291 Captain Henry Bedinger
b. Henry Bedinger
c. G. Horn; J. Hedges, 1828

S-0828 1000a A:334 X-0660 WARR:WASH
a. W-1387 Captain Ferdinand O'Neal
b. Ferdinand O'Neal
c. None

S-0829 1000a C:11 X-0750 X-0110 UNIO:LEES
a. W-0659 Captain Thomas Bowyer
b. Thomas Bowyer
c. Unknown; Manley S. Butler, 1836

S-0830 1000a A:437 X-0660 GREE:SILV CLIN:RICH
a. W-1357 William Ware, 100a
W-1727 Thomas Burk, 100a
W-1744 Mosby Childress, 100a
W-1770 William Smith, 200a
W-0571 Womack Blankenship, 200a
W-0820 James Cooley, 100a
W-0709 Cole Robinson, 200a; *all the above warrants to* Robert Draffen [assignee?]
b. Robert Draffin
c. None

S-0831* 667a -- -- LOGA:PERR
a. --
b. William Sample
c. --
*Apparently not listed in Source A.

S-0834 700a A:233 X-0030 CLER:WASH
a. W-1892 Captain Alexander Parker
b. Alexander Parker
c. -- Pegman? & -- Barkley; S. Weaver, 1826; J. Pigman; A. Stokes, 1835; M. Bonner; George Gregg, 1841

S-0834 700a A:235 X-0030 CLER:WASH
a. W-1892 Captain Alexander Parker
b. Alexander Parker
c. None

S-0835 640a B:222 X-1000 DELA:SCIO
a. W-1623 Lieutenant Javin Miller
b. James Miller
c. L. Sullivant; Lyne Starling, 1826; S. Beattie & M. Beattie, 1839

S-0836 1000a A:438 X-0840 FAYE:JEFF GREE:SILV CLIN:RICH
a. W-0300 Captain Abraham Hite
b. Abraham Hite
c. Amers.? Jackson; J. N. Renton, 1832

S-0837 1400a A:445 X-0840 CLIN:RICH
a. W-0018 Colonel Presley Nevill
b. Presley Nevill*
c. Alexander McLaughlin; Cama? Rigdon, 1824; C. B. Harlan; R. B. Harlan, 1835; J. Tagart, trustee; G. Fallis, 1836; trustee of -- Holmes & -- Rogers; J. Haws & J. Floyd; J. W. Hackney, 1841
*Source B spells Neville; notation: "Sabina."

S-0841 1000a A:438 X-0840 FAYE:JEFF GREE: --* CLIN:RICH
a. W-1792 Lieutenant Colonel Edward Carrington
b. Edward Carrington
c. S. Winston, 1826; John O'Bannon; Samuel McCune, 1829; J. Fife & L. Fitzhugh, 1831
*Source B does not mention Greene County.

S-0842 667a C:30 X-0750 LOGA:PERR LOGA:BOAK
a. W-2211 Lieutenant Daniel Bedinger
b. Daniel Bedinger
c. L. B. Wysong, 1835

S-0843 715a B:187 X-0840 FAYE:UNIO
a. W-2655 William Lawson, heir to C. Lawson
b. William Lawson
c. None

S-0844 1000a F:118 X-0840 CLIN:RICH
a. W-0285 Captain Lieutenant Ambrose Bohannon; Thomas Shaw [assignee?]
b. Griffith Foos*
c. Carter B. Harlan; A. E. Strickle, 1838; E. Woodland; Jeremiah McLane?; Warren Sabin, 1831; Robert Means
*Source B shows Thomas Shaw.

S-0845 2516a A:390 X-1000 ROSS:DEER
a. W-1925* --
b. Francis Gray
c. None
*This warrant number must be in error, as it was issued to James Hawkins for 100a only. *See* S-1233.

S-0846 1000a B:191 X-0840 FAYE:UNIO
a. W-1751 Captain Hughes Woodson
b. Hughes Woodson
c. None

S-0847 1000a A:243 X-0800 CLER:OHIO*
a. W-0198 Captain Robert Beale
b. Robert Beale
c. H. Hardin; J. D. Morris? 1824; S. Palmer; William Wainwright, 1826; E. Roberts; T. Morris, 1823; P. Twiner; R. D. Donham, 1825?; T. Ashburn; J. M? [W?] Brown, 1827; John A. Creekbaum; Robert McFarland, 1841
*Source B notation: "New Richmond."

S-0849 1000a A:435 X-0660 CLIN:GREE
a. W-0753 Major John Willis; Clement Biddle [assignee?]
b. Clement Biddle
c. None

S-0850 500a A:524 X-0663 BROW:PERR
a. W-0075 Lieutenant Benjamin Moseley
b. Benjamin Mosby*
c. James Machir; -- Butt & -- Shepherd, 1823; James Walsh
*Source B spells Moseley.

S-0850 500a A:525 X-0663 BROW:PERR
a. W-0075 Lieutenant Benjamin Moseley
b. Benjamin Mosby*
c. None
*Source B spells Moseley.

S-0851 75a C:382 X-1000 CLER:WASH
a. W-2226 Richard Taylor; George Robertson & Terry Galloway [assignees?]
b. George Robertson
c. None

S-0851* 200a -- -- CLER:WASH
a. --
b. James Robertson
c. None
*Listed in Source B, but not in Source A.

S-0851 200a C:383 X-0030 X-0800 CLER:WASH
a. W-1101 John Riley
b. John Ryly
c. None

S-0851 60a* F:252 X-0030 CLER:WASH
a. W-1022 Jacob Smock
b. Allen Latham*
c. Mary Ogden; A. Latham, 1833; Harvey Irwin, 1835
*Source B says Jacob Smock & otherwise differs in acreage.

S-0851 200a C:382 X-0030 CLER:WASH
a. W-2231 James Robinson
b. James Robertson*
c. None
*Source B says John Spruce.

S-0851 41a* F:201 X-0805 CLER:WASH
a. W-1142 Henry Skinner
b. E. P. Kendrick*
c. None
*Source B says Henry Spencer for 200 acres.

S-0852 1000a B:386 X-1301 HIGH:SALE
a. W-2223 Captain Patrick Carnes
b. Patrick Carnes
c. Samuel Bell, 1828; Thomas Carneal

S-0853 1000a A:435 X-0660 CLIN:GREE
a. W-1663 Samuel Merritt, 100a
W-1586 John Davis, heir to John Davis, 100a
W-1618 John Brown, 200a
W-1779 James Dunn, 200a
W-1630 Thomas Tapley, 200a
W-1645 Thomas Hill, 200a; *all of the above warrants to* Clement Biddle [assignee?]
b. Clement Biddle
c. Sarah McConnel; S. Hodgson, 1832; Jonathan? Gustin; J. Cole, 1837

S-0854 1000a A:439 X-0840 CLIN:RICH
a. W-0240 Lieutenant Colonel Thomas Posey
b. Thomas Posey
c. H. L. Akin [*also* Aikin]; J. Dakin, 1828; Job Sperry; J. Fyfe, 1833; Elias Dakin; G. D. Haworth, 1831; James Dakin; George Bruce, 1833; W. Sabin; A. E. Strickle, 1838; James Doan; S. Hodge; Isaac Jacks

S-0855 600a A:440 X-0840 CLIN:RICH
a. W-0398 Captain Thomas Pemberton
b. Thomas Pemberton
c. R. Barclay Haslaw, 1830; J. Fife; T. Pemberton, heirs; A. E. Strickle, 1841; Grif[fith?] G. Perkins

S-0856 667a A:513 X-0660 WARR:WASH
a. W-0342 Lieutenant Albert Russell
b. Albert Russell
c. None

S-0862 1000a? B:395 X-0180 GREE:SILV
a. W-2262 Lieutenant Ambrose Gordon
b. Ambrose Gordon
c. None

S-0863 1000a A:460 X-0840 FAYE:UNIO FAYE:MADI
a. W-0206 Captain Samuel Eddens
b. Samuel Eddins
c. None

S-0865 700a B:245 X-0840 FAYE:UNIO
a. W-1670 Phillip Barbour, heir to James Robertson; Albert Gallatin [assignee?]
b. Albert Gallatin
c. None

S-0866 400a A:233 X-0030 CLER:WASH
a. W-1842 William Jones; John Hammelton [assignee?]
b. John Hamilton
c. None

S-0866 200a A:233 X-0030 CLER:WASH
a. W-1078 Peter McCartney; Colonel John Campbell [assignee?]
b. John Campbell
c. None

S-0866 400a A:234 X-0030 CLER:WASH
a. W-1844 Robert McQuillen? [McQuitten?]; William Smith [assignee?] 200a
W-2729 William Trabue; William Smith [assignee?] 200a
b. William Smith
c. None

S-0867 1000a A:241 X-1120 BROW:UNIO
a. W-2270 Lieutenant Stephen Southall
b. Stephen Southall
c. David Bradford; William Shepherd, 1824; Archibald Hamilton; George Shultz, 1825; Martha Hodgkins; J. Philips; L? [S?] Pangburn, 1842; W. Rogers; J. S. Beasley, 1842

S-0868 1000a A:435 X-0840 FAYE:JEFF GREE:SILV
a. W-0564 James Cary, 100a
W-1554 Benoni Perryman, 100a
W-1633 Nicholas Wood, 200a
W-1568 Charles Dobbins, 200a
W-0843 William Davidson, 200a
W-1397 James Lynch, 200a; *all of the above warrants to* Clement Biddle [assignee?]
b. Clement Biddle
c. None

S-0870 130a B:183 X-0660 GREE:XENI
a. W-0812 Colonel William Dark
b. William Dark
c. None

S-0872 1000a A:439 X-0840 PICK: --* FAYE:JEFF CLIN:RICH
a. W-1935 Lieutenant George Carrington
b. George Carrington
c. James Taylor
*Source A does not mention Fayette County; Source B does not mention Pickaway County.

S-0874 667a B:3 X-0360 PICK:DARB PICK:MORG MADI:PLEA FAYE: --*
a. W-0305 Captain Thomas Bell
b. Thomas Bell
c. James Welsh; J. N. Jones, 1839
*Source B does not mention Fayette County.

S-0875 644a B:481 X-1000 FRAN:FRAN
a. W-0215 Doctor David Holmes; [assignee*]
b. William Wilson
c. James Foley; E. Backus, 1838
*Name of assignee for 1000a illegible.

S-0876 1000a B:19 X-0663 CLIN:JEFF
a. W-0152 Captain Lieutenant Thomas Dix
b. Thomas Dix
c. William Bohannon; Isaiah Clark, 1831

S-0877 1300a A:439 X-0840 FAYE:JEFF
a. W-0025 Major William Croghan
b. William Croghan
c. James Woods, 1830

S-0878 1000a B:214 X-0840 FAYE:JEFF FAYE:CONC
a. W-2246 Lieutenant Isaac Webb
b. Isaac Webb
c. R. Douglas, 1832

S-0879 1000a B:136 X-0660 GREE:MIAM GREE:XENI
a. W-0298 Colonel James Wood
b. James Wood
c. None

S-0880 1000a A:436 X-0840 FAYE:JEFF CLIN:RICH
a. W-1384 Lieutenant Thomas Burford; Edward Dowse [assignee?]
b. Edward Dowse
c. Ab. Ditmers?; James Davis, 1826; William Piggott; B. Hinkson, 1823; Jesse Tomlinson; William R. Cole, 1824; John Baldwin, heirs; Thomas Babb, 1830; W. P. Hunicut; J. Nicholas; James Worthington, 1832 (Fayette County); Thomas Robb; M. M? [W?] Hale, 1837; James Moorman; G. Foos, 1837; A. E. Strickle, 1839; Daniel Parish; J. Hale, Junior, 1842; J. Wood, 1842

S-0882 1200a B:24 X-0340 FRAN:BROW
a. W-0712 Doctor William Brown
b. William Brown
c. Unknown; Lyne Starling, 1828; M. L. Sullivant, 1834; Jacob Francis

S-0883 667a A:236 X-0800 SCIO:WASH
a. W-2270 Lieutenant Stephen Southall
b. Stephen Southall
c. William Roby; D. McArthur, 1834; David Bradford, heirs; Thomas Morgan, 1824; David Ghackey? Junior, 1827; Stephen Kendall, 1837

S-0884 1200a A:351 X-0420 ADAM:LIBE
a. W-2360 Colonel Charles Harrison
b. Charles Harrison
c. None

S-0885 1334a A:448 X-0660 CLIN:UNIO CLIN:RICH
a. W-0209 Colonel Theodorick Bland
b. Theodorick Bland
c. None

S-0886 1000a A:447 X-0660 CLIN:UNIO CLIN:RICH
a. W-2366 Richard Eggleston, heir to W. Eggleston
b. Richard Eggleston
c. A. O. Eggleston & W. H. Eggleston; James Wilson, 1825

S-0887 2221a A:448 X-0660 CLIN:RICH
a. W-2260 Major Richard Call
b. Richard Call
c. None

S-0888 1667a A:311 X-0950 BROW:UNIO
a. W-0598 Captain James Williams
b. James Williams
c. None

S-0889 2667a A:446 X-0660 FAYE:JEFF GREE:SILV
a. W-0123 Lieutenant John Hardyman; Richard Claiborne [assignee?]
b. Richard Claiborne
c. Unknown; John Dodd, 1828

S-0891 1000a A:440 X-0840 CLIN:RICH
a. W-1887 Captain Joseph Scott, Junior
b. Joseph Scott
c. None

S-0892 964a A:236 X-0800 CLER:FRAN CLER:WASH
a. W-0187 Lieutenant Robert Cradduck
b. Robert Craddock
c. None

S-0895 1000a A:440 X-0840 FAYE:CONC CLIN:RICH
a. W-2121 Lieutenant William Whitaker
b. William Whitaker
c. None

S-0896 1200a A:463 X-1130 FAYE:GREE
a. W-2417 Colonel Benjamin Temple
b. Benjamin Temple
c. None

S-0898 1000a B:192 X-1301 HIGH:SALE
a. W-1652 Lieutenant Henry Boyer
b. Henry Bowyer*
c. None
*Source B spells Bowyier.

S-0899 290a B:212 X-0840 FAYE:CONC FAYE:UNIO
a. W-0011 James Baush? [Brush? Banks?]
b. Andrew Dunscomb
c. None

S-0900 720a A:450 X-0840 FAYE:CONC CLIN:RICH
a. W-1792 Lieutenant Colonel Edward Carrington
b. Edward Carrington
c. William Lytle; Timothy Kirby; P. F. Birchfield & C. B. Harlan, 1831

S-0901 1000a B:49 X-1300 BROW:SCOT
a. W-2331 Captain Lewis Booker
b. Lewis Booker
c. Fred Bingaman, 1823; Unknown; H. H. Bingaman; P. L. Wilson, 1841

S-0902 1000a A:228 X-1150 ADAM:SPRI
a. W-0827 Captain John Holcomb; Richard James [assignee?]
b. John McDowell
c. None

S-0903 1000a B:28 X-1000 PICK:JACK PICK:SCIO
a. W-0199 Captain Lawrence Butler
b. Lawrence Butler
c. None

S-0904 1000a A:488 X-0660 GREE:SUGA
a. W-1007 Lieutenant John Crittendon
b. John Crittendon
c. None

S-0905 667a A:236 X-0800 CLER:FRAN
a. W-0596 Lieutenant John Hackley
b. John Hackley
c. J. H. Scofield; G. Crawford, 1840

S-0907 1200a A:441 X-0840 FAYE:CONC CLIN:RICH
a. W-0192 Lieutenant Colonel John Jameson
b. John Jameson
c. -- Gamble & -- Brooks; James Brooks, 1829; J. & D. Brown; W. P. Hunicut [*also* Hunnicut] 1832; S. Frazier; B. Ballard, 1835; A. Grantham, 1837

S-0908 1000a A:438 X-0840 FAYE:JEFF
a. W-0073 Captain Samuel Hogg; Colonel Edward Carrington [assignee?]
b. Edward Carrington
c. David Harland; James Weal, 1836; James Doan, Junior; James Bloomer, 1840; H. J. Pyle

S-0909 1000a B:131 X-0663 BROW:STER
a. W-2349 Captain Henry Whiting
b. Henry Whiting
c. Thomas Middleton, 1826; N? [U?] S. Bank; D. G. Devore, 1834; J. Taylor, Junior, 1831

S-0910 800a A:497 X-0663 CLER:WILL*
a. W-1137 John Brean, 200a
W-1508 James Slate, 400a
W-1520 William Bailey, 200a; *all the above warrants to* Captain F. Paskie [assignee?]
b. Frederick Paskey
c. None
*Source B notation: "By Williamsburg."

S-0910 200a A:497 X-0663 CLER:WILL
a. W-1539 William Zimmerman
b. William Zimmerman
c. None

S-0911 900a A:446 X-0840 FAYE:CONC
a. W-1882 Peter Collins; Levi Hollingsworth [assignee?] 200a
W-1926 Rush Hudson; John Barret [assignee?] 400a
W-1881 William Bedworth; Levi Hollingsworth [assignee?] 200a
W-1594 William Bransford; Esten? Barrett & William Bigbie [assignees?] 200a
b. John Barrett & William Bigby
c. Jacob Miller; Richard Douglas, 1827; Allen Trimble; James Brooks, heirs; B. Brooks, 1836; Albert Stevens; R. Burnett, 1835

S-0912 1000a A:228 X-1160 ADAM:SPRI
a. W-2052 Captain Abraham Kirkpatrick
b. Abraham Kirkpatrick
c. None

S-0913 1000a A:277 X-0910 CLER:MONR
a. W-1387 Captain Ferdinand O'Neal
b. Ferdinand O'Neal
c. Thomas Morris; B. Morris, 1839

S-0914 700a B:296 X-1000 PICK:JACK
a. W-0223 Captain Uriah Springer
b. Uriah Springer
c. Hy. Brush; James Olds, 1826; Guy W. Doan, 1833; John W? [M?] Fallon; J. D. Lutz, 1838; A. Glatsmith? 1835

S-0914 300a B:296 X-1000 PICK:JACK
a. W-0223 Captain Uriah Springer
b. Uriah Springer
c. None

S-0915 1400a A:228 X-1150 ADAM:SPRI
a. W-688 Lieutenant Colonel Samuel Hopkins
b. Samuel Hopkins
c. P. Pence; L. Cole, 1842

S-0916 160a B:60 X-0660 HAMI:ANDE
a. W-1820 William Moore
b. William Moore
c. Jesse Stephens; William Orr, 1826

S-0917 600a D:82 X-1203 HIGH:DODS
a. W-0350 Captain Samuel K. Bradford
b. Samuel K. Bradford
c. James Jennings; Elisha Riley; John Berans, 1834; William Hayden; Mahlon Elwell, 1831

S-0918 400a D:58 X-1005 PIKE:NEWT
a. W-1296 Timothy Peyton, heir to V. Peyton
b. Timothy Peyton
c. None

S-0919 1000a A:241 X-0800 BROW:PLEA BROW:LEWI
a. W-2242 Lieutenant John Roney
b. John Roney
c. Michael Young, heirs; Fred Kirkwald, 1832; R. Mefford; J. T. Smiley, 1841

S-0921 1000a A:279 X-0910 CLER:MONR
a. W-2556 Lieutenant Claiborne Vaughan; Richard J. Waters [assignee?]
b. Richard J. Waters
c. James Light; Samuel Robb; James Robb, 1841

S-0923 1000a B:133 X-0130 HIGH:CONC
a. W-0111 Captain Clough Shelton
b. Clough Shelton
c. John Phibbs; John Jones, 1833; D. Boatman; T. Shockley, 1836

S-0925 1333a A:442 X-0660 X-0840 FAYE:JEFF GREE:SILV
a. W-0046 Clement Read, heir to Colonel -- Read
b. Clement Read
c. John Gist; Alfred Trader, 1832; Benjamin Benum?; E. D. L. Graham, 1836

S-0926 2000a A:375 X-0663 CLER:TATE*
a. W-1331 Captain Lieutenant Richard Waters
b. Richard Waters
c. John Watson; A. Stark, 1832
*Source B notation: "By Bantam."

S-0927 1000a A:441 X-0840 FAYE:JEFF CLIN:RICH
a. W-0236 Lieutenant John Harrison; Alexander Fowler [assignee?]
b. Alexander Balmain
c. David Lupton; James Fife, 1830

S-0928 1333a A:375 X-0663 CLER:BATA CLER:TATE* CLER:MONR
a. W-0904 Lieutenant Thomas Pearson**
b. Thomas Pierson**
c. W. Sterrett; W. Dillon, 1824; Z? Chapman, 1826; W. Ross; A. Leeds, 1826; John Justus; Lott Halick [*also* Hulick] 1836; Josiah Leeds; A. Starks, 1835
*Source B notation: "By Bantam."
**So spelled.

S-0929 1000a B:184 X-0740 GREE:XENI
a. W-0345 Captain Arthur Lind; John Fowler [assignee?]
b. John Fowler
c. None

S-0930* 1000a -- -- CLIN: --
a. --
b. Daniel Duvall
c. Arthur O'Neal; William M. Sabin, 1825
*Source B entry cancelled.

S-0931 1200 C:8 X-0340 PICK:DARB FRAN:PLEA
a. W-0351 Lieutenant Colonel Charles Simms
b. Charles Simmes*
c. -- Olds & -- Ludwig, 1826; C. Symmes; Andrew Huston, 1832; -- Symmes & -- Martin; E. Converse, 1837 (Franklin County)
*Source B spells Simms.

S-0932 1000a A:444 X-0840 FAYE:CONC FAYE:JEFF CLIN:RICH
a. W-0194 James Galt, heir to Doctor P. Galt
b. James Galt, heir*
c. William Dice, heirs; Absalom Carr, 1841
*Source B spells Gault.

S-0933 1000a A:512 X-0040 ADAM:TIFF
a. W-0241 Captain Thomas Barbee
b. Thomas Barbee
c. None

S-0934 738a A:453 X-0663 CLER:BATA CLER:TATE CLER:MONR
a. W-1889 Captain Peter Jones; Colonel Joseph Jones [assignee?]
b. Joseph Jones
c. L. Doughty; W. McCune? 1836; D. Tewell

S-0935 667a A:448 X-0663 CLIN:LIBE
a. W-1935 Lieutenant George Carrington
b. George Carrington
c. Carlisle B. Williams, 1825; Benjamin Williams; B. Hinkson, 1823

S-0936 1333a A:442 X-0660 GREE:SILV
a. W-1386 Major Joseph Eggleston
b. Joseph Eggleston
c. None

S-0937 1000a A:453 X-0660 CLER:MONR
a. W-2117 Captain John B. Johnson
b. John B. Johnson
c. Jesse Hart? [Hant?]; Shadrack Lane; Jesse Hunt; David Dyal, 1830; W. Reeves; Isaac N. Morris, 1834; W. Beers; G. Chapman, 1836; D. Deal; A. Stark, 1835

S-0938 785a A:413 X-1120 BROW:UNIO
a. W-0617 Captain Alexander Brackenridge*
b. Alexander Breckenridge*
c. None
*So spelled.

S-0939 120a C:443 X-0310? CLER:TATE
X-0320? CLER:MONR
a. W-0154 Captain Beaverley Roy
b. Beverly Roy
c. Rebecca Dailey; Vincent Cordery; John Slade, 1841

S-0939 940a C:443 X-0663 CLER:TATE
CLER:MONR
a. W-0154 Captain Beaverley Roy
b. Beverly Roy
c. None

S-0941 1400a B:293 X-0840 HIGH:NEWM
a. W-1912 Doctor Thomas Cristie
b. Thomas Christie
c. H. Massie; G. W. Barriere, 1826

S-0942 1000a B:214 X-0840 FAYE:JEFF
FAYE:PAIN
a. W-0649 Captain Lawrence Trent
b. Lawrence Trent
c. None

S-0943 283a C:16 X-0270 CLER:WILL
CLER:TATE
a. W-0096 Captain Baylor Hill
b. Baylor Hill
c. Charles L. Bahne? [Bahner?]; R. W. Clar, 1836

S-0943 230a C:16 X-0270 CLER:WILL
CLER:TATE
a. W-0096 Captain Baylor Hill
b. Baylor Hill
c. None

S-0947 1200a C:22 X-0340 FRAN:PLEA
a. W-0351 Lieutenant Colonel Charles Simms
b. Charles Simmes*
c. John Lewis; Land.? Shipman, 1827; C. Sims; John Tipton, 1832; Justin Smith; J. Chinioth? [Chenowith?] 1832
*Source B spells Simms.

S-0948 1000a A:498 X-0663 CLER:WILL
a. W-1889 Captain Peter Jones; Colonel Joseph Jones [assignee?]
b. Joseph Jones
c. None

S-0949 1333a A:501 X-0663 CLER:WILL
CLER:JACK
BROW: --*
a. W-0115 Major William Moseley
b. William Mosley**
c. John Barrett; John Washburn; Samuel Vail, 1830 (Clermont County); J. Haight, 1820; C. H. Huber, 1835 (Clermont County); C. B. Huber; Jacob Hite; John Patton; G. Ashton; H. Ellison; Samuel Hadley; D. Wassel? [Warrel?]; H. Tice, 1842?
*Source B does not mention Brown County.
**Source B spells Moseley.

S-0950 666a A:498 X-0663 CLER:WILL
a. W-0146 Lieutenant W[illiam] S. Smith
b. William S. Smith
c. William Greaves; John T. Ross, 1836? [1826?]

S-0951 1000a A:441 X-0660 GREE:SILV
CLIN:RICH
a. W-1386 Major Joseph Eggleston
b. Joseph Eggleston
c. A. E. Strickle, 1836

S-0953 400a B:314 X-0840 ROSS:TWIN
a. W-1450 Major Samuel Finley
b. Samuel Finley
c. None

S-0954 1000a A:502 X-0663 BROW:STER
CLER:JACK
a. W-1296 Timothy Peyton, heir to V. Peyton
b. Timothy Peyton
c. Robert Campbell, 1828; George Fryman; O. T. Fishback, 1837 (Clermont County); Martin Gats; M. F. H. Veitch, 1835 (Clermont County); E. Chichester, heirs; J. W. Low, 1840

S-0955 1000a A:502 X-0663 CLER:WILL
CLER:JACK
a. W-0702 Lieutenant William B. Wallace
b. William B. Wallace
c. Edward Wilson; James Perin, 1836; Henry Wharton; Isaac Patterson

S-0956 1667a C:100 X-0663 CLIN:CLAR
a. W-2329 Lieutenant Thomas Martin
b. Thomas Martin
c. None

S-0957 1000a A:503 X-0663 CLER:JACK
a. W-2655 William Lawson, heir to C. Lawson
b. William Lawson
c. None

S-0958 910a A:271 X-0663* CLER:MIAM
a. W-0771 Lieutenant Peter Higgins
b. Peter Higgins
c. None
*Source A notation: "Upper side."

S-0961 1000a A:434 X-0660 CLIN:UNIO
a. W-2235 Lieutenant Nathaniel Anderson
b. Nathaniel Anderson
c. None

S-0963 1000a A:434 X-0840 FAYE:CONC
CLIN:RICH
a. W-1199 Captain William Lindsay
b. William Lindsay*
c. Elizabeth Lindsey*; William R. Sewell, 1828; William Woodruff; George Fallis, 1830; H. Hinkston* 1832; Derta? B. Stark; James Brook, 1829; W. P. Hunnicutt; Benjamin Hinkson*; R. Stark; W. V. Rawlings, 1842 (Fayette County)
*So spelled.

S-0964 583a A:369 X-0270 CLER:TATE
a. W-0147 Colonel Nathaniel Gist
b. Nathaniel Gist
c. M. Ellsberry; R. Tweed, 1826; John Ellrod; J. D. Morris, 1835; M. Ellrod; L? [S?] Pease, 1837

S-0968 1200a A:502 X-0663 BROW:STER BROW:PERR
a. W-2417 Colonel Benjamin Temple
b. Benjamin Temple
c. A. T. & B. F. Sweet; A. McLain, 1837; Mary Williamson; J. Sweet

S-0969 1500a A:503 X-0663 CLER:JACK
a. W-2262 Lieutenant Ambrose Gordon
b. Ambrose Gordon
c. Thomas Kerr; James Pirken* 1836; C. Cooper; James Pickens*; D. H. Nowland; T. J. Buckannon? [Buchannan?] 1842
*So spelled.

S-0970 667a B:152 X-0840 FAYE:CONC
a. W-0012 Joseph Holmes, heir to Lieutenant T? Holmes; Clement Biddle [assignee?]
b. Clement Biddle
c. John Brown; R. Douglas, 1827; James? Y. Green, 1831

S-0971 1000a B:13 X-1000 FRAN:FRAN
a. W-0217 Doctor John Knight
b. John Knight
c. L. Sullivant, heirs; Lyne Starling; M. L. Sullivant; Sarah Smith; E. Backus, 1836; N. Smith; S. M? [W?] White, 1839

S-0972 1000a A:257 X-0663 CLER:MIAM
a. W-0172 Lieutenant Colonel Jonathan Clark
b. Colonel Jonathan Clark
c. None

S-0973 1000a A:259 X-0663 CLER:MIAM
a. W-0633 Captain Thomas Holt
b. Thomas Holt
c. F. P. Ramsey

S-0974 890a B:213 X-0840 FAYE:JEFF* FAYE:CONC
a. W-0060 Captain Samuel Jones
b. Samuel Jones
c. T. Kirley? 1823; Henry Phelps & James Woods, 1828; Samuel Jones; J. S. Bereman? 1833; Abraham Bush? 1837; Phebe Smith; John Smith, 1839; B. Hinkson
*Source B also lists Clinton County, but without township.

S-0975 1000a B:182 X-0660 GREE:SUGA GREE:BEAV
a. W-0198 Captain Robert Beale
b. Robert Beale
c. Daniel Staley, heirs; J. A. Scott, 1838

S-0976 1000a A:258 X-0663 CLER:MIAM
a. W-2578 Cadwallader Jones
b. Cadwallader Jones
c. None

S-0978 1200a B:489 X-0340 FRAN:PLEA
a. W-0289 Doctor Cornelius Baldwin
b. Cornelius Baldwin
c. None

S-0979 930a B:279 X-0660 CLAR:GREE CLAR:MADI GREE:ROSS
a. W-0560 Captain Peter Garland
b. Peter Garland
c. None

S-0980 334a B:173 X-0660 WARR:SALE
a. W-1007 Lieutenant John Crittendon
b. John Crittendon
c. James R. Taylor; William Bennett, 1832

S-0980 333a B:173 X-0660 WARR:SALE
a. W-1007 Lieutenant John Crittendon
b. John Crittendon
c. None

S-0981 1000a A:258 X-0660 CLER:MIAM CLER:GOSH CLER:STON
a. W-2117 Captain John B. Johnson
b. Captain John B. Johnston*
c. None
*Source B spells Johnson.

S-0982 1000a B:153 X-0846 FAYE:CONC
a. W-2133 Captain Nathaniel Burwell
b. Nathaniel Burwell
c. J. Jameson & J. Wall, 1835

S-0986* 1367a A:449 X-0660 CLIN:UNIO
a. W-0073 Captain Samuel Hogg; Colonel Edward Carrington [assignee?] 1000a
W-1792 Lieutenant Colonel Edward Carrington, 367a
b. Edward Carrington
c. Jesse M. Wood, 1825; George Bruce, 1826
*See also S-2433.

S-0987 376a D:41 X-0663 CLER:STON
a. W-0153 Captain John Overton
b. John Overton
c. G. Rust; J. Hill, 1836; William Wainwright, 1826

S-0987 514a C:259 X-0663 CLER:STON
a. W-0153 Captain John Overton
b. John Overton
c. None

S-0988 1000a B:150 X-0840 FAYE:CONC
a. W-2309 Captain John H. Fitzgerald
b. John H. Fitzgerald
c. H. Massie; Hecter* McNeil; John L. Taylor, 1831
*So spelled.

S-0989 260a B:510 X-0663 CLER:BATA CLER:UNIO
a. W-0044 Captain Thomas Overton
b. Thomas Overton
c. James Taylor; S. Maham, 1835

S-0991 1000a A:258 X-0660 CLER:MIAM
a. W-1889 Captain Peter Jones; Colonel Joseph Jones [assignee?]
b. Joseph Jones
c. James Jones; S? [L?] Winston 1823; S? [L?] B. Cleveland, 1825; John H. James; W. C. Moore, 1826; John Main; C. Eversole, 1823; William Megrew; B. Brown, 1827; A. J. Patton, 1827; John Bills; A. Stark, 1835; Andrew Patton

S-0992 1000a A:258 X-0660 CLER:MIAM
a. W-0152 Captain Lieutenant Thomas Dix
b. Thomas Dix
c. T. Combs; W. Waynewright, 1826; S. Hooper; J. Duckwall, 1826; William Insley; John Main, 1824; C. Eversole, 1823; W? [M?] Highland

S-0993 1767a B:137 X-0200 HIGH:CLAY BROW: --*
a. W-0051 Captain Joseph Scott, Senior, 1767a
W-2230 Jesse Bolling, with John Barrett Cott** 100a
b. Joseph Scott & Jesse Bolling
c. Erastus Custis, 1828; Samuel Jones; Fred Bingaman, 1833
*Source B does not mention Brown County.
**This might be an abbreviation of the word Colonel.

S-0994 1200a A:533 X-0665 CLIN:GREE
a. W-2417 Colonel Benjamin Temple
b. Benjamin Temple
c. J. L. Barret; J. Morris, 1825

S-0995 500a A:242 X-0800 BROW:HUNT
a. W-0244 Captain Reuben Field
b. Captain Reuben Field
c. John Barret? [Basset?] 1823; John Brown; M. Weaver, 1827

S-0996 1000a A:531 X-0660 CLIN:WASH
a. W-0125 Captain Lieutenant Thomas Fenn
b. Thomas Fenn
c. None

S-0997 1000a A:414 X-1120 BROW:BYRD BROW:PLEA
a. W-1653 Lieutenant Robert Brackenridge*
b. Robert Breckenridge
c. None
*So spelled.

S-0998 1000a B:71 X-0663 CLER:BATA
a. W-0196 Lieutenant James Mabon*
b. James Mabone*
c. George Clark; T. Kirby, 1823; J. Gray, heirs
*So spelled.

S-0999 1400a A:352 X-0420 BROW:BYRD* ADAM: --
a. W-0688 Lieutenant Colonel Samuel Hopkins
b. Samuel Hopkins
c. Sarah Shaw; 'Robert Allen, 1823
*Source B notation: "Decatur;" does not mention Adams County.

S-1002 1000a B:150 X-0840 FAYE:CONC
a. W-2309 Captain John H. Fitzgerald
b. John H. Fitzgerald
c. Hector McNiel; N. F. Jones, 1833; Thomas P. Watkins; J. Jameson, 1837

S-1003 1000a B:170 X-0420 BROW:JACK
a. W-2669 Lieutenant Daniel Ball
b. Daniel Ball
c. Mary Spears; W? [M?] Spears, 1842

S-1005 907a A:280 X-0910 CLER:MONR CLER:OHIO
a. W-0224 Captain Benjamin Biggs
b. Captain Benjamin Biggs
c. J. Bonner; R. Denham, 1826; W. Sell

S-1008 1000a A:530 X-0660 CLIN:WASH
a. W-0067 William Giles, heir to John Giles
b. William Giles
c. John Wilkins, Junior; Christopher Hiatt; S. Moore? [Moon?]; A. E. Strickle, 1839

S-1009 1000a A:447 X-0660 CLIN:WASH
a. W-0060 Captain Samuel Jones
b. Samuel Jones
c. David Carter, 1828; S. Jones; William Barrett; J. Fyfe, 1836

S-1010 1000a A:383 X-0133 ADAM:FRAN HIGH: --*
a. W-0290 Captain Abraham Shepherd
b. Abraham Shepherd
c. None
*Source B does not mention Highland County.

S-1013 275a B:180 X-0660 WARR:WAYN GREE:SUGA*
a. W-2331 Captain Lewis Booker
b. Lewis Booker
c. None
*Source A does not mention Greene County or Sugar Creek Township.

S-1014 1000a A:383 X-0020 ADAM:FRAN HIGH: --*
a. W-0290 Captain Abraham Shepherd
b. Abraham Shepherd
c. None
*Source B does not mention Highland County.

S-1015* 100a -- -- ROSS:UNIO
a. --
b. Thomas Shore
c. --
*Source A does not list this entry.

S-1015* 467a -- -- ROSS:UNIO
a. --
b. Eleanah Tharp
c. --
*Source A does not list this entry.

S-1016 711a B:138 X-1301 HIGH:CLAY
a. W-0369 James Tutt, heir to Charles Tutt
b. James Tutt, heir
c. -- Ball & -- Collins, 1825

S-1017 1111a A:268 X-0660* CLER:MIAM
a. W-0302 Lieutenant Phillip Eslen? [Easlin?]; Robert Todd [assignee?]
b. Robert Todd
c. L. Buckingham; S. West; James W. Robinson; C. Vail, 1828; E. Holmes; O. T. Fishback, 1834
*Source A notation: "East side."

S-1019 667a B:295 X-0340 FRAN:PLEA PICK: --*
a. W-0074 Lieutenant James Morton
b. James Morton
c. James Malton; William Mooberry, 1829
*Source B does not mention Pickaway County.

S-1020 1000a B:320 X-0360 MADI:UNIO
a. W-0222 Captain Uriah Springer
b. Uriah Springer
c. None

S-1023 1000a A:447 X-0660 CLIN:WAYN
a. W-2121 Lieutenant William Whitaker
b. William Whitaker
c. Dinah Bray; William Walker; G. D. Hayworth, 1841

S-1024 1000a A:454 X-0230 ADAM:WAYN
a. W-0610 Captain John Winston
b. John Winston
c. None

S-1025 2000a A:296 X-0420 X-1120 BROW:FRAN
a. W-0707 Captain Nathaniel Fox
b. Nathaniel Fox
c. John Fowler; Josiah Pritchard, 1825; Simon Kratzer; John S? [L?] Wills, for H. R. Shaw, 1824 (not patented); George Marshall; Benjamin Wills, 1826; Peter Shaw, 1827; Mason Fox *et al*; N. Ellis, 1828; C. Whipple; Unknown; A. Wells, 1837

S-1027 1000a B:80 X-0840 CLIN:WAYN FAYE:GREE HIGH:FAIR*
a. W-0167 Captain Thomas Ransdale
b. Thomas Ransdale? [Rausdale?]
c. Nicholas Newlin; Israel Woodruff, 1828; James St. Clair; R. M. Ross
*Source A does not mention Highland County or Fairfield Township.

S-1027* 488a E:283 X-0840 HIGH: -- FAYE: --
a. W-0167 Captain Thomas Ransdale
b. Thomas Ransdale? [Rausdale?]
c. --
*Source B does not list this entry.

S-1029 1000a B:82 X-1150 BROW:HUNT
a. W-1296 Timothy Peyton, heir to V. Peyton
b. Timothy Peyton, heir
c. Robert Campbell, 1828; Elijah Martin; Timothy Payne; William Sellman, 1831; -- Parker & -- Wright; P. S? [L?] Wilson

S-1032 1000a B:198 X-1080 CLIN:MARI WARR: --* CLER: --* BROW: --*
a. W-2271 Captain Holman Minnis
b. Holman Minnis
c. Samuel Ayres; T. Kirby, 1823; S. Reed; J. Taylor; Uriah Biggs, 1824; H. Avery; John Lyon, 1831; C. Minnis; George Bruce, 1833; John Hadley, 1835; G. Foos, 1839
*Source B does not mention Warren, Clermont, and Brown counties.

S-1033 836a A:414 X-0800 X-1120 BROW:UNIO
a. W-0308 Lieutenant John Crawford
b. John Crawford
c. None

S-1035 919a A:414 X-1120 X-0950 BROW:UNIO
a. W-1843 Lieutenant William Smith
b. William Smith
c. None

S-1036 900a A:311 X-0420 X-0950 BROW:UNIO
a. W-2402 Lieutenant Jordan Harris
b. Jordan Harris
c. J. Louden, 1828

S-1038 380a C:146 X-0800 ADAM:SPRI
a. W-0815 Brigadier General Charles Scott
b. Charles Scott
c. R. Brooks; H. Rape? 1829; Andrew Boyd; William McCoy; T. Huston, 1841

S-1038 900a B:59 X-0800 ADAM:SPRI*
a. W-0815 Brigadier General Charles Scott
b. Charles Scott
c. None
*Source B notation: "Manchester."

S-1038 600a B:179 X-0800 ADAM:SPRI
a. W-0815 Brigadier General Charles Scott
b. Charles Scott
c. None

S-1038 120a D:29 X-0800 ADAM:SPRI
a. W-0815 Brigadier General Charles Scott
b. Charles Scott
c. None

S-1039 1000a B:211 X-0840 FAYE:GREE CLIN:WAYN
a. W-2347 Lieutenant Richard Claiborne
b. Richard Claiborne
c. Walter Dun, ex[ecutor of] -- Graham; Alexander Douglas; J. Y. Greene

S-1041 200a A:418 X-0420 BROW:UNIO
a. W-1288 Thomas Groves
b. Thomas Groves
c. None

S-1041 400a A:418 X-0420 BROW:UNIO
a. W-1965 Francis Dawson
b. Francis Dawson
c. None

S-1041 100a A:418 X-0420 BROW:UNIO
a. W-2143 Samuel Kenny, heir to Joseph Kenny
b. James Kenney
c. Nathan Sidwell, 1828

S-1041 100a A:418 X-0420 BROW:UNIO
a. W-1027 John Chinworth
b. John Chenoweth*
c. None
*Source B spells Chinworth.

S-1041 200a A:418 X-0420 BROW:UNIO
a. W-2268 James Dishman
b. James Deshman*
c. Daniel Hitchcock, 1828
*Source B spells Dishman.

S-1043 1000a A:305 X-0134 ADAM:WINC ADAM:SCOT BROW:EAGL
a. W-1811 Captain Thomas Blackwell
b. Thomas Blackwell
c. David Johnson; Francis Duffy; William Butt, 1823; Thomas Lueques?; M. Kincaid, 1826; James Greathouse; J. Davidson, 1830; W. Crawford; J. Fenton, 1829

S-1044 1000a A:335 X-0182 GREE:CAES
a. W-0206 Captain Samuel Eddens
b. Samuel Eddins
c. None

S-1045 1000a A:422 X-0180 WARR:WAYN
a. W-1391 Captain Nathaniel Pendleton
b. Nathaniel Pendleton
c. None

S-1046 1000a B:25 X-0340 FRAN:BROW
a. W-0812 Colonel William Dark
b. William Dark
c. Lyne Starling [*also* Sterling] 1828; John Brown; C. Higgins, 1835; W. S. Sullivant; M. L. Sullivant, 1827; James Sullivant

S-1048 1000a B:247 X-0180 WARR:WAYN
a. W-0614 Captain Henry Moss
b. Henry Moss
c. Joel Wright, heirs; A. G. Wright, 1834

S-1049 500a B:71 X-0840 CLIN:WAYN FAYE: --*
a. W-2425 Stephen Petters, heir to John Petters; William Hendrick [assignee?]
b. William Hendricks**
c. Adam Woolard; B Hinkson, 1831
*Source B does not mention Fayette County.
**So spelled.

S-1051 867a B:285 X-0640 HIGH:FAIR
a. W-0228 Lieutenant Jacob Springer
b. Jacob Springer
c. None

S-1053 1000a B:61 X-1300 BROW:WASH BROW:PIKE BROW:SCOT
a. W-1820 William Moore
b. William Moore
c. None

S-1055 1000a B:132 X-0150 ROSS:BUCK
a. W-0701 Lieutenant Luke Cannon
b. Luke Cannon
c. John Hemphill; James McConnell, 1825

S-1056 1000a A:62 X-1300 BROW:SCOT BROW:PIKE
a. W-2497 Bennett Tompkins
b. Bennett Tompkins
c. James McCall; -- Shepherd & -- Masterson; John Strange; M. Weaver, 1827; [*one illegible name*]

S-1057 2820a A:488 X-1170 CLIN:UNIO*
a. W-0240 Lieutenant Colonel Thomas Posey
b. Thomas Posey
c. B. R. Cincin?; B. Hinkson, 1823; S? Bosworth; John Fales, 1823; J. Akin; A. E. Strickle, 1838; Robert Hooten; Warren Saben; Aquilla Jones, 1841; M? [W?] Walker; D. F. Walker, 1841; H. Babb, heirs; F. Casto, 1842; W. J. Scott; T. L. Carruthers, 1842
*Source B notation: "Wilmington."

S-1058. *See also* S-0630

S-1058 1197a B:455 X-0840 FAYE:WAYN
a. W-0347 Major David Stephenson
b. David Stephenson
c. None

S-1059 825a E:62 X-1300 BROW:SCOT
a. W-1375 Tarpley White
b. Tarpley White
c. Robert Campbell; Moses Reynolds; F. Bingaman, 1830

S-1060 1000a A:312 X-0950 BROW:UNIO BROW:BYRD
a. W-0290 Captain Abraham Shepherd
b. Abraham Shepherd
c. None

S-1061 2500a A:445 X-0660 CLIN:WAYN CLIN:RICH FAYE: --*
a. W-0019 Brigadier General -- Morgan
b. Daniel Morgan
c. Samuel Mordoch; A. Jones & W. Mellikan, 1827; Thomas Hallam; J. Morris, 1832; James Rude; John Carman? [Casmon?] 1834; Thomas Palmer; J. Hadley, Junior; Warren Sabin, 1840
*Source B does not mention Fayette County.

S-1063 1000a B:206 X-0840 FAYE:PAIN
a. W-0310 Lieutenant David Miller
b. David Miller
c. Mary & Martha Baskerville; -- Phelps & -- Woods, 1823; E. T. Eastman; H. Phelps, 1839; William Hotchkiss, 1833; E. F. Eastman; I? [J?] Y. Greene; A. Kirkendall; Ezekiel F. Eastman; L. P. Reed, 1831

S-1064 1000a A:237 X-0800 CLER:FRAN*
a. W-0154 Captain Beaverley Roy
b. Beverly Roy
c. G. Richards; W. S. Patterson, 1835
*Source B notation: "Felicity."

S-1064 1000a A:248 X-0800 CLER:WASH
a. W-0154 Captain Beaverley Roy
b. Beverly Roy
c. D. Fisher; M. Mullen, 1842

S-1065 1000a B:72 X-0840 CLIN:WAYN
a. W-4041 Edmond? [Edward?] Shacklett, 100a
W-0902 Daniel Cumbo, 100a
W-1403 George Oust? 400a
W-1389 William Townsend, 200a
W-0185 Aaron Smith, 200a; *all the above warrants* to Doctor James Currie [assignee?]
b. James Curry*
c. C. B. Harlan, 1832; J. Gordon; E. Adams, 1835
*Source B spells Currie.

S-1066 533a A:238 X-0800 CLER:FRAN
a. W-1963 William Taliaferro, heir to Colonel [William] Taliaferro
b. William Taliaferro, heir
c. John Pyle; A. Hall, 1835; Unknown; J. R. Prather, 1836; S. English, 1838; W? [M?] Pyle & J. Kendal; John Hull, 1841; T. Clark; A. C. Medary, 1842; J. Clark; W. Lynn; M. Mullen & O. Pearce?

S-1067 657a A:239 X-0800 CLER:FRAN*
a. W-1652 Lieutenant Henry Boyer
b. Henry Bowyer
c. None
*Source B notation: "Chilo." [possibly meaning Chillicothe].

S-1069 1667a A:429 X-0360 ROSS:UNIO* PICK:WAYN
a. W-0131 Lieutenant Francis Whiting
b. Francis Whiting
c. Thomas Ozewell; William Thompson, 1827; J. Tarlton, 1827; J. B. Clark; S. S. Frame, 1839 (Pickaway County); -- Bartlett & -- Coates; E. W. Smith, 1840; Dilly H. Bartlett; D. A. Woodbridge; A. Richart, Junior; A. McCoy, 1842; J. Waterman; E. Bixler, 1842
*Source B notation: "Yellow Bud."

S-1071 1000a A:526 X-0660 CLIN:GREE
a. W-1935 Lieutenant George Carrington
b. George Carrington
c. J. Larow; L? [S?] Williamson, 1842

S-1073 1000a A:527 X-0660 CLIN:GREE
a. W-0051 Captain Joseph Scott, Senior
b. Joseph Scott
c. Isaac Miller; J. Darbyshire, 1840; W? [M?] Barnes; A. E. Strickle, 1841; G. Lamb; C. Atkinson, 1842

S-1078 1480a B:47 X-0660 HIGH:FAIR HIGH:UNIO CLIN:GREE CLIN:WAYN
a. W-2272 Captain Callohill Minnis
b. Callohill Minnis
c. William Vanmetre; John Hogsett, 1836; Joshua Muzzy; James Fyfe, 1833 (Clinton County)

S-1079 1150a C:88 X-0840 GREE:SILV
a. W-1850 Doctor Robert Rose
b. Robert Rose
c. Alexander F. Rose; James Galloway, Junior, 1833; -- Watson & -- Johnson; Aaron Harlan, 1841

S-1080 1000a A:238 X-0800 CLER:FRAN
a. W-1623 Lieutenant Javin Miller
b. Javire? [Javier?]* Miller
c. T. Wells; M. Mullen, 1842
*Source B spells Javin.

S-1081 140a B:213 X-0840 FAYE:JEFF GREE:SILV
a. W-0060 Captain Samuel Jones
b. Samuel Jones
c. W? [M?] Wymans, 1828

S-1082 500a B:72 X-0840 HIGH:FAIR CLIN: --* FAYE:GREE
a. W-0028** --
b. Abraham Hite
c. None
*Source B does not mention Clinton County.
**Source C does not list W-0028.

S-1084 1000a B:92 X-0180 GREE:SILV
a. W-0240 Lieutenant Colonel Thomas Posey
b. Thomas Posey
c. None

S-1085 1100a A:489 X-1170 CLIN:UNIO
a. W-2162 Colonel William Heth
b. William Hith*
c. None
*Source B spells Heth.

S-1087 1000a A:237 X-0800 CLER:FRAN CLER:WASH
a. W-2273 Captain Thomas Buckner
b. Thomas Buckner
c. W. Lynn; W. Johnson, 1827; M. Miller; J. C. Dyal, 1823; William Johnson; S. Mahan? [Maham?] 1832; S. G. Clark, 1834; James Cook; William S. Patterson, 1835; C. C. Leroy; T. Rush, 1836

S-1088 900a A:530 X-0660 CLIN:UNIO
a. W-0597 Captain John Spotswood
b. John Spotswood
c. None

S-1089 143a C:464 X-1080 CLER:STON
a. W-0596 Lieutenant John Hackley
b. John Hackley
c. None

S-1089 100a C:464 X-1080 CLER:STON
a. W-0596 Lieutenant John Hackley
b. John Hackley
c. None

S-1090 1000a A:519 X-0663 HIGH:UNIO CLIN:GREE
a. W-0398 Captain Thomas Pemberton
b. Thomas Pemberton
c. Joseph Anthony, 1830; William G. Botts; J. W. Hackney, 1841

S-1092 1200a B:120 X-0180 GREE:SILV GREE:ROSS
a. W-0286 Reverend Alexander Balmain
b. Alexander Balmain
c. Margaret Baldwin; W. G. Sanders, 1827; Russell Rice, 1828; David Stewart; Josiah Davidson, 1834?

S-1093 1000a B:157 X-0840 FAYE:PAIN FAYE:JEFF MADI:STOK
a. W-0674 Captain William Epps; Colonel A. Buford [assignee?]
b. Alexander Buford
c. None

S-1094 800a B:120 X-0180 GREE:ROSS
a. W-1707 Adam Rutter, 200a
W-1699 William Plummer, 200a
W-1595 David Boils, 200a
W-1643 Christopher Hopkinstock, 200; *all four warrants to* -- Pickering & -- Hodgdon [assignees?]
b. -- Pickering & -- Hodgdon*
c. James Bruce; John Dodd, 1838; L. Groves? [Grover?] & John Ankeny, 1831
*Source B spells Hodgden.

S-1095 740a B:113 X-1180 MADI:MONR
a. W-0850* --
b. Robert Vance
c. None
*Source C does not list W-0850.

S-1096 1000a A:534 X-0660 CLIN:UNIO
a. W-0105 Doctor John Roberts
b. John Roberts
c. None

S-1097 370a F:63 X-1145 PIKE:PEBB
a. W-1653 Lieutenant Robert Brackenridge*
b. Robert Breckenridge*
c. John Henry Brown; Dickerson Burt, 1823; -- Burt & -- Chinowith; Arthur Chinowith, 1829; A. Ellison; Peter Spurk? 1833; E. H. Smith, 1835; E. Smith, heirs; James Moore, 1838
*So spelled.

S-1098 1000a B:139 X-1300 HIGH:SALE HIGH:CLAY
a. W-2219 Captain John F. Mercer [assignee of?] Rawleigh Colson
b. John F. Mercer
c. William Scott; John Lee; -- Harris & -- Hopkins

S-1101* 800a -- -- CLER? --
a. --
b. Francis Muir
c. --
*Entry in Source B only; appears to be incomplete.

S-1102 800a D:449 X-0800 CLER:FRAN
a. W-1468* --
b. Benjamin Mosley**
c. Daniel Cameron; S. Barclay [*also* Barklay] 1832; Demaris Joslin; George Gregg
*Source C does not list W-1468.
**Source B spells Mosely.

S-1105 610a B:27 X-1000 FRAN:JACK
a. W-0172 Lieutenant Colonel Jonathan Clark
b. Jonathan Clark
c. D. Adams, 1832

S-1108 1200a B:27 X-1000 PICK:SCIO FRAN:JACK
a. W-1850 Doctor Robert Rose
b. Robert Rose
c. Unknown (forfeited) 1836

S-1111 1000a A:384 X-0180 CLIN:CHES
a. W-2499 Lieutenant William McGuire
b. William McGuire
c. M. Baker, heirs; H. Hall, 1823; J. Arnold; A. E. Strickle, 1838

S-1112 1175a A:530 X-0660 CLIN:GREE CLIN:WAYN
a. W-1937 Major Francis Taylor
b. Henry Lee
c. Hezekiah Sanders; William McMillan, 1831; D. Smith; C. Atkinson, 1842; John Fallis, 1823; Eli McGregor, 1826; John Haugham; George Bruce, 1823; William Kiff; Richard Hodgson; J. Owens, 1823; M. Howard, 1826; J. Morris, 1823; George R. Fitzgerald; John Frazier, 1829; Samuel Gibson; Israel Woodruff, 1827; A. E. Strickle, 1829; H. Leeky; William Darby, 1827; William Dixon; William Decker, 1831; B. Hinkson, 1831; M. Howard; E. J. Lee, 1832; P. West, 1835; W. Dickey; William Hardesty; E. Adams, 1836

S-1115 1000a A:257 X-0660 HAMI:ANDE CLER:UNIO
a. W-0115 Major William Moseley
b. Major William Mosley*
c. Richard Hodgson; O. T. Fishback**; T. L. Shields, 1834**; John? T? Haines**; C. A. Warren, 1834**
*Source B spells Mosely.
**It is thought that these names belong to this entry, rather than to S-1112 above, but it is not entirely certain.

S-1116 984a B:138 X-0663 CLER:BATA
a. W-2631 Captain James Gray
b. James Gray
c. B. Crumell; J. Taylor, 1823; J. Slade, 1825; P. H. Loop; N. Reeves; S. Medary, 1829; Henry Loop; Samuel Vail, 1830; John Hill, 1832

S-1117 1667a B:74 X-0663 CLIN:MARI CLIN:JEFF BROW: --*
a. W-2601 Captain Nathaniel Terry
b. Nathaniel Terry
c. William Lytle; John Watts, "original proprietor"; Tin? Kirley, 1823
*Mentioned in Source B only.

S-1118 500a B:398 X-0340 CHAM:WAYN CHAM:RUSH
a. W-0091 General George Weedon
b. George Weedon
c. George Lewis; James Campbell, 1827

S-1118 500a B:398 X-0340 CHAM:WAYN
a. W-0091 General George Weedon
b. George Weedon
c. None

S-1118 500a B:398 X-0340 CHAM:WAYN
a. W-0091 General George Weedon
b. George Weedon
c. None

S-1118 500a B:399 X-000* CHAM:WAYN
a. W-0091 General George Weedon
b. George Weedon
c. None
*Source A does not give watercourse; probably X-0340.

S-1119 1000a B:189 X-0840 FAYE:UNIO
a. W-0811 Captain Robert Randolph
b. Robert Randolph
c. None

S-1121 2000a B:74 X-1070 CLIN:MARI*
a. W-1619 Doctor George Munroe
b. George Monroe**
c. None
*Source B notation: "Blanchester."
**Source B spells Munroe.

S-1122* 1333a — — FAYE:--**
a. --
b. Theodoric Bland
c. -- Phelps & -- Woods, 1828; R. Douglas, 1829; William Dangerfield
*Listed in Source B only, but out of sequence (before S-1094 therein).
**Source B does not give township.

S-1124 1000a B:19 X-1300 BROW:LEWI
a. W-0105 Doctor John Roberts
b. John Roberts
c. William Kendall; J. McCormick, 1831; S. Glaze; P. L. Wilson, 1840; J. & E. Ambrose; M. Day, 1842; J. F. Foos

S-1125 333a B:166 X-0870 PIKE:PEEP
a. W-1144 Samuel McCord, 200a
W-1098 Thomas McElevin [McElwain?], 200a; *both warrants to* Captain Alexander Fowler [assignee?]
b. Alexander Fowler
c. Unknown; James Penniston, 1836; D. L. Hodges, 1838; Van S. Murphey, 1840; A. Fowler, heirs

S-1125 667a B:166 X-0870 PIKE:PEEP
a. W-1042 William Coxon, 200a
W-1057 William Smith, 200a
W-1069 Thomas Craig, 200a
W-1098 Thomas McElevin? [McElwain?], 200a; *all four warrants to* Alexander Fowler [assignee?]
b. Alexander Fowler
c. R. Clark, heirs; C. McCollister, 1836; D. L. Hodges, 1838

S-1126 1000a A:282 X-0660 HAMI:ANDE
a. W-0113 Captain James Pendleton
b. James Pendleton
c. C. Webb; R. Powell; G. W. Jones, 1826; Stephen Simpson; Vincent Goldsmith, 1833

S-1129 1200a B:12 X-0840 ROSS:TWIN
a. W-1886* Francis Ramsey; Joseph Watkins & William R. Bernard [assignees?]
b. Joseph Watkins
c. David Breedlove; Joshua Seney? [Leney?] 1839
*W-1886 was issued for 200a only; this entry may be erroneous or incomplete.

S-1131 1000a B:269 X-0840 HIGH:NEWM HIGH:UNIO
a. W-0660 Captain Hezekiah Morton
b. Hezekiah Morton
c. W. Doyle; J. Jones, 1824

S-1133 1000a B:207 X-0840 MADI:STOK FAYE: --*
a. W-0398 Captain Thomas Pemberton
b. Thomas Pemberton
c. M. Bonner, 1833; R. Douglas; Alexander Douglas, 1838; T. Pemberton, heirs; Peter Douglas, 1840; C. Pancake, 1842
*Source B does not list Fayette County.

S-1134 1000a A:256 X-0260 CLER:UNIO*
a. W-2311 Captain Churchill Jones
b. Churchill Jones
c. C. H. Everett; W. Thomas, 1831? [1836?]; D. Pease
*Source B notation: "Withamsville."

S-1135 1000a B:65 X-0130 HIGH:NEWM HIGH:CONC
a. W-0753 Major John Willis
b. Clement Biddle
c. John Jordan & -- Lights; G. W. Barriere, 1828; Unknown; John M. Barriere, 1838; Abel Wood; John Purdy, 1839; M. Eder? [Caer?]; M. M. Bunnion, 1842

S-1136 1000a A:256 X-0660 CLER:UNIO
a. W-1382 Lieutenant James Merriwether
b. James Merriwether
c. -- Kyle & -- McKay; John Whetstone, 1824; J. Yeo, 1826; Shadrack Lane, 1827; Z. Chapman, 1829; C. L. Mathews; -- Kyle & -- McKay, heirs; John Walker, 1837

S-1137 400a B:26 X-0800 ADAM:SPRI
a. W-0291 Captain Henry Bedinger
b. Hendry Bedinger
c. None

S-1138 1778 A:257 X-0660 CLER:UNIO
a. W-1934 Colonel George Matthews
b. George Matthews
c. None

S-1139 750a C:2 X-0110 UNIO:LEES
a. W-0070 Lieutenant Francis Smith
b. Francis Smith
c. James Taylor, 1826; James Sill; J. Woodrow, Junior, 1837

S-1140 1000a* F:59 X-1300 BROW:PLEA
a. W-2331 Captain Lewis Booker
b. Lewis Booker
c. William Kendall; Michael Pritchett, 1826; M. Levi; D. Johnson, 1839; D. G. Devore, 1841
*Source A notation: "333-1/3 [acres] withdr[awn]."

S-1144 1000a B:11 X-0010 CLIN:CHES GREE: --
a. W-1880* John Corbett; Levi Hollingsworth [assignee?]
b. Joseph Watkins**
c. John Bush; J. Fyfe, 1836
*W-1880 was issued for 200a, according to Source C.
**Source B shows Charles Fleming, but stricken out.

S-1146 1000a A:422 X-0180 WARR:WAYN CLIN:CHES*
a. W-0207 Robert Gibins, heir to Major E. Dickinson
b. Robert Gibbons
c. David Harvey; E. Stowell, 1838; John Satterthwaite, heirs; B. Hathaway, 1839
*Source A does not mention Clinton County, Chester Township.

S-1147 1000a B:401 X-0340 CHAM:RUSH*
a. W-0224 Captain Benjamin Biggs
b. Benjamin Biggs
c. Ezra Reed, 1831; Ebenezer Mathews
*Source B notation: "Lewisburg."

S-1148 500a B:455 X-0840 FAYE:WAYN
a. W-0225 Captain Benjamin Biggs
b. Benjamin Biggs
c. None

S-1149 500a A-417 X-0040 ADAM:TIFF
a. W-0110 David Clark, assignee of W. Bunch; Bowling Clark [assignee?] 100a
W-2107 William Mosby; Bowling Clark [assignee?] 200a
W-2123 Bowling Clark; assignee of Ch[ristopher?] Stoakes, 200a
b. Bolling Clark
c. William Crawford, deceased; Daniel P. Wilkins, 1826; Sarah Yeocum [*also* Yocum]; John Bayless; Mary Crawford, 1831; William Crawford, heirs; D. Malkeney [*also* Matheney] 1835; T. Houston, 1828

S-1149* 300a A:417 X-0040 ADAM:TIFF
a. W-1360 John Jones; Thomas Conn [assignee?] 200a
W-1362 Daniel Grant; Thomas Conn [assignee?] 100a
b. Thomas Conn*
c. David Flournoy; L. Cole, 1835
*Source B shows another entry under S-1149 in the name of John Wallace for 200a (no location given). The entry is crossed out, however.

S-1151 1000a B:275 X-0840 HIGH:UNIO
a. W-2647 William Worsham, heir to J. W[orsham?]
b. William Worsham
c. None

S-1152 1000a B:120 X-0840 FAYE:JEFF
a. W-0619 Captain Larkin Smith
b. Larkin Smith
c. None

S-1153 850a C:334 X-1120 BROW:FRAN
a. W-1468 Lieutenant Benjamin Moseley
b. Benjamin Moseley
c. Philip Baker; George Shultz; J. Bander? & C. Buck*; Uriah Springer, 1826; Jonah? [Josiah?] Lucas; John Ernst, 1832; S. Work, 1834
*Source B could also read J. & C. Buck.

S-1156 2475a A:278 X-0800 CLER:MONR CLER:WASH
a. W-1606 John Woodford, heir to General -- Woodford
b. John Woodford
c. M? [W?] Allen; W. Dowdney, 1826; G. Barclay; [continued]

D. Hawkins, 1823; Joseph? Evans; William Johnson, 1824; John Duckwall, 1826; William McCarty; E. Salt, 1823; E. Shaw, 1826; A. Stewart; W. Stewart; W. C. Moore, 1826; R. Denham, 1826; J. D. Morris, 1831; R. Naylor

S-1158 600a B:140 X-0660 GREE:ROSS
a. W-1519 Nicholas Neil; James Wilson [assignee?] 467a
W-1354 Patrick Hagerly; James Wilson [assignee?] 400a
b. James Wilson
c. None

S-1160 525a A:450 X-0310 or X-0320 CLER:OHIO
a. W-0019 Brigadier General -- Morgan
b. John Crawford
c. None

S-1161 83a B:407 X-0800 SCIO:WASH
a. W-0660 Captain Hezekiah Morton
b. Hezekiah Morton
c. None

S-1161 57a B:407 X-0800 SCIO:WASH
a. W-0660 Captain Hezekiah Morton
b. Hezekiah Morton
c. None

S-1162 1000a A:527 X-0660 CLIN:UNIO
a. W-2273 Captain Thomas Buckner
b. Thomas Buckner
c. None

S-1163 1400a B:170 X-0420 BROW:BYRD*
a. W0688 Lieutenant Colonel Samuel Hopkins
b. Samuel Hopkins
c. Rodman Gardner; Robert Allen, 1823; L. L. Haines; J. Louden? [London?] 1828; James Lansbury? [Sansbury?]; L? L? [S? S?] Tucker, 1831
*Source B notation: "By Russelville."

S-1164 1000a A:229 X-1150 ADAM:SPRI
a. W-0598 Captain James Williams
b. James Williams
c. None

S-1165 500a B:74 X-1073 BROW:PERR CLIN:MARI CLIN:JEFF
a. W-2279 Colonel Christian Febeger
b. Christian Febiger
c. Randall Brewer; B. Hinkson, 1823; W. J. Berry; John Hadley, Junior, 1840; J. Doherty, heirs; William Farquhar; D. C. Hinman, 1840

S-1166 1000a B:87 X-0180 GREE:SILV
a. W-1936 Captain Reuben Taylor
b. John Watts
c. None

S-1169 1000a A:312 X-0420 BROW:JACK
a. W-0404 William Tompkins, heir to Robert Tompkins
b. William Tompkins
c. James Middleswart; J. Middleton, 1826; Nathan Patton; Thomas Middleton, 1826; James Barnes, 1835; John Ellison; John S. Beasley, 1839; J. & T. Reynolds; J. W. Reynolds, 1841

S-1170 1500a A:527 X-0660 CLIN:UNIO
a. W-0765 Colonel Thomas Gaskins
b. Thomas Gaskins
c. W. K. Wood; T. L. Caruthers, 1842

S-1171 1000a B:120 X-0180 GREE:SILV
a. W-0814 David Walker, heir to Captain -- Walker
b. David Walker
c. D. Browder; J. Browder, 1823

S-1172 1667a B:75 X-0663 CLIN:JEFF
a. W-0389 Lieutenant John Lapsley
b. John Lapsley
c. William Barr; H. R. Gedding, 1824; Charles Thompson; -- Sewell & -- Melliken, 1824; Jeremiah Hadley, 1834; Isaiah Clark*; William P. Hunnicut, 1833; J. C. Morris
*Land forfeited in 1838.

S-1174 1000a B:128 X-1080 CLIN:MARI BROW: --*
a. W-0056 Captain John Peyton
b. John Peyton
c. -- Duncan, -- Howell, & -- Lam; William R. Cole, 1827; William R. Sewell, 1828; E. May; C. B. Harlan, 1832; William Woodruff; Levi Gustin, 1834; D. Fisher; S. Soloman, 1836; J. Darbyshire, 1837; G. Tribbey, 1839; Gilbert Terril [*also* Terrill]; Lewis Webber; A. E. Strickle, 1839; G. Fooz, 1839; John Dunkins & L. L. Howell & R. P Howell, 1827

S-1175 800a* B:12 X-0841 ROSS:CONC
a. W-1880** John Corbett; Levi Hollingsworth [assignee?]
b. Joseph Watkins
c. None
*Source B shows 1000a.
**W-1880 issued for 200a only; this entry incomplete or erroneous; *see also* S-1144.

S-1176 667a B:75 X-1173 CLIN:WASH
a. W-1495 John Gratton, heir to Lieutenant J. Gratton, deceased
b. John Gratton
c. Jacob Swoop; W. P. Hunnicut, 1835

S-1177 1000a B:241 X-0663 BROW:PERR CLIN: --*
a. W-0096 Captain Baylor Hill
b. Baylor Hill
c. William Lytle; David G. Devore, 1833; E. L? [S?] Haines
*Source B does not show Clinton County.

S-1185 *or* S-1186 1000a B:140 X-0660 CLAR:GREE GREE:MIAM GREE:ROSS
a. W-0014 Samuel Oldham, heir to Captain C. Oldham
b. Samuel Oldham
c. None

S-1187 800a B:216 X-0340 MADI:CANA
a. W-0351 Lieutenant Colonel Charles Simms
b. Charles Simms
c. Alexander Cormer? [Conner?] 1832; C. Simms, heirs; D. K. Bigelow, 1837

S-1188 2167a B:154 X-0660 GREE:SILV
a. W-0101 Colonel George Baylor
b. George Baylor
c. H. Siscoe?; J. George, 1820-1826

S-1189 1630a B:32 X-1000 PICK:SCIO
a. W-0019 Brigadier General -- Morgan
b. Daniel Morgan
c. None

S-1190 1000a A:440 X-0660 CLIN:GREE CLIN:WAYN
a. W-1845 John Walker, 200a
W-1799 William O'Neal, 100a
W-1812 John Howard, 100a
W-1800 Joseph Bishop, 100a
W-2196 Henry Childress, 100a
W-1876 Thomas Tunstall, 200a
W-4774 George Hill, 200a: *all seven warrants to* -- Montgomery & -- Allen [assignees?]
b. -- Montgomery & -- Allen
c. John Henry; Isaiah Morris, 1828

S-1192 1000a B:47 X-0663 CLIN:GREE
a. W-1963 William Taliaferro, heir to Colonel [William] Taliaferro
b. William Taliaferro
c. None

S-1194 867a B:27 X-1000 PICK:SCIO
a. W-2162 Colonel William Heth
b. William Heth
c. None

S-1197 1000a A:246 X-0800 CLER:MONR
a. W-1386 Major Joseph Eggleston
b. Joseph Eggleston
c. None

S-1198 1000a A:429 X-1000 PICK:WAYN
a. W-0303 Captain Robert White
b. Robert White
c. John Keen; William Henry, 1827; E. Langham; John Osenbaugh, 1827

S-1199 880a D:119 X-0910 CLER:MONR CLER:TATE
a. W-0199 Captain Lawrence Butler
b. Lawrence Butler
c. None

S-1203 1000a A:291 X-0130 HIGH:JACK
a. W-0241 Captain Thomas Barbee
b. Thomas Barbee
c. None

S-1204 1000a B:207 X-0840 FAYE:JEFF
a. W-0113 Captain James Pendleton
b. James Pendleton
c. None

S-1205 1000a B:282 X-0840 FAYE:JEFF FAYE:PAIN
a. W-1375 Captain Tarpley White
b. Tarpley White
c. R. Wilson, heirs; Elain Hinton, 1839

S-1209 1067a B:45 X-0663 BROW:PERR CLER:JACK
a. W-2199 Captain William Johnson
b. William Johnson
c. Plat Evans; Timothy Kirby, 1826; Robert Dickey; James Perin, 1836; Unknown; C. B. Huber, 1836 (Clermont County); C. Conklin, 1842 (Brown County)

S-1211 1067a A:420 X-1170 WARR:WASH
a. W-2012 Major General Charles Scott; Stephen T. Mason [assignee?]
b. Stephen T. Mason
c. William Snider; John Kitchen, 1831; E. Stowel, 1837

S-1213 1333a B:243 X-1300 BROW:SCOT*
a. W-1273 John Burton, heir to H. Burton
b. John Burton
c. John McBeth; David Johnson, 1823; Henry Purviance; William Lee, and George Shultz, 1824; John Wilkins, Junior; George W. Jouett, 1824; James McDaniel; G. Kimball, 1830; Lawrence Rose; R. D. Tomb, 1830; John Rice, 1833; J. Foster; John A. Gage, 1831; James McCall; Robert? [Richard?] Campbell, 1831
*Source B notation: "Near Hope."

S-1214 1000a B:17 X-0663 BROW:PERR
a. W-0067 William Giles, heir to John Giles
b. William Giles
c. J. S. Beasley, 1839; J. M. Trimble

S-1216 1000a B:207 X-0840 FAYE:CONC
a. W-0113 Captain James Pendleton
b. James Pendleton
c. -- Todd & -- Gatewood; J. Jamison? [Jameson?] 1839

S-1219 500a B:75 X-0663 BROW:PERR
a. W-0074 Lieutenant James Morton
b. James Morton
c. James McNutt; George Shultz, 1825; Robert Campbell, 1830; D. Foy; P. L. Wilson, 1841

S-1219 500a B:75 X-0663 BROW:PERR
HIGH: --*
a. W-0074 Lieutenant James Morton
b. James Morton
c. None
*Source B does not mention Highland County.

S-1223 1000a B:87 X-0840 FAYE:JEFF
a. W-0300 Captain Abraham Hite
b. Abraham Hite
c. Jonathan Wait; Thomas M. Garraugh, 1835

S-1227 1500a B:40 X-1000 PICK:JACK
a. W-0009 Lieutenant Colonel Samuel F? Cabell
b. Samuel J. Cabell
c. None

S-1228 1200a B:154 X-0660 GREE:SILV
a. W-0753 Major John Willis; Clement Biddle [assignee?]
b. Clement Biddle
c. None

S-1231 1000a B:47 X-0840 CLIN:GREE
a. W-1963 William Taliaferro, heir to Colonel [William] Taliaferro
b. William Taliaferro
c. John Fisher; J. Morris & C. Hiatt, 1824; Job Ellis; B. Bollard, 1835

S-1233 200a B:137 X-1300 HIGH:CLAY
a. W-2151 John Payne
b. John Payne
c. William Scott, 1833

S-1233 200a B:137 X-1300 HIGH:CLAY
a. W-2100 Patrick Glason
b. Patrick Glasser
c. None

S-1233 100a B:137 X-1300 HIGH:CLAY
a. W-1925 James Hawkins
b. James Hawkins
c. William Scott; J. E. Stretcher, 1835; Joseph Hawkins

S-1233 117a D:372 X-0460 HIGH:CLAY
a. W-2241 Samuel Hunt
b. William Handley
c. None

S-1233 117a D:372 X-0460 HIGH:CLAY
a. W-2241 Samuel Hunt
b. R. G. Leonard & A. Latham*
c. None
*Source B mentions only R. G. Leonard.

S-1233 100a D:137 X-1300 HIGH:CLAY
a. W-1898 Joseph Hughes
b. Joseph Huges*
c. William Scott; J. E. Stretcher, 1835; Joseph Hawkins
*Source B spells Hughes.

S-1234 410a B:417 X-1000 PICK:SCIO
a. W-2162 Colonel William Heth
b. William Heth
c. None

S-1235 1000a B:38 X-0440 HIGH:JACK
a. W-0598 Captain James Williams
b. James Williams
c. -- Latham & -- Leonard*; William Hunnicut, 1831*; "Part of Gaines' tract in Clinton [County] No. 1203."*
*These notations were marked out in Source B.

S-1236 1000a A:489 X-1170 CLIN:UNIO
CLIN:LIBE
a. W-2367 Captain John Anderson
b. John Anderson
c. Benjamin Anderson; B. Hinkson, 1823; Joel Holson, 1827; John Frazier, 1824; Amos Hodson, 1831

S-1238 667a B:281 X-0840 MADI:STOK
a. W-2014 Lieutenant Archibald Campbell; Thomas Shelton [assignee?]
b. Thomas Shelton, Junior
c. None

S-1239 1310a A:265 X-0800 CLER:TATE
X-0910
a. W-0855 Lieutenant Colonel Oliver Towles
b. Oliver Towles
c. O. E. Denham; -- Barber & -- Bryan, 1823; Joseph Henderson; D. Dickerson, 1824; John Boggess? 1825; Peter Machir; J. Noble; Chapman Archer, 1824; Samuel Sly; S. Mahon, 1833; William West; G. Clark, 1834; Joseph Altman? [Attman?]; R. McFarland, 1835

S-1239 1000a A:266 X-0800 CLER:MONR
X-0910
a. W-0855 Lieutenant Colonel Oliver Towles
b. Oliver Towles
c. Peter Machir; T. Kirby, 1826; John Boggess, 1825; S. Slye; Z. Chapman, 1835; Thomas Morris; J. D. Morris, 1839

S-1240 667a A:345 X-0180 GREE:XENI
X-0740
a. W-1822 Lieutenant John Heth; Robert Baylor & William McGuire [assignees?]
b. William McGuire
c. Daniel Dean, 1830

S-1241 1000a B:209 X-0840 MADI:STOK
a. W-2601 Captain Nathaniel Terry
b. Nathaniel Terry
c. William B. Rowand; S. B. Baskerville, 1833; R. Douglas; Alexander Douglas, 1838; J. Johnson

S-1242 1000a B:138 X-0663 CLER:BATA
a. W-2631 Captain James Gray
b. James Gray
c. None

S-1244 1000a B:281 X-0840 MADI:STOK
a. W-0056 Captain John Peyton
b. John Peyton
c. David Ross; S. B. Gorley, 1835

S-1248 1200a A:351 X-0800 ADAM:LIBE
a. W-2360 Colonel Charles Harrison
b. Charles Harrison
c. Thomas Foote; Jonas Carl, 1823; Elijah Hendricks; William Armstrong, 1823; James Brownfields; Thomas? Huston, 1834; T. Reese

S-1249 1000a B:87 X-0840 FAYE:JEFF
a. W-1498 Ephraim Cooper; Clement Biddle [assignee] 400a
W-1852 John Stith; Doctor James Currie [assignee?] Clement Biddle [assignee?] 200a*
W-1665 Robert Hart; Clement Biddle [assignee?] 400a
b. Clement Biddle
c. None
*This warrant number may be in error. *See* S-1250.

S-1250 1000a B:121 X-0840 FAYE:JEFF
a. W-1852 Captain John Stith; Doctor James Currie [assignee?]
b. James Currie
c. J. Jamison; W. V. Rawlings, 1841

S-1252 1000a A:300 X-0130 ADAM:WINC
a. W-2323 Captain Colin Cocke? [Cooke?]
b. Colin Coke*
c. None
*Source B spells Cocke.

S-1253 1265a B:211 X-0840 FAYE:JEFF
a. W-0101 Colonel George Baylor
b. George Baylor*
c. Walker Bayler*; Benjamin Greathouse, 1827; John Brown; John Rankin, 1829; Thomas Rankin "deeded Sept. 5, 1833"; John Batterton; Lawson P. Reed, 1830; J. A. Rankin, 1838
*So spelled.

S-1256 1000a B:88 X-0840 FAYE:JEFF
MADI: --*
a. W-2223 Captain Patrick Carnes
b. Patrick Carns**
c. Thomas Carneal; -- Phelps & -- Woods, 1828; R. Douglas, 1827; J. Y. Green, 1831***
*Source B does not mention Madison County.
**Source B spells Carnes.
***"27 Dec. 1831 deeded J. Y. Green & James Green, assignees of Douglas."

S-1260 1000a A:402 X-0840 ROSS:SCIO
a. W-2655 William Lawson, heir to C. Lawson
b. William Lawson
c. None

S-1262 1111a B:88 X-0840 FAYE:JEFF
a. W-2242 Lieutenant John Roney
b. John Roney
c. Jesse McKay; Andrew Hardway? 1828; Luke Arnold; Alexander Douglas, Junior, 1838; R. Douglas; A. S. Dickey, 1839; N. Robinson; James Henton, 1841

S-1264 1000a B:247 X-0134 ADAM:SCOT
a. W-0614 Captain Henry Moss
b. Henry Moss
c. None

S-1265 1000a B:12 X-0010 CLIN:LIBE
CLIN:CHES
a. W-1880* --
b. Joseph Watkins**
c. Mayo C. Watkins; Joseph? [James?] Owen; John Chapman, 1830; J. Morris, 1835
*Warrant W-1880 was issued to John Corbett for 200 acres; the above entry may be incorrect.
**Source B also shows the name Charles Fleming crossed out.

S-1267 1000a B:88 X-0840 FAYE:JEFF
a. W-0389 Lieutenant John Lapsley
b. John Lapsley
c. Michael Creamer, 1829; D. Dougherty; W. Loofborrow, 1839

S-1269 200a A:384 X-0133 HIGH:JACK
a. W-0719 Samuel McCall
b. Samuel McCall*
c. James Perry; James M. Trimble, 1831
*Source B spells McCaul.

S-1269* 200a A:398 X-0133 HIGH:JACK
a. W-1134 Thomas Jones
b. Thomas Jones**
c. John Machir; R. Moberley, 1826; J. M. Trimble, 1831
*Source B says not patented.
**Source B notation: "Shelby County, Kentucky" but is not clear to whom the notation pertains.

S-1269* 200a A:398 X-0133 HIGH:JACK
a. W-1084 Laughlin McClean
b. Laughlin McClain
c. Stephen Mooberry; J. M. Trimble, 1833
*Source B says not patented.

S-1269* 200a A:398 X-0133 HIGH:JACK
a. W-1073 Michael Kairns
b. Michael Kairnes
c. E. Murfin; S. Swartz; J. W. Trimble, 1840
*Source B says not patented.

S-1270 1000a A:424 X-0800 SCIO:WASH
X-1000 SCIO:UNIO
a. W-0145 Captain William Fowler
b. William Fowler
c. J. M. Nelson; John A. Trimble, 1827; G. D. H. Wilcoxon; J. D. Smith, 1839

S-1271 2000a B:88 X-0840 FAYE:JEFF*
a. W-0586 Doctor Edward Duff
b. Edward Duff
c. Samuel Herold; Aaron Johnston, 1824; Edward Fulk; Amos Woods, 1831; John Harness; George Benson, 1831; P. Harness; Henry Phelps, 1831; H. McCanless, 1833; J. H. Green, 1834; Susanna Rowe; L. P. Reid, 1830; Stephen Fulk; James Shavers, 1835; A. Douglas, Junior; Joseph [or James] Barrett; J. Jamison, 1838; Abel Armstrong; James [or Joseph?] Bloomer, 1840
*Source B notation: "Jeffersonville."

S-1272 1333a B:89 X-0840 FAYE:JEFF
a. W-2560 Major Everard Meade*
b. Everard Mead*
c. J. N. & N. Huston; Lawson P. Reid [or Reed] 1830; John L. Avery; Abraham? Bush, 1837
*So spelled.

S-1273 & S-12353 1200a E:295 X-0660 GREE:SILV
a. W-2377 Doctor John Trezevant; John Tench, Cadwallader Wallace, & Thomas J. McArthur [assignees?]
b. Cadwallader Wallace, *et al**
c. — McGregor & — McCune; G. Stevens, 1840; J. & T. Smith; James Snodgrass, 1840; Elias Roley? [Robey?] 1841
*Source B lists grantee as John Tench.

S-1274 1200a B:155 X-0660 GREE:SILV GREE:CAES
a. W-0286 Reverend Alexander Balmain
b. Alexander Balmain
c. J. Owens; S. W. McCracken, 1823; John Wicks; J. Dodd, 1828; Unknown; T. J. Freeman, 1830

S-1275 1867a A:352 X-0420 ADAM:LIBE
a. W-2360 Colonel Charles Harrison
b. Charles Harrison
c. William Black, heirs; John Askew* 1826; Z. Black, 1827; Charles Johnson; Thomas Hill; John Askreen* 1832; John Watts; Thomas Huston, 1832
*So spelled.

S-1276 1000a A:414 X-1120 BROW:FRAN
a. W-0685 Lieutenant Obadiah Smith
b. Obadiah Smith
c. None

S-1278 1035a B:211 X-0840 FAYE:JEFF
a. W-0101 Colonel George Baylor
b. George Baylor
c. Charles Holleman; D. McLane, 1827

S-1279 350a B:29 X-0800 FRAN:FRAN FAYE:JEFF*
a. W-0307 Captain John Clarke
b. John Clark
c. None
*Source A does not mention Fayette County, Jefferson Township.

S-1280 500a B:122 X-0840 FAYE:JEFF
a. W-1384* Lieutenant Thomas Burford
b. Abraham Hite
c. Philip Gossard; D. McLane, 1827; N. F. Jones, heirs; William Holt, 1841; Samuel F. Kerr, assignee of -- Philps** "deeded 22 February 1833."
*Erroneous warrant number?; see following entry.
**So spelled.

S-1280 167a B:122 X-0840 FAYE:JEFF
a. W-1384 Lieutenant Thomas Burford ; Edward Dowse [assignee?]
b. Philip Henry, 1829; Amos Jones; — Hite & — Dowse; H. Phelps, 1831

S-1281 677a A:395 X-0180 GREE:SUGA CLIN:CHES WARR:WAYN
a. W-1476 Captain Leroy Edwards
b. Leroy Edwards
c. None

S-1283 1000a B:89 X-0840 FAYE:JEFF
a. W-0089 Captain Abraham Murry
b. Abraham Maury
c. G. Wardway; W. B. Wright

S-1284 2000a B:89 X-0840 FAYE:JEFF MADI:STOK*
a. W-2263 Lieutenant William Washington
b. William Washington
c. Bailey Washington; Robert Porter, 1833; Carr F. Porter
*Source A does not mention Madison County, Stokes Township.

S-1285 400a A:239 X-0800 CLER:FRAN
a. W-1065* Nicholas Carter
b. Nicholas Carter
c. None
*Warrant is for 200a only.

S-1286 2000a B:8 X-0340 PICK:DARB
a. W-0587 Captain John Blackwell
b. John Blackwell
c. None

S-1287 1400a A:295 X-0800 BROW:BYRD
a. W-0688 Lieutenant Colonel Samuel Hopkins
b. Samuel Hopkins
c. Arthur Fox, heirs; John Chapman, 1824; James London, 1826

S-1289 1000a C:225 X-1000 PICK:SCIO
a. W-0057 Captain Robert Porterfield
b. Robert Porterfield
c. J. Fulson & E. Williams, 1823

S-1293 1333a B:90 X-0840 FAYE:JEFF MADI:STOK
a. W-0046 Clement Read
b. Clement Read
c. Michael Swing?; J. Y. Green, 1831; E. Hunt, heirs; Samuel N. Kerr, 1838 (Madison County); Unknown; R. Douglas, 1836 (Madison County); William Hudson

S-1294 2222a B:33 X-1000 PICK:SCIO FRAN:JACK
a. W-0020 Brigadier General -- Morgan
b. Daniel Morgan
c. Robert Leeds; Edward Williams, 1823; Jacob Castleman; James Reid [or Reed]; J. L. Taylor (Franklin County); J. Tunney, 1838; Mary Smith; Unknown (Pickaway County); T. Akin; Lyne Starling, 1831

S-1295 1000a A:395 X-0180 GREE:SUGA
a. W-0207 Robert Gibins, heir to Major E. Dickinson
b. Robert Gibbons
c. None

S-1297 667a B:376 X-0180 GREE:SUGA
a. W-0075 Lieutenant Benjamin Moseley
b. Benjamin Mosley*
c. None
*Source B spells Moseley.

S-1298 130a D:95 X-0340 PICK:JACK
a. W-0814 David Walker, heir to Captain -- Walker
b. David Walker
c. None

S-1299 890a C:87 X-0340 PICK:SCIO
a. W-1570 Lieutenant Reuben Long
b. Reuben Long
c. Robert? Means; William Martin, 1829; James Bronson; George Botkin, 1834; Samuel Kinnear, 1831; W. Reed, 1837

S-1300 700a B:167 X-0870 PIKE:PEEP
a. W-0610 Captain John Winston
b. John Winston
c. None

S-1301 460a C:69 X-1000 PICK:JACK
a. W-1396 Captain John Stokes
b. John Stokes
c. None

S-1301 106a C:69 X-1000 PICK:JACK
a. W-1396 Captain John Stokes
b. John Stokes
c. None

S-1301 500a C:115 X-1005 PICK:JACK
a. W-1396 Captain John Stokes
b. John Stokes
c. None

S-1302 200a D:47 X-1005 PICK:JACK
a. W-1396 Captain John Stokes
b. John Stokes
c. None

S-1302 214a D:47 X-1005 PICK:JACK
a. W-1396 Captain John Stokes
b. John Stokes
c. None

S-1302 56a D:47 X-1005 PICK:JACK
a. W-1396 Captain John Stokes
b. John Stokes
c. None

S-1304 1000a A:301 X-0134 ADAM:WINC ADAM:SCOT
a. W-2323 Captain Colin Cocke? [Cooke?]
b. Colin Coke*
c. Robert Craig; D. P. Wilkins, 1823; B. Robuck; A. D. Beasley, 1828; J. Bailey, heirs
*Source B spells Cocke.

S-1306 1000a A:302 X-0134 ADAM:SCOT ADAM:WINC BROW:EAGL
a. W-0638 Captain Robert Morrow
b. Robert Morrow
c. Elias Boatman, heirs; Mathew Kincaid, 1826

S-1307 1000a B:50 X-0750 UNIO:MILL
a. W-0727 Lieutenant Robert Dandridge
b. Robert Dandridge
c. James Watkins; S. G. Strong, 1828

S-1309 1000a B:187 X-0840 FAYE:UNIO FAYE:CONC
a. W-2321 Captain William Parsons
b. William Parsons
c. George Coil; Humphrey Fulliston? 1825; Thomas Coil; Edward Turner, 1839

S-1310 1000a B:90 X-0840 MADI:STOK FAYE: --*
a. W-0350 Captain Samuel K. Bradford
b. Samuel K. Bradford
c. None
*Source B does not mention Fayette County.

S-1313 450a B:6 X-0340 PICK:DARB
a. W-0069 Captain Philip Slaughter
b. Philip Slaughter
c. -- Taylor, -- Webster, & -- Berry; Richard Seymour, 1831

S-1315 1000a B:3 X-0360 MADI:PLEA
a. W-2311 Captain Churchill Jones
b. Churchill Jones
c. None

S-1316 1000a B:191 X-0840 FAYE:UNIO
a. W-1376 Lieutenant John White
b. John White
c. William Miller; J. Woods, 1826; Benjamin Dawson, heirs; Robert Robinson, 1828; W. Loofborrow, 1829; David Loofborrow; John White; James Fife; N. F. Jones, 1833

S-1317 1000a A:415 X-1120 BROW:PLEA
a. W-1894 Captain Henry Heth
b. Henry Hith*
c. James Thompson; W. Hewitt, 1834
*Source B spells Heth.

S-1318 1100a B:48 X-0800 CLER:WASH
a. W-2613 David Hambick? [Hambrick?] 200a
W-2630 W. Young, 200a
W-2616 Samuel Cox, 100a
W-2620 James Bailey, 200a
W-2625 Thomas Miller, 100a
W-2627 Alexander Patton, 100a
W-2618 Dawson Burgers, 200a; *all the above warrants assigned to* Daniel Flowerre
b. Daniel Flowers*
c. E. Jones; J. Duckwall, 1826
*Source B spells Flowerree.

S-1320 1200a A:528 X-0660 CLIN:GREE
a. W-0192 Lieutenant Colonel John Jameson
b. John Jameson
c. J. Woodrow; R. B. Harlan, 1837

S-1321 1200a A:291 X-0133 HIGH:JACK*
a. W-2199 Captain William Johnson
b. William Johnson
c. J. Noland; A. Grantham, 1826
*Source B notation: "Belfort."

S-1324 1000a B:131 X-0660 CLAR:GREE GREE:ROSS
a. W-0096 Captain Baylor Hill
b. Baylor Hill
c. William Lytle; John F. Stewart; Frederick Johnson, 1828; Stephen Wilson; John Dodd, 1838 (Greene County)

S-1326 1333a B:443 X-0133 HIGH:JACK
a. W-0235 Lieutenant Josiah Tannehill
b. Josiah Tawnyhill*
c. Andrew Gilmore; J. M. Trimble, 1833; James G. Strean; Jared Hopkins; J. A. Smith, 1840
*Source B spells Tawneyhill.

S-1327* 910a -- -- PICK: --
a. --
b. Strothers Jones
c. --
*This entry cancelled in Source B.

S-1329* 1200a -- -- --
a. --
b. William Johnson
c. --
*This entry cancelled in Source B.

S-1330 870a B:144 X-0660 MADI: -- GREE: --
a. W-1396 Captain John Stokes
b. John Stokes
c. None

S-1332 200a B:488 X-0730 CHAM: --* CLAR:PLEA
a. W-0685 Lieutenant Obadiah Smith
b. Obadiah Smith
c. Shad[rack?] Harrison; George Nedsker? [Medsker?] 1823
*Source B does not mention Champaign County.

S-1335 667a B:62 X-1000 FRAN:NORW
a. W-2235 Lieutenant Nathaniel Anderson
b. Nathaniel Anderson
c. Smith Slaughter; Andrew Jameson, 1826; Robert Brotherton, 1827; William Brown

S-1336 1000a B:213 X-0180 GREE:SILV
a. W-1383 Lieutenant Robert Kirk
b. Robert Kirk
c. None

S-1338 1000a A:396 X-1170 CLIN:UNIO
a. W-0176 General P. Muhlenberg
b. Peter Muhlenburg
c. None

S-1341 200a B:277 X-0840 MADI:STOK
a. W-1732 Robert Jones
b. Robert Jones
c. None

S-1342 1667a B:90 X-0840 FAYE:JEFF
a. W-0285 Captain Lieutenant Ambrose Bohannon; Thomas Shaw [assignee?]
b. Thomas Shaw
c. R. Means; Michael Christie, 1829; R. Douglas, 1831; H. McLaughlin; William Clark, 1833

S-1343 1000a B:121 X-0840 FAYE:JEFF
a. W-0350 Captain Samuel K. Bradford
b. Samuel K. Bradford
c. Jer[emiah?] Scott; Henry Phelps, 1829; Hugh McLaughlin; William Popejoy, 1830; Thomas W. Lee; M. B. Wright, 1837; Joseph? [James?] Parrott, Junior, 1838; J. N. Green, 1837; Henry Bramer; James? [Joseph?] Bloomer

S-1344 867a B:89 X-0840 FAYE:JEFF
a. W-0089 Captain Abraham Murry
b. Abraham Murry*
c. John Clemons; James? [Joseph?] Paret; Z. Brewster; A. S. Dickey, 1839; R. Douglas
*Source B also spells Maury.

S-1347 1667a B:7 X-0340 PICK:MUHL
a. W-0176 General P. Muhlenberg
b. Peter Muhlenburgh
c. None

S-1348 932a B:323 X-0800 BROW:UNIO*
a. W-0814 David Walker, heir to Captain -- Walker
b. David Walker
c. Samuel Houghten; A. Ligget, 1826; David Johnston; Nathaniel? H. Masterson, 1826; Anania Rollings; F. Shaler? 1824; Jacob Roup? [Rouse?]; Elijah Walls; John Johnson; J. Davidson, 1831; J. & J. Jordan; -- Wilson & -- Middleton, 1842
*Source B notation: "Sevanna? [Levanna?]."

S-1349 667a A:259 X-0663 CLER:MIAM CLER:STON
a. W-2433 Lewis Starke, assignee of B. Starke & W. Starke
b. Lewis Starke
c. A. Conrad, heirs

S-1351 1000a C:183 X-0663 HIGH:DODS
a. W-1199 Captain William Lindsay
b. William Lindsay*
c. Peter Crigger, 1831; Samuel Bell, 1833
*Source B spells Lindsey.

S-1352 700a B:450 X-0740 GREE:ROSS
a. W-1751 Captain Hughes Woodson CLAR: --*
b. Hugh Woodson
c. None
*Source B does not mention Clark County.

S-1354 1000a A:289 X-0130 ADAM:MEIG
a. W-0305 Captain Thomas Bell
b. Thomas Bell
c. Robert Gamble; Sand? [Land?] Treat, 1824

S-1355 800a B:249 X-1000 ROSS:UNIO
a. W-2629 Captain Simon Morgan
b. Simon Morgan
c. H. Brush; W. H. Douglas, 1841

S-1357 240a B:370 X-0570 CLER:WASH
a. W-0199 Captain Lawrence Butler
b. Lawrence Butler
c. None

S-1358 1000a A:301 X-0134 ADAM:WINC
a. W-0040 Captain Thomas Edmunds
b. Thomas Edmonds
c. John Kincaid, 1828; Peter Machir; James D. Darlington, 1828

S-1359 667a B:192 X-0840 FAYE:UNIO
a. W-2504 Captain William White
b. William White
c. None

S-1360 1400a A:428 X-1000 ROSS:UNIO
a. W-0937 Colonel John Nevill
b. John Neville
c. None

S-1361 1000a B:121 X-0840 FAYE:JEFF
a. W-0456 Captain Lieutenant William F. Gaines
b. Henry Gaines
c. -- Melliken & -- Latham; B. Latham, 1826; Carter B. Page [*also* Paige]; D. McSene? [McLene?], 1827; Jesse Millikan, 1830; T. B. Dawson; Jesse Melliken* heirs, 1845
*So spelled.

S-1362 1000a B:90 X-0840 MADI:STOK
a. W-0146 Lieutenant W. S. Smith
b. William S. Smith
c. None

S-1365 1000a B:63 X-1000 FRAN:JACK
a. W-0014 Samuel Oldham, heir to Captain C. Oldham
b. Samuel Oldham
c. None

S-1366 1000a A:454 X-0663 CLER:OHIO
a. W-0206? Captain Samuel Eddens
b. Samuel Eddins
c. None

S-1367 1000a A:527 X-0660 CLIN:WASH
a. W-1583 Aaron Ball, 100a
W-1815 Richard Jenkins, 200a
W-1644 Daniel Bunn, 200a
W-0645 Robert Angel, 100a
W-1641 Robert Doyle, 200a
W-1658 Harrison Pearman, 200a; *all six of these warrants assigned* to Colonel Edward Carrington
b. Edward Carrington
c. J. Brown, 1825; Lewis Wright, 1826

S-1368 1500a B:133 X-0840 HIGH:JACK
X-0130
a. W-2279 Colonel Christian Febeger
b. Christian Febiger
c. N. Jarnigan? [Jamigan?]; T. Groves, 1824

S-1371 1000a B:63 X-1000 FRAN:JACK
a. W-0014 Samuel Oldham, heir to Captain C. Oldham
b. Samuel Oldham
c. None

S-1373 1100a D:384 X-0186* GREE:CAES
GREE:SILV
a. W-1849 Major John Belfield
b. John Belfield**
c. W. Cline; J. Galloway, 1826
*"Right-hand fork of Caesar's Creek."
**Source B spells Bellfield.

S-1375 1000a A:295 X-0800 BROW:UNIO
BROW:HUNT
a. W-0635 Captain Archibald Denholm; John Harvie & Edward Lyne [assignees?]
b. Edmund Lyne
c. Charles C. Dorsey; George Shultz, 1824; Ignatius Mitchell; V. S. Masterson, 1826; Robert Savage; Allen Butt, 1826; William Hewitt, 1833; -- Oursler & -- Mitchell; H. Hall; -- Wilson & -- Middleton, 1842

S-1376 1000a B:407 X-0180 GREE:CAES
GREE:SILV
a. W-1735* John Newhall; Doctor James Guthrie [assignee?]
b. Tarpley White
c. Jesse Coffitt; R. D. Forsman, 1831; William Neiley; J. Bails, 1832
*Warrant number apparently erroneous; it was issued for 200a only.

S-1378 1200a B:154 X-0660 GREE:CAES
a. W-0753 Major John Willis; Clement Biddle [assignee?]
b. Clement Biddle
c. Unknown; John Beales, 1836

S-1379 1000a B:214 X-0840 FAYE:JEFF
a. W-0597 Captain John Spotswood
b. John Spotswood
c. None

S-1380 1000a B:91 X-0840 FAYE:JEFF FAYE:PAIN
a. W-0115 Major William Moseley
b. William Mosley*
c. W. B. Iron? F. Warner; Jeremiah Bowyer, 1840
*Source B spells Moseley.

S-1382 1000a A:525 X-0660 CLIN:WASH CLIN:CLAR
a. W-0329 Captain Joseph Blackwell
b. Joseph Blackwell
c. J. Pennington; G. Fallis, 1836

S-1383 2222a B:33 X-1000 FRAN:JACK
a. W-0020 Brigadier General -- Morgan
b. Daniel Morgan
c. Horton Howard, heirs; C. Higgins, 1836; -- Holmes & -- Rogers; J. L. Taylor, 1836; R. Douglas, 1837; J. Tunney, 1838; J. Tagart; Daniel Wood; R. Brotherton, 1835; N. Wood; R. Wickson

S-1384 1000a B:91 X-0840 FAYE:PAIN FAYE:JEFF
a. W-2239 Ensign Clement Carrington
b. Clement Carrington
c. James Carrington; Richard Baughan, 1833; Edward Janes? [Jones?]; J. Janes, 1835

S-1385 1000a B:91? X-0840 FAYE:PAIN
a. W-0732 Captain Thomas Parker
b. Thomas Parker
c. Solomon Flesher; William Fitzhugh; Joseph Bloomer, 1831

S-1386 400a B:489 X-0730 CHAM:UNIO
a. W-0341 Captain Joseph Swerringen
b. Joseph Swearingen
c. W. R. Ganson

S-1387 100a B:489 X-0840 MADI:RANG
a. W-0194 James Galt, heir to Doctor P. Galt
b. James Galt
c. None

S-1388 1420a E:4 X-1000 FRAN:JACK
a. W-2263 Lieutenant Colonel William Washington
b. Bailey* Washington, heirs of
c. Bayley Washington; David Collins, 1828; Andrew Grant; W. Worthington; *S. L. White, 1827*; John Goldsmith, 1833; Washington Bailey
*Source B says William Washington, heirs.

S-1389 1000a B:34 X-1000 FRAN:JACK FRAN:FRAN
a. W-2052 Captain Abraham Kirkpatrick
b. Abraham Kirkpatrick
c. Peter Lee

S-1390 52a B:480 X-1004 FRAN:FRAN
a. W-0307 Captain John Clarke
b. John Clark
c. None

S-1391 2500a A:338 X-0180 GREE:XENI
a. W-1606 John Woodford, heir to General -- Woodford
b. John Woodford
c. None

S-1393 1000a B:29 X-1000 FRAN:FRAN*
a. W-0850**
b. Robert Vance
c. L. Sullivant, heirs; Lyne Starling, 1826
*Source B notation: "Franklinton."
**Warrant 0850 is not listed in Source C.

S-1394 1111a B:332 X-0750 UNIO:MILL
a. W-2248 & W-1376 Lieutenant John White
b. John White
c. David Wilton; David? Markley, 1830

S-1396 1000a B:34 X-1000 FRAN:FRAN
a. W-1332 Lieutenant James De la Plane; William Semple [assignee?]
b. William Semple
c. Unknown; Lyne Starling, 1829; Nicholas Demarast [*also* Demerest]; Elijah Bachus, 1833; Isaac Demerast

S-1397 1000a A:415 X-1300 BROW:PLEA
a. W-0348 Captain James Curry
b. James Curry
c. Hugh McFall; William Butt, 1823

S-1402 667a B:145 X-0840 FAYE:JEFF
a. W-0187 Lieutenant Robert Cradduck
b. Robert Craddock
c. None

S-1405 1300a B:270 X-0340 PICK:DARB FRAN:PLEA*
a. W-0586 Doctor Edward Duff
b. Edward Duff
c. Lyne Starling, 1828; Unknown; J. D. Lutz, 1838 (Pickaway County); C. Chinioth [*also* Chinoweth) 1832
*Source B does not mention Franklin County, Pleasant Township.

S-1406 1000a B:191 X-1004 FRAN:NORW
a. W-2601 Captain Nathaniel Terry
b. Nathaniel Terry
c. None

S-1407 1333a A:291 X-0133 ADAM:MEIG
a. W-0234 Lieutenant Josiah Tannehill
b. Joseph Tawnihill*
c. James McArthur
*Source B spells Tawneyhill.

S-1408 1000a B:214 X-0840 FAYE:JEFF
a. W-0599* Captain Thomas Fox
b. John Spotswood
c. None
*There is an apparent discrepancy here; the original warrant for 4000a was used entirely in S-0700.

S-1410 667a B:479 X-1180 MADI:JEFF
a. W-2446 Captain Clough Shelton
b. Clough Shelton
c. John Concklin; R. Douglas, 1836

S-1411 1000a B:210 X-0840 FAYE:JEFF
a. W-1849 Major John Belfield
b. John Belfield*
c. None
*Source B spells Bellfield.

S-1412 2667a A:422 X-0134 ADAM:WAYN ADAM:SCOT
a. W-0138 & W-2555 John Leigh
b. John Leigh
c. Addison Dryden; Samuel Dryden, 1831; George Lynch; T. Huston, 1837

S-1414 1000a A:290 X-0130 ADAM:MEIG
a. W-0310 Lieutenant David Miller
b. David Miller
c. -- James & -- McArthur; T. Huston, 1837

S-1415 200a B:76 X-0663 BROW:PERR
a. W-2103 James Reatley? [Beatley?]
b. James Reatley
c. James Chaquin?; T. Kirby, 1826

S-1415 200a B:76 X-0663 BROW:PERR
a. W-2102 Walter Hooper
b. Walter Hooper
c. H. McDonald; J. Lake, 1842

S-1415 200a B:76 X-0663 BROW:PERR
a. W-0910 William Death
b. William Death
c. Jesse Gould; Phineas Allen, 1825

S-1415 100a B:76 X-0663 BROW:PERR
a. W-0977 William McKnight
b. William McKnight
c. None

S-1415 100a B:76 X-0663 BROW:PERR
a. W-0924 Christopher Becks
b. Christopher Beck
c. James Bell; Timothy? Kirby, 1826; Thomas Kelly; J. Taylor, Junior, 1837

S-1415* 100a B:76 X-0663 BROW:PERR
a. W-0961 Jeremiah Lahaw
b. Jeremiah Lahaw
c. None
*Source B notation: "Not patented."

S-1415 100a B:76 X-0663 HIGH: --* BROW:PERR
a. W-0935 William Jacobs
b. William Jacobs
c. None
*Source B does not mention Highland County.

S-1418 1000a B:200 X-1000 ROSS:UNIO ROSS:SCIO
a. W-2252 Lieutenant John Harris
b. John Harris
c. None

S-1419 1778a A:423 X-0840 ADAM:WAYN
a. W-0107 Colonel John Green
b. John Greene*
c. Samuel McClure; James L. McVey, 1826; John H. Wood, 1823
*Source B spells Green.

S-1421 1200a B:216 X-1004 DELA:CONC
a. W-0289 Doctor Cornelius Baldwin
b. Cornelius Baldwin
c. None

S-1423 1000a A:229 X-0420 ADAM:LIBE
a. W-1894 Captain Henry Heth
b. Henry Heth
c. John Sloop; George Bryan, 1825; James Carson, 1823; J. Bryan, 1827; T. Payne, 1829; Joseph Wade

S-1424 2000a A:509 X-0840 ROSS:PAIN
a. W-0815 Brigadier General Charles Scott
b. Charles Scott
c. None

S-1425 1000a B:15 X-1000 FRAN:FRAN FRAN:PRAI
a. W-2271 Captain Holman Minnis
b. Holman Minnis
c. Joseph Grate; Lyne Starling, 1824; -- Hill? [Kill?] widow; M? [W?] L. Sullivant; W? [J?] J. Gilbert, 1841

S-1426 200a A:230 X-0420 ADAM:LIBE
a. W-0555 Charles Anderson
b. Charles Anderson
c. John Street; John Francis, 1824

S-1426 100a A:230 X-0420 ADAM:LIBE
a. W-2205 William Powers
b. William Powers
c. -- Rownalds & -- Brown; James Hood, 1842

S-1426 100a A:230 X-0420 ADAM: --*
a. W-0001 James Askew
b. James Askew
c. None
*Source B does not give township.

S-1426 100a A:230 X-0420 ADAM:LIBE
a. W-1829 Nicholas Fitzsimmons
b. Nicholas Fitzsimmons
c. John L. Francis, 1828

S-1426 100a A:230 X-0420 ADAM:LIBE
a. W-2206 William Soles
b. William Soles
c. None

S-1426 100a A:230 X-0420 ADAM:LIBE
a. W-2204 Richard Williams; John Barrett [assignee?]
b. John Barrett
c. Thomas Francis, 1828

S-1426 100a A:231 X-0420 ADAM:LIBE
a. W-2228 George Slaughter, heir to N. S[laughter]
b. Jacob Alford
c. Henry Asbury, 1828; J. Bartholomew, 1834

S-1426 100a A:230 X-0420 ADAM:LIBE BROW: --*
a. W-2207 Mag Shackelford
b. Mag Shackelford
c. Robert Means; William Francis, 1824; A. Blair; J. C. Scott, 1840
*Source B does not mention Brown County.

S-1426 100a A:231 X-0420 ADAM:LIBE
a. W-2208 Henry Shackelford
b. Henry Shackelford
c. George Bryan, 1825

S-1429 1000a A:495 X-0180 FAYE:JEFF GREE: --*
a. W-0030 Captain John Marshall
b. John Marshall
c. Stephen Corkwell? [Cockwell?]; John Dawson; James Currie; James Bloomer, 1840; Thomas Mormen
*Source B does not mention Green County.

S-1431 500a B:263 X-0420 BROW:BYRD
a. W-0018 Colonel Presley Nevill
b. Presley Nevill*
c. Charlotte Redmond; -- Shepherd & -- Masterson, 1823
*Source B spells Neville.

S-1432 1000a A:496 X-0180 GREE:ROSS FAYE: --*
a. W-0030 Captain John Marshall
b. John Marshall
c. John Smith, 1828; Thomas Underwood; M. Wynand, 1828; Anthony Walke; David Davis, 1838; -- King (Fayette County?)
*Source B does not mention Fayette County.

S-1434 1000a C:7 X-1000 FRAN:JACK
a. W-2052 Captain Abraham Kirkpatrick
b. Abraham Kirkpatrick
c. None

S-1435 930a A:407 X-0840 ROSS:PAXT HIGH: --*
a. W-1174 Major Thomas Massey
b. Thomas Massie
c. None
*Source B does not mention Highland County.

S-1436 1000a B:63 X-0340 FRAN:PRAI
a. W-2000 James Hockaday, heir to Phillip Hockaday
b. James Hockaday
c. William L. Casey, 1832

S-1440 1000a B:459 X-0340 UNIO:JERO
a. W-0348 Captain James Curry
b. James Curry
c. None

S-1441 1000a B:224 X-1004 DELA:CONC
a. W-0069 Captain Phillip Slaughter
b. Philip Slaughter
c. Susanna Carpenter (forfeited 1839)

S-1445 1657a* B:38 X-0841 ROSS:UNIO
a. W-0812 Colonel William Dark
b. William Darke
c. None
*Source B says 1557a.

S-1445 1010a B:37 X-1000 ROSS:SCIO
a. W-0812 Colonel William Dark
b. William Darke
c. None

S-1446 2000a B:121 X-0180 GREE:ROSS
a. W-1619 Doctor George Munroe
b. George Munroe
c. None

S-1447 1974a A:429 X-0360 ROSS:UNIO PICK:WAYN
a. W-1249 Captain Thomas Chilton, heir
b. Thomas Chilton
c. Thomas M. Marshall; P. N. White, 1825; William Thompson, 1827

S-1448 1000a B:63 X-0340 FRAN:PLEA
a. W-0014* Samuel Oldham, heir to Captain C. Oldham
b. Samuel Oldham
c. None
*This may represent an overpayment in land. W-0014 was issued in the amount of 4000a (4666a, according to Gwathmey); but see entries S-0148, S-1185, S-1365, and S-1371.

S-1449 1200a A:438 X-0660 CLIN:RICH CLIN:WAYN
a. W-1792 Lieutenant Colonel Edward Carrington
b. Edward Carrington
c. William Barret; W? D. Reed, 1824; William Lytle; B. Hinkson, 1823; John Cobelton? 1823; L. Reed; William Melliken, 1826; James Reed, Junior; S. Winston, 1826; Thomas Stitt; J. Hadley, Junior, 1840; A. Mason; W. Sabin, 1840

S-1450 667a B:93 X-0180 MADI:STOK
GREE:ROSS
FAYE: --*
a. W-0404 William Tompkins, heir to Ro[bert] Tompkins
b. William Tompkins
c. None
*Source B does not mention Fayette County.

S-1451 1000a B:122 X-0840 FAYE:JEFF
a. W-0064 Thomas Bowne
b. Thomas Bowne
c. Nathan McGill, "deeded 23 Feb 1833;" Wade Loofborrow [or Loofborough] "deeded 7 Feb 1829"

S-1453 600a B:402 X-1000 PICK:WAYN
a. W-0088 Captain Strothers Jones
b. Strothers Jones
c. Asahel Heath, Junior, administrator; Andrew? White; Asahel Reanick? 1823; E. Sittler? [Littler?]; Joseph? [James?] Hedges, 1826; J. Radcliff, heirs; A. C. McArthur; J. Olds, 1842

S-1454 1000a C:29 X-1000 FRAN:FRAN
a. W-0853 Captain Robert Beall
b. Robert Beall
c. Robert Brotherton; C. Thomas, 1832; John Gotchins

S-1455 833a A:413 X-1000 SCIO:UNIO
SCIO:MORG
a. W-0815 Brigadier General Charles Scott
b. Charles Scott
c. Henry Utt; S? [L?] W. Tracy, 1827; Thomas Graham; George Herdeth, 1836; -- Merritt; D. Kittle, 1842

S-1456 1000a B:12 X-0840 ROSS:TWIN
a. W-1880*
b. Joseph Watkins**
c. None
*Warrant probably in error; it was issued to John Corbett for 200a.
**Source B shows Charles Fleming, but is cancelled out.

S-1457 1000a A:526 X-0660 CLIN:WASH*
a. W-0329 Captain Joseph Blackwell
b. Joseph Blackwell
c. William Brigs?; J. Morris, 1826; John Dale; William R. Cole, 1826; James Machir; George Mann, 1825; Thomas Thatcher, administrator of William Ward; L? [S?] McCune, 1825; Anthony Brandt; Thomas Woodmanse, 1829; T. Pennington; J. Fife, 1830; Rachel Ward; -- Bruce & -- Fyfe
*Source B notation: "Cuba."

S-1458 1000a A:531 X-0660 CLIN:WASH
a. W-0602 John Steel
b. John Steel
c. H. Caste; G. Foos, Junior, 1835; J. Fleming; L. Gustin, 1837; E. McCune; J. Fyfe, 1835

S-1460 600a B:257 X-1140 PIKE:PEBB
X-1000
a. W-0198 Captain Robert Beale
b. Robert Beale
c. Gilbert Hamilton; Abraham Carter & J. Sargent, 1830

S-1462 1000a B:63 X-0340 FRAN:PRAI
a. W-2610 Lieutenant John Foster
b. John Foster
c. Samuel Shepherd, 1823; John Hickman; G. H. Foster; M. L. Sullivant, 1831; F. W. Defany? [Defarry?]; E. Backus, 1838

S-1464 569a B:110 X-1000 SCIO:MORG
a. W-0145 Captain William Fowler
b. William Fowler
c. Samuel W? [M?] Tracy, 1827; John Waller, 1840; M. Gregory, 1842

S-1465 1000a B:157 X-1301 HIGH:CLAY*
a. W-0674 Captain William Epps; Colonel A. Buford [assignee?]
b. Abraham Buford
c. G. F. Hawkins; Ensign Mitchell
*Source B notation: "Near Buford."

S-1466 667a B:35 X-0340 FRAN:PLEA
PICK: --*
a. W-1382 Lieutenant James Meriwether
b. James Merriwether
c. J. W. Trimble
*Source B does not mention Pickaway County.

S-1467 1000a B:35 X-0340 FRAN:PLEA
PICK: --*
a. W-2331 Captain Lewis Booker
b. Lewis Booker
c. A. J. McDowell, 1824
*Source B does not mention Pickaway County.

S-1467 595a B:33 X-0340 FRAN:PLEA
PICK: --*
a. W-2700 Doctor? Miles King
b. Miles King
c. Robert Burton; A. J. McDowell, 1824; John P. Holloway; William Mooberry, 1829; D. Nicholls? [Nicholas?]; J. Bryden, 1829
*Source B does not mention Pickaway County.

S-1469 1200a A:386 X-0841 ROSS:CONC
a. W-1174 Major Thomas Massey
b. Thomas Massie
c. None

S-1472 1000a B:35 X-0340 FRAN:PLEA
a. W-2219 Captain John F. Mercer
b. John F. Mercer
c. None

S-1473 1000a B:64 X-0360 FRAN:PRAI
a. W-1186 Captain Whitehead Coleman
b. Whitehead Coleman
c. None

S-1474 1000a B:15 X-1000 FRAN:PRAI
a. W-2271 Captain Holman Minnis
b. Holman Minnis
c. Abitha Ann Higgins; D. D. Warren, 1839

S-1475 1000a B:274 X-0840 HIGH:UNIO
a. W-0588 Captain John Gillison
b. John Gillison
c. None

S-1478 1200a B:117 X-0340 MADI:CANA FRAN:BROW
a. W-0712 Doctor William Brown
b. William Brown
c. James Fuller; J. Tunney, 1838; S. Fuller; M. J. Gilbert; H. Gorton; Joel Harris; Ananias Harris; A. Stone; S. Sullivant, heirs; R. Douglas (Madison County); D. D. Warren, 1839; James? [Joseph?] Francis

S-1479 1200a B:117 X-0340 MADI:CANA MADI:DARB
a. W-0351 Lieutenant Colonel Charles Simms
b. Charles Simms
c. E. Heard; John H. Norton, 1829; C. Simms, heirs; D. K. Bigelow, 1837

S-1480 667a A:259 X-0663 CLER:MIAM CLER:STON
a. W-0827 Captain John Holcomb; Richard James [assignee?]
b. John McDowell
c. None

S-1482 1000a B:16 X-1000 FRAN:FRAN
a. W-0043 Archibald Blair, heir to Captain -- Blair
b. Archibald Blair
c. None

S-1484 1000a B:16 X-1000 FRAN:PRAI
a. W-2120 Captain Anthony Singleton
b. Anthony Singleton
c. M. Robinson & E. Robinson; R. Brotherton, 1838

S-1485 850a B:352 X-0424 BROW:BYRD
a. W-0635 Captain Archibald Denholm; John Harvie & Edward Lyne [assignees?]
b. Edmund Lyne
c. None

S-1486 200a B:301 X-0420 BROW:UNIO
a. W-1518 James Cowherd
b. James Cowherd
c. None

S-1488 2000a B:315 X-0840 HIGH:MADI
a. W-1984 Captain William George
b. William George
c. John Thornton

S-1488 1400a B:432 X-0841 ROSS:CONC FAYE: --*
a. W-3252 --**
W-2955 James Davis; William George [assignee?]
W-2946 --***
W-1984 Captain William George
W-4205 Jacob Phillips; William George & Duncan McArthur [assignees?]
b. William George
c. None
*Source B does not mention Fayette County.
**Source C shows Conrad Peterson, 100a, but the name is stricken out and rewritten as W-3253. Thus, W-3252 has, in effect, been left blank.
***Blank in Source C.

S-1493 1111a B:187 X-0750 DELA:SCIO
a. W-1414 Lieutenant Thomas Coverley; Stephen T. Mason [assignee?]
b. Stephen T. Mason
c. John G. Mason; Anthony Walker, 1829

S-1494 4000a A:355 X-0660 WARR:SALE*
a. W-0171 Captain John Taylor Harrison
b. John P. Harrison
c. Enoch Baldwin; Joel A? Stokes, 1835; Robert Hughes; S. Suydam, 1835; H. M. Stokes, 1837; Sarah Ann Thomas; J. Taylor; J. H. Burrows; H. B. Thompson; J. Woodruff, 1839; T. R. Gaskill; D. Hopewell, heirs; C. Roach, heirs; A. G. Wright, 1840; J. Snyder; Obed Stowell, 1840; Theodore Tea; S. E. Stone, 1840; J. Pickens, heirs; J. Egbert, 1841; D. Mercer; J. W? [M?] Roosa, 1842; S. Parker; J. H. Patterson; S. Baldwin, 1842; S. White, heirs
*Source B notation: "Rochester."

S-1495 2667a A:511 X-1170 WARR:SALE
a. W-2843 & W-2844 Lieutenant Roger Nelson
b. Roger Nelson
c. William Lytle; E. Thomas, 1825; James S. R. Gilman; William Steward, 1832; R. R. Fielding; Joel A. Stokes, 1835; Obed? [Ebad?] Stowell, 1837; R. K. Fielding; B. Smith, 1839; R. W. R. Fielding; E. Baldwin, 1841

S-1496 1500a A:335 X-0660 WARR:HAMI
a. W-2999 Den? Campbell, 200a
W-2961 Milton Fordd?; G. Hailey*, 200a
W-2994 Alexander Williams, 100a
W-1281 James Sample, 200a
W-2995 Maximilian Rector, 100a
W-2976 William Haley, 100a
W-2989 A. Bennett; William Reynolds, 100a
W-2978 John Cannor, 100a
W-2990 A. Kent; William Reynolds, 100
W-2936 Moses Wright, 100a
W-1298 John A. Reep, 200a; *all eleven warrants were assigned to John A. Binns [assignee?]*
b. John A. Binns
c. T. Forshee; J. Mountz? [Monntz?] 1824; Zerubabel Wells; A. H. Denlavy? [Dunlavy?] 1832
*It seems probable that G. Hailey [Haley] was the actual veteran, and that Milton Fordd? was an assignee.

S-1497 800a B:45 X-0660 WARR:HAMI
a. W-2942 Jonathan Potts, 100*
W-0940 William Mardis; William Ellzey [assignee?] 100a
W-2940 William Thomas, 100a*
W-2943 John Wotter? 100a*
W-2939 David Potts, 100a*
W-2970 John Cleveland; William Taylor & -- McIlhany [assignees?] 100a
W-2945 Isaac Rose, 200a*
b. James McIllhaney, *et al* [James McIlhaney, William Elzy, William Thomas, William Wolfler, David Potts, William Taylor, Isaac Rose**]
c. None
*Apparent assignment to -- McIlhaney.
**According to Source B.

S-1498 1000a B:253 X-1170 WARR:SALE
a. W-1416 Peyton Powell; John Wise [assignee?]
b. John Wise
c. R. Boutz, heirs; Francis? Dunlavy, 1832; J. Sertin; J. Mounts, 1842

S-1499 1167a B:457 X-0660 WARR:SALE CLER: --*
a. W-2957 William Moxley; John Binns & Charles Binns [assignees?]
b. William Modley**
c. None
*Source B does not mention Clermont County.
**Source B spells Moxley.

S-1499 1500a B:457 X-0660 WARR:SALE CLER: --*
a. W-2957 William Moxley; John Binns & Charles Binns [assignees?]
b. John Binns & Charles Binns
c. John Fulks; William Stokes; J. P. Chapman; George Kesling, 1836; Zela Conklin; A. G. Wright, 1840
*Source B does not mention Clermont County.

S-1500 200a B:42 X-0660 WARR:SALE
a. W-2959 Edward Rinker?; Alexander McIntire [assignee?]
b. Alexander McIntire
c. None

S-1501 2867a A:398 X-0130 ADAM:TIFF
a. W-0165 & W-1485 Robert Rankin
b. Robert Rankin
c. None

S-1502 300a B:444 X-0340 CHAM: --* UNIO:ALLE LOGA: --*
a. W-0275**
W-2755 George Jones; Walter E. Strong & James Denny [assignees?]
b. James Denny
c. Unknown; Thomas Collins, 1823; John Yarborough; S. G. Strong, 1826; Samuel Hawkins
*Source B notation: "Lies in Champaign County;" Logan County not mentioned.
**W-0275 is not listed in Source C.

S-1503 420a B:110 X-1000 SCIO:WASH
a. W-1611 Farale O'Neale; John Harl [assignee?]
W-2904 John Chatham; John Harl [assignee?]
b. John Harle
c. None

S-1505 1067a A:419 X-0660 WARR:WASH
a. W-2900 James Hooper; Stephen T. Mason [assignee?]
b. Stephen T. Mason
c. James Welch, 1825

S-1506 1000a A:420 X-1170 CLIN:VERN WARR:WASH
a. W-2743 Thomas Grissett, 100a*
W-3036 Thomas Jones, 100a*
W-3048 John Brawner; William Reynolds & Edward Dowse [assignees?] 200a
W-3051 Edward Valentine, 100a*
W-3052 Elisha Rodes, 100a*
W-3098 W. McClure, 200a*
W-3388 Peter Levins; Matthew Pate & Edward Dowse [assignees?] 200a
b. Stephen T. Mason
c. Thomas Kelsey; S. Winston, 1826; John T. Mason; James Harris, 1827; -- Chapman & -- Walker, 1829; -- Bruce & -- Walker, 1832; J. Morris, 1834; B. Hinkson, 1831; J. Jones, 1836; W. Snyder; J. Carman, 1837; J. Riddle, 1836; J. Hadley, Junior; E. Stowel, 1840 (Warren County); L. S. Howard; A. G. Wright, 1842 (Warren County)
*Edward Dowse [assignee?]

S-1507 1000a A:345 X-1170 CLIN:VERN
a. W-2705 James Buford, 400a
W-2738 Philip Kengore, 200a
W-2281 John Addeson, 200a
W-2766 James Herrald, 200a; *all four warrants* to Stephen T. Mason [assignee?]
b. Stephen T. Mason
c. None

S-1509 1700a C:286 X-1140 PIKE:BENT
a. W-3039 Major John Swan
b. John Swan
c. John Swan, heirs; J. Wickoff, 1836; James Miller; James Penniston, 1841; J. Robinson; M. Thomas; L. Byington, 1842; J. Watts

S-1510 250a C:287 X-1140 PIKE:PEBB PIKE:SUNF
a. W-3039 Major John Swan
b. John Swan
c. A. Winkoop, 1823; John S. Wells; H. Hempstead, 1829

S-1512 400a A:382 X-0660 X-0800 HAMI:ANDE
a. W-0463 John Jowett [Jouett?] heir to Mat[thew] Jowett [Jouett]; Nathaniel Massie [assignee?]
b. Nathaniel Massie
c. None

S-1514 50a D:253 X-0133 HIGH:BRUS
a. W-3383 Samuel Dedman
b. Samuel Dedman
c. None

S-1515 200a A:291 X-0130 ADAM:TIFF
a. W-3178 John Barber? [Barbee?]
b. John Barbee
c. None

S-1515 200a A:292 X-0130 ADAM:TIFF
a. W-3179 Joshua Barbee
b. Joshua Barbee
c. None

S-1515 100a A:292 X-0130 ADAM:TIFF
a. W-3180 William Barbee
b. William Barbee
c. None

S-1515 200a A:292 X-0130 ADAM:TIFF
a. W-3181 Daniel Barbee
b. Daniel Barbee
c. None

S-1515 200a A:292 X-0130 ADAM:TIFF
a. W-1915 Jesse Kelly; Robert Roberts [assignee?]
b. Abraham Shepherd
c. None

S-1515* 100a A:312 X-0130 ADAM:TIFF
a. W-1885 Joseph Hoofman
b. Joseph Hoffman
c. Unknown; William Philips, 1828
*Source B notation: "Not patented."

S-1517 215a A:245 X-0800 CLER:OHIO
a. W-2675 Robert Jouit; N. Massie [assignee?]
b. Robert Jouitt
c. Isaac Ferguson; N? [T?] Kirby, 1823; J? Ferguson; Robert Dunham, 1825; Hugh Ferguson, 1827

S-1519 995a A:335 X-0660 WARR:WASH
a. W-0559 Captain Benjamin Taliaferro
b. Benjamin Taliaferro
c. S. H. Woodson; Samuel Nixon, 1825

S-1520 2000a A:312 X-0133 HIGH:BRUS HIGH:JACK
a. W-0007 Captain John Marks
b. John Marks*
c. R. Carlisle; Robert Patton; James A. Trimble, 1824; John Wade & Josiah Wade; -- Kirby & -- Starling, 1831
*Source B also lists Pat[rick] Moore & Mary Moore.

S-1521 1906a A:313 X-0440 X-0133 HIGH:JACK
a. W-0007 Captain John Marks
b. John Marks*
c. I. Miller; Amos Evans; A. Evans, Junior, 1823; S. Mahaffy; J. Smith, 1826; W. Nesbit; John Purdy, 1831; James M. Trimble, 1831; B. Shannon; J. L. Hughes, 1842
*Source B also lists Pat[rick] Moore & Mary Moore.

S-1523 1000a A:396 X-0660 WARR:WASH
a. W-0180 Captain Robert Woodson
b. Robert Woodson
c. T. R. Foulk; S. Roger, 1836

S-1524 2000a A:290 X-0133 ADAM:MEIG*
a. W-0180 Captain Robert Woodson
b. Robert Woodson
c. John Ellison & Co.; Thomas McCan, 1826; W. Thomas, heirs
*Source B notation: "Jacksonville."

S-1525 1000a A:396 X-1170 WARR:WASH
a. W-0180 Captain Robert Woodson
b. Robert Woodson
c. None

S-1526 500a B:200 X-0841 ROSS:UNIO
a. W-2962 Zephaniah Posey, 100a
W-2783 William Tyler, 200a
W-2781 Martin Watts, 200a; *all three warrants to* James Ewell [assignee?]
b. James Ewell
c. None

S-1527 400a B:26 X-1000 PIKE:NEWT
a. W-2780 Joseph Veronay, 200a*
W-2782 James Clarke, 100a**
W-2785 James Carlick, 100a***
b. Jesse Ewell
c. None
*Jesse Ewell [assignee?]
**James Ewell [assignee?]
***Jesse Ewell & Michael Thomas [assignees?]

S-1530 800a B:51 X-0980 HIGH:JACK
a. W-1261 Stacey Wilson, 400a*
W-0913 James Gassaway, 100a*
W-0964 John Tomlin, 100a*
W-1921** General Robert Lawson, 100a
W-1855 James Grimsley; John Brown [assignee] 100a
b. Charles Lee
c. None
*Charles Lee [assignee?]
**This warrant number appears to be incorrect, as it was issued to General Lawson for 10,000a.

S-1532 950a A:288 X-0133 ADAM:MEIG
a. W-3396 Leven Powell
b. Leven Powell
c. -- James & -- McArthur

S-1536 1500a E:146 X-0420 BROW:UNIO BROW:HUNT BROW:BYRD
a. W-3885*
b. James Taylor
c. James Jones; Allen Butt; John? Woods, 1824; John McIntire; William Dixson, 1826; Michael Wood; John W. Tibetts, 1826; N. Ellis, 1829; Josiah Dixon, 1830; O. Young, 1841; J. Ellis; P. L. Wilson & J. Middleton, 1842; J. Bartholomew, heirs; John Baird, 1842
*This warrant number apparently in error, as it was issued to William Hamilton for 100a only.

S-1536* 2000a -- -- BROW: --
a. --
b. Simon Sowers
c. Jacob Bartholomew, heirs
*Source B (top of page, above S-1512) shows this incomplete entry, which does not appear in Source A.

S-1539 & S-1563 333a A:246 X-0800 CLER:OHIO
a. W-2201 John Drew; David Jackson [assignee?]
b. David Jackson
c. W. Dunham; David John, 1836

S-1540 240a C:235 X-0130 ADAM:GREE
a. W-1918 General Edward Stevens
W-2548 John Scott; Andrew Woodrow [assignee?] 100a
W-3076 Thomas Hanson; John Ellison, Stephen Beach, [illegible] & Andrew Woodrow [assignees?]
b. Andrew Woodrow
c. John Aldred, heirs; William Armstrong, heirs, 1840; J. Ellis; L? [S?] Cole, 1841

S-1543 515a A:281 X-0800 CLER:MONR
a. W-3221 William Reynold, assignee of John Fauntleroy, heir to Captain -- Fauntleroy
b. John Harrison
c. S? [Z?] Chapman; Benjamin Brown, 1831

S-1543 545a A:281 X-0800 CLER:TATE
a. W-3221 William Reynold, assignee of John Fauntleroy, heir to Captain -- Fauntleroy
b. John Harrison
c. None

S-1544 400a A:415 X-0660 BROW:UNIO
a. W-3568 Charles Lewis; John Harrison [assignee?]
b. John Harrison
c. John Allen; W. Dixon, 1828; John Dixon, 1835

S-1545 & S-2195 400a B:254 X-0660 CLER:MIAM
a. W-1911 Elisha King
b. Elisha King
c. T. H. Breeding

S-1546 1080a A:504 X-0660 WARR:HAMI
a. W-1911 Elisha King
b. Elisha King
c. John Dugan; A. H. Dunlevy, 1824; R. Wilson; C. Snyder, 1825; M. B. Neely; J. M. Sind; J. Sertin? [Sirtin?]; W. Sinnard, 1831; D. C. Shillan?; T. Ireland, 1832; S. Gregg, 1836; E. Stowell, 1840

S-1547 1333a A:504 X-0660 WARR:HAMI*
a. W-0687 Lieutenant James Hamilton; Elisha King [assignee?]
b. Elisha King
c. John Fulks; Abel J? [I?] Thomas
*Source B notation: "By Hopkinsville & Deerfield."

S-1548 1533a A:504 X-0660 WARR:HAMI
a. W-1363 Holman Snead, 100a
W-2445 James Barton, 100a
W-0687 Lieutenant James Hamilton, 1333a; *all three warrants to* Elisha King [assignee?]
b. Elisha King
c. N. Fisher; J. Hopkins, 1824; Owen Legg; A. G. Wright, 1833; R. Harshman; E. Stowell, 1840

S-1549 1000a A:505 X-0660 WARR:HAMI
a. W-3384 Samuel McCraw, 200a
W-1497 Hugh Robertson, 200a
W-3370 Henry Pendleton, 100a
W-3371 Timothy O'Connor, 100a
W-1597 William Hunt, 200a
W-3409 Mat[thew] Pate, 100a; *all six warrants to* Sackville King [assignee?]*
b. Elisha King**
c. None
*One warrant number, in the amount of 100a, appears to be missing.
**Source B says Sackville King.

S-1550 & S-2375 400a A:432 X-0660 CLER:MIAM
a. W-3966 John Gunnell; Robert Todd [assignee?] 200a
W-3229 Robert Todd, 100a
W-3761 William Layne; William Lytle [assignee?] 100a
b. Robert Todd
c. N. Hughes; E. Williams, 1823; J. Millspaugh, 1829; Alexander Brannon; G. Brannon, 1831

S-1551 500a B:300 X-0130 ADAM:MEIG
a. W-3492 Richard McKess, 200a
W-3495 William Sudduth, 200a
W-3453 Charles Milton, 100a; *all three warrants to* Robert Boggers [assignee?]
b. Robert Boggess
c. J. Thomas, heirs; A. Latham, 1840

S-1551 100a B:300 X-0130 ADAM:MEIG
a. W-3499 Jesse Pinker; Thomas Brown & Andrew Specht [assignees?]
b. Andrew Speht*
c. None
*Source B spells Specht.

S-1552 2667a C:215 X-1170 WARR:SALE WARR:WASH
a. W-3788 May Rodes; E. Hitchcock, Cornelius Skinner [assignees?]
b. Cornelius Skinner
c. G. W. Trickey; J. Mills, 1835; R. Terry; S? [L?] Rogers, 1835; H. B. Thompson; J. S. Tuttle; J. A. Stokes, 1837; B. Hathaway, 1839; J. Menley, heirs; J. Egbert, 1841

S-1553 1175a B:49 X-0130 HIGH*:CONC
a. W-3496 James Hutchins, 200a
W-3629 Leven Powell, 200a**
W-3787 John Smith, 200a
W-3613 Henry Stringfellow, 200a
W-3774 Thomas Collins, 200a
W-2473 John Elmore, 200a
W-3785 George Nelson, 200a; *all seven warrants to*

Cornelius Skinner [assignee?]
b. Cornelius Skinner
c. John Beekman; William Scott, 1838; John Skinner; A. Baskin, 1836 (Highland County); Henry O'Neal; John Penwell, 1831
*Source B mentions Greene County, bu says "*His* in Highland . . ."
**This warrant number may be redundant, as it results in an overage.

S-1554 2000a A:342 X-1170 CLIN:UNIO CLIN:CHES
a. W-0802 General Horatio Gates
b. Horatio Gates
c. None

S-1556 2000a A:342 X-1170 CLIN:UNIO
a. W-0805 General Horatio Gates
b. Horatio Gates
c. A. Garrison; John Wilson, 1826

S-1557 1000a A:342 X-0180 CLIN:CHES
a. W-0807 General Horatio Gates
b. Horatio Gates
c. None

S-1558 1000a A:343 X-1170 CLIN:UNIO
a. W-0806 General Horatio Gates
b. Horatio Gates
c. None

S-1559 1500a A:411 X-1000 PIKE:JACK
a. W-0808 General Horatio Gates
b. Horatio Gates
c. None

S-1560 2500a A:343 X-0180 X-0740 GREE:XENI
a. W-0810 General Horatio Gates
b. Horatio Gates
c. None

S-1561 1000a A:343 X-1170 CLIN:UNIO CLIN:VERN
a. W-0809 General Horatio Gates
b. Horatio Gates
c. None

S-1562 500a A:281 X-1080 CLER:STON
a. W-0015 Sally Phillips; Aaron Denney [assignee?]
b. Aaron Denny
c. M. Williams; J. McKenney [McKinney] 1826; James Johnson; James Porter; T. Baldwin; J. Fletcher, 1831; C. Zugg, 1835; C. Porter; M. F. H. Veitch, 1835; C. Smith; J. Harvey

S-1563* 333a A:246 X-0800 CLER: --
a. W-2201 John Drew; David Jackson [assignee?]
b. David Jackson**
c. None
*Source B notation: "Should be 1653 on patent." *See also* S-1539
**Source B lists Reuben Taylor.

S-1566 1000a A:354 X-0133 HIGH:JACK
a. W-3222 William Mountjoy [Mountjoir?]
b. William Mountjoy
c. John Beasley; James M. Trimble, 1831; William McCutcheon; Amos Grantham, 1831

S-1567 1000a A:292 X-0130 ADAM:TIFF
a. W-3222 William Mountjoy [Mountjoir?]
b. William Mountjoy
c. None

S-1568 2000a A:397 X-0020 HIGH:BRUS ADAM:FRAN PIKE: --*
a. W-3222 William Mountjoy [Mountjoir?]
b. William Mountjoy
c. Elizabeth Fry; W. Markland, 1837; Andrew Ellison; M. Fellows & R. Fellows; T. Huston, 1841 (Adams County); William Scott, 1833 (Highland County)
*Source B does not list Pike County.

S-1570 200a B:300 X-0420 BROW:UNIO
a. W-4265 Joseph Brady
b. Joseph Brady*
c. None
*Source B notation: "Patented Cornelius Brady, 1803, or rather C. Lafferty--s.t.old [meaning unknown]."

S-1571 200a C:502 X-0340 FRAN:PRAI
a. W-0640 Joseph Harden?; William Henry [assignee?]
b. William Henry
c. Lyne Starling, 1826; Unknown; Henry Clover, 1829

S-1572 200a A:242 X-0800 BROW:HUNT
a. W-3106 Sarah Moore; John Roder Ragland [assignee?]
b. John R. Ragland
c. None

S-1573 400a B:65 X-0750 UNIO:MILL DELA:CONC
a. W-3077 Sydnor Cosby
b. Sydnor Cosby
c. Jesse Parick?; M. D. Pettibone; W. Dearth, 1827; Thomas Bradford, 1829; James Bradford, 1831; James Martin; Charles Humber, 1833; James Matthews; D. Smith; P. Goodrich, 1837; Robert Brown; M. S. Butler, 1836; M. James, forfeited (Delaware County); William Duval; P. B. Cole, 1839 (Delaware County)

S-1573* 100a -- -- BROW: --
a. W-[not given] Thomas Ermine
b. --
c. H. Apple, 1828
*This partial entry in Source B does not appear in Source A.

S-1575 & S-1769 700a A:270 X-0660 HAMI:ANDE CLER: --*
a. W-0919 --**
W-1593 James Swart; John Parker [assignee?] 200a
W-0849 William Mitchell, 200a

W-2829 Richard Harrison, heir to James Harrison; Richard Clough Anderson [assignee?]***
b. John Parker, William Mitchell, & David Mullins
c. None
*Source B does not mention Clermont County.
**Source C does not list W-0919.
***It seems doubtful that this warrant number is correct, as it was issued for 2667a.

S-1575 168a B:343 X-0800 BROW:HUNT
a. W-4028 George Roberts
b. George Roberts
c. Mathew Gray; W. Hewitt, 1834

S-1576 100a B:255 X-0420 ADAM: --*
a. W-3056 John Anthony; Robert Todd [assignee?]
b. Robert Todd
c. None
*Source B does not list township.

S-1579 200a B:161 X-1303 HIGH:WHIT BROW: --*
a. W-2522 Nicholas Long
b. Nicholas Long
c. None
*Source B does not list Brown County.

S-1581 1000a A:281 X-0130 ADAM:TIFF
a. W-2868 Major John Fitzgerald
b. John Fitzgerald
c. Thomas Kincaid

S-1583 200a A:412 X-1000 SCIO:UNIO
a. W-3884 Benjamin Tyler
b. Benjamin Tyler
c. David Moore; W. Kendall, 1826; John Noel, 1827

S-1616 1000a A:451 X-0800 CLER:WASH CLER:MONR
a. W-3548 Henry Balis?
b. Henry Bayles
c. William Lytle; T. Kirby, 1823; Joseph? [James?] Stover; W. P. Lakin, 1828; James Sarver; D. Duff; A. C. Medary, 1842

S-1617 156a B:169 X-1003* ADAM:MEIG X-0130 ADAM:JEFF
a. W-3167 William Bayly
b. William Bayles
c. None
*Southeast branch.

S-1617 134a B:169 X-1190 ADAM:MEIG
a. W-3167 William Bayly
b. William Bayles
c. None

S-1617 247a B:169 X-1190 ADAM:MEIG
a. W-3167 William Bayly
b. William Bayles
c. None

S-1617 118a B:169 X-1190 ADAM:MEIG ADAM:JEFF
a. W-3167 William Bayly
b. William Bayles
c. None

S-1617 175a B:169 X-1190 ADAM:MEIG
a. W-3167 William Bayly
b. William Bayles
c. None

S-1618 467a C:155 X-0340 MADI:DARB FRAN: --*
a. W-3548 Henry Balis?
b. Henry Bayles
c. Peter Hoover; D. Adams, 1830; Unknown; Simeon Hager, Junior, 1836 (Madison County)
*Source B does not list Franklin County.

S-1619 1000a B:64 X-0020 HIGH:BRUS
a. W-3167 William Bayly
b. William Bayles
c. None

S-1620 400a B:302 X-0800 BROW:HUNT
a. W-3828 John Hopper
b. John Hooper*
c. None
*Source B spells Hopper.

S-1621 1000a B:39 X-0800 ADAM:MONR
a. W-0769 Francis Minnis; -- Davies, -- O'Bannon, & -- Johnson [assignees?]
b. Walter Davis & John O'Bannon
c. John Barret; William Armstrong, 1823

S-1622 490a B:60 X-0800 ADAM:MONR
a. W-0769 Francis Minnis; -- Davies, -- O'Bannon, & -- Johnson [assignees?]
b. Walter Davis & John O'Bannon
c. None

S-1623 347a A:247 X-0800 ADAM:GREE*
a. W-3530 Stephen Goodwin; Thomas Perkins & John Armstrong [assignees?]
b. John Armstrong
c. None
*Source B notation: "By Rockville."

S-1624 614a A:246 X-0800 SCIO:NILE
a. W-1968 Nancy Due, heir[ess] to Jonathan Due; John Bradshaw & John Armstrong [assignees?]
b. John Armstrong
c. John Cain, heirs; J. R. Walker, 1834; J. Kendall, 1839

S-1625 180a A:247 X-0800 SCIO:NILE
a. W-3474 Lewis Cooper; Samuel Brady & A. M. Dunn [assignees?]
W-0769 Francis Minnis; -- Davies, -- O'Bannon, & -- Johnson [assignees?]
b. Abner Dun, Walter Davis, & John O'Bannon
c. None

S-1626 95a A:246 X-0800 SCIO:NILE
a. W-0777 Henry Moss; David Williams & Richard C. Anderson [assignees?]
b. Richard C[lough] Anderson
c. William Byer, 1824

S-1627 270a A:247 X-0800 SCIO:NILE
a. W-3474 Leonard Cooper; Samuel Brady & A. M Dunn [assignees?]
b. Abner M? [W?] Dun
c. None

S-1629 400a A:290 X-0130 ADAM:JEFF
a. W-2675 Robert Jouit
b. Robert Jouett
c. None

S-1630 400a B:60 X-0130 ADAM:TIFF
a. W-2675 Robert Jouit; N. Massie [assignee?]
b. Nathaniel Massie
c. None

S-1631 837a A:397 X-0130 ADAM:TIFF ADAM:MONR
a. W-2868 Major John Fitzgerald
b. John Fitzgerald
c. J. H. Piatt; J. M. Smith, 1842

S-1632 1000a A:341 X-1170 CLIN:VERN
a. W-0803 General Horatio Gates
b. Horatio Gates
c. J. Garrison; E. McGregor, 1826; John McGregor; E. Fugate; A. E. Strickle, 1837; E. McGregor, 1826; T. Wilkerson; W. P. Hunnicut, 1835; G. Foos, 1839; J. Grooms; J. Morris, 1841

S-1633 1100a A:512 X-0130 ADAM:JEFF ADAM:MONR
a. W-0463 John Jowett, heir to Mat [Jowett?]; N. Massie [assignee?]
b. John Jouett
c. None

S-1634 2000a A:353 X-0420 ADAM:WINC X-0130 BROW:JACK BROW:EAGL
a. W-4083 Nathan Lamme
b. Nathan Lamme
c. Francis Duffield; J. Riggs, 1823; M. M. Parker; Jonathan? [Jonah?] Vandike; John Wilkinson; Alfred Beasley, 1828; A. Cradet; William Hewitt, 1832; James Brewell?; J. A. Moore, 1837; James Mills; J. Crawford, 1839; Samuel Masters; P. L. Wilson, 1840; B. J. Moore; J. S. Beasley, 1840

S-1635. *See* S-1982

S-1636 917a A:405 X-0150 ROSS:BUCK
a. W-1330 John Tibbs
b. John Tills* heir
c. William Nesbit; R. Adam? [Adair?] 1837
*Source B spells Tibbs.

S-1637 1795a A:328 X-0133 HIGH:JACK
a. W-2540 John Hawkins
b. John Hawkins
c. J. Bereman; J. Smith, 1824; E. Johnson; J. Marquise?; Z. Wade, 1826; — Kirby & — Sterling [*or* Starling]; J. M. Trimble, 1833; Peter Sole; Thomas John; William Vinsonhaller

S-1637 1000a A:353 X-0180 WARR:WASH WARR:WAYN CLIN:CHES*
a. W-4083 Nathan Lamme
b. Nathan Lamme
c. None
*Source A does not list Clinton County.

S-1638 2000a A:313 X-0133 HIGH:BRUS
a. W-2540 & W-3829 John Hawkins
b. John Hawkins
c. None

S-1639 & S-1640 130a B:258 X-0420 BROW:UNIO
a. W-3401 & W-3402 John Pitt; Benjamin Cleft [assignee?]
b. Benjamin Clift
c. None

S-1640 23a B:259 X-0420 BROW:UNIO
a. W-3402 John Pitt; Benjamin Cleft [assignee?]
b. Benjamin Clift
c. None

S-1640 23a B:259 X-0420 BROW:UNIO
a. W-3402 John Pitt; Benjamin Cleft [assignee?]
b. Benjamin Clift
c. None

S-1640 24a B:259 X-0420 BROW:UNIO
a. W-3402 John Pitt; Benjamin Cleft [assignee?]
b. Benjamin Clift
c. None

S-1641 200a B:259 X-0420 BROW:UNIO
a. W-2185 James McCant
b. Benjamin Clift
c. Horatio Blanchard; G. W. King

S-1642* 200a — — BROW: —
a. —
b. Richard Graves
c. George Boherer? [Bokerer?] 1828
*This incomplete entry in Source B only.

S-1645 100a B:272 X-0420 BROW:HUNT
a. W-2115 Samuel Young; Adam Penewell? [assignee?]
b. Adam Pennywith*
c. None
*Source B spells Peneywith.

S-1646 1000a A:260 X-0800 CLER:FRAN BROW:LEWI*
a. W-3427 William Reynolds, 200a
W-3440 William Reynolds, 200a
W-3417 John Croxton, 100a
W-3434 --**, [100a?]
W-3311 Welcome Louchtmiller, 100a
W-3665 Henry Banks, 100a
W-1860 Richard Epple, 200a; *all seven warrants to* -- Davis & -- O'Bannon [assignees?]
b. Walter Davis & John O'Bannon
c. John Layman, 1824; Z. Chapman, 1825; J. Laymond; J. Osborn, 1829
*Brown County not mentioned in Source A.
**This warrant number is probably erroneous, as Source C shows a blank for it; however, W-3436, in the name of James Fair for 100a (Davis & O'Bannon, assignees) is probably meant.

S-1647 1000a A:260 X-0800 BROW:LEWI CLER:FRAN
a. W-0769 Francis Minnis; -- Davis & -- O'Bannon [assignees?]
b. Walter Davis & John O'Bannon
c. None

S-1649 4000a A:276 X-0800 BROW:LEWI
a. W-1033 Henry Willis
b. Robert C. Jacobs
c. -- Haywood & Co.; John Hillicort, 1826; Robert C. Jacobs; Willis Lee, 1824; Willis Lee & George Shultz, 1824; Z. Donaldson; P. L. Wilson, 1839; J. Cochran; J. S. Beasley, 1840; J. Patterson

S-1650 839a A:239 X-0800 CLER:FRAN
a. W-3753 General George Washington, assignee
b. George Washington
c. None

S-1651 634a A:238 X-0800 CLER:FRAN
a. W-1968 Nancy Due, heir[ess] to Jonathan Due; John Bradshaw & John Armstrong [assignees?]
b. John Armstrong
c. None

S-1652 1000a A:253 X-0800 CLER:FRAN
a. W-1936 Captain Reuben Taylor
b. Reuben Taylor
c. C. Harman; Richard Pemberton, 1824; M. Perkins; J. Utter, 1828

S-1653* 1000a A:254 X-0800 CLER:FRAN
a. W-1936 Captain Reuben Taylor
b. Reuben Taylor
c. R[ichard] C[lough] Anderson; W. Wainwright, 1826; C. Hill; Otho Pearre, 1829
**See also* S-1563.

S-1654 1000a A:248 X-0800 CLER:FRAN
a. W-1937 Major Francis Taylor
b. Francis Taylor
c. Andrew Miller; Daniel Hawkins, 1823

S-1655 1000a A:249 X-0800 CLER:FRAN
a. W-2214 Colonel James Innis
b. James Innis
c. None

S-1656 1000a A:249 X-0800 CLER:FRAN
a. W-2214 Colonel James Innis
b. James Innis
c. Samuel Haffer; John Duckwall, 1826; B. Rodgers; Z. Chapman, 1825; Nathaniel Bonsers? heirs; W. Glaney, 1831

S-1657 1000a A:248 X-0800 BROW:LEWI CLER:FRAN
a. W-1937 Major Francis Taylor
b. Francis Taylor
c. None

S-1658 1000a A:251 X-0800 BROW: --* CLER:FRAN
a. W-1937 Major Francis Taylor
b. Francis Taylor
c. -- Shepherd, -- Johnston, & -- Masterson, 1823; W. Bradley; D. S. Smith, 1826; Abraham? Miller; S. Weaver, 1826; D. Whitman? [Whiteman?]; William Johnson, 1823
*Source B notation: "Lies in Clermont [County]."

S-1659 1000a A:249 X-0800 BROW:LEWI CLER: --*
a. W-1937 Major Francis Taylor
b. Francis Taylor
c. None
*Source B does not list Clermont County.

S-1660 1000a A:250 X-0800 BROW:LEWI
a. W-0877 Lieutenant Colonel Richard K. Meade
b. Richard K. Meade
c. None

S-1661 1000a A:260 X-0800 BROW:LEWI
a. W-0877 Lieutenant Colonel Richard K. Meade
b. Richard K. Meade
c. None

S-1662 1000a A:251 X-0800 BROW:LEWI
a. W-0877 Lieutenant Colonel Richard K. Meade
b. Richard K. Meade
c. None

S-1663 1000a A:252 X-0800 BROW:LEWI CLER: --*
a. W-0877 Lieutenant Colonel Richard K. Meade
b. Richard K. Meade
c. None
*Source B does not list Clermont County.

S-1664 1000a A:251 X-0800 BROW:LEWI
a. W-0877 Lieutenant Colonel Richard K. Meade
b. Richard K. Meade
c. Stephen Colvin; William Butt, 1823; John Williams; John Bals? & Jesse Miller, 1826

S-1665 1000a A:252 X-0800 BROW:LEWI
a. W-0877 Lieutenant Richard K. Meade
b. Richard K. Meade
c. None

S-1668 1041a A:273 X-0160 BROW:LEWI CLER:FRAN
a. W-2214 Colonel James Innis
b. James Innis
c. None

S-1669 1000a A:250 X-0800 BROW:LEWI CLER:FRAN
a. W-1917 General Edward Stevens
b. Edward Stevens
c. John Weaver, heirs; Benjamin Wells, 1825; Th. G. Hampton; P. Emry, 1826; A. Osborn; S. Waterman, 1840' -- Wilson & -- Middleton, 1842

S-1670 1000a A:250 X-0800 BROW:LEWI CLER:FRAN
a. W-1918 General Edward Stevens
b. Edward Stevens
c. Christian Gray; James Taylor, 1823

S-1671 & S-1672 & S-1673 2262a A:265 X-0800 CLER:BATA* CLER:OHIO
a. W-1917 & W-1918 General Edward Stevens
b. Edward Stevens
c. Elijah Mattex; Z. Chapman, 1826; Henry Avery; R. McFarland, 1839; J. Whitaker, Junior; William Dillon, 1840
*Source B notation: "By Withamsville."

S-1674 1000a A:263 X-0660 HAMI:ANDE
a. W-1917 General Edward Stevens
b. Edward Stevens
c. M. Sharrow; L. H. Hall, 1826

S-1675 & S-1676 1900a A:272 X-0663 CLER:MIAM CLER:STON
a. W-1917 General Edward Stevens
b. Edward Stevens
c. W. Fletcher; Z. Chapman, 1826; E. Porter, Junior; James McKinney, 1826; P. Malott; S. Medary, 1829; James Taylor; James Stevens; John Hill, 1831; Jacob Dunham; James Perins, 1836; J. Holford; J. W. Kain [*also* Cain]; J. Hoffard; W. S. Patterson, 1837; Mary Neil; S. Ewing, 1836; Robert Dun, heirs

S-1677* 454a -- -- HAMI:ANDE CLER:OHIO
a. --
b. Richard C[lough] Anderson
c. D. John; William Waynewright, 1826; Stephen Lindsey; John M. Tucker, 1823; William Greenlee; Z. Chapman, 1827; Lem[uel] John; William John; David Dyal, 1829; James John, 1834; Daniel Hawkins; Jonathan D. Morris, 1831; S. J. John, 1834; J. W. John; Thomas John, 1831; J. John, heirs, & S. John; David John, 1836
*This incomplete entry does not appear in Source A.

S-1678 2372a C:389 X-0340 PICK:DARB
a. W-2752 Arthur Gordon; John Clemson [assignee?]
b. John Clemson
c. None

S-1679 400a A:244 X-0800 HAMI:ANDE CLER: --*
a. W-3356 John Middlebrook; Edmond Clark [assignee?] 200a
W-3357 Edmond Clarke; Eliz[abeth] Dicky? [assignee?] 200a**
b. Edmund Clark
c. C. Young; W. Baxter, 1826
*Source B does not list Clermont County.
**It seems likely that Edmund Clark was the assignee and Elizabeth Dicky? was the heiress of the original warrant holder.

S-1680* 200a A:244 X-0800 HAMI:ANDE
a. W-2559** John Cowgall; John Hume [assignee?]
b. Joseph Neville
c. None
*Source B notation: "Not patented."
**Warrant number is probably erroneous, since it was originally issued for only 100a.

S-1681 200a A:244 X-0800 HAMI:ANDE
a. W-3551 Samuel Sandowskie; Abraham Hite [assignee?]
W-2825 James Robertson
b. Abraham Hite & James Robertson
c. None

S-1682 434a A:245 X-0800 HAMI:ANDE
a. W-1441 Martin Murphy; John Nancarro [assignee?]
W-1462 Henry Perry; John Nancarro [assignee?]
b. John Nancarro
c. S? [L?] Rose; W. Baxter, 1826; Unknown; Jacob Moore; N. Longworth, 1827

S-1683 510a B:323 X-0800 CLER:WASH
a. W-3438 Valentine Peyton; John McDougal [assignee?]
b. John McDougal
c. None

S-1683* & S-4400 & S-5067 437a B:455 X-0800 CLER: --
a. W-3438 Valentine Peyton; John McDougal [assignee?] 37a
W-4535 John Curtis; John McDougal [assignee?] 200a
W-2027 Richard Richardson; William Roberts [assignee?] 200a
b. -- McDougal & -- Ralston
c. None
*This entry not listed in Source B.

S-1684 573a B:322 X-0800 CLER:WASH
a. W-3438 John Peyton; John McDougal [assignee?]
b. John McDougal
c. R. Buchannon, heirs

S-1685 400a A:262 X-1150 ADAM:SPRI
a. W-3091 John Lee, 100a
W-2549 Joseph Scott, 100a
W-1689 John Simpson, 100a
W-0742 Barnabas Mars, 100a; *all four warrants assigned to* Richard Edwards
b. Richard Edwards
c. None

S-1686 & S-1759 1333a A:262 X-0800 BROW:HUNT
a. W-3123 Isaac Hite
b. Isaac Hite
c. Lewis Jones; Thomas Middleton, 1826; J. Long; -- Wilson & -- Middleton, 1842

S-1686 1334a A:262 X-0800 ADAM:SPRI BROW:HUNT
a. W-3123 Isaac Hite
b. Isaac Hite
c. None

S-1687 1000a A:261 X-0800 ADAM:SPRI BROW: --*
a. W-3033 Samuel Gill; Humphrey Brooke [assignee?]
b. Humphrey Brooks**
c. D. Buchannan; T. Huston, 1837; James Clark, 1839
*Source B does not list Brown County.
**Source B spells Brooke.

S-1688 1000a A:261 X-0800 ADAM: -- BROW: --
a. W-3033 Samuel Gill; Humphrey Brooke [assignee?]
b. Humphrey Brooks*
c. Phillip Smalley; Henry Rape, 1823
*Source B spells Brooke.

S-1689 700a A:263 X-1150 ADAM:SPRI
a. W-3474 Leonard Cooper; A. M. Dunn & Samuel Brady [assignees?]
b. Samuel Brady
c. Van S. Brady; William Armstrong, 1823

S-1690 1000a A:261 X-0800 ADAM:SPRI BROW:HUNT
a. W-3033 Samuel Gill; Humphrey Brooke [assignee?]
b. Humphrey Brook*
c. John S. Wills? [Wells?] 1823
*Source B spells Brooke.

S-1691 1000a A:261 X-0800 ADAM:SPRI
a. W-3033 Samuel Gill; Humphrey Brooke [assignee?]
b. Humphrey Brook*
c. C. Wallace
*Source B spells Brooke.

S-1692 1000a B:255 X-0800 BROW:UNIO
a. W-0628 Captain Walker Baylor
b. Walker Baylor
c. Alexander Campbell; G. W. King, 1826; John Henny, heirs, by P. N. Wiles; Robert Conn, 1823; James Higgins; Thomas Middleton, 1826; Joseph D. McCarty; John W. Tibbetts, 1826; -- Shepherd & -- McCarty; -- Humphrey & -- Campbell, 1824; P. M. Wiles; George W. King; James Stephenson, 1831

S-1693 & S-1695 2000a A:328 X-0130 ADAM:WINC ADAM:SCOT HIGH: --*
a. W-3554 William Vanse**
b. William Vanse
c. William Naylor; John Patterson, 1823; Edward Inlow (Adams County); Thomas Huston, 1834 (Adams County); John D. Robin; Andrew Davidson; S. Campbell, 1837 (Adams County); S. Beam; J. McCullough, 1842
*Source B does not mention Highland County.
**Vause, according to Gwathmey.

S-1694 1000a A:269 X-1120 BROW:UNIO BROW:BYRD BROW:PLEA
a. W-3554 William Vanse*
b. William Vanse
c. None
*Vause, according to Gwathmey.

S-1695. *See* S-1693

S-1696 1000a A:367 X-0130 BROW:EAGL ADAM: --*
a. W-3554 William Vanse**
b. William Vanse
c. Samuel Kirkpatrick; Joseph? [James?] Kirkpatrick, 1826
*Source B does not mention Adams County.
**Vause, according to Gwathmey.

S-1697 121a C:68 X-0800 BROW:UNIO
a. W-0628 Captain Walker Baylor
b. Walker Baylor
c. -- Shepherd & -- King, 1823; William John Hull

S-1698 1000a B:255 X-0800 BROW:UNIO
a. W-0629 Captain Walker Baylor
b. Walker Baylor
c. Moses Potter, 1824; Abel Little; Vachael H. Masterson, 1823; Joseph McCarty; Moses P. McCarty, 1823; G. W. King, 1826; J. Armstrong, 1827; James Stephenson, 1831

S-1700 577a D:69 X-0955 BROW:BYRD
a. W-3320 Isham Keith
b. Isham Keith
c. None

S-1700 423a B:527 X-0955 BROW:BYRD
a. W-3320 Isham Keith
b. Isham Keith
c. None

S-1701 944a B:193 X-0663 CLER:BATA
a. W-3320 Isham Keith
b. Isham Keith
c. T. S. Shields, 1823; J? [I?] Keith; S? [L?] Maham; D. Morgan; C. Zugg; W. C. Duckwall; M? [W?] Groves, 1841

S-1702 220a B:308 X-0420 BROW:UNIO
a. W-3320 Isham Keith
b. Isham Keith
c. None

S-1703 510a D:213 X-0950 BROW:UNIO
a. W-1920 Colonel Josiah Parker
b. Josiah Parker
c. Stephen Willis; John S. Wills, 1824; G. Moore; E. Kreaghbaum, 1828

S-1703 490a B:466 X-0950 BROW:UNIO
a. W-1920 Colonel Josiah Parker
b. Josiah Parker
c. None

S-1707 965a B:21 X-1120 BROW:PLEA
a. W-1921 General Robert Lawson; Nathaniel Massie & John O'Bannon [assignees?]
b. John O'Bannon
c. Mathew Rea; Samuel Tucker, 1826

S-1708 2000a A:499 X-0660 CLIN:WAYN
a. W-3451 Samuel Ball Green
b. Samuel B. Green
c. F. Allen; G. Breece, 1826; John Dixon; A. Underwood, 1825; E. Evans; -- Bruce & -- Strickle, 1825; John Elliot; M. Howard, 1826; M. Petters; J. C. Smith, 1826; David Stokesberry; George Bruce; Matilde Shrialkill?; O. Morris, 1826; Even Evans; Ab[raham?] Strickle; A. Underwood; John Woodberry, 1828; W. Hunnicutt; G. Bruce & A. Walker, 1832; P. R. Thompson; J. Woodruff; Joel Woodruff, 1833; T. Dailey, 1836; W. Holloway; V. Hart, 1837; J. Cummings; Edward Willey, 1838

S-1709 450a B:278 X-0840 FAYE:CONC
a. W-2157 William Eustace
b. William Eustace
c. Willis Feagins; -- Waddle, 1826; William Suddoth; -- Mellikin? [Millikan] 1823; R. Douglas, 1829; James Brooks, heirs; J. Jameson; Wade Loofboro

S-1709 300a B:278 X-0840 FAYE:CONC
a. W-2157 William Eustace
b. William Eustace
c. Albert Steven; R. Douglas; J. Y. Green

S-1710 333a B:281 X-0840 FAYE:CONC
a. W-3111 Samuel Davis; David Ross [assignee?] 200a
W-3135 James Fair; David Ross [assignee?] 133a
b. David Ross
c. None

S-1712 68a C:39 X-0420 BROW:UNIO
a. W-3518 James Bailey
b. James Bailey
c. None

S-1713 100a B:302 X-0420 BROW:HUNT
a. W-3704 James Watson; Alexander McIntire [assignee?]
b. Alexander McIntire
c. None

S-1715 1000a A:253 X-0800 BROW:LEWI
a. W-1921 General Robert Lawson
b. Robert Lawson
c. Hugh Morrow; Samuel Ross, 1824; E. W. Bassett, 1825

S-1716 1000a A:252 X-0800 BROW:LEWI
a. W-1921 General Robert Lawson
b. Robert Lawson
c. John Sergeant; David Ferguson, 1825

S-1720 1000a A:301 X-0134 ADAM:WINC
a. W-1936 Captain Reuben Taylor
b. Reuben Taylor
c. Patsey Johnson; Thomas Huston, 1832; John A. Porter

S-1721 1000a A:302 X-0134 ADAM:WINC
BROW: --*
a. W-1936 Captain Reuben Taylor
b. Reuben Taylor
c. None
*Source B notation: "Winchester;" does not mention Brown County.

S-1723 222a A:274 X-0660* HAMI:ANDE
a. W-0602 John Steel
b. John Steele**
c. None
*"East side."
**Source B spells Steel.

S-1724 200a A:239 X-0800 CLER:FRAN
a. W-0694 William Brown; Morgan Bryan [assignee?] 100a
W-3114 Thomas Warren; C. Morgan Bryan [assignee?] 100a
b. Morgan Bryan
c. None

S-1725 1000a A:253 X-0800 CLER:FRAN
a. W-2214 James Innis
b. James Innis
c. None

S-1726 1000a A:254 X-0800 CLER:TATE
CLER:FRAN
a. W-2214 James Innis
b. James Innis
c. J. Day, heirs; John Bayne, 1824; Joseph? [James?] Johnson; R. McFarland, 1830; A. Coffman; M. F. H. Veitch, 1835; John Coffman

S-1727 1000a B:2 X-0360 MADI:PLEA
a. W-2214 James Innis
b. James Innis
c. William Radford; J. Jones; Stephen Moore, 1828

S-1728 1000a A:490 X-0012 CLIN:LIBE
a. W-3209 Captain Carter Page
b. Carter Page
c. M. Jenkins; A. E. Strickle

S-1729 1000a A:490 X-0010 GREE:SILV GREE:CAES CLIN:LIBE
a. W-3209 Captain Carter Page
b. Carter Page
c. None

S-1730 434a A:240 X-0800 CLER:FRAN
a. W-1968 Nancy Due, heir to Jonathan Due; John Bradshaw & John Armstrong [assignees?]
b. Richard Allison
c. None

S-1731 1000a A:491 X-0010 GREE:CAES CLIN:LIBE
a. W-3209 Captain Carter Page
b. Carter Page
c. None

S-1732 1000a A:491 X-0010 GREE:SILV CLIN:LIBE
a. W-3209 Captain Carter Page
b. Carter Page
c. Solomon Wood; John Atkinson, 1827; Michael Man; Ab[raham?] Trader, 1833; Isaac Williams; John Dodd, 1838

S-1733 1000a A:394 X-0180 CLIN:LIBE
a. W-2213 William Nelson
b. William Nelson
c. None

S-1734 880a A:394 X-0010 CLIN:LIBE
a. W-2213 William Nelson
b. William Nelson
c. S. Garwood; B. Hinkson, 1832; A. E. Strickle, 1836; J. Woolman

S-1735 880a A:394 X-0010 CLIN:UNIO CLIN:LIBE
a. W-2213 William Nelson
b. William Nelson
c. None

S-1747 822a A:245 X-0800 HAMI:ANDE CLER:OHIO CLER:UNIO
a. W-1448 John Tillery, 200?a
W-0547 —* 100a
W-0915 Edward Clavenger, 100a
W-0922 John Kelley, 100a
W-1723 Joshua Hundley, 100a
W-1905 Thomas Johnston, 200a
W-1462? Henry Perry, 22a; *all seven warrants to* John Nancarrow [assignee?]
b. John Nancarrow
c. T. Littleton (Clermont County); Z. Chapman, 1826
*Source C does not list W-0547.
**W-1462 had already been used in S-1682.

S-1748 230a A:271 X-0663 CLER:MIAM*
a. W-3930 William Reynolds, 100a
W-3931 William Reynolds, 100a
W-3932 William Reynolds, 30a; *all three warrants to* John Nancarrow [assignee?]
b. John Nancarro
c. William Imley; L. Gatch, 1824; -- Hart; S. Vail, 1828; S. Medaris; E. Holmes, 1827; J. Parker; C. Pierson; C. Rust, 1827?; E. Tuttle; Green Marmaduke; John Bills, 1831; Thomas Morris, 1830; S. Thompson; J. Dennison, 1837; J. Wood; D. Jenkins, 1839; A. Fairchild; H. Simon ton; John Hull, 1841

S-1749 100a B:18 X-0800 BROW:HUNT
a. W-1021 Henry Anderson; John Loveless [assignee?]
b. John Lovelace
c. None

S-1751 2000a A:516 X-0800 ADAM:SPRI
a. W-1919 General Edward Stevens
b. Edward Stevens
c. William Smith; William Bradford, 1824; Charles C. Chum; John O'Bannon; W. McColm, 1831; T. Huston, 1833; -- Walls & -- Yates; R. N. Carder, 1841

S-1752 2000a A:277 X-0800 ADAM:SPRI BROW:HUNT
a. W-2368 Major James Munroe*
b. James Munroe
c. -- King & -- Payne
*James Monroe, U.S. President.

S-1753 1000a A:276 X-0770 CLER:OHIO
a. W-3263 Nathaniel Lucust
b. Nathaniel Lucas
c. D. Hawkins; E. Ward, 1826; Henry Gollison; Z. Chapman, 1823; S? [L?] Lindsey; J. Payne; W. Ashton, 1826; S. Winston; P. L? [S?] Sever? [*or* Lever?]; T. Kingman, 1827

S-1753 2045a A:280 X-0800 CLER:OHIO
a. W-3263 Nathaniel Lucust
b. Nathaniel Lucas
c. -- Corothers, -- Patton, & -- Corothers; John Payne, 1824; L. Huff; Z. Chapman, 1826

S-1759 200a A:293 X-0130 ADAM:TIFF
a. W-1106 Peter Mallory, heir to John Mallory
b. Peter Mallory
c. None

S-1760 1064a A:266 X-0800 CLER:MONR CLER:OHIO
a. W-4155 James Busby, 100a
W-4139 Beriah West, 200a
W-4141 James Hoof, 400a
W-4104 Thomas Camp, heir to James [Camp?], 100a
W-1310 Edward Driver, 200a
W-4136 William Reynolds, 64a; *all six warrants to* Samuel McCraw [assignee?]
b. Samuel McCraw
c. None

S-1761 734a A:266 X-0800 CLER:MONR CLER:OHIO
a. W-4142 Jacob Gore, 400a
W-4156 James Busby, heir to John [Busby?] 100a
W-4124 Sherwood Naughan? [Vaughan?] 200a

S-1761 [continued]
W-4136 William Reynolds, 34a; *all four warrants to* Samuel McCraw [assignee?]
b. Samuel McCraw
c. J. Brown; S. B. Cleveland, 1825; John Weeks; R. Haynes, 1824; Otho Pierce, 1831

S-1762 1000a A:259 X-0663 CLER:BATA*
a. W-2753 Lewis Thomas
b. Lewis Thomas
c. None
*Source B notation: "By Amelia."

S-1763 400a A:265 X-0800 CLER:OHIO
a. W-3498 James Jackson; Samuel Finley [assignee?]
b. Samuel Finley
c. None

S-1765 1000a A:267 X-0663* CLER:BATA**
a. W-0769 Francis Minnis; -- Davies & -- O'Bannon [assignees?]
b. William Johnston
c. E. Dimmet [*or* Dimmett] 1839
*"Lower side."
**Source B notation: "By Batavia."

S-1765 1235a A:268 X-0133 ADAM: --* CLER:MIAM
a. W-3753 General George Washington, assignee
b. Ezekiel Howell**
c. None
*Source B does not mention Adams County.
**Source B says George Washington.

S-1766 400a B:60 X-0133 ADAM:FRAN
a. W-2047 Christopher McConnor; Richard Easton [assignee?]
b. Ezekiel Howell
c. William Sterrett

S-1767 800a A:377 X-0660 CLER:MIAM
a. W-1038 Thomas Hosfield, 400a
W-1286 John Lewis, 200a
W-3602 John Cross, 200a; *all three warrants to* Ezekiel Howell [assignee?]
b. Ezekiel Howell
c. J. W. Branch; C. Branch; W? [M?] Elstern, 1842; M. Branch; A. Branch

S-1768 667a A:276 X-0800 CLER:MONR
a. W-3438 Valentine Peyton; John McDougal [assignee?]
b. John McDougal
c. None

S-1769* 200a A:272 X-0575 CLER:WASH
a. W-2109 John Woods; George Lewis [assignee?]
b. George Lewis
c. None
**See also* S-1575

S-1770 200a A:271 X-0663* CLER:MIAM
a. W-3581 John McCawley; Edward Simpson [assignee?]
b. Edward Simpson
c. None
*"Upper side."

S-1771 1295a A:273 X-0663* CLER:BATA CLER:UNIO
a. W-0239 Joseph Winlock
b. Joseph Winlock
c. James Sealey; Z. Chapman, 1829; Henry Davis, heirs; J. Davis, 1834; Thomas Davis? [David?] 1831; O. T. Fishback, 1833; Samuel West; B. Brown, 1833; M. F. H. Veitch, 1835; J. Stewart; S. Lane, 1839; S. Medary, 1839
*"Lower side."

S-1772* 1150a -- -- CLER: --
a. --
b. John Bradshaw
c. Richard Malot; -- Bryan & -- Bailer? 1823
*This incomplete entry appears in Source B only.

S-1773 441a A:271 X-0663* CLER:STON
a. W-1968 Nancy Due, heir[ess] to Jonathan Due; John Bradshaw & John Armstrong [assignees?]
W-0769 Francis Minnis; -- Davies & -- O'Bannon [assignees?]
b. Richard Allison
c. Henry Allison; Samuel West; C. Rust; S. Ewing, 1835; H. Allison, heirs
*"Upper side."

S-1774 1000a A:270 X-0663* CLER:BATA**
a. W-0769 Francis Minnis, -- Davies & -- O'Bannon [assignees?]
b. William Johnston
c. A. Bull; D. Hawkins, 1824?; -- Bryan & -- Hawkins; S. Lane, 1825; R. Tweed, 1825; Able [Abel?] Cox; D. Kidd, 1823; W. White, 1825; Edward Kinnan; T. Keezer; A. Cutrite, 1824; E. Shaw, 1826; J. Grant, 1826; J. B. Mix; D. C. Bryan, 1823; John Miles; J. Johnston, 1823; Benjamin Munn; -- Miley & -- Armstrong; F. White, 1824; T. Everhart, 1825; J. B. Mix; G. S. Bryan, 1826; H. Cox; C. Rust, 1827; Timothy Keizer; A. Foote, 1830; J. D. Morris, 1831; S. Medary, 1833; John Whetstone; D. B. Leeds, 1833; D. C. Bryan; J. Hill, 1836; J. Osborn, 1837; W. S. Patterson, 1836; Bank Jones; S. Mahan, 1832; -- Bettz & -- Biggle, 1834 [*or* Betts & Beagle]; J. Hawkins; M. F. H. Veitch, 1835; W. Lytle; George S. Lee, 1837; B. Field; J. Whitstone [*or* Whetstone] heirs; O. T. Fishback, 1835; E. Frazier, 1838; A. Blair; W. M. Vorhees; W. Wayland; J. White; A. Hulick; John Dimmitt; James Holliday; E. & E. Blair; B. R. Blair; H. Tise? [Tire?] 1840; S. Burroughs; John Hall? [Hull?] 1841
*"Upper side."
**Source B notation: "Batavia."

S-1775 977a A:270 X-0660 CLER:UNIO HAMI:ANDE
a. W-3753 General George Washington, assignee, 877a
W-3670 Thomas Cope; William Croghan & George Washington [assignees?] 100a
b. George Washington
c. Unknown; J. Beagle, 1842; Bank Jones; S. Mahan, 1832; -- Bettz & -- Biggle [*also* Betts & Beagle] 1834; Z. Chapman

S-1784 25a D:82 X-0420 BROW:BYRD
a. W-4270 Jonas Morgan
b. Jonas Morgan
c. William Bennett; Franklin Shaler, 1824; D. F. Barney, 1826

S-1785 2667a A:297 X-0800 BROW:JACK BROW:FRAN
a. W-3288 Lewis Lunford
b. Lewis Lunsford
c. Z. Delaney; Stephen Reynolds, 1833; J. Reynolds; E. West, 1835

S-1786 200a B:300 X-0650 ADAM:TIFF
a. W-3996 Benjamin Smithers; John Tristoe [assignee?]
b. John Fristoe
c. None

S-1787 200a B:525 X-0423 ADAM:LIBE
a. W-4364 Richard Harris
b. Richard Harris
c. None

S-1788 1200a A:499 X-0420 BROW:JACK
a. W-0116 John Webb; Andrew Gatewood [assignee?]
b. Andrew Gatewood
c. Casey Emmons; Mathew Tomb, 1834

S-1789 1300a A:499 X-0230 ADAM:WAYN
a. W-0016 John Webb; Andrew Gatewood [assignee?]
b. James McEittrick, heirs; John T. Wright, 1831

S-1790 1500a A:498 X-0230 ADAM:WAYN
a. W-0116 John Webb; Andrew Gatewood [assignee?]
b. Andrew Gatewood
c. Steele F. Randolph; J. Riggs, 1823

S-1791 640a A:499 X-0230 ADAM:WAYN
a. W-0116 John Webb; Andrew Gatewood [assignee?]
b. Andrew Gatewood
c. James Clark; James Young, 1824; William Ellison, 1831

S-1792 1000a B:82 X-0420 ADAM:WAYN BROW:JACK
a. W-4108 John Bell: John Buck, Junior [assignee?]
b. John Buck
c. William Bennett; Archibald Lewis, 1826; John Husband, 1823; Jeremiah Walker; W. Markland, 1837 (Adams County); P. Campbell, 1837; H. Guthrie

S-1793 100a B:168 X-0420 BROW:BYRD
a. W-0781 Wyatt Elliott; Andrew Gatewood [assignee?]
b. Andrew Gatewood
c. None

S-1794 250a B:426 X-0663 CLER:BATA
a. W-0369 James Tutt, heir to Charles Tutt
b. William Crogan*
c. None
*Source B spells Croghan.

S-1795 290a B:430 X-1300 BROW:SCOT
a. W-1203 Captain Beverly Stubblefield
b. Beverly Stubblefield
c. H. Meharry; J. Meharry, 1827

S-1795 650a B:430 X-1300 BROW:SCOT
a. W-1203 Captain Beverly Stubblefield
b. Beverly Stubblefield
c. Thomas Carneal; Joseph Davidson, 1825; Lewis Werry; G. Anderson, 1831

S-1820 500a B:303 X-0420 BROW:BYRD
a. W-0657 James Mackrill, 200a
W-1690 Ralph Murray, 100a
W-2832 Charles Botkins, 100a
W-2823 Caleb Haild, 100a; *all four warrants to* John Wilson [assignee?]
b. John Wilson
c. A. Mehaffy, heirs; R. L. Wilson, 1840

S-1830 2000a A:474 X-0940* HIGH:MADI
a. W-0859 David Riddick
b. -- Reddick, -- Hardin, -- Gray, & -- Mercer
c. J. McCalm; -- Jones & -- Kirby, 1825; D. Strain, heirs; T. M. Strain, 1824; D. Strain; A. Farquhar, 1826
*"Rattle Snake f[or]k P[aint Creek]."

S-1831 2000a A:474 X-0940* HIGH:MADI
a. W-0859 David Riddick
b. -- Reddick, -- Hardin, -- Gray, & -- Mercer
c. Andrew Reddick; A. Baskin, 1824; James Harbour, 1834; Henry Snuvely; James M. Trimble, 1831; David Reddick, deceased; -- Kirby & -- Starling
*"Rattle Snake f[or]k, P[aint Creek]."

S-1832 2000a A:475 X-0940* HIGH:PAIN HIGH:FAIR
a. W-3437 David Riddick
b. -- Reddick, -- Hardin, -- Gray, & -- Mercer
c. Mary Grim; John R. Thurman, 1833; H. Reddick, heirs, & Co.; Abraham Welty, 1834; A. Malcom; J. Simpson, 1838
*"Rattle Snake f[or]k, P[aint Creek]."

S-1833 2067a A:475 X-0940* HIGH:FAIR HIGH:MADI**
a. W-3437 David Riddick, 667a
W-4025 David Reddick, & assignee, 200a
W-2877 David Riddick, 200a
W-3807 David Reddick & assignee, 300a
W-3922 David Reddick, 100a
W-4026 David Reddick & assignee, 200a
W-3941 David Reddick & assignee, 200a
W-3954 David Reddick & assignee, 100a
W-3942 David Reddick & assignee, 100a
b. -- Reddick, -- Hardin, -- Gray, & -- Mercer
c. William Capps; S. Bell, 1828; J. M. Combs; J. Smith, 1829; Philip Grim; John Gosset, 1830; Elijah Capps
*"Rattle Snake f[or]k, P[aint Creek]."
**Source B notation: "Centrefield."

S-1837 1000a A:476 X-0940* HIGH:FAIR HIGH:MADI
a. W-3528 William Finnie (Resolution); John Hardin & David Gray [assignees?]
b. John Hardin & David Gray
c. J. Kirby, 1825; B. Ratcliff; R. Cherry, 1826
*"Rattle Snake f[or]k, P[aint Creek]."

S-1838 1000a A:476 X-0940* HIGH:FAIR**
a. W-1982 William Cherry
b. William Cherry
c. Samuel? Bell, 1831
*"Rattle Snake f[or]k, P[aint Creek]."
**Source B Notation: "Monroe."

S-1839 1000a A:476 X-0940* HIGH:FAIR**
a. W-1982 William Cherry
b. William Cherry
c. John Cherry; Amos Grantham, 1829
*"Rattle Snake f[or]k, P[aint Creek]."
**Source B notation: "By Monroe."

S-1840 1000a A:476 X-0940* HIGH:FAIR
FAYE:GREE
a. W-1982** William Cherry; John Askew [assignee?]
b. William Cherry
c. John Cherry; Henry Phelps, 1829
*"Rattle Snake f[or]k, P[aint Creek]."
**Probably W-1981 is meant.

S-1841 400a A:474 X-0940* HIGH:MADI
a. W-3729 Fielding Barrom; Philip Hupp [assignee?]
b. Philip Hipp**
c. None
*"Rattle Snake f[or]k, P[aint Creek]."
**Source B spells Hupp.

S-1850 112a B:411 X-1000 ROSS:SCIO
a. W-1133 Isaac Halfpenny; James Robinson [assignee?]
b. Daniel Stull
c. None

S-1852 1000a A:466 X-0840 FAYE:UNIO
a. W-3526 William Finne [Finnie?]; Mark Harden [assignee?]
b. Mark Hardin
c. Luke Freeland; A. Latham, 1823; Abraham Grim? [Gum?]; B. Latham, 1826; Daniel Stull, heirs; H. Phelps, 1829

S-1913 800a B:338 X-0750 UNIO:PARI
a. W-1769 James Bell, 200a
W-1866 Samuel Davis, 100a
W-2794 Thomas Bushop, 100a
W-3456 [Original warrantee not given], 400a; *all four warrants to* Thomas Kennon [assignee?]
b. Thomas Kennon
c. Benjamin Cummings; S. S. Bennett, 1824; William Gregg; S. G. Strong, 1830; Lewis Wheeler; A. Pollock; C. Comegys; John Mathiat [Mathias?] 1835; William Gregg; B. Cissel, 1837; Thomas Barret; H. Campbell

S-1914 1826a A:410 X-0840 ROSS:PAIN
ROSS:PAXT
a. W-2858 Strother Sittle? [Settle?]
b. Strother Suttle
c. Daniel Edminston; J. Tarlton, 1827; John Newland; John Watts, 1840; Peter Douglas, 1831; W. H. Douglas, 1842

S-1931 800a C:38 X-0480 DELA:THOM
UNIO: --*
a. W-3680 William Reynolds, 200a
W-3682 William Reynolds, 100a
W-3683 William Reynolds, 100a
W-3684 William Reynolds, 200a
W-3685 William Reynolds, 100a
W-3688 William Reynolds, 100a; *all six warrants to* Henry Bedinger [assignee?]
b. Henry Bedinger
c. Samuel Stroud; Silvester Root, 1820-1826; Samuel Davenport; William M. Warren, 1839
*Source B does not list Union County.

S-1935 250a A:302 X-0663* CLER:UNIO
a. W-0860 David Williams, 50a; John Hardin [assignee?]
W-1108 John Robertson, 200a; John Hardin [assignee?]
b. John Hardin
c. None
*"Lower side."

S-1936 530a A:407 X-0840 HIGH:PAIN
ROSS: --*
a. W-3326 William S. Hawkins, heir
b. William S. Hawkins
c. James Reighley; John Hogsett, 1836
*Source B does not mention Ross County.

S-1938 500a B:267 X-0950 BROW:BYRD
a. W-3487 Henry Hughes
b. Henry Hughes
c. None

S-1938 37a B:267 X-0950 BROW:BYRD
X-1120
a. W-3487 Henry Hughes
b. Henry Hughes
c. None

S-1938 22a B:267 X-1120 BROW:BYRD
a. W-3487 Henry Hughes
b. Henry Hughes
c. None

S-1939 4221a B:239 X-0663 CLIN:GREE
CLIN:CLAR
CLIN:WASH
a. W-0023 Captain Thomas H. Drew; John T. Griffin [assignee?] 2110a*
W-0296 William Eskridge; Richard Throckmorton [assignee?] 2111a
b. Richard Throckmorton
c. Jesse Hunt & Oby's?; S. Winston, 1826; James McKibbon; R. Cole, 1825; James Dakin, 1828; D. Stratton, 1832; J. Shepherd, 1834; A. Edgington; J. Jones, 1836; J. Miller; A. E. Strickle, 1837; R. Philips; J. H. Moon? [Moore?]
*Acreage may be incorrect.

S-1942 860a A:403 X-1120 BROW:FRAN
BROW:PLEA
a. W-1330 John Tibbs
b. John Tibbs
c. William Powell; Joseph Stableton, 1824; Jacob Hewitt; Nathan Ellis, 1832; D. G. Devore, 1834

S-1942 400a B:245 X-0136 SCIO:BRUS
a. W-3044 Henry Stringfellow; John Gerard [assignee?]
b. John Garrard
c. None

S-1947 1000a B:173 X-0650 ADAM:TIFF*
a. W-4087 Walter Ashmore
b. Walter Ashmore
c. William Russel; L. Cole, 1836
*Source B notation: "West Union."

S-1965 200a A:492 X-0180 GREE:XENI GREE:CAES
a. W-3700 William Moffett; William Smalley [assignee?] 100a
W-4152 John Fox; John G. McDowell [assignee?] 100a
b. William Smalley
c. None

S-1966 20a B:461 X-0660 CLER:MIAM
a. W-3924 John Garrett
b. John Garrett
c. None

S-1973 1000a A:287 X-0133 ADAM:FRAN
a. W-3396 Leven Powell
b. Levin Powell
c. None

S-1974 1000a A:287 X-0133 ADAM:FRAN
a. W-3397 Leven Powell
b. Levin Powell
c. -- James & -- McArthur; T. Huston, 1835

S-1975 1000a A:287 X-0133 ADAM:FRAN ADAM:MEIG
a. W-3397 Leven Powell
b. Levin Powell
c. J. Heistand; J. Huston, 1829

S-1976 964a A:288 X-0133 ADAM:JEFF
a. W-3396 & W-3398 Leven Powell
b. Levin Powell
c. None

S-1977 683a A:288 X-0133 ADAM:JEFF
a. W-3398 Leven Powell
b. Levin Powell
c. None

S-1978 200a A:288 X-0130 ADAM:TIFF ADAM:JEFF
a. W-4051 Thomas Sewell; Alexander Dunlap [assignee?]
b. Alexander Dunlap
c. Thomas Lewis; A. Ellison, 1823; John Means & Co.; James McCullough, 1842

S-1979 1000a A:289 X-0130 ADAM:FRAN
a. W-0325 Marquis Calmes
b. Marquis Calmes
c. James Morrison; A. Lafferty, 1823; Aquilla Partee; Henry Rape, 1823

S-1980 1000a A:416 X-0133 ADAM:FRAN HIGH: --*
a. W-0325 Marquis Calmes
b. Marquis Calmes
c. L. Cole, 1836
*Source B does not mention Highland County.

S-1981 500a A:397 X-0130 ADAM:MEIG
a. W-4259 William Willis, 200a
W-3391 Macy Consoller, representative, 100a
W-2015 William Stanley, 100a
W-0842 Thomas Puryens? [Puryear?] 100a; *all four warrants to* Joseph Watkins [assignee?]
b. Joseph Watkins
c. None

S-1982 & S-1635 2000a A:402 X-1120 BROW:PLEA
a. W-1330 John Tibbs
b. John Tibbs
c. Elijah Hall; David Johnston, 1823; James Taylor; Nathan Ellis, 1829; Nancy Hall; D. G. Devore, 1834

S-1983 690a A:416 X-1120 BROW:PLEA
a. W-1452 Matthey Rhea
b. Mathew Rhea
c. Allen Butt, 1826

S-1984 892a A:416 X-1120 BROW:PLEA
a. W-1452 Matthey Rhea
b. Mathew Rhea
c. None

S-1988 250a A:302 X-0690* CLER:BATA
a. W-4107 John Bell; Martin Harden [assignee?]
b. Martin Harden
c. None
*"Branch of East Fork."

S-1989 95a C:193 X-0663 CLER:MONR
a. W-2753 Lewis Thomas
b. Lewis Thomas
c. None

S-1990 138a B:454 X-0663 CLER:UNIO
a. W-1108 John Robertson; John Hardin [assignee?]
b. John Hardin
c. None

S-1992 & S-2430* 1400a A:406 X-1120 BROW:BYRD BROW:PLEA
a. W-3421 Thomas Jones, 200a
W-1637 William Taylor, 467a
W-3716 Richard Johnston, 100a
W-0647 John Legg, 100a
W-0383 Philip Daw, assignee, 100a
W-0384 Philip Daw, assignee, 200a
W-0382 Philip Daw, assignee, 200a
W-1654 Joseph Payne; -- Roberts & -- Massie [assignees?]**; *first four listed warrants have assignments to* Philip Daw
b. Philip Dawe
c. -- Wilson & -- Higgins, 1842
*Which see, for additional names mentioned.
**Warrant number probably erroneous.

S-1993 2033a A:354 X-0133 HIGH:BRUS
HIGH:JACK
ADAM: --*
a. W-0425 Thomas Winslow, heir to Benjamin Winslow
b. Thomas Winston
c. None
*Source B does not list Adams County.

S-1994 4000a A:337 X-0180 CLIN:CHES
a. W-2089 James Crain
b. James Craine*
c. David Cleaver; G. Foos, 1834; A. E. Strickle, 1837; John Kay; J. Fyfe, 1835; W. Harlan
*Source B spells Crain.

S-1995 1333a A:336 X-0180 GREE:XENI
GREE:CAES
a. W-3286 John McAdams
b. John McAdams
c. S. Payne; R. Dean, 1824; Ann S. Sally; James Payne; Daniel Dean, 1828

S-1996 4750a B:203 X-0130 HIGH:CONC
a. W-3394 James Frisby Leith
b. James Frisby Leitch
c. H. Massie; J. Smith, 1826; G. W. Barriere, 1826; J. Ross; R. Collins, 1826; L. Whitley; A. Wilkins; M. Whitley; David Whitley; James Walker; E. Moore; L? [S?] B. Collins, 1825; Charles C. Patterson; William Nevin, 1833; John Gossett, 1830; William Whitley, 1831; J. White; T. Shockley, 1837; John Hare? [Hase?]; John Delany; Morris Call, 1840; J. S. Shane; Richard Collins; J. M. Trimble, 1831; James Corothers; William Scott, 1833

S-1997 400a A:313 X-0420* BROW:JACK
a. W-1452 Matthey Rhea
b. Matthew Rhea
c. None
*"Hd. drains Eagle Creek."

S-1999 1000a A:314 X-0420 BROW:JACK
a. W-3943 John Dent
b. John McAllister & James McAllister
c. Andrew Ellison; Stephen Parker, 1834; C. Baird, 1840

S-2017 2300a* B:43 X-0663 BROW:PERR
a. W-1650 William Fleming, 400a
W-2950 Richard Claiborne, 100a
W-2405 John Williams, 200a
W-3164 Samuel Murphy, 100a
W-1956 Abraham Pigott, 100a
W-3086 Jesse Armstrong, 200a
W-2181 Lewis Ford, assignee? 100a
W-2880 Peter Howard, 200a
W-3163 Randolph West, 100a
W-1705 Richard Bonner, 200a
W-3147 John Powell, 400a
W-3346 Martha Pate, assignee of William Arnold, 100a
b. William Payne
c. Obed Burman; Timothy Kirby, 1823; William Lytle; William Boyle, 1825
*Might be erroneous, since warrants total 2200a only.

S-2018 1300a A:314 X-0137 ADAM:JEFF
a. W-1737 Michael Murphy, 200a
W-0817 James Hines, 200a
W-2949 Richard Claiborne, assignee, 100a
W-2408 John Jones, 200a
W-3162 Charles Broadfield, 100a
W-3166 William Meacham, 200a
W-3251 Edward Crew, 100a
W-2582 Lewis Ford, 200a
b. William Payne
c. J. McCall; T. Huston, 1840

S-2019 500a A:376 X-0790 CLER:MIAM
WARR: --*
a. W-0776 Robert Wright, 100a
W-0591 James Duffey, 200a
W-2008 Gideon Watts, 100a
b. William Lytle
c. None
*Source B does not mention Warren County.

S-2020 200a B:417 X-0130 ADAM:JEFF
a. W-2531 Bernard Rogers
b. Bernard Rogers
c. J. Rogers; J. C. Scott, 1826

S-2021 700a A:521 X-0130 ADAM:MEIG
a. W-0697 Hamlin Coles, 200a
W-1778 Robert Scott, 200a
W-2051 George Bond, 100a
W-4076 Colorop? Freeman, 200a
b. John W. Johnston
c. John Jourdan; Joseph Curry, 1824

S-2022 200a B:83 X-1110 ADAM:GREE
a. W-3571 William Graves
b. William Hord
c. Daniel Carroll; John Young, 1823; William Cole; D. P. Wilkins, 1823; George H. Panteney? [Punteney?] 1824

S-2023 100a C:57 X-0130 ADAM:GREE
a. W-1863 John Armond; John Blackwell [assignee?]
b. Thomas McClannahan
c. John Pike; Thomas Huston? [Haston?] 1831

S-2024 100a B:85 X-1110 ADAM:GREE
a. W-3177 Joseph Thomas
b. John Beasley
c. None

S-2025 200a A:505 X-0130* ADAM:WAYN
a. W-4261 Edward Larkin
b. Thomas Crawford
c. Jane Brown, deceased; John Linton
*"Ch. f[or]k of . . ."

S-2026 1000a A:532 X-0660 CLIN:WASH
a. W-2127 Thomas Ridley
b. Thomas Ridley
c. None

S-2027 1000a A:532 X-0660 CLIN:UNIO CLIN:WASH
a. W-2127 Thomas Ridley
b. Thomas Ridley
c. S. Winston

S-2028 1000a A:532 X-0660 CLIN:WASH
a. W-2127 Thomas Ridley
b. Thomas Ridley
c. James Machir; Thomas Woodmantle? [Woodmanse?] 1827; -- Bruce & -- Walker, 1832; James? Carmony, 1834

S-2029 1000a A:532 X-0660 CLIN:WASH
a. W-2127 Thomas Ridley
b. Thomas Ridley
c. None

S-2030 1000a A:533 X-0660 CLIN:VERN
a. W-2127 Thomas Ridley
b. Thomas Ridley
c. P. Titus; F. Caste? 1842

S-2031 & S-2032 2000a A:505 X-0134 ADAM:WAYN ADAM:SCOT
a. W-3235 Francis Peyton, heir to -- Dade
b. Francis Peyton
c. James Criswell; John Criswell, 1826; Andrew Ellison; George Bryan, 1826; William Melligen; D. P. Wilkins, 1826; George Morris; Charles Wylie? [Wislie?]; R. Johnson, 1827; J. Coles, 1827; S. Oldson, 1828

S-2040 667a B:168 X-0420 BROW:BYRD
a. W-1468 Lieutenant Benjamin Moseley
b. Benjamin Moseley
c. Arthur Fox, heirs; Thomas Baird, 1831; Silas Bayne, 1831

S-2041 667a A:453 X-0130* ADAM:WAYN
a. W-2201 John Drew
b. David Jackson
c. None
*"Ch. f[or]k of . . ."

S-2042 400a A:304 X-1300 HIGH:WHIT
a. W-3762 John Emmons, 200a
W-3771 Thomas Burns, 200a
b. George Francisco
c. Thomas L? [S?] Lewis; J. A. Trimble, 1824; J. Smith, 1826; J. Lewis; Elizabeth Lewis; J. Hogsett, 1835

S-2043 1000a A:301 X-0134 ADAM:WINC*
a. W-1937 Major Francis Taylor
b. Francis Taylor
c. Lauban? [Sanborn?] Bramble; T. Huston, 1835
*Source B notation: "By Winchester."

S-2044 200a A:304 X-1300 HIGH:WHIT
a. W-4336 Charles King
b. John Ritchie
c. Samuel Bell, 1832

S-2045 1000a A:302 X-0134 ADAM:WINC BROW: --*
a. W-3174 John Jameson
b. John Jamison**
c. Francis Shinn; T. Huston, 1833; John Payne; David Dyal, 1831
*Source B does not mention Brown County.
**Source B and Source C spell Jameson.

S-2046 200a A:304 X-1300 HIGH:WHIT
a. W-3109 Josiah Martin
b. Robert Nourse
c. None

S-2047 600a* A:304 X-1300 HIGH:WHIT
a. W-2472 Francis Peyton, assignee of Benjamin? Rankin? 100a
W-2471 Daniel Feagan? assignee of John Roach, 200a
W-2474 Daniel Feagan? assignee of John Hopper, 200a
W-3633 Francis Peyton, assignee of Adam Goff, 200a
b. Jacob Spears
c. Andrew Badgley; Amos Grantham, 1828
*Might be in error, as the warrants total 700a.

S-2048 2000a A:368 X-0130 ADAM:WINC ADAM:SCOT HIGH: --*
a. W-1934 Colonel George Matthews
b. George Matthews
c. John Burns; Joseph Blair, 1826; William Blair; James? [Joseph?] Briggs, 1823; Robert Glascoe; Joseph? [James?] Riggs, 1823; Alexander McClure; James Campbell, 1826; Halbert McLure; John H. Wood, 1823; Alexander McLure; Timothy Williamson; William Williamson, 1824; Jesse McKay; D. Boyle, 1828; Thomas Huston, 1828; Joseph Glasgo, heir; Edward Hoge; W. McColm? 1831; J. McKay, heirs; W. Baldridge, 1834; J. L. Beveridge, 1837; L. Cole, 1836; Asa Williamson, 1839; A. Barnes, 1842

S-2049 2000a A:369 X-0130 ADAM: --* BROW: --* HIGH:CONC
a. W-1934 Colonel George Matthews
b. George Matthews
c. None
*Source B does not mention Adams or Brown counties.

S-2050 667a A:304 X-1300 HIGH:WHIT*
a. W-2323 Captain Colin Cocke
b. Colin Cocke
c. R. Marz
*Source B notation: "Mourytown."

S-2051 200a A:315 X-1300 HIGH:WHIT
a. W-1314 Reuben Griffin, 100a
W-1011 Andrew Lawson, 100a
b. Philip Buckner
c. J. Miller

S-2055 600a A:382 X-1080 CLER:STON
a. W-3840 John Lutrell, heir, 400a
W-3839 John Lutrell, heir, 200a

S-2055 [continued]
b. Original Young
c. Robert Hall; J. Pickett, 1826; F. Shumard; Levi Buckingham; Thomas South, 1841

S-2057 1444a A:374 X-0663 CLER:BATA
a. W-1299 Nathaniel Darby
b. Nathaniel Darby
c. S. Estell; John Harden; John Mason; J. Duckwall, 1826; -- Barr & -- Lytle; O. T. Fishback, 1833; T. L. Shields, 1833; M. F. Veitch, 1831; John Hill, 1836; D. C. Brian; William Price, Junior; M. Groves, 1841

S-2058 1033a B:71 X-0663 CLER:BATA CLER:UNIO
a. W-1299 Nathaniel Darby
b. Nathaniel Darby
c. None

S-2058 634a B:71 X-0663 CLER:UNIO
a. W-1299 Nathaniel Darby
b. Nathaniel Darby
c. J. A. Armstrong; M? [W?] Hulick; S. King; S. Ewing, 1837; S. W. Lane; R. McFarland, 1836

S-2059 1000a A:305 X-0134 BROW:EAGL
a. W-1811 Captain Thomas Blackwell
b. Thomas Blackwell
c. None

S-2060 1000a A:305 X-0134 BROW:EAGL
a. W-1811 Captain Thomas Blackwell
b. Thomas Blackwell
c. None

S-2062 1000a A:306 X-0134 HIGH:WHIT BROW:EAGL
a. W-1811 Captain Thomas Blackwell
b. Thomas Blackwell
c. L. D. Woods; J. J. Higgins, 1841

S-2065 1073a A:391 X-0841 ROSS:CONC
a. W-1159 William Mercer, heir to General H. Mercer
b. Smith Snead
c. None

S-2066 1500a B:145 X-0660 CLAR:MADI GREE:ROSS
a. W-1159 William Mercer, heir to General H. Mercer
b. Smith Snead
c. None

S-2068 560a B:146 X-0660 CLAR:MADI GREE:ROSS
a. W-1159 William Mercer, heir to General H. Mercer
b. Smith Snead
c. James Browder; Jonathan Ward, 1834; -- Dun & -- Waddle

S-2069 1000a B:192 X-0840 FAYE:UNIO
a. W-1159 William Mercer, heir to General H. Mercer
b. Smith Snead*
c. James? [Joseph?] Kile; R. Waddle, 1826; James? [Joseph?] Coil, heirs; D. McLane; John Rankin
*Source B notation: "Patented to Charles Snead."

S-2070 560a B:146 X-0660 GREE:ROSS
a. W-1159 William Mercer, heir to General H. Mercer
b. Smith Snead
c. None

S-2071 1200a B:142 X-1303 BROW:WASH
a. W-2926 Captain Custes Kendall
b. Curtis Kendall
c. John Shultz; William L? [S?] Thorp, 1829; Mark Day; Hill D. Slaton, 1838; William Jameson; Solomon Bingaman; A. F. Sisco, 1831

S-2073 1040a B:161 X-1303 BROW:WASH
a. W-2926 Captain Custes Kendall
b. Custis Kendall
c. James Riley; A. Ligget, 1824

S-2074 1200a C:384 X-1060 BROW:GREE BROW:PIKE
a. W-2926 Captain Custes Kendall
b. Custis Kendall
c. Samuel Houghton; Robert Allen, 1823; Allen B. Hughes; John Allen & Robert Hix, [*also* Hicks] 1824; John Still; T. Handley; E. Bingaman & -- Towerton, 1830; Jesse Ellis; A. C. Stewart, 1831; William Russell; J. M. Smith; W. P. Burt, 1830; W. Hewitt, 1833; James N. Smith; Willis Burt, 1832; D. Kethler, 1837; S. Slade, heirs; John Vandyke, 1837

S-2075 260a B:488 X-1150 BROW:HUNT
a. W-3794 John Hardy, 200a
W-1706 Peter Jones; [mentions] John O'Bannon, 60a
b. Jacob Boone
c. None

S-2076 69a C:185 X-1150 BROW:HUNT
a. W-1706 Peter Jones [mentions] John O'Bannon, 36a
W-1892 Captain Alexander Parker, 33a
b. John O'Bannon & Alexander Parker
c. None

S-2079 1000a A:490 X-0010 CLIN:LIBE
a. W-2894 Lieutenant William Porter
b. William Porter
c. Cyrus Ball, 1827; James Dakin; David Fairfield, Senior; W. P. Hunnicutt, 1834

S-2080 667a A:516 X-0010 CLIN:LIBE
a. W-2894 Lieutenant William Porter
b. William Porter
c. -- Corothers, -- Patton, & -- Corothers; Samuel McGill, 1825; Menon Miles; Amos Underwood, 1827; John Crawford; John Atkinson, 1829; William Ireland, 1828; C. D. Dorsey; C. G. Dorsey; Samuel Iredell, 1829; Az[ariah?] Wall, 1828; A. E. Strickle, 1837; H. Robins

S-2081 1000a A:490 X-0010 CLIN:LIBE
a. W-2894 Lieutenant William Porter
b. William Porter
c. Hugh Adair; A. E. Strickle

S-2104 1000a B:306 X-0980 HIGH:PAIN
a. W-1457 Thomas Wilkins, 200a
W-1764 John Brett; Dr. James Currie [assignee?] 200a*
W-3465 Thomas Figgs, 100a
W-4392 William Russell, assignee, 200a; William Reynolds [assignee?] 200a
W-4449 William Reynolds, assignee, 200a
W-4453 William Reynolds, assignee, 100a
b. William Reynolds
c. None
*Information probably erroneous, because the warrant was used on S-0771. However, the number might have been used also for a John Gardner, mentioned only at the beginning of Source C.

S-2015 100a F:252 X-0850 LOGA: --*
a. W-4493 George Rice, assignee [of?] Edmund Rice
b. Robert** [Clough] Anderson
c. None
*Source B says ROSS:PAXT.
**Source B says Richard Clough Anderson.

S-2187 100a B:83 X-0420 BROW:BYRD
a. W-4394 Leroy Beasley, heir
b. Thomas Kerlin
c. John Glendening [*also* Glendenning]; Greenleaf Norton, 1828; John Lane; John Sand, 1831; G. H. Borer, 1831; J. Baird, Junior; -- Wilson & -- Middleton, 1842

S-2188 633a A:314 X-0138 ADAM:TIFF
a. W-0425 Thomas Winslow, heir to Benjamin Winslow
b. Thomas Winslow
c. David Dunwoody; William Parks, 1824

S-2189 1893a A;356 X-1170 CLIN:UNIO
a. W-1168 Ambrose Dudley, heir to Robert Dudley
b. Ambrose Dudley
c. T. C. Blake; James Elliot, 1823; John Stackhouse; J. Morris, 1823

S-2190 200a A:376 X-0790 CLER:GOSH CLER:MIAM WARR: --*
a. W-1284 Robert Thompson
b. William Lytle
c. A. Brannon; G. Brannon, 1831
*Source B does not mention Warren County.

S-2192 1100a A:376 X-0660 WARR:HAMI CLER:GOSH
a. W-1453 Jacob Smith, 100a
W-1454 John Baines, 100a
W-3126 Daniel Delany, 200a
W-3127 Lewis Yancy, 100a
W-3128 Joshua Bartley, 200a
W-3129 Daniel Long, 100a
W-3130 John Wetherall, 100a
W-3131 Francis L. Slaughter, 200a
b. William Nall
c. J. Mooney, 1825; William Simonton; Samuel Paxton, 1840 (Clermont County)

S-2193 400a A:375 X-0790 WARR: --* CLER:GOSH
a. W-2550 William Broughton, "with Flaughertys"
b. William Broughton
c. None
*Source B does not mention Warren County.

S-2194 667a A:377 X-0790 WARR: --* CLER:MIAM
a. W-3132 Robert Yancy
b. Martin Nall
c. None
*Source B does not mention Warren County.

S-2195. *See* S-1545

S-2196 400a A:375 X-0790 WARR: --* CLER:GOSH
a. W-1094 James Lane
b. Robert Campbell
c. None
*Source B does not mention Warren County.

S-2197 1000a A:314 X-0300 ADAM:FRAN
a. W-1561*
b. Aaron Denny
c. Andrew Cipinger? [Cissinger?]; David P. Wilkins, 1823; Elizabeth Rich; Abraham Lafferty, 1826; L. Carter, heirs; J. G. Reed, 1842
*Source C does not list this warrant number.

S-2198 1000a A:329 X-0133 ADAM:FRAN
a. W-0015 Sally Phillips
b. Aaron Denny
c. -- James & -- McArthur; T. Huston, 1835

S-2199 50a B:167 X-1110 ADAM:GREE
a. W-4566 John Warren
b. John Warren
c. None

S-2200 167a B:259 X-0420 BROW:JACK
a. W-0015 Sally Phillips
b. Aaron Denny
c. None

S-2201 600a A:315 X-0130 ADAM:TIFF
a. W-3943 John Dent, [*mentions*] John McAllister
b. James McAllister
c. None

S-2202 200a A:315 X-0800 BROW:HUNT ADAM: --*
a. W-3943 John Dent, [*mentions*] John McAllister
b. James McAllister
c. None
*Source B does not mention Adams County.

S-2203 200a A:315 X-0130 ADAM:TIFF
a. W-3943 John Dent, [mentions] John McAllister
b. James McAllister
c. J. & J. McAllister; Thomas Huston; Thomas Smart? [Swart?]; A. Compton, 1838

S-2204 400a A:328 X-0800 HAMI:ANDE
a. W-0145 Captain William Fowler, 200a
W-4268 James Howard, 200a
b. Nathaniel Wilson & William Fowler
c. William Deseresy; J. B. Miller, 1829

S-2205 250a B:123 X-0420 BROW:BYRD BROW:JACK
a. W-2367 Captain John Anderson
b. John Anderson
c. None

S-2208 400a A:403 X-1000 PIKE:PEEP
a. W-0463 John Jowett, heir to Mat[thew] Jowett
b. Nathaniel Massie
c. None

S-2210 200a B:179 X-0423 ADAM:LIBE
a. W-1154 Charles Crawford
b. William Wood
c. None

S-2212 954a A:416 X-1120 X-1300 BROW:PLEA
a. W-3533 Peter Talbot, heir to William Worsham
b. Peter Talbert
c. John Dawning; James Woods, 1824; John Holman; William Shepherd, 1825

S-2213 340a B:170 X-0420 BROW:BYRD
a. W-4169 John Thompson
b. John Hook
c. None

S-2214 1000a A:330 X-1300 HIGH:WHIT BROW: --*
a. W-3527 William Finne [Finnie?]
b. Adrian Valck
c. George Rinechar; James Smith, 1829
*Source B does not mention Brown County.

S-2215 1000a A:330 X-1300 HIGH:CONC
a. W-3527 William Finne [Finnie?]
b. Adrian Valck
c. None

S-2216 1400a A:400 X-0840 ROSS:SCIO ROSS:HUNT
a. W-2898 Thomas Lewis, representative
b. Thomas Lewis
c. John Haines; R. Long, 1827

S-2216 534a A:400 X-0840 ROSS:SCIO ROSS:HUNT
a. Thomas Lewis, representative
b. Thomas Lewis
c. None

S-2217 1490a B:69 X-0841 ROSS:SCIO
a. W-0854 Lieutenant Nicholas Taliaferro
b. Nicholas Taliaferro
c. D. McArthur; W. S. Murphy; R. Stewart

S-2220 100a B:381 X-0610 LOGA:MONR
a. W-1019 John McKenny
b. Henry Delay
c. Alexander Basset; Joseph Strothers, 1824

S-2225 3671a A:336 X-0660 WARR:SALE WARR:WASH
a. W-0559 Captain Benjamin Taliaferro
b. Benjamin Taliaferro
c. S. Dougherty; W. Sinnard, 1825; H. German; J. Hopkins, 1824; John James; E. B. Wright, 1832; Enoch Baldwin; Joel A. Stokes, 1835; Thomas Thompson; J. Martin; H. M. Stokes, 1837; E. Thomas; M. Mills; S. Stowel; R. Burns; J. Egbert, 1842

S-2226 1601a A:397 X-1170 WARR:SALE WARR:WASH CLIN: --*
a. W-2900 James Hooper
b. Stephen T. Mason
c. W. Penquite; A. E. Strickle, 1836; E. Fleming; J. M. Roosa (Warren County); L. S. Howard; A. G. Rice; William Penquite, Junior
*Source B mentions Clinton County, but says "lies in Warren County."

S-2227 1000a A:344 X-1173 CLIN:VERN*
a. W-3671 William Boyce
b. William Boyce
c. Jaw? Longstreth; J. Morris, 1825; Aaron? Oxley; James Dakin; J. Bagmiller; J. Morrow, 1827; John Wakley; G. Bruce, 1830; H. Work; L? [S?] Gastin? [Gustin?] 1834; John Combs; A. E. Strickle; W. Oxley; W. P. Hunnicut, 1840

S-2228 1000a A:345 X-0660 WARR:WASH CLIN:CHES CLIN:VERN
a. W-1721 Jesse Headin, 200a
W-0863 Robert Bacon, 200a
W-1589 George Grimes, 200a
W-2099 William Binns, 200a
W-2906 Edward Valentine, heir Mary Minton, 200a
b. Stephen T. Mason
c. None

S-2229 1000a A:341 X-1170 WARR:WASH CLIN:VERN
a. W-0803 General Horatio Gates
b. Horatio Gates
c. None

S-2230 1000a A:341 X-1170 WARR: --* CLIN:CHES
a. W-0804 General Horatio Gates
b. Horatio Gates
c. J. Falles; George Bruce, 1826; J. Carpenter; William Falles, 1840
*Source B does not mention Warren County.

S-2231 1000a A:341 X-0180 WARR: --* CLIN:CHES
a. W-0804 General Horatio Gates
b. Horatio Gates
c. A. Garrison; E. Dakin, 1826; Ralph Myers; William R. Cole, 1826; George Bruce, 1826
*Source B does not mention Warren County.

S-2232 1000a A:3432 X-1170 X-0180 WARR: --* CLIN:CHES
a. W-0807 General Horatio Gates
b. Horatio Gates
c. None
*Source B does not mention Warren County.

S-2233 900a A:395 X-0180 GREE:SUGA GREE:CAES
a. W-4190 Edward Lewis, heir [mentions -- Jackson, assignee]
b. Aaron Mercer
c. None

S-2234 1000a A:337 X-0180 GREE:CAES
a. W-2763 Warner Lewis & Addison Lewis
b. Warren Lewis & Addison Lewis
c. None

S-2235 1000a A:337 X-0180 GREE:XENI GREE:CAES
a. W-2763 Warner Lewis & Addison Lewis
b. Warren Lewis & Addison Lewis
c. None

S-2236 1000a A:337 X-0180 GREE:XENI
a. W-2763 Warner Lewis & Addison Lewis
b. Warren Lewis & Addison Lewis
c. None

S-2237 1000a A:337 X-0180 GREE:XENI
a. W-2763 Warner Lewis & Addison Lewis
b. Warren Lewis & Addison Lewis
c. None

S-2238 1000a A:339 X-0180 GREE:CAES
a. W-2763 Warner Lewis & Addison Lewis
b. Warner Lewis & Addison Lewis
c. None

S-2239 1000a A:339 X-0180 GREE:XENI
a. W-2763 Warner Lewis & Addison Lewis
b. Warren Lewis & Addison Lewis
c. Margaret Snavely; William H. Good, 1824

S-2240 1000a A:339 X-0180 GREE:XENI
a. W-2763 & W-2764 Warner Lewis & Addison Lewis
b. Warner Lewis & Addison Lewis
c. None

S-2241 1000a A:340 X-0500 GREE:XENI*
a. W-2764 Warner Lewis & Addison Lewis
b. Warner Lewis & Addison Lewis
c. None
*Source B notation: "By Xenia."

S-2242 1000a A:339 X-0500 GREE:XENI
a. W-2764 Warner Lewis & Addison Lewis
b. Warner Lewis & Addison Lewis
c. None

S-2243 1000a A:340 X-0500 GREE:XENI*
a. W-2764 Warner Lewis & Addison Lewis
b. Warner Lewis & Addison Lewis
c. None
*Source B notation: "Xenia."

S-2244 1000a A:340 X-0180 GREE:XENI GREE:CAES
a. W-2764 Warner Lewis & Addison Lewis
b. Warner Lewis & Addison Lewis
c. None

S-2245 1000a A:344 X-1170 CLIN:VERN WARR:WASH
a. W-3671 William Boyce
b. William Boyce
c. None

S-2246 667a A:344 X-1170 CLIN:UNIO CLIN:CHES
a. W-3671 William Boyce
b. William Boyce
c. B. D. Disbrow; J. Hampstead? 1823

S-2247 1333a A:336 X-0180 GREE:XENI GREE:CAES GREE:ROSS
a. W-3286 John McAdams
b. John McAdams
c. J. Anderson; G. Moss, 1826; S. Payne; T. Watson, 1824; Anns? [Amos?] Sally; B. Payne & James Payne; J. Galloway, 1829

S-2248 1000a A:343 X-1170 CLIN:UNIO CLIN:LIBE
a. W-0806 General Horatio Gates
b. Horatio Gates
c. None

S-2249 1000a A:345 X-1170 CLIN:VERN
a. W-3001 Archibald Campbell, heir to Richard [Campbell]
b. Archibald Campbell
c. Andrew Christie; J. Christie, 1824; J. Galloway, Junior; J. Morris, 1823

S-2250 1000a A:346 X-1173 CLIN:VERN
a. W-3001 Archibald Campbell, heir to Richard [Campbell]
b. Archibald Campbell
c. S. Winston; C. B. Harlan & R. B. Harlan, 1830

S-2251 1000a A:346 X-1170 CLIN:VERN
a. W-3001 Archibald Campbell, heir to Richard [Campbell]
b. Archibald Campbell
c. Levi Hughes; E. Smith, 1823; William M. Woodward; Samuel? Winston, 1826; D. Manning; J. Woodruff, 1828; Andrew Christie; Jean Mills;

S-2251 [continued]
James Christie, 1829; J. Morris, 1829; John J. Reeder; George Fallis, 1838

S-2252 1000a A:346 X-1173 CLIN:VERN
a. W-3001 Archibald Campbell, heir to Richard [Campbell]
b. Archibald Campbell
c. S. Winston; C. B. Harlan & R. B. Harlan, 1830

S-2253 1000a A:408 X-0840 HIGH:PAIN ROSS: --*
a. W-0892 John Karne; Matthew Black? [assignee?] 100a
W-1710 Jesse Punerer? [Purrear? Puryear?] 100a
W-2765 Isham Valentine, 100a
W-2737 George Coats, 100a
W-2801 Jacob Luckelle? [Luckette?] 100a
W-2768 Patrick Martin? [Marlin?] 100a
W-1856 Robert Kimble [mentions John Brown] 100a
W-2661 James Bedford, 100a
W-2594 William Reynolds, assignee, 100a
W-2713 Thomas Aslin, 100a
b. Edward Dowse
c. None
*Source B does not mention Ross County.

S-2254 1000a B:134 X-0750 UNIO:PARI
a. W-2652 Samuel Trower; A? Guthbert, assignee, 200a
W-2799 Thomas Cain, heir to Thomas Cain, 400a
W-1877 William Beale, 400a
b. Edward Dowse
c. Mathew Carey; S. G. Strong, 1828

S-2255 1000a* A:408 X-0840 HIGH:PAIN
a. W-2636 Obadiah Nunally, heir to John Nunally, 100a
W-2602 John Depriest; John Flowers, assignee, 200a
W-2673 Charles Neal, 200a
W-0190 John Gamble, 200a
b. Edward Dowse
c. None
*Warrants rendered in payment are insufficient for this acreage.

S-2256 1000a B:134 X-0750 UNIO:PARI
a. W-2715 Thomas Aslin; Aaron? Gibson representative, 200a
W-2734 William Linchiers? [Sirchier?] 200a
W-2762*
W-2695 Martin Hawkins; John Mather, assignee, 100a?
W-1430? William Smith, 200a
b. Edward Dowse
c. John F. Mason; John Jolley, 1828; J. B. Krautline
*Source C does not list this warrant number.

S-2262 500a A:408 X-0840 ROSS:PAIN
a. W-2592 Francis Graves, 100a
W-2702 Francis Graves; assignee Joel Bragg, 100a
W-2645*
W-2634 Daniel Vasser, heir to Joel Vasser, 100a
W-2635 Obadiah Nunally, heir to John Nunally, 100a
b. Edward Dowse
c. None
*Source C does not list this warrant number.

S-2263 965a A:494 X-0500 GREE:XENI
a. W-3347 Samuel C. Sanderson, 100a
W-3350 John Ritchie, 100a
W-3351 Timothy Contey? [Conely?] 200a
W-3352 John Brookes, 200a
W-3353 William Weldy, 200a
W-3349 Edward Stephens, 200a
b. Jacob Brown
c. None

S-2264 1000a A:346 X-0500 GREE:XENI
a. W-3001 Archibald Campbell, heir to Richard [Campbell]
b. Archibald Campbell
c. J. Baker, heirs of; J. Galloway (no date)

S-2265 1000a A:347 X-0740 GREE:XENI
a. W-3101 Archibald Campbell, heir to Richard [Campbell]
b. Archibald Campbell
c. J. Baker, heirs of; J. Browder, 1825

S-2266 500a A:344 X-1170 CLIN:CHES
a. W-0809 General Horatio Gates
b. Horatio Gates
c. James Conger; W. P. Hunnicut, 1831

S-2267 1200a* A:419 X-0740 GREE:XENI
a. W-0636 George Robertson, 100a
W-3061 Milton Ford, assignee [of?] Robert Archer, 100a
W-3392 Thomas B. Adams, assignee [of[William Kemp, 200a
W-3040 Newton Philips, 100a
b. Stephen T. Mason
c. None
*Warrants submitted are insufficient for this acreage.

S-2269 1720a B:132 X-0840* HIGH:LIBE
a. W-3073 William Reynolds, assignee [of] John Suddeth, 100a
W-2863 Adam Loudon, assignee [of] Burwell Jackson, 200a
W-1909** Philip Langfelt, 100a
W-2697 Robert Waysoan? assignee Stephen T. Mason, 33a
W-2451?***
b. Tarlton Fleming
c. None
*"R.K. f[or]k of . . ."
**Warrant number probably erroneous, as it was used in S-0452 by Clement Biddle.
***Source C does not list this warrant number.

S-2270 64a B:271 X-0660* HAMI:ANDE
a. W-1654 Joseph Payne
b. Nathaniel Massie
c. None
*"Island in L[ittle] Miami [River]."

S-2272 1000a A:340 X-0740 GREE:XENI
a. W-2764 Warner Lewis & Addison Lewis
b. Warner Lewis & Addison Lewis
c. None

S-2273 200a A:352 X-0133 ADAM:FRAN
a. W-1969 Charles Morgan, heir
b. Charles Morgan
c. James Taylor; Joseph Zumalt, 1827

S-2274 100a A:353 X-0133 ADAM:FRAN
a. W-1197 Frederick Coones
b. John Fishback
c. None

S-2275 100a A:353 X-0133 ADAM:FRAN
a. W-1194 Harmon Button
b. Harmond Button
c. None

S-2276 600a A:381 X-0260 HAMI:ANDE
a. W-0463 John Jowett, heir to Mat[thew] Jowett
b. Nathaniel Massie
c. L. Cooper; G. W. Jones, 1826; S. Sutton; A. McGill; P. Miller, 1842

S-2277 1000a A:396 X-0740 GREE:XENI
a. W-4467 Charles Bradford
b. Charles Bradford
c. None

S-2278 1200a A:421 X-0740 GREE:XENI
a. W-4467 Charles Bradford
b. Charles Bradford
c. None

S-2279 778a A:515 X-1170 CLIN:UNIO CLIN:CHES
a. W-4576 John Hurt
b. Thomas Banks
c. None

S-2280 1000a A:394 X-0180 CLIN:CHES
a. W-0394 Nathan Hughs, 100a
W-2691 Martin Hawkins; assignee [of?] Benjamin Head, 100a
W-2699 George Tey? [Try?] heir . . .? 100a
W-2692 Benjamin Beyanan?; assignee [of?] W. Sexton, 100a
W-2693 Martin Hawkins; assignee [of?] Thomas Coleman, 200a
W-2690 Martin Hawkins; assignee [of?] Thomas Loyd, 100a
W-2694 Martin Hawkins; assignee [of?] W. Lardwick, 200a
W-2696 James Lewis; assignee [of?] Robert Armsted, 100a
b. William H. Sergeant
c. None

S-2282* 200a -- -- --
a. --
b. John Cox
c. James Taylor; Adam Reed, 1824
*This partial entry does not appear in Source A. In Source B it appears out of sequence at top of page before S-2267.

S-2283 100a A:376 X-0790 CLER:GOSH
a. W-4248 Edward Wood
b. James McCardell
c. None

S-2284 & S-2469 181a C:406? X-0600 ADAM:MONR
a. W-1654 Joseph Payne, 81a?
W-4087 Walter Ashmore, 100a?
b. Nathaniel Massie
c. Benjamin Bowman, heirs; Edward Bowman, 1831; R. Holerness, 1839

S-2285 500a A:403 X-0130 ADAM:TIFF
a. W-3865 John Shaver, 100a
W-3864 George Shaver, 100a
W-1634 Jonathan Tinsley, 200a
W-3607 Dennis McKinney, 100a
b. William Lytle
c. None

S-2286 & S-2948 356a C:443 X-0660 CLER:MIAM*
a. W-2830 James Wilson, 200a
W-3705 William McElroy; [mentions] Evan Francis, 100a
W-0347 Major David Stephenson, 56a
b. William Lytle & D. Stephenson
c. None
*Source B shows Williamsburg Township crossed out.

S-2287 1000a A:381 X-0131 BROW:EAGL
a. W-0227 Lieutenant Jacob Coleman
b. Jacob Coleman
c. Henry O'Neal; Mathew Kincaid, 1826; R. Kincaid, 1828

S-2288 1333a A:472 X-0640 HIGH:FAIR
a. W-4008 Peregrine Fitzhugh
b. Peregrine Fitzhugh
c. S. F. Randolph; A. Trimbel, 1823

S-2289 1426a A:482 X-0980 HIGH:PAIN
a. W-3455 Lieutenant Peregrine Fitzhugh
b. Peregrine Fitzhugh
c. J. Criger; A. Browse, 1826; J. Welsh; Isaac West

S-2289* 15a E:338 X-1080 CLIN: --
a. W-3455 Lieutenant Peregrine Fitzhugh
b. John Jones
c. None
*This entry not shown in Source B.

S-2289* 24a E:366 X-0195 PIKE: --
a. W-3455 Lieutenant Peregrine Fitzhugh
b. James Starr
c. None
*This entry not shown in Source B.

S-2289* 10a E:366 X-1145 PIKE: --
a. W-3455 Lieutenant Peregrine Fitzhugh
b. John Bromley
c. None
*Source B does not show this entry.

S-2290 311a C:306 X-0150 ROSS:BUCK
a. W-1627 Lieutenant Joseph Conway
b. Joseph Conway
c. James Bell, 1825

S-2291 1333a B:133 X-0150 ROSS:BUCK
a. W-0238 Joseph Winlock
b. Eli Williams
c. None

S-2292 1000a A:409 X-0150 ROSS:BUCK
a. W-4320 William Hatcher, 400a
W-4351 William Cosby, 400a
W-4333 Jesse Bayles, 100a
W-4404 Francis Ravenscraft, 100a
b. John Wilson
c. None

S-2293 360a A:458 X-0150 ROSS:BUCK ROSS:PAIN
a. W-3889 James Wood
b. John Wilson
c. None

S-2294 200a A:462 X-0150 ROSS:PAIN
a. W-4395 George Wills
b. Joseph Swearingen
c. Robert Greenleaf; Emor Bail? [Boil?]; W? [M?] Greenlee & R. Greenlee; A. Carlisle, 1841

S-2295 400a A:511 X-0150 ROSS:BUCK
a. W-3916 Richard Pile
b. Richard Evans
c. None

S-2297* 50a — — —
a. --
b. James Craig
c. --
*This entire entry crossed out in Source B.

S-2298 1333a A:475 X-0840 HIGH:FAIR FAYE:GREE
a. W-4578 Severn Teagle
b. Severn Teagle
c. D. Terry, heirs

S-2299 600a A:406 X-0840 ROSS:PAIN
a. W-3422 George Tennell? [Fannell? Ferrell?] 200a
W-3450 Richard Turner, 200a
W-3364 James Fear, 200a
b. John Barrett? [Bassett?]
c. None

S-2300 1000a A:408 X-0840 ROSS:PAIN
a. W-3455 Lieutenant Peregrine Fitzhugh
b. Peregrine Fitzhugh
c. Moses Glasscock; A. Latham, 1823; R. Stewart, 1827

S-2301 1333a B:252 X-0840 HIGH:PAIN
a. W-2960 Nathan Smith
b. Nathan Smith
c. A. Sharp; Abner Jessop, 1829; Samuel Acres; James Murdock, 1832; A. Hewitt, 1831

S-2302 1333a A:478 X-0840 HIGH:PAIN
a. W-2960 Nathan Smith
b. Nathan Smith
c. A. Sharp; A. Jessup, 1826; A. Cooley

S-2303 1500a B:188 X-1300 HIGH:NEWM HIGH:SALE HIGH:WHIT
a. W-3029 Thomas Parker
b. Thomas Parker
c. James Murphy; J. M? [W?] Trimble, 1832; J. Hays, heirs; William Malcom, 1840

S-2304 1500a B:194 X-1300 HIGH:NEWM
a. W-3029 Thomas Parker
b. Thomas Parker
c. William Beard; William Scott

S-2305 1000a A:470 X-0250 HIGH:LIBE
a. W-3029 Thomas Parker
b. Thomas Parker
c. None

S-2306 1000a A:471 X-0250 HIGH:LIBE ROSS: --*
a. W-4578 Severn Teagle
b. Severn Teagle
c. Demus Adams; A. Trimble, 1839
*Source B does not mention Ross County.

S-2307 1083a B:64 X-0980 HIGH:JACK
a. W-2744 Anthony Singleton, heir
b. Anthony Singleton
c. Anthony Singleton, heirs; -- Kirley & -- Starling, 1831

S-2308 1000a A:392 X-0841 ROSS:CONC ROSS:BUCK
a. W-2744 Anthony Singleton, heir
b. Antony Singleton
c. None

S-2309 1000a A:392 X-0841 ROSS:BUCK
a. W-2744 Anthony Singleton, heir
b. Anthony Singleton
c. None

S-2310 1150a A:392 X-0841 ROSS:CONC
a. W-4501 Thomas Wallace
b. Thomas Wallace
c. None

S-2311 1150a A:392 X-0841 ROSS:BUCK
a. W-4501 Thomas Wallace
b. Thomas Wallace
c. T. Marshall, heirs; C. Wallace, 1839

S-2312 640a A:488 X-0010 GREE:CAES
a. W-2213 William Nelson
b. William Nelson
c. None

S-2312 1640a A:491 X-0010 GREE:CAES
FAYE: --*
CLIN:LIBE
a. W-2213 William Nelson
b. William Nelson
c. Henry Welsh; O. Wall, 1835
*Source B does not mention Fayette County, but does mention Clinton County, Liberty Township.

S-2313 2790a A:420 X-0180 WARR:WASH
X-0660
a. W-0176 General P. Muhlenberg
b. Peter Muhlenburg
c. William Moon; J. A. Stokes, 1838

S-2313 1120a A:521 X-0180 WARR:WASH
X-0660 CLIN: --*
a. W-0176 General P. Muhlenberg
b. Peter Muhlenburg
c. Is.? [J?] Harvey; J. Egbert, 1841
*Source B does not mention Clinton County.

S-2314 1333a A:478 X-0840 HIGH:PAIN
a. W-0204 Major John Hay
b. John Hays
c. None

S-2315 1000a A:478 X-0840 HIGH:LIBE
HIGH:PAIN
a. W-0204 Major John Hay
b. John Hays
c. None

S-2316 1000a A:478 X-0840 HIGH:LIBE
HIGH:PAIN
a. W-0204 Major John Hay
b. John Hays
c. R. Cunningham, heirs; J? [I?] Simpson, 1840; John Beeson; James Farley, 1840

S-2317 1000a A:479 X-0840 HIGH:LIBE
HIGH:FAIR
a. W-0204 Major John Hay
b. John Hays
c. Thomas Burgess; Isaac Simpson, 1838

S-2318 1000a A:479 X-0520 HIGH:FAIR
a. W-0204 Major John Hay
b. John Hays
c. None

S-2319 1000a A:470 X-0250 HIGH:LIBE
a. W-0176 General P. Muhlenberg
b. Peter Muhlenburg
c. None

S-2320 2000a A:479 X-0840 HIGH:LIBE
a. W-2741 Captain John Hughes
b. John Hughs*
c. None
*Source B spells Hughes.

S-2321 1333a A:479 X-0840 HIGH:LIBE
HIGH:FAIR
a. W-2741 Captain John Hughes
b. John Hughs*
c. J. F. Liverton? [Siverton?]
*Source B spells Hughes

S-2322 1333a A:480 X-0840 HIGH:FAIR
a. W-2741 Captain John Hughes
b. John Hughs*
c. J. Watkins, heirs; T. M? [W?] Sanders, 1826; Benjamin Watkins; Jesse Johnson, 1832
*Source B spells Hughes.

S-2323 1333a A:480 X-0520 HIGH:FAIR
a. W-4427 Michael Feely
b. Michael Feeley
c. S. M. Tracy; Peter Clark, 1840

S-2324 1333a A:480 X-0840 HIGH:FAIR
a. W-4427 Michael Feely
b. Michael Feeley
c. James Dailey; Allen Trimble, 1831; J. Van Pelt; A. Moore, 1842

S-2325 1000a A:480 X-0840 HIGH:LIBE
a. W-1564 Captain James Baytop
b. James Baytop
c. Thomas Riley; William Mathews

S-2326 1000a A:473 X-0840 HIGH:LIBE
HIGH:FAIR
a. W-1564 Captain James Baytop
b. James Baytop
c. Asa Hunt, heirs; N. Swadley, Junior

S-2327 1000a A:473 X-0840 HIGH:FAIR
a. W-1564 Captain James Baytop
b. James Baytop
c. None

S-2328 1000a A:473 X-0840 HIGH:FAIR
a. W-1564 Captain James Baytop
b. James Baytop
c. J. Hyatt

S-2334 1000a B:64 X-0840 HIGH:NEWM
a. W-3176 Alexander Skinner
b. Adam Hoops
c. None

S-2335 1000a B:185 X-0250 HIGH:LIBE
HIGH:PAIN
a. W-3223 Robert Boyd; Thomas Cocke [assignee?]
b. John Graham
c. G. Roads; J. Smith, 1826; Walter Dun; William Boestler? 1831

S-2336 253a B:409 X-0840 ROSS:PAIN HIGH:PAIN
a. W-3223 Robert Boyd; Thomas Cocke [assignee?]
b. John Graham
c. None

S-2337 1000a B:283 X-0360 ROSS:UNIO ROSS:DEER
a. W-3223 Robert Boyd; Thomas Cocke [assignee?]
b. John Graham
c. None

S-2338 1000a B:185 X-0160 BROW:LEWI
a. W-3223 Robert Boyd: Thomas Cocke [assignee?]
b. John Graham
c. William Beer; David Johnston, 1823; James Hanna; Peter Barr, 1825; Thomas Murphy; David Johnson; James Vanscoge; -- Shepherd & -- Masterson, 1823; W. Dun; S. Pangburn, 1829; R. Chalfant, 1830

S-2339 600a B:50 X-1001* ADAM:FRAN
a. W-1632 Valentine Ross; David Anderson [assignee?] 200a
W-1783 William Cook; David Anderson [assignee?] 200a
W-1857 Robert Belcher; James Jenkins [assignee?] 100a
b. Francis Graves
c. Benjamin Day; Jesse Edwards, 1824; D. Boyle, 1828; B. Day, heirs; Thomas Huston, 1833; C. Cannon, heirs; L. Cole, 1839
*"N[orth] f[or]k Scioto Br[ush] Cr[eek]."

S-2340 700a B:69 X-1001 ADAM:FRAN
a. W-1868 James Culvertson, 100a
W-3007 Hugh Gillam; David Anderson [assignee?] 200a
W-1907 George Somerson; David Anderson [assignee?] 200a
W-3020 Benjamin McDonald; David Anderson & S. McCargo [assignees?] 200a
b. Francis Graves
c. Benjamin Day; Isaac Smalley, 1824
*"N[orth] f[or]k Scioto Br[ush] Cr[eek]."

S-2341 700a B:69 X-1001* ADAM:MEIG SCIO:BRUS**
a. W-3006 Littlebury Scott; David Anderson [assignee?] 200a
W-3104 Francis Graves; David Anderson & W. Golson [assignees?] 400a
W-2544 Robert Smithie; David Anderson [assignee?] 100a
b. Francis Graves
c. None
*"N[orth] f[or]k Scioto Br[ush] Cr[eek]."
**Source A does not list Scioto County, Brush Creek Township.

S-2342 200a B:67 X-1001* ADAM:FRAN
a. W-3013 Benoni Overstreet
b. David Walker
c. John Matthews; John Copeland, 1825
*"N[orth] f[or]k Scioto Br[ush] Cr[eek]."

S-2345 600a B:69 X-1001* SCIO:BRUS ADAM:--**
a. W-1671 Ralph Moore, 400a
W-1686 James Dickinson, 200a
b. Nathaniel Irish
c. John Boleman; James? [Joseph?] Moore, 1823; Peter Randle; John Fisher, 1823; Enoch Randolph; William Burkit? 1826; Wyly Noland, 1826; Thomas Worthington; -- McDaid & -- Wilkins, 1826; L? [S?] Randell; J. Cole, 1827; J. Newland, 1828
*"N[orth] f[or]k Scioto Br[ush] Cr[eek[."
**Source B mentions Adams County, but says tract "lies in Scioto County . . ."

S-2351 2000a A:472 X-0250 HIGH:LIBE HIGH:FAIR HIGH:UNIO
a. W-3295 Robert Ballard
b. Robert Ballard
c. None

S-2352 1000a A:468 X-0250 HIGH:LIBE
a. W-3295 Robert Ballard
b. Robert Ballard
c. None

S-2353 1000a A:468 X-0250 HIGH:LIBE*
a. W-3295 Robert Ballard
b. Robert Ballard
c. Samuel D. Hoge; L? [S?] Collins, 1830
*Source B notation: "Hillsboro."

S-2354 1050a A:492 X-0010 GREE:CAES
a. W-3990 Nancy Grimes, heir[ess]
b. Nancy Grymes
c. None

S-2358 1480a B:252 X-0180 GREE:XENI
S-2359 GREE:CAES
S-2475
S-2476
a. W-3765 Benjamin Spiller
b. Benjamin Spiller
c. Thomas Carneal; Mathias Wynans, 1828; Robert Clark; J. Leaman? [Seaman?] 1829; Arthur Oniel

S-2365 667a B:64 X-1004 UNIO:JERO DELA:CONC
a. W-3030 Thomas Parker
b. Thomas Parker
c. Mease Smith; Manly S. Butler, 1836

S-2366* 500a -- -- UNIO:MILL
a. --
b. Isaac Hite
c. None
*Listed in Source B but not in Source A.

S-2369 750a B:56 X-1000 PIKE:JACK
a. W-3889 James Wood
b. John Wilson
c. None

S-2371 2000a A:418 X-1170 CLIN:CHES
a. W-3099 Thomas Baytop
b. Thomas Baytop
c. John Jones; J. Morris, 1826; James? [Joseph?] Townsend; B. Hinkson, 1831; Eli Hovey? [Havey?]; A. E. Strickle, 1837

S-2372 2000a A:419 X-1170 CLIN:CHES CLIN:VERN
a. W-3099 Thomas Baytop
b. Thomas Baytop
c. J. Harvey

S-2373 4000a A:431 X-0270 CLER:TATE*
a. W-0147 Colonel Nathaniel Gist
W-2509 Captain John Jordan
b. John Breckenridge
c. John S. Beck; Calvin A. Warren, 1834; A. Branland; L. T. Pease, 1837; A. Patterson; J. Perin, 1836; W. Robinson; J. D. Morris, 1836; Levi Rogers; R. W. Clark, 1836; J. L. Beck; E. L. Rogers; J. Church; W. South, 1842; D. Mefford; J. Quinlan, 1842
*Source B notation: "Bethel."

S-2374 100a A:432 X-0790 CLER:GOSH
a. W-2851 William Foster; William Lytle [assignee?]
b. Henry Voder
c. J. Reader; S. B. Cleveland, 1825; S. Winston; Z. Chapman, 1825

S-2375. *See* S-1550

S-2376 300a A:431 X-0790 CLER:GOSH*
a. W-3550 Samuel Dunlap, heir, 200a
W-3868 William Gillaspy, 100a
b. Joseph Gerrard
c. J. Wood; B. Brown, 1828; J. Strout, 1831
*Source B notation: "By Goshen."

S-2377 500a A:431 X-0790 CLER:MIAM CLER:GOSH*
a. W-3513 John Casey, 200a
W-3407 Samuel Brooking; Allen Stubbs [assignee?] 100a
W-2535 Samuel Brooking; Allen Stubbs [assignee?] 200a
b. William Lytle
c. W. Clark; Isaac? Challer, 1825; John Cotterel; John Duckwall, 1826; J. Hunt; C. Gatch, 1824; E. Poudens; M. A. Bryan, 1826; Jesse Wood; S. Winston, 1823; J. Atherton; J. W. Brown, 1827; C. Burrows; B. Brown, 1828; S. Pray; James Taylor; Z. Chapman, 1828; R. E. Hale? [Hall?]; Eber[hard?] Fritz; B. M. Jackson, 1831; G. Kerns; E. Pruden; T. Morris, 1830; D. M. Jackson, 1830; J. Emery; J. Randle, 1837

S-2378 470a C:358 X-0800 CLER:FRAN
a. W-4297 David Gray, 100a
W-4564 James Sculley, 200a
W-4295 Daniel Smith, 200a
b. John O'Bannon
c. J. Jones; M. Mullen, 1842; E. Pruden; J. Randle, 1837; F. Snyder; B. Brown

S-2379 590a A:450 X-0800 CLER:FRAN
a. W-3305 John Colbert, 100a
W-3937 John Lyne, 100a
W-3938 David Spang, 100a
W-3951 James Barnwell, 100a
W-3952 Moses Oliver, 200a
b. John O'Bannon
c. J. McClanahan; A. C. Day, 1836

S-2380 700a A:384 X-0133 ADAM:MEIG
a. W-2402 Lieutenant Jordan Harris
b. Jordan Harris
c. Stacey Storer; John Liston? [Linton?] 1823

S-2381 400a A:384 X-0841 ROSS:CONC
a. W-3467 James Davies; John Rork, assignee, 200a
W-3447 John Alfred, 200a
b. Jacob Warrick
c. None

S-2382 1000a B:61 X-0180 WARR:WAYN
a. W-4645 Richard C[lough] Anderson
b. Richard C[lough] Anderson
c. None

S-2383 2533a B:535 X-0180 GREE:XENI GREE:CAES
a. W-0736 Doctor Alexander Skinner
W-1938*
W-3944 John Dent; Fleming Tarlton, assignee, 667a
b. Richard C[lough] Anderson
c. Unknown; Samuel Herod, 1827
*This warrant number must be erroneous, as it was issued to Jeremiah Walker and assigned to Clement Biddle, and used on S-0452.

S-2384 300a* A:431 X-0790 CLER:GOSH
a. W-4167 David Harris, assignee, 100a
W-4236 Jeremiah Bolling, heir, 100a
b. John W. Johnson
c. Jesse Wood; John Randell, 1830
*Acreage may be erroneous, as warrants are for 200a.

S-2385 560a B:163 X-0790 CLER:GOSH
a. W-4592 Samuel O. Pettus
b. Richard C[lough] Anderson
c. None

S-2386* 2000a A:529 X-0660 CLIN:UNIO CLIN:GREE CLIN:WASH
S-2386* 2000a A:529 X-0660 CLIN: --
S-2386* 2000a A:529 X-0660 CLIN: --
a. W-4189 George Johnson
b. Archibald Johnston & Patrick Moores [by devise]
c. William Anderson; W. H. Skinner, 1826; U. Biggs; William A. Skinner, 1826; Samuel Daniels; B. Hinkson, 1823; S? [L?] Davis, 1825; William R. Cole, 1825; T? [S? L?] Gibson, 1825; J. Stout; J. Hays & J. Haynes, 1824; J. Stewart; James Spencer; Elizabeth Daniels; W. P. Hunnicut, 1832; George Johnson; William Kinworthy [*also* Kenworthy]; W. Roberts, 1833; Aaron Oaley [*also* Oxley]; -- Skinner & -- Fife, 1832; Rosanna Oaley; G. Y. Wilkinson; A. Boring? J. Pyle, 1835; J. Fyfe, 1835; D. S. Murray; Samuel

S-2386* [continued]
McCray, heirs; Francis? Dunlavy; R. Roberts; A. Johnson, P. Moore & wife? descendants? [devisees?] of George Johnson; J. Roberts, 1835; Samuel Wasson? [Warron?]; A. E. Strickle; W. Morris; F. Casto, 1842
*Apparently, names mentioned in part c pertain to all three surveys.

S-2387 667a A:449 X-0660 GREE:SILV CLIN:LIBE
a. W-3451 Samuel Ball Green
b. Samuel B. Green
c. William Beauford; Cyrus Ball, 1827; T. Kennedy; A? Grantham, 1837; James H. Thompson; A. E. Strickle, 1841

S-2388 1756a C:17 X-0660 CLIN:GREE
a. W-0026 John? Shetth?*
b. Andrew Mead
c. John B. Beard; James Howe, 1828; John Hall; James? [Joseph?] Philips; Lewis Wright, 1828; James Shields, Ellen Shields, & Elizabeth Shields; William McDaniels, 1829; John Hall; G. Bruce & A. Walker, 1832; Joel Rynard, 1834; David Karnes; J. Johnson, 1832; Paul Hultz, 1832; E. Roberts, heirs; John Roberts
*There is a major discrepancy here, as this warrant was for 100a only.

S-2389 & S-2390 1300a D:115 X-0663* CLIN:GREE CLIN:CLAR
a. W-1608 William Haynes, 200a
W-3390 Benjamin Lockett, 100a
W-3444 James Dawson, 200a
W-4034 John Stockdill, 200a
W-4035 Alexander Wiley, 200a
W-4066**
W-1121 James Beham, 200a
W-4015 Benjamin Lockett, 100a
b. David Bradford
c. None
*"H[ea]d waters of . . ."
**Source C does not show this warrant number.

S-2390* 190a E:20 X-0845 ROSS:PAIN
a. W-4033 Jesse White; David Bradford, assignee, 100a
W-3998 William Pettyjohn; David Bradford, assignee, 100a
b. Cadwallader Wallace
c. None
*This may duplicate the survey immediately above. According to Source B, there was a third grant under S-2390 in the amount of 200a in the same county and township; it is not listed in Source A.

S-2390 50a E:16 X-0845 ROSS:PAIN
a. W-3998 William Pettyjohn; David Bradford, assignee
W-4015 Benjamin Lockett, David Bradford, assignee
b. Cadwallader Wallace
c. None

S-2391 1700a A:517 X-0660 CLIN:CLAR*
a. W-4043 Samuel McCraw, assignee, 400a
W-4088 Alexander Wiley, 200a
W-4002 William Pettyjohn, 200a
W-4003 William Pettyjohn, 100a
W-4006 Joshua Humphreys, 200a
W-4007 Joshua Humphreys, 200a
W-4010 Henry Banks, 100a
W-4011 Henry Banks, 100a
W-4150 Charles Lewis, 200a
b. David Bradford
c. William Lytle; J. Jackson, 1827; A. Cowgill, 1829; John Shields; -- Fife, -- Bruce, & -- Strickle, 1829; Aaron Betts, 1831; James? [Joseph?] Moore, Senior; Levi Gustin, 1834; Isaac Moore; J. Hadley, 1837; J. Hadley, Junior, 1840; A. E. Strickle, 1842
*Source B notation: "Martinsville."

S-2392 200a A:518 X-0663 CLIN:CLAR
a. W-4291 William Obannon, heir
b. William Obannon
c. None

S-2393 200a A:518 X-0663 CLIN:CLAR
a. W-1697 William Vanse, 100a
W-3552 Michael Pough, 100a
b. William Vanse*
c. None
*So spelled in both Source A & Source B.

S-2394 400a A:518 X-0663 CLIN:CLAR
a. W-3981 William Davis
b. John Richardson
c. George W. Berrere; P. West, 1826

S-2395 200a A:518 X-0663 CLIN:GREE CLIN:CLAR
a. W-3314 Job Wigley, 100a
W-3846 James Beckham, 100a
b. Isaac Hornback
c. R? [B?] Hinkson; J. McGrew; J. E. Dalton, 1836; J. Ratcliff; A. E. Strickle

S-2396 600a A:518 X-0663 CLIN:CLAR
a. W-1064 Jacob Conrod, 200a
W-1068 Samuel Osborn, 200a
W-1041 John Smith, 200a
b. John Moyland
c. John Lawson; J. Taylor; J. Bealls, 1842

S-2397* 400a A:518 X-0663 HIGH:UNIO CLIN:GREE
a. W-4294 James Carpenter, 200a
W-4296 William Hillings, 100a
W-4304 Philip Baker? 100a
b. James Ireland
c. J. Robinson; A. Farquahar, 1824; C. Botts (G. B. Moore); George B. Moore (Clinton County); L. Gustin, 1836
*Source B notation: "Not patented."

S-2398* 400a A:519 X-0663 HIGH:UNIO CLIN:GREE
a. W-1445 William Coram
b. William Hume
c. None
*Source B notation: "Not patented."

S-2400 300a B:193 X-0663 HIGH:DODS
a. W-1702 Robert Gilbreath; "with Flaugherty's" 200a
W-3231 James Marney; assignee Benjamin Deans 100a
b. David Hogg
c. R. Barr; J. M. Trimble, 1840

S-2401 200a B:193 X-0663 HIGH:DODS
a. W-3555 Joseph Vanmeter, 100a
W-3556 Joseph Vanmeter, 100a
b. Joseph Vanmeter
c. G. Hughs, 1826; H. P. Herine; George Smith, 1837

S-2402 400a B:193 X-0663 HIGH:DODS
a. W-2934 George Moxley
b. George Moxley
c. W. Terrell; A. Farquahar? [Forquahar?] 1826

S-2404 100a A:432 X-0790 CLER:GOSH
a. W-3655 Benjamin Hawkins
b. Samuel Shackleford*
c. None
*Source B spells Shackelford.

S-2405 850a B:197 X-0663 CLER:GOSH CLER:STON
a. W-4024* William Reynolds, assignee
b. Francis Graham
c. T. S. Foot; David Dixon, 1824
*Warrant number may be in error, as it was issued for 100a only.

S-2406 200a B:199 X-0790 CLER:GOSH
a. W-0966 Dennis Boush, 100a
W-0938 Joseph Vance, 100a
b. Andrew Vance
c. None

S-2407 775a D:10 X-1000 ROSS:UNIO
a. W-1880* John Corbett
b. Joseph Watkins
c. None
*Warrant number probably erroneous.

S-2408 135a A:402 X-0133 ADAM:FRAN
a. W-0903 Captain Robert Powell
b. Robert Powell
c. None

S-2409 400a A:403 X-0133 HIGH:JACK*
a. W-0903 Captain Robert Powell
b. Robert Powell
c. None
*Source B notation: "Belfort."

S-2410 410a A:407 X-0840 ROSS:PAIN
a. W-1174 Major Thomas Massey
b. Thomas Massie
c. None

S-2411 840a A:409 X-0840 ROSS:PAIN
a. W-1173 Mordecai? Barber, heir to James Barber
b. John Thompson
c. E. Wade; W. H. Douglas, 1842

S-2412 1100a A:409 X-0150 ROSS:BUCK
a. W-1173 Mordecai? Barber, heir to James Barber
b. John Thompson
c. P. Douglas; N. Massie, 1833; John Perry; Peter Douglas

S-2413 727a A:406 X-0841 ROSS:CONC
a. W-1173 Mordecai? Barber, heir to James Barber
b. John Thompson
c. Lewis? [Samuel?] Corey, heirs; N. Corey, 1827

S-2414 600a B:56 X-0250 HIGH:LIBE
a. W-3853 John George, 100a
W-4332 William Colgin, 100a
W-4275 Joseph Stillwell, 100a
W-3854 Robert Taylor, 100a
W-3770 Levi Bridgewater, 100a
W-3945 William Reynolds [assignee?] 100a
b. Hugh Evans & Amos Evans
c. None

S-2415 400a B:56 X-0250 HIGH:LIBE
a. W-1126 Thomas Jackson, 200a
W-4276 Drury Covey, 200a
b. David* Evans
c. None
*Source B says Daniel Evans.

S-2416 400a B:56 X-0250 HIGH:LIBE?
a. W-4272 John Smith, 100a
W-4273 George Harlen? [Harlan?] 100a
W-3851 Andrew Susang, 100a
W-3769 Thomas Whitaker, 100a
b. Samuel Evans
c. None

S-2417 289a B:188 X-1004 FRAN:NORW
a. W-0679 Seymour Powell, heir
b. Seymour Powell
c. John Sawyer? [Lawqier?]; William Moobery, Junior, 1828; William Mooberry; D. Scott, 1833

S-2417 600a B:188 X-1004 FRAN:NORW
a. W-0679 Seymour Powell, heir
b. Seymour Powell
c. None

S-2418 889a B:30 X-1004 FRAN:WASH FRAN:NORW
a. W-0679 Seymour Powell, heir
b. Seymour Powell
c. None

S-2421 300a B:294 X-1300 BROW:SCOT
a. W-1521 John Dillyard, 200a
W-1545 Phillip Bowers, 100a
b. David Lambert
c. None

S-2422 200a B:199 X-0980 HIGH:NEWM
a. W-2340 Richard Noell
b. Richard Noill*
c. None
*Source B spells Noell.

S-2423 100a B:295 X-1120 BROW:FRAN
a. W-3202 John Rice
b. John Rice
c. Daniel Malot; Jesse R. Grant, 1823; John Rice; Michael Pinder, 1828

S-2424 200a A:494 X-0180 GREE:XENI
a. W-2987 David Price, heir, 100a
W-3767 Cornelius Johnson, 100a
b. David Price
c. None

S-2425 400a B:174 X-0180 GREE:SUGA GREE:XENI
a. W-3245 Benjamin Athey, 100a
W-3246 James Corner, 200a
W-3247 Thomas Athey, 100a
b. John Gibson
c. None

S-2426 733a A:495 X-0180 GREE:SUGA GREE:CAES GREE:XENI
a. W-2188 Spencer Simpson, 100a
W-2189 James Tasker, 100a
W-2191 James Aldridge, 100a
W-3249 David Atcheson, 233a
W-3799 Peter Bumback, 200a
b. Alexander Henderson
c. None

S-2427 223a A:405 X-0130* ADAM:TIFF
a. W-1330 John Tibbs
b. John Tibbs
c. Willoughby Tibbs; Henry Rape, 1831; T. Huston, 1833; J. Hempleman, 1835
*"Lk. f[or]k of . . ."

S-2428 400a A:406 X-0840 ROSS:TWIN
a. W-4017 Reuben Finny; Robert Todd [assignee?] 200a
W-0463 John Jowett, heir to Mat[thew Jowett] 200a
b. -- Parker & Nathaniel Massie
c. C. W. Smith; A. Carlisle, 1829

S-2429 1000a B:58 X-0130 X-0840 PIKE:PERR
a. W-3373 William Jones, 400a
W-3358 Travis Wren, 100a
W-1678 Lewis Hoomes [Holmes?] 100a
W-3359 Edward Vauce; Francis Milton, assignee, 200a
W-3369 Peter Glasscock; Derby McGannon, assignee, 200a
b. Robert Nicholson
c. James? [Joseph?] Taylor; J. Penniston & J. Sargeant, 1830; Hecter? McNeil; James Sargeant, 1831

S-2430* 33a -- -- BROW: --
a. --
b. Philip Daw
c. George Shultz, 1825
*Listed with S-1992 in Source A.

S-2432 100a A:432 X-0790 CLER:GOSH
a. W-4550 Samuel Coleman
b. Samuel Coleman
c. C. B. Huber

S-2433* 67a -- -- CLIN: --
a. W-1792? Edward Carrington
b. Edward Carrington
c. J. M. Wood, 1825; George Bruce, 1826
*Not listed in Source A; Source B shows at top margin of page preceding S-2429.

S-2434 1100a A:449 X-0663 CLER:UNIO HAMI: --*
a. W-1792 Edward Carrington
b. Edward Carrington
c. Lewis Furlong; W. Wainwright, 1826; B. Smith; James C. Morris; T. Kirby, 1823; C. Beagle; R. McFarland, 1836; Josiah Cross; Z. Chapman, 1836; E. A. Davis
*Source B does not mention Hamilton County.

S-2435 667a A:451 X-0010 GREE:CAES
a. W-0002 Lieutenant Willis Wilson
b. Willis Wilson
c. None

S-2436 700a A:453 X-0663 CLER:WILL CLER:TATE
a. W-0083 Doctor Joseph Davis
b. Thomas Overton
c. James? [Joseph?] Higbee; W. Johnson, 1824; G. Johnson; R. Tweed, 1827; William Johnson; J. Moss, 1831; J. Burnett; L? [S?] Pease, 1837

S-2437 470a A:499 X-0134 ADAM:SCOT ADAM:MEIG
a. W-0116 John Webb
b. Andrew Gatewood
c. None

S-2438 260a A:498 X-0420 BROW:JACK
a. W-0116 John Webb
b. Andrew Gatewood
c. George H. Bohrer, 1828

S-2439 200a A:500 X-0130* ADAM:WAYN
a. W-4626 James Taylor
b. David Duncan
c. None
*"Ch. f[or]k of . . ."

S-2440 100a B:168 X-0130 ADAM:WAYN
a. W-3869 James McKinney
b. Nathaniel Allen
c. None

S-2442 463a C:281 X-1000 FRAN:FRAN
a. W-3221 William Reynold, assignee of John Fauntleroy, heir to Captain -- Fauntleroy
b. John Harrison
c. Nicholas Demarest; James Knight; John McWilliams, 1828; D. Demerest

S-2442 394a C:281 X-1000 FRAN:FRAN
a. W-3221 William Reynold, assignee of John Fauntleroy, heir to Captain [Griffin?] Fauntleroy
b. John Harrison
c. A. Latham, 1826; John Loring; Jacob Grub, 1826; J. Harrison; C. Harrison; William Harrison, 1838; Paul Jones; M. L. Sullivant, 1837

S-2442 51a C:281 X-1000 FRAN:FRAN
a. W-3221 William Reynold, assignee of John Fauntleroy, heir to Captain [Griffin?] Fauntleroy
b. John Harrison
c. Nicholas Demarest; Jacob Grub, 1824; Daniel Demarest; R. Brotherton, 1830; Robert Brotherton; Unknown; C. Higgins, 1836

S-2445 1000a B:68 X-1180 MADI: --* MADI:JEFF
a. W-0221 Colonel John Gibson
b. John Gibson
c. None
*Source B does not mention Madison County.

S-2446 2000a B:28 X-1000 PICK:SCIO
a. W-2829 Richard Harrison, heir to James Harrison
b. Richard C[lough] Anderson
c. -- Gray & -- Taylor; Peter West, 1831

S-2447 200a B:228 X-1040 SCIO:UNIO
a. W-4608 Representatives of Daniel Sanders
b. Representatives of Daniel Saunders
c. None

S-2448 437a B:290 X-1120 BROW:BYRD BROW:FRAN
a. W-0200 Lieutenant Ballard Smith
b. Ballard Smith
c. J. Graham; J. H. Shepherd, 1828; Rolley B. Calvin, heirs

S-2450 625a B:233 X-1000 PIKE:JACK ROSS: --*
a. W-1415 Lieutenant Peyton Powell
b. Peyton Powell
c. None
*Source B does not mention Ross County.

S-2451 400a B:480 X-1180 MADI:JEFF
a. W-1415 Lieutenant Peyton Powell
b. Peyton Powell
c. M. L? [S?] Sullivant, 1831

S-2452 86a B:124 X-1000 SCIO:UNIO
a. W-4490 William Dark
b. William Dark
c. None

S-2452 400a B:124 X-1000 SCIO:UNIO
a. W-4490 William Dark
b. William Dark
c. S? S? [L? L?] Clark; S? [L?] Noel, 1838; Robert Lucas; C. Overturf, 1840

S-2452 250a B:124 X-1000 SCIO:UNIO
a. W-4490 William Dark
b. William Dark
c. None

S-2453 118a B:123 X-1000 SCIO:MORG
a. W-4478 Joseph Swearingen
b. Joseph Swearingen
c. Ora Crane, 1827

S-2454 633a B:123 X-1000 SCIO:MORG
a. W-4321 George Yates
b. George Yates
c. None

S-2455 456a B:123 X-1000 PIKE:CAMP SCIO:MORG
a. W-1415 Lieutenant Peyton Powell
b. Peyton Powell
c. W. Campbell; A. Winkoop, 1828; William Campbell, heirs; Loyd Howard, 1834; E. Campbell; Jeptha Parrill, 1832; Daniel Kirkendoll; J. Penniston, 1834; Benjamin Hoffman; Samuel J. McLoud; J. Lay, 1836

S-2456 600a B:123 X-1000 PIKE:CAMP
a. W-4321 George Yates
b. George Yates
c. J. Leath, 1826

S-2457 336a B:171 X-1000 SCIO:UNIO
a. W-4321 George Yates
b. George Yates
c. G. Beloat? heirs; C. Overturf, 1840

S-2458 150a D:373 X-0805 ADAM:GREE
a. W-4527 David McDorman
b. David McDorman
c. William White; -- McDaid & -- Wilkins, 1826

S-2458* 50a F:308 X-0135 ADAM: --
a. W-4527 David McDorman
b. James A. Trimble
c. None
*Source B does not list this entry.

S-2459 & S-2558 1550a A:509 X-0800 SCIO:NILE*
a. W-1687 Charles Powell, 200a
W-3619 George Morrow, 100a
W-3977 Shadrack Pickstone, 100a
W-4504 Samuel Payne, 100a
W-4524 Willis Gwen, 100a
W-4599 John Whitt, 200a
W-4595 John Allen, 200a
W-4620 Samuel Sorton? [Lawton? Lowton?] 200a
W-4618 James Gum, 250a
W-4651 Charles Carter, 100a

S-2459 [continued]
b. -- O'Bannon, -- Graham, & -- Massie
c. Jonathan Ridgway; A. Tucker, 1839; G. Mitchell; A. Noel, 1841
*Source B notation: "Rockville."

S-2460 1900a B:36 X-0841 ROSS:TWIN
a. W-4592 Samuel O. Pettus
b. Richard C[lough] Anderson
c. None

S-2461 2000a A:482 X-0840 ROSS:TWIN*
a. W-1580 Captain Valentine Harrison; George Underwood & Oldham? Shepherd, assignees
W-4087 Walter Ashmore
b. Nathaniel Massie
c. None
*Source B notation: "Bounville? [Bownville?]."

S-2462 1900a B:57 X-1000 X-0840 ROSS:SCIO*
a. W-2675 Robert Jouit
W-3398 Leven Powell
W-4642 Nathaniel Massie, assignee of John Tucker, [heir?] of Thomas Payne
b. Nathaniel Massie
c. John Carlisle; A. Carlisle, 1836; J. Carlisle & Co; C. Wallace
*Source B notation: "Chillicothe."

S-2462 & S-3037 & S-3570 1580a B:177 X-1000 ROSS:SCIO*
a. W-4328 Mary Walker, heir[ess] to J. W[alker?] 100a
W-3206 Albion Throckmorton, Junior? 1000a
W-4642 Nathaniel Massie, assignee of John Tucker, [heir?] of Thomas Payne [280a?]
W-1089 Benjamin Brooke, 200a
b. Nathaniel Massie
c. None
*Source B notation: "Near Chillicothe."

S-2463 & S-2900 1117a B:57 X-1000 PIKE:JACK*
a. W-1921 General Robert Lawson
W-0233 Henry Dawson
b. Nathaniel Massie
c. None
*Source B notation: "Near Sharonville."

S-2464 600a A:495 X-0660 WARR:WAYN*
a. W-4087 Walter Ashmore
b. Nathaniel Massie
c. None
*Source B notation: "By Waynesville."

S-2465 400a A:512 X-0130 X-0420 ADAM:TIFF
a. W-4087 Walter Ashmore
b. Nathaniel Massie
c. None

S-2466 & S-3360 1430a B:178 X-0840 ROSS:TWIN*
a. W-1921 General Robert Lawson
W-4697 William Bawcalt
b. Nathaniel Massie
c. A. H. Cochran; J. Somerville & J. McMullen, 1827
*Source B notation: "Cattail."

S-2466 & S-3360 500a B:178 X-0840 ROSS:TWIN
a. W-1921 General Robert Lawson
W-4697 William Bawcalt
W-4808 Peyton Powell
b. Nathaniel Massie
c. None

S-2467 & S-2899 851a B:57 X-0840 PIKE:PEEP
a. W-2675 Robert Jouit
W-George Holland; Charles Lynch [assignee?]
b. Nathaniel Massie
c. None

S-2468 & S-2782 & S-3569 690a B:177 X-0130 ADAM:TIFF ADAM:MONR
a. W-4358 Dudley Ballard, 100a
W-0145 Captain William Fowler, 200a?
W-4087 Walter Ashmore, 100a?
W-3096 John Hasty; Charles Lynch [assignee?] 100a
W-0815 Brigadier General Charles Scott, 190a?
b. Nathaniel Massie
c. Charles Fields, representatives; William Armstrong, 1823; Thomas Lewis; Olive? [Oliver?] Smith, 1823; John Raider

S-2468 200a B:177 X-0040 ADAM:TIFF
a. W-4161 Jesse Ewell, assignee [of?] Richard Stonell (Stonerell) *alias* Stoner
b. Nathaniel Massie
c. None

S-2469* & S-2933 200a -- -- ADAM:MONR
a. --
b. Nathaniel Massie
c. --
*This entry is not listed in Source A. *See* S-2284

S-2470 720a A:513 X-0130 ADAM:TIFF ADAM:JEFF
a. W-4087 Walter Ashmore
b. Nathaniel Massie
c. None

S-2471 1177a A:489 X-1170 CLIN:UNIO
a. W-2483 Captain Daniel Duvall
b. Daniel Duval*
c. D. H. Bardsall; James Burdsall, 1824; James? [Joseph?] Woodrow; I. Morris, 1832; J. Cowgill; D. Stratton, 1835; J. Fleming, heirs; G. Fallis; T. Kimbrow; L. Gustin, 1836; Rebecca Vanhorn
*Source B could spell Dural.

S-2472 900a B:185 X-0130 ADAM:FRAN
a. W-2162 Colonel William Heth
b. William Hith*
c. None
*Source B spells Heth.

S-2473 1000a A:492 X-0010 GREE:CAES
a. W-3990 Nancy Grimes, heir[ess]; Seth Smith [*mentioned*]
b. Nancy Grymes
c. None

S-2474 & S-2526 1740a B:353 X-0180 GREE:CAES
a. W-3990 Nancy Grimes, heir[ess]; Seth Smith [*mentioned*]
b. Nancy Grymes
c. James Risk; Magdalene Shoock, 1832

S-2475. *See* S-2358

S-2476. *See* S-2358

S-2477 180a B:186 X-0133 HIGH:JACK
a. W-0240 Lieutenant Colonel Thomas Posey
b. Thomas Posey
c. Jesse Wood; James Bell, 1831

S-2480 1000a A:470 X-0980 HIGH:LIBE
a. W-4644 Temple Elliott
b. Temple Elliott
c. None

S-2481 1000a A:470 X-0980 HIGH:LIBE HIGH:NEWM
a. W-4644 Temple Elliott
b. Temple Elliott
c. M? [W?] Gray; A. Browse, 1826

S-2482 1000a A:469 X-0980 HIGH:LIBE HIGH:NEWM
a. W-4644 Temple Elliott
b. Temple Elliott
c. J. Shoffner; A. Grantham, 1826; Jacob Myres; John Pardy? [Purdy?] 1839

S-2483 420a D:339 X-0840 ROSS:TWIN
a. W-4644 Temple Elliott
b. Temple Elliott
c. Thomas Scott; William Creighton, Junior, 1824

S-2484 200a A:511 X-0840 ROSS:BUCK
a. W-4138 Daniel Delozier
b. Andrew Valck*
c. None
*Source B Says Adrian Valck.

S-2485 1870a A:473 X-0250 HIGH:LIBE HIGH:FAIR
a. W-4618 James Gum
b. John Graham
c. None

S-2486 & S-2556 1750a A:508 X-0250 HIGH:LIBE HIGH:FAIR
a. W-4618 James Gum
b. John Graham
c. John Baskin; A. Trimble, 1839; Allen Trimble & John Trimble; J. M. Trimble, 1840

S-2488 200a B:185 X-0133 HIGH:JACK
a. W-4557 Charles Jones
b. Charles Jones
c. Jacob Bower; John Hogsett, 1836; A. Frazier; J? [I?] L. Hughes, 1842

S-2493 250a A:515 X-0130 ADAM:TIFF ADAM:MEIG
a. W-0463 John Jowett, heir to Mat[thew Jowett]
b. John Jouitt
c. None

S-2493 250a A:513 X-0130* ADAM:TIFF
a. W-0463 John Jowett, heir to Mat[thew Jowett]
b. John Jouitt
c. None
*"Lk. f[or]k of . . ."

S-2494 100a B:83 X-1110 ADAM:GREE
a. W-2888 Anthony Coon
b. Belteshazar Draggool? [Draggoe?]
c. Joshua Truitt; Sawmill & gristmill; T. Huston, 1837

S-2495 & S-3260 150a B:297 X-0800 ADAM:MONR
a. W-4343 Gordon Kelly, 100a
W-3986 John Etherington? 100a
b. Andrew Ellison
c. None

S-2496 400a A:500 X-0800 SCIO:NILE
a. W-0083 Captain Thomas Overton, assignee of Doctor Joseph Davis
b. Thomas Overton
c. William Higby; Joseph Orr, 1824; John Lewis; H. Burrows; Ignatius Burrows, 1841

S-2497 765a A:500 X-0800 CLER:MONR
a. W-0083 Captain Thomas Overton, assignee of Doctor Joseph Davis
b. Thomas Overton
c. T. Dixon; W. Waynwright, 1824; Isaac Mitchell; T. K. Hollman, 1833

S-2498 190a B:340 X-0380* HIGH:DODS
a. W-3728 Andrew McMahan
b. Joshua Dodson
c. None
*"Dodson's f[or]k, E[ast] f[or]k . . ."

S-2499 250a B:340 X-0380* HIGH:DODS
a. W-4056 Ambrose McGinnis, 100a
W-3728 Andrew McMahan, 150a
b. Joshua Dodson
c. Unknown; J. S. Crawford, 1832

S-2500 200a B:340 X-0663 HIGH:DODS CLIN: --*
a. W-3763 James Simpkins, 100a
   W-3674 Garrett Simpkins, 100a
b. Richard Wolfolk**
c. None
*Source B does not mention Clinton County.
**Source B spells Woolfolk.

S-2501 400a A:455 X-0980 HIGH:PAIN
a. W-1156 George Draper; R. Butler [assignee?]
b. John Moyland
c. None

S-2502 1333a A:456 X-0980 HIGH:PAIN HIGH:JACK
a. W-1156 George Draper; R. Butler [assignee?]
b. John Moyland
c. None

S-2503 1333a A:456 X-0980 HIGH:LIBE HIGH:PAIN HIGH:JACK
a. W-1156 George Draper; R. Butler [assignee?]
   W-1157 George Draper; R. Butler [assignee?]
b. John Moyland
c. S. Blount

S-2504 755a A:456 X-0250 HIGH:LIBE
a. W-1157 George Draper; R. Butler [assignee?]
b. John Moyland
c. None

S-2505 1600a A:457 X-0250 HIGH:PAIN
a. W-1158 George Draper; R. Butler [assignee?]
b. John Moyland
c. None

S-2506 578a A:457 X-0980 HIGH:JACK
a. W-1157 George Draper; R. Butler [assignee?]
   W-1158 George Draper; R. Butler [assignee?]
b. John Moyland
c. Mary Butler; J. M. Trimble, 1832; S. P. Adams; J. A. Trimble, 1840

S-2507 2400a A:471 X-0640 HIGH:FAIR
a. W-1627 Lieutenant Joseph Conway
b. Joseph Conway
c. William Gulick; A. Malcom, 1835; D. L. Davis

S-2508 2000a A:472 X-0250 HIGH:LIBE HIGH:FAIR
a. W-2790 Anthony New, heir to John Baynham
b. Thomas Streshley
c. T. W. Rayburn

S-2509 667a A:482 X-0980 HIGH:PAIN
a. W-2790 Anthony New, heir to John Baynham
b. Thomas Streshley
c. None

S-2510 1000a A:469 X-0980 HIGH:LIBE HIGH:NEWM
a. W-4644 Temple Elliott
b. Temple Elliott
c. None

S-2511 1000a A:469 X-0980 HIGH:NEWM
a. W-4644 Temple Elliott
b. Temple Elliott
c. None

S-2512 1000a A:469 X-0980 HIGH:LIBE HIGH:NEWM
a. W-4644 Temple Elliott
b. Temple Elliott
c. None

S-2513 1000a A:468 X-0980 HIGH:LIBE*
a. W-3295 Robert Ballard
b. Robert Ballard
c. J. Ellicot; Isaac Sams
*Source B notation: "Near Hillsboro."

S-2514 1000a A:468 X-0980 HIGH:LIBE HIGH:NEWM
a. W-3295 Robert Ballard
b. Robert Ballard
c. J. W. Price

S-2515 4255a A:481 X-0980 HIGH:LIBE
a. W-3367 Colonel Otway Byrd, "resolution"
b. Ottaway* Byrd
c. N. Massie; J. Smith, 1826; Polly Barnett; John Hogsett, 1836; W. Mullinux, heirs; Joseph H. Mullinux, 1840; J. M. Trimble; John A. Smith, 1840; N. Massie, heirs
*Source B spells Otway.

S-2516 1745a B:13 X-0840 HIGH:LIBE*
a. W-3367 Colonel Otway Byrd, "resolution"
b. Ottaway** Byrd
c. J. Smith; A. Grantham, 1829
*Source B notation: "Near Hillsboro."
**Source B spells Otway.

S-2517 1750a A:471 X-0250 HIGH:LIBE HIGH:UNIO
a. W-4442 Matthew Myer, heir to Christopher Myer
b. Augustine Davis
c. None

S-2518 1667a A:477 X-0640 X-0520 HIGH:FAIR
a. W-4578 Severn Teagle
b. Severn Teagle
c. Demus Adams; Moses Milner, 1840

S-2520 1767a A:431 X-0980 HIGH:PAIN
a. W-2450 Doctor George Evans, "resolution"
b. George Evans
c. None

S-2521 720a A:483 X-0980 HIGH:PAIN
a. W-2450 Doctor George Evans, "resolution"
b. George Evans
c. None

S-2522 1000a A:477 X-0945 HIGH:FAIR FAYE: --*
a. W-3601 John Bartlett; William Stroud, assignee, 400a
W-3782 James Johnston, 200a
W-3796 John Townsend, 200a
W-4389 William Reynolds, assignee of John Madder? 100a
W-0327 William Burns, 100a
b. James Ewell
c. J. Taylor; J. Stooks, 1824; Margaret Ann Turry; A. Malcom, 1835
*Source B does not mention Fayette County.

S-2523 2000a A:496 X-1300? X-1120 BROW:PLEA*
a. W-1921 General Robert Lawson
b. Robert Lawson
c. Andrew Donaldson; T. L. Harner? [Hamer?] 1826; R. Crostwait; P. Hickman, 1829; P. Buckner, Junior; R. Allen, 1831; A. Woods & H. Clark; R. Campbell & P. L. Wilson, 1830; J. P. Hickman; P. L? [S?] Wilson, 1837; C. Lovenguire; R. McComb; H. B. Payne; G. H. Bohrer? 1831; James Henny, 1831
*Source B notation: "Georgetown."

S-2524 1260a A:467 X-0840 ROSS:BUCK FAYE:WAYN
a. W-2450 Doctor George Evans, "resolution"
b. George Evans
c. None

S-2526. *See* S-2474

S-2527 1187a A:42 X-0660 WARR:SALE
a. W-1911 Elisha King
b. Elisha King
c. W. Boyd; J. Mountz, 1825

S-2528 167a A:501 X-0663 CLER:WILL
a. W-2262 Lieutenant Ambrose Gordon
b. Ambrose Gordon
c. William Lytle; John Kain, 1825

S-2529 667a B:43 X-0660 WARR:SALE
a. W-0728 Lieutenant Andrew Lewis; John Campbell & Richard Archer [assignees?]
b. William Nall
c. W. Boyd; J. Mountz, 1825

S-2530 1000a B:92 X-0840 FAYE:JEFF
a. W-0202 Captain Robert Yancey
b. Robert Yancy
c. Jacob Hosier; Richard Baughan, 1833; Joseph? [James?] Hidy, 1838; W. Loofborough, 1837

S-2531 750a A:512 X-0841 ROSS:UNIO
a. W-3497 Richard Carter, heir, 200a
W-4589 Philip Harrison, 400a
W-1894 Captain Henry Heth, 100a
W-1930 George Belvin; Clement Biddle, assignee, 50a
b. Nathaniel Massie
c. None

S-2532 & S-3361 & S-3658 1370a B:202 X-0841 ROSS:UNIO ROSS:TWIN
a. W-4802 Benoni Lipscomb, 100a
W-2006 William McIntire, 200a
W-1921 General Robert Lawson, --a?
W-4697* William Bawcalt, --a?
W-4662 Robert Means, assignee [of?] H. Young, --a?
b. Nathaniel Massie
c. None
*This warrant already used in S-2466.

S-2533 370a B:58 X-1000 ROSS:FRAN
a. W-1921 General Robert Lawson; John Obannon [assignee?]
b. Nathaniel Massie
c. None

S-2534 200a B:411 X-0800* BROW:HUNT
a. W-1929 Francis King; Clement Biddle, assignee
b. Nathaniel Massie
c. None
*"Northwest bank of . . ."

S-2535 1500a B:294 X-1120 BROW:FRAN
a. W-3482 Francis Graves, assignee [of?] Mat[thew] R--? 200a
W-3483 Francis Graves, assignee [of?] Jeremiah Walker, 200a
W-3589 Nathaniel Gray, assignee [of?] Daniel Allen, 200a
W-3479 Philip Jameson, 200a
W-4355 James White, 400a
W-4650 Thomas More, assignee [of?] Jeffery Palmer, 100a
W-2695* Martin Hawkins, assignee [of?] John Mather; Edward Dowse [assignee?] 100a?
W-4818 John Savage, heir, 100a
b. John Graham
c. None
*This warrant number may be in error; *see* S-2256.

S-2542 889a B:31 X-1004 FRAN:WASH*
a. W-1797 James Holt
b. James Holt
c. Bryce Hays; George Jeffries, 1837; B. Sells; C. Higgins, 1835; John Sells; C. Rogers, 1837; J. King, heirs; D. D. Warner, 1839
*Source B notation: "Dublin."

S-2543 889a B:31 X-1004 FRAN:WASH
a. W-1797 James Holt
b. James Holt
c. None

S-2544 889a B:31 X-1004 FRAN:WASH
a. W-1797 James Holt
b. James Holt
c. None

S-2545 889a B:32 X-1004 FRAN:WASH DELA:CONC
a. W-4338 Robert Cooper
b. Robert Cooper
c. Lucas Sullivant; Nathaniel Hull, 1835; Milo D. Pettibone, 1839; Charles Sweetser, 1839; Edward Dulin

S-2546 889a B:32 X-1104 DELA:CONC
a. W-4338 Robert Cooper
b. Robert Cooper
c. Lucas Sullivant; Charles Sweetser, 1834; John Dodd, 1839, forfeited

S-2547 889a B:32 X-1004 DELA:CONC
a. W-4338 Robert Cooper
b. Robert Cooper
c. Lucas Sullivant; Nathaniel Hull, 1835; T. Foster, heirs, 1839, forfeited; Mary Peters, 1839, forfeited; Milo D. Pettibone

S-2548 250a A:500 X-0130* ADAM:WAYN
a. W-0116 John Webb
b. Andrew Gatewood
c. None
*"Ch. f[or]k Brush Creek."

S-2549 380a A:500 X-0130 ADAM:SCOT
a. W-0116 John Webb
b. Andrew Gatewood
c. None

S-2550 240a B:263 X-0490 ADAM:SCOT
a. W-3234 Francis Peyton, heir to Henry [Peyton]
b. Francis Peyton
c. None

S-2551 1380a A:507 X-0134 ADAM:WAYN ADAM:SCOT ADAM:WINC
a. W-3234 Francis Peyton, heir to Henry [Peyton]
b. Francis Peyton
c. William A? Luckett; D. P. Wilkins, 1824; T. Clifford; T. Huston, 1829; James Young; Thomas Clifton, heirs; John Criswell, 1831; A. D. Smith, 1834; Thomas Huston, 1833

S-2552 2300a A:506 X-0420 ADAM:WAYN ADAM:WINC BROW:JACK
a. W-3234 & W-3235 Francis Peyton, heir to Henry [Peyton]; . . . heir to Dade [Peyton]
b. Francis Peyton
c. -- Shepherd & -- Masterson, 1823; John Graham; John Meharry, 1834; John Follan; T. Huston (Adams County); M. Pitchett, 1835; John Fulton; L. Cole (Adams County); G. H. Bohrer, 1840; Arthur Fox; Russell Shaw, 1831; J. Bennington; A. Liggett, 1842

S-2553 580a A:503 X-0130* ADAM:WINC
a. W-3235 Francis Peyton, heir to Dade [Peyton]
b. Francis Peyton
c. George Edgington; Thomas Scott, 1826; John Pendle; James S? [L?] McVey
*"Ch. f[or]k Brush Creek."

S-2554 667a B:84 X-0420 BROW:BYRD
a. W-2222 Richard Waters
b. John Smith
c. None

S-2555 468a A:501 X-0940 HIGH:MADI
A. W-0083 & W-1908 Doctor Joseph Davis; Thomas Overton [assignee?]
b. Thomas Overton
c. None

S-2556. *See* S-2486

S-2558. *See* S-2459

S-2557 200a A:511 X-0520 HIGH:FAIR
a. W-4560 Jacob Parker, heir to John [Parker]
b. Jacob Parker
c. C. Bentley; George Collings, 1835

S-2559 917a A:510 X-0841 ROSS:CONC
a. W-4442 Matthew Myer, heir to Christopher Myer
b. Augustine Davis
c. None

S-2560 400a A:510 X-0840 HIGH:PAIN HIGH:MADI
a. W-1300 Augustine Weeden, 200a
W-3616 Richard Marshall, 200a
b. Philip Dawe
c. J. Collins, 1824; Henry Elwood

S-2561 1000a A:514 X-1170 WARR:SALE
a. W-2868 Major John Fitzgerald
b. John Fitzgerald
c. John Machir; J. Keenan, 1824

S-2562 1000a A:514 X-1170 WARR:SALE CLIN:MARI
a. W-2868 Major John Fitzgerald
b. John Fitzgerald
c. J. Baldwin; J. P. R. Nailer; George Stephenson, 1832; J. & J. Corothers & John Patton; J. Fyfe & Isaiah Morris, 1831

S-2563 1497a A:514 X-1170 WARR:SALE CLIN: --*
a. W-2868 Major John Fitzgerald
b. John Fitzgerald
c. Isaac Goodplaster; W. Sinnard, 1831; Hugh Meharry; H. King, 1834
*Source B does not mention Clinton County.

S-2564 2277a A:513 X-1170 WARR:SALE CLIN:VERN CLIN:MARI
a. W-3630 Pamelia Russell & Penelope Russell
b. Parmelia Russell & Penelope Russell
c. William Ellzey; William R. Cole, 1823; John Doctor; A. E. Strickle; J. Brannon; M. M. Hale, 1840

S-2565 1730a A:515 X-1170 GREE:SUGA GREE:XENI
a. W-3631 Pamelia Russell & Penelope Russell
b. Parmelia Russell & Penelop Russell
c. J. Galloway, Junior, 1824

S-2566 500a A:516 X-1170 GREE:SUGA
a. W-3631 Pamelia Russell & Penelope Russell
b. Parmelia Russell & Penelope Russell
c. None

S-2567 826a A:515 X-1170 GREE:XENI
a. W-3630 & W-3631 Pamelia Russell & Penelope Russell
b. Parmelia Russell & Penelope Russell
c. None

S-2568 1297a A:516 X-0250 HIGH:LIBE HIGH:PAIN
a. W-4604 William Begger [Bigger?] assignee [of?] Stephen? Scott, 200a
W-4605 William Begger [Bigger?] assignee [of?] Nathaniel Wallace, 200a
W-4618 James Gum, 897a
b. John Graham
c. G. Nicholas, heirs; J. Jones, 1825

S-2570 233a B:198 X-0660 CLER:MIAM
a. W-1582 Lewis Flemister
b. Francis Baldwin
c. Patience Irwin

S-2571 200a B:198 X-0790 CLER:GOSH
a. W-4460 Mary Brittain, widow of Samuel [Brittain]
b. Mary Brittain*
c. None
*Source B notation: "S.T. old patented Joseph Kyle 1805, sent to General -- Taylor."

S-2572 207a B:165 X-0800 ADAM:GREE
a. W-4099 William Triplett; -- Davis & -- Duncan [assignees?]
b. Andrew Ellison
c. None

S-2575 400a B:84 X-0420 ADAM:WAYN ADAM:WINC
a. W-3735 Osborn Flinn
b. Osborn Flinn
c. John H. Shepherd; John Kincaide, 1825

S-2576 200a B:110 X-1110* ADAM:GREE
a. W-1978 John Colvin, heir
b. Joseph Allen
c. None
*"L[ef]t h[an]d f[or]k Stout's Run."

S-2577 333a B:148 X-0130 ADAM:WAYN
a. W-4099 William Triplett; Andrew Ellison, assignee
b. -- Davis & -- Duncan
c. None

S-2584 100a B:430 X-0342 MADI:PIKE CHAM:GOSH
a. W-4418 William Reynolds; assignee James McGraw
b. Daniel Morris
c. None

S-2586 1000a B:58 X-0250 HIGH:LIBE
a. W-0325 Marquis Calmes
b. Marquis Calmes
c. None

S-2687 400a B:255 X-0940 HIGH:PAIN*
a. W-4289 John Blokemore? Hofferling [assignee?] 200a
W-4387 John Slaughter; John Blohemore? [assignee?] 100a
W-4391 James Kemp; John Blohemore? [assignee?] 100a
b. John Blackmon**
c. J. Conrad; J. Roads, 1829; James Hague; J. Boyd, 1832; Joseph? [James?] Serain; R. D. McClure; J. Simpson, 1838; J. Plummer; W. Piggett
*Source B notation: "Petersburg."
**Source B spells Blackmore.

S-2588 50a C:418 X-0663 BROW:PERR CLER: --*
a. W-1930 George Belvin; Clement Biddle, assignee
b. John Parker
c. William Lytle; John Hardin, 1824; N? S. Bank; S. Strimple, 1834
*Source B does not give township, although Clermont County is mentioned.

S-2589 1000a A:520 X-0663 BROW:PERR
a. W-2383 Lieutenant Archelus Perkins
b. Archelus Perkins
c. John Chamberlain; Allen Butt, 1826; George C. Light; John Jones, 1826; John Mahon; Mathew Kincaid, 1826; Joel Curless, 1826; Seneca Palmer; John Oconner, 1826; -- Bishop & -- Boyle, 1827; Eddie Bishop; P. L? [S?] Wilson, 1840

S-2590 1000a A:520 X-0663 BROW:PERR
a. W-2383 Lieutenant Archelus Perkins
b. Archelus Perkins
c. A. Pagan; John Pattridge; M? [W?] Bishop, 1838; S. Shumard; William Boyle; Martin Bishop, 1839; Rebecca Lewis; R. W. Dittoe, 1839; Thomas McCarr? [McCann?]; E. McCune; T. C. Bamber, 1840; A. Hollstead, 1842; A. White; D. G. Devore, 1842

S-2591* 100a -- -- A.S.? --
a. --
b. Isaac Taylor
c. --
*This partial survey listed in Source B only, but notation says "not found."

S-2592 100a B:164 X-1190 SCIO:NILE
a. W-4279 Jeremiah Archer
b. Nathaniel Beasley
c. None

S-2593 250a B:260 X-0920 SCIO:UNIO
a. W-2883 Thomas Brownlee, 100a
W-1043 John Head, 200a
b. Robert Ellison
c. David Rupe; E. Osborn, 1830

S-2594 185a C:462 X-0920 SCIO:UNIO
a. W-3690 John Hays
b. John Ellison
c. None

S-2595 889a B:224 X-0340 FRAN:PLEA PICK: --*
a. W-4601 John Massenburg
b. John Massenburg
c. None
*Source B does not mention Pickaway County.

S-2596 & S-2597 996a C:18 X-0340 FRAN:PLEA
a. W-4601 John Massenburg
b. John Massenburg
c. T. C. Flournoy, 1824

S-2597 29a C:18 X-0340 FRAN:PLEA
a. W-4601 John Massenburg
b. John Massenburg
c. None

S-2598 100a B:230 X-0340 UNIO:ALLE
a. W-3595 John Hefferlin
b. John Hefferlin*
c. None
*Source B notation: "Patented to him in 1831 [;] sent Lyne Starling.

S-2599 100a B:230 X-0340 MADI:JEFF FRAN:BROW
a. W-4593* Robert Dudley
b. Robert Dudley
c. L. M. Sullivant; L. Sullivant, heirs; M. L. Sullivant; W? [M?] J. Gilbert, 1842
*Warrant of this number grated for 200a.

S-2601 667a B:23 X-0340 FRAN:PLEA*
a. W-3800 David Airell
b. George Gilpin
c. None
*Source B notation: "Georgesville."

S-2602 667a B:23 X-0340 FRAN:PLEA
a. W-3800 David Airell
b. George Gilpin
c. Robert Robb; Thomas Lord, 1824

S-2603 667a B:23 X-0340 FRAN:PLEA
a. W-3800 David Airell
b. George Gilpin
c. Edward Tiffin; D. D. Warner, 1841

S-2604 667a B:23 X-0340 FRAN:PRAI
a. W-3800 David Airell
b. George Gilpin
c. John W. Graham; Robert Pollock; M. L. Sullivant, 1831

S-2605 667a B:24 X-0340 FRAN:PRAI
a. W-3800 David Airell
b. George Gilpin
c. John W. Graham; Robert Pollock, 1827; R. Osborn, 1831

S-2606 667a B:24 X-0340 FRAN:PRAI
a. W-3800 David Airell
b. George Gilpin
c. Robert Robb; William Mooberry, 1829; John Bigart; E. Backus, 1837

S-2607 800a B:115 X-0340 PICK:MUHL
a. W-4569 William Carter, Senior
b. William Carter
c. None

S-2608 800a B:115 X-0340 PICK:MUHL
a. W-4569 William Carter, Senior
b. William Carter
c. None

S-2609 1200a B:115 X-0340 PICK:MUHL
a. W-4569 William Carter, Senior
b. William Carter
c. None

S-2611* 200a -- -- PICK: --
a. --
b. John Darke
c. --
*Listed in Source B only; notation says: "not found."

S-2612 & S-2622 330a B:337 X-1040* ADAM:JEFF
a. W-4531 John Brent, 200a
W-4848 John Stewart, 200a
b. Benjamin Goodin
c. None
*"Left h[an]d f[or]k S[outh] Brush Creek."

S-2614 400a B:165 X-0210 ADAM:JEFF
a. W-4099 William Triplett; -- Davis & -- Duncan [assignees?]
b. Andrew Ellison
c. None

S-2615 1000a B:10 X-0130 ADAM:JEFF
a. W-4099 William Triplett; Andrew Ellison & -- Duncan [assignees?]
b. David Davis
c. T. James & Co; E. Nichols, 1837; T. Huston, 1840

S-2616 500a B:26 X-0800 ADAM:SPRI
a. W-4099 William Triplett; -- Davis & -- Duncan [assignees?]
b. Andrew Ellison
c. David? [Daniel?] Lee

S-2617 & S-3529 250a B:165 X-0130* ADAM:TIFF
a. W-3709 Nicholas Decker, 100a
W-3296 John Ray, heir to David Ray; -- Edie [assignee?] 100a
W-2528 Jesse Hilhiby; Robert Elleson [assignee?] 100a
b. Andrew Ellison
c. None
*"Lk. f[or]k Brush Creek."

S-2618 300a B:293 X-1043 ADAM:JEFF
a. W-3203 Thomas Rice, 100a
W-4285 Charles Lewis, assignee, 200a
b. Benjamin Goodwin
c. None

S-2620 1200a B:446 X-0941 FAYE:GREE
a. W-4659 Robert Means, assignee [of?] F. Graves, 400a
W-1654 Joseph Payne; -- Roberts [assignee?] 800a
b. Nathaniel Massie
c. None

S-2621 & S-3979 125a B:271 X-1240 SCIO:NILE
a. W-4615 William Gray, 100a
W-1089 Benjamin Brooke, 25a
b. Nathaniel Massie
c. John Tucker, 1824

S-2622. *See* S-2612

S-2623 100a B:338 X-1000 X-0130 ADAM:JEFF
a. W-2786 Isaac Smith; Benjamin Goodin [assignee?]
b. Michael Thomas
c. None

S-2624* 100a C:337 X-1190 SCIO:NILE
a. W-4152** John Fox
b. John G. McDowell
c. None
*Source B notation: "Not patented."
**This warrant already used for S-1965.

S-2625 124a B:25 X-1140 PIKE:NEWT
a. W-1870 William Tugler? [Zigler?]*
b. Benjamin** Beasley
c. W. Moore; J. Devoss? [Deross?] 1825; C. Wallace; S. Wallace, 1842
*Source D says Tugler.
**Source B says John Beasley.

S-2627 200a B:85 X-1150 BROW:HUNT
a. W-2186 Isham Hogen
b. Benjamin Beasley
c. None

S-2628 200a B:299 X-1040* ADAM:JEFF
a. W-3473 Leonard Cooper
b. Samuel McCullock
c. None
*Southeast fork.

S-2629 285a B:9 X-1042 SCIO:BRUS
a. W-3473 Leonard Cooper
b. Samuel McCullock
c. None

S-2630 550a B:8 X-1000 X-0130 SCIO:UNIO
a. W-3957 William Reynolds, assignee [of?] Samuel Yealey, 200a
W-3946 Thomas Pelley, 200a
W-3947 George Peay, rep[resentative] 200a
b. Samuel McCullock
c. None

S-2631 1000a B:82 X-0880 PIKE:PEBB
a. W-3956 Thomas Ogden, 200a
W-3959 John Sullevis? heir, 200a
W-3963 George Pair? [Pain?] 200a
W-3524 Richard Jones, 100a
W-3758 John Clarke, 100a
W-3958 William Maddox, 100a
W-3964 Anthony Junian? 100a
b. Samuel McCullock
c. Philip Acton; J. Penniston & J. Goodwin, 1833; Daniel Dunlavy; John Goodwin, 1833; R. Douglas; James? [Joseph?] Penniston, 1836

S-2632 1000a B:8 X-1140 PIKE:NEWT
a. W-4500 Thomas Seayres? [Scayres?] heir
b. Samuel McCullock
c. Ashbel? Tuttle; J. Penniston & William Mitten, 1830; William Robinson; James B. Turner, 1831; William McKirnan? [McKinnan?]; John Brown, 1831?

S-2632 2000a B:8 X-1140 PIKE:NEWT
a. W-4500 Thomas Seayres? [Scayres?] heir
b. Samuel McCullock
c. S. Reed; A. Reynolds, 1823; Thomas Johnson; Chauncey Beman? 1828; C. Wallace, 1832; John Sloan; R. Douglas, 1842; -- Penniston & -- Willis; J. Jones, 1842; William Reed, 1839; B. McDaniel; N. S. Murphy, 1841; J. Brown, heirs; L. Brown, 1842

S-2633 1000a B:9 X-1140 PIKE:NEWT
a. W-4500 Thomas Seayres? [Scayres?] heir
b. Samuel McCullock
c. J. Penticost; P. N. White, 1826; William Moore; Reuben Beeman, 1831; C. Wallace; S. Wallace, 1842

S-2634 1000a B:9 X-1140 PIKE:NEWT
a. W-4500 Thomas Seayres? [Scayres?] heir
b. Samuel McCullock
c. None

S-2635 1000a B:9 X-1140 PIKE:NEWT
a. W-4500 Thomas Seayres? [Scayres?] heir
b. Samuel McCullock
c. R. Douglas; Henry Bliss, 1828; James B. Turner, 1830; P. Wills & John Hopper, 1833; William Robinson; John Sargeant, 1831

S-2636* 300a -- -- ADAM:JEFF
a. --
b. William Humphreys
c. None
*This partial entry listed in Source B only.

S-2642 340a B:225 X-1004 DELA:CONC
a. W-3187 John Scott
b. John Scott
c. Nathaniel Hull, 1835; John Watts

S-2648 1000a B:22 X-0340 PICK:DARB
a. W-3207 Albion Throckmorton
b. Joseph Holmes
c. L. Sullivant, heirs; E. B. Heath, 1836

S-2649 1067a B:23 X-0340 PICK:DARB PICK:MONR
a. W-3478* William Stribling
b. Joseph Holmes
c. J. N. Holmes; Henry Rudy? [Rydy?] 1833; L. Sullivant, heirs; M? [W?] Parker, 1836; Z. Fowler, 1838
*Warrant number may be wrong, as it was issued for 400a only.

S-2651 200a B:433 X-1000 X-0130 ADAM:JEFF
a. W-0230 John Mills
b. Benjamin Goodin
c. None

S-2652 280a B:337 X-0130* ADAM:JEFF
a. W-0230 John Mills
b. Benjamin Goodin
c. None
*Southeast fork.

S-2653 88a B:337 X-0130* ADAM:JEFF
a. W-0230 John Mills
b. Benjamin Goodin
c. None
*Southeast fork.

S-2656 100a B:166 X-0130 ADAM:JEFF
a. W-3697 James McMullin
b. Joseph Stewart
c. None

S-2659 1000a A:525 X-0663 BROW:PERR
a. W-4647 Nicholas Carrele, John Obannon [assignee?]
b. Abraham Claypole & Peter Hull
c. Phineas Allen, 1824; John Jones, 1828; W. R. Hull; Joel Careless, 1833; J. M? [W?] Trimble, 1837; J. Gross; G. D. Brannon; J? [I?] Lake, 1842; T. L. Shields

S-2660 1000a A:525 X-0663 BROW:PERR
a. W-4312 John Bourne, 100a
W-4647 Nicholas Carrele; John Obannon [assignee?] 900a
b. Abraham Claypole & Peter Hull
c. -- Thompson & -- Lindsey, 1824; P. Hull, heirs, & Peter O'Conner; Rebecca Potter; S. A. Pegg, 1839; Benjamin Ryder; Abner Jurg? 1831

S-2661 600a B:439 X-0346 FRAN:PLEA
a. W-0205 Captain Thomas Thucutt?
b. Thomas Thweatt
c. Robert Dyer; Noah Hardwick? [Hardsuck?] 1840

S-2662 200a B:433 X-1000 X-0130 ADAM:JEFF
a. W-0230 John Mills
b. Benjamin Goodin
c. Parker? Truitt, 1828

S-2663 250a B:337 X-0130* ADAM:JEFF
a. W-0231 John Mills
b. Benjamin Goodin
c. None
*Lefthand fork.

S-2664 300a B:433 X-1350 ADAM:JEFF
a. W-0231 John Mills
b. Benjamin Goodin
c. None

S-2666 100a B:337 X-0130* ADAM:JEFF
a. W-0231 John Mills
b. Benjamin Goodin
c. J. T. Hamer; T. Huston, 1841
*Lefthand fork.

S-2668 2000a B:225 X-1004 FRAN:FRAN
a. W-2988 Richard Stephenson, heir to Hugh [Stephenson?]
b. Richard Stephenson
c. None

S-2669 1000a B:226 X-0340 UNIO:ALLE CHAM:RUSH
a. W-2988 Richard Stephenson, heir to Hugh [Stephenson?]
b. Richard Stephenson
c. L. Sullivant, heirs; J. Bigelow, 1837

S-2670 1000a B:24 X-0340 FRAN:BROW
a. W-2988 Richard Stephenson, heir to Hugh [Stephenson?]
b. Richard Stephenson
c. C. M. Shepherd; Dennis Adams, 1832; J. Turney, 1838

S-2671 1000a B:226 X-0340 UNIO:DARB
a. W-2988 Richard Stephenson, heir to Hugh [Stephenson?]
b. Richard Stephenson
c. L. Sullivant; Maly S. Butler, 1836

S-2673 1000a B:216 X-1004 DELA:CONC*
a. W-2753 Lewis Thomas; Lucas Sullivant [assignee?]
b. Lewis Thomas
c. Lucas Sullivant; Jacob Swartz, 1831; J? [I?] Iniks? [Juiks?] 1839, forfeited; J. Reese, 1839, forfeited
*Source B notation: "Bellepoint."

S-2674 667a B:401 X-0730 LOGA:JEFF
X-0750
a. W-4640 Thomas Holt
b. Thomas Holt
c. D. McArthur; Samuel Newell, 1828

S-2675 1000a B:116 X-0340 UNIO:UNIO
UNIO:DARB
a. W-2753 Lewis Thomas
b. Lucas Sullivant
c. None

S-2676 1000a B:25 X-0340 FRAN:PLEA
MADI: --*
a. W-0855 Lieutenant Colonel Oliver Towles
b. Oliver Towles
c. Andrew Lewis; Thomas Roberts, 1841
*Source B does not mention Madison County.

S-2677 1000a B:25 X-0340 FRAN:PRAI
MADI: --*
a. W-0855 Lieutenant Colonel Oliver Towles
b. Oliver Towles
c. Andrew Lewis; Thomas Roberts, 1841
*Source B does not mention Madison County.

S-2678 690a B:24 X-0340 MADI:JEFF
FRAN:PRAI*
a. W-0855 Lieutenant Colonel Oliver Towles
b. Oliver Towles
c. L. Sullivant, heirs; Lyne Starling, 1827; C. Towles; M. L. Sullivant, 1834; Israel Lucas; Alexander Fulton, 1838 (Delaware County)
*Source A does not mention Franklin County.

S-2679 956a B:21 X-0340 MADI:PLEA
FRAN:PRAI*
FRAN:BROW*
a. W-0021** John Crawford, heir
b. John Crawford
c. William Winship, heirs; Orvin Atkinson; L. N. Kerr (Madison County); J? [I?] Olney; D. Dunkin, 1842
*Source A does not mention Franklin County.
**Source C does not list this warrant.

S-2680 955a B:21 X-0340 MADI:JEFF
FRAN:BROW*
a. W-0021** John Crawford, heir
b. John Crawford
c. S. Springer; R. Francis, 1823; N. Cone, 1832; John Peters, heirs; John Moore, 1834; Francis Downing; Robert Brotherton, 1835 (Franklin County); J. Patterson, heirs; Daniel Cone; J. N. Jones, 1839; S. Downing, heirs; S. N. Kerr, 1839
*Source A does not mention Franklin County.
**Source C does not list this warrant.

S-2681 956a B:22 X-0340 MADI:JEFF
MADI:CANA
a. W-0021* John Crawford, heir
b. John Crawford
c. T. Clark; J. Harrell, 1823; John Kerr; Alexander Conner, 1832; L. Sullivant; Paul Smith, 1832; John Kerr, heirs; M. Sly, 1838; J. Lacompt; H. Warner, 1836; Unknown
*Source C does not list this warrant.

S-2682 1200* B:69 X-1180 MADI:JEFF
a. W-0221 Colonel John Gibson; Captain -- Paschk--? [assigner?]
b. John Gibson
c. None
*Source A says 1000a.

S-2686 1000a A:533 X-0660 CLIN:VERN
CLIN:UNIO
a. W-2127 Thomas Ridley, 333a
W-4676 Thomas Ridley, 667a
b. Thomas Ridley
c. L? [S?] Winston, 1826

S-2687 1000a B:19 X-0663 BROW:PERR
a. W-0105 Doctor John Roberts
b. John Roberts
c. P. Vanderwort; P. L? [S?] Wilson, 1841

S-2688 926a A:534 X-0660 CLIN:CLAR
CLIN:WASH
a. W-1541 John Lowe, 200a
W-1260 William Roach, 467a
W-1621 Daniel McCormack, 200a
W-1236 Joseph Bridgeman, 200a
b. Robert Harvie
c. W. McDaniel; F. Casto, 1842

S-2689 216a B:1 X-0660 CLIN:CLAR
a. W-1254 George Haines
b. Moses Coallier
c. None

S-2689 184a B:1 X-0660 CLIN:CLAR
a. W-1254 George Haines
b. Moses Coallier
c. None

S-2690 1383a A:535 X-0660 CLIN:UNIO
a. W-3326 William S. Hawkins, heir
b. William S. Hawkins
c. John Saterthwaite; James Fife, 1826; William Dillon; James? [Joseph?] W. Hackney, 1841

S-2691 1000a B:19 X-0663 CLIN:JEFF
a. W-3326 William S. Hawkins, heir
b. William S. Hawkins
c. John Sheets; Jacob Burnet, 1825

S-2692 895a A:535 X-0663 CLIN:UNIO
a. W-3326 William S. Hawkins, heir
b. William S. Hawkins
c. None

S-2693 715a A:535 X-0663 CLIN:UNIO
a. W-1918 General Edward Stevens
b. Edward Stevens
c. -- Smith & -- Jenkins; A. E. Strickle, 1842

S-2694 530a A:531 X-0663 CLIN:UNIO
a. W-0125 Captain Lieutenant Thomas Fenn, 330a
W-4295* Daniel Smith; John Obannon [assignee?] 200a
b. Thomas Fenn & John Obannon
c. George Cotten, executor; J. Morris, 1825
*This warrant number may be wrong, as it was used in S-2378.

S-2696 667a B:2 X-0360 MADI:UNIO
a. W-2214 Colonel James Innis
b. James Innis
c. William Radford; J. Farrer, 1833

S-2697 1850a B:1 X-0660 CLIN:CLAR CLIN:WASH
a. W-0104 Major General Baron F. W. H. F. [von] Steuben
b. Baron -- von Steuben
c. N. Massie, heirs; Samuel Hiatt, 1827; James Stone; Joel Rynard, 1834; J. Richards; J. Riddle, 1836; Joel Wright; A. E. Strickle, 1836; Asa Cowgill; William Wickersham, 1831

S-2698 1150a B:2 X-0360 MADI:PLEA
a. W-0104 Major General Baron F. W. H. F. [von] Steuben
b. Baron -- [von] Steuben
c. James Brown (Kentucky), *see* [S-] 6298; C. B. Harlan, 1830

S-2699 785a B:3 X-0360 PICK:MONR
a. W-2260 Major Richard Call
b. Richard Call
c. None

S-2700 667a B:5 X-0360 PICK:PERR FAYE: --*
a. W-2309 Captain John H. Fitzgerald
b. John H. Fitzgerald
c. Daniel Hanson; A. Latham; Jacob K. Lutz, 1830
*Source B does not mention Fayette County.

S-2701 200a B:2 X-0360 PICK:MONR
a. W-3719 Richard Moore
b. William West
c. K. Cath & J. Slouff; Richard Seymour, 1833

S-2702 100a B:1 X-0360 PICK:MONR
a. W-0578 Benjamin Kelley
b. Joseph Pirkman
c. G. W. Doan, 1827; John Parkman; M. O'Brian, 1829; J. Sharp, 1831; Samuel Swindler, 1833

S-2704 100a B:2 X-0360 PICK:MONR
a. W-4549 John Hamilton
b. Samuel McFerran*
c. None
*Source B spells McFerrin.

S-2705 2000a B:73 X-0660 CLIN: --*
a. W-4675 Alexander Spotswood
b. Alexander Spottswood**
c. Andrew Mart?; John Murphey, 1826; George C. Hite; W. S? Bruce, 1837
**See* next entry.
**Source B spells Spotswood.

S-2705 2000a B:73 X-0660 CLIN:MARI CLIN:VERN CLIN:JEFF CLIN:WASH
a. W-4675 Alexander Spotswood
b. Alexander Spottswood*
c. Phebe Smith**; J. Morris, 1841**; George C. Hite**; J. W. Hacknewy, 1841**
*Source B spells Spotswood.
**Names mentioned pertain also to following entry.

S-2705 2000a B:73 X-0660 CLIN:JEFF CLIN:WASH
a. W-4675 Alexander Spotswood
b. Alexander Spottswood*
c. [See preceding entry]
*Source B spells Spotswood.

S-2706 752a C:204 X-1173 CLIN:VERN
a. W-2126 Abrington Jones
b. Albridgton* Jones
c. P. Carrison; N. Boums, 1836
*Source B spells Albridgeton.

S-2708 889a B:77 X-0663 CLIN:JEFF
a. W-2126 Abrington Jones
b. Albridgton* Jones
c. John Obannon; William Gaskill, 1827; C. B. Harlan, 1833
*Source B spells Albridgeton.

S-2709 180a B:453 X-1150 BROW:HUNT
a. W-4647 Nicholas Carrele; -- Claypoole & -- Hull [assignees?]
b. John Obannon
c. Benjamin Perry; Thomas Middleton, 1826

S-2710 100a B:527 X-0800 BROW:HUNT
a. W-4187 John Mitchell
b. Elizabeth Boone
c. James Brown; Thomas Middleton, 1826; J. King; -- Wilson & -- Middleton, 1842

S-2711 100a B:528 X-0800 BROW:HUNT
a. W-4219 James Obrian
b. James Obrian
c. -- Shepherd & -- Masterson, 1823; J. H. Shepherd, 1826

S-2712 100a B:528 X-0800 BROW:HUNT
a. W-4324 Martin Sutton
b. William Love
c. Samuel H. Helm; Thomas Middleton, 1826

S-2713 100a B:153 X-0800 BROW:HUNT
a. W-1510 Patrick Stewart
b. William Ritchey
c. None

S-2713 100a B:153 X-0800 BROW:HUNT
a. W-4463 Patrick Lockhart; assignee [of?] George Fielder
b. William Ritchey
c. None

S-2713 100a B:153 X-0800 BROW:HUNT
a. W-4464 Patrick Lockhart; assignee [of?] William Millisons
b. William Ritchey
c. None

S-2714 1450a A:526 X-0660 CLIN:UNIO CLIN:LIBE
a. W-0174 Captain William White
b. William White
c. John Hughs; G. Hartman, 1832; Samuel Evans; J. Hadley, Junior, 1840; James? [Joseph?] W. Hackney, 1841

S-2715 282a B:80 X-1170 CLIN:VERN
a. W-0043 Archibald Blair, heir to Captain -- Blair
b. Archibald Blair
c. Harvey Stearns, 1826

S-2716 560a B:72 X-0845 HIGH:FAIR CLIN:WAYN
a. W-1788 John Bates, 200a
W-1929* Francis King, 200a
W-1962 John Depriest; Richard Edmonton, assignee, 160a; *all three warrants to* Clement Biddle [assignee?]
b. Clement Biddle
c. S? [L?] Carey? [Casey?]; James? [Joseph?] H. Dunlavy, 1826

S-2717 757a B:212 X-0840 FAYE:CONC FAYE:GREE
a. W-2637 Lieutenant John Eustes
b. John Eustace
c. John Harbinson, 1828; William R. Archley? [Ashley?]; I? [J?] Y. Greene, 1836; Joel Rogers, deeded 13 May 1830

S-2718 573a B:287 X-1140 PIKE:MIFF
a. W-2273 Captain Thomas Buckner
b. Thomas Buckner
c. Abraham Peters; Samuel Skander? 1830; A. Powelson; James O'Brien, Junior, 1841

S-2720 600a B:210 X-0840 FAYE:GREE
a. W-0350 Captain Samuel K. Bradford
b. Samuel K. Bradford
c. Thomas Bradford; Richard Douglas, 1829; C. Safford; A. J. Huff, 1842 (Highland County)

S-2721 290a B:294 X-0663 CLER:UNIO
a. W-2722 William Sebry, 200a
W-0868 Alexander Chambers, 100a
b. John Obannon
c. R. Cazel? [Cozel?]; R. Townsley, 1826

S-2722 360a B:176 X-0130 ADAM:MONR ADAM:GREE
a. W-4653 William Rippolo? [Rippito?]
b. Nathaniel Massie
c. John McHenry, heirs; R. Holliday, 1840

S-2723 1000a C:237 X-0040 ADAM:MONR
a. W-4672 Bartholomew Yates, representative of
b. Nathaniel Massie
c. Elijah Collins; Robert Johnson, 1826; James Newland; Z. Wade, Junior, 1831

S-2724 1267a B:271 X-0841 ROSS:UNIO
a. W-4672 Bartholomew Yates, representative of
b. Nathaniel Massie
c. None

S-2725 1065a B:84 X-0420 ADAM:LIBE ADAM:WAYN BROW:BYRD BROW:JACK
a. W-3432 John M. Galt, "resolution"
b. Abraham Shepherd
c. George Knight; D. P. Wilkins, 1823; J. Machir; R. Johnson, 1827; J. L. Cunningham; E. Nicholas, 1837

S-2726 1200a* B:84 X-0420 ADAM:LIBE
a. W-1413* Thomas Coverley
b. Abraham Shepherd
c. None
*W-1413 is for 200a only; thus, there is a discrepancy in this entry.

S-2727* 500a -- -- PIKE: --
a. --
b. Abra[ha]m Shepherd
c. A. Winkoop, 1823; E. O'Brien; J. Dunham, 1832; John Hopper, Junior; -- Penniston & -- Jones, 1838
*This partial entry appears only in Source B, at top of page before S-2723.

S-2728 300a B:84 X-0420 ADAM:LIBE
a. W-3432 John M. Galt
b. Abraham Shepherd
c. None

S-2729, S-2829, S-2845 400a B:85 X-0423 ADAM:LIBE
a. W-4123 George Richards, 100a
W-3672 Thomas William[s?] 100a
W-2826 James Maloy, 100a
W-3239 Hamlin Tomlinson, heir to Herbert Tomlinson, 100a
b. John Beasley
c. None

S-2731 100a B:110 X-0130 ADAM:LIBE
a. W-1987 Richard Marshall
b. Richard Marshall*
c. None
*Source B says Andrew Ellison.

S-2732* 266a -- -- ADAM:LIBE
a. --
b. Richard Marshall
c. None
*This partial entry listed in Source B only. Warrant number could have been W-1987.

S-2733 200a B:25 X-0230 ADAM:WAYN
a. W-1987 Richard Marshall
b. Richard Marshall
c. None

S-2734 50a B:167 X-0130 ADAM:GREE
a. W-4566 John Warren
b. John Warren
c. None

S-2735 150a B:83 X-0423 ADAM:LIBE
a. W-1844* Robert Mc Quillen
b. Richard Spear
c. None
*Warrant already used on S-0866.

S-2736 100a B:166 X-1190 SCIO:NILE
a. W-4635* --
b. William Huddleston
c. None
*Source C shows no warrant issued under this number.

S-2737 1300a B:186 X-0570 BROW:CLAR CLER:FRAN
a. W-2025 Major James Knox
b. James Knox
c. James Kox? [Knox?]; Allen Butts, 1826; N. Ellis, 1828; J. Baird; William Shepherd, 1831 (Brown County)

S-2739 & 4567a B:55 X-0130 HIGH:JACK
S-3015 X-0980 HIGH:LIBE
a. W-1756 Richard Murry; Clement Biddle [assignee?] 100a*
W-0901 Claiborne Andrews, 100a
W-1460 Nutley? [Natley?] Maddox, 200a
W-1661 William Cox, 200a
W-4105 George Estes, 100a
W-4506 John Harris, 100a
W-4532 Thomas Creed, 467a
W-4534 Jacob Fishback, 200a
W-4542 Thomas Goodman, 200a
W-4553 William Begger? [Bigger?]; assignee John Langston, who married Mary Gabriel, 100a
W-4554 William Begger? [Bigger?]; assignee [of?] Salley Frails, representative, 100a
W-4555 William Begger? [Bigger?]; assignee [of?] George Turner, 100a
W-4558 William Begger? [Bigger?]; assignee [of?] Reubin Samson, representative, 100a
W-4567 Robert Means; assignee [of?] James Vaughan, assignee of James Smith, 100a
W-4572 Christ[opher] McKaunen, 400a
W-4575 Robert Means; assignee [of?] James Dealake, 200a
W-4582 William Begger? [Bigger?]; assignee [of?] Caleb Hill, 100a
W-4584 David Stern, 400a
W-4587 Francis Graves; assignee [of?] Lewis Lee, heir to Bartlett Lee, 200a
W-4588 Hannah Hawkins, representative [of?] Michael Hogan, 200a
W-4593 Robert Dudley; [assignee? of?] Nathaniel Wills, 200a**
W-4623 Robert Means; assignee [of?] F[rancis] Graves, assignee [of?] James Stewart, 200a
W-4667 Robert Means; assignee [of?] Thomas Pears, representative of William Pears, 100a
W-1851 Reuben Plunket, 200a
W-3652 John Farmer, 200a
b. Robert Means
c. Samuel Beard; J. Smith, 1838
*This warrant already used on S-0727.
**Apparently two warrants issued with same number--one for 100a, the second for 200a.

S-2740 667a B:295 X-1140 PIKE:MIFF
a. W-4670 Thomas Pemberton
b. Thomas Pemberton
c. G. Ellison; J. Dunham, 1823; James Sargent? [Sargint?] 1824; S. Read, *et al*, 1830; T. Pemberton, heirs; Cad[wallader?] Wallace, 1834; E. H. Davis; T. B. Anderson, 1841; A. Powelson; J. O'Brien, Junior, 1841; G. G. Perkins

S-2741 400a C:229 X-1120 BROW:FRAN
a. W-0398 Captain Thomas Pemberton
b. Thomas Pemberton
c. [Names mentioned in S-2740 also apply here.]

S-2743 270a B:240 X-1140 PIKE:MIFF
a. W-2213 William Nelson
b. William Nelson
c. None

S-2744 553a C:126 X-0040 ADAM:MONR ADAM:TIFF
a. W-3398 Leven Powell
W-1930 George Belvin; Clement Biddle, assignee*
b. Nathaniel Massie
c. None
*This warrant was already used on S-2531 and S-2588.

S-2745 189a B:244 X-0663 CLER:UNIO
a. W-2576 Cadwalader Jones
b. John Graham
c. None

S-2748 600a B:343 X-0663 HIGH:DODS
a. W-4256 Mary Randolph, representative of Frank Poythess, 400a
W-4482 Jesse Chandler, 200a
b. Robert Watkins
c. None

S-2749 400a B:173 X-1000 PIKE:PEEP
a. W-3200 John Clough
b. Thomas McCoy
c. None

S-2751 100a B:416 X-0840 ROSS:PAXT
a. W-1303 Demsey Eastwood
b. Richard C[lough] Anderson
c. None

S-2752 533a C:498 X-0940 FAYE:GREE
a. W-4668 Francis Graves, assignee [of?] Samuel Hubbard
b. Francis Graves
c. James Woods, 1828; Thomas Grear; -- Parey? [Parrey?] 1834; James Hyatt, deeded 23 Dec 1829; Samuel Shepherd, 1830; T. Childers

S-2753 1000a B:43 X-0790 CLER:GOSH CLER:MONR
a. W-0137 Richard Starke
b. Richard Starke
c. H. B. Parker; D. Roude? [Roudecash?] 1826

S-2754 1000a* B:43 X-1170 WARR:WASH CLIN:VERN
a. W-0137 Richard Starke
b. Richard Starke
c. None
*Source B says 800a.

S-2755, S-3174, S-3240[2] 1622a D:367 X-1005 PIKE:NEWT BROW: --[1]
a. W-1328 Edward Harris, 400a
W-1759 John Miller, heir to John Miller, deceased; assignee [of?] Alexander Petrie, 200a
W-3653 John Hopper; Charles Lee [assignee?] 400a
W-5821[3] Ellison E. Adams; Duncan McArthur [assignee?] 400a
W-6014 Benjamin Harrison, representative[4]
W-6217 -- Triplett; -- Wallace & -- Dun [assignees?][4]
W-6537 Thomas Parramore; Peter P. Mayo? [Mays?] [assignee?][4]
W-1375 Captain Tarpley White[4]
b. Alexander Tarte[5], John Miller, & -- Wallace
c. Alexander Tate; David Johnston, 1823; -- Wallace, *et al*; S. Wallace, 1842 (Pike County)
[1]Source A does not mention Brown County.
[2]Source B says S-13174 and S-13240.
[3]Warrant number may be wrong and W-3821 meant. W-3821 was issued to Samuel Aubry, *alias* Avery; William George [assignee?].
[4]Acreage assignable to this land grant is unknown.
[5]Source B spells Taite.

S-2756 100a B:260 X-1040 ADAM:FRAN
a. W-4571 James Hines
b. James Hines
c. Curtis Cannon, 1825

S-2757 200a B:183 X-1120 BROW:BYRD
a. W-3501 Lawrence Everhart
b. Lawrence Everhart
c. John H. Shepherd, 1828; James Sansbury? [Lansbury?]; S? S? [L? L?] Tucker, 1831

S-2758 100a B:265 X-1040 ADAM:FRAN
a. W-1809 Aaron Darnold
b. Alexander Parker & James Parker
c. None

S-2759 200a B:171 X-0130 ADAM:TIFF
a. W-1085 Edward McDonald
b. James Huntly
c. None

S-2760 100a B:174 X-0133 HIGH:JACK
a. W-2599 Henry Brown
b. Samuel Ayres
c. Joshua Smart, 1828

S-2762 200a B:246 X-0020 HIGH:BRUS
a. W-4429 Turner Morris, assignee, 100a
W-4430 Turner Morris, assignee, 100a
b. Joseph Kerr & John Stealey
c. Charles W. Byrd; Joel Butler, 1833

S-2763 300a B:305 X-0130 ADAM:TIFF
a. W-1547 Jesse Andrews; John North [assignee?] 200a
W-1550 Edward Cannafax; John North [assignee?] 100a
b. Nathaniel Massie
c. None

S-2765 300a B:250 X-1120 BROW:BYRD BROW:PLEA
a. W-1551 Josiah Learwood; John North [assignee?] 100a
W-1549 Nathaniel Cunningham; John North [assignee?] 200a
b. Nathaniel Massie
c. William Lyon; James Loudon, 1826

S-2766 333a B:273 X-0150 ROSS:PAIN
a. W-4639 John Dandridge
b. John Watkins* & Nathaniel Massie
c. None
*Source C says Joseph Watkins.

S-2769 2000a B:38 X-0130 HIGH:JACK HIGH:LIBE
a. W-1523 Higgins Coppinger, 200a
W-1679 Francis Woolfolk, 200a
W-1920 Colonel Josiah Parker, [200a]
W-3454 William Waggoner, 200a
W-3681 William Reynolds; assignee [of?] Nathaniel Jackson, 200a
W-3849 Patrick Brumagem, 200a
W-3856 John Smith, 200a
W-3898 William Reynolds, 200a
W-3899 William Reynolds, 200a
W-3900 William Reynolds, 200a
b. John Clemson
c. John Smith; John Hogsett, 1836; W. Dun; John L. Hughes, 1840

S-2770 1433a B:38 X-0130 HIGH:JACK HIGH:LIBE
a. W-1885* Joseph Hoofman, 233a
W-3443 Archibald McCloud, 200a
W-3903 William Reynolds, 200a
W-3904 William Reynolds, 200a
W-3906 William Reynolds, 200a
W-3908 William Reynolds, 200a
W-3914 Joseph Toat? 200a
b. John Clemson
c. None
*Warrant already used in S-1515.

S-2771 1434a B:39 X-0130 HIGH:JACK
a. W-3915 George Wikle, 400a
W-3919 David Buckley, 200a
W-3920 William Askew, 200a
W-3923 James Griffin, 200a
W-4100 John Kerney, 400a
W-3914* Joseph Toat? 200a
b. John Clemson
c. None
*Warrant already used in S-2770.

S-2772 500a B:179 X-0250 HIGH:LIBE
a. W-4612 Jacob Johnson, 100a
W-4613 Benjamin Johnson, 200a
W-4614 George Bozzell, 200a
b. John Florence & Nathaniel Massie
c. None

S-2773 400a C:128 X-1280 FAYE:GREE
a. W-2563 Thomas Camp, heir, 100a
W-3376 Richard Croxton, 100a
W-4127 Thomas Camp, heir, 200a; *all three warrants to* Ebenezer Scrogs [assignee?]
b. Ebenezer Scroggs
c. Isaac Henderson, deeded 28 May 1832

S-2774 100a B:245 X-0020 HIGH:BRUS
a. W-3430 Richard Harvie
b. Richard Harvie
c. Fred[erick?] Bougher; James Smith, 1830

S-2775 231a B:49 X-0130 ADAM:TIFF
a. W-0145 Captain William Fowler
b. Nathan[iel?] Massie
c. None

S-2782. *See* S-2468

S-2786 100a B:249 X-0130 ADAM:TIFF
a. W-4669 Christopher Nead? [Neal?]
b. Robert Pollard
c. None

S-2787 3338a B:20 X-1120 BROW:UNIO X-0950 BROW:BYRD
a. W-1920 Colonel Josiah Parker
b. Josiah Parker
c. John Edwards? [Edwardsley?] [&] Alexander Jolley, ag[ent?]; William Shepherd, 1823; James Johnson; Vachel H. Masterson, 1823; Man Lyner? [Syner?]; John S. Wills, 1823; John Moore, 1824; John Thompson, heirs; J. Jacobs, 1828; L. Mann

S-2789 1340a B:17 X-1300 BROW:PLEA BROW:LEWI
a. W-0821 Colonel Samuel Hawes
b. Samuel Hawes
c. James Baker; Job Egbert, 1823; Henry Oakwood, 1825; D. Ferguson; P. L. Willson, 1841

S-2790 1667a B:18 X-0663 BROW:PERR CLIN:JEFF
a. W-0821 Colonel Samuel Hawes
b. Samuel Hawes
c. William Brooks; James Taylor, 1823; Thomas Hart; David Johnson [*also* Johnston] 1823; John W. Tibbatts, 1826; N. Ellis, 1833; A. C. Stewart; Thomas Watson

S-2791 1667a B:18 X-0663 BROW:PERR HIGH:DODS CLIN:JEFF
a. W-0821 Colonel Samuel Hawes
b. Samuel Hawes
c. George Gratten; David Johnson, 1823; James Rush; James Taylor, 1823; William Lytle; N. Ellis, 1832; D. G. Devore, 1834; S. Waterman, 1831; John Smith; F. Bingaman, 1830; Thomas McCan? [McCar? McCaw?]; R. Alexander; J. Lake; -- Mossman? [Morsman?]; -- Allen & -- Lake, 1842

S-2792 800a E:87 X-0663 CLIN:JEFF
a. W-0821 Colonel Samuel Hawes
b. James Taylor
c. Robert Means; Samuel Hawes; J. Fyfe & Isaiah Morris, 1831

S-2793 1062a B:466 X-0950 BROW:BYRD
a. W-1920 Colonel Josiah Parker
b. Josiah Parker
c. James Gilleland; John S? [L?] Wills, 1824; A. Leggett, 1825; D. Pickerell; W. Hewitt, 1835

S-2794 200a C:185 X-0950 BROW:UNIO
a. W-1921 General Robert Lawson
b. John Obannon
c. None

S-2795 240a C:393 X-0800 BROW:UNIO
a. W-1921 General Robert Lawson
b. John Obannon
c. None

S-2796 830a B:254 X-1300 BROW:PLEA
a. W-1921 General Robert Lawson
b. John Obannon
c. H. White; J. J. Higgins, 1827

S-2797 400a B:307 X-0420 BROW:UNIO
a. W-1921 General Robert Lawson
b. John Obannon
c. Henry Apple, 1828; G. W. Jones, 1831

S-2798 1867a B:308 X-1150 BROW:HUNT
X-0420
a. W-3442 William Reynolds, assignee [of?] Richard Christian, 400a
W-3530 Stephen Goodwin; John Armstrong [assignee?] 1467a
b. Thomas Perkins
c. Sarah Carrigan; Thomas Middleton, 1826; George T. Cotton; S. H. Helm, 1831; J. Harsh; -- Wilson & -- Middleton, 1842

S-2799 133a B:72 X-1150 BROW:HUNT
a. W-1324 John Bartlett
b. John Bartlett
c. Benjamin Applegate; Allen Butt, 1826; Daniel Moore; W. McDowell, 1829

S-2799 133a B:72 X-1150 BROW:HUNT
a. W-1324 John Bartlett
b. John Bartlett
c. None

S-2799 133a B:72 X-1150 BROW:HUNT
a. W-1324 John Bartlett
b. John Bartlett
c. None

S-2800 280a B:18 X-0660 CLER:MIAM
a. W-0821 Colonel Samuel Hawes
b. Samuel Hawes
c. None

S-2801 240a E:95 X-1040 SCIO:UNIO
a. W-2629 Captain Simon Morgan
b. Simon Morgan
c. John Noel

S-2802 400a B:125 X-1040* SCIO:BRUS
a. W-1095 John Hull
b. Thomas Rardin
c. Hugh Brown; S. S. Brown, 1826
*"Northwest fork of . . ."

S-2803 300a B:85 X-1040* SCIO:BRUS
a. W-1123 Edward Walker, 200a
W-3693 Charles McKinley, 100a
b. Charles Morgan
c. None
*"Northwest fork of . . ."

S-2804 200a B:125 X-1040* SCIO:BRUS
a. W-4352 William Merrick, heir to John Merrick
b. William Merrick
c. J. Armstrong; A. Armstrong; J. Willson? 1824; J. Wallace, 1826
*"Northwest fork of . . ."

S-2805 200a B:167 X-1040 SCIO:BRUS
ADAM:MEIG
a. W-0607 James Wyant
b. Alexander Dunlap
c. None

S-2810 2000a B:44 X-0663 CLER:WILL*
a. W-4660 Daniel de Benneville
b. Daniel Debeneville
c. John McAdams, heirs; E. McAdams, 1823; A? V. Hopkins; Jesse E. Dozier; Thomas J. Buchannan, 1841
*Source B notation: "By Williamsburg."

S-2810 1500a B:44 X-0663 CLER:WILL*
a. W-4660 Daniel de Benneville
b. Daniel Debeneville
c. J. McAdams; E. [Mc]Adams, 1827; E. Adams, 1829
*Source B notation: "Williamsburg."

S-2811 1000a B:44 X-0663 CLER:WILL
a. W-4660 Daniel de Benneville
b. Daniel Debeneville
c. Thomas S. Shields, 1841

S-2811 1000a B:44 X-0663 CLER:WILL
a. W-4660 Daniel de Benneville
b. Daniel Debeneville
c. None

S-2819 1000a B:92 X-0840 FAYE:JEFF
a. W-0202 Captain Robert Yancey
b. Robert Yancy
c. Samuel Loofborough, 1835; Joseph? [James?]Parrott, deceased? 1835; I? [J?] Y. Green, 1836; James Hatfield, 1837; H. Sanderson, 1837; Joseph Hydy [*also* Hidy] 1838; William Hogue, 1839; Alexander Torbet, 1841

S-2820 150a B:164 X-0130 ADAM:JEFF
a. W-4133 Michael Moore
b. John Barrett
c. None

S-2822 300a B:244 X-1040 ADAM:JEFF
a. W-3812 John Eubank; Jesse Edwards & Peter Wykoff [assignees?] 200a?
W-3797 John Tally? [Fally?] Senior; Joseph Moore & Elisha Chapman [assignees?] 200a?
b. Benjamin Goodin
c. None

S-2823 & S-4026 200a B:420 X-1043* ADAM:JEFF
a. W-4047 William Taylor, heir, 100a
W-3822 Henry Ethel, assignee of Benjamin Ethel, 100a
b. George Rogers
c. None
*"Branch of . . ."

S-2828 100a B:316 X-0136 ADAM:GREE
a. W-2833 William Campbell
b. Robert Morrison
c. None

S-2829. *See* S-2729

S-2830 100a B:85 X-0423 ADAM:LIBE
a. W-4649 John Penny, assignee; representative of Daniel Haggard
b. Andrew Ellison
c. None

S-2830 80a B:86 X-0423 ADAM:LIBE
a. W-1062 Samuel Smith
b. Andrew Ellison
c. None

S-2831 126a B:110 X-0423 ADAM:LIBE
a. W-4099 William Triplett
b. Andrew Ellison
c. None

S-2832 1000a B:223 X-0110 UNIO:YORK
a. W-4583 Peter Manifeld, assignee of David Hopkins
b. Peter Manifold
c. None

S-2833 1000a B:117 X-0340 UNIO:ALLE CHAM:RUSH
a. W-4583 Peter Manifeld, assignee of David Hopkins
b. Peter Manifold
c. T. McLung; Levi Wells, 1840

S-2835 700a B:325 X-0841 ROSS:CONC
a. W-1841 Ensign John Gibson
b. Duncan McArthur
c. None

S-2836 1000a B:114 X-1180 MADI:JEFF*
a. W-2217 Isaac Morris, 200a
W-3588 Goodrich Lightfoot, assignee, 200a
W-3534 John Keen, 200a
W-3486 Linny Arnold, assignee, 200a
W-3503 Robert W. Chavers, 100a
W-3520 Francis Graves, 100a
b. Jacob Woolston
c. M. L. Sullivant; S? [L?] Jones, heirs; R. Douglas, 1836; S. Sullivant, heirs
*Source B notation: "Jefferson."

S-2842 2180a B:39 X-0890 HIGH:BRUS HIGH:JACK
a. W-4465 James Armstrong
b. John Graham
c. None

S-2843 300a* B:52 X-0130 HIGH:BRUS
a. W-4665 James Armstrong
b. John Graham
c. W. Dun; J. Roads, 1831
*Source B says 1300a.

S-2844 300a B:168 X-1190 SCIO:NILE
a. W-0227 Lieutenant Jacob Coleman
b. Richard C[lough] Anderson
c. None

S-2845. *See* S-2729

S-2846 100a B:164 X-1190 SCIO:NILE
a. W-3070 Ludwell Yancey
b. Ezekiel Beasley
c. None

S-2847 200a B:82 X-0870 PIKE:PEBB
a. W-3082 Benjamin May, heir to William [May]
b. Samuel Henry
c. J. Beasley; John Farnsler, 1826; Samuel Means; James Candy, 1840

S-2848 200a B:82 X-0220 PIKE:SUNF
a. W-3214 William Gallay
b. Samuel Henry
c. None

S-2849 76a B:25 X-0420 BROW:BYRD
a. W-1870 William Tugler? [Zigler? Hughes?]; Clement Biddle [assignee?]
b. John Beasley
c. None

S-2850 300a B:171 X-1040 SCIO:BRUS
a. W-0405 William Tompkins, heir to H. Tompkins
b. William Tompkins
c. None

S-2850 150a B:171 X-0930 SCIO:BRUS ADAM:FRAN
a. W-0405 William Tompkins, heir to H. Tompkins
b. William Tompkins
c. None

S-2851 100a B:303 X-1000 PIKE:NEWT
a. W-0604 Samuel McDonnan?
b. James Trenor
c. Steele F. Randolph; R. Lucas, 1823; James Sargent, 1835; William Reed; Van S. Murphy, 1841

S-2851 100a B:303 X-1000 PIKE:NEWT
a. W-1526 Robert Welch
b. James Trenor
c. None

S-2851 100a B:303 X-1000 PIKE:NEWT
a. W-1526 Robert Welch
b. James Trenor
c. None

S-2852 100a B:301 X-1000 PIKE:NEWT
a. W-3078 John Gunter
b. John Grinter
c. Jacob Loy, 1830; H. Hempstead, 1834

S-2852 100a B:301 X-1000 PIKE:NEWT
a. W-3078 John Gunter
b. John Grinter
c. None

S-2852 100a B:301 X-1000 PIKE:NEWT
a. W-4174 Moses Mills
b. John Grinter
c. None

S-2853 100a B:111 X-1140 PIKE:NEWT
a. W-3722 Elizabeth Stadler, heir[ess] to John Kaerns
b. Elizabeth Stadler
c. James Weaver; Samuel Shepherd, 1823

S-2853 100a B:111 X-1140 PIKE:NEWT
a. W-3722 Elizabeth Stadler, heir[ess] to John Kaerns
b. Elizabeth Stadler
c. None

S-2854 100a B:111 X-1140 PIKE:NEWT
a. W-1350 Thomas McClain
b. Thomas McClain
c. C. Wallace; S. Wallace; John Beasley, patented 1805

S-2855 200a B:170 X-0870 PIKE:PEEP
a. W-1602 Archibald Taylor
b. Knight Bowles
c. Abraham Chenowith & J. Loy, 1830

S-2856 200a B:302 X-0870 PIKE:PEEP
a. W-3648 Moses Rawlins
b. Moses Rawlins
c. J. Sewall, 1830

S-2858 100a D:361 X-0425 BROW:JACK
a. W-3055 William Carter
b. William Carter
c. John Machir; Henry Apple, 1828

S-2859 200a B:83 X-1140 PIKE:SUNF
a. W-1127 Charles Morgan
b. Joseph McCune
c. J. Beasley; Loyd Howard, 1826

S-2860 200a B:83 X-1140 PIKE:SUNF
a. W-3161 Henry Clark
b. Henry Clark
c. None

S-2861 477a B:26 X-0420 ADAM:WAYN
a. W-2629 Captain Simon Morgan
b. Simon Morgan
c. None

S-2862 300a B:70 X-0420 BROW:BYRD
a. W-0019 Brigadier General [Daniel] Morgan
b. John Crawford
c. John Johnson; Philip Miller, 1826; I? [J?] Dean; J. S. Beasley, 1841

S-2863 200a B:171 X-0870 PIKE:PEEP
a. W-1917 General Edward Stevens
b. William Hulse
c. None

S-2866 300a B:109 X-1000 SCIO:WASH
a. W-0232 Henry Dawson
b. Joseph Winlock
c. C. Potts; S. G. Jones, 1828; G. Graves, heirs; Samuel Coil, 1840; S. Moss; W? [N?] V. Peck, 1842; L. Moss

S-2867 400a B:109 X-1040 SCIO:UNIO
a. W-0232 Henry Dawson
b. Joseph Winlock
c. William Dever? [Derer?]; William Ghacky? [Gharky?] 1832; William Kendall; Robert Steele; A. & R. Steele; W. Gharky? or G. Henry; G. Herdeth, 1836; W. Kinney; Aaron Noel, 1840

S-2868 300a B:85 X-1140 PIKE:SUNF
a. W-0232 Henry Dawson
b. Joseph Winlock
c. D. Pollock; J. Dunham, 1823

S-2869 300a B:109 X-1140 PIKE:PEBB
a. W-0232 Henry Dawson
b. Joseph Winlock
c. Henry White; H. Hempstead, 1829

S-2873 580a B:472 X-1090 LOGA:LAKE
a. W-3195 Samuel Wallace, heir
b. Samuel Wallace
c. None

S-2875 1000a B:117 X-0340 UNIO:ALLE
a. W-3195 Samuel Wallace, heir
b. Samuel Wallace
c. L. Sullivant; Lyne Starling, 1826

S-2879 1000a B;116 X-0340 UNIO:DARB
a. W-4731 Lawrence Harrison
b. Lucas Sullivant
c. Lyne Sterling [Starling?]

S-2881 750a B:481 X-1180 MADI:MONR
a. W-3196 Samuel Wallace, heir
b. Samuel Wallace
c. Hugh Glen; George Harris, 1828

S-2882 628a B:458 X-1180 MADI:MONR
a. W-3196 Samuel Wallace, heir
b. Samuel Wallace
c. None

S-2883 657a B:458 X-1180 MADI:MONR
a. W-3196 Samuel Wallace, heir
b. Samuel Wallace
c. None

S-2884 985a B:458 X-1180 MADI:MONR
a. W-3196 Samuel Wallace, heir
b. Samuel Wallace
c. Hugh Glen; R. Douglass, 1825

S-2885 689a B:531 X-0340 FRAN:PRAI
a. W-3194 Samuel Wallace, heir
b. Samuel Wallace
c. Daniel Lambert; M. L. Sullivant; D. Adams, 1837

S-2886 689a B:531 X-0340 FRAN:PRAI
a. W-3194 Samuel Wallace, heir
b. Samuel Wallace
c. Isaac Corothers [Caruthers?]; Jeremiah McLane; C. Davis, 1834; J. McLure? J. Galloway; Thomas Bevans, 1833; William Wise

S-2887 689a B:532 X-0340 FRAN:PRAI
a. W-3194 Samuel Wallace, heir
b. Samuel Wallace
c. Isaac Caruthers; William Jamison, 1830

S-2890 46a E:226 X-1120 BROW:PLEA
a. W-4551 Harmon Nash, heir
b. Harman Nash
c. None

S-2890 136a C:403 X-1120 BROW:PLEA
a. W-4551 Harmon Nash, heir
b. Harman Nash
c. William Dixon, 1828; William V. Powell; Levi Mordecai, 1831

S-2891 1000a B:54 X-0130 HIGH:NEWM HIGH:CONC
a. W-1325 Captain Erasmus Gill
b. Erasmus Gill
c. None

S-2892 1000a B:54 X-0840 HIGH:NEWM
a. W-1325 Captain Erasmus Gill
b. Erasmus Gill
c. H. McNiel; G. W. Barriere? 1825; H. Massie; John Gossit, 1832

S-2893 1000a B:54 X-0130 HIGH:NEWM HIGH:CONC
a. W-1325 Captain Erasmus Gill
b. Erasmus Gill
c. H. Massie; G. W. Barriere, 1830

S-2894 750a B:62 X-0980 HIGH:BRUS HIGH:JACK
a. W-2518 Lieutenant James Brodus
b. James Brodus
c. None

S-2895 1000a B:183 X-0980 HIGH:PAIN*
a. W-0197 Lieutenant William Pointer; N. Johnson [assignee?]
b. Daniel Clark
c. A. Myers; F. Johnson, 1824
*Source B notation: "Rainsboro."

S-2896 1467a B:183 X-0840 HIGH:PAIN
a. W-0197 Lieutenant William Pointer; N. Johnson [assignee?]
b. Daniel Clark
c. E. Van Pelt; J. Rhodes, 1828

S-2897 617a B:62 X-1005 DELA:CONC
a. W-2518 Lieutenant James Brodus
b. James Brodus
c. None

S-2898 100a B:62 X-0250 HIGH:LIBE
a. W-3676 Richard Broadus*, heir
b. Richard Brodus*
c. None
*So spelled in Sources C & A.

S-2899. *See* S-2467

S-2900. *See* S-2463

S-2901 1300a B:271 X-1000 ROSS:UNIO
S-2905
S-3663
S-3978
a. W-4809 William Porter, 444a
W-3198 John Stockdell; Charles Lynch [assignee?] 100a
W-3097 William Burke; Charles Lynch [assignee?] 200a
W-3714 James Aihen? [Aekin? Ackin? Arkin?] heir to George [Aihen?] 200a
W-4662 Robert Means; H. Young [assignee?]*
W-4087 Walter Ashmore*
W-2373 George Holland; Charles Lynch [assignee?]*
b. Nathaniel Massie
c. None
*Acreage undetermined.

S-2904 100a B:410 X-0840 ROSS:PAXT ROSS:TWIN
a. W-3095 James Soirel? [Sorrell?]
b. Nathaniel Massie
c. None

S-2905. *See* S-2901

S-2906 1000a B:65 X-0130 HIGH:BRUS HIGH:JACK
a. W-0233 Henry Dawson
b. Joseph Winlock
c. Fielding Coppage; Daniel Zink, 1831

S-2907 867a B:52 X-0980 HIGH:BRUS
a. W-4704 Samuel Eddins, 667a
W-1026 William McMeans, 100a
W-3606 John Knight, heir to William [Knight] 100a
b. John Graham
c. None

S-2908 727a B:409 X-1000 PIKE:JACK
S-4705 PIKE:PEEP
a. W-4706 Benjamin Hoomes*
W-2938 Thomas Glascock*
b. John Graham
c. John McClure; C. McCollister, 1836; E. Smith, heirs; J. Moore, 1838; Daniel Davis; L? [S?] Byington, 1839
*Acreage undetermined.

S-2909 444a B:159 X-0150 ROSS:BUCK
a. W-4646 Philip Clayton
b. John Graham
c. None

S-2910 200a B:242 X-0840 ROSS:HUNT
a. W-1629 William Elliott
b. James Herron
c. None

S-2911 100a B:242 X-0840 ROSS:HUNT
a. W-3026 John Araenate? [Arcenate?]
b. John Arrenate*
c. None
*Source B spells Arenate.

S-2912 1000a B:241 X-0840 ROSS:HUNT
S-3816 ROSS:TWIN
a. W-4300 Zachariah Hendrick, heir to Benjamin [Hendrick?] 100a
W-4700 Aaron Smith; Benjamin Bartlett [assignee?] 100a
W-1736 Francis Turner; Robert Marshal [assignee?] 100a
W-4709 Jacob Valentine; William Lipscomb [assignee?] 100a
W-4712 Thomas Dix, 600a
b. James Herron
c. Isaac Bradford; A. Chesnut, 1830; George Kerr, heirs

S-2914 250a C;526 X-0020 ADAM:FRAN
a. W-4057 William Hayes, 200a
W-4284 Daniel Deskin? 100a
b. John Dolaldson? [Donaldson?]
c. John Linton, 1826; H? [M?] & R. Fellows; T. Huston, 1841

S-2918 100a B:320 X-0840 ROSS:TWIN
a. W-3710 Philip Finn
b. Cornelius R. Sedam
c. None

S-2919 333a B:507 X-0840 ROSS:HUNT
a. W-3654 William Tyree, heir to John [Tyree?] 100a
W-4495 Henry Christian; Alexander Woods [assignee?] 233a
b. Furgus Moore
c. None

S-2925 667a B:65 X-1004 UNIO:JERO
a. W-4730* --
b. Beverly Roy
c. None
*Source C shows no assignment of this warrant number.

S-2926 1290a B:181 X-0840 FAYE:WAYN
a. W-3133 William Randolph, representative
b. Richard Bibb
c. John Linch; George Yeoman, 1826; Jared Benjamin; B. Yeoman; Polly Benjamin; N. Coffman, 1840

S-2928 1140a B:70 X-0940 HIGH:FAIR
a. W-4663 James Lovell
b. John Wilkins, Junior
c. -- Beard & -- Winegar; J. Gunn, 1824; Mary Worley; John Hogsett, 1836; P. Stooks; J. H. Patton, 1842

S-2928 936a B:70 X-0940 HIGH:PAIN
a. W-4663 James Lovell
b. John Wilkins, Junior
c. None

S-2929 80a B;469 X-0670 ROSS:TWIN
a. W-0635 Captain Archibald Denholm
b. John Harvie
c. None

S-2929 200a B:469 X-0670 ROSS:TWIN
a. W-0635 Captain Archibald Denholm
b. John Harvie
c. None

S-2933 200a C:404 X-0800 ADAM:SPRI
or ADAM:MONR
a. W-3149 James Bland
b. Nathaniel Massie
c. None

S-2933. *See also* S-2469

S-2936 1000a B:46 X-0270 BROW:CLAR
a. W-2739 Charles Petteson*, heir to Thomas Patteson*; W[illiam] Lytle [assignee?]
b. Charles Patterson
c. John Dawson; Michael Kennedy, 1825; C. Patterson; William Niel, 1828; James Ross; John S. Beasley, 1839; T. Allen, 1841; J. Carless; P. L. Wilson, 1841; H. McGuier? [McGuinn?]; J. Rounds, Junior; J. J. Higgins
*So spelled in Source C.

S-2937 820a B:46 X-0270 BROW:CLAR
CLER: --*
a. W-2739 Charles Petteson**, heir to Thomas Patteson**; W[illiam] Lytle [assignee?]
b. Charles Patterson
c. Moses Bradbury; John Boals [Bolles?] 1823; Benjamin Bradley; John Palmer, 1826; Daniel F. Barney, 1826; Alexander Donaldson; James Woods, 1823; Nathan Eldon; James Rounds, 1824; -- Watts & -- Palmer, 1826; John Terell; John Walker, 1826; W. Watts; A. Michaelree? 1834; John Park
*Source B does not mention Clermont County.
**So spelled in Source C.

S-2938 1100a B:46 X-0270 CLER:TATE
BROW:CLAR*
a. W-4754 Jones Allen; James Garland [assignee?] 100a
W-4756 Jones Allen; assignee of James Bates, representative of Thomas Bates, 200a
W-4757 Jones Allen; Robert Wilkins [assignee?] 200a
W-4764 John Allen; assignee of Thomas Grubbs, 100a
W-4762 Jones Allen; assignee of William Murray, 100a
W-4761 Jones Allen; assignee of Reubin Beverly, 200a
W-4765 Abraham Scott, 200a
b. George F. Straws
c. William Lytle; T. Kirley, 1823; Z. Chapman, 1825; James Carter; George Hunt, 1827; S. Danbury, 1829; J. Johnson, 1833; W. S. Patton, 1835
*Source A does not mention Brown County.

S-2939 1000a B:45 X-0270 CLER:WILL BROW:CLAR BROW:PIKE
a. W-2739 Charles Petteson*, heir to Thomas Patteson*
b. William Lytle
c. A. Earley; N. L. Boyd, 1842
*So spelled in Source C.

S-2940 1250a B:46 X-0270 BROW:CLAR BROW:PIKE
a. W-2882 Peter McCune, 200a
W-2878 Arthur Hagen, heir, 400a
W-1530 James Dailey, 200a
W-2889 Jeremiah Simpson, 200a
W-2891 David Porter, 100a
W-2751 Patrick Hearagas? [Hargis?] 100a
W-2899 Alexander Read, 50a
b. James Morrison
c. -- Heldrick, *et al*; Alfred Ogden, 1828; Jacob Shane; John Thompson, 1827; Richard Spinney; J. Rilea, 1838; David Dunwoodie; J. S. Beasley, 1840; W. Robins; A. C. H. Cotterill, 1842

S-2941 1333a B:75 X-0663 BROW:PERR HIGH: --*
a. W-4191 Edward Lewis, heir
b. Edward Lewis
c. Timothy Kirley; S? [L?] Hopkins; Robert Chalfant, 1828; Unknown; F? [H?] Bingaman, 1832; John O'Brien; P. L. Wilson, 1840; S. S. Liggett; J. S. Beasley, 1841
*Source B does not mention Highland County.

S-2942 1000a B:77 X-0270 CLER:WILL BROW:PIKE
a. W-2739 Charles Petteson*, heir to Thomas Patteson*
b. William Lytle
c. Daniel Bryan; Archibald Lewis, 1826
*So spelled in Source C.

S-2944 445a B:45 X-0663 CLER:WILL BROW: --*
a. W-4692 Samuel Coleman
b. Samuel Coleman
c. William Lytle; William Waters, 1825; J. Johnson, 1829; N. Sinks; S? [L?] Brown, 1828; C. B. Huber, 1836
*Source B does not mention Brown County.

S-2945 100a B:45 X-0663 CLER:WILL BROW: --*
a. W-3723 James Thompson, assignee [of?] Spencer Edwards
b. James Thompson
c. William Lytle; Jonathan Johnston, 1823; C. B. Huber, 1836
*Source B does not mention Brown County.

S-2946 100a B:46 X-0663 CLER:WILL BROW: --*
a. W-0978 Bartholomew Ragan
b. Alexander Humphreys
c. Thomas L? [S?] Foot; F. White, 1824; T. Kain, 1826; John Jameson, 1827; W. Blazier; E. B. Huber, 1840
*Source B does not mention Brown County.

S-2947 200a B:78 X-0663 CLER:WILL
a. W-3110 Thomas McGlen, heir to John Gray
b. William Chambers
c. None

S-2948. *See* S-2286

S-2949 525a B:77 X-0270 CLER:TATE CLER:WILL BROW:PIKE
a. W-2352 Martin Hawkins; assignee [of?] William Irving, 200a
W-2356 Martin Hawkins; assignee [of?] John Humphreys, 100a
W-2386 Martin Hawkins; assignee [of?] Joseph Dill, 100a
W-2384 Martin Hawkins; assignee [of?] Thomas Haldrop, 100a
W-3705 William McElroy; Evan Francis [assignee?] 100a*
b. William Lytle
c. T. Morgan; J. Johnson, 1828
*Warrant already used for S-2286.

S-2950 800a E:151 X-0663 CLER:WILL
a. W-2387 Martin Hawkins; assignee [of?] Absalom? Woodson, 100a
W-2389 Martin Hawkins; assignee [of?] Francis Allen, 200a
W-2394 Martin Hawkins; assignee [of?] W. Bryant, 200a
W-2399 Thomas Aslin; [assignee?] Henry Tugle, Martin Hawkins, 100a
W-2400 Martin Hawkins; assignee [of?] W. Blyse, 100a
W-2401 Martin Hawkins; assignee [of?] W. Wiloby, 100a
b. Martin Hawkins
c. W. Johnston, 1824; P. Brewer; R. Tweed, 1826

S-2951 884a B:78 X-0270 CLER:TATE
a. W-1507 John Madden, 200a
W-1452 Matthey Rhea, 684a
b. Mathew Rhea
c. -- Hunt, -- Pyatt, & Company; J. D. Morris, 1828; E. Downing; E. Frazier, 1839; J. P. Myers

S-2952 774a B:77 X-0270 CLER:TATE
a. W-1168 Ambrose Dudley, heir to Robert Dudley
b. Ambrose Dudley
c. None

S-2953 180a B:199 X-0663 BROW:PIKE
a. W-2739 Charles Petteson*, heir to Thomas Patteson*
b. Charles Patterson
c. D. M. Shotwell, 1828; J. Bennett & J. Thomas; F. Bingaman, 1834
*So spelled in Source C.

S-2954 500a B:78 X-0270 CLER:TATE
a. W-3662 William Johnson, 100a
W-3755 David Henderson, heir to John [Henderson] 100a
W-4505 Henry Barton, 100a
W-4434 Samuel Derossett, 200a

S-2954 [continued]
b. John Clay
c. S. A. Combs; Jonathan D. Morris, 1832; M. Hutchings; T. L? [S?] Shields, 1833; D. Osborn; -- Maham, 1832; G. Hampton; R. McFarland, 1837; George R. Noble; R. W. Clark, 1836

S-2955 205a B:78 X-0270 CLER: --* BROW:CLAR
a. W-2540 John Hawkins
b. John Hawkins
c. William Lytle; W. Penn, 1824; B. Penn; S. Wert, 1826; G. Hunt, 1827; C. Darsey? [Dorsey?]; D. M. Shotwell, 1828; Robert Rachford, 1832; Unknown; S? [L?] Rounds, 1837
*Source B mentions Clermont County but says "lies in Brown [County]."

S-2956 540a B:195 X-0660 WARR:HAMI*
a. W-0137 Richard Stark
b. Richard Starke
c. None
*Source B notation: "Hopkinsville."

S-2957 500a B:127 X-0666 CLER:WILL
a. W-4660 Daniel de Benneville
b. Daniel de Benneville
c. William Lytle; William C. Moore, 1826; J. Taylor; Thomas John, 1831; -- Huber & -- Pease, 1837

S-2958 375a B:47 X-1120 BROW:PLEA
a. W-1963 William Taliaferro, heir to Colonel [William] Taliaferro
b. William Taliaferro
c. None

S-2959 287a B:136 X-1301 BROW:WASH
a. W-0785 John Barnett [Bernard?] heir to W. Bernard
b. John Bernard
c. Unknown; S? [L?] Wardlow, 1830; P. Vance, 1832; A. Singleton; S. McCune, 1834; -- Wilson & -- Middleton, 1842

S-2960 580a B:48 X-0840 HIGH:FAIR CLIN:GREE
a. W-4585 Anthony Singleton
b. Anthony Singleton
c. S. McCune; A. E. Strickle, 1838

S-2961 672a C:125 X-0800 CLER:FRAN CLER:WASH
S-3616
S-7362
a. W-4647 Nicholas Carrele*
W-1921 General Robert Lawson*
W-5941 William Higganbotham; George Galloway, David Gwynne, William Keys [assignees?]*
b. John Obannon
c. W. Lyme; A. C. Day, 1836; J. Pigman, heirs
*Acreage assignable could not be determined.

S-2962 1000a B:350 X-0740 GREE:ROSS
a. W-2740 Captain James Wright
b. James Wright
c. None

S-2965 200a B:351 X-1170 CLIN:VERN
a. W-2724* John Cheseround?; John Kirkwood? [Kirkweel? assignee?]
b. Stephen Tomlin
c. None
*This warrant good for 100a only, according to Source C.

S-2966 200a B:352 X-0663 HIGH:UNIO CLIN:CLAR
a. W-4361 Daniel Williams
b. Lewis Jennings
c. None

S-2970 1011a B:357 X-0640 CLIN:GREE CLIN:WAYN
a. W-1820 William Moore
b. William Moore
c. S. Harrod; Lewis Wright, 1837

S-2971 175a B:110 X-0423 ADAM:LIBE
a. W-0019 Brigadier General [Daniel] Morgan
b. John Crawford
c. None

S-2972 100a B:260 X-1040 ADAM:FRAN
a. W-3985 William Rowe
b. David Edie
c. E. Worthington; A. Parker & D. Eddie; Thomas Huston, 1832

S-2973 1000a B:125 X-0420 BROW:JACK
S-3100
a. W-3874 Charles Morgan, heir to John Morgan
b. Charles Morgan
c. John Cox; Abraham Evans, 1826; Rachel McMannis; Joseph White, 1826; William Donaldson; J. Meharry, 1835 "error"; T. Butt; J. H. Johnston, 1842

S-2975 667a B:125 X-0760 PIKE:BENT
a. W-3874 Charles Morgan, heir to John Morgan
b. Charles Morgan
c. F. Stokes, 1830

S-2976 444a B:166 X-0130 ADAM:TIFF ADAM:MEIG
a. W-4729 Robert Rankin
b. Robert Rankin
c. None

S-2977 600a B:116 X-0340 UNIO:DARB
a. W-3108 Robert White, 100a
W-3241 William Putty, 100a
W-3560 Humphrey Arnold, heir to Elijah [Arnold?] 100a
W-4731 Lawrence Harrison; Lucas Sullivant [assignee?] 300a
b. Samuel Robertson
c. None

S-2979 1300a B:116 X-0340 UNIO:ALLE
a. W-4731 Lawrence Harrison
b. Lucas Sullivant
c. John Coolidge; Alexander Reed; R. P. Mann, 1831

S-2980 800a B:114 X-0340 UNIO:ALLE
a. W-4594 John Munford Gregory, heir to John Gregory
b. John Munford Gregory
c. Unknown; S. G. Strong, 1836

S-2981 1000a B:113 X-0340 UNIO:ALLE
a. W-4792 Andrew Torborn, heir to Peter Duncan
b. Andrew Torborn
c. Hector McNiel; Lyne Starling, 1826; Unknown; M. S. Butler, 1836; L. Sullivant; J. W. Evans, 1839; -- Starling & -- Kirby

S-2982 1000a B:215 X-0110 UNIO:YORK
a. W-4792 Andrew Torborn, heir to Peter Duncan
b. Andrew Torborn
c. None

S-2983 1000a B:113 X-0340 UNIO:ALLE
a. W-4792 Andrew Torborn, heir to Peter Duncan
b. Andrew Torborn
c. Unknown; Adam Miller, 1824; N. McWilliams; Lucas Sullivant; S. McWilliams

S-2984 1000a B:215 X-0110 UNIO:YORK
a. W-4594 John Munford Gregory, heir to John Gregory
b. John M[unford] Gregory
c. None

S-2985 1667a B:114 X-1180 MADI:JEFF
a. W-4792 Andrew Torborn, heir to Peter Duncan
b. Andrew Torbone*
c. Thomas D. Harris; Lyne Starling, 1828; J. Johnson, heirs; Thomas Morris, 1840
*Source B spells Torborn.

S-2986 178a D:104 X-1005 FRAN:NORW FRAN:PRAI
a. W-1985 William Bussell
b. William Bussell*
c. James Taylor, 1826; Unknown
*Source B spells Russell.

S-2988 225a D:105 X-1005 FRAN:NORW FRAN:PRAI
a. W-3045 William Southerland
b. John Seddon
c. Unknown; Lyne Starling, 1829; E. Bachus; J. C. Brodrick, 1833

S-2989 1070a B:66 X-0750 UNIO:MILL DELA:CONC
a. W-0127 Lieutenant Jonathan Smith
b. John Philips
c. Orris Parish; P. B. Wilcox, 1826; John Wilkins, Junior; John Keesler; W. Bell, 1829; Harvey Johnson, 1829; Susan Bickley; Sydney Gilbert, 1836 (Union County); Daniel? [David?] Duvall; Hiram Bickley; Benjamin F. Allen, 1833 (Delaware County)

S-2990 666a B:66 X-1005 UNIO:JERO DELA:CONC
a. W-0127 Lieutenant Jonathan Smith
b. John Philips
c. John Wilkins, Junior; M. D. Pettibone, 1824; Otis Millington

S-2991 1330a B:66 X-1005 UNIO:JERO
a. W-0671 Ebenezer Branham, 200a
W-2184 Thomas Cooke, heir, 200a
W-0127 Lieutenant Jonathan Smith, 930a
b. John Philips
c. John Adams; John Wilkins; Lyne Starling, 1831

S-2992 1100a B:68 X-0750 UNIO:MILL DELA:CONC
a. W-2668 James Tompkins, [heir?] of Daniel Tompkins
b. William Croghan
c. Levi Hinton; Christ[ian? -opher?] Myers; Daniel Long; Thomas Bradford, 1833

S-2993 860a B:68 X-0750 DELA:SCIO
a. W-1977 Samuel Yowell, 100a
W-4218 Stephen Smith, heir to Richard Smith, 100a
W-4217 Charles Smith, 100a
W-0025 Major William Croghan, 560a
b. William Croghan
c. G. Houston

S-2994 667a B:68 X-0750 DELA:SCIO
a. W-4237 Edward Jackson, 100a
W-2668 James Tompkins, [heir?] of Daniel Tompkins, 567a
b. William Croghan
c. John Graham; Nathaniel Hull, 1827; Milo D. Pettibone, 1839

S-2995 800a B:48 X-1005 UNIO:MILL DELA:CONC
a. W-4598 Isaac Jeffries, representative[s] of
b. Isaac Jeffries* representatives [of]
c. None
*Source B spells Jefferies.

S-2996 727a B:49 X-1004 UNIO:MILL
a. W-4598 Isaac Jeffries, representative[s] of
b. Isaac Jeffries* representatives [of]
c. None
*Source B spells Jefferies.

S-2997 1140a B:48 X-1004 UNIO:MILL DELA:CONC
a. W-4598 Isaac Jeffries, representative[s] of
b. Isaac Jeffries* representatives [of]
c. None
*Source B spells Jefferies.

S-2998 1086a B:53 X-0750 UNIO:MILL
a. W-2291 Lieutenant Samuel Seldon
b. Samuel Seldon
c. Isaac Smith Brewer; Newton Logan, John C. Burns

S-2999 464a B:52 X-1005 FRAN:WASH
a. W-2291 Lieutenant Samuel Seldon
b. Samuel Seldon
c. None

S-3000 450a B:53 X-1005 FRAN:NORW
a. W-2291 Lieutenant Samuel Seldon
b. Samuel Seldon
c. None

S-3001 540a B:56 X-1005 FRAN:NORW
a. W-4690 William Price, assignee [of?] Ephraim Hunt, 200a
W-4703 Reuben Jackson, 200a
W-4705 Bartlett Hawkins, 140a
b. William Price
c. None

S-3002 560a B:56 X-1005 FRAN:NORW
a. W-3008 Frederick Nance, 200a
W-4630 Patrick Macmahon, 100a
W-4691 David Walch; John Hume [assignee?] 200a
W-4705 Bartlett Hawkins, 60a
b. William Price
c. Robert Shouff; W. Francher, 1838

S-3003 174a C:217 X-1005 UNIO:JERO DELA:CONC
a. W-0025 Major William Croghan
b. William Croghan
c. None

S-3004 667a B:55 X-1005 FRAN:WASH
a. W-4009 James Adams, heir to John Adams, deceased, 200a
W-4405 William Carswell, 100a
W-4562 John Jones, heir to James Jones, 100a
W-2850 John Stockdell, 100a
W-4563 John Jones, heir to Richard Jones, 100a
W-3763 --*
b. Robert Means
c. James Condrin? [Cendrin? Codrin?]; B. Sells, 1827; J. Condrin? & -- Kias; E. Ellis, 1828; R. Brotherton, 1833; Jacob Rodgers; S. S. Davis, 1834
*This warrant number not assigned in Source C.

S-3005 667a B:53 X-1005 UNIO:JERO
a. W-3533 Peter Talbot, heir to William Worsham
b. Peter Talbot
c. Samuel Symon? [Lymon?]; M. L? [S?] Butler, 1836; William Magill

S-3006 1000a B:53 X-1005 UNIO:MILL
a. W-3533 Peter Talbot, heir to William Worsham
b. Peter Talbot
c. J. P. Edwards; M. S. Butler, 1836; Robert White; E. P. Johnson; J. Layman; W. McCarty, *et al*

S-3007 1087a B:52 X-0750 UNIO:DOVE DELA:SCIO
a. W-4702 Philip Sausum? [Sausiun?] 667a
W-4606 William Higgin Colhame? [Coltrame?] 400a
W-4665 James Armstrong, 20a?
b. John Graham, "Washington City"*
c. Margaret Baley; Elem Vining, "error"; Unknown; Andrew Young, 1827; J. W. C. Graham; R. Broome? 1833
*Source B notation.

S-3008 590a B:52 X-0750 DELA:SCIO
a. W-4665 James Armstrong*
W-4706 Benjamin Hoomes*
b. John Graham
c. William Radford; Ray Thomas, 1835
*Acreage not given.

S-3009 233a B:60 X-1005 FRAN:WASH
a. W-2708 Elizabeth Burk, representative of John Burk, deceased, 100a
W-3766 John Barns, 133a
b. Robert Means
c. Unknown; Samuel Shipman; M. L. Sullivant, 1831

S-3010 805a B:50 X-1005 FRAN:WASH
a. W-4526 Hincha Gilliam, heir
b. Hincha Gilliam
c. Stephen Grace; E. Converse, 1837; Thomas Harris; C. Higgins, 1835

S-3011 605a B:50 X-1005 FRAN:WASH
a. W-4526 Hincha Gilliam, heir
b. Hincha Gilliam
c. B. W. Ladd; Henry Huston, 1829; Hugh Hastings; William Davis, 1834; Jeremiah McLene, 1832; C. Higgins, 1837; T. Harris; Thomas Hawes; E. Converse, 1837; B. Ladd, heirs; C. Rogers, 1837; D. D. Warner, 1839

S-3012 617a B:50 X-1005 FRAN:WASH FRAN:NORW
a. W-4526 Hincha Gilliam, heir
b. Hincha Gilliam
c. Elias Pegg; J. P. Ladd; Jeremiah McLane; James? [Joseph?] Siberson; R. Brotherton, 1833

S-3013 440a B:50 X-1005 FRAN:NORW
a. W-4526 Hincha Gilliam, heir
b. Hincha Gilliam
c. John P. Ladd; Henry Huston, 1829; Hugh Hasting; C. Davis, 1834

S-3014 199a B:50 X-1005 DELA:CONC UNIO: --*
a. W-4526 Hincha Gilliam, heir
b. Hincha Gilliam
c. M. Wright, forfeited 1839
*Source B does not mention Union County.

S-3015* 400a -- -- HIGH: --
a. --
b. R. Means
c. W. Murfin, 1823
*Mentioned in Source B only (at top of page above S-3012). *See also* S-2739

S-3016 1000a B:58 X-0133 ROSS:PAXT PIKE:PERR
a. W-4494 Moore Fauntleroy
b. Robert Pollard
c. Austin Buchannon; William Reed, 1831; -- Graham & -- Dun; L? [S?] Byington; J. Silcott; T. Reid, 1842

S-3017 1000a B:58 X-0133 PIKE:PERR
a. W-4494 Moore Fauntleroy
b. Robert Pollard
c. None

S-3018 1000a B:59 X-0133 PIKE:PERR HIGH:PAIN ROSS: --*
a. W-1617 Lieutenant John Perry
b. Benjamin Wynkoop
c. None
*Source B does not mention Ross County.

S-3019 850a B:59 X-0133 PIKE:PERR HIGH: --*
a. W-1617 Lieutenant John Perry
b. Benjamin Wynkoop
c. H. Eubanks; J. Dunham, 1826
*Source B mentions Highland County but corrects to Pike County; notation: "Cynthiann."

S-3020 2667a B:399 X-1004 DELA:THOM
a. W-4744 Leonard Cooper
b. Jonathan Clark
c. James W. Crawford; William Gold, 1830; John Bacon; H. Bedinger; Deemas Adams; -- Baum & -- Perry, 1839

S-3021 2000a B:400 X-1005 DELA:THOM
a. W-4744 Leonard Cooper
b. Jonathan Clark
c. Elijah Bowditch?; William M. Warren, 1833; Samson Russell; -- Baum & -- Perry, 1839

S-3022 617a B:59 X-1005 FRAN:NORW
a. W-1617 Lieutenant John Perry
b. Benjamin Wynkoop
c. None

S-3023 200a B:59 X-0840 HIGH:PERR
a. W-1617 Lieutenant John Perry
b. Benjamin Wynkoop
c. C. Benner; J. M. Johnson, 1836; Samuel Beard; -- Kirley & -- Starling, 1831

S-3024 767a B:133 X-1300 BROW:PLEA BROW:CLAR BROW:SCOT
a. W-4770 Robert Gamble, 667a
W-4204 Jacob Philips; William George, Duncan McArthur [assignees?] 100a*
b. Robert Gamble
c. James Smith; William Wall? 1825; T. C. Leming? [Seming?]; J. S? [L?] Beasley, 1842
*This warrant already used on S-1488.

S-3025 200a B:65 X-0840 ROSS:PAXT HIGH: --*
a. W-1067 --**
b. Henry Van***
c. Henry Vance***; Adam Brouse, 1828; -- Kirley & -- Starling, 1831
*Both counties mentioned, but on wrong line.
**Source C does not show that this warrant number was used.
***So spelled.

S-3026 1000a B:67 X-1000 FRAN:PRAI
a. W-1986 Lieutenant John Townes
b. John Townes
c. John Gilmore; M. L. Sullivant, 1837

S-3027 1000a B:67 X-0340 FRAN:PLEA
a. W-1986 Lieutenant John Townes
b. John Townes
c. None

S-3028 652a D:324 X-0070 FRAN:PLEA
a. W-1986 Lieutenant John Townes
b. John Gilmore
c. None

S-3029 400a B:135 X-0250 HIGH:LIBE
a. W-0325 Marquis Calmes
b. Marquis Calmes
c. None

S-3034 340a B:173 X-0250 HIGH:LIBE
a. W-0325 Marquis Calmes
b. Marquis Calmes
c. None

S-3036 1300a B:164 X-1000 ROSS:UNIO
a. W-2452 Colonel William Davies
b. William Davis
c. None

S-3037. *See* S-2462

S-3040 400a B:250 X-1120 BROW:PLEA
a. W-0635 Captain Archibald Denholm; Edward Lynen? [assignee?]
b. John Harvie
c. None

S-3041 600a B:189 X-1000 ROSS:FRAN
a. W-0815 Brigadier General Charles Scott
b. Charles Scott
c. None

S-3043 575a B:78 X-0663 BROW:PERR
a. W-3784 George Burroughs, assignee of John Hughes, 200a
W-4058 Thomas Waddy, 200a
W-4335 Francis Litchfield, 100a
W-4059 Beacham Hull, 125a
W-4713 Norman Harvey, 100a
b. John Breckenridge

S-3043 [continued]
c. Robert Campbell, 1828; John Scanlon [*also* Scanline]; John Vogle; M. Dennison; P. L. Wilson, 1839; J? [I?] Slatterman, heirs

S-3043 575a B:78 X-0663 BROW:PERR HIGH: --*
a. W-4075 Elizabeth Davis, representative of Arthur Davis, 200a
W-4062 Benjamin Powell, 200a
W-4059 Beacham Hull, 75a
b. John Breckenridge
c. None
*Source B does not mention Highland County.

S-3044 394a D:341 X-0663 BROW:PERR
a. W-4727 Samuel Eddins
b. John Breckenridge
c. Isaac Haines; John Bingaman, 1834; J? [I?] Breckenridge, heirs; D. Crawford, 1841; M. Haines; T. C. Bomber? 1841; G. Haines; P. L? [S?] Wilson

S-3045 1336a D:346 X-0663 BROW:PERR CLIN:JEFF
a. W-4743 George Raiborne, 200a
W-4771 Stephen Woodrum, 200a
W-4783 George Rose, representative of, 200a
W-4711 Isaac Procter, 200a
W-4780 Austin Gilliam, representative of, 100a
W-4719 William G. Payne [assignee?]; John Evans, heir to John McDowell, 100a
W-4777 Daniel Ellis, representative of, 100a
W-4735 Henry Moss, 236a?
b. John Breckenridge
c. Robert Campbell, 1828; John Breckenridge, heirs; G. H. Bohrer, 1832; F. Bingaman, 1834; Nathaniel Batson, 1827; W. H. Trimble, 1839 (Brown County); F. Casto (Clinton County)

S-3046 1089a B:79 X-0663 BROW:PERR
a. W-4726 William B. Wallace, 889a
W-4748 Jones Allen, assignee [of?] John Riscrop? 200a
b. John Breckenridge
c. John Breckenridge, heirs; W. Humber, 1833, forfeited 1838

S-3047 200a B:360 X-0663 BROW:PIKE
a. W-4719* William G. Payne, assignee [of?] John Evans, heir to John McDowel, deceased
b. John Breckenridge
c. Timothy Kirby; John Breckenridge, heirs; N. Ellis, 1833
*This warrant, for 100 acres only, was used in S-3045; but see W-4720, however.

S-3048 200a B:361 X-0663 BROW:PIKE
a. W-4747 James Jenkins
b. William Lytle
c. Unknown; J. M. Trimble, 1837; J. Pedan; P. L? [S?] Wilson, 1841

S-3049* 100a -- -- --
a. --
b. Samuel Steel
c. -- Smock & -- Steele; Alfred Beasley, 1828
*Not listed in Source A, but is shown in Source B in proper sequence.

S-3050 333a B:199 X-1080 CLER:WAYN
a. W-1937 Major Francis Taylor
b. Francis Taylor
c. Z. Chapman, 1823; F. Taylor; S? [L?] B. Cleveland, 1825; James Taylor; C. Smith, 1837

S-3052 2800a B:178 X-0423 ADAM:LIBE
S-3571
a. W-1730 Lieutenant Charles Yarborough, 2000a?
W-4722 Jasper Hughes, 444a?
W-0815 Brigadier General Charles Scott, 356a?
b. Nathaniel Massie
c. Thomas Robertson; Joseph? [James?] Riggs, 1823; J. Currie

S-3053 1000a B:132 X-0150 ROSS:BUCK
S-3074
a. W-0701 Lieutenant Luke Cannon
b. Luke Cannon
c. N? [M?] Cochran; A. Cochran, 1842; J. McArthur, heirs

S-3054 210a B:174 X-0423 ADAM:LIBE
a. W-2452 Colonel William Davies
b. William Davis
c. None

S-3054 700a B:174 X-0423 ADAM:LIBE
S-3567
a. W-2452 Colonel William Davies
b. William Davis
c. A. March; James Hood, 1840

S-3054 430a B:175 X-0423 ADAM:LIBE
S-3055
a. W-2452 Colonel William Davies
b. William Davis
c. None

S-3058 570a B:177 X-0130 ADAM:TIFF
a. W-0815 Brigadier General Charles Scott*
W-4801 Hilman Minnis, representative of*
W-4722 Jasper Hughes*
b. Nathaniel Massie
c. Percival Lovejoy; G. D. Darlington, 1834
*Acreage undeterminable.

S-3059 400a C:114 X-0130 ADAM:TIFF
a. W-1928 Major Tarlton Woodson
b. Tarlton Woodson
c. George Purtee, heirs; A. Ellison, 1823; Samuel Thoroman, 1828

S-3061 100a C:125 X-0130 ADAM:TIFF
a. W-0463 John Jowett, heir to Mat[thew Jowett]
b. John Jouitt
c. Samuel Black, 1826; John Linton

S-3062 200a B:176 X-0040 ADAM:TIFF
a. W-0463 John Jowett, heir to Mat[thew Jowett]
b. John Jouitt
c. None

S-3065 700a B:159 X-0980 HIGH:BRUS PIKE: --*
a. W-3504 John Stackhouse, 100a
W-2530 Thomas Gaines, 200a
W-2559 John Cowgall, 100a**
W-4491 David Walch, 200a?
W-4509 John Hume, assignee of Frank Graves, assignee of Benjamin [Graves] 100a
b. John Hume
c. None
*Source B does not mention Highland County.
**Warrant also listed on S-1680, probably in error.

S-3066 200a B:243 X-0570 CLER:TATE CLER:FRAN
a. W-0841 John Collins; John W. Semple [assignee?] 100a
W-3815 Mary King; William Lytle [assignee?] 100a
b. Richard C[lough] Anderson
c. None

S-3067 1691a B:202 X-1000 ROSS:UNIO
a. W-3155 Henry Salmons, 100a
W-3436 James Fair, 100a*
W-3468 Christopher Francis, 100a
W-4579 John Coffin, representative [of?] 100a
W-4580 Samuel Coffin, representative [of?] 100a
W-4581 Edward Davis; Theodorick Nowell, assignee [of?] Larkin Branson, heir at law to John Branson, 200a
W-4616 Thomas Sweeney, 200a
W-4624 Francis Graves; assignee [of?] Major Merritt, 200a
W-4663 James Lovell, 591a?
b. John Wilkins, Junior
c. H. Brush; W. H. Douglas, 1841
*Warrant was also used on S-1646, probably incorrectly.

S-3072 100a B:433 X-1350 ADAM:JEFF
a. W-0231 John Mills
b. Benjamin Goodin
c. None

S-3073 100a B:433 X-1042 ADAM:JEFF
a. W-0231 John Mills
b. Benjamin Goodin
c. None

S-3074. *See* S-3053

S-3075 300a B:273 X-0150 ROSS:PAIN
a. W-4801 Hilman Minnis, representative of
b. Nathaniel Massie
c. None

S-3077 667a C:375 X-0130 ADAM:FRAN
a. W-4721 Erasmus Gill
b. Benjamin Temple
c. A. Ellison, Junior, 1826

S-3078 100a B:194 X-1300 BROW:CLAR
a. W-1151 William Martin
b. Benjamin J. Brice
c. None

S-3079 700a B:188 X-1300 BROW:FRAN BROW:PLEA BROW:SCOT
a. W-3261 Aaron, Reynolds, 200a
W-3256 Joseph Strother, assignee, 200a
W-3254 Thomas Thornhill, 200a
W-3650 Matthew Sulser, 100a
b. Benjamin Strother
c. Lucas Sullivant; Samuel Tucker, 1826

S-3080 1000a B:92 X-0180 GREE:ROSS
a. W-0240 Lieutenant Colonel Thomas Posey
b. Thomas Posey
c. W. Browder; J. Browder, 1825; John Sheely, Junior [*also* Shealey]; R. Nesbit, 1827; James Johnson, 1830; J. M. Renton? [Ruston?] 1832

S-3081 1000a B:92 X-0180 GREE:SILV*
a. W-0240 Lieutenant Colonel Thomas Posey
b. Thomas Posey
c. W. A. G. Posey & A. Posey; David Dean, 1831; Benjamin Shealey; Jonathan Bayles; Elizabeth Cullens; John Weaver, 1831
*Source B notation: "By Jamestown."

S-3083 50a B:83 X-0423 ADAM:LIBE
a. W-1844* Robert McQuillen
b. Richard Spear
c. None
*This warrant already completely used on S-0866 and S-2735.

S-3084 100a B:258 X-0420 BROW:HUNT
a. W-2604 John Rowman
b. [Nathaniel?] Beasley & [William] Ledom*
c. None
*Source B spells Leedom; Source C spells Leedon.

S-3085 100a B:166 X-0800 ADAM:SPRI
a. W-4039 Thomas Hull
b. David Edie
c. None

S-3086 800a B:266 X-0130 ADAM:WAYN ADAM:WINC
a. W-0303 Captain Robert White
b. Robert White
c. James McKee; L? [S?] Cole, 1839

S-3088 85a B:165 X-1100 ADAM:GREE
a. W-1062 Samuel Smith
b. Andrew Ellison
c. None

S-3089 100a D:161 X-0420 BROW:BYRD
a. W-0781 Wyatt Elliott
b. Andrew Gatewood
c. None

S-3090 150a B:168 X-0800 ADAM:SPRI
a. W-2629 Captain Simon Morgan
b. Simon Morgan
c. None

S-3091 100a B:167 X-0800 ADAM:GREE SCIO:NILE
a. W-3696 Martin Madder
b. Martin Madder
c. G. Mitchell; George Corwine, 1841

S-3092 200a B:265 X-0420 BROW:UNIO BROW:HUNT
a. W-3080 William Johnson
b. Caleb Tate
c. None

S-3093 100a B:262 X-0420 BROW:HUNT
a. W-3696 Martin Madder
b. Martin Madder
c. None

S-3094* 500a -- -- BROW: --
a. --
b. Abraham Shepherd
c. Benjamin Bayless, 1824
*Listed in Source B only (at top of page, before S-3084).

S-3097 700a B:265 X-1040* ADAM:FRAN
a. W-1203 Captain Beverly Stubblefield
b. Beverly Stubblefield
c. Jacob Tener, 1824
*"Northwest fork [of] . . ."

S-3099 200a B:410 X-0660 GREE:XENI
a. W-1203 Captain Beverly Stubblefield
b. Beverly Stubblefield
c. None

S-3100. *See* S-2973

S-3107 100a B:526 X-0800 ADAM:GREE
a. W-4254 Anthony W. White
b. Alexander Parker
c. Fitch Ives; William Parks, 1826

S-3108* 100a -- -- SCIO:BRUS
a. --
b. Alexander Parker
c. John Smith; James Wallace, 1824
*Listed in Source B only (in proper sequence).

S-3112 100a C:291 X-1110 ADAM:GREE
a. W-1863* John Armond; John Blackwell [assignee?]
b. Thomas McClanahan
c. None
*This warrant already used in S-2023.

S-3117 50a B:390 X-0420 ADAM:LIBE
a. W-1043* John Head
b. Robert Ellison
c. William Silcott; James Hood, 1841
*Warrant already used in S-2593.

S-3118 150a C:205 X-0300 PIKE:JACK
S-6460
a. W-1691 Anthony Chavalier; Samuel Tannen? [assignee?] 50a
W-1050 John Britton, 50a
W-3986 John Etherington? 50a
b. Andrew Ellison
c. None

S-3120 500a B:159 X-0150 ROSS:BUCK
a. W-4627 Henry Bedinger
b. Henry Bedinger
c. None

S-3122 1000a B:248 X-0150 X-0840 ROSS:BUCK
a. W-4793 William Pyle
b. Thomas Worthington
c. None

S-3130 100a B:235 X-0840 ROSS:TWIN
a. W-3258 John Wood
b. James Kerr & D[uncan] McArthur
c. J? [I?] Hanes; James McMullen, 1825

S-3132 100a B:235 X-0840 ROSS:TWIN
a. W-3604 James Sargent
b. James Sargeant
c. None

S-3133 160a B:240 X-0133 PIKE:PERR
a. W-4267 John Smith
b. Thomas Hoff
c. None

S-3133 1260a B:240 X-0133 PIKE:PERR
a. W-4415 Richard Burnell; assignee of representative of Thomas Talley, 100a
W-4413 John Bailey, assignee of representative of Mathieu Cain, 200a
W-4411 Patrick Punet? [Prenit? Pruit?] 200a
W-4416 William Reynolds, 400a
W-4267 John Smith, 360a?
b. Thomas Hoff
c. None

S-3134 400a B:159 X-0133 PIKE:PERR
a. W-3485 Francis Graves, 200a
W-4420 William Reynolds, 200a
b. Thomas Flowers*
c. J. Dunham, 1823
*Source C spells Flower.

S-3135 400a B:158 X-0980 HIGH:BRUS
a. W-3974 Samuel Couch, 100a
W-4396 James Hines, 100a
W-4412 Bartlett Holmes, 200a
b. William McDonald
c. None

S-3136 300a B:401 X-0730 LOGA:JEFF
a. W-4012 Henry Banks; assignee [of?] Peter Jones, 100a
W-4032 John Phillips, 100a
W-4238 Jacob Antill? 100a
b. David Bradford
c. Ira Brown, 1830

S-3137 1000a B:218 X-0830 LOGA:JEFF*
a. W-4799 James Calderwood, representatives of
b. James Calderwood, representatives of
c. R. Armstrong; D[uncan] McArthur, 1823; R. Marmon; Unknown; Isaac Zane, Junior
*Source B notation: "Zanesfield."

S-3138 780a B:218 X-0830 LOGA:JEFF
X-0730*
a. W-4799 James Calderwood, representatives of
b. James Calderwood, representatives of
c. None
*"Head branch of . . ."

S-3139 1500a B:219 X-0830 LOGA:JEFF
X-0730*
a. W-4799 James Calderwood, representatives of
b. James Calderwood, representatives of
c. None
*"Head branch of . . ."

S-3150 400a B:400 X-1004 DELA:THOM
a. W-2871 Charles Moorehead
b. Charles Moorhead
c. John Machir; F. H. Cook, 1820-1826; G. C. Knight, forfeited, 1839; O. G. Pettibone, forfeited, 1839; Isaac Meed?

S-3151 1000a B:115 X-0340 UNIO:ALLE
a. W-4569 William Carter, Senior
b. William Carter
c. -- Allen & -- Ellis; Silas G. Strong, 1831

S-3152 200a B:115 X-0340 UNIO:ALLE
a. W-4569 William Carter, Senior
b. William Carter
c. Amaziah Davidson; James Taylor, 1829

S-3153 667a B:114 X-1180 MADI:PIKE
a. W-4594 John Munford Gregory, heir to John Gregory
b. John Munford Gregory
c. L? [S?] W. Sullivant; A. L? [S?] Stone, 1838

S-3154* 1000a B:116 X-0050 LOGA:ZANE
LOGA:PERR
a. W-4590 Joseph Valentine, 100a
W-4602 Armstead Long, 200a
W-3759 James Hepkenstall, 200a
W-3561 John Sinah, 100a
W-0069 Captain Philip Slaughter, 400a
b. Philip Slaughter
c. Isaac B. Dillon; J. W. Marmon, 1827; N. Z. McCulloch, 1837; Notty Thrasher
*Source B notation: "Not patented."

S-3155 1000a B:114 X-0050 LOGA:ZANE*
a. W-0169 John King, 100a
W-4673 Caleb White, 200a
W-4728 William Mosely, 700a
b. George McCredy
c. None
*Source B notation: "Middlebury."

S-3156 200a B:117 X-0340 UNIO:ALLE
a. W-4610 Henry Baumgartner
b. Henry Bumgartner
c. None

S-3157* 20a F:248 X-1140 PIKE: --
a. W-1147 Samuel Cruswell; Joseph Davesson [assignee?]
b. C. Wallace
c. None
*This entry shown in Source A only.

S-3157 100a D:494 X-0345 ROSS:FRAN
MADI: --*
a. W-1147 Samuel Cruswell; Joseph Davesson [assignee?]
b. Joseph Davidson**
c. None
*Source B does not mention Madison County
**Source B spells Davisson.

S-3157* 80a E:53 X-1000 ROSS:FRAN
a. W-1147 Samuel Cruswell; Joseph Davesson [assignee?]
b. Joseph Davidson
c. None
*Source B does not list this survey.

S-3159 150a B:225 X-0050 LOGA:ZANE
a. W-0069 Captain Philip Slaughter
b. Philip Slaughter
c. None

S-3160 467a B:230 X-0050 LOGA:ZANE
a. W-1490 Andrew McGuire, 200a
W-1879 Joseph Robinett, 233a
b. Levi Hollingsworth
c. None

S-3161 189a B:215 X-0050 LOGA:ZANE
LOGA:PERR
a. W-4728 William Moseley
b. George McCradie
c. None

S-3162 640a B:227 X-0340 UNIO:DARB
a. W-4790 Josiah Osborn, representative of George [Osborn] 100a
W-0579 Joseph Carter, 100a
W-4731 Lawrence Harrison, 440a
b. Lucas Sullivant
c. None

S-3163 800a B:226 X-0340 UNIO:ALLE LOGA:ZANE
a. W-2988 Richard Stephenson
b. Richard Stephenson
c. Lyne Sterling [Starling]; Isaac Biegelow, 1837; L. Sullivant

S-3164 667a B:229 X-0050 LOGA:PERR
a. W-4322 George Yates
b. Philip Clayton
c. John Woolman, heirs

S-3168 1575a B:156 X-1301 HIGH:CLAY*
a. W-0173 Francis Cowherd
b. Abraham Buford
c. J. Ackles; W? [M?] Call, 1840; Ensign Mitchell; C. W. Winter
*Source B notation: "Buford."
**Some warrant numbers presumably missing, as W-0173 is for 400 acres only.

S-3171 300a B:166 X-0130 ADAM:JEFF
a. W-1657 Jacob Dener
b. Clement Biddle
c. None

S-3174. *See* S-2755

S-3175 150a B:298 X-0470 SCIO:WASH
S-3530
a. W-0948 Cornelius Burgett, 100a
W-2528 Jesse Wilhiby, 50a
b. Andrew Ellison
c. None

S-3176 500a B:107 X-0660 GREE:ROSS
a. W-1963 William Taliaferro, heir to Colonel [William] Taliaferro
b. William Taliaferro
c. None

S-3177 200a B:301 X-1140 PIKE:SUNF
a. W-1412 William McIntosh
b. Clement Biddle
c. None

S-3181 352a C:166 X-0130 ADAM:WAYN
a. W-4254 Anthony W. White
b. Alexander Parker
c. Andrew Robinson, heirs; D. P. Wilkins, 1826; John Linton? [Sinton?] 1827

S-3183* 167a -- -- SCIO:NILE
a. W-4254? Anthony W. White
b. Alexander Parker
c. T. Morgan, 1824
*This survey listed in Source B only (at proper sequential place).

S-3184 75a B:299 X-1190 SCIO:NILE
a. W-4254 Anthony W. White
b. Alexander Parker
c. None

S-3185 120a B:299 X-1040* ADAM**:JEFF
a. W-4254 Anthony W. White
b. Alexander Parker***
c. John Weldon; J. Kendall, 1837? [1839?]
*"Southeast fork of . . ."
**Source B shows county as S? [L?] which could mean Scioto or Logan.
***Source B originally showed William McDonald, 400a, but entry is crossed out.

S-3186 100a C:233 X-1040* SCIO:BRUS
a. W-4254 Anthony W. White
b. Alexander Parker
c. P. Wyckoff, 1824
*"Southeast fork of . . ."

S-3187 150a D:437 X-0030 SCIO:MORG
a. W-4254 Anthony W. White
b. R. B. Parker & M. W. Crittendon
c. James Miller; William Kendall, 1826

S-3187* 100a -- -- SCIO:MORG
a. W-4254? Anthony W. White
b. A[lexander?] Parker
c. None
*Entry shown in Source B only (at sequential place).

S-3191 125a B:263 X-1040* ADAM:FRAN
a. W-4254 Anthony W. White
b. Alexander Parker
c. E. Worthington; A. Parker & D. Eddie; Thomas Huston, 1832
*"Northwest fork of . . ."

S-3195* 200a B:169 X-1040 ADAM:FRAN
a. W-4406 James Arnold, 100a
W-3502 Thomas Hough, 100a
b. -- Arnold & -- Hough
c. None
*Source B says "not patented."

S-3196 100a B:459 X-0540 UNIO:DARB
a. W-0140 Warren Cash
b. Warren Cash
c. Unknown; H. W. Perkins, 1831 (Union County)

S-3199 100a B:296 X-1120 BROW:FRAN
a. W-2881 William Boyd, heir
b. William Roberts
c. James Edwards, 1834

S-3200 100a B:243 X-0423 ADAM:LIBE
a. W-1151 William Martin
b. Benjamin J. Brice
c. None

S-3202* 40a -- -- ADAM:WAYN
a. --
b. John H. Norton
c. None
*Survey listed in Source B only (at sequential place).

S-3203* 200a C:384 X-0130** ADAM:TIFF
a. W-1359 William Jones
b. John H. Norton
c. None
*Source B notation: "Not patented."
**"Lk. fork of . . ."

S-3206 300a B:363 X-0570 CLER:TATE CLER:MONR
a. W-4742 Samuel Landrum
b. William Sewell*
c. None
*Source C says William Lowell.

S-3207 453a C:68 X-0800 BROW:UNIO
a. W-0629 Captain Walker Baylor
b. Walker Baylor
c. Robert McCormick; Willis Lee, 1824; Wallace Lee; Michael Pritchard, 1831

S-3207 139a C;68 X-0800 BROW:UNIO
a. W-0629 Captain Walker Baylor
b. William Baylor
c. None

S-3208 31a C:68 X-0800 BROW:UNIO
a. W-0629 Captain Walker Baylor
b. Walker Baylor
c. G. W. King, 1823; William J. Hull? [Hall?]

S-3209 525a B:159 X-0840 ROSS:TWIN
a. W-4267 John Smith
b. Thomas Hoff
c. None

S-3209 825a B:159 X-0840 ROSS:TWIN
a. W-4267? [W-4207?] John Smith
b. Thomas Hoff
c. Benjamin Purdam; Walter Purdam, 1830

S-3211 600a B:236 X-0150 ROSS:PAIN
a. W-3845 Rodham K. Cralle, 100a
W-4042 Benjamin Canidear? [Kennedy?] 200a
W-4049 Thomas Hill, heir at law of James Hill, 100a
W-4790* Josiah Osborn, representative of George [Osborn] 100a
W-4793 William Pyle, 100a
b. Thomas Worthington
c. None
*This warrant already used in S-3162.

S-3213 500a B:312 X-0133 HIGH:BRUS
a. W-4627 Henry Bedinger
b. Henry Bedinger
c. None

S-3215 50a B:326 X-0570 ROSS:HUNT
a. W-4525 James Smith; Samuel Davis [assignee?]
b. Thomas McDonald
c. None

S-3216 350a B:372 X-0730 LOGA:JEFF
a. W-4525 James Smith
b. Samuel Davis
c. None

S-3217 100a B:160 X-0840 ROSS:TWIN
a. W-1872 William Grey
b. Duncan McArthur
c. None

S-3218 100a B:270 X-0840 ROSS:TWIN
a. W-2903 William Tanner
b. Silas Johnston
c. None

S-3219 400a B:270 X-0840 ROSS:PAIN ROSS:TWIN
a. W-4288 Lewis Lunford*
W-0623 Robert Shearman, 200a
W-2529 --**
b. James Spear
c. Jacob Myres; F. Edwards, 1833
*Acreage not determinable.
**This warrant number not used in Source C.

S-3220 1000a B:372 X-0060 X-0730 LOGA:JEFF
a. W-1224 Alexander Spotswood Dandridge
b. Alexander S. Dandridge
c. None

S-3220 1000a B:373 X-0730 LOGA:JEFF
a. W-1225 Alexander Spotswood Dandridge
b. Alexander S. Dandridge
c. None

S-3221 640a B:221 X-0730 LOGA:MONR
a. W-2804 Holland Haney
b. Holland Haney
c. None

S-3222 640a B:221 X-0730 LOGA:MONR
a. W-2804 Holland Haney
b. Holland Haney
c. W. Dun; M. Bonner, 1827

S-3223 640a B:222 X-0730 LOGA:MONR
a. W-2804 Holland Haney
b. Holland Haney
c. W. Dun; M. Bonner, 1827; William Thompson, 1831; William Bayless, 1833; J. McLaughlin, 1835

S-3224 640a B:222 X-0730 LOGA:MONR
a. W-2804 Holland Haney
b. Holland Haney
c. Lyne Starling; D. W? [M?] Trader, 1836; Lucas Sullivant

S-3225 640a B:231 X-0730 LOGA:MONR
a. W-4695 Augustine J. Smith, representative of Matt[hew Smith]
b. Augustine J. Smith
c. None

S-3226 640a B:231 X-0730 LOGA:MONR
a. W-4695 Augustine J. Smith, representative of Matt[hew Smith]
b. Augustine J. Smith
c. None

S-3227 640a B:231 X-0730 LOGA:MONR
a. W-4695 Augustine J. Smith, representative of Matt[hew Smith]
b. Augustine J. Smith
c. None

S-3228 640a B:232 X-0730 LOGA:MONR
a. W-4695 Augustine J. Smith, representative of Matt[hew Smith]
b. Augustine J. Smith
c. None

S-3229 640a B:232 X-0730 LOGA:MONR CHAM:WAYN
a. W-4695 Augustine J. Smith, representative of Matt[hew Smith]
b. Augustine J. Smith
c. J. A. Vasse; Simon Ensom? [Enion?] 1828

S-3230 640a B:232 X-0730 LOGA:MONR CHAM:WAYN
a. W-4695 Augustine J. Smith, representative of Matt[hew Smith]
b. Augustine J. Smith
c. None

S-3231* 640a -- -- CHAM:WAYN
a. --
b. Benjamin Stubblefield
c. D[uncan] McArthur, 1823
*Listed in Source B only.

S-3234 1000a B:216 X-0110 UNIO:YORK
a. W-3142 Robert Alexander, heir to George Deut...? Alexander
b. George Bexley* & [Joseph] Merriman
c. William Murphy; L? [S?] G. Strong, 1826
*Source B spells Baxley.

S-3235 1000a B:216 X-0110 UNIO:YORK
a. W-3142 Robert Alexander, heir to George Deut...? Alexander
b. George Bexley* & Joseph Merriman
c. None
*Source B spells Baxley.

S-3236 1000a B:217 X-0110 UNIO:YORK
a. W-3142 Robert Alexander, heir to George Deut...? Alexander
b. George Bexley* & Joseph Merriman
c. None
*Source B spells Baxley.

S-3237 1000a B:217 X-0110 UNIO: --
a. W-3142 Robert Alexander, heir to George Deut...? Alexander
b. George Bexley* & Joseph Merriman
c. Unknown; J. McLain, 1823; L. Sterling [Starling]; L? [S?] G. Strong, 1837; Jeremiah McLene
*Source B spells Baxley

S-3238 1000a B:217 X-0110 UNIO:YORK
a. W-3142 Robert Alexander, heir to George Deut...? Alexander
b. George Bexley* & Joseph Merriman
c. None
*Source B spells Baxley.

S-3239 1000a B:217 X-0110 UNIO:YORK
a. W-3142 Robert Alexander, heir to George Deut...? Alexander
b. George Bexley* & Joseph Merriman
c. Nicholas Fast; Aurora Buttles, 1823; J. Freer; P[eter] Manifold
*Source B spells Baxley.

S-3240* 200a B:228 X-0340 MADI:DARB
a. W-1208 Robert Brumley, 100a
W-4451 Drury Cross, heir to Richard [Cross]; Barnet Hughes, assignee, 100a
b. Lucas Sullivant
c. None
See also S-2755

S-3241 200a B:231 X-0340 UNIO:ALLE
a. W-1283 Bennett McGuy
b. Obediah R. Harrison
c. None

S-3242 107a B:222 X-0730 LOGA:MONR
a. W-2804 Holland Haney
b. Holland Haney
c. W. Dun; M. Bonner, 1827

S-3243 100a D:309 X-0345 FRAN:PRAI
a. W-2310 Stephen Mallett
b. Joseph Bennett
c. Unknown; M. L. Sullivant, 1831; David Scott, 1833

S-3244 200a B:490 X-1004 UNIO:JERO
a. W-4577 Robert Carrell Appleby, heir to Samuel [Appleby]
b. William Annes*
c. P. A. Annis; Samuel Farnham, 1833
*Source B spells Annis.

S-3245 160a B:231 X-0340 MADI:DARB
a. W-4695 Augustine J. Smith, representative of Matt[hew Smith]
b. Augustine J. Smith
c. J. B. D. Smith; William Battern, 1831

S-3249 275a B:124 X-0920 SCIO:UNIO
a. W-4490 William Dark
b. William Dark
c. None

S-3254 260a B:261 X-0760 PIKE:BENT*
S-3255
a. W-3635 John Green, heir to Thomas [Green] 100a
W-4737 William Bailey, 100a
W-3718 James McGraw, 60a
b. Simon Morgan
c. None
*Mifflin Township crossed out in Source B.

S-3255 142a C:211 X-0760 PIKE:BENT*
a. W-4738 Simon Bailey, representative of
b. Simon Morgan
c. None
*Mifflin Township crossed out in Source B.

S-3255* 253a B:261 X-0760 PIKE:BENT**
a. W-4739 James Hudnell, representative of, 200a
W-4738 Simon Bailey, representative of, 53a
b. Simon Morgan
c. None
*Source B notation: "Not patented."
**Mifflin Township crossed out in Source B.

S-3255 145a B:261 X-0760 PIKE:BENT*
a. W-4269 James McGraw, 100a
W-3718 James McGraw, 40a
W-4738 Simon Bailey, representative of, 5a
b. Simon Morgan
c. None
*Mifflin Township crossed out in Source B.

S-3258 100a B:298 X-1140 PIKE:MIFF
a. W-3317 Henry Millions
b. Andrew Ellison
c. None

S-3258 80a B:298 X-1140 PIKE:MIFF
a. W-1971 Charles Murphey
b. Andrew Ellison
c. None

S-3258 120a B:298 X-1140 PIKE:MIFF
S-3954
a. W-1971 Charles Murphey, 20a
W-3105 Thomas Miller; Didier Collin [and?] A. Foulds? assignees, 100a
b. Andrew Ellison
c. None

S-3259 100a B:298 X-0760 PIKE:BENT*
a. W-4216 Thomas Campbell
b. Michael Hogg
c. None
*Mifflin Township crossed out in Source B.

S-3260. *See* S-2495

S-3261 633a B:244 X-1300 BROW:SCOT
a. W-4666 Robert Forsythe & John Forsythe
b. John Brown
c. Jonathan Atwood; Allen Butt, 1826; Jacob Vanderment [Vandamant] 1826

S-3262 100a B:244 X-1140* PIKE:MIFF
a. W-4666 Robert Forsythe & John Forsythe
b. John Brown
c. None
*"Main fork of . . ."

S-3267 200a B:290 X-1140* PIKE:MIFF
a. W-3826 John Hanson Crowson, 100a
W-3816 Mary McDonald, heir[ess] to Angus [McDonald] 100a
b. Abraham Wyckoff
c. None
*"Main fork of . . ."

S-3268 100a B:435 X-0130 ADAM:TIFF
a. W-3354 Anthony Whitson
b. Henry Massie
c. None

S-3272 100a C:501 X-0340 UNIO:DARB
a. W-4830 James Linn, representative of
b. Lucas Sullivant
c. None

S-3279 500a B:122 X-0840 FAYE:JEFF
GREE:SILV
a. W-0060 Captain Samuel Jones
b. Samuel Jones
c. H? [W?] Wynans, 1828; Doctor A. Wynans; Arthur Cryfield, 1831 (Fayette County)

S-3280 1500a B:122 X-0180 GREE:SILV
a. W-0732 Captain Thomas Parker
b. Thomas Parker
c. James Watson, heirs; John Watson, 1835

S-3281 1000a B:165 X-0130 ADAM:MEIG
a. W-4846 Simon Morgan, assignee of representative of Allen Walker
b. John Beasley & A[ndrew] Ellison
c. None

S-3282 70a C:224 X-1003 ADAM?: --*
a. W-4254 Anthony W. White
b. Alexander Parker
c. None
*Source B says "S[cioto] not found," presumably referring to the township.

S-3283 200a B:405 X-0740 GREE:XENI
GREE:ROSS
a. W-4516 James Ryalls
b. James Ryalls
c. None

S-3284 540a B:126 X-1040 SCIO:UNIO
a. W-3039 Major John Swan
b. John Swan
c. B. McLaughlin; D. Pollock, 1836

S-3285 127a B:127 X-0700 SCIO:UNIO
a. W-3039 Major John Swan
b. John Swan
c. B. McLaughlin; G. Gwathmey, 1836

S-3287 200a B:305 X-0841 ROSS:SCIO
a. W-4829 Edwin Long, assignee [of?] Spratley Simmons
b. Nathaniel Massie
c. None

S-3289 200a B:263 X-0420 BROW:BYRD
a. W-4254 Anthony W. White
b. Alexander Parker
c. None

S-3290 150a B:263 X-0420 BROW:BYRD
a. W-0018 Colonel Presley Nevill
b. Presley Nevill
c. None

S-3290 550a B:263 X-0420 BROW:BYRD
a. W-0018 Colonel Presley Nevill
b. Presley Nevill
c. None

S-3290* 150a -- -- BROW:BYRD
a. [W-0018? Colonel Presley Nevill]
b. Presley Neville
c. None
*Mentioned in Source B only.

S-3299* 50a -- -- ADAM:--**
a. --
b. Michael Hogg
c. None
*Mentioned in Source B only.
**Source B says township "not found."

S-3300 500a B:164 X-0420 BROW:UNIO
a. W-4846 Simon Morgan, assignee of representative of Allen Walker
b. John Beasley & A[ndrew] Ellison
c. None

S-3303 870a B:262 X-0840 X-1140 ROSS:HUNT
a. W-0019 Colonel Daniel Morgan
b. Daniel Morgan
c. James? [Joseph?] Beckett; R. Stewart, 1830

S-3304 200a B:266 X-0870 ROSS:HUNT
a. W-1074 Richard Sharraw
b. Thomas Wilson
c. Robert Stewart, 1827; P. Douglas, 1830; S? [L?] Downey?; W. Cassan, 1838; S. Devinny; W. Cochran, 1842

S-3304 200a B:266 X-0870 ROSS:HUNT ADAM: --*
a. W-1077 John Tinney
b. Thomas Wilson
c. Thomas Williamson; Paul Kerr, 1824
*Source B says also Adams County, township not given.

S-3306 200a D:359 X-1040* PIKE:SUNF ADAM:--**
a. W-4842 Jeremiah Davis
b. Jeremiah Davis
c. Samuel Reed, 1830
*"Waters of the northwest branch of . . ."
**Source B does not mention Adams County.

S-3310 300a B:127 X-0360 --*
a. W-4165 Isham Browder, 100a
W-4250 Thomas Gist, 100a
W-4664 William Donaldson, 100a
b. Nathaniel Randolph
c. None
*Pencilled notation in Source A says "not found." Source B states Pickaway County, township "not found."

S-3311 200a B:226 X-0340 UNIO:DARB UNIO:UNIO
a. W-4849 James Johnson, assignee of Andrew A. Gilchrist, representative of George [Gilchrist]
b. Lucas Sullivant
c. None

S-3312 122a B:228 X-0340 UNIO:DARB
a. W-4849 James Johnson, assignee of Andrew A. Gilchrist, representative of George [Gilchrist]
b. Lucas Sullivant
c. None

S-3312 151a B:228 X-0340 UNIO:DARB
a. W-4849 James Johnson, assignee of Andrew A. Gilchrist, representative of George [Gilchrist]
b. Lucas Sullivant
c. None

S-3313 100a B:228 X-0340 UNIO*:CANA
a. W-4849 James Johnson, assignee of Andrew A. Gilchrist, representative of George [Gilchrist]
b. Lucas Sullivant
c. None
*Source B says Madison County.

S-3314 1000a B:215 X-0750 LOGA:RUSH
a. W-4776 George Long, 100a
W-2840 Larkin Ferguson, 100a*
W-4753 Thomas Adams, representative of, 100a
W-4814 Herbert Owen, representative of, 100a
W-4782 Nathaniel Kearn, representative of, 100a
W-4778 James Stewart, representative of, 100a
W-4812 Nathaniel Hubbard, representative of, 100a
W-4813 Charles Sammons, representative of, 100a
W-2839 Thomas Fraser, heir to Fal[vey] Fraser, 200a
b. George McCredie
c. Benjamin Dawson; James? [Joseph?] Kilpatrick; Archibald Boyd, 1831; Noah Z. McCulloch, 1840
*Entry contains the words "error" and "state" and is nearly illegible. Stephen T. Mason [assignee?]

S-3316 889a B:480 X-1000 FRAN:FRAN
a. W-4852 James Parks, representative of
b. James Parks, representative of
c. Mary Kellar; M. L. Sullivant, 1838

S-3317 889a B:439 X-1000 LOGA:LAKE
a. W-4852 James Parks, representative of
b. James Parks, representative of
c. None

S-3320 500a B:229 X-1000 LOGA:RUSH
a. W-2921 Layton Yancey
b. Layton Yancey
c. None

S-3321 889a B:229 X-1000 LOGA:RUSH
a. W-2921 Layton Yancey
b. Layton Yancey
c. Henry King; J. B. Hunnicut, 1834

S-3322 889a B:229 X-0660 LOGA:LAKE
a. W-2921 Layton Yancey
b. Layton Yancey
c. J. Smith, heirs; J. S. Gardner, 1835

S-3323 1400a B:222 X-0750 LOGA:RUSH
a. W-0196 Lieutenant James Mabon
b. James Maybon
c. R. Wilson, heirs; George C. Clark; Lyne Starling, 1831

S-3324 1000a B:223 X-0660 LOGA:LAKE
a. W-0151 Captain William Miller
b. William Miller
c. Michael Crosby, 1824; Robert Gratton; Lawson Curtis? [Custis?] 1828; M[ichael] Crosby *et al*; Benjamin S. Brown, 1832

S-3325 1000a B:223 X-0750 LOGA:JEFF LOGA:RUSH
a. W-0151 Captain William Miller
b. William Miller
c. None

S-3326 1000a B:223 X-0750 LOGA:JEFF LOGA:RUSH
a. W-0151 Captain William Miller
b. William Miller
c. John Jameson? heirs; John Swan *et al*; H. Hendrickson, 1831

S-3327 1000a B:223 X-1000 LOGA:JEFF LOGA:RUSH
a. W-0151 Captain William Miller
b. William Miller
c. None

S-3329 / S-5252 2667a D:114 X-0063* CLER:BATA CLER:WILL CLER:JACK
a. W-4848 Susanna Armstead, late Susanna Christian, [heiress] of John Blair (deceased); William Lytle [assignee?]
b. James Johnson
c. William Davis; Ralph Sharp, 1823; James Johnston, heirs?; William Walker, 1825; G. Seiber; Z. Chapman, 1828; L? [S?] Burrows; W. P. Marshall; John Hile? [Hill?] 1833; John Bridges; C. B. Huber; F? [T?] Curtis; J. T. Brush, 1836; L. Boswel? 1835; J. Osborn; J. Perin, 1836; James Williamson, 1831; S. See, 1837; L? [S?] Bonnel; T. Carless; James Johnson
*"Waters of . . ."

S-3331 500a B:196 X-0664 CLER:JACK
a. W-4848 Susanna Armstead, (late Susanna Christian) [heiress] of John Blair (deceased); James Johnson [assignee?]
b. William Lytle
c. None

S-3332 500a B:196 X-0660 CLER:MIAM CLER:GOSH
a. W-4848 Susanna Armstead (late Susanna Christian) [heiress] of John Blair (deceased); James Johnson [assignee?]
b. William Lytle
c. J. Wood; L? [S?] Winston, 1823

S-3333 630a B:196 X-0270 CLER:WILL
a. W-4848 Susanna Armstead (late Susanna Christian) [heiress] of John Blair (deceased); James Johnson [assignee?] 333a
W-4858 John Hays, 297a
b. William Lytle
c. F. Hise? [Hire?] heirs; L. T. Pease, 1839

S-3334 3333a D:120 X-0665 WARR:HAMI
a. W-2368 Major James Munroe, "resolution"
b. William Lytle
c. B. M. Fall?; B. McFall?; J. Hopkins, 1824; Reuben Bond, heirs; John Kitchen, 1831; A. & J. Farris; J? [I?] A. Stokes, 1833; F. Moss; G. King, 1831; -- Taylor, -- Lytle, & Company; William Bennett, 1832

S-3335 300a B:195 X-0663 BROW:STER CLER: --*
a. W-4095 William Gehagan, heir to John [Gehagan] 200a
W-2004 John Griffin, heir to Thompson [Griffin] 100a
b. Charles Lee
c. None
*Source B does not list Clermont County.

S-3336 300a B:196 X-0663 BROW:PIKE
a. W-4796 William Cocke, representative of, 200a
W-4768 Charles Stewart, 100a
b. Robert Campbell
c. None

S-3337 4500a B:129 X-1080 CLER:WAYN WARR: --*
a. W-0306 Captain John C. Carter**
W-0635 Captain Archibald Denholm; Edward Lynen? [assignee?]**
W-0699 Captain Tarlton Payne**
W-1533 Robert Brown, 100a
W-1170 John Hackett, 233a
W-1276 Isaac Taylor, 467a
b. John Harvie & Thomas Fenn***
c. L? [S?] Smith; L? [S?] West, 1826; Richard Wood;

S-3337 [continued]
J. Fletcher, 1832; J. S. Richards; J. S. Wood, 1835; W. H. Lever; T. R. Wallace; Thomas Carneal; Joseph? [James?] Brown; Samuel Perine; J. H. Jackson & -- Hait, 1831; H. Irwin; A. McNeall, 1842
*Source B does not mention Warren County.
**Assigned acreage could not be determined.
***Source A does not list Fenn.

S-3337 4500a B:130 X-1080 CLER:GOSH CLER:WAYN BROW: --*
a. W-1277 William Hodges, 200a
W-1837 Phillip Duvall, assigeen [of?] David Mitchell, 100a
W-1447 William Cornal, 200a
W-1286 John Lewis; Ezekiel Howell [assignee?]** 200a
W-1659 Nathan Fortune, 200a
W-1680 John Jones, 200a
W-0699 Captain Tarlton Payne, 1400a?
W-1677 Lieutenant William Winston, 1000a?
W-0125 Captain Lieutenant Thomas Fenn, 1000a?
b. John Harvie & Thomas Fenn
c. None
*Source B does not mention Warren County.
**This warrant already used for S-1767.

S-3338 733a B:163 X-1080 CLER:WAYN BROW: --*
a. W-1458 George Rice, 400a
W-0009 Lieutenant Colonel Samuel F? Cabell, 233a
W-1631 Richard Curl, 100a
b. James Currie
c. None
*Source B does not list Brown County.

S-3339
S-3340 1467a B:163 X-1080 CLER:GOSH CLER:WAYN BROW: --*
a. W-1470 James Hodge, 200a
W-1869 Daniel Gray, 200a
W-1584 Thomas Bridgman, 200a
W-0009 Lieutenant Colonel Samuel F? Cabell, 767a
W-1631 Richard Curl, 100a
b. James Currie
c. William Wood, 1826; John Gerrard?; J. Emery, 1833
*Source B does not list Brown County.

S-3341 167a B:163 X-1080 CLER:WAYN BROW: --*
a. W-0125 Captain Lieutenant Thomas Fenn
b. Thomas Fenn
c. Stephen McFarland; J. Dunlap, 1823; Stephen B. Cleveland, 1831
*Source B does not list Brown County.

S-3342 1000a B:130 X-1080 WARR: --* CLIN:MARI
a. W-0079 Captain Philip Mallory
b. John Harvie
c. William Lytle; A. Underwood, 1825; David Morton & William Morton; A. T. Tewell? [Terrell?] 1829; William Clark; A. E. Strickle, 1837; G. Fallis, 1836
*Source B does not mention Warren County.

S-3343 2000a B:129 X-0663 BROW:STER BROW:PIKE BROW:CLAR CLER: --*
a. W-0079 Cpatain Philip Mallory
b. John Harvie
c. M. Prater; Allen Butt, 1824; Joab Smith; F. Barney, 1826; B. Bosworth; Robert Chalfant, 1828; S. Herrod; R. Campbell, 1828; Jesse Chambers, heirs; John Kains; John Mahaffy; John H. Blair, 1831
*Source B does not mention Clermont County.

S-3344 1000a B:131 X-0663 BROW:STER
a. W-0699 Captain Tarlton Payne
b. John Harvie
c. Curtis? [Custis?] Wilson; Peter Berry, 1832; R. E. Irvin [Irwin?]; James Kelley; George H. Bohrer, 1831; P. L. Wilson, 1842

S-3345 833a B:103 X-0663 BROW:STER CLER:WILL
a. W-0699 Captain Tarlton Payne, 500a?
W-1677 Lieutenant William Winston, 333a?
b. John Harvie
c. William Lytle; A? [H?] Patten, 1826; D. C. Richardson

S-3346 400a B:194 X-0270 BROW:PIKE
a. W-2507 Colonel Holt Richerson
b. Holt Richison*
c. Thomas Carneal; James Taylor, Junior, 1831
*Source B spells Richeson.

S-3347 400a B:194 X-0270 BROW:PIKE
a. W-2507 Colonel Holt Richerson
b. Holt Richison*
c. Thomas Carneal; James Taylor, Junior, 1831
*Source B spells Richeson.

S-3347 400a B:194 X-0270 BROW:PIKE
a. W-2507 Colonel Holt Richerson
b. Holt Richison
c. Thomas Carneal; James Taylor, Junior, 1831
*Source B spells Richeson.

S-3349 1200a B:135 X-0750 UNIO:MILL
a. W-2198 John Evans, 200a
W-2772 James Jenkins, 100a?
W-2457 James Jenkins, assignee [of?] Richard Aldridge, 100a
W-2770 James Jenkins, assignee [of?] James McCoum? 100a
W-2771 James Jenkins, assignee [of?] John Smith, 100a
W-2773 James Jenkins, assignee [of?] William Seymore, 100a
W-2774 James Jenkins, assignee [of?] Henry Tunstall, 200a
W-2775 James Jenkins, assignee [of?] John Wilmington, 200a
W-2776 James Jenkins, assignee [of?] Jacob Seay, 100a
b. James Jenkins
c. None

S-3350 1087a B:134 X-0750 UNIO:PARI
a. W-2644 John Ashley, 200a
W-2671 Francis Graves, assignee [of?] Thomas Mooney, 200a
W-1499 James Taylor, 200a
W-2812 Eppa Hubbard, 200a
W-2585 Tarrell? [Fanell?] O'Neal, assignee [of?] James Aylett, 200a
W-2670 Francis Graves, assignee [of?] Thomas Wooley, 87a
b. Edward Dowse
c. None

S-3351 1087a B:134 X-0750 UNIO:PARI*
a. W-1552 James Tucker, 200a
W-2611 Richard Claiborne, assignee [of?] John Thomson, 200a
W-2651 Samuel Trower, assignee [of?] W. Quigley, 200a
W-2650 Samuel Trower, assignee [of?] M. Whitlow, 200a
W-2670 Francis Graves, assignee [of?] Thomas Wooley, 100a
b. Edward Dowse
c. Margaret Bailey; Robson Broome, 1833; R. L. Broome; O. B. Cissell, 1837; Randolph Sells; James Thornton, 1824
*Source B notation: "Marysville."

S-3352 800a B:134 X-0750 UNIO:PARI
a. W-2598 William Herbert, 233a
W-2595 John Depriest, assignee [of?] Thomas Raines? 200a
W-2269 Colonel Christian Febeger, 200a?*
W-2597 Anthony Leider? 100a
W-2579 James Bedford, assignee [of?] W. Waller, 67a
b. Edward Dowse
c. John F. Mason; John Jolley, 1825
*W-2269 may duplicate W-2279.

S-3353 800a B:135 X-0750 UNIO:PARI*
a. W-1307 William Martin, 200a
W-2757 John Watkins, 200a
W-2828 George Sims, representative of Thomas [Sims] 200a
W-2584 Farrell O'Neal, assignee [of?] John Doil, 200a
b. Edward Dowse
c. William Myres; S. G. Strong, 1826; Peter Machir
*Source B notation: "By Marysville."

S-3354 1087a B:135 X-0750 UNIO:PARI
a. W-2718 Francis Graves, assignee [of?] William Gray, 100a
W-2703 Francis Graves, assignee [of?] Edward Dwane, 100a
W-2612 George Pickett? [Puckett?] assignee [of?] George Allen, 100a
W-2588 Francis Graves, assignee [of?] Mg? 100a
W-2646 --*
W-2706 John Depreast, assignee [of?] Thomas Epps? 100a
W-2701 John Ross, 100a
W-2717 Robert Gray, 100a
W-2714 Thomas Aslin, 100a
W-2707 Stephen Stacy, 100a
W-2597 Anthony Leider, 100a?
b. Edward Dowse
c. None
*Source C does not give name of warrantee.

S-3355 372a B:204 X-0750 UNIO:DOVE
a. W-1729 John Smith, 106a?
W-1496 Ferguson Taylor, 100a
W-2670 Francis Graves, assignee [of?] Thomas Wooley, 33a
W-2579 James Bedford, assignee [of?] W. Waller, 133a
b. Edward Dowse
c. None

S-3356 96a C:279 X-1000 FRAN:FRAN
a. W-4798 William Throckmorton
b. John Harrison
c. Benjamin Houghes, heirs; A[llen] Latham, 1826

S-3357 700a B:204 X-1303 BROW:WASH
a. W-4666 Robert Forsythe & John Forsythe
b. Peter Shenkle? [Shinkle?] 1826

S-3358 410a B:307 X-0420 BROW:UNIO
a. W-3623 Robert Sayers, "resolution"
b. Robert Sayers
c. Joseph Lane; George Shultz, 1825

S-3358 300a B:307 X-0420 BROW:UNIO
a. W-3623 Robert Sayers, "resolution"
b. Robert Sayers
c. None

S-3359* 1146a -- -- HIGH:NEWM HIGH:LIBE
a. --
b. Tarlton Fleming
c. None
*Mentioned only in Source B (in sequential place).

S-3360. *See* S-2466

S-3361. *See* S-2532

S-3365 1930a C:83 X-0020 ADAM:FRAN
S-4708 HIGH:BRUS
a. W-3244 Francis Hogan, 100a
W-1950 Richard Jenkins, 100a
W-4682 Robert Young; Charles Copeland, Timothy Dogan [assignees?] 200a
W-1279 Patrick Murphey, 233a
W-2938 Thomas Glascock, 1000a?
W-2576 Captain Cadwallader Jones, 297a?
b. John Graham
c. J. Kisling; J. Jones, 1825; W. Dun; William Elliott, 1837; John Smith, 1831; J. L? [S?] Hughes, 1842

S-3366 814a B:138 X-1301 HIGH:CLAY BROW: --*
a. W-0369 James Tutt, heir to Charles Tutt
b. James Tutt
c. J. Florence; R. Collins, 1824; Nicholas Sinks; Robert Davidson, 1833
*Source B does not mention Brown County.

S-3367 142a B:282 X-0460 HIGH:CLAY BROW:WASH
a. W-0369 James Tutt, heir to Charles Tutt
b. James Tutt
c. None

S-3368 1000a B:157 X-0461? X-1301? HIGH:CLAY HIGH:SALE BROW: --*
a. W-0673 Colonel Abraham Buford
b. Abraham Buford
c. None
*Source B does not mention Brown County.

S-3369 85a B:156 X-0461? X-1301? HIGH:CLAY BROW: --*
a. W-0173 Francis Cowherd**
b. Abraham Buford
c. None
*Source B does not mention Brown County.
**Warrant number may be in error and possibly should read W-0673, as in S-3368 above.

S-3370 200a B:139 X-1300 BROW:EAGL
a. W-0094 Benjamin Dillon, heir to Jesse Dillon
b. Benjamin Dillon
c. John W. Odell; Mathew Kincaid, 1830; J? [I?] Hagle; P. L? [S?] Wilson, 1841

S-3371* 150a C:442 X-1060 BROW:GREE
a. W-2237 William Andrews
b. William Andrews
c. None
*Source B notation: "Not patented."

S-3372 100a B:192 X-1300 BROW:WASH
a. W-0193 John Chavers
b. John Chavers*
c. -- Chavers & -- Slaughter; Uriah Springer, 1828; Hill D. Staton, 1838; M. Day, 1840
*Source B spells Chaver.

S-3372* 100a B:192 X-1300 BROW:WASH
a. W-2228** George Slaughter, heir to N. [Slaughter]
b. George Slaughter
c. S. F. Randolph; James? [Joseph?] Newman, Junior, 1828; William Sims; W. Brown, 1834; Mathew Day, 1840
*Source B notation: "Not patented."
**Warrant already used on S-1426.

S-3373 200a B:242 X-1301 HIGH:CLAY
a. W-2828* George Sims, representative of Thomas [Sims]
b. Jeremiah Pierce
c. None
*Warrant already used in S-3353.

S-3373 100a B:242 X-1301 HIGH:CLAY
a. W-4005 Thomas Rosson, heir to William [Rosson]
b. John Lemon
c. None

S-3374 200a B:139 X-1300 BROW:WASH
a. W-2122 Daniel Keith
b. James Young
c. Jonathan Hopkins; G. W. King, 1826; William Lyne; William Butt, 1823

S-3375 200a B:138 X-1300 BROW:WASH
a. W-2952 -- Mtchel & -- Barnes
b. J. & E. Mitchell & G. & E. Barnes
c. Andrew Woodfield [*also* Woodfill]; W? [M?] Tomb? 1838; W. Frazer; P. L? [S?] Wilson, 1841

S-3376 200a B:139 X-0740 GREE:XENI*
a. W-3757 Edmund Foster
b. James Lemmon
c. Benjamin Stephens; J. Miller, 1830
*Source B notation: "By Milford."

S-3376 200a B:139 X-0740 GREE:XENI GREE:ROSS
a. W-4193 George Friskell
b. George Freskett*
c. None
*Source B spells Friskett.

S-3378* 250a B:140 X-0660 GREE: --
a. W-1519 Nicholas Neil
b. James Wilson
c. None
*This survey not listed in Source B.

S-3380 173a B:141 X-1301 HIGH:SALE
a. W-0818 Lieutenant J. William Ludeman
b. William Ludiman
c. John Davidson, 1828

S-3381 151a B:141 X-0660 HIGH:SALE
a. W-1925* James Hawkins
b. Francis Gray
c. John Baird
*Warrant already used in S-1233.

S-3382 274a B:141 X-0660 HIGH:SALE
a. W-1889 Captain Peter Jones
b. Joseph Jones
c. John Baird; -- Kirby & -- Starling, 1831

S-3383 451a B:142 X-0660 HIGH:SALE
a. W-0630 Lieutenant Jacob Brown
b. Jacob Brown
c. None

S-3384 262a B:141 X-1300 HIGH:SALE
a. W-1889 Captain Peter Jones
b. Joseph Jones
c. John Baird; Andrew Baskin? [Raskin?] 1831

S-3386 50a B:143 X-1301 HIGH:SALE
a. W-2272 Captain Calohill Minnis
b. Calohill Minnis
c. Robert Means; T. Colvin, Senior, 1837; Unknown

S-3387 112a B:142 X-1301 HIGH:SALE
a. W-2260 Major Richard Call
b. Richard Call
c. None

S-3388* 200a B:143 X-1301 HIGH:SALE
a. W-1071 John Gossett
b. Sealey Rawlings
c. None
*Source B notation: "Not patented."

S-3389 500a B:143 X-1303 BROW:WASH*
a. W-4182 Thomas Waring, heir to Henry [Waring]
b. Thomas Warring**
c. None
*Source B notation: "Sardinia."
**Source B spells Waring.

S-3390 500a B:162 X-1303 BROW:WASH
HIGH: --*
a. W-4182 Thomas Waring, heir to Henry [Waring]
b. Thomas Warring**
c. W. B. Logan; J. S. Beasley, 1841
*Source B mentions Highland County, but does not give township.
**Source B spells Waring.

S-3391 500a B:162 X-1303 BROW:WASH
a. W-4182 Thomas Waring, heir to Henry [Waring]
b. Thomas Warring*
c. None
*Source B spells Waring.

S-3392 200a B:386 X-1300 BROW:WASH
a. W-3491 George Eskridge
b. George Eskridge
c. None

S-3393 270a B:509 X-0800 HAMI:ANDE
a. W-1182 John Guille, 100a
W-0929 Abraham Buckley, 100a
W-3932 William Reynolds, assignee, 70a
b. John Nancarrow
c. None

S-3394 90a B:509 X-0800 HAMI:ANDE
a. W-0771 Lieutenant Peter Higgins
b. Peter Higgins
c. William Vincent; M. Wright, 1832

S-3395 100a B:512 X-0800 HAMI:ANDE
a. W-1841 Ensign John Gibson
b. James Young
c. None

S-3396 16a C:185 X-0800 BROW:UNIO
a. W-1519 Nicholas Neil
b. James Wilson
c. James Wilkins; Job Egbert, 1828

S-3400 528a B:394 X-0660 GREE:ROSS
a. W-1912 Doctor Thomas Christie
b. Thomas Christie
c. None

S-3401 400a B:144 X-1303 BROW:EAGL
BROW:WASH
a. W-1396 Captain John Stokes
b. John Stokes
c. None

S-3402 500a B:490 X-0110 DELA:SCIO
UNIO: --*
a. W-2759 Benjamin Welch, 100a
W-2758 Silvester Welch, 100a
W-2760 Benjamin Lawson, 100a
W-2789 Charles Charity, 200a
b. John Barrett**
c. None
*Source B does not mention Union County.
**Source B spells Barritt.

S-3405 529a C:390 X-0400 MADI:PLEA
FAYE: --*
a. W-1159 William Mercer, heir to General H. Mercer
b. Smith Snead
c. Thomas Compton; John Kious, 1838
*Source B mentions Fayette County, but does not give township.

S-3406 167a B:213 X-0663 CLER:UNIO
a. W-4676 Thomas Ridley
b. Thomas Ridley
c. None

S-3407 133a B:212 X-0663 CLER:UNIO
a. W-2162 Colonel William Heth
b. William Hith*
c. None
*Source B spells Heth.

S-3408 36a B:300 X-0800 BROW:HUNT
a. W-0187 Lieutenant Robert Craddock
b. Robert Craddock
c. None

S-3409 150a B:303 X-0800 BROW:HUNT
a. W-0174 Captain William White
b. William White
c. M. Kincaid, 1828

S-3411 1000a B:286 X-0640 HIGH:FAIR
a. W-4182 Thomas Waring, heir to Henry [Waring]
b. Thomas Warring*
c. David Terril, Junior
*Source B spells Waring.

S-3412 1000a B:149 X-0130 ADAM:WAYN
ADAM:WINC
a. W-4846 Simon Morgan, assignee of [the] representative of Allen Walker
b. John Beasley & A[ndrew] Ellison
c. William McIntire, 1828

S-3414 380a B:526 X-0420 BROW:BYRD
S-6087 ADAM: --*
a. W-4254 Anthony W. White
b. Alexander Parker
c. N. Sidwell, 1828
*Source B does not mention Adams County.

S-3417 350a B:160 X-0150 ROSS:BUCK
X-0840
a. W-0248 William Evans
b. Duncan McArthur
c. None

S-3421 310a B:270 X-0840 FAYE:UNIO
a. W-0247 William Evans
b. William Evans
c. None

S-3423 400a B:234 X-0840 ROSS:PAIN
a. W-0248 William Evans
b. William Evans
c. None

S-3425 200a B:248 X-0840 ROSS:PAIN
GREE: --*
a. W-3201 Jacob? Dowch? [Deutsch?], assignee [of?] Robert Chambers
b. William Ross
c. W. Wynans, 1828
*Source B mentions Greene County, but not the township.

S-3426* 200a -- -- PIKE: --
a. --
b. John Smith
c. C. Cisna; -- Miller & -- Penniston, 1830
*Listed in Source B only (at top of page, before S-3375).

S-3427 100a B:314 X-0980 HIGH:PAIN
a. W-3146 Joseph Smith
b. Bartholomew Fitzgerald
c. None

S-3428 500a B:313 X-0730 CHAM:UNIO
a. W-4533 William McClung, assignee [of?] William Coffle, 200a
W-3406 Samuel Brooking, assignee [of?] John Warner, 200a
W-1876* Thomas Tunstall; -- Montgomery & -- Allen [assignees?] 200a?
b. William Clendennen & William McClung
c. None
*This warrant almost certainly listed in error. It was used in S-1190 and results in an overage here.

S-3429 1000a B:151 X-0840 FAYE:CONC
a. W-3037 Thomas Hall, heir to John [Hall] 200a
W-1886* Francis Ramsey, 200a
W-4154 James Ramsey, 100a
W-4112 Thomas Camp, heir; Ebenezer Scrots [assignee?] 200a
W-2227 Thomas Barnett, 200a
W-4629 Richard Mason, heir to James [Mason] 200a
b. Joseph Watkins, Hector McNeil,** & William R. Bernard
c. James? [Joseph?] Watkins; Phelps Woods, 1828; Adley Gregory, 1828; Joseph? [James?] Foster; J. Jameson, 1835; John B. Allen & Samuel Allen (by County Auditor); Benjamin Allen & Juhel? Allen, 1831
*Warrant already used in S-1129.
**Source B spells McNeal.

S-3430 250a B:385 X-0663 CLIN:GREE
a. W-3220 Alexander McKinsey
b. Alexander McKinzie*
c. None
*Source B spells McKinsey.

S-3431 950a B:280 X-0840 FAYE:GREE
a. W-4696 Robert Moore, heir to William [Moore]
b. Robert Moore
c. None

S-3432 136a B:280 X-0840 FAYE:CONC
a. W-4696 Robert Moore, heir to William [Moore]
b. Robert Moore
c. None

S-3433 850a B:280 X-0840 FAYE:CONC
a. W-4696 Robert Moore, heir to William [Moore]
b. Robert Moore
c. None

S-3434 200a B:279 X-0840 FAYE:GREE
a. W-3038 John Forehand, 100a
W-3885 John Forehand, "representative of daddy," 100a
b. William Hamilton
c. None

S-3434 100a B:279 X-0840 FAYE:GREE
a. W-4407 John Irvine
b. William Patton
c. None

S-3435 200a B:155 X-1300 HIGH:WHIT
a. W-0286 Reverend Alexander Balmain
b. Alexander Balmain
c. None

S-3436* 1000a B:217 X-0750 LOGA:JEFF
a. W-0055 Captain Thomas Payne
b. William Cochran
c. Lucas Sullivant, heirs; Lyne Starling, 1833
*Source B notation: "Not patented."

S-3437 1000a B:218 X-0750 LOGA:JEFF
a. W-0055 Captain Thomas Payne
b. William Cochran
c. Ruth Kenton; John G. Parkinson, 1823; Eliza Kenton; John Kenton; Martin Marmon, 1823; Daniel Butler; Martin Dewill?

S-3438 1000a B:218 X-0730 LOGA:JEFF
a. W-0055 Captain Thomas Payne
b. William Cochran
c. None

S-3439 1000a B:218 X-0730 LOGA:JEFF
a. W-0055 Captain Thomas Payne
b. William Cochran
c. None

S-3441 889a B:225 X-1000 LOGA:JEFF
a. W-3187 John Scott
b. John Scott
c. Samuel Cox; R. Dout? [Doud?] 1837; N. Stillwell; J. McLaughlin, 1835

S-3442 889a B:225 X-1000 LOGA:JEFF LOGA:LAKE
a. W-3187 John Scott
b. John Scott
c. None

S-3443 1000a B:219 X-0110 UNIO:YORK
a. W-0214 Doctor David Holmes
b. David Duncan
c. Lucas Sullivant; -- Strong, for L. Starling, 1826; M. S. Butler, 1836; Unknown; I? [J?] Dean

S-3444 1000a B:219 X-0750 UNIO:LIBE
a. W-0214 Doctor David Holmes
b. David Duncan
c. Lucas Sullivant; Lyne Starling; J. January; R. Dorsey

S-3445 200a C:50 X-0340 FRAN:BROW
a. W-3741 Thomas Bird
b. Thomas Bird
c. Unknown; Lyne Starling, 1829

S-3446 200a C:455 X-1000 FRAN:NORW
a. W-3738 John Roberts
b. John Roberts
c. None

S-3446 200a C:455 X-1000 FRAN:NORW
a. W-3738 John Roberts
b. John Roberts
c. Lyne Starling, 1827

S-3446* 200a -- -- FRAN:NORW
a. --
b. John Roberts
c. None
*Listed in Source B only (at sequential place).

S-3446* 1000a -- -- UNIO:LIBE
a. --
b. Richard Lee
c. None
*Listed in Source B only (at sequential place).

S-3447* 1000a -- -- UNIO:LIBE
a. --
b. Richard Lee
c. None
*Listed in Source B only (at sequential place).

S-3448* 1000a -- -- UNIO:LIBE
a. --
b. Richard Lee
c. None
*Listed in Source B only (at sequential place).

S-3449* 1000a -- -- UNIO:LIBE
a. --
b. Richard Lee
c. None
*Listed in Source B only (at sequential place).

S-3450 525a B:380 X-0730 CHAM:UNIO
a. W-0631 Samuel Baskerville
b. John Kean
c. None

S-3450 300a B:380 X-0730 CHAM:UNIO
a. W-0631 Samuel Baskerville
b. John Kean
c. None

S-3451 500a D:34 X-1005 HARD:TAYL
a. W-3975 Thomas Brown, assignee [of?] Richard Powell, 100a
W-3976 Thomas Brown, assignee [of?] Daniel Simpson, 200a
W-3675 Thomas Patterson, assignee, 100a
W-3500 John Hiller, 100a
b. Thomas Brown
c. -- Templeton & -- Elder, 1831 (Logan County)

S-3452 650a C:50 X-1005 FRAN:WASH
a. W-3211 William Barksdale, heir to John [Barksdale]
b. William Barksdale
c. Unknown; John Vastine, 1832; M. A. Sayers, 1834; Henry Highland; L. Sterling, Junior, 1838; P. Sharp; H. B. Curtis? [Custis?] 1836

S-3452 350a C:50 X-1005 FRAN:NORW UNIO:JERO
a. W-3211 William Barksdale, heir to John [Barksdale]
b. William Barksdale
c. Thomas Robinson; Thomas Wasson, 1833; John Vastine; Peter Sharp; S. G. Strong, 1836

S-3453 650a C:50 X-1005 FRAN:WASH FRAN:NORW
a. W-3211 William Barksdale, heir to John [Barksdale]
b. William Barksdale
c. Unknown; Benjamin Sell? [Sills?] 1828; M. L. Sullivant, 1831; A. Galloway, 1831; John Marcey, 1833; Peter Sells, Junior, 1830

S-3453 561a C:50 X-1005 FRAN:WASH
a. W-3211 William Barksdale, heir to John [Barksdale]
b. William Barksdale
c. Unknown; Jeremiah McLene, 1827

S-3453 456a C:50 X-1005 FRAN:NORW
a. W-3211 William Barksdale, heir to John [Barksdale]
b. William Barksdale
c. John Marcey; M. L. Sullivant, 1835

S-3459 400a B:504 X-0340 UNIO:PARI
a. W-1848 James Waters
b. James Waters
c. L[ucas] Sullivant

S-3460 467a C:496 X-0340 MADI:DARB
a. W-3731 James Casady
b. James Cassaday
c. Unknown; Simeon Hagen, 1836

S-3462 666a C:240 X-0750 UNIO:LIBE
a. W-3414 John Scarbrough
b. John Scarborough
c. John R. Turner; James Taylor, 1829; John N. Turner

S-3462 150a D:436 X-0750 UNIO:LIBE
a. W-3414 John Scarbrough
b. Duncan McArthur
c. None

S-3464* 400a B:230 X-0340 MADI:DARB
a. W-1666 Mary Bradley
b. Robert Cochran
c. Daniel R. Bigelow, 1837
*Source B notation: "Not patented."

S-3468 889a --* -- UNIO:YORK**
a. W-0741 Lieutenant John Bowen
b. John Bowen
c. None
*No citation given for this survey, but probably C:115 with the two tracts immediately following.
**Source B notation: "Somerville."

S-3469 889a C:115 X-0110 UNIO:YORK
a. W-0741 Lieutenant John Bowen
b. John Bowen
c. John Johnson

S-3470 889a C:115 X-0110 UNIO:YORK
a. W-0741 Lieutenant John Bowen
b. John Bowen
c. John Keener? [Keenes?]; R. L? [S?] Judy, 1836

S-3472 400a B:221 X-0750 LOGA:RUSH
a. W-4856 William Coats
b. Charles Humphreys
c. None

S-3473 400a D:369 X-0135 UNIO:JACK
a. W-1036 John Williams
b. John Williams
c. None

S-3474* 81a E:389 X-0345 FRAN:BROW MADI:--**
a. W-3213 William Hackney; Michael Burk [assignee?]
b. Kendall Thomas
c. *See* S-3474 which follows
*Source B shows 300a to Michael Burk.
**Source B does not mention Madison County.

S-3474* 219a E:416 X-0345 FRAN:BROW MADI:--**
a. W-3410 David Shepherd, 100a
W-3590 John Kearns, 100a
W-3213 William Hackney, 19a; *all three warrants assigned to* Michael Burke
b. Kendall Thomas
c. B. Boyd, 1837; Unknown; C. Higgins, 1835
*Source B shows 300a granted to Michael Burk; evidently the grant was split and reregistered.
**Source B does not mention Madison County.

S-3475 400a C:462 X-1000 UNIO:JERO
a. W-2912 William Hendrin
b. Robert Woodcock
c. None

S-3476 750a B:417 X-0340 CHAM:RUSH
a. W-1981* William Cherry
b. John Askew
c. None
*This warrant already used in S-1840.

S-3480 700a C:252 X-0750 UNIO:LIBE
a. W-0822 John Martin, 100a
W-1598 John Purcell, 200a
W-2821 James Hawkins; Stockline Hayley [assignee?] 400a
b. Samuel Bayley
c. John McLain; John Custar, 1837; Edgar Sherk & -- Moore

S-3481 136a C:366 X-0340 FRAN:PLEA
a. W-4849 James Johnson, assignee of Andrew A. Gilchrist, represenative of George [Gilchrist]
b. Lucas Sullivant
c. None

S-3482 567a B:226 X-0340 UNIO:DARB
a. W-2988 Richard Stephenson, heir to Hugh [Stephenson]
b. Richard Stephenson
c. None

S-3483 450a B:226 X-0340 UNIO:DARB
a. W-2988 Richard Stephenson, heir to Hugh [Stephenson] 300a
W-4849 James Johnson, assignee of Andrew A. Gilchrist, representative of George [Gilchrist] 150a
b. Richard Stephenson & L[ucas] Sullivant*
c. None
*Source B does not mention Lucas Sullivant.

S-3484 800a B:227 X-0340 UNIO:DARB UNIO:JERO
a. W-4732 Battle Harrison, representative
b. Lucas Sullivant
c. None

S-3485 267a C:264 X-0340 FRAN:PLEA
a. W-0205 Captain Thomas Thucutt? [Thewait? Thweatt?]
b. Thomas Thiveath*
c. None
*Source B spells Thiveatt.

S-3487* 400a D:106 X-0755 UNIO:LIBE
a. W-3615 William Dangerfield
b. William Dangerfield
c. None
*Source B notation: "Not patented."

S-3487 200a D:106 X-0755 UNIO:LIBE
a. W-3365 Joel Jones
b. Joel Jones
c. None

S-3487 191a D:106 X-0755 UNIO:LIBE
a. W-4135 Thomson Davis
b. Thomas Davis*
c. None
*Source B says Thompson Davis.

S-3489* 200a -- -- UNIO?: --
a. --
b. Robert Rains
c. --
*Not listed in Source A; Source B notation: "Not found."

S-3489* 100a -- -- UNIO: --
a. --
b. Abraham Richie
c. --
*Not listed in Source A; Source B notation: "Not found."

S-3490 100a D:106 X-0755 UNIO:LIBE
a. W-3706 William Ritchie
b. William Richie
c. None

S-3490 100a D:106 X-0755 UNIO:LIBE
a. W-3558 Samuel Hoffer
b. John Hoopwood*
c. None
*Source B spells Hopwood.

S-3498* 200a -- -- UNIO?: --
a. --
b. Hugh Parkinson
c. --
*Listed in Source B only (in sequential place).

S-3498* 200a -- -- UNIO?: --
a. --
b. Jacob Campbell
c. --
*Listed in Source B only; notation says "not found."

S-3498* 233a -- -- UNIO?: --
a. --
b. Michael Buckley
c. --
*Listed in Source B only (at sequential place).

S-3501 300a B:235 X-0570 ROSS:HUNT
a. W-4807 John King, 100a
W-4720 William G. Payne, assignee [of?] John Evans, heir to John McDowell, 100a
W-3189 Sylvester? Coburn? 100a
b. John McDonald
c. None

S-3505 367a B:236 X-0840 ROSS:BUCK
a. W-4793 William Pyle
b. Thomas Worthington
c. None

S-3509 100a B:372 X-1370 PICK:WAYN
a. W-0248 William Evans
b. William Evans
c. None

S-3511 472a B:222 X-1004 DELA:SCIO
a. W-1623 Lieutenant Javin Miller
b. James Miller
c. L[ucas] Sullivant; Lyne Starling, 1826

S-3512 125a B:180 X-0570 CLER:FRAN
a. W-2829 Richard Harrison, heir to James Harrison
b. Richard C[lough] Anderson
c. None

S-3513 1000a B:180 X-0570 CLER:TATE
a. W-1963 William Taliaferro, heir to Colonel [William] Taliaferro
b. Richard C[lough] Anderson
c. J. Barrett; E. Salt, 1823; Wright Donnelly; Thomas Kain, 1824; Thomas Early; Z. Chapman, 1824; J. Higgenbotham; Eleazar Williams, 1823; William Hiland; T. Morris, 1823; David Hyland; R. Tweed, 1825; A. Jones; W. Waynwright, 1826; N. Kyle; William C. Moore, 1826; W. Reddick; E. Shaw, 1825; D. Holmes; C. Dennison, 1833; C. Davidson; W. S. Patterson, 1835

S-3514 200a B:162 X-1303 BROW:HUNT
a. W-3459 Elizabeth Carr
b. Elizabeth Carr
c. W. Higgins; P. L. Wilson, 1841

S-3515 200a B:162 X-1303 HIGH:WHIT BROW: --*
a. W-3459 Elizabeth Carr
b. Elizabeth Carr
c. None
*Source B does not mention Brown County.

S-3516 770a B:162 X-1303 HIGH:WHIT BROW: --*
a. W-0628 Captain Walker Baylor
b. Walker Baylor
c. J. Miller
*Source B does not mention Brown County.

S-3517 80a B:205 X-1303 HIGH:WHIT
a. W-0628 Captain Walker Baylor
b. Walker Baylor
c. None

S-3518 365a B:161 X-1303 BROW:WASH BROW:SCOT
a. W-2926 Captain Custes Kendall
b. Curtis Kendall
c. None

S-3519 670a B:161 X-1303 BROW:WASH BROW:SCOT
a. W-2926 Captain Custes Kendall
b. Curtis Kendall
c. R. Davis; Gabriel Pindle, 1828

S-3520 192a B:161 X-1300 BROW:WASH
a. W-2926 Captain Custes Kendall
b. Curtis Kendall
c. None

S-3522 150a B:258 X-0800 ADAM:SPRI
a. W-0796 Henry Holdcraft Norvell
b. John Beasley & William Lucas
c. W. Kenney; Aaron Noel, 1840

S-3523 50a B:258 X-0130* SCIO:UNIO
a. W-0796 Henry Holdcraft Norvell
b. John Beasley & William Lucas
c. William Kendall (grist & sawmill); W. Gharkey, 1831
*"Scioto Brush Creek."

S-3524 140a B:261 X-0800 ADAM:SPRI
a. W-1083 James Cunningham
b. John Morgan
c. None

S-3525 96a B:263 X-0420 BROW:BYRD
a. W-4254 Anthony W. White
b. Alexander Parker
c. None

S-3527 68a B:524 X-0420 BROW:UNIO BROW:BYRD
a. W-4199 Sampson Henderson; Frederich Dyche [Deutsch] assignee
b. Jeptha Beasley
c. None

S-3529. *See* S-2617

S-3530. *See* S-3175

S-3531 300a B:167 X-0130 ADAM:TIFF ADAM:MEIG
a. W-0610 Captain John Winston
b. John Winston
c. None

S-3532 550a B:171 X-0130 ADAM:MEIG
a. W-0405 William Tompkins, heir to H. Tompkins
b. William Tompkins
c. William Tompkins, heirs; L? [S?] Treat, 1824

S-3538 160a B:261 X-0420 BROW:UNIO BROW:BYRD
a. W-3708 Henry Lawson, 100a
W-1083 James Cunningham, 60a
b. John Morgan
c. J. Ellis; -- Wilson & -- Middleton, 1842

S-3540 100a B:525 X-0424 BROW:BYRD BROW:JACK
a. W-0949 William Kingere?
b. John Machin*
c. None
*Source B spells Machir.

S-3541 100a F:200 X-0420 BROW:JACK
a. W-1196 John Pulham
b. Benjamin Kendrick
c. None

S-3542 167a B:258 X-0133 ADAM:TIFF
a. W-4846 Simon Morgan, assignee of the representative of Allen Walker
b. John Beasley & A[ndrew] Ellison
c. J. Key; Henry Rape? [Rasse?] 1827

S-3543 100a B:301 X-0133 ADAM:TIFF
a. W-1657 Jacob Dener
b. Clement Biddle
c. None

S-3544 33a B:297 X-0760 PIKE:BENT
a. W-1062 Samuel Smith
b. Andrew Ellison
c. John Groves, heirs; James? [Joseph?] Penniston, 1831

S-3546 965a B:262 X-0130 ADAM:WINC
a. W-3948 Presley Roley, 400a
W-3947* George Peay, representative, 200a
W-3473 Leonard Cooper, 365a
b. Samuel McCullock
c. R. Smith; T. Huston, 1829; Benjamin Medough; John Robinson, heirs; James Robinson, 1833; Henry Rape, 1831
*Warrant already used in S-2630.

S-3549 450a D:213 X-1300 BROW:PLEA
a. W-1920 Colonel Josiah Parker
b. Josiah Parker
c. None

S-3551 1700a B:243 X-0570 CLER:TATE
a. W-1963 William Taliaferro, heir to Colonel [William] Taliaferro, 700a?
W-2829 Richard Harrison, heir to James Harrison, 793a?
W-4592 Samuel O[verton] Pettus, 207a?
b. Richard C[lough] Anderson
c. L? [S?] Thompson; Charles Hunt, 1824; G. C. Light; T. Canter, 1828; O. T. Fishback, 1827; John Harvie, heirs; John Boggess, 1822

S-3552 100a B:253 X-0570 CLER:WASH
a. W-4854 John Williamson
b. John Graham
c. None

S-3553 100a B:290 X-0840 ROSS:PAXT
a. W-1761 John Randolph
b. David Rees
c. None

S-3554 100a B:303 X-0134 ADAM:SCOT
a. W-4661 Thomas Peers
b. Robert H. Sanders
c. None

S-3555 333a B:376 X-0840 ROSS:PAXT ROSS:TWIN
a. W-2190 Samuel Hodgins, 233a
W-3300 John Maden Wilson, 100a
b. [Samuel] Hodgins & [John Maden] Wilson
c. None

S-3556 100a C:125 X-0134 ADAM:SCOT
a. W-1493 James Crawley
b. John Elliott
c. None

S-3557 80a C:518 X-0840 FAYE:GREE
a. W-4245 Hugh Donaghe, exe[cutor] to John Massie
b. Hugh Donaghe
c. J? Hutton

S-3560* 100a — — PIKE:PERR DELA:SCIO**
a. —
b. Moses Caruthers
c. —
*Listed in Source B only (at sequential place).
**Source B notation in pencil appears to refer to this survey.

S-3561 100a D:60 X-1005 HARD:DUDL
a. W-4833 John Lee
b. John See*
c. None
*Source B may spell Lee.

S-3562 667a B:472 X-0840* FAYE:PAIN
a. W-4693 Presley Thorton
b. James Taylor
c. None
*"East fork of main fork of . . ."

S-3563* 400a — — FAYE: —
a. —
b. William Price
c. William Radford; R. Douglas, 1832
*Listed in Source B (at sequential place) but crossed out.

S-3564* 200a B:313 X-0840 ROSS:TWIN
a. W-1072 Charles Brooks
b. Henry Clines
c. None
*Source B notation: "Not patented."

S-3565 100a B:200 X-1000 ROSS:FRAN
a. W-3760 Thomas Prichard
b. John Fowler
c. None

S-3567. *See* S-3054

S-3568 650a B:179 X-0130 ADAM:GREE ADAM:MONR
a. W-0815 Brigadier General Charles Scott, 350a?
W-2452 Colonel William Davies, 300a?
b. N[athaniel] Massie & [W.] Davis
c. William Smith; Robert E. Lockhart, 1824; William Smith, heirs; L? [S?] Cole, 1842

S-3569. *See* S-2468

S-3570. *See* S-2462

S-3571. *See* S-3052

S-3752 100a B:176 X-1120 BROW:BYRD
a. W-0468* —
b. John Jouitt
c. S. T. Masterson & — Middleton, 1823
*Source C does not show that this warrant number was used.

S-3573 1120a B:181 X-0840 HIGH:MADI
a. W-3069 William Randolph, representative
b. Richard Bibb
c. — Kirley? [Kirby?] & — Starling, 1831

S-3574 1390a B:181 X-0840 HIGH:MADI
a. W-3069 William Randolph, representative, 1347a
W-3133 William Randolph, representative, 43a
b. Richard Bibb
c. — Kirley? [Kirby?] & — Starling, 1831

S-3575 200a B:181 X-0840 FAYE:WAYN
a. W-3133* William Randolph, representative
b. Richard Bibb
c. None
*Almost certainly, W-3069 is meant, as W-3133 was completely used elsewhere.

S-3576 475a B:180 X-0500 GREE:SUGA GREE:XENI
a. W-2331 Captain Lewis Booker
b. Lewis Booker
c. None

S-3577 250a B:180 X-0180 GREE:SUGA GREE:XENI
a. W-2331 Captain Lewis Booker
b. Lewis Booker
c. None

S-3578 233a B:190 X-1000 ROSS:FRAN
a. W-0815 Brigadier General Charles Scott
b. Charles Scott
c. None

S-3579 1016a B:284 X-0640 HIGH:FAIR
a. W-0205 Captain Thomas Thucutt? [Thewait? Thweatt?] 950a?
W-0227 Lieutenant Jacob Coleman, 66a?
b. Richard C[lough] Anderson
c. David Swain; Jacob Chalfant, 1831; J. Green; W. Scott, 1838; William Scott

S-3582 1016a -- -- HIGH:BRUS
a. --
b. -- Douglas & -- Haynes
c. Nathan Douglas; S. A. Keys, 1828; William Keys, 1831

S-3583 280a B:175 X-0660 GREE:SUGA
a. W-2374 Lieutenant George Holland
b. George Holland
c. M. Wynans, 1828

S-3584 230a B:175 X-0660 GREE:SUGA
a. W-2374 Lieutenant George Holland
b. George Holland
c. M. Wynans, 1828

S-3585 240a B:176 X-0660 GREE:SUGA
a. W-2374 Lieutenant George Holland
b. George Holland
c. None

S-3586 250a B:176 X-0660 GREE:XENI
a. W-2374 Lieutenant George Holland
b. George Holland
c. None

S-3587 260a B:180 X-0133 ADAM:FRAN HIGH: --*
a. W-0325 Marquis Calmes
b. Marquis Calmes
c. None
*Source B does not mention Highland County.

S-3593 300a B:244 X-0134 ADAM:SCOT HIGH:CONC
a. W-4844 Levi Phillips, 200a
W-4845 Joseph Williamson, 100a; *both warrants assigned to* Joseph Foreman
b. Joseph Foreman
c. Joseph Robbins; James Campbell, 1826; Thomas Williamson; Hy. Landress; S. Campbell, 1837; Thomas Huston; Unknown; -- Kirby & -- Starling, 1831 (Highland County)

S-3595 200a B:408 X-1270 HIGH: --* FAYE:GREE
a. W-3408 Henry Goran
b. Daniel Brown & Company
c. None
*Source B does not mention Highland County.

S-3596 1000a B:288 X-1303 HIGH:SALE
a. W-4688 Charles Lewis, deceased, the representative of
b. Charles Lewis, representative of
c. A. E. Carver; J. Davidson, 1828; J. Donaho; John McFarland; Isaac Woods, 1833

S-3598 300a B:247 X-1140 PIKE:MIFF
S-3770
a. W-3170 Duncan Young, 200a
W-4725 Lawrence Vancamp, 100a
b. Henry Massie
c. J. Davis; G. Taylor, 1826; "patented to Joseph Kerr"

S-3601 1000a B:201 X-0133 ADAM:FRAN
a. W-4688 Charles Lewis, deceased, the representative of
b. Charles Lewis, representative of
c. Robert Murphey; Absalom Lafferty, 1826; William Armstrong; T. Francis, 1829; Thomas Reid; Joseph Darlington, 1828

S-3602* 150a C:261 X-0840 ROSS:BUCK
a. W-0852 John Beck
b. John Beck
c. John Beck, heirs; R. Stewart; George Batain? [Batam?] 1835
*Source B notation: "Not patented."

S-3604 110a B:271 X-1000 ROSS:SCIO
a. W-1921 General Robert Lawson, 55a?
W-3809 Richard Baker, 55a?
b. Nathaniel Massie
c. None

S-3606 1000a B:201 X-1300 BROW:LEWI BROW:CLAR
a. W-3475 Leonard Cooper
b. John Wilkins
c. Thomas Middleton, 1824; John Wilkins, Junior; John Herter? 1826; Unknown; M. Weaver, 1827; John McGuire; F. Bingaman, 1834; Hugh Kennedy, 1831

S-3607 100a B:344 X-0450 BROW:HUNT
a. W-3837 Reuben Odel
b. John Parker
c. George Boherer, 1828; Mathew Gray; William Hewitt, 1834

S-3608 460a B:190 X-0840 ROSS:PAXT
a. W-3221 William Reynolds, assignee of John Fauntleroy, heir to Captain -- Fauntleroy, 315a?
W-3809 Richard Baker; Nathaniel Massie [assignee?] 145a?

S-3608 [continued]
b. John Stealy & James Kerr
c. None

S-3609 100a B:246 X-0840 ROSS:PAXT
a. W-0635 Captain Archibald Denholm
b. John Harvie
c. None

S-3610 780a B:251 X-0660 GREE:SUGA
a. W-0815 Brigadier General Charles Scott
b. Alexander Parker & James Parker
c. None

S-3612 285a B:279 X-0840 FAYE:CONC
a. W-2655 William Lawson, heir to C. Lawson
b. William Lawson
c. None

S-3614 240a B:279 X-1301 BROW:BYRD
a. W-2610 Lieutenant John Foster
b. John H. Foster
c. Peter Machir; Hugh Maharry, 1823

S-3615 1000a B:190 X-0840 FAYE:UNIO
a. W-3626 Robert Sayers, "resolution"
b. Robert Sayers
c. None

S-3616* 207a -- -- CLER: --
a. --
b. John Obannon
c. James Forsythe; J. Sargeant, 1824; James Galbreath [*also* Gilbreath]; S. Weaver, 1826; Z. Chapman, 1823; R. Tweed; Betsy Bagby; Stirling Bagby, 1831; J. Biddle, 1832; J. Battle, 1834; A. Miller, heirs; J. O. Prather, 1836; A. C. Day; B. South; W. Pollard, 1839; J. Hull, 1841
*Listed in Source B only (at top of page preceding S-3606). *See also* S-2961

S-3618 192a B:204 X-0840 FAYE:CONC
a. W-3326 William S. Hawkins, heir
b. William S. Hawkins
c. William Harper; Thomas Coil, 1831; S. Jones; James Hogue, 1839

S-3619 367a B:292 X-1130 FAYE:UNIO
a. W-4666 Robert Forsythe & John Forsythe
b. John Brown
c. -- Hopkins & -- McLane, 1827; John Brown; David Wright, 1833; J. Jameson, 1835; "deeded David Wright, asignee of -- McLean & -- Hopkins, 14 Dec 1831"

S-3620 137a B:286 X-0840 FAYE:UNIO
a. W-1856* Robert Kimble, 100a
W-1855** James Grimsley, 100a
b. John Brown
c. None
*This warrant already used in S-2253.
**This warrant already used in S-1530.

S-3621 560a B:197 X-0660 CLER:MIAM
a. W-1677 Lieutenant William Winston, 280a?
W-0137 Richard Stark, 280a?
b. John Harvie & Richard Stark
c. None

S-3622 400a B:198 X-0663 BROW:STER
a. W-1635 John Scott, 200a
W-3544 William Day, 100a
W-4283 Thomas Cooper, 100a; *latter two warrants assigned to* William Lytle
b. Archibald McIlvain
c. Benjamin Wells, 1824

S-3623 200a B:197 X-0660 CLER:MIAM CLER:GOSH
a. W-4603 John Tale? administrator of Matt[hew] Lattimore
b. Joseph Lindsay
c. None

S-3624 150a B:197 X-0790 CLER:GOSH
a. W-0942 Thomas Hall
b. Francis Graham
c. None

S-3625 300a B:199 X-0663 BROW:PIKE
a. W-3277 Samuel Blundel, 100a
W-3579 Ewell Townsend, 200a
b. S[amuel] Blundil & E[well] Townsend
c. None

S-3626 220a B:321 X-1370 PICK:WAYN
a. W-0088 Captain Strether Jones
b. -- Patton, -- Hackley, & -- Thompson
c. A. Latham; P. H. Junior; James Evans, 1827; P. R. Julian, 1829; John Evans, 1827; Isaac W. Julian, 1833; W. J. Julian

S-3627 1000a B:200 X-0170 BROW:CLAR
a. W-2507 Captain Holt Richerson
b. Holt Richerson*
c. William Lytle; T. Kirby, 1823; Alexander Mitchell; Benjamin Bayless, 1824; William H. Allen; G. Bingaman, 1832
*Source B spells Richeson.

S-3628 200a B:200 X-0800 BROW:CLAR
a. W-2507 Captain Holt Richerson
b. Holt Richerson*
c. John Jones, 1826; M. Moss; M. Weaver; James Moss; C. White, 1835
*Source B spells Richeson.

S-3629 150a B:209 X-1303 BROW:EAGL
a. W-0649 Captain Lawrence Trent
b. Lawrence Trent
c. Unknown; Aaron F. Siscoe, 1831

S-3630 88a B:205 X-1303 HIGH:WHIT
a. W-2630?* Daniel Flowerre; W. Young [assignee?]
W-2632?* John Redwood
b. Benjamin Grimes
c. None
*Both warrants previously used (S-1318 and S-0540).

S-3631 300a B:205 X-1303 BROW:EAGL
a. W-0745 Peter Casey, heir to Benjamin Casey
b. Peter Casey
c. Charles G. Dorsey; George Shultz, 1824; James Thomas, 1828; Mathew Kincaid, 1830; Griffin W. Jones

S-3632 200a B:206 X-1303 HIGH:WHIT
a. W-3506 Braddock Vaden
b. Anthony Hayden*
c. A. Wills; G. W. Barriere, 1826
*Source B spells Haden.

S-3633 100a B:208 X-1303 HIGH:WHIT
a. W-0597 Captain John Spotswood
b. John Spottswood*
c. William Mahon, 1828
*Source B spells Spotswood.

S-3634 116a B:208 X-1303 BROW:EAGL BROW:WASH
a. W-2443 Captain William Pierce
b. William Pierce
c. James Taylor; Thomas Adams, 1827; Orange Hamilton; E. Mannon, 1838; R. Kincaid; P. L? [S?] Wilson, 1841

S-3642 650a B:210 X-0840 MADI:STOK
a. W-0174 Captain William White
b. William White
c. S. Herrod, 1834

S-3643 600a B:284 X-1170 CLIN:VERN
a. W-0033 Dennis Reddy, 200a
W-0907 Robert Stokes, 200a
W-3535 George Scott, 100a
W-3953 Job Jenkins, 100a
b. William Barlow
c. None

S-3644 267a B:283 X-1170 CLIN:UNIO CLIN:WASH
a. W-3135 James Fair, assignee
b. David Ross
c. None

S-3645 133a B:285 X-1170 CLIN:VERN
a. W-4182 Thomas Waring, heir to Henry [Waring]
b. Thomas Waring
c. M. Barlow; S? [L?] Duval; S? [L?] Daniel; L? [S?] Shepherd, 1825

S-3646 194a B:206 X-0840 FAYE:JEFF
a. W-0060 Captain Samuel Jones
b. Samuel Jones
c. -- Phelps & -- Woods, 1828; Richard Douglas, 1829; R. Douglas; J? [I?] Y. Green, 1831

S-3647 276a B:206 X-0840 FAYE:JEFF GREE: --*
a. W-0060 Captain Samuel Jones
b. Samuel Jones
c. -- Phelps & -- Woods, 1829; Griffith Foos, 1833; "deeded heirs of Henry Phelps, 15 Sep 1838"
*Source B does not mention Greene County.

S-3648 500a B:205 X-0840 FAYE:PAIN
a. W-2157 William Eustace
b. William Eustace
c. None

S-3649 1000a B:206 X-0840 MADI:STOK FAYE: --*
a. W-2157 William Eustace
b. William Eustace
c. J. Obannon; A. Douglas, 1838
*Source B does not mention Fayette County.

S-3654 267a B:208 X-0840 FAYE:JEFF
a. W-2570 Lieutenant William Quarles
b. William Quarles
c. None

S-3655 222a B:208 X-1303 BROW:WASH HIGH: --*
a. W-2570 Lieutenant William Quarles
b. William Quarles
c. None
*Source B does not list township, although Highland County is mentioned.

S-3656 178a B:208 X-1303 HIGH:CLAY BROW: --*
a. W-2570 Lieutenant William Quarles
b. William Quarles
c. William Scott, 1833
*Source B does not mention Brown County.

S-3657 33a B:282 X-1303 BROW:WASH
a. W-4182 Thomas Waring, heir to Henry [Waring]
b. Thomas Waring
c. William Barlow, heirs; Levi Estell, 1823; Unknown; Gabriel Pendel, 1831

S-3658. *See* S-2532

S-3659 1600a B:202 X-1303 HIGH:NEWM*
a. W-4871 William Bunberry
b. Henry Massie
c. None
*Source B notation: "New Market."

S-3660 1000a B:201 X-1300 HIGH:SALE
a. W-4871 William Bunberry
b. Henry Massie
c. G. Jackson; J. Davidson, 1828

S-3661 1000a B:201 X-0133 ADAM:FRAN
a. W-4688 Charles Lewis, deceased, representative of
b. Charles Lewis, representative of
c. Unknown; D. Boyle, 1828; T. Francis; T. Huston, 1841; J. Owens; G. Leman, 1842

S-3662 583a B:203 X-1300 BROW:LEWI
a. W-3394 James Frisby Leith*
b. James Frishby Leitch
c. J. Patterson; T. L. Hamer, 1827
*Source B spells Frisby.

S-3663. *See* S-2901

S-3665 667a B:505 X-0360 PICK:DEER
a. W-3477 Abraham Shepherd; Joseph Petty, Nathaniel Massie, Duncan McArthur [assignees?]
b. Ralph Morgan
c. None

S-3666 683a D:506 X-1300 BROW:PLEA
S-3915 BROW:LEWI
a. W-2938 Thomas Glascock
b. Walter Dun
c. D. Crawford, 1840; John Graham

S-3667* 52a C:523 X-0042 ADAM:MONR
a. W-0067 William Giles, heir to John Giles
b. William Giles
c. James Moore; John McDaide, 1826
*Source B notation: "Not patented."

S-3669* 1000a B:233 X-0130** ADAM:JEFF
a. W-1049 William Barr? [Marr?] 200a
W-1066 Henry Vann, 200a
W-1081 Daniel Easterwine, 200a
W-1087 Thomas Moose? [Moore?] 200a
W-1139 John Morrison, 200a
b. Alexander Fowler
c. G. H. Punteney? [Pernteney?] Junior, 1828
*Source B notation: "Not patented."
**"Scioto Brush Creek."

S-3669 1000a B:233 X-0130* ADAM:GREE
a. W-1046 Garrel Cavennear, 200a
W-1105 John Rooke, 200a
W-1113 John Doherty, 200a
W-1140 John Guthrey, 200a
W-1149 Jonathan Welch, 200a
b. Alexander Fowler
c. None
*"Scioto Brush Creek."

S-3670 260a* C:278 X-0301 PIKE:JACK
ROSS:—**
a. W-0911 Michael Dean; Elias Langheim*** [assignee?]
W-3969 George Blackmore, heir to Thomas [Blackmore] 100a
b. Elias Laugham***
c. None
*Source B says 200 acres.
**Source B does not list township, although Ross County is mentioned.
***So spelled.

S-3671 300a B:349 X-0540 PICK:DEER
a. W-0946 George Black, 100a
W-0952 George Wafield? [Mafield?] 100a
W-0984 Thomas Pollock, 100a
b. Andrew Wolf
c. None

S-3672* 200a -- -- CHAM: --
a. --
b. Adam Dean
c. Thomas Stewart; William? Barrett
*Listed in Source B only (at top of page before entry S-3654).

S-3673 90a B:282 X-0840 FAYE:JEFF
a. W-0174 Captain William White
b. William White
c. None

S-3674 710a B:277 X-0840 MADI:STOK
a. W-0011* --
b. Andrew Dunscomb
c. F. Andrick; George Linson? [Sinson?] 1826
*This warrant number probably is erroneous.

S-3675 550a B:282 X-0840 FAYE:UNIO
a. W-2433 Lewis Starke, assignee of B. Starke & W. Starke
b. Lewis Starke
c. None

S-3677 100a B:285 X-0640 HIGH:FAIR
FAYE: --*
a. W-1850 Doctor Robert Rose
b. Robert Rose**
c. None
*Source B does not mention Fayette County.
**Source B might read Rape.

S-3678 111a B:354 X-0946 FAYE:GREE
a. W-2265 Lieutenant Francis Brooke
b. Francis Brooke
c. None

S-3679 200a B:214 X-0340 MADI*:UNIO
a. W-4594 John Munford Gregory, heir to John Gregory
b. John M. Gregory
c. Thomas Harris; M. L. Sullivant, 1831
*Source B also has pencilled notation possibly naming Franklin County.

S-3680 2000a B:224 X-0050 LOGA:ZANE
a. W-1775 Lieutenant Robert Power
b. Robert Power
c. Robert Powers; Lyne Starling, 1831

S-3681 1000a B:227 X-0340 UNIO:DARB
UNIO:ALLE
LOGA: --*
a. W-4868 Alvin Mountjoy
b. Lucas Sullivant
c. L. Starling; S. G. Strong, 1836
*Source B does not mention Logan County, but does Champaign County.

S-3682 311a B:228 -- UNIO:DARB
a. W-1775 Lieutenant Robert Power, 111a
W-2154 Andrew Knight, 100a
W-3136 William Buford, 100a
b. [Robert] Power & [Lucas] Sullivant
c. None

S-3683 1000a B:231 X-0660 LOGA:JEFF
LOGA:LAKE
a. W-1775 Lieutenant Robert Power
b. Robert Power
c. Lot T. Janney; William Charles, 1830; R. McMullen; Anthony Casad, 1835; R. S? [L?] Canbey, 1841

S-3684 720a B:219 X-0340 CHAM:WAYN
LOGA: --*
a. W-4799 James Calderwood, representative of
b. James Calderwood, representative of**
c. Caleb Russell, heirs; W. Turner? 1833; Lydia Russel; Thomas Hunter; S. G. Strong; R. L. Broome, 1840; Jae? [Jacob?] Woolston
*Source B does not mention Logan County.
**Source B lists as James Caldwell, representatives [of].

S-3685 667a B:227 X-0340 MADI:DARB
UNIO:JERO
a. W-4868 Alvin Mountjoy
b. Lucas Sullivant
c. None

S-3686 1000a B:227 X-0340 UNIO:JERO
a. W-4868 Alvin Mountjoy
b. Lucas Sullivant
c. None

S-3687 549a B:224 X-0340 UNIO:DARB
a. W-3187 John Scott
b. John Scott
c. None

S-3688 389a B:229 X-0340 LOGA:ZANE
a. W-2921 Layton Yancey
b. Layton Yancey
c. None

S-3689 600a B:229 X-1330 UNIO:LIBE
a. W-3485* Francis Graves; Thomas Flower [assignee?] 200a
W-3484 Francis Graves, assignee, 200a
W-3481 Francis Graves, assignee, 200a
b. Jacob Woolston
c. John Barnes; S. G. Strong, 1836; C. Allen; R. L. Broome, 1840
*This warrant already completely used on S-3134.

S-3690 1000a B:220 X-0110 UNIO:YORK
a. W-4791 Falvery Frazer, representative of W. Frazer, deceased
b. Falvery Frazer
c. Robert Means; J. S. Watkins, 1839

S-3691 1000a B:220 X-0110 UNIO:LEES
a. W-4791 Falvery Frazer, representative of W. Frazer, deceased
b. Falvery Frazer
c. H. W. Perkins, 1831

S-3692 1000a B:220 X-0110 UNIO:LEES
a. W-4791 Falvery Frazer, representative of W. Frazer, deceased
b. Falvery Frazer
c. None

S-3693 1000a B:220 X-0110 UNIO:LEES
a. W-4791 Falvery Frazer, representative of W. Frazer, deceased
b. Falvery Frazer
c. None

S-3694 1000a B:220 X-0110 UNIO:LEES
a. W-2839 Thomas Frazer, heir to Fal[very] Frazer
b. Thomas Frazer
c. John R. Parish; S. G. Strong, 1825; Unknown; Robert Gordon

S-3695 667a B:221 X-0730 CHAM:WAYN
a. W-2839 Thomas Frazer, heir to Fal[very] Frazer
b. Thomas Frazer
c. J. Wicklam; E. Thomas, 1828; Nicholas D. Scott, 1828

S-3696 1000a B:221 X-0110 UNIO:LEES
DELA: --*
a. W-2839 Thomas Frazer, heir to Fal[very] Frazer
b. Thomas Frazer
c. Unknown; Samuel Hughes, 1820-1826
*Source B mentions Delaware County, but does not give township.

S-3697 100a B:215 X-0340 UNIO:ALLE
MADI: --*
a. W-4781 George Moseley, representative of
b. George McCredie
c. Unknown; A. S? [L?] Stone, 1836; M. S. Butler (Union County); S. Hager? [Hagen?] 1840 (Madison County)
*Source B mentions Madison County, but does not give township.

S-3698 822a B:235 X-0150 ROSS:BUCK
a. W-0633 Captain Thomas Holt
b. Duncan McArthur
c. None

S-3699 50a B:233 X-0840 ROSS:BUCK
a. W-0633 Captain Thomas Holt
b. Duncan McArthur
c. None

S-3700 300a B:235 X-0840 ROSS:TWIN
a. W-0248 William Evans, 150a?
W-0633 Captain Thomas Holt, 150a?
b. Duncan McArthur
c. None

S-3701 765a B:309 X-0840 FAYE:UNIO
FAYE:PAIN
a. W-4796 Alexander Cummins
b. George Matthews*
c. Henry M. Surlinger? [Swilinger?]; A. Stewart, 1823; Michael Blue; J? [I?] Y. Green, 1832; N. F. Jones, 1834; M. Blue, heirs; J. M. Willis, 1840
*Source B spells Mathews and has notation: "Bloomingburg."

S-3702 545a B:309 X-0840 FAYE:UNIO
a. W-1935* Lieutenant George Carrington, 310a?
W-4795 Alexander Cummins, 135a?
W-2918 Michael Barret, 100a
b. George Matthews**
c. None
*This warrant already completely used in S-0872, S-0935, and S-1071.
**Source B spells Mathews.

S-3703 1200a B:236 X-0840 FAYE:PAIN
a. W-4793 William Pyle
b. Thomas Worthington
c. Samuel Gillespie; C. B. Woodruff, 1831

S-3704 600a B:234 X-0840 FAYE:PAIN
a. W-4267 John Smith
b. Thomas Hoff
c. None

S-3705 500a B:234 X-0840 FAYE:PAIN
a. W-4203* -- [100a]
W-2807 Griffith Haynes, 200a
W-1964 George Loyd, 200a
b. Thomas Hoff
c. None
*Source C does not show that this warrant number was used.

S-3706 500a B:234 X-0840 FAYE:PAIN
a. W-4898 Joseph Higdon, 400a?
W-4882 Basil Carlile, 100a?
b. Henry Bedinger
c. Jacob Funk; James Brooks, 1823; John Kleber; Thomas Turner, 1826

S-3707 400a B:235 X-0840 FAYE:PAIN
a. W-4804 Joshua Jenkins
b. John McClean
c. None

S-3708 400a B:235 X-0840 FAYE:PAIN
a. W-4419 William Reynolds, 200a
W-4464 Patrick Lockhart, assignee [of?] William Millisons; William Ritchey, assignee, 100a*
W-4421 Patrick Lockhart, assignee [of?] William Turner, 100a
b. Thomas Hoff
c. Adam Funk; Archibald? Stewart, 1824
*This warrant already completely used in S-2713.

S-3709 121a B:234 X-0840 ROSS:TWIN
a. W-3717 James Chavers, 100a
W-4267 John Smith, 21a
b. Thomas Hoff
c. Rebecca Loveless; John Adams, 1824

S-3710 67a B:322 X-0840 ROSS:TWIN
a. W-4874 Joseph White, Duncan McArthur
b. Joseph White
c. James McMullen, 1827

S-3711 33a C:272 X-0860 ROSS:FRAN
a. W-4874 Joseph White, Duncan McArthur
b. Duncan McArthur
c. None

S-3712 400a B:320 X-0150 ROSS:BUCK
a. W-1093 Peter Brandon, 200a
W-4119 John Milligan, 200a
b. John Robins
c. None

S-3713 200a B:321 X-0840 FAYE:WAYN
a. W-1088 William Craig
b. George Troughtes*
c. None
*Source B spells Troughs.

S-3714 800a B:328 X-0360 PICK:MONR
a. W-1674 Matthew Bayling, 200a
W-2243 Francis Bundy, 200a
W-1262 John Kairns, 400a
b. Valentine Kinder
c. None

S-3715 600a B:314 X-0360 PICK:MONR
PICK:DEER
a. W-1450 Major Samuel Finley
b. Samuel Finley
c. J. Tevebaugh; J. D. Caldwell, 1829; Isaac Davis; William McArthur, 1830

S-3716 1382a B:310 X-0360 PICK:DEER
a. W-4795 Alexander Cummins
b. George Matthews*
c. None
*Source B spells Mathews.

S-3717 1000a B:310 X-0360 PICK:DEER
ROSS:DEER
a. W-4795 Alexander Cummins
b. George Matthews*
c. None
*Source B spells Mathews.

S-3718 1085a B:310 X-0360 PICK:DEER
a. W-1934 Colonel George Matthews, 1000a?
W-4795 Alexander Cummins, 85a?
b. George Matthews*
c. R. Shanton [Stanton?] heirs; G. Botkin, 1835; T. S? [L?] Hines; James Gill, 1840; Harmon Skiles; Daniel Hanson, 1831
*Source B spells Mathews.

S-3719 393a B:372 X-0420 BROW:HUNT
a. W-4627 Henry Bedinger, 333a?
W-0291 Captain Henry Bedinger, 60a?
b. Henry Bedinger
c. D[uncan] McArthur; J. M. Trimble, 1837; -- Wilson & -- Middleton, 1842

S-3720 230a B:248 X-0840 ROSS:HUNT
a. W-4892 George Minzies, representative of
b. Hugh Boyle
c. Charles Martin, 1831

S-3721 58a B:248 X-0840 ROSS:HUNT
a. W-4892 George Minzies, representative of
b. Hugh Boyle
c. Charles Martin, 1831

S-3724 70a B:248 X-0840 ROSS:HUNT
S-3904
a. W-4892 George Minzies, representative of
b. Hugh Boyle
c. Pleasant Thurman, 1831

S-3725 400a B:320 X-0360 MADI:SUMM
a. W-1741 James Gray
b. James Steel
c. None

S-3726 200a B:314 X-0360 MADI:SUMM
a. W-3134 William Tiller; Thomas Huffard [assignee?]
b. Thomas Hoff & [Isaac] Taylor
c. G. Marday? [Marclay?]; D. Thompson, 1826

S-3727* 200a -- -- HARD:DUDL MARI**
a. --
b. Claiborne Maddox
c. D[uncan] McArthur, 1831 (Logan County)
*Listed in Source B only (at sequential place).
**Source B says: "Marion [County], lies in Hardin [County] Dudley [township]."

S-3729 100a B:257 X-0136* ADAM:TIFF
a. W-4883 John Popp
b. Joseph Barnes**
c. None
*"Right fork of Lk. fork . . ."
**Source B spells Barns.

S-3731 300a B:259 X-1040 SCIO:UNIO
a. W-0812 Colonel William Dark
b. William Dark
c. Samuel Garvin; J. Clark, 1840

S-3733 100a B:526 X-0423 ADAM:LIBE
a. W-4117 Thomas Smith; Benjamin Goodin [assignee?]
b. John Beasley
c. None

S-3734 267a B:264 X-0136* ADAM:TIFF
a. W-4254 Anthony W. White
b. Alexander Parker
c. None
*"Lk. fork . . ."

S-3735 100a B:257 X-0760 PIKE:MIFF
a. W-4117 Thomas Smith; Benjamin Goodin [assignee?]
b. John Beasley
c. None

S-3739 100a B:264 X-0190 PIKE:CAMP
a. W-4254 Anthony W. White
b. Alexander Parker
c. None

S-3739* 60a E:403 X-0195 PIKE: --
a. W-4254 Anthony W. White; Alexander Parker [assignee?]
b. Henry Starr, heirs [of?]
c. None
*This entry not shown in Source B.

S-3740 300a B:258 X-0134 ADAM:SCOT
S-3932
a. W-4929 Joseph Garner, 200a
W-4857 Clement Green; John Bailey [assignee?] 100a
b. John Beasley
c. None

S-3741* 100a B:228 X-0340 UNIO:ALLE
a. W-1241 James Wilson
b. James Wilson
c. Cyprian Lee; William Thompson
*Source B notation: "Not patented."

S-3742 200a B:228 X-0340 UNIO:ALLE
a. W-1025 Patrick Shannon
b. James Wilson
c. None

S-3743 600a B:224 X-0340 UNIO:JERO MADI:DARB
a. W-4192 William Hackworth, 200a
W-4860* William Roads? 200a
W-4861 James Collier, 200a
b. Robert Means
c. Unknown; D. Bigelow, 1837; J. Galloway, Junior
*Another warrant of the same number may have been issued, according to a footnote in Source C.

S-3744 100a B:228 X-0340 MADI*:DARB
a. W-1846 Jonathan Brown
b. William Taylor, Junior
c. Thomas Cornelius; Orris Parrish, 1823; Unknown; L. Stone, 1836 (Madison County)
*Source B says: "Union [County], lies in M[adison County] Darby [Township]."

S-3745 100a B:351 X-0740 GREE:XENI
a. W-0404 William Tompkins, heir to Robert Tompkins
b. William Tompkins
c. J. Newport; J. Galloway, 1824

S-3746 900a B:351 X-0740 GREE:MIAM GREE:XENI
a. W-0404 William Tompkins, heir to Robert Tompkins
b. William Tompkins
c. None

S-3747 100a B:242 X-1301 HIGH*:SALE
a. W-4348 George Knox
b. Robert Patterson
c. Job Egbert, 1828
*Source B notation: "Brown [County], lies in H[ighland County] Salem [Township]."

S-3748 200a B:232 X-0340 UNIO:ALLE
a. W-4731 Lawrence Harrison, 170a
W-4849 James Johnson, assignee of Andrew A. Gilchrist, representative of George [Gilchrist] 30a
b. Lucas Sullivant
c. Unknown

S-3749 600a B:230 X-0340 UNIO:ALLE
a. W-4876 James Longest, deceased, representative of 200a
W-4877 Joseph Fleppo [Flippo?] 100a
W-4106 Rowland Estes, 100a
W-3378 William Buifolk? [Burfoke?]*; Lucas Sullivant [assignee?] 100a
W-4146 John White, heir at law to Benjamin White; David White [assignee?] 100a
b. James Coleman, *et al*
c. James Bell; M. S. Butler, 1836; Ester Rolland; Unknown; R. L? [S?] Browne
*Jillson (*The Kentucky Land Grants: A Systematic Index to All of the Land Grants Recorded in the State Land Office in Frankfort, Kentucky, 1782-1924*) reads Burfott; Gwathmey (*Historical Register of Virginians in the Revolution: Soldiers, Sailors, Marines, 1775-1783*) reads Burfoot.

S-3750 100a B:232 X-0340 UNIO:JERO
a. W-2838 Thomas Sneed
b. Thomas Sneed
c. None

S-3751* 200a -- -- FRAN:BROW
a. --
b. Thomas Sanders, representatives of
c. Clark Higgins; J. Bryden, 1837; Unknown
*Listed in Source B only.

S-3752 100a B:230 X-0340 UNIO:ALLE
a. W-3692 George Custard
b. George Custard
c. Newton Sagar? 1837; L? [S?] Sterling

S-3753 1000a B:232 X-0050 LOGA:ZANE
a. W-4732 Battle Harrison, representative
b. Lucas Sullivant
c. None

S-3754 400a B:233 X-0340 UNIO:JERO
a. W-0351 Lieutenant Colonel Charles Simms
b. Charles Simms
c. None

S-3757* 200a C:26 X-0980 HIGH:LIBE
a. W-4330 William Brian
b. William R. Bernard
c. William Martin, 1831
*Source B says: "Not patented."

S-3758* 375a -- -- CLIN: --
a. --
b. E. Read
c. John Brown; W. McClary?; T. Davis, 1826; William McChesney; James Dakin, 1826
*Listed in Source B only (at top of page, preceding S-3751.

S-3762 400a B:316 X-0840 MADI:SUMM
a. W-1449 William Wedabar [Wedeburn?] 200a
W-4887 Andrew Coon, 200a
b. Peter Leonbarger*
c. Jessup N. Couch; John Kious, 1831; Abner Armstrong; Stephen Moore, 1839
*Source B spells Lionbarger.

S-3768 230a B:270 X-0840 FAYE:UNIO
a. W-0247 William Evans, 130a?
W-0248 William Evans, 100a?
b. William Evans
c. None

S-3770. *See* S-3598

S-3772 100a B:238 X-0130* ADAM:TIFF
a. W-4875 Peter Seaburn, administrator of [the] estate of John [Seaburn]
b. Henry Line
c. A. D. Beasley, 1828; John Baird, 1831
*"Lk. branch of . . ."

S-3774 100a C:207 X-0760 PIKE:BENT*
a. W-4341 John Campbell
b. Andrew Ellison
c. John Groven? [Groom?] heirs; James? [Joseph?] Penniston, 1831
*Source B shows Mifflin Township crossed out.

S-3775 517a F:140 X-0660 CLER:GOSH
a. W-2899 Alexander Reed, 417a
W-4652 William Anderson, 100a
b. James Morrison & John Donnel*
c. David Wade; S? [L?] Harvie, 1831
*Source B spells Dennel.

S-3776 150a C:425 X-0660 CLER:GOSH
a. W-4170 Thomas Parker, Thomas P. Massie [assignee?] 50a
W-4249 James Chambers; Thomas P. Massie [assignee?] 100a
b. James Taylor
c. Jesse Wood; S. Winston, 1823; J. Bishop

S-3776 200a C:426 X-0665 CLER:GOSH
a. W-4810 Benjamin Lockett, 100a
W-4816 Daniel Wooldridge, 100a
b. James Smith
c. None

S-3776 150a C:426 X-0665 CLER:GOSH
a. W-4170 Thomas Parker, 50a
W-4249 James Chambers, 100a; *both warrants to* James Taylor [assignee?]
b. Thomas P. Massie
c. None

S-3776 200a C:425 X-0665 CLER:MIAM CLER:GOSH
a. W-3304 John Smith
b. John Higgins
c. T. Shaw; W. Wainwright, 1826; J. Wood; J. S. Wood, 1835; P. Bishop; H. Simonton, 1840; Giles Richards; John Higgan, *et al*; Jesse Woods

S-3777 300a C:338 X-0665 CLER:GOSH
a. W-3004 Smith Thompson, 100a
W-3418 William Branham, 200a
b. Alexander Humphreys & [William?] Brannon
c. William Lytle; T. Kirby, 1823; Jess Fletcher, 1825; S. Medary, 1829; Timothy Kirby; Jesse Woods, 1831

S-3778 325a B:370 X-0800 CLER:TATE
a. W-0154 Captain Beaverley Roy
b. Beverly Roy
c. None

S-3779 650a B:341 X-0270 BROW:CLAR*
a. W-1936 Captain Reuben Taylor
b. John Watts
c. J. O. Butler & H. Jaugan?; E. Moore, 1839; T. Kennedy; J. S. Beasley
*Source B notation: "Homersville."

S-3780 463a D:113 X-0275 BROW:CLAR CLER: --*
a. W-1936 Captain Reuben Taylor
b. John Watts
c. A. Poe; J. S. Beasley, 1842
*Source B does not mention Clermont County.

S-3781 667a B:341 X-0160 BROW:CLAR
a. W-1936 Captain Reuben Taylor, 67a?
W-4083 Nathan Lamme, 400a?
W-4046 Thomas Sears; David Bradford [assignee?] 200a
b. -- Watts, -- Smith, & -- Robertson
c. R. Allen; P. L? [S?] Wilson, 1842

S-3782 140a E:337 X-0663* HIGH:UNIO
a. W-6647 William Christian, 40a?
W-5809 Thomas McKindley, heir to John [McKindley]; George Dawson [assignee?] 100a?
b. Allen Latham**
c. R. C. Anderson
*"Waters of east fork . . ."
**Source B says John Nelson.

S-3783 200a B:281 X-1301 BROW:GREE
a. W-1869* Daniel Gray; Doctor James Currie [assignee?]
b. Benjamin Marten**
c. J? [I?] Hardesty; -- Sroufe? [Soonfe?] 1842; J. Workman, 1842
*Warrant number probably wrong; already used in S-3339.
**Source B spells Martin.

S-3784 1150a B:283 X-0840 FAYE:GREE
a. W-3237 Charles West
b. Charles West
c. James Barret; J? Hoyle, 1824; James? [Joseph?] Burges; J. Jones, 1826; Sam Shepherd; Reece Moor, 1825; Thomas Southerland; R. Douglas, 1826; David Terry; H. Phelps, 1829; Philip Syford? [Lyford?]; I. Y. Green, 1836; Charles West; J. West; L. Algren? 1838

S-3785 1150a B:286 X-0840 FAYE:GREE
a. W-3237 Charles West
b. Charles West
c. Philip Olinger?; S? [L?] Shepherd, 1825; Reece Moore, 1825; Robert Adam; James? [Joseph?] Burgess; Levi Rodgers, 1834; O. Bonum?; C. Bently, 1834; Amos Jones; N. F. Jones, 1833; John Morris; I? [J?] Y. Green, 1831; S. Shepherd, heirs; David Pavey, 1840; C. West; L. Alligra? 1840

S-3789 176a B:240 X-0840 FAYE:PAIN
a. W-4267 John Smith
b. Thomas Hoff
c. Absalom Funk; Wade Loofborough [*also* Loofborrow] 1826; William Douglas; R. Douglas, 1829; C. Wallace; A. Douglas, Junior, 1838; "Deeded Richard Douglas, 1833"

S-3790 1767a B:338 X-0790 WARR:HAMI CLER:GOSH
a. W-4905 James Taylor, assignee [of] John Nelson, 667a
W-4888 James Taylor, assignee [of] Eppa Fielding, 200a
W-4902 James Taylor, assignee [of] Henry Rose, heir to Reubin [Rose] 100a
W-4899 James Taylor, assignee [of] John Hollaway, heir to Martin [Hollaway] 100a
W-4903 William Plunkett, heir to James [Plunkett] 100a
W-4828 John Whaley, representative of, 200a
W-3583 Olive Mann? [Manns?] representative, 200a
W-4617 Francis Graves, assignees Edward Davis, Robert Nash, James Doran, Robert Underwood, 200a
b. James Taylor, William Lytle, & -- Underwood
c. Ab[raham?] Morgan; Z. Chapman

S-3792* 125a C:413 X-0660 WARR:SALE
a. W-4831 William Peake
b. James Morrison
c. None
*Source A notation: "GLO-0244." [GLO presumably means General Land Office.]

S-3793 1000a B:339 X-0660 WARR:SALE WARR:HAMI
a. W-4911 John Taylor
b. John Taylor
c. J. Hannah; S? [L?] C. Chamberlin, 1824

S-3794 1215a B:338 X-1170 WARR:SALE
a. W-4911 John Taylor
b. John Taylor
c. John Simmons; H. B. Mellen? [Udlen?] 1832

S-3795 1215a B:339 X-0663 WARR:SALE
a. W-4911 John Taylor
b. John Taylor
c. Eli Collins; Joel A. Stokes, 1835; Enoch Ross, heirs; J? [I?] Holmes; J? [I?] M? [W?] Roosa, 1842

S-3796 115a C:464 X-0660 CLIN:CLAR
a. W-4911 John Taylor
b. John Taylor
c. None

S-3797 689a B:361 X-0660 WARR:SALE WARR:WASH
a. W-4911 John Taylor
b. John Taylor
c. None

S-3798 1840a B:339 X-0790 WARR:SALE
a. W-4889 Richard Taylor, 840a
W-4904 Richard Taylor, 1000a
b. Richard Taylor
c. Joseph? [James?] Hanna; William Stokes, 1833; H. Snell; S. Craig, 1839

S-3799 816a C:251 X-0790 WARR:SALE CLER: --*
a. W-4891 George Minzies, representative of
b. Samuel P. Ninzes? [Minzes?]**
c. J. Mooney, 1825
*Source B does not mention Clermont County.
**Source B spells Menzies.

S-3800 1667a B:360 X-0790 CLER:GOSH
a. W-4863 Henry Vowler? [Vawles?]
b. Henry Vowler*
c. J. Dunham; S. Winston, 1824; W. Carrender?; J. Cassiday; R. Leah; John Randall, 1827; John Hite; C. A. Warren, 1834
*Source B spells Vowles.

S-3801 1000a B:360 X-0790 CLER:GOSH WARR:SALE
a. W-4863 Henry Vowler? [Vawles?]
b. Henry Vowler*
c. A. Darke; S. Winston, 1824; E. Wood; William Lyman [*also* Layman]; B. M. Jackson, 1830; A. Drake; C. Zugg, 1835; Pleasant Smell; Lott Hulick; W. Hill; E. Baldwin, 1839; I? [J?] Hendiman; H. Simonton, 1840
*Source B spells Vowles.

S-3802 600a B:361 X-1170 WARR:SALE
a. W-4900 James Taylor, assignee [of?] William B. Harrison, allowing in fact for Sillas Johnson, heir to Jacob [Johnson] 200a
W-4901 James Taylor, assignee [of?] Jonathan Sanders, heir to Reubin [Sanders] 400a
b. James Taylor
c. Bartlet Simmons; A. I? [J?] Thomas, 1834; George King, 1831; B. Lemons; John Probasco, Junior, 1836; R. T. Kirby; J. W? [M?] Williams, 1837; J. A. Stokes, 1839; J. D. Thomas; E. Stowel, 1839; Jacob Egbert, 1841

S-3803 1000a B:362 X-1080 CLER:GOSH CLER:WAYN CLER:STON
a. W-4912 Oliver Fowler
b. James Taylor & -- Towles
c. O. Towles; John Boggess, 1825; S. McFarland; Elijah Jameson; S. Anderson, Junior, 1839

S-3804 667a B:361 X-0790 CLER:GOSH WARR:SALE WARR:HAMI
a. W-4907 James Taylor, assignee of Beverly Stubblefield
b. James Taylor
c. E. Morgan; Z. Chapman, 1826

S-3805 667a B:362 X-0663* CLER:STON
S-4235
a. W-4906 Thomas Fox
b. James Taylor & Thomas Fox
c. A. Moore; Z. Chapman, 1826; Thomas Fox; S. Medary, 1829; S. McFarland; J. McFarland, 1830; T. S? [L?] Bryan, 1833; J. Taylor, Junior, 1834; John Hill, 1835; James Moore; -- Fox & -- Taylor
*"Stone fork of . . ."

S-3806 500a B:363 X-0270 BROW:CLAR
a. W-4890 George Minzies, representative of
b. James Taylor
c. William Lytle; James Taylor, 1823

S-3808 100a B:247 X-0133 HIGH:BRUS PIKE: --*
a. W-1692 George Ward
b. Andrew Woodrow
c. None

S-3809 1500a B:288 X-0340 FRAN:PLEA
a. W-2450 Doctor George Evans, "resolution"
b. George Evans
c. George Leonard; Samuel Shipman, 1827; Unknown; James Bryden, 1829; Thomas Carpenter, 1830; C. Thomas, 1832; D. Layton; N. Medbury, 1832; R. Parish; William Marble, 1831; C. Higgins, 1834; W. L? [S?] Casey, 1836

S-3811 753a B:287 X-0340 FRAN:PLEA
a. W-2450 Doctor George Evans, "resolution"
b. George Evans
c. -- Renick & -- McLene; N. Medbury, 1832

S-3812* 200a -- -- ADAM:SCOT
a. --
b. Daniel Clark
c. Unknown; James Robinson, 1833
*Entry appears in Source B only (at sequential place).

S-3813 125a B:504 X-0840 GREE:SILV
a. W-3785* George Nelson
b. Cornelia** Skinner
c. W? [M?] Wynans, 1828
*This warrant already used in S-1553.
**Source C spells Cornelius.

S-3814 667a B:245 X-0663 CLER:UNIO
a. W-4678 Thomas Bowne
b. James Heron
c. None

S-3815 200a D:202 X-0845 ROSS:HUNT
a. W-2895 Thomas Porter
b. Thomas Porter
c. None

S-3816. *See* S-2912

S-3817 100a D:95 X-0805 HAMI:ANDE
a. W-3298 John Temple
b. John Hann
c. None

S-3818 1000a B:399 X-1250 HAMI: --*
FAYE: --*
a. W-0291 Henry Bedinger
b. Henry Bedinger
c. None
*Source B says Highland County, Madison Township; does not mention Hamilton or Fayette counties.

S-3819 100a C:523 X-0040 ADAM:MONR
a. W-0679 Seymour Powel, heir
b. Nathaniel Massie
c. None

S-3820 480a B:408 X-0660 WARR:WAYN
S-4706
a. W-3223 Robert Boyd, Thomas Cocke, 240a?
W-2938 Thomas Glascock, 240a?
b. John Graham
c. None

S-3821 467a B:254 X-0020 HIGH:BRUS
S-3909
a. W-0673 Colonel Abraham Buford
b. Abraham Buford
c. Fred Brougher; James Smith, 1830; S. B. Finley; G. W. Smith, 1838

S-3823 100a B:442 X-1144 PIKE:MIFF
a. W-4225 Reuben Long
b. Gregory* Sly
c. A. McCay; L. Howard, 1826; A. McCay, heirs; Van S. Murphy, 1841
*Source B says George Sly. Source C says George Sly, Senior.

S-3824 300a C:26 X-0130 ADAM:TIFF
a. W-0230 Benjamin Mills, 100a?
W-0231 Benjamin Mills, 200a?
b. Benjamin Goodin
c. None

S-3825 690a B:240 X-1080 CLER:STON
a. W-2213 William Nelson
b. William Nelson
c. Richard Hall, 1824; John Hall, heirs; K. Westerfield, 1824; J. Duckwall, 1826; John Pickett; S. Shumard? 1824; T. Cook; S. Brown, 1829; Eleazar Campbell; John Hull, 1841; C. Durst, 1842

S-3827* 100a -- -- BROW:PIKE
a. --
b. Charles Nelms**
c. None
*Entry appears in Source B only (in sequential place); says "not patented."
**So spelled.

S-3827* 100a -- -- BROW:PIKE
a. --
b. Charles Nelms**
c. None
*Entry appears in Source B only (in sequential place); says "not patented."
**So spelled.

S-3829* 200a -- -- SCIO:MORG
a. --
b. T. Martin
c. J. Taylor; A. Noel, 1841
*Entry appears in Source B only (at top of page, above S-3825).

S-3830 100a B:268 X-1301 HIGH:SALE
a. W-0592 John Trackle
b. John Treakle*
c. George W. Doggett, 1828
*Source B spells Treckle; says "not patented."

S-3831 100a B:268 X-1301 HIGH:SALE
a. W-0667 Dawson Treacle
b. Dawson Treckle*
c. Adam Brouse, 1828
*Source B spells Treacle; says "not patented."

S-3832 57a B:461 X-0660 CLER:MIAM
a. W-3924 John Garrett
b. John Garret*
c. William Miley? [Smiley?]; L. Gatch & J. Main, 1824
*Source B spells Garrett; has additional note "Gerrard."

S-3838 100a B:347 X-0301* ROSS:HUNT
a. W-4834 Charles Arnold, represenative of
b. Adam Dunn
c. Andrew Dunbar; Thomas J. Tarlton, 1827; T. Shearer; State of Ohio
*"Branch of . . ."

S-3844 775a C:93 X-0360 MADI:PLEA
MADI:UNIO
a. W-4878 James McNutt
b. James McNutt
c. A. Davidson; W. J. Davidson, 1841

S-3845 400a B:246 X-0980 HIGH:NEWM
a. W-1287 Henry Klung, 200a
W-2503 Henry R. Laey? [Lacy?] 100a
W-3381 Eddy Holbrock, 100a
b. Henry Massie & Joseph Kerr
c. None

S-3846 300a B:246 X-1303 HIGH:NEWM
a. W-3827 Edward Harvey, 100a
W-4176 Benjamin Cook, 100a
W-4177 Richard Cleineal, 100a
b. Henry Massie & Joseph Kerr
c. None

S-3847 544a B:246 X-0980 HIGH:NEWM
a. W-4172 George Fritts, 100a
W-4896 Richard Clairborne [Claiborne?] 444a
b. Henry Massie
c. None

S-3849 1000a B:289 X-1303 HIGH:WHIT
a. W-4920 James Heard [Herd]
b. H. Massie & James Kerr
c. Doctor? John Jones; G. W. Barriere, 1830; J. Collins, F. Davidson, E. Collins, & J. Borden; J. Hogsett, 1835

S-3850 500a B:289 X-1303 HIGH:SALE HIGH:WHIT
a. W-4920 James Heard [Herd]
b. Henry Massie & Joseph Kerr
c. None

S-3851 500a B:291 X-0663 HIGH:SALE
a. W-4920 James Heard [Herd]
b. Henry Massie & Joseph Kerr
c. None

S-3854 300a B:433 X-1303 HIGH:SALE BROW: --*
a. W-1097 Moses Ware
b. Leonard Chobe**
c. None
*Source B does not mention Brown County.
**Source B spells Chobs.

S-3855 200a C:27 X-1301 HIGH:SALE
a. W-2480 John Martin
b. Tarlton Fleming
c. None

S-3856 600a B:290 X-0663 CLER:UNIO
a. W-3234 Francis Peyton, heir to Henry [Peyton]
b. Francis Peyton
c. C. Bugle [*also* Beagle] 1824; P. Emry, 1827

S-3857 100a B:440 X-0134 ADAM:SCOT
a. W-1097 Moses Ware
b. Leonard Chobe
c. None

S-3859 700a B:294 X-1300 BROW:CLAR BROW:SCOT
a. W-1670 Phill[ip] Barbour, heir to James Robertson
b. Albert Gallatin
c. H. H. Bingaman; A. C. H. Cotterell, 1841; R. Allen; P. L. Wilson, 1842

S-3862 900a B:289 X-1300 BROW:CLAR BROW:SCOT
a. W-3234 Francis Peyton, heir to Henry [Peyton]
b. Francis Peyton
c. James Watkins, heirs; John Hillegas, 1828

S-3865 25a B:372 X-0570 ROSS:FRAN
a. W-0348 Captain James Curry
b. James Curry
c. None

S-3868 500a -- — BROW:EAGL
a. --
b. Catesby Jones
c. Unknown; James Callesby; James Loudon, 1827

S-3870 200a B:442 X-0133 HIGH:JACK
a. W-3995 George Paskill
b. John Sinns*
c. T. W? [M?] Sanders, 1828
*Source B spells Sims.

S-3872 400a B:244 X-1300 BROW:SCOT
a. W-4666 Robert Forsythe & John Forsythe
b. John Brown
c. Rachel Smith; J. M. Padden, 1833

S-3873 60a D:371 X-1305 BROW:WASH HIGH: --*
a. W-4169 John Thompson
b. John Hook**
c. Unknown; S. Kerr, 1839
*Source B shows Highland County only as a pencilled notation.
**Source B says "Heirs of John Hook;" and further states "John Hook lived in Franklin County . . . [illegible abbreviated word] in 1791."

S-3874 90a C:387 X-1300 BROW:WASH
a. W-0176 General P[eter] Muhlenberg
b. Peter Muhlenberg
c. Unknown; P. Mallary; Mathew Day, 1831

S-3875 73a D:72 X-1305 HIGH:SALE
a. W-2483 Captain Daniel Duvall
b. Daniel Duvall
c. None

S-3876 100a B:303 X-0340 MADI:DARB
a. W-4811 Richard Jones
b. George McCredie
c. Unknown; E. Ellis, 1836; J. Bigelow* 1838; K. Bigelow* 1840; D. K. Bigalow* 1842
*So spelled.

S-3877 123a B:510 X-0663 CLER:UNIO
a. W-1918 General Edward Stevens
b. Edward Stevens
c. None

S-3878 100a B:508 X-0663 CLER:UNIO
a. W-4274 John Aldridge
b. John Aldridge
c. None

S-3878 100a B:509 X-0663 CLER:UNIO
a. W-3768 James Gunner
b. James Gunner
c. "Patented to William Nash, 1815. Sent to Gov[ernor] Morrow."

S-3879* 9a -- -- CLER:MONR
a. --
b. John Obannon
c. None
*Entry appears in Source B only (at sequential place).

S-3880* 20a -- -- ADAM: --*
a. --
b. John Obannon
c. S. G. Clark, 1834
*Entry appears in Source B only (at sequential place).
**Source B shows Clermont County in pencil, but without giving township.

S-3881 345a C:500 X-0340 UNIO:DARB
a. W-4940 John Knight
b. John Knight
c. None

S-3884 667a C:108 X-1004 DELA:SCIO
a. W-4938 Uriah Springer
b. Uriah Springer
c. Lucas Sullivant; Milo D. Pettibone, 1839

S-3888 50a D:362 X-0350 MADI:JEFF
a. W-2153 James Baines; Thomas Beatleys? [Bralleys?] [assignee?]
b. Matthew Bonner
c. None

S-3898 1000a B:311 X-0344 CHAM:GOSH
a. W-4931 Matthew Arbuckle, deceased, representative of
b. Mathew Arbuckle, representative of
c. None

S-3899 1000a B:324 X-0131* ROSS:CONC
a. W-4931 Matthew Arbuckle, deceased, representative of
b. Mathew Arbuckle, representative of
c. W. Jones, 1823; T. Shields; J. Moore, 1824

S-3901 900a B:311 X-0360 MADI:DEER*
a. W-4931 Matthew Arbuckle, deceased, representative of
b. Mathew Arbuckle, representative of
c. I? [J?] Jones; R. McLaughlin, 1824; A. Winchester, 1826
*Source B notation: "Lafayette."

S-3902* 600a B:319 X-0360 MADI:DEER
a. W-1785 -- [200a?]**
W-4821 Cornelius Organ, 100a
W-4822 William Bullery, 100a
W-4823 Samuel Callender, 100a
W-4824 Thomas Maddin, 100a
b. Ebenezer Owen, Junior
c. None
*Source B says "not patented."
**Source C does not show this warrant number as having been used.

S-3903 400a B:319 X-0360 MADI:DEER
a. W-4926 Zachariah Pigman, representative of
b. John Perill* & James Thompson
c. B. Garrett; W? [M?] Garrett 1826
*Sources B and C spell Parill.

S-3904. *See* S-3724

S-3905 90a D:132 X-0845 ROSS:HUNT
a. W-4892 George Minzies, representative of
b. Hugh Boyle
c. Pleasant Thurman, 1831

S-3908 4222a B:249 X-0010 GREE:CAES
CLIN:CHES
a. W-4494 Moore Fauntleroy
b. Robert Pallard*
c. George Pickett; George Beal, 1827; John Bush; J. Fyfe, 1836 (Clinton County)
*Source B spells Pollard.

S-3909. *See* 3821

S-3910 1300a B:252 X-0180 GREE:SILV
GREE:ROSS
a. W-3765 Benjamin Spiller
b. Benjamin Spiller
c. Thomas Carneal; M. Wynans, 1828; Benjamin Moorman, heirs; John Ankeny? [Aukeny?] 1831

S-3911 1220 B:253 X-0180 GREE:SILV
GREE:ROSS
a. W-3765 Benjamin Spiller
b. Benjamin Spiller
c. Thomas Carneal; M. Wynans, 1828; Reuben Moorman, heirs; Alfred Trader, 1833; Joel Harris, 1837

S-3912 750a B:266 X-0180 GREE:XENI
a. W-2203 George Mitchell, 200a
W-2369 Richard Hazlewood, 100a
W-3137 Robert Pollard, assignee, 100a
W-3139 Robert Pollard, assignee, 100a
W-4179 John Jones, 100a
W-2125 Richard Johnson, 150a
b. William [Pennock*] Croghan
c. None
*Middle name given in Source C.

S-3913 950a B:266 X-0010 GREE:SILV
GREE:CAES
a. W-2002 William Lewis, 200a
W-2010 Robert Doil, 200a
W-2011 John Connant, 200a
W-2108 Francis McGraw, heir, 100a
W-2110 John Depriest, 200a
W-2125 Richard Johnson, 50a
b. William Croghan
c. S. Galloway, 1825; M. Wynans, 1828; Thomas Walden; George Galloway, 1831

S-3914 490a B:254 X-0163 BROW:LEWI
a. W-3509 Richard Thorn, 200a
W-3511 William Kelly, 200a
W-1613 Obediah Roberts, 90a?
b. James Heron
c. None

S-3915. *See* S-3666

S-3916 800a B:272 X-0010 GREE:CAES
CLIN:CHES
a. W-0815 Brigadier General Charles Scott
b. Charles Scott
c. David Connely; James Fisher, 1829; John Arnold, 1829; -- Fife & -- Fitzhugh, 1831

S-3917 560a B:308 X-0160 BROW:LEWI
S-4100 CLER: --*
a. W-4843 Wyatt Collier, 200a
W-4847 Richard Davis, 200a
W-4855 Benjamin Rush? 100a
W-2938 Thomas Glascock, 60a
b. John Graham
c. None
*Source B does not list Clermont County.

S-3920 200a B:328 X-0390 ROSS:UNIO
a. W-4800 Charles Nichols
b. H[enry] Massie & Isaac Davis
c. None

S-3922 500a B:267 X-0840 ROSS:PAXT
a. W-4927 Robert White; Henry Massie [assignee?]
b. John S. Wills
c. None

S-3924 52a B:267 X-0840 ROSS:PAXT
a. W-4927 Robert White; John S. Wills [assignee?]
b. Henry Massie
c. None

S-3927 400a B:257 X-0760 PIKE:MIFF
a. W-0198 Captain Robert Beale
b. Robert Beale
c. None

S-3928 57a B:259 X-1040 SCIO:UNIO
a. W-0812 Colonel William Dark
b. William Dark
c. William Kendall; J. A. Hitchcock, 1831; W. Kinney; A. Noel, 1840

S-3929 200a B:258 X-0420 BROW:JACK
a. W-4701 John Poe
b. William Leedom & Nathaniel Beasley
c. None

S-3930 340a B:261 X-0420 BROW:JACK
a. W-1092 John Bready, 200a
W-0917 William Jenkins, 140a
b. Charles Morgan
c. Daniel Morgan; John Anderson, Junior, 1832

S-3931* 280a B:261 X-0420 BROW:JACK
a. W-0917 William Jenkins, 60a
W-1092 John Bready [220a?]
b. Charles Morgan
c. None
*Source B says "not patented."

S-3932. *See* S-3740

S-3933 100a B:265 X-0130 ADAM:SCOT
a. W-0303 Captain Robert White
b. Robert White
c. None

S-3934 940a B:264 X-0230 ADAM:WINC
a. W-4254 Anthony W. White
b. Alexander Parker
c. None

S-3935 480a B:262 X-0134 ADAM:WINC
a. W-3874 Charles Morgan, heir to John Morgan
b. Charles Morgan
c. James L. McVay? [McNay?]; James Ramsey, 1834; L. Cole, 1836

S-3935* 480a -- -- ADAM: --
a. --
b. Charles Morgan
c. Cornelius Dougherty; James L. McVay? [McNay?] 1826
*This entry (which may be a duplicate of the preceding one) appears at the top of page, preceding S-3929 in Source B.

S-3936 360a B:265 X-0134 ADAM:WINC
a. W-4254 Anthony W. White
b. Alexander Parker
c. None

S-3937 300a B:262 X-0420 BROW:JACK
a. W-3874 Charles Morgan, heir to John Morgan
b. Charles Morgan
c. Andrew Meharra; Archibald Leggett, 1826

S-3938 360a B:260 X-1000 SCIO:UNIO
a. W-0812 Colonel William Dark
b. William Dark
c. Henry Utt, Junior; T. Utt, 1831; S. Lucas; S. M. Tracy, 1827

S-3939 253a B:260 X-0136* ADAM:TIFF
a. W-0812 Colonel William Dark
b. William Dark
c. None
*"Lk. fork of . . ."

S-3940 1600a B:264 X-0190 PIKE:CAMP
X-1140
a. W-4254 Anthony W. White
b. Alexander Parker
c. J. Currie? [Carrie?]; H. Hemstead, 1826; Richard Tucker; Daniel Lee, 1832; John Beasley, heirs; James Sargeant, 1831; J. & M. Eakins; L. Byington, 1842; J. S. Eakins; S. Blizzard, 1842; A. Parker

S-3941 330a B:526 X-0800 X-1040 ADAM:FRAN
a. W-4254 Anthony W. White
b. Alexander Parker
c. None

S-3942 50a B:297 X-0420 BROW:HUNT
a. W-3105 Thomas Miller; Didier Collin, A. Foulds? [assignees?]
b. John Beasley
c. None

S-3943 76a B:257 X-0700 SCIO:BRUS
a. W-4117 Thomas Smith; Benjamin Goodin [assignee?]
b. John Beasley
c. None

S-3946 100a B:296 X-1000 SCIO:WASH
a. W-4117 Thomas Smith; Benjamin Goodin [assignee?]
b. John Beasley
c. S? [L?] M. Stillwell; J. Pyles & R. Crane, 1838; L. Moss; W. V. Peck, 1842

S-3950 100a B:391 X-0133 ADAM:TIFF
a. W-3105 Thomas Miller; Didier Collin, A. Foulds? [assignees?]
b. Andrew Ellison
c. None

S-3953 200a B:262 X-0133 ADAM:TIFF
a. W-0018 Colonel Presley Nevill
b. Presley Nevill
c. Daniel Boyle, 1828; Unknown

S-3954. *See* S-3258

S-3956 1000a B:333 X-0750 UNIO*:MILL
a. W-1376 Lieutenant John White
b. John White
c. Unknown; Hez[ikia]h Kilbourn, 1820-1826
*Apparently thought to have been in Delaware County originally.

S-3964 1000a B:345 X-0841* FAYE:MADI
a. W-4867 Archibald Armstrong, representative of
b. Robert Armstrong
c. Joel Walker; R. Douglas, 1831; S? [L?] Reed, 1831
*"Branch of . . ."

S-3965 364a B:315 X-0841 FAYE:MADI
a. W-4867 Archibald Armstrong, representative of
b. Robert Armstrong
c. John Barnes; W. Loofborrow, 1827

S-3967 400a B:313 X-0841 FAYE:MADI
a. W-4932 Edward Demaster
b. Edward Demasters
c. James Mulkenin; A. Latham, 1828

S-3968 200a B:313 X-0841 FAYE:MADI
a. W-4933 James Demas[ters]
b. James* Demasters
c. None
*Pencilled notation in Source B says "John."

S-3969 200a B:311 X-0841 FAYE:MADI
a. W-4934 Samuel Bibbe
b. Samuel Bibee
c. None

S-3971 800a B:331 X-0366 MADI:PLEA
a. W-3994 Captain Alexander Rose
b. David Bradford
c. W? [M?] Bonner, 1828

S-3972 1000a B:331 X-0366 MADI:RANG
a. W-3994 Captain Alexander Rose
b. David Bradford
c. None

S-3973 400a B:468 X-0360 MADI:UNIO MADI:FAIR
a. W-4001 William Pettyjohn, 200a
W-4021 William Reynolds [assignee?] 200a
b. David Bradford
c. J. Erwin; C. Meloin, 1825

S-3974 75a C:115 X-0423 BROW:HUNT
a. W-2156 Simon Baley; Benjamin Goodin [assignee?]
b. Nathaniel Ellis
c. None

S-3975 830a B:319 X-0150 ROSS:CONC ROSS:BUCK
a. W-3472 Leonard Cooper
b. Thomas Patterson
c. None

S-3978. *See* S-2901

S-3979. *See* S-2621

S-3981 300a B:316 X-1210 ROSS:TWIN
a. W-4853 Charles Calley, 100a
W-4850 Michael Eckhart, 100a
W-2174 George Gray, 100a
b. Duncan McArthur
c. None

S-3982* 100a B:277 X-0845 MADI: --
a. W-0650 George Brooks
b. George Brooks
c. --
*This entry not listed in Source B.

S-3983* 100a B:277 X-0845 MADI: --
a. W-0182 Nathaniel Brooks
b. Nathaniel Brooks
c. --
*This entry not listed in Source B.

S-3984* 100a B:277 X-0845 MADI: --
a. W-2129 Josiah Cornelius
b. Josiah Cornelius
c. --
*This entry not listed in Source B.

S-3985* 100a B:277 X-0845 MADI: --
a. W-1179 William Aaron
b. William Aaron
c. --
*This entry not listed in Source B.

S-3986 546a B:280 X-0845 FAYE:GREE
a. W-4696 Robert Moore, heir to William [Moore]
b. Robert Moore
c. None

S-3987 185a B:280 X-0845 FAYE:GREE
a. W-4696 Robert Moore, heir to William [Moore]
b. Robert Moore
c. None

S-3988 640a B:278 X-1300 BROW:FRAN
a. W-2157 William Eustace
b. William Eustace
c. J. B. Gibson; J. B. Crist, 1840; M? [W?] A. Chilton; P. S. Wilson, 1841

S-3989 560a B:278 X-1300 BROW:WASH
a. W-2157 William Eustace
b. William Eustace
c. John B. Gibson; G. H. Bohrer, 1840

S-3990 400a B:278 X-1300 BROW:WASH
a. W-2157 William Eustace
b. William Eustace
c. John Morlin; Hugh Meharry, 1823; Samuel Fleming; John Davidson, 1830; J? B. Gibson; John Erst, 1840

S-3991 150a B:279 X-0840 FAYE:CONC
a. W-2157 William Eustace
b. William Eustace
c. Wade Loofborrow, 1828; John Mann; Thomas Maddox, 1837; "deeded John Mann, 13 May 1830"

S-3992 720a B:276 X-1300 BROW:WASH
a. W-2256 Captain William Barrett
b. William Barrett
c. Nathan Ellis, 1831

S-3993 130a B:275 X-0840 FAYE:CONC
a. W-2256 William Barrett
b. William Barrett
c. None

S-3994 250a B:383 X-0530 HIGH:FAIR
a. W-0228 Lieutenant Jacob Springer
b. Jacob Springer
c. James P. Johnson

S-3995 183a B:285 X-0940 HIGH:FAIR
a. W-0228 Lieutenant Jacob Springer
b. Jacob Springer
c. None

S-3996 60a B:316 X-0150 ROSS:BUCK
a. W-4965 Henry Crook
b. Duncan McArthur
c. None

S-4001 94a C:125 X-0130 HIGH:BRUS PIKE: --*
a. W-0007 Captain John Marks
b. John Marks
c. Fred. Brougher; James Morrow, 1830
*Source B does not mention Pike County.

S-4003 1533a B:286 X-0640 HIGH:FAIR*
a. W-3237 Charles West
b. Charles West
c. John Pike; Ephraim Worthington; L. George; J. Simpson, 1836
*Source B notation: "New Lexington."

S-4004 612a B:284 X-0640 HIGH:FAIR CLIN:WAYN
a. W-3263 Nathaniel Lucas
b. Nathaniel Lucas
c. John Surface; William Dailey, 1827; Susanna Chiles; Israel Woodruff, 1828; Solomon Hodgson; John Owens, 1828; James Lewis; James Roberts, 1827; Jones Lewis; Lewis Wright, 1828; N. Lucas; J. McGrew; W. Fuller; C. Atkinson, 1838; Joel Woodruff; John McCraw, 1833?

S-4005 343a B:284 X-0640 FAYE:GREE HIGH: --*
a. W-3263 Nathaniel Lucas
b. Nathaniel Lucas
c. None
*Source B does not mention Highland County.

S-4006 200a B:285 X-0640 HIGH:FAIR
a. W-1850 Doctor Robert Rose
b. Robert Rose
c. Andrew Baskin, 1836

S-4008 50a D:244 X-0920 SCIO:UNIO
a. W-4886 Matthew Johnson
b. William Lucas, Junior*
c. None
*According to Source C.

S-4009 50a C:197 X-1040 SCIO:UNIO
a. W-4886 Matthew Johnson
b. William Lucas, Junior
c. None

S-4010 100a E:414 X-0926* SCIO:UNIO
a. W-4886 Matthew Johnson
b. William Lucas, Junior
c. None
*"Right hand fork of . . ."

S-4011 667a B:287 X-1000 ROSS:FRAN
a. W-4865 Thomas Fenn
b. Abraham Baldwin
c. None

S-4012 1000a B:296 X-1000 PICK:MUHL
a. W-2742 Jasper Hughes
b. Thomas Pemberton
c. James H. Doyle, 1830; T. Pemberton, heirs; James Allen, 1840

S-4013 1000a B:291 X-1000 PICK:SCIO
a. W-1893 Doctor William McMeehin
b. William McMehen*
c. James Sample; Peter West, 1829; Thomas Sample; S. Hunter, 1837; William Wilson, 1841
*Source B spells McMechen; McMahon.

S-4014 700a B:291 X-1000 PICK:SCIO
a. W-1893 Doctor William McMeehin
b. William McMechen
c. None

S-4015 444a B:292 X-0360 ROSS:DEER PICK: --*
a. W-1681 Thomas Altop, 100a
W-1667 Jacob Decker, 100a
W-1605 Stephen Fletcher, 100a
W-1668 Robert Hart, 144a
b. John S. Wills
c. None
*Source A says Pickaway County; Source B says Ross County, Deerfield Township.

S-4016 800a B:490 X-0360 PICK:DEER*
a. W-1681 Thomas Altop, 100a
W-1667 Jacob Decker, 100a
W-1605 Stephen Fletcher, 100a
W-1668 Robert Hart, 56a
b. John S. Wills
c. None
*Source B notation: "Williamsport."

S-4017 175a B:292 X-1000 PIKE:JACK ROSS: --*
a. W-4927 Robert White
b. John S. Wills
c. None
*Source B does not mention Ross County.

S-4018 50a D:136 X-1140 PIKE:MIFF
a. W-0230 John Mills; Benjamin Goodin [assignee?]
b. -- Massie & -- Kerr
c. None

S-4019 1000a B:292 X-1120 BROW:FRAN
a. W-4688 Charles Lewis, deceased, representative of
b. Charles Lewis, representative of
c. John Prickett; U. Springer, 1832

S-4020 200a B:294 X-1120 BROW:FRAN
a. W-4873 Joshua Worsham
b. James Heron*
c. None
*Source B spells Herron.

S-4021 200a C:337 X-0663 HIGH:UNIO
a. W-4918 John Hilbert
b. Andrew Boyd
c. None

S-4022 1000a B:336 X-1303 HIGH:WHIT
a. W-4955 Reubin Briscoe
b. Joseph Kerr
c. None

S-4023 100a B:291 X-1140 PIKE:MIFF
a. W-4916 Thomas Howle
b. H[enry] Massie & Joseph Kerr
c. None

S-4024 400a B:291 X-0133 HIGH:BRUS
a. W-0673 Colonel Abraham Buford
b. -- Buford & -- Worthington
c. J. Kniseley [*also* Kinsley]; J. Jones, 1824; S. B. Finley; G. W. Smith, 1838; J. Hogsett, 1836; J. A. Roads

S-4026. *See* S-2823

S-4028 300a B:293 X-0980 HIGH:NEWM
a. W-0218 Colonel John Gibson
b. Thomas Franklin
c. None

S-4031 389a B:513 X-0663 CLER:BATA
a. W-0129 Albert Gordon, 200a
W-3290 Simmons Lee, 100a
W-0868 Alexander Chambers* 100a
W-0875 Royal Eubank, 100a
b. John Obannon
c. None
*This warrant already completely used in S-2721.

S-4032 400a B:317 X-0840 ROSS:TWIN*
a. W-0586 Doctor Edward Duff
b. Duncan McArthur
c. None
*Source B notation: "Near Sattesville? [Lattesville?]."

S-4033 200a B:317 X-0840 ROSS:TWIN
a. W-0586 Doctor Edward Duff
b. Duncan McArthur
c. None

S-4034 120a B:329 X-0360 PICK:DEER
S-4216
a. W-0586 Doctor Edward Duff, 100a
W-0633 Captain Thomas Holt, 20a
b. Duncan McArthur
c. Thomas Williams; Conrad Funk, 1831; James Baker; Z. Fowler, 1838

S-4036 400a B:317 X-0150 ROSS:BUCK
X-0151
a. W-1885 Joseph Hoofman* 100a
W-5002 William McGlochlin, 100a
W-5004 William Davis, 100a

S-4036 [continued]
b. Duncan McArthur
c. None
*This warrant already completely used, twice over, in S-1515 and S-2770.

S-4037 80a B:416 X-0576* ROSS:FRAN
a. W-0348 Captain James Curry
b. James Curry
c. None
*"Second branch below . . ."

S-4038 250a B:412 X-1000 ROSS:FRAN
a. W-4805 Frederick Seigle, representative of
b. Frederick Siegle* representative of
c. None
*Source B spells Seigle.

S-4040 86a B:297 X-1040 ADAM:JEFF SCIO: --*
a. W-4992 Thomas Mills, representative of
b. John Beasley
c. None
*Source B mentions Scioto County, but says tract "lies in A[dams County]."

S-4041 50a B:297 X-1043 ADAM:JEFF
a. W-4992 Thomas Mills, representative of
b. John Beasley
c. None

S-4042 140a B:297 X-1190 SCIO:NILE
a. W-4992 Thomas Mills, representative of
b. John Beasley
c. None

S-4043 46a B:297 X-0420 ADAM:LIBE
a. W-4992 Thomas Mills, representative of
b. John Beasley*
c. None
*Source B lists David Duncan.

S-4047 107a B:299 X-1190 SCIO:NILE
a. W-4254 Anthony W. White
b. Alexander Parker
c. A. Morley, heirs; L. Bradford, *et al*, 1832

S-4048 175a B:299 X-1190 SCIO:NILE
a. W-4254 Anthony W. White
b. Alexander Parker
c. S. Veitch; H. Devore & O. Crane, 1824; William Harbert? [Hasbert?]; J. Kendall, 1839

S-4049 180a B:299 X-1040 SCIO:BRUS ADAM: --*
a. W-4254 Anthony W. White
b. Alexander Parker
c. William Newman; Thomas Huston, 1832; J. P. Newman, 1838
*Source B lists Adams County, but does not give township.

S-4050* 84a SCIO:UNIO
a. --
b. Alexander Parker
c. None
*Entry appears in Source B only (at sequential place).

S-4051 200a C:208 X-0130 ADAM:MEIG
a. W-1145 James Amberson
b. Andrew Ellison
c. None

S-4053 50a B:391 X-0130 ADAM:JEFF
a. W-1117 Clement McGilleham; Alexander Fowler [assignee?]
b. Andrew Ellison
c. None

S-4055 150a C:151 X-0130 ADAM:MEIG
a. W-5001 Matthew Macey? 100a
W-1117 Clem[ent?] McGilleham; Alexander Fowler [assignee?] 50a
b. Andrew Ellison
c. None

S-4056 56a B:298 X-0130 ADAM:MONR
a. W-3531 Richard Tryar? [Fryar?]
b. Andrew Ellison
c. Francis Campbell; William Parks, 1824; Jacob Machir; John Baird, 1831; Noah Whitlatch; Robert Johnson, heirs, 1838

S-4057 100a B:524 X-0420 ADAM:LIBE BROW: --*
a. W-4992 Thomas Mills, representative of
b. John Beasley
c. None
*Source B does not mention Brown County.

S-4059* 28a -- -- SCIO:UNIO
a. --
b. John Beasley
c. --
*Entry appears in Source B only (at sequential place).

S-4061 600a C:204 X-0130 ADAM:MEIG
a. W-0215 Doctor David Holmes
b. David Holmes
c. None

S-4064 150a B:335 X-0840 X-0130 ROSS:PAIN
a. W-0218 Colonel John Gibson
b. Thomas Franklin
c. John Williams, heirs; J. Rockhold, 1830

S-4065 1000a B:333 X-0750 UNIO:DOVE
a. W-0153 Captain John Overton
b. John Overton
c. S. G. Strong, 1836; Abram Deppo? [Deppe?]; C. Wallace; R. L. Broome, 1840

S-4066 751a B:333 X-0750 UNIO:PARI
a. W-0153 Captain John Overton, 84a?
W-4956 John Overton, 667a?
b. John Overton
c. Abraham Armim? [Armine?]; George Diron, 1830; R. Elliott, heirs; M. Wasson, 1839

S-4067 1120a B:333 X-0750 UNIO:DARB
a. W-2245 Elizabeth Rickman Wedon
b. Elizabeth Reckman*
c. D. Copeland; S. G. Strong, 1826; J. Taylor, 1829; D. O. Copeland; J. Bigelow, 1837; D. C. Copeland
*Source B spells Rickman.

S-4068 1120a B;474 X-1000 DELA:SCIO
a. W-2245 Elizabeth Rickman Wedon
b. Elizabeth Reckman*
c. Jesse Bills; Emry Moore, 1833; E. Beckman; John Ferguson; E. Richmond; James McCune, 1831; Martha Black, 1836
*Source B spells Rickman.

S-4069 1000a B:334 X-0750 UNIO:PARI
a. W-2245 Elizabeth Rickman Wedon
b. Elizabeth Reckman**
c. D. Copland*; S. G. Strong, 1826; C. Copland*; J. B. Baird, heirs; B. O. Copeland*; Susan Copeland*; James Galloway, Junior, 1831
*So spelled.
**Source B spells Rickman.

S-4070 1080a B:475 X-0110 DELA:SCIO
a. W-2245 Elizabeth Rickman Wedon
b. Elizabeth Reckman*
c. None
*Source B spells Rickman.

S-4071 1080a B:335 X-0340 UNIO:UNIO
a. W-2245 Elizabeth Rickman Wedon
b. Elizabeth Reckman*
c. Samuel Fisher; John Hawley, 1830; William Porter
*Source B spells Rickman.

S-4072 600a B:335 X-0750 UNIO:PARI
a. W-2245 Elizabeth Rickman Wedon
b. Elizabeth Reckman*
c. John Mings? [Minge?]; Demas Adams, 1831
*Source B spells Rickman.

S-4073 667a B:334 X-0750 UNIO:ALLE
a. W-2245 Elizabeth Rickman Wedon
b. Elizabeth Reckman*
c. Thomas Cowen; Hollis S? Anry, 1828
*Source B spells Rickman.

S-4074 600a B:332 X-0750 UNIO:PARI
a. W-4648 John Green, 400a
W-4514 Thomas Ogle, 200a
b. Benjamin Biggs
c. S. G. Strong; Henry Massie; Ezra Reed, 1831

S-4075 667a B:332 X-0750 UNIO:PARI
a. W-4628 Benjamin Biggs
b. Benjamin Biggs
c. None

S-4080 144a B:391 X-0136* ADAM:TIFF
a. W-3531 Richard Tryar? [Fryar?] 44a
W-1117 Clem[ent] McGilleham; Alexander Fowler [assignee?] 100a
b. Andrew Ellison
c. None
*"Lk. fork of . . ."

S-4081 1860a B:305 X-0980 HIGH:BRUS HIGH:PAIN
a. W-3658 Jos[eph] Staples, 200a
W-3752 Josiah Puckett, 200a
W-4060 William Dennis, 200a
W-4063 Jacob Riggs, 200a
W-4073 George Dicks, 200a
W-4074 William Taylor, 200a
W-4677 Alexander Montgomery; Thomas Molloy? Richard Rees [assignees?] 200a
W-4061 Arthur Bloxem, representative of A. Blo[xem] deceased, 200a
W-4098 John Lemay, 100a
W-4684 Thomas Marshall, 200a
W-1613 Obediah Roberts, 60a
b. James Heron
c. None

S-4082 217a B:308 X-0980 HIGH:BRUS
a. W-4347 Henry Pilkerton, 100a
W-1613 Obediah Roberts, 50a
W-4712 Thomas Dix, 67a
b. James Heron
c. None

S-4083 800a B:305 X-0940 HIGH:MADI
a. W-4706 Benjamin Hoomes
b. John Graham
c. None

S-4084* 1153a E:495 X-0980 ROSS: -- HIGH: --
a. W-3585 Simon Sommers
b. James Taylor
c. --
*This survey does not appear in Source B (but see following entry).

S-4084* 1386a -- -- HIGH:PAIN
a. [W-3585 Simon Sommers]
b. Simon Sommers
c. J. Taylor; John Boyd, 1829
*This entry appears in Source B, but not in Source A.

S-4085 114a D:45 X-0980 HIGH:PAIN
a. W-3585 Simon Sommers
b. Simon Sommers
c. None

S-4086 200a B:389 X-1260 X-0780 MADI:UNIO
a. W-1229 John Minnes; with John Barrett; William Ellett [assignee?]
b. Tunstal Quarls*
c. None
*Source B spells Quarles.

S-4087 1a B:393 X-0660 GREE:BEAV
a. W-1020 Nathan Young
b. Alexander Armstrong
c. None

S-4089 S-4188 700a B:324 X-0130 HIGH:BRUS
a. W-4921 James Herd, 500a?
W-1841 Ensign John Gibson, 200a?
b. Duncan McArthur
c. None

S-4090 210a B:325 X-0840 ROSS:TWIN
a. W-4921 James Herd
b. Duncan McArthur
c. H. Shaver; M. Lewis, 1842

S-4091 63a B:306 X-0420 BROW:JACK
a. W-4921 James Herd
b. Charles Morgan
c. None

S-4092 52a B:306 X-0420 BROW:JACK
a. W-4921 James Herd
b. Charles Morgan
c. None

S-4093 400a B:307 X-0420 BROW:HUNT
a. W-1614 William Clift, 200a
W-0885 John Farrell, 200a
b. James Poage
c. None

S-4094 153a B:306 X-0420 BROW:HUNT
a. W-4921 James Herd
b. Charles Morgan
c. None

S-4095 185a B:307 X-0420 BROW:HUNT
a. W-4921 James Herd
b. Charles Morgan
c. None

S-4096 300a B:307 X-0420 BROW:HUNT
a. W-4921 James Herd
b. Charles Morgan
c. None

S-4097 100a B:354 X-0423 BROW:HUNT
a. W-1045 John Lockart
b. Charles Morgan
c. Archibald Oursler; William Hunt, 1833

S-4098 100a B:525 X-0420 BROW:HUNT
a. W-1045 John Lockart
b. Charles Morgan
c. None

S-4099 47a B:306 X-0420 BROW:HUNT
a. W-4921 James Herd
b. Charles Morgan
c. None

S-4100. *See* S-3917

S-4101 300a B:308 X-0980 HIGH:PAIN
a. W-4450 William Reynolds [assignee?] 200a
W-4454 William Reynolds [assignee?] 100a
b. William Reynolds
c. None

S-4102 300a B:327 X-0366 ROSS:DEER
a. W-4993 Ann McKnight, widow
b. Duncan McArthur
c. None

S-4103 1000a B:327 X-0841 ROSS:CONC ROSS:BUCK
a. W-4993 Ann McKnight, widow
b. Duncan McArthur
c. None

S-4104 137a B:328 X-0840 ROSS:TWIN
a. W-4993 Ann McKnight, widow
b. Duncan McArthur
c. None

S-4105 100a B:317 X-0840 ROSS:TWIN
a. W-4993 Ann McKnight, widow
b. Duncan McArthur
c. None

S-4106 230a B:327 X-0366 ROSS:DEER
a. W-4993 Ann McKnight, widow
b. Duncan McArthur
c. William Clark; R. Douglas; James V. Hill; Robert Stewart, 1830

S-4107 300a B:317 X-0366 ROSS:UNIO ROSS:DEER
a. W-4993 Ann McKnight, widow
b. Duncan McArthur
c. None

S-4108 100a B:317 X-0840 ROSS:TWIN
a. W-4993 Ann McKnight, widow
b. Duncan McArthur
c. None

S-4109 300a B:374 X-0360 ROSS:UNIO
a. W-4993 Ann McKnight, widow
b. Duncan McArthur
c. None

S-4110 533a B:318 X-0840 ROSS:CONC ROSS:BUCK
a. W-4993 Ann McKnight, widow
b. Duncan McArthur
c. None

S-4113 100a C:234 X-1043 ADAM:JEFF
S-5033
a. W-4990 Thomas Mills, representative of
b. Michael Freeman
c. None

S-4116 200a B:356 X-0940 FAYE:GREE
a. W-4893 Thomas Dixon, representative of
b. Thomas Dixon, representative of
c. S. Crispen; W? [M?] B. Rawlings, 1842

S-4117 200a B:383 X-0530 HIGH:FAIR
a. W-0011* James Brush
b. James Brush
c. None
*This warrant has been used completely twice over in S-0899 and S-3674.

S-4119 170a B:320 X-0841 ROSS:CONC
a. W-3472 Leonard Cooper
b. Thomas Patterson
c. None

S-4120 458a B:321 X-0841 ROSS:CONC
a. W-4976 Jonathan Snowdon
b. James Thompson
c. None

S-4122 1333a B:322 X-0840 FAYE:WAYN ROSS:CONC ROSS:BUCK
a. W-4976 Jonathan Snowdon
b. James Thompson
c. None

S-4124 1076a B:314 X-0360 MADI:UNIO MADI:FAIR
a. W-0247 William Evans, 560a?
W-0248 William Evans, 516a?
b. William Evans
c. J. Boswell; A. G. Thompson, 1823; A. Erwin; J. F. Chinowith, 1827

S-4125 667a B:312 X-0360 MADI:SUMM
a. W-0852 John Beck
b. John Beck
c. None

S-4126 200a B:321 X-0360 MADI:SUMM
a. W-2521 Evans Long; Nimrod Long [assignee?]
b. Philip Roots Thompson
c. None

S-4127 100a B:312 X-0841 FAYE:MADI
a. W-4882 Basil Carlile
b. Henry Bedinger
c. None

S-4128 450a B:318 X-0841 FAYE:MADI
a. W-4997 Ann McKnight, widow
b. Duncan McArthur
c. Mark Morris, heirs; Rob Robinson, 1828; Thomas Morris; W. Loofborrow, 1839

S-4129 200a B:344 X-0841* FAYE:MADI
a. W-3881 Patrick Dunn, 100a
W-4797 Hugh Allen, assignee of William Sutton, 100a
b. Samuel Dew, Junior
c. None
*"West branch of . . ."

S-4130 240a B:318 X-0841* PICK:PERR FAYE:WAYN FAYE:MADI ROSS: --**
a. W-4981 William Richmond, 100a
W-4982 Simon Cooper, 100a
W-4965 Henry Crook, 40a
b. Duncan McArthur
c. None
*"East branch of . . ."
**Source B does not mention Ross County.

S-4131 328a B:325 X-0841 ROSS:CONC FAYE: --*
a. W-0633 Captain Thomas Holt
b. Duncan McArthur
c. None
*Source B does not mention Fayette County.

S-4132 110a B:325 X-0841* FAYE:WAYN ROSS:--** PICK:--**
a. W-0633 Captain Thomas Holt
b. Duncan McArthur
c. T. Rittenhouse
*"East branch of . . ."
**Source B mentions Ross County but does not give township. Source B does not mention Pickaway County.

S-4133 320a B:329 X-0150 ROSS:BUCK
a. W-0633 Captain Thomas Holt
b. Duncan McArthur
c. None

S-4134 250a B:318 X-0840 ROSS:TWIN
a. W-4999 Ann McKnight
b. Duncan McArthur
c. None

S-4136 125a B:318 X-0130 HIGH:BRUS PIKE: --*
a. W-4983 David Jameson, 100a
W-4986 Samuel Jameson, 100a
b. Duncan McArthur
c. None
*Source B does not mention Pike County.

S-4137 50a B:319 X-0362 ROSS:DEER
a. W-4997 Ann McKnight
b. Duncan McArthur
c. None

S-4138 200a B:315 X-0841* PICK:PERR
a. W-4973 Godrell Lively
b. Goodrill Lively
c. None
*"East branch of . . ."

S-4139 200a B:319 X-0840 ROSS:BUCK
a. W-4964 Matthew Pigman
b. Duncan McArthur
c. None

S-4140* 100a -- -- ROSS:BUCK
a. --
b. John Williams
c. None
*Entry in Source B only (at sequential place).

S-4142 100a B:375 X-0360 ROSS:UNIO
a. W-3292 William Bockham
b. James Rolstone
c. None

S-4143 215a B:329 X-0840 ROSS:TWIN
S-4209
a. W-0633 Captain Thomas Holt, 15a?
W-4986 Samuel Jameson* 100a?
W-4921 James Herd, 100a?
b. Duncan McArthur
c. None
*Warrant already completely used in S-4136.

S-4144 50a B:326 X-0840 ROSS:BUCK ROSS:TWIN
a. W-0633 Captain Thomas Holt
b. Duncan McArthur
c. None

S-4145 300a B:311 X-0360 PICK:MONR
a. W-2919 John Smith, 100a
W-2918 Michael Barret* 100a
W-1868 James Culverson, 100a
b. George Mathews & James Culbertson
c. None
*This warrant already completely used in S-3702.

S-4146 200a B:330 X-0360 PICK:DEER
a. W-1868 James Culverson
b. James Culbertson
c. Reuben Heath; George Botkin, 1836; C. Williamson, 1838

S-4147 80a -- X-0800 SCIO:NILE
S-14072
a. W-1868 James Culverson, 34a?
W-6645 Alexander Brownlee, heirs, 46a?
b. James Culbertson & -- Kendrick
c. E. P. Kendrick; R. Hamilton, 1842

S-4148 100a B:371 X-0740 GREE:XENI
a. W-1868 James Culverson
b. James Culbertson
c. None

S-4149 550a B:371 X-0740 GREE:XENI
a. W-1868 James Culverson
b. James Culbertson
c. None

S-4151 442a B:346 X-0300 ROSS:HUNT
a. W-4943 Thomas Hungerford; James Stephenson [assignee?]
b. William Rector
c. John Janny; C. Wallace, 1832

S-4152 424a B:348 X-0300 ROSS:HUNT
a. W-4988 Samuel Smith
b. Samuel Smith
c. C. W. Hoffman; R. Stewart, 1829

S-4153 200a B:347 X-0301 ROSS:HUNT
a. W-4966 Andrew Dunbar, heir to Hamilton Dunbar
b. Andrew Dunbar
c. E. H. Dewey; Aaron Vanscoy, 1836

S-4154 200a B:347 X-0841* PICK:PERR FAYE:--**
a. W-3057 Peter Pritchett
b. Wilkins Ogburn
c. A. W. Richey; J. Gill, 1838
*"Right hand fork of . . ."
**Source B does not mention Fayette County.

S-4156 1080a B:348 X-0840 MADI:RANG FAYE?: --*
a. W-4988 Samuel Smith
b. Samuel Smith
c. W. Gallup; Daniel Kountz, 1829
*Source B does not mention Fayette County.

S-4157 1000a B:348 X-0730 CHAM:UNIO
a. W-4988 Samuel Smith
b. Samuel Smith
c. None

S-4160 300a B:476 X-0960 ROSS:HUNT
a. W-4998 Ann McKnight
b. Samuel McKnight
c. William McCarrol, 1825; John Robertson, 1825; William Jenkins; John Fulton, 1830

S-4161 1000a B:477 X-0960 ROSS:HUNT
a. W-4995 Ann McKnight, later Ann Fullerton, widow and de[visee?] of Doctor Humphrey Fullerton, deceased, 500a
W-4996 Ann McKnight, late Ann Fullerton, widow and de[visee?] of Doctor Humphrey Fullerton, deceased, 500a
b. Ann McKnight
c. James Fulton; Mary Selig; Jacob Selig, 1831

S-4163 2290a B:340 X-0663 HIGH:DODS CLIN:CLAR
a. W-3624 Robert Sayers, "resolution" 1000a
W-3625 Robert Sayers, "resolution" 1000a
W-3623 Robert Sayers, "resolution" 290a
b. Robert Sayers

S-4163 [continued]
c. Thomas Revel [*also* Reveal]; R. Collins, 1826; J. Saunderson; A. Grout? [Grant?]; T. Shockley, 1837; John Owens, 1828; J. Maston? [Marton?] 1831; Unknown; Carter B. Harlan; Clinton Cox; H. and W. Taylor; I? [J?] L. Hughes

S-4164 200a B:341 X-0663 CLIN:CLAR
a. W-3751 John Spitzfathom
b. John Swearing Williams
c. None

S-4165 500a B:340 X-0663 CLIN:CLAR* HIGH:DODS
a. W-4241 John Brownley
b. Elisha Williams
c. Abraham Gibler; Peyton West, 1835; Samuel H. Hale, 1841
*Source B notation: "Lynchburg."

S-4166* 159a -- -- CLER:WASH
a. --
b. John McDougal
c. None
*Entry in Source B only (at sequential place).

S-4167 136a B:391 X-0300 PIKE:PEEP
a. W-4921 James Herd
b. John Beasley
c. None

S-4168 57a D:210 X-0300 PIKE:PEEP
a. W-4921 James Herd
b. John Beasley
c. None

S-4170* 100a D:67 X-1045 SCIO:UNIO
a. W-4921 James Herd
b. John Beasley
c. John Wright, heirs; J. B. Clingman, 1830; John Noel, 1828
*Source B notation: "Not patented."

S-4173 50a B:506 X-1040* ADAM:JEFF
a. W-4992 Thomas Mills, representative of
b. John Beasley
c. None
*"Southwest fork of . . ."

S-4174* 57a -- -- SCIO:NILE
a. [W-4992 Thomas Mills, representative of]
b. John Beasley
c. John Beasley, heirs; J. R. Walker, 1831; J. Pyles [*also* Piles] 1839
*Not listed in Source A.

S-4175 100a C:384 X-1230 ADAM:GREE
a. W-4992 Thomas Mills, representative of
b. William Russell
c. None

S-4176 984a B:448 X-0130 ADAM:FRAN
a. W-3432 John M. Galt
b. Abraham Shepherd
c. James Boyd, heirs; William Parks, 1826

S-4176 200a B:448 X-0130 ADAM:FRAN
a. W-3432 John M. Galt
b. Abraham Shepherd
c. J. McCagus?; J. Cole, 1827

S-4180 200a D:35 X-1005 HARD:TAYL
a. W-4775 Thomas Cook, representative of William Cook
b. John Doherty
c. Lyne Starling, 1831 (Logan County)

S-4181 1000a B:348 X-0730 CHAM:UNIO
a. W-4988 Samuel Smith
b. Samuel Smith
c. G. Swisher; L. Collins, 1826; Isaac Parker

S-4182 1000a B:349 X-0730 CHAM:WAYN
a. W-4988 Samuel Smith
b. Samuel Smith
c. Richard? Jones; Nicholas Niles, 1831

S-4183 357a B:346 X-0570 ROSS:HUNT
a. W-0199 Captain Lawrence Butler
b. Lawrence Butler
c. None

S-4185 200a B:347 X-0730 CHAM:UNIO
a. W-2225 Alexander Petrie
b. Alexander Petre
c. Thomas Stewart, 1823

S-4186 700a B:379 X-0730 CHAM:UNIO
a. W-4872 John Belfield, representative of
b. John Belfield, representative of*
c. None
*Source B spells Bellfield.

S-4188. *See* S-4089

S-4189 200a B:325 X-0360 X-0390 ROSS:UNIO
a. W-1841 Ensign John Gibson
b. Duncan McArthur
c. None

S-4190 120a B:326 X-0360 ROSS:UNIO
a. W-1841 Ensign John Gibson
b. Duncan McArthur
c. None

S-4191 127a B:326 X-0841* FAYE:WAYN FAYE:MADI
a. W-1841 Ensign John Gibson
b. Duncan McArthur
c. None
*"Branch of . . ."

S-4192 60a B:416 X-1000 ROSS:SCIO
a. W-1841 Ensign John Gibson
b. Duncan McArthur
c. None

S-4193 880a B:330 X-0360 MADI:UNIO MADI:FAIR
a. W-4878 James McNutt
b. James McNutt
c. E. DeLashmutt; O. W. DeLashmutt, 1826; W. Jameson; J. F. Chinowith, 1823; A. Jameson

S-4195 197a B:418 X-0730 LOGA:JEFF
S-4604
a. W-4878 James McNutt
b. James McNutt
c. None

S-4196 160a B:326 X-0840 ROSS:TWIN
a. W-2710 Barnabas Wilkinson
b. John McDonald
c. None

S-4197 70a B:326 X-0840 ROSS:TWIN
a. W-4686 Peter Francisco
b. John McDonald
c. None

S-4199 100a B:437 X-0342 CHAM:GOSH
a. W-0088 Captain Strether Jones
b. -- Thompson, -- Patton, & -- Hackley
c. None

S-4200 802a B:375 X-0360 MADI:SUMM CLAR:HARM
a. W-0341 Captain Joseph Swerringen, 253a? W-4478 Joseph Swearengen, 549a?
b. Joseph Swearingen
c. None

S-4201 500a B:327 X-0390 ROSS:UNIO
a. W-4991 Thomas Mills, representative of
b. Joseph Tiffin
c. James? [Joseph?] Wampler; M. Purdam, 1831

S-4202 45a B:327 X-0390 ROSS:UNIO
a. W-4991 Thomas Mills, representative of
b. Isaac Davis
c. None

S-4203 200a B:328 X-0570 ROSS:SCIO
a. W-4944 Thomas Hungerford
b. Jacob Shepherd
c. None

S-4204 200a C:80 X-1370 PICK:WAYN
a. W-3832 Joseph Gibbs
b. Joseph Tiffin
c. None

S-4207 750a B:328 X-0360 ROSS:UNIO ROSS:DEER
a. W-4805 Frederick Seigle, representative of
b. Frederick Seigle, representative of
c. James Briggs, heirs; A. Richhart, 1835; A. Richart, Junior; A. McCoy, 1842

S-4208 200a B:331 X-0366 MADI:STOK MADI:PLEA
a. W-3994 Captain Alexander Rose
b. David Bradford
c. Jacob Kirk, heirs; Samuel N. Kerr, 1831

S-4209. *See* S-4143

S-4210 1000a C:1 X-0750 LOGA:PERR UNIO: --*
a. W-0088 Captain Strether Jones
b. Strother Jones
c. "Patented to -- Patton, -- Hackley, & -- Thompson;" S. Strong, 1820-1826; Lawson Curtis, 1830
*Source B mentions Union County, but not the township.

S-4211 1200a B:331 X-0730 X-0340 CHAM:UNIO
a. W-4867 Archibald Armstrong, representative of
b. Philip F. Lee* representative of
c. Benjamin Cheney, 1823; P. R. Lee and F. Lee, representatives of
*Source B says Philip Richard Lee, representatives of.

S-4212 2000a B:332 X-0730 X-0340 CHAM:GOSH
a. W-4867 Archibald Armstrong, representative of
b. Philip F. Lee* representative of
c. Jones Mason; L? [S?] Hogg, 1826; Aaron Deevers
*Source B says Philip R. F. Lee, representative of.

S-4213 800a B:331 X-0730 CHAM:UNIO
a. W-4867 Archibald Armstrong, representative of
b. Philip F. Lee* representative of
c. None
*Source B says Philip R. F. Lee, representative of.

S-4214 400a B:375 X-0366 MADI:SUMM CLAR:HARM
a. W-4928 James Sawyer
b. Joel Stokes
c. C. McDonald; J. Moore, 1835; T. Turner; I? [J?] Gerrard, 1842

S-4215 100a B:329 X-0840 ROSS:TWIN
a. W-0633 Captain Thomas Holt
b. Duncan McArthur
c. None

S-4216. *See* S-4034

S-4217 1200a B:336 X-0980 HIGH:LIBE HIGH:NEWM
a. W-4339 Samuel Smith, elder brother of William [Smith] deceased
b. Henry Massie
c. S. K. Stivers; A. Grantham, 1825; James? [Joseph?] Brice; J. M. Trimble, 1831

S-4221 600a B:335 X-0840 ROSS:TWIN ROSS:HUNT
a. W-4954 Reubin Briscoe, 500a
W-4998 Ann McKnight, 100a
b. George Vinsonhaller*
c. John Kilbourne, heirs; William Bussard, 1839
*Source B spells Vinsonhaler.

S-4222 586a B:336 X-0360 ROSS:DEER PICK: --*
a. W-4953 Reubin Briscoe
b. Henry Massie
c. None
*Source B does not mention Pickaway County.

S-4223 100a B:434 X-1030 ADAM:JEFF
a. W-0231 John Mills
b. Benjamin Goodin
c. None

S-4224 300a B:336 X-0133 HIGH:BRUS
a. W-0218 Colonel John Gibson
b. Thomas Franklin
c. L. Reed, 1823; George Woods, 1826

S-4225 80a B:335 X-1300 BROW:PLEA BROW:CLAR
a. W-0218 Colonel John Gibson
b. Thomas Franklin
c. E. Ross; N. Wall, 1827; A. Thompson, 1831

S-4226 50a B:432 X-0800 ADAM:MONR
a. W-0218 Colonel John Gibson
b. Thomas Franklin
c. None

S-4227 50a B:432 X-0040 ADAM:MONR
a. W-0218 Colonel John Gibson
b. Thomas Franklin
c. None

S-4229 200a B:343 X-0663 HIGH:DODS
a. W-1817 Hugh Morrison; Toliver Craig & Joseph Kerr [assignees?]
b. Joseph Kerr
c. None

S-4230 70a B:432 X-1140 PIKE:MIFF
a. W-0218 Colonel John Gibson
b. Thomas Franklin
c. None

S-4232 1111a B:364 X-0663 CLIN:CLAR
a. W-4946 John Tibbs
b. John Tibbs
c. William Lytle; T. Kirby, 1823

S-4233 510a B:436 X-0663 HIGH:UNIO
a. W-4922 Whitehead Coleman, representative of
b. Whitehead Coleman, representative of
c. W. Lytle; Z. Chapman, 1823

S-4234 667a B:365 X-0663 CLIN:CLAR HIGH: --*
a. W-4923 William Miller, representative of
b. William Miller, representative of
c. None
*Source B does not mention Highland County.

S-4235. *See* S-3805

S-4236 2000a B:364 X-1080 CLER:GOSH
S-4447 CLER:STON
a. W-4950 John Mountjoy
b. John Mountjoy
c. J. Knott; D. Hawkins, 1823; Z. Chapman, 1825; John Lytle & William Lytle; S. Winston, 1823; James Taylor, 1830; John Hill, 1832; N. Dumford; A. J. Pruden, 1842

S-4237 889a B:362 X-1080 CLER:STON
a. W-4947 William Taylor
b. William Taylor
c. Michael Morgan; Levi Moore, 1826; S. Smith; S? [L?] West? [Weston?] 1826; R. Marsh, 1827; George Durham; James Ewing, 1833; J. Nash? 1831; S. Ewing; J. Fletcher

S-4239 700a B:367 X-0660 WARR:HAMI
a. W-4969 Francis Taylor
b. Francis Taylor
c. None

S-4240 200a B:363 X-1070 CLER:STON
a. W-0378 Nathaniel Quarles, "state line taken out by James Taylor, 6 Jul 1800"
b. Nathaniel Quarles
c. None

S-4241 200a B:363 X-0660 CLER:STON CLER:JACK
a. W-1528 James Span, 100a
W-3592 William Whitmore, 100a
b. George Standard & Benjamin Johnson
c. William Lytle; S. Winston, 1823; S. B. Cleveland, 1825; J? [I?] Taylor; T. Everhart, 1824; John Hill, 1836; S? [L?] Bonnel? 1837

S-4242 150a E:45 X-0665 CLIN:CLAR BROW:PERR
a. W-4946 John Tibbs
b. -- Taylor & -- Tibbs
c. Willoughby Tibbs; Z. Chapman, 1828; James Taylor; John Donnell; E. L? [S?] Haines, 1828; William Lytle; John Tibbs; N. Ellis, 1833; John Hill, 1831; T. Kirley? [Kirby?] 1826

S-4243 189a C:441 X-0800 CLER:OHIO HAMI: --*
a. W-4969 Francis Taylor
b. Francis Taylor
c. None
*Source B does not mention Hamilton County.

S-4244 100a C:440 X-0790 CLER:GOSH
a. W-4924 James Taylor, assignee of John Sale
b. James Taylor
c. None

S-4246 600a B:424 X-1020 BROW:STER
S-4447
a. W-4716 Peter Thomas, 200a
W-4717 John Sudthard, 200a
W-4718 Nathaniel Dobbs, 200a
b. [Peter] Thomas, [John] Southard; & [Nathaniel] Dobbs
c. John Brown; D. Crawford, 1840

S-4247 667a B:422 X-0663 CLER:WILL
BROW: --*
a. W-4945 Thomas Hungerford; William Lytle [assignee?]
b. William Lytle
c. William Smith, 1823
*Source B mentions Brown County, but says "lies in Clermont [County]."

S-4248 1500a B:362 X-0660 WARR:HAMI
CLER: --*
a. W-3487 Henry Hughes
b. William Lytle
c. None
*Source B does not mention Clermont County.

S-4249 500a B:422 X-0663 BROW:PIKE
CLER:WILL
a. W-3487 Henry Hughes
b. William Lytle
c. William Norris, 1824; Daniel F. Barney, 1826; Elias Walling; William Lytle (Clermont County); T. Kirby, 1823; J. Owen & E. Owen, 1833; L? [S?] McCullock; L? [S?] Davis (Clermont County); Smith J. Cowdry; A. McLain, 1837; J. S. Beasley, 1840

S-4250 207a E:373 X-0663 BROW:STER
CLER:WILL
a. W-4080 William Fullin, 100a
W-3487 Henry Hughes, 107a
b. William Lytle
c. None

S-4251 600a B:424 X-0663 BROW:STER
a. W-4772 Henry Carver, representative of, 200a
W-3712 William Beverly Fitzhugh, 100a
W-4714 William Foster, 100a
W-4393 James Loyd, 100a
b. James Morrison
c. William Morrison; T. Kirby, 1826; George H. Bohrer, 1831

S-4252 1000a B:425 X-0663 BROW:STER
CLER: --*
a. W-4946 John Tibbs
b. John Tibbs
c. Willoughby Tibbs; N. Ellis, 1831; William Lytle; E. Mannon? [Marmon?] 1838
*Source B does not mention Clermont County.

S-4253 950a B:434 X-1120 BROW:FRAN
a. W-1693 Captain Robert Higgins
b. Robert Higgins
c. Thomas Pindel, Junior; John Lindsey, 1833

S-4254 503a B:356 X-0663 HIGH:DODS
a. W-3320 Isham Keith
b. Isham Keith
c. Arthur O'Neal, Junior; Jacob Barnes, 1831

S-4255 60a B:356 X-0663 HIGH:DODS
CLIN:CLAR
a. W-3728 Andrew McMahan
b. Joshua Dodson
c. Isaac Jones; Peyton West, 1826

S-4256 200a B:358 X-0663 HIGH:DODS
CLIN:CLAR
a. W-3530 Stephen Goodwin
b. Thomas Perkins
c. Andrew Smith; William Darby, 1827; G. Hartman; J. Riddle, 1831; E. Adams, 1836 [crossed out]; S? [L?] Darbyshire, 1838; I? [J?] Burton; W? W? [M? M?] Hale, 1840

S-4257 70a B:343 X-1300 HIGH:SALE
a. W-0560 Captain Peter Garland
b. Peter Garland
c. John Overton; Thomas Shockley, 1836

S-4258 150a B:359 X-0663 CLIN:CLAR
HIGH: --*
a. W-0174 Captain William White
b. William White
c. None
*Source B does not mention Highland County.

S-4259* 200a -- -- CLAR:PLEA
a. --
b. Thomas Turk
c. None
*Entry in Source B only (at sequential place); notation: "Not patented."

S-4260 187a B:357 X-0663 HIGH:DODS
a. W-2272 Captain Calohill Minnis
b. Calohill Minnis
c. None

S-4261 68a B:358 X-0663 HIGH:DODS
a. W-0814 David Walker
b. David Walker
c. None

S-4262 330a B:341 X-0270 BROW:CLAR
a. W-1936 Captain Reuben Taylor, 130a?
W-3188 John Scott, 100a?
W-3264 Richard Harrison, 100a
b. -- Watts, -- Carrington, & Joseph Nichols
c. Nathaniel Moore; Benjamin Smith, 1824; John Watts; S. Glaze, 1838

S-4263 1333a C:64 X-0841* ROSS:DEER PICK:PERR
a. W-4609 John Kelly
b. John Holmes
c. J. Parkins; John Troutner, 1823
*"Hay Run of . . ."

S-4264 1333a B:342 X-0750 UNIO:LEES
a. W-4609 John Kelly
b. John Holmes
c. Unknown; John R. Parish, 1823; Joshua Mathcut [Northcut?] 1837

S-4265 1334a B:342 X-0750 UNIO:LIBE
a. W-4609 John Kelly
b. John Holmes
c. B. H. Lathrop, 1823; Joshua Mathcut [Northcut?] 1837

S-4266 700a B:396 X-1004 DELA:SCIO
a. W-1325 Captain Erasmus Gill
b. Erasmus Gill
c. None

S-4267 967a B:397 X-1004 DELA:SCIO
a. W-1325 Captain Erasmus Gill
b. Erasmus Gill
c. A. Stephens

S-4271 100a B:391 X-1140 PIKE:PEBB
a. W-4979 Phillip Hammond
b. Andrew Ellison
c. None

S-4273 100a B:445 X-0040 ADAM:TIFF
a. W-4978 James Ketcher
b. John Ellison, Junior
c. None

S-4275 100a B:375 X-0840 ROSS:BUCK
a. W-4998 Ann McKnight
b. Thomas Worthington
c. None

S-4277 367a C:366 X-0340 UNIO:UNIO
a. W-0556 Robert Hays? [Kays?]*
b. Robert Kays* & -- Sullivants**
c. None
*Kays and Hays may be the same person (both listed in Gwathmey).
**Source B mentions only Robert Kays and states "patented to Swepson? Whitehead."

S-4278 2000a B:481 X-0340 UNIO:UNIO*
a. W-0556 Robert Hays? [Kays?]**
b. Robert Kays
c. None
*Source B notation: "By Milford."
**Kays and Hays may be the same person (both listed in Gwathmey).

S-4279 100a B:350 X-1170 CLIN:VERN
a. W-3632 Henry Rains
b. Cornelius Skinner
c. H. Stearns; I? [J?] Morris, 1834

S-4280 100a B:350 X-1170 CLIN:VERN
a. W-3113 John Ferrol
b. Nimrod Long
c. None

S-4281 100a B:354 X-0940 FAYE:GREE HIGH: --*
a. W-1698 John Beaver, heir to William Beaver
b. James Currie
c. None
*Source B does not mention Highland County.

S-4282 600a B:344 X-0400 FAYE:MADI
a. W-4867 Archibald Armstrong, representative of
b. Robert Armstrong
c. None

S-4283 261a B:346 X-0360 PICK:MONR
a. W-4837 James Elliott, representative of Archibald [Elliott] 100a
W-4838 Robert Armstrong, representative of John [Armstrong] 161a
b. Robert Armstrong
c. None

S-4284 742a B:344 X-0730 CHAM:SALE CHAM:WAYN
a. W-4867 Archibald Armstrong, representative of, 703a
W-4838 Robert Armstron[g], representative of John [Armstrong] 39a
b. Robert Armstrong
c. None

S-4285 43a B:352 X-1000 ROSS:SCIO
a. W-4971 Jonathan Snowdon
b. Elias Rector
c. None

S-4287 150a B:352 X-0360 PICK:PERR
a. W-4971 Jonathan Snowdon
b. Elias Rector
c. None

S-4288 260a B:347 X-0841* FAYE:MADI
a. W-4971 Jonathan Snowdon
b. Elias Rector
c. None
*"Branch of . . ."

S-4289 2000a B:350 X-1320 PICK:MONR
a. W-1580 Captain Valentine Harrison
b. Adam Shepherd*
c. Gilbert Fields; E. M. Carpenter, 1826; Jacob Clover; Joshua Brownell, 1832; Charles Oliver; W. Y. Emmitt, 1837
*Source C says Old[ha]m Shepherd.

S-4290 1051a B:349 X-0360 PICK:MONR
a. W-4988 Samuel Smith
b. Samuel Smith
c. None

S-4291 183a B:346 X-0735 CHAM:WAYN CHAM:SALE
a. W-0199 Captain Lawrence Butler
b. Lawrence Butler
c. W. L? Meredith, 1825

S-4292 191a B:346 X-0360 PICK:MONR
a. W-0199 Captain Lawrence Butler
b. Lawrence Butler
c. None

S-4293 445a B:349 X-0841 PICK:PERR
a. W-4988 Samuel Smith
b. Samuel Smith
c. None

S-4294 455a B:411 X-0570 ROSS:HUNT
a. W-4944 Thomas Hungerford
b. Elias Langham? [Laugham?]
c. None

S-4295 56a B:377 X-0540 ROSS:DEER
a. W-4943 Thomas Hungerford
b. Nathaniel Cox
c. None

S-4297 500a B:447 X-0180 CLIN:CHES
a. W-3432 John M. Galt, "resolution"
b. Abraham Shepherd
c. J. Dakin; E. Dakin, 1826

S-4303 310a B:410 X-0660 WARR:WAYN
S-4703
a. W-1814 Claiborne Davenport, 100a
W-3477 Abraham Shepherd, 210a
b. Nathaniel Massie
c. None

S-4304 400a C:291 X-0130 ADAM:MEIG
a. W-3477 Abraham Shepherd
b. Nathaniel Massie
c. None

S-4306 40a B:410 X-0130* ADAM:TIFF
a. W-4801 Hilman Minnis, representative of
b. Nathaniel Massie
c. None
*"Lk. fork of . . ."

S-4307* 850a — — FAYE:UNIO
a. --
b. Ephraim Ralph
c. —
*Entry shown in Source B only (at sequential place).

S-4308 200a C:404 X-1303 HIGH:WHIT BROW:WASH
a. W-4465 John Lee
b. John Sturrell*
c. None
*Source B says Charles Sturritt.

S-4309 200a C:37 X-1000 PICK:JACK
a. W-3477 Abraham Shepherd
b. Ralph Morgan
c. None

S-4310* 100a — — ADAM:FRAN
a. --
b. Richard Bibb
c. --
*Entry shown in Source B only (at sequential place); notation: "Not patented."

S-4311* 30a -- — FRAN:JACK
a. [W-3967 John Yager]
b. Michael Fisher
c. None
*Entry shown in Source B only (at sequential place).

S-4312 70a B:407 X-1000 FRAN:JACK
a. W-3967 John Yager
b. Michael Fisher
c. None

S-4315 208a B:377 X-1320 PICK:MONR
S-4358
a. W-4971 Jonathan Snowdon
b. Elias Rector
c. None

S-4316 50a C:78 X-1370 PICK:WAYN
a. W-4944 Thomas Hungerford
b. John Evans
c. None

S-4324* 100a — — ADAM:FRAN
a. --
b. Charles Kean
c. None
*Entry shown in Source B only (at sequential place); notation: "Not patented."

S-4325* 100a — — ADAM:FRAN
a. —
b. Alexander McNutt
c. None
*Entry shown in Source B only (at sequential place); notation: "Not patented."

S-4327 50a B:443 X-1140 PIKE:MIFF
a. W-4927 Robert White
b. John S. Wills
c. None

S-4328 25a B:443 X-0020 HIGH:BRUS
a. W-4927 Robert White
b. John S. Wills
c. A. Evans, 1823; J. Kirby, 1825; J. Kerr

S-4330* 200a -- -- ADAM:FRAN
a. --
b. George McCredie
c. None
*Entry shown in Source B only (at sequential place).

S-4331 460a B:388 X-0730 CHAM:SALE
S-4332 LOGA: --*
a. W-1642 David Price, 360a
W-0900 Francis Merriman, 100a
b. Alexander Dunlap
c. Aaron Brown, 1823
*Source B does not mention Logan County.

S-4333* 7a -- -- PICK:DARB
a. --
b. Elias Rector
c. None
*Entry shown in Source B only (at sequential place).

S-4335 100a B:388 X-0730 CHAM:SALE
a. W-4619 Henry Wilson
b. Alexander Dunlap
c. Niel Gunn, 1823

S-4340 250a B:410 X-0660 GREE:XENI
S-4442? [4422?]
a. W-0079 Captain Phillip Mallory, 100a?
W-1280 Williamson Simmons, 100a?
W-1203 Captain Beverly Stubblefield, 50a?
b. [John] Harvie & [Beverly] Stubblefield
c. None

S-4342 100a C:204 X-0760 PIKE:MIFF
a. W-0215 Doctor David Holmes
b. David Holmes
c. None

S-4343 50a B:420 X-0630 PIKE:MIFF
a. W-0215 Doctor David Holmes
b. David Holmes
c. None

S-4344 50a C:204 X-0760 PIKE:BENT*
a. W-0215 Doctor David Holmes
b. David Holmes
c. None
*Source B shows Mifflin Township crossed out.

S-4345 200a B:392 X-0130 ADAM:MEIG
a. W-0215 Doctor David Holmes
b. David Holmes
c. None

S-4348 100a B:392 X-0130* ADAM:TIFF
a. W-4921 James Herd
b. Andrew Ellison
c. None
*"Lk. fork of . . ."

S-4349 50a B:391 X-1140 PIKE:MIFF
a. W-4921 James Herd
b. Andrew Ellison
c. None

S-4353 200a B:392 X-1140 PIKE:MIFF
a. W-0215 Doctor David Holmes
b. David Holmes
c. None

S-4355 100a B:373 X-0841 ROSS:CONC
a. W-4972 Jonathan Snowdon
b. Duncan McArthur
c. None

S-4356 200a B:373 X-0841 ROSS:CONC
a. W-4972 Jonathan Snowdon
b. Duncan McArthur
c. None

S-4357 95a B:374 X-0550 ROSS:CONC
S-4412
a. W-1841 Ensign John Gibson, 45a?
W-5037 John Manning Murphey, 50a
b. Duncan McArthur
c. None

S-4358. *See* S-4315

S-4359 47a B:356 X-0663 HIGH:WHIT
CLIN:CLAR*
a. W-0821 Colonel Samuel Hawes
b. Samuel Hawes
c. John John, Senior; William Cole, 1826; Samuel Hawes; John Smith, 1828
*Source A does not show Clinton County, Clark Township.

S-4360 170a B:357 X-0663 CLIN*:CLAR
a. W-1820 William Moore
b. William Moore
c. W. Liggett; J. A. Trimble, 1824; John Rees; William Moore; Elias Dakin, 1828
*Source B corrected from Highland County.

S-4361 185a B:357 X-0663 HIGH:UNIO
CLIN:CLAR
a. W-1820 William Moore
b. William Moore
c. William George; William Millikan [*also* Milligan] 1827; A. E. Stickler [Strickle!] 1832

S-4362 160a B:359 X-0663 HIGH:DODS
CLIN: --*
a. W-0174 Captain William White
b. William White
c. None
*Source B does not mention Clinton County.

S-4363 460a B:358 X-0663 HIGH:UNIO
HIGH:DODS
a. W-2740 Captain James Wright
b. James Wright
c. C. Butler; A. Grantham, 1828; P. Drais, 1833

S-4364 530a B:358 X-1170 CLIN:MARI WARR:SALE*
a. W-2740 Captain James Wright
b. James Wright
c. William Barlow; William Stockdale, 1827; W. Fuller
*Source A does not list Union County.

S-4365 115a B:359 X-1170 CLIN:MARI WARR:SALE*
a. W-2740 Captain James Wright
b. James Wright
c. None
*Source A does not list Union County.

S-4366 955a B:414 X-0010 CLIN:LIBE*
a. W-2740 Captain James Wright
b. James Wright
c. J. Shambough; I? [J?] Thomas, 1832
*Source B notation: "Port William."

S-4367 250a B:385 X-0740 GREE:XENI
a. W-0174 Captain William White
b. William White
c. J. Galloway, 1824

S-4368 45a B:359 X-0663 CLIN:CLAR
a. W-2740 Captain James Wright
b. James Wright
c. Samuel Jones; Samuel Winston, 1826

S-4369 160a B:359 X-0663 CLIN:CLAR
a. W-2740 Captain James Wright
b. James Wright
c. Samuel Jones; S. Winston, 1826; John John, Junior; William R. Cole, 1826

S-4370 106a B:359 X-0663 CLIN:CLAR
a. W-2740 Captain James Wright
b. James Wright
c. Isaac Jones; P. West, 1826

S-4371 130a B:386 X-0740 GREE:XENI
a. W-2740 Captain James Wright
b. James Wright
c. None

S-4372 140a B:357 X-0741 GREE:XENI GREE:ROSS
a. W-1820 William Moore
b. William Moore
c. None

S-4373 360a B:355 X-0663 HIGH:UNIO
a. W-2312 Captain Francis Dade
b. Francis Dade
c. Unknown; James Wright, 1829

S-4374 260a B:355 X-0663 HIGH:UNIO
a. W-2312 Captain Francis Dade
b. Francis Dade
c. None

S-4375 700a B:355 X-0940 FAYE:GREE HIGH: —*
a. W-2312 Captain Francis Dade
b. Francis Dade
c. Edward Conway; Samuel Shepherd, 1825; Samuel Gregory; James Taylor, 1826; Wade Loofborrow [*also* Loofborough] 1827; Samuel Winston
*Source B does not mention Highland County.

S-4376 120a B:385 X-0946* HIGH:FAIR
a. W-2312 Captain Francis Dade
b. Francis Dade
c. None
*"Hardin's Branch of . . ."

S-4377 220a B:355 X-0180 GREE:CAES
a. W-2312 Captain Francis Dade
b. Francis Dade
c. Lawrence L. Dade; M. Wynans, 1828

S-4378 455a B:386 X-0660 GREE:MIAM
S-4554 GREE:XENI GREE:ROSS
a. W-0174 Captain William White
b. William White
c. None

S-4380 185a B:360 X-0663 HIGH:UNIO CLIN: —*
a. W-0174 Captain William White
b. William White
c. None
*Source B does not list Clinton County.

S-4387 1158a B:378 X-1260 MADI:UNIO
a. W-5036 Peter Helphenstine, representative of
b. Peter Helphenstine, representative of
c. J. Minchel; S. Watson, 1825; W. Watson; G. Grover, 1827; W. Watson, heirs; A. Conner, 1831; A. Freshour, heirs; S. N. Kerr, 1839; Daniel Freshour

S-4387 800a B:378 X-1260 MADI:UNIO
a. W-5036 Peter Helphenstine, representative of
b. Peter Helphenstine, representative of
c. None

S-4393* 15a — — SCIO:—** ADAM:—**
a. —
b. Nathaniel Massie
c. None
*Entry shown in Source B only (at sequential place).
**Source B says: "S[cioto] or A[dams counties] not found."

S-4394 149a C:81 X-1370 PICK:DEER*
a. W-4991 Thomas Mills, representative of
b. Joseph Tiffin
c. None
*Source B notation: "Wolf Run."

S-4395 296a C:80 X-1370 PICK:WAYN PICK:DEER
a. W-4991 Thomas Mills, representative of
b. Joseph Tiffin
c. None

S-4397 600a B:384 X-0663 CLIN:GREE
a. W-0673 Colonel Abraham Buford
b. Abraham Buford
c. None

S-4398 400a B:384 X-0663 HIGH:UNIO
a. W-0673 Colonel Abraham Buford
b. Abraham Buford
c. None

S-4399 207a B:403 X-0060 LOGA:JEFF LOGA:LAKE
a. W-4972 Jonathan Snowdon
b. Thomas Worthington
c. Lawson Curtis, 1823

S-4400* 437a -- -- CLER:WASH
a. --
b. J. McDougal, J. Roston, & M. Roston
c. None
**See also* S-1683 *and* S-5067.

S-4401 100a B:386 X-0663 CLER:BATA
a. W-3882 Spencer Hill
b. James Mitchel*
c. None
*Source B spells Mitchell.

S-4402 87a B:386 X-0663 CLER:BATA
a. W-4585 Anthony Singleton
b. Anthony Singleton
c. None

S-4403* 94a C:26 X-0420 ADAM:TIFF
a. W-4573 Benjamin Wood, representative of
b. Francis Ayres
c. Moses McFadden; John M. Haslip, 1825; George Baker; John Hemphill, 1831; Thomas Huston, 1833; Samuel Ross
*Source B notation: "Not patented."

S-4404 1333a B:353 X-0750 UNIO:LIBE
a. W-5027 Benjamin Grimes, 1000a
W-5030 Benjamin Grimes, 333a
b. Benjamin Grimes
c. None

S-4404 1333a B:353 X-0750 UNIO:LIBE
a. W-5028 Benjamin Grimes, 1000a
W-5030 Benjamin Grimes, 333a
b. Benjamin Grimes
c. W? [M?] Baughan; Adam Brake; William M? [W?] Baughan, 1840

S-4405 1334a B:352 X-0750 UNIO:LEES
a. W-5029 Benjamin Grimes, 1000a
W-5030 Benjamin Grimes, 334a
b. Benjamin Grimes
c. L? [S?] Ashton

S-4406 200a B:390 X-0230 ADAM:WAYN
a. W-1106 John Inglish? [English?]
b. John Stephenson*
c. None
*Source C spells Stevenson.

S-4407 170a B:377 X-0730 CHAM:UNIO
a. W-5031 Peter Helphenstine, representative of
b. John Haines
c. S. Gibbs, 1823

S-4408 500a B:377 X-0841* FAYE:MADI
a. W-5031 Peter Helphenstine, representative of
b. John Haines
c. None
*"Branch of . . ."

S-4410 575a B:374 X-0841 ROSS:CONC ROSS:BUCK
a. W-4976* James Thompson
b. Duncan McArthur
c. None
*Inasmuch as this warrant was good only for 267a, it would appear that an additional warrant number should have been listed.

S-4411 100a B:374 X-1240 ROSS:PAIN
a. W-5037 John Manning Murphey
b. Duncan McArthur
c. None

S-4412. *See* S-4357

S-4413 65a B:417 X-0730 LOGA:JEFF
a. W-5037 John Manning Murphey
b. Duncan McArthur
c. None

S-4415 273a B:467 X-0420 BROW:HUNT
a. W-1920 Colonel Josiah Parker
b. Josiah Parker
c. None

S-4416 104a B:465 X-0420 BROW:BYRD
a. W-0635 Captain Archibald Denholm
b. Nathaniel Beasley
c. None

S-4417 46a B:465 X-0424 BROW:BYRD
a. W-0635 Captain Archibald Denholm
b. Nathaniel Beasley
c. None

S-4418 200a B:466 X-0420 BROW:BYRD
a. W-1473 Charles Duncan, 100a
W-3876 Peter Cutright, 100a
b. Elijah Cuchin
c. None

S-4419 100a B:527 X-0080 BROW:HUNT
a. W-3125 John Harrison
b. John Harrison
c. None

S-4421 94a B:467 X-0080 BROW:HUNT
a. W-1920 Colonel Josiah Parker
b. Josiah Parker
c. John S. Wills [*also* Mills]; William Sellenan? [Sellonan?] 1831

S-4422. *See* S-4442

S-4423 140a B:375 X-0360 MADI:SUMM
a. W-4376 William Reynolds, assignee of John Depinta? [Depriest?], [assignee?] of W. Darville
b. William Reynolds
c. None

S-4424 450a* B:373 X-0360 MADI:UNIO
a. W-4930 Isaac Fisher, 100a
W-5000 Matthew Murry, 100a
W-5018 Elizabeth Lambert, late E[lizabeth] McDaniel, 100a
b. Robert Means
c. None
*Additional warrants needed to cover acreage granted.

S-4425 100a B:355 X-0940 FAYE:GREE
a. W-0348 Captain James Curry
b. James Curry
c. None

S-4426 50a B:383 X-0940 FAYE:GREE
a. W-0348 Captain James Curry
b. James Curry
c. None

S-4428 275a B:384 X-0663 HIGH:UNIO
S-4557
a. W-2312 Captain Francis Dade
b. Francis Dade
c. None

S-4429 200a B:385 X-0663 HIGH:UNIO
a. W-2194 Nathaniel Ralls
b. Nathaniel Ralls
c. Aaron Betts

S-4430 30a B:402 X-1000 SCIO:MORG
a. W-4535 John Curtis
b. Duncan McArthur
c. None

S-4431* 50a — — ROSS:FRAN
a. —
b. Elias Rector
c. None
*Entry shown in Source B only (in sequential place).

S-4434 150a B:383 X-0663 CLIN:GREE
a. W-3220 Alexander McKinsey
b. William Barlow
c. William Compton? [Campton?] 1825

S-4435 367a B:385 X-0940 FAYE:GREE
a. W-4501 Thomas Wallace
b. Thomas Wallace
c. S. Crispen; W? [M?] R. Rawlings, 1842

S-4436 60a C:294 X-0840 ROSS:BUCK
S-8946
a. W-4866 Thomas Hankens, representative of, 30a?
W-5838 William Kempin, assignee[s] Joseph Ladd, Robert Townsley, 30a?
b. John McDonald
c. None

S-4438 60a C:179 X-0840 ROSS:TWIN
a. W-4866 Thomas Hankens, representative of
b. John McDonald
c. None

S-4439 700a B:365 X-0660 WARR:SALE
a. W-1841 Ensign John Gibson
b. William Lytle
c. None

S-4440 1500a B:366 X-1080? CLER:WAYN* CLER:STON
a. W-1578 Ephraim Elder; John Collett [assignee?], 200a
W-1841 Ensign John Gibson, 800a?
W-4992 Thomas Mills, representative of, 500a?
b. William Lytle
c. J. Dunlap; J. McKinney, 1826; S? [L?] McFarland; Benjamin Evason, 1824; Z. Chapman, 1828; J. McKinzey, 1829; James Taylor; Isaac McFarland, 1830; B. Everson; H. Bigham [*also* H. A. Bigam] 1831; T. S. Bryan, 1833; S. Whitcher; J. McKenner, 1836; S? [L?] Ewing, 1835; W. Vancamp
*Source B notation: "Boston."

S-4441 300a B:366 X-1080? CLER:STON CLER:JACK
a. W-3462 Moses Parry, 200a?
W-0386 John Pritchett, 100a?
b. William Lytle
c. None

S-4442* 667a B:365 X-1080? CLER:STON CLER:JACK
a. W-4975 James Culbertson
b. John Donnell
c. D. Hunter & R. Hunter; S. B. Cleveland, 1825; J. B. Cleveland; S. Medary, 1829; S. McFarland; James McKinney, 1831; J. Needham & J. Hunter, 1833; James Taylor; John Bills, 1831; E. S. Haines
*See also S-4340.

S-4443 200a B:363 X-0790 WARR:HAMI
a. W-1289 David Morgan; Peter Smith [assignee?]
b. William Lytle
c. None

S-4444 200a B:364 X-1080 CLER:STON
CLER:JACK
a. W-1596 Thomas Fisher
b. Jonathan Donel*
c. None
*Source B spells Donnel.

S-4445 200a B:365 X-1080 CLER:JACK
a. W-3703 William Jenkins, 100a
W-3872 Phillip Conolly, 100a
b. John Irwin*
c. None
*Source C spells Irwine.

S-4446 200a B:367 X-1080 CLER:JACK
a. W-3634 Weedon Smith, 100a
W-3817 Moses Spencer, 100a
b. John Payne
c. John James Smith

S-4447. *See* S-4236 *and* S-4246

S-4448 2000a B:367 X-1080 CLER:WILL
CLER:JACK
a. W-4950 John Mountjoy
b. John Mountjoy
c. William Lytle; S. Winston, 1823; E. Moorhead; John Smith, 1830; James Taylor; John Hill, 1831; David Dyar; S. Mahan? [Maham?] 1835; Joseph? [James?] Holliday, heirs; William Patterson; John D. Moorhead, 1841

S-4449 2116a B:368 X-1080 CLER:STON
a. W-4908 James Taylor, assignee of John W. Williams, 889a?
W-4913 James Taylor, assignee of John Jones, 100a
W-4914 James Taylor, assignee of John Jones, 200a
W-4915 James Taylor, assignee of John Self, heir to Ben Vaughter, 100a
W-4904 Richard Taylor, 160a?
W-5039 Robert Morrow, representative of, 667a
b. J. Taylor, R. Taylor, and representatives of R. Morrow
c. James Taylor; John Hill, 1833; Z. Dooley; S. Hill, Junior; J. Hare; W. Wayland, Junior, 1839; W. Wood; James? [Joseph?] Derrow; W. Patterson

S-4450 500a B:368 X-1083 CLER:STON
a. W-4890 George Minzies, representatives of
b. James Taylor
c. John Hill, 1831

S-4451 500a B:421 X-0663 BROW:STER
a. W-3150 John Sanders, 200a
W-4149 Miles Travis, 100a
W-1110 John Berry, 200a
b. [James] Oharra* and [Nicholas] Bowsman
c. James Marrison; Timothy Kirby, 1826
*Source B spells O'Harra; Source C spells O'Hara.

S-4452 100a B:368 X-1080 CLER:JACK
a. W-4909 George Walden
b. George Walden
c. None

S-4453 349* D:364 X-0663 CLER:BATA
a. W-5019 Ferdinand Oneal; John Watts [assignee?]
b. George Mathews & Charles L. Mathews
c. T. Patterson; C. Harsh; B. Combs; S? [L?] Mayhan, 1842
*Source B says 340a.

S-4454 750a B:369 X-0663 BROW:PERR
CLIN:MARI
a. W-0147 Colonel Nathaniel Gist
b. Nathaniel Gist
c. John W. Tibatts [*also* Tibbatts] 1826; Benjamin Temple; John Weeks; E. Barcroft; R. Chalfant, 1828; D. Sutton; William Hillicost; S. Reynolds, 1830; W. Hewett, 1832; A. C. Stewart, 1831; William Hewit; George Curtis; L? [S?] Kimbley, 1839; A. Miller; J. Lake (Brown County); H. Weeks; A. Liggett, 1842

S-4455 500a C:338 X-0663 CLER:UNIO
S-5957
S-7090
a. W-5866 Abraham Bowman, 200a?
W-5254 John Mountjoy, 200a?
W-2753 Lewis Thomas, 100a?
b. -- Bowman, -- Mountjoy, & -- Thomas
c. John Tunis [crossed out]; A. Bowsman; H. Apple; M. F. H. Neith? [Veitch?] 1835

S-4455 200a B:511 X-0663 CLER:BATA
a. W-2753 Lewis Thomas
b. Lewis Thomas
c. John Prickett; William Johnson, 1824

S-4455 20a B:511 X-0663 CLER:BATA
a. W-2753 Lewis Thomas
b. Lewis Thomas
c. None

S-4456 467a B:368 X-0663 BROW:PIKE
a. W-4467 Charles Bradford
b. Charles Bradford
c. None

S-4457 200a B:367 X-0663 CLER:BATA
a. W-3216 William Woodfold
b. Nicholas Smith
c. None

S-4457 200a B:367 X-0663 CLER:BATA
a. W-2150 William Gimbo
b. William Gimbo
c. None

S-4458* 675a B:366 X-0570 CLER:TATE
a. W-0386 William Pritchett, 100a?
W-1037 Thomas Tawnehill, 200a?
W-4742 Samuel Landrum? [Landium?] 100a
W-4831 William Peake, 275a
b. [William] Lytle, [Thomas] Tawnihill, -- Sewell,** & [James] Morrison
c. J? [I?] Hoover; J? [I?] McDougal; Edward Salt, 1823
*Source B says "not patented."
**Source C says William Lowell.

S-4459 1000a B:426 X-0663 CLER:BATA
a. W-2417 Colonel Benjamin Temple
b. Benjamin Temple
c. J. Dennis & E. Dennis; James? [Joseph?] Kidd, 1839

S-4460 175a C:183 X-0270 CLER:TATE
a. W-0154 Captain Beaverley Roy
b. Beverly Roy
c. None

S-4461 350a D:148 X-0663* CLIN:JEFF HIGH:--**
a. W-4946 John Tibbs
b. John Tibbs
c. Willoughby Tibbs; -- Bruce, -- Davis, -- Strickle, 1825; J. Taylor, 1831; I? [J?] Morris, 1833
*"Waters of . . ."
**Source B does not mention Highland County.

S-4462 100a B:368 X-0663 CLIN:CLAR
a. W-4911 John Taylor
b. John Taylor
c. None

S-4463 200a B:369 X-1070 CLER:STON
a. W-1704 Walter Gregory
b. Walter Gregory
c. None

S-4464 200a B:366 X-1070 CLER:STON
a. W-4715 Zephaniah Farrel
b. [William] Lytle & [John] Whetstone
c. J. Seal, 1824

S-4465 100a B:369 X-1070 CLER:JACK
a. W-1703 Walter Gregory
b. Walter Gregory
c. None

S-4466 50a B:445 X-0650 ADAM:TIFF
a. W-4989 Thomas Alsberry
b. John Ellison, Junior
c. None

S-4467 50a B:390 X-0650 ADAM:TIFF
a. W-4989 Thomas Alsberry
b. John Ellison, Junior
c. None

S-4469 150a C:204 X-0000* ADAM:FRAN
S-8259
a. W-0215 Doctor David Holmes
b. David Holmes
c. None
*"Scioto Brush [Creek]."

S-4470 175a C:309 X-0655 ADAM:MEIG
a. W-0215 Doctor David Holmes
b. David Holmes
c. None

S-4471 300a B:391 X-1040* ADAM:FRAN
a. W-4794 John Nutt, 200a
W-4992 Thomas Mills, representative of, 100a
b. John Beasley
c. None
*"Northwest fork of . . ."

S-4473 500a B:395 X-0740 GREE:MIAM
S-4624 GREE:ROSS
a. W-1382 Lieutenant James Meriwether
b. James Merriwether*
c. None
*Source B spells Meriwether.

S-4475 1a B:371 X-0660 GREE:MIAM
a. W-1382 Lieutenant James Meriwether
b. James Merriwether*
c. None
*Source B spells Meriwether.

S-4477 500a B:373 X-0660 X-0730 LOGA:JEFF
a. W-1227 Alexander Spotswood Dandridge
b. Alexander S[potswood] Dandridge
c. None

S-4478 500a B:401 X-0060 LOGA:JEFF LOGA:LAKE
a. W-1227 Alexander Spotswood Dandridge
b. Alexander S[potswood] Dandridge
c. None

S-4479 800a B:403 X-0610 LOGA:MONR
a. W-4972 Jonathan Snowdon
b. Thomas Worthington
c. None

S-4480 500a B:419 X-0732 CLAR:HARM*
a. W-3035 Martha Lewis (representative) 200a
W-2709 Thomas Wilkinson, 100a
W-1112 Joseph Fowler, 200a
b. George Wallace
c. None
*Source B notation: "Brighton."

S-4481* 200a B:374 X-0360 MADI:SUMM
a. W-4970 Richard Priddy
b. George Priddy
c. Alexander Brady; Valentine Wilson, 1831
*Source B says "not patented."

S-4482 100a B:401 X-0841* FAYE:WAYN
a. W-4093 Frederick Shibler
b. Henry Bedinger
c. None
*"Waters of . . ."

S-4483 200a B:374 X-0843 FAYE:UNIO
a. W-4976 James Thompson
b. Duncan McArthur
c. None

S-4484 143a B:418 X-1000 PICK:WAYN
S-4704 X-0340
a. W-4976 James Thompson, 100a?
W-4535 John Curtis, 43a?
b. Duncan McArthur
c. A. C. McArthur; I? [J?] W. Julian, 1842

S-4492 2000a B:451 X-0730 LOGA:MONR
CHAM:SALE
a. W-5053 Jesse Davis, 1000a
W-5054 Jesse Davis, 1000a
b. Jesse Davis
c. Robert Fields; Samuel Newell, 1823

S-4493 900a B:453 X-0730 LOGA:MONR
S-4525
a. W-1450 Major Samuel Finley
b. Samuel Finley
c. None

S-4497 492a B:436 X-0730 LOGA:JEFF
LOGA:MONR
a. W-0732 Captain Thomas Parker
b. Thomas Parker
c. None

S-4498 415a B:453 X-0060 LOGA:JEFF
LOGA:LAKE
a. W-0660 Captain Hezekiah Morton
b. Hezekiah Morton
c. None

S-4499 60a B:382 X-0180 GREE:SUGA
a. W-5044 Thomas Woodlief, representative of Francis
Epps, deceased
b. James Fowler*
c. None
*Source B spells Towler.

S-4502 200a B:393 X-0660 GREE:XENI
a. W-5045 Thomas Woodlief, representative of Francis
Epps, deceased
b. Thomas Browder
c. None

S-4503 340a B:376 X-0660 GREE:ROSS
a. W-5045 Thomas Woodlief, representative of Francis
Epps, deceased
b. Thomas Browder
c. None

S-4504 199a B:396 X-0743 GREE:ROSS
a. W-1382 Lieutenant James Meriwether
b. James Merriwether*
c. None
*Source B spells Meriwether.

S-4507 110a B:393 X-0620 CHAM:WAYN
a. W-5045 Thomas Woodlief, representative of Francis
Epps, deceased
b. Thomas Browder
c. H. Warner; D[uncan] McArthur, 1823

S-4510 200a B:380 X-0780 MADI:UNIO
a. W-4448 John Hill
b. William Geddy
c. J. Moore, 1824

S-4511 160a B:389 X-0780 MADI:UNIO
a. W-5038 Francis Ratliff
b. Francis Ratliff
c. None

S-4512 600a B:380 X-0621 CHAM:WAYN
a. W-0631 Samuel Baskerville CLAR: --*
b. John Kean
c. None
*Source B does not mention Clark County.

S-4513 1207a B:378 X-0360 MADI:UNIO
a. W-5035 Peter Helphinstine, representative of
b. Peter Helphenstine, representative of
c. B. Kirkpatrick; — Mason & -- Kirkpatrick, 1826;
J. Timmons; H. Warner, 1823

S-4514 615a B:379 X-1260 MADI:UNIO
a. W-5034 Peter Helphinstine, representative of, 447a?
W-5033 Peter Helphinstine, representative of, 168a?
b. Peter Helphinstine, representative of
c. None

S-4515 884a B:378 X-0780 MADI:UNIO
a. W-5032* Peter Helphinstine, representative of
b. Peter Helphenstine, representative of
c. J. Timmons; -- Lewis & -- Phifer, 1823; G. Batie;
S. N. Karr, 1829; G. Crawford; W. Simpkins, 1829;
Jacob Gerrard, 1827; John Beatley, heirs; S. B.
Baskerville, 1832
*Warrant insufficient for acreage granted.

S-4516 1064a B:380 X-0621 CHAM:WAYN
a. W-2274 Doctor Basil Middleton
b. John Campbell
c. None

S-4517 136a B:377 X-0360 PICK:MONR
a. W-4971 Jonathan Snowdon
b. Elias Rector
c. None

S-4518 146a B:389 X-1260 MADI:UNIO
a. W-4971 Jonathan Snowdon
b. Elias Rector
c. None

S-4519 225a B:381 X-0730 CLAR:PLEA
a. W-1482 William Davis, 200a
W-3997 Shadrach Pinkstone, 25a
b. Richard Osburn
c. None

S-4520 675a B:381 X-0730 CHAM:WAYN CHAM:SALE LOGA: --*
a. W-0997 Robert Howard, 100a
W-1481 John Evans, 100a
W-2941 Lodwick Miller, 100a
W-3228 James Brown, 200a
W-2974 George Ryan, 100a
W-3997 Shadrach Pinkstone, 75a
b. Richard Osburn
c. G. Martin & B. Martin; J. Thompson, 1827
*Source B does not mention Logan County.

S-4524 400a B:431 X-0730 CHAM:SALE
a. W-5055 Jesse Davis
b. Jesse Davis
c. None

S-4525. *See* S-4493

S-4526 300a B:395 X-0730 CLAR:PLEA
a. W-1382 Lieutenant James Meriwether
b. James Merriwether*
c. None
*Source B spells Meriwether.

S-4532 500a B:394 X-0730 CLAR:PLEA
a. W-5041 John Cole
b. John Cole
c. B. Hough, heirs; Thoda Norton, 1826

S-4533 200a B:524 X-0423 ADAM:LIBE
a. W-3795 Reuben Cooper
b. Nolley* Cohn
c. None
*Source C spells Notley.

S-4534 1200a B:431 X-0730 CHAM:SALE CHAM:WAYN
a. W-0226 Lieutenant Jacob Coleman
b. Gahiel* Peterson
c. Joseph? [James?] Tallman
*Source B and C spell Gabriel.

S-4538 380a B:431 X-0730 CHAM:SALE
a. W-5055 Jesse Davis
b. Jesse Davis
c. None

S-4539 213a B:389 X-0730 CLAR:PLEA
a. W-4943 Thomas Hungerford, 113a?
W-4944 Thomas Hungerford, 100a?
b. William Rector
c. None

S-4540 200a B:379 X-0780 MADI:UNIO
a. W-1456 William Willis
b. Charles Buck*
c. T. Bond, 1824; E. Langham? [Laugham?] 1826; W. Wilson, 1827
*Source C may spell Burk.

S-4541 189a B:388 X-0730 CLAR:PLEA
a. W-4872 John Belfield, representative of
b. John Bellfield, representative of
c. None

S-4542* 222a -- -- CLAR: -- CHAM: --
a. --
b. Alexander Petrie?
c. George Medsker; Solomon Scott, 1825; J. Thompson, 1828
*Entry in Source B only (at top of page above S-4497).

S-4543 75a B:389 X-0730 CHAM:SALE
a. W-0631 Samuel Baskerville
b. John Kean
c. James? [Joseph?] Stewart, 1823

S-4544 1200a B:379 X-0730 CHAM:SALE CHAM:WAYN
a. W-2274 Doctor Basil Middleton
b. John Campbell
c. None

S-4545 266a B:393 X-0730 CLAR:PLEA CHAM: --*
a. W-1020 Nathan Young, 66a
W-1099 William Overlin? [Overton?] 200a
b. Alexander Armstrong
c. None
*Source B does not list Champaign County.

S-4546 133a B:392 X-0180 GREE:SILV
a. W-1020 Nathan Young
b. Alexander Armstrong
c. None

S-4551 350a B:393 X-0730 CLAR:PLEA
a. W-5045 Thomas Woodlief, representative of Francis Epps, deceased
b. Thomas Browder
c. -- Hudson; J. Cooper, 1826; Enoch Henry

S-4552 200a B:394 X-0663 HIGH:DODS CLIN:CLAR HAMI: --*
a. W-5041 John Cole
b. John Cole
c. Jacob Ratcliff; Thomas Woodmanse, 1827; Ann Smith; Jeremiah Hadley, 1827
*Source A does not list Highland County; Source B does not list Hamilton County.

S-4553 400a B:383 X-0450 BROW:HUNT
a. W-4647 Nicholas Carrele, 200a?
W-3952* Moses Oliver, 100a?
W-1706 Peter Jones, 100a?
b. John Obannon
c. George T. Cotton, heirs; S. Rankin, 1833
*This warrant already entirely used in S-2379.

S-4554. *See* S-4378

S-4555 100a B:384 X-0663* CLIN:GREE
a. W-4746 Mathew Crowder
b. William Barbour**
c. A. Coats; James Fyfe, 1835
*"Waters of . . ."
**Source B spells Barlow.

S-4556 260a? B:384 X-0663 HIGH:UNIO
a. W-2312 Captain Francis Dade
b. Francis Dade
c. None

S-4557. *See* S-4428

S-4558* 35a -- -- CLIN:UNIO
a. [Probably W-2312 Captain Francis Dade]
b. Francis Dade
c. Thomas Osburn; J? [I?] W. Hackney, 1841
*Entry in Source B only (at sequential place).

S-4559 250a B:436 X-0663 HIGH:UNIO
a. W-2312 Captain Francis Dade
b. Francis Dade
c. None

S-4561 125a B:413 X-0743 GREE:XENI
a. W-2312 Captain Francis Dade
b. Francis Dade
c. None

S-4564 140a B:403 X-0366 MADI:RANG
a. W-4972 Jonathan Snowdon
b. Thomas Worthington
c. None

S-4568 100a D:392 X-1185 CHAM:RUSH
a. W-5008 Edward Stokes? [Stoker?]
b. Edward Stokes
c. None

S-4569 500a D:19 X-1000 UNIO:JACK
a. W-1118 James Parlor, 200a
W-1091 Thomas Haley, 200a
W-0782 Thomas Ravenscraft, 100a
b. Maria Bella Scott & William Bernard Scott
c. William Myres; S. S. Bennett, 1826; Bela? [Beta?] Croyle; A. Kerns, 1833; Joshua Mathiott, 1835; Joshua Northcut, 1837

S-4570 3000a C:387 X-0730 LOGA:ZANE
X-0340 LOGA:MONR
a. W-4958 Richard Kennon, 1000a
W-4959 Richard Kennon, 1000a
W-4960 Richard Kennon, 500a
W-4961 Richard Kennon, 500a
b. Richard Kennon
c. J. Galloway, Junior, 1831

S-4571* 500a -- -- LOGA: --
a. [Probably W-4962 Richard Kennon]
b. Richard Kennon
c. Samuel Hawkins, 1823
*Entry shown in Source B only (in sequential place).

S-4572* 1000a -- -- UNIO:CLAI
a. --
b. Robert Patton
c. Unknown; M? [W?] S. Butler, 1836
*Entry shown in Source B only (in sequential place).

S-4573 100a -- -- MADI:CANA
a. --
b. James Winkfield, representative of
c. None
*Entry shown in Source B only (in sequential place).

S-4575* 100a C:99 X-0340 MADI:CANA
a. W-4925 James Winkfield, representative of
b. James Winkfield, representative of
c. None
*Not shown in Source B, but see S-4573.

S-4578 260a B:387 X-0663 BROW:STER
BROW:PERR
a. W-4752 John Allen, assignee Robert Brower, 100a
W-4727 Samuel Eddins, 100a?
W-4713 Norman Earvey, 60a?
b. John Breckenridge
c. Timothy Kirby, 1826; John Breckenridge, heirs; G. H. Bohrer, 1832; William Hunt, 1834; F. Bingaman, 1834

S-4585* 100a -- -- CHAM:UNIO
a. --
b. James Harris
c. William Sells, 1829
*Entry shown in Source B only (in sequential place).

S-4588* 116a -- -- CLAR:PLEA**
a. --
b. Jordan Harris
c. None
*Entry shown in Source B only (in sequential place).
**Source B notation: "Newburg."

S-4589* 20a -- -- ROSS:UNIO
a. --
b. Jordan Harris
c. None
*Entry shown in Source B only (in sequential place).

S-4590* 13a C:354 X-1260?** MADI:UNIO
a. W-1574 Samuel Flournoy
b. James Harris
c. None
*Source B says "Not patented."
**Does not state which Walnut River is meant.

S-4592 1501a B:507 X-0660 CLIN:CHES
S-4715 WARR:WAYN
S-5656
S-5657
S-5658
S-5858
a. W-5058 Henry Field, representative of
b. Henry Fields, representative of
c. None

S-4595 200a B:409 X-0180 GREE:SUGA
a. W-4773 Jesse Gaskins; Sanford Bradwell, Jacob B. Miller [assignees?]
b. Ichabod B. Miller
c. None

S-4596 250a C:101 X-0420 ADAM:TIFF
S-5340
a. W-4984 Jonathan Howard, representative of; Jacob Traber [assignee?] 100a
W-4985 Simon Akers; Frederick Brautier [assignee?] 100a
W-5112 Henry Aldred, 50a?
b. Andrew Ellison
c. None

S-4598 25a B:392 X-1110 ADAM:GREE
a. W-4050 John Posey Newman; Jacob Edwards, John Brown [assignees?]
b. Andrew Ellison
c. None

S-4599 25a B:390 X-1110 ADAM:GREE
a. W-4050 John Posey Newman; Jacob Edwards, John Brown [assignees?]
b. Andrew Ellison
c. None

S-4600 100a B:420 X-0130* ADAM:TIFF
a. W-0215 Doctor David Holmes
b. David Holmes
c. Andrew Willock; T. Huston, 1834
*"Lk. fork of . . ."

S-4601 50a B:392 X-0130 ADAM:MONR
a. W-0215 Doctor David Holmes
b. David Holmes
c. None

S-4602 667a B:419 X-0340 CHAM:WAYN
S-4741 CHAM:RUSH
a. W-2418 Lieutenant Thomas Sears
b. Thomas Sears*
c. None
*Source B notation: "Patented to Swefson Whitehead."

S-4604. *See* S-4195

S-4605 63a C:500 X-0340 UNIO:DARB
a. W-0556 Robert Hays? [Kays?]
b. Robert Kays
c. None

S-4606 320a D:196 X-0345 LOGA:ZANE
UNIO: --*
a. W-1495 John Gratton, heir to Lieutenant J. Gratton
b. John Gratton
c. Lucas Sullivant, heirs; Martin Hill, 1830
*Source B does not list Union County.

S-4607* 185a -- -- CHAM: --
a. --
b. Nath[aniel] Tyler
c. E. Hovey, 1828
*Entry in Source B only (at top of page above S-4555).

S-4608* 889a -- -- CHAM: --
a. --
b. Nath[aniel] Tyler
c. William Vance? [Nance?] 1828
*Entry in Source B only (at top of page above S-4555).

S-4609* 888a -- -- CHAM: --
a. --
b. Nath[aniel] Tyler
c. Samuel Franklin, 1828
*Entry in Source B only (at top of page above S-4555).

S-4610 481a B:501 X-0340 UNIO:UNIO
a. W-4583 Peter Manifeld? [Mansfeld?] assignee of David Hopkins
b. Peter Manifold
c. W. W. Irwin; W? [N?] Massie, 1840

S-4613 400a B:394 X-1170 CLIN:UNIO
a. W-5064 Lewelling Jones, representative of
b. Daniel Bailey
c. Susanna Bailey; J? [I?] Morris; G. Bruce, 1832

S-4620 294a D:12 X-0180 GREE:SILV
GREE:ROSS*
a. W-5065 Lewelling Jones, representative of
b. Thomas Browder
c. W. Marshall; J. Galloway, 1826; T. Sheely; B. McClelland, 1841
*Source B notation: "Jamestown."

S-4624. *See* S-4473

S-4626* 266a B:406 X-1010 GREE:XENI
S-4651
a. W-5042 John Cole
b. James Fowler
c. None
*Source B does not show this entry, but does show at S-4651.

S-4634 60a B:406 X-1170 CLIN:UNIO
a. W-5042 John Cole
b. James Fowler
c. None

S-4636 150a B:454 X-0730 CHAM:SALE
a. W-3707 Matthias Sheener
b. William Tidball
c. None

S-4637 100a B:431 X-0340 MADI:DARB
a. W-0226 Lieutenant Jacob Coleman
b. Gahiel* Peterson
c. James? [Joseph?] Lacompt; H. Warner, 1836
*Source B and C say Gabriel.

S-4638 1300a B:398 X-0980 HIGH:LIBE
a. W-4339 Samuel Smith
b. Henry Massie
c. H. Miller; J. Smith, 1826

S-4639 1000a B:400 X-0980 HIGH:JACK*
a. W-4927 Robert White, 500a
W-4954 Reuben Briscoe, 500a
b. Henry Massie
c. D. Scott; Eli Murphin, 1841
*Source B notation: "Marshall."

S-4640 350a B:398 X-0840 ROSS:HUNT
a. W-4953 Reuben Briscoe
b. Henry Massie
c. None

S-4641 264a B:397 X-1000 FRAN:JACK
a. W-4953 Reuben Briscoe, 64a
W-3567 John Dedman, heir to R. Dedman, 200a
b. Henry Massie
c. None

S-4642 94a B:397 X-0840 ROSS:FRAN
a. W-4339 Samuel Smith, elder brother of William [Smith] deceased
b. Henry Massie
c. None

S-4643 37a B:398 X-0840 ROSS:TWIN
a. W-3724 William Pope
b. John Teeters
c. None

S-4644 104a B:397 X-0840 ROSS:TWIN
a. W-4339 Samuel Smith, elder brother of William [Smith] deceased, 73a?
W-4927 Robert White, 31a?
b. Henry Massie
c. John Reeves; James H. Myres, 1840

S-4651. *See* S-4626

S-4655 620a B:405 X-0050* LOGA:PERR
a. W-5063 Lewelling Jones, representative [of?]
b. Lewelling Jones, representative [of?]
c. Herbert Beard; John D. Elbert, 1839
*Source B says "Reaver [Beaver?] run . . ."

S-4658 500a B:404 X-0340 LOGA:ZANE
S-4678 CHAM:RUSH
a. W-5023 Henry Tatum
b. Benjamin Rosseau*
c. James? [Joseph?] Spain; J. D. Elbert, Junior, 1838; Lyne Starling, 1831
*Source B spells Bosseau; Source C spells Boisseau.

S-4661 500a B:453 X-0730 LOGA:JEFF
LOGA:PERR
a. W-0205 Captain Thomas Thucutt? [Thewait? Thweatt?]
b. Thomas Thweatt
c. None

S-4666 1000a B:404 X-0340 CHAM:WAYN
CHAM:RUSH
LOGA: --*
a. W-5047 Thomas Woodlief, legal representative of Francis Epps
b. Thomas Browder, Junior
c. Jacob Frankaberger; M. W. Ward, 1824
*Source B does not list Logan County.

S-4667 50a B:403 X-0180 GREE:ROSS
a. W-5065 Lewelling Jones, representative of
b. Thomas Browder, Junior*
c. None
*Source B omits Junior.

S-4670* 10a -- -- GREE:XENI
a. --
b. James Towler
c. --
*Entry listed in Source B only (at sequential place).

S-4671 1059a C:410 X-0180 GREE:ROSS
S-6564
S-6565
S-10183
S-10184
S-10185
a. W-5499 Thomas Ruffin, deceased, representative of, 500a
W-5817 John Goodrich, heir, 500a
W-5042 John Cole, 59a?
b. [James] Galloway & -- Fowler*
c. None
*Source B spells Towler.

S-4672 400a B:405 X-0730 CLAR:HARM
a. W-5059 Peter Minor, representative of
b. Peter Minor, representative [of?]
c. Simon Dickey, heirs; Gilka Wallingford, 1833

S-4673 600a B:405 X-0730 CLAR:PLEA
a. W-5059 Peter Minor, representative of
b. Peter Minor, representative [of?]
c. V. Bowen; T. Browder; C. Arbogard, 1829; Richard Sweeney; Richard Bodkin, 1833; I? [J?] Asher; G. Messenger, 1842

S-4674 1000a B:414 X-0342 CHAM:GOSH
a. W-5054 Peter Minor, representative of
b. Peter Minor, representative of
c. Jacob Frankaberger

S-4675 800a B:415 X-0010 GREE:SILV
a. W-5046 Thomas Woodlief, legal representative of Francis Epps
b. Frederick Stanton
c. Michael Man[n]; Alfred Trader, 1833

S-4676 800a B:404 X-0730 LOGA:ZANE
X-0340 LOGA:MONR
LOGA:PERR
a. W-5025 Henry Tatum, 300a?
W-5023 Henry Tatum, 500a?
b. Benjamin Rosseau*
c. R. M. McMunnon? [Munnon?] 1830
*Source B spells Bosseau; Source C spells Boisseau.

S-4678. *See* S-4658

S-4686 100a C:212 X-1000 PIKE:JACK
a. W-0958 Peter Haines
b. Andrew Wolff*
c. S. Holliday; H. Hempstead, 1829; R. Douglas
*Source B spells Wolf.

S-4687 296a C:411 X-0730 CHAM:UNIO
S-4772
S-4773
S-10158
a. W-0194 James Galt, heir to Doctor P. Galt, 196a?
W-5817* John Goodrich, 100a?
b. James Galt
c. D. Marsh; William Silver, 1831; James McDonald, 1831
*Warrant already used entirely in S-4671.

S-4689 800a B:429 X-0830 LOGA:PERR*
a. W-0211 Robert Baines; John Lockley, assignee, 100a
W-1437 William Gregory, 100a
W-0369 James Tutt, heir to Charles Tutt, 600a
b. William Croghan
c. None
*Source B notation: "East Liberty."

S-4690 85a B:417 X-1240 ROSS:TWIN
a. W-1450 Major Samuel Finley
b. Duncan McArthur
c. Jacob Myres; S. Edwards & F. Edwards, 1833

S-4691 150a B:417 X-0845 ROSS:TWIN
a. W-1450 Major Samuel Finley
b. Duncan McArthur
c. None

S-4692 165a B:418 X-1000 PICK:SCIO
a. W-1450 Major Samuel Finley
b. Duncan McArthur
c. None

S-4693 175a C:52 X-1170 CLIN:UNIO
a. W-2312 Captain Francis Dade
b. Francis Dade
c. None

S-4694 100a B:414 X-1170 WARR:SALE
CLIN: --*
a. W-1810 Joseph Parker
b. Joseph Parker
c. William Barlow
*Source B does not mention Clinton County.

S-4695 100a C:46 X-1180 CHAM:GOSH
a. W-1810 Joseph Parker
b. Joseph Parker
c. None

S-4696 1111a B:408 X-0663 BROW:PERR
a. W-4860* John Scarburg, 444a
W-3414 John Scarbrough, 667a
b. John Lytle
c. William Cox; Fred[erick] Bingaman, 1823; William Curry; Timothy Kirby; William Bamber, 1826; -- Hawk & -- Lytle; United States Bank; Robert Rallston; Richard Holden? [Holders?]
*A warrant of the same number was issued to William Roads, according to Source C, and used in S-3743.

S-4697 667a B:430 X-0340 LOGA:ZANE
CHAM:WAYN
a. W-4870 John Stith
b. Peter Pelham
c. J. H. Piatt [*also* Pyatt] heirs; Samuel Newell, 1826

S-4703. *See* S-4303

S-4704 460a B:410 X-0660 GREE:SUGA
a. W-1226 Alexander S. Dandridge
b. Nathaniel Massie
c. None

S-4704. *See* S-4484

S-4705. *See* S-2908

S-4706. *See* S-3820

S-4708. *See* S-3365

S-4709 100a B:411 X-1310 ROSS:TWIN
a. W-3432 John M. Galt, "resolution"
b. Abraham Shepherd
c. None

S-4710 50a B:411 X-1230 ROSS:PAIN
a. W-3432 John M. Galt, "resolution'
b. Abraham Shepherd
c. None

S-4711 50a C:493 X-0710 ROSS:TWIN
a. W-4992 Thomas Mills, representative of
b. Nathaniel Massie
c. None

S-4713 410a C:26 X-0841 ROSS:UNIO
a. W-4992 Thomas Mills, representative of, 260a?
W-1226 Alexander S. Dandridge, 200a?
b. Nathaniel Massie
c. None

S-4714 266a B:506 X-0840* HIGH:PAIN
S-5828
a. W-5058 Henry Field, representative of
b. Henry Fields, representative of
c. None
*"R[ight] h[and] fork of . . ."

S-4715. *See* S-4592

S-4716 98a B:437 X-0570 ROSS:HUNT
a. W-4943 Thomas Hungerford
b. George Girvins*
c. None
*Source B spells Givens.

S-4717 200a B:437 X-0570 ROSS:SCIO
a. W-4943 Thomas Hungerford
b. James Stevenson*
c. None
*Sources B and C spell Stephenson.

S-4718 70a B:413 X-0570 ROSS:SCIO
a. W-4943 Thomas Hungerford
b. David Richie*
c. None
*Source B spells Ritchie.

S-4719 750a B:413 X-0360 ROSS:UNIO
X-0841 PICK: --*
a. W-4805 Frederich Seigle, representative of
b. Frederick Seigle, representative [of?]
c. None
*Source B does not mention Pickaway County.

S-4720 662a B:412 X-1370 PICK:DEER
a. W-4805 Frederich Seigle, representative of
b. Frederick Seigle, representative [of?]
c. John Hulsted, heirs; Andrew Huston, 1832

S-4721 3500a B:412 X-0360 ROSS:UNIO
ROSS:DEER
PICK:WAYN
PICK:DEER
a. W-4805 Frederich Seigle, representative of
b. Frederick Seigle, representative [of?]
c. Jessup N. Couch, heirs; T. P. Brown, 1831; William McDowell; John Lybran, 1832; John Rector, heirs; Stephen Horsey, 1833; John Richart; Jonathan Craybill; P. N. White, 1836; George Bennett, 1841

S-4722 75a B:411 X-1000 ROSS:UNIO
a. W-4805 Frederich Seigle, representative of
b. Frederick Seigle, representative [of?]
c. None

S-4723 13a F:311 X-1375 PICK:DEER
a. W-4805 Frederich Seigle, representative of
b. Frederick Seigle, representative [of?]
c. J? [I?] Davis, heirs; John Mills, 1836

S-4724 60a C:503 X-0360 PICK:DEER
a. W-1420 Ning Bell
b. James Miskimins
c. None

S-4725 73a D:473 X-1375 PICK:DEER
a. W-4787 Jacob Price
b. Jeremiah Joskin*
c. Daniel Hanson, 1831; Robert Lee Richardson
*Sources B and C spell Joslin.

S-4726 359a D:381 X-1385 PICK:DEER
a. W-4917 John Steed
b. John Beauchamp
c. None

S-4727 200a C:232 X-0841 ROSS:SCIO
a. W-4917 John Steed
b. John Miskimins* & William Miskimins*
c. None
*Source B spells Miskimon; Source C spells Miskemen, Mishemen.

S-4728 100a D:447 X-1375 PICK:WAYN
PICK:DEER
a. W-4417 William Reynolds, assignee
b. Alexander Gibson
c. G. W. Doan, 1827

S-4729 79a B:527 X-0130* ADAM:TIFF
S-6096
a. W-3092 Samuel Decker; W? Russell [assignee?]
b. Joseph Darlington
c. None
*"Lk. f[ork] of . . ."

S-4730 50a B:416 X-0660 GREE:MIAM
GREE:XENI
a. W-5042 John Cole
b. James Towler
c. None

S-4731 300a B:497 X-0342 CHAM:GOSH
a. W-5044 Thomas Woodlief, representative of Francis Epps, deceased, 135a?
W-5042 John Cole, 165a?
b. James Towler
c. None

S-4735 283a B:427 X-0351 UNIO:UNIO
CHAM: --*
a. W-5046 Thomas Woodlief, representative of Francis Epps, deceased, 183a
W-5064 Lewelling Jones, representative of, 100a
b. Frederick Stanton & -- Bailey
c. None
*Source B does not mention Champaign County.

S-4741. *See* S-4602

S-4742 130a B:437 X-0342 MADI:JEFF
a. W-5072 Isaac Browning
b. Duncan McArthur
c. None

S-4743 667a B:437 X-0342 CHAM:GOSH*
a. W-5072 Isaac Browning
b. Duncan McArthur
c. None
*Source B notation: "By Mechanicsburg."

S-4744 77a B:418 X-0840 ROSS:TWIN
a. W-5072 Isaac Browning
b. Duncan McArthur
c. None

S-4747 382a B:419 X-0342 CHAM:GOSH*
a. W-4376 William Reynolds, [assignee?] of John Depinta? [Depriest?], [assignee?] of W. Darville
b. William Reynolds
c. H. Barrett? [Bassett?]; W. S. Jones, 1827; Hy [Henry?] Neil; Isaac Putnam
*Source B notation: "Mechanicsburg."

S-4748 250a B:436 X-0342 CHAM:GOSH
a. W-1981 William Cherry
b. John Askew
c. None

S-4749 90a B:438 X-0342 CHAM:GOSH
a. W-4878 James McNutt
b. James McNutt
c. None

S-4750* 80a C:311 X-0342 CHAM:GOSH
a. W-0088 Captain Strether Jones
b. Strother Jones
c. Robert Patten & Company; S. N. Kerr, 1831
*Source B says "not patented."

S-4751 200a B:418 X-0360 MADI:DEER
a. W-4878 James McNutt
b. James McNutt
c. None

S-4752 605a C:228 X-0342 MADI:PLEA
FRAN:PLEA
a. W-2162 Colonel William Heth
b. William Heth
c. W. Dun; James Bryden, 1831; C. Thomas, 1832; C. Higgins, 1834; R. Douglas; A. Douglas, 1838 (Madison County); P. Douglas, 1840

S-4753 590a B:469 X-0342 CHAM:WAYN
a. W-2162 Colonel William Heth
b. William Hith*
c. William Heath; James Stewart & W. Stewart, 1831
*Source B spells Heth.

S-4755 125a B:418 X-0840 ROSS:TWIN
a. W-2710 Barnabas Wilkinson, 40a
W-4686 Peter Francisco, 30a
W-4866 Thomas Hankens, representative of, 55a
b. John McDonald
c. None

S-4756 433a B:419 X-0130 ADAM:MEIG
a. W-1587 John Roe, 200a
W-1664 James Hynes, 200a
W-1412 William McIntosh, 33a
b. Clement Biddle
c. None

S-4758 75a C:152 X-0130 ADAM:MONR
a. W-1141 Edward Shepherd
b. Stephen Beech
c. None

S-4759 200a B:444 X-0340 LOGA:ZANE
CHAM:RUSH
a. W-2793 Baker Hagard
b. Thomas Campbell
c. David Rees; John Mays, 1832; Gary Gray

S-4763 100a B:469 X-0342 CHAM:GOSH
a. W-5072 Isaac Browning
b. Duncan McArthur
c. None

S-4766 400a B:524 X-0340 PICK:JACK
a. W-1984 Captain William George
b. Duncan McArthur
c. J. Hall; H. White, 1827; A. Hull; John Stroup, 1831; W. Forsman; John Walker, 1840

S-4769 200a B:523 X-0342 MADI:PIKE
UNIO: --*
a. W-1984 Captain William George
b. Duncan McArthur
c. None
*Source B does not mention Union County.

S-4771 145a B:438 X-0840 ROSS:TWIN
a. W-0348 Captain James Curry
b. Benson Goldsberry
c. None

S-4772. *See* S-4687 *(not separately listed in Source A)*

S-4773* 40a — — CHAM**:--
a. --
b. James Galt
c. James Galt, heirs; James McDonald, 1831
**See* S-4687 (not separately listed in Source A).
**Source B could also read Clark County.

S-4778* -- -- -- PICK:DARB MADI:--**
a. --
b. James Gault
c. Abel Westfall; Joseph Crisman, 1828
*Not listed in Source A.
**Source B does not list township.

S-4779 190a C-368 X-0730 --*
a. W-0194 James Galt, heir to Doctor P. Galt
b. James Galt
c. D. Marsh, 1826
*Source C says: "Not found [in] Clark, Champaign, or Logan [counties]. Source B says Champaign County.

S-4780 621a B:422 X-0663 CLER:JACK
a. W-0772 John Gresham, 100a
W-5090 James Taylor, assignee of James McGeorge, 100a
W-3015 Leven Joins, 300a?
W-5075 James Taylor, assignee of Tarpley White, 121a?
b. William Lytle
c. W? [M?] McGinley

S-4781 50a B:423 X-0663 CLER:WILL
a. W-5075 James Taylor, assignee of Tarpley White
b. William Lytle
c. James Taylor; Z. Chapman

S-4782* 67a B:422 X-0665 CLER:JACK
a. W-5075 James Taylor, assignee of Tarpley White
b. William Lytle
c. J. Taylor; Z. Chapman, 1828
*In Source B entry is at top of page above S-4753, as well as at sequential place. *See also* S-5259, S-4800, and S-5258

S-4783 667a B:423 X-1070 CLER:BATA CLER:STON CLER:JACK
a. W-5083 William Merideth
b. James Taylor & William Lytle
c. James Taylor; John Hill, 1831; W. Baird; J. McKinner, 1836; J. Dryden; J. McKinnie [*also* McKinney]

S-4784 200a B:422 X-0663 CLER:JACK
a. W-1146 James Karr
b. James Karr
c. William Lytle; S. Winston, 1823; S. B. Cleveland, 1825; James Taylor; Z. Chapman, 1828; James Taylor, 1830

S-4785 1556a B:425 X-0663 BROW:STER
a. W-5077 Thomas Martin
b. Thomas Martin
c. -- Canfield & -- Bliss; J. S. Beasley, 1841

S-4786 445a B:425 X-0663 BROW:STER BROW:PERR
a. W-5078 Thomas Pearson
b. Thomas Pearson
c. William Lytle; Thomas Perkins; T[imothy] Kirby, 1826; United States Bank; N. Ellis, 1832

S-4787 445a B:423 X-0663 BROW:STER BROW:PERR
a. W-5079 Henry Bowyer
b. -- Bowyers* & James Taylor
c. William Lytle; John W. Tibatts, 1826; T. C. Bomber? [Boneber?] 1841
*Source B spells Bowyer.

S-4788 333a B:425 X-0663 BROW:PERR
a. W-5076 Tarpley White
b. Tarpley White
c. Robert Means; J. H. Price, 1840; William Lytle; James Taylor, Junior, 1831; P. L. Wilson, 1842

S-4789 1000a B:421 X-1300 BROW:STER
a. W-5082 Abraham Buford
b. Abraham Buford
c. William Lytle; T[imothy] Kirby, 1826; Robert Chalfant; Thomas Ross; J[ames] Taylor, Junior, 1831

S-4790 111a B:421 X-0663 BROW:STER BROW:PERR
a. W-5082 Abraham Buford
b. Abraham Buford
c. William Lytle; Timothy Kirby, 1826; N. Ellis, 1832; J. Taylor; -- Snell & -- Woods; T. C. Bomber, 1841

S-4791 667a B:424 X-0663 CLER:JACK
a. W-5081 James Taylor, assignee of John Gillison
b. James Taylor
c. William Lytle; Samuel Winston, 1823; S. B. Cleveland, 1825; Phillip Stoner; James Perin, 1836

S-4792 667a B:421 X-0663 BROW:STER
a. W-5080 Thomas Bowyer, representative of
b. Thomas Bowyer, representative [of?]
c. William Lytle; T[imothy] Kirby, 1826; Nathan Sidwell; Nathan Ellis, 1828; D. C. Devore, 1834; United States Bank; E. Marmon? 1838; C. Hess; W. Parker, 1841

S-4793 667a B:423 X-0663 BROW:STER
a. W-5084 Robert Sayers & James Taylor
b. Robert Sayers & James Taylor
c. None

S-4795 889a C:425 X-0770 CLER:OHIO
a. W-5086 James Knox
b. James Knox
c. None

S-4797 500a D:197 X-1060 BROW:PIKE
a. W-5091 Thomas Overton & James Taylor
b. Thomas Overton & James Taylor
c. Joseph? [James?] Keethler

S-4798 200a B:421 X-0663 BROW:STER
a. W-5088 James Bell
b. James Bell
c. J. Roney, 1827; James Taylor; N[athan] Ellis, 1833; A. R. Snell; J[ames] Taylor, Junior, 1841

S-4799 100a B:421 X-0663 BROW:STER
a. W-5087 James Borne, representative of
b. Jesse Borne, representative of
c. Adam Snell; Nathan Ellis, 1829

S-4800* 100a B:424 X-0663 CLER:JACK
a. W-4831 William Peake
b. James Morrison
c. None
*See also S-4782, S-5258, & S-5259

S-4801 17a B:423 X-0663 CLER:WILL
a. W-5075 James Taylor, assignee of Tarpley White
b. William Lytle
c. William Wainwright, 1824; J. Jameson? 1826; James Taylor; Z. Chapman, 1828; W. Wainwright & V. Wainwright; -- Maham? 1833; H. Broadwell

S-4802 200a C:429 X-0663 CLER:BATA
a. W-2417 Colonel Benjamin Temple
b. Benjamin Temple
c. None

S-4804 324a B:430 X-0341 CHAM:GOSH
UNIO: --*
a. W-5042 John Cole
b. James Towler
c. None
*Source B does not mention Union County.

S-4805 400a B:444 X-0350 UNIO*:UNIO
a. W-1379 Daniel Blair, 200a
W-2532 Peter Batchelor; John Taylor [assignee?] 200a
b. Abraham Bainbridge**
c. -- Bonner & -- Galloway, 1825; Alexander Comer, 1831; Ira Wood, 1831
*Survey originally thought to have been in Madison County.
**Source B says Absalom Bainbridge.

S-4806 30a C:38 X-0570 ROSS:HUNT
a. W-0199 Captain Lawrence Butler
b. Lawrence Butler
c. None

S-4807 467a B:445 X-0350 MADI*:UNIO
UNIO*:UNIO
a. W-0685 Lieutenant Obediah Smith
b. Obediah Smith
c. J. B. Andrews, 1829; H. Tunney? [Turney?] heirs; Adam Reister; L[ucas] Sullivant, 1831 (Madison County)
*Source B entry unclear as to whether survey was in one or both counties.

S-4809 178a C:409 X-0180 GREE:SILV
a. W-4974 Richard Cale? [Call?]
b. Richard Call
c. Jacob Evans; Gasper Clemons, 1835

S-4810 711a B:428 X-0820 LOGA:PERR
a. W-4974 Richard Cale? [Call?]
b. Richard Call
c. George Mathews; J. McLain, 1823; James Garwood; Jeremiah McLain; Adam Brown, 1831

S-4811 533a B:427 X-0050 LOGA:PERR
LOGA:ZANE
UNIO:JERO
a. W-5024 Henry Tatum
b. Benjamin Boisseau*
c. William Warrel
*Source B seplls Bosseau.

S-4812 833a B:427 X-0340 UNIO:ALLE
LOGA: --*
a. W-5023 Henry Tatum, 366a
W-5024 Henry Tatum, 467a
b. Benjamin Boisseau**
c. None
*Source A does not mention Union County; Source B does not mention Logan County.
**Source B spells Bosseau.

S-4813 500a B:429 X-0750 LOGA:PERR
a. W-5062 Peter Minor, representative of
b. James Galloway
c. None

S-4814 1100a B:429 X-0340 CHAM:RUSH
a. W-5066 Lewelling Jones, representative of
b. Lewelling Jones, representative [of?]
c. Elias Ellicott

S-4815 1380a B:429 X-0750 UNIO:LIBE
LOGA: --*
a. W-5063 Lewelling Jones, representative of
b. Lewelling Jones, representative [ov?]
c. W. Skidmore & J. Skidmore; M? [W?] S. Butler, 1836

S-4818 100a B:428 X-0340 UNIO:UNIO*
a. W-5041 John Cole
b. John Cole
c. Orris Parrish, 1823; S. G. Strong, 1825; Unknown
*Source B notation: "By Milford."

S-4819 17a B:427 X-0240 GREE:XENI
a. W-5064 Lewelling Jones, representative of
b. Daniel Bailey
c. J. Galloway, 1828

S-4820 667a B:472 X-0342 MADI:PIKE
S-4945 UNIO: --*
S-5207
a. W-5069 Joseph Swearingen
b. Joseph Swearingen
c. None
*Source B does not list Union County.

S-4821* -- -- -- UNIO:UNIO
a. --
b. George Young
c. None
*Not listed in Source A.

S-4825 23a B:461 X-0840 FAYE:JEFF
a. W-3924 John Garrett
b. John Garrett
c. None

S-4826 100a C:115 X-0800 BROW:HUNT
a. W-5022 Amos Spencer; Gideon Dunham [assignee?]
b. Nathan Ellis
c. None

S-4832 50a D:330 X-0135 ADAM:GREE
a. W-1141 Edward Shepherd
b. John McHenry
c. None

S-4833 50a C:250 X-0420 ADAM:LIBE
a. W-4990 Thomas Mills, representative of
b. Alexander Mahary
c. None

S-4834 750a B:465 X-0420 BROW:JACK
BROW:EAGL
a. W-5060 Peter Minor, representative of
b. Robert Mack*
c. None
*Source C may spell Mark.

S-4835 39a B:465 X-0420 BROW:UNIO
a. W-5060 Peter Minor, representative of
b. Robert Mack*
c. None
*Source C may spell Mark.

S-4837 550a B:434 X-0133 ADAM:SCOT
HIGH: --*
a. W-0107 Colonel John Green
b. Joseph Kerr
c. Philip Noland; John Linton, 1826; A. Kirkpatrick (Adams County); J. R. Lancer? [Sancer?] 1829
*Although Highland County is listed, Source B says tract lies in Adams County.

S-4838 1080a B:434 X-1300 HIGH:WHIT
a. W-1476 Captain Leroy Edwards
b. Joseph Kerr
c. P. Gates; A. Baskin, 1824

S-4839 667a B:435 X-0180 GREE:SILV
a. W-3158 Captain Leroy Edwards
b. Joseph Kerr
c. None

S-4840 500a B:435 X-1303 HIGH:WHIT
a. W-0107 Colonel John Green
b. Joseph Kerr
c. None

S-4841 200a B:432 X-0663 CLER:UNIO
a. W-4977 Malcom McCown; John G. McCan? [Macan?] [assignee?]
b. Henry Massie
c. None

S-4842 67a B:436 X-0130* ADAM:TIFF
a. W-4971 Jonathan Snowdon; Elias Rector [assignee?]
b. Henry Massie
c. None
*"Lk. br[anch] of . . ."

S-4843 67a B:435 X-1140 PIKE:MIFF
a. W-2930 William Reynolds, assignee [of] J. Shackleford; David Anderson [assignee?]
b. Joseph Kerr
c. J. Sconton? [Scouton?]; C. Cisna, 1823

S-4844 100a B:434 X-1043 ADAM:JEFF
a. W-0230 John Mills
b. Benjamin Goodin
c. None

S-4845 243a B:441 X-0690 CLER:BATA
a. W-1476 Captain Leroy Edwards
b. Joseph Kerr
c. None

S-4846 200a B:440 X-1120 BROW:JACK
BROW:FRAN
a. W-0107 Colonel John Green
b. Joseph Kerr
c. None

S-4847 839a B:441 X-0800 CLER:FRAN
a. W-0937 Colonel John Nevill
b. John Nevill
c. None

S-4848 1061a B:441 X-0660 CLER:MIAM
a. W-0937 John Nevill
b. John Nevill
c. None

S-4849 275a D:59 X-1305 BROW:FRAN
X-1125 BROW:PLEA
a. W-0368 Captain Andrew Nixon
b. Andrew Nixon
c. Unknown; Richard Brown, 1827; F. Osborn; S. Waterman, 1840

S-4850 280a E:344 X-1303* HIGH:CONC
a. W-0368 Andrew Nixon
b. Andrew Nixon
c. John Gossit [*also* Gossett]; G. W. Barriere, 1834; Unknown
*"Branch of . . ."

S-4851 300a B:440 X-1300 BROW:CLAR
BROW:SCOT
a. W-2331 Captain Lewis Booker
b. Joseph Kerr
c. None

S-4852 789a B:442 X-1004 FRAN:WASH
a. W-0937 Colonel John Nevill
b. John Nevill
c. None

S-4854 600a B:441 X-1004 FRAN:NORW
a. W-0738 Doctor Mace Clements
b. Joseph Kerr
c. Benjamin Grace; Adam Brotherlin; W. Dun; C. Thomas, 1822; M. J. Gilbert, 1834; Unknown; L. Starling, 1833

S-4855 150a B:441 X-1140 PIKE:MIFF
a. W-0738 Doctor Mace Clements
b. Joseph Kerr
c. None

S-4858 550a B:439 X-0663 CLER:BATA
a. W-4666 Robert Forsythe & John Forsythe
b. John Brown
c. W. Allston; S. Shaw, 1826; T. Allston

S-4859 550a B:473 X-0340 LOGA:ZANE CHAM: --*
a. W-1122 Pat[rick?] Thornton, 200a
W-1489 John Smith, 200a
W-1880** John Corbett, 150a
b. Levi Hollingsworth
c. H. Massie; William Baylis? [Bayles?] 1833
*Source B mentions Champaign County but corrects to Logan County.
**This warrant used six times on land surveys, even though completely used up on the first of the six!

S-4862 977a B:443 X-0660 HAMI:ANDE CLER:UNIO
a. W-0107 Colonel John Green
b. Henry Massie
c. None

S-4865 100a C:173 X-0663 HIGH:DODS
a. W-4994 Ann McKnight, widow
b. Henry Massie
c. None

S-4866 373a B:474 X-0960 ROSS:HUNT
a. W-0107 Colonel John Green, 73a?
W-4994 Ann McKnight, widow, 300a?
b. Henry Massie
c. None

S-4871 500a B:506 X-0660 GREE:SUGA
a. W-5058 Henry Field, representative of
b. Henry Fields, representative of
c. None

S-4872 100a C:332 X-1125 HIGH:CONC
a. W-2826* James Maloy
b. William Vause? [Vanse?]**
c. Hy [Henry?] Palmer; J. M. Trimble, 1835; Unknown; Mahlon Elwell, 1831; W. Wilson
*This warrant already completely used on S-2729.
**Source B spells Vance.

S-4873 100a C:37 X-1040 ADAM:MEIG
a. W-4803 William Hensley
b. Andrew Smalley
c. None

S-4874 200a C:135 X-1301* HIGH:SALE
a. W-5049 John Bau? [Barr?]
b. John Barr
c. None
*"Waters of . . ."

S-4876* 85a -- -- ADAM:JEFF
a. --
b. Benjamin Goodin
c. None
*Entry in Source B only (at sequential place).

S-4880 250a C:45 X-0340 UNIO:ALLE LOGA: --*
a. W-4858 John Hays
b. John Hays
c. None
*Source B does not mention Logan County.

S-4881 125a B:449 X-0663 CLIN:GREE
a. W-4858 John Hays
b. John Hays
c. None

S-4883 600a B:449 X-0663 HIGH:UNIO
a. W-2735 John Lewis, 100a
W-2923 Nicholas Payne; Elijah Walden [assignee?] 100a
W-2922 Nicholas Payne; John Johnson [assignee?] 100a
W-2929 Charles Burrage, 100a
W-1297 Samuel Courtney, 200a
b. Thomas Brown
c. J. Crawford; A. Hait, 1823; T. Brown; Jacob Beshare, 1828; Jeremiah Thompson, 1833

S-4884 300a C:4 X-0640 CLIN:WAYN
a. W-4880 John Higdon, 200a
W-4881 Edward Jenkins, 100a
b. Henry Bedinger
c. None

S-4885* 200a C:51 X-0340 MADI:JEFF
a. W-1469 Hanley? [Stanley?] Chaffin
b. Stanley Chaffin
c. J. Galloway, 1828
*"Patent sent Samuel Shepherd, Elotown? [Ecotown?] Kentucky."

S-4886 100a C:51 X-0840 CLAR:MADI
a. W-1972 Robert McMeehan
b. John Coones
c. Caleb Lewis; Thomas Jones, 1831

S-4887* 100a C:52 X-0010 GREE:SILV
a. W-3079 Duncan Camson? [Camron?] heir to Hugh [Camson? Camron?]
b. Duncan Cameron
c. None
*Source B says "not patented."

S-4888 445a B:503 X-0740 GREE:ROSS MADI:STOK
a. W-4819 John Robins, representative of
b. John Robbins,* representative [of?]
c. None
*Source B spells Robins.

S-4889 25a C:177 X-0840 FAYE:PAIN
a. W-3727 Michael Feagle
b. Michael Feagle
c. James Woods, 1828

S-4890 100a C:52 X-0840 MADI:STOK
a. W-0982 Archibald Finley
b. Archibald Finley
c. None

S-4891 200a C:429 X-1300 BROW:PIKE
a. W-4068 William Hanson, heir to Shadrack [Hanson]
b. Robert Gamble
c. Temple Gothney; John Shofe, 1829; John Scroufe; David Morgan, 1834

S-4892* 200a -- -- BROW:SCOT
a. --
b. Joseph Holmes
c. Henry Apple; Mathew Day, 1831; Unknown; I? [J?] Counts? [Courts?] 1842
*Entry listed in Source B only (at sequential place).

S-4895 200a B:450 X-0663 HIGH:UNIO
a. W-5020 Thomas Purcell
b. Francis Johnston
c. William McNiel; S. S. Bennett, 1824; Francis Johnson; John Smith, 1828; Joel Hart, 1833

S-4896 100a C:8 X-0640 CLIN:WAYN
a. W-1865 Jesse Rose
b. Jesse Rose
c. Michael Fry; S? [L?] Shepherd; Samuel Shepherd, 1828; J. Rose; W. P. Hunnicutt, 1832; J. Fife; D. Carter, 1838

S-4897* 100a -- -- BROW:BYRD *or* BROW:JACK
a. --
b. John Lewis
c. William Smith
*Entry listed in Source B only (at sequential place).

S-4898 65a C:69 X-0420 BROW:JACK
a. W-4185 Mary Hoye & Elizabeth Hoye
b. Mary Hoy* & Elizabeth Hoy*
c. William Barlow, heirs; James Taylor, 1823; Unknown; P. L? [S?] Wilson, 1841
*Source B spells Hoye.

S-4899 200a C:260 X-0010 CLIN:LIBE
a. W-3257 Thomas Thurman, 100a
W-3260 Joseph Boan, 100a
b. Garrett* Smock
c. Gerrard Smock; William Hoblett, 1825; John Falles, 1824; John Atkinson, 1826
*Source B spells Garnett.

S-4901 100a C:260 X-0010 CLIN:LIBE
a. W-3431 John Murphey
b. John Murphey
c. William Townsley; A. E. Strickle, 1836

S-4902 100a B:450 X-1170 CLIN:MARI WARR:SALE
a. W-3811 Mason Owens
b. Mason Owens
c. John Woodyard, 1825

S-4903 100a C:46 X-0340 UNIO:DARB
a. W-4162 William Petty
b. John* Petty
c. None
*Source B says William John Petty.

S-4904 200a C:57 X-0340 MADI:PIKE
a. W-3089 James Vaughan
b. James Rice
c. None

S-4905 100a C:93 X-0010 GREE:SILV
a. W-3659 Thomas Ray
b. Thomas Ray
c. S. W. McCracken, 1823

S-4906 100a D:341 X-1301* HIGH:CLAY
a. W-3694 James Rankin
b. James Rankin
c. John Florence? [Flounce?] Senior, 1836; Robert Davidson; John A. Smith, 1840; I? [J?] Hogsett, 1842**
*"Waters of . . ."
**Names in section c may pertain to S-4907 instead.

S-4907 100a E:257 X-1301* HIGH:CLAY**
a. W-3867 William Shaw
b. William Shaw
c. William Townsley; William Smith; William Shaw; James Rankin; John Hotsenpillar, 1833 (Highland County)
*"Waters of . . ."
**Apparently thought to have been in Brown County.

S-4908* 100a -- -- HIGH:CLAY
a. --
b. Henry Spencer
c. Samuel Herod; H. Massie; John Smith, 1828
*In Source B only.

S-4910 100a C:529 X-1120 BROW:JACK BROW:FRAN
a. W-4078 Christopher Fosil
b. Edmond Read
c. None

S-4910 300a C:529 X-1120 BROW:JACK BROW:FRAN
a. W-2080 John Jackson, 200a
W-4078 Christopher Fosil, 100a
b. Edmond Read
c. None

S-4911* 200a B:503 X-1303 HIGH:WHIT
a. W-3831 William Smith
b. William Smith
c. None
*Source B says "not patented."

S-4917 170a B:446 X-0840 ROSS:PAXT
S-5020
a. W-3749 Andrew Dunbar; A. C. Locke? [assignee?] 70a?
W-4851 George Breech; A. C. Locke [assignee?] 100a?
b. Elias Langham
c. None

S-4919 500a C:47 X-0663 CLER:BATA
X-0800 CLER:MONR
CLER:OHIO
a. W-0107 Colonel John Green
b. John Green
c. H. Steinchfield; Z. Chapman, 1823; James Taylor; R. McFarland, 1836; A. Leeds

S-4920 430a C:47 X-1000 ROSS:SCIO*
S-6721
S-6722
a. W-2319 Captain William Merideth
b. Nathaniel Massie
c. None
*Source B notation: "Near Chillicothe."

S-4921 633a B:527 --* ADAM:TIFF
ADAM:MIEG
a. W-2319 Captain William Merideth
b. Andrew Ellison
c. None
*"Ohio Brush [Creek?]."

S-4922 150a B:451 X-0730 CHAM:WAYN
a. W-5067 John Bareth
b. John Barrett*
c. None
*Source B appears to spell Barreth.

S-4932 500a B:470 X-0340 CHAM:WAYN
LOGA: --*
a. W-5101 William Bird, assignee [of] Philip Courtney
b. Robert Means
c. None
*Source B does not list Logan County.

S-4933 500a B:439 X-0340 LOGA:ZANE
UNIO:ALLE
a. W-2418 Lieutenant Thomas Sears
b. Thomas Sears
c. None

S-4937* 403a C:261 X-0840 ROSS: --
S-5329
S-8233
a. W-5104** Samuel Marsh, assignee [of?] Joseph Smith, 310a?
W-5072 Isaac Browning, 93a?
b. [Duncan] McArthur & [Henry] Massie
c. --
*Entry not shown in Source B.
**Warrant number repeated, probably erroneously.

S-4938 200a B:468 X-0342 MADI:PIKE
a. W-4318 Richard Webster, 100a
W-4319 Henry Davis, 100a
b. Caswell* Gardner
c. W. Marquis; W. K. Marquis, 1826
*Sources B and C spell Carswell.

S-4939 200a B:468 X-0342 MADI:PIKE
a. W-4314 Nathaniel Potter, 100a
W-4316 Michael Caswell, 100a
b. Caswell* Gardner
c. None
*Source B spells Carswell.

S-4940 200a B:469 X-0340 MADI:PIKE
a. W-4315 Caswell Gardner
b. Caswell Gardner
c. *N. Sawyer, 1828*

S-4942 300a B:467 X-0342 MADI:PIKE
a. W-2234 Robert Richardson, 100a
W-1075 Michael Smith; Barny Carter, Nicholas Carter [assignees?] 200a
b. Richard C[lough] Anderson
c. None

S-4943 400a E:64 X-0065 HARD*:TAYL
a. W-2120 Captain Anthony Singleton
b. Anthony Singleton
c. James Curry; Luquine [Suquinie?] Rawson, 1832; Gamela Gordon, heirs; C. W. Stevenson, 1842
*Source B originally said tract located in Logan County.

S-4944 85a D:256 X-0810 MADI:JEFF
X-0340 FRAN:PLEA*
a. W-2120 Captain Anthony Singleton
b. Anthony Singleton
c. C. Higgins, 1835; E. Backus, 1837
*Source A does not list Franklin County.

S-4945. *See* S-4820

S-4946 200a B:444 X-0350 UNIO:UNIO
a. W-2162 Captain William Heth
b. William Heth
c. None

S-4948 870a D:54 X-0735 LOGA:JEFF
S-9423
S-9876
a. W-5101 William Bird, assignee [of?] Philip Courtney, 270a?
W-5617 Nathaniel G. Morris, 100a
W-5618 Nathaniel G. Morris, 100a
W-5338 Matthew Clay, 400a?
b. [Robert] Means & [Duncan] McArthur
c. None

S-4952 100a C:133 X-1000 ROSS:FRAN
S-6858 ROSS:TWIN
a. W-5072 Isaac Browning
b. Duncan McArthur
c. None

S-4953 500a B:438 X-0340 LOGA:ZANE
a. W-5072 Isaac Browning
b. Duncan McArthur
c. None

S-4957 465a B:452 X-0730 LOGA:JEFF
LOGA:MONR
a. W-0107 Colonel John Green, 355a?
W-4892 George Minzies, representative [of?] 110a?
b. James Denney
c. S. McCullock, heirs; Lawson Curtis, 1827

S-4958 500a B:452 X-0730 CHAM:WAYN
LOGA: --*
a. W-1450 Major Samuel Finley, 200a?
W-0107 Colonel John Green, 250a?
W-5067 John Bareth, 50a
b. -- Finley, -- Denney, & -- Barrith**
c. None
*Source B does not mention Logan County.
**Source B spells Barreth.

S-4963 333a C:137 X-0134 BROW:EAGL
a. W-2742 Jasper Hughes
b. Thomas Pemberton
c. J. Edgington, 1830; J. M. Trimble, 1837; A. Crenshaw; P. L. Wilson, 1841

S-4964 200a* B:439 X-1120 BROW:JACK
X-0420
a. W-4666 Robert Forsythe & John Forsythe
b. John Brown
c. None
*Source B says 550a.

S-4965 220a B:440 X-0134 ADAM:SCOT
a. W-4666 Robert Forsythe & John Forsythe
b. John Brown
c. Michael Maddox; T. Huston, 1831

S-4966 250a B:440 X-0130 BROW:EAGL
a. W-4666 Robert Forsythe & John Forsythe
b. John Brown
c. Jonas Sams; George Shultz, 1825

S-4967 293a B:440 X-0134 BROW:EAGL
a. W-4666 Robert Forsythe & John Forsythe, 193a
W-1856* Robert Kimble, 100a
b. John Brown
c. Unknown; P. L. Wilson, 1840
*This warrant already completely used twice (S-2253 & S-3620)!

S-4968 100a B:442 X-0150 ROSS:PAIN
a. W-3873 Samuel Blair
b. William Nevan
c. None

S-4969 43a B:443 X-0590 ADAM:SPRI
a. W-2331 Captain Lewis Booker, 20a?
W-0738 Doctor Mace Clements, 23a?
b. Joseph Kerr
c. None

S-4974* 100a -- -- ADAM:LIBE
a. --
b. William Bryan
c. --
*Listed in Source B only; note says "not patented."

S-4977 100a B:459 X-0730 CLAR:PLEA
a. W-2755 George Jones
b. James Denney
c. None

S-4982 100a B:462 X-0540 UNIO:DARB
a. W-4053 John Jeffcoat
b. Balzar King
c. None

S-4989 200a C:108 X-1004 DELA:SCIO
DELA:CONC
a. W-4939 Samuel Glen
b. Samuel Glenn
c. None

S-4990 400a D:171 X-1095 LOGA:LAKE
a. W-3195 Samuel Wallace, heir
b. Samuel Wallace
c. Richard S. Canby, 1831

S-4995 260a D:295 X-0750 LOGA:PERR
a. W-0850 --*
b. Robert Vance
c. None
*Source C does not list the name of a warrantee under this number.

S-4998 350a D:71 X-0345 UNIO:DARB
a. W-4583 Peter Manifold, assignee of David Hopkins
b. Peter Manifold
c. Unknown; S. G. Strong, 1831

S-5002 180a C:461 X-0340 FRAN:PRAI
a. W-2904 John Harle, assignee [of?] John Chatham
b. John Harle
c. M. L. Sullivant, 1831; Unknown

S-5005* 200a B:479 X-0340 UNIO:DARB
a. W-4515 Richard Smyth, assignee
b. Richard Smyth
c. Unknown; Isaac Bigelow, 1837
*Source B says "Not patented; good land."

S-5006 200a B:502 X-0340 UNIO:UNIO
UNIO:PARI
a. W-4522 Bazaleel Norris
b. Bazaleel Norris
c. State [of Ohio?]

S-5007 400a C:55 X-0940 FAYE:GREE
a. W-1039 James Adams
b. William Hicman*
c. Richard Douglas, 1827; J. W. Pumphrey, 1829; "4 January? 1832 deeded John Pumphrey, assignee of [--] Douglas."
*Source B spells Hickman.

S-5008* 657a B:451 -- UNIO: --
a. W-1751 Captain Hughes Woodson
b. Hughes Woodson
c. --
*Source B does not list this entry.

S-5009 265a B:451 X-0340 UNIO:DARB
a. W-1751 Captain Hughes Woodson
b. Hughes Woodson
c. None

S-5011 1290a B:446 X-0840 ROSS:PAXT*
a. W-2319 Captain William Merideth
b. Nathaniel Massie
c. None
*Source B notation: "Bainbridge."

S-5012 1000a C:336 X-0600 ADAM:MONR
a. W-5017 John Pain, 100a
W-1546 Walter Harris; John North [assignee?] 100a
W-0463 John Jowett, heir to Mat[thew Jowett] 460a?
W-1226 Alexander S. Dandridge, 340a?
b. Nathanial Massie
c. Charles W. Byrd; Thomas Huston, 1829; James Clark, 1834

S-5013 200a B:448 X-0150 ROSS:PAIN
a. W-3432 John M. Galt, "resolution"
b. Abraham Shepherd
c. None

S-5014 333a B:447 X-0150 ROSS:PAIN
a. W-4639 John Dandridge
b. Joseph Watkins & Nathaniel Massie
c. E. J. Nuckles; A. Cochran, 1842; A. Nuckles; R. A. Nuckles

S-5015 250a B:447 X-0150 ROSS:PAIN
a. W-3432 John M. Galt, "resolution"
b. Abraham Shepheard*
c. None
*Source B spells Shepherd.

S-5016 280a B:448 X-0150 ROSS:PAIN
a. W-3432 John M. Galt
b. Abraham Shepheard*
c. None
*Source B spells Shepherd.

S-5019 1300a B:447 X-0020 HIGH:BRUS*
a. W-4679 Benjamin Temple, 1000a?
W-2319 Captain William Merideth, 300a?
b. [Benjamin] Temple & [Nathaniel] Massie
c. S. B. Finley; B. Temple; G. W. Smith, 1838; I? [J?] A. Roads
*Source B notation: "By Sinking Springs."

S-5020. *See* S-4917

S-5021 50a C:360 X-0040 ADAM:MONR
a. W-3477 Abraham Shepherd
b. Nathaniel Massie
c. None

S-5023 120a B:449 X-0663 HIGH:UNIO
a. W-4858 John Hays
b. John Hays
c. None

S-5024 240a B:450 X-0663 HIGH:UNIO
a. W-2556 Lieutenant Claiborne Vaughan
b. Richard J. Waters
c. S. Shepherd; G. W. Barriere, 1825; S. Bell, 1826

S-5026 60a C:192 X-0663 HIGH:UNIO
a. W-2854 James Lemaster
b. Richard J. Waters
c. None

S-5027 33a D:355 X-1205 HIGH:UNIO
a. W-1297 Samuel Courtney
b. Thomas Brown
c. John Brown; S. Shepherd, 1826; Samuel Shepherd; N. Walton, 1830; Joel Hart, 1833

S-5028 40a C:192 X-1120 BROW:UNIO
a. W-2854 James Lemaster
b. Richard J. Waters
c. None

S-5029 100a B:449 X-0840 FAYE:GREE
a. W-3691 Hezekiah Clark
b. Hezekiah Clark
c. Milcher? Barlow; Samuel Shepherd, 1825

S-5030 97a B:449 X-0840 FAYE:GREE
a. W-4858 John Hays
b. John Hays
c. John Davis; Jacob Jameson, 1837; A. S. Dickey, 1842; I. Pavey

S-5033* 126a -- -- --
a. --
b. Peter Manifold
c. --
*Entry appears only in Source B (at sequential place) but is crossed through. *See also* S-4113

S-5034 50a C:360 X-0090 ADAM:JEFF
a. W-4990 Thomas Mills, representative of
b. Joseph Freeman
c. None

S-5035 250a B:451 X-0740 GREE:ROSS
a. W-1751 Captain Hughes Woodson
b. Hughes Woodson
c. None

S-5038 80a B:460 X-0340 UNIO:UNIO
a. W-5044 Thomas Woodlief, representative of Francis Epps, deceased
b. James Galloway*
c. John Davis; R. R. Phelps, 1824; Unknown; R. Gabriel, 1823
*Source B says James Galloway, Junior.

S-5042 270a B:452 X-0730 LOGA:MONR
a. W-3661 Peter Whirley, 100a
W-1450 Major Samuel Finley, 120a?
W-0205 Captain Thomas Thucutt? [Thewait? Thweatt?] 50a?
b. [James] Denney, [Samuel] Finley, & -- Prewitt*
c. James Stewart, 1823
*Source B spells Periwitt.

S-5044 125a B:453 X-0730 CHAM:SALE
a. W-0205 Captain Thomas Thucutt? [Thewait? Thweatt?]
b. Byrd Prewitt*
c. None
*Source B may spell Perewitt.

S-5045 100a B:453 X-0060 LOGA:LAKE
a. W-0205 Captain Thomas Thucutt? [Thewait? Thweatt?]
b. Byrd Prewitt*
c. Lawren[ce?] Curtis, 1823
*Source B may spell Perewitt.

S-5046 525a B:470 X-0500 MADI:UNIO
a. W-5106 Samuel Marsh, assignee [of?] Joseph Smith
b. Robert Means
c. None

S-5049 200a B:462 X-0340 CHAM:WAYN
a. W-4443 William Ballinger
b. John McKinney
c. None

S-5050 200a B:464 X-0340 CHAM:WAYN
a. W-2795 Peter Fullom, 100a
W-5093 Samuel Elliott, 100a
b. Jacob Poe
c. Thomas Leeper; Elisha Reynolds, 1831

S-5051 100a B:455 X-0360 ROSS:UNIO
a. W-4972 Jonathan Snowdon
b. Thomas Toolle*
c. None
*Source B spells Tootle.

S-5053 42a C:35 X-0340 UNIO:DARB
a. W-4583 Peter Manifold, assignee of David Hopkins
b. Peter Manifold
c. None

S-5053 126a C:35 X-0345 UNIO:PARI
a. W-4583 Peter Manifold, assignee of David Hopkins
b. Peter Manifold
c. None

S-5054 567a B:470 X-0342 CHAM:GOSH
a. W-5109 Robert Means, assignee of Thomas Blackwell
b. Robert Means
c. None

S-5056 475a B:469 X-0841* FAYE:MADI
a. W-4878 James McNutt
b. Duncan McArthur
c. None
*"West fork of . . ."

S-5057 50a B:454 X-0730 CHAM:WAYN
a. W-3707 Matthias Sheener
b. William Tidball
c. Gray Garey? 1823

S-5059 26a B:467 X-1150 BROW:HUNT
a. W-1920 Colonel Josiah Parker
b. Josiah Parker
c. John S. Mills, 1823; Edward Francis, 1831

S-5063 500a B:473 X-0840 FAYE:WAYN
a. W-0702 Lieutenant William B. Wallace
b. William B. Wallace
c. None

S-5064 167a B:505 X-1050 MADI:MONR
a. W-0702 William B. Wallace
b. William B. Wallace
c. None

S-5067. *See* S-1683 *and* S-4400

S-5075 160a D:329 X-1120 BROW:JACK
a. W-5100 David Scott
b. Joseph Kerr
c. None

S-5076 200a B:528 X-1140 PIKE:MIFF
a. W-5100 David Scott
b. Joseph Kerr
c. None

S-5077 200a B:529 X-1300 BROW:CLAR
a. W-5099 David Scott
b. David Scott
c. None

S-5078 300a B:529 X-1301 HIGH:SALE
a. W-5099 David Scott
b. David Scott
c. None

S-5079 117a B:529 X-0663 HIGH:NEWM
a. W-5097 David Scott
b. David Scott
c. None

S-5080* 200a -- -- HIGH: --
a. --
b. John Wilkins, Junior
c. John Roads, 1828
*Entry shown in Source B only (at top of page, above S-5046).

S-5081 233a* B:529 X-0133 ADAM:FRAN
a. W-5097 David Scott
b. David Scott
c. I? [J?] Gustin; I? [J?] Hood, 1841
*Source B says 283a [which is probably incorrect, based upon total of grants made under this warrant number].

S-5082 200a B:529 X-0133 ADAM:FRAN
a. W-5097 David Scott
b. David Scott
c. A. Ellison; A. Hemphill, 1831

S-5083 200a B:530 X-0133 ADAM:FRAN
a. W-5097 David Scott
b. David Scott
c. William Parks, 1824

S-5084 250a B:530 X-0133 ADAM:SCOT
a. W-5097 David Scott
b. David Scott
c. John Berreman? [Beneman?]; Wesley? Noland, 1826

S-5085 500a B:530 X-0133 ADAM:FRAN
a. W-5098 David Scott
b. David Scott
c. Abraham Rhodes; Jerop? [Ieross?] Carson? [Caison?] 1823

S-5086 500a B:530 X-0134 HIGH:CONC
a. W-5098 David Scott
b. David Scott
c. William Thomas; George W. Barriere, 1832; Unknown; A. Baskin, 1836; A. Abrams, 1838; Amos Grantham

S-5087 500a B:530 X-0134 ADAM:SCOT
HIGH: --*
a. W-5099 David Scott
b. David Scott
c. None
*Source B does not mention Highland County.

S-5088 500a B:534? X-0730 LOGA:JEFF
X-0750 LOGA:PERR
a. W-4784 Benjamin Nelson, representative of William [Nelson]
b. John McDonald
c. None

S-5089 1067a B:534? X-0750 LOGA:JEFF
LOGA:PERR
a. W-4784 Benjamin Nelson, representative of William [Nelson]
b. John McDonald*
c. A. W. Burnsides; Z. McCulloch, 1835; S. G. Hoge, 1841
*Source B has notation: "McDougal."

S-5091 1050a B:471 X-0750 LOGA:JEFF
LOGA:PERR
a. W-5109 Robert Means, assignee [of] Thomas Blackwell; George Weedon [assignee?]
b. Robert Means
c. W. Dun; M. Bonner, 1827; Robert Hamilton; L. P. Burton, 1840

S-5092 1333a C:1 X-0750 LOGA:PERR
UNIO: --*
a. W-5110 Robert Means, assignee of Thomas Blackwell
b. Robert Means
c. Henry Clay; J. S. Dawson, 1839
*Source B does not mention Union County.

S-5094 100a C:2 X-0340 PICK:JACK
a. W-4784 Benjamin Nelson, representative of William [Nelson]
b. Duncan McArthur
c. None

S-5095 300a B:473 X-1004 DELA:THOM
a. W-5104 Samuel Marsh, assignee of Joseph Smith
b. Nathaniel Massie
c. Stephen Barnaby, 1827; J. & J. Tipton; D. Heffner, 1828; Jacob Swartz; J. J. Swartz

S-5097 150a C:32 X-0340 MADI:CANA
a. W-5105 Samuel Marsh, assignee of Joseph Smith
b. Robert Means
c. None

S-5104 150a C:150 X-0400 FAYE:MADI
a. W-2274 Doctor Basil Middleton
b. John Campbell
c. None

S-5106 885a B:480 X-0340 FRAN:PRAI
a. W-0307 Captain John Clarke
b. John Clark
c. C. Higgins; W. Stirewalt

S-5111 80a D:196 X-0340 UNIO:DARB
UNIO:JERO
a. W-4583 Peter Manifold, assignee of David Hopkins
b. Lucas Sullivant
c. Unknown; Isaac Bigelow, 1837

S-5113 100a C:30 X-0660 HAMI:ANDE
a. W-0360 John Woodcock
b. John Steel
c. None

S-5118* 44a -- -- ROSS:UNIO
a. --
b. Thomas Worthington
c. None
*Shown in Source B only.

S-5122 100a B:464 X-0340 UNIO:DARB
a. W-3517 Minor Smith
b. Minor Smith
c. J. Galloway, Junior

S-5123 200a B:461 X-0620 CHAM:WAYN
a. W-1053 William Herbert
b. William Herbert
c. None

S-5124 400a B:460 X-0340 UNIO:DARB
a. W-5044 Thomas Woodlief, representative of Francis Epps, deceased
b. James Galloway, Junior
c. None

S-5125 130a B:460 X-0340 MADI:DARB
a. W-5041 John Cole
b. James Galloway, Junior
c. None

S-5126 470a B:462 X-0340 UNIO:JERO
a. W-3016 Leven Joins
b. Alexander Kerr
c. None

S-5127 150a B:462 X-0340 UNIO:UNIO*
a. W-3016 Leven Joins
b. Alexander Kerr
c. None
*Source B notation: "Milford."

S-5128 80a B:462 X-0340 UNIO:JERO MADI: --*
a. W-3016 Leven Joins
b. Alexander Kerr
c. S. N. Kerr, 1831
*Source B does not give township.

S-5129 100a B:462 X-0340 MADI:CANA
a. W-3016 Leven Joins
b. Alexander Kerr
c. None

S-5131 80a B:460 X-0180 GREE:SUGA
a. W-5041 John Cole
b. James Galloway, Junior
c. None

S-5132 600a B:460 X-0340 UNIO:JERO
a. W-3016 Leven Joins, 200a?
W-5042 John Cole, 76a?
W-0712 Doctor William Brown, 324a?
b. James Galloway, Junior
c. Michael King; Thomas Robinson, 1830; E. W. H. Reid, 1831

S-5133 190a B:461 X-0340 UNIO:JERO
a. W-5041 John Cole, 40a?
W-5044 Thomas Woodlief, representative of Francis Epps, deceased, 50a?
W-5061 Peter Minor, representative of, 100a?
b. James Galloway, Junior, and John Goode
c. James Conner, heirs; William Bethard, 1830

S-5134 533a B:463 X-0340 UNIO:JERO
a. W-1500 John Pride, heir to William Pride
b. John Pride
c. Benjamin Boysan [*also* Borsam?]; Samuel Reid; Joseph? [James?] Carter, 1827

S-5135 1000a B:463 X-0750 UNIO:DOVE
a. W-1500 John Pride, heir to William Pride
b. John Pride
c. Thomas F? Gray; Coats Thornton, 1826; William Richie [*also* Richey]; S. Dysert? 1830; Thomas E. Gray, heirs

S-5136 800a B:463 X-0750 UNIO:PARI
a. W-1500 John Pride, heir to William Pride
b. John Pride
c. T. F. Gray; Cyprian Lee, 1826; Thomas E. Gray, heirs; Chapman Lee, 1828

S-5137* 655a D:424 X-0340 UNIO:DARB
S-7964
S-7218
a. W-1500 John Pride, heir to William Pride, 134a?
W-5759 Peter Garland, representative of, 521a?
b. James Galloway*
c. None
*Source B says James Galloway, Junior.

S-5138 667a B:461 X-0750 UNIO:PARI
a. W-4820 Baylor Hill
b. Baylor Hill
c. None

S-5139 1000a B:475 X-0340 UNIO:DARB
a. W-0205 Captain Thomas Thucutt? [Thewait? Thweatt?]
b. Richard C[lough] Anderson
c. H. M. Perkins, 1831; Thomas Robinson, 1833; Judith Kellog

S-5140 433a B:475 X-0750 UNIO:DARB UNIO:PARI
a. W-4583 Peter Manifold, assignee of David Hopkins
b. Richard C[lough] Anderson
c. None

S-5141 100a C:317 X-0750 UNIO:DARB
a. W-5107 James Tate & William Steel
b. William Steel
c. James Taylor, 1829

S-5141 100a C:317 X-0750 UNIO:DARB
a. W-5107 James Tate & William Steel
b. William Steel
c. None

S-5142 200a B:475 X-0750 UNIO:DARB
a. W-1615 John Arnold
b. John Arnold
c. H. M. Perkins, 1831

S-5143* 100a B:460 X-0340 UNIO:JERO
a. W-1948 Terence Doren
b. Terence Doren
c. Unknown; H. M? [W?] Perkins, 1831
*Source B says "not patented."

S-5144 50a B:475 X-0340 UNIO:JERO
a. W-2258 Richard Jones
b. Richard C[lough] Anderson
c. Unknown; D. Burnham

S-5144 50a B:475 X-0340 UNIO:JERO
a. W-2258 Richard Jones
b. Richard Jones
c. David Burnham, 1831; Unknown

S-5145 200a B:463 X-0730 CHAM:UNIO
a. W-5120 Robert Means, assignee [of?] David Carmichal, as attorney in fact for Lowell Harrison
b. Robert Means
c. None

S-5148 100a B:478 X-1180 MADI:MONR
a. W-5119 Robert Means, assignee [of?] Lowell Harrison, representative of Andrew Harrison
b. Robert Means
c. Joseph? [James?] Carter; W. W. Warren, 1831

S-5149 50a C:214 X-0740 GREE:ROSS
a. W-4305 Joseph Brand
b. Samuel Harrod & James Hillis*
c. None
*Source B may read Haller.

S-5150 370a B:461 X-0340 CHAM:WAYN
LOGA: --*
a. W-5061 Peter Minor, representative of
b. John Goode
c. None
*Source B does not mention Logan County.

S-5158 400a B:464 X-0340 CHAM:WAYN
X-0620
a. W-1338 Thomas Marshal
b. George Pomroy
c. Trustees, Methodist Church

S-5162 800a B:477 X-1004 FRAN:WASH
UNIO: --*
DELA: --*
a. W-5125 Robert Means, assignee of John Stokely, who was assignee of James Neal
b. Robert Means
c. None
*Source B does not mention Union or Delaware counties; *but see* S-5166.

S-5166 2000a B:477 X-0340 UNIO:JERO
DELA:CONC
a. W-5127 Robert Means, assignee of John Stokely, [who was] assignee of David Steel
b. Robert Means
c. James Galloway, Junior, 1831

S-5167* 200a B:476 X-0340 UNIO:DARB
MADI:--**
a. W-3991 Reuben Toney, 100a
W-3992 Archibald Toney, 100a
b. -- Galligo*** & -- Heric***
c. Unknown; J. Crisman, 1836
*Source B says "not patented."
**Source B does not mention Madison County.
***Source B spells Gallego & Therie; Source C spells Galleo.

S-5169 393a B:483 X-0730 CHAM:SALE
CHAM:WAYN
a. W-0660 Captain Hezekiah Morton
b. Hezekiah Morton
c. William Downs, heirs; James Inskip, 1838

S-5171 150a C:122 X-0940 HIGH:MADI
FAYE: --*
a. W-5131 William McKee
b. William McKee
c. None
*Source B does not give township.

S-5176 100a B:465 X-0230 ADAM:WAYN
a. W-5060 Peter Minor, representative of
b. Robert Mack*
c. None
*Source B may spell Mark.

S-5177 111a B:464 X-0230 ADAM:WAYN
a. W-5060 Peter Minor, representative of
b. Robert Mack*
c. None
*Source B may spell Mark.

S-5178 33a B:465 X-0420 BROW:BYRD
a. W-4199 Sampson Henderson; Frederick Dyche [assignee?]
b. Jeptha Beasley
c. None

S-5179 80a B:527 X-0420 BROW:FRAN
X-1120
a. W-4085 William Ward
b. Isham Kendrick
c. William Butt, 1823; Mathew Gardner, 1825

S-5180 200a B:526 X-1120 BROW:BYRD
a. W-0580 Matt[hew] Anderson, 100a
W-1421 Elijah Smith, 100a
b. Edmond Wooldridge
c. None

S-5181 200a C:532 X-0420 BROW:JACK
a. W-3747 John Gisner
b. John Gesner
c. William Hannah, 1828; N. Beasley; P. L. Wilson, 1840

S-5182* 233a D:355 X-0805 ADAM:SPRI
a. W-3732 Peter Armond
b. Peter Armond
c. J. Machir; William Ellison, 1827
*Source B says "not patented."

S-5183* 110a -- -- ADAM:SPRI
a. --
b. George Lear
c. None
*Entry appears in Source B only (at sequential place).

S-5185 200a C:166 X-0420 BROW:HUNT
a. W-4512 Joseph Evans
b. Joseph Evans
c. None

S-5186 100a C:166 X-0420 BROW:HUNT
a. W-3313 Lawrence Ward
b. Lawrence Ward
c. Samuel Neel; Elijah Baldwin, 1825; J? [I?] Carr; P. L. Wilson, 1841; J? [I?] Donaldson

S-5187 330a B:467 X-0490 ADAM:SCOT
a. W-4987 Jesse Bland, 100a
W-0057 Captain Robert Porterfield, 230a
b. Abraham Shepherd
c. None
*Source B says Abraham Shepherd, Junior.

S-5190 200a C:311 X-0680 MADI:PLEA
a. W-5113 John Copin, representative of
b. Henry Flesher
c. M. L. Sullivant, 1831

S-5191 100a C:133 X-0840 FAYE:PAIN
a. W-5070 Henry Tuggle
b. John Kittaman
c. None

S-5192 100a F:312 X-0365 MADI:DEER
a. W-4980? [W-4986?] John Shull, representative of
b. John Shull, representative of
c. None

S-5193* 200a C:7 X-0340 MADI:FAIR
a. W-1124 James Low
b. James Low
c. D. Thompson, 1823
*Source B says "not patented."

S-5194 900a B:470 X-0840 HIGH:MADI
a. W-5131 William McKee
b. Duncan McArthur
c. None

S-5195 1200a C:202 X-0500 MADI:DEER
a. W-5131 William McKee
b. Duncan McArthur
c. None

S-5197 678a C:176 X-0340 PICK:JACK
S-6446 X-1000
S-7207
S-7658
a. W-5692 Joseph Woodson, 125a?
W-5693 Joseph Woodson, 125a?
W-5698 Joseph Woodson, 125a?
W-5836 Ann Shepherd, heir to Major -- [Shepherd?] who was heir to Solomon Shepherd, deceased, 50a?
W-4793 William Pyle, ?a
W-5131 William McKee, ?a
b. [Benjamin] Hough & [Duncan] McArthur
c. T. McCollister; R. Hall, 1828; Thomas Luke; Thomas McCollister, heirs; James Cook, 1838? [1831?]

S-5198 830a B:471 X-0363 MADI:SUMM
a. W-5105 Samuel Marsh, assignee [of?] Joseph Smith, 400a?
W-5106 Samuel Marsh, assignee [of?] Joseph Smith, 30a?
W-5109 Robert Means, assignee [of?] Thomas Blackwell, 400a?
b. Robert Means
c. None

S-5205 500a C:150 X-0360 MADI:UNIO
a. W-1171 Benjamin Stubblefield, heir to George Stubblefield
b. Benjamin Stubblefield
c. N. Bond, 1823

S-5206 140a C:230 X-0122 MADI:RANG
a. W-1642 David Price; Joseph Moore [assignee?] 40a
W-3754 Charles Cooper, 100a
b. Alexander Dunlap & James Dunlap
c. None

S-5207. *See* S-4820

S-5209 500a B:537 X-0750 LOGA:PERR
a. W-0225 Captain Benjamin Biggs
b. Benjamin Biggs
c. None

S-5216* 500a -- -- UNIO: --
a. --
b. David Williams
c. D. McArthur; Thomas Bowyer; J. McLain, 1823; M. S. Butler
*Entry appears in Source B only (at top of page above S-5158).

S-5218 175a B:512 X-0840 MADI:RANG FAYE:PAIN*
a. W-5131 William McKee
b. William McKee
c. None
*Listed in Source B only.

S-5219 200a B:512 X-0841 FAYE:PAIN MADI: --*
a. W-5131 William McKee
b. William McKee
c. None
*Not mentioned in Source B.

S-5220 175a B:512 X-0841 MADI:RANG
a. W-5131 William McKee
b. William McKee
c. None

S-5223 150a C:388 X-0540 PICK:DEER
S-7370
a. W-5051 Elias Wingate, 100a
W-5740 Elias Langham; A. C. Lodna? [assignee?] 50a
b. Sylvester Ralston* & [Elias?] Langham
c. None
*Source C spells Rowlson.

S-5226 180a C:315 X-0540 PICK:DEER
a. W-2274 Doctor Basil Middleton
b. John Campbell
c. None

S-5227 244a B:481 X-0340 FRAN:PRAI
a. W-4936 Joseph Winlock
b. Joseph Winlock
c. W. Steinwalt; William Mooberry, Junior, 1829; Daniel Harrington; B. Sells, 1832; C. Higgins, 1834; D. Howard; E. Backus, 1838; Isaac Maharry? [McMaharry?]; M. L. Sullivant, 1836; W. S. Sullivant

S-5229 1833a C:419 X-0663 BROW:PERR CLER:WAYN CLIN:MARI*
a. W-0009 Lieutenant Colonel Samuel F? Cabell
b. Samuel J. Cabell
c. James Taylor, 1823; Henry Brackman; Isaac Chapman, 1837; Charles Cunninger [*also* Gerriswinigin? Glemmenger?]; L. E. Cartwright; J. Brucker, 1839 (Clermont County); James Picken, 1839; S. J. Cabell; J. Taylor, Junior, 1831 (Brown County); P. L. Wilson, 1842 (Brown County)
*Mentioned in Source B only.

S-5230 1833a C:251 X-0663 HIGH:DODS
a. W-0009 Lieutenant Colonel Samuel F? Cabell
b. Samuel J. Cabell
c. Z. Chapman, 1823; L. L. Cartwright

S-5231 1000a B:510 X-0663 CLIN:CLAR
a. W-5094 James Taylor, assignee of Robert Elliott
b. James Taylor
c. None

S-5232 269a C:191 X-0840 FAYE:PAIN
S-6112
S-6113
a. W-1906 John Morris, ?a
W-1984 Captain William George, ?a
W-2019 William Turvey, ?a
b. [Duncan] McArthur & [J.] McDonald
c. None

S-5234 450a C:501 X-0340 FRAN:PRAI
a. W-3196 Samuel Wallace, heir
b. Lucas Sullivant
c. M. L. Sullivant, 1834; E. M. Shanks; M. I? [J?] Shanks; M. I? [J?] Gilbert, 1842

S-5234 *or* S-5235* 600a B:504 X-1004 UNIO:JERO
a. W-0303 Captain Robert White
b. Robert White
c. None
*Source B lists entry as S-5235.

S-5236 100a C:501 X-0340 UNIO:DARB FRAN: --*
a. W-4936 Joseph Winlock
b. Lucas Sullivant
c. L. Sullivant, heirs; M. L. Sullivant, 1836
*Mentioned in Source B, but says in Union County.

S-5237 186a C:101 X-0340 FRAN:BROW
a. W-1415 Lieutenant Peyton Powell
b. Peyton Powell
c. None

S-5238 200a C:501 X-0340 UNIO:JERO FRAN: --*
a. W-3196 Samuel Wallace, heir
b. Lucas Sullivant
c. M. L. Sullivant
*Mentioned in Source B, but says in Union County.

S-5239* 448a D:104 X-1005 FRAN:NORW
S-5241
a. W-4583 Peter Manifold, assignee of David Hopkins, ?a
W-4732 Battle Harrison, representative of, ?a
b. Lucas Sullivant
c. None
**Also see* S-5339

S-5240 320a C:501 X-0340 FRAN:PRAI
a. W-4732 Battle Harrison, representative of
b. Lucas Sullivant
c. None

S-5241. *See* S-5239

S-5242 133a C:502 X-0340 FRAN:PRAI
a. W-0205 Captain Thomas Thucutt? [Thewait? Thweatt?]
b. Thomas Thweatt
c. Unknown; Adam Brotherton, 1829

S-5243 200a D:309 X-0345 FRAN:PRAI
a. W-2092 Samuel Eakin
b. Samuel Eakin*
c. Unknown; Adam Brotherton
*Source B spells Eaken.

S-5244 81a D:105 X-1005 FRAN:PRAI
a. W-0989 William Powle
b. William Powle*
c. Unknown; Dimus Adams, 1829
*Source B spells Poole.

S-5245 240a B:468 X-1090 LOGA:LAKE
a. W-0629 Captain Walker Baylor
b. Walker Baylor
c. None

S-5248 100a B:509 X-0663 CLER:BATA
a. W-4836 Moses Parish
b. Zachariah Massena* & William Lytle
c. O. T. Fishback, 1836
*Sources B and C spell Massina.

S-5249 400a B:503 X-0750 UNIO:LIBE
a. W-2963 Matthew Whisley, 100a
W-2964 William Briant, 100a
W-3087 John Kennady, 200a
b. Nathan Reed*
c. None
*Source B spells Reid.

S-5251 100a B:513 X-0663 CLER:BATA
a. W-4660 Daniel De Benneville
b. Daniel De Benneville
c. None

S-5252. *See* S-3329

S-5253 222a E:205 X-0665 CLER:BATA CLER:JACK
a. W-5019 Ferdinand Oneal
b. John Watts, representative [of?]
c. N. Wainwright, 1824; -- Taylor, -- Winston, & -- Berry; Levi Bannel, 1837

S-5254 100a B:509 X-0270 CLER:WILL BROW: --*
a. W-2830 James Wilson
b. William Lytle
c. None
*Source B does not mention Brown County.

S-5255* 350a -- -- HIGH:UNIO
a. --
b. Benjamin Mosely
c. W. Moseley; J. West (Clinton County); Unknown; A. Ratcliff, Junior, 1842 (Highland County)
*Listed in Source B only.

S-5256 80a B:511 X-0663* CLER:BATA
a. W-1206 John Straughan
b. William Tibbs
c. William Lytle; John Weaver, 1825
*"Waters of . . ."

S-5257 400a B:510 X-0663* BROW:STER
a. W-3050 John Clemens, 200a
W-4574 John Tapicott, representative of, 200a
b. John Savary**
c. William Lytle; T. Kirby, 1823; James Taylor; A. McLain, 1837; P. L. Wilson, 1841; Unknown
*"Waters of . . ."
**Source B spells Savay, Savacy.

S-5258* 120a B:509 X-0663** CLER:JACK
a. W-0199 Captain Lawrence Butler
b. Lawrence Butler
c. I? [J?] Moorhead; William Lytle, Junior, 1839
**See also* S-4782, S-4800, & S-5259
**"Waters of . . ."

S-5259* 305a D:461 X-0663** CLER: --
a. W-2753 Lewis Thomas
b. Jesse Taylor***
c. L. Butler; R. Tweed, 1824; William Lytle; Lewis Thomas; John Hill, 1831
**See also* S-4782, S-4800, & S-5258
**"Waters of . . ."
***Source B says James Taylor.

S-5259* 652a -- -- CLER?: --
a. --
b. [Lewis] Thomas, -- Morrison, [William] Lytle, & [L?] Butler
c. S. McCune, 1826; Z. Chapman, 1824; D. Arthur? 1826; O. T. Fishback, 1829; S. Butler; John Osburn; I? [J?] Vail, 1830; I? [J?] Moorhead; William Lytle, Junior, 1839
**See also* S-4782, S-4800, & S-5258. This specific entry in Source B only (at sequential place) and may have been cancelled.

S-5260 16a C:252 X-0663* BROW:PERR
a. W-2631 Captain James Gray
b. James Taylor
c. None
*"Waters of . . ."

S-5261 467a B:499 X-1000 UNIO:JERO
a. W-2856 Henry Bedinger
b. Henry Bedinger
c. None

S-5263 356a B:476 X-1180 MADI:MONR
a. W-5130 Henry Tatum
b. John Baird
c. None

S-5265 700a B:478 X-1180 UNIO:UNIO
a. W-5125 Robert Means, assignee of John Stokely, who was assignee of John Neal
b. Robert Means
c. Otis Dunlap & Company

S-5266* 600a -- -- UNIO:YORK
a. --
b. -- Danley, -- Jones, & -- Fautz
c. None
*Entry in Source B only (at sequential place).

S-5267 100a D:105 X-0345 UNIO:LIBE
a. W-0998 George Solomon
b. George Solomon
c. Unknown; M. S. Butler, 1836; B. Simons, *et al* [crossed out]

S-5267 100a D:105 X-0345 UNIO:LIBE
a. W-2149 James Baldwin
b. James Baldwin
c. Unknown; M. S. Butler, 1836

S-5267 100a D:105 X-0345 UNIO:LIBE
a. W-1002 Bryan Simmons
b. Bryan Simmons
c. Unknown; M. S. Butler, 1836

S-5267* 200a -- -- UNIO:LIBE
a. --
b. Charles Calpey
c. None
*Entry in Source B only (at sequential place).

S-5270 200a D:104 X-0345 UNIO:LIBE
a. W-2911 Daniel Perryman, assignee [of?] Charles Nicholas, 100a
W-2916 Thomas Vernon, 100a
b. William Russell
c. Unknown; M. S. Butler, 1836

S-5270* 100a D:104 X-0345 UNIO:LIBE
a. W-0642 George Winter
b. George Winters
c. Unknown; M. S. Butler
*Source B says "not patented."

S-5271* 100a -- -- UNIO:LIBE
a. --
b. Reuben Atkinson
c. None
*Entry in Source B only (at sequential place).

S-5271* 100a -- -- UNIO:LIBE
a. --
b. Benjamin Dickie
c. None
*Entry in Source B only (at sequential place).

S-5271* 100a -- -- UNIO:LIBE
a. --
b. Terence McDonald
c. --
*Entry in Source B only (at sequential place).

S-5272* 100a -- -- LOGA:ZANE
a. --
b. James Barrett? [Barnett?]
c. None
*Entry in Source B only (at sequential place).

S-5272* 100a -- -- LOGA:ZANE
a. --
b. Joshua Wayland
c. None
*Entry in Source B only (at sequential place).

S-5273 200a C:51 X-0345 FRAN:BROW
a. W-3741 Thomas Bird
b. Thomas Bird
c. Lucas Sullivant, heirs; I? [J?] Clover, 1829; Unknown; L. Starling, 1829

S-5274* 40a -- -- BROW: --
a. --
b. M. Hawkins
c. --
*Entry in Source B only (at sequential place) but crossed out.

S-5275 100a D:103 X-0345 LOGA:PERR
a. W-1763 Francis Turner
b. Robert Marshall
c. J. Asher, 1842

S-5275* 100a D:103 X-0345 LOGA:PERR
a. W-3562 Anthony Garnett
b. Anthony Garrett**
c. J. Asher, 1842
*Source B says "not patented."
**Source B may spell Garnett.

S-5275 200a D:103 X-0345 LOGA:PERR
a. W-1152 Michael Murphy
b. Michael Murphey
c. John H. Hanson, 1824; Lucas Sullivant; R. P. Mann, 1833

S-5275* 100a D:103 X-0345 LOGA:PERR
a. W-1867 William Jais? [Jaes? Inis?]; William Halliday [assignee?]
b. John Jordan**
c. James Bell; M. S. Butler, 1836; W. Butler; R. L. Broome, 1839; J. Asher, 1842
*Source B says "not patented, no . . .? of warrant."
**Source B may spell Jordain.

S-5279 235a C:123 X-0342* CHAM:RUSH
a. W-0891 John Warner, 200a?
W-1121 James Beham, ?a
b. David Bradford
c. None
*"Branch of . . ."

S-5280 300a C:311 X-0410 MADI:FAIR
a. W-3578* Leonard Botts
b. David Bradford
c. James Bradford; Alexander Comer, 1831
*Warrant number may be wrong, as acreage exceeds amount assignable under this warrant.

S-5281 400a B:478 X-1182 MADI:MONR
a. W-5115 Robert Means, assignee of John Blackwell, administrator of James Bassett, deceased, 100a
W-5116 Robert Means, assignee of John Blackwell, administrator of James Barrett [!] deceased, 200a
W-5117 Robert Means, assignee of John Blackwell, administrator of Malcomb McGeorge, deceased, 100a
b. Robert Means
c. None

S-5286 800a* E:436 X-0663 HIGH:DODS
a. W-2377 Doctor John Trezevant; Thomas J. McArthur, John Tench [assignees?]
b. W[allace] M. Anderson, et al*
c. B. Ladd & J. Ladd; Joel Hart, 1831; William Lytle, 1808; B. W. Ladd, 1809
*Source B says patented to John Tench and that tract "contains 1217 acres, or 515 acres not sold to Hart."

S-5287 800a B:469 X-0841 ROSS:CONC
a. W-0633 Captain Thomas Holt
b. Thomas Holt
c. None

S-5288* 1000a B:537 X-0750 LOGA:PERR LOGA:BOAK LOGA:RUSH
a. W-0659 Captain Thomas Boyer
b. Thomas Bowyer
c. None
*Source B says "not patented."

S-5289* 1000a B:537 X-0110 UNIO:YORK
a. W-0659 Captain Thomas Boyer
b. Thomas Bowyer
c. D. McArthur; Thomas Collins, 1823; John H. Houser; Ira Wood, 1833
*Source B says "not patented."

S-5290* 1000a C:11 X-0110 UNIO:YORK
a. W-0659 Captain Thomas Boyer
b. Thomas Bowyer
c. D. McArthur; Orris Parrish, 1823; James Taylor, 1826; Ezra Reed, 1831
*Source B says "not patented."

S-5291 200a C:228 X-0342 UNIO:UNIO
a. W-0633 Captain Thomas Holt
b. Thomas Holt
c. None

S-5292 440a D:423 X-0340 UNIO:UNIO
S-12398 UNIO:PARI
a. W-5123 Francis Lewis, administrator of [the] estate of William [Lewis?] 240a
W-6463 Thomas Osuley? [Ousley?]; Robert D. Farmer? [Farnum?] assignee, 200a
b. James Galloway, Junior
c. None

S-5294 150a C:5 X-0340 MADI:FAIR
a. W-5096 John Lawrence
b. William Bond
c. None

S-5297 55a E:165 X-0270 CLER:TATE
a. W-0107 Colonel John Green
b. James Taylor
c. None

S-5298 120a B:499 X-1180 MADI:MONR
a. W-0630 Lieutenant Jacob Brown
b. Jacob Brown
c. J. Downing; J. Moore, 1823

S-5300 207a C:411 X-1180 CHAM:RUSH
S-5976
a. W-5136 David Mason, 100a
W-5123 Francis Lewis, administrator of [the?] estate of William [Lewis?] 107a?
b. -- Mason & -- Means
c. H. Cushman; Jacob Lane

S-5301 200a B:478 X-1180 MADI:PIKE*
UNIO:UNIO
a. W-5125 Robert Means, assignee of John Stokely, who was assignee of James Neal
b. Robert Means
c. W. Dun; John Kious, 1831
*Source B notation: "Home."

S-5304 100a B:479 X-1180 CHAM:GOSH
a. W-5114 Simon Morgan
b. Robert Means
c. None

S-5308 125a C:148 X-1000 PICK:WAYN
a. W-5104 Samuel Marsh, assignee of Joseph Smith
b. Duncan McArthur
c. None

S-5309 100a C:382 X-0970 FAYE:WAYN
a. W-5108 Robert Throckmorton
b. Thomas Carter
c. None

S-5311 10a E:351 X-0845 ROSS:TWIN
a. W-5072 Isaac Browning
b. Duncan McArthur
c. None

S-5313 50a C:289 X-0840 ROSS:BUCK
a. W-5072 Isaac Browning
b. Duncan McArthur
c. None

S-5314 100a B:479 X-0750 DELA:CONC
a. W-3493 John Craig
b. Robert Means
c. None

S-5323 300a B:490 X-1004 DELA:SCIO
a. W-5104 Samuel Marsh, assignee [of?] Joseph Smith
b. Henry Massie
c. None

S-5326 400a C:172 X-0750 DELA:SCIO
a. W-0307 Captain John Clarke
b. John Clark
c. Joseph P. Smith; Milo D. Pettibone, 1839

S-5327 300a B:474 X-0840 ROSS:HUNT
a. W-5104 Samuel Marsh, assignee [of?] Joseph Smith
b. Henry Massie
c. None

S-5328 200a C:64 X-0663 HIGH:DODS
a. W-5104 Samuel Marsh, assignee [of?] Joseph Smith
b. Henry Massie
c. None

S-5329* 403a -- -- ROSS:HUNT
a. --
b. D. McArthur & H. Massie
c. None
**See also* S-4937

S-5339* 50a C:216 X-0130 ADAM:MONR
a. W-5112 Henry Aldred
b. Andrew Ellison
c. None
*Source B entry says S-5239, but is in correct sequential place to be S-5339.

S-5340. *See* S-4596

S-5342 112a C:265 X-0510 PIKE:MIFF
S-8262
a. W-1910 Smith Kent; David Anderson [assignee?] ?a
W-3105 Thomas Miller; Didier Collin & A. Foulds? [assignees?] ?a
b. Andrew Ellison
c. James Jones, 1836

S-5343 200a C:151 X-0130* ADAM:TIFF
a. W-5118 John Hughes
b. Andrew Ellison
c. None
*"Lk. fork of . . ."

S-5344 100a B:206 X-0130* ADAM:TIFF
a. W-1696 William Copeland
b. Andrew Ellison
c. None
*"Lk. fork of . . ."

S-5347 200a C:260 X-0010 CLIN:LIBE
a. W-5129 Simpson Foster, representative of
b. Simpson Foster, representative [of?]
c. None

S-5348 400a C:21 X-0840* FAYE:GREE
a. W-5129 Simpson Foster, representative of
b. Simpson Foster, representative [of?]
c. S. Shepherd; Reece? Moore, 1825; John Holliday; J. G. Green, 1831; A. Jones; N. F. Jones, 1833
*"Right fork of . . ."

S-5349 185a C:21 X-0640 FAYE:GREE
a. W-5129 Simpson Foster, representative of
b. Simpson Foster, representation [of?]
c. I? [J?] Davis, representative [of?]; J. Jameson, 1837; John Davis; W. V. Rawlins, 1841

S-5350 410a C:20 X-1303 HIGH:WHIT
a. W-5129 Simpson Foster, representative of
b. Simpson Foster, representatives [of?]
c. None

S-5351 465a C:101 X-0840* FAYE:JEFF
a. W-5129 Simpson Foster, representative of
b. Simpson Foster, representative [of?]
c. Lambert Kimble; George Kimble, 1826; John Warrenburg; Robert Hogue, 1840
*"Right fork of . . ."

S-5352 100a C:21 X-0741 GREE:ROSS
a. W-5129 Simpson Foster, representative of
b. Simpson Foster, representative [of?]
c. None

S-5353 250a C:21 X-0741 GREE:ROSS
a. W-5129 Simpson Foster, representative of
b. Simpson Foster, representative [of?]
c. S. W. McCracken, 1823; J. Y. Bacon; T. Marshall, 1838

S-5354 60a C:117 X-0663 HIGH:UNIO
a. W-5129 Simpson Foster, representative of
b. Simpson Foster, representative [of?]
c. Samuel Shepherd; J. Thompson, 1828; H. Walton; William Scott, 1836; William Wilkinson, 1840

S-5355 347a C:20 X-0640 CLIN:WAYN
a. W-5129 Simpson Foster, representative of
b. Simpson Foster, representative [of?]
c. J. B. Lemans, 1827; James Roberts; Samuel Wilson, 1833; S. Miller; A. E. Strickle, 1837

S-5356 129a C:152 X-0423 ADAM:TIFF
a. W-4992 Thomas Mills, representative of
b. Robert Ellison
c. Absalom Lafferty; T. Huston, 1834

S-5357 41a D:319 X-0425 ADAM:TIFF
a. W-4992? Thomas Mills, representative of
b. Robert Ellison
c. None

S-5362 300a C:224 X-0133 ADAM:FRAN
a. W-0083 Captain Thomas Overton, assignee [of?] Doctor Joseph Davis
b. Thomas Overton
c. Cyrus Strong; John Wood, 1826; T. Huston, 1834

S-5363 50a D:171 X-0425 ADAM:MONR
a. W-1566 Charles Stern
b. Michael Hogg
c. Walter Smith, 1824

S-5364 200a D:342 X-1005 DELA:SCIO
a. W-1010 Richard Routen
b. Joseph Dickson
c. Lucas Sullivant; N. Hull, 1835

S-5365* 116a -- -- ROSS:TWIN
a. --
b. Robert Means
c. None
*Entry in Source B only (at sequential place).

S-5375 1500a D:21 X-0150 PICK:DARB
S-6907 PICK:MONR
a. W-5137 Thomas D. Harris, assignee of David Mason
b. Robert Means
c. S. Morton & B. C. Morton; W. Y. Emmitt, 1837; Clement Parker; S. Timmons; A. Grady, 1841

S-5376* 541a -- -- MADI:FAIR
FRAN:PLEA
a. --
b. Thomas Chilton
c. None
*Entry in Source B only (at sequential place).

S-5378* 142a -- -- FRAN:FRAN
a. --
b. Robert Means
c. None
*Entry in Source B only (at sequential place).

S-5379* 333a -- -- PICK:JACK PICK:SCIO
a. --
b. Robert Means
c. None
*Entry in Source B only (at sequential place).

S-5386 990a C:33 X-0110 UNIO:LEES
a. W-5149 John Stokely, assignee of Jacob Springer, 444a
W-5150 John Stokely, assignee of John Beck, 444a
W-5152 John Stokely, assignee of Philip Hupp, 102a
b. Robert Means
c. S. G. Strong, 1833; Unknown; H. W? [M?] Perkins, 1831

S-5387 1000a C:2 X-0750 X-0110 UNIO:YORK
a. W-5153 John Stokely, assignee of Lazarus Rhine, 200a
W-5154 John Stokely, assignee of Hazett Laear, 200a
W-5155 John Stokely, assignee of Joseph Fuller, 200a
W-5156 John Stokely, assignee of Richard Davis, 100a
W-5152 John Stokely, assignee of Philip Hupp, 98a
W-5139 Robert Means, assignee of James Smith, 202a
b. Robert Means
c. Adam Miller; George Custard; William Knox

S-5388 667a D:22 X-1000* PICK:WAYN
a. W-5139 Robert Means, assignee of James Smith
b. Robert Means
c. A. C. McArthur; I? [J?] Olds, 1842
*"Lk. Run of . . ."

S-5390 667a B:485 X-0750 UNIO:PARI
a. W-5114 Simon Morgan, 567a
W-5123 Francis Lewis, administrator of [the?] estate of William [Lewis] 100a
b. Robert Means
c. None

S-5392 642a B:486 X-0750 UNIO:PARI
a. W-5126 John Stokely, assignee of James Neal
b. Robert Means
c. William Shelpman, 1828

S-5398 130a C:235 X-0840 ROSS:TWIN ROSS:HUNT
a. W-5026 David Meriwether
b. Thomas Worthington
c. None

S-5399 45a D:371 X-0845 ROSS:TWIN ROSS:HUNT
a. W-5026 David Meriwether
b. Thomas Worthington*
c. None
*Source B says "Heirs of Thomas Worthington."

S-5408 S-5485 300a B:492 X-1180 CHAM:GOSH
a. W-5041 John Cole
b. John Cole
c. None

S-5415 50a B:500 X-1180 CHAM:GOSH
a. W-0205 Captain Thomas Thucutt? [Thewait? Thweatt?]
b. Alexander Kerr
c. None

S-5416 500a B:493 X-0750 UNIO:PARI
a. W-4083 Nathan Lamme
b. Nathan Lamme
c. John Bowen, heirs

S-5417 300a B:495 X-0340 UNIO:JERO
a. W-4083 Nathan Lamme
b. Nathan Lamme
c. None

S-5418 200a B:496 X-0340 CHAM:GOSH
a. W-4083 Nathan Lamme
b. Nathan Lamme
c. None

S-5421 100a B:483 X-0900 PICK:DARB
a. W-3779 Mourning Richardson
b. Thomas Carneal
c. None

S-5423 334a C:517 X-0360 MADI:UNIO
a. W-1203 Captain Beverly Stubblefield
b. Beverly Stubblefield
c. None

S-5425 167a C:47 X-0663 HIGH:UNIO
a. W-1203 Captain Beverly Stubblefield
b. Beverly Stubblefield
c. None

S-5426* 100a -- -- MADI:PLEA
a. --
b. Henry Brush
c. None
*Entry in Source B only (at sequential place).

S-5429 650a C:327 X-0360 MADI:UNIO*
a. W-0176 General P[eter] Muhlenberg
b. Peter Muhlenburg
c. J. Warner, 1823
*Source B notation: "By London."

S-5431 1000a C:69 X-0980 FAYE:GREE
a. W-5160 John Moore
b. John Moore
c. None

S-5432* 450a C:70 X-0940 FAYE: --
a. W-5160 John Moore
b. John Moore
c. --
*Marginal notation in Source A: "Emsherd? See [S]-9910." The entry number is then crossed out. Entry does not appear in Source B.

S-5433 2740a C:49 X-0360 MADI:PLEA MADI:FAIR
a. W-5134 Richard Apperson
b. Richard Apperson
c. D. Denison; J. D. Denison, 1826; J. Oxford, 1823; -- Crismans, 1827; T. Carneal; Jacob Fowler, 1828; Jonathan Harner? [Farner?] 1831; James Corder, heirs; R. Douglas, 1836; Unknown; J. Taylor, Junior, 1837

S-5435 210a C:8 X-0342 MADI:SUMM CHAM:GOSH
a. W-1203 Captain Beverly Stubblefield
b. Beverly Stubblefield
c. None

S-5436 109a C:8 X-0342 CHAM:GOSH MADI: --*
a. W-1203 Captain Beverly Stubblefield
b. Beverly Stubblefield
c. None
*Source B does not mention Madison County.

S-5439 160a C:8 X-0342 MADI:SUMM CHAM: --*
a. W-1203 Captain Beverly Stubblefield
b. Beverly Stubblefield
c. None
*Source B does not mention Champaign County.

S-5444 80a C:8 X-0342 CHAM:GOSH
a. W-5134 Richard Apperson
b. Richard Apperson
c. T. Stewart, 1823? [1826?]

S-5447 593a B:491 X-0010* DELA:SCIO
a. W-5170 Thomas D. Harris, assignee of Albridgeton Jones
b. John Baird
c. None
*Called Blue Creek in Source A.

S-5451* 15a -- -- PICK:DARB
a. [W-1203? Captain Beverly Stubblefield]
b. Beverly Stubblefield
c. None
*Entry in Source B only.

S-5452 333a C:150 X-0730 CLAR:PLEA
a. W-5174 John White
b. James Knight
c. William H. Fyffe, 1828; Bazil Harrison; Sampson Mason, 1828

S-5454 100a C:176 X-0120 MADI:RANG
a. W-5111 Robert Means, assignee of John Blackwell
b. Thomas Worthington
c. None

S-5456 2739a C:175 X-0120 MADI:RANG
S-6824
S-7112
S-7612
a. W-5006 James McDaniel, 200a
W-5639 Michael Bowyer, 416a
W-5736 Thomas Gaskins, 229a
W-5738 Thomas Gaskins, deceased, 229a
W-5111 Robert Means, assignee of John Blackwell, 197a?
W-5739 Thomas Gaskins, deceased, 229a
W-5917 Anderson Claybrook, 200a
W-5793 Richard C. Waters, deceased, 300a
W-5846 Charles Stockly, deceased; Oliver Simpson, William Fulton [assignees?] 370a?
W-4859 Leven Joyner, 100a?
W-5026 David Meriwether, 269a?
b. Thomas Worthington
c. None

S-5458 603a B:496 X-1180 CHAM:GOSH
a. W-4601 John Massenburg
b. John Massenburg
c. None

S-5460 310a C:146 X-0843 FAYE:PAIN MADI: --*
a. W-1936 Captain Reuben Taylor
b. John Stokes
c. A? C. Funk; L. Loofborough [*also* Loofburrow] 1826; William Douglas; R. Douglas, 1829
*Source B does not mention Madison County.

S-5461 400a C:114 X-0810 PICK:DARB MADI:PLEA
a. W-1936 Captain Reuben Taylor
b. John Stokes
c. D. Mantle; C. Everson, 1837; E. Waldo; G. R. Anderson, 1837 (Pickaway County)

S-5468 237a B:489 X-0841 MADI:RANG
a. W-5138 Thomas D. Harris, assignee of Alexander Rose
b. William Creighton, Junior
c. None

S-5469 180a B:483 X-0730 CHAM:GOSH CHAM:WAYN
a. W-0205 Captain Thomas Thucutt? [Thewait? Thweatt?] 60a?
W-0660 Captain Hezekiah Morton, 60a?
W-0732 Captain Thomas Parker, 60a?
b. James Denny, [Hezekiah] Morten* & [Thomas] Parker*
c. None
*These patentees not listed in Source B.

S-5475 100a B:484 X-1180 UNIO:UNIO
a. W-5151 Hugh Montgomery
b. Hugh Montgomery
c. R. Means; Sanford S. Bennett, 1824; S. G. Strong, 1827

S-5476 830a C:9 X-0840 MADI:RANG*
S-5672
a. W-5160 John Moore, 400a
W-5138 Thomas D. Harris, assignee of Alexander Rose, 430a
b. [John] Moore & [William] Creighton [Junior]
c. None
*Source B notation: "Willow Spring."

S-5477 1600a B:492 X-0750 UNIO:MILL
a. W-5041 John Cole
b. John Cole
c. Samuel Carnvine?; Edward Hollycross; Samuel Farnam; George Dean; S. Gilbert, 1826? [1836?]

S-5478 100a B:500 X-1180 MADI:SUMM
a. W-5217 David Drummond, representative of
b. David Drummond, representative [of?]
c. Charles Rigdon [*also* Bigdon] 1831; D. Dromgoole, representative [of?]

S-5479 100a B:499 X-1180 MADI:SUMM
a. W-5209 Thomas M. Bailey, assignee of Stephen Moore
b. Thomas M. Bailey
c. None

S-5480 100a B:499 X-1180 CHAM:GOSH
a. W-5210 Thomas M. Bailey, assignee of Mathias Phillips
b. Thomas M. Bailey
c. None

S-5481 200a B:500 X-1182 MADI:MONR
a. W-5189 William Care? [Case?] representative of
b. William Case, representative [of?]
c. None

S-5482 200a B:500 X-1182 MADI:MONR
a. W-5190 John Carr? [Case?] representative of
b. John Case, representative [of?]
c. Thomas M. Bailey; Amos Howard, 1830

S-5483 200a B:503 X-1182 MADI:MONR
S-5484
a. W-5197 William Raleigh
b. William Raleigh
c. Thomas M. Bailey

S-5485. *See* S-5408

S-5491 100a B:483 X-0840 GREE*:SILV
a. W-5186? Thomas M. Bayly, assignee of Samuel Waple
b. Thomas M. Bayley
c. E. Nance? [Vance?]; A. Johnson, 1824; John Osborn; Joel Harris, 1837 (Greene County)
*Source B also mentions Clark County, but apparently this was erroneous.

S-5495 25a* B:484 X-0841 ROSS:CONC
a. W-5186 Thomas M. Bayly, assignee of Samuel Waple
b. Thomas M. Bayley
c. None
*Source B says 250a.

S-5497 1358a B:486 X-0100 UNIO:DOVE
a. W-5126 John Stokely, assignee of James Neal
b. Robert Means
c. I? [J?] Peck

S-5498 1358a B:486 X-0100 UNIO:DOVE
a. W-5128 John Stokely, assignee of David Steel
b. Robert Means
c. None

S-5499 1358a B:486 X-0100 UNIO:DOVE
DELA:SCIO
a. W-5121 Thomas D. Harris, assignee of Robert Means; assignee of James Bayless?; estate of Beverly Whiting
b. Robert Means
c. James Carter; J. S. Carter; S. G. Strong; J. Southgate; R? [K?] L. Broome, 1833

S-5500 1000a B:487 X-0100 DELA:SCIO
a. W-5121 Thomas D. Harris, assignee of Robert Means; assignee of James Bayless? estate of Beverly Whiting
b. Robert Means
c. John Snowden; Perus Dex, 1838; T. Burr? [Burn?] (forfeited 1839)

S-5501 800a B:487 X-0750 UNIO:DOVE
DELA:SCIO
a. W-5128 John Stokely; assignee of David Steel; David Means [assignee?] 491a
W-5121 Thomas D. Harris, assignee of Robert Means; assignee of James Bayless? estate of Beverly Whiting, 309a
b. Robert Means
c. David Dix, 1828; R. P. Mann; S. G. Strong, 1839 (Union County); M. D. Pettibone, 1839 (Delaware County)

S-5502 800a B:487 X-0750 UNIO:DOVE
a. W-5132 William Glenn, representative of, 200a
W-5144 Robert Means, assignee of Thomas D. Harris; assignee of William Simmons, 200a
W-5125 Robert Means, assignee of John Stokely; assignee of James Neal
W-5123 Francis Lewis, administrator of [the?] estate of William [Lewis] 200a
b. Robert Means
c. Anthony Newhart, 1826; John W. [U? M?] Pomroy; Joshua Mathcott, 1835 (Union County)

S-5503 540a B:487 X-0750 UNIO:PARI
a. W-5140 John Stokely, assignee of Robert Vaner? [Waner?]
b. Robert Means
c. James Watkins; R. Graham, 1839

S-5504 428a B:487 X-0750 UNIO:DOVE
a. W-5121 Thomas D. Harris, assignee of Robert Means; assignee of James Bayless? estate of Beverly Whiting, 101a
W-5140 John Stokely, assignee of Robert Vaner? [Waner? Warner?] 127a
W-5141 John Stokely, assignee of Thomas Givin? 100a

S-5504 [continued]
W-5142 John Stokely, assignee of John Givin? 100a
b. Robert Means & -- Stokely*
c. Joseph Carter; James Martin; B. Selman; R. L. Broome, 1840
*Source B does not mention Stokely.

S-5505 255a C:45 X-0100 UNIO:DOVE
a. W-5143 Robert Means, assignee of Samuel Marsh; assignee of William Flong? [Florey?] 100a
W-5123 Francis Lewis, administrator of [the?] estate of William [Lewis] 100a?
W-5140 John Stokely, assignee of Robert Vaner? [Waner? Warner?] 55a?
b. Robert Means & -- Stokely*
c. -- Blackburn & -- Brown; B. Hill
*Source B does not mention Stokely.

S-5505 200a C:45 X-0100 UNIO:DOVE
a. W-5133 Salley Orion? [Onions?] representative of
b. Selby Onions, representative [of?]
c. None

S-5506 1796a B:496 X-0100 UNIO:LEES
a. W-0026 John? Shetth?
b. Andrew Meade
c. None

S-5507 390a B:495 X-0100 UNIO:LEES
a. W-0096 Captain Baylor Hill
b. Baylor Hill
c. None

S-5508 97a B:494 X-0660 CLAR:MADI
a. W-0096 Captain Baylor Hill
b. Baylor Hill
c. None

S-5515 145a B:484 X-0660 GREE:ROSS
a. W-5188 Thomas M. Bayly, assignee of John Curtis, administrator of [the?] estate of George Oldham, deceased
b. Thomas M. Bayley
c. None

S-5521 200a C:201 X-0840 FAYE:PAIN
a. W-5162 Peter Manifold, assignee of Matthew Irvine
b. Duncan McArthur
c. None

S-5526 200a C:149 X-0330 MADI:UNIO
a. W-5164 Peter Manifold, assignee of Matthew Irvine
b. John Shearer
c. None

S-5527 160a C:314 X-0365 FAYE:MADI
a. W-5164 Peter Manifold, assignee of Matthew Irvine
b. John Shearer
c. None

S-5532 695a C:198 X-0120 MADI:RANG
a. W-5187 Thomas M. Bayly, assignee of John Drummond
b. Joseph Harness
c. None

S-5533 1133a C:199 X-0840 MADI:STOK
S-5797
S-5798
S-8212
a. W-5187 Thomas M. Bayly, assignee of John Drummond
b. Joseph Harness
c. None

S-5537 180a B:523 X-0841* FAYE:MADI
a. W-5072 Isaac Browning
b. Duncan McArthur
c. None
*"West branch of . . ."

S-5539 100a C:131 X-0360 MADI:SUMM
a. W-4356 Whitmore Mail; Richard Taylor [assignee?]
b. Thomas Springer
c. None

S-5540* 10a -- -- WARR:WAYN
a. --
b. Nancy Grimes
c. None
*Entry in Source B only (at sequential place).

S-5541* 30a -- -- WARR:WAYN
a. --
b. Nancy Grimes
c. None
*Entry in Source B only (at sequential place).

S-5542 100a C:47 X-0140 PICK:DEER
a. W-5193 Thomas M. Bayly, assignee of George Harman
b. Charles A. Stewart
c. None

S-5543 100a C:331 X-0360 PICK:DEER
a. W-5193 Thomas M. Bayly, assignee of George Harman
b. Charles A. Stewart
c. E. Davidson; W. Davidson, 1836

S-5546 300a B:490 X-0840 MADI:STOK
a. W-5196 Thomas M. Bayly, assignee of Leven Hyshop [Hyslop?] 200a
W-5205 Thomas M. Bayly, assignee of Caleb Massey, 100a
b. Charles A. Stewart*
c. None
*Source B also spells Stuart.

S-5551 200a C:116 X-0840 MADI:STOK
S-5675
a. W-5164 Peter Manifold, assignee of Matthew Irvine 100a?
W-5332 William Eskridge, 100a?
b. John Shearer
c. None

S-5552 200a C:148 X-0840 MADI:UNIO
S-5676 X-0360
a. W-5164 Peter Manifold, assignee of Matthew Irvine 100a?
W-5332 William Eskridge, 100a?
b. John Shearer
c. None

S-5553 1000a C:65 X-0340 PICK:MUHL
a. W-5191 Solomon Parks, 200a
W-5192 Levi Annis, 200a
W-5195 Daniel Richardson, 200a
W-5213 --* Thornton, 100a
W-5214 William Lillerton, 100a
W-5215 Thomas Elliott, 100a
W-5216 Susanna Heath, administratrix of Joseph [Heath?] 100a; *all of the above warrants assigned to* Thomas M. Bayly
b. Henry Massie
c. None
*Name blotted out.

S-5554 200a B:505 X-0360 PICK:DEER
a. W-5100 David Scott
b. Joseph Kerr
c. None

S-5555 200a D:436 X-0380 HIGH:DODS
a. W-3309 Robert Wakins? [Watkins?]
b. John Wilkins, Junior, heirs [of?]
c. Unknown; J. Watkins, Junior; James Hultz, 1831

S-5555 100a D:436 X-0380 HIGH:DODS
a. W-4031 Simon Barry
b. John Wilkins, Junior, heirs [of?]
c. None

S-5558 1333a B:494 X-0840* FAYE:GREE** HIGH: --***
a. W-2638 John McAdams, heir to Jo[seph?] McAdams
b. Benjamin Grimes
c. None
*"R[ight?] fork of . . ."
**Source B notation: "Martinsburg."
***Source B does not mention Highland County.

S-5559 200a B:494 X-0340 CHAM:RUSH
a. W-2638 John McAdams, heir to Jo[seph?] McAdams
b. Benjamin Grimes
c. None

S-5562 370a B:488 X-0180 WARR:WAYN
a. W-5104 Samuel Marsh, assignee of Joseph Smith
b. Henry Massie
c. None

S-5563 300a B:488 X-0663 HIGH:NEWM
a. W-5201 Solomon Russell, 100a
W-5202 William Cennchorn? [Kennchorn?] 100a
W-5216 Susanna Heath, administratrix of Joseph [Heath?] 100a; *all three warrants assigned to* Thomas M. Bayly
b. Henry Massie
c. None

S-5564 150a B:488 X-0840 ROSS:TWIN
a. W-5211 John Ross, 100a
W-5212 Robert Davis, 50a?; *both warrants assigned to* Thomas M. Bayly
b. Henry Massie
c. None

S-5570* 10a -- -- WARR:WAYN
a. --
b. Joseph Chinowith
c. None
*Entry in Source B only (at sequential place).

S-5572 52a C:531 -- CHAM:UNIO
S-10905
a. W-3749 Andrew Dunbar; A. C. Locke [assignee?] ?a
W-4851 George Breech; A. C. Locke [assignee?] ?a
b. Elias Langham
c. None

S-5578 188a B:502 X-1186 MADI:MONR
a. W-4432 William Diven
b. Simon Nicholson
c. None

S-5580 350a C:403 X-0310 CLER:OHIO
a. W-5257 Thomas Martin & James Taylor, 175a?
W-5260 Robert Kirk & James Taylor, 175a?
b. [James] Taylor, [Thomas] Martin, & [Robert] Kirk
c. John Snyder; James Snyder, 1832; Daniel Snyder, 1833

S-5581 555a B:510 X-0800 HAMI:ANDE
a. W-5255 James Taylor
b. James Taylor
c. None

S-5582 300a D:402 X-0663* CLER:TATE
a. W-5254 John Mountjoy
b. John Mountjoy
c. None
*"Waters of . . ."

S-5583 888a B:491 X-0340 CHAM:RUSH
a. W-5236 William Benlly? [Bently?] 555a
W-5237 William Benley? [Bently?] 333a
b. John Baird
c. None

S-5585 199a B:495 X-0663 HIGH:UNIO
a. W-1890 Lieutenant David Walker
b. Joseph Jones
c. None

S-5586 1000a B:501 X-0110 UNIO:LEES
a. W-5148 John Stokely, assignee of Abraham Shepherd
b. Robert Means
c. None

S-5591 236a B:506 X-0841 FAYE:PAIN
a. W-0347 Major David Stephenson
b. David Stephenson
c. None

S-5592 300a C:37 X-0360 MADI:UNIO
a. W-0347 Major David Stephenson
b. David Stephenson
c. James Trotter; William Battern, 1831; William Button [*also* Batten, Batton]; John Moore, 1835; Henry Warner, 1837; C. Mills; H. W. Smith, 1842

S-5593 360a C:36 X-0840 MADI:STOK
a. W-0347 Major David Stephenson
b. David Stephenson
c. None

S-5596 830a B:489 X-0340 CHAM:RUSH CHAM:GOSH CHAM:UNIO
a. W-2263 Lieutenant Colonel William Washington
b. William Washington
c. Aaron Pierce

S-5601 300a B:503 X-1186 MADI:PIKE
a. W-5102 Michael McGraw
b. John Patterson
c. Alexander Conner, 1832

S-5602 100a B:502 X-0340 UNIO:UNIO
a. W-5102 Michael McGraw
b. John Patterson
c. None

S-5606 760a? B:497 X-1180 MADI:MONR
a. W-5188 Thomas M. Bayly, assignee of John Curtis, administrator of [the?] estate of George Oldham, deceased
b. Thomas M. Bailey
c. None

S-5607 912a B:498 X-1180 CHAM:GOSH
a. W-5188 Thomas M. Bayly, assignee of John Curtis, administrator of [the?] estate of George Oldham, deceased
b. Thomas M. Bailey
c. None

S-5609 690a B:497 X-1004 UNIO:MILL
a. W-5186 Thomas M. Bayly, assignee of Samuel Waple
b. Thomas M. Bailey
c. None

S-5610 700a B:498 X-1004 UNIO:JERO
a. W-5267 Levin Hyslop, representative of Abner Hyslop, 200a
W-5268 Easter Holon? representative of Major -- Johnson, ?a
W-5269 [page torn]
W-5271 [page torn]; *first three warrants assigned to* Thomas M. Bayly
b. Thomas M. Bailey
c. None

S-5611 360a B:513 X-0340 UNIO:JERO
a. W-5270 [page torn] [200a?]
W-5274 Daniel Richardson, representative of William Richardson, 100a
W-5325 Southy Bailey, 60a; *last two warrants assigned to* Thomas M. Bayly
b. Thomas M. Bailey
c. None

S-5613 1000a B:499 X-0756 UNIO:LEES
a. W-5286 [manuscript torn]
b. Thomas M. Bailey
c. None

S-5626 153a B:493 X-0743 GREE:XENI GREE:ROSS
a. W-2638 John McAdams, heir to Jo[seph?] McAdams, 103a?
W-4433 Robert Diven; John Handley, Simon Nicholson [assignees?] 50a?
b. Benjamin Grimes & -- Galloway
c. None

S-5629 1867a C:34 X-0750 UNIO:LEES
S-6493
a. W-5147 Isaac Israel, 400a?
W-5240 Presley Nevill, [assignee?] of John Nevill, 1467a?; *both warrants assigned to* John Stokely
b. Robert Means
c. Nathan Reeves; Thomas P. Head; M. S. Butler, 1836

S-5630 900a C:33 X-0110 UNIO:LEES
S-6510
a. W-5105 Samuel Marsh, assignee of Joseph Smith, 450a?
W-5147 John Stokely, assignee of Isaac Israel, 450a?
b. Robert Means
c. Means Masson? 1833; S. G. Strong

S-5633 200a C:272 X-1360 PIKE:JACK
S-8775 ROSS: --*
a. W-5262 Duncan McArthur
b. Duncan McArthur
c. None
*Source B does not mention Ross County.

S-5635* 650a -- -- UNIO:YORK
a. --
b. John Gilmore
c. James Gilmore; Sanford S. Bennett, 1824
*Entry in Source B only (at sequential place).

S-5637 1118a C:10 X-0360 MADI:FAIR
a. W-5245 Robert Means, assignee of Thomas D. Harris, assignee of [the?] representatives of John Cobb, heir to Samuel Cobbs
b. Robert Means
c. I? [J?] N. Jones, 1839

S-5640 95a D:357 X-0730 X-0660 CLAR:HARM
a. W-5231 Henry Lee, [--] of Alexander Skinner
b. Robert Means
c. D[uncan] McArthur; Jacob Dougherty, 1838

S-5641. *See* S-5778

S-5643 500a C:88 X-0290 FAYE:MADI FAYE:PAIN
a. W-5235 John Stith
b. Robert Means
c. Ganet? Blue, 1828

S-5645 300a C:313 X-0342 MADI:PIKE CHAM: --*
a. W-5231 Henry Lee, --? of Alexander Skinner
b. Robert Means
c. None
*Source B does not mention Champaign County.

S-5646 750a C:2 X-0110 UNIO:LEES
a. W-2211 Lieutenant Daniel Bedinger
b. Thomas Worthington
c. None

S-5647 200a C:30 X-0360 PICK:PERR
a. W-1653 Lieutenant Robert Brackenridge
b. Elias Rector
c. None

S-5648 357a C:29 X-0780 MADI:UNIO
S-6322
a. W-1653 Lieutenant Robert Brackenridge, ?a
W-4851 George Breech; Elias Langham, A. C. Locke [assignees?] ?a
b. Elias Rector
c. J. Humbert; W. Warner, 1823

S-5652 260a D:57 X-0500 MADI:DEER
a. W-5240 John Stokely, assignee of Presley Nevill, [assignee?] of John Nevill
b. Robert Means
c. None

S-5656. *See* S-4592

S-5657. *See* S-4592

S-5658. *See* S-4592

S-5660 100a C:219 X-0540 ROSS:DEER
a. W-4207 Robert Ogilsby; William George [assignee?]
b. Duncan McArthur
c. None

S-5661 50a C:276 X-0570 ROSS:HUNT
a. W-5169 William Smith; William George [assignee?]
b. Robert Means
c. None

S-5662* 40a C:210 X-0130 ADAM:TIFF
a. W-4740 Elijah Ford, representative of; Simon Morgan, Andrew Ellison [assignees?]
b. Paul Kerr
c. None
*Source B says "not patented."

S-5663 50a C:102 X-0130 ADAM:JEFF DELA:SCIO*
a. W-1567 John Waller; Thomas Coleman, David Reese [assignees?]
b. Andrew Ellison
c. None
*Source B shows Delaware County, Scioto Township, but other abbreviations in entry are not understood.

S-5665 800a D:23 X-1000 MARI:BOWL
a. W-2275* David Murry
b. Callohill Minnis
c. None
*Warrant number may be wrong, as it is for 200a only.

S-5670 300a C:288 X-0360 MADI:RANG
a. W-5138 Thomas D. Harris, assignee of Alexander Rose
b. William Creighton, Junior
c. None

S-5672. *See* S-5476

S-5673 150a C:9 X-1260 MADI:UNIO
a. W-5346 William Arbuckle, 100a
W-4878 James McNutt, 50a
b. [William] Arbuckle & -- Stewart
c. None

S-5675. *See* S-5551

S-5676. *See* S-5552

S-5677 252a D:232 X-0135 CLAR:PLEA
a. W-5332 William Eskridge
b. John Shearer
c. George Medsker; Solomon Scott, 1825; Henry Armacosh, 1829; J. Shearer, heirs; William H. Lafferty, 1837

S-5684 300a C:64 X-0340 PICK:SCIO
a. W-0857 William Dowell, 100a
W-1762 Moses Daulton, 200a
b. John Foggy
c. Helen Massie; W. P. Darst & P. N. White, 1840; H. Massie; D. Prindle, 1842

S-5689 1000a C:307 X-1000* X-0340* PICK:SCIO
a. W-2349 Henry Whiting
b. Henry Whiting
c. Samuel Holmes & L? [S?] R. Becket; -- Olds & -- McCrea, 1826; James Morrison; H. Patrick, 1833 (Union County)
*Between the two streams.

S-5697 125a C:278 X-0840 ROSS:TWIN
a. W-1912 Doctor Thomas Cristie
b. Thomas Christie
c. None

S-5699* 47a -- -- ROSS:DEER
a. --
b. David Walker
c. None
*Entry in Source B only (at sequential place).

S-5705 1023a C:15 X-1170 CLIN:MARI
a. W-1450 Major Samuel Finley, 23a?
W-5250 Major Samuel Finley, 1000a?
b. Samuel Finley
c. Francis Dunlavy [*also* Dunlavey]; J. H. Dunlavey, 1826; J. Morris, 1827

S-5706 815a B:500 X-0740 MADI:STOK
CLAR: --*
a. W-5251 George Mathews
b. George Mathews**
c. None
*Source B does not mention Clark County.
**Source B spells Matthews.

S-5708 200a B:492 X-1180 UNIO:UNIO
a. W-5044 Thomas Woodlief, representative of Francis Epps, deceased
b. James Galloway, Junior
c. None

S-5714 300a B:492 X-0660 CLAR:GREE
CLAR:MADI
a. W-5096 John Lawrence; William Bond [assignee?] 50a
W-5130 Henry Tatum; John Baird [assignee?] 24a?
W-5288 Thomas M. Bayly, assignee of George Cristofer? & George Wilson, representative of Bartholomew Fisher, 100a
W-5287 Thomas M. Bayly, assignee of Thomas Evans, representative of Thomas Evans, 100a
W-0712 Doctor William Brown, 26a?
b. -- Galloway & -- Bailey*
c. None
*Source B spells Bayley.

S-5716 242a C:410 X-1180 CHAM:RUSH
S-5748 UNIO: --*
S-5754
a. W-0712 Doctor William Brown, 200a?
W-4601 John Massenburg, 42a?
b. -- Galloway & [John] Massenburg
c. None
*Source B does not mention Union County.

S-5717 225a B:491 X-0840 MADI:STOK
a. W-0712 Doctor William Brown, 105a?
W-5230 John Stith, 120a?
b. [James] Galloway & [John] Baird
c. None

S-5719 661a B:493 X-0840 MADI:STOK
a. W-0712 Doctor William Brown, 61a?
W-5170 Thomas D. Harris, assignee of Albridgton Jones, 100a?
W-5289 George Christofor & George Williams, representative of John Fisher, 100a
W-5291 Micajah Annis, representative of Jesse Annis, 100a
W-5292 Thomas Kelly, representative of Thomas Bloxam, 100a
W-5293 Thomas Kelly, representative of Woodsman Bloxam, 100a
W-5294 Thomas Kelly, representative of John Bloxam, 100a; *the last five of the above-listed warrants assigned* to Thomas M. Bayly
b. -- Galloway & [Thomas M.] Bailey*
c. None
*Source B spells Bayly.

S-5723 670a C:40 X-0660 CLAR:MADI
X-0740
a. W-0026 John? Shetth? [Stith?] 470a
W-5239 Ebenezer Minton, 200a
b. [Andrew] Mead* & -- Baird
c. Henry Miller; S. W. Wheeler, 1838
*Source B spells Meade.

S-5724 295a B:491 X-0340 UNIO:JERO
a. W-5230 John Stith
b. John Baird
c. None

S-5725. *See* S-5717

S-5726 1000a B:522 X-1180 UNIO:UNIO
a. W-5247 Robert Young, representative of
b. Robert Young, representative [of?]
c. None

S-5728 1567a B:502 X-0750 UNIO:ALLE
X-0340
a. W-5147 John Stokely, assignee of Isaac Israel, 1000a?
W-5148 John Stokely, assignee of Abraham Shepherd, 333a?
W-5139 Robert Means, assignee of James Smith, 234a?
b. Robert Means
c. None

S-5729 1000a B:501 X-0750 UNIO:LIBE
a. W-5147 John Stokely, assignee of Isaac Israel
b. Robert Means
c. None

S-5733 750a B:498 X-0730 CLAR:PLEA
a. W-5320 Stephen Moore, representative of Levi Moore, 100a
W-5323 Joshua Riggs, 100a
W-5324 John Huchison, representative of -- Huchison, 100a
W-5326 Henry Sterling, representative of Richard Sterling, 100a
W-5286 [manuscript torn]; *first four of the above-listed warrants assigned* to Thomas M. Bayly
b. Thomas M. Bailey
c. None

S-5734 100a B:495 X-0660 WARR:HAMI
a. W-5038 Francis Ratliff? 40a
W-5246 James Taylor, assignee of Peter Evans, 40a?
W-5130 Henry Tatum, 20a?
b. [Ralph] Hunt & [Jacob D.] Lowe
c. J. Stubbs; J. M. Roosa, 1842

S-5735* 304a -- -- WARR:HAMI
a. [W-2126? Abrington Jones]
b. Albridgton Jones
c. --
*Entry in Source B only (at sequential place).

S-5738 400a B:504 X-0060 LOGA:JEFF
X-0730
a. W-5337 Joseph Bohannon, assignee [of?] William Beatty? assignee of Henry Moss
b. Charles Spencer
c. Thomas S? [L?] Foote; Lyne Starling, 1831

S-5740 255a B:521 X-1180 UNIO:UNIO*
a. W-5250 Samuel Finley
b. Samuel Finley
c. None
*Source B entry shows Allen Township crossed out.

S-5741 100a B:522 X-1180 CHAM:GOSH
a. W-5337 Joseph Bohannon, assignee of William Beatty? assignee of Henry Moss
b. Charles Spencer
c. None

S-5742 400a C:427 X-1000 FRAN:PRAI
S-9221
a. W-5316 John Lurton? representative of Leven Lurton, 100a
W-5317 John Lurton? representative of William Lurton, 100a
W-5188 John Curtis, administrator of George Oldham, deceased, 200a; *all three warrants assigned to* Thomas M. Bayly
b. Thomas M. Bayley
c. None

S-5743 200a B:492 X-0350 MADI:PIKE UNIO:UNIO
a. W-1429 Charles Ballard
b. James Galloway
c. A. Sabin

S-5744 270a B:493 X-1160 MADI:CANA
a. W-4432 William Diven; Simon Nicholson [assignee?] 12a
W-4433 Robert Diven; Simon Nicholson & John Handley [assignees?] 150a
W-0712 Doctor William Brown, 108a?
b. James Galloway
c. None

S-5745 400a C:66 X-1000 FRAN:FRAN
a. W-0091 General George Weedon
b. George Weedon
c. George Lewis; Peter Hoover, 1828; James Bryden, 1830

S-5746 360a B:493 X-0990 UNIO:PARI
a. W-1183 Alexander McLardy, 200a
W-5281 Jesse? Bunting, representative of Smith Bunting, 100a
W-5282 [manuscript torn] representative of Benjamin Burton, 60a?; *last two warrants probably assigned to* Thomas M. Bayly
b. James Galloway, Junior
c. None

S-5747 340a B:493 X-1186 MADI:MONR
a. W-5279 Elijah Bloscom, representative of Charles Stuart, 100a
W-5280 --? & John Lurton? representative of Richard Bunting, 100a
W-5282 [manuscript torn] . . . representative of Benjamin Burton, 40a; *all three warrants probably assigned to* Thomas M. Bayly
b. James Galloway, Junior
c. J. Wingate; D. Bradley, 1823

S-5748. *See* S-5716

S-5749 204a B:501 X-1160 MADI:CANA
a. W-5251 George Mathews
b. George Mathews
c. T. Patterson, heirs; H. Warner, 1836

S-5750 1646a B:520 X-1006* DELA:THOM
a. W-5219 Jonathan Clark, 667a
W-0172 Lieutenant Colonel Jonathan Clark, 979a
b. Jonathan Clark
c. None
*"Waters of . . ."

S-5751 411a B:520 X-1180 CHAM:GOSH
a. W-0172 Lieutenant Colonel Jonathan Clark
b. Jonathan Clark
c. None

S-5753 73a* C:412 X-1180 CHAM:RUSH
a. W-1751 Captain Hughes Woodson
b. Hughs Woodson
c. None
*Source B says 53 acres.

S-5754. *See* S-5716

S-5756 150a B:513 X-1180 CHAM:GOSH
a. W-5318 Elijah Lillerton, representative of John Lillerton? [Lilleston?] 100a
W-5317 John Lurton? representative of William Lurton, 50a?; *both warrants assigned to* Thomas M. Bayly
b. Thomas M. Baily*
c. None
*Source B spells Bailey.

S-5765 1000a B:523 X-0340 PICK:WAYN PICK:JACK
a. W-4748*
b. John McDonald
c. A. C. McArthur; J. Olds, 1842
*Warrant number seems definitely to be in error.

S-5766 1167a C:103 X-0810 MADI:FAIR MADI:PLEA FRAN:PLEA PICK: --*
a. W-5387 Margaret Brownley? [Bromley?] widow of Ralph Falkner
b. Robert Means
c. None
*Source B does not mention Pickaway County.

S-5777 300a C:34 X-1340 UNIO:LIBE
a. W-5169 Thomas D. Haines, assignee of Erasmus Gill, administrator of Peter Minor
b. Robert Means
c. None

S-5778 1829a C:33 X-0750* UNIO:LIBE
S-5641 X-0110*
S-5806
S-6495
a. W-5228 Henry Lee, 300a
W-5169 Thomas D. Haines, assignee of Erasmus Gill, administrator of Peter Minor, 200a?
W-5240 John Stokely, assignee of Presley Nevill, [assignee?] of John Nevill, 262a?
W-0293 William Palmer, 200a
W-5470 Robert Means, assignee of Edward Smith, 267a?
W-5101 William Bird, assignee of Philip Courtney, 280a?
W-5184 Samuel Coleman, 370a
b. Robert Means
c. None
*Between the two watercourses.

S-5779 502a B:116 X-1000 PICK:JACK
a. W-5162 Peter Manifold, assignee of Matthew Irvine, 250a?
W-5072 Isaac Browning, 252a?
b. Duncan McArthur
c. None

S-5780 1035a C:132 X-0840 FAYE:JEFF
S-6859 FAYE:PAIN
S-7043
a. W-0606 James Browser; John Allen [assignee?] 200a
W-5131 William McKee, 200a?
W-5782 John Hull, in his own right & as assignee, 200a?
W-5752 John Walker, deceased, heirs of, 200a?
W-5821 Ellis L. Adams, 100a
W-5072 Isaac Browning, 135a?
b. Duncan McArthur
c. Benjamin Harper; Amos Wood, 1830; Isaac Harness; Solomon Carr, 1834

S-5781 150a C:145 X-0840 MADI:STOK
a. W-1517 John Hudson; Lewis Craig [assignee?]
b. Francis Ayers
c. None

S-5782 130a C:145 X-0296 FAYE:UNIO
S-6338
a. W-1517 John Hudson, 30a?
W-5677 Joseph Woodson, 100a?
b. [Francis] Ayers & [Duncan] McArthur
c. Hiland Seminary

S-5783* 200a D:62 X-1005 HARD:DUDL
a. W-1843 Lieutenant William Smith
b. John Wallace
c. James Tagart? [crossed out]; Duncan McArthur, 1831 (Logan County)
*Source B says "not patented."

S-5791 162a C:313 X-0360 MADI:SUMM
a. W-5228 Henry Lee
b. Robert Means
c. None

S-5792 50a C:35 X-0360 MADI:SUMM
a. W-5228 Henry Lee
b. Robert Means
c. None

S-5793 83a C:134 X-0140 PICK:DEER
S-6823
a. W-5200 Thomas M. Bayly, assignee of Samuel Russell, 40a?
W-5534 Peter Manifold, assignee of Lawrence Manning, administrator of Laurence [Manning?] deceased, 43a?
b. [Elias] Langham & [George] Hoffman
c. None

S-5795 500a C:48 X-0330 MADI:UNIO
a. W-1249 Captain Thomas Chilton, heir, 250a?
W-0347 Major David Stephenson, 250a?
b. -- Chitten & -- Stephenson
c. R. Gragg; A. Evans, 1827

S-5796* 400a -- -- MADI: --
a. --
b. C. Baldwin
c. E[lias] Langham, 1829
*Entry in Source B only (at top of page above S-5756).

S-5797. *See* S-5533

S-5798. *See* S-5533

S-5799 1000a C:292 X-0360 MADI:PLEA
a. W-3528 William Finnie, "resolution"; John Hardin & David Gray [assignees?]
b. Martin B. Hardin & [David?] Gray
c. E. Langham, heirs; Hugh Ganey? [Garrey?] 1833; M. L. Sullivant, 1831

S-5801 667a C:76 X-0360 MADI:DEER
a. W-5339 Sigmond Stribling
b. Nathan Sitter*
c. W. Lytle; D. Thompson, 1824; J. Woods; -- Warner & -- Thompson, 1826; William Woods; William Jones
*Source B may spell Sitler; Source C may spell Litler.

S-5802 1667a C:77 X-0360 MADI:UNIO
MADI:DEER
a. W-0996 Captain Sigismond Stribling
b. Sigismond Stribling
c. W. Lytle; R. McLaughlin, 1824; J. Sittler; W. Jones, 1826; J. Moore; S. Talbert; -- Thompson & -- Lewis, 1823; I? [J?] Hull, 1826; G. Cooper; M. Baum; E. Langham, 1828; M. Baum, heirs; J. B. Croney, 1835; Samuel S. Kerr, 1838; J. W. Blackley & O. B. Blackley; J. Crisman, 1842

S-5803 157a D:504 X-0365 MADI:RANG
a. W-5339 Sigmond Stribling
b. Nathan Sitter* heirs [of?]
c. S. N. Kerr, 1831; J. Crisman, 1834
*Source B spells Sitler; Source C may spell Litler.

S-5804 23a C:257 X-0250 HIGH:LIBE
a. W-5200 Thomas M. Bayly, assignee of Samuel Russell
b. Elias Langham
c. None

S-5806. *See* S-5778

S-5808 200a B:519 X-0340 CHAM:RUSH
a. W-3237 Charles West
b. John Baird
c. None

S-5809 2000a C:18 X-0480 UNIO:CLAI
a. W-5175 John Nicholas, 500a
W-5176 John Nicholas, 500a
W-5177 John Nicholas, 500a
W-5178 John Nicholas, 500a
b. John Nicholas
c. George Sutton; Joshua Mathiott [*or* Mathcott?]; Joseph Nicholas

S-5812 80a B:519 X-0730 LOGA:JEFF
a. W-5181 Beetley Barret
b. Benjamin Rosseau*
c. Thomas Freer
*Sources B and C spell Boisseau.

S-5814 400a B:517 X-0180 WARR:WASH
a. W-5366 Nancy McGee, representative of Archibald [McGee] 200a
W-5373 Patience Bunting, representative of Sacher [Bunting] 200a; *both warrants assigned to* Thomas M. Bayly
b. James Galloway, Junior
c. None

S-5817 150a B:521 X-1180 CHAM:GOSH
a. W-5263 Irby Hudson, administrator of estate of
b. Theodoric Spain
c. None

S-5818 50a B:522 X-1180 CHAM:GOSH
a. W-5263 Irby Hudson, administrator of estate of
b. Theodoric Spain
c. None

S-5819 35a B:521 X-1180 CHAM:GOSH
a. W-5263 Irby Hudson, administrator of estate of
b. Theodoric Spain
c. None

S-5820 50a B:522 X-0730 CHAM:GOSH
a. W-5263 Irby Hudson, administrator of estate of
b. Theodoric Spain
c. None

S-5821 15a B:522 X-1180 MADI: --*
a. W-5263 Irby Hudson, administrator of estate of
b. Theodoric Spain
c. None
*Source A says "not found;" Source B says Madison County, but township not found.

S-5822 20a C:106 X-0730 CHAM:UNIO
a. W-5263 Irby Hudson, administrator of estate of
b. Theodoric Spain
c. None

S-5823 64a C:370 X-0841 FAYE:PAIN
a. W-0347 Major David Stephenson
b. David Stephenson
c. None

S-5824 300a C:149 X-0810 PICK:DARB
a. W-5163 Peter Manifold, assignee of Matthew Irvine
b. George Renick
c. None

S-5825 105a B:507 X-0135 ADAM:TIFF
X-0425
a. W-3477 Abraham Shepherd, 85a?
W-4653 William Rippolo? 40a
W-1089 Benjamin Brooke, 175a?
b. Nathaniel Massie
c. None

S-5826 100a B:506 X-0770 HIGH:BRUS
a. W-4815 Thomas Summersett
b. Henry Lyne
c. None

S-5827 200a B:505 X-0770 HIGH:BRUS
a. W-4841 Thomas Polloch? [Pollack?]
b. Henry Bedinger
c. None

S-5828. *See* S-4714

S-5829 400a B:506 X-0770 HIGH:BRUS
a. W-5058 Henry Field, representative of
b. Henry Fields, representative [of?]
c. None

S-5830 730a C:23 X-0840 ROSS:BUCK
a. W-4569 William Carter, Senior
b. William Carter, Senior
c. None

S-5831 430a C:23 X-0840* HIGH:PAIN**
S-5832
a. W-4569 William Carter, Senior
b. William Carter, Senior
c. Abner Jessup; James Moore, 1832; Joseph Sevim? [Levim?] 1834; Daniel Edwards; James? [Joseph?] Hull; J? [I?] Simpson, 1840; Andrew Johnson; -- Kirby & -- Starling, 1831; Pleasant Thurman; Peter Weaver; William Nevins, 1833
*R[attle?] S[nake?] fork of . . ."
**Source B notation: "Near Petersburg."

S-5833 370a C:249 X-0150 ROSS:PAIN
a. W-4569 William Carter, Senior
b. William Carter, Senior
c. Moses McCune; Peter Douglas, 1830

S-5836 600a C:125 X-0134 ADAM:SCOT
a. W-0635 Captain Archibald Denholm
b. John Harvie
c. None

S-5839 250a C:127 X-0840 HIGH:PAIN
S-7368
a. W-5229 Lawrence Butler
b. Nathaniel Pope
c. None

S-5840 1000a C:128 X-1290* FAYE:GREE
a. W-3432 John M. Galt, "resolution" 500a?
W-4569 William Carter, Senior, 500a?
b. [Abraham] Shepherd & [William] Carter [Senior]
c. None
*"Walnut Run of S[outh?] Fork . . ."

S-5843 200a C:128 X-0130 ADAM:FRAN
a. W-3432 John M. Galt, "resolution"
b. Abraham Shepheard*
c. None
*Sources B and C spell Shepherd.

S-5844 400a C:128 X-0300 ADAM:FRAN
a. W-3432 John M. Galt, "resolution"
b. Abraham Shepheard*
c. John Davis; William Parks, 1826; C. Hoskins; A. D. Beasley, 1829; William Ogle, heirs; B? Ogle, 1835
*Sources B and C spell Shepherd.

S-5846 136a C:128 X-0300 ADAM:FRAN
a. W-3432 John M. Galt, "resolution"
b. Abraham Shepheard*
c. None
*Sources B and C spell Shepherd.

S-5847 445a C:34 X-0840 FAYE:PAIN
a. W-5171 Robert Means, assignee of Thomas D. Harris, assignee of John Crawford
b. Robert Means
c. None

S-5848 200a B:518 X-0730 CLAR:PLEA CHAM: --*
a. W-0348 Captain James Curry
b. James Galloway, Junior
c. James Hunt; James Wallace, 1839
*Source B does not mention Champaign County.

S-5849 200a C:126 X-0640 FAYE:GREE
a. W-5239 Ebenezer Minton
b. Ebenezer Minton
c. Noble Crawford; J. Jameson, 1837

S-5850 277a C:129 X-0640 FAYE:GREE DELA:SCIO*
a. W-5238 John Watts
b. John Watts
c. None
*Shown in Source B only.

S-5856* 100a D:2 X-1005 MARI:BOWL
a. W-5011 David Stafford
b. David Stafford
c. E. Scroggin; E. W. H. Reed, 1831; D. Spafford
*Source B says "not patented."

S-5856* 100a C:536 X-1000 MARI:BOWL
a. W-5014 Ephraim Scoggins**
b. Ephraim Scroggins**
c. E. Scroggin; E. W. H. Reed, 1831; D. Spafford
*Source B says "not patented."
**So spelled.

S-5856* 100a D:2 X-1000 MARI:BOWL
a. W-5012 Henry Meacham
b. Harvey Meachain? [Meacham?]
c. E. Scroggin; E. W. H. Reed, 1831; D. Spafford
*Source B says "not patented."

S-5857* 100a D:1 X-1000 MARI:BOWL
a. W-5010 James Cook, representative of
b. James Cook, representative [of?]
c. None
*Source B says "not patented."

S-5857* 200a D:1 X-1000 MARI:BOWL
a. W-5009 Holmes Jones, representative of
b. Holmes Jones, representative [of?]
c. Lyne Starling
*Source B says "not patented."

S-5857* 100a D:1 X-1000 MARI:BOWL
a. W-5013 John Scoggins**
b. John Scroggins**
c. None
*Source B says "not patented."
**So spelled.

S-5858. *See* S-4592

S-5861 100a C:131 X-0360 MADI:SUMM
a. W-5263 Irby Hudson, administrators of estate of
b. Theodoric Spain
c. None

S-5862 750a B:514 X-1180 CHAM:GOSH MADI: --*
a. W-5300 [manuscript torn] [100a?]
W-5301 John Nork? representative of William Nork? 100a
W-5302 Richard Parker, representative of Leven Parker, 100a
W-5303 Susanna Potter, representative of John Potter, 100a
W-5304 John Ross, representative of Elijah Ross, 100a
W-5305 Tabetha Simpson, representative of Drummond Simpson, 100a
W-5306 Hancock Simpson, representative of Elisha Simpson, 50a; *all warrants assigned to* Thomas M. Bayly
b. Thomas M. Bailey**
c. None
*Source B does not mention Madison County.
**Source B spells Bayley.

S-5863 550a B:514 X-1180 CHAM:RUSH UNIO: --*
a. W-5307 Elizabeth Scott, representative of Sacker? Scott, 100a
W-5308 John Read, representative of Henry Window, 100a
W-5309 Coluna Watkinson, representative of Leven Watkinson, 100a
W-5310 James Thornton, representative of Henry Jones, 100a
W-5311 William Henman; representative of Elijah Henman, 100a
W-5306 Hancock Simpson, representative of Elisha Simpson, 50a; *all warrants assigned to* Thomas M. Bayly

S-5863 [continued]
b. Thomas M. Bailey**
c. None
*Source B does not mention Union County.
**Source B spells Bayley.

S-5864 833a B:514 X-0730 LOGA:JEFF
a. W-5295 Thomas Kelly, representative of Leven Bloxam, 100a
W-5296 William Dameson, representative of Jacob Dameson, 100a
W-5297 Elizabeth Dickerson, representative of Edward Dickerson, 100a
W-5298 Tabetha Simpson, representative of Leven? [Severn?] Dailey, 100a
W-5312 Jacob Kelley, representative of John Harman, 100a
W-5313 Jacob Kelley, representative of Leven Harman, 100a
W-5314 Jacob Kelley, representative of Ezekiel Harman, 100a
W-5322 Francis Savage, executor of Robinson Long, 133a; *all warrants assigned to* Thomas M. Bayly
b. Thomas M. Bailey*
c. None
*Source B spells Bayley.

S-5866 730a B:513 X-0840 FAYE:JEFF
a. W-5186 Thomas M. Bayly, assignee of Samuel Waple
b. Thomas M. Bailey*
c. None
*Source B spells Bayley.

S-5868 1458a B:515 X-1004 DELA:SCIO
a. W-5186 Thomas My Bayly, assignee of Samuel Waple, 1123a?
W-5286 [manuscript torn] [335a?]
b. Thomas M. Bailey*
c. None
*Source B spells Bayley.

S-5869 1000a B:517 X-1000 UNIO:DOVE DELA:SCIO
a. W-5185 William B. Bunting, representative of
b. William B. Bunting, representative [of?]
c. None

S-5870 1000a B:517 X-0090* X-0010* UNIO:LEES
a. W-5185 William B. Bunting, representative of
b. William B. Bunting, representative [of?]
c. Nathaniel Benton; M. S. Butler, 1836
*Blue's Creek. It is not clear which of the above watercourses is meant.

S-5871 667a B:517 X-1000 PICK:SCIO
a. W-5185 William B. Bunting, representative of
b. William B. Bunting, representative [of?]
c. None

S-5872 2222a B:518 X-0360 CLAR:PLEA CHAM: --*
a. W-5327 Thomas M. Bayly, assignee of John Cropper
b. John Cropper
c. None
*Source B does not mention Champaign County.

S-5873 1063a B:520 X-1000 DELA:THOM
a. W-5173 William Carter, deceased, representative of
b. William Carter, representative [of?]
c. Margaret Kent; John Hawkins, 1838; C. Swelser? (forfeited 1839); George Wolf; Jacob Swartz, 1833

S-5874 354a C:117 X-0340 MADI:CANA
a. W-5173 William Carter, deceased, representative of
b. William Carter, representative [of?]
c. None

S-5875 200a B:519 X-0830 LOGA:PERR
a. W-5467 John Baird, assignee of Robert Gwathmey; assignee of Henry Young
b. John Baird*
c. John B. Beard*; Sanson? [Lanson?] Curtis? [Custis?] 1828
*So spelled.

S-5581 236a* C:218? *or* X-0560 FAYE:WAYN
S-8197 C:278
a. W-3821 Samuel Aubry, *alias* Avery; William George [assignee?] 100a**
W-5162 Peter Manifold, assignee of Matthew Irvine, 36a?
W-5851 Osbourne Coffey; John A. Fulton [assignee?] 100a
b. Duncan McArthur
c. None
*Source B says 230a.
**Warrant may also have been used in S-2755.

S-5882 111a C:313 X-0841 FAYE:WAYN
a. W-5358 James Harman & John Potts, representatives of William Rogers
b. Robert Means
c. None

S-5883 54a D:46 X-0835 LOGA:PERR
a. W-5470 Robert Means, assignee of Edward Smith
b. Robert Means
c. None

S-5884 300a C:35 X-0290* FAYE:MADI
a. W-5470 Robert Means, assignee of Edward Smith
b. Robert Means
c. None
*"Dew's Run of . . ."

S-5886 100a C:385 X-0130 PIKE:CAMP
a. W-0981 Henry Oram
b. Henry Oram
c. J. Penniston & W. Mittin, 1830; E. Smith, heirs; J. Moore, 1838; "Patented Amelia Shoemaker [*et al*] 1838"

S-5888 106a D:178 X-0130 ADAM:TIFF
S-9685 X-0420
a. W-1910 Smith Kent; David Anderson [assignee?] ?a
W-5555 Samuel Booker, heirs; S. Donaldson, David Bradford [assignees?] ?a
b. David Bradford
c. None

S-5889* 160a C:151 X-0130** ADAM:TIFF
a. W-4741 Edwin Fielding, representative of; Simon Morgan, Andrew Ellison [assignees?] 100a
W-4740 Elijah Ford, representative of; Simon Morgan, Andrew Ellison [assignees?] 60a
b. Andrew Boyd
c. A. Ellison; J. Cole, 1829; T. Huston, 1831; A. Boyd, heirs
*Source B says "not patented."
**"Lk. branch of . . ."

S-5890 300a C:147 X-0120 MADI:RANG
S-7623
a. W-5340 Thomas Parker, 200a
W-6039 John Cramp? [Crane?]; Joseph Ladd, Benjamin W. Ladd [assignees?] 100a
b. Jesse McKay & -- Ladd
c. B. W. Ladd; -- Bond & -- Rhea, 1823

S-5891* 250a C:105 X-0120 MADI:RANG
a. W-5340 Thomas Parker
b. Jesse McKay
c. None
*Source B says "not patented."

S-5892* 105a C:149 X-0120 MADI:PLEA
a. W-5340 Thomas Parker
b. Jesse McKay
c. Benjamin Pike, 1828
*Source B says "not patented."

S-5893* 4a -- -- FAYE:MADI
a. --
b. Jesse McKay
c. None
*Entry in Source B only (at sequential place).

S-5893* 26a F:217 X-1040 ADAM: --
a. W-5405 Philip Mallory; Jesse McKaye [assignee?]
b. A. D. Kendrick & -- Massie
c. None
*Entry in Source A only (at sequential place).

S-5896 150a C:321 X-0360 PICK:PERR
a. W-4125 Edward Howard, heir to Charles [Howard]
b. Robert Sharp
c. None

S-5897 150a C:135 X-0780 MADI:UNIO
a. W-4459 Robert Sharp, heir to Jona [Sharp] 100a
W-4125 Edward Howard, heir to Charles [Howard] 50a
b. Robert Sharp
c. None

S-5898 200a C:179 X-0360 MADI:RANG
a. W-5131 William McKee
b. William McKee
c. None

S-5899 145a C:179 X-0120 MADI:RANG
a. W-5131 William McKee
b. William McKee
c. None

S-5900 172a C:375 X-0841 MADI:RANG
a. W-5131 William McKee
b. William McKee
c. None

S-5901 176a C:392 X-0841 MADI:RANG
a. W-5229 Lawrence Butler; Jacob Poe, Nathaniel Pope [assignees?] 100a?
W-5131 William McKee, 76a?
b. Daniel Countz & [Jesse?] McKee
c. None

S-5957. *See* S-4455

S-5958 300a B:511 X-0663 CLER:BATA
a. W-5094 James Taylor, assignee of Robert Elliott
b. James Taylor
c. John Tunis; Josiah Birdsall, 1832

S-5959 800a B:511 X-0790 CLER:GOSH
a. W-5094 James Taylor, assignee of Robert Elliott
b. James Taylor
c. N. Smith, heirs; S. Winston, 1824; W. Jones; T. Jones; J. Duckwall, 1826; B. M. Jackson, 1830; W. D. Tripp; John Hill, 1835

S-5960 400a C:441 X-1170 WARR:SALE
CLER: --*
a. W-5094 James Taylor, assignee of Robert Elliott
b. James Taylor
c. Robert Dodge; S. Winston, 1824; William Lytle; Z. Chapman, 1824; Caleb Smith; W. Simard? 1824; Robert McFarland; I? [J?] Wood; Jesse Wood; J. S. Wood
*Source B mentions Clermont County but says tract in Warren County.

S-5961 48a C:399 X-0663* CLIN:MARI
a. W-5094 James Taylor, assignee of Robert Elliott
b. James Taylor
c. S. Jackson; S. Winston, 1823; John Slade, 1825; John Hill, 1831
*"West fork of . . ."

S-5962 45a C:412 X-0790 CLER:GOSH
a. W-1206 John Straughan, 20a?
W-2830 James Wilson, 25a?
b. -- Tibbs & William Lytle
c. None

S-5964 118a* C:62 X-0841 ROSS:DEER
a. W-5388 Margaret Bromley, widow of Ralph Falkner
b. George Clark
c. None
*Source B says 48a.

S-5966 140a C:9 X-0360 PICK:DEER
a. W-5163 Peter Manifold, assignee [of?] Mathew Irvine
b. George Renick
c. None

S-5967 200a C:88 X-0290 FAYE:MADI
a. W-5405 Philip Mallory
b. Jesse McKay
c. None

S-5968 50a C:48 X-0360 PICK:DEER
a. W-5405 Philip Mallory
b. Jesse McKay
c. None

S-5969* 52a -- -- PICK:DEER
a. --
b. Jesse McKay
c. None
*Entry in Source B only (at sequential place).

S-5972 100a D:132 X-0085 ADAM:SPRI
a. W-2272 Captain Calohill Minnis
b. Callohill Minnis
c. Henry Gutridge?; Joseph? [James?] Riggs? [Biggs?] for H[enry] G[utridge] 1823; Ellis Palmer; John Francis, 1824

S-5973 90a* F:121 X-0130 ADAM:GREE
a. W-1896 Thomas Shelton
b. John Wilkins, Junior
c. James? [Joseph?] Nash; J. Williams, Junior; L. Cole, 1836
*Source B says 100a.

S-5974 100a C:337 X-1150 ADAM:SPRI
a. W-2272 Captain Calohill Minnis
b. Callohill Minnis
c. John Lodwick; -- McDade? & -- Wilkins, 1826

S-5976. *See* S-5300

S-5977 400a B:521 X-0010 GREE:SILV
a. W-5136 David Mason
b. David Mason
c. J. G. Lee; William W. Perkins, 1826

S-5979 870a C:17 X-0840* FAYE:GREE
a. W-5136 David Mason
b. David Mason
c. None
*"R[attle?] S[nake?] fork of . . ."

S-5981 296a B:522 X-0010 GREE:SILV
a. W-5419 Henry Tatum
b. Henry Tatum
c. None

S-5982 222a C:34 X-0840 MADI:STOK
a. W-5169 Thomas D. Haines, assignee of Erasmus Gill, administrator of Peter Minor
b. Robert Means
c. T. Cooper, heirs; J. T. Price, 1842

S-5985 1221a B:515 X-0340 FRAN:BROW
a. W-5368 Thomas M. Bayly, assignee of Lucretia Teagle, administratrix of Levern? [Severn?] Teagle, deceased
b. Thomas M. Bailey
c. None

S-5990 420a B:512 X-0660 X-0180 WARR:WASH
a. W-5179 John Nicholas
b. James Galloway, Junior
c. None

S-5991 347a B:513 X-1170 CLIN:UNIO
a. W-5179 John Nicholas, 247a
W-5284 [page torn] [100a]
b. James Galloway, Junior
c. None

S-5992 112a C:348 X-0660 CLER:MIAM
a. W-5336 William Mosley, 52a?
W-5246 James Taylor, assignee [of?] Peter Evans; Jacob D. Lowe, Ralph Hunt, Samuel Robinson [*or* Robertson] assignees, 60a?
b. William Moseley & Samuel Robison
c. James W. Robinson; -- Robertson & -- Todd; O. T. Fishback, 1834

S-5993 333a C:500 X-0840 X-0660 GREE:ROSS FAYE: --*
a. W-5341 William S. Smith, representative of
b. William S. Smith, representative of
c. Philip Gatch; Moses Hall, 1829; Jonathan Wade, 1834; I? [J?] Parrot, Junior (Fayette County); T. Maddox, 1837 (Fayette County); Thomas Lucas, 1840 (Fayette County)
*Source B does not mention Fayette County.

S-5993 815a C:514 X-0840 GREE:ROSS FAYE:JEFF MADI: --*
a. W-4789 James Morton, 444a
W-5345 James Morton, 370a
b. James Morton
c. Aaron Maston? [Marton?]; Benjamin Styles, 1834; John Gist; John Andrews, 1837; Conduce Gatch; Michael Swing; B. McClelland, 1841
*Source B does not mention Madison County.

S-5994* 100a -- -- GREE:ROSS** FAYE:JEFF**
a. --
b. Patrick Stewart
c. None
*Entry in Source B only (at sequential place).
**In either Green or Fayette counties.

S-5995* 178a -- -- CLER:MIAM
a. --
b. William Moseley
c. None
*In Source B only (at sequential place).

S-5996 100a B:518 X-1180 MADI:MONR
a. W-0712 Doctor William Brown
b. James Galloway, Junior
c. None

S-5998 1000a B:515 X-0360 CLAR:PLEA
a. W-5369 Thomas M. Bayly, assignee of William Joynes [Joyner?], representative of Reubin Joynes [Joyner?], deceased
b. Thomas M. Bailey*
c. None
*Source B spells Bayley.

S-5999 574a B:514 X-0360 CLAR:HARM CLAR:PLEA MADI: --*
a. W-5369 Thomas M. Bayly, assignee of William Joynes [Joyner?], representative of Reubin Joynes [Joyner?], deceased
b. Thomas M. Bailey**
c. None
*Source B does not mention Madison County.
**Source B spells Bayley.

S-6000 1093a B:516 X-1180 MADI:JEFF
a. W-5369 Thomas M. Bayly, assignee of William Joynes [Joyner?], representative of Reubin Joynes [Joyner?], deceased
b. Thomas M. Bailey*
c. None
*Source B spells Bayley.

S-6001 560a B:516 X-0731 CLAR:PLEA
a. W-5186 Thomas M. Bayly, assignee of Samuel Waple
b. Thomas M. Bailey*
c. None
*Source B spells Bayley.

S-6003 270a B:516 X-0840 FAYE:UNIO
a. W-5272 Thomas M. Bayly, assignee of Isaac Dix, representative of Walter Metcalfe, 200a
W-5294 Thomas M. Bayly, assignee of Thomas Kelly, representative of John Bloxam, 70a
b. Thomas M. Bailey*
c. None
*Source B spells Bayley.

S-6006 200a B:516 X-1180 MADI:SUMM
a. W-5285 [page torn] [100a]
W-5315 Thomas M. Bayly, assignee of William Hogshire? representative of Robert Hogshire, 100a
b. Thomas M. Bailey*
c. None
*Source B spells Bayley.

S-6007 100a B:518 X-0740 GREE:ROSS
a. W-5371 Thomas M. Bayly, assignee of John Benson, representative of George [Benson]
b. James Galloway, Junior
c. None

S-6009 711a C:7 X-0840 HIGH:MADI FAYE:WAYN
a. W-5394 Samuel Arnold
b. James D. Ladd
c. None

S-6010 711a C:7 X-0090 *or* X-0010 UNIO:LEES
a. W-5393 Samuel Arnold
b. Benjamin W. Ladd
c. John Hunt; S. G. Strong, 1836; William Morford

S-6014 1067a B:519 X-360 MADI:SUMM CLAR: --*
a. W-5135 James Claiborne, Robert Claiborne, Sterling Claiborne, Lucy Claiborne (Wright, late Livey?) who . . .? heirs of Buller Claiborne, deceased
b. Buller** Claiborne, heirs [of]
c. None
*Source B does not mention Clark County.
**Source B spells Butler.

S-6018 461a C:91 X-0360 MADI:SUMM CLAR:PLEA
a. W-5290 Thomas M. Bayly, assignee of William Andrews, 100a?
W-5375 Thomas M. Bayly, assignee of Major Andrews, representative of William Andrews, 361a?
b. Thomas Scott
c. A[llen] Latham, 1825; D. Walling; J. Walling, 1826

S-6021 530a B:521 X-0342* CHAM:GOSH
a. W-5136 David Mason
b. David Mason
c. None
*"Waters of . . ."

S-6022 201a B:519 X-1180 MADI:SUMM
a. W-5299 Thomas M. Bayly, assignee of Leven Gray, representative of Thomas Gray, 100a
W-5186 Thomas M. Bayly, assignee of Samuel Waple, 101a
b. Thomas M. Bailey*
c. None
*Source B spells Bayley.

S-6023 333a C:135 X-0360 MADI:UNIO
a. W-5481 Samuel Baskerville
b. Samuel Raskenville*
c. Isaac Evans; W. Waddle, 1828
*Source B spells Baskerville.

S-6024 7a C:131 X-1004 SCIO:MORG
a. W-5342 Joseph Swearingen
b. Robert Lucas
c. J. A. Bingham, 1829

S-6027 15a C:132 X-0920 SCIO:UNIO
a. W-5342 Joseph Swearingen
b. Robert Lucas
c. David Rape; J. R. Turner, 1830

S-6028 25a D:464 X-0640 CLIN:GREE*
a. W-5355 John Fox, representative of Drury Ragsdale, deceased
b. James Galloway, Junior
c. None
*Source B notation: "Snow Hill."

S-6029 525a C:15 X-0360 MADI:UNIO
S-6302
a. W-5355 John Fox, representative of Drury Ragsdale, deceased, 125a
W-5516 Andrew Moore [illegible: reso.? to Will. Isa[a]c? Leat heir [or Leather], 400a
b. James Galloway, Junior
c. R. McLaughlin; E. Turner, 1827

S-6030 50a C:6 X-1184 MADI:DEER
a. W-5355 John Fox, representative of Drury Ragsdale, deceased
b. James Galloway, Junior
c. None

S-6031 1500a C:5 X-1104 UNIO:LEES DELA:SCIO
a. W-5496 Sally Jordan, late Sally Smith, representative of Arthur Smith, deceased
b. Edward Dromgoole
c. Charles Sweetser, 1836

S-6033 1000a C:4 X-0110 X-0480 UNIO:LEES
a. W-5165 Peter Manifold, assignee of Matthew Irvine, 500a
W-5166 Peter Manifold, assignee of Matthew Irvine, 500a
b. John Baird
c. S. G. Strong, 1831

S-6046 200a C:3 X-0540 ROSS:DEER PIKE: --*
a. W-5158 Anne B. West, representative of Charles [West] who was representative of Thomas [West]
b. Ann B. West
c. None
*Source B does not mention Pike County.

S-6049 746a D:136 X-0841* FAYE:PAIN MADI:RANG
a. W-5399 William Sanford, representative of
b. William Robinson
c. Joseph? [James?] Bell, 1831
*"Waters of . . ."

S-6049 274a D:136 X-0841* FAYE:PAIN MADI:RANG**
a. W-5403 William Sanford, representative of
b. William Robinson
c. Daniel Kountz, 1829
*"Waters of . . ."
**Source A does not mention Madison County.

S-6050 1000a D:99 X-0843* MADI:RANG MADI:UNIO
a. W-5398 William Sanford, representative of
b. William Robinson
c. None
*"Waters of . . ."

S-6051 492a C:217 X-0840 MADI:UNIO
a. W-5402 William Sanford, representative of
b. William Robinson
c. None

S-6052 446a D:131 X-0365 MADI:RANG
S-9803
a. W-5400 William Sanford, representative of, 246a?
W-5401 William Sanford, representative of, 200a?
b. William Sanford, representative of
c. None

S-6054 200a C:113 X-0841* FAYE:PAIN
S-6186
a. W-5400 William Sanford, representative of, 100a
W-5573 William Cocke Holt, heir to James Holt, 100a
b. -- Sanford & William Robinson
c. None
*"East fork of . . ."

S-6058 490a* C:389 X-0843 FAYE:PAIN
S-6059 MADI: --*
a. W-5409 John Hays
b. John Hays
c. William Douglas; Peter Douglas, 1829; Reuben Grigsby; C. Wallace; "deeded Richard Douglas, 6 April 1838"
*Source B says 492a; does not mention Madison County.

S-6060 100a C:328 X-0360 PICK:DEER
a. W-5409 John Hays
b. John Hays
c. None

S-6061 540a C:107 X-0840 MADI:STOK
a. W-2263 Lieutenant Colonel William Washington
b. William Washington
c. None

S-6062 310a C:274? X-0330 MADI:UNIO
a. W-0289 Doctor Cornelius Baldwin
b. Cornelius Baldwin
c. G. Frizler; S. Morris, 1825; George Trisler [*also* Triceler]; William B. Baskerville, 1830; John Stroup, 1837

S-6063 468a C:107 X-0840 MADI:STOK
S-6140 MADI:UNIO
S-7184
a. W-5695 Joseph Woodson, 75a?
W-5273 Thomas M. Bayly, assignee of Daniel Richardson, representative of Zerubabel Richardson, 100a?
W-5526 John Moore? Verell? [Levell?], assignee of John [Verell?], assignee of Jacob Morgan, Samuel Stuart, & Charles Stuart; John Hamlin, original proprietor, 200a
W-2263 Lieutenant Colonel William Washington, 93a
b. Charles A. Stuart & -- Washington
c. None

S-6064 100a C:309 X-0365 MADI:UNIO
a. W-4884 Philip McDade
b. John McDonald
c. None

S-6065 200a C:31 X-0340 FRAN:PLEA
X-0810 PICK: --*
a. W-5182 Simon Cochran
b. Simon Cochran
c. None
*Source B does not mention Pickaway County.

S-6068 200a C:85 X-0120 MADI:RANG
a. W-5198 William Russell, representative of
b. William Russell, representative of
c. None

S-6070 200a C:85 X-0120 MADI:RANG
a. W-5198 William Russell, representative of
b. William Russell, representative of
c. None

S-6072 350a B:528 X-1303 HIGH:WHIT
a. W-5100 David Scott
b. Joseph Kerr
c. J. Roads; G. W. Barriere, 1826

S-6075 225a C:63 X-0360 ROSS:DEER
a. W-5388 Margaret Bromley? [Brownley?] widow of Ralph Falkner
b. George Clark
c. None

S-6077 250a B:529 X-0360 ROSS:DEER
a. W-5104 Samuel Marsh, assignee of Joseph Smith, 200a
W-5212 Thomas M. Bayly, assignee of Robert Davis, 50a
b. Henry Massie
c. None

S-6078 200a D:185 X-1305 BROW:SCOT
a. W-5057 John Page
b. Jacob Roth
c. M? [W?] Bonner, 1828

S-6083 39a D:122 X-0345 PICK:JACK
a. W-5473 Calohill Minnis
b. George Clarke
c. None

S-6084 667a C:102 X-0120 MADI:RANG
a. W-5508 Daniel Call, decree? in fact? of Robert Means, assignee of Thomas Lipscomb
b. Daniel Call
c. None

S-6087* 280a -- -- BROW:BYRD
a. --
b. Alexander Parker
c. E. Francis; -- Wilson & -- Middleton, 1842; J. Francis; W. Parker; J. Baird, 1842
*Entry in Source B only (at top of page above S-6031). *See also* S-3414

S-6088 350a B:525 X-0423 ADAM:LIBE
a. W-4254 Anthony W. White
b. Alexander Parker
c. None

S-6089 100a B:524 X-0420 ADAM:LIBE
BROW: --*
a. W-4944 Thomas Hungerford
b. John Beasley, heirs
c. None
*Source B does not mention Brown County.

S-6090 174a B:524 X-0423 ADAM:LIBE
a. W-4992 Thomas Mills, representative of, 100a
W-4117 Thomas Smith, 24a?
W-3105 Thomas Miller, 50a?
b. John Beasley
c. James? [Joseph?] Brownfield, heirs; D. Meharry, 1835

S-6091* 20a -- -- BROW:HUNT
a. --
b. Isham Kendrick
c. Job Egbert, 1828
*Entry in Source B only (at sequential place).

S-6092 120a B:528 X-0420 BROW:UNIO
a. W-3745 Michael Sellar
b. Michael Sellars
c. William Kirkpatrick, 1823; Samuel Fitch; William Hewitt, 1834

S-6093 80a F:97 X-0420 BROW:UNIO
a. W-3745 Michael Sellar
b. Michael Sellars
c. None

S-6094 54a D:318 X-0423** ADAM:TIFF
S-8066*
a. W-1141 Edward Shepheard; Nathaniel Massie, John Inglish, Stephen Beach, John McHenry [assignees?
b. Andrew Woodrow
c. None
*Source B says S-8006.
**"Waters of . . ."

S-6096. *See* S-4729

S-6097 300a C:192 X-0290 FAYE:MADI
a. W-5389 Thomas Golford? [Galford?] 200a
W-5390 James Reddin? [Keddin?] 100a
b. John Core*
c. Christian Kore, heirs; John Smith
*Source B spells Kore.

S-6098 100a C:134 X-0840 FAYE:PAIN
a. W-3637 William Crosley? [Crosby?]
b. Edward D. Rowe
c. None

S-6099 100a D:41 X-1045 ADAM:MEIG
a. W-4936 Joseph Winlock
b. Henry Massie & — Vinsonhaller*
c. C. Cannon, 1828
*Source B spells Vinsonhaler.

S-6101 236a C:306 X-0360 MADI:UNIO
a. W-5474 Holman Minnis, representative of
b. Daniel Brown
c. Matthew Bonner, 1831

S-6101* 200a -- -- CLAR: --
a. --
b. H. Twede
c. Ezekiel Palmer; Samuel McMillen, 1826
*Entry in Source B only (at sequential place).

S-6107 633a C:64 X-0480 UNIO:CLAI
X-0110
a. W-5527 Leven Joynes? [Jaynes? Joyner?] representative of
b. Levin Joynes, representative of
c. -- Wallace & -- Watts; Robson Broome, 1833

S-6110 511a C:85 X-0125 MADI:RANG
a. W-5198 William Russell, representatives of
b. William Russell, representatives of
c. None

S-6111 200a C:85 X-0125 MADI:RANG
a. W-5198 William Russell, representatives of
b. William Russell, representatives of
c. None

S-6112. *See* S-5232

S-6113. *See* S-5232

S-6114 75a C:390 X-0840 ROSS:TWIN
S-6529
a. W-2019 William Turvey; William George [assignee?] 50a?
W-5563 Edmund Goode, 25a?
b. John McDonald & Joshua McFarland*
c. None
*Sources B and C spell McFarlin.

S-6115 3900a* B:532 X-1000 PICK:SCIO
FRAN:JACK
a. W-5501 John Smith Sneed, heir to Thomas Sneed, deceased, 1000a
W-5502 John Smith Sneed, heir to Thomas Sneed, deceased, 1000a
W-5503 John Smith Sneed, heir to Thomas Sneed, deceased, 1333a
W-5504 John Verell, assignee [of?] John Evans; Moses Trader, James Galloway, Junior [assignees?] 200a
b. John Smith Snead
c. -- Gray & -- Taylor; Robert Pollock, 1827; Alexander McLoughlin; James? [Joseph?] Tagart; J. McLene, 1831; E. Bachus, 1832; J. Crosby, 1834; S. Crosby, 1834; Samuel Hunter, 1833 (Pickaway County); United States Bank; J. Stone & S. Stone, 1836; -- Boggs & Company; J. L. Taylor, 1836; C. Higgins, 1836; Jesse Stone; J. Turney, 1838; John Haines, 1838; Isaac Borrow, 1838; Unknown; W. Bowles, 1836; S. Hinton, 1835 (Pickaway County); William Reed, 1839 (Pickaway County); William Rolls
*Warrants submitted are less than acreage granted.

S-6116 1000a B:533 X-0841 ROSS:CONC
a. W-5535 Peter Manifold, assignee of Matthew Irvine
b. Peter Manifold
c. None

S-6117 1333a X-533 X-0841 FAYE:WAYN
ROSS: --*
a. W-5535 Peter Manifold, assignee of Matthew Irvine
b. Peter Manifold
c. None
*Source B does not mention Ross County.

S-6118 875a B:534 X-0840 FAYE:WAYN
ROSS: --*
a. W-5537 Peter Manifold, assignee of George Hardy? [Handy?]
b. Peter Manifold
c. Stephen Whitney; Isaac Smith, 1829
*Source B does not mention Ross County.

S-6120 370a C:31 X-0340 FRAN:PLEA
PICK: --*
a. W-5233 John Morris, assignee of Thomas Coverly
b. John Morris
c. Asa Lee, 1829; William Mooberry, 1830
*Source B does not mention Pickaway County.

S-6121 333a C:31 X-0730 LOGA:JEFF
a. W-5234 John Morris, assignee of Peyton Powell
b. John Morris
c. John Bishop, heirs; Z. Brown, 1837; Lyne Starling, 1831

S-6126 1500a B:533 X-0840 FAYE:WAYN
a. W-4583 Peter Manifold, assignee of David Hopkins
b. Peter Manifold
c. None

S-6129 407a C:25 X-1004 DELA:THOM
UNIO: --*
a. W-5425 John Quarles, executor of John Peyton
b. Joseph Tagart, Alexander McLaughlin, Edward Gray, & Robert Taylor
c. John Kerr; Stephen Barnaby, 1827; Wheeler Whitney, 1831; I? [J?] Horr [*also* Hott] heirs; Milo D. Pettibone, 1838
*Source B does not mention Union County.

S-6134 100a C:38 X-0480 DELA:THOM
a. W-5241 Nathan? Walling? [Welling?]*
b. Joseph Tagart, Alexander McLaughlin, Edward Gray, & Robert Taylor
c. Alexander McLaughlin; Thadeus Newcomb, 1826
*Source C entry is mutilated and reading is doubtful.

S-6135 276a C:58 X-1000 PICK:SCIO
a. W-5385 Thomas Taylor, administrator of John McAdams
b. Joseph Tagart, Alexander McLaughlin, Edward Gray, & Robert Taylor
c. None

S-6136 444a C:25 X-1004 DELA:THOM
a. W-5243 Alexander Rose
b. Joseph Tagart, Alexander McLaughlin, Edward Gray, & Robert Taylor
c. None

S-6138 667a C:99 X-0480 DELA:THOM
a. W-5480 Thomas Redley
b. Joseph Tagart, Alexander McLaughlin, Edward Gray, & Robert Taylor
c. Alexander McLaughlin; Pardon Sprague, 1820-1826; Demas Adams, 1831; T. Taggart; Charles Sweetser, 1839; John B. Delsaver

S-6140. *See* S-6063

S-6145 150a C:105 X-0360 PICK:DEER
a. W-5495 Francis Cowherd
b. Jesse McKay
c. None

S-6147 133a C:171 X-0900 PICK:PERR
S-6148
S-7887
a. W-5495 Francis Cowherd, 72a?
W-3531 Richard Tryar? [Fryar?]; Andrew Ellison [assignee?] 60a?
b. Jesse McKay
c. None

S-6149 174a C:149 X-0360 PICK:PERR
a. W-5495 Francis Cowherd
b. Jesse McKay
c. None

S-6151 456a C:150 X-0360 CLAR:PLEA
a. W-1774 Cornet William B. Harrison
b. William B. Harrison
c. William Berry, 1837

S-6152 5a* E:202 X-0660 CLER:MIAM
a. W-4818 William Hubard
b. Green K. Hubbard
c. None
*An entry for 100 acres to the same patentee was crossed out.

S-6154 1700a C:1 X-0750 LOGA:BOAK
X-0110
a. W-5478 Ramon? [Ransom?] Bridges, 200a
W-5387 Margaret Brownley? [Bromley?] widow of Ralph Falkner, 1500a
b. Robert Means
c. None

S-6156 250a C:3 X-0110 UNIO:LEES
a. W-2211 Lieutenant Daniel Bedinger
b. Thomas Worthington
c. J. Brundidge

S-6158 120a C:192 X-1220 ROSS:PAIN
a. W-2019* William Turvey; William George [assignee?] 30a?
W-4866** Thomas Hankens, representative of, 55a?
W-5391 John Slaven, 35a?
b. John McDonald & John Kore
c. None
*Appears to read W-20194 (which does not exist).
**Appears to read W-0866.

S-6159 40a C:192 X-1220 ROSS:PAIN
a. W-5391 John Slaven
b. John Kore
c. None

S-6160 25a C:192 X-1220 ROSS:TWIN
a. W-5391 John Slaven
b. John Kore
c. None

S-6161 823a C:25 X-1005 UNIO:CLAI
a. W-5533 David Hopkins
b. John Cronse? [Crouse?]*
c. None
*Source B spells Crouse.

S-6162 250a C:26 X-1005 DELA:THOM
UNIO: --*
a. W-5533 David Hopkins
b. John Kerr
c. Stephen Barnaby, 1827; Clark H. Dwinnell, 1837; John Hern, heirs; Milo D. Pettibone, 1838
*Source B does not mention Union County.

S-6165 125a C:320 X-0360 ROSS:DEER*
PICK:DEER*
a. W-5543 Christopher Moon, heir to Jacob [Moon]
b. George Hoffman
c. None
*Source B notation: "By Clarksburg."

S-6166 100a C:62 X-0140 PICK:DEER
PICK:PERR
a. W-5543 Christopher Moon, heir to Jacob [Moon]
b. George Hoffman
c. None

S-6167 50a C:60 X-0540 PICK:PERR
a. W-5543 Christopher Moon, heir to Jacob [Moon]
b. George Hoffman
c. None

S-6168 100a C:61 X-0540 PICK:DEER
a. W-5543 Christopher Moon, heir to Jacob [Moon]
b. George Hoffman
c. None

S-6169 107a C:134 X-0780 MADI:UNIO
a. W-5543 Christopher Moon, heir to Jacob [Moon]
b. George Hoffman
c. None

S-6170 100a C:6 X-0340 PICK:DARB
a. W-5321 Thomas M. Bayly, assignee of Smith Milliner, representative of Henry Milliner
b. James Galloway, Junior
c. None

S-6171 50a C:5 X-0180 GREE:ROSS
a. W-1259 Samuel Burch
b. John Campbell
c. None

S-6172 25a C:8 X-0180 GREE:ROSS
a. W-1259 Samuel Burch
b. Reuben McDaniel
c. None

S-6173 150a C:9 X-0180 GREE:ROSS
a. W-5504 John Verell, assignee [of?] John Evans
b. Moses Trader
c. None

S-6174 50a C:14 X-0180 GREE:ROSS
a. W-5504 John Verell, assignee [of?] John Evans
b. James Galloway, Junior
c. None

S-6176 266a C:67 X-1000 PICK:SCIO
a. W-5547 Sarah Gunn, devisee? of James [Gunn]
b. Walter Dun
c. Norris Loyd, 1838

S-6178 1500a C:4 X-0340 FRAN:PLEA
a. W-5161 Peter Manifold, assignee of Matthew Irvine, 1000a
W-5168 Peter Manifold, assignee of Matthew Irvine, 500a
b. John Baird
c. John Andrews; E. Backus, 1834; -- Bragg & -- Jones; Lyne Starling, 1831

S-6179* 1414a E:431 X-1300 HIGH:SALE?
S-13566
S-13583
S-13727
S-14359
a. W-5573 William Cock Holt, heir to James Holt, ?a
W-6539 William Withers, ?a
W-1413 Thomas Coverley, ?a
W-2744 Anthony Singleton, heir, ?a
W-8678** --
b. Cad[wallader?] Wallace
c. None
*Source B shows 40 acres to the Executor of William Robinson; this may be another survey entirely, not listed in Source B.
**Warrant numbers in Source C run to S-6726 only.

S-6183 200a B:535 X-0340 PICK:MUHL
a. W-1203 Captain Beverly Stubblefield
b. Beverly Stubblefield
c. None

S-6186. *See* S-6054

S-6189 750a C:329 X-0130 HIGH:CONC
HIGH:JACK
a. W-5218 Robert D. Fowke, heir at law of John Fowke
b. William Phillips, heirs [of?]
c. William Hager; George Smith, 1836; C. Wallace, by S. Bell, 1831

S-6191 167a C:331 X-0663 HIGH:DODS
a. W-5218 Robert D. Fowke, heir at law of John Fowke
b. William Phillips, heirs [of?]
c. None

S-6192 400a C:277 X-0360 PICK:PERR
a. W-5218 Robert D. Fowke, heir at law of John Fowke
b. William Phillips, heirs [of?]
c. T. J. Timmons, 1831

S-6193 200a C:277 X-0840 FAYE:WAYN
a. W-5218 Robert D. Fowke, heir at law of John Fowke
b. William Phillips, heirs [of?]
c. None

S-6194 180a C:310 X-0663 CLER:BATA
S-7120
S-7121
a. W-5336 William Mosley
b. William Mosley*
c. None
*Source B spells Moseley.

S-6195 2600a C:39 X-0730 CHAM:GOSH
X-1180 CHAM:UNIO
a. W-5499 Thomas Ruffin, deceased, representative of
b. Thomas Ruffin, representative [of?]
c. William Fithian, 1828; William Hunt; Israel Hamilton, 1833; Samuel Jack; J. R. James

S-6196 200a C:46 X-1186 MADI:PIKE
a. W-5499 Thomas Ruffin, deceased, representative of
b. Thomas Ruffin, representative [of?]
c. None

S-6197 592a C:18 X-0340 PICK:DARB
S-6254
a. W-5396 Francis Whiting, 333a
W-5643 Albert Russell, 159a
b. James Russell & Albert Russell
c. G. Botkin, 1836

S-6199 400a C:5 X-0110 UNIO:LEES
X-0480 DELA: --*
a. W-5167 Peter Manifold, assignee of Matthew Irvine, 300a?
W-5467 John Baird, assignee of Robert Gwathmey, assignee of Henry Young, 100a?
b. John Baird
c. None
*Source B does not mention Delaware County.

S-6200 200a C:5 X-0360 MADI:SUMM
a. W-5467 John Baird, assignee of Robert Gwathmey, assignee of Henry Young
b. John Baird
c. None

S-6201 131a C:6 X-1186 MADI:SUMM
a. W-0308 Lieutenant John Crawford
b. John Crawford
c. James Brundage; H. Warner, 1837

S-6202 100a C:6 X-1180 MADI:JEFF
a. W-5393 Samuel Arnold
b. James Galloway
c. None

S-6203 298a C:6 X-0740 CLAR:MADI
a. W-5393 Samuel Arnold, 78a
W-5394 Samuel Arnold, 177a
W-5181 Beetly Barret, 20a
W-5373 Thomas M. Bayly, assignee of Daniel Richardson, representative of Zerubabel Richardson, 23a?
b. James Galloway, Junior
c. None

S-6204 335a C:7 X-0840 MADI:STOK
a. W-5516 Andrew Moore, reso.? to Will. Isa[a]c? Leat? [Leather?] heir
b. James Galloway, Junior
c. None

S-6205 65a C:7 X-0740 CLAR:MADI
a. W-5516 Andrew Moore, reso.? to Will. Isa[a]c Leat? [Leather?] heir
b. James Galloway, Junior
c. None

S-6210 400a C:19 X-0340 PICK:DARB
a. W-5522 Joseph Ladd, assignee of Robert S. Ware, executor of the estate of John Hockaday, deceased
b. James Barnett
c. James Galloway, [Junior?]; G. Botkin, 1835

S-6211 640a C:51 X-0480 UNIO:LEES
a. W-5522 Joseph Ladd, assignee of Robert S. Ware, executor of the estate of John Hockaday, deceased, 540a
W-5546 Benjamin W. Ladd, assignee of William Ladd, who was heir at law to James Ladd, deceased, 100a
b. James Barnett
c. S. G. Strong, 1836; J. G. Carter; John Unglesby; William Unglesby

S-6214 444a C:51 X-0340 FRAN:PRAI
a. W-5509 John Bowen, representative of
b. John Bowen, representative [of?]
c. Cornelius Thomas; C. Higgins, 1834; Christian Deardorf; Jacob Davis; E. Bachus, 1834; John Gardner

S-6215 111a C:20 X-0840 CLIN:RICH
a. W-5509 John Bowen, representative of
b. John Bowen, representative [of?]
c. None

S-6216 100a C:37 X-1000 PICK:JACK
a. W-5582 Margaret Lingo, representative of Jedediah White, deceased
b. Benjamin Hough
c. None

S-6219 311a C:12 X-0800 X-0663 CLER:MONR
a. W-2753 Lewis Thomas
b. Lewis Thomas
c. None

S-6220 9a C:12 X-0663 CLER:BATA
a. W-2753 Lewis Thomas
b. Lewis Thomas
c. None

S-6222 160a D:210 X-0805 CLER:MONR
a. W-5548 Abraham Hite
b. Abraham Hite & James Taylor
c. James Dawson; Z. Chapman, 1826; R. McFarland, 1830; William Lytle; John Hill, 1831

S-6223 620a C:3 X-0340 PICK:JACK
a. W-5158 Anne B. West, representative of Charles [West] who was representative of Thomas [West]
b. Ann B. West
c. None

S-6224 750a C:67 X-0540 PICK:DEER PICK:PERR
a. W-5158 Anne B. West, representative of Charles [West] who was representative of Thomas [West]
b. Ann B. West
c. John Derorse*; Walter Thrall, 1831
*So spelled.

S-6225 1300a C:3 X-0340 PICK:DARB
a. W-5158 Anne B. West, representative of Charles [West] who was representative of Thomas [West]
b. Ann B. West
c. Thomas Reynolds; James Burgit; James? [Joseph?] Morris

S-6226 980a C:3 X-0540 PICK:PERR
a. W-5158 Anne B. West, representative of Charles [West] who was representative of Thomas [West]
b. Ann B. West
c. None

S-6227 150a C:68 X-0360 PICK:DEER
a. W-5158 Anne B. West, representative of Charles [West] who was representative of Thomas [West]
b. Ann B. West
c. None

S-6228 500a C:123 X-1000 UNIO:CLAI
a. W-5532 David Hopkins
b. John Evans & Edward Owens*
c. Unknown; Aurora Buttles? [Buttler?] 1823; J. Evans; Ruth Wetsell
*Source B spells Owings.

S-6230 100a C:30 X-1000 ROSS:UNIO
a. W-2954 Saban? [Laban?] Ship, assignee of Maximilian Robinson
b. Edward Tiffin
c. None

S-6232 400a C:22 X-0830 LOGA:PERR UNIO: --*
a. W-5264 Tuttle Hudson and? Co[mpany?] administrators of William Hudson, deceased
b. Tuttle Hudson
c. C. Grubbs
*Source B does not mention Union County.

S-6233 100a C:22 X-1180 MADI:PIKE UNIO:UNIO
a. W-5264 Tuttle Hudson and? Co[mpany?] administrators of William Hudson, deceased
b. Tuttle Hudson
c. M. L. Sullivant

S-6235 93a C:31 X-0300 PIKE:PEEP
a. W-5547 Sarah Gunn, devisee? of James [Gunn]
b. Walter Dun
c. None

S-6238 1000a C:61 X-0620 CHAM:WAYN
a. W-5523 Joseph Ladd, assignee of Robert S. Ware, executor of John Hockaday, deceased
b. George Hoffman
c. P. L? [S?] Osborn & D. Osborn

S-6240 400a C:322 -- CHAM:GOSH
a. W-5534 Peter Manifold, assignee of Laurence Manning, administrator of Laurence [Manning] deceased
b. George Hofman
c. E. B. Soller, 1831

S-6242 200a C:322 X-0730 CLAR:PLEA CHAM: --*
a. W-5534 Peter Manifold, assignee of Laurence Manning, administrator of Laurence [Manning] deceased
b. George Hoffman
c. None
*Source B does not mention Champaign County.

S-6243 104a C:61 X-0360 MADI:DEER
a. W-5534 Peter Manifold, assignee of Laurence Manning, administrator of Laurence [Manning] deceased
b. George Hoffman
c. A. Toland, 1826

S-6244 130a C:221 X-0360 MADI:SUMM
a. W-5521 Joseph Ladd, assignee of Robert S. Ware, executor of John Hockaday, deceased
b. George Hoffman
c. None

S-6245 500a C:62 X-0360 MADI:UNIO
a. W-5521 Joseph Ladd, assignee of Robert S. Ware, executor of John Hockaday, deceased
b. George Hoffman
c. A. Toland, 1826

S-6246 300a C:62 X-0360 MADI:UNIO
a. W-5521 Joseph Ladd, assignee of Robert S. Ware, executor of John Hockaday, deceased
b. George Hoffman
c. None

S-6247 400a C:62 X-0780 MADI:UNIO
a. W-5520 Joseph Ladd, assignee of Robert S. Ware, executor of John Hockaday, deceased
b. George Hoffman
c. H. Brush; Samuel Brush, 1837; W. Rowe, 1841

S-6248 200a C:62 X-0360 MADI:UNIO
a. W-5520 Joseph Ladd, assignee of Robert S. Ware, executor of John Hockaday, deceased
b. George Hoffman
c. None

S-6249 300a C:134 X-0780 MADI:UNIO
a. W-5520 Joseph Ladd, assignee of Robert S. Ware, executor of John Hockaday, deceased
b. George Hoffman
c. None

S-6251 407a C:31 X-0750 LOGA:BOAK
a. W-5528 William Evans
b. William Evans
c. Lanson? [Sanson?] Curtis, 1828

S-6252 400a C:10 X-0840 MADI:STOK
a. W-5164 Peter Manifold, assignee of Matthew Irvine, 300a?
W-5200 Thomas M. Bayly, assignee of Samuel Russell, 100a?
b. William H. Puthuff & Elias Langham
c. None

S-6253 333a C:67 X-0340 PICK:DARB
a. W-5506 Thomas Lipscomb
b. John Graham
c. None

S-6254. *See* S-6197

S-6256 300a C:22 X-0640 CLIN:WAYN
a. W-0243 Lieutenant William Gray
b. William Gray
c. None

S-6258 797a C:187 X-0540 PICK:PERR
S-6477
S-7306
S-8025
a. W-5968 William Poyner, 67a?
W-5940 George Mallow, 200a?
W-5542 Christopher Moon, son & heir to Jacob [Moon] 130a?
W-5949 William Pullen, 300a?
W-5532 David Hopkins, 100a?
b. John Evans & Edward Owings
c. None

S-6260* 100a -- -- MADI:PLEA
a. --
b. John Bryant
c. C. Bryant; M. L. Sullivant, 1831
*Entry in Source B only (at sequential place).

S-6260 550a E:77 X-0365 MADI:PLEA
a. W-5134 Richard Apperson, 100a?
W-1606 John Woodford, heir to General -- Woodward, 450a?
b. -- Apperson & -- Woolford*
c. None
*Source B spells Woodford.

S-6260 720a E:78 X-0365 MADI:PLEA
a. W-5134 Richard Apperson, 520a?
W-5016 George Guthry, representative of, 200a?
b. -- Apperson & -- Guthery* representatives [of?]
c. George Guthrie; M. L. Sullivant, 1831
*Source B spells Guthrie.

S-6263 190a C:278 X-0840 ROSS:TWIN
a. W-5525 James Dowden, 100a
W-5597 Thomas Howell, heir to Robert [Howell] deceased, 90a
b. George Clark
c. None

S-6265 600a C:295 X-0360 MADI:STOK
S-8119 MADI:UNIO
S-8174
a. W-5494 Francis Cowherd, 300a
W-6129 Harad Gibbs, 300a
b. W. Baffenbaugh; George Senson? [Lenson?] 1826

S-6267 222a C:82 X-0360 MADI:RANG
a. W-5494 Francis Cowherd
b. Jesse Dungan
c. None

S-6268 200a C:86 X-0360 MADI:STOK
a. W-5494 Francis Cowherd
b. Elisha Scott
c. None

S-6274 200a D:109 X-0540 PICK:PERR
a. W-5553 John Wright, representative of
b. Joseph Ladd
c. None

S-6276 667a C:21 X-0130 ADAM:FRAN
a. W-3529 William Finnie? [Finne?]
b. Daniel Stull
c. J. Crisman, 1828; E. Taylor; J. Horn, 1828

S-6277 88a C:29 X-0840 HIGH:LIBE
a. W-1133 Isaac Halfpenny; James Robinson [assignee?]
b. Daniel Stull*
c. James Swearingen, 1829; Daniel Still*
*So spelled.

S-6281 1440a C:126 X-0640 FAYE:CONC
S-6332
a. W-5349 John Nicholas
b. John Nichols*
c. Henry Phelps, 1829; Benjamin Clark; George W. Cook, 1829; Ed[ward] Davis; I? [J?] Jameson [*also* Jamison] 1836; Nicholas Newland; Gilbert Yeoman? [Leoman?]; D. McLain, 1840; Josiah Hilliard, assignee of -- Phelps, November 1832; "Deeded G. W. Cook, 13 Nov 1832"
*Source B spells Nicholas.

S-6282 444a C:106 X-0360 PICK:MONR
a. W-5529 Nathan Reid
b. Nathaniel Reid
c. None

S-6285 905a E:214 X-0810 MADI:FAIR
S-13258 FRAN: --*
a. W-5549 Benjamin Green, ?a
W-6331? John Sturdivant, by the administrator, John Manlove, ?a
W-6647 William Christian, ?a
b. Allen Latham
c. None
*Source B does not mention Franklin County.

S-6286 643a D:453 X-0360 MADI:FAIR
a. W-5549 Benjamin Green
b. Cadwallader Wallace
c. None

S-6287 1000a C:79 X-0360 PICK:DARB
X-0340
a. W-5549 Benjamin Green
b. Berryman Green
c. Hector McNiel; Henry Rudy, 1837

S-6288 727a C:148 X-0360 MADI:SUMM*
a. W-5134 Richard Apperson
b. Richard Apperson
c. Jacob Fowler, 1828
*Source B notation: "Somerford."

S-6289 100a C:37 X-1000 PICK:WAYN
a. W-5584 William R. Finney, heir to John [Finney] deceased
b. Richard R. Finney*
c. Andrew Nichols, heirs [of?]; Robert Campbell, 1828
*Source B says William R. Finney.

S-6290 100a C:372 X-0360 MADI:RANG
a. W-5333 Jacob Poe, assignee of William Kerner
b. Andrew Poe
c. W. Hall, 1823

S-6291 150a C:153 X-0840* HIGH:PAIN
S-6867
a. W-5583 Robert Broadwater, heir to Caleb [Broadwater] deceased, 100a
W-5801 John Norvell, deceased, 50a
b. [Robert] Broadwater & [Jesse] Millikan
c. None
*"Rk. fork of . . ."

S-6292 78a C:273 X-0840 ROSS:TWIN
a. W-5542 Christopher Moon, son & heir to Jacob [Moon]
b. John Evans
c. None

S-6293 1267a C:14 X-0480 UNIO:CLAI
DELA:THOM
a. W-5135 James Claiborne, Robert Claiborne, Sterling Claiborne, & Lucy Claiborne (Wright, late Livey?) who . . . ? heirs of Buller Claiborne, deceased
b. Buller* Claiborne, heirs of
c. Sarah Lindsey; A. Hall, 1836; H. Ayres; C. Morse; David Garland, Junior; David Gregory, 1831; Lucy Wright (Delaware County); John Evans, 1831 (Delaware County)
*Source B spells Butler.

S-6295 120a C:13 X-0340 UNIO:ALLE
a. W-5586 Zadock Bailey, 60a
W-5590 James Crapper? [Cropper?] 60a
b. [Zadock] Bailey & [James] Cropper
c. None

S-6296 348a C:13 X-0840 FAYE:GREE
a. W-5599 William Croghan, 148a?
W-5589 Agnes Lingo, representative of Thomas Lingo, 100a?
W-5591 Anthony Matthew, representative of Thomas Bennett, 100a?
b. [William] Croghan, -- Lingo, & [Anthony] Mathews
c. Henry Phelps, 1829

S-6297 592a C:13 X-0340 MADI:FAIR FRAN:PLEA
a. W-5599 William Croghan
b. William Croughan*
c. Peter Hoover, 1828; D. Adams, 1830; C. Higgins, 1835; W. Crawford; R. Douglas, 1837; Unknown; A. Douglas, 1838
*Source B spells Croghan.

S-6298 309a C:13 X-0840 CLIN:RICH CLIN:WAYN
a. W-5578 Benjamin Leach, heir to William [Leach] deceased; Andrew Ellison [assignee?] 200a?
W-5589 Agnes Lingo, representative of Thomas Lingo, 109a?
b. -- Bagwell & -- Lingo
c. James Brown (Kentucky); J. Woodruff, 1833; C. B. Harlan, 1830; R. B. Harlan, 1833; J. B. Posey, 1835; A. S. Strickle, 1838; J. K. Brown

S-6299 461a C:16 X-1180 MADI:JEFF
a. W-5588 Jesse Gladden, representative of John Delastation? [Delastatious?] 261a
W-5580 John Tappins? [Toppins?]; Thomas James [assignee?] 200a
b. Jesse Gladden & -- Bailey
c. None

S-6300 312a C:16 X-1180 MADI:JEFF
a. W-5515 Joseph Ladd, assignee of William Phillips; James Barnett [assignee?] 200a?
W-5546* Benjamin W. Ladd, assignee of William Ladd, who was heir at law to James Ladd, deceased, ?a
W-5589 Agnes Lingo, representative of Thomas Lingo, 112a?
b. -- Galloway & -- Lingo
c. I? [J?] Powers; H. McMillan, 1842
*Warrant already entirely used on S-6211.

S-6301 400a C:40 X-0480 UNIO:YORK
a. W-5499 Thomas Ruffin, deceased, representative of
b. Thomas Ruffin, representative [of?]
c. None

S-6302. *See* S-6029

S-6304 100a C:16 X-0730 CLAR*:PLEA
a. W-5488 Benjamin W. Ladd, assignee of the heirs of Berskin? Shearman & John W. Shearman
b. Joseph Ladd
c. None
*Source B says Clark County.

S-6305 600a C:60 X-0340 MADI:FAIR FRAN:PLEA
a. W-5552 Richard C[lough] Anderson
b. Richard C[lough] Anderson
c. None

S-6306 133a C:59 X-1180 MADI:JEFF
a. W-5552 Richard C[lough] Anderson
b. Richard C[lough] Anderson
c. William Myres; James Taylor, 1829

S-6307 1200a C:41 X-0480 UNIO:CLAI
a. W-5659 William Pelham
b. William Pelham
c. None

S-6307 1200a C:41 X-0480 UNIO:CLAI*
a. W-5660 William Pelham
b. William Pelham
c. Increase Mather; S. G. Strong, 1836; A. Hodge; William Surplus? [Surplen?]; H. Swartz
*Source B notation: "Richland."

S-6307 380a C:41 X-1000 UNIO:CLAI
a. W-5662 William Pelham
b. William Pelham
c. None

S-6307* 1200a C:41 X-1000 UNIO: --
a. W-5661 William Pelham; James Galloway [assignee?]
b. William Pelham
c. --
*Source B does not list this entry; possibly Source A is in error.

S-6308 280a C:4 X-0480 DELA:THOM UNIO: --*
a. W-5663 William Pelham
b. William Pelham
c. Jesse Miller; Jacob Swartz, 1831
*Source B does not mention Union County.

S-6309 640a C:4 X-0340 FRAN:PLEA
S-6582
a. W-5663 William Pelham
b. William Pelham
c. James Bryden; Isaac Helmick, 1833; Hiram Lakins

S-6310 280a C:41 X-1000 UNIO:JERO
a. W-5663 William Pelham
b. William Pelham
c. Eli Fox; S. G. Strong, 1827

S-6312 300a C:12 X-1180 UNIO:UNIO MADI: --*
a. W-5134 Richard Apperson
b. Richard Apperson
c. None
*Source B does not mention Madison County.

S-6313 227a D:146 X-1005 HARD*:TAYL
a. W-5134 Richard Apperson
b. Richard Apperson
c. Robert Pollock; Edward Mead, 1831
*Source B mentions Logan County, but corrects to Hardin.

S-6315 120a D:138 X-1005 HARD:TAYL
a. W-0635 Captain Archibald Denholm
b. John Harvey
c. C. Wallace; M. Bonner, 1838; Craud.? Wallace, 1840; Mathew Bonner, 1831 (Logan County)

S-6316 354a X:12 X-1180 UNIO:UNIO
a. W-5134 Richard Apperson, 200a?
W-1203 Captain Beverly Stubblefield, 154a?
b. [Richard] Apperson & [Beverly] Stubblefield
c. G. Weaver

S-6317 287a C:19 X-0360 MADI:DEER
a. W-1203 Captain Beverly Stubblefield
b. Beverly Stubblefield
c. T. Shields; J. Moore, 1824

S-6320 180a C:15 X-1180* MADI:MONR MADI:PIKE
a. W-5378 Thomas M. Bayly, assignee of Rachel Richards, representative of Preston Richards
b. James Galloway, Junior
c. J. Falless; R. Douglas, 1825; Alexander Ross; H. Warner, 1834
*"Sp. fork of . . ."

S-6321 658a C:14 X-1170 CLIN:MARI
a. W-5319 Edward Martin, representative of James Martin, 100a
W-5374 John Taylor, representative of George Filby? dec[ease]d, 60a
W-5381 Jabez? Cheshire, representative of John Cheshire, 261a
W-5378 Rachel Richards, representative of Preston Richards, 81a
W-5186 John Bryan? [Bigan?] 81a
W-5287* Thomas Evans, representative of Thomas Evans, ?a; *all warrants to* Thomas M. Bayly
b. James Galloway, Junior
c. None
*This warrant entirely used in S-5714.

S-6322. *See* S-5648

S-6323 52a C:29 X-0780 MADI:UNIO
a. W-5495 Francis Cowherd
b. Jesse McKay
c. None

S-6324 146a C:29 X-0780 MADI:UNIO
a. W-5495 Francis Cowherd
b. Jesse McKay
c. J. Humbert; W. Warner, 1824

S-6328 410a C:19 X-1170 WARR:SALE
a. W-5516 Andrew Moore, reso[lution?] to Will. Isa[a]c? Leat [,] heir [or Leather?] ?a
W-5370 Thomas M. Bayly, assignee of John Warrington; Thomas Scott [assignee?] 261a?
W-5591 Anthony Matthew, representative of Thomas Bennett, 61a?
b. James Galloway, Junior, & Anthony Mathews
c. None

S-6332. *See* S-6281

S-6337 175a C:202 X-0841* FAYE:MADI
a. W-5676 Joseph Woodson, 100a
W-5636 James Barnett, 75a
b. Duncan McArthur
c. None
*"Branch of . . ."

S-6338. *See* S-5782

S-6339 90a C:124 X-0841* FAYE:WAYN
a. W-5678 Joseph Woodson
b. Duncan McArthur
c. None
*"Waters of . . ."

S-6342 130a C:203 X-0841 FAYE:UNIO
a. W-5681 Joseph Woodson, 100a
W-5677 Joseph Woodson, 20a?
W-5678 Joseph Woodson, 10a
b. Duncan McArthur
c. None

S-6343 100a C:520 X-0841 FAYE:MADI
a. W-0874 Carter Hanney
b. Thomas McDonald
c. None

S-6345* 1233a -- -- --
a. --
b. Benjamin W. Ladd
c. --
*Entry in Source B only (at sequential place) but is crossed out and has "WD" [withdrawn?] notation in margin.

S-6347 480a C:24 X-0840 MADI:STOK
a. W-5716 William Hibson, *et al*, heirs of Nicholas [Hibson]
b. Nicholas Hobson, heirs [of?]
c. W. Buffenbergh; George Lenson, 1826

S-6348 630a C:24 X-0360 MADI:SUMM CLAR:PLEA CHAM: --*
a. W-5715 William Hibson, *et al*, heirs of Nicholas [Hibson]
b. Nicholas Hobson, heirs [of?]
c. A. Williams; J. Gallispie, 1826; T. Gillespie; J. S. Halsey, 1836 (Clark County)
*Source B does not mention Champaign County.

S-6349 2000a C:267 X-0730 CHAM:GOSH X-0340 CLAR:PLEA
a. W-5713 William Hibson, *et al*, heirs of Nicholas [Hibson] 1000a
W-5714 William Hibson, *et al*, heirs of Nicholas [Hibson] 1000a
b. Nicholas Hobson, heirs [of?]
c. James S. Duval; Ira Paige, 1833

S-6350 450a C:25 X-0360 MADI:SUMM
X-0340
a. W-5716 William Hibson, *et al*, heirs of Nicholas [Hibson]
b. Nicholas Hobson, heirs [of?]
c. None

S-6353 160a C:339 X-0360 PICK:DEER
a. W-5598 Archelaus Mitchell; John Evans [assignee?]
b. Michael Conn
c. None

S-6358 200a C:81 X-0150* PICK:DARB
S-6952
a. W-5564 Willis Wilson
b. Willis Wilson
c. David Henderson; Alexander McKinley, 1826; R. Seymour, 1831
*Listed only as Buckskin Run; may not be the same as stream coded.

S-6365 514a C:124 X-0970* FAYE:WAYN
a. W-5679 Joseph Woodson, 100a
W-5680 Joseph Woodson, 100a
W-5338 Matthew Clay, 314a
b. Duncan McArthur
c. William Stockdale; D[uncan] McArthur
*Listed only as Ridge Run; may not be the same as stream coded.

S-6366 1067a C:56 X-1000 FRAN:WASH
FRAN:NORW
a. W-5550 John Meanly
b. Peter Pelham
c. R. Closson; C. Higgins, 1837; J. Febril? [Ferril?]; John B. Pelham; J. Galloway, 1836

S-6367 100a C:46 X-0180 GREE:ROSS
a. W-5665 Joseph Woodson
b. Peter Pelham
c. None

S-6376* 75a C:86 X-1000 PICK:JACK
a. W-5519 Thomas Harris
b. Asahel Renick
c. None
*Source B says "not patented."

S-6377 700a C:79 X-0843 FAYE:UNIO
FAYE:PAIN
a. W-5549 Berryman Green
b. Berryman Green
c. None

S-6379 100a C:171 X-0360 PICK:DEER
a. W-5549 Berryman Green
b. Berryman Green
c. None

S-6380 111a C:81 X-0366 FAYE:MADI
a. W-5529 Nathan Reid
b. Nathan Reid
c. Zach[ariah?] Galespie; Solomon Soward, 1823

S-6380 114a C:81 X-0360 FAYE:MADI
a. W-5564 Willis Wilson
b. Willis Wilson
c. John Level, 1824

S-6382 100a C:518 X-0840 FAYE:PAIN
a. W-5701 Joseph Woodson, 50a
W-5702 Joseph Woodson, 50a
b. Thomas McDonald
c. None

S-6383 195a C:203 X-0843 MADI*:RANG
a. W-5554 William Bryant
b. Singleton Foster
c. James Woods, 1828; S. Foster; Arch[ibald] Stewart, 1834
*Source B also mentions Fayette County, but apparently erroneously.

S-6384 750a C:223 X-0360 MADI:UNIO
a. W-5497 Sally Jordan, representative of Arthur Smith; John F. Price [assignee?]
b. Peter Pelham
c. None

S-6384 750a C:223 X-0360 CLAR:HARM
MADI: --*
a. W-5497 Sally Jordan, representative of Arthur Smith; John F. Price [assignee?]
b. Peter Pelham
c. None
*Source B does not mention Madison County.

S-6385 400a C:306 X-0665 CLAR:HARM
a. W-5669 Joseph Woodson, 100a
W-5670 Joseph Woodson, 100a
W-5671 Joseph Woodson, 100a
W-5672 Joseph Woodson, 100a
b. John Emmitt*
c. None
*Source B spells Emmett.

S-6386 100a C:306 X-0841 MADI:RANG
a. W-5686 Joseph Woodson
b. William Robinson
c. None

S-6388 480a C:116 X-0843* FAYE:PAIN
S-7053
a. W-5720 William Price; Angus Lewis Langham [assignee?] 330a
W-5687 Joseph Woodson, 150a
b. William Robinson
c. None
*"Big Run branch of . . ."

S-6390 340a C:304 X-0301 ROSS:HUNT
S-8981 PIKE:PEBB*
a. W-5615 Nathaniel G. Morris; Angus Lewis Langham [assignee?] 100a
W-6122 Thomas Hopper, 200a?
W-2945** Isaac Rose, with -- McIlhany,40a?
b. William Robinson
c. Jacob Shepherd; G. Porter, 1831; P. Spurck, 1833
*Source A does not mention Pike County.
**Warrent entirely used in S-1497.

S-6391 1600a C:391 X-0841 MADI:RANG
S-7894
S-9651
S-9697
a. W-5723 William Price; Angus Lewis Langham [assignee?] 200a
W-5638 James Barnett; Angus Lewis Langham [assignee?] 444a
W-5877 William Triplett; Benjamin W. Ladd, Joseph Ladd, Thomas Norvell [assignees?] 167a?
W-5631 Nathaniel G. Morris; George Renick, -- Ladd & -- Ladd, -- Norvell [assignees?] 100a?
W-5621 Nathaniel G. Morris; Angus Lewis Langham [assignee?] 200a
W-5828 William Cunningham, heirs and . . .?; Joseph Ladd, Benjamin W. Ladd, & Thomas Norvell [assignees?] 100a?
W-5825 Richard Foster, heir to, 167a?
W-5619 Nathaniel G. Morris, 100a
W-5978 John E. Scott, representative of; James Dunlap, Elias Langham, Nathan Wood, -- Fulton [assignees?] 122a?
b. Wallace Dunlap
c. None

S-6392 100a C:83 X-0120 MADI:RANG
a. W-5596 Thomas Hill, heir of Samuel [Hill]
b. Daniel Gambriel*
c. None
*Source B spells Gambril.

S-6401 1056a C:27 X-0840* HIGH:LIBE HIGH:JACK
a. W-5641 Robert Beall, representative of
b. Henry Massie
c. None
*"Rk. fork of . . ."

S-6404 667a C:257 X-0841 ROSS:UNIO
a. W-2024 Captain James Craig
b. James Craig
c. William Cary; P. Douglas, 1836

S-6405 61a* E:231 X-0841 ROSS:CONC
a. W-0230 John Mills, 30a
W-0231 John Mills, 31a
b. Benjamin Goodin
c. Robert Stewart, 1827; W. J. Hewitt; N. Massie, 1839; W. Hewitt, Junior; T. Goldsberry, 1841
*Source B says 150a.

S-6406 566a C:28 X-0840* HIGH:LIBE
a. W-5500 John Smith Sneed, heir to Thomas Sneed, deceased
b. John S. Snead
c. None
*"Rk. fork of . . ."

S-6407 650a C:27 X-0840* HIGH:JACK
a. W-0307 Captain John Clarke, 350a?
W-5606 William Aylett & Phillip Aylett, 300a?
b. John Clarke & George Clarke
c. John Morrow, 1831
*"Rk. fork of . . ."

S-6408 113a C:28 X-0840 ROSS:HUNT
a. W-5092 Adam Jones, representative of, 100a
W-3724 William Pope, 13a
b. Henry Massie
c. None

S-6409 100a C:173 X-0840 ROSS:HUNT ROSS:TWIN
a. W-5989 John Yancey; Henry Massie, Nathan Beeves, Benj[amin] Bowman, & Christian Ma---? [assignees?]
b. Henry Massie
c. None

S-6410 100a C:173 X-0840 ROSS:TWIN
a. W-5989 John Yancey; Henry Massie, Nathan Beeves, Benj[amin] Bowman, & Christian Ma---? [assignees?]
b. Henry Massie
c. None

S-6414 267a C:66 X-1000 PICK:SCIO
a. W-5500 John Smith Sneed, heir to Thomas Sneed, deceased
b. John S. Snead
c. P. N. White, 1838

S-6415* 106a C:58 X-1000 PICK:SCIO
a. W-4573 Benjamin Wood, representative of
b. Francis Ayers
c. Morris Howe, 1827
*Source B say "not patented."

S-6416 110a C:58 X-1000 PICK:SCIO
a. W-0153 Captain John Overton
b. John Overton
c. None

S-6420 437a C:49 X-1000 UNIO:JERO
a. W-3363 Henry Hendley; John Rogers [assignee?] 200a
W-4362 Mallory Adams; John Rogers [assignee?] 100a
W-4576 John Hurt; Thomas Banks [assignee?] 37a?
W-4307 Daniel Gilder; John Rogers [assignee?] 100a
b. William Barlow
c. Unknown; William Barksdale; John Vastine [*also* Vastein] 1827; Thomas Robinson, 1830; J. Bigelow; John Carter

S-6422 300a -- -- FAYE: --
a. --
b. John Nicholas
c. John Cohorn? [Chorn?]; James M. Davis, 1824

S-6423 325a D:71 X-0845 FAYE:WAYN
a. W-2024 Captain James Craig
b. James Craig
c. Richard Douglas, 1829; J. Y. Green, 1831; "deeded R. Douglas, 26 Apr 1833"

S-6431 500a C:30 X-0540 PICK:PERR
a. W-5624 Nathaniel G. Morris, 200a
W-5628 Nathaniel G. Morris, 200a
W-5601 Isham White, 100a
b. William Rector
c. William Henry, 1827; W. R. Rodman; Isaac Davis, 1840

S-6432 3200a C:32 X-0360 MADI:RANG
a. W-5630 Nathaniel G. Morris, 500a
W-5632 Nathaniel G. Morris, 500a
W-5635 James Barnett, 1000a
W-5636 James Barnett, 200a?
W-5637 James Barnett, 1000a?
b. Benjamin W. Ladd
c. -- Bond & -- Ray, 1823

S-6434 100a C:278 X-0810 PICK:DARB
a. W-5636 James Barnett
b. Duncan McArthur
c. None

S-6436 221a C:37 X-1000 PICK:JACK
a. W-5634 Nathaniel Morris
b. Benjamin Hough
c. None

S-6437 222a D:4 X-1000 HARD:HALE
a. W-5742 Marks Vandawall, representative
b. Mark Vandawall, representative
c. Lyne Starling, 1831 (Logan County)

S-6440 1333a C:95 X-0840 FAYE:CONC CLIN:RICH CLIN:WAYN
a. W-5545 John Moss
b. John Moss
c. Edward Drumgole [*also* Doramgole; Drumgoole]; James Brooks, 1829; C. B. Harlan, 1830 (Clinton County); J. Hadley, Junior, 1840 (Clinton County)

S-6441 233a C:45 X-0340 FRAN:PLEA
a. W-5644 John Galloway
b. John Galloway
c. None

S-6442 300a C:44 X-1180 CHAM:GOSH
a. W-5644 John Galloway
b. John Galloway
c. None

S-6444* 943a C:44 X-1180 CHAM:GOSH
a. W-5644 John Galloway
b. John Galloway
c. William Vance, 1828
*Entry at S-6451 in Source B.

S-6446. *See* S-5197

S-6447 200a C:42 X-0730 LOGA:JEFF
a. W-5664 Joseph Woodson, 100a
W-5683 Joseph Woodson, 100a
b. William Thorn
c. None

S-6448 817a C:42 X-1180 CHAM:GOSH
a. W-5540 Christopher Moon, son & heir of Jacob [Moon] 667a
W-5684 Joseph Woodson, 150a
b. William Thorn
c. None

S-6449 400a C:44 X-0730 LOGA:JEFF
a. W-5644 John Galloway
b. John Galloway
c. None

S-6450 340a C:45 X-0730 LOGA:JEFF
a. W-5644 John Galloway
b. John Galloway
c. Unknown

S-6451. *See* S-6444

S-6452 594a C:99 X-0841 ROSS:CONC FAYE:WAYN
a. W-5622 Nathaniel G. Morris, 200a
W-5629 Nathaniel G. Morris, 200a
W-5573 William Cocke Holt, heir . . .? to James Holt, 194a?
b. William Robinson
c. Moses Williams; David Hays, 1834

S-6453 500a C:83 X-1000 PICK:SCIO
a. W-5545 John Moss
b. John Moss
c. None

S-6454 500a C:83 X-0840 ROSS:PAIN
a. W-5545 John Moss
b. John Moss
c. None

S-6460. *See* S-3118

APPENDIX

Other Primary Source Materials of Value to Genealogical Researchers

I. Manuscripts in the Illinois Historical Survey Collections, University of Illinois Library at Urbana-Champaign, Urbana, Illinois 61801.

Genealogical researchers should keep in mind that, in addition to the 28 registers listed hereinafter, there are 169 folders, containing an estimated 10,000 items, in this collection. The typed inventory runs to 536 pages in length, obviously making it too long for reproduction here. The 28 bound volumes, all original records of the Virginia Military District of Ohio land office, consist of:

1. *Surveying accounts with index, 1796-1811.* Colonel Richard C. Anderson. Leather-bound account book, 10" x 17"; 271 pages with index.

2. *Surveying accounts with index, 1811-1826.* Colonel Richard C. Anderson. Leather-bound account book, 10" x 17"; 310 double pages with index.

3. *Lands delinquent for taxes: List of proprietors in the Virginia Military District, 1804-1811, and list of lands twice returned delinquent for taxes, 1811-1812.* On the reverse: *Ledger of surveying fees, 1829-1840.* Allen Latham. Volume 10¼" x 6½"; 245 double pages.

4. *List of surveys arranged alphabetically by owner.* Allen Latham. Leather-bound volume, 6½" x 16".

5. *Cash account book, 1784-1799.* Colonel Richard C. Anderson.

Leather-bound volume 9½" x 15¼"; 181 double pages. [Index by Clifford Neal Smith published in the *National Genealogical Society Quarterly*, vol. 61, no. 1, pp. 16-27.]

6. *List of persons making entries in the Virginia Military District, entries [surveys] 102-15763, arranged numerically.* Colonel Richard C. Anderson, continuing into Allen Latham's administration. Backbone stamped "Record Book". Leather-bound volume, 10¼" x 15¼". [This volume is the primary source summarized in volume 4 of the *Federal Land Series*.]

7. *Survey record book: Description of survey with maps, 1815-1822.* In reverse: *Entries, memoranda of land surveyed, list of taxable lands, etc., 1818-1824.* Colonel Richard C. Anderson. Leather-bound volume.

8. *Index of surveys in Ohio.* Leather-bound volume.

9. *[Bounty-land warrants] 1-3115, with names of persons, number of acres granted, to whom transferred, etc.* Richard C. Anderson and Allen Latham. Leather-bound notebook, 4½" x 7½". [This notebook has been used in volume 4 of the *Federal Land Series*.]

10. *[Bounty-land warrants] 1849-1939, 3116-6729, with names of persons, number of acres granted, to whom transferred, etc.* Richard C. Anderson and Allen Latham. Leather-bound notebook, 4½" x 7½". [This notebook has also been used in volume 4 of the *Federal Land Series*.]

11. *Benjamin Hough's Book, 1800-1812.* Cardboard-bound volume. [A statement of the U.S. Military District, as divided into quarter townships, with the contents of each, showing also those quarter-townships settled, by whom, and those remaining unlocated, 31 March 1804. Also a list of lands located for the refugees from Canada and Nova Scotia by Act of Congress, 1 February

1801. This volume does not belong in the Anderson Collection, as it pertains to the U.S. Military District of Ohio, rather than to the Virginia Military District of Ohio. It has been used extensively in volume 2 of the *Federal Land Series*.]

12. *Alphabetical index of Virginia officers and men entitled to Virginia bounty-land grants: Names beginning with A and B only.* Colonel Richard C. Anderson.

13. *List of non-residents' lands entered by the auditor [for the] territorial tax of 1802.* John Carlyle, collector of the Virginia Army lands.

14. *Cash book, 1853-1854.* Cardboard-bound volume.

15. *Letter-book of John R. Anderson, Chillicothe, 1851-1852.* Cloth-bound journal.

16. *Copies of entries, Virginia District B, 1787-1814: Entries 386-7896, with original proprietor, acreages, warrant [survey number], watercourses, and other data.* Leather-bound volume, 19" x 12".

17. *Ohio surveys, 1818-1821.* A. C. Looker. Field notebook, 4" x 6½".

18. *Ohio surveys, 1817-1819.* Allen Latham? Field notebook, 4" x 6½".

19. *Ross County, Ohio: Entries by post office.* Allen Latham? Miscellaneous notebook, many pages blank. [Pasted inside front and back covers are printed lists of names, dated 8 August 1838.]

20. *Entries by name and place.* Allen Latham. Several field notebooks hinged together; 4" x 6½".

21. *Number 1 [quality] Ohio lands registered for sale at Allen Latham's office . . . Chillicothe.* Printed list, 1822?. Notebook.

22. *Field notebook, 1817-1818.* Allen Latham.

23. *Entries for various land parcels, 1801-1840: By name, with many notes on persons and transfers of title; indexed.* Allen Latham. Pocket notebook.

24. *Entry book: township 10, range S, [dated] 1805.* Allen Latham. Notebook; 4" x 8".

25. *Entry book: township 9, range S, [dated] 1805.* Allen Latham. Notebook; 4" x 8".

26. *List of land entries by township.* Allen Latham. Notebook; 4" x 8".

27. *Account book, 9 June 1819.* John M. Moore, Clerk, General Land Office, Washington [D.C.]. No cover; 4" x 7".

28. *A. Latham Library: Listed under general subject areas.* Allen Latham. Notebook; 63 numbered pages, many blank; 10¼" x 8¼".

II. Manuscripts in the office of the Auditor of State, Ohio State Land Office, 88 East Broad Street, Columbus, Ohio 43215.

Materials in the Ohio State Land Office are of three kinds: original manuscripts, secondary card files and indexes, and microfilms. The most important items pertaining to the Virginia Military District of Ohio are as follows:

1. *Entry books.* Contain dates of entry, entry numbers, names of entrymen (or their assignees), number of acres entered, military [bounty-land] warrant numbers used, brief general description of the land claimed.

2. *Survey books.* Contain survey numbers, plats of surveys, for whom surveyed (including their assignees), number of acres in the

surveys, military [bounty-land] warrant numbers used, metes-and-bounds descriptions of the surveyed lands, names of chainmen, markermen, and deputy surveyors, dates of surveys, dates recorded.

3. *Source volumes (both Ohio and Kentucky): [Bounty-land] warrants 13 to 8956.* Give warrant numbers, names of warrantees, the surveys for which the warrants were used, names of warrantees and their assignees.

4. *Card index to the Virginia Military District records: Arranged by surname.* Lists survey numbers and warrant numbers used to claim land; indicates entry books where complete information can be found.

5. *Typed list of withdrawals.* Lists survey numbers, original proprietors, original acreage, acreage withdrawn.

6. *Works Progress Administration plat books of Ohio counties in the Virginia Military District.* These volumes contain plats of townships. No plats were completed for townships in Adams, Brown, Clermont, Pike, Ross, or Scioto counties.

7. Original records (Record Group XXXVII):
    a. *Numerical abstract, Virginia military bounty-land warrants.*
    b. *Virginia military bounty-land warrants located in Ohio and Kentucky issued to Virginia soldiers of the Revolutionary War.*
    c. *Entry books, volumes 2, 4, 5, 6.* Allen Latham.
    d. *Entry books, volumes A, A-2, A-3, B, C. C-2, D, E.*
    e. *Entry book, volume 1.* Allen Latham.
    f. *Miscellaneous entries, 1801-1815, 1816-1842, 1826-1852, 1847-1857.*
    g. *Survey locations.*
    h. *Survey books, volumes A, A-2, B, B-2, B-3, C, D, E, F.*
    i. *Surveys by townships, Auglaise - Highland.*

j. *Surveys by townships, Logan - Warren.*

k. *Surveys.* Not inked.

l. *Entries and surveys, Delaware County, various townships.* Contains material not pertaining to the Virginia Military District.

m. *Survey books, volumes C-1, D-2, E-3, F-4, G-5, H-6.* A. Latham.

n. *Survey book, volume 1.* A. Latham.

8. The following items are available on microfilm:

Roll number 81:

a. *Survey locations in the Virginia Military District of Ohio.*

b. *Virginia military warrants located in Ohio and Kentucky issued to Virginia soldiers of the American Revolution.* (Continues at beginning of next roll.)

Roll number 82:

a. *Numerical abstract of Virginia military land warrants.*

b. *Entry books, volumes 1, 2, 4, 5.* A. Latham. (Continues at beginning of next roll.)

Roll number 83:

a. *Entry books, volumes 6, A, A-2.* A. Latham. (Continues at beginning of next roll.)

Roll number 84:

a. *Entry books, volumes A-3, B.* A. Latham. (Continues at beginning of next roll.)

Roll number 85:

a. *Entry books, volumes C, C-2, D.* A. Latham. (Continues at beginning of next roll.)

Roll number 86:

a. *Entry book, volume E.* A. Latham.

b. *Survey book, volume A (with index) and survey book, volume A (without index).* (Continues at beginning of next roll.)

Roll number 87:

a. *Survey books, volumes A-2, B.* (Continues at beginning of next roll.)

Roll number 88:

a. *Congress lands, U.S. Reserves, volume 19.* [Material not pertinent to the Virginia Military District land grants.]

b. *Survey books, volumes B-2, B-3.* (Continues at beginning of next roll.)

Roll number 89:

a. *Survey books, volumes C, D.*

Roll number 90:

a. *Survey books, volumes E, F.*

b. *Virginia military warrants located in Ohio and Kentucky issued to Virginia soldiers in the Revolutionary War.* (Continues at beginning of next roll.)

Roll number 91:

a. *Virginia military entries, book* A.

b. *Index to survey books A and B.*

c. *Index to survey books 1 and 2.* (Continues at beginning of next roll.)

Roll number 92:

a. Completes *Index of survey book 2* and contains additional material not pertinent to the land grants in the Virginia Military District of Ohio.

Roll number 18-A:

Applications for land and sales of lands, Cincinnati Land Office, 1801-1810; includes Virginia Military District land surveys; ends with VMD survey district number 17, 1805-1806.

III. Manuscripts in the Western Reserve Historical Society, Manuscript Collections, Cleveland, Ohio.

The papers in this collection include seven entry books, an estimated 4,400 to 4,800 surveys, and one index to entries. The manuscripts are as follows:

Group A:

Container 1: Surveys #102-1899.
Container 2: Surveys #1900-3899.
Container 3: Surveys #3900-5099.
Container 4: Surveys #5100-7099.
Container 5: Surveys #7100-8699.
Container 6: Surveys #8700-10699.
Container 7: Surveys #10700-14409; warrants and other papers.

Group B:

Volume 1: Index to surveys, #143-15370.
Volume 2: Entries, 1787-1808, #455-2998.
Volume 3: Entries, 1801-1810, #3981-6798.

IV. Manuscripts of the Virginia Land Office in the Archives Division, Virginia State Library, Richmond, Virginia 23219.

The material in this collection pertains almost entirely to proof of military service in the American Revolution. There is little or no information regarding the location of actual land grants themselves. Items listed hereinafter are record groups 95 through 108 in the Archives Division.

95. *Military Certificates, A-Z.* 213 boxes. Upon examination and approval of documentation of Revolutionary War military service, the executive issued a certificate on which the Land Office register then issued a warrant for bounty lands. These certificates

are printed forms filled in with the name of the individual, his rank, the line in which he served, and the length of such service. They are dated and signed. They, along with supplemental papers presented with the claim (other than those actually proving military service), are filed in individual folders. For accepted documentation of the military service, see the Executive Papers series identified as Bounty Warrants.

96. *Military Certificates, 1-9926.* 3 volumes, 5 books. Arranged numerically; separate index. Recorded copies of certificates issued in Executive Council to persons entitled to bounty lands for Revolutionary War military service, either in their own right or as heirs or assignees. The certificates, dated and signed by the clerk to the executive, give the name of the soldier, his rank, period of service in years. Appended to the certificates are notations that the warrant was issued for a stated quantity of land. Most of those warrants after 1850 lack the certificate and have only the notation regarding the issuance of the warrant. Many of the loose certificates are filed among the papers identified in the series entitled Military Certificates, record group 95. For the index to this series, see entry 98.

97. *Index to Land Office Military Certificates, volumes 1-3 (in one volume).* Typescript arranged by surname initial. In columns under the number of each volume are given the name of the soldier, the number of acres to which he was entitled, and the page number on which his certificate was recorded. The names are entered in the order in which they appear in the volumes, prepared from a similarly arranged manuscript roll. This index has been replaced by entry 98.

98. *Index to Land Office Military Certificates, volumes 1-3, in one volume.* An alphabetical listing of men who received bounty-land certificates for Revolutionary War military service. In columns are given the name of the soldier, his rank, the volume and page on which the certificate is recorded, the number of the certificate, the number of acres allowed, and the date on which the certificate (warrant, if the former is undated) was issued. The volume was compiled from a card index. The cards contain the additional data of the name of the heir or assignee to whom the warrant was issued. This item replaces entry 97 above. It has not been microfilmed.

99. *Register of Military Certificates Located in Ohio and Kentucky, 1-6899, 8701-8850.* One volume, arranged numerically; no index. Volume locating the area in which bounty land awarded for Revolutionary War military service might have been taken up. In columns are recorded the number of the warrant, the name of the person for whose service it was issued, the quantity of acres, the number of those acres located in Ohio or Kentucky, and any remarks. Not all columns are filled in for every number. An authoritative source for proving that the acreage was located where stated is not available. (This register has been microfilmed and is available on interlibrary loan.)

100. *Military Warrants, 1-1320, 1328-5020, 8780-9969.* In eight volumes, arranged numerically; no index. Recorded copies of warrants issued by the Land Office on the basis of certificates from the executive proving Revolutionary War military service and thus eligibility for bounty lands. The warrants contain the names of the warrantee, the quantity of land to which he was entitled, the name of the person for which service the land was due, the rank and period of service. The date recorded is

that on which the warrant was issued. A note that the warrants have been issued is entered in the certificate volumes, item 96.

101. *Register of Military Warrants, 1331-1553, 4057-5478,* and *Preemption Warrants 2363-2738.* One volume, arranged numerically; no index. Volume recording, in separate sections, warrants issued both under military and preemption claims. In the military section, the name of the warrantee, his rank, the number of acres allotted, the years of service, the line in which service was performed, the date of issue of the warrant, and its number are given in columns on a folio page. Between numbers 4312 and 4652 the line of service is omitted and beginning with number 5092 fees received are registered. This register fills in a portion of the gap caused by the lack of warrant books for numbers 5021-8779 (see item 100 above). Columns in the preemption section record the name of the warrantee, note the quantity of land due, the amount of composition money paid, the date the warrant was issued, and its number.

102. *Register of Bounty Land Warrants, 5479-9914.* In three volumes, arranged numerically; no index. Volume listing warrants issued between 1808 and 1870 for Revolutionary War military service. In columns are recorded the name of the person to whom the warrant was issued, the fee charged for the warrant, the rank of the person on whose service the warrant was issued, the line in which he served, the number of acres allotted, the length of service, the date, and the number of the warrant. During the period 1832-1839 (warrants 7124-8688) various columns are not filled in. This register fills in a portion of the gap created by the lack of warrant books for numbers 5021-8779 (see item 100 above). Clippings reciting congressional acts passed in 1814 and 1826 extending the time to locate Virginia military land are attached to the front cover.

103. *List of Military Bounty Land Warrants, 1 September 1833 to 1 Deptember 1834.* One volume, arranged numerically; no index. Volume listing by month the recipients of Revolutionary War bounty land warrants 7394-8018. Warrants issued in exchange during this one year period are entered also. There is a gap of several hundred numbers. In columns are recorded the number of the warrant, the date of issue, the number of acres allotted, the name of the warrantee, the name of the person who performed the service, the nature of that service, and remarks.

104-108. Small registers containing miscellaneous listings of Revolutionary War military certificates. They appear not to be very valuable, but should be searched by persons not finding warrants listed in items 96 through 103 above.

INDEX BY
COUNTY AND TOWNSHIP

INDEX TO WATERCOURSES

NAME INDEX

Federal Land Series

Federal Land Series

A CALENDAR OF ARCHIVAL MATERIALS ON THE LAND PATENTS ISSUED BY THE UNITED STATES GOVERNMENT, WITH SUBJECT, TRACT, AND NAME INDEXES

Volume 4 • Part 2

GRANTS IN THE VIRGINIA MILITARY DISTRICT OF OHIO

Clifford Neal Smith

Contents

Introduction

Part two of volume four of the Federal Land Series continues the tabular listing of land grants in the Virginia Military District of Ohio begun in part one. The user of part two will want to refer to the Introduction to part one for a fuller discussion of the archival sources used herein.

In the Introduction to part one it was stated that the summary and indexes to the land grants in the Virginia Military District of Ohio would be covered in two parts. However, an additional manuscript has since come to light, listing still more early settlers, which will make a third part necessary.

Entry Format

Entries in both parts one and two have been compiled from several source documents. No one of these original registers contains all of the data herein, and discrepancies between source documents are frequent. Entries are presented in the following format:

```
1              2          3                  4              5
S-0102         740a       C:163      X-0340         UNIO:ALLE
                                                    CHAM:RUSH
6 → a.  W-2349 Captain Henry Whiting
7 → b.  Henry Whiting
8 → c.  Rhoda Askew;  Thomas Dunn, 1833
```

1. *Survey Number*. This is the key by which references to a land tract were made in all the records. The researcher will note large gaps between survey numbers; no explanation of these gaps is to be found in any of the extant registers, and the method by which survey numbers were originally assigned is unknown. Survey numbers appearing in the registers seem to be the only ones which actually resulted in land patents, however, so that missing numbers probably are not of importance. The consecutive listing of survey numbers, with its gaps, is taken from Register 6 (called Source A in textual footnotes) and has been compared with the Kendrick "smooth copy" in the National Archives (called Source B in the footnotes). Notebooks 9 and 10 are called Source C in these footnotes.

2. *Acreage in the Grant or Parcel*. Separate parcels to the same patentee frequently bear the same survey number, and the description of each parcel will normally be found within the same survey book.

3. *Survey Book and Page Number Citation*. The description of the land surveyed was entered in one of several survey books, designated by letters of the alphabet, and can be found on the page indicated: For example, C:163 means Survey Book C, page 163. Since the land grants were not in the rectangular

system typical of federal grants but in the ancient English metes-and-bounds system customary in Virginia, researchers must refer to the original survey books in the Illinois Historical Survey Collection if they wish to know the shapes of the grants, often irregular and complicated to describe in words.

4. *Watercourses.* In order to conserve space (and to facilitate computer indexing) the names of watercourses have been reduced to numerical coding preceded by an X. The first three numbers of the coding designate the stream name; the last (or fourth) digit designates the branch thereof. For example, X-0340 breaks down to mean: 034 = Darby's Creek, 0 = no branch listed. The complete watercourse coding is set forth in the Index to Watercourses at the back of this volume. As a practical matter, genealogical researchers may find watercourse designations of slight significance, excepting that during the period before the organization of counties and townships the watercourse may have been the only descriptive locational device. Likewise, it may be that the earliest residents settled along navigable watercourses, in the absence of roads, and that early commercial and social relationships among them can be posited from a knowledge of the watercourses near which they lived. This writer suggest that, having located the place of settlement of an ancestor of interest, genealogical researchers should refer to the Index to Watercourses to determine who the ancestor's contemporary neighbors might have been. In this manner eventual familial relationships can probably be determined.

5. *County and Township.* It will be seen that many grants extended beyond county and township limits, a phenomenon rare in the rectangular federal system of land division. The name of the county, reduced to the first four letters thereof, appears first, followed by the name of the township, similarly abbreviated. For example: UNIO:ALLE means Union County, Allen Township. Researchers should remember that these designations are the original historical ones. No doubt, county and township lines have been redefined in later years, so that Ohio maps of the 1810-1830 period should be compared with modern ones to determine the exact location of grants. Here, again, the researcher should refer to the special Index by County and Township in the back of this volume for insight into possible relationships among early settlers, as determined by propinquity. The code used for county (cty) and township (twp) designations is as follows:

ADAM	Adams Cty
ALLE	Allen Twp
ANDE	Anderson Twp
BATA	Batavia Twp
BEAV	Beaver Creek Twp
BENT	Benton Twp
BOAK	Boake's Creek Twp
BOWL	Bowling Green Twp
BROW	Brown Cty & Twp
BRUS	Brush Creek Twp
BUCK	Buckskin Twp
BYRD	Byrd Twp
CAES	Caesar's Creek Twp
CAMP	Camp Creek Twp
CANA	Canaan Twp
CHAM	Champaign Cty
CHES	Chester Twp
CLAI	Claiborne Twp
CLAR	Clark Cty & Twp
CLAY	Clay Twp
CLER	Clermont Cty
CLIN	Clinton Cty
CONC	Concord Twp
DARB	Darby Twp
DEER	Deer Creek Twp
DELA	Delaware Cty
DODS	Dodson Twp
DOVE	Dover Twp
DUDL	Dudley Twp
EAGL	Eagle Twp
FAIR	Fairfield Twp
FAYE	Fayette Cty
FRAN	Franklin Cty & Twp
GOSH	Goshen Twp
GREE	Green Cty & Twp
HALE	Hale Twp
HAMI	Hamilton Cty & Twp

HARD	Hardin Cty
HARM	Harmony Twp
HIGH	Highland Cty
HUNT	Huntington Twp
JACK	Jackson Twp
JEFF	Jefferson Twp
JERO	Jerome Twp
LAKE	Lake Twp
LEES	Leesburg Twp
LEWI	Lewis & Clark Twp
LIBE	Liberty Twp
LOGA	Logan Twp
MADI	Madison Cty & Twp
MARI	Marion Cty & Twp
MCAR	McArthur Twp*
MCDO	McDonald Twp*
MEIG	Meigs Twp
MIAM	Miami Twp
MIFF	Mifflin Twp
MILL	Mill Creek Twp
MONR	Monroe Twp
MORG	Morgan Twp
MUHL	Muhlenberg Twp
NEWM	Newmarket Twp
NEWT	Newton Twp
NILE	Nile Twp
NORW	Norwich Twp
OHIO	Ohio Twp
PAIN	Paint Twp
PARI	Paris Twp
PAXT	Paxton Twp
PEBB	Pebble Twp
PEEP	Pee Pee Twp
PERR	Perry Twp
PICK	Pickaway Cty
PIKE	Pike Cty & Twp
PLEA	Pleasant Twp
PRAI	Prairie Twp
RANG	Range Twp
RICH	Richland Twp
ROSS	Ross Cty & Twp
ROUN	Roundhead Twp
RUSH	Rush Twp
SALE	Salem Twp
SCIO	Scioto Cty & Twp
SCOT	Scott Twp
SILV	Silver Creek Twp
SPRI	Sprig Twp
STER	Sterling Twp
STOK	Stokes Twp
STON	Stonelick Twp
SUGA	Sugar Creek Twp
SUMM	Summerford Twp
SUNF	Sunfish Twp
TATE	Tate Twp
TAYL	Taylor Creek Twp
THOM	Thompson Twp
TIFF	Tiffin Twp
TWIN	Twin Twp
UNIO	Union Cty & Twp
VERN	Vernon Twp
WARR	Warren Cty
WASH	Washington Twp
WAYN	Wayne Twp
WHIT	White Oak Twp
WILL	Williamsburg Twp
WINC	Winchester Twp
XENI	Xenia Twp
YORK	York Twp
ZANE	Zane Twp

* New twp; not listed in part one

6. *Warrant Number and Warrantee.* Since all the land grants were made for service with Virginia military units in the American Revolution (with a few warrants perhaps including prior service in Indian skirmishes), the first step in the land-granting process was the presentation of a valid military bounty-land warrant. The warrant numbers appear in both Register 6 and in the Kendrick "smooth copy." The names of the corresponding warrantees and their assignees have been taken from Registers 9 and 10 of the Illinois Historical Survey collection. As mentioned above, Registers 9 and 10 are poorly written and partly illegible. The spelling of names is often primitive and not in agreement with other extant lists of veterans. Indeed, it is clear that Registers 9 and 10 were not always consistent as to who was the original warrantee and who was his assignee or heir.

7. *Patentee.* The patentee was the person to whom the land grant was actually made by the Virginia Land Office. Very frequently, this was not the war veteran, and occasionally the warrant itself may have been made out in the name of the patentee. For example, Duncan McArthur was the patentee of numerous land grants in which he is also shown as the warrantee; probably he simply bought up the rights to the warrants from veterans or their heirs and assignees and had the warrants made out in his own name.

8. *Unidentified Names.* The right-hand pages of Register 6 contain lists of names corresponding to most survey numbers. It is thought that these are the names of actual settlers on the

land, purchasers or lessees of portions thereof, possibly squatters or persons having preemptive rights by reason of having settled on the land before it was granted to the patentee. Wherever a date appears in Register 6 it is reproduced herein, even though its significance can only be conjectured. It seems likely that most patentees did not themselves take up residence on their grants, and that they authorized the Virginia Land Office to sell, lease, or rent land, either in entirety or in parcels, to actual settlers. Thus, despite the difficulty of determining the business relationships between patentees and these unidentified persons, it is obvious that the latter are of significance to researchers. Probably, the only way to determine the nature of these relationships is to study the corresponding survey records and deeds recorded in the county seats. No doubt, reference to early federal censuses for the county and township, and to tax records, would shed additional light.

SUMMARIES OF LAND GRANT ENTRIES

S-6456 200a C:151 X-0360 MADI:UNIO
a. W-5625 Natnaniel G. Morris
b. Elias Barcroft
c None

S-6457 100a? C:107 X-0840 MADI:STOK
a. W-5647 Stokes? Seldon, heir to G. A. Seldon or --? of Samuel (Seldon), deceased
b. Charles A. Stewart
c. None

S-6358. See S-6952

S-6460. See S-3118 (in volume 4, part 1)

S-6461 50a? D:331 X-0655 ADAM:TIFF
a. W-5610 Nathaniel G. Morris
b. Andrew Ellison
c. None

S-6462
S-8735 225a C:226 X-0650 ADAM:MONR
a. W-5726 Benjamin M. Ladd, representative of William Price
W-5781 Joseph Crockett
b. Andrew Ellison
c. None

S-6463 75a C:101 X-0040 ADAM:MONR
a. W-3987 John Littlepage
b. Andrew Ellison
c. Noah Whitlatch; Robert Johnson, 1838

S-6464 50a C:361 X-0600 X-0420 ADAM:SPRI
a. W-3987 John Littlepage
b. Andrew Ellison
c. None

S-6465 50a C:208 X-0600 ADAM:MONR
a. W-3987 John Littlepage
b. Andrew Ellison
c. None

S-6466* 25a -- -- PIKE:PEEP
a. --
b. Andrew Ellison
c. None
* Listed in Source A only.

S-6467
S-7715 100a C:209 X-0590 ADAM:SPRI
a. W-4094 Philip Main
W-5972 Edward Wills? (Wells?)
b. John Ellison, Junior
c. None

S-6468 100a C:523 X-0600 ADAM:SPRI
a. W-5647 Stokes? Seldon, heir to G. A. Seldon, --? to Samuel (Seldon), deceased
b. John Ellison & Robert Ellison
c None

S-6469 50a D:210 X-0135 ADAM:GREE ADAM:MONR
a. W-5616? Nathaniel G. Morris
b. Moses Lockhart
c. None

S-6470 50a C:291 X-0650 ADAM:GREE
a. W-5611 Nathaniel G. Morris
b. Israel Donaldson
c. None

S-6471 150a C:210 X-0301 PIKE:PEEP
a. W-5614 Nathaniel G. Morris
W-5611 Nathaniel G. Morris
b. Israel Donaldson
c. None

S-6472
S-7555
S-8384 52a C:234 X-0650 ADAM:TIFF
a. W-5699 Joseph Woodson
W-5947 William Pullen
W-5122 John Wright
b. John Raider*
c. None
* Source A says: -- Raider, J. Ellison, & A. Ellison.

S-6473 50a C:123 X-0130 ADAM:MONR
a. W-5700 Joseph Woodson
b. John Raider
c. None

S-6474 30a C:102 X-0040 ADAM:MONR
a. W-5699 Joseph Woodson
b. John Raider
c. None

S-6475 250a C:106 X-0841 FAYE:MADI
a. W-5486 Hezekiah Morton
b. John Watts
c. I. Y. Green? 1836

S-6477. See S-6258 (in volume 4, part 1)

S-6479 52a C:78 X-0540 PICK:PERR
a. W-5542 Christopher Moon, son & heir of Jacob (Moon), deceased
W-5598 Archelaus Mitchell
W-5532 David Hopkins
b. John* Evans & Edward* Owings
c. None
* Per Source C.

S-6480
S-10547 84a D:228 X-1005 PICK:WAYN
a. W-5598 Archelaus Mitchell
W-6417 Joseph Britton
b. John Evans
c. None

S-6482 200a C:79 X-0360 MADI:PLEA
a. W-5728 Charles Scott

b. Charles Scott
c. Asa K. Lewis; Henry Buchannan, 1828

S-6483
S-6945 190a C:80 X-0360 MADI:PLEA
a. W-5728 Charles Scott
b. Charles Scott
c. Asa K. Lewis; C? Lewis; Lyne Sterling, 1828

S-6487 46a C:42 X-0735 LOGA:MONR
a. W-5404 William Sanford, representatives of
b. James Galloway (Junior*)
c. None
* Per Source A.

S-6488 100a C:42 X-0740 CLAR:MADI
a. W-5404 William Sanford, representatives of
b. James Galloway (Junior*)
c. None
* Per Source A.

S-6492 70a C:34 X-0110 UNIO:YORK
a. W-5184 Samuel Coleman
b. Robert Means
c. J. S. Bennett, 1824; M. S. Butler, 1836

S-6493. See S-5629 (in volume 4, part 1)

S-6495. See S-5778 (in volume 4, part 1)

S-6496 150a C:86 X-1000 ROSS:FRAN
a. W-5724 William Price
b. Joseph Foster
c. None

S-6497 570a C:36 X-0360 MADI:RANG
a. W-4859 Leven Jaynes? (Joyner?)
b. Thomas Worthington
c. None

S-6498 900a C:36 X-0120 MADI:RANG
a. W-5111 Robert Means, assignee of James? Blackwell
b. Thomas Worthington
c. None

S-6499 160a C:36 X-0122 MADI:RANG
a. W-4972 Jonathan Snowden
W-4859 Leven Jaynes? (Joyner?)
b. Thomas Worthington
c. None

S-6502 200a C:103 X-0290 FAYE:PAIN
a. W-5749 David Williams
b. Abraham J. Williams
c. None

S-6502*
S-6547 102a C:103 X-0290 FAYE:PAIN
a. W-5554 William Bryant
W-5749 David Williams
b. Duncan McArthur & -- Williams
c. None
* Listed in Source A at S-6547.

S-6508 367a C:35 X-0340 MADI:CANA
a. W-5160 John Moore
b. John Moore
c. None

S-6510. See S-5630 (in volume 4, part 1)

S-6512
S-7341
S-7342
S-7969
S-7970 446a C:180 X-0290 FAYE:PAIN
a. W-4583 Peter Manifold
W-5636 James Barnett
W-5162 Peter Manifold, representative of Matthew Irvine
b. -- Manifold & -- McArthur
c. None

S-6516 400a C:109 X-0730 LOGA:MONR
a. W-5512 John Hardeman
b. Zadock Walker
c. None

S-6517 133a D:95 X-0365 MADI:UNIO
a. W-5740 Elias Langham
b. Elias Langham
c. None

S-6519 100a C:171 X-0360 PICK:PERR FAYE:---*
a. W-5740 Elias Langham
b. Elias Langham
c. None
* Source A does not mention Fayette County.

S-6521 100a C:326 X-0841 FAYE:MADI
a. W-5631 Nathaniel G. Morris
b. George Renick
c. None

S-6522 100a C:326 X-0841 FAYE:MADI
a. W-5631 Nathaniel G. Morris
b. George Renick
c. None

S-6525 100a C:171 X-0360 PICK:DARB
a. W-5483 -- Williams, representative of
b. John Shearer
c. Lyne Starling, 1831

S-6526* 100a C:349 X-1260 MADI:UNIO
a. W5466 William Tinsley
b. James Armstrong
c. None
* Source A says by Palestine.

S-6527 50a C:490 X-0840 ROSS:TWIN
a. W-5563 Edmund Goode
b. Joshua McFallin*
c. None
* Source A says Joshua McFarlin.

S-6528 25a C:490 X-0840 ROSS:TWIN
a. W-5553 John Wright, representatives of
b. Joshua McFallin*
c. None
* Source A says Joshua McFarlin.

S-6529. See S-61114 (in volume 4, part 1)

S-6531 100a C:240 X-0847 HIGH:MADI
a. W-5647 Stiles? (Stokes?) Seldon, heir to G. A. Seldon, --? of Samuel (Seldon)
b. Jesse Millikan
c. None

S-6532 50a E:89 X-0660 HAMI:ANDE
a. W-1136 James Stark
b. John English
c. T. V. Swearingen; G. W. Jones, 1826

S-6538 1500a C:89 X-0840 FAYE:PAIN MADI:STOK
a. W-5743 William Green?
b. Edward Stubblefield
c. Richard Douglas; Wade Loofborrow; William Douglas; John Stubblefield; J. Blue?, 1827; R. Winegarner; S. Case, 1834; J. McLain, 1832; I. Y. Green, 1831; John McLain; J. Jameson, 1839

S-6538 1300a C:515 X-0840 FAYE:PAIN
a. W-5743 William Green?
b. Edward Stubblefield
c. Heirs of William Mumford; R. Douglas; L. Rankin; J. Hays, 1842; "440 deeded Richard Douglas, assignee T. J. Timmore, 4 Oct 1831 & 24 Dec 1836"

S-6538 100a* C:498 X-0840 FAYE:PAIN
a. W-5743 William Green?
b. Edward Stubblefield
c. None
* Source A says 120 acres.

S-6538 100a C:497 X-0840 FAYE:PAIN
a. W-5743 William Green?
b. Edward Stubblefield
c. James Kirkpatrick, 1837

S-6538 437a C:497 X-0840 FAYE:PAIN
a. W-5743 William Green?
b. Edward Stubblefield
c. R. Douglas; H. Paul, 1835; Alexander Douglas; Hugh Paul; deeded R. Douglas, 24 Sep 1836

S-6538 410a C:497 X-0840 FAYE:PAIN
a. W-5743 William Green?
b. Edward Stubblefield
c. A. Bush, 1837

S-6540
S-6889 418a C:77 X-0480 DELA:THOM UNIO:---*
a. W-5224 Colin? Cocke
W-5225 Colin? Cocke
b. -- Tagart, -- McLaughlin, -- Gray, & -- Taylor
c. None
* Source A does not mention Union County.

S-6541 581a C:58 X-1000 PICK:SCIO
a. W-3790 Barnet? Armstrong, representative? of James Armstrong
W-5227 John Pryor
W-5384 Thomas Taylor, administrator? of John McAdams
b. -- Tagart, -- McLaughlin, -- Gray, & -- Taylor
c. John Stephenson; John Thompson, 1826; A. McLaughlin; William Renick, 1827

S-6542 866a C:49 X-0340 FRAN:NORW
a. W-5608 William Aylett
b. Andrew Alexander
c. None

S-6543 200a C:48 X-0340 UNIO:UNIO
a. W-5608 William Aylett
b. Andrew Alexander
c. None

S-6545 160a C:56 X-0360 MADI:CANA
a. W-3737 William Moody
b. William Moody
c. None

S-6547
S-6502
S-6550 150a C:43 X-0743 GREE:XENI
a. W-5666 Joseph Woodson
W-5667 Joseph Woodson
b. James Galloway, Junior
c. None

S-6547. See S-6502

S-6550* 150a -- -- GREE:XENI
a. --
b. James Galloway, Junior
c. None
* Entry in Source A only.

S-6550. See also S-6547

S-6551 200a C:103 X-0663 CLER:MIAM
a. W-5646 Charles Pelham & James Taylor, assignees
b. -- Pelham & -- Taylor
c. William Lytle; Samuel Veal & Saul Perrine?, 1831

S-6552 1000a C:138 X-0840 FAYE:UNIO
a. W-5545 Nicholas Taliaferro
b. John Moss
c. Elizabeth Titsworth; James Henton, 1841

S-6554
S-7029 132a C:333 X-1000 FRAN:NORW
a. W-5225 William Boyer?
W-5244 John C. Cobbs, heir? of Samuel (Cobbs)
b. -- Tagart, -- McLaughlin, -- Gray, & -- Taylor
c. Robert Brotherton; William Mooberry? 1837

S-6556* 125a C:86 X-1000 PICK:SCIO
a. W-5518 Thomas Dowden
W-5519 Thomas Haine? (Dowden?)
b. Asahel Renick
c. None
* Source A says not patented.

S-6557 600a C:85 X-1000 PICK:SCIO
a. W-5560 Francis Preston, assignee of Henry Conway
b. Francis Preston
c. James Hannah

S-6558 160a C:82 X-0570 ROSS:HUNT
a. W-3389 John Sturdevan(t)
b. Edward Drongoole* Junior
c. Heirs of Redman Condon; P. Thurman, 1839; J. A. Fulton
* Source A spells Dromgoole.

S-6558 40a C:82 X-0570 ROSS:HUNT
a. W-3389 John Sturdevan(t)
b. Edward Drongoole* Junior
c. None
* Source A spells Dromgoole.

S-6559 200a C:294 X-1120 BROW:FRAN
a. W-5559 Francis Preston, assignee of Henry Conway
b. Francis Preston
c. George C. Light, 1836; George Bohrer & G. H. Bohrer

S-6560 200a C:202 X-0360 ROSS:DEER
a. W-5752 John Walker, deceased, heirs of
b. Duncan McArthur
c. None

S-6561 73a C:202 X-0360 ROSS:---*
PICK:DEER
a. W-5752 John Walker, deceased, heirs of
b. Duncan McArthur
c. None
* Source A does not list Ross County.

S-6563
S-6776 880a C:201 X-0750 UNIO:LIBR
a. W-5752 John Walker, deceased, heirs of
b. Duncan McArthur
c. Thomas Taylor; John Custer, 1837; D. Potts

S-6564 & S-6565. See S-4671 (in volume 4, part 1)

S-6570 820a C:42 X-1180 MADI:FAIR
MADI:JEFF
FRAN:----
a. W-5662 William Pelham
b. William Pelham
c. William Long, 1829; Charles Blagrove; J. B. Andrews, 1828

S-6579 67a C:396 X-0296 FAYE:MADI
a. W-5731 John Begent
b. Solomon Smith
c. None

S-6581 450a C:45 X-1000 UNIO:JERO
a. W-5644 John Galloway
b. John Galloway
c. None

S-6582. See S-6309 (in volume 4, part 1)

S-6583 150a E-72 X-0845 FAYE:PAIN
a. W-5747 Henry Flasher
b. David Sayers
c. -- Loofborrow & -- Roebuck; William Williams, 1829; Lemuel? Connelly; J. Sayers; J. Calender

S-6584 50a D:499 X-0843 FAYE:PAIN
a. W-5747 Henry Flasher
b. Thomas McDonald
c. R. Douglas; W. Loofborrow, 1827; William Douglas

S-6585 100a C:84 X-0840 ROSS:PAXT
a. W-5545 John Moss
b. John Moss
c. Robert Stewart, 1837; J. McNeil, 1830; heirs of Michael Markee; T. J. Campbell; J. A. Fulton

S-6585 150a C:84 X-0840 ROSS:PAXT
a. W-5545 John Moss
b. John Moss
c. None

S-6586 138a C:151 X-0139 HIGH:BRUS
a. W-5122 John Wright
b. Andrew Ellison
c. None

S-6588 50a C:369 X-0845 ROSS:PAXT
a. W-5754 Sally Evans, representative of Jess (Evans)
b. Nathan Reeves
c. P.? Douglas, 1836

S-6590* 13a -- -- --
a. --
b. James Harris
c. --
* Listed in Source A only.

S-6591* 42a -- -- HIGH:LIBE
a. --
b. John Graham
c. --
* Listed in Source A only.

S-6592 45a C:107 X-0846 HIGH:BRUS
a. W-5694 Joseph Woodson
b. Jesse Millikan
c. None

S-6595 278a C:57 X-1000 UNIO:JERO FRAN:---*
a. W-5587 Thomas Parker, son of George (Parker)
b. Thomas Parker
c. Reas? (Pleas(ant)?) Smith, 1829
* Listed only in Source A.

S-6596 278a C:51 X-1000 UNIO:JERO
a. W-5587 Thomas Parker, son of George (Parker)
b. Thomas M. Bailey
c. None

S-6597 348a C:53 X-0740 MADI:STOK CLAR:---*
a. W-5124 Robert Means, assignee of Lovell Harrison, heir at law
W-5275 Thomas Bagly? (Bayly?), assignee of Daniel Richardson, representatives of
W-5396 Francis Whiting
W-5643 Albert Russell Jones
b. -- Galloway & James Russell
c. James Kilgore; S. Harrod, 1832; heirs of J. Rowland; S. N. Kerr, 1835
* Source A does not mention Clark County.

S-6598 25a C:293 X-1230 ROSS:TWIN
a. W-2019 William Turvey
b. John McDonald
c. None

S-6599* 83a -- -- FAYE:PAIN
a. --
b. Thomas McDonald
c. Alexander McMullen; I? Y. Green, 1831; Jesse McKay; John McLain, 1831; N. F. Jones, 1833
* Listed in Source A only.

S-6600 250a C:217 X-0841 FAYE:MADI
a. W-5562 James Curry
b. James Curry
c. William S. Williams; I. Y. Green, 1838

S-6602 683a C:53 X-0340 UNIO:UNIO X-1180 UNIO:DARB
a. W-5682 Joseph Woodson
W-5685 Joseph Woodson
W-5608 William Aylett
W-5550 John Meanly
W-5667 Joseph Woodson
b. James Galloway, Junior
c. None

S-6604* 150a -- -- GREE:XENI
a. --
b. Ephraim Ralph
c. --
* Listed in Source A only.

S-6610* 600a -- -- LOGA:PERR
a. --
b. Robert Means
c. Richard Kennon; B. Stanton, 1836
* Listed in Source A only.

S-6614 1000a C:82 X-0840 FAYE:JEFF
a. W-5357 James Harmon & John Potts? (Potter?), assignee of William Rogers, deceased
W-5642 Josiah Payne, heir to Thomas (Payne), deceased
b. Walter Dun
c. --

S-6615 133a C:54 X-0840 MADI:STOK
a. W-5541 Christopher Moor(e), son & heir to Jacob (Moore)
b. W. Galloway & G. Galloway
c. None

S-6616 200a C:54 X-0340 FRAN:BROW
a. W-5541 Christopher Moor(e), son & heir to Jacob (Moore)
b. W. Galloway & G. Galloway
c. None

S-6620 540a C:57 X-0840 GREE:SILV
a. W-2556 Claiborne Vaughan
b. Richard J. Waters
c. None

S-6621 360a C:93 X-0010 CLIN:LIBE
a. W-2556 Claiborne Vaughan
b. Richard J. Waters
c. Samuel Daniels? (David?), 1833

S-6623 850a C:84 X-0840 FAYE:CONC CLIN:---*
a. W-5545 John Moss
b. John Moss
c. Edward Drumgole; J. P. Andrews, 1828
* Source A does not mention Clinton County.

S-6624
S-6625 500a C:91 X-0840 ROSS:TWIN
a. W-5545 John Moss
b. John Moss
c. Thomas? P. Scott; William Creighton, Junior, 1824; James Goodman; R. Stewart, 1827

S-6635 450a C:56 X-0340 FRAN:NORW
a. W-5136 David Mason
b. David Mason
c. None

S-6636 667a C:54 X-0340 FRAN:PRAI
a. W-5541 Christopher Moor(e), son & heir of Jacob (Moore)
W-5493 John C. Carter
b. W. Galloway & G. Galloway
c. Robert Pollock, 1827

S-6637 967a C:57 X-0340 FRAN:BROW
a. W-5607 William Aylett
b. Elizabeth Moore
c. James Boyd; Robert Brotherton, 1827; Benjamin Morris; H. Miller; William B. Brown; M. J. Gilbert, 1834; David Scott, 1833?; O. T. Reeves;

Valentine Simpson; M. S. Sullivant, 1832; L. Starling; D. Nelson, 1836; Elias Roberts; B. Boyd, 1837

S-6638 300a C:48 X-0340 FRAN:NORW
a. W-5605 William Aylett
W-5609 William Aylett
W-5607 William Aylett
b. -- Aylett, Joseph B. Lapsley, & Elizabeth* Moore
c. None
* Per Source C.

S-6639 200a* C:48 X-0340 FRAN:BROW
a. W-5605 William Aylett
b. William Aylett
c. Philip Clover; William Mooberry, 1837
* Source A says 266a.

S-6640 967a C:49 X-0340 FRAN:BROW
a. W-5605 William Aylett
b. William Aylett
c. Joseph B. Lapsley; Demus Adams, 1828; Lyne Starling, 1831

S-6641 266a C:56 X-0340 FRAN:NORW
a. W-5609 William Aylett
b. Joseph B. Lapsley
c. William G. Swearingen; D. D. Warner, 1839

S-6642 350a C:55 X-0340 FRAN:PRAI FRAN:NORW
a. W-5609 William Aylett
b. Joseph B. Lapsley
c. Demus Adams, 1828; M. J. Gilbert, 1836; M. L. Sullivant

S-6643 617a C:56 X-0340 MADI:JEFF
a. W-5609 William Aylett
b. Joseph B. Lapsley
c. M. L. Sullivant; John Parker, 1833; R. Douglas; Alexander Douglas, 1838; Mary Downing; S. N. Kerr, 1839; P. Douglas, 1840; A. Douglas

S-6644 300a C:55 X-0500 MADI:DEER
a. W-5404 William Sanford, representative of
b. Lincoln Goodale
c. --

S-6645 300a C:54 X-1180 CHAM:GOSH
a. W-5404 William Sanford, representatives of
b. Lincoln Goodale
c. None

S-6646 200a C:51 X-0360 MADI:DEER
a. W-5167 Peter Manifold, assignee of Matthew Irvine
b. John Baird
c. M. L. Sullivant, 1831

S-6647 130a C:53 X-0360 MADI:DEER
a. W-5550 John Meanly
W-3737 William Moody
b. -- Galloway & -- Moody
c. --

S-6648 60a C:53 X-0340 MADI:CANA
a. W-5550 John Meanly
b. James Galloway, Junior
c. None

S-6649 100a C:53 X-1050 MADI:SUMM
a. W-5668 Joseph Woodson
b. James Galloway, Junior
c. None

S-6650 100a C:54 X-0660 CLAR:MADI
a. W-5370 Thomas M. Bayley, assignee of John Warrington?
b. James Galloway, Junior
c. None

S-6651 367a -- X-0660 CLAR:HARM
a. W-5498 Sally Jordan, representative of Arthur Smith
b. James Galloway, Junior
c. None

S-6652 100a C:54 X-0360 MADI:DEER
a. W-5498 Sally Jordan, representative of Arthur Smith
b. James Galloway, Junior
c. None

S-6653 100a C:54 X-0360 MADI:JEFF MADI:DEER
a. W-5498 Sally Jordan, representative of Arthur Smith
b. James Galloway, Junior
c. None

S-6654 100a C:59 X-1180 MADI:JEFF
a. W-5498 Sally Jordan, representative of Arthur Smith
b. James Galloway, Junior
c. None

S-6655 266a C:56 X-0740 CLAR:MADI
a. W-5607 William Aylett
b. Elizabeth Moore
c. None

S-6656 100a D:156 X-1005 HARD:DUDL
a. W-1037 Thomas Tawnehill
b. William Hickman
c. None

S-6657* 100a D:26 X-1306 BROW:PIKE
a. W-3383 Samuel Dedman
b. Samuel Dedman
c. Daniel? (David?) Keethen?
* Source A says not patented.

S-6657 50a D:26 X-1306 BROW:PIKE
a. W-3383 Samuel Dedman
b. Samuel Dedman
c. None

S-6658 483a C:152 X-0650 ADAM:WAYN
S-7721
a. W-5122 John Wright
W-5356 William Rogers
b. Andrew Ellison
c. None

S-6660 50a C:208 X-0130 ADAM:TIFF
a. W-5356 William Rogers
b. Andrew Ellison
c. None

S-6661* 65a -- -- ADAM:MONR
a. --
b. Andrew Ellison
c. None

S-6662 50a C:151 X-0130 ADAM:TIFF
a. W-5356 William Wright
b. Andrew Ellison
c. None

S-6663 100a C:405 X-1190 ADAM:MEIG
a. W-912 Joseph Dean
b. Joseph Dean
c. None

S-6664* 100a D:339 X-0650 ADAM:TIFF
a. W-968 William Berkley
b. Spencer Berkley
c. William Bakley (so spelled); James Clark, 1832
* Source A says not patented.

S-6666 50a C:336 X-0040 ADAM:MONR
a. W-1567 John Waller
b. Andrew Ellison
c. None

S-6673* 544a -- -- FRAN:WASH
a. --
b. John Graham
c. None
* Listed in Source A only.

S-6680 648a D:448 X-0750 UNIO:YORK
X-0110
a. W-4798 William Throckmorton
b. Burgess Ball, representative of
c. E. W. H. Reed, 1831

S-6681 350a C:350 X-0360 PICK:MONR
a. W-1850 Doctor Robert Rose
b. John Rose
c. Alexander Rose; Joseph Johnson, 1833; C. Williamson, 1838

S-6696
S-10656 279a C:503 X-0840 FAYE:UNIO
a. W-5733 Thomas Gaskins
W-6366 Andrew Chilton
b. -- Dun & -- Latham
c. None

S-6702 100a D:490 X-1305 BROW:SCOT
a. W-5703 Archibald Moon?
b. John Hill
c. William Hinton & -- Strain?; J. Mellikan, 1823; E. Popejoy & -- Erwin; B. Walker; H? Fullerton, 1825; John McMannit? (McMannis?); J. Hinton, 1832; N. F. Jones, 1834; heirs of J. McMannis; W. Dun; I. Y. Green, 1831; J. Jameson, 1838

S-6702 350a E:68 X-1305 BROW:SCOT
a. W-5703 Archibald Moon?
b. Joseph Kerr
c. Sarah Fields; P. R. Rice, 1833; Samuel? McBeth; Solomon Rich, 1833; John Forsythe; J. Kerr; T. S. Harris? 1831

S-6703 100a E:187 X-1305 BROW:CLAR
a. W-5703 Archibald Moon?
b. James M. Trimble
c. None

S-6704* 75a -- -- BROW:CLAR
a. --
b. Joseph Kerr
c. None
* Listed in Source A only.

S-6709 175a C-135 X-1301 HIGH:SALE
a. W-5704 Archibald Moon?
b. Joseph Kerr
c. None

S-6710 100a C:135 X-1146 PIKE:MIFF
a. W-5703 Archibald Moon?
b. Joseph Kerr
c. J. Johnson; L? (S?) Howard, 1826

S-6711 40a C:135 X-1140 PIKE:MIFF
a. W-5704 Archibald Moon?
b. Joseph Kerr
c. None

S-6712 200a C:136 X-0145 ADAM:SCOT
HIGH:---*
a. W-5704 Archibald Moon?
b. Joseph Kerr
c. Thomas Williamson; James Campbell, 1826; John Linton? 1829; J. Dulty & G. Dulty; J. S. Patton, 1833; J. Kerr; George W. Doggett, 1828; T. Huston
* Source A does not mention Highland County.

S-6713 400a C:136 X-1301 HIGH:SALE
a. W-5704 Archibald Moon?
b. Joseph Kerr
c. John Moler; Beniah Feris, 1834; Lewis Moler

S-6714 200a E:91 X-0134 BROW:EAGL
a. W-5705 Archibald Moon?
b. James M. Trimble
c. None

S-6717 100a C:136 X-0423 ADAM:LIBE
a. W-5704 Archibald Moon?
b. Joseph Kerr
c. None

S-6719 181a C:512 X-0847 HIGH:PAIN
a. W-5490 Jesse Witt? (Will? Wall?)
W-5576 William Crouch
b. -- Johns* & -- Watts**
c. None
* Source A says Johnson; Source C says James Johnson.
** Source C says John Watts.

S-6719 20a C:512 X-0847 HIGH:PAIN
a. W-5490 Jesse Witt? (Will? Wall?)
W-5576 William Crouch
b. -- Johns* & -- Watts**
c. None
* Source A says Johnson; Source C says James Johnson.
** Source C says John Watts.

S-6720 70a C:240 X-0150 ROSS:PAIN
a. W-2319 Captain William Meredith
b. Nathaniel Massie
c. None

S-6721 & S-6722. See S-4920 (in volume 4, part 1)

S-6729 200a C:316 X-0575 ROSS:SCIO
a. W-5721 William Price
b. A. L. Langham*
c. None
* Source C says Angus Langham.

S-6730 100a C:153 X-0575 ROSS:SCIO
a. W-5719 William Price
b. A. L. Langham*
c. None
* Source C says Angus Lewis Langham.

S-6731* 15a -- -- PICK:JACK
a. --
b. A. L. Langham
c. None
* Listed in Source A only.

S-6733 100a C:107 X-0840 MADI:STOK
a. W-5696 Joseph Woodson
W-5695 Joseph Woodson
b. Charles A. Stewart*
c. None
* Source A spells Stuart.

S-6735 82a C:326 X-0841 FAYE:MADI
a. W-5612 Nathaniel G. Morris
b. Gabriel Coile
c. None

S-6741 100a C:519 X-0360 FAYE:MADI
a. W-5627 Nathaniel G. Morris
b. A. L. Langham*
c. W. Loofborrow, 1828
* Source A says Angus L. Langham; Source C says Angus Lewis Langham

S-6745
S-10622? 140a C:521 X-0134 ADAM:WAYN
a. W-3987 John Littlepage
W-6425 George Purcell
b. Andrew Ellison
c. None

S-6746 135a C:55 X-0340 FRAN:BROW
a. W-4185 Mary Hayes & Elizabeth Hayes
b. Mary Hoye? (Hays?) & Elizabeth Hoye? (Hays?)*
c. Heirs of William Barlow; E. Bachus, 1832; C. Higgins, 1834; A. Barger & C. Barger; S. Shepherd; J. Turney, 1838?
* Source A spells Hoge.

S-6747 438a D:357 X-1060 BROW:PIKE
a. W-1 James Askew
b. M. S. Holmes & Benjamin Holmes*
c. Thomas Carneal; John Allen, 1824; Benjamin Homans; James Thompson; Reuben Fight, 1826; William Keither; Vincent Crabb, 1834; S. B. Allen; J. W. Allen, 1838; J. D. Allen; P. Russel(1)
* Source A spells Hoomes.

S-6747 363a D:358 X-1060 BROW:PIKE
a. W-1 James Askew
b. -- Ball, -- Dabney, & -- Holmes*
c. James Thompson; Benjamin Homens; S. B. Allen; A. Goodin; Hugh Binkley?; Charles White, 1831; C. Wallace; S. E. Beasley; Edward Francis, 1831; J. Bowen; A. C. H. Cottrell, 1841; N. Pedicord, 1841
* Source A spells Hoomes.

S-6748 555a C:60 X-1000 FRAN:WASH UNIO:---*
a. W-5745 Benjamin Anderson, heir to John (Anderson) deceased
b. Benjamin Anderson
c. Charles Bradshaw; Robert Pollock, 1828; W. C. Casey, 1834; Simon Depp; M. J. Gilbert, 1838; M. Depp; Z. Hutchinson, 1838; William Depp; Pocahontas Depp; E. Depp
* Source A does not mention Union County.

S-6749 100a C:60 X-0340 FRAN:BROW
a. W-4492 Robert Belvin
b. Richard C. Anderson
c. None

S-6757 200a C:180 X-0841 FAYE:WAYN FAYE:PAIN
a. W-5801 John Norvell? (Nowell?)

b. Benjamin Hough
c. None

S-6759 97a C:86 X-0840 ROSS:TWIN
a. W-5370 Thomas M. Bayley, assigee of John Warrington
b. Thomas Scott
c. None

S-6760 160a C:91 X-0840 ROSS:TWIN
a. W-5559 Francis Preston, assignee of Henry Conway
b. Francis Preston
c. Thomas Scott; William Creighton, Junior, 1824

S-6762 50a C:139 X-0730 LOGA:MONR
a. W-5547 Sarah Gunn, devisee of James (Gunn)
b. Walter Dun
c. M. Bonner, 1827

S-6771 100a C:385 X-0423 ADAM:LIBE
a. W-5468 Ephraim Andrews
b. Ephraim Andrews
c. None

S-6772 192a C:58 X-1005 PICK:SCIO
a. W-5244 John C. Cobbs? --? of Samuel (Cobbs)
b. -- Tagart, -- McLaughlin, -- Gray, & -- Taylor
c. None

S-6773 250a C:67 X-1000 PICK:SCIO
a. W-5244 John C. Cobbs? --? of Samuel (Cobbs)
b. -- Tagart, -- McLaughlin, -- Gray, & -- Taylor
c. James Tagart

S-6774 200a C:77 X-0340 PICK:DARB
X-1000
a. W-5244 John C. Cobbs? --? of Samuel (Cobbs)
b. -- Tagart, -- McLaughlin, -- Gray, & -- Taylor
c. J. McLain, 1838

S-6775 100a C:95 X-1000 PICK:SCIO
a. W-5595 William McEroy
b. Samuel Prebles
c. R. Layman, 1831

S-6776. See S-6563

S-6780 640a C:327 X-0360 MADI:SUMM
a. W-1899 Thomas Walen? (Waters?)
W-1234 Henry Lipscomb
W-750 William Crallon? (Challon?)
b. David Ross
c. Lyne Starling, 1828

S-6781 1111a C:124 X-0360 MADI:DEER
a. W-3414 John Scarbrough*
b. John Scarborough*
c. None
* So spelled.

S-6782 407a C:273 X-0811 MADI:PLEA
a. W-5485 John Crute, alias John L. Crute
b. Charles Woodson
c. None

S-6783 240a C:124 X-0360 MADI:FAIR
a. W-5782 John Hull
b. Duncan McArthur
c. S. M. McDonald; G. G. McDonald, 1839

S-6790 1120a C:59 X-0340 PICK:JACK
PICK:MUHL
a. W-2312 Francis Dade
b. Francis Dade
c. Lyne Starling, 1831; "redeemed"

S-6791 100a C:63 X-0340 PICK:JACK
a. W-2312 Francis Dade
b. Francis Dade
c. Henry Mapes; J. Julian, 1829; H. Massie; Isaac Julian, 1831

S-6792
S-8472
S-8501
S-8807 300a D:303 X-0845 ROSS:TWIN
a. W-5545 John Moss
W-6160 Thomas Ray?
W-6158 Thomas Ray
b. -- Moss & -- Fulton
c. None

S-6798 15a D:150 X-1145 HIGH:---*
FAYE:MADI
a. W-5743 William Green, representatives of
b. Duncan McArthur
c. None
* Source A does not mention Highland County.

S-6799 100a C:293 X-0342 CHAM:GOSH
MADI:---*
a. W-5581 Priscilla Harmon, heir to Zorobabel (Harmon)
b. Edward Tiffin
c. None
* Source A does not mention Madison County.

S-6800 100a C:60 X-0340 MADI:CANA
a. W-5552 Richard C. Anderson
b. Richard C. Anderson
c. None

S-6801 30a C:95 X-0840 ROSS:TWIN
a. W-1691 Anthony Chavalier (Chevalier)
b. Samuel Turner
c. None

S-6803 150a C:59 X-0660 CLAR:MADI
a. W-5074 James Morgan, representatives of
b. Thomas* Antrim & James* Curle
c. None
* Per Source C.

S-6808 100a C:84 X-0840 ROSS:SCIO
a. W-5545 John Moss
b. John Moss
c. None

S-6809 750a C:109 X-1180 CHAM:GOSH
a. W-5807 Thomas McKinley, heir to John (McKinley)
W-5808 Thomas McKinley, heir to John (McKinley)
b. George Dawson
c. D. Springer; J. Cheney, 1823; J. Springer; Dennis Springer; Benjamin Cheney, 1831

S-6812 50a C:94 X-0340 PICK:DARB
a. W-5559 Francis Preston, assignee of Henry Conway
b. Francis Preston
c. J. Keplar; W. P. Darsh & P. N. White, 1840; J. Olds, 1842

S-6815 110a C:86 X-0841 FAYE:MADI
a. W-1570 Lieutenant Reuben Long
b. Reuben Long
c. Reuben King; J? Hagler, 1829; Robert Means; R. Douglas, 1833

S-6816 250a C:113 X-0130 PIKE:PERR
X-1140
a. W-5649? Not listed in Source C
W-5763 William Thorman? heir to Leven (Thorman?)
W-5754 Sally Evans, representative of Jess (Evans)
W-5003 John Thompson
b. Nathan* Reeves & -- Massie
c. None
* Per Source C.

S-6823. See S-5793 (in volume 4, part 1)

S-6824. See S-5456 (in volume 4, part 1)

S-6825 200a C:60 X-1000 PICK:SCIO
a. W-5790 Obadiah Watson & --? heir of David (Watson)
b. John Kerr
c. None

S-6827 166a C:404 X-0840 ROSS:TWIN
a. W-5853 Henry Massie, assignee of James Craig
b. Henry Massie
c. None

S-6828
S-8328 247a C:219 X-1000 ROSS:SCIO
a. W-5803 John Remay? representatives of
W-5734 Thomas Gaskins
b. F. Renick & W. Dun
c. None

S-6829* 50a C:77 X-1000 PICK:SCIO
a. W-1620 Luke Brady
b. John Kerr
c. A McLaughlin; W. Renick, 1827
* Source A says not patented.

S-6830* 150a C:66 X-1000 PICK:SCIO
a. W-1620 Luke Brady
b. Patrick Feny? (Finy?)**
c. G. Justus, 1829; Patrick Terry (Ferry?); Jesse Justus, Junior, 1831; Ferry Justus; John Lee; S. S. Frame, 1839
* Source A says not patented.
** Sources A & C spell Ferry.

S-6831 550a C:87 X-0150 ROSS:BUCK
X-1220 ROSS:PAIN
a. W-5072 Isaac Browning
W-4205 Conrad Michael
b. Duncan McArthur
c. None

S-6833 200a C:87 X-0296 FAYE:MADI
a. W-5162 Peter Manifold, assignee of Matthew Irvine
b. Duncan McArthur
c. None

S-6834 1150a C:64 X-0540 ROSS:DEER
a. W-32 John C---? (illegible)
W-627 Duncan Muray (Murray)
W-573 John Snow?
W-864 Joseph Norwood?
W-1880 John Corbett
W-1881 William Bedworth
W-1882 Peter Collins
b. Levi Hollingsworth
c. None

S-6835 700a C:63 X-0540 PICK:PERR
a. W-5388 Margaret Bromley, widow of Ralph (Bromley)
b. George Clarke
c. None

S-6836 600a C:63 X-0540 ROSS:DEER
PICK:PERR
a. W-5388 Margaret Bromley, widow of Ralph (Bromley)
b. George Clarke
c. None

S-6837 800a C:65 X-0841 ROSS:CONC
ROSS:DEER
a. W-5104 Samuel March? assignee of Joseph Smith
W-4994 Ann McKnight, widow
b. Henry Massie
c. None

S-6838 1100a C:63 X-0360 ROSS:DEER
a. W-5388 Margaret Bromley, widow of Ralph (Bromley)
W-5420 John P. Hungerford, assignee of Reuben Briscoe?
b. George Clarke*
c. None
* Source A spells Clark.

S-6839 700a C:65 X-1000 FRAN:JACK
a. W-5500 John Smith Sneed, heir to Thomas Sneed, deceased
W-5853 Henry Massie, assignee of James Craig
b. -- Snead & -- Massie
c. John Stranahan; D. Morgan; Jacob Grub, 1826; William McMullen; J. McLene, 1831; C. Higgins; J. Turney, 1833; David McMullen; R. Douglas, 1837; J. L. Taylor, 1836

S-6840 1892a C:200 X-1005 FRAN:JACK
a. W-5505 Thomas Lipscomb
W-5476 John Brown
W-5473 Calohill Minnis
W-5606 William Aylett
W-5420 John P. Hungerford, assignee of Reuben Briscoe?
b. George Clarke*
c. James L. Holten; J. McLene
* Source A spells Clark.

S-6841 100a C:66 X-0340 PICK:SCIO
a. W-5500 John Smith Sneed, heir to Thomas (Sneed)
b. John S. Snead
c. Isaac Julian; George Botkin; P. N. White, 1838

S-6842 300a C:281 X-1000 PICK:JACK
a. W-5853 Henry Massie, assignee of James Craig
b. Henry Massie
c. Peter Suddith; William McArthur, 1830

S-6843 117a C:65 X-1000 FRAN:JACK
a. W-5853 Henry Massie, assignee of James Craig
b. Henry Massie
c. None

S-6844 100a C:65 X-1000 PICK:SCIO
a. W-5853 Henry Massie, assignee of James Craig
b. Henry Massie
c. None

S-6845 500a C:215 X-1000 PICK:MUHL
a. W-814 David Walker, heir to Captain -- Walker
b. David Walker
c. Lyne Starling; C. F. Dresbach? 1833; D. Walker

S-6849
S-7565
S-7566 500a C:146 X-0360 CLAR:HARM
a. W-5846 Charles Stockley, deceased
W-5767 John Small? deceased
b. Oliver Simpson
c. Ira Delano; Saul Henkle, 1826; Zeph Platt; J. Delano, 1823; L. Mason, 1837; Gus Swan; S. McMillan (error) 1827; Alexander Simpson heirs; James L? (S?) Elsey, 1829

S-6851 25a C:399 X-0540 ROSS:DEER
a. W-5803 John Remay, representative of
b. Henry Massie
c. None

S-6854
S-8065 66a C:531 X-0840 ROSS:DEER ROSS:PAXT ROSS:PAIN
a. W-5104 Samuel March? assignee of Joseph Smith
W-5989 John Yancy?
b. Henry Massie
c. None

S-6855 150a C:109 X-1000 PICK:SCIO
a. W-5244 John C. Cobbs, --? of Samuel (Cobbs)
b. -- Tagart, -- McLaughlin, -- Gray, & -- Taylor
c. J. Tagart; J. P. Brown, 1829; Philip Cherry, 1832; S? (L?) Tully, 1838

S-6856 80a C:88 X-1230 ROSS:TWIN
a. W-5072 Isaac Browning
b. Duncan McArthur
c. None

S-6858. See S-4952 (in volume 4, part 1)

S-6859. See S-5780 (in volume 4, part 1)

S-6860 105a C:313 X-0732 CLAR:HARM
a. W-5857 William Jolley, heir to Joseph (Jolley)
b. Duncan McArthur
c. William Berry, 1837

S-6860 95a C:313 X-0732 CLAR:HARM
a. W-5857 William Jolley, heir to Joseph (Jolley)
b. Duncan McArthur
c. None

S-6865 157a C:109 X-0847 HIGH:PAIN
a. W-5811 Thomas McKinley, heir to John (McKinley)
W-5809 Thomas McKinley, heir to John (McKinley)
b. George Dawson
c. None

S-6867 15a D:157 X-0847 HIGH:PAIN
a. W-5694 Joseph Woodson
b. Jesse Millikan
c. None

S-6867. See S-6291

S-6868 150a C-176 X-1000 PICK:WAYN
a. W-5801 John Norvell? (Nowell])
b. Benjamin Hough
c. None

S-6869 10a C:93 X-0840 ROSS:TWIN
a. W-5809 Thomas McKinley, heir to John (McKinley)
b. George Dawson
c. None

S-6877 722A C:112 X-0340 MADI:PIKE CHAM:GOSH
a. W-5538 William White

b. Jesse McKay
c. Lemuel Mann? (Mane?)

S-6878 580a C:131 X-0663 CLER:BATA
a. W-3200 John Clough
W-5071 Peter Lampkin
b. -- Martin & Joseph* Stokeley
c. None
* Per Source C.

S-6881 80a C:99 X-0730 CHAM:GOSH CHAM:UNIO
a. W-5263 Irby Hudson, administrators of the estate of
b. Benjamin Cheney
c. None

S-6883 100a F:200 X-0230 ADAM:WINC
a. W-1188 Daniel Kendrick
b. Daniel Kendrick
c. -- McDaid & -- Lafferty, 1826

S-6884 50a C:294 X-0840 ROSS:TWIN
a. W-5838 William Renfrow?
b. Joseph Ladd
c. None

S-6888 100a D:204 X-0135 ROSS:PAXT
a. W-4654 Philip Philips, representatives of
b. John Graham
c. None

S-6889. See S-6540

S-6901 200a D:296 X-0843 FAYE:PAIN MADI:RANG
a. W-5879 Benjamin Porter
b. John* Hobson & Matthew* Hobson
c. None
* Per Source C.

S-6907. See S-5375 (in volume 4, part 1)

S-6908
S-6909 570a C:369 X-0841 FAYE:---* MADI:RANG
a. W-5534 Peter Manifold, assignee of Lawrence Manning
b. George Hoffman
c. None
* Source A does not mention Fayette County.

S-6910 200a C:134 X-0840 MADI:RANG
a. W-5534 Peter Manifold, assignee of Lawrence Manning
b. George Hoffman
c. None

S-6912* 235a C:70 X-0732 CLAR:----
a. W-5782 John Hull
b. Duncan McArthur
c. None
* Not listed in Source A.

S-6913* 255a C:70 X-0730 CLAR:----
a. W-5878 John Graves
b. John Hobson & Matthew Hobson
c. None
* Not listed in Source A.

S-6914* 312a C:70 X-0730 CLAR:----
a. W-5878 John Graves
b. John Hobson & Matthew Hobson
c. None
* Not listed in Source A.

S-6915* 270a C:71 X-0730 CLAR:----
a. W-5878 John Graves
b. John Hobson & Matthew Hobson
c. None
* Not listed in Source A.

S-6919* 1240a C:70 X-0145 CHAM:----
a. W-5856 James Bullifant
W-5743 William Green Munford, representative of W-5782 John Hull
b. Duncan McArthur
c. None
* Not listed in Source A.

S-6922* 6220a C:71 X-0730 LOGA:---- CHAM:----
a. W-5878 John Graves
W-5879 Benjamin Porter
b. John Hobson & Matthew Hobson
c. None
* Not listed in Source A.

S-6927* 1300a C:76 X-0146 CHAM:----
a. W-5868 Abraham Bowman
b. Abraham Bowman
c. None
* Not listed in Source A.

S-6928* 700a C:76 X-0063 CHAM:----
a. W-5867 Abraham Bowman
b. Abraham Bowman
c. None
* Not listed in Source A.

S-6929* 600a C:76 X-0063 CHAM:----
a. W-5867 Abraham Bowman
b. Abraham Bowman
c. None
* Not listed in Source A.

S-6936 400a C:132 X-0841 ROSS:CONC
a. W-5604 John Rice, representative of David (Rice)
b. Latham Stanton*
c. None
* Source C spells Staunton.

S-6938 1467a C:122 X-0840 HIGH:MADI FAYE:GREE

a. W-5157 James Gilmore (assignee? of) Thomas D. Garr--?
b. James Gilmore
c. M. Brown; S? (L?) Hinton, 1829; Mathew Brown; Jacob Chalfant, 1831; Adam Waybill; James Morrow, 1830

S-6939 500a C:314 X-0150 ROSS:BUCK ROSS:PAIN
a. W-5568 Tarlton Woodson
b. Tarlton Woodson
c. None

S-6941 125a C:81 X-0841 FAYE:MADI
a. W-5486 Hezekiah Morton
b. John Watts
c. None

S-6942 125a C:81 X-1385 PICK:DEER
a. W-5486 Hezekiah Morton
b. John Watts
c. None

S-6943 927a C:80 X-0240 X-0150 PICK:MONR
a. W-5728 Charles Scott
b. Charles Scott
c. Lyne Sterling, 1831

S-6944 350a C:80 X-0360 PICK:MONR
a. W-5728 Charles Scott
b. Charles Scott
c. None

S-6945. See S-6483

S-6946 203a C:79 X-0145 PICK:MONR
a. W-5549 Berryman Green
b. Berryman Green
c. Isaac Davis; Joseph Hodges, 1826

S-6948 62a C:259 X-0663 CLER:BATA
a. W-5838 William Renfrow?
b. Robert Townsley
c. None

S-6949 35a C:105 X-0663 CLER:BATA
a. W-5838 William Renfrow?
b. Robert Townsley
c. H. McGill; J. McKinney, 1836; David Duckwall; Daniel Duckwall, 1841

S-6952*
S-6358
S-6953 1180a C:101 X-1004 FRAN:----
a. W-5727 Anthony Dixon, representatives of
b. Anthony T. Dixon, representatives of
c. None
* Not listed in Source A.

S-6954 320a C:100 X-1004 UNIO:---* FRAN:WASH
a. W-5727 Anthony Dixon, representatives of
b. Anthony T. Dixon, representatives of
c. Demus Adams, 1829
* Source A does not mention Union County.

S-6957 260a C:117 X-0340 FRAN:BROW
a. W-5794 Tully Rogers
b. Thomas M. Bayley
c. None

S-6959
S-8022 225a* C:187 X-1385 PICK:DEER
a. W-5542 Christopher Moon, son & heir to Jacob (Moon)
W-5961 Barnabas Arthur
b. John Evans
c. A. Birt; J. Olds, 1842
* Source A says 325a.

S-6960*
S-7785
S-8127 103a -- -- PICK:WAYN
a. --
b. John Evans
c. A. Kerns; R. Campbell, 1827
* Listed in Source A only. See also S-6969

S-6969*
S-7775*
S-8127 103a C:199 X-1370 PICK:WAYN
a. W-5542 Christopher Moon, son & heir to Jacob (Moon)
W-5940 George Mallow
W-6130 Richard M. Owen
b. John Evans
c. A. Kerns; R. Campbell, 1827
* Source A says S-6960 & S-7785.

S-6962
S-7305 286a C:188 X-0360 PICK:MONR
a. W-5532 David Hopkins
W-5960 John Carroll
b. John* Evans & Edward* Owings
c. None
* Per Source C.

S-6965 300a C:186 X-0342 MADI:PIKE
a. W-5810 Thomas McKinley, heir to John (McKinley)
b. George Dawson
c. None

S-6966
S-7024 300a C:92 X-0620 X-0340 CHAM:WAYN
a. W-4796 William Cocke, representatives of
W-5793 Richard C. ---? deceased
b. James Galloway, Junior
c. None

S-6969 116a C:90 X-0340 MADI:CANA
a. W-5793 Richard C. ---? deceased
b. James Galloway, Junior
c. G. Kean; R. Douglas, 1825

S-6971 140a C:90 X-1180 MADI:JEFF
a. W-5894 Thomas Moore
b. James Galloway, Junior
c. None

S-6972 600a C:90 X-0740 GREE:ROSS CLAR:---*
a. W-5874 William Triplett
b. James Galloway, Junior
c. None
* Source A does not mention Clark County.

S-6973 100a C:96 X-0340 MADI:DARB UNIO:---*
a. W-5874 William Triplett
b. James Galloway, Junior
c. None
* Source A does not mention Union County.

S-6975 65a C:90 X-0180 GREE:CAES GREE:SILV
a. W-5875 William Triplett
b. James Galloway, Junior
c. None

S-6976 60a C:92 X-0180 GREE:ROSS
a. W-5875 William Triplett
b. James Galloway, Junior
c. None

S-6985 150a C:117 X-0340 CHAM:WAYN
a. W-5864 Henry Scott
b. David Black
c. None

S-6987 150a C:215 X-0663 HIGH:NEWM
a. W-5706 Archibald Moon? (Moore?)
b. Joseph Kerr
c. Jeremiah Fenner, 1831

S-6987 100A C:215 X-0663 HIGH:SALE
a. W-5706 Archibald Moon? (Moore?)
b. Joseph Kerr
c. None

S-6988 150a C:90 X-0730 CLAR:PLEA
a. W-5875 William Triplett
b. James Galloway, Junior
c. None

S-6994 40a D:428 X-0420 BROW:HUNT
a. W-3656 John Whealer*
b. Robert West
c. None
* So spelled.

S-6998 63a C:91 X-1004 DELA:CONC
a. W-5547 Sarah Gunn, devisee of James (Gunn)
W-5493 John C. Carter
W-5862 Jacob Daviss? heir?
b. Walter Dun
c. None

S-7000 150a C:127 X-0844 FAYE:GREE
a. W-5229 Lawrence Butler
b. Nathaniel Pope*
c. None
* Source C says Rose.

S-7001 150a B:527 X-0600 ADAM:SPRI ADAM:MONR
a. W-1114 Jacob Burker? (Burk?)
b. Andrew Ellison
c. None

S-7002 100a C:205 X-0600 ADAM:SPRI
a. W-1050 John Britton
b. Andrew Ellison
c. None

S-7003* 40a -- -- PIKE:JACK
a. --
b. Andrew Ellison
c. None
* Listed in Source A only.

S-7004 80a B:58 X-0040 ADAM:MONR
a. W-4992 Thomas Wills? (Wells?), representatives of
b. David Satterfield*
c. None
* Source A spells Saterfield.

S-7005 50a C:152 X-1007 ADAM:JEFF
a. W-4990 Thomas Wills? (Wells?), representatives of
b. Robert Ellison
c. None

S-7006 10a E:65 X-0840 ROSS:TWIN
a. W-1691 Anthony Chavalier (Chevalier)
b. Samuel Turner
c. None

S-7007 50a C:206 X-0300 PIKE:PEEP
a. W-1114 Jacob Burker (Burk?)
b. Andrew Ellison
c. None

S-7008 2400a B:531 X-0480 UNIO:CLAI
a. W-5516 Andrew Moore
b. William Caruthers & J. Caruthers
c. B. H. Lathrop, 1823; Christopher Cummings

S-7009 800a B:531 X-0480 UNIO:CLAI
a. W-5516 Andrew Moore
b. Andrew Moore
c. Heirs of James McCollum; William Little, 1820-1826; Robson L. Broome, 1835; C. Kazar; P. Plummer; John McColm (so spelled); Benjamin Thompson, 1831; Thomas Smith, 1833

S-7011 70a C:15 X-0660 GREE:MIAM GREE:XENI
a. W-5516 Andrew Moore
b. James Galloway, Junior
c. None

S-7015 100a C:464 X-0995 BROW:PERR
a. W-5492 John Wyatt
b. John Wyatt
c. None

S-7020 1000a C:92 X-1303 HIGH:SALE
a. W-5524 James Crain
b. Joseph Kerr
c. G. W. Barriere, 1833

S-7021 250a C:92 X-0010 GREE:SILV CLIN:LIBE
a. W-5129 Simpson Foster
b. Simpson Fa---?*, representative of
c. None
* Source A says Simpson Foster.

S-7022 867a C:93 X-0340 X-0750 UNIO:ALLE
a. W-5795 Rice Haggard & Nancy (Haggard) his wife
b. R. Haggard & N. Haggard
c. Rick Haggard; Henry Eemerine? 1823; N. Benton; H. Bates; R. L. Broome, 1840

S-7023 200a C:92 X-0110 X-0480 DELA:THOM
a. W-5795 Rice Haggard & Nancy (Haggard) his wife
b. R. Haggard & N. Haggard
c. Anthony Walker, 1824

S-7024. See S-6966

S-7025 40a C:92 X-0740 GREE:ROSS CLAR:---*
a. W-5793 Richard C. ---?
b. James Galloway, Junior
c. None
* Source A does not mention Clark County.

S-7026 50a C:102 X-0130 ADAM:CREE
a. W-4990 Thomas Wills? (Wells?) representative of
b. Robert Ellison
c. James Newland; C. Stephenson, 1837

S-7027 50a C:233 X-1007 ADAM:JEFF
a. W-4990 Thomas Wills? (Wells?) representative of
b. Robert Ellison
c. None

S-7028 50a C:209 X-0040 ADAM:MONR
a. W-5356 William Rogers
b. Andrew Ellison
c. None

S-7029. See S-6554

S-7031* 83a -- -- CHAM:RUSH FRAN:NORW
a. --
b. Walter Dun
c. J. S. Cowgill
* Listed in Source A only.

S-7034 100a C:129 X-1240 ROSS:TWIN
a. W-181 Robert Woodson
b. R. Woodson & S. Woodson
c. None

S-7035 100a C:129 X-1240 ROSS:TWIN
a. W-181 Robert Woodson
b. R. Woodson & S. Woodson
c. None

S-7037 600a C:113 X-0840 FAYE:UNIO
a. W-5354 Thomas Hungerford, deceased
b. William Robinson
c. Heirs of James Patterson; I Y. Green, 1836; William Allen

S-7038 944a C:110 X-0840 FAYE:UNIO
a. W-5889 Thomas Moore
W-5897 Henry Dawson
b. George Dawson
c. None

S-7039 100a* C-94 X-0841 FAYE:MADI
a. W-5559 Francis Preston, assignee of Henry Conway
b. Francis Preston
c. None
* Source A says 160a.

S-7040 428a C:94 X-0840 FAYE:JEFF
a. W-5559 Francis Preston, assignee of Henry Conway
W-5560 Francis Preston, assignee of Henry Conway
b. Francis Preston
c. None

S-7041 69a E:267 X-1300 BROW:PIKE
a. W-5559 Francis Preston, assignee of Henry Conway
b. Francis Preston
c. George C. Light, 1836

S-7043. See S-5780 (in volume 4, part 1)

S-7051 747a C:113 X-0840 FAYE:UNIO
a. W-5688 Joseph Woodson
W-5689 Joseph Woodson
W-5690 Joseph Woodson
W-5354 Thomas Hungerford, deceased, executors of
b. William Robinson
c. Joseph? (James?) Brown; J. Melliken, 1826

S-7052 422a C:113 X-0840 FAYE:UNIO FAYE:PAIN
a. W-5536 George Handy
b. Jesse McKay
c. None

S-7053. See S-6388 (in volume 4, part 1)

S-7055 306a C:459 X-0340 MADI:FAIR
a. W-5727 Anthony Dixon, representatives of
b. Anthony T. Dixon, representatives of
c. None

S-7056 167a C:98 X-0340 MADI:DARB
a. W-5795 Rice Haggard & Nancy (Haggard) his wife
b. R. Haggard & N. Haggard
c. D. Chapman; R. Douglas, 1836

S-7057 100a C:98 X-0340 MADI:CANA
a. W-5795 Rice Haggard & Nancy (Haggard) his wife
b. R. Haggard & N. Haggard
c. None

S-7058 400a C:97 X-1000 X-0340 UNIO:JERO
a. W-5717 John Spilfatham? (Spelfatham?)
b. James M. Galloway
c. None

S-7059 220a C:98 X-0340 MADI:CANA MADI:DARB
a. W-5717 John Spilfatham? (Spelfatham?)
b. George Galloway
c. None

S-7060 180a C:98 X-0840 CLAR:---* MADI:STOK
a. W-5717 John Spilfatham? (Spelfatham?)
b. George Galloway
c. M. L. Sullivant, 1831
* Source A does not mention Clark County.

S-7061 100a C:98 X-0340 MADI:JEFF
a. W-5717 John Spilfatham? (Spelfatham?)
b. Samuel Galloway
c. None

S-7062 50a C:96 X-0340 MADI:CANA
a. W-5864 Henry Scott
b. James Galloway (Junior*)
c. None
* Per Source A.

S-7063 60a C:96 X-0340 UNIO:---* MADI:DARB
a. W-5717 John Spilfatham? (Spelfatham?)
b. James Galloway
c. None
* Source A does not mention Union County.

S-7064 120a C:96 X-0340 MADI:DARB
a. W-5875 William Triplett
b. James Galloway
c. None

S-7065 350a C:118 X-1000 FRAN:NORW
a. W-5875 William Triplett
b. James Galloway
c. Hugh McGill; C. Higgins, 1837; G. Jefferis? (Jefferies?) 1835

S-7066 150a C:97 X-0340 FRAN:BROW FRAN:PRAI
a. W-5875 William Triplett
b. James Galloway
c. Ezekiel Hellor*; M. L. Sullivant, 1831
* So spelled.

S-7067 55a C:96 X-0340 MADI:CANA
a. W-5875 William Triplett
b. James Galloway
c. None

S-7068 329a C:97 X-0340 FRAN:PRAI
a. W-5830 John Middlebrook
W-5737 Thomas Gaskins, deceased
b. James Galloway
c. None

S-7069 133a C:97 X-0840 MADI:STOK
a. W-5717 John Spilfatham? (Spelfatham?)
b. James Galloway
c. None

S-7070 140a C:97 X-0340 MADI:CANA
a. W-5717 John Spilfatham? (Spelfatham?)
b. James Galloway
c. None

S-7071 340a C:97 X-0340 FRAN:BROW
a. W-5827 William Cunningham
b. James Galloway
c. R. Jones; E. Jones, 1842

S-7073 527a C:98 X-1000 UNIO:JERO
a. W-2556 Lieutenant Claiborne Vaughan
b. Richard J. Waters
c. H. W. Perkins, 1836?

S-7074 800a C:95 X-1000 X-0340 MADI:DARB FRAN:---*
a. W-308 Lieutenant John Crawford
b. John Crawford
c. H. W. Perkins, 1831; William Woods; Titus Dart, 1835; John D. Elbert; S. Hager, 1840; J. D. Elbert, Junior; R. L. Broome, 1840; John Beard; Joseph? (James?) Chesman, 1831 (Madison County)
* Source A says Union County, Jerome Township; does not mention Franklin County.

S-7075 200a C:96 X-0340 MADI:CANA
a. W-308 Lieutenant John Crawford
b. John Crawford
c. None

S-7076
S-7078 400a C:268 X-0360 PICK:PERR
a. W-5823 William Darke, representatives of
W-4710 Thomas Smith, representatives of
b. John McCormick
c. Mathew Bonner, 1831

S-7079 493a C:326 X-0360 MADI:UNIO
a. W-5806 Daniel Bedinger
b. Daniel Bedinger
c. None

S-7083 600a C:110 X-1301 HIGH:SALE
a. W-5421 Reuben Briscoe
W-5808 Thomas McKinley, heir to John (McKinley)
b. George Dawson
c. None

S-7084 300a C:110 X-0381 HIGH:DODS
a. W-5811 Thomas McKinley, heir to John (McKinley)
W-5808 Thomas McKinley, heir to John (McKinley)
b. George Dawson
c. None

S-7085 1634a? C:112 X-1301 HIGH:SALE
a. W-5829 William Cunningham, heirs (of)
W-5569 James Pendleton
W-5822 William Higgenbotham
b. John Hobson & Matthew Hobson
c. J. Faust; A. Cunningham, 1824

S-7087 236a C:224 X-0663 HIGH:UNIO
a. W-5673 Joseph Woodson
W-5674 Joseph Woodson
W-5675 Joseph Woodson
b. Thomas Scott
c. None

S-7088 860a C:99 X-0570 CLER:WASH
a. W-5866 Abraham Bowman
b. Abraham Bowman
c. None

S-7090. See S-4455 (in volume 4, part 1)

S-7091 485a C:412 X-0790 CLER:GOSH CLER:WAYN
a. W-5866 Abraham Bowman
b. Abraham Bowman
c. William Lytle; S? (L?) Winsten, 1823; J. Garrison; E. Frazier, 1839

S-7092 500a E-147 X-0790 CLER:GOSH CLER:WAYN CLER:STON
a. W-5866 Abraham Bowman
b. -- Taylor & -- Kirby
c. H. Irwin; Jacob Beagle, 1842

S-7093 200a C:412 X-0790 CLER:GOSH
a. W-5866 Abraham Bowman
b. Abraham Bowman
c. None

S-7097* 4a -- -- BROW:STER
a. --
b. John Crittenden, representatives of
c. None
* Listed in Source A only.

S-7101* 184a -- -- HIGH:DODS
a. --
b. Samuel P. Minzie
c. S. Spencer, 1824; John McClure; George Smith, 1836; Stephen Spencer; George Charles, 1831; John Smith, 1831
* Listed in Source A only.

S-7102* 100a -- -- --
a. --
b. Green K. Hubbard
c. None
* This entry, which appears in Source A only, has been stricken out.

S-7103 2a* E:403 X-0663 CLER:MONR CLER:BATA
a. W-5071 Peter Lamkin
b. James Taylor**
c. None
* Source A says 23a.
** Source A says Joseph Stokeley.

S-7104* 42a -- -- HIGH:CLAY
a. --
b. Joseph Stokeley
c. None
* Entry in Source A only.

S-7105
S-10420
S-13934 220a E:43 X-1070 CLER:STON
a. W-5055 Jesse Davis
b. Jesse Davis
c. None

S-7105. See also S-13934

S-7106
S-8561* 43a C:258 X-0663 CLER:BATA
a. W-5838 William Renfrow
b. Robert Townsley
c. James McKinney
* Source A says S-8567.

S-7111 100a C:131 X-1045 SCIO:UNIO
a. W-5831 Jeremiah Kendall
b. Jeremiah Kendall
c. None

S-7112. See S-5456 (in volume 4, part 1)

S-7113 60a C:176 X-0120 MADI:RANG
a. W-5846 Charles Stockley
b. Thomas Worthington
c. None

S-7114
S-7115
S-8024 380a C:188 X-0360 PICK:DEER
a. W-5542 Christopher Moone, son & heir of Jacob Moon
W-5961 Barnabas Arthur
b. -- Evans & -- Owings
c. None

S-7116 19a C:199 X-1370 PICK:WAYN
a. W-5564 Willis Wilson
b. Willis Wilson
c. None

S-7117 930a D:385 X-0345 LOGA:ZANE CHAM:---*
a. W-5661 William Pelham
b. James Galloway (Junior**)
c. None
* Source A does not mention Champaign County.
** Per Source A.

S-7119 57a C:131 X-0130 ADAM:JEFF
a. W-3656 John Whealer*
b. Benjamin Wood
c. Thomas Lewis; Joseph Biggs, 1823
* So spelled.

S-7120*
S-7121* 180a -- -- CLER:BATA
a. --
b. William Moseley
b. David Duckwall; Daniel Duckwall, 1841
* Listed in Source A only (at top of page beginning with S-7076).

S-7120 & S-7121. See S-6194 (in volume 4, part 1)

S-7122 200a C:171 X-0840 ROSS:HUNT
a. W-5539 William White
b. Jesse McKay
c. None

S-7123 148a C:265 X-0134 ADAM:SCOT
a. W-5578 Benjamin Leach, heir to William (Leach)
b. Andrew Ellison
c. None

S-7125 79a C:166 X-1189 SCIO:NILE
a. W-4145 Edward W. Clement
b. Abraham Bibby
c. None

S-7126 21a C:166 X-1189 SCIO:NILE
a. W-4145 Edward W. Clement
b. Abraham Bibby
c. None

S-7127
S-7439 55a C:209 X-0130 ADAM:WAYN
a. W-5356 Thomas D. Harris, assignee of Francis Smith
W-5947 William Pullen
b. Andrew Ellison
c. None

S-7128
S-8257 68a C:208 X-0130 ADAM:GREE
a. W-5577 Benjamin Leach, heir to John (Leach) deceased
W-5768 Samuel Blair?
b. Andrew Ellison
c. None

S-7129 50a C:102 X-0600 ADAM:MONR
a. W-4990 Thomas Wills? (Wells?) representative of
b. Robert Ellison
c. None

S-7132* 10a -- -- ADAM:TIFF
a. --
b. Andrew Ellison
c. None
* Listed in Source A only.

S-7141 100a C:104 X-1180 CHAM:GOSH
a. --
b. James Galloway, Junior
c. None

S-7142 100a C:104 X-1180 UNIO:---* MADI:--** CHAM:--**
a. W-5661 William Pelham
b. James Galloway, Junior
c. None
* Township illegible in Source A.
** Source A does not mention Madison or Champaign counties.

S-7143 100a C:105 X-1180 CHAM:RUSH
a. W-1771 William Gentry
b. William Townsley
c. None

S-7146 264a C:105 X-0360 PICK:DEER
a. W-5405 Philip Mallory
W-5531 Robert Beale
b. Jesse McKay
c. John Locum; David Montgomery, 1831; W. H. Leffinwell* 1837
* So spelled.

S-7149 50a C:189 X-0360 ROSS:DEER
a. W-5549 Berryman Green
b. Berryman Green
c. None

S-7152 300a C:112 X-1000 PICK:JACK PICK:DEER
a. W-387 Captain Samuel Lapsley
b. Samuel Lapsley
c. John Thompson; Isaac Julian, 1832

S-7155* 106a -- -- FRAN:PRAI
a. --
b. Walter Dun
c. None
* Listed in Source A only.

S-7159* 13a -- -- DELA:SCIO
a. --
b. Walter Dun

c. None
* Listed in Source A only.

S-7161 296a D:19 X-0991 LOGA:BOAK
a. W-5232 Richard Call, representatives of
b. Richard Call, representatives of
c. George Mathews; T. James & J. Garwood, 1830; John Mays, 1832; heirs of John Wilder; Jacob R. Hall, 1839

S-7162 74a C:114 X-0840 MADI:STOK
a. W-5232 Richard Call, representatives of
b. Richard Call, representatives of
c. None

S-7164 74a C:315 X-0845 ROSS:SCIO
a. W-5495 Francis Cowherd
b. Jesse McKay
c. None

S-7165
S-7166 300a C:120 X-0840 ROSS:TWIN
a. W-5349 John Nicholas
b. John Nicholas
c. None

S-7168 100a C:108 X-0600 ADAM:SPRI
a. W-5349 John Nicholas
b. John Nicholas
c. None

S-7169
S-11923*
S-12254* 276a D:276 X-0845 ROSS:PAIN
a. W-5555 Samuel Booker's heirs S. Donaldson (&) David Bradford
W-5989 John Yancey
W-6539 William Withers?
b. -- James, -- Massie, & -- Withers
c. None
* Source A says S-10923 & S-12259.

S-7172 65a C:106 X-1040 ADAM:JEFF
a. W-1914 Benjamin Hughes
b. John Ellison, Junior
c. None

S-7173 75a C:206 X-1045 SCIO:BRUS
a. W-5577 Benjamin Leach, heir to John (Leach)
W-5578 Benjamin Leach, heir to John (Leach)
b. Andrew Ellison
c. None

S-7174 50a C:197 X-0840 ROSS:PAIN
a. W-5555 Samuel Booker's heirs S. Donaldson (&) David Bradford
b. Thomas James
c. None

S-7175 180a C:218 X-0290 FAYE:MADI
a. W-5954 Richard Hooper
W-5691 Joseph Woodson
b. William Robinson
c. George Dunkle; R. Waddle, 1826

S-7176 200a C:349 X-0840 MADI:UNIO
a. W-4685 Wyatt Smith
b. Henry Brush
c. Heirs of Stephen Cessna; John Moore, 1835

S-7181 200a C:108 X-1004 UNIO:JERO
a. W-5903 Leroy Edwards' devisees
b. Walter Dun
c. None

S-7183 100a C:107 X-0840 MADI:---*
a. W-5574 Joseph Dunlap
b. Jacob Lease
c. E. Langham; H. Warner, 1826
* Source A does not mention township.

S-7184. See S-6063 (in volume 4, part 1)

S-7185 200a C:518 X-0360 PICK:DARB
a. W-5395 Robert Eager, representatives of
b. Robert Eager, representatives of
c. J. Olds & D. Adams, 1831

S-7187 10a C:108 X-0840 ROSS:PAIN
a. W-5903 Leroy Edwards' devisees
b. Walter Dun
c. None

S-7188 200a C:193 X-0846 HIGH:BRUS
HIGH:PAIN
a. W-5555 Samuel Booker's heirs S. Donaldson (&) David Bradford
b. Jesse Baldwin
c. C. Benner? (Bonner?); J. M. Johnson, 1836

S-7195 60a C:333 X-1000 PICK:SCIO
a. W-5244 John C. Cobbs, --? to Samuel (Cobbs)
b. -- Tagart, -- McLaughlin, -- Gray, & -- Taylor
c. S? (L?) Tully, 1838

S-7196 40a C:333 X-1000 PICK:DARB
PICK:SCIO
a. W-5244 John C. Cobbs, --? to Samuel (Cobbs)
b. -- Tagart, -- McLaughlin, -- Gray, & -- Taylor
c. Thomas C. Reber, 1838

S-7197 17a C:409 X-0663 CLER:BATA
a. W-5336 William Mosley*
b. William Moseley*
c. None
* So spelled.

S-7198 100a C:144 X-0840 ROSS:TWIN
a. W-5925 Jenn? Pea, heir to Thomas Pea
b. Cadwallader Wallace
c. None

S-7200
S-8258 200a C:205 X-0136 ADAM:JEFF
a. W-5555 Samuel Booker's heirs S. Donaldson (&) David Bradford
W-3105 Thomas Miller
b. Andrew Ellison
c. None

S-7201 54a C:206 X-0130 ADAM:MEIG
a. W-5841 Samuel Scruggs
b. Andrew Ellison
c. None

S-7202 25a C:523 X-0130 ADAM:GREE
a. W-6425 George Purcell, heirs (&) assignees (of)
b. Robert Whitlatch
c. None

S-7204 50a D:99 X-0650 ADAM:TIFF
a. W-5555 Samuel Booker's heirs S. Donaldson (&) David Bradford
b. Andrew Ellison
c. None

S-7205 50a C:151 X-0130 ADAM:JEFF
a. W-5555 Samuel Booker's heirs S. Donaldson (&) David Bradford
b. Andrew Ellison
c. John Rodgers; John Fisher, 1823

S-7206 13a D:200 X-0650 ADAM:TIFF
a. W-3092 Samuel Decker
b. William Russell
c. T. Huston, 1836; William Russell; William Allen, 1838

S-7207. See S-5197 (in volume 4, part 1)

S-7209 38a C:501 X-0340 UNIO:JERO
a. W-5265 Tuttle Hudson et al, administrators of William Hudson
b. Lucas Sullivant
c. None

S-7210 100a D:9 X-0135 ADAM:FRAN
a. W-5915 Peggy Moors? heir to Francis Downing
b. Peggy Meen
c. James Lewis; -- Adams; William Parks, 1826

S-7211 221a C:139 X-0846 FAYE:JEFF
a. W-5493 John C. Carter
b. Walter Dun
c. None

S-7214 540a C:559 X-0540 ROSS:DEER
ROSS:PERR
a. W-5711 Andrew A. Gilchrist, heir to George (Gilchrist)
b. Thomas James
c. None

S-7215 50a D:301 X-0365 ROSS:DEER
a. W-5592 John Hart, assignee of John (Hart?)
b. Thomas James
c. None

S-7216 185a C:117 X-0340 MADI:JEFF
a. W-5918 Ballard Smith, representatives of
b. James Barrett*
c. None
* Sources A & C spell Barnett.

S-7218 593a C:121 X-0340 UNIO:DARB
a. W-5759 Peter Garland, representative of
b. Benjamin W. Ladd
c. J. R. Parish; Joseph? (James?) Hutten; Means? Wasson, 1833; Lyne Starling; T. Robinson, 1833; Oliver C. Kanady, 1831?

S-7218. See also S-5137 (in volume 4, part 1)

S-7219 100a D:81 X-0365 MADI:RANG
GREE:---*
a. W-5845 Margaret Neill*, heir to Hugh Griffen?
b. Margaret Neil*
c. Napoleon Lucas; John Kaious, 1831
* So spelled.

S-7223 100a C:300 X-0730 CHAM:SALE
a. W-5489 Thomas Dove
b. Christopher Bartlett
c. None

S-7225 70a C:111 X-1000 PICK:JACK
a. W-5895 Thomas Moore
b. John A. Fulton
c. None

S-7226 250a C:111 X-0663 HIGH:NEWM
a. W-5849 Richard Crafton
W-5846 Charles Stockly, deceased
W-5545 John Moss
b. J. A.* Fulton & J.* Moss
c. Benjamin Thomas, 1838?
* Per Source A.

S-7227 775a D:248 X-0663 HIGH:UNIO
a. W-5421 Reuben Briscoe
W-5809 Thomas McKindley* heir to John (McKindley)
b. George Dawson
c. None
* Probably McKinley is meant.

S-7228 125a C:320 X-0840 ROSS:TWIN
a. W-5967 William Poyner
b. Moses Dewitt*
c. Heirs of J. Pancake; H. Fullerton, 1841
* Source A may spell Demitt; Source C spells Demmitt.

S-7230 500a C:111 X-0350 MADI:PIKE
a. W-5892 Thomas Moore
b. John A. Fulton
c. None

S-7231 60a C:111 X-0360 PICK:DEER
a. W-5895 Thomas Moore
b. John A. Fulton
c. None

S-7232 50a C:111 X-0663 HIGH:DODS
a. W-5846 Charles Stockly
b. William Fulton
c. None

S-7233 30a C:111 X-0570 ROSS:SCIO
a. W-5895 Thomas Moore
b. John A. Fulton
c. None

S-7234 50a C:237 X-0540 ROSS:DEER
a. W-5895 Thomas Moore
W-5820 William Adams
b. John A. Fulton
c. None

S-7235 50a C:178 X-0900 ROSS:DEER
a. W-5820 William Adams
b. John A. Fulton
c. William Clark; Richard Douglas, 1828?

S-7236
S-8468 200a C:242 X-1300 HIGH:SALE
HIGH:CLAY
a. W-5820 William Adams
W-5539 William White
W-6130 Richard H? Owen
b. John A. Fulton
c. None

S-7237
S-7269
S-8198
S-8955* 1300a C:218 X-0841 FAYE:MADI
FAYE:PAIN
a. W-6121 Thomas Hopper
W-5769 Robert Hai--?
W-6122 Thomas Hopper
W-5954 Richard Hoopes? (Hooper?)
W-5964 William Poyner
b. William Robinson
c. Jesse? Davis; E. Waddle, 1826; Fontley Muse; E. Allen, 1830
* Source A says S-8055.

S-7238 70a C:213 X-0366 PICK:DEER
a. W-5539 William White
b. John A. Fulton
c. None

S-7239 637a C:142 X-0340 MADI:DARB
a. W-5792 James Johnston
b. James Johnston
c. W. Dun; H. Warner, 1836

S-7240 192a C:142 X-0340 MADI:CANA
a. W-5792 James Johnston
b. James Johnston
c. None

S-7241 78a C:142 X-0340 MADI:DARB
a. W-5792 James Johnston
b. James Johnston
c. None

S-7242 45a C:225 X-0740 GREE:ROSS
a. W-5547 Sarah Gunn, devisee of James (Gunn)
b. Walter Dun
c. None

S-7243 197a C:157 X-0340 MADI:DARB
a. W-5547 Sarah Gunn, devisee of James (Gunn)
W-5792 James Johnston
b. -- Dun & -- Johnston
c. W. Dun; W. McCoy, 1828

S-7245 543a C:137 X-0340 UNIO:DARB
a. W-5792 James Johnston
W-5755 William Price
b. James* Johnston & John* Graham
c. L. Sullivant; J. Bigelow
* Per Source C.

S-7247 100a D:108 X-1005 FRAN:PLEA
PICK:---*
a. W-5900 David Scott, heir to John (Scott)
b. David Scott
c. A. Boring?
* Source A does not mention Pickaway County.

S-7249* 1000a C:154 X-0841 PICK:PERR
a. W-5891 Thomas Moore
W-5893 Thomas Moore
b. Thomas Moore
c. John Lindsey; Henry Ely, 1829
* Source says "by Holland."

S-7250 126a C:164 X-0843 FAYE:PAIN
a. W-5971 Edward Wills? (Wells?)
b. Cadwallader Wallace
c. Absalom? Funk; L. Loofborrow, 1826; R. Douglas; W. Loofborrow, 1827; William Douglas

S-7251 150a C:164 X-0843 FAYE:PAIN
a. W-5971 Edward Wills? (Wells?)
b. Cadwallader Wallace
c. Ab(salom?)(Abraham?) Funk; L. Loofborrow, 1826; R. Douglas, 1831; A. Douglas, Junior, 1838

S-7255 100a C:217 X-0841 ROSS:DEER
a. W-5757 Solomon Tracy
b. Solomon Tracy
c. None

S-7256 150a C:178 X-1000 ROSS:HUNT
a. W-5941 William Higginbotham
b. William Keys
c. None

S-7257 200a C:532 X-0841 ROSS:CONC
a. W-5964 William Poynor*
b. William Robinson
c. None
* So spelled.

S-7260 370a C:173 X-0840 MADI:STOK
a. W-5953 Richard Hooper
b. William Creighton, Junior
c. W. Buffenbergh; G. Lenson, 1826

S-7262 250a C:287 X-0360 MADI:UNIO
a. W-5953 Richard Hooper
b. William Creighton, Junior
c. None

S-7263
S-7799 517a D:100 X-0846 MADI:RANG
a. W-5978 John E. Scott, representative of
W-5953 Richard Hooper
b. -- Robinson & -- Creighton
c. Richard Douglas; -- Robinson & -- Slaughter; M. Sullivant, 1831

S-7264 100a C:134 X-0360 MADI:DEER
a. W-5941 William Higginbotham
b. Thomas Gwynne & David Gwynne
c. None

S-7265 220a C:191 X-0841 MADI:RANG
a. W-5944 William Higginbotham
b. Mathew Hobson
c. James Woods, 1828 (Fayette County)

S-7267
S-7567
S-7890 600a C:218 X-0840 FAYE:---*
MADI:RANG
a. W-6026 John Stokes, representatives of
W-6028 John Stokes, representatives of
W-6030 John Stokes, representatives of
W-5954 Richard Hooper
b. William Robinson
c. Absalom Funk; Richard Douglas, 1831

S-7268
S-8147 200a C:217 X-0290 FAYE:PAIN
a. W-5954 Richard Hooper
W-6129 Herod Gibbs
b. William Robinson
c. None

S-7269. See S-7237

S-7270 25a D:493 X-0290 FAYE:MADI
a. W-5954 Richard Hooper
b. William Robinson
c. None

S-7271 250a C:239 X-0290 FAYE:MADI
a. W-5956 John Carroll
b. Hugh Stewart
c. None

S-7272
S-8139 500a C:239 X-0841 FAYE:MADI
a. W-5956 John Carroll
W-5969 Edward Wills? (Wells?)
b. Hugh Stewart
c. None

S-7273 100a C:167 X-0290 FAYE:MADI
a. W-5963 Barnabas Arthur
b. John A. Fulton
c. None

S-7275 100a C:143 X-0300 PIKE:JACK
a. W-5007 Humphrey Beckett
b. Vatchel Howard
c. None

S-7276 90a C:139 X-0300 PIKE:JACK
a. W-5493 John C. Carter
b. Walter Dun
c. None

S-7277 333a C:349 X-0840 MADI:UNIO
CLAR:---*
a. W-5935 Robert Thelaball
b. Henry Brush
c. None
* Source A does not mention Clark County.

S-7278* 300a D:195 X-0365 MADI:RANG
a. W-5934 Robert Thelaball
b. Henry Brush
c. None
* Source A says not patented.

S-7279 150a C:349 X-0120 MADI:UNIO
a. W-5934 Robert Thelaball
b. Henry Brush
c. None

S-7280 40a C:120 X-0660 GREE:XENI
a. W-5941 William Higginbotham
b. George Galloway
c. None

S-7281 450a C:118 X-0340 FRAN:PLEA
a. W-5960 John Carroll
b. James Galloway, Junior
c. Samuel Gosley; James Bryden, 1827

S-7285 70a C:119 X-0340 MADI:CANA
a. W-5957 John Carroll
b. James Galloway, Junior
c. R. Knox; K. Bailey, 1825

S-7288 175a C:119 X-0756 LOGA:PERR
a. W-5958 John Carroll
b. James Galloway, Junior
c. None

S-7291 165a C:274 X-1260? MADI:UNIO
a. W-4944 Thomas Hungerford

W-5878 John Graves
b. E. Langham, J. Hobson, & M. Hobson
c. W. Coberly; A. G. Thompson, 1824; E. T. Langham; S. N. Kerr, 1831

S-7292 180a C:121 X-0740 CLAR:GREE
a. W-5970 Edward Wills? (Wells?)
b. George Townsley
c. None

S-7295 50a C:144 X-0840 ROSS:TWIN
a. W-5936 Robert Dugar
b. Joseph Westbrook
c. None

S-7296 50a C:144 X-1226 ROSS:TWIN
a. W-5936 Robert Dugar
b. Joseph Westbrook
c. None

S-7303 150a C:322 X-0360 FAYE:MADI MADI:PLEA
a. W-5474 Holman Minnis, representatives of
W-5475 Benjamin Minnis, representatives of
b. Daniel Brown
c. James Woods, 1828; M. S. Cook & J. Webb

S-7305. See S-6962

S-7306. See S-6258 (in volume 4, part 1)

S-7308
S-7914
S-7915 400a C:442 X-0360 PICK:PERR
a. W-5965 William Poyner
b. Stephen Timmons
c. None

S-7309 100a C:530 X-1000 PICK:WAYN
a. W-5968 William Poyner
b. Thomas Bowdle
c. None

S-7311 1955a C:118 X-1180 CHAM:RUSH CHAM:WAYN
a. W-5712 John Monroe
W-5730 John? (Jesse?) Merryman
W-5966 William Poyner
W-5957 John Carroll
W-5958 John Carroll
W-5970 Edward Wills? (Wells?)
b. James Galloway, Junior
c. J. Faurote?; S. Collings, 1826

S-7313 125a C:458 X-1000 PICK:WAYN
a. W-5354 Thomas Hungerford, deceased, executor of
b. William Robinson
c. None

S-7318 340a C:119 X-0730 LOGA:JEFF LOGA:MONR
a. W-5827 William Cunningham, heirs of
W-5973 Edward Wills? (Wells?)
b. James Galloway, Junior
c. None

S-7319 50a C:120 X-0740 CLAR:MADI
a. W-5973 Edward Wills? (Wells?)
W-5970 Edward Wills? (Wells?)
b. -- Galloway & -- Townsley
c. None

S-7320 250a C:119 X-0665 GREE:MIAM GREE:XENI
a. W-5973 Edward Wills? (Wells?)
b. James Galloway, Junior
c. None

S-7321 100a C:119 X-0660 CLAR:MADI
a. W-5955 Richard Hooper
b. James Galloway, Junior
c. None

S-7323 310a C:119 X-1180 CHAM:RUSH
a. W-5955 Richard Hooper
b. James Galloway, Junior
c. None

S-7324* 300a C:120 X-0740 GREE:ROSS CLAR:MADI
a. W-5955 Richard Hooper
b. James Galloway, Junior
c. None
* Source A says "Woodstock."

S-7325 50a C:120 X-1000 FRAN:FRAN
a. W-5955 Richard Hooper
b. James Galloway, Junior
c. None

S-7326 360a C:120 X-1000 FRAN:PRAI
a. W-5955 Richard Hooper
W-5974 Edward Wills? (Wells?)
b. James Galloway, Junior
c. None

S-7330 50a* C:184 X-0660 WARR:WAYN
a. W-5975 Edward Wills? (Wells?)
b. James Galloway, Junior
c. None
* Source A says 150a.

S-7336 60a C:120 X-0660 CLAR:MADI
a. W-5941 William Higginbotham
b. George Galloway
c. None

S-7341 & S-7342. See S-6512

S-7344 36a C:224 X-0840 ROSS:TWIN
a. W-5708 John Poulson? deceased, executor of
b. Thomas Scott
c. None

S-7345 30a C:123 X-0130 ADAM:MONR
a. W-5947 William Pullen
b. Robert Moore
c. None

S-7346 20a C:123 X-0130 ADAM:SCOT ADAM:JEFF
a. W-5947 William Pullen
b. John Raider
b. None

S-7347 200a C:183 X-0136 ADAM:JEFF
a. W-5947 William Pullen
b. Robert Moore
c. Robert Means; Samuel Treat? 1824 "error, should be Moore"; T Jarvis & Co.; T. Huston, 1837

S-7348 50a C:206 X-0130 PIKE:SUNF
a. W-5761 Barnabas Arthur
b. Andrew Ellison
c. None

S-7349 50a C:206 X-0239 ADAM:MONR
a. W-5761 Barnabas Arthur
b. Andrew Ellison
c. Lydia Miller; L. Cole, 1836

S-7351 50a C:206 X-0042 ADAM:TIFF
a. W-5761 Barnabas Arthur
b. Andrew Ellison
c. None

S-7352 35a C:183 X-1045 ADAM:JEFF
a. W-1914 Benjamin Hughes
b. John Ellison, Junior
c. None

S-7353 32a D:130 X-0545 PICK:PERR ROSS:DEER
a. W-5963 Barnabas Arthur
b. John A. Fulton
c. None

S-7355. See S-7175

S-7358 100a C:290 X-0841 ROSS:DEER PICK:PERR
a. W-5952 Richard Hooper
b. Richard Eggleston
c. D. Kinnear, 1833

S-7359 333a C:290 X-0841 FAYE:MADI
a. W-5952 Richard Hooper
b. Richard Eggleston
c. None

S-7361 100a C:187 X-0515 PICK:PERR
a. W-5949 William Pullen
b. John Evans
c. None

S-7362. See S-2961 (in volume 4, part 1)

S-7363 200a C:338 X-0795 CLER:GOSH
a. W-4799 James Calderwood, representatives of
b. William Lytle
c. None

S-7364 240a C:129 X-0840 FAYE:GREE
a. W-5778 Tucker M. Woodson, heir to Robert (Woodson)
b. Tucker M. Woodson
c. None

S-7365 800a C:127 X-0640 X-0847 FAYE:CONC
a. W-5349 John Nicholas
b. John Nicholas
c. John Watts; J. Jameson, 1837

S-7366 760a C:127 X-0640 FAYE:GREE
a. W-5349 John Nicholas
b. John Nicholas
c. Thomas Embrel; Thomas Thorn, 1830; "deeded to Thomas Emmery, 21 Nov 1831"

S-7367 626a C:129 X-0130 ADAM:FRAN
a. W-5778 Tucker M. Woodson, heir to Robert (Woodson)
W-5779 Tucker M. Woodson, heir to Robert (Woodson)
W-181 Robert Woodson
b. T. M. Woodson & R. S. Woodson*
c. Colin Thompson, 1824; A. D. Beasley, 1828; John Davis, 1828; J. A. Andrews; J. Hood, 1841
* Source A says T. M. Woodson, R. Woodson, & S. Woodson.

S-7368. See S-5839 (in volume 4, part 1)

S-7369 133a C:128 X-0847 HIGH:PAIN
a. W-5229 Lawrence Butler
b. Nathaniel Pope
c. None

S-7370. See S-5223 (in volume 4, part 1)

S-7372 550a C:127 X-1120 PIKE:MIFF ADAM:---*
a. W-2742 Jasper Hughes
b. Thomas Pemberton
c. None
* Source A does not mention Adams County.

S-7375 200a D:35 -- UNIO:WASH
a. W-3644 Thomas Byens? (Byers?)
b. Squire Grant
c. None

S-7376 115a C:254 X-0130 ADAM:FRAN
a. W-3432 Thomas M. Galt
b. Abraham Shepheard
c. None

S-7378 30a C:261 X-1005 ADAM:SPRI
a. W-5946 William Pullen
b. Isrial* Donaldson
c. None
* So spelled.

S-7379 28a D:354 X-0595 ADAM:SPRI
a. W-5946 William Pullen
b. James Lang
c. None

S-7382 60a C:147 X-0840 ROSS:TWIN ROSS:PAXT
a. W-5732 Thomas Jackson, deceased
b. Benjamin W. Ladd
c. None

S-7385 82a C:140 X-0340 MADI:DARB
a. W-5786 Edwin Hull
b. John Graham
c. None

S-7386 100a C:140 X-0340 MADI:CANA
a. W-5786 Edwin Hull
b. John Graham
c. None

S-7387 70a C:140 X-0340 MADI:DARB
a. W-5786 Edwin Hull
W-5787 Edwin Hull
b. John Graham
c. None

S-7388 91a C:157 X-0340 UNIO:DARB MADI:DARB
a. W-5787 Edwin Hull
b. John Graham
c. None

S-7389 42a C:140 X-0340 MADI:CANA
a. W-5786 Edwin Hull
b. John Graham
c. None

S-7390 45a C:141 X-0340 UNIO:JERO MADI:---*
a. W-5787 Edwin Hull
b. John Graham
c. M. L. Sullivant, 1831
* Source A does not mention Madison County.

S-7391 226a C:156 X-1180 MADI:DARB
a. W-5791 George Lee Turberville
W-5493 John C. Carter
b. -- Graham & -- Dun
c. None

S-7392 230a C:141 X-1180 MADI:DARB
a. W-5791 George Lee Turberville
W-5786 Edwin Hull
b. John Graham
c. None

S-7393 313a C:141 X-0340 UNIO:DARB MADI:---*
a. W-5791 George Lee Turberville
b. John Graham
c. None
* Source A does not mention Madison County.

S-7394 181a C:143 X-0340 MADI:CANA
a. W-5792 James Johnston
b. James Johnston
c. None

S-7395 128a C:143 X-0340 MADI:DARB
a. W-5792 James Johnston
b. James Johnston
c. D. Chapman; R. Douglas, 1836

S-7397 100a C:143 X-0340 UNIO:DARB
a. W-5792 James Johnston
b. James Johnston
c. None

S-7398
S-12878
S-12948 232a D:276 X-0340 MADI:CANA
a. W-2365 John Hall
W-5139 Robert Means, assignee of James Smith
b. -- Chambers & -- Dun
c. None

S-7398 96a D:279 X-0340 MADI:DARB
a. W-2365 John Hall
b. Joseph Chambers
c. None

S-7398 69a C:280 X-0340 MADI:DARB
a. W-2365 John Hall
b. Joseph Chambers
c. None

S-7399 86a C:139 X-0340 MADI:---* UNIO:DARB
a. W-2365 John Hall
b Joseph Chambers
c. None
* Source A does not mention Madison County.

S-7400 100a C:139 X-0340 MADI:---* UNIO:DARB
a. W-2365 John Hall
b. Joseph Chambers
c. James Boals, 1824; William Lechey; H. S. Amy, 1827
* Source A does not mention Madison County.

S-7401 140a C:143 X-1180 MADI:DARB
a. W-5792 James Johnston
b. James Galloway, Junior*
c. F. Bond; P. Douglas, 1840
* Source A says James Johnston.

S-7402 360a C:130 X-1180 MADI:MONR MADI:PIKE
a. W-5976 Edward Wills? (Wells?)
b. James Galloway, Junior
c. None

S-7403 350a C:130 X-1180 MADI:SUMM
a. W-5976 Edward Wills? (Wells?)
W-5974 Edward Wills? (Wells?)
b. James Galloway, Junior
c. None

S-7404 400a C:130 X-1186 MADI:SUMM
a. W-5970? (5974?) Edward Wills? (Wells?)
W-5962 Barnabas Arthur
W-5975 Edward Wills? (Wells?)
b. James Galloway, Junior
c. None

S-7405 367a C:130 X-0730 CLAR:HARM
a. W-5975 Edward Wills? (Wells?)
W-5960 John Carroll
b. James Galloway, Junior
c. Heirs of T. Hull; H. Rungan? (Runyan? Rungase?) & W. H. Lafferty, 1835

S-7406 200a C:129 X-1180 UNIO:UNIO
a. W-5949 William Pullen
b. David Comer*
c. None
* Source A may spell Camer.

S-7407 100a C:130 X-0340 UNIO:WAYN
a. W-5566 Dennis Ferrall
b. Alexander Reed
c. None

S-7408
S-8275
S-8406 130a C:227 X-0250 HIGH:LIBE
a. W-5960 John Carroll
W-4305 Joseph Brand
b. James Galloway, Junior
c. J. D. Scott; J. A. Trumble, 1823

S-7409 200a C:219 X-0840 ROSS:CONC
a. W-5933 Robert Thelable (Thelaball?) deceased, representatives of
b. Duncan McArthur
c. None

S-7410
S-8623 320a C:257 X-0365 MADI:PLEA
a. W-5933 Robert Thelable (Thelaball?) deceased, representatives of
W-5718 John Spelfathom (Spilfathom?)
b. Duncan McArthur
c. A. Comer & Co., 1830; George Pew, 1833

S-7416 109a C:143 X-0340 MADI:DARB
a. W-5792 James Johnston
b. James Johnston
c. None

S-7417 88a C:133 X-1000 ROSS:UNIO
a. W-1391 Captain Nathaniel Pendleton
b. Nathaniel Pendleton
c. None

S-7418 422a C:133 X-0360 MADI:FAIR
a. W-1391 Captain Nathaniel Pendleton
b. Nathaniel Pendleton
c. None

S-7420 170a C:281 X-1000 PICK:JACK
a. W-5709 Nathaniel Darby
b. Thomas James
c. H. Massie; Walter Thrall, 1830

S-7422 100a C:203 X-0841 FAYE:MADI
a. W-5933 Thomas Gaskins
b. Duncan McArthur
c. None

S-7423 7a C:139 X-0800 SCIO:NILE
a. W-5493 John C. Carter
b. Walter Dun
c. None

S-7424 200a C:188 X-0366 PICK:JACK PICK:MONR
a. W-5968 William Poyner
b. Elizabeth Evans
c. None

S-7426 100a E:63 X-0179 PICK:MONR
a. W-5965 William Poyner
b. John Evans
c. None

S-7427 254a C:188 X-0366 PICK:PERR
a. W-5549 Berryman Green
b. Berryman Green
c. None

S-7428 113a C:161 X-1006 PIKE:JACK ROSS:---*
a. W-5792 James Johnston
W-13440 --**
W-16063 --**
b. James Johnston
c. None
* Source A does not mention Ross County.
** Source C does not list this warrant number.

S-7432
S-7756 191a C:159 X-0340 MADI:DARB
a. W-5791 George Lee Turberville
W-5755 John Walker, deceased, heirs of
W-5792 James Johnston
b. Graham Johnston*
c. None
* Source A says -- Graham & -- Johnston.

S-7433 97a C:142 X-1137 ROSS:FRAN
a. W-5792 James Johnston

W-5791 George Lee Turberville
b. Graham Johnston*
c. None
* Source A says -- Graham & -- Johnston.

S-7434* 134a -- -- FRAN:PLEA
a. --
b. John Stokes
c. None
* Listed in Source A only.

S-7435 67a C:178 X-0841 ROSS:DEER
a. W-5963 Barnabas Arthur
b. John A. Fulton
c. None

S-7437 37a C:360 X-0230 ADAM:WAYN
a. W-5947 William Pullen
b. Robert Moore
c. John Morton & Samuel Treat, 1824; John Moore, 1826

S-7438* 44a -- -- ADAM:JEFF
a. --
b. Andrew Ellison
c. None
* Listed in Source A only.

S-7439. See S-7127

S-7440 21a C:210 X-0420 ADAM:TIFF
a. W-5946 William Pullen
b. David Bradford
c. None

S-7441 25a E:438 X-0130 ADAM:MEIG
a. W-5947 William Pullen
b. Henry Fry
c. None

S-7442 50a C:308 X-0130 ADAM:MEIG SCIO:---*
a. W-5946 William Pullen
b. William Creighton, Junior
c. None
* Source A mentions Scioto County, but says "lies in" ADAM:MEIG.

S-7443 100a D:60 X-0145 HIGH:CONC
a. W-5524 James Crain
b. Joseph Kerr
c. None

S-7444 200a C:136 X-1300 BROW:PLEA
a. W-5524 James Crain
b. Joseph Kerr
c. Thomas Harris, 1823

S-7445 75a C:136 X-1140 PIKE:MIFF
a. W-5703 Archibald Moon, representative of
b. Joseph Kerr
c. None

S-7446
S-9605* 150a C:386 X-0840 ROSS:HUNT
a. W-5951 William Pentecost
W-5828 William Cunningham, heirs of
b. -- Keys & -- Dun
c. None
* Source A says S-9665.

S-7447 100a C:150 X-0130 ADAM:TIFF
a. W-5524 James Crain
b. Joseph Kerr
c. None

S-7448 100a C:360 X-0130 ADAM:TIFF
a. W-5524 James Crain
b. Joseph Kerr
c. None

S-7449 650a D:479 X-1305 HIGH:---* BROW:GREE
a. W-5872 Francis M. Boykin & Ann Johnson, heirs of F(rancis) Boykin
b. -- James, -- Woodbridge, & -- Bond
c. D. Scott & D. Read? (Reed?)
* Source A does not mention Highland County

S-7449 350a D:479 X-1305 BROW:GREE
a. W-5872 Francis M. Boykin & Ann Johnson, heirs of F(rancis) Boykin
b. -- James, -- Woodbridge, & -- Bond
c. None

S-7449*
S-8466* 1467a -- -- --
a. --
b. -- Boykin & -- Johnston**
c. None
* This entry stricken out in Source A & does not appear in Source B.
** So spelled.

S-7459 100a D:406 X-1000 PICK:SCIO
a. W-980 Lewis Frame? (France?)
b. Ephraim Doolittle
c. None

S-7460 50a D:383 X-0841 ROSS:UNIO
a. W-5950 William Pullen
b. William Robinson
c. None

S-7461 200a C:154 X-1000 PICK:JACK
a. W-5948 William Pullen
W-5950 William Pullen
b. John A. Fulton
c. None

S-7465 105a C:141 X-1180 MADI:PIKE
a. W-5791 George Lee Turberville
b. John Graham
c. None

S-7466 100a C:326 X-0841 PICK:PERR

a. W-5942 William Higginbotham
b. James Dunlap
c. None

S-7467 800a C:374 X-0360 MADI:RANG
a. W-5942 William Higginbotham
W-5943 William Higginbotham
b. James Dunlap
c. Hallam? Hempstead, 1828

S-7472
S-7677 172a C:239 X-1180 UNIO:UNIO
a. W-5836 Ann Shepherd, heir to Major, who was heir to ---?
W-6006 Moore Lumpkin
b. Benjamin Hough
c. None
* Source A does not mention Madison County.

S-7473 312a C:142 X-1186 MADI:MONR
a. W-5783 Edward Hull, deceased, son of John (Hull), heir
W-5785 Edward Hull
b. John Gaham*
c. J. McLain; C(adwallader) Wallace; E. Langham, 1825
* Source A spells Graham.

S-7474 640a C:140 X-1180 UNIO:UNIO MADI:PIKE
a. W-5785 Edward Hull
W-5792 James Johnston
W-5493 John C. Carter
b. -- Graham, -- Johnston, & -- Dun
c. W. Dun; James Gardner, 1828; Hariet* Rice; Ira? Wood, 1828; heirs of Silas Kent
* So spelled.

S-7476* 20a -- -- FRAN:FRAN
a. --
b. Lucas Sullivant
c. None
* Listed in Source A only.

S-7477 9a D:226 X-1000 FRAN:FRAN
a. W-5265 Tuttle Hudson, administrator of William Hudson
b. Robert Culbertson
c. None

S-7478* 40a -- -- FRAN:FRAN
a. --
b. Lucas Sullivant
c. L. Starling, 1826

S-7479* 40a -- -- FRAN:FRAN
a. --
b. Lucas Sullivant
c. L. Starling
* Listed in Source A only.

S-7482 233a C:141 X-1180 MADI:PIKE
a. W-5785 Edward Hull
W-5784 Edward Hull
b. John Graham
c. Jonas Snyder; John Kious, 1831

S-7483 560a C:153 X-0841 FAYE:MADI
a. W-5571 John Langden? (Longden?)
b. Benjamin Adamson
c. None

S-7484 60a C:177 X-0340 MADI:JEFF
a. W-6014 Benjamin Harrison? (Harman? Hammon?), representative of
b. William Fulton
c. None

S-7490* 50a -- -- ADAM:JEFF
a. --
b. William Fulton
c. T. Huston, 1832; Peter Warnsley? (Wamsley?), 1836

S-7491 1500a C:177 X-1180 CHAM:RUSH UNIO:UNIO
a. W-5890 Thomas Moore
W-5894 Thomas Moore
W-5896 Thomas Moore
b. Thomas Moore
c. Heirs of Andrew Kimball; Bela Kimball, 1831

S-7492
S-9461 500a C:348 X-1180 UNIO:UNIO
a. W-5950 William Pullen
W-6194 Robert Hanson Harrison, heirs of
b. -- Robinson & -- Fulton
c. None

S-7493 60a C:177 X-0340 PICK:DARB
a. W-6014 Benjamin Harrison, representative of
b. William Fulton
c. Joshua Brownell, 1832

S-7494* 10a -- -- MADI:JEFF
a. --
b. William Fulton
c. None
* Listed in Source A only.

S-7498 200a C:144 X-0150 ROSS:BUCK
a. W-5971 Edward Wills? (Wells?)
b. Cadwallader Wallace
c. None

S-7500 32a C:158 X-0800 BROW:LEWI
a. W-5791 George Lee Turberville
b. John Graham
c. None

S-7504
S-8541 203a C:336 X-0230 ADAM:WAYN
a. W-5871 Francis M. Boykin & Ann Johnson, heirs & administrators to F(rancis) Boykin
W-5991 John Price, heirs of
b. John Ellison, Junior
c. None

S-7505 100a C:209 X-0210 ADAM:JEFF
a. W-5947 William Pullen
b. Andrew Ellison
c. None

S-7508 100a C:138 X-0660 CLAR:MADI
a. W-5937 Daniel Cochran
b. Charles T. Arthur
c. None

S-7509* 1000a -- -- PICK:MONR
a. --
b. S. McGrew
c. None
* This entry appears in Source A only (entered at top of page beginning with S-7476 therein).

S-7511
S-8269 72a C:207 X-0130 ADAM:MONR
a. W-5761 John Hart?
W-5768 Samuel Blair?
b. Andrew Ellison
c. None

S-7512
S-12324
S-12698 501a E:83 X-0190 SCIO:MORG
PIKE:---*
a. W-6504 Allen ---?
W-6537 Thomas Passmore?
W-5871 William Triplett
b. Thomas Mountjoy
c. None
* Source A does not mention Pike County.

S:-7513 12a C:291 X-1110 ADAM:GREE
a. W-5871 Francis M. Boykin & Ann Johnson, heirs & administrators of F(rancis) Boykin
b. John Ellison, Junior
c. None

S-7514 50a C:207 X-0130 ADAM:TIFF
ADAM:LIBE
a. W-5760 William Thorp, deceased
b. Andrew Ellison
c. None

S-7515 50a C:210 X-0130 ADAM:MONR
a. W-5947 William Pullen
b. Jonathan Pollard
c. None

S-7516 100a C:147 X-0806 ADAM:MEIG
ADAM:GREE
a. W-5871 Francis M. Boykin & Ann Johnson, heirs & administrators of F(rancis) Boykin
b. John Thompson
c. None

S-7517 50a C:207 X-1140 PIKE:PEBB
a. W-5760 William Thorp, deceased
b. Andrew Ellison
c. James Emmitt, 1834

S-7518 100a C:209 X-0423 ADAM:TIFF
a. W-5871 Francis M. Boykin & Ann Johnson, heirs & administrators of F(rancis) Boykin
b. John Ellison
c. None

S-7519 257a C:200 X-0360 PICK:DEER
a. W-5531 Robert Beale
b. Jesse McKay
c. None

S-7520 97a C:137 X-0400 FAYE:MADI
a. W-5405 Philip Mallory
b. Jesse McKay
c. None

S-7521
S-9739
S-10138 206a C:414 X-0360 PICK:PERR
ROSS:---*
a. W-5998 William Triplett
W-2855 Will(iam) Bell
W-5873 William Triplett
b. -- Langham, -- Bell, & -- Wallace
c. William Voss; J. Defebaugh, 1837
* Source A does not mention Ross County.

S-7523
S-7607 1055a C:168 X-0841 FAYE:MADI
a. W-5746 Robert Rose, heir & executor (of?)
W-5571 John Longdon? (Langdon?)
b. Benjamin Adamson
c. None

S-7526 40a D:484 X-1370 PICK:WAYN
ROSS:---*
a. W-1420 Ning Bell
b. James Miskiman
c. Thomas Bowdle, 1831
* Source A does not mention Ross County.

S-7527 108a F:311 X-1370 PICK:DEER
a. W-4917 John Steed
b. John Steed
c. John Beauchamp, 1831

S-7528 190a C:158 X-1180 MADI:MONR
a. W-5791 George Lee Turberville
b. John Graham
c. None

S-7529 145a C:158 X-1180 MADI:MONR
a. W-5791 George Lee Turberville
b. John Graham
c. None

S-7530
S-7827 90a C:159 X-1180 MADI:DEER
a. W-5791 George Lee Turberville
b. John Graham
c. None

S-7532 150a C:147 X-1180 MADI:JEFF
a. W-5784 Edward Hull? (Hall?), deceased
W-5755 William Price
b. John Graham
c. None

S-7535 70a C:155 X-1180 MADI:DEER MADI:MONR
a. W-5863 Dolly Davis, Judith Davis, & Nancy, wife of Godfrey (Davis), heirs of Jacob (Davis?)
b. Walter Dun
c. H. Lappin?; S. Moore, 1826

S-7540 295a C:138 X-0841 FAYE:MADI PICK:---*
a. W-2752 Arthur Gordon
b. John Clemson
c. James Woods, 1828; A. Ramsey, 1829; John Thompson; R. Douglas, 1837; Norman F. Jones, 1831; deeded to -- Ramsey in 1829
* Source A does not mention Pickaway County.

S-7541
S-7637 235a C:157 X-0340 FRAN:PLEA
a. W-5784 Edward Hull? (Hall?) deceased
W-5862 Jacob Davis, heirs of
W-5863 Dolly Davis, Judith Davis, & Nancy, wife of Godfrey (Davis), heirs of Jacob (Davis)
W-5547 Sarah Gunn, devisee of James (Gunn?)
W-5792 James Johnston
b. -- Graham, -- Dun, & -- Johnston*
c. None
* Source C says John Graham, Walter Dun, & James Johnston.

S-7544
S-7671
S-8222 517a C:216 X-0360 FAYE:MADI
a. W-5978 John E. Scott, representatives of
W-5127 Robert Means, assignee of John Stokely
W-5895 Thomas Moore
W-5539 William White
W-6129 Harod Gibbs
W-5950 William Pullen
b. -- Fulton & -- Robison*
c. None
* Source A says W. Fulton, J. A. Fulton, & W. Robinson (so spelled).

S-7545 85a C:189 X-0360 X-0540 PICK:DEER
a. W-5549 Berryman Green
b. Berryman Green
c. None

S-7546 125a C:138 X-0660 CLAR:GREE
a. W-5321 Thomas M. Bailey, assignee of Smith Milliner
W-1257 Roman Fromaget
b. James Galloway, Junior
c. None

S-7550 100a C:144 X-0840 X-1220 ROSS:PAIN
a. W-5732 Thomas Gaskins, deceased
b. Cadwallader Wallace
c. None

S-7553* 200a -- -- ADAM:MEIG
a. --
b. John Ellison, Junior
c. None
* Listed in Source A only.

S-7554 50a C:211 X-0130 ADAM:GREE
a. W-5871 Francis M. Boykin & Ann Johnson, heirs & administrators of F(rancis) Boykin
b. John Stickler
c. None

S-7555. See S-6472

S-7556 12a C:233 X-0130 ADAM:JEFF
a. W-5871 Francis M. Boykin & Ann Johnson, heirs & administrators of F(rancis) Boykin
b. Daniel Collier
c. None

S-7557 50a C:313 X-0841 FAYE:MADI
a. W-5939 John Murphy
b. Thomas McDonald
c. Thomas Jones, 1831

S-7558 150a D:153 X-0841 FAYE:MADI
a. W-5939 John Murphy*
b. John Murphey*
c. None
* So spelled.

S-7559
S-7575 1057a C:146 X-1000 ROSS:UNIO
a. W-5784 Edward Hull? (Hall?) deceased
W-5783 Edward Hull? (Hall?) deceased, now (reversion to?) John('s) heirs
W-5797 James Dillard
W-5755 William Price
b. John Graham
c. None

S-7559. See S-7575

S-7560 246a C:158 X-0360 MADI:DEER
a. W-5783 Edward Hull? (Hall?) deceased, now (reversion to?) John('s) heirs
b. John Graham
c. None

S-7565 & S-7566. See S-6849

S-7567. See S-7267

S-7568 1100a C:168 X-0360 PICK:MONR
a. W-5987 William McCraw
b. -- Scott, -- Medley, & -- Green*
c. None
* Source C says Joseph W. Scott, Isaac Medley, & Berryman Green.

S-7569 830a D:410 X-0360 PICK:MONR
a. W-5987 William McCraw
b. Isaac Medley
c. William McCean? (McClean? McLean?); G. W. Doan, 1827; William McCraw; P. Douglas, 1829; heirs of William McCraw; S. S. Frame, 1838

S-7570 260a C:168 X-0360 PICK:MONR
a. W-5987 William McCraw
b. -- Scott, -- Medley, & -- Green*
c. John Evans; C. Williams, 1838; J. Hedges; G. Botkin, 1835; John Watts; James Hedges, 1831
* Source C says Joseph W. Scott, Isaac Medley, & Berryman Green.

S-7571 80a C:216 X-1370 PICK:WAYN
a. W-5987 William McCraw
b. -- Scott, -- Medley, & -- Green*
c. None
* Source C says Joseph W. Scott, Isaac Medley, & Berryman Green.

S-7572 300a C:169 X-0360 PICK:MONR
a. W-5987 William McCraw
b. -- Scott, -- Medley, & -- Green*
c. None
* Source C says Joseph W. Scott, Isaac Medley, & Berryman Green.

S-7573 134a C:169 X-0240 PICK:MONR
a. W-5987 William McCraw
b. -- Scott, -- Medley, & -- Green*
c. William McCean? (McClean? McLean?); G. W. Doan, 1827; William McCraw; J. D. Caldwell, 1829; heirs of William McCraw; Joseph Olds, 1831; Thomas Hubbard, 1831
* Source C says Joseph W. Scott, Isaac Medley, & Berryman Green.

S-7575*
S-7576
S-7559* 380a** C:182 X-1000 ROSS:UNIO
a. W-5916 Gross Scruggs
b. Gross Scruggs
c. J. Work & A. Work; William Fulton, 1838
* Source A does not mention S-7575 & S-7559.
** Source A says 580a.

S-7575. See also S-7559

S-7577 225a C:164 X-0840 ROSS:---* FAYE:WAYN
a. W-5788 David Wallace, representatives of
W-5971 Edward Wills? (Wells?)
W-5732 Thomas Gaskin, deceased
b. Cadwallader Wallace
C. None
* Source A does not mention Ross County.

S-7578 75a C:389 X-0841 MADI:RANG
a. W-5992 John Johnson?
b. Joseph Ladd & Benjamin W. Ladd*
c. None
* Source A also mentions -- Norvell.

S-7587
S-7608 290a C:147 X-0360 FAYE:MADI
a. W-6614 --*
W-6211 Robert Bolling
W-5571 John Langdon? (Longdon?)
b. -- Fulton's & -- Adamson**
c. None
* Not listed in Source C.
** Source A lists J. A. Fulton, W. Fulton, & B. Adamson.

S-7588 100a C:165 X-0660 CLAR:MADI
a. W-5938 Maximilian Rector
b. John Turner
c. None

S-7589
S-8273 112a C:212 X-0759 ADAM:WAYN
a. W-5871 Francis M. Boykin & Ann Johnson, heirs & administrators of F(rancis) Boykin
W-5768 Samuel Blair? heirs? of
b. Jesse Stout
c. -- Barrett & -- Lotsip? (Lotrip?)

S-7590 50a C:291 X-1140 PIKE:MIFF
a. W-5871 Francis M. Boykin & Ann Johnson, heirs & administrators of F(rancis) Boykin
b. John Ellison, Junior
c. None

S-7591* 30a -- -- PIKE:----
a. --
b. John Ellison, Junior
c. None
* Listed in Source A only; says "not found."

S-7598* 100a -- -- HIGH:DODS
a. --
b. Joseph Kerr
c. None
* Listed in Source A only.

S-7607. See S-7523

S-7608. See S-7587

S-7609 100a C:237 X-0360 PICK:PERR
a. W-5920 Peter Kelly*, representatives of
b. Peter Kelley*, representatives of
c. None
* So spelled.

S-7610 500a C:191 X-0841 FAYE:MADI
a. W-5851 Osborne Coffey
W-6129 Harod Gibbs
b. William Fulton & John A. Fulton
c. None

S-7612. See S-5456 (in volume 4, part 1)

S-7619* 250a -- -- CHAM:UNIO

a. --
b. -- Johnson & -- Moore
c. None
* Listed in Source A only.

S-7620 239a C:178 X-0840 FAYE:PAIN
a. W-3740 Philip Faint
W-3742 George Faint
W-3727 Michael Teagle? (Feagle?)
b. -- Teant's & -- Feagle*
c. None
* Source A says P. Feant, G. Feant, & M. Teagle.

S-7621 500a C:232 X-0360 PICK:PERR
a. W-5914 Kendall Hyslop, heir of Smith Hyslop
W-5919 Thomas Wyatt, representatives of
W-5920 Peter Kelly, representatives of
b. -- Kendall*, -- Hyslop*, -- Wyatt, & -- Kelley**
c. Seymour G. Renick, 1832; K. Hyslop; G. Botkin, 1836
* Almost certainly, this is one person, Kendall Hyslop.
** Source A spells Kelly.

S-7624 100a C:234 X-0420 ADAM:TIFF
a. W-5871 Francis M. Boykin & Ann Johnson, heirs & administrators of F(rancis) Boykin
b. John Ellison, Junior
c. None

S-7625* 10a -- -- ADAM:TIFF
a. --
b. Ralph McClure
c. None
* Listed in Source A only.

S-7628 200a C:161 X-0500 MADI:UNIO
a. W-5916 Gross Scruggs
b. Gross Scruggs
c. None

S-7630 706a C:195 X-1040 SCIO:UNIO
a. W-6033 Jacob Moore
b. William Kendall
c. W. B. Belnap; J. M. Merrell, 1842

S-7631 34a C:195 X-0910 SCIO:NILE
a. W-6035 Jacob Moore
b. William Kendall
c. None

S-7633 20a C:350 X-0800 SCIO:NILE
a. W-6035 Jacob Moore
b. William Kendall
c. Harvey Beard; J. Kendall, 1839

S-7634 12a C:196 X-1040 SCIO:UNIO
a. W-6035 Jacob Moore
b. William Kendall
c. None

S-7636 88a C:159 X-0360 MADI:DEER
a. W-5792 James Johnston
b. James Johnston
c. None

S-7637. See S-7541

S-7641 100a D:62 X-0840 FAYE:UNIO
a. W-4204 Jacob Philips
b. Duncan McArthur
c. None

S-7642 400a C:261 X-0150 ROSS:BUCK
a. W-4175 John Martin
W-4208 Robert Ogilsby
W-1984 Captain Will(iam) George
b. Duncan McArthur
c. None

S-7650 254a* C:196 X-1040 SCIO:UNIO
a. W-6035 Jacob Moore
b. William Kendall
c. B. McLaughlin; John Noel, 1831; T. Musgrove, 1834
* Source A says 250a.

S-7652 321a C:223 X-0133 ADAM:FRAN
a. W-5861 Henry Bell
b. James Pemberton
c. None

S-7654 163a C:519 X-0360 PICK:DARB
MADI:---*
a. W-1203 Captain Beverly Stubblefield
b. Beverly Stubblefield
c. Daniel F. McCoy
* Source A does not give township.

S-7656 400a C:309 X-0400 FAYE:MADI
a. W-5266 Tuttle Hudson, administrator of William Hudson
b. Lucas Sullivant
c. None

S-7657 400a D:170 X-0841 FAYE:PAIN
a. W-5266 Tuttle Hudson, administrator of William Hudson
b. Lucas Sullivant
c. None

S-7658. See S-5197 (in volume 4, part 1)

S-7659
S-8986
S-8987 95a E:2 X-1000 PIKE:JACK
ROSS:---*
a. W-5978 John E. Scott, representatives of
W-5200 Thomas M. Bayly, assignee of Samuel Russell
W-3749 Andrew Dunbar
b. Cadwallader Wallace
c. None
* Source A does not mention Ross County.

S-7660 80a E:10 X-1000 ROSS:PAXT
a. W-5978 John E. Scott, representatives of
b. Cadwallader Wallace
c. None

S-7661* 100a -- -- MADI:----
a. --
b. Elias Langham
c. James Woods, 1828
* Listed in Source A only, wherein crossed out.

S-7662 50a E:503 X-0360 MADI:UNIO
a. W-5978 John E. Scott, representatives of
b. Elias Langham, heirs of
c. J. W. Simpkins, 1828

S-7663 150a C:353 X-0360 PICK:DEER
a. W-5405 Philip Mallory
W-5531 Robert Beale
b. Jesse McKay
c. None

S-7667 100a C:170 X-1375 PICK:DEER
a. W-5987 William McCraw
b. -- Scott, -- Medley, & -- Green*
c. None
* Source C says Joseph W. Scott, Isaac Medley, & Berryman Green.

S-7669 78a C:196 X-1040 SCIO:BRUS
a. W-6035 Jacob Moore
b. William Kendall
c. None

S-7670
S-9460 400a C:532 X-0841 FAYE:WAYN
a. W-5978 John E. Scott
W-6194 Robert Hanson Harrison
b. -- Robinson & -- Fulton*
c. John Chom; James Stewart, 1824; John A. Fulton; Richard Douglas, 1831
* Source C says John A. Fulton.

S-7671. See S-7544

S-7674 40a C:196 X-1040 SCIO:UNIO
a. W-6033 Jacob Moore
b. William Kendall
c. None

S-7676 100a C:342 X-1180 MADI:PIKE UNIO:---*
a. W-348 Captain James Curry
b. John Erwine**
c. None
* Source A does not mention Union County.
** Source A spells Erwin.

S-7677. See S-7472

S-7681
S-7891 305a C:171 X-1370 PICK:WAYN
a. W-5987 William McCraw
b. -- Scott, -- Medley, & -- Green*
c. None
* Source C says Joseph W. Scott, Isaac Medley, & Berryman Green.

S-7682 65a C:170 X-0140 PICK:DEER
a. W-5987 William McCraw
b. -- Scott, -- Medley, & -- Green*
c. None
* Source C says Joseph W. Scott, Isaac Medley, & Berryman Green.

S-7689
S-8370 60a C:222 X-0133 ADAM:FRAN
a. W-5708 John Poulson? deceased, ---? G? P. Bagwell
b. George Vinsonhaller*
c. None
* Source A spells Vinsonhaler.

S-7691 100a C:190 X-0133 ADAM:SCOT ADAM:FRAN
a. W-5948 William Pullen
W-5708 John Poulson? deceased, ---? G? P. Bagwell
b. -- Scott* & -- Vinsonhaller**
c. John Peterson; Ab(raham?) Lafferty, 1826
* Source C says Thomas Scott.
** Source A spells Vinsonhaler.

S-7693 695a C:162 X-1004 FRAN:BROW MADI:---*
a. W-5852 Edward Carrington, John Marshall
b. -- Carrington, -- Marshall, & -- Heths**
c. Edward Carrington; Onis Parish, 1829; John C. Brodrick; G. W. Brodrick, 1831; M. L. Sullivant, 1837; W. Heth
* Source A does not mention Madison County.
** Source C says Henry Heth & Henry G. Heth, executors? of Will(iam) Heth, deceased.

S-7696
S-7866
S-8402 198a C:227 X-0840 ROSS:HUNT
a. W-5765 John Spelfatham? (Spilfatham?)
W-6027 John Stokes, representatives of
W-5800 James Dillard
b. -- Graham & -- Hough
c. None

S-7709 100a C:153 X-0381 ADAM:MONR
a. W-2024 Captain James Craig
b. James Craig
c. None

S-7710
S-10157 350a C:499 X-0190 PIKE:CAMP SCIO:---*
a. W-5871 Francis M. Boykin & Ann Johnson, heirs & administrators of F(rancis) Boykin
b. Thomas Mountjoy
c. R. Wood, 1826; J. Wilson; R. Douglas, 1842
* Source A does not mention Scioto County.

S-7711 25a C:260 X-0030 SCIO:MORG
a. W-5871 Francis M. Boykin & Ann Johnson, heirs & administrators to F(rancis) Boykin
b. Thomas Bevin
c. William Currie; J. Cockrell, 1832

S-7712 25a C:261 X-0195 PIKE:CAMP
a. W-5871 Francis M. Boykin & Ann Johnson, heirs & administrators to F(rancis) Boykin
b. Nehemiah Walls
c. None

S-7714
S-8781 120a D:67 X-0420 ADAM:TIFF
a. W-5871 Francis M. Boykin & Ann Johnson, heirs & administrators of F(rancis) Boykin
W-5991 John Price, heirs to
b. John Ellison, Junior
c. None

S-7714. See S-8781

S-7715. See S-6467

S-7718 262a C:152 X-0600 ADAM:SPRI
a. W-5972 Edward Wills? (Wells?)
W-5577 Benjamin Leach, heir to John (Leach) deceased
W-5760 William Thorp? (Tharp?) deceased
b. Andrew Ellison, Junior*
c. Benjamin Bowman, heirs of; Benjamin Bowman, Junior; T. Huston, 1833; E. Bowman, 1835; R. Holderness, 1839
* Source A says Andrew Ellison.

S-7721. See S-6658

S-7723 100a C:378 X-0130 ADAM:MEIG
a. W-290 Captain Abraham Shepherd
b. John Machir
c. None

S-7724 59a C:211 X-0939 SCIO:BRUS ADAM:FRAN
a. W-290 Captain Abraham Shepherd
b. John Machir
c. E. Mustard; Thomas Huston

S-7725 50a C:205 X-0220 PIKE:SUNF
a. W-1696 William Copeland
W-5578 Benjamin Leach, heir to William (Leach) deceased
b. Andrew Ellison
c. None

S-7726 50a C:234 X-0130 ADAM:TIFF
a. W-290 Captain Abraham Shepherd
b. Thomas Lewis
c. A. Ellison, 1823

S-7727 50a C:211 X-0130 ADAM:MEIG
a. W-290 Captain Abraham Shepherd
b. John Machir
c. None

S-7732 34a C:196 X-1040 SCIO:UNIO
a. W-6035 Jacob Moore
b. William Kendall
c. None

S-7734 100a C:184 X-0340 UNIO:UNIO
a. W-5962 Barnabas Arthur
b. James Galloway, Junior
c. None

S-7737 30a C:153 X-1180 CHAM:---* UNIO:UNIO
a. W-5962 Barnabas Arthur
b. James Galloway, Junior
c. None
* Source A does not mention Champaign County.

S-7738 200a C:331 X-0120 MADI:RANG
a. W-6008 John M. Gregory, heir to William (Gregory)
b. Joseph Ladd
c. B. W. Ladd; -- Bond & -- Rea, 1823

S-7742 250a C:164 X-0360 ROSS:DEER
a. W-6008 John M. Gregory, heir to William (Gregory)
W-4792 Andrew Torborn, heir to Peter Dunn
W-4793 William Pyle
b. Cadwallader Wallace
c. None

S-7743 200a C:238 X-0840 FAYE:PAIN
a. W-5865 Shadrach Henson
b. Thomas Browder
c. Edward Stokes; Richard Douglas, 1831

S-7744 200a C:238 X-0840 FAYE:PAIN
a. W-5826 James Williams
W-5843 James Williams, heir of Reuben (Williams)
b. James Williams
c. -- James & -- Wood; J. Millikan, 1826; William Hays, 1827; Charles Davis; deeded to William Hays, 27 Jan? 1831

S-7745 200a C:279 X-0540 PICK:PERR
a. W-5762 John Gladding, deceased
b. Thomas James
c. None

S-7747 847a C:51 X-0270 CLER:TATE
a. W-5994 Nathaniel Gist, representatives of
b. Nathaniel Gist, representatives of
c. James Taylor; John Hill, 1831

S-7749
S-13517 81a D:438 X-0841 FAYE:WAYN
a. W-5978 John E. Scott, representatives of
W-5403 William Sanford, representatives of
b. William Robinson, executor
c. None

S-7750 60a D:228 X-0841 FAYE:WAYN
a. W-5978 John E. Scott, representatives of
b. William Robinson, executor*
c. James Woods, 1828
* Source A does not mention executor.

S-7751
S-7774 447a C:156 X-0340 MADI:DARB UNIO:---*
a. W-6075 Joseph Parrott
W-6076 Joseph Parrott
b. Walter Dun
c. None
* Source A does not mention Union County.

S-7752 310a C:156 X-0340 MADI:CANA
a. W-6075 Joseph Parrott
b. Walter Dun
c. None

S-7753 220a C:155 X-0340 MADI:DARB
a. W-6075 Joseph Parrott
b. Walter Dun
c. None

S-7754 220a C:155 X-0340 MADI:DARB
a. W-6075 Joseph Parrott
b. Walter Dun
c. None

S-7756. See S-7432

S-7757 100a C:157 X-0340 MADI:DARB
a. W-5916 Gross Scruggs
W-5493 John C. Carter
b. -- Scruggs & -- Dun*
c. None
* Source C says Walter Dun.

S-7758
S-7830 168a C:160 X-0340 MADI:DARB UNIO:JERO
a. W-5765 John Spelfatham? (Spilfatham?)
W-5758 -- (illegible)
W-5791 George Lee Turberville
W-5916 Gross Scruggs
b. -- Graham & -- Scruggs*
c. S? (L?) King; J. W. Simpkins, 1828; C. Brown; K. Bailey, 1828
* Source C says John Graham & Gross Scruggs.

S-7759 168a C:161 X-0340 UNIO:JERO MADI:DARB
a. W-5916 Gross Scruggs
b. -- Gross & -- Scruggs*
c. None
* Source A says Gross Scruggs (one person).

S-7762. See S-7766

S-7763 100a C:173 X-0540 PICK:DEER
a. W-6008 John M. Gregory, heir to William (Gregory)
b. John Hoffman
c. None

S-7764 150a C:254 X-0360 PICK:DEER
a. W-6008 John M. Gregory, heir to William (Gregory)
b. John Hoffman
c. None

S-7765 50a C:238 X-0540 ROSS:---* PICK:DEER
a. W-6008 John M. Gregory, heir to William (Gregory)
b. John Hoffman
c. None
* Source A does not mention Ross County.

S-7766
S-7762 500a C:180 X-0360 PICK:DEER
a. W-6008 John M. Gregory, heir to William (Gregory)
b. John Hoffman
c. None

S-7767 200a C:216 X-0841 FAYE:UNIO
a. W-6008 John M. Gregory, heir to William (Gregory)
b. John Hoffman
c. R. Douglas, 1829

S-7770
S-7836 284a C:176 X-0340 UNIO:UNIO
a. W-6050 James Price, representatives of
b. Anthony Walker*
c. None
* Possibly Anthony Walke is meant.

S-7771 80a C:155 X-0340 UNIO:UNIO
a. W-6075 Joseph Parrott
b. Walter Dun
c. None

S-7772 83a C:156 X-0340 CHAM:RUSH UNIO:---* LOGA:---*
a. W-6075 Joseph Parrott
W-6076 Joseph Parrott
b. Walter Dun
c. None
* Source A does not mention Union or Logan counties.

S-7774. See S-7751

S-7775. See S-6969

S-7776 117a C:186 X-0360 PICK:JACK
a. W-5940 George Mallow
b. John Evans
c. None

S-7777 150a C:170 X-0390 PICK:MONR
a. W-5987 William McCraw
b. -- Scott, -- Medley, & -- Green*
c. H. Lewis; G. E. Wolfley, 1836; J. Fowler, 1838;

Hy Lewis; J. Evans
* Source C says Joseph W. Scott, Isaac Medley & Berryman Green

S-7778 100a C:170 X-1375 PICK:WAYN
a. W-5987 William McCraw
b. -- Scott, -- Medley, & -- Green*
c. None
* Source C says Joseph W. Scott, Isaac Medley, & Berryman Green.

S-7781
S-7782 100a C:174 X-0360 FAYE:MADI
a. W-6008 John M. Gregory, heir to William (Gregory)
b. -- Hoffman & -- Wallace*
c. None
* Source C says John Hoffman, Joseph? Ladd, & Cad-(wallader) Wallace

S-7785. See S-6960 & S-6969

S-7786 100a C:174 X-0840 FAYE:MADI
a. W-6008 John M. Gregory, heir to William (Gregory)
b. John Hoffman
c. Michael Hawk; G. H. Freeman, 1823; George H. Creamer; Bonner Lockead, 1828

S-7788 140a C:388 X-0400 FAYE:MADI
a. W-5978 John E. Scott, representatives of
b. Elias Langham
c. None

S-7789 800a C:163 X-1180 UNIO:UNIO
a. W-6076 Joseph Parrott
b. Joseph Parrott
c. None

S-7790 95a C:163 X-1180 UNIO:UNIO
a. W-6050 James Price, representives of
b. Anthony Walke
c. None

S-7791 3200a C:185 X-0340 X-1180 MADI:CANA
a. W-6016 Strother G. Settle, representatives of
b. Nathan Haines
c. R. McLaughlin; N. Sawyer, 1826; E. Bidwell; J. Bidwell; R. Douglas, 1825; S. Buckman; K. Briley? (Bailey?), 1825; -- Brannon & -- Thompson; H. Warner, 1834; George Pew, 1832; Russell Bidwell, 1830; E. McCumber; heirs of R. Bidwell

S-7794
S-7795
S-10768 300a C:516 X-0130 ADAM:FRAN
a. W-2024 Captain James Craig
b. James Craig
c. John Kees, 1828

S-7796 100a C:516 X-0130 ADAM:FRAN
a. W-2024 Captain James Craig
b. James Craig
c. None

S-7797 50a C:516 X-0133 ADAM:FRAN
a. W-2024 Captain James Craig
b. James Craig
c. None

S-7798* 40a -- -- HIGH:BRUS
a. --
b. James Craig
c. John Smith, 1828
* Listed in Source A only.

S-7799. See S-7263

S-7800 50a C:225 X-0841 PICK:PERR
a. W-6014 Benjamin Harrison, representatives of
b. William Fulton
c. None

S-7801 50a C:189 X-0841 FAYE:MADI
a. W-6014 Benjamin Harrison, representatives of
b. William Fulton
c. None

S-7802 30a C-226 X-0841 FAYE:MADI
a. W-6014 Benjamin Harrison, representatives of
b. William Fulton
c. None

S-7805 150a C:286 X-0841 FAYE:MADI
a. W-6014 Benjamin Harrison, representatives of
b. Benjamin Harrison, representatives of
c. None

S-7805 100a C:286 X-0841 FAYE:MADI
a. W-6014 Benjamin Harrison, representatives of
b. Benjamin Harrison, representatives of
c. None

S-7806 600a C:305 X-0841 FAYE:MADI
a. W-6014 Benjamin Harrison, representatives of
b. Benjamin Harrison, representatives of
c. None

S-7808 100a C:222 X-1040 SCIO:BRUS
a. W-5708 John Poulson, by his executor, G. P. Bagwell
b. George Vinsonhaller*
c. None
* Source A spells Vinsonhaler.

S-7809 100a C:224 X-1045 ADAM:MEIG
a. W-5407 Thomas M. Bayly, assignee of Ben(jamin) Phillips
W-5948 William Pullen
b. Thomas Scott
c. None

S-7812 117a C:162 X-0360 MADI:UNIO
a. W-5916 Gross Scruggs
b. Gross Scruggs
c. None

S-7813 100a C:162 X-0360 MADI:FAIR
a. W-5916 Gross Scruggs
b. Gross Scruggs
c. None

S-7814 216a C:159 X-0360 MADI:FAIR
a. W-5916 Gross Scruggs
W-5881 Edmund? Farrell, heir to Thomas (Farrell)
W-5791 George Lee Turberville
b. -- Scruggs & -- Graham*
c. None
* Source C says Gross Scruggs & John Graham.

S-7817
S-7879 150a C:172 X-0360 PICK:PERR
a. W-5972 Edward Wills? (Wells?)
W-6008 John M. Gregory, heir to William (Gregory)
b. -- Wallace & -- Hoffman
c. None

S-7821 300a C:164 X-0840 ROSS:BUCK
a. W-6008 John M. Gregory, heir to William (Gregory)
b. Cadwallader Wallace
c. None

S-7822 3337a C:194 X-0340 UNIO:UNIO UNIO:ALLE CHAM:RUSH
a. W-6050 James Price, representative of
W-2126 Abrington Jones
b. -- Walke* & -- Jones
c. None
* Source C says Anthony Walke.

S-7823 260a C:160 X-0340 MADI:CANA MADI:DARB
a. W-5792 James Johnston
b. James Johnston
c. None

S-7824 135a C:161 X-1000 PIKE:JACK ROSS:---*
a. W-5792 James Johnston
b. James Johnston
c. None
* Source A does not mention Ross County.

S-7825 112a C:158 X-0660 CLAR:MADI
a. W-5791 George Lee Turberville
b. John Graham
c. None

S-7826 200a C:158 X-1180 MADI:MONR
a. W-5916 Gross Scruggs
b. John Graham
c. None

S-7827. See S-7530

S-7828 550a C:162 X-0360 MADI:DEER
a. W-5916 Gross Scruggs
b. Gross Scruggs
c. None

S-7829 345a C:159 X-0500 MADI:DEER
a. W-5765 John Spelfatham? (Spilfatham? Spitfatham?)
W-5916 Gross Scruggs
b. -- Graham & -- Scruggs
c. None

S-7831 400a C:162 X-0380 HIGH:DODS
a. W-5916 Gross Scruggs
b. Gross Scruggs
c. J. Pancake; A. Cunningham, 1824

S-7831. See also S-7758

S-7832 400a C:157 X-0340 MADI:CANA
a. W-5787 Edwin Hull? (Hall?)
W-5784 Edwin Hull? (Hall?)
W-5755 William Price
W-5791 George Lee Turberville
b. John Graham
c. W. Dun; L. Bramblet, 1832

S-7833 880a C:160 X-0500 MADI:SUMM
a. W-5792 James Johnston
b. James Johnston
c. None

S-7835 500a C:161 X-1004 FRAN:WASH MADI:---*
a. W-5916 Gross Scruggs
b. Gross Scruggs
c. A. McCollough, 1836; Isaac Bigelow, 1838
* Source A mentions Madison County but does not give township.

S-7836. See S-7770

S-7842 150a C:247 X-0660 CLAR:MADI
a. W-5916 Gross Scruggs
b. Gross Scruggs
c. W. Dun; Justis Cooper, 1826

S-7846 100a C:191 X-1000 PICK:WAYN
a. W-6006 Moore Lumpkin
b. Benjamin Hough
c. None

S-7850 300a D:28 X-0840 FAYE:PAIN
a. W-6076 Joseph Parrott
b. Joseph Parrott
c. William McCormick; W. McBride, 1826; Aaren Thomas; J. House, 1826

S-7854 267a C:165 X-0230 ADAM:WAYN
a. W-290 Captain Abraham Shepherd
b. John Beasley, heirs of
c. Adam Kirkpatrick; William Finley, 1825

S-7855 50a C:165 X-0910 SCIO:NILE
a. W-290 Captain Abraham Shepherd
b. John Beasley, heirs of
c. None

S-7856 18a C:166 X-0470? SCIO:WASH
a. W-290 Captain Abraham Shepherd
b. John Beasley, heirs of
c. Roswell Craine, 1824

S-7857* 100a -- -- HIGH:----
a. --
b. James Craig
c. John Smith, 1828
* Listed in Source A only (at top of page beginning with S-7854).

S-7860 210a C:240 X-0150 ROSS:BUCK
a. W-6008 John M. Gregory, heir to William (Gregory)
b. Cadwallader Wallace
c. None

S-7861 100a C:178 X-0570 ROSS:SCIO
a. W-5944 William Boughten? (Boughton?)
b. Mathews* Hobson
c. None
* Source A spells Matthew.

S-7862 367a C:323 X-0360 FAYE:MADI
a. W-6001 William Triplett
W-1653 Lieutenant Robert Breckenridge
b. -- Langham & -- Rector*
c. None
* Source A has additional notation: "Patented to Nathaniel Massie."

S-7863 100a D:144 X-1000 UNIO:JACK
a. W-1233 John? (Jesse?) Jones
b. John Woodsides
c. M. S. Butler, 1836; J. Beaven, 1840; Fa? Woodside & -- Conner; R. Douglas; I. Y. Green, 1831

S-7863* 100a D:144 X-1000 UNIO:JACK
a. W-4040 Hopewell Hull? (Hall?)
b. William Conner
c. None
* Source A says "not patented."

S-7865 133a C:198 X-0360 FAYE:MADI
a. W-4792 Andrew Torborn, heir to Peter Dunn
b. Elisha Winn
c. None

S-7866. See S-7696

S-7868 500a C:167 X-0360 X-0841 PICK:PERR
a. W-5989 John Yancey
W-5482 John Gibson
b. -- Massie & -- Gibson
c. None

S-7869 400a C:167 X-0480 UNIO:YORK
a. W-5482 John Gibson
b. John Gibson
c. George Wallace; Joshua Matheat? 1837; R. M. Dawson; -- McElwain & -- Hariot, 1840

S-7869 400a C:167 X-0480 UNIO:YORK
a. W-5482 John Gibson
b. John Gibson
c. None

S-7874 306a C:169 X-0360 PICK:MONR
a. W-5987 William McCraw
b. -- Scott, -- Medley, & -- Green*
c. John Watt; Henry Rudy, 1835; Q. B. Richey & W. B. Richey
* Source C says Joseph W. Scott, Isaac Medley, & Berryman Green.

S-7875 100a C:170 X-1370 PICK:DEER
a. W-5987 William McCraw
b. -- Scott, -- Medley, & -- Green*
c. None
* Source C says Joseph W. Scott, Isaac Medley, & Berryman Green.

S-7876 130a C:247 X-1180 MADI:JEFF
a. W-5916 Gross Scruggs
b. Gross Scruggs
c. None

S-7878 100a C:172 X-0340 PICK:PERR FAYE:---*
a. W-5972 Edward Wills? (Wells?)
b. Cadwallader Wallace
c. None
* Source A does not mention Fayette County.

S-7879. See S-7817

S-7882 100a C:328 X-0360 PICK:DEER
a. W-5772 Thomas Hill, representatives of
b. Thomas Hill, representatives of
c. None

S-7883 110a C:241 X-0360 MADI:PLEA
a. W-5901 Ann Garnett? (Garrett?), heir to Benjamin (Garnett? Garrett?)
b. Ann Garrett
c. None

S-7886 100a C:174 X-0840 FAYE:MADI
a. W-6008 John M. Gregory, heir to William (Gregory)
b. -- Hoffman $ -- Wallace*
c. None
* Source C says John Hoffman, Joseph? Ladd, & Cadw(allader) Wallace.

S-7887. See S-6147 in volume 4, part 1)

S-7889 100a C-200 X-0840 ROSS:PAXT
a. W-6016 Strother G. Settle, representatives of
b. Nathan Hains*
c. None
* Sources A & C spell Haines.

S-7890. See S-7267

S-7891. See S-7681

S-7893 225a C-375 X-0841 MADI:RANG
a. W-6019 John Baldwin
b. John Baldwin
c. None

S-7894. See S-6391 (in volume 4, part 1)

S-7895 25a E:348 X-0841 MADI:RANG
a. W-5992 John Jefson (Jeffries?), heir to Randolph? (Jefson? Jeffries?)
b. James Dungan
c. None

S-7897 660a C:220 X-0840 MADI:STOK MADI:RANG
a. W-2483 Captain Daniel Duvall
b. Daniel Duvall
c. David Collins; M. Bonner, 1829; D. Duval

S-7898 96a C:173 X-0540 PICK:DEER ROSS:---*
a. W-5989 John Yancey
b. Henry Massie
c. None
* Source A does not mention Ross County.

S-7899 250a C:195 X-0843 MADI:RANG
a. W-5945 William Higginbotham
b. William Robinson
c. None

S-7900 100a C:392 X-0841 MADI:RANG
a. W-6046 William Freeman
b. Thomas Worthington
c. None

S-7903
S-9256 130a C:324 X-0840 FAYE:WAYN
a. W-5901 Ann Garnett? (Garrett?), heir to Benjamin (Garnett? Garrett?)
b. Andrew Garrett
c. None

S-7905 150a C:184 X-1180 CHAM:RUSH CHAM:WAYN
a. W-5962 Barnabas Arthur
W-308 Lieutenant John Crawford
b. -- Galloway & -- Crawford
c. None

S-7910 500a C:363 X-0360 X-1385 PICK:JACK
a. W-5248 Cornelius Baldwin
b. Cornelius Baldwin
c. M. O. Brien (possibly O'Brien); heirs of C. Baldwin; Walter Thrall, 1830; Jonathan Carlisle, 1831; -- Craybill, 1835; Archibald Stewart; Lyne Starling, 1831

S-7910 200a C:363 X-0360 X-1385 PICK:JACK
a. W-5418 Thomas Jones
b. Thomas Jones
c. W. Reed, 1837

S-7913 200a C:178 X-1180 CHAM:RUSH
a. W-5963 Barnabas Arthur
W-5978 John E. Scott, representatives of
b. John A. Fulton
c. None

S-7914 & S-7915. See S-7308

S-7916 800a C:231 X-0340 X-1180 MADI:---* UNIO:DARB
a. W-5792 James Johnston
W-5791 George Lee Turberville
b. -- Johnston & -- Graham
c. None
* Source A does not mention Madison County.

S-7917 112a C:229 X-1186 MADI:PIKE
a. W-6050 James Price, representatives of
b. Anthony Walke
c. None

S-7924
S-8441
S-8442 480a C:245 X-1186 MADI:MONR
a. W-6086 Thomas Colter, representatives of
W-6089 Thomas Colter, representatives of
W-6126 Stephen Young
W-5493 John C. Carter
W-5547 Sarah Gunn, devisee of James Gunn
W-5916 Gross Scruggs
W-5791 George Lee Turberville
W-5832 Edmund Fauel? (Favel?)
b. -- Dun, -- Scruggs, & -- Graham
c. None

S-7926 260a C:231 X-1180 UNIO:UNIO
a. W-5791 George Lee Turberville
W-5916 Gross Scruggs
b. -- Graham & -- Scruggs
c. None

S-7927 100a C:247 X-1180 MADI:FAIR
a. W-5791 George Lee Turberville
b. John Graham
c. None

S-7928 90a C:247 X-1180 MADI:FAIR
a. W-5971 Edward Wills? (Wells?)
b. John Graham
c. None

S-7929 120a C:229 X-0340 MADI:DARB
a. W-5791 George Lee Turberville
b. John Graham
c. None

S-7937 15a C:210 X-1000 SCIO:UNIO
a. W-5871 Francis M. Boykin & Ann Johnson, heirs & administrators of F(rancis) Boykin
b. William Campbell
c. None

S-7939 25a C:209 X-1042 SCIO:BRUS
a. W-5871 Francis M. Boykin & Ann Johnson, heirs & administrators of F(rancis) Boykin
b. John Ellison, Junior
c. J. Wallace, 1824

S-7940 50a C:499 X-0030 SCIO:MORG
a. W-5871 Francis M. Boykin & Ann Johnson, heirs & administrators of F(rancis) Boykin
b. Thomas Mountjoy
c. J. Pyles, 1824; R. Pandy, 1836

S-7941* 10a -- -- SCIO:MORG
a. --
b. Hezekiah Merritt
c. None
* Listed in Source A only.

S-7943 600a C:240 X-0360 MADI:UNIO CLAR:HARM
a. W-5534 Peter Manifold, assignee of Lawrence Manning, administrator of Lawrence (Manning)
W-5520 Joseph Ladd, assignee of Robert Hockaday, executor of John Hockaday
b. George Hoffman
c. E. Langham; heirs of Dennis Lane; S. N. Kerr, 1832; heirs of E. Langham; William W. Warner, 1831

S-7944 300a C:181 X-0540 PICK:PERR
a. W-6089 Thomas Colter, representatives of
W-6008 John M. Gregory, heir to William (Gregory)
b. Cadwallader Wallace
c. None

S-7945
S-8448 1000a C:395 X-0360 MADI:UNIO
a. W-6045 William Berry
b. Levi Springer
c. None

S-7946 640a C:293 X-1180 MADI:PIKE
a. W-6045 William Berry
b. Levi Springer
c. None

S-7947 1067a C:189 X-1000 PICK:JACK
a. W-5932 Robert Thelaball, deceased, representatives of
b. Hance Baker
c. Heirs of B(enjamin) Hough; Andrew Huston, 1827

S-7948
S-7997 999a C:182 X-0120 MADI:RANG
a. W-5978 John E. Scott, representatives of
W-6045 William Berry
W-5932 Robert Thelaball, deceased, representatives of
b. John A. Fulton
c. None

S-7953 50a C:232 X-1000 ROSS:FRAN
a. W-6091 Lewis Guthrie, representatives of
b. Walter Dun
c. None

S-7955 1251a C:181 X-0360 PICK:PERR
a. W-4894 Leighton Yancey*
b. Leighton Yancy*
c. None
* So spelled.

S-7956 285a C:181 X-0360 PICK:PERR
a. W-6074 Layton Yancey*
b. Leighton Yancy*
c. None
* So spelled.

S-7964. See S-5137 (in volume 4, part 1)

S-7965 51a C:186 X-0740 CLAR:MADI
a. W-1500 John Pride, heir to William (Pride)
b. John Pride
c. None

S-7966 527a C:184 X-0847 FAYE:CONC
a. W-323 Lieutenant Robert Green
b. Robert Green
c. None

S-7967 195a C:184 X-1180 UNIO:UNIO
a. W-323 Lieutenant Robert Green
b. Robert Green
c. James Taylor, 1829

S-7969 & S-7970. See S-6512

S-7971* 15a -- -- HIGH:BRUS HIGH:PAIN
a. --
b. Jesse Baldwin
c. None
* Listed in Source A only.

S-7972 15a C:525 X-0846 HIGH:PAIN
a. W-5567 Edward Herndon
b. Isaac Waters
c. None

S-7974 220a C:192 X-0780 MADI:UNIO
a. W-6065 Thomas Conner
W-6066 William Bowden
W-6008 John M. Gregory, heir to William (Gregory)
b. Cadwallader Wallace
c. J. McLain; E. Langham, 1825

S-7976 400a C:266 X-0360 MADI:UNIO

a. W-5901 Ann Garnett? (Garrett?), heir to Benjamin (Garnett? Garrett?)
b. Ann Garrett
c. M. Bonner, 1828; Peter Hammond; C. Wallace, 1834; Morris O'Brien; J. Hammond; J. Crisman, 1842

S-7981 150a C:253 X-0841 FAYE:WAYN
a. W-6071 George Ryan
b. George Ryan
c. None

S-7986 100a C:181 X-0130 X-1140 PIKE:PERR
a. W-5989 John Yancey
b. Nathan Reeves
c. None

S-7995 1233a C:248 X-0110 LOGA:BOAK
a. W-6058 John Morriss?
W-6038 John Hargus? (Hargess?)
b. George Dawson
c. None

S-7997. See S-7948

S-7998
S-8146 167a C:213 X-0870 ROSS:HUNT
a. W-5944 William Higginbotham
W-6129 Harod Gibbs
b. -- Hobson & -- Fulton
c. None

S-8005 550a C:266 X-1260? MADI:UNIO
a. W-5901 Ann Garnett? (Garrett?), heir to Benjamin (Garnett? Garrett?)
b. Ann Garrett
c. John Moore, 1828

S-8008 280a C:186 X-0010 GREE:SILV CLIN:LIBE
a. W-323 Lieutenant Robert Green
b. Robert Green
c. None

S-8009 50a C:189 X-0360 PICK:DEER
a. W-6002 Daniel Keith
b. Daniel Kieth*
c. None
* Source A spells Keith.

S-8010 50a C:189 X-0360 PICK:DEER
a. W-6002 Daniel Keith
b. Daniel Kieth*
c. A. Burt
* Source A spells Keith.

S-8011. See S-8023

S-8013 191a C:403 X-0660 CLAR:MADI
a. W-5335 Richard Kennon, representatives of
b. Richard Kennon, representatives of
c. None

S-8017 50a C:198 X-0360 FAYE:MADI PICK:---*
a. W-6008 John M. Gregory, heir to William (Gregory)
b. Cadwallader Wallace
c. None
* Source A does not mention Pickaway County.

S-8018 100a C:182 X-0840 ROSS:TWIN ROSS:HUNT
a. W-5989 John Yancey
b. Henry Massie
c. None

S-8019 50a C:182 X-0840 ROSS:TWIN ROSS:HUNT
a. W-5989 John Yancey
b. Henry Massie
c. None

S-8020* 29a -- -- ROSS:DEER
a. --
b. Henry Massie
c. None
* Listed in Source A only.

S-8021 67a C:442 X-0841 PICK:---* ROSS:DEER
a. W-5961 Barnabas Arthur
b. John Evans
c. None
* Source A does not mention Pickaway County.

S-8023
S-8011
S-8872
S-8196*
S-8126** 332a D:77 X-0515 PICK:PERR
a. W-5961 Barnabas Arthur
W-6130 Richard H? (M?) Owen
W-5837 Zachariah --? (illegible)
W-5953? (W-5952?) Richard Hooper
b. John Evans
c. None
* Source A does not list S-8196.
** This warrant number appears in Source A only.

S-8024. See S-7114

S-8025. See S-6258 (in volume 4, part 1)

S-8026 116a C:193 X-1055 PICK:PERR
a. W-5549 Berryman Green
b. Benjamin Green
c. None

S-8037 100a C:288 X-0360 MADI:PLEA
a. W-4795 Alexander Cummins
b. Joseph Bohannan*
c. None
* Source A spells Bohannon.

S-8037 200a C:288 X-0360 MADI:PLEA

a. W-5572 William Palmer
b. William Palmer
c. None

S-8037 200a C:288 X-0360 MADI:PLEA
a. W-4794 John Nutt
b. Philip Sneed
c. None

S-8039 262a C:358 X-0360 PICK:MONR
a. W-5772 Thomas Hill, representatives of
b. Thomas Hill, heirs (of)
c. Joseph Olds & D. Adams, 1831

S-8041 35a C:184 X-1180 MADI:SUMM
a. W-5575 Joseph Hooker?
b. James Galloway (Junior*)
c. None
* Per Source A.

S-8044 400a C:194 X-0120 MADI:RANG
a. W-6117 Thomas Hopper
b. John A. Fulton
c. None

S-8045
S-8824 210a C:441 X-0841 MADI:RANG
a. W-6117 Thomas Hopper
W-6130 Richard H? (M?) Owen
W-6099 Harry Terrell
b. John A. Fulton
c. None

S-8053 150a C:225 X-1000 PICK:JACK
a. W-6118 Thomas Hopper
b. Benjamin Hough
c. None

S-8054 150a C:190 X-1000 PICK:JACK
a. W-6118 Thomas Hopper
b. Benjamin Hough
c. None

S-8056 100a C:396 X-0840 MADI:RANG
a. W-6123 Thomas Hopper
b. William Fulton
c. None

S-8057 200a C:210 X-0420 ADAM:LIBE
a. W-6102 James Collier
b. William Leedom
c. None

S-8058 1223a D:448 X-0360 MADI:PLEA
a. W-6036 John Hargus? (Hargess?)
W-6037 John Hargus? (Hargess?)
W-6063 William Conner?
b. George Dawson & John Dawson
c. Jonathan Farrar; Samuel N. Kerr, 1841

S-8060 20a C:226 X-0360 PICK:JACK
a. W-6123 Thomas Hopper
b. William Fulton
c. None

S-8062
S-8063 100a C:396 X-0366 PICK:PERR
a. W-6118 Thomas Hopper
b. Hugh Young
c. None

S-8065. See S-6854

S-8066. See S-6094 (in volume 4, part 1)

S-8070 325a C:214 X-0660 CLAR:MADI
a. W-5960 John Carroll
W-5955 Richard Hopper
W-5962 Barnabas Arthur
b. James Galloway, Junior
c. None

S-8071* 150a -- -- MADI:----
a. --
b. Jeremiah McLem?
c. None
* Listed in Source A only.

S-8073 80a C:226 X-0841 FAYE:MADI
a. W-6123 Thomas Hopper
b. William Fulton
c. None

S-8074
S-8432 165a C:282 X-0840 FAYE:UNIO
a. W-6118 Thomas Hopper
W-5694 Joseph Woodson
b. Jesse Millikan
c. None

S-8075 30a C:514 X-0136 ADAM:MEIG
a. W-5871 Francis M. Boykin & Ann Johnson, heirs & administrators of F(rancis) Boykin
b. Patrick Montgomery
c. None

S-8077 30a C:274 X-0730 CLAR:HARM
a. W-6014 Benjamin Harrison, representatives of
b. Alexander Simpson
c. None

S-8081 170a C:231 X-0340 MADI:FAIR
a. W-5791 George Lee Turberville
W-5916 Gross Scruggs
b. -- Graham & -- Scruggs
c. None

S-8082 200a C:344 X-0360 MADI:FAIR
a. W-5791 George Lee Turberville
W-5786 Edwin Hull? (Hall?)
W-5881 Edmund Farrell, heir to Thomas (Farrell)
W-5787 Edwin Hull? (Hall?)

W-5784 Edward Hull? (Hall?)
W-5735 Thomas Gaskins, deceased
b. -- Graham & -- Dun
c. None

S-8083 200a C:242 X-0340 MADI:FAIR
a. W-5707 Edmond Edmondson
b. Robertson Burge
c. William Johnson; M. S. Sullivant, 1831

S-8084 100a C:339 X-0366 MADI:DEER
a. W-6042 Edward Hall
b. William Erwin
c. D. Thomas, 1826

S-8085
S-8086 137a C:505 X-1375 PICK:JACK
a. W-6130 Richard H? (M?) Owen
b. John Evans
c. None

S-8089 33a C:404 X-0847 HIGH:MADI
HIGH:PAIN
a. W-5753 John Walker, deceased, heirs of
b. Thomas M. Bayley
c. None

S-8090 162a C:404 X-0840 HIGH:PAIN
a. W-5753 John Walker, deceased, heirs of
b. Thomas M. Bayley
c. None

S-8094 200a C:342 X-0340 FRAN:PLEA
a. W-1915 John? (James?) Kelly
b. Robert Roberts
c. J. L. Taylor, 1836

S-8100 98a C:190 X-0133 ADAM:MEIG
a. W-5708 John Poulson, by his executor, G? P. Bagwell
b. George Vinsonhaller*
c. None
* Source A spells Vinsonhaler.

S-8101 100a C:190 X-0134 ADAM:MEIG
a. W-5913 William Mag? Porter
b. George Vinsonhaller*
c. None
* Source A spells Vinsonhaler.

S-8102 116a C:190 X-0130 ADAM:SCOT
a. W:5948 William Pullen
b. George Vinsonhaller*
c. None
* Source A spells Vinsonhaler.

S-8103 53a C:190 X-0134 ADAM:SCOT
a. W-5708 John Poulson, by his executor, G. P. Bagwell
W-5948 William Pullen
b. George Vinsonhaller*
c. None
* Source A spells Vinsonhaler.

S-8104 45a C:222 X-1040 SCIO:---*
ADAM:JEFF
a. W-5708 John Poulson, by his executor, G. P. Bagwell
b. George Vinsonhaller**
c. None
* Source A does not mention Scioto County.
** Source A spells Vinsonhaler.

S-8106 94a C:254 X-1040 SCIO:BRUS
a. W-5708 John Poulson, by his exector, G. P. Bagwell
b. George Vinsonhaller*
c. None
* Source A spells Vinsonhaler.

S-8107 267a C:222 X-0133 ADAM:FRAN
a. W-5592 John Hart, representative of John (Hart?)
W-5708 John Poulson, by his executor, G. P. Bagwell
b. George Vinsonhaller*
c. J. Gustin; J. Wood, 1841
* Source A spells Vinsonhaler.

S-8114 150a C:190 X-0340 PICK:JACK
a. W-6130 Richard H? (M?) Owen
b. Benjamin Hough
c. None

S-8117. See S-8338

S-8118 333a C:340 X-0360 MADI:UNIO
a. W-6045 William Berry
b. Levi Springer
c. None

S-8119. See S-6265 (in volume 4, part 1)

S-8120. See S-7610

S-8121 800a C:195 X-0840 MADI:UNIO
X-0340
a. W-6129 Harod Gibbs
b. John A. Fulton
c. None

S-8122 200a C:429 X-0360 MADI:UNIO
a. W-6129 Harod Gibbs
b. John A. Fulton
c. None

S-8124 100a C:213 X-0840 ROSS:HUNT
a. W-6129 Harod Gibbs
b. John A. Fulton
c. None

S-8126. See S-8023 (footnote)

S-8127. See S-6969 & S-6960

S-8130. See S-8321

S-8131 1016a C:518 X-0360 MADI:RANG
a. W-6083 Thomas Collier, representatives of
W-6084 Thomas Collier, representatives of
W-6087 Thomas Collier, representatives of
W-6106 James Dunn, representatives of
W-5980 George Thomas
W-6141 Claiborne Morris
b. Thomas Worthington
c. None

S-8133 50a C:233 X-1149 ADAM:JEFF
a. W-5871 Francis M. Boykin & Ann Johnson, heirs & administrators of F(rancis) Boykin
b. James Anderson
c. J. H. Hanar? & brothers; T. Huston, 1841

S-8134
S-12962
S-12997
S-12998
S-12999
S-13007
S-13011 601a D:264 X-0840 ROSS:PAXT PIKE:BENT
a. W-6128 Stephen Young
W-6719 William Price
W-6720 William Price
W-6668 George Barker? (Backer?)
b. -- McLene, -- Wallace, & -- Clark
c. J. Potts; C. McCollister, 1840; C. Wallace; George W. Reynolds, 1841

S-8135 100a C:348 X-1180 MADI:PIKE UNIO:---*
a. W-6005 George Godby
b. George Hovoer (Hoover?)**
c. None
* Source A does not mention Union County.
** Source A spells Hoover.

S-8136 200a C:213 X-0841 FAYE:PAIN
a. W-6129 Harod Gibbs
b. John A. Fulton
c. None

S-8137 42a D:476 X-0360 MADI:JEFF
a. W-6110 Coleman May
b. Thomas Worthington, heirs (of)
c. None

S-8137 8a D:476 X-1000 PIKE:PEEP
a. W-6110 Coleman May
b. Thomas Worthington, heirs (of)
c. None

S-8137 250a C:472 X-0120 MADI:RANG
a. W-6094 William Toomes? (Toomer?)
W-6110 Coleman May
b. Thomas Worthington, heirs (of)
c. None

S-8138 220a C:223 X-1042 MADI:---*
a. W-6095 Thomas Thorp? (Sharp?)
W-6096 John Hutchson? (Hutcheson?)
b. William Creighton, Junior
c. None
* Source A does not mention Madison County.

S-8139. See S-7272

S-8140 50a C:226 X-0840 ROSS:HUNT
a. W-6129 Harod Gibbs
b. William Fulton
c. Dickerson Bart, 1824

S-8141 100a C:304 X-0870 PIKE:PEEP
a. W-6129 Harod Gibbs
b. William Robinson
c. None

S-8142 15a C:197 X-0180 WARR:WAYN
a. W-3349 Edward Shepherd
b. Jacob Brown
c. None

S-8143 50a C:236 X-0300 ROSS:HUNT
a. W-5941 William Higginbotham
b. William Keys
c. Samuel Reed, 1830

S-8144 30a C:226 X-0300 ROSS:HUNT
a. W-6129 Harod Gibbs
b. William Fulton
c. J. C. Sweney, 1831

S-8145 50a C:213 X-1000 ROSS:HUNT
a. W-6129 Harod Gibbs
b. John A. Fulton
c. None

S-8146. See S-7998

S-8147. See S-7268

S-8148 94a C:193 X-0730 CHAM:GOSH CHAM:UNIO
a. W-5570 Isaiah Corbin
b. Benjamin Cheney
c. None

S-8149 6a C:193 X-0730 CHAM:UNIO
a. W-5570 Isaiah Corbin
b. Benjamin Cheney
c. None

S-8150 50a C:226 X-1000 ROSS:HUNT
a. W-6123 Thomas Hopper
b. William Fulton
c. Moses McClelland; James B. Turner, 1831

S-8151 120a C:249 X-1180 UNIO:UNIO

a. W-6016 Strother G. Settle, representatives of
W-2349 Captain Henry Whiting
b. -- Haines & -- Whiting
c. None

S-8152 220a C:229 X-1180 UNIO:UNIO
a. W-2349 Captain Henry Whiting
b. Henry Whiting
c. None

S-8153 94a C:247 X-0340 UNIO:UNIO
a. W-5791 George Lee Turberville
b. John Graham
c. None

S-8159 150a C:233 X-0130 ADAM:JEFF
a. W-5871 Francis M. Boykin & Ann Johnson, heirs & administrators of F(rancis) Boykin
b. John Burley
c. None

S-8160 176a C:211 X-0590 X-0600 ADAM:SPRI
a. W-290 Captain Abraham Shepherd
b. John Macher*
c. None
* So spelled.

S-8162* 25a -- -- ROSS:DEER
a. --
b. John Evans
c. None
* Listed in Source A only.

S-8163. See S-10516

S-8164 18a C:193 X-0840 ROSS:TWIN
a. W-6016 Strother G. Settle, representatives of
b. Nathan Haines
c. None

S-8166 70a C:208 X-0130 ADAM:MEIG
a. W-5871 Francis M. Boykin & Ann Johnson, heirs & administrators of F(rancis) Boykin
b. Andrew Ellison
c. None

S-8167 100a C:244 X-0340 UNIO:DARB
a. W-5799 James Dillard
b. Walter Dun
c. Alpheus Bigelow; S. G. Strong, 1827

S-8171 598a C:255 X-0663 CLER:JACK
a. W-5961 Barnabas Arthur
W-6008 John M. Gregory, heir to William (Gregory)
W-6074 Layton Yancey
b. -- Wallace & -- Young
c. T. L? (S?) Foote? (Forte?); Holly Raper (Roper?) 1824

S-8171 83a C:255 X-0663 CLER:JACK
a. W-4894 Leighton Yancey*
b. Layton Yancy*
c. None
* So spelled.

S-8172 25a C:198 X-0840 ROSS:PAIN
a. W-6008 John M. Gregory, heir to William (Gregory)
b. Cadwallader Wallace
c. None

S-8173 50a C:257 X-0840 FAYE:MADI
a. W-5901 Ann Garnett? (Garrett?), heir to Benjamin (Garnett? Garrett?)
b. Ann Garrett
c. Heirs of C. Kore

S-8174. See S-6265 (in volume 4, part 1)

S-8176 675a C:304 X-1180 MADI:PIKE
a. W-5335 Richard Kennon, representatives of
b. Richard Kennon, representatives (of)
c. John Kious; L. Starling, Junior

S-8177 13a C:210 X-0130 ADAM:TIFF
a. W-5947 William Pullen
b. James Davis
c. None

S-8178 65a C:351 X-1000 SCIO:WASH
a. W-6035 Jacob Moore
b. William Kendall
c. None

S-8179 60a C:349 X-1190 SCIO:NILE
a. W-6007 Robert Martin? (Marlin?)
b. James Andrews
c. None

S-8180 73a C:349 X-1000 SCIO:WASH
a. W-6007 Robert Martin? (Marlin?)
b. James Andrew
c. None

S-8181 67a C:351 X-1000 SCIO:WASH
a. W-6007 Robert Martin? (Marlin?)
b. Robert Lucas
c. L. M. Sullivant; R. Craine, 1838

S-8182 144a C:197 X-1040 SCIO:UNIO
a. W-6035 Jacob Moore
b. William Kendall
c. None

S-8183 69a C:196 X-1040 SCIO:UNIO
a. W-6035 Jacob Moore
b. William Kendall
c. None

S-8189. See S-8989

S-8196
S-8639 216a C:272 X-0841 FAYE:WAYN
a. W-5551 John Meanly
W-5718 John Spilfatham
b. Duncan McArthur
c. None

S-8196. See S-8023

S-8197. See S-5581 (in volume 4, part 1)

S-8198. See S-7237

S-8200 50a C:226 X-0570 ROSS:HUNT
a. W-6123 Thomas Hopper
b. William Fulton
c. None

S-8201 25a E:10 X-1000 ROSS:SCIO
a. W-6127 Stephen Young
b. John A. Fulton
c. I. Y. Green, 1835

S-8202 25a D:408 X-0840 ROSS:HUNT
a. W-6128 Stephen Young
b. Jeremiah McLene*
c. None
* Source A notation: "Patented to Daniel Gregg."

S-8203
S-8205 450a C:274 X-0840 ROSS:HUNT
a. W-6116 George Greenway
b. George Greenway
c. John Campbell; Gus Scott, 1831; John Chapman; H. Fullerton, 1836; J. P. Cisna; S. D. Wesson, 1840; A. Hunt; B. Malone, 1842

S-8204 78a C:275 X-0760 PIKE:BENT
a. W-6116 George Greenway
b. George Greenway
c. Michael Mackey; Loyd Howard, 1826

S-8205. See S-8203

S-8206 139a C:241 X-1000 PICK:WAYN
a. W-6116 George Greenway
b. George Greenway
c. Isaac Terwilliger, 1827

S-8207 1000a C:241 X-0360 MADI:PLEA
a. W-6115 George Greenway
b. George Greenway
c. John Kyas (Kious?) 1828

S-8208 200a C:237 X-0870 ROSS:HUNT
PIKE:PEBB
a. W-6127 Stephen Young
b. John A. Fulton
c. William Murphey; A. G. Thurman, 1831; A. L. S. Thurman; John R. Anderson; A. Latham, 1837; Henry Bliss, 1831

S-8211 310a C:228 X-0660 CLAR:MADI
a. W-6016 Strother G. Settle, representative of
b. Nathan Haines
c. None

S-8212. See S-5533 (in volume 4, part 1)

S-8213 100a C:200 X-0180 GREE:ROSS
a. W-5839 William Newell
b. Reuben McDaniel
c. None

S-8215 50a C:264 X-0030 SCIO:MORG
a. W-5871 Francis M. Boykin & Ann Johnson, heirs & administrators of F(rancis) Boykin
b. Cornelius Shellman*
c. None
* Source A spells Shelpman.

S-8216 40a D:107 X-0420 BROW:FRAN
X-1120
a. W-5871 Francis M. Boykin & Ann Johnson, heirs & administrators of F(rancis) Boykin
b. Thomas Mountjoy
c. None

S-8217 100a C:233 X-0130 ADAM:MEIG
a. W-5904 Bernard Houchings
b. Andrew Ellison
c. None

S-8218 200a D:263 X-0870 PIKE:PEEP
a. W-6128 Stephen Young
b. Jeremiah McLene
c. None

S-8222. See S-7544

S-8223 200a C:271 X-0840 MADI:---*
X-0660 CLAR:HARM
a. W-6101 Harry Terrell
b. John A. Fulton
c. None
* Source A does not mention Madison County.

S-8226 150a E:109 X-0400 FAYE:MADI
a. W-5895 Thomas Moore
b. Thomas Moore, representatives of
c. R. Douglas; J. F. Chenwith (Chenowith?)(Madison County) 1827; I. Y. Green, 1834; J. T. Cook, 1838

S-8227 510a C:330 X-0660 MADI:STOK
GREE:ROSS
CLAR:----
a. W-387 Captain Samuel Lapsley
b. Samuel Lapsley
c. R. Douglas, 1825; -- Herod? & -- Harpole? (Haspole?) 1829; Paul Herod; J. Hively, 1827; S? (E?) Herod, 1827

S-8228 69a C:201 X-0420 BROW:UNIO
a. W-6041 Ishmael Bailey

b. John Fisher
c. J. Ellis; -- Wilson & -- Middleton, 1842

S-8230 323a C:201 X-0540 ROSS:DEER PICK:---*
a. W-814 David Walker, heir to Captain -- Walker
b. David Walker
c. None
* Source A does not mention Pickaway County; notation: "By Clarksburg."

S-8231 1150a C:201 X-1000 FRAN:JACK
a. W-5989 John Yancey
b. Henry Massie
c. Ira Delano; D. Adams, 1831

S-8232 160a C:290 X-0540 ROSS:DEER
a. W-5989 John Yancey
b. Henry Massie
c. G. Lewis; William Brown, 1842

S-8233. See S-4937 (in volume 4, part 1)

S-8234
S-8249 284a C:229 X-0847 PIKE:PERR HIGH:BRUS
a. W-6097 Jacob Daniel
W-6069 William Fleming
W-6124 Thomas Hopper
W-5852 Edward Carrington, John Marshall, Henry Heth, & Henry G. Heth, executor of Will(iam) Heth, deceased
b. -- Dun, -- Carrington, -- Marshall, & -- Heth
c. None

S-8235 90a C:229 X-0130 PIKE:PERR
a. W-6069 William Fleming
W-6148 William McGeorge
b. Walter Dun
c. None

S-8236 57a C:203 X-0130 PIKE:PERR HIGH:---*
a. W-6148 William McGeorge
b. Walter Dun
c. None
* In Source A, Highland County shown in pencilled notation only.

S-8237 90a C:203 X-0840 PIKE:PERR
a. W-6016 Strother G. Settle, representatives of
W-6148 William McGeorge
b. -- Dun & -- Haines
c. None

S-8238
S-8740
S-8865
S-8705 400a C:285 X-0570 X-0840 ROSS:HUNT
a. W-6098 Harry Terrell
W-6016 Strother G. Settle, representatives of
b. -- Dun & -- Haines
c. None

S-8240
S-8869 550a C:287 X-1000 PICK:JACK
a. W-6114 George Greenway
b. George Greenway
c. Isaac Terwilliger, 1827

S-8242* 200a -- -- ADAM:----
a. --
b. James H. Wilson
c. None
* Entry in Source A only, where crossed out.

S-8243 267a C:355 X-0841 FAYE:MADI
a. W-6057 James Tallman, representatives of
W-6113 Robert Mitchell?
b. P. Tallman & representatives (of) J. Tallman
c. J. Wood, 1824

S-8245 100a C:304 X-1240 ROSS:PAIN
a. W-4825 Isaac Kemmey
b. James Mahan
c. None

S-8246* 75a -- -- ROSS:DEER
a. --
b. Jeremiah McLene
c. None
* Entry in Source A only.

S-8249. See S-8234

S-8251* 70a -- -- ROSS:HUNT
a. --
b. John A. Fulton
c. None
* Entry in Source A only.

S-8252 107a C-207 X-0760 PIKE:BENT
a. W-5768 Samuel Blair, heirs of
b. Andrew Ellison
c. None

S-8253 74a C:207 X-0423 ADAM:TIFF
a. W-5768 Samuel Blair, heirs of
b. Andrew Ellison
c. None

S-8254 50a C:205 X-0800 ADAM:GREE
a. W-3105 Thomas Miller
b. Andrew Ellison
c. None

S-8255 100a C:209 X-0136 ADAM:MEIG
a. W-4325 Ann, Elizabeth, Catharine, Mary, & Eppa Simmons, heirs to James A--? Allen
b. Andrew Ellison
c. John Chapman, 1826

S-8256 73a C:204 X-0130 ADAM:MEIG
a. W-215 Doctor David Holmes
b. David Holmes
c. None

S-8257. See S-7128

S-8258. See S-7200

S-8259. See S-4469 (in volume 4, part 1)

S-8260   20a   C:212   X-0130   ADAM:TIFF
a. W-4992 Thomas Wells? (Wills?), representatives of
b. Henry Young
c. None

S-8261   150a   C:208   X-0650   ADAM:WAYN
a. W-3870 Jacob Beerly? (Beesly?)
W-5841 Samuel Scruggs
W-5356 William Rogers
b. Andrew Ellison
c. None

S-8262. See S-5342 (in volume 4, part 1)

S-8263   131a   C:207   X-0590   ADAM:SPRI
X-0600
a. W-5768 Samuel Blair, heirs of
b. Andrew Ellison
c. None

S-8265   100a   C:212   X-0340   MADI:DARB
a. W-6146 James Blake, heirs of
b. Jesseup* N. Conch
c. None
* Source A spells Jessup.

S-8266   100a   C:211   X-1040   ADAM:JEFF
a. W-4992 Thomas Wells? (Wills?) representatives of
b. William McClarin
c. None

S-8267   50a   C:292   X-0381   ADAM:MONR
a. W-5871 Francis M. Boykin & Ann Johnson, heirs & administrators of F(rancis) Boykin
b. Thomas Mountjoy, Junior
c. None

S-8268   200a   C:212   X-1040   ADAM:JEFF
a. W-3105 Thomas Miller
b. Elijah Walden
c. None

S-8269. See S-7511

S-8273. See S-7589

S-8274   120a   C:213   X-0740   MADI:STOK
CLAR:MADI
a. W-4305 Joseph Brand
b. James Galloway, Junior
c. None

S-8275. See S-7408

S-8277   450a   C:271   X-0730   CHAM:---*
CLAR:PLEA
a. W-6060 William Connor
b. John Dawson
c. None
* Source A does not mention Champaign County.

S-8278   40a   E:92   X-1055   SCIO:---*
a. W-5871 Francis M. Boykin & Ann Johnson, heirs & administrators of F(rancis) Boykin
b. Thomas Mountjoy, Junior
c. T. Huston, 1837
* Source A shows Jefferson Township, but is marked out.

S-8279   140a   E:148   X-0133   HIGH:BRUS
a. W-5706 Archibald Moon, representatives of
b. Joseph Kerr
c. Hugh West, 1831

S-8280   50a   E:239   X-0133   HIGH:BRUS
a. W-5706 Archibald Moon, representatives of
b. James M. Trimble*
c. John Gosset, 1831
* Source A says Joseph Kerr.

S-8281   100a   C:217   X-1303   HIGH:WHIT
a. W-5706 Archibald Moon, representatives of
b. Joseph Kerr
c. None

S-8282   150a   E:187   X-0134   HIGH:CONC
a. W-5706 Archibald Moon, representatives of
b. James M. Trimble
c. Joseph Kerr; William Rodgers, 1831

S-8283   150a   C:217   X-1303   HIGH:WHIT
a. W-5706 Archibald Moon, representatives of
b. Joseph Kerr
c. Jacob Kirby; J. M. Trimble, 1835

S-8284*   75a   --   --   HIGH:WHIT
a. --
b. Joseph Kerr
c. S. Gibler & W. Gibler; G. Smith, 1837
* Entry in Source A only.

S-8285   100a   F:78   X-0134   ADAM:SCOT
a. W-5706 Archibald Moon, representatives of
b. Joseph Kerr
c. Mary Van Polt? (Pelt?); T. Huston, 1835

S-8287   300a   C:425   X-0663   BROW:STER
BROW:PERR
a. W-5866 Abraham Bowman
b. Abraham Bowman
c. John W. Tibbats, 1826

S-8289 344a C:406 X-0663 CLER:WILL
a. W-5544 James Hirt? (Hart? Hurt?)
W-3056 John Anthony
W-6109 William Porter
b. -- Lytle & -- Porter
c. None

S-8291 94a C:228 X-1000 PICK:WAYN
a. W-5800 James Dillard
b. Benjamin Hough
c. None

S-8292 250a C:241 X-0340 X-1385 PICK:JACK
a. W-5800 James Dillard
b. Benjamin Hough
c. None

S-8294 400a E:253 X-0130 ADAM:TIFF
a. W-368 Captain Andrew Nixon
b. Andrew Nixon
c. None

S-8295* 150a -- -- HIGH:DODS
a. --
b. Joseph Kerr
c. None
* Entry in Source A only.

S-8296* 243a -- -- HIGH:SALE
a. --
b. Joseph Kerr
c. None
* Entry in Source A only.

S-8297* 200a -- -- BROW:JACK
a. --
b. Joseph Kerr
c. None
* Entry in Source A only.

S-8298 200a E:265 X-1120 BROW:JACK
a. W-5705 Archibald Moon, representatives of
W-5704 Archibald Moon, representatives of
W-5706 Archibald Moon, representatives of
b. Joseph Kerr
c. None

S-8299 85a* F:213 X-0133 ADAM:SCOT
a. W-5705 Archibald Moon, representatives of
W-5706 Archibald Moon, representatives of
b. Joseph Kerr
c. None
* Source A says 95 acres.

S-8300 66a D:363 X-0800 SCIO:WASH
a. W-6061 William Connor
b. James Bradford
c. None

S-8301 20a C:459 X-1196 SCIO:NILE
a. W-6061 William Connor*
b. William Conner*
c. None
* So spelled.

S-8302 313a C:350 X-0030 SCIO:MORG
a. W-6061 William Connor*
b. William Conner*
c. Levi Walls, 1830; Joseph? (James?) Swearingen; -- Gregory & -- Delong, 1829
* So spelled.

S-8303 230a C:243 X-0730 LOGA:JEFF LOGA:MONR
a. W-6081 John Collier
W-6125 Stephen Young
b. Walter Dun
c. M. Bonner, 1827; William Bayless, 1833

S-8304 13a C:263 X-0340 FRAN:PLEA
a. W-6125 Stephen Young
b. Walter Dun
c. None

S-8305 240a C:244 X-0340 MADI:DARB
a. W-6125 Stephen Young
W-6089 Thomas Collier, representatives of
b. Walter Dun
c. None

S-8308 175a C:355 X-0841 FAYE:PAIN
a. W-6057 James Tallman, representatives of
W-6111 John Bevan
b. Peter Tallman & representatives of James Tallman
c. Jonah Van Pelt; L? (S?) P. Reed, 1831

S-8309 58a C:393 X-0841 FAYE:MADI
a. W-6113 Robert Mitchell?
W-6111 John Bevan
b. Thomas McDonald
c. None

S-8310 165a C:264 X-0840 ROSS:PAIN
a. W-6089 Thomas Collier, representatives of
W-5787 Edwin Hull? (Hall?)
W-5916 Gross Scruggs
b. -- Dun, -- Graham, & -- Scruggs
c. None

S-8311 25a C:235 X-0130 ADAM:GREE
a. W-5946 William Pullen
b. Robert Whitlatch
c. None

S-8312 36a C:235 X-0130 ADAM:GREE
a. W-5768 Samuel Blair, heirs of
b. James Scott
c. A. Ellison, 1823

S-8313* 15a -- -- ADAM:--**
a. --
b. Andrew Ellison
c. None

* Entry in Source A only.
** Source A notation: "Not found."

S-8314
S-9210 40a C:308 X-0130 ADAM:GREE
a. W-1567 John Waller
W-5781 Joseph Crockett
b. Andrew Ellison
c. None

S-8315 200a C:310 X-0841 FAYE:MADI
a. W-6014 Benjamin Harrison, representatives of
b. William Fulton
c. None

S-8316 200a C:237 X-0841 FAYE:MADI
a. W-5978 John E. Scott, representatives of
W-6123 Thomas Hopper
b. J. A. Fulton & William Fulton
c. None

S-8319 100a C:280 X-0840 ROSS:PAIN
a. W-6160 Thomas Ray
b. John A. Fulton
c. None

S-8321
S-8130 216a C:290 X-0679 PICK:DEER
a. W-6130 Richard H? (M?) Owen
b. John Evans
c. Eliza Parot; John Tiffin

S-8322
S-10544
S-10545
S-10546
S-12337
S-12610 300a D:242 X-1385 PICK:WAYN
a. W-6524 Richard Dorsey, heirs of
W-6489 Robert Wilmott
W-5949 William Pullen
W-6417 Joseph Britton
b. John Evans
c. None

S-8323
S-8861 143a C:290 X-1000 PICK:WAYN
a. W-6127 Stephen Young
W-6130 Richard H? (M?) Owen
b. John Evans
c. M. Tawnehill; J. Olds, 1842

S-8325* 2a -- -- PICK:WAYN
a. --
b. John Evans
c. None
* Entry in Source A only.

S-8326 200a C:371 X-0360 MADI:UNIO
a. W-6040 George Wright
b. Conrad Kramer*
c. T. Chapman, 1823
* Source A may spell Kromer.

S-8328. See S-6828

S-8329 150a C:227 X-1303 HIGH:SALE
a. W-6159 Thomas Ray
b. John A. Fulton
c. D. H. Murphy; John Purdy, 1839

S-8330 100a C:242 X-1303 HIGH:SALE
HIGH:WHIT
a. W-6159 Thomas Ray
b. John A. Fulton
c. Joseph Rankin; Samuel Woodmansee, 1833

S-8333 200a C:219 X-0730 CLAR:PLEA
a. W-1864 William Rose
W-1238 Thomas Turk, heir to James Turk
b. -- Collins & -- Turk
c. None

S-8337 200a C:295 X-0840 FAYE:MADI
FAYE:PAIN
a. W-6160 Thomas Ray
b. William Robinson
c. G. Hammond

S-8338
S-8117 533a C:227 X-0660 CLAR:MADI
a. W-5962 Barnabas Arthur
W-5575 Joseph Hawkins
W-5960 John Carroll
W-5902 Leroy Edwards, devisees of
b. James Galloway, Junior
c. None

S-8339
S-9292 100a C:339 X-0663 HIGH:UNIO
a. W-6123 Thomas Hopper
W-6194 Robert Hanson Harrison, heirs of
b. William Fulton & J. A. Fulton
c. Benjamin Thomas, 1831

S-8340
S-9291 95a C:339 X-0663 HIGH:DODS
a. W-6123 Thomas Hopper
W-6194 Robert Hanson Harrison, heirs of
b. William Fulton & J. A. Fulton
c. None

S-8341 132a C:385 X-0800 SCIO:WASH
a. W-6035 Jacob Moore
b. William Kendall
c. None

S-8342 200a C:300 X-1130 MADI:STOK
a. W-2274 Doctor Basel Middleton
b. John Campbell
c. None

S-8345 33a C:230 X-0670 ROSS:TWIN
a. W-6125 Stephen Young
b. Walter Dun
c. None

S-8352 400a C:220 X-0360 MADI:SUMM
a. W-6151 William B. Thornton
b. James L. Markham*
c. Joseph? (James?) Crisman, 1828
* Source A says James S. Markham.

S-8361 102a C:254 X-0040 ADAM:TIFF
a. W-5708 John Poulson, by his executor G? P. Bagwell
b. George Vinsonhaller*
c. None
* Source A spells Vinsonhaler.

S-8362 212a C:223 X-0134 ADAM:FRAN
a. W-5861 Henry Bell
b. James Pemberton
c. None

S-8363 80a C:224 X-1045 SCIO:BRUS
a. W-6096 John Hutchson (Hutcheson?)
b. William Creighton, Junior
c. None

S-8364 97a C:222 X-0133 ADAM:MEIG
a. W-5861 Henry Bell
b. George Vinsonhaller*
c. None
* Source A spells Vinsonhaler.

S-8365 52a C:224 X-0133 ADAM:SCOT
a. W-5675 Joseph Woodson
b. Thomas Scott
c. None

S-8366 12a C:254 X-0840 ROSS:HUNT
a. W-5675 Joseph Woodson
b. Thomas Scott
c. None

S-8367 53a C:222 X-1044 ADAM:SCOT
a. W-6088 Thomas Collier, representatives of
b. George Vinsonhaller*
c. None
* Source A spells Vinsonhaler.

S-8368 170a C:222 X-0133 ADAM:SCOT
a. W-6088 Thomas Collier, representatives of
b. George Vinsonhaller*
c. None
* Source A spells Vinsonhaler.

S-8369 41a C:255 X-0133 HIGH:BRUS PIKE:---*
a. W-5861 Henry Bell
W-5708 John Poulson, by his executor G? P. Bagwell
b. George Vinsonhaller**
c. None
* Source A does not mention Pike County.
** Source A spells Vinsonhaler.

S-8370. See S-7689

S-8371 70a C:327 X-0360 MADI:UNIO
a. W-5521 Joseph Ladd, assignee of Robert S. Ware, executor of John Hockaday, deceased
b. George Hoffman
c. None

S-8372 78a C:221 X-0360 ROSS:DEER
a. W-6156 Christopher Bland
W-6155 George Thompson
b. Cadwallader Wallace
c. None

S-8373
S-9485 400a C:358 X-0360 MADI:UNIO MADI:DEER
a. W-6033 Jacob Moore
W-6049 John Story
W-6032 Peter Triplett
W-6047 William Lampkin
b. James Markham
c. None

S-8374
S-8792 1760a C:277 X-0360 MADI:DEER
a. W-6165 William Royall*
b. William Royal*
c. None
* So spelled.

S-8377* 31a -- -- BROW:BYRD
a. --
b. Noble Melvin
c. None
* Entry in Source A only.

S-8378 19a C:229 X-0670 ROSS:TWIN
a. W-6125 Stephen Young
b. Walter Dun
c. None

S-8382* 200a -- -- CLAR:HARM
a. --
b. Thomas Scott
c. Peter Douglas, 1828
* Entry in Source A only.

S-8384. See S-6472

S-8385* 73a -- -- ROSS:HUNT
a. --
b. -- Dun & -- Graham
c. None
* Entry in Source A only.

S-8390 200a C:250 X-0150 ROSS:PAIN
a. W-6165 William Royall
b. -- Wallace & -- Woodbridge
c. None

S-8391 76a C:238 X-0360 PICK:PERR FAYE:MADI
a. W-6165 William Royall

b. -- Wallace & -- Woodbridge
c. C. Wallace; R. Douglas, 1829; I. Y. Green, 1831; J. McCoy, 1837

S-8396 100a C:287 X-0360 PICK:PERR
a. W-5883 William Allen
b. William Allen
c. James Renick, 1830

S-8397 111a C:268 X-0366 PICK:PERR
a. W-310 Lieutenant David Miller
b. David Miller
c. None

S-8399 100a C:230 X-0846 ROSS:TWIN
a. W-6125 Stephen Young
b. Walter Dun
c. None

S-8400 239a C:275 X-0840 ROSS:HUNT
a. W-6017 Reuben Field
b. Anthony Sheriff
c. E. P. Kendrick; A. Latham, 1829; W. W. Irwin; B. S. Wentworth, 1840

S-8401 123a C:277 X-0840 ROSS:HUNT
a. W-6027 John Stokes, representatives of
W-5836 Ann Shepherd, heir to Major (Shepherd?), who was heir to Solomon Shepherd, deceased
W-6006 Moore Lumpkin
W-5800 James Dillard
b. Benjamin Hough
c. None

S-8402. See S-7696

S-8403 53a D:454 X-0840 ROSS:SCIO
a. W-6129 Harod Gibbs
b. William Robinson
c. None

S-8404 40a C:280 X-0570 ROSS:SCIO
a. W-6129 Harod Gibbs
b. William Robinson
c. None

S-8406. See S-7408

S-8408 800a C:228 X-0848 FAYE:UNIO FAYE:CONC
a. W-5104 Samuel March? assignee of Joseph Smith
W-5853 Henry Massie, assignee of James Craig
W-5989 John Yancey
b. Henry Massie
c. None

S-8410 30a C:340 X-1300 HIGH:WHIT
a. W-6099 Harry Terrell
b. John A. Fulton
c. None

S-8412
S-8413 210a C:305 X-0300 PIKE:PEBB
a. W-6099 Harry Terrell
b. John A. Fulton
c. William Downing; C. M. McCollister, 1840; Jacob Loy, 1831

S-8414 368a C:230 X-1180 MADI:PIKE UNIO:UNIO
a. W-6120 Thomas Hopper
W-6092 Thomas Collier, representative of
W-6079 Jeremiah Pickett, heirs of
b. Walter Dun
c. Heirs of Andrew Burnham; M. S? Sullivant, 1831

S-8415 500a C:232 X-1180 MADI:---* UNIO:UNIO
a. W-6050 James Price, representatives of
W-6016 Strother G. Settle, representatives of
W-5852 Edward Carrington, John Marshall, Henry Heth, & Henry G. Heth, executor of Will(iam) Heth, deceased
b. -- Walke, -- Hains**, -- Carrington, -- Heth, & -- Marshall
c. None
* Source A does not mention Madison County.
** Source A spells Haines.

S-8416 640a C:231 X-1180 MADI:PIKE
a. W-5916 Gross Scruggs
W-5792 James Johnston
W-6089 Thomas Collier, representatives of
b. -- Scruggs, -- Johnston, & -- Dun
c. None

S-8417 355a C:236 X-0340 MADI:CANA
a. W-6076 Joseph Parrott
W-6089 Thomas Collier, representatives of
b. Walter Dun
c. A. McElvain; S. Moore, 1826

S-8418 170a C:243 X-0847 HIGH:BRUS
a. W-6089 Thomas Collier, representatives of
b. Walter Dun
c. None

S-8420 300a C:231 X-0340 FRAN:PLEA
a. W-5791 George Lee Turberville
b. John Graham
c. None

S-8422 110a C:247 X-0360 CHAM:RUSH
a. W-5916 Gross Scruggs
b. Gross Scruggs
c. None

S-8423 721a C:246 X-0340 MADI:FAIR FRAN:PLEA
a. W-5787 Edwin Hull? (Hall?)
W-5784 Edward Hull? (Hall?)
W-5832 Edmund Fairel? (Fauel? Ferrell?)
W-5786 Edwin Hull? (Hall?)
W-5791 George Lee Turberville
W-6126 Stephen Young

W-5916 Gross Scruggs
b. -- Graham, -- Dun, & -- Scruggs
c. Joseph? (James?) Walker, 1836

S-8424 231a C:247 X-1180 MADI:JEFF
a. W-5787 Edwin Hull? (Hall?)
W-5791 George Lee Turberville
b. John Graham
c. None

S-8425 221a C:346 X-0340 MADI:JEFF
a. W-5735 Thomas Gaskins, deceased
W-6124 Thomas Hopper
W-5791 George Lee Turberville
W-5916 Gross Scruggs
W-5792 James Johnston
b. -- Dun, -- Graham, -- Scruggs, & -- Johnston
c. None

S-8425
S-9502 138a C:342 X-1180 MADI:PIKE
a. W-6079 Jeremiah Pickett, heirs of
W-6217 Thomas Triplett
b. Walter Dun
c. None

S-8428 130a C:243 X-0340 MADI:CANA
a. W-6072 William Allman
W-6079 Jeremiah Pickett, heirs of
b. Robert Dun
c. None

S-8429 64a D:50 X-1370 PICK:DEER
a. W-5949 William Pullen
b. John Mills
c. None

S-8432. See S-8074

S-8433 25a C:360 X-1044 SCIO:BRUS
a. W-5799 James Dillard
b. Aaron Brown
c. Thomas Brown; S? S? (L? L?) Brown, 1826

S-8439 120a C:244 X-0340 MADI:CANA
a. W-6089 Thomas Collier, representatives of
b. Walter Dun
c. None

S-8440 300a C:243 X-0340 FRAN:PLEA
a. W-6089 Thomas Collier, representatives of
W-5735 Thomas Gaskins, deceased
b. Walter Dun
c. Charles L? (S?) Hunter; D. D. Warner, 1839

S-8441 & S-8442. See S-7924

S-8443 70a C:245 X-1186 MADI:MONR
a. W-5547 Sarah Gunn, devisee of James (Gunn?)
b. Walter Dun
c. None

S-8446
S-8476*
S-9293 150a C:339 X-0360 ROSS:DEER
a. W-6099 Harry Terrell
W-6194 Robert Hanson Harrison, heirs of
b. John A. Fulton
c. None
* Source A says S-8776.

S-8448. See S-7945

S-8449 210a C:234 X-0590 ADAM:SPRI
a. W-5799 James Dillard
W-5789 John Yancey
b. -- Ellison & -- Mowry
c. None

S-8450 100a C:234 X-0600 ADAM:MONR
a. W-5871 Francis M. Boykin & Ann Johnson, heirs & administrators of F(rancis) Boykin
b. Isaac Foster
c. None

S-8451 200a C:235 X-1040 ADAM:MEIG
a. W-4466 John Vincent
b. Abraham Kirkpatrick
c. T. Huston, 1836; Robert Calvert, 1840

S-8456
S-8459
S-8474 188a C:238 X-0040 ADAM:MONR
a. W-4671 Nelson Cosby, representatives of
W-4050 John Posey Newman
W-6056 Anyer? (Anger?) Price
b. Andrew Ellison
c. None

S-8457 100a C:238 X-0130 ADAM:MONR
X-0800
a. W-4362 Mallory Adams
b. Thomas Mountjoy, Junior
c. None

S-8458*
S-12025* 140a D:413 X-0190 PIKE:----
a. W-6425 George Purcell, heirs of
W-5871 Francis M. Boykin & Ann Johnson, heirs & administrators of F(rancis) Boykin
b. Thomas Mountjoy, Junior
c. None
* Entry not shown in Source A; see also S-12025.

S-8459. See S-8456

S-8461 160a E:489 X-0840 MADI:JEFF
a. W-6165 William Royall
b. Cad(wallader) Wallace
c. None

S-8461 40a D:486 X-0840 FRAN:PRAI

a. W-6165 William Royall

b. Cad(wallader) Wallace
c. None

S-8462
S-8571 200a C:252 X-1180 CHAM:GOSH
a. W-6080 Hugh Cameron, heirs of
W-5899 Peter Dager
b. James Galloway, Junior
c. None

S-8463 200a C:299 X-0840 ROSS:HUNT
a. W-6133 Dennis Ready
W-6025 Jesse? Binger? heirs of
b. Jesse Spencer
c. None

S-8465
S-8466
S-13639*
S-13732*
S-14644* 4017a E:245 X-1300 HIGH:SALE
X-0663 BROW:WASH
a. W-5872 Francis M. Boykin & Ann Johnson, heirs & administrators of F(rancis) Boykin
W-1451 Lieutenant Charles Jones
W-5052 Jesse Davis
W-6515 Daniel Barnett
W-8591**
W-8660**
W-8665**
W-8657**
W-8656**
W-8611**
b. Cadwallader Wallace
c. James Elliott, 1839; D. Scott & R. Reed; J. S. Beasley, 1840; J. Hall; W. Moore, 1842
* Source A does not list these survey numbers at this place.
** Source C does not list these warrant numbers.

S-8466. See also S-7449

S-8468. See S-7236

S-8469 150a C:244 X-0840 ROSS:HUNT
a. W-6125 Stephen Young
b. Walter Dun
c. J. T. Burks; B. Malone, 1842

S-8470 140a C:245 X-0340 MADI:DARB
a. W-5797 James Dillard
b. Walter Dun
c. None

S-8471 50a C:335 X-1040 ADAM:JEFF
a. W-6056 Anyer? (Anger?) Price
b. Andrew Ellison
c. None

S-8473
S-8915 134a C:291 X-0130 ADAM:MONR
X-0800
a. W-5871 Francis M. Boykin & Ann Johnson, heirs & administrators of F(rancis) Boykin
W-5781 Joseph Crockett
b. Lewis Bible
c. None

S-8474. See S-8456

S-8475 100a C:238 X-0760 PIKE:BENT
a. W-5 Lieutenant Charles Vowles
b. Abraham Kirkpatrick
c. None

S-8476. See S-8446

S-8478 356a C:340 X-0360 PICK:DARB
a. W-5840 Nathaniel Fox? --? heirs
b. -- Fox*, -- Abbott, -- Pumphrey, & -- Conner
c. N. Fox; Pleasant Southard, 1827? (1829?)
* Source A says "Fox's" (presumably plural).

S-8478 356a C:340 X-0360 PICK:DARB
a. W-5840 Nathaniel Fox? --? heirs
b. -- Fox*, -- Abbott, -- Pumphrey, & -- Conner
c. N. Fox & H. Fox; Lyne Starling, 1831
* Source A says "Fox's" (presumably plural).

S-8478 355a C:340 X-0340 PICK:DARB
a. W-5840 Nathaniel Fox? --? heirs
b. -- Fox*, -- Abbott, -- Pumphrey, & -- Conner
c. None
* Source A says "Fox's" (presumably plural).

S-8478 355a C:340 X-0340 PICK:DARB
a. W-5840 Nathaniel Fox? --? heirs
b. -- Fox*, -- Abbott, -- Pumphrey, & -- Conner
c. None
* Source A says "Fox's" (presumably plural).

S-8479 356a C:341 X-1180 MADI:JEFF
a. W-5840 Nathaniel Fox? --? heirs
b. -- Fox*, -- Abbott, -- Pumphrey, & -- Conner
c. N. Fox; S? (L?) Moore, 1825; H. Fox; Isaac N. Crisman, 1828
* Source A says "Fox's" (presumably plural).

S-8479 68a C:341 X-1180 MADI:JEFF
a. W-5840 Nathaniel Fox? --? heirs
b. -- Fox*, -- Abbott, -- Pumphrey, & -- Conner
c. None
* Source A says "Fox's" (presumably plural).

S-8480 197a C:341 X-1180 MADI:JEFF
a. W-5840 Nathaniel Fox? --? heirs
b. -- Fox*, -- Abbott, -- Pumphrey, & -- Conner
c. N. Fox; J. Burnam? 1825
* Source A says "Fox's" (presumably plural).

S-8481 90a C:249 X-0340 MADI:DARB
a. W-5840 Nathaniel Fox? --? heirs
b. -- Fox*, -- Abbott, -- Pumphrey, & -- Conner
c. N. Fox; J. Moore, 1825
* Source A says "Fox's" (presumably plural).

S-8482 240a C:244 X-0840 PIKE:PERR ROSS:---*
a. W-5797 James Dillard
b. Walter Dun
c. None
* Source A does not mention Ross County.

S-8484 200a C:243 X-0340 MADI:DARB
a. W-6103 Richard Newcomb, heirs of
W-5799 James Dillard
W-6079 Jeremiah Pickett, heirs of
W-6125 Stephen Young
b. Walter Dun
c. W. McCoy, 1828; Daniel F. McCoy, 1833

S-8489 181a C:288 X-0360 MADI:PLEA
a. W-5774 Thomas Hill, deceased, representatives of
b. Sewell* Osgood
c. None
* Source A says Saul.

S-8492*
S-10356 467a C:492 X-0841 MADI:----
a. W-6311 John Poe
W-5551 John Meanly
b. -- Poe & -- Scott
c. None
* Source A does not list this entry.

S-8493 570a C:239 X-0290 FAYE:UNIO FAYE:MADI
a. W-5797 James Dillard
W-5752 John Walker, deceased, heirs of
b. Duncan McArthur
c. None

S-8495 45a C:339 X-0841 ROSS:DEER
a. W-6099 Harry Terrell
b. John A. Fulton
c. None

S-8501. See S-6792

S-8502 244a C:280 X-0840 ROSS:TWIN
a. W-6101 Harry Terrell
b. John A. Fulton
c. None

S-8503 400a C:267 X-0360 MADI:SUMM
a. W-5534 Peter Manifold, assignee of Lawrence Manning, administrator of Lawrence Manning, deceased
b. George Hoffman
c. A. Toland, 1826; E. W. Guin, 1828

S-8505 67a C:358 X-0841 MADI:RANG
a. W-5884 Worden Burge
b. Richard C. Baron
c. None

S-8505 267a C:358 X-0840 MADI:RANG
a. W-4797 Hugh Allen, assignee of William Sutton
b. -- Bryder* & -- Hurt
c. C. Brider**; -- Culbert & -- Smith, 1826?
* Source A spells Beyder.
** So spelled.

S-8506 255a C:241 X-0840 ROSS:SCIO
a. W-6165 William Royall
b. -- Wallace & -- Woodbridge
c. None

S-8507 160a C:244 X-0340 MADI:CANA
a. W-6119 Thomas Hopper
b. Walter Dun
c. None

S-8508 80a C:245 X-0360 UNIO:DARB MADI:---*
a. W-6119 Thomas Hopper
b. Walter Dun
c. E. W. H. Reed; George Parmenter
* Source A does not mention Madison County.

S-8510 50a C:335 X-0136 ADAM:GREE
a. W-6056 Anyer? (Anger?) Price
b. John Aldrid
c. None

S-8512* 10a -- -- ADAM:GREE
a. --
b. William G. Wilson
c. John Ellison, Junior; Levi Mattison; T. Huston, 1829
* Entry listed in Source A only.

S-8513 67a D:199 X-1138 ADAM:GREE
a. W-5172 Robert Williams
b. Peter Walker
c. None

S-8514 100a C:240 X-0840 ROSS:TWIN
a. W-5561 William Connor, heirs of
b. Benjamin Turner
c. None

S-8515
S-8543 103a C:250 X-0150 ROSS:PAIN
a. W-6142 Charles Lamberth
W-6008 John M. Gregory, heir to William (Gregory)
b. Cadwallader Wallace*
c. None
* Source A says "-- Wallace & -- Woodbridge."

S-8516 100a C:242 X-0150 ROSS:PAIN
a. W-5853 Henry Massie, assignee of James Craig
b. Christian Benner
c. None

S-8517 15a C:350 X-0870 PIKE:PEEP
a. W-5800 James Dillard
b. Benjamin Hough
c. None

S-8518 60a C:335 X-0590 ADAM:SPRI
a. W-4671 Nelson Cosby, representatives of
W-5871 Francis M. Boykin & Ann Johnson, heirs & administrators of F(rancis) Boykin
b. Andrew Ellison
c. None

S-8521 33a C:292 X-0136 ADAM:TIFF
a. W-5172 Robert Williams
b. Peter Walker
c. None

S-8523 870a C:246 X-1180 X-0340 UNIO:UNIO
a. W-5792 James Johnston
W-5916 Gross Scruggs
W-5791 George Lee Turberville
W-6125 Stephen Young
b. -- Johnston, -- Scruggs, -- Graham, & -- Dun
c. Job Pew; S. S. Bennett, 1824; Hollis Amy, 1827

S-8524 160a C:245 X-0500 MADI:DEER
a. W-6125 Stephen Young
W-5786 Edwin Hull? (Hall?)
W-5792 James Johnston
b. -- Dun, -- Graham, & -- Johnston
c. None

S-8526 900a C:287 X-1385 PICK:JACK
a. W-6017 Reuben Field
b. Anthony Sheriff
c. W. W. Irwin; Lyne Starling, 1831

S-8534* 32a -- -- BROW:UNIO BROW:BYRD
a. --
b. George Fisher
c. None
* Entry in Source A only.

S-8535* 38a -- -- BROW:BYRD
a. --
b. Joseph Redman
c. None
* Entry in Source A only.

S-8536 29a D:163 X-1385 BROW:UNIO PIKE:---*
a. W-6070 Reuben Puryear
b. Horatio Blanchard
c. None
* Source A does not mention Pike County.

S-8537 150a C:263 X-0840 PIKE:PERR
a. W-6124 Thomas Hopper
W-6125 Stephen Young
b. Walter Dun
c. None

S-8538 75a C:264 X-0840 ROSS:PAXT PIKE:---*
a. W-6125 Stephen Young
W-5791 George Lee Turberville
b. -- Dun & -- Graham
c. R. Wood, 1826?
* Source A also mentions Pike County but does not list township.

S-8539 280a C:264 X-0340 MADI:DARB
a. W-5791 George Lee Turberville
W-5786 Edwin Hull? (Hall?)
W-5916 Gross Scruggs
W-5792 James Johnston
b. -- Graham, -- Scruggs, & -- Johnston
c. None

S-8540 462a C:246 X-0340 MADI:CANA
a. W-5791 George Lee Turberville
W-5787 Edwin Hull? (Hall?)
W-5792 James Johnston
b. -- Graham & -- Johnston
c. None

S-8541. See S-7504

S-8542
S-8624 91a C:360 X-0136 ADAM:TIFF ADAM:MEIG
a. W-5990 John Price, heirs of
W-5991 John Price, heirs of
b. -- Wilson & -- Ellison
c. John W. Campbell; John Ellison, Junior; Thomas Huston, 1834; John Hayslip

S-8543. See S-8515

S-8544 83a C:250 X-0840 ROSS:PAXT
a. W-6165 William Royall
b. -- Wallace & -- Woodbridge
c. None

S-8546 200a C:253 X-0133 ADAM:FRAN
a. W-4644 Thomas? Elliott
b. Temple Elliott
c. Amos Guston; William Parks, 1826; J. S. Busuck?; J. Guston, 1827; T. Guston; T. Huston, 1829; S. J. Gustin; S? (L?) Cole, 1838; B. Guston

S-8549
S-8725 100a C:264 X-0660 CLAR:MADI
a. W-6125 Stephen Young
W-6098 Harry Terrell
W-5791 George Lee Turberville
b. -- Dun & -- Graham
c. None

S-8550 50a C:343 X-1360 ROSS:---* PIKE:JACK
a. W-6098 Harry Terrell
b. Walter Dun
c. None
* Source A mentions Ross County but does not list township.

S-8557 38a C:254 X-0360 ROSS:UNIO

a. W-6098 Harry Terrell
b. Cadwallader Wallace
c. None

S-8561* 255a C:458 X-1000 PIKE:NEWT
a. W-5342 Joseph Swearingen
b. Robert Lucas
c. None
* See also S-7106

S-8562 140a C:462 X-0800 ADAM:MONR
a. W-6098 Harry Terrell
b. Walter Dun
c. None

S-8564 103a C:263 X-1180 MADI:DARB
a. W-6098 Harry Terrell
b. Walter Dun
c. None

S-8565 500a C:284 X-0340 CHAM:RUSH UNIO:ALLE
a. W-6119 Thomas Hopper
W-6125 Stephen Young
W-6086 Thomas Collier, representatives of
W-6016 Strother G. Settle, representatives of
b. -- Dun & -- Haines
c. W. L. Sullivant; William Dun

S-8567. See S-7106

S-8568 100a C:252 X-1240 ROSS:PAIN
a. W-6098 Harry Terrell
b. Cadwallader Wallace
c. None

S-8569
S-8843 151a C:285 X-1220 ROSS:BUCK ROSS:PAIN
a. W-6098 Harry Terrell
W-6503 Allen Walker, devisees of
b. -- Wallace & -- Garrett*
c. None
* Source A may spell Garnett.

S-8571. See S-8462

S-8575
S-12688 196a D:412 X-0119 PIKE:PEEP
a. W-5871 Francis M. Boykin & Ann Johnson, heirs & administrators of F(rancis) Boykin
W-6503 Allen Walker, devisees of
b. Thomas Mountjoy
c. None

S-8576 59a C:499 X-0870 X-0779 PIKE:PEBB
a. W-5871 Francis M. Boykin & Ann Johnson, heirs & administrators of F(rancis) Boykin
b. Thomas Mountjoy
c. None

S-8578 300a C:276 X-1000 PIKE:JACK
a. W-6133 Dennis Ready
b. Ralph Osborn
c. Heirs of H. Keen; L. Byington, 1842

S-8579 100a C:335 X-0590 ADAM:SPRI
a. W-6096 John Hutchson (Hutcheson?)
b. William Creighton
c. None

S-8580 67a C:253 X-0350 MADI:PLEA FRAN:PLEA
a. W-6098 Harry Terrell
b. Walter Dun
c. None

S-8581 100a C:254 X-0660 CLAR:MADI
a. W-6098 Harry Terrell
b. Cadwallader Wallace
c. None

S-8582 1000a C:253 X-0840 MADI:STOK
a. W-649 Captain Lawrence Trent
b. Lawrence Trent*
c. Ann Burley; Samuel M. Kerr, 1833
* Source A spells Trant.

S-8584
S-9605 107a C:521 X-1140 PIKE:SUNF ADAM:---*
a. W-5946 William Pullen
W-5950 William Pullen
b. Andrew Ellison
c. None
* Source A does not mention Adams County.

S-8586
S-8698 441a C:263 X-0340 UNIO:DARB
a. W-6098 Harry Terrell
W-5791 George Lee Turberville
b. -- Dun & -- Graham
c. None

S-8589 165a C:262 X-0340 MADI:CANA
a. W-6098 Harry Terrell
b. Walter Dun
c. None

S-8590 104a C:262 X-0340 MADI:CANA
a. W-6098 Harry Terrell
b. Walter Dun
c. None

S-8591 110a C:257 X-0340 MADI:CANA
a. W-5800 James Dillard
b. Benjamin Hough
c. None

S-8592 25a C:256 X-0840 ROSS:TWIN
a. W-6090 John Webly, representatives of
b. Cadwallader Wallace
c. None

S-8593 100a C:256 X-0840 ROSS:TWIN
a. W-6090 John Webly, representatives of
b. Cadwallader Wallace
c. None

S-8595* 85a -- -- ADAM:SCOT
a. --
b. Abraham Shepherd
c. None
* Entry in Source A only.

S-8597 55a* C:255 X-0840 ROSS:PAIN
a. W-5967 William Poyner
b. Moses Demitt
c. None
* Source A says 53 acres.

S-8597
S-8598 172a C:255 X-0840 ROSS:PAIN ROSS:TWIN
a. W-5967 Will(iam) Poyner
W-6090 John Webly, representative of
W-6098 Harry Terrell
b. -- Demitt & -- Wallace
c. None

S-8601 100a C:304 X-0840 FAYE:CONC PICK:WAYN
a. W-6157 Thomas Ray
b. William Robinson
c. None

S-8602 30a C:256 X-0840 ROSS:TWIN
a. W-6156 Christopher Bland
b. Cadwallader Wallace
c. None

S-8605 37a C:284 X-0840 ROSS:PERR
a. W-5718 John Spelfatham? (Spilfatham?)
b. Cadwallader Wallace
c. None

S-8608 22a C:289 X-0340 CHAM:WAYN
a. W-6098 Harry Terrell
b. James Galloway, Junior
c. None

S-8609 25a C:335 X-1040 ADAM:JEFF SCIO:---*
a. W-5946 William Pullen
b. William Creighton
c. None
* Source A mentions Scioto County but does not list township.

S-8614 75a C:263 X-0340 FRAN:PLEA
a. W-5718 John Spelfatham? (Spilfatham?)
b. Walter Dun
c. None

S-8615 175a C:256 X-0660 CLAR:MADI
a. W-4797 Hugh Allen, assignee of William Sutton
W-5884 Warden Burge
W-6008 John M. Gregory, heir to William (Gregory)
b. Cadwallader Wallace
c. E. Barks; A. Johnston, 1826

S-8616 80a C:256 X-0660 CLAR:MADI
a. W-6091 Lewis Guthrie, deceased, representative of
W-5735 Thomas Gaskins, deceased
b. Cadwallader Wallace
c. None

S-8617 55a C:256 X-0660 CLAR:MADI
a. W-6091 Lewis Guthrie, deceased, representative of
W-6167 John Valentine
b. Cadwallader Wallace
c. J. Cooper, 1826

S-8621 200a C:258 X-0130 ADAM:MEIG
a. W-6126 Stephen Young
b. Duncan McArthur
c. None

S-8622 200a C:257 X-0841 FAYE:MADI
a. W-5718 John Spelfatham? (Spilfatham?)
b. Duncan McArthur
c. None

S-8623. *See* S-7410

S-8624. *See* S-8542

S-8629 45a C:258 X-0133 ADAM:SCOT
a. W-4897 George Tucker
b. George Vinsonhaller*
c. None
* Source A spells Vinsonhaler.

S-8630 110a C:258 X-0134 ADAM:SCOT
a. W-4897 George Tucker
b. George Vinsonhaller*
c. None
* Source A spells Vinsonhaler.

S-8631 23a C:258 X-0130 ADAM:JEFF
a. W-4897 George Tucker
b. George Vinsonhaller*
c. None
* Source A spells Vinsonhaler.

S-8633 32a C:258 X-1220 ROSS:TWIN
a. W-6098 Harry Terrell
W-6167 John Valentine
b. Cadwallader Wallace
c. None

S-8636 90a C:263 X-0340 MADI:DARB
a. W-5718 John Spelfatham? (Spilfatham?)
b. Walter Dun
c. None

S-8639. See S-8196

S-8641 25a C:331 X-0840 ROSS:TWIN
a. W-6167 John Valentine
b. Cadwallader Wallace
c. None

S-8642
S-8671 83a C-274 X-0840 FAYE:PAIN
a. W-6172 Banks Dudley, heirs of
b. Cadwallader Wallace
c. A. McMullen; J. Y. Taylor, 1831; N. F. Jones, 1833; Joseph? (James?) McLain (also McLane)

S-8645 100a C:259 X-0660 CLAR:MADI
a. W-4827 Momas? Pope
b. William Beancham? (Beaneham?)
c. None
* Source A may spell Beaucham.

S-8646 280a C:277 X-0840 ROSS:PAXT
a. W-6165 William Royall
b. William Royal*
c. Chapman Johnson; Robert Stewart, 1829
* Source A spells Royall.

S-8647 100a C:259 X-0840 ROSS:TWIN
a. W-181 Robert Woodson
b. R. Woodson & S. Woodson
c. John Somerville, 1827

S-8648 50a D:405 X-0847 HIGH:PAIN
a. W-6159 Thomas Ray
b. John A. Fulton
c. None

S-8649 200a C:463 X-0136 ADAM:TIFF
a. W-6140 James Johnson
b. Andrew Ellison
c. None

S-8650* 13a C:308 X-1140 PIKE:MIFF
a. W-5799 James Dillard
b. Andrew Ellison
c. None
* See also S-8941

S-8651* 12a -- -- ADAM:TIFF
a. --
b. Andrew Ellison
c. None
* Entry in Source A only.

S-8653* 5a -- -- BROW:UNIO
a. --
b. Thomas S? (L?) Foote
c. James Lytle**, 1824; Abel Little**; Moses P. McCarty, 1823; William Hillicort, 1826
* Entry in Source A only.
** So spelled.

S-8658
S-8769 670a C:271 X-0130 ADAM:FRAN
a. W-6158 Thomas Ray
W-6157 Thomas Ray
b. -- Fulton & -- Robertson*
c. Heirs of Thomas Holten; S? (L?) Cole, 1838
* Source A spells Robinson.

S-8660* 25a -- -- PIKE:PEEP
a. --
b. Robert Lucas
c. None
* Entry in Source A only.

S-8662 180a C:262 X-0841 ROSS:UNIO
S-8717 ROSS:TWIN
a. W-5718 John Spelfatham? (Spilfatham?)
W-1451 Lieutenant Charles Jones
b. Duncan McArthur
c. None

S-8663* 24a -- -- ADAM:--**
a. --
b. John Ellison, Junior
c. None
* Entry in Source A only.
** Source A says: "Not found."

S-8665 75a C:260 X-1186 CHAM:GOSH
MADI:---*
a. W-6166 Henry Hern
b. Abraham Shepheard**
c. J. B. Andrew, 1828; J. B. Anderson; Henry Warner, 1834
* Source A mentions Madison County but does not list township.
** Source A spells Shepherd.

S-8666 75a C:260 X-0010 CLIN:LIBE
a. W-6166 Henry Hern
W-5411 John Bowden? (Bowdin?)
b. James Galloway, Junior
c. None

S-8667 50a C:260 X-0010 CLIN:LIBE
CLIN:VERN
a. W-5411 John Bowden? (Bowdin?)
b. James Galloway, Junior
c. James Hutchinson; Willis Crane, 1827; H(enr)y Work; John Carnion (possibly Cannon), 1834; A. E. Strickle, 1836; J. Carman

S-8668 50a C:289 X-0730 CHAM:SALE
a. W-6077 Sampson Clark
b. James Galloway, Junior
c. None

S-8669 50a C:318 X-0180 GREE:XENI
X-0740
a. W-6077 Sampson Clark
b. James Galloway, Junior
c. None

S-8671. See S-8642

S-8672 100a C:407 X-0840 MADI:STOK
a. W-5985 John --?
b. Jacob Vandeventer
c. None

S-8673 50a C:437 X-0840 MADI:STOK
a. W-5985 John --?
b. Jacob Vandeventer
c. None

S-8674 50a C:437 X-0840 MADI:STOK
a. W-5985 John --?
b. Jacob Vandeventer
c. None

S-8675 600a C:272 X-0846 HIGH:JACK
a. W-5710 Charles Snead, heir to Smith (Snead)
b. Thomas James
c. None

S-8677 100a C:272 X-0420 ADAM:LIBE
a. W-5420 John P. Hungerford, assignee of Reuben Briscoe
b. John Barrett
c. None

S-8678
S-8895 253a C:290 X-0841 MADI:---*
FAYE:MADI
a. W-6130 Richard H? Owen
W-6158 Thomas Ray
b. John A. Fulton
c. None
* Source A does not mention Madison County.

S-8679* 150a -- -- ADAM:MEIG
a. --
b. Andrew Ellison
c. None
* Entry in Source A only.

S-8680*
S-8682 375a -- -- ADAM:MEIG
a. --
b. Andrew Ellison
c. None
* Entry in Source A only.

S-8681 100a C:336 X-0210 ADAM:MEIG
a. W-5781 Joseph Crockett
b. Andrew Ellison
c. None

S-8682. See S-8680

S-8684 74a C:442 X-0590 ADAM:SPRI
a. W-5781 Joseph Crockett
b. Andrew Ellison
c. A. Boyd; B. Bowman, 1827

S-8691 100a C:265 X-0840 ROSS:PAIN
a. W-6172 Banks Dudley, heirs of
b. Cadwallader Wallace
c. None

S-8694 200a C:276 X-0840 ROSS:PAIN
a. W-5986 (illegible)
b. Benjamin W. Ladd
c. None

S-8695 15a C:265 X-0840 HIGH:MADI
a. W-6172 Banks Dudley, heirs of
b. Walter Dun
c. John Kingery; John Coffey, Junior, 1833

S-8696 240a C:262 X-0340 MADI:CANA
a. W-6098 Harry Terrell
b. Walter Dun
c. None

S-8698. See S-8586

S-8700 200a C:293 X-1370 PICK:DEER
a. W-6015 Jesse Nicholson
b. Jessup N. Conch
c. None

S-8701 94a C:365 X-1385 PICK:DEER
a. W-4134 Jesse Nicholson
b. Jessup N. Conch
c. None

S-8702 50a C:269 X-0730 CLAR:HARM
a. W-6120 Thomas Hopper
b. Walter Dun
c. D. McArthur; Joseph? (James?) Myres, 1838; James? Myres; Reuben Miller, 1840

S-8703
S-8764 194a C:269 X-0730 CHAM:GOSH
a. W-6120 Thomas Hopper
W-6098 Harry Terrell
W-5718 John Spelfatham? (Spilfatham?)
b. Walter Dun
c. None

S-8705. See S-8238

S-8707 67a C:393 X-0841 FAYE:MADI
a. W-6113 Robert Mitchell?
b. Thomas McDonald
c. None

S-8708 200a C:383 X-0841 ROSS:CONC
a. W-5159 Robert Quillen
b. William Wickerham
c. None

S-8711 115a C:270 X-1180 CHAM:GOSH
a. W-6098 Harry Terrell

b. Walter Dun
c. None

S-8712 90a D:241 X-1140 PIKE:PERR
a. W-6014 Benjamin Harrison, representatives of
b. Benjamin Harrison, representatives of
c. None

S-8717. See S-8662

S-8718
S-8892
S-8969 452a C:294 X-0130 ADAM:MEIG
a. W-70 Lieutenant Francis Smith
W-5536 George Handy
b. -- Smith & -- Handy
c. None

S-8720* 5a -- -- ADAM:MEIG
a. --
b. Andrew Ellison
c. None
* Entry in Source A only.

S-8721 50a D:413 X-0030 SCIO:---*
PIKE:CAMP
a. W-5871 Francis M. Boykin & Ann Johnson, heirs & administrators of F(rancis) Boykin
b. Thomas Mountjoy
c. None
* Source A does not mention Scioto County.

S-8723 410a C:327 X-0360 MADI:UNIO
a. W-176 General P(eter) Muhlenberg
b. Peter Mu(h)lenberg
c. William Kirkpatrick; J. F. Chenowith, 1827; John W. Sumpkins? (Lumpkins?) 1831

S-8725. See S-8549

S-8728 47a C:309 X-0570 CLER:WASH
a. W-6143 Harry Cramsell?
b. John Watts
c. T. Rush, 1836; W. Pollard, 1839

S-8731 150a C:275 X-0840 ROSS:HUNT
a. W-5800 James Dillard
b. Benjamin Hough
c. Anthony Williams; C. Martin, 1834

S-8732 79a C:280 X-0840 ROSS:HUNT
a. W-5800 James Dillard
b. Benjamin Hough
c. John Donnel; W. P. Wheaton, 1840

S-8733* 100a C:280 X-0840 ROSS:----
a. W-5800 James Dillard
b. Benjamin Hough
c. None
* This entry is not listed in Source A.

S-8734 300a C:265 X-0136 ADAM:TIFF
ADAM:WAYN
a. W-4921 James Herd? (Heard?)
W-1567 John Waller
W-5781 Joseph Crockett
b. Andrew Ellison
c. None

S-8735. See S-6462

S-8736* 50a -- -- --**
a. --
b. Andrew Ellison
c. None
* Entry in Source A only.
** Source A says: "Not found."

S-8738 20a D:164 X-1120 BROW:UNIO
a. W-2908 Abner Howell
b. Thomas Foot
c. None

S-8740. See S-8238

S-8741
S-8866 185a C:286 X-0340 PICK:JACK
a. W-6097 Jacob Daniel
W-5933 Richard Hooper
b. William Creighton (Junior*)
c. None
* Per Source A.

S-8741. See also S-8866

S-8742 1531a C:269 X-0780 MADI:UNIO
a. W-6165 William Royall
b. -- Wallace & -- Woodbridge
c. None

S-8743 190a C:327 X-0360 MADI:UNIO
a. W-5543 Peter Manifold, assignee of Lawrence Manning, administrator of Lawrence (Manning), deceased
W-5534 Christopher Moon? (Moor?), assignee & heir of Jacob (Moon? Moor?)
b. George Hooffman*
c. None
* Source A spells Hoffman; notation says: "By London."

S-8745 850a C:268 X-1260 MADI:UNIO
a. W-176 General P(eter) Muhlenberg
b. Peter Muhlenburgh*
c. A. Toland, 1823
* So spelled.

S-8746 25a C:521 X-1042 ADAM:JEFF
a. W-5781 Joseph Crockett
b. David Hoppe
c. J. T. Hamer & Co.; T. Huston, 1841

S-8747 25a C:308 X-1042 ADAM:JEFF
a. W-5946 William Pullen
b. William Creighton, Junior*
c. None
* Source A says William Creighton.

S-8749 440a C:267 X-0360 MADI:UNIO
a. W-5715 William Hobson, et al, heirs to Nicholas (Hobson)
W-5716 William Hobson, et al, heirs to Nicholas (Hobson)
b. Nicholas Hobson, heirs of
c. None

S-8750 109a C:268 X-0360 HIGH:---* PICK:PERR
a. W-5718 John Spelfatham? (Spilfatham?)
W-6008 John M. Gregory, heir to William (Gregory)
b. Cadwallader Wallace
c. None
* Source A does not mention Highland County.

S-8751 1050a C:266 X-0360 MADI:UNIO
a. W-5901 Ann Garnett? (Garrett?), heir to Benjamin (Garnett? Garrett?)
b. Ann Garrett*
c. None
* Source A may read Ann Garnett.

S-8752 100a C268 X-0360 PICK:DEER
a. W-6008 John M. Gregory, heir to William (Gregory)
b. John Hoffman
c. None

S-8753 100a C:268 X-0360 PICK:PERR
a. W-6008 John M. Gregory, heir to William (Gregory)
b. John Hoffman
c. None

S-8758 362a C:288 X-0360 PICK:PERR
a. W-5771 Thomas Hill, representatives of
b. Thomas Hill, representatives of
c. Heirs of Thomas Hill; Mathew Bonner, 1831

S-8761 50a D:301 X-0840 ROSS:HUNT
a. W-6159 Thomas Ray
b. John A. Fulton
c. C. Palmer et al; R. Curry, 1842

S-8762 640a C:270 X-0622 CHAM:SALE CHAM:WAYN
a. W-5734 Thomas Gaskins, deceased
W-6098 Harry Terrell
W-6089 Thomas Collier, representatives of
W-6092 Thomas Collier, representatives of
W-5718 John Spelfatham? (Spilfatham?)
W-6016 Strother G. Settle, representatives of
b. -- Dun & -- Hains
c. Adam Rader; Israel Hamilton, 1841

S-8763 330a C:269 X-0730 CHAM:UNIO
a. W-6098 Harry Terrell
W-6093 Thomas Collier, representatives of
W-5718 John Spelfatham? (Spilfatham?)
b. Walter Dun
c. None

S-8764. See S-8703

S-8765 10a C:342 X-1004 FRAN:WASH
a. W-5718 John Spelfatham? (Spilfatham?)
b. Walter Dun
c. None

S-8767 544a C:297 X-1180 MADI:DEER
a. W-6062 William Connor
W-6060 William Connor
b. George Dawson & John Dawson
c. None

S-8769. See S-8658

S-8772
S-8789 650a C:276 X-0360 CLAR:PLEA
a. W-5218 Robert D. Fowke, heir at law to John Fowke
b. William Philips, heirs of
c. John L. Fout; -- Davidson & -- Curl, 1828; George Sharp; Russel A Daton* 1832; -- Rungan & -- Lafferty, 1835; G. Messenger, 1842
* So spelled.

S-8774
S-8841 101a C:284 X-0340 CHAM:UNIO
a. W-5901 Ann Garnett? (Garrett?), heir to Benjamin (Garnett? Garrett?)
b. Ann Garrett*
c. C. Wallace; L? (S?) Hogg
* Source A may read Ann Garnett.

S-8775. See S-5633 (in volume 4, part 1)

S-8776 250a C:273 X-0342 CHAM:GOSH
a. W-5240 --*
b. Robert Means
c. None
* Manuscript torn.

S-8776. See also S-8446 (footnote)

S-8777 170a C:273 X-0346 CHAM:GOSH
a. W-5147 John Stokely, assignee of Abraham Shepherd
b. Robert Means
c. None

S-8778 130a C:279 X-0841 ROSS:CONC
a. W-6071 George Ryan
b. George Ryan
c. None

S-8780 170a C:274 X-0740 CLAR:MADI
a. W-3990 Nancy Gaines (heir)
b. Seth Smith
c. None

S-8781. See S-7714

S-8781
S-7714
S-8782 30a* C:367 X-0590 ADAM:TIFF
a. W-5991 John Price, heirs of
b. John Ellison, Junior**
c. Thomas Mountjoy; James Hood, 1840
* Source A says 20 acres.
** Source A says John Ellison.

S-8782* 30a -- -- ADAM:SPRI
a. --
b. John Ellison, Junior
c. None
* Entry in Source A only.

S-8783 350a C:283 X-0340 UNIO:DARB
a. W-6098 Harry Terrell
b. Walter Dun
c. None

S-8785 70a C:284 X-1180 MADI:SUMM
CHAM:---*
a. W-6098 Harry Terrell
W-5718 John Spelfatham? (Spilfatham?)
b. Walter Dun
c. None
* Source A does not mention Champaign County.

S-8786 50a C:284 X-0840 PIKE:PERR
X-0130
a. W-6013 John Williams, representatives of
b. John Williams, representatives of
c. J. Sargent, 1830

S-8787 33a D:260 X-0230 ADAM:WAYN
a. W-5990 John Price, heirs of
b. James Wilson
c. None

S-8788* 11a -- -- FRAN:WASH
a. --
b. Benjamin Sells
c. None
* Entry in Source A only.

S-8789. See S-8772

S-8792. See S-8374

S-8793 300a C:357 X-0350 CHAM:UNIO
a. W-5886 William Bonniface (Boniface)
b. William Bonniface
c. None

S-8795
S-15980 26a F:120 X-0040 ADAM:MONR
a. W-5871 Fancis M. Boykin & Ann Johnson, heirs & administrators of F(rancis) Boykin
ex W-421 No name given
b. -- Dillon* & -- Robe
c. None
* Source A says Joseph Dillin (so spelled).

S-8796 200a C:295 X-0840 ROSS:PAXT
a. W-5977 Georege Pritchett
b. John Pritchett, representatives of
c. None

S-8798 110a C:281 X-0840 ROSS:TWIN
a. W-4937 John Harrison
b. John Harrison*
c. None
* Source A says: "-- Hough & -- Harrison;" notation therein says* "Patented to -- Hough."

S-8800 1278a C:314 X-0360 MADI:PLEA
X-0810
a. W-5568 Tarlton Woodson
b. Tarlton Woodson
c. None

S-8805 70a D:344 X-0660 CLAR:HARM
X-0840
a. W-6157 Thomas Ray
b. William Robinson, heirs of
c. None

S-8806 200a C:348 X-0660 CLAR:HARM
a. W-6157 Thomas Ray
b. William Robinson
c. None

S-8807. See S-6792

S-8808* 200a -- -- MADI:UNIO
a. --
b. Jeremiah McLene
c. None
* Entry in Source A only.

S-8819 50a C:330 X-0660 CLAR:MADI
a. W-6154 Hugh Norvell? (Nowell?)
b. Cadwallader Wallace
c. None

S-8819 100a C:330 X-0660 CLAR:MADI
MADI:STOK
GREE:ROSS
a. W-5886 William Bonniface (Boniface)
b. William Bonniface*
c. None
* Source A spells Boniface.

S-8821 80a C:422 X-0870 PIKE:PEBB
a. W-1984 Captain Will(iam) George
b. Benjamin Hough
c. David Downs; John R. Anderson, 1836

S-8823 356a C:300 X-0870 PIKE:PEBB
ROSS:---*

a. W-215 Doctor David Holmes
b. William Wilson
c. None
* Source A does not mention Ross County.

S-8826 90a C:343 X-0300 PIKE:JACK
a. W-5905 Joseph Gregory, heir to Naphtalem? (Gregory)
b. Joseph Gregory
c. None

S-8827
S-8858 140a C:342 X-0300 ROSS:---* PIKE:JACK
a. W-5903 Leroy Edwards, devisees of
W-5735 Thomas Gaskins, deceased
W-5862 Jacob Davis, heirs of
W-5755 William Price
W-5791 George Lee Turberville
b. -- Dun & -- Graham
c. None
* Source A does not mention Ross County.

S-8828 75a C:282 X-0360 PICK:DEER
a. W-5878 John Graves
b. John Hoffman
c. None

S-8829 150a C:373 X-0840 MADI:STOK CLAR:---*
a. W-6098 Harry Terrell
W-6008 John M. Gregory, heir to William (Gregory)
W-6154 Hugh Norvell? (Nowell?)
W-5878 John Graves
b. Cadwallader Wallace
c. None
* Source A does not mention Clark County.

S-8833 50a C:514 X-0379 ADAM:TIFF
a. W-5781 Joseph Crockett
b. William Wilkinson
c. Sharleton King; Patrick C. May, 1831; John Sampson; Williams Wilkins; T. Huston, 1838

S-8834 50a C:292 X-0130 X-0800 ADAM:MONR
a. W-5781 Joseph Crockett
b. Henry Malone
c. None

S-8838 550a C:403 X-0660 CLAR:MADI
a. W-3167 William Bayles? (Baylis?)
b. William Bayles
c. Henry Bayles; -- Anderson, -- Holloway, et al, 1831

S-8840 553a C:282 X-0830 X-0570 ROSS:HUNT
a. W-3221 Will(iam) Reynolds, assignee of John Fantleroy (Fauntleroy), heir to Griffin Fantleroy (Fauntleroy)
W-4937 John Harrison
b. John Harrison
c. Henry March? (Mauk? Marsh?); John Robinson, 1825

S-8841. See S-8774

S-8842 130a C:285 X-1220 ROSS:PAIN
a. W-5901 Ann Garnett? (Garrett?), heir to Benjamin (Garnett? Garrett?)
b. Ann Garrett*
c. None
* Source A may read Ann Garnett.

S-8843. See S-8569

S-8844 25a C:300 X-1240 ROSS:TWIN
a. W-5901 Ann Garnett? (Garrett?), heir to Benjamin (Garnett? Garrett?)
b. Ann Garrett*
c. None
* Source A may read Ann Garnett.

S-8845 200a C:376 X-0130 ADAM:FRAN
a. W-2856 Henry Bedinger
b. Henry Bedinger
c. Samuel Treat, 1824; -- Wilkins & -- McDaide, 1826

S-8846 1300a C:283 X-0780 MADI:UNIO
a. W-5802 George Norvell? (Nowell?), deceased
W-5800 James Dillard
W-6126 Stephen Young
W-6119 Thomas Hopper
W-5791 George Lee Turberville
W-5916 Gross Scruggs
b. -- Dun, -- Graham, & -- Scruggs
c. None

S-8850 50a C:385 X-0590 ADAM:SPRI
a. W-5781 Joseph Crockett
b. Christian Mowry
c. None

S-8851 50a C:522 X-1040 SCIO:UNIO
a. W-5781 Joseph Crockett
b. David Smith
c. None

S-8852 25a E:426 X-1040 SCIO:BRUS
a. W-5781 Joseph Crockett
b. William Peyton*
c. William Payton*; James Wallace, 1824
* So spelled; Source A says Poythress.

S-8853 100a C:492 X-0840 ROSS:PAIN FAYE:---*
a. W-3433 Archibald McCloud
b. Nathan Hays
c. A. McArthur, 1828
* Source A mentions Fayette County but does not give township.

S-8854 740a C:283 X-1180 MADI:PIKE
a. W-6126 Stephen Young
W-5547 Sarah Gunn, devisee of James (Gunn)
W-5862 Jacob Davis, heirs of
W-6093 Thomas Collier, representatives of

W-6086 Thomas Collier, representatives of
W-6125 Stephen Young
W-6089 Thomas Collier, representatives of
W-6098 Harry Terrell
W-5718 John Spelfatham? (Spilfatham?)
W-5916 Gross Scruggs
W-5905 Joseph Gregory, heir to Naphtalen? (Gregory)
b. -- Dun, -- Gregory, & -- Scruggs
c. None

S-8857 150A C:285 X-1000 PICK:WAYN
a. W-6147 Nathaniel Wells? (Walls?)
b. Samuel Beaven*
c. None
* Source A spells Bevers.

S-8858. See S-8827

S-8859 25a C:293 X-1240 ROSS:PAIN
a. W-181 Robert Woodson
b. Edward Keran
c. None

S-8860 30a C:393 X-1240 ROSS:TWIN
a. W-181 Robert Woodson
b. Edward Keran
c. None

S-8861. See S-8323

S-8862
S-8883 200a C:341 X-0300 PIKE:PEEP
a. W-6098 Harry Terrell
W-5844 William Boughton
b. Walter Dun
c. None

S-8863 157a D:454 X-0360 MADI:UNIO
a. W-5187 Thomas M. Bayly, assignee of John Drummond
b. -- Harness, -- Voss, & -- Vanmeter
c. None

S-8864 280a D:455 X-0780 MADI:UNIO
a. W-5187 Thomas M. Bayly, assignee of John Drummond
b. -- Harness, -- Voss, & -- Vanmeter
c. None

S-8865. See S-8238

S-8866. See S-8741

S-8867
S-10891 1040a D:8 X-0841 FAYE:MADI
a. W-6014 Benjamin Harrison, representatives of
b. Benjamin Harrison, representatives of
c. None

S-8868 50a C:341 X-0840 PIKE:PERR
a. W-6013 John Williams, representatives of
b. John Williams, representatives of
c. None

S-8869. See S-8240

S-8870 200a C:289 X-0810 PICK:DARB MADI:PLEA
a. W-852 John Beck
b. John Beck
c. W. Leffin? (Seffin?) 1837; E. Fitzgerald, 1839 (Madison County)

S-8871 150a C:289 X-0840 FAYE:PAIN
a. W-852 John Beck
b. John Beck
c. None

S-8872. See S-8023

S-8874*
S-9214
S-10541
S-10542
S-12612
S-13772
S-13691 381a E:62 X-0679 PICK:----
a. W-5952 Richard Hooper
W-6524 Richard Dorsey, heirs of
W-6418 Vashel? (Vachel?) D. Howard
b. John Evans
c. None
* This entry not listed in Source A.

S-8874. See also S-9214

S-8875 75a C:351 X-0870 PIKE:NEWT
a. W-6061 William Connor
b. Robert Lucas
c. None

S-8876 181a C:321 X-0360 MADI:PLEA
a. W-5774 Thomas Hill, deceased, representatives of
b. Thomas Hill, heirs of
c. R. Douglas, 1825; Thomas Hill; E. Langham, 1826; Thomas Compton; T. Bell; John Kious, 1838

S-8876 181a C:323 X-0360 MADI:PLEA
a. W-5775 Thomas Hill, representatives of
b. Thomas Hill, heirs of
c. Richard Douglas; Mathew Bonner, 1831

S-8878 100a C:394 X-0840 MADI:RANG
a. W-6012 Charles Harris, representatives of
b. James Clarke
c. None

S-8880 270a C:301 X-0360 MADI:UNIO
a. W-5878 John Graves
b. Cadwallader Wallace
c. None

S-8881 30a C:301 X-0300 PIKE:PEEP
a. W-5878 John Graves
b. Cadwallader Wallace
c. None

S-8883. See S-8862

S-8884 88a C:341 X-0300 PIKE:PEEP
a. W-6098 Harry Terrell
W-5791 George Lee Turberville
b. -- Dun & -- Graham
c. J. Graham; C. Cisna, 1824

S-8886 100a C:325 X-0360 MADI:UNIO
a. W-5802 George Norvell? (Nowell?), deceased
b. Thomas Worthington
c. J. Murfen (also Murfin); J. Moon, 1826; J. Moore, 1827

S-8887
S-9262* 410a C:325 X-0841 PICK:PERR
a. W-5802 George Norvell? (Nowell?), deceased
b. Thomas Worthington
c. None
* Mentioned in Source A only.

S-8888 75a C:300 X-0360 MADI:RANG
a. W-5802 George Norvell? (Nowell?)
b. Thomas Worthington
c. None

S-8890 33a C:301 X-0840 ROSS:PAIN
a. W-5802 George Norvell? (Nowell?), deceased
b. Thomas Worthington
c. None

S-8892. See S-8718

S-8893 10a D:374 X-0130 ADAM:MEIG
a. W-5946 William Pullen
b. Andrew Ellison
c. None

S-8895. See S-8678

S-8896 100a C:298 X-0841 FAYE:MADI
a. W-5536 George Handy
b. George Handy
c. R. Douglas, 1827; "deeded to R. Douglas, 26 Feb 1830"

S-8898 170a C:298 X-0840 FAYE:UNIO
a. W-5536 George Handy
b. George Handy
c. None

S-8899
S-10806 140a C:29 X-0840 FAYE:PAIN
a. W-5536 George Handy
b. George Handy
c. None

S-8900 150a C:298 X-0840 ROSS:PAIN
a. W-5536 George Handy
b. George Handy
c. None

S-8901 200a C:309 X-0270 BROW:CLAR
a. W-6144 John Repley? (Ripley?)
b. John Watts
c. George C. Light, 1836; heirs of A. Newkirk, 1836; Levi Wilson, 1841; R. T. McKee; Jonas Murphey, 1841

S-8902 100a C:309 X-0663 BROW:PIKE
a. W-6144 John Repley? (Ripley?)
b. John Watts
c. John Patridge; A. McIlree, 1839

S-8903 27a C:295 X-0800 HAMI:ANDE
a. W-6176 Edward Shepherd, heirs of
b. George C. Light
c. None

S-8904 8a C:296 X-0663 CLER:WILL
CLER:TATE
a. W-6176 Edward Shepherd
b. George C. Light
c. Isaac Higby, Junior; J. T. Brush, 1835

S-8905 20a C:296 X-0910 CLER:OHIO
a. W-6176 Edward Shepherd
b. George C. Light
c. John Weeks; J. T. Donham? 1824

S-8907 15a C:384 X-0800 CLER:OHIO
a. W-6176 Edward Shepherd
W-6145 John Gramsell
b. George C. Light
c. None

S-8909 380a C:350 X-0133 ADAM:SCOT
HIGH:---*
a. W-2199 Captain William Johnson**
b. William Johnston**
c. None
* Source A does not mention Highland County.
** So spelled.

S-8912 60a D:373 X-0800 ADAM:MONR
a. W-2199 Captain William Johnson*
b. William Johnson*
c. None
* So spelled.

S-8914 25a C:292 X-1040 ADAM:JEFF
a. W-5781 Joseph Crockett
b. Jesse Matheney*
c. None
* Source A spells Manatheny.

S-8915. See S-8473

S-8916 50a C:360 X-0130 ADAM:MONR
a. W-5781 Joseph Crockett
b. John Raider
c. None

S-8917* 34a -- -- ADAM:TIFF
a. --
b. Adam Hempleman
c. None
* Entry in Source A only.

S-8918* 25a -- -- HIGH:UNIO
a. --
b. Andrew Boyd
c. None
* Entry in Source A only.

S-8919
S-9017
S-9263 537a C:325 X-0841 FAYE:MADI
a. W-5802 George Norvell? (Nowell?), deceased
b. Thomas Worthington
c. William Motter; John David, 1823

S-8921 75a C:300 X-0840 ROSS:TWIN
a. W-5802 George Norvell? (Nowell?), deceased
b. Thomas Worthington
c. None

S-8922 200a C:300 X-0360 MADI:UNIO
a. W-5802 George Norvell? (Nowell?), deceased
b. Thomas Worthington
c. None

S-8924* 48a -- -- ADAM:WAYN
a. --
b. John Ellison, Junior
c. None
* Entry in Source A only.

S-8925 10a D:374 X-0130 ADAM:MONR
a. W-5781 Joseph Crockett
b. John Ellison, Junior
c. None

S-8926
S-8927
S-9391 347a C:347 X-1180 MADI:JEFF
a. W-6126 Stephen Young
W-5887 Thomas Wallace? (Weihart?), representatives of
W-1451 Lieutenant Charles Jones
b. -- Dun & -- Jones
c. None

S-8930 36a C:299 X-0340 PICK:JACK
a. W-3221 Will(iam) Reynolds, assignee to John Fantleroy (Fauntleroy), heir to Griffin Fantleroy (Fauntleroy)
b. John Harrison
c. None

S-8932* 510a -- -- PICK:WAYN
a. --
b. John Swan
c. None
* Entry in Source A only.

S-8933 240a C:299 X-1000 PICK:JACK
a. W-3039 Major John Swan
b. John Swan
c. None

S-8934 55a C:295 X-0360 PICK:MUHL
a. W-6158 Thomas Ray
b. John A. Fulton
c. None

S-8935 90a C:295 X-0360 PICK:MUHL
a. W-6158 Thomas Ray
b. John A. Fulton
c. N. Franklin, 1828; Abraham? Hasselton, 1830

S-8936 467a C:306 X-0390 PICK:MONR
a. W-6158 Thomas Ray
W-6157 Thomas Ray
b. John A. Fulton
c. George Botkin, 1835

S-8937 25a C:299 X-0840 FAYE:PAIN
a. W-5536 George Handy
b. George Handy
c. None

S-8938 100a C:489 X-0841 FAYE:MADI
a. W-3221 Will(iam) Reynolds, assignee of John Fantleroy (Fauntleroy), heir to Griffin Fantleroy (Fauntleroy)
b. John Harrison*
c. None
* Source A notation: "Patented to Benjamin Hough."

S-8939 98a C:294 X-0841 FAYE:MADI
a. W-3221 Will(iam) Reynolds, assignee of John Fantleroy (Fauntleroy), heir to Griffin Fantleroy (Fauntleroy)
b. John Harrison
c. None

S-8941*
S-8650 21a -- -- ADAM:MEIG
a. --
b. Andrew Ellison
c. None
* Entry in Source A only.

S-8942 90a C:343 X-0300 PIKE:PEEP
a. W-6098 Harry Terrell
b. Walter Dun
c. None

S-8946. See S-4436 (in volume 4, part 1)

S-8947* 37a -- -- PICK:MONR
a. --
b. John Evans
c. None
* Entry in Source A only.

S-8948 55a D:75 X-0360 X-0841 PICK:PERR
a. W-5952 Richard Hooper
b. John Evans
c. None

S-8950 200a C:318 X-0340 CHAM:---* MADI:SUMM CLAR:---*
a. W-5517 William Anderson, executor of
b. William Anderson
c. J. Mitchell, 1840; W. S? (L?) Bates, 1842
* Source A does not mention Champaign or Clark counties.

S-8951 135a C:393 X-0841 HIGH:PAIN
a. W-5567 Edward Herndon
b. John* Baldwin
c. None
* Source A says Jesse Baldwin.

S-8952 110a* C:294 X-0300 ROSS:HUNT
a. W-3221 Will(iam) Reynolds, assignee of John Fantleroy (Fauntleroy), heir to Griffin Fantleroy (Fauntleroy)
b. John Harrison
c. None
* Source A says 100 acres.

S-8953 17a C:299 X-0840 ROSS:TWIN
a. W-5536 George Handy
b. George Handy
c. None

S-8955. See S-7237

S-8956 100a C:293 X-1000 PICK:WAYN
a. W-6138 William Speak? (Speake?)
b. Samuel Spencer
c. Thomas Bowdle, 1831

S-8957 200a C:357 X-0660 CLAR:MADI CLAR:HARM
a. W-6159 Thomas Ray
W-6130 Richard H? Owen
b. John A. Fulton
c. Samuel McMillan, 1825

S-8963 25a* E:35 X-0847 HIGH:PAIN
a. W-5567 Edward Herndon
b. Christian Benner
c. None
* Source A says 34-1/4 acres.

S-8964 120a C:343 X-0730 CHAM:SALE
a. W-708 Nathan Gammells? (Gammetts?)
b. Walter Dun
c. None

S-8965
S-10927 275a D:14 X-0500 MADI:DEER MADI:JEFF
a. W-5513 Thomas Bowyer, assignee of Martha? Lanier, widow, Bart? Rahlings? & Lucy, his wife, late? L. Lanier, children of Thomas Lanier
W-708 Nathan Gammells? (Gammetts?)
b. -- Clark & -- Dun
c. None

S-8969. See S-8718

S-8970 155a C:298 X-1140 HIGH:BRUS
a. W-5536 George Handy
b. George Handy
c. None

S-8971* 170a -- -- ADAM:FRAN
a. --
b. George Handy
c. D. McArthur; T. Huston, 1829
* Entry in Source A only.

S-8972 65a C:294 X-0841 FAYE:MADI
a. W-6082 Robert Green
b. Benjamin Hough
c. None

S-8973
S-9133
S-9351 245a C:352 X-0840 ROSS:HUNT
a. W-5620 Nathaniel G. Morris
W-5638 James Barnett
W-6082 Robert Green
b. -- Ladd, -- Norvill, & -- Hough*
c. None
* Source A notation: "Patented to Benjamin Hough."

S-8974 60a C:299 X-0304 ROSS:HUNT
a. W-3221 Will(iam) Reynolds, assignee of John Fantleroy (Fauntleroy), heir to Griffin Fantleroy (Fauntleroy)
b. John Harrison
c. None

S-8975 50a C:496 X-0841 FAYE:MADI
a. W-3221 Will(iam) Reynolds, assignee of John Fantleroy (Fauntleroy), heir to Griffin Fantleroy (Fauntleroy)
b. John Harrison
c. Joseph Godfrey; I. Y. Green, 1836

S-8976 66a D:202 X-0663 CLER:UNIO
a. W-5336 William Mosley
b. William Mosley*
c. None
* Source A spells Moseley or Maseley.

S-8977 25a C:323 X-0840 ROSS:PAIN

a. W-5802 George Norvell? (Nowell?), deceased
b. Thomas Worthington
c. None

S-8978 75a C:323 X-0840 ROSS:PAIN
a. W-5802 George Norvell? (Nowell?), deceased
b. Thomas Worthington
c. None

S-8980 45a C:297 X-0840 ROSS:TWIN
a. W-3221 Will(iam) Reynolds, assignee of John Fantleroy (Fauntleroy), heir to Griffin Fantleroy (Fauntleroy)
b. John Harrison
c. None

S-8981. See S-6390 (in volume 4, part 1)

S-8982 100a -- X-0660 CLAR:MADI
a. W-139 Lieutenant Markes* Vandewall*
b. Mark* Vanderwall*
c. So spelled.

S-8983 400a C:297 X-0660 CLAR:MADI
a. W-139 Lieutenant Markes* Vandewall
b. Mark* Vandewall
c. None
* So spelled.

S-8984 67a C:330 X-0660 CLAR:MADI
a. W-139 Lieutenant Markes* Vandewall*
b. Mark* Vanderwall*
c. None
* So spelled.

S-8985 100a C:324 X-0840 ROSS:TWIN
a. W-139 Lieutenant Markes* Vandewall*
b. Mark* Vanderwall*
c. Joseph Boulenger; T. H. Davis, 1831
* So spelled.

S-8986 & S-8987. See S-7659

S-8989
S-8189* 157a C:343 X-0301 PIKE:JACK PIKE:PEBB
a. W-708 Nathan Gammells? (Gammetts?)
W-6079 Jeremiah Pickett, heirs of
W-6064 William Connor
b. Walter Dun
c. H. Brown; L? (S?) Byington, 1842
* Source A says S-9189.

S-8990 687a C:296 X-0730 CHAM:---* CLAR:PLEA
a. W-6037 John Hargus
W-6064 William Connor
b. George Dawson
c. None
* Source A does not mention Champaign County.

S-8994 13a C:301 X-0843 FAYE:PAIN
a. W-1232 Andrew Cypress?
b. Cadwallader Wallace
c. None

S-8996
S-9649 260a C:371 X-0660 CLAR:MADI UNIO:---*
a. W-1232 Andrew Cypress?
W-57 Captain Seth Porterfield
b. -- Wallace & -- Porterfield
c. Caleb Lewis; George Messinger, 1840
* Source A mentions Union County but does not list township.

S-8997
S-9680 700a C:400 X-0620 CHAM:WAYN
a. W-5880 Thomas Porter
b. -- Ladd's* & - Norvill
c. Heirs of J. Smith; James Parker; Henry Reynolds, 1831; John Organ; Wesley Hough, 1831
* Probably Ladds (in the plural) is meant.

S-8998 85a C:318 X-0660 CLIN:CHES
a. W-5880 Thomas Porter
b. -- Ladd's* & -- Norvill
c. None
* Probably Ladds (in the plural) is meant.

S-8999 55a C:401 X-0340 MADI:DARB
a. W-5880 Thomas Porter
b. -- Ladd's* & -- Norvill
c. None
* Probably Ladds (in the plural) is meant.

S-9000 700a C:362 X-0660 CLAR:MADI
a. W-5880 Thomas Porter
b. -- Ladds & -- Norvill
c. None

S-9002 200a C:318 X-1180 CHAM:RUSH
a. W-5880 Thomas Porter
b. -- Ladds & -- Norvill
c. None

S-9003 80a C:318 X-0750 UNIO:DARB
a. W-5880 Thomas Porter
b. -- Ladds & -- Norvill
c. None

S-9005 13a C:318 X-0340 UNIO:DARB
a. W-5880 Thomas Porter
b. -- Ladds & -- Norvill
c. None

S-9007
S-9812
S-10099
S-10327 366a C:428 X-0730 X-0340 CHAM:WAYN
a. W-5880 Thomas Porter
W-5633 Nathaniel G. Morris
b. -- Ladds & -- Norvill
c. None

S-9008 130a C:319 X-0740 MADI:STOK
a. W-5880 Thomas Porter
b. -- Ladds & -- Norvill
c. None

S-9009 50a C:319 X-1170 CLIN:MARI
a. W-5880 Thomas Porter
b. -- Ladds & -- Norvill
c. Isaac Riggs; George B. Moore, 1826

S-9014 220a C:305 X-1180 CHAM:RUSH
a. W-5335 Richard Kennon, representatives of
b. Richard Kennon, representatives of
c. Ezekiel Thomas, 1828

S-9017. See S-8919

S-9018 390a C:305 X-0400 MADI:---* FAYE:MADI
a. W-6014 Benjamin Harrison, representatives of
b. Benjamin Harrison, representatives of
c. None
* Source A does not mention Madison County.

S-9020 120a C:319 X-1180 UNIO:UNIO
a. W-5633 Nathaniel G. Morris
b. -- Ladds & -- Norvill
c. None

S-9022 15a C:301 X-0360 ROSS:UNIO ROSS:DEER
a. W-1232 Andrew Cypress?
b. Cadwallader Wallace
c. None

S-9023 1600a C:303 X-0660 MADI:STOK CLAR:MADI
a. W-2274 Dr. Basel Middleton
W-2510 Ambr(ose) Lipscomb, assignee of John Sneed
W-728 Lieutenant Andrew Lewis
b. John Campbell
c. Joseph? (James?) Kirby; Russel A. Daton, 1832

S-9024 560a C:303 X-0847 HIGH:PAIN
a. W-2274 Dr. Basel Middleton
b. John Campbell
c. None

S-9025 350a C:303 X-0840 ROSS:HUNT
a. W-728 Lieutenant Andrew Lewis
W-2274 Dr. Basel Middleton
b. John Campbell
c. T. S. Hinds; Peter Douglas, 1831; C. Palmer et al; R. Curry, 1842

S-9026 146a C:315 X-0840 ROSS:HUNT
a. W-2274 Dr. Basel Middleton
b. John Campbell
c. None

S-9027 1876a C:302 X-0730 CHAM:UNIO
a. W-6130 Richard H? Owen
W-6127 Stephen Young
W-6159 Thomas Ray
b. Thomas S. Hinde*
c. None
* So spelled.

S-9028 1000a C:301 X-0750 UNIO:DOVE
a. W-2247 Reverend John Hurt
b. John Hurt
c. John Hart*; John H. Harrison, 1824; William Badley; S. G. Strong, 1830
* So spelled.

S-9029 350a D:72 X-0840 MADI:---* CLAR:MADI
a. W-2247 Reverend John Hurt
b. John Hurt**
c. None
* Source A does not mention Madison County.
** Source A may spell Hurst.

S-9029* 200a C:333 X-0840 CLAR:MADI
a. W-1339 John Edwards
b. John Edwards
c. David Harrold, 1831
* Source A notation: "Not patented."

S-9030 600a C:302 X-0841 ROSS:CONC
a. W-1734 Lieutenant Colonel Richard Taylor
b. Thomas S. Hinde
c. None

S-9031 1159a C:302 X-0663 CLER:UNIO
a. W-1734 Lieutenant Colonel Richard Taylor
W-6159 Thomas Ray
b. Thomas S. Hinde
c. John Martin

S-9032 900a C:315 X-0840 MADI:STOK
a. W-1928 Major Tarlton Woodson
W-5410 Moses Atkinson, representatives of
W-5412 Benjamin Parnell, representatives of
W-5413 John Montgomery, representatives of
W-5414 Jesse Braden? (Borden?), representatives
W-5415 Elisha Atkinson, representatives of
b. Thomas S. Hinde
c. W. Buffenbergh; G. Lenson, 1826

S-9033 400a C:315 X-0840 ROSS:PAXT PIKE:PERR
a. W-5360 Thomas M. Bayley, assignee of -- Bloxom's executor
W-5361 Thomas M. Bayley, assignee of John Madison's executor
W-5362 Thomas M. Bayley, assignee of John Bull's representatives
W-5530 Thomas Bowden
b. Thomas S. Hinde
c. J. Bales; J. Richeson, 1826

S-9034 931a D:47 X-0840 FAYE:UNIO
a. W-1968 Nancy Deer? heir to Jonathan Deer?
W-3530 Stephen G. Owen
b. John Bradshaw
c. Ann Inglish; S. Loofborough, 1835; John Rease; J. Jameson, 1837; William S. Cockrill, 1840

S-9034 200a D:47 X:0840 FAYE:UNIO FAYE:GREE
a. W-2274 Dr. Basel Middleton
b. John Campbell
c. Richard Douglas, 1831

S-9035 71a D:72 X-0360 PICK:PERR
a. W-2274 Dr. Basel Middleton
b. John Campbell
c. None

S-9039 100a C:386 X-0360 MADI:UNIO
a. W-6168 William Champ
b. William Champ
c. J. Jones, 1833

S-9040* 2a -- -- CLIN:WASH
a. --
b. Thomas S. Foote
c. None
* Entry in Source A only.

S-9041 40a D:168 X-0800 ADAM:MONR
a. W-2199 Captain William Johnson*
b. William Johnston*
c. None
* So spelled.

S-9043 30a D:281 X-1110 ADAM:GREE
a. W-5781 Joseph Crockett
b. William Russell
c. None

S-9044 40a D:67 X-1040 ADAM:JEFF
a. W-5781 Joseph Crockett
b. John Ellison
c. None

S-9045 50a D:44 X-0847 HIGH:LIBE
a. W-5781 Joseph Crockett
b. James Wilson
c. None

S-9047 100a C:365 X-1385 PICK:JACK
a. W-6177 Edward Thomas, --? assignee of
b. James Goldsby
c. G. W. Doan, 1827; J. Goldsberry; P. Douglas, 1829; P. Richardson, 1837; H. Ruby? 1835; J. & J. Goldsberry; J. Olds, 1842

S-9048 100a D:492 X-0570 ROSS:HUNT
a. W-6165 William Royall
b. Cadwallader Wallace
c. None

S-9050* 50a -- -- PIKE:PEBB
a. --
b. George Dawson
c. Joseph Sewell; E. H. Smith, 1835; heirs of E. H. Smith; J. Moore, 1838; John A. Fulton
* Entry in Source A only.

S-9051* 100a -- -- PIKE:PEEP
a. --
b. Jeffrey Russell**
c. None
* Entry in Source A only.
** Source A notation: "Entry Cabell County, Va., 1812."

S-9053 250a D:229 X-0841 FAYE:MADI MADI:RANG
a. W-5969 Edward Wells? (Wills?)
b. Hugh Stewart*
c. None
* Source A spells Smart.

S-9054 200a C:368 X-0870 PIKE:PEEP
a. W-5906 John Wells
b. Henry S. Halley*, Junior
c. A. S? (L?) Holley*; Henry J. Holley*; E. Hall, 1828; heirs of E. H. Smith; J. Moore, 1838
* So spelled.

S-----* 368a C:310 X-0840 PIKE:--** ROSS:--**
a. W-6079 Jeremiah Pickett, heirs of
b. Walter Dun
c. None
* Says: "200? should be 9054 to 9060."
** Source A does not list this entry.

S-9058* 11a -- -- PIKE:PERR
a. --
b. Walter Dun
c. None
* Entry in Source A only.

S-9059* 20a -- -- SCIO:NILE
a. --
b. James Cross
c. Joseph? (James?) Nicholas; J. R. Walker, 1833
* Entry in Source A only.

S-9060 160a C:354 X-1140 PIKE:BENT
a. W-3039 Major John Swan
b. John Swan
c. J. Wyckoff, 1836

S-9061 150a C:354 X-0840 X-0570 ROSS:HUNT
a. W-3039 Major John Swan
b. John Swan
c. W. J. Gilbert; G. Scott, 1842

S-9062 50a C:306 X-0300 ROSS:HUNT
a. W-5638 James Barnett
b. -- Ladds & -- Norvell
c. None

S-9063* 125a -- -- ROSS:CONC ROSS:DEER
a. --
b. -- Ladds & -- Norvell
c. None
* Entry in Source A only.

S-9064* 100a -- -- ROSS:HUNT
a. --
b. -- Ladds & -- Norvell
c. None
* Entry in Source A only.

S-9066 30a C:354 X-1000 PICK:WAYN
a. W-3039 Major John Swan
b. John Swan
c. Thomas Bowdle, Senior, 1830

S-9067 40a C:352 X-0870 PIKE:PEBB
a. W-5631 Nathaniel J. Morris
b. -- Ladds & -- Norvell*
c. B. Hough; P. N. White, 1826; Joseph Penniston, 1828; H. Boswell, 1830; J. R. Anderson; A. Latham, 1837; heirs of J. Boswell
* Source A notation: "Patented to heirs (by name) of Benjamin Hough."

S-9068 10a D:257 X-0130 ADAM:JEFF
a. W-3076 Thomas Hanson
b. Stephen Beach
c. None

S-9076 200a C:355 X-0841 FAYE:MADI
a. W-5888 David Wallace
b. David Wallace, representatives of
c. A. C. Looker, 1824; Henry Phelps, 1829; James H. Looker; I. Y. Green, 1835

S-9078 60a C:331 X-0360 MADI:UNIO
a. W-5873 William Triplett
b. Cadwallader Wallace
c. H. Montgomery; J. F. Chinowith, 1823

S-9081 200a C:307 X-0150 ROSS:PAIN
a. W-5781 Joseph Crockett
b. Joseph Crockett
c. None

S-9082 289a C:307 X-0840? X-0150 ROSS:PAIN
a. W-5781 Joseph Crockett
b. Joseph Crockett
c. None

S-9083 200a C:307 X-1000 X-0340 PICK:SCIO
a. W-5606 William Aylett
b. George Clarke*
c. None
* Source A spells Clark.

S-9087 400a C:307 X-0847 HIGH:NEWM
a. W-5580 William Tappins
W-5709 Nathaniel Darby
b. Thomas James
c. J. Wasson; G. W. Barriere, 1826

S-9096
S-9641 80a C:372 X-0841 MADI:RANG
a. W-5798 James Dillard
b. -- Ladds & -- Norvell
c. None

S-9099 240a C:424 X-0300 ROSS:HUNT
a. W-5877 William Triplett
b. -- Ladds & -- Norvell
c. None

S-9100* 60a -- -- PIKE:PEBB
a. --
b. -- Ladds & -- Norvell
c. None
* Entry in Source A only.

S-9101* 60a -- -- PIKE:PEBB
a. --
b. -- Ladds & -- Norvell
c. None
* Entry in Source A only.

S-9102* 70a -- -- ----:----
a. None
b. -- Ladds & -- Norvell
c. None
* Entry in Source A only; says "not found."

S-9103* 45a -- -- PIKE:PEBB
a. --
b. -- Ladds & -- Norvell
c. None
* Entry in Source A only.

S-9105* 40a -- -- ROSS:SCIO
a. --
b. -- Ladds & -- Norvell
c. None
* Entry in Source A only.

S-9107* 209a -- -- UNIO:UNIO
a. --
b. Joshua Poythress
c. None
* Entry in Source A only.

S-9111 70a C:311 X-0130 ADAM:FRAN
a. W-5869 Abraham Bowman
b. Abraham Bowman
c. D. McArthur; T. Huston, 1829

S-9112 90a C:328 X-0841 FAYE:MADI
a. W-176 General P(eter) Muhlenberg
b. Peter Muhlenberg
c. Foster Pries; James Wood, 1830

S-9121 135a C:319 X-0740 CLAR:MADI
a. W-5880 Thomas Porter
b. -- Ladds & -- Norvell
c. None

S-9123 20a C:371 X-0840 ROSS:TWIN
a. W-6167 John Valentine
b. Cadwallader Wallace
c. None

S-9124 69a C:332 X-0840 MADI:STOK
a. W-5967 Will Poyner
b. Moses Demmitt
c. None

S-9125 38a C:332 X-0840 FAYE:JEFF
a. W-5967 Will Poyner
b. Moses Demmitt
c. None

S-9126 18a C:332 X-0663 CLER:STON
a. W-5967 Will Poyner
b. Moses Demmitt
c. None

S-9128 250a C:352 X-0841 FAYE:MADI
a. W-5722 William Price
b. -- Ladds & -- Norvell
c. T. J. Timmons, 1828

S-9129 165a C:352 X-0841 FAYE:MADI
a. W-5621 Nathaniel G. Morris
b. -- Ladds & -- Norvell
c. None

S-9130* 40a -- -- ROSS:HUNT
a. --
b. -- Ladds & -- Norvell
c. None
* Entry in Source A only.

S-9131
S-9142
S-9143 725a C:312 X-0841 ROSS:CONC FAYE:WAYN
a. W-5536 George Handy
W-5805 Joseph Hite? (Hile?)
b. -- Handy & -- Hite
c. None

S-9132 45a C:381 X-1000 PICK:JACK
a. W-5536 George Handy
b. George Handy
c. A. C. McArthur; J. Olds, 1842

S-9133
S-8973
S-9351 245a C:352 X-0840 ROSS:HUNT
a. W-5620 Nathaniel G. Morris
W-5638 James Barnett
W-6082 Robert Green
b. -- Ladds, -- Norvell, & -- Hough*
c. D. Collins; P. N. White, 1825; T. S? (L?) Hinds; E. P. Kendrick; S. Lawqier? 1829; N. Lawqier? (Sawyer?)
* Source A says: "Patented to heirs (by name) of Benjamin Hough."

S-9133. See also S-8973

S-9134 20a C:352 X-0840 ROSS:HUNT
a. W-5623 Nathaniel G. Morris
b. -- Ladds & -- Norvell
c. Benjamin Hough; E. P. Kendrick, 1827

S-9135 60a C:526 X-0840 ROSS:HUNT
a. W-5623 Nathaniel G. Morris
b. -- Ladds & -- Norvell
c. D. Collins; P. N. White, 1825; B(enjamin) Hough's heirs; E. P. Kendrick; N. Lawqier? (Sawyer?) 1829

S-9138 160a C:348 X-1185 MADI:SUMM
a. W-6045 William Berry
b. Levi Springer
c. None

S-9139 500a C:328 X-0663 HIGH:DODS
a. W-5218 Robert D. Fowke? (Fouke?) heir at law to John Fowke? (Fouke?)
b. William Philips, heirs of
c. John Gossett

S-9142; S-9143. See S-9131

S-9144 100a C:310 X-0659 FAYE:MADI
a. W-5963 Barnabas Arthur
b. Walter Dun
c. None

S-9152 35a C:346 X-0130 HIGH:BRUS
a. W-6125 Stephen Young
b. Walter Dun
c. None

S-9153 17a C:346 X-0130 PIKE:PERR
a. W-6125 Stephen Young
W-6199 Reuben Davenport
b. Walter Dun
c. None

S-9154 82a C:345 X-0840 ROSS:PAXT
a. W-6199 Reuben Davenport
b. Walter Dun
c. None

S-9157 509a C:312 X-1040 ADAM:MEIG
ADAM:FRAN
a. W-5367 Charles Harrison, representatives of
b. Robert Means
c. D. McArthur

S-9158 800a C:365 X-0215 ADAM:MEIG
ADAM:FRAN
a. W-5536 George Handy
W-5869 Abraham Bowman
b. -- Handy & -- Bowman
c. Isaac Addis; Thomas Huston, 1841

S-9159* 280a -- -- ROSS:HUNT
a. --
b. -- Ladds & -- Norvell
c. None
* Entry in Source A only.

S-9162 300a C:346 X-1186 MADI:PIKE
a. W-5749 David Williams
W-5718 John Spelfatham? (Spilfathom?)
W-6098 Harry Terrell
W-6086 Thomas Collier, representatives of
W-6200 George Langston, heirs of
b. Walter Dun
c. None

S-9163* 90a -- -- MADI:DEER
a. --
b. Joshua Poythress
c. None
* Entry in Source A only.

S-9165* 100a -- -- MADI:DEER
a. --
b. Joshua Poythress
c. None
* Entry in Source A only.

S-9166* 60a -- -- MADI:MONR
a. --
b. Joshua Poythress
c. None
* Entry in Source A only.

S-9167* 400a C:323 X-0360 PICK:----
a. W-1627 Lieutenant Joseph Conway
b. Joseph Conway
c. None
* Entry not listed in Source A.

S-9168* 600a -- -- MADI:JEFF
a. --
b. Joshua Poythress
c. None
* Entry in Source A only.

S-9169* 115a -- -- MADI:JEFF
a. --
b. Joshua Poythress
c. None
* Entry in Source A only.

S-9176* 400a -- -- PICK:MONR
a. --
b. Joseph Conway
c. Lyne Starling, 1831
* Entry in Source A only. This is probably the same as entry S-9167.

S-9177
S-9179 165a C:329 X-0663 HIGH:NEWM
a. W-57 Captain Seth Porterfield
b. Robert Porterfield
c. None

S-9178 50a C:322 X-0840 ROSS:PAXT
a. W-57 Captain Seth Porterfield
b. Robert Porterfield
c. None

S-9179. See S-9177

S-9180 140a C:373 X-0663 HIGH:SALE
HIGH:DODS
a. W-57 Captain Seth Porterfield
b. Robert Porterfield
c. C. Wallace; William O. Collins, 1840

S-9183 50a D:164 X-0540 PICK:DEER
a. W-2483 Captain Daniel Duvall
b. Daniel Duvall
c. Walter Thrall, 1831

S-9184 290a D:72 X-1300 BROW:EAGL
X-0130
a. W-2483 Captain Daniel Duvall
b. Daniel Duvall
c. None

S-9185 250a C:33 X-0360 MADI:UNIO
a. W-6182 Robert Hanson Harrison, heirs of
b. Charles Cutts
c. None

S-9189. See S-8989 (footnote)

S-9197 136a C:400 X-1000 FRAN:FRAN
a. W-5633 Nathaniel G. Morris
b. -- Ladds & -- Norvell
c. None

S-9198 100a C:362 X-0750 LOGA:PERR
X-0730
a. W-5633 Nathaniel G. Morris
b. -- Ladds & -- Norvell
c. None

S-9200 37a C:345 X-1180 MADI:JEFF
a. W-6064 William Connor
b. Walter Dun
c. None

S-9205* 200a -- -- MADI:UNIO
a. --
b. A. L. Laugham? (Langham?)
c. R. Douglas, 1828; Levi Warner, 1831
* Entry in Source A only.

S-9206* 100a -- -- PICK:DARB
a. --
b. A. L. Laugham? (Langham?)
c. None
* Entry in Source A only.

S-9207 100a D:371 X-0810 PICK:DARB MADI:PLEA
a. W-5876 William Triplett
b. Cadwallader Wallace
c. None

S-9209 200a C:336 X-0133 HIGH:JACK
a. W-5781 Joseph Crockett
b. Andrew Ellison
c. None

S-9210. See S-8314

S-9211* 50a -- -- PIKE:PEEP
a. --
b. Andrew Ellison
c. None
* Entry in Source A only.

S-9212 50a C:337 X-0600 ADAM:MONR
a. W-5989 John Yancy
b. Benjamin Bowman
c. E. Bowman, 1835; heirs of B. Bowman; R. Holerness* 1839
* So spelled. Probably Holderness is meant.

S-9213 10a E:316 X-0390 PICK:MONR
a. W-5952 Richard Hooper
b. James Bonner*
c. None
* Source A says John Evans.

S-9214
S-8874
S-10541
S-10542
S-12612
S-13772
S-13691 381a E:62 X-0679 PICK:DEER
a. W-5952 Richard Hooper
W-6524 Richard Dorsey, heirs of
W-6418 Vashel? (Vachel?) D. Howard
b. John Evans
c. T. Williams; W. N. Hedges, 1840

S-9214. See also S-8874; S-13770

S-9216
S-9811 730a C:401 X-0840 MADI:STOK
a. W-5880 Thomas Porter
b. -- Ladds & -- Norvell
c. None

S-9217 25a C:319 X-1180 CHAM:---* MADI:PIKE
a. W-5880 Thomas Porter
b. -- Ladds & -- Norvell
c. None
* Source A mentions Champaign County but does not give township.

S-9218 20a C:319 X-0620 CHAM:WAYN
a. W-5880 Thomas Porter
b. -- Ladds & -- Norvell
c. None

S-9219* 100a -- -- FRAN:BROW
a. --
b. -- Ladds & -- Norvell
c. C. Higgins, 1836
* Entry in Source A only.

S-9221. See S-5742 (in volume 4, part 1)

S-9222
S-10326 600a C:427 X-0620 CHAM:---* FRAN:PRAI
a. W-5188 Thomas M. Bayley, representative of John Custis? (Curtis?), administrator
b. Thomas M. Bailey
c. None
* Source A does not mention Champaign County.

S-9224 200a C:322 X-0840 ROSS:TWIN
a. W-6618 --*
b. Cadwallader Wallace
c. Jacob Callar; Pleasant Thurman, 1831
* Warrantee not listed in Source C.

S-9226 250a C:362 X-0740 MADI:STOK GREE:ROSS
a. W-6185 Robert Hanson Harrison, heirs of
b. Sarah Easton
c. S. Herod; J. Hiveling, 1829

S-9232 90a C:345 X-0360 MADI:JEFF
a. W-5887 Thomas Wallace? (Weinhart?), representatives of
b. Walter Dun
c. None

S-9242 100a C:317 X-0570 ROSS:HUNT
a. W-5828 William Cunningham, heirs of
b. -- Ladds & -- Norvell*
c. None
* Source A notation: "No warrant."

S-9249 180a C:393 X-0841 MADI:RANG
a. W-6164 Joseph Lett? (Leck? Leckader?), administrator
b. Walter Dun
c. John A. Fulton; Richard Douglas, 1832

S-9250* 70a -- -- HIGH:DODS
a. --
b. John A. Fulton
c. None
* Entry in Source A only.

S-9251
S-13241 565a D:496 X-1000 PIKE:SUNF
X-1140
a. W-654 Abraham Coff, heir to Samuel Coff
W-666 John Treacle
W-1819 John Aspenwall
W-6159 Thomas Ray
W-2274 Dr. Basel Middleton
b. -- Jenkins, -- Campbell, & -- Hinde
c. J. Jenkins; Adam Johnston, 1828; R. Douglas, 1829; C. Wallace et al; S. Wallace, 1842

S-9252
S-9732 187a C:408 X-0381 ADAM:MONR
a. W-215 Dr. David Holmes
b. David Holmes
c. None

S-9253 100a C:367 X-0600 ADAM:SPRI
a. W-5781 Joseph Crockett
b. Daniel Whittenmyer*
c. Everet Tacker; T. Huston
* Also spelled Wettenmyre.

S-9256. See S-7903

S-9257 55a C:324 X-0840 FAYE:WAYN
a. W-5783 William Triplett? (Treplett?)
W-5901 Ann Garnett? (Garrett?), heir to Benjamin Garnett? (Garrett?)
b. -- Wallace & -- Garrett
c. None

S-9258 30a C:324 X-0840 ROSS:BUCK
a. W-5783 William Triplett? (Treplett?)
b. Cadwallader Wallace
c. None

S-9259 47a C:324 X-0840 ROSS:PAXT
a. W-5802 George Norvell? (Nowell?), deceased
b. Thomas Worthington
c. Heirs of N. Reeves; P. Douglas, 1836; C. Wallace

S-9260 153a C:324 X-0840 ROSS:PAXT
a. W-5802 George Norvell? (Nowell?), deceased
b. Thomas Worthington
c. None

S-9261 250a C:534 X-1000 HARD:TAYL
a. W-6181 Robert Hanson Harrison, heirs of
b. Charles Cutts
c. Lyne Starling, 1831 (Logan County)

S-9262. See S-8887

S-9263. See S-8919

S-9264 46a D:310 X-1000 FRAN:JACK
a. W-6128 Stephen Young
b. Orris Parish
c. William Miller, 1829

S-9268 400a C:333 X-1301 HIGH:CLAY
a. W-5931 Cawfield Taylor
W-5993 John Taylor, heirs of
b. Samuel Bell
c. None

S-9269 320a C:368 X-0810 MADI:PLEA
PICK:DARB
a. W-5805 Joseph Hite
b. Joseph Hite
c. D. McArthur; Samuel Kinnear, 1831; John J. Mantle; G. Botkin, 1835; heirs of J(ohn) J. Mantle

S-9270 225a C:368 X-0810 MADI:---*
PICK:DARB
a. W-5805 Joseph Hite
b. Joseph Hite
c. Heirs of J. Bridge; W. Mills, 1836
* Source A does not mention Madison County.

S-9271 80a C:380 X-0810 PICK:DARB
a. W-5147 John Stokely, assignee of Abraham Shepherd
W-5240 --*
b. Robert Means
c. None
* Manuscript torn.

S-9272 350a C:381 X-0810 PICK:DARB
a. W-6034 Jacob Moore
b. George Dawson
c. None

S-9273 200a C:371 X-1000 ROSS:HUNT
X-0570
a. W-1231 George Greg? (Grey?)
b. Cadwallader Wallace
c. None

S-9274 304a C:321 X-0841 FAYE:MADI
a. W-6165 William Royall*
b. William Royal*
c. Fielding Clavenger; W. Loofborough, 1831; James Hudson; I. Y. Green, 1836; Thomas? M. Garrough, 1835; J. S. Dickey, 1838; C. Wallace; John Jackson, 1831
* So spelled; Source A spells Royall.

S-9275 100a C:357 X-0360 FAYE:MADI
a. W-6165 William Royall*
b. William Royal*
c. Richard Cafferty; James Woods, 1828; C. Wallace; Calvin B. Woodruff, 1831
* So spelled; Source A spells Royall.

S-9276 90a C:322 X-1000 ROSS:SCIO
X-0570
a. W-5873 William Triplett
b. Cadwallader Wallace
c. None

S-9277 60a C:359 X-1000 X-0570 ROSS:HUNT
a. W-5873 William Triplett
b. Cadwallader Wallace
c. None

S-9278 250a C:386 X-0360 MADI:UNIO
a. W-6186 Robert Hanson Harrison, heirs of
b. Alexander Kerr
c. M. Bonner, 1831

S-9280 285a C:408 X-0800 ADAM:SPRI
a. W-5796 James Jones
W-5593 Henry Sterling? (Starling?), representative of William Sterling? (Starling?)
W-5711 Andrew A. Gilchrist, heir to George (Gilchrist)
b. Thomas James
c. None

S-9283* 20a -- -- ADAM:MEIG
a. --
b. John Ellison, Junior
c. None
* Entry in Source A only.

S-9285
S-10626 100a C:462 X-1186 MADI:SUMM
a. W-5910 Weedon Smith
b. Archibald E. Mickle
c. Robert Farris, 1828

S-9287 25a C:334 X-0010 CLIN:LIBE
a. W-5880 Thomas Porter
b. -- Ladds & -- Norvell
c. None

S-9288 208a C:350 X-1000 SCIO:WASH
a. W-6035 Jacob Moore
b. William Kendall
c. William Curtis? (Custis?); J. Andrews, 1832; J. J. Collins; N. K. Clough, 1824; heirs of G. Graves; Samuel Coil, 1840; G. Calvert; W. V. Peck, 1842

S-9290 500a C:378 X-0841 FAYE:MADI
a. W-6197 Robert Hanson Harrison, heirs of
b. Abraham Bradley, Junior
c. Samuel Myers, 1827

S-9291. See S-8340

S-9292. See S-8339

S-9293. See S-8446

S-9294 25a D:255 X-0841 FAYE:MADI
a. W-6194 Robert Hanson Harrison, heirs of
b. John A. Fulton
c. None

S-9295* 30a -- -- SCIO:MORG
a. --
b. John A. Fulton
c. None
* Entry in Source A only.

S-9300 140a C:356 X-0360 PICK:DEER
a. W-5996 Samuel Collins, representatives of
b. M. Baker & J? (I?) Baker
c. Isaac Baker

S-9301 205a D:35 X-1000 HARD:TAYL
a. W-5534 Peter Manifold, assignee of Lawrence Manning (Junior), administrator of Lawrence (Manning), deceased
W-5543 Christopher Moon? (Moor?), son & heir to Jacob Moon? (Moor?)
b. George Hoffman
c. None

S-9302 125a C:370 X-0360 PICK:MONR
a. W-5967 Will Poyner
b. Moses Demitt
c. Richard Douglas, 1831

S-9303 181a C:321 X-0841 FAYE:WAYN ROSS:---*
a. W-5776 Thomas Hill, representatives of
b. Thomas Hill, heirs of
c. James Woods, 1828; Henry Phelps, 1829
* Source A does not mention Ross County.

S-9304 181a C:321 X-0360 PICK:DEER
a. W-5777 Thomas Hill, representatives of
b. Thomas Hill, heirs of
c. None

S-9305 50a C:320 X-0841 FAYE:MADI
a. W-5802 George Norvell? (Nowell?), deceased
b. Thomas Worthington
c. None

S-9306 500a C:320 X-0360 PICK:PERR FAYE:MADI
a. W-5798 James Dillard
b. -- Ladds & -- Norvell
c. None

S-9311 300a C:424 X-0876 PIKE:PEBB
a. --
b. Anthony Walke*
c. David Murphey; Jacob Lay? (Say?), 1831; John Smith; J. Penniston, 1839
* Source A says "patented to representatives of Benjamin Hough."

S-9313 100a C:354 X-1140 PIKE:MIFF
a. W-5803 John Ramsey, representatives of
b. Anthony Walke
c. None

S-9318 25a* F:4 X-0663 CLIN:CLAR
a. W-5336 William Mosley
b. -- Haworth & -- Garrner**
c. William McChesney, 1823; Israel Woodruff, 1828; Thomas West, 1835
* Source A says 31 acres.
** So spelled. Source A says William Moseley.

S-9319* 14a -- -- CLIN:CLAR
a. --
b. William Moseley
c. William McChesney, 1823; John Hartman, 1828
* Entry in Source A only.

S-9320 230a C:311 X-0841 FAYE:WAYN
a. W-5869 Abraham Bowman
b. Abraham Bowman
c. D. McArthur; D. Wickle, 1828

S-9321*
S-9418 197a C:440 X-0810 PICK:----
a. W-5101 William Bird, assignee of Philip Courtney W-5805 Joseph Hite
b. -- Means & -- Hite
c. None
* Entry not listed in Source A; see S-9418, however.

S-9322 90a C:354 X-0841 FAYE:MADI
a. W-5803 John Remay, representatives of
b. Anthony Walk*
c. A. Bowman; J. Wood, 1830
* Source A spells Walke.

S-9324 55a C:355 X-0841 FAYE:MADI
a. W-5803 John Remay, representatives of
b. Anthony Walk*
c. None
* Source A spells Walke.

S-9331* 108a -- -- MADI:FAIR
a. --
b. Joseph Hite
c. None
* Entry in Source A only.

S-9333 19a C:355 X-0360 PICK:DEER
a. W-5373 Thomas M. Bayley, assignee of Patience Bunting, representative of Sacher (Bunting)
b. Cadwallader Wallace
c. Noah Justis; W. P Durst & P. N. White, 1840

S-9334 150a C:328 X-0663 HIGH:DODS
a. W-111 Captain Clough Shelton*
b. Clough Sheldon*
c. None
* So spelled.

S-9335 175a C:328 X-0663 HIGH:UNIO
a. W-111 Captain Clough Shelton*
b. Clough Sheldon*
c. None
* So spelled.

S-9336 161a C:330 X-0360 MADI:UNIO
a. W-111 Captain Clough Shelton*
b. Clough Sheldon*
c. None
* So spelled.

S-9337 276a D:491 X-0780 MADI:UNIO
a. W-111 Captain Clough Shelton
b. Valentine Wilson
c. None

S-9338 150a C:357 X-0360 FAYE:MADI
MADI:---*
a. W-111 Captain Clough Shelton
b. Clough Shelton
c. None
* Source A does not mention Madison County.

S-9339 100a C:332 X-0130 ADAM:SCOT
a. W-5802 George Norvell? (Nowell?), deceased
b. Thomas Worthington
c. J. Campbell; L. Cole, 1842

S-9348 40a C:353 X-0570 ROSS:HUNT
a. W-5877 William Triplett
b. -- Ladds & -- Norvell
c. None

S-9349* 20a -- -- PIKE:PEBB
a. --
b. -- Ladds & -- Norvell
c. None
* Entry in Source A only.

S-9350* 70a -- -- ROSS:HUNT
a. --
b. -- Ladds & -- Norvell
c. None
* Entry in Source A only.

S-9351. See S-8973; S-9133

S-9353 200a D:383 X-0840 FAYE:PAIN
a. W-5403 William Sanford, representatives of
b. William Robinson
c. Mathaias Smith; J. McLain*, 1831; John McLane*, 1833
* So spelled.

S-9354 50a D:13 X-1000 PICK:JACK
a. W-5810 Thomas McKinley, heir to John (McKinley)
b. John A. Fulton
c. None

S-9355 200a D:195 X-1301 HIGH:SALE
a. W-5922 Jacob Rodes (his son George)
b. James McManaway*
c. None
* Source A spells McManamay.

S-9360 50a C:344 X-0660 CLAR:MADI
a. W-6202 Robert Balleu? (Ballen? Rollen? Bolling?), heirs of
b. Walter Dun
c. Justis Cooper, 1826

S-9363 10a D:396 X-0190 PIKE:CAMP
a. W-5871 Francis M. Boykin & Ann Johnson, heirs & administrators to F(rancis) Boykin
b. Thomas Mountjoy
c. None

S-9365 43a C:334 X-0180 GREE:SUGA
a. W-6025 Jesse? Binger? heirs to
b. James Galloway, Junior
c. None

S-9366
S-10096 65a C:407 X-0840 MADI:STOK
a. W-6025 Jesse? Binger? heirs to
W-5812 John Goodrich? heir
b. James Galloway, Junior
c. G. Linson? (Sinson?) 1826

S-9367
S-10614 149a C:461 X-0340 UNIO:JERO
a. W-5899 Peter Dager
W-712 Dr. William Brown
b. James Galloway, Junior
c. None

S-9368 100a C:334 X-1186 MADI:MONR
a. W-6208 Robert Bolling
b. James Galloway, Junior
c. J. Bradley, 1823

S-9370 150a C:362 X-0730 X-0750 LOGA:JEFF
a. W-6204 Robert Bolling
W-6205 Robert Bolling
b. Thomas Perkins
c. None

S-9371
S-12174 200a D:58 X-0730 X-0750 LOGA:PERR
a. W-6205 Robert Bolling
W-6206 Robert Bolling
W-6520 William Onell? (O'Neal?), heirs of
b. -- Perkins, -- Aldridge*, & -- Dun
c. W? (M?) Bonner, 1827
* Source A spells Ardridge.

S-9372 150a C:361 X-0730 X-0750 LOGA:JEFF LOGA:PERR
a. W-6207 Robert Bolling
W-6206 Robert Bolling
b. -- Littleberry & -- Aldridge*
c. None
* Source A says Littleberry Aldridge (one person).

S-9374* 133a -- -- BROW:CLAR
a. --
b. -- Carrol & -- Carris? (Carrs)
c. Thomas Carneal? (Carreal?); Benjamin Stubblefield; Hugh Maharry, 1823

S-9375 42a C:338 X-0663 CLER:TATE
a. W-2700 Dr. Miles King
b. Miles King
c. James? (Joseph?) A. Ware; C. A. Warren, 1834

S-9376 30a C:419 X-0800 BROW:PLEA
a. W-2700 Dr. Miles King
b. Miles King
c. None

S-9377* 213a -- -- BROW:SCOT
a. --
b. Richard C. Anderson
c. None
* Entry in Source A only.

S-9382 500a C:418 X-1080 CLER:WAYN
a. W-6196 Robert Hanson Harrison, heirs of
b. Young Felix Gresham
c. R. E. Hall, 1828; C. A. Warren, 1834; John Hill, 1833; F. Y. Graham; T. L. Shields, 1839

S-9383 250a E:79 X-1080 CLER:JACK
a. W-6180 Robert Hanson Harrison, heirs to
b. Vanzandt Meigs*
c. D. Wainwright, 1824; S? (L?) West, 1826; Samuel West, 1827
* Source A says -- Van Zandt & -- Meigs.

S-9385 220a C:419 X-0663 BROW:PERR CLER:---*
a. W-5260 Robert Keck? (Kirk?) & James Taylor
b. -- Taylor & -- Kirk
c. None
* Source A does not mention Clermont County.

S-9386 125a C:418 X-0663 CLER:JACK
a. W-5866 Abraham Bowman
b. Abraham Bowman
c. -- Shaw & -- Harris, 1824; W. Aslaton? (A. Slaton?) 1826; William Lytle; Z. Chapman, 1826; John Hill, 1832

S-9388 333a E:37 X-1159 ADAM:SPRI
a. W-1921 General Robert Lawson
b. Elizabeth Taylor
c. J. O'Bannon (Obannon); W. McColm? 1831; Thomas Huston, 1833

S-9389 50a C:347 X-0360 MADI:DEER
a. W-5887 Thomas Herbert? representatives of
b. Walter Dun
c. None

S-9390 95a C:347 X-0340 UNIO:UNIO
a. W-5887 Thomas Herbert? representatives of
b. Walter Dun
c. None

S-9391. See S-8926

S-9396* 100a -- -- HARD:TAYL
a. --
b. -- Ladd & -- Norvell
c. Defunct**
* Entry in Source A only.
** Presumably one of the Ladds was defunct.

S-9399 400a C:535 X-1000 MADI:---* MARI:GREE
a. W-2140? (2146?) John Wilson or Daniel Donnakin
W-4416 William Reynolds
W-4568 Thomas Hopkins assignee**
b. Thomas Hopkins
c. Mathew Bonner, 1831
* Source A does not mention Madison County.
** Ambiguous.

S-9401 150a C:357 X-0350 CHAM:WAYN
a. W-111 Captain Clough Shelton
b. Clough Shelton
c. None

S-9403 50a C:357 X-0360 FAYE:MADI
a. W-5543 Christopher Moon? (Moor?), heir to Greg? (Moon? Moor?)
b. George Hoffman
c. None

S-9411* 215a -- -- HARD:----
a. --
b. George Clark
c. Defunct
* Entry in Source A only; township not given.

S-9416 30a C:381 X-0810 PICK:DARB
a. W-5536 George Handy
b. George Handy
c. None

S-9418 197a C:440 X-0810 PICK:DARB
a. W-5101 William Bird, assignee of Philip Courtney
W-5805 Joseph Hite
b. Means Hite*
c. D. McArthur; D. Wickle, 1828
* Source A says -- Means & -- Hite.

S-9419 25a E:351 X-0841 FAYE:MADI PICK:---*
a. W-5613 Nathaniel G. Morris
b. Duncan McArthur
c. H. McDonald, 1829; George Handy; James Renick, 1833
* Source A does not mention Pickaway County.

S-9423. See S-4948 (in volume 4, part 1)

S-9424 100a C:379 X-0840 FAYE:PAIN
a. W-5616 Nathaniel G. Morris
b. Duncan McArthur
c. None

S-9435
S-9436 340a C:380 X-1180 MADI:JEFF
a. W-5536 George Handy
b. George Handy
c. B. Jones & wife; -- Price & -- Cosey? 1826

S-9437 260a C:380 X-0360 PICK:DARB
X-0810 MADI:PLEA
a. W-5536 George Handy
b. George Handy
c. D. McArthur; Samuel Kinnear, 1831; R. Douglas, 1836 (Madison County); W. I? Emmitt, 1837; P. Douglas, 1840 (Madison County); S? (L?) Andrews, 1842 (Madison County)

S-9439 15a C:380 X-0841 FAYE:MADI
a. Robert Means, assignee of Edward Smith
b. Robert Means
c. None

S-9440
S-9479 161a C:359 X-0360 MADI:PLEA
a. W-57 Captain John Peyton
W-6217 Thomas Treplett? (Triplett?)
b. -- Wallace & -- Porterfield
c. None

S-9441 15a C:356 X-0840 ROSS:UNIO
a. W-57 Captain John Peyton
b. Robert Porterfield
c. None

S-9442 40a C:356 X-0360 PICK:DEER
a. W-5996 Samuel Collins, representatives of
b. M. Baker & J. Baker
c. None

S-9443 20a C:373 X-0360 PICK:PERR
a. W-5996 Samuel Collins, representatives of
b. M. Baker & J. Baker
c. None

S-9444 300a C:464 X-0275 CLER:TATE BROW:---*
a. W-3980 Peter F. Sheldon
W-3933 William Reynolds, assignee
b. John Nancarrow
c. J. Taylor; Levi Bonnel, 1837
* Source A does not mention Brown County.

S-9445* 70a -- -- CLER:MIAM
a. --
b. --Chambers & -- Pollock
c. P. D. Bills, 1824
* Entry in Source A only.

S-9446* 356a -- -- CLER:----
a. --
b. Benjamin Beasley
c. None
* Entry in Source A is crossed out.

S-9447 170a C:409 X-0080 BROW:HUNT
a. W-1296 Timothy Peyton, heir to V(alentine) Peyton
b. Benjamin Beasley
c. None

S-9448 30a C:427 X-0080 BROW:HUNT
a. W-1296 Timothy Peyton, heir to V(aletine) Peyton
b. Benjamin Beasley
c. None

S-9449 44a C:58 X-0080 BROW:HUNT
a. W-1296 Timothy Peyton, heir to V(alentine) Peyton
b. Benjamin Beasley
c. None

S-9450 291a D:55 X-0663 CLIN:---* BROW:PERR
a. W-2126 Abrington** Jones
b. Albridgeton** Jones
c. -- Forman & -- White?; Thomas Haggerty, 1839; U.S. Bank; P. O. Conner, 1839; Benjamin Harpar** 1831 (Clermont County)
* Source A does not mention Clinton County.
** So spelled.

S-9451* 24a -- -- ADAM:SPRI
a. --
b. William Johnston
c. None
* Entry in Source A only.

S-9452* 200a -- -- ADAM:--**
a. --
b. William Johnson***
c. A. D. Beasley, 1828; Davis Beattie, 1834
* Entry in Source A only.
** Source A does not mention township.
*** So spelled.

S-9454* 220a -- -- BROW?:-**
a. --
b. William Johnston***
c. H. J. De Buen? (Breen?) 1834
* Entry in Source A only, where crossed out.
** Source A may mention Brown County, but without township.
*** So spelled.

S-9455 200a D:73 X-0730 CHAM:WAYN
a. W-2247 Reverend John Hurt
b. John Hurt
c. None

S-9456* 100a -- -- HIGH:CLAY
a. --
b. John Hurt**
c. John Hart**; Lanner? B. Collins, 1828
* Entry in Source A only.
** So spelled.

S-9457* 63a -- -- HIGH:CLAY
a. --
b. Lawrence Butler
c. None
* Entry in Source A only.

S-9458 40a D:387 X-0840 ROSS:TWIN
a. W-5731 John Begent
W-2019 William Turvey
b. John McDonald
c. None

S-9460. See S-7670

S-9461. See S-7492

S-9465
S-9577 1133a C:377 X-1300 BROW:FRAN BROW:SCOT
a. W-5885 William Mosby, deceased, by Ann W. Chamberlayn
W-6216 William Holt
b. Cadwallader Wallace
c. None

S-9471 68a C:359 X-0360 MADI:UNIO
a. W-6217 Thomas Treplett? (Triplett?)
b. Cadwallader Wallace
c. David Groves, 1828

S-9472 110a C:359 X-0360 MADI:DEER
a. W-6217 Thomas Treplett? (Triplett?)
b. Cadwallader Wallace
c. None

S-9473 225a C:359 X-0360 MADI:UNIO
a. W-6217 Thomas Treplett? (Triplett?)
b. Cadwallader Wallace
c. None

S-9474 59a C:374 X-0019 GREE:CAES
a. W-6217 Thomas Treplett? (Triplett?)
b. Cadwallader Wallace
c. None

S-9476 100a C:371 X-0841 FAYE:WAYN
a. W-6217 Thomas Treplett? (Triplett?)
b. Cadwallader Wallace
c. George Ralls; D. McLane, 1827

S-9477*
S-16065 192a F:246 X-1360 X-0300 ROSS:----
a. W-6217 Thomas Treplett? (Triplett?)
W-442 --*
b. Cadwallader Wallace
c. None
* Warrantee not listed in Source C.

S-9479. See S-9440

S-9481 45a C:364 X-0360 ROSS:DEER

a. W-6217 Thomas Treplett? (Triplett?)
b. Cadwallader Wallace
c. John Trontner? 1823

S-9482 250a C:363 X-0840 ROSS:TWIN
a. W-6217 Thomas Treplett? (Triplett?)
b. Cadwallader Wallace
c. None

S-9485. See S-8373

S-9489 139a C:390 X-0360 PICK:PERR
a. W-111 Captain Clough Shelton
b. Clough Shelton
c. None

S-9490 56a C:347 X-0500 MADI:JEFF
a. W-6216 William Holt
b. Walter Dun
c. None

S-9492 210a C:346 X-1180 MADI:DEER
a. W-6216 William Holt
b. Walter Dun
c. None

S-9494 400a C:343 X-0340 UNIO:UNIO
a. W-6216 William Holt
b. Walter Dun
c. None

S-9496* 53a -- -- MADI:CANA
a. --
b. Walter Dun
c. None
* Entry in Source A only.

S-9499 240a C:346 X-0659 PICK:WAYN
a. W-6217 Thomas Treplett? (Triplett?)
b. Walter Dun
c. Alexander Beard; James Hedges, 1830

S-9500 380a C:342 X-0360 MADI:UNIO
a. W-6217 Thomas Treplett? (Triplett?)
b. Walter Dun
c. None

S-9502. See S-8425

S-9503
S-12574 46a D:205 X-0300 PIKE:JACK
a. W-5825 Richard Foster, heirs of
W-5139 Robert Means, assignee of James Smith
b. Walter Dun
c. Isaac Owen; A. G. Thurman, 1833
* Source A does not mention Ross County.

S-9511 60a C:353 X-0570 ROSS:HUNT
a. W-5631 Nathaniel G. Morris
W-5621 Nathaniel G. Morris
b. -- Ladds & -- Norvell
c. None

S-9512 45a C:351 X-0840 ROSS:TWIN
a. W-5638 James Barnett
b. -- Ladds & -- Norvell*
c. None
* Source A says: "Patented to heirs (by name) of Benjamin Hough."

S-9513 150a C:353 X-0870 PIKE:PEBB
a. W-5631 Nathaniel G. Morris
b. -- Ladds & -- Norvell
c. B(enjamin) Hough; P. N. White, 1826; F. Mitchel; Esbridge Hall, 1828; -- Phelps & -- Woods, 1828

S-9515* 50a -- -- ROSS:HUNT
a. --
b. -- Ladds & -- Norvell
c. None
* Entry in Source A only.

S-9516 55a C:495 X-0570 ROSS:HUNT
a. W-5803 John Remay, representatives of
b. Anthony Walke*
c. None
* Source A says: "Patented to heirs of Benjamin Hough."

S-9518 220a C:423 X-0870 ROSS:HUNT
PIKE:PEBB
a. W-5803 John Remay, representatives of
b. Anthony Walke
c. None

S-9519 533a D:356 X-0879 PIKE:PEBB
a. W-5888 David Wallace, representatives of
b. Jonah Halton*
c. B. Wallace; Isaac Quin; David Wallace; J. Penniston, 1832; C. M. McCollister, 1840
* Source A spells Hatton.

S-9519 204a E:47 X-0879 PIKE:PEBB
a. W-5888 David Wallace, representatives of
b. Isaac Quin
c. None

S-9522* 4a -- -- PICK:WAYN
a. --
b. John Harrison
c. None
* Entry in Source A only.

S-9525* 319a -- -- MADI:UNIO
a. --
b. Thomas M. Bayly
c. --
* Entry in Source A only.

S-9530 300a C:378 X-0340 MADI:CANA
a. W-5265 Tuttle Hudson, et al, administrators of William Hudson

b. Lucas Sullivant
c. None

S-9531* 63a -- -- FRAN:FRAN
a. --
b. John Clark
c. None
* Entry in Source A only.

S-9532 550a C:420 X-1070 CLER:GOSH
CLER:WAYN
a. W-2443 Captain William Pierce
b. William Pierce
c. None

S-9534 500a C:413 X-0663 CLIN:CLAR
a. W-2860 Thomas Knox
W-3182 William Smith
W-3197 Peter McNeal
W-3348 William McCoy
b. John Nancarrow
c. William Lytle; T? Kirley? (Kirby?), 1823; William Millikan, 1827; Joseph? (James?) Jennings; G. Fallis, 1830; B. Ballard, 1835; J. Hadley, 1835; James Taylor; L. Fitzhugh, 1837; E. Hayworth; C. Hendrickson; R. Hendrickson, 1840; John Hadley, 1842

S-9535 200a C:413 X-0663 BROW:PERR
HIGH:DODS
a. W-3893 Robert Rankin, assignee of
W-3929 William Reynolds, assignee
b. John Nancarrow
c. William Lytle; James Taylor, 1823; J. Riley, 1838; G. Smith, 1837 (Highland County); James Riley, 1840

S-9536 300a C:413 X-1170 WARR:SALE
a. W-3695 Thomas Holloway
W-3480 James Fear
b. John Nancarrow
c. None

S-9539 370a C:463 X-0660 GREE:ROSS
a. W-617 Captain Alexander Breckenridge
b. Alexander Breckenridge
c. None

S-9540 370a C:463 X-0660 GREE:ROSS
a. W-617 Captain Alexander Breckenridge
b. Alexander Breckenridge
c. None

S-9545 5a C:428 X-0663 CLER:BATA
a. W-5336 William Mosley
b. William Mosley*
c. None
* Source A spells Moseley.

S-9546 8a C:428 X-0663 CLER:BATA
a. W-5336 William Mosley
b. William Mosley
c. None

S-9547* 59a -- -- HIGH:DODS
a. --
b. -- Williams, -- Boyce, & -- Stokes
c. None
* Entry in Source A only.

S-9550 18a D:435 X-1080 CLER:STON
a. W-5222 William Boyce
b. William Boyce
c. James Taylor

S-9566 100a C:367 X-0423 ADAM:TIFF
a. W-5847 Moses Stanley
b. John Ellison, Junior
c. J. P. Hamilton; James Hood, 1842

S-9567 75a D:28 X-0570 ADAM:MONR
a. W-5972 Edward Wills? (Wells?)
b. Robert Ellison
c. None

S-9569 50a C:370 X-1000 PIKE:NEWT
a. W-6216 William Holt
b. Cadwallader Wallace
c. J. Bateman; L. Hodges, 1826; P. Boswell; Loyd Howard, 1824

S-9570* 73a -- -- FAYE:--**
PICK:PERR
a. --
b. C(adwallader) Wallace
c. George Hollinger; James N. Davis, 1824
* Entry in Source A only.
** Source A does not mention township.

S-9571 350a C:392 X-1300 HIGH:WHIT
a. W-6216 William Holt
W-6155 George Thompson
b. Cadwallader Wallace
c. N. Reck; A. Farquahar, 1824; J. Harvey; J. Hogsett, 1836

S-9572 65a C:364 X-0060 LOGA:LAKE
a. W-6217 Thomas Treplett? (Triplett?)
b. Cadwallader Wallace
c. None

S-9574 220a C:364 X-0360 PICK:DEER
a. W-6217 Thomas Treplett? (Triplett?)
b. Cadwallader Wallace
c. Leonard Beercyl?; Joseph? (James?) Hedges, 1826

S-9575 165a C:364 X-0360 ROSS:DEER
PICK:DEER
a. W-6217 Thomas Treplett? (Triplett?)
W-5725 William Price
b. Cadwallader Wallace
b. None

S-9577. See S-9465

S-9579
S-9646
S-9666 1417a C:376 X-1300 BROW:EAGL
X-0130
a. W-5719 William Price
W-5756 Lewis Powers
W-5626 Nathaniel G. Morris
W-5721 William Price
W-5798 James Dillard
W-5885 William Mosby, deceased, by Ann W. Chamberlayn
W-6237 William Yates, heirs of
b. Cadwallader Wallace
c. Henry Boatman; David Johnson, 1823; John McKnight; John Hillicost, 1826; Isaac Edgington; M. Kincaid, 1830

S-9579* 400a -- -- BROW:EAGL
a. --
b. C(adwallader) Wallace
c. None
* Entry in Source A only

S-9580*
S-9581
S-9582 1500a C:377 X-1124 BROW:FRAN
a. W-6220 William Yates, heirs of
W-6221 William Yates, heirs of
W-6223 Richard Hays
W-6216 William Holt
b. Cadwallader Wallace
c. William Prickett; David Johnson, 1823; Ann Boling?; Mordecai Levi, 1829; J. Prickett; L. Pangburn, 1829
* Source A does not mention S-9580.

S-9584 380a C:370 X-0340 PICK:MUHL
a. W-5825 Richard Foster, heirs of
b. Cadwallader Wallace
c. None

S-9585
S-9660 563a C:374 X-0660 MADI:STOK
CLAR:MADI
a. W-5825 Richard Foster, heirs of
W-6217 Thomas Treplett? (Triplett?)
b. Cadwallader Wallace
c. Isaac Atkinson; S? (L?) M. Wheeler, 1838

S-9587 160a C:369 X-0660 CLAR:MADI
a. W-5840 Nathaniel Fox, Senior?, heirs of
b. Walter Dun
c. None

S-9589 800a C:369 X-0840 ROSS:PAXT
a. W-6219 William Yates, heirs of
W-5840 Nathaniel Fox, Senior?, heirs of
b. Walter Dun
c. George Batam, 1835; N. Massie

S-9591 100a C:369 X-0340 UNIO:UNIO
a. W-6222 Charles Walden
b. Walter Dun
c. None

S-9592
S-10075
S-9618 560a C:408 X-0730 LOGA:MONR
a. W-6222 Charles Walden
W-6217 Thomas Treplett? (Triplett?)
W-5885 William Mosby, deceased, by Ann W. Chamberlayn
W-6218 William Yates
b. Walter Dun
c. M. Bonner, 1827

S-9594* 269a -- -- UNIO:UNIO
a. --
b. -- Poythress & -- Dun
c. None
* Entry in Source A only.

S-9599* 25a -- -- FRAN:WASH
a. --
b. Jeremiah McClean
c. None
* Entry in Source A only.

S-9600 65a C:367 X-0130 ADAM:GREE
a. W-5848 William Mitchell
b. Andrew Ellison, Junior
c. None

S-9601 35a C:367 X-0130 ADAM:GREE
a. W-5848 William Mitchell
b. Andrew Ellison, Junior
c. None

S-9602 50a C:367 X-0040 ADAM:TIFF
a. W-5848 William Mitchell
b. George R. Fitzgerald
c. None

S-9605. *See* S-7446; S-8584

S-9606 60a C:406 X-0650 ADAM:TIFF
a. W-5750 John Pollet
b. Andrew Ellison
c. None

S-9607
S-10895 150a D:168 X-1045 SCIO:BRUS
ADAM:MEIG
a. W-3088 James Vaughn, assignee
W-3984 Arthur Leath, representative of Peter (Leath)
b. Alexander Fowler
c. George Williams; A. Ellison, 1826

S-9612 100a C:376 X-0300 ADAM:FRAN
a. W-111 Captain Clough Shelton
b. Clough Shelton
c. None

S-9614 75a C:376 X-0847 HIGH:FAIR
a. W-5907 Richard Savage, heirs of
b. Isaac Laronse*
c. None
* Source A spells Larouse.

S-9618. See S-9592

S-9620 350a D:59 X-0380 HIGH:NEWM
a. W-4107 John Bell
b. -- Stealey* & -- Kerr
c. None
* Source A spells Steeley.

S-9621 100a E:33 X-0130 HIGH:WHIT
X-1300 HIGH:CONC
a. W-4107 John Bell
b. John Stealey*
c. Philip Roush; -- Stealey & -- Kerr; John Hogsett, 1836
* Source A spells Steeley.

S-9621 100a D:469 X-1300 HIGH:CONC
a. W-4107 John Bell
b. Philip Roush
c. -- Stealey & -- Kerr; William Rodgers, 1831

S-9622 120a D:59 X-1300 HIGH:SALE
a. W-4107 John Bell
b. -- Stealey* & -- Kerr
c. None
* Source A spells Steeley.

S-9623 100a C:459 X-1186 CHAM:GOSH
a. W-5487 Frederick Hentze
b. Harry Beame
c. None

S-9624 300a C:370 X-0870 PIKE:PEEP
a. W-5885 William Mosby, deceased, by Ann W. Chamberlayn
W-5825 Richard Foster, heirs of
W-6216 William Holt
b. Cadwallader Wallace
c. S. Butler; L. Hodges, 1823; J. Sewell, 1826; H. Hemstead, 1823; P. Boswell; Jane Hodges, 1829

S-9625 80a C:370 X-0870 PIKE:PEEP
a. W-6217 Thomas Treplett? (Triplett?)
W-6216 William Holt
b. Cadwallader Wallace
c. None

S-9626* 60a -- -- LOGA:MONR
a. --
b. Walter Dun
c. None
* Entry in Source A only.

S-9627 90a C:372 X-0360 PICK:PERR
a. W-5885 William Mosby, deceased, by Ann W. Chamberlayn
b. Cadwallader Wallace
c. None

S-9628 400a C:373 X-0779 PIKE:PERR
a. W-5885 William Mosby, deceased, by Ann W. Chamberlayn
b. Cadwallader Wallace
c. E. Perrill; James Sergent, 1830; W. How; N. S. Murphey, 1842

S-9629 10a C:508 X-1000 ROSS:SCIO
a. W-5805 Joseph Hite
b. Joseph Hite
c. None

S-9631* 20a -- -- ADAM:----
a. --
b. William Johnston
c. Job Vining, 1823; Foster Hubank; Thomas Huston, 1831
* Entry in Source A only, where cancelled as "wdn." (withdrawn?).

S-9632* 40a -- -- PIKE:PEBB
a. --
b. Benjamin Hough**
c. P. N. White, 1826; William P. Cook; A. G. Thurman, 1833; J. R. Anderson; A. Latham, 1837; N. S. Murphy, 1841
* Entry in Source A only.
** Source A says: "Patented to heirs of Benjamin Hough."

S-9636 230a C:424 X-0570 ROSS:HUNT
a. W-6253 William Yates, representatives of
W-6254 William Yates, representatives of
b. John Watkins
c. None

S-9637 90a C:424 X-0570 ROSS:HUNT
a. W-6255 William Yates, representatives of
b. John Watkins
c. None

S-9638 70a C:423 X-0304 ROSS:HUNT
a. W-6234 William Yates, representatives of
b. Ann Gholson
c. None

S-9639 45a -- -- PIKE:PEBB
a. --
b. Ann Gholson
c. A. G. Thurman, 1833; John R. Anderson; A. Latham, 1837; Heirs of Benjamin Hough

S-9640 85a C:424 X-0570 ROSS:HUNT
a. W-6234 William Yates, representatives of
b. Ann Gholson
c. None

S-9641. See S-9096

S-9642 220a C:372 X-0841 MADI:RANG
a. W-5798 James Dillard
b. -- Ladds & -- Norvell
c. None

S-9646. See S-9579

S-9647
S-9663 340a C:375 X-1120 PIKE:MIFF ADAM:---*
a. W-6218 William Yates
W-6217 Thomas Treplett? (Triplett?)
W-6237 William Yates, heirs of
b. Cadwallader Wallace
c. None
* Source A does not mention Adams County.

S-9649. See S-8996

S-9651. See S-6391 (in volume 4, part 1)

S-9653 30a C:531 X-1180 CHAM:GOSH
a. W-6242 William Yates, heirs of
b. Benjamin Cheney
c. None

S-9654 70a D:10 X-0730 CHAM:UNIO
a. W-6242 William Yates, heirs of
b. Benjamin Cheney
c. A. Washington; S? (L?) Hogg, 1826

S-9655 160a C:422 X-0570 ROSS:HUNT
a. W-6238 William Yates
W-6239 William Yates
b. Benjamin Hough
c. None

S-9656 100a C:387 X-0670 ADAM:GREE
a. W-5723 William Price
b. Walter Dun
c. None

S-9657
S-9740 331a C:402 X-0340 X-0730 LOGA:ZANE
a. W-5638 James Barnett
W-5631 Nathaniel G. Morris
W-5621 Nathaniel G. Morris
W-5877 William Triplett? (Treplett?)
W-5825 Richard Foster, heirs of
b. Walter Dun
c. None

S-9658 75a C:379 X-0841 PICK:PERR
a. W-5613 Nathaniel G. Morris
b. Duncan McArthur
c. None

S-9659 100a D:21 X-0840 FAYE:UNIO
a. W-5764 Patrick Boyd
b. Duncan McArthur
c. None

S-9660. See S-9585

S-9661 60a C:376 X-0130 PIKE:MIFF
a. W-111 Captain Clough Shelton
b. Clough Shelton
c. None

S-9663. See S-9647

S-9665. See S-7446

S-9666. See S-9579

S-9669 400a C:383 X-0640 HIGH:FAIR
a. W-5349 John Nicholas
b. -- Sanders & -- Pope
c. T. M. Sanders, 1826; C. M. Bentley; G. Ladd, 1837; E. Johnson; J. E. Johnson, 1842

S-9672* 110a -- -- GREE:CAES
a. --
b. William Bayles
c. Robert D. Forsman, 1831
* Entry in Source A only.

S-9676 80a C:402 X-0730 LOGA:PERR
a. W-6203 Robert Bolling
b. Edward Watts
c. None

S-9679 500a C:437 X-0340 X-0730 LOGA:ZANE
a. W-5880 Thomas Porter
b. -- Ladds & -- Norvell
c. None

S-9680. See S-8997

S-9681 22a C:399 X-0730 CLAR:HARM
a. W-5880 Thomas Porter
b. -- Ladds & -- Norvell
c. None

S-9682 35a C:400 X-0730 CLAR:HARM
a. W-5880 Thomas Porter
b. -- Ladds & -- Norvell
c. None

S-9684* 50a -- -- PIKE:CAMP
a. --
b. William Johnston**
c. P. Spunck? (Spurck?), 1833; W. Johnson**; Jacob Lay, 1836
* Entry in Source A only.
** So spelled.

S-9685. See S-5888 (in volume 4, part 1)

S-9686 40a D:68 X-0040 ADAM:MONR
a. W-352 Reverend David Griffith
b. John H. Norton
c. Robert Ellison, 1826

S-9687* 60a -- -- ADAM:MONR
a. --
b. John H. Norton
c. Robert Ellison, 1826
* Entry in Source A only.

S-9688* 70a -- -- ADAM:TIFF
a. --
b. John H. Norton
c. Robert Ellison, 1826
* Entry in Source A only.

S-9689 12a D:323 X-0800 ADAM:GREE
a. W-6104 Hardin Woodroof
b. George R. Fitzgerald
c. John McDaide; S. Smith; J. P. Smith, 1841

S-9690 156a C:405 X-0130 ADAM:MEIG
a. W-237 Lieutenant John Harrison
b. Andrew Ellison
c. None

S-9691 50a C:405 X-0130 ADAM:JEFF
a. W-237 Lieutenant John Harrison
b. Andrew Ellison
c. None

S-9692 39a C:405 X-0130 ADAM:MEIG
a. W-3105 Thomas Miller
W-237 Lieutenant John Harrison
b. Andrew Ellison
c. None

S-9693 65a C:405 X-0381 ADAM:MONR
a. W-237 Lieutenant John Harrison
b. Andrew Ellison
c. None

S-9694 135a C:405 X-0420 ADAM:TIFF
a. W-1696 William Copeland
W-2264 Thomas? Jones
b. Andrew Ellison
c. None

S-9696 401a C:392 X-0360 MADI:RANG
a. W-6237 William Yates, heirs of
W-5873 William Triplett? (Treplett?)
b. Cadwallader Wallace
c. None

S-9697. See S-6391 (in volume 4, part 1)

S-9703* 363a -- -- ROSS:----
a. --
b. John Watkins**
c. None
* Entry in Source A only, where crossed out.
** Source A says* "Patented to heirs of Benjamin Hough."

S-9704* 100a -- -- LOGA:----
a. --
b. David? Aikin
c. L? (S?) J. Sewell, 1823
* Entry in Source A only.

S-9709 40a C:423 X-1000 ROSS:FRAN
a. W-5719 William Price
b. Angus L. Langham
c. None

S-9710 100a D:350 X-0590 ADAM:SPRI
a. W-352 Reverend David Griffith
b. John H. Norton
c. John Patterson, 1823; John Ellison; W. Ellison, 1831?

S-9712 46a E:236 X-0040 ADAM:MONR
a. W-5781 Joseph Crockett
b. Robert Johnston, deceased, heirs of*
c. None
* Source A says John Ellison.

S-9713 200a C:384 X-0420 BROW:BYRD
a. W-6225 Alexander Monroe
b. Nathaniel Beasley
c. E. Francis; -- Wilson & -- Middleton, 1842; W. Parker; J. Baird, 1842

S-9714 85a C:382 X-1140 HIGH:BRUS
PIKE:---*
a. W-5805 Joseph Hite
b. Joseph Hite
c. None
* Source A does not mention Pike County.

S-9717 150a C:381 X-0360 MADI:FAIR
a. W-6034 Jacob Moore
b. George Dawson
c. None

S-9718 300a C:381 X-0500 MADI:DEER
a. W-6034 Jacob Moore
b. George Dawson
c. None

S-9721 2160a C:388 X-0841 FAYE:PAIN
FAYE:MADI
MADI:RANG
a. W-5825 Richard Foster, heirs of
W-6217 Thomas Treplett? (Triplett?)
W-6155 George Thompson
W-6019 John Baldwin
b. -- Wallace & -- Baldwin
c. J. Baldwin; S? (L?) Moore, 1826; heirs of Robert Mortimore; W. T. Reeves, 1841; C. Wallace; James Bell, 1831; John Baldwin; Samuel Lydy, 1834

S-9723* 100a -- -- MADI:FAIR
a. --
b. John Smith
c. None
* Entry in Source A only.

S-9724 500a C:390 X-0340 UNIO:UNIO
CHAM:RUSH
a. W-5850 Tarlton Payne
b. B. Forsyth, dev(isees of)
c. Heirs of Benjamin Forsyth; John B. Cranston, 1841

S-9731 105a D:211 X-0136 ADAM:TIFF
a. W-215 Doctor David Holmes
W-2264 Thomas? Jones
b. -- Holmes & -- Ellison
c. None

S-9732. See S-9252

S-9733* 100a -- -- ADAM:CREE
a. --
b. Roley Jacobs
c. A. Ellison; William Ellison, 1827
* Entry in Source A only.

S-9734 160a C:423 X-0570 ROSS:HUNT
a. W-5719 William Price
W-5354 Thomas Hungerford, deceased, executors of
b. -- Langham & -- Robinson
c. B(enjamin) Hough; P. N. White, 1825; E. P. Kendrick; N. Lawqier? (Sawyer?), 1829

S-9736 407a C:399 X-0340 UNIO:JERO
a. W-5874 William Triplett? (Treplett?)
W-5875 William Triplett? (Treplett?)
W-5827 William Cunningham, heirs of
W-5729 Peter Garland, representatives of
b. -- Galloway, -- Ladd, & -- Robinson*
c. J. Galloway; John Low, 1840
* Source A says: "-- Galloway, -- Ladd, & -- Barnett."

S-9737* 25a -- -- FRAN:WASH
a. --
b. -- Kerr & -- Steeley
c. James Kerr; Orris Parish, 1823
* Entry in Source A only.

S-9738* 100a -- -- MADI:FAIR
a. --
b. John Smith
c. None
* Entry in Source A only.

S-9739. See S-7521

S-9740. See S-9657

S-9741*
S-12235 750a D:70 X-0840 HIGH:FAIR
a. W-5825 Richard Foster, heirs of
W-5885 William Mosby, deceased, by Ann W. Chamberlayn
W-6520 William Terrell, heirs of
W-6522 William Terrell, heirs of
b. Walter Dun
c. None
* Source A notation: "Near Leesburg."

S-9742 87a C:504 X-0600 ADAM:MONR
a. W-6104 Hardin Woodroof
b. George R. Fitzgerald
c. None

S-9743* 40a -- -- ADAM:MONR
a. --
b. John H. Norton
c. John Carl, 1823
* Entry in Source A only.

S-9744 150a F:207 X-0420 ADAM:MONR
a. W-352 Reverend David Griffith
b. Joseph McCormick
c. Robert Ellison, 1826

S-9751 18a C:395 X-0360 PICK:DEER
a. W-5612 Nathaniel G. Morris
b. Gabriel Coil*
c. None
* Source A may spell Cail.

S-9755 60a C:402 X-1180 UNIO:UNIO
a. W-6218 William Yates
b. Walter Dun
c. R. P. Mann, 1833

S-9756 100a C:395 X-0841 FAYE:MADI
a. W-5959 John Carroll
b. Joseph Evans
c. James Woods, 1828

S-9757 250a C:396 X-0660 CREE:---*
CLAR:MADI
a. W-5959 John Carroll
b. Joseph Evans
c. None
* Source A does not mention Green County.

S-9760 150a C:396 X-0360 MADI:PLEA
a. W-5959 John Carroll
b. Joseph Evans
c. None

S-9761 90a C:395 X-0841 FAYE:MADI
a. W-6130 Richard M. Owen
b. James Dunlap
c. None

S-9762* 60a -- -- ROSS:HUNT
a. --
b. John Watkins
c. None
* Entry in Source A only.

S-9765 300a C:400 X-1000 PICK:DEER
a. W-6244 Churchill Gibbs
b. Henry Beatty
c. None

S-9771* 50a -- -- PIKE:PEBB
a. --
b. John Watkins
c. None
* Entry in Source A only.

S-9780 100a C:398 X-0360 PICK:DEER
a. W-6130 Richard M. Owen
b. Martin Baker
c. None

S-9781 100a C:415 X-1120 BROW:FRAN
a. W-6130 Richard M. Owen
b. Silvanus Bourne
c. None

S-9782 57a C:395 X-0840 MADI:RANG
a. W-5131 William McKee
b. William McKee*
c. None
* Source A says: "Patented to the heirs of Benjamin Hough."

S-9783* 90a -- -- PIKE:PEBB
a. --
b. Angus L. Langham**
c. B(enjamin) Hough; P. N. White, 1826; A. G. Thurman, 1833; J. R. Anderson
* Entry in Source A only.
** Source A says: "Patented to heirs of Benjamin Hough."

S-9785 30a C:423 X-0840 ROSS:HUNT
a. W-5719 William Price
b. Angus L. Langham
c. None

S-9793 70a C:402 X-0730 LOGA:MONR
a. W-6218 William Yates
b. Walter Dun
c. M. Bonner, 1827

S-9796 200a D:18 X-0340 UNIO:ALLE
a. W-5828 William Cunningham, heirs of
W-5885 William Mosby, deceased, by Ann W. Chamberlayn
b. Walter Dun
c. None

S-9798 1024a C:431 X-1180 X-0340 UNIO:UNIO
a. W-6209 Robert Bolling
W-5887 Thomas Herbert, representatives of
b. Joshua Poythress
c. None

S-9802* 200a -- -- CLER:WILL
a. --
b. John Preston
c. None
* Entry in Source A only.

S-9803 335a D:132 X-0360 MADI:UNIO
a. W-6157 Thomas Ray
W-5494 Francis Cowherd
W-5744 Meshack? Wakefield?
W-5978 John E. Scott, representatives of
b. William Robinson
c. None

S-9803. See also S-6052 (in volume 4, part 1)

S-9804 145a D:302 X-1300 HIGH:CLAY
a. W-5791 George Lee Turberville
b. William Fulton
c. A. Baskin, 1824; Jane W. Marsh; P. Roush, 1828; Samuel Woodmansee, 1833

S-9809 401a C:431 X-1000 ROSS:FRAN
a. W-5187 Thomas M. Bayly, assignee of John Drummond
b. Joseph Harness
c. None

S-9811. See S-9216

S-9812. See S-9007

S-9820 50a D:40 X-0840 MADI:STOK
a. W-3879 Charles Forklin? (Focklin?), heirs of
b. Cadwallader Wallace
c. W. Buffenbergh; G. Lenson? (Leuson?), 1826

S-9821 1241a C:397 X-0660 X-0360 X-0840 CLAR:HARM MADI:UNIO
a. W-2858 Strother Settle
W-3049 John Branham*
b. -- Settle & -- Branhan*
c. None
* So spelled.

S-9822* 1400a -- -- FAYE:PAIN
a. --
b. John Tench
c. Richard Douglas, 1831
* Entry in Source A only.

S-9823 170a C:416 X-0639 LOGA:RUSH
a. W-2742 Jasper Hughes
b. Thomas Pemberton
c. None

S-9827 730a C:527 X-0360 PICK:MONR
a. W-6014 Benjamin Harrison, representatives of
b. Benjamin Harrison, representatives of
c. H. Reedy, 1840

S-9829
S-10466 62a C:511 X-0800 ADAM:SPRI
a. W-5781 Joseph Crockett
W-6184 Robert Hanson Harrison
b. Richard Rounsaville*
c. None
* Source A spells Roansaville.

S-9831* 45a -- -- FRAN:NORW
a. --
b. Jeremiah McLene
c. None
* Entry in Source A only.

S-9832 25a C:401 X-0840 MADI:STOK
a. W-5880 Thomas Porter
b. -- Ladds & -- Norvell
c. None

S-9833 9a C:407 X-0730 LOGA:JEFF
a. W-5880 Thomas Porter
b. -- Ladds & -- Norvell
c. None

S-9834 39a C:428 X-1180 CHAM:GOSH
a. W-5633 Nathaniel G. Morris
b. -- Ladds & -- Norvell
c. T. Stewart, 1823; William McCanesey?; J. Galloway

S-9835 20a C:437 X-1180 MADI:SUMM
a. W-5633 Nathaniel G. Morris
b. -- Ladds & -- Norvell
c. None

S-9836 80a C:411 X-0740 GREE:ROSS
a. W-5633 Nathaniel G. Morris
b. -- Ladds & -- Norvell
c. None

S-9837 150a C:411 X-0840 MADI:---* CLAR:MADI
a. W-6203 Robert Bolling
b. Edward Watts
c. None
* Source A does not mention Madison County.

S-9838 50a C:412 X-0660 MADI:---* CLAR:MADI
a. W-6203 Robert Bolling
b. Edward Watts
c. None
* Source A does not mention Madison County.

S-9839
S-10619 383a C:460 X-0360 MADI:DEER
a. W-5812 John Goodrich, heir (of?)
W-4919 Nathaniel Rowland, representative of Burwell (Rowland)
W-5123 Francis Lewis, administrator of the estate of William (Lewis)
W-5136 David Mason
W-6203 Robert Bolling
b. -- Galloway, -- Means, -- Mason, & -- Watts
c. None

S-9841 50a D:10 X-1180 MADI:DEER
a. W-5812 John Goodrich, heir (of?)
b. James Galloway*
c. None
* Source A says James Galloway, Junior.

S-9842 75a C:401 X-0730 X-1180 CHAM:GOSH
a. W-5817 John Goodrich, heir (of?)
b. James Galloway*
c. None
* Source A says James Galloway, Junior.

S-9846 25a C:508 X-0840 ROSS:HUNT
a. W-5338 Mathew Clay
b. Duncan McArthur
c. None

S-9847 144a C:401 X-0840 ROSS:HUNT
a. W-6244 Churchill Gibbs
b. Henry Beatty
c. William Buzzard, 1840

S-9848
S-10872 270a D:304 X-0360 PICK:MONR
a. W-5627 Nathaniel G. Morris
W-6064 William Connor
b. John A. Fulton
c. G. C. Wolfley, 1836; J. D. Lutz, 1838

S-9851*
S-10718
S-10719
S-12697 368a D:395 X-0870 X-0779 PIKE:----
a. W-587 Captain John Blackwell
W-6503 Allen Walker, devisee of
W-6504 Allen Walker, devisee of
b. Thomas Mountjoy
c. None
* Entry not listed in Source A.

S-9851. See also S-12697

S-9852* 126a C:409 X-0640 HIGH:FAIR
a. W-5907 Richard Savage, heirs of
b. -- Pope & -- Sanders
c. R. Cherry, 1826
* Source A notation: "Near Leesburg."

S-9854
S-13189 100a D:335 X-0841 MADI:RANG
a. W-6130 Richard M. Owen
b. Burton Blizzard
c. None

S-9858
S-10116 240a C:414 X-0840 HIGH:---* ROSS:PAXT
a. W-6160 Thomas Ray
W-5873 William Triplett? (Treplett?)
W-5870 Wood Baldwin, heirs of
b. -- Dunlap, -- Wallace, -- Ladd, & -- Norvell
c. None
* Source A does not mention Highland County.

S-9865* 55a -- -- PIKE:PEBB
a. --
b. John Harrison
c. None
* Entry in Source A only.

S-9866 40a D:110 X-0800 SCIO:NILE
a. W-6059 Jeremiah Kendall
b. Jeremiah Kendall
c. None

S-9867 10a D:110 X-0800 SCIO:NILE
a. W-6059 Jeremiah Kendall
b. Jeremiah Kendall
c. None

S-9868 90a D:66 X-0860 ROSS:HUNT
a. W-6218 William Yates
b. Walter Dun
c. None

S-9876. See S-4948 (in volume 4, part 1)

S-9877 18a C:407 X-1120 BROW:PLEA
a. W-4551 Harmon Nash (heir)
b. Harmon Nash
c. None

S-9878
S-10109
S-10718
S-10719 502a C:511 X-0730 LOGA:MONR
a. W-5885 William Mosby, deceased, by Ann W. Chamberlayn
W-5749 David Williams
W-6124 Thomas Hopper
W-5887 Thomas Herbert, representative of
W-5963 Barnabas Arthur
W-6064 William Connor
W-6765 --*
W-5916 Gross Scruggs
W-6173 Francis Thompson, heirs of
b. Walter Dun
c. M. Bonner, 1827
* Warrantee not listed in Source C.

S-9881 1000a C:453 X-0060 LOGA:MCAR
a. W-6260 Billy H. Avery
b. Hubbard Wyatt, executor
c. None

S-9883 1000a C:483 X-0229 LOGA:MCAR
a. W-3526 William Finne
b. Mark Hardin
c. James Hays, 1830

S-9884 1000a C:483 X-0229 LOGA:MCAR
a. W-5805 Joseph Hite
b. Joseph Hite
c. James Hays, 1830; George Irwin (Irwine?), 1832

S-9885 867a D:390 X-0130 LOGA:MCAR
a. W-5885 William Mosby, deceased, by Ann W. Chamberlayn
b. Walter Dun
c. M. Bonner, 1827

S-9887 208a C:466 X-0991 LOGA:RUSH
a. W-5437 John Jameson
b. John Jemison*
c. None
* Source A spells Jamison.

S-9887 792a C:467 X-0991 LOGA:RUSH
a. W-5437 John Jameson
W-5423 Lewis Booker
W-5548 Abraham Hite & James Taylor, assignee of said (Abraham) Hite
b. -- Jemison*, -- Booker*, -- Hite, & -- Taylor
c. Heirs of John Jameson; James Taylor, 1833; William Robinson; H. Hendrickson, 1830; Samuel Smith
* Source A may read -- Jameson & -- Bookes.

S-9888 1000a C:432 X-0750 LOGA:RUSH
a. W-5455 Charles Porterfield*, representatives of
b. Charles Potterfield*
c. John Porterfield; Nathan Hockett, 1841
* So spelled.

S-9889 180a D:148 X-0750 LOGA:RUSH
a. W-5447 James Taylor, assignee of John Spotswood
W-1474 Captain Francis Muir?*
b. -- Taylor & -- Minor*
c. Abraham Dearduff
* Possibly the same person or surname.

S-9889 106a D:24 X-0750 LOGA:RUSH
a. W-4785 Harriet? Starke & Maria Starke, representatives of Richard (Starke)
W-5513 Thomas Bowder? assignee of Batha? (Martha?) Lanier, widow, Barabas? Rowlings, & Lucy, his wife, late L. Lanier, --? of Thomas Lanier
b. -- Means & -- Clarke
c. None

S-9890 1000a C:465 X-0110 LOGA:BOAK
a. W-5444 Luke Cannon & James Taylor
W-6161 Thomas Ray
W-5646 Charles Pelham & James Taylor, assignee
b. -- Cannon, -- Taylor, -- Wilson, & -- Pelham
c. None

S-9891 999a C:433 X-0110 LOGA:BOAK
a. W-2027 Richard Richardson
W-2030 --*
W-2158 Lieutenant John Robinson
W-44 Captain Thomas Overton
b. -- Roberts, -- Robertson, & -- Overton
c. None
* Name illegible in Source C.

S-9892 1000a C:475 X-0110 LOGA:BOAK
a. W-5434 James Taylor, assignee of Francis Swain & John Graff
b. James Taylor
c. None

S-9893 472a C:474 X-0110 UNIO:WASH
LOGA:---*
a. W-5426 Maria & John Ransdale, heirs of Thomas Ransdale, deceased
b. M. Ranidale**, J. C. Ranidale**, & -- Taylor
c. Maria Ransall***; James Taylor, 1824
* Source A does not mention Logan County.
** Source A may read Ransdale.
*** Probably Ransdale is meant.

S-9893 528a C:474 X-0110 UNIO:WASH LOGA:---*
a. W-5426 Maria & John Ransdale, heirs of Thomas Ransdale, deceased
W-5436 Charles Scott
b. -- Ranidale**, -- Taylor, & -- Scott
c. None
* Source A does not mention Logan County.
** Presumably, Ransdale is the correct spelling.

S-9894 1000a C:472 X-0110 UNIO:WASH
a. W-5451 John Swan & James Taylor
b. -- Swan & -- Taylor
c. John Swan; John H. Hanson, 1824; M. S. Butler, 1836

S-9895 1000a C:467 X-0110 UNIO:WASH
a. W-5459 James Wallace, deceased, representatives of, & James Taylor
W-979 David Rumage
b. -- Wallace, -- Taylor, & -- McPherson
c. None

S-9896 364a D:5 X-0991 UNIO:WASH
a. W-5551 John Meanly
b. Thomas Scott
c. None

S-9896 100a D:5 X-0991 UNIO:WASH
a. W-2558 James Fitzpatrick, heir to So(lomon) Fitzpatrick
b. James Fitzpatrick
c. Ezra Reed, 1831

S-9897 815a C:472 X-1000 UNIO:WASH
a. W-5256 Robert Sayers & James Taylor
W-5645 Nicholas Taliaferro & James Taylor, assignee
W-4922 Whitehead Coleman, representatives of
b. -- Sayers, -- Taylor, -- Taliaferro, & -- Coleman
c. None

S-9897 185a C:472 X-1000 UNIO:WASH
a. W-5645 Nicholas Taliaferro & James Taylor, assignee
b. -- Taliaferro & -- Taylor
c. Nicholas Taliaferro; George H. Houser, 1824

S-9898 800a C:452 X-0991 UNIO:JACK
a. W-6235 William Yates, heirs of
W-6236 William Yates, heirs of
b. Ann Gholson
c. None

S-9898 200a C:452 X-0991 UNIO:JACK
a. W-3039 Major John Swan
b. John Swan
c. None

S-9899 833a C:453 X-0991 UNIO:JACK
a. W-6210 Robert Bolling
W-6211 Robert Bolling
W-6212 Robert Bolling
W-6213 Robert Bolling
W-6214 Robert Bolling
W-6215 Robert Bolling
b. Peyton Mason
c. None

S-9899 167a C:454 X-0991 UNIO:JACK
a. W-3039 Major John Swan
b. John Swan
c. None

S-9900 1000a C:534 X-1000 MARI:GREE UNIO:JACK
a. W-6248 Edward Garland, representatives of
b. John Neilson
c. N. W. Silence; E. Hardy, 1840

S-9901 1300a C:515 X-0991 UNIO:JACK
a. W-5743 William Green (illegible), representative of
b. Edward Stubblefield
c. None

S-9902 1000a C:488 X-0229 LOGA:MCAR
a. W-6310 Michael Rudolph
b. Michael Rudolph, representatives of
c. Allen Latham; Samuel Newell, 1826; William H. Beard, 1831

S-9903
S-9928 1600a D:25 X-0229 LOGA:MCAR
a. W-6187 Robert Hanson Harrison, heirs of
W-6188 Robert Hanson Harrison, heirs of
W-6189 Robert Hanson Harrison, heirs of
W-6190 Robert Hanson Harrison, heirs of
W-6195 Robert Hanson Harrison, heirs of
W-6194 Robert Hanson Harrison, heirs of
b. William H. Beard
c. None

S-9904 275a C:509 X-0229* LOGA:MCAR
a. W-1494 Captain Robert Gamble
b. Robert Gamble
c. W. Dun; R. Sample; M. Bonner, 1827
* North fork of.

S-9904 725a C:509 X-0060 LOGA:MCAR
a. W-1494 Captain Robert Gamble
b. Robert Gamble
c. None

S-9905 250a C:478 X-0060 LOGA:MCAR
a. W-6198 Simon Sommers
b. Simon Sommers
c. None

S-9905 500a C:479 X-0060 LOGA:MCAR
a. W-3585 Simon Sommers
b. Simon Sommers
c. J. Elder & C. Elder; O. L. Insurance & Trust Co., 1842

S-9905 246a C:479 X-0060 LOGA:MCAR
a. W-6198 Simon Sommers
b. Simon Sommers
c. None

S-9906 333a C:480 X-0060 LOGA:MCAR
a. W-5448 Thomas Pearson
b. Thomas Pearson
c. T. Jones; John Harrod, 1826; -- Pearson & -- Ralph; H. Hendrickson, 1831; J. Taylor

S-9907 700a C:447 X-0060 LOGA:RUSH
a. W-64 --*
b. Thomas Bowne
c. Lyne Starling, 1831
* Warrantee's name is illegible in Source C.

S-9907 272a C:447 X-0060 LOGA:MCAR
a. W-64 --*
b. Thomas Bowne
c. Henry Massie; S. Walker, 1835
* Warrantee's name is illegible in Source C.

S-9908 481a C:450 X-0991 X-0060 LOGA:RUSH
a. W-2257 Captain Chiswell Barrett
b. Chiswell Barrett
c. None

S-9908 481a C:450 X-0991 LOGA:RUSH
a. W-2257 Captain Chiswell Barrett
b. Chiswell Barrett
c. None

S-9909 472a C:474 X-0991 LOGA:RUSH
a. W-5491 Nathaniel Pendleton & James Taylor
b. Nathaniel Pendleton
c. None

S-9909 487a C:474 X-0991 LOGA:RUSH
a. W-5491 Nathaniel Pendleton & James Taylor
W-4951 Matthew Griggs? (Gregg?)
W-4922 Whitehead Coleman, representatives of
b. -- Pendleton, -- Taylor, -- Gregg, & -- Coleman
c. None

S-9910 450a D:435 X-0991 LOGA:RUSH
a. W-5160 John Moore
b. John Moore, representatives of
c. None

S-9910 550a D:345 X-0991 LOGA:RUSH
a. W-5157 Thomas D. Harris & James Gilmore, assignees of David Mason
b. James Gilmore
c. Lyne Starling, 1831

S-9911 100a D:324 X-0750 LOGA:RUSH
a. W-2968 Charles Barker
b. John Griffith, assignee of -- Barker
c. Charles Barker; Lyne Starling

S-9911* 223a -- -- LOGA:RUSH LOGA:MILL
a. W-2898 Thomas Lewis, representatives of
b. William M. Kenton, assignee
c. None
* Entry in Source A only.

S-9911* 200a -- -- LOGA:BOAK LOGA:RUSH
a. W-4483 Isham Turner
b. William M. Kenton, assignee
c. None
* Entry in Source A only.

S-9912* 1000a -- -- LOGA:BOAK
a. W-854 Lieutenant Nicholas Taliaferro
b. Nicholas Taliaferro
c. None
* Entry in Source A only (after S-9914)

S-9913 50a C:473 X-0110 LOGA:BOAK
a. W-5145 George Henning
b. George Henning
c. None

S-9913 294a C:473 X-0110 LOGA:BOAK
a. W-5465 John Swan & James Taylor
b. -- Willis, -- Henning, & -- Plodd
c. None

S-9913 100a C:473 X-0110 LOGA:BOAK
a. W-5855 John Plodd
b. John Plodd
c. None

S-9913 258a C-473 X-0110 LOGA:BOAK
a. W-5451 John Swan & James Taylor
b. -- Swan & -- Taylor
c. John Swan; James Taylor, 1831

S-9913* 258a C:473 X-0110 LOGA:BOAK
a. W-5451 John Swan & James Taylor
b. -- Swan & -- Taylor
c. None
* Duplicate entry?

S-9914 983a C:468 X-0991 X-0110 LOGA:BOAK
a. W-5440 James Taylor, assignee of Joshua Barber, legal representative of Thomas Barber
b. James Taylor
c. None

S-9915 959a C:467 X-0110 UNIO:---* LOGA:BOAK
a. W-5461 Representatives of Willoby Tibbs? (Tebbs?) & John Tibbs? (Tebbs?), deceased, & James Taylor
W-4946 John Tibbs? (Tebbs?)
W-139 Lieutenant Markes Vandewall
b. -- Tibbs & -- Vandewall**
c. W. Tibbs; H. Hendrickson, 1834
* Source A does not mention Union County.
** Source A says: "-- Tibbs, -- Tibbs, & -- Vandawall (so spelled)."

S-9916 833a D:4 X-0991 UNIO:WASH
a. W-5823 William Darke*, representatives of
b. William Dark*, representatives of
c. James Taylor, 1831
* So spelled.

S-9917 400a C:445 X-0991 UNIO:WASH
a. W-5789 Rowland Madison
b. Rowland Madison, representatives of
c. J. Biegelow, 1837; L. Curtis

S-9917 600a C:445 X-0991 UNIO:WASH
a. W-5789 Rowland Madison
b. Rowland Madison, representatives of
c. None

S-9918 667a D:198 X-0991 UNIO:WASH
a. W-4036 Lieutenant James Berwick
b. James Berwick
c. Lyne Starling, 1831

S-9919 1000a D:24 X-0991 UNIO:JACK
a. W-5048 Thomas Woodlief, representative of Francis Epps
b. Thomas Miller
c. None

S-9920 1000a C:454 X-0991 UNIO:JACK
a. W-3039 Major John Swan
W-5048 Thomas Woodlief, representative of Francis Epps
b. John Swan
c. M. S. Butler, 1836

S-9921 400a C:450 X-0991 UNIO:JACK
a. W-2050 Nathaniel Triplett? (Treplett?)
b. Nathaniel Triplett
c. None

S-9921 600a C:450 X-0991 UNIO:JACK
a. W-91 General George Weedon
b. George Weedon
c. None

S-9922 1000a C:434 X-0991 UNIO:JACK
a. W-5462 John Blackwell, Junior, & James Taylor
W-617 Captain Alexander Breckenridge
b. -- Blackwell, -- Taylor, & -- Breckenridge
c. Heirs of J. Blackwell

S-9923 333a C:438 X-1000 MARI:GREE
a. W-5556 Henry Conway
b. Francis Preston
c. Abra(ha)m Hardin, 1829; Aaron Markle; G. W. Bartlett, 1838; D. Markle; R. Patten, 1840

S-9923 333a C:438 X-1000 MARI:GREE
a. W-5556 Henry Conway
b. Francis Preston
c. E. S. Haines; Charles L. Boalt, 1828; John G. Clark, 1841

S-9923 333a C:438 X-1000 MARI:GREE
a. W-5556 Henry Conway
b. Francis Preston
c. E. S. Haines; George H. Busby, 1828

S-9925
S-9946
S-10121 1050a C:417 X-0060 LOGA:WASH
a. W-6202 Simon Sommers
W-5877 William Triplett? (Treplett?)
W-6217 Thomas Triplett? (Treplett?)
W-5840 Nathaniel Fox, Senior? heirs of
W-6218 William Yates
W-5718 John Spelfatham? (Spilfatham?)
W-6120 Thomas Hopper
W-6124 Thomas Hopper
W-6222 Charles Walden
W-5825 Richard Foster, heirs of
W-6216 William Holt
W-5828 William Cunningham, heirs of
b. Walter Dun
c. M. Bonner, 1827

S-9927 500a C:488 X-0229 LOGA:MCAR
a. W-6246 Edward Garland, heirs of
b. Nathan Rewes? (Reeves?)*
c. W. Dun; M. Bonner, 1827
* Source A spells Reeves.

S-9928. See S-9903

S-9929 100a* C:486 X-0060 LOGA:MCAR
a. W-5351 Cole Digges
b. Robert Means
c. John P. Cothon; Adcock Carter, 1833; James Carter; S. Walker, 1836; J. B. Clagg, 1836
* Source A says 1000 acres.

S-9930 1000a C:449 X-0060 LOGA:MCAR
a. W-4688 Charles Lewis, deceased, representatives of
b. Charley* Lewis
c. None
* Source A says Charles.

S-9931 1000a C:436 X-0060 LOGA:MCAR
a. W-5392 Samuel Arnold
W-5376 Thomas M. Bayly, assignee of Rachel Richardson, representative of William Richards(on?)
W-5372 Thomas M. Bayly, assignee of Jonathan Bunting, representative of Holloway Bunting
b. James Taylor
c. H. Hendrickson, 1831

S-9932 1000a C:447 X-0060 LOGA:MCAR
a. W-5194 Thomas M. Bayly, assignee of Arthur Chenix?
W-5199 Thomas M. Bayly, assignee of Southey Copis? (Copes?)
W-4069 James Ewing, Junior, heir to Edward (Ewing)
W-5203 Thomas M. Bayly, assignee of George Justice
W-5204 Thomas M. Bayly, assignee of Thomas Bagwell

W-5208 Thomas M. Bayly, assignee of George Nock
W-5364 Thomas M. Bayly, assignee of Soneth? Nelson?
W-5207 Thomas M. Bayly, assignee of Micajah Annis
W-5372 Thomas M. Bayly, assignee of Jonathan Bunting, representative of Holloway Bunting
b. Henry Massie
c. J. Smith; R. Dow, 1837

S-9933 400a C:449 X-0060 LOGA:RUSH
a. W-6044 Thomas Christie, heirs of
b. Thomas Christie, representatives of
c. None

S-9933* 200a D:42 X-0060 LOGA:RUSH
a. W-3838 Leonard Helm
b. Thomas Miller
c. None
* Source A lists this entry and the following one together.

S-9933* 400a D:42 X-0060 LOGA:RUSH
a. W-5513 Thomas Bowder? assignee of Batha? (Martha?) Lanier, widow, Barabas? Rallings? & Lucy, his wife, late L. Lanier's, the --? of Thomas Lanier
W-6044 Thomas Christie, heirs of
b. -- Clarke & -- Christie
c. None
* Source A lists this entry together with the preceding one.

S-9934 4a C:454 X-0991 LOGA:RUSH
a. W-3039 Major John Swan
b. John Swan
c. None

S-9934* 717a -- -- LOGA:RUSH
a. W-5888 David Wallace, representatives of
b. David Wallace, representatives of
c. None
* Entry in Source A only.

S-9934* 280a -- -- LOGA:RUSH
a. W-6262 Billy H. Avery
W-6263 Billy H. Avery
b. Hubbard Wyatt, executors of
c. None
* Entry in Source A only.

S-9935 1000a C:482 X-1000 HARD:TAYL
a. W-4937 John Harrison
W-6098 Harry Terrell
W-5999 William Triplett? (Treplett?)
W-6000 William Triplett? (Treplett?)
W-5998 William Triplett? (Treplett?)
W-3221 William Reynold(s), assignee of John Fantleroy (Fauntleroy), heir to --? Fantleroy (Fauntleroy)
b. -- Dun & -- Harrison
c. M. Bonner, 1827

S-9936 1000a D:198 X-0991 LOGA:RUSH
a. W-4036 Lieutenant James Berwick
b. James Burwick*
c. None
* Source A spells Berwick.

S-9937 1000a C:435 X-1000 LOGA:RUSH
a. W-5460 Elizabeth Morrow, administrator? of David Morrow, heir to Robert Morrow, deceased
W-5456 James Taylor, assignee of James Williams, executor
b. -- Morrow & -- Taylor
c. None

S-9938 600a C:446 X-0991 LOGA:BOAK
a. W-5789 Rowland Madison
b. Rowland Madison, representatives of
c. None

S-9938 400a C:446 X-0991 LOGA:BOAK
a. W-5789 Rowland Madison
b. Rowland Madison, representatives of
c. None

S-9940 400a D:342 X-0991 UNIO:JACK
a. W-5471 Edward Smith
b. Edward Smith
c. J. S. Gregory, 1831

S-9941 533a C:453 X-0991 MARI:BOWL
a. W-1474 Captain Francis Muir?
b. Francis Muire*
c. None
* Source A spells Muir.

S-9941 267a C:453 X-0991 MARI:---* UNIO:JACK
a. W-3039 Major John Swan
b. John Swan
c. M. S. Butten, 1836
* Source A does not mention Marion County.

S-9941 200a C:453 X-0991 MARI:---* UNIO:JACK
a. W-6054 Keda? Hobbs
b. Phineas Sanborn
c. James Taylor, 1826
* Source A does not mention Marion County.

S-9942 278a C:466 X-0991 UNIO:JACK
a. W-5422 Mayo Carrington, representatives of
b. Mayo Carrington
c. James Taylor, 1826; John Stokes; Thomas Taylor, 1833

S-9942 278a C:466 X-0991 UNIO:---* MARI:BOWL
a. W-5422 Mayo Carrington, representatives of
b. Mayo Carrington
c. None
* Source A does not mention Union County.

S-9942 194a C:466 X-0991 MARI:BOWL
a. W-5261 Abraham Buford

b. Abraham Buford
c. None

S-9942 194a C:466 X-0991 MARI:---*
a. W-5261 Abraham Buford
b. Abraham Buford
c. None
* Source A does not give location; might be a duplication of the preceding entry.

S-9942 57a -- -- UNIO:JACK
a. W-1396 Captain John Stokes
b. John Stokes
c. None

S-9943 111a C:465 X-1000 MARI:---* UNIO:JACK
a. W-5406 Anthony Singleton, representatives of
b. Anthony Singleton
c. None
* Source A does not mention Marion County.

S-9943 888a C:465 X-1000 UNIO:JACK MARI:---*
a. W-5331 David Stephenson & James Taylor
W-5406 Anthony Singleton, representatives of
b. -- Taylor, -- Stephens**, & -- Singleton
* Source A does not mention Marion County.
** Source A says Stephenson.

S-9943* 111a -- -- ----:----
a. W-5406 Anthony Singleton, representatives of
b. Anthony Singleton
c. None
* Entry in Source A only; no location given.

S-9944 1000a C:432 X-1000 MARI:GREE
a. W-5455 Charles Porterfield, representatives of
b. Charley Potterfield*
c. James Taylor; Edmond S. Eubanks, 1828
* Source A spells Porterfield.

S-9945 583a C:476 X-1000 MARI:GREE
a. W-5452 Richard Taylor
W-5350 Reverend Alexander Balmain
b. -- Taylor & -- Balmain
c. None

S-9945 417a C:476 X-1000 MARI:GREE
a. W-5350 Reverend Alexander Balmain
b. Alexander Balmain
c. None

S-9946. See S-9925

S-9947 1000a C:448 X-0060 LOGA:MCAR
a. W-5382 Thomas Taylor, administrator of the estate of John McAdam
b. George Clark
c. A. H. Mefford; William Clagg, 1841; George K. Mefford; Peter Leister, 1841

S-9948 1000a C:488 X-0060 LOGA:MCAR
a. W-5382 Thomas Taylor, administrator of the estate of John McAdam
W-5514 Thomas Lanier, representatives of
b. George Clark
c. None

S-9949 1000a C:444 X-0060 LOGA:MCAR
a. W-3224 Michael Bowyer
b. Michael Bowyer
c. None

S-9950 1000a C:445 X-0060 LOGA:MCAR
a. W-3224 Michael Bowyer
b. Michael Bowyer
c. Abraham Ammine?

S-9951 1000a C:445 X-0060 LOGA:MCAR
a. W-3224 Michael Bowyer
b. Michael Bowyer
c. Joel Ryster; William Leese, 1832

S-9952 690a C:509 X-0060 LOGA:MCAR
a. W-5221 Thomas D. Harris, assignee of John Peyer?
W-5226 Thomas D. Harris, assignee of John Peyer?
b. Robert Means
c. None

S-9952 288a C:509 X-0060 LOGA:MCAR
a. W-5101 William Bird, assignee of Philip Courtney
b. Robert Means
c. L. B. Wysong, 1835

S-9953* 300a C:482 X-0060 LOGA:RUSH
a. W-2558 James Fitzpatrick, heir to So(lomon) Fitzpatrick
b. James Fitzpatrick
c. Duncan McArthur, 1831
* Source A notation: "Not patented."

S-9953 700a C:482 X-0060 LOGA:RUSH
a. W-850 --*
b. Robert Vance
c. William McDonald, 1840
* Warrantee not listed in Source C.

S-9954 1000a C:475 X-0060 LOGA:RUSH
a. W-5440 James Taylor, assignee of Joshua Barber, legal representative of Thomas Barber
W-5453 William Taylor
b. James William Taylor
c. D. Woods & A. Savage

S-9954* 17a -- -- ROSS:----
a. --
b. George Handy
c. David Breedlove; Joshua Seney, 1839
* Entry in Source A only, where crossed out.

S-9955* 500a C:448 X-0060 LOGA:RUSH
a. W-6053 James Burton
b. James Burton
c. Francis Goodrich; N. Z. McCulloch, 1837
* Source A notation: "Big Spring."

S-9955 500a C:447 X-0060 LOGA:RUSH
a. W-6053 James Burton
b. James Burton
c. None

S-9956 1000a C:439 X-1000 LOGA:RUSH
a. W-2740 Captain James Wright
b. James Wright
c. Ezekiel S. Haines; Sanson? Curtis, 1828

S-9957 300a D:53 X-1000 HARD:DUDL
a. W-2338 Lieutenant Philip Stewart
b. Philip Stewart
c. W. Dun; M. Bonner, 1827

S-9957 700a D:54 X-1000 HARD:DUDL
a. W-2338 Lieutenant Philip Stewart
b. Philip Stewart
c. W. Dun; M. Bonner, 1827; Henry Ramo? 1830; Jacob Dick; Daniel Barron, 1837; E. Fisher, 1842

S-9958 1000a C:488 X-0991 LOGA:BOAK
a. W-735 Captain Alexander Parker, heir to Colonel -- Parker
b. Alexander Parker
c. None

S-9959 1000a C:486 X-0991 LOGA:BOAK
a. W-5359 Thomas D. Harris, assignee of Francis Smith
W-5351 Cole Digges
b. Robert Means
c. William Collins, 1834

S-9960
S-10042 2000a C:533 X-0991 UNIO:WASH
HARD:HALE
LOGA:---*
a. W-6310 Michael Rudolph
b. Michael Rudolph, representatives of
c. Lyne Starling, 1831

S-9963 1000a C:475 X-0991 MARI:BOWL
a. W-4911 John Taylor
b. John Taylor
c. None

S-9964 1000a C:472 X-0991 MARI:BOWL
a. W-5449 Thomas Overton & James Taylor
W-5450 Beverley Stubblefield
b. -- Overton, -- Taylor, & -- Stubblefield
c. None

S-9965 333a C:439 X-1000 MARI:GREE
a. W-5557 Henry Conway
b. Francis Preston
c. E. S? (L?) Haines; George H. Busby, 1828; Hugh Cummings; Elisha Hardy, 1835

S-9965 333a C:439 X-1000 MARI:GREE
a. W-5557 Henry Conway
b. Francis Preston
c. E. S? (L?) Haines; Charles L. Boalt, 1828

S-9965 333a C:439 X-1000 MARI:GREE
a. W-5557 Henry Conway
b. Francis Preston
c. E. S? (L?) Haines; Charles L. Boalt, 1828

S-9966 1000a C:433 X-1000 MARI:GREE
a. W-5247 Robert Young, representatives of
b. Robert Young, representatives of
c. E. Arris & M. Arris; E. Hardy, 1840

S-9967 333a C:438 X-1000 MARI:GREE
a. W-5558 Henry Conway
b. Francis Preston
c. George H. Busby, 1828

S-9967 333a C:438 X-1000 MARI:GREE
a. W-5558 Henry Conway
b. Francis Preston
c. None

S-9967 333a C:438 X-1000 MARI:GREE
a. W-5558 Henry Conway
b. Francis Preston
c. None

S-9968 611a E:147 X-0060 LOGA:MCAR
a. W-5431 Churchill Jones & James Taylor
b. James Taylor
c. None

S-9968* 1000a -- -- ----:----
a. W-5431 Churchill Jones & James Taylor
W-5443 John Steel
b. -- Jones, -- Taylor, & -- Steel
c. None
* Entry in Source A only.

S-9969 1000a C:436 X-0060 LOGA:MCAR
a. W-5445 Francis Taylor, deceased, representatives of
W-5276 James Taylor, assignee of Shadrach Pierson
W-5372 Thomas M. Bayly, assignee of Jonathan Bunting, representative of Holloway Bunting
b. Francis Taylor & J. Taylor, representatives of
c. None

S-9970 1000a C:434 X-0060 LOGA:MCAR
a. W-5247 Robert Young, representatives of
b. Robert Young, representatives of
c. James Morton, 1840

S-9971 572a C:479 X-0060 LOGA:MCAR
a. W-5417 Benjamin Temple, representatives of
W-5834 Nathaniel Beall
W-5835 Nathaniel Beall
W-5859 John Crittenden*
b. -- Temple, -- Beale, & -- Crittendon*
c. James Taylor; H. Hendrickson, 1831; heirs of John Crittendon*
* So spelled.

S-9971 278a C:479 X-0060 LOGA:MCAR
a. W-5417 Benjamin Temple

b. Benjamin Temple, representatives of
c. Nathaniel Beall; H. Hendrickson, 1830; J. Taylor?

S-9971 150a C:479 X-0060 LOGA:MCAR
a. W-5835 Nathaniel Beall*
b. Nathaniel Beale*
c. Solomon McCullock, 1827
* So spelled.

S-9972 778a C:471 X-0060 LOGA:MCAR
a. W-5457 John Gilleson, representatives of
W-5146 Robert Kirk & James Taylor
b. -- Gillison*, -- Taylor, & -- Kirk
c. None
* Source A spells Gilleson.

S-9972 222a C:472 X-0060 LOGA:MCAR
a. W-5146 Robert Kirk & James Taylor
b. Robert Kirk
c. None

S-9973 675a C:486 X-0060 LOGA:MCAR
a. W-5383 Robert Means, assignee of Thomas D. Haris, who was assignee of Thomas Taylor, administrator of John McAdam
W-5184 Samuel C. Leman
W-5169 Thomas D. Harris, assignee of Erasmus Gill, administrator of Peter Minor
b. Robert Means
c. None

S-9974 550a C:483 X-0060 LOGA:RUSH
a. W-5637 James Barnett
W-5104 Samuel March?, assignee of Joseph Smith
b. Duncan McArthur
c. Isaac Zane, Junior, 1831

S-9974 390a C:516 X-0060 LOGA:RUSH
a. W-5743 William Green (illegible), representatives of
b. Duncan McArthur
c. None

S-9975 1000a C:435 X-0060 LOGA:RUSH
a. W-5439 William Miller, representatives of
W-5089 John Green, representatives of
W-5257 Thomas Martin & James Taylor
W-5363 Thomas M. Bayly, assignee of George Wright, executor of Abel Wright
W-5408 or W-5418 Thomas M. Bayly, assignee of the representatives of Benjamin Phillips or Thomas Jones
b. -- Miller, -- Martin, -- Green, & -- Taylor
c. James Stephenson; H. Hendrickson, 1834; Samuel Mason, Junior

S-9976 1000a C:431 X-0060 LOGA:RUSH
a. W-1474 Captain Francis Muir
b. Francis Muire*
c. None
* Source A spells Muir.

S-9977 1000a C:486 X-1000 LOGA:RUSH
a. W-5351 Cole Digges
b. Robert Means
c. None

S-9978 333a C:470 X-1000 LOGA:RUSH
a. W-5446 John Spotswood, representatives of
b. John Spotswood, representatives of*
c. James Taylor, 1831
* Sold to Charles Lofland at judgment sale of 8 February 1827 (per schedule bound in Source A register, S-10012). "Lands are all north of Indian boundary."

S-9978 667a C:471 X-1000 LOGA:RUSH HARD:---*
a. W-5085 Robert Porterfield
b. -- Potterfield** & -- Taylor
c. James Taylor; H. Hendrickson, 1832; William Kinney, Junior; E. M. McCulloch, 1840
* Source A does not mention Hardin County.
** Source A spells Porterfield.

S-9979 1000a D:24 X-1000 MARI:BOWL HARD:---*
a. W-5043 Thomas Woodlief?, representative of Francis Epps, deceased
b. Thomas Miller
c. None
* Source A does not mention Hardin County.

S-9980 1000a D:24 X-1000 MARI:BOWL
a. W-4688 Charles Lewis, deceased, representatives of
b. Charles Lewis, representatives of
c. None

S-9981 417a C:437 X-1000 MARI:BOWL
a. W-5347 Edward Carrington
b. Edward Carrington
c. James Taylor, 1827

S-9981 584a C:437 X-1000 MARI:BOWL
a. W-5347 Edward Carrington
W-5091 Thomas Overton & James Taylor
b. -- Carrington, -- Overton, & -- Taylor
c. E. Carrington; Edmond S. Eubank, 1828

S-9982 999a C:467 X-1000 MARI:BOWL
a. W-5548 Abraham Hite & James Taylor, assignee of said (Abraham) Hite
W-5442 James Pendleton & James Taylor
W-5447 James Taylor, assignee of John Spotswood
b. -- Hite, -- Taylor, -- Pendleton, & -- Taylor
c. James Pendleton; E. W. H. Reed, 1831

S-9983 1000a C:536 X-1000 MARI:BOWL
a. W-6310 Michael Rudolph
b. Michael Rudolph, representatives of
c. Lyne Starling, 1831

S-9984 1000a D:43 X-1000 MARI:GREE
a. W-735 Captain Alexander Parker, heir to Colonel -- Parker
b. Alexander Parker
c. None

S-9985 548a C:439 X-1000 MARI:GREE
a. W-5252 James Knox
b. James Knox
c. None

S-9985 243a C:440 X-1000 MARI:GREE
a. W-5252 James Knox
W-4951 Matthew Griggs (Gregg?)
b. -- Knox & -- Gregg
c. None

S-9985 209a C:440 X-1000 MARI:GREE
a. W-5222 William Boyce
b. William Boyce
c. None

S-9987 445a C:468 X-0060 LOGA:MCAR
a. W-5330 William Robertson* & James Taylor
b. -- Taylor & -- Robinson*
c. None
* So spelled.

S-9987 551a C:468 X-0060 LOGA:RUSH LOGA:MCAR
a. W-5330 William Robertson* & James Taylor
W-5343 Andrew Waggoner
b. -- Taylor, -- Morrison, & -- Robison*
c. John Whisler; H. Hendrickson, 1836
* So spelled.

S-9988
S-9997 353a C:502 X-0060 HARD:---* LOGA:MCAR
a. W-1348 Lieutenant David Allen
b. John Beal**
c. None
* Source A does not mention Hardin County.
** Source A spells Beale.

S-9988 361a C:478 X-0060 LOGA:MCAR
a. W-5348 Nathaniel Burwell, representatives of
b. Nathaniel Burwell, representatives of
c. John Bealle; Henry H. Hendrickson, 1832; James Taylor

S-9988 361a C:478 X-1000 LOGA:MCAR
a. W-5348 Nathaniel Burwell, representatives of
b. Nathaniel Burwell, representatives of
c. None

S-9989 1000a C:432 X-0060 HARD:---* LOGA:MCAR
a. W-44 Captain Thomas Overton
b. Thomas Overton
c. None
* Source A does not mention Hardin County.

S-9990* 1000a -- -- ----:----
a. W-4906 Thomas Fox
b. Ephraim Rolple? (Ralph?)
c. None
* Entry in Source A only.

S-9990* -- -- -- ----:----
a. W-4906 Thomas Fox
b. Ephraim Ralph
c. None
* Entry in Source A only.

S-9990* -- -- -- ----:----
a. W-4906 Thomas Fox
b. Ephraim Ralph
c. None
* Entry in Source A only.

S-9991 1000a C:435 X-0060 HARD:TAYL LOGA:MCAR
a. W-5854 William Grayson?, representatives of
W-5548 Abraham Hite & James Taylor, assignee of said (Abraham) Hite
W-5646 Charles Pelham & James Taylor, assignee
b. -- Grayson, -- Hite, -- Taylor, & -- Pelham
c. James Taylor; H. Hendrickson, 1832

S-9992 1000a C:432 X-1000 X-0060 HARD:TAYL LOGA:---*
a. W-5455 Charles Porterfield, representatives of
b. Charley Potterfield**, representatives of
c. None
* Source A does not mention Logan County.
** Source A spells Porterfield.

S-9993 1000a C:434 X-1000 X-0060 HARD:TAYL
a. W-5458 James Taylor, assignee of George W. B. Spooner, executor of Gustavus B. Wallace
W-4922 Whitehead Coleman, representatives of
b. -- Taylor & representatives of -- Coleman
c. None

S-9994 1000a C:434 X-1000 HARD:TAYL
a. W-5430 James Taylor, assignee of Lipscomb Norvell? (Nowell?)
W-5441 James Taylor, assignee of Robert Craddock
W-5329 James Taylor, assignee of William H. Cabell, attorney in fact for Henry Read
W-5095 James Taylor, assignee of James McGuire
W-5436 Charles Scott
W-5432 Francis Gray
b. -- Taylor, -- Scott, & -- Gray
c. None

S-9995 900a E:336 X-1000 HARD:DUDL
a. W-681 Captain Lieutenant Will(iam) Brownlee
b. William Brownlee, heirs of
c. Lyne Starling, 1831 (Logan County)

S-9996 1000a C:469 X-0060 HARD:---* MARI:BOWL
a. W-5253 Oliver Towle & James Taylor
W-5249 Robert Gamble

b. -- Febiger**, -- Taylor, & -- Morrison
c. None
* Source A does not mention Hardin County.
** Source A spells Febeger.

S-9997. See S-9988

S-9998 500a C:470 X-0060 HARD:MCDO LOGA:---*
a. W-5253 Oliver Towle** & James Taylor
W-5249 Robert Gamble
b. -- Towles**, -- Taylor, & -- Gamble
c. O. Towles**; Solomon McCullock, 1827; James Taylor; H. Hendrickson, 1831; -- Burwell & -- Beall
* Source A does not give township.
** So spelled.

S-9998 375a C:470 X-0060 HARD:MCDO
a. W-5353 Oliver Towle* & James Taylor
b. -- Towles*, & -- Taylor
c. None
* So spelled.

S-9998 125a C:470 X-0060 HARD:MCDO
a. W-5249 Robert Gamble
b. Robert Gamble
c. None

S-9999 1000a C:475 X-0060 HARD:TAYL
a. W-5427 James Taylor, assignee of Robert Baylor, executor of Whitehead (Baylor?)
W-5435 William B. Wallace
W-5430 James Taylor, assignee of Lipscomb Norvell? (Nowell?)
b. James Taylor
c. None

S-10000 445a C:477 X-1000 HARD:TAYL LOGA:---*
a. W-5261 Abraham Buford
b. Abraham Buford
c. H. Hendrickson, 1832
* Source A does not give township.

S-10000 167a C:477 X-1000 HARD:TAYL
a. W-1348 Lieutenant David Allen
b. John Beale
c. None

S-10001 889a C:470 X-1000 HARD:TAYL LOGA:---*
a. W-5328 Joseph Scott, Senior
W-5428 Thomas Fox & James Taylor
b. -- Fox, -- Taylor, & -- Scott
c. James Taylor; H. Hendrickson, 1831
* Source A does not give township.

S-10001 111a C:470 X-1000 HARD:TAYL
a. W-5428 Thomas Fox & James Taylor
b. -- Fox & -- Taylor
c. None

S-10004 980a C:485 X-1000 HARD:HALE
a. W-5101 William Bird, assignee of Philip Courtney
W-5470 Robert Means, assignee of Edward Smith
W-5424 Thomas D. Harris, assignee of John Quailes, executor of John Peyton, deceased
b. -- Means & -- Harris
c. None

S-10005 1000a D:343 X-1000 HARD:HALE
a. W-196 Captain James Mabon*
b. James Mabin*
c. L. Sterling*; Lyne Starling* (Logan County), 1831
* So spelled.

S-10006* 1000a C:507 X-1000 HARD:DUDL
a. W-2052 Captain Abraham Kirkpatrick
b. Abraham Kirkpatrick
c. A. Kirk**
* Sold to A. Latham at judgment sale of 8 February 1827 (per schedule bound in register, Source A, S-10012). "Lands are all north of Indian Boundary."
** May be partially erased.

S-10009 500a C:449 X-1000 HARD:ROUN
a. W-5513 Thomas Bowyer, assignee of Martha? Lanier, widow, Barnabas? Rallings? & his wife Lucy, late L. Lanier, children of Thomas Lanier
b. George Clarke*
c. None
* Source A spells Clark.

S-10010 1000a D:343 X-1000 HARD:MCDO HARD:ROUN
a. W-5089 John Green, representatives of
b. John Green, representatives of
c. None

S-10011 1000a D:43 X-0060 HARD:MCDO LOGA:---*
a. W-6053 James Burton
b. James Burton
c. Henry Hendrickson, 1828; Nancy Brown; William Taylor, 1832; heirs of William Taylor
* Source A does not give township.

S-10012 1000a C:477 X-0060 HARD:TAYL LOGA:---*
a. W-821 Colonel Samuel Hawes
b. Samuel Hawes
c. James Taylor; H. Hendrickson, 1831
* Source A does not give township.

S-10013 660a C:454 X-1000 HARD:TAYL
a. W-1159 William Mercer, heir to General H. Mercer
b. Smith Sneed*
c. Smith Snead*; Lyne Starling, 1831 (Logan County); patented to Sarah Y? Snead*
* So spelled.

S-10013 320a C:455 X-1000 HARD:TAYL
a. W-6269 Billy H. Avery
b. Hubbard Wyatt
c. None

S-10014 555a C-471 X-1000 HARD:TAYL
a. W-5259 Robert Porterfield & James Taylor
b. -- Potterfield* & -- Taylor
c. None
* Source A spells Porterfield.

S-10014 223a C:471 X-1000 HARD:TAYL
a. W-5454 Samuel Hopkins
b. Samuel Hopkins
c. None

S-10014 222a C:471 X-1000 HARD:TAYL
a. W-5454 Samuel Hopkins
b. Samuel Hopkins
c. None

S-10015 250a C:476 X-1000 HARD:TAYL LOGA:---*
a. W-9 Lieutenant Colonel Samuel J. Cabell
b. Samuel J. Cabell
c. James Taylor
* Source A does not give township.

S-10015* 250a C:476 X-1000 HARD:TAYL
a. W-9 Lieutenant Colonel Samuel J. Cabell
b. Samuel J. Cabell
c. James Taylor; -- Cabell & -- Cline; H. Hendrickson, 1831
* Owner was Frederick Cline; sold to Charles Lofland at judgment sale of 8 February 1827 (per schedule, Source A at S-10012). "Lands are all north of Indian Boundary."

S-10015 500a C-476 X-1000 HARD:TAYL
a. W-5479 Nathaniel Fox
b. Frederick Cline
c. None

S-10016 1000a* C:483 X-1000 HARD:HALE
a. W-3167 William Bayles
W-3548 Henry Bales**
b. William Bayles & Henry Bayles**
c. A. C. Barnes; A. McConnel, 1840; Lyne Starling, 1831; Eli Arnold, 1831
* Five hundred acres sold to Harvey D. Evans at judgment sale of 8 February 1825 (per schedule, Source A, at S-10012). "Lands all north of the Indian Boundary."
** So spelled.

S-10017* 1000a -- -- ----:----
a. W-5803 John Remay, representatives of
b. Anthony Walk, assignee
c. None
* Entry in Source A only.

S-10018* 1000a -- -- ----:----
a. W-5803 John Remay, representatives of
b. Anthony Walk
c. None
* Entry in Source A only.

S-10019 1000a C:485 X-1000 HARD:HALE
a. W-5245 Robert Means, assignee of Thomas D. Harris, who was assignee of John Cobbs, heir to Samuel Cobbs
b. Robert Means
c. None

S-10020 1000a D:199 X-1000 HARD:DUDL
a. W-4036 Lieutenant James Berwick
b. James Berwick
c. Lyne Starling; James Berwick

S-10021 1000a D:61 X-1000 HARD:DUDL
a. W-5470 Robert Means, assignee of Edward Smith
b. Robert Means
c. None

S-10022 1000a C:469 X-1000 HARD:DUDL
a. W-5860 Christian Febiger* & James Taylor
b. -- Febeger* & -- Taylor
c. None
* So spelled.

S-10025* 1000a -- -- ----:----
a. W-2443 Captain William Pierce
b. William Pierce
c. None
* Entry in Source A only.

S-10026 333a* D:42 X-0060 X-1000 HARD:TAYL
a. W-3224 Michael Bowyer
b. Michael Bowyer
c. Lyne Starling, 1831 (Logan County)
* Source A says 667 acres.

S-10026 333a D:42 X-0060 X-1000 HARD:TAYL
a. W-3224 Michael Bowyer
b. Michael Bowyer
c. None

S-10026* 334a C:444 X-0060 HARD:----
a. W-3224 Michael Bowyer
b. Michael Bowyer
c. None
* This third entry is not shown in Source A but no doubt indicates the halving of the penultimate entry for 667 acres.

S-10027
S-10247
S-10293 997a D:156 X-1000 HARD:TAYL
a. W-5223 Robert Means, assignee of Thomas D. Harris, who was assignee of (Doctor) Bazel Middleton
W-5424 Thomas D. Harris, assignee of John Quailes, executor of the estate of John Peyton, deceased
b. -- Means & -- Harris
c. None

S-10029 1000a C:489 X-1000 HARD:TAYL
a. W-1171 Benjamin Stubblefield, heir to George Stubblefield
b. Benjamin Stubblefield
c. Lyne Starling, 1831 (Logan County)

S-10030 1000a D:56 X-1000 HARD:PLEA
a. W-5223 Robert Means, assignee of Thomas D. Harris, who was assignee of (Doctor) Bazel Middleton
b. Robert Means
c. Lyne Starling, 1831 (Logan County)

S-10031 667a D:26 X-1000 HARD:PLEA
a. W-6053 James Burton
b. James Burton
c. Ann E. Burton; Hugh Letson, 1839

S-10032 400a C:446 X-1000 HARD:DUDL
a. W-5789 Rowland Madison
b. Rowland Madison, representatives of
c. John Paver; C. Garlough (Gerlach?), 1839

S-10032 400a C:446 X-1000 HARD:DUDL
a. W-5789 Rowland Madison
b. Rowland Madison, representatives of
c. None

S-10035 400a D:161 X-1000 HARD:MCDO
a. W-91 General George Weedon
b. George Weedon
c. None

S-10036 500a D:160 X-1000 HARD:MCDO
a. W-1171 Benjamin Stubblefield, heir to George Stubblefield
b. Benjamin Stubblefield
c. Lyne Starling

S-10036 500a D:160 X-1000 HARD:MCDO
a. W-6178 Robert Hanson Harrison, heirs of
W-6179 Robert Hanson Harrison, heirs of
b. Sarah Easton
c. None

S-10037 1000a C:452 X-1000 HARD:TAYL
a. W-5888 David Wallace, representatives of
b. David Wallace, representatives of
c. Jacob Coons*; heirs of D. Wallace; Jacob Koons*, 1840
* So spelled.

S-10039* 100a -- X-1000 ----:----
a. --
b. Samuel Cole**
c. None
* Entry in Source A only.
** Sold to Lyne Sterling at judgment sale of 8 February 1827 (per schedule bound in Source A at S-10012). "Lands are all north of Indian Boundary."

S-10039* 200a -- X-1000 ----:----
a. --
b. William Carter**
c. None
* Entry in Source A only.
** Sold to Lyne Sterling at judgment sale of 8 February 1827 (per schedule bound in Source A at S-10012). "Lands are all north of Indian Boundary."

S-10039* 200a -- X-1000 ----:----
a. --
b. Aquilla Norvell**
c. None
* Entry in Source A only.
** Sold to Lyne Sterling at judgment sale of 8 February 1827 (per schedule bound in Source A at S-10012). "Lands are all north of Indian Boundary."

S-10040*
S-10292 970a D:56 X-1000 HARD:PLEA
a. W-5386 Robert Means, assignee of John Bryan
W-5397 William D. Wren? (Oren?), assignee of Daniel Carmichael, assignee of Peter R? Garland, administrator of the estate of W. Belfield
W-5470 Robert Means, assignee of Edward Smith
b. Robert Means
c. None
* "By Kenton."

S-10041 1000a C:484 X-0991 LOGA:RUSH
a. W-4962 Richard Kennon
W-4963 Richard Kennon
b. Richard Kennon
c. James Kilpatrick, 1831; William Ross; Walter Slicer, 1841

S-10042. *See* S-9960

S-10044* 1000a -- X-1000 ----:----
a. W-5803 John Remay, representatives of
b. Anthony Walk, assignee
c. None
* Entry in Source A only.

S-10045 500a C:446 X-1000 HARD:MCDO
a. W-5789 Rowland Madison
b. Rowland Madison, representatives of
c. Jacob Lauch? (Laub?); R. S. Madison; J. Jackson

S-10046 750a C:506 X-1000 HARD:TAYL
a. W-6191 Robert Hanson Harrison, heirs of
W-6192 Robert Hanson Harrison, heirs of
W-6193 Robert Hanson Harrison, heirs of
b. Charles Cutts
c. Lyne Starling, 1831 (Logan County)

S-10046 100a C:506 X-1000 HARD:TAYL
LOGA:---*
a. W-3028 Abel Armstrong
b. Robert Gamble
c. John Watts; Joseph Clark, 1832
* Source A does not give township.

S-10047
S-10663
S-10870 2400a* D:7 X-1000 HARD:HALE
a. W-5803 John Remay, representatives of
W-6201 Abraham Davenport
W-6249 Edward Garland, heirs of
W-5981 John Daws?
W-6247 Edward Garland, heirs of
W-5887 Thomas Herbert, representatives of

b. -- Wallace, -- Davenport, & -- Bourne
c. None
* Source A says 800 acres to Anthony Walk but does not give location.

S-10047. See also S-10663

S-10048 992a C:436 X-1000 HARD:HALE
a. W-5434 James Taylor, assignee of Francis Swain & John Graff, executors of (the estate of) Peter Muhlenberg
W-5438 James Taylor, assignee of Robert Elliot
W-5372 Thomas M. Bayly, assignee of Jonathan Bunting, representative of Holloway Bunting
W-5429 John Green, deceased, representatives of
b. -- Taylor & -- Green, representatives of*
c. P. Muhleberg & Hetty Heester
* Representatives of Green but not Taylor.

S-10050 417a C:469 X-0060 HARD:MCDO
a. W-5258 Thomas Posey & James Taylor
b. -- Posey & -- Taylor
c. None

S-10050 417a C:469 X-0060 HARD:MCDO
a. W-5258 Thomas Posey & James Taylor
b. -- Posey & -- Taylor
c. None

S-10051 1000a D:146 X-1000 MARI:BOWL
a. W-5866 Abraham Bowman
b. Abraham Bowman
c. None

S-10053 720a C:468 X-1000 MARI:---* HARD:TAYL
a. W-5352 Thomas Den? (Dix?)
W-5183 James Taylor, assignee of Jacob C. Leman
b. -- Taylor & -- Dix
c. None
* Source A does not mention Marion County.

S-10054 750a C:478 X-1000 HARD:TAYL
a. W-5455 Charles Porterfield, representatives of
b. Charley Potterfield*
c. Edwin Fisher, 1840
* Source A spells Porterfield.

S-10056 500a C:477 X-1000 MARI:---* HARD:MCDO
a. W-1348 Lieutenant David Allen
W-1405 Thomas Stephens
b. John Beale
c. None
* Source A mentions Logan County (no township) but not Marion County.

S-10056 500a C:477 X-1000 HARD:MCDO
a. W-1356 Francis Cox, heir to William Cox, deceased
W-1588 James League
W-1405 Thomas Stephens
b. John Beale
c. None

S-10059 700a C:447 X-0991 MARI:BOWL
a. W-5789 Rowland Madison
b. Rowland Madison, representatives of
c. None

S-10060 889a C:436 X-0991 LOGA:BOAK
a. W-5465 James Taylor, assignee of Richard Hawes, executor of Samuel (Hawes)
W-5858 William Pierce, heirs of
b. -- Taylor & -- Pierce
c. None

S-10061 200a C:487 X-1000 HARD:HALE
a. W-5842 Margaret Bidgood, heir to Philip Bidgood
b. William Moore
c. Daniel Campbell, 1837

S-10061 200a C:487 X-1000 HARD:HALE LOGA:---*
a. W-6243 Anthony? Talley?, heirs of
b. Charles Tulley**
c. None
* Source A does not mention township.
** Source A spells Talley.

S-10063 800a C:503 X-0840 ROSS:PAXT PIKE:---*
a. W-5555 Samuel Booker, heirs of
W-5003 John Thompson
W-5697 Joseph Woodson
W-6246 Edward Garland, heirs of
b. Nathan Reeves
c. None
* Source A does not mention Pike County.

S-10064* 300a D:161 X-1000 HARD:PLEA
a. W-91 General George Weedon
b. George Weedon
c. None
* Forfeited to State, 1837.

S-10065 300a D:23 X-1000 MARI:BOWL
a. W-91 General George Weedon
b. George Weedon
c. T. Holmes, 1826; Daniel D. Tompkins, 1827; -- Bennett & -- Hardy; Elisha Hardy, 1834

S-10066 464a C:408 X-0840 PIKE:BENT X-0760 ROSS:TWIN
a. W-5379 Thomas M. Bayly, assignee of Henry Stevens, representative of Elijah Heckman? (Hickman?)
W-5380 Thomas M. Bayly, assignee of Nancy Stevens?, representative of Ezekiel Heckman? (Hickman)
W-5362 Thomas M. Bayly, assignee of John Bull, representative of Henry Garnet? (Garrett?)
W-5361 Thomas M. Bayly, assignee of John Madiax?, representative of Elisha? Madiax?
W-5514 Thomas Lanier, representatives of
b. -- Massie & -- Clark
c. D. Burgess; -- Penniston & -- Murphy

S-10068 416a C:449 X-1000 HARD:MCDO
a. W-5640 Michael Bowyer
b. George Clark
c. None

S-10070 201a C:503 X-1000 MARI:GREE
a. W-5436 Charles Scott
W-5094 James Taylor, assignee of Robert Elliott
W-979 David Rumage
b. -- Taylor, -- Scott, & -- McPherson
c. None

S-10071 200a C:495 X-0840 FAYE:MADI
a. W-6259 William Diamond? (Drummond?)
b. -- Lewis & -- Drummond*
c. None
* Source A says Drummonds (presumably plural).

S-10072* 71a -- -- SCIO:UNIO
a. --
b. William Kendall
c. None
* Entry in Source A only.

S-10075. See S-9592

S-10076 20a C:426 X-0840 ROSS:SCIO
a. W-5803 John Remay, representatives of
b. Anthony Walke
c. None

S-10081
S-10605
S-10984
S-10858
S-12171 458a D:68 X-0340 MADI:CANA
a. W-5870 Wood Baldwin, heirs of
W-6417 Joseph Britton
W-6489 Robert Wilmott
W-6428 Vachel Howard
b. -- Dun & -- Chapman
c. None

S-10083 10a* E:349 X-1040 SCIO:BRUS
a. W-6056 Anger? Price
b. Andrew D. Kendrick*
c. Isaac Wright; J. Wallace, 1826; A. Wallace, 1827
* Source A says 25 acres to Andrew Ellison.

S-10083 10a* E:350 X-0090 or X-0100 ADAM:--** SCIO:BRUS
a. W-6056 Anger? Price
b. Andrew D. Kendrick*
c. None
* Source A says 25 acres to Andrew Ellison.
** Source A does not mention Adams County.

S-10083 5a* E:353 X-0840 ROSS:--** SCIO:BRUS
a. W-6056 Anger? Price
b. Andrew D. Kendrick*
c. None
* Source A says 25 acres to Andrew Ellison.
** Source A does not mention Ross County.

S-10084
S-10093 60a D:20 X-0840 SCIO:BRUS
a. W-6056 Anger? Price
W-5781 Joseph Crockett
b. Andrew Ellison
c. None

S-10086
S-10198 88a C:415 X-1090 LOGA:LAKE
a. W-5870 Wood Baldwin, heirs of
b. -- Ladd & -- Norvell
c. None

S-10090
S-10202
S-10213 375a C:418 X-0663 BROW:PERR CLER:JACK
a. W-5873 William Treplett? (Triplett?)
W-6172 Banks Dudley, heirs of
W-5878 John Graves
W-1232 Andrew Hynes?
W-6130 Richard M. Owen
W-5870 Wood Baldwin, heirs of
b. -- Wallace, -- Dunlap, -- Ladd, & -- Norvell
c. None

S-10091 130a C:416 X-0730 LOGA:MONR
a. W-5873 William Treplett? (Triplett?)
b. Cadwallader Wallace
c. None

S-10095 200a C:407 X-0840 MADI:STOK
a. W-2747 Joseph Newman
b. Peter Vandeventer*
c. None
* Source A spells Vandevanter.

S-10096. See S-9366

S-10097 150a C:410 X-0660 MADI:STOK
a. W-5812 John Goodrich, heirs of
b. James Galloway, Junior
c. None

S-10099. See S-9007

S-10103 1000a C:487 X-1000 HARD:PLEA
a. W-6331 John Sturdivant
W-6333 John Sturdivant
b. John Manlove*
c. Lyne Starling, 1831 (Logan County)
* Source A says John Malone, administrator. However, in a schedule bound in Source A at S-100012, it is stated that the owners of record were the representatives of John Manlove; property sold to Jere(miah?) McLene at a judgment sale of 8 February 1827. "Lands are all north of the Indian Boundary."

S-10104 1000a C:487 X-1000 HARD:TAYL
a. W-6332 John Sturdivant
W-6333 John Sturdivant
b. John Manlove*
c. Wray Thomas; Jacob Coons; Lyne Starling, 1831

(Logan County)
* Source A says John Malone, administrator. However, in a schedule bound in Source A at S-10012, it is stated that the owners of record were the representatives of John Manlove; property sold to Jere(miah?) McLene at a judgment sale of 8 February 1827. "Lands are all north of the Indian Boundary."

S-10109. See S-9878

S-10114
S-10141 84a C:417 X-0840 ROSS:PAIN
a. W-5870 Wood Baldwin, heirs of
W-6130 Richard M. Owen
b. -- Ladd, -- Norvell, & -- Dunlap*
c. None
* Source A does not mention Dunlap.

S-10115 100a C:494 X-0840 ROSS:PAIN
a. W-5870 Wood Baldwin, heirs of
b. -- Ladd & -- Norvell
c. None

S-10116. See S-9858

S-10119 200a D:158 X-0380 HIGH:DODS
a. W-6273 Stephen Thompson, heirs of
b. James Thompson
c. None

S-10121. See S-9925

S-10122
S-10248
S-10249 1095a C:481 X-0060 LOGA:MCAR
a. W-5870 Wood Baldwin, heirs of
W-6218 William Yates
W-6202 Robert Ballen? heirs of
W-6217 Thomas Treplett? (Triplett?)
W-6124 Thomas Hopper
W-6126 Stephen Young
W-6147 Nathaniel Wells? (Wills?)
W-5749 David Williams
W-3167 William Bayles
b. -- Dun & -- Bayles
c. W. Dun; M. Bonner, 1827

S-10124 500a C:506 X-1000 HARD:ROUN
a. W-6330 John Sturdivant
b. Joshua Poythress
c. John Dunlap; John F. Hinkle, 1838

S-10125* 200a -- -- ----:----
a. W-5344 Robert Means, assignee of John Stokeley, assignee of Andrew Waggener
b. Robert Means, assignee
c. None
* Entry in Source A only.

S-10137 135a C:414 X-0840 FAYE:GREE
a. W-5873 William Treplett? (Triplett?)
W-5802 George Norvell? (Nowell?)
b. -- Wallace & -- Worthington
c. None

S-10138. See S-7521

S-10140* 180a -- -- ROSS:PAIN
a. --
b. James Dunlap
c. None
* Entry in Source A only.

S-10141. See S-10114

S-10143 100a C:440 X-1303 HIGH:WHIT
a. W-6226 David Jones, heirs of
b. Samuel Bell
c. None

S-10144 100a C:440 X-1300 HIGH:CLAY
a. W-2081 Godfrey Jones
b. Thomas Jones
c. George Barngrove; Samuel Bell, 1832; Isaac Garretson, 1839

S-10147 700a C:420 X-1000 PICK:WAYN
a. W-6325 Edward Beeson
W-6020 John Baldwin
b. -- Springer & -- Beeson
c. None

S-10154 50a D:353 X-0590 ADAM:SPRI
a. W-5871 Francis M. Boykin & Ann Johnson, heirs & administrators of F(rancis) Boykin
W-4671 Nelson Cosby, representatives of
b. Andrew Ellison
c. None

S-10155 25a D:169 X-0040 ADAM:MONR
a. W-5799 James Dillard
b. Andrew Ellison
c. Noah Whitlatch; Robert Johnson, 1838

S-10156 85a E:100 X-0381 ADAM:MONR
a. W-4671 Nelson Cosby, representatives of
W-1050 John Britton
b. Andrew Ellison, heirs of
c. John Ellison, Junior; Levi Mattison, 1824; T. Huston, 1829

S-10157. See S-7710

S-10158. See S-4687 (in volume 4, part 1)

S-10159 8a C:409 X-0663 CLER:BATA
a. W-5336 William Mosley
b. William Mosley
c. None

S-10164 60a C:463 X-0650 ADAM:TIFF
ADAM:MEIG

a. W-6098 Harry Terrell
b. Walter Dun
c. None

S-10165 100a C:521 X-0650 ADAM:WAYN
a. W-6098 Harry Terrell
b. Walter Dun
c. None

S-10166 250a C:462 X-0760 PIKE:PEBB
a. W-6183 Robert Hanson Harrison, heirs of
b. Andrew Ellison
c. J. A. Penniston, 1837; heirs of A. Ellison; L? (S?) Byington, 1839

S-10171 1000a C:488 X-1000 HARD:HALE
a. W-6170 Daniel Worsham, heirs of
W-6240 William Yates, heirs of
W-6241 William Yates, heirs of
W-5887 Thomas Herbert, representatives of
b. Joshua Poythross*
c. None
* So spelled.

S-10172 667a C:507 X-1000 HARD:DUDL
a. W-2338 Lieutenant Philip Stewart
b. Philip Stewart
c. James Scott; J. James; John M. Drew?, 1840; Allen Owen; Lyne Starling, 1831 (Logan County); John Parver? Joseph? Scott, 1831 (Logan County); W. Carter, 1842 (Hardin County)

S-10173 667a C:507 X-1000 HARD:TAYL
a. W-2052 Captain Abraham Kirkpatrick
b. Abraham Kirkpatrick*
c. None
* Sold to A. Latham at judgment sale of 8 February 1827 (per schedule bound in Source A at S-10012). "Lands are all north of the Indian Boundary."

S-10176 384a D:6 X-1000 HARD:HALE LOGA:---*
a. W-5748 David Williams
b. David Williams
c. Saquino? (Laquino?) Rawson; W. T. Layton, 1838 (Hardin County)
* Source A does not give township.

S-10176 384a D:6 X-1000 LOGA:---* HARD:HALE
a. W-5748 David Williams
b. David Williams
c. None
* Source A does not mention Logan County.

S-10176 384a D:6 X-1000 LOGA:---* HARD:HALE
a. W-5748 David Williams
b. David Williams
c. None
* Source A does not mention Logan County.

S-10176 384a D:6 X-1000 HARD:HALE
a. W-5748 David Williams
b. David Williams
c. Daniel Baldwin

S-10176 522a D:345 X-0991 UNIO:WASH
a. W-5749 David Williams
b. Abraham J. Williams
c. None

S-10179
S-10404 888a C:484 X-0991 LOGA:RUSH
a. W-5817 John Goodrich, heirs of
W-1451 Lieutenant Charles Jones
W-5344 Robert Means, assignee of John Stokeley, assignee of Andrew Waggener
W-5169 Thomas D. Harris, assignee of Erasmus Gill, administrator of Peter Minor
W-5470 Robert Means, assignee of Edward Smith
W-5805 Joseph Hite
W-5867 Abraham Bowman
W-5536 George Handy
W-6071 George Ryan
b. -- McArthur, -- Means, -- Hite, et al*
c. None
* Source A says -- McArthur, -- Means, -- Hite, -- Bowman, -- Handy, & -- Ryan

S-10180 388a D:5 X-1000 HARD:HALE
a. W-196 Captain James Mabon*
b. James Mabin*
c. Lyne Starling, 1831 (Logan County)
* So spelled. Sold to Lyne Sterling at judgment sale of 8 February 1827 (per schedule bound in Source A at S-10012). "Lands are all north of the Indian Boundary."

S-10181 181a -- -- ROSS:FRAN
a. --
b. George Dawson
c. None
* Entry in Source A only.

S-10183; S-10184; S-10185. See S-4671 (in volume 4, part)

S-10186 100a C:409 X-0663 CLER:BATA
a. W-1937 Major Francis Taylor
b. Henry Lee
c. None

S-10187
S-10785 75a C:521 X-0840 ROSS:TWIN ROSS:PAIN
a. W-6071 George Ryan
W-5867 Abraham Bowman
b. -- Ryan & -- Bowman
c. None

S-10188* 50a -- -- ADAM:--** BROW:HUNT
a. --
b. Simon Reeder
c. John Fisher, 1823
* Entry in Source A only.
** Source A does not mention township.

S-10189* 10a -- -- ADAM:--** BROW:HUNT
a. --
b. Jacob Boone
c. Heirs of J. Boone; T. J. Lockhart, 1833
* Entry in Source A only.
** Source A does not mention township.

S-10190 500a D:483 X-0663 MARI:---* CLIN:CLAR
a. W-6020 John Baldwin
b. John Hoy
c. James Fyfe, 1838; Peyton West, 1840
* Source A does not mention township.

S-10192* 1600a -- -- MARI:BOWL
a. W-3034 Boswell Bridgeman
W-332 Henry Punter
W-750 William Crallon?
W-1234 Henry Lipscomb
W-1427 Jacob Hutts?
W-1585 William Bartley
W-1592 John Nichols
W-1404 William Harris
b. David Ross, assignee
c. Heirs of D. Ross; Daniel Ross; Lyne Starling, 1831
* Entry in Source A only; says "not patented."

S-10193 200a D:19 X-1000 UNIO:JACK
a. W-3739 Alexander Drummond
b. Alexander Drummond
c. James Galloway, Junior, 1831

S-10194 200a D:468 X-1000 UNIO:JACK
a. W-3736 John Welch
b. John Welsh*
c. James Galloway, 1831
* Source A spells Welch.

S-10195 200a D:469 X-1000 UNIO:JACK
a. W-3081 Sawney Whistler
b. Sawney Whistler
c. James Galloway, 1831

S-10196 100a D:469 X-1000 UNIO:JACK
a. W-686 Lewis Fox
b. Lewis Fox
c. None

S-10197 100a D:469 X-1000 UNIO:JACK
a. W-3744 William Hooks
b. William Hooks
c. James Galloway, Junior, 1831

S-10198. See S-10086

S-10199
S-10796 380a D:73 X-0841 FAYE:MADI PICK:PERR
a. W-5870 Wood Baldwin, heirs of
W-6130 Richard M. Owen
W-5802 George Norvell? (Nowell?), deceased
W-6160 Thomas Ray
W-6374 John Emmerson
b. -- Ladd, -- Norvell, & -- Dunlap*
c. Rease Young; I. Y. Green, 1836; James Dunlap; J. L. Taylor, 1831; L. P. Reed, 1831
* Source A says -- Ladd, -- Norvell, -- Dunlap, -- Wallace, & -- Worthington

S-10202. See S-10090

S-10204* 100a -- -- CLIN:CLAR
a. --
b. Nicholas Cassell? (Carrell?)
c. None
* Entry in Source A only; says "not patented."

S-10205* 500a -- -- CLER:STON CLER:JACK
a. --
b. Nicholas Cassell? (Carrell?)
c. None
* Entry in Source A only; says "not patented."

S-10206* 1067a -- -- CLER:JACK BROW:PERR
a. None
b. Nicholas Carrell
c. John S. Herring, 1824
* Entry in Source A only; says "not patented."

S-10207* 40a -- -- BROW:HUNT
a. --
b. Jonathan Reed
c. None
* Entry in Source A only.

S-10213. See S-10090

S-10217 200a D:58 X-0420 BROW:HUNT
a. W-6023 Thomas Pears, representatives of
b. Ebenezer Melvin*
c. S. Brown; J. S. Beasley, 1842; J. Seeks; A. Liggett, 1842
* Source A spells Melven.

S-10218* 69a -- -- ROSS:PAIN
a. --
b. John A. Fulton
c. Charles Crozier, 1824
* Entry in Source A only.

S-10220 85a C:500 X-0270 BROW:CLAR
a. W-5531 Robert Beale
W-5495 Francis Cowherd
b. Jesse McKay
c. George C. Light; E. Owen, 1834; J. Derry? 1841

S-10221
S-10310
S-10360 678a C:485 X-1000 HARD:MCDO

a. W-5367 Charles Harrison, representatives of
W-5231 Henry Lee, devisee of Alexander Skinner
W-5072 Isaac Browning
W-5551 John Meanly
W-5104 Samuel March?, assignee of Joseph Smith, deceased
b. -- Means & -- McArthur
c. None

S-10224* 55a -- -- ROSS:HUNT
a. --
b. John Harrison
c. None
* Entry in Source A only.

S-10230* 222a -- -- ----:----
a. --
b. Joseph Scott
c. None
* Entry in Source A only, where crossed out.

S-10232 170a C:421 X-0663 CLER:STON CLER:JACK
a. W-5870 Wood Baldwin, heirs of
b. -- Ladds* & -- Norvell
c. None
* Plural.

S-10233 100a C:495 X-0360 MADI:UNIO
a. W-6344 Zachariah Taylor
b. John Aiken
c. E. Langham? (Laugham?), 1823

S-10234 607a D:3 X-1000 HARD:DUDL LOGA:---*
a. W-6021 Benjamin Baldwin
W-5766 John Spilfatham
W-5850 Tarlton Payne
b. Benjamin Forsyth
c. David Camper, 1831
* Source A does not give township.

S-10239 1808a D:4 X-1000 LOGA:---* HARD:HALE
a. W-6285 Robert Slaughter
W-6277 Alexander Keeth**
W-6327 John Roberts
b. Nathaniel Sawyer
c. None
* Source A does not mention Logan County.
** So spelled.

S-10240 3665 C:535 X-1000 MARI:GREE UNIO:---*
a. W-5873 William Treplett? (Triplett?)
W-5813 John Goodrich, heirs of
W-5814 John Goodrich, heirs of
W-5815 John Goodrich, heirs of
W-5816 John Goodrich, heirs of
W-5818 John Goodrich, heirs of
W-5819 John Goodrich, heirs of
W-6224 Abraham Goff?
W-6231 Benjamin Jacobs
W-111 Captain Clough Shelton
b. -- Wallace, -- Watts, -- Wallace, & -- Shelton
c. None
* Source A does not mention Union County.

S-10242 100a D:4 X-1000 HARD:HALE
a. W-6336 Jacob Garvey
b. Daniel McPayne*
c. J. McDowall; Adam Snoddy, 1836; C. Wallace
* Sold to A. J. McDowell at judgment sale of 8 February 1827 (per schedule bound in Source A at S-10012). "Lands are all north of Indian Boundary."

S-10244*
S-10851 281a D:55 X-0790 CLER:GOSH
a. W-2740 Captain James Wright
W-137 Richard Clark
b. -- Write** & -- Starke
c. None
* May not have been patented.
** Source A spells Wright.

S-10244. See also S-12483

S-10246
S-10267
S-10268
S-10428
S-10463
S-10464
S-10438 2820a C:481 X-1000 HARD:TAYL
a. W-5825 Richard Foster, heirs of
W-5828 William Cunningham, heirs of
W-6217 Thomas Treplett? (Triplett?)
W-5870 Wood Baldwin, heirs of
W-5887 Thomas Herbert, representatives of
W-5749 David Williams
W-6288 Presley Davis, representatives of
W-5885 William Mosby, deceased, by Ann W. Chamberlayn
W-6216 William Holt
W-5963 Barnabas Arthur
W-5984 Thomas Meadow
W-6202 Robert Ballen? heirs of
W-2162 Colonel William Heth*
b. -- Dun & -- Hith*
c. None
* So spelled.

S-10247. See S-10027

S-10248; S-10249. See S-10122

S-10267; S-10268. See S-10246

S-10270
S-10344
S-10436
S-10677
S-10678 591a C:500 X-1000 HARD:TAYL
a. W-5335 Richard Kennon, representatives of
W-6217 Thomas Treplett? (Triplett?)
W-6218 William Yates
W-6098 Harry Terrell
W-5887 Thomas Herbert, representatives of

b. -- Dun & -- Kennon
c. None

S-10270. See also S-10678

S-10271 50a C:524 X-0130 PIKE:PERR
a. W-5749 David Williams
b. Walter Dun
c. None

S-10276* 1000a C:510 X-1000 HARD:TAYL HARD:MCDO
a. W-5220 James Mabon, representatives of W-5510 Thomas Herde?
b. -- Tagart, --McLaughlin, -- Grey, & -- Taylor
c. James Tagart; -- Templeton & -- Elder, 1831 (Logan County)
* Source A says "not patented."

S-10278* 200a -- -- HARD:MCDO
a. --
b. Robert Means
c. Benjamin Henry
* Entry in Source A only.

S-10282 100a C:426 X-0080 BROW:HUNT
a. W-6334 John Allen
b. Benjamin Beasley
c. None

S-10286 333a D:348 X-1000 PIKE:SUNF
a. W-6217 Thomas Treplett? (Triplett?)
b. Cadwallader Wallace
c. None

S-10290* 100a D:115 X-0350 CHAM:GOSH MADI:--**
a. W-3789 Bennett Armstrong, representive of James Armstrong
b. Edward Tiffin
c. Ezra Reed, 1831
* Source A says "not patented."
** Source A does not mention Madison County.

S-10293. See S-10027

S-10294* 85a -- -- LOGA:MCAR
a. --
b. George Dawson
c. None
* Entry in Source A only.

S-10295 200a C:429 X-0360 MADI:DARB
a. W-6175 Benjamin Archer, heirs of
b. Samuel Smith
c. Joseph Chrisman, 1831 (crossed out); John W. Warner, 1831

S-10296 388a C:474 X-1000 HARD:TAYL
a. W-5454 Samuel Hopkins
b. Samuel Hopkins*
c. None
* Sold to Lyne Sterling at judgment sale of 8 February 1827 (per schedule bound in Source A at S-10012). "Lands are all north of Indian Boundary."

S-10298 800a C:465 X-1000 MARI:GREE
a. W-5459 James Wallace, deceased, representatives of
b. -- Wallace & -- Taylor, representatives of
c. None

S-10299 629a C:480 X-0991 MARI:BOWL
a. W-5247 Robert Young, representatives of W-5435 William B. Wallace
b. -- Young & -- Wallace, representatives of
c. None

S-10300 370a C-478 X-1000 HARD:ROUN
a. W-5463 James Smith
b. James Smith
c. None

S-10301* 250a -- -- HARD:TAYL
a. --
b. Samuel J. Cabell
c. None
* Entry in Source A only.

S-10302 250a D:146 X-0060 HARD:MCDO
a. W-5455 Charles Porterfield, representatives of
b. Charles Porterfield, representatives of
c. None

S-10302 480a E:44 X-0060 HARD:MCDO
a. W-5183 James Taylor, assignee of Jacob Coleman W-5459 James Wallace, deceased, representatives of
b. -- Taylor & -- Wallace
c. None

S-10303* 300a -- -- BROW:PERR
a. --
b. Nicholas Cussel (Carrell?), heirs of
c. James Cox, 1829; James Fencick? 1838
* Entry in Source A only.

S-10304* 100a -- -- CLER:STON CLER:JACK
a. --
b. Nicholas Cussell (Carrell?), heirs of
c. J. S. Herring, 1824
* Entry in Source A only.

S-10305 500a C:463 X-1170 CLIN:CLAR CLIN:WASH
a. W-9 Lieutenant Colonel Samuel J. Cabell
b. Samuel J. Cabell
c. None

S-10306 278a C:480 X-0229 LOGA:MCAR
a. W-5749 David Williams
b. Abraham J. Williams
c. None

S-10307 722a C:484 X-0229 LOGA:MCAR
a. W-5338 Mathew Clay
W-5551 John Meanly
W-5805 Joseph Hite
b. -- McArthur & -- Hite
c. None

S-10308* 450a -- X-1000 ----:----
a. W-860 Lieutenant David Williams
b. David Williams**
c. Lyne Starling, H. G. B. Goodin? 1837
* Entry in Source A only.
** Sold to Lyne Sterling at judgment sale of 8 February 1827 (per schedule bound in Source A at S-10012). "Lands are all north of the Indian Boundary."

S-10310. See S-10221

S-10311 600a D:64 X-1000 HARD:MCDO
a. W-5344 Robert Means, assignee of John Stokeley, assignee of Andrew Waggener
W-5383 Robert Means, assignee of Thomas D. Harris, assignee of Thomas Taylor, administrator of John McAdam
b. Robert Means
c. None

S-10312 1000a C:532 X-1000 HARD:MCDO
a. W-6285 Robert Slaughter
b. Walter Dun
c. James Scott

S-10315* 87a D:4 X-1000 MARI:BOWL HIGH:--**
a. W-1574 Samuel Flouronoy (Flournoy)
b. James Harris
c. J. Armstrong; T? A. Holmes, 1826
* Source A says "not patented."
** Source A does not mention Highland County.

S-10320 533a C:430 X-1300 BROW:WASH
a. W-6325 Edward Beeson
b. Dennis Springer
c. None

S-10321 485a C:430 X-0841 FAYE:UNIO
a. W-6325 Edward Beeson
W-6020 John Baldwin
b. -- Springer & -- Dawson
c. Rachel Looker; N. F. Jones, 1837

S-10322 175a C:430 X-0841 FAYE:MADI
a. W-6325 Edward Beeson
W-6020 John Baldwin
b. -- Springer & -- Dawson
c. A. Bourne; H. Core, 1830

S-10326. See S-9222

S-10327. See S-9007

S-10328 35a C:427 X-1000 FRAN:PRAI
a. W-4919 Nathaniel Rowland, representative of Burwell (Rowland)
b. James Galloway, Junior
c. None

S-10332 500a D:311 X-1385 PICK:WAYN
a. W-678 Thomas Asselin
W-1857 Robert Belcher
W-2777 James Jenkins, assignee of Elijah Siles? (Liles?)
W-2778 James Jenkins, assignee of Basdell Price
b. James Jenkins
c. L? L? (S? S?) Denny, 1832; Samuel Jenkins; Henry Rector, 1834

S-10337 286a D:151 X-0060 HARD:MCDO LOGA:---*
a. W-4359 William Hopkins?
W-5222 William Boger? (Boyer? Bogen? Boyce?)
W-5336 William Mosley
b. -- Pankey, -- Boyce, & -- Mosley**
c. Philip Pankey; Henry Hendrickson, 1828; William Boyce; James Taylor
* Source A does not mention Logan County.
** Source A spells Moseley.

S-10338 200a C:428 X-1180 UNIO:UNIO
a. W-617 Captain Alexander Breckenridge
W-5222 William Boger? (Boyer? Bogen? Boyce?)
b. -- Breckenridge & -- Boyce
c. None

S-10339* 170a -- -- SCIO:NILE
a. --
b. Anthony Walk
c. None
* Entry in Source A only.

S-10340 150a C:492 X-1120 BROW:FRAN
a. W-4227 James McGovern
b. David Miller
c. W. Springer, 1832

S-10342* 100a -- X-1000 ----:----
a. W-6289 James Dickin? (Dickins?), representatives of
b. James Dicken
c. None
* Entry in Source A only.

S-10344. See S-10270; S-10678

S-10348 216a D:83 X-1300 BROW:CLAR
a. W-5921 Richard Taylor, heirs of
b. Mary Reddick & Mills Reddick
c. Henry Apple, 1828; James? (Joseph?) Owen, 1832; Josiah Boothby, 1831; E. Owen; Heirs of J. Boothby

S-10350 40a C:489 X-0840 ROSS:TWIN
a. W-6162 James Whaley

b. Allison C. Looker
c. None

S-10351* 100a -- X-1000 ----:----
a. --
b. J. Rutherford**
c. None
* Entry in Source A only.
** Sold to Lyne Sterling at judgment sale of 8 February 1827 (per schedule bound in Source A at S-10012). "Lands are all north of Indian Boundary."

S-10353 100a D:405 X-0060 HARD:TAYL
a. W-3720 Margaret Barns*, heir
b. Margaret Barnes*
c. Lyne Starling, 1831 (Logan County)
* So spelled.

S-10354 400a D:1 X-0710 MARI:BOWL
a. W-6364 William McDonald
W-6365 James McCracken
b. William McDonald
c. D. McArthur; John Bartrand, 1835

S-10356
S-8492 467a C:492 X-0841 MADI:RANG
a. W-6311 John Poe
W-5551 John Meanly
b. -- Poe & -- Scott
c. None

S-10356. See also S-8492

S-10357 40a C:517 X-0360 MADI:RANG
a. W-5026 David Meriwether
b. William Creighton*
c. None
* Source A says William Creighton, Junior.

S-10360. See S-10221

S-10362 66a C:444 X-0250 HIGH:LIBE
a. W-6245 Newman Landman
b. William A. Trimble
c. None

S-10363*
S-12934 300a D:334 X-0663 BROW:----
a. W-6696 --**
W-154 Captain Beaverley*** Roy
b. Timothy Kirby
c. None
* This entry does not appear in Source A.
** Warrantee's name not listed in Source C.
*** So spelled.

S-10363* 100a -- -- ----:----
a. --
b. Beverly Roy
c. None
* Entry in Source A only.

S-10363. See S-12934

S-10364 15a D:113 X-0663 BROW:PERR
a. W-154 Captain Beaverley* Roy
b. Beverly Roy**
c. William Lytle; T. Kirby, 1826
* So spelled.
** Source A says Beverly Le Roy.

S-10365 25a D:114 X-0663 BROW:PERR
a. W-154 Captain Beaverly* Roy
b. Beverly Roy**
c. None
* So spelled.
** Source A says Beverly Le Roy.

S-10366 10a D:114 X-0663 CLIN:JEFF
a. W-154 Captain Beaverly* Roy
b. Beverly Roy**
c. None
* So spelled.
** Source A says Beverly Le Roy.

S-10367 10a C:497 X-1173 CLIN:CLAR
a. W-154 Captain Beaverly* Roy
b. Beverly* Roy
c. William R. Cole, 1824
* So spelled.

S-10369 50a C:530 X-0663 BROW:PERR
CLIN:---*
a. W-154 Captain Beaverly** Roy
b. Beverly** Roy
c. M. Howard; Thomas Haggerty (Brown County)
* Source A does not give township.
** So spelled.

S-10370. See S-10459

S-10373 120a C:505 X-0360 MADI:UNIO
a. W-6325 Edward Beeson
b. Dennis Springer
c. S. S. Kerr, 1838

S-10374 200a C:494 X-1000 PICK:SCIO
a. W-5803 John Remay, representatives of
b. Anthony Walke
c. None

S-10376 300a C:490 X-0840 FAYE:GREE
a. W-5803 John Remay, representatives of
b. Anthony Walke
c. None

S-10377
S-10378 215a C:499 X-0150 PICK:DARB
a. W-5803 John Remay, representatives of
b. Anthony Walke
c. C. Wallace; David Montgomery, 1831

S-10383 200a D:97 X-1000 UNIO:WASH
MARI:---*
a. W-6288 Presley Davis, representatives of
b. Presley Davis, representatives of
c. N. Sawyer, 1826; J. Bigelow, 1837
* Source A does not give township.

S-10384* 100a -- X-1000 ----:----
a. W-6278 John Forrester**
b. John Forester**
c. None
* Entry in Source A only.
** So spelled.

S-10387
S-10388 500a C:534 X-0991 LOGA:BOAK
a. W-6009 David Aiken? (Aikens?), representatives of
W-6010 David Aiken? (Aikens?), representatives of
b. David Aikens*, representatives of
c. James Taylor, 1836; George L? Aiken*; Walter Slicer, 1841
* So spelled.

S-10389 40a C:496 X-0870 PIKE:PEBB
a. W-6239 William Yates
b. Benjamin Hough*
c. None
* Source A says: "Patented to heirs of Benjamin Hough."

S-10390* 30a -- -- PIKE:PEBB
a. --
b. Anthony Walke
c. B. Hough; P. N. White, 1826; A. G. Thurman, 1833; J. R. Anderson; A. Latham
* Entry in Source A only.

S-10391* 30a -- -- ROSS:HUNT
a. --
b. -- Watkins & -- Hough
c. B. Hough; P. N. White, 1825; John Wakins**; John Renshaw, 1824; E. P. Kendrick; N. Lawquier? (Sawyer?), 1829; Aaron Vans Coy? (Vanscoy?)
* Entry in Source A only.
** So spelled.

S-10392 50a D:209 X-0870 PIKE:PEBB
a. W-5877 William Treplett? (Triplett?)
b. -- Ladds* & -- Norvell
c. B. Hough; P. N. White, 1826; James Sargeant, 1831
* Plural.

S-10393* 40a -- -- PIKE:PEBB
a. --
b. Anthony Walke
c. B. Hough; P. N. White, 1826
* Entry in Source A only.

S-10394* 60a -- -- PIKE:PEBB
a. --
b. Anthony Walke
c. B. Hough; P. N. White, 1826; A. G. Thurman, 1833; J. R. Anderson; A. Latham, 1837
* Entry in Source A only.

S-10395* 30a -- -- ROSS:HUNT
a. --
b. Anthony Walke
c. None
* Entry in Source A only.

S-10396 46a E:64 X-0360 MADI:RANG
a. W-6325 Edward Beeson
b. Levi Springer
c. None

S-10399 250a C:464 X-1173 CLIN:CLAR
a. W-9 Lieutenant Colonel Samuel J. Cabell
b. Samuel J. Cabell
c. None

S-10402 200a C:443 X-1303 HIGH:WHIT
a. W-6358 Peter Emmons
b. Samuel Williams*
c. G. W. Barriere, 1830
* Source A says Samuel S. Williams.

S-10403; S-10404. See S-10179

S-10407 200a C:492 X-0360 PICK:MONR
a. W-6230 Valentine Leach
b. Valentine Leach
c. None

S-10408 1000a D:3 X-1000 UNIO:JACK
MARI:BOWL
a. W-6378 Hedgeman Triplett
W-6379 Hedgeman Triplett
b. Nathaniel Sawyer
c. R. R. Maise; S. G. Strong, 1837; Adam Hayt? (Haysh?)

S-10412 100a C:441 X-0841 FAYE:MADI
a. W-5978 John E. Scott, representatives of
b. James Dunlap
c. None

S-10413 100a C:441 X-0841 FAYE:MADI
a. W-5978 John E. Scott, representatives of
b. James Dunlap
c. None

S-10414 100a C:458 X-0360 FAYE:MADI
a. W-5978 John E. Scott, representatives of
b. James Dunlap
c. John Jackson, 1831

S-10415 200a C:489 X-0570 ROSS:HUNT
a. W-6292 Henry Ayres
b. John McClean
c. Heirs of A. C. Looker; John McLene? (McLane?), 1827

S-10417 320a D:74 X-0663 BROW:PERR
a. W-6270 Billy H. Avery, executor of
b. -- Hartwell & -- Mitchell
c. None

S-10417 80a D:74 X-0663 BROW:PERR
a. W-6264 Billy H. Avery, executor of
b. -- Hartwell & -- Mitchell
c. None

S-10420. See S-7105

S-10421* 400a -- -- BROW:STER
a. --
b. Nicholas Cassell? (Cussell? Carrell?), heirs of
c. Archibald Oursler, 1831
* Entry in Source A only; says "not patented."

S-10422 24a C:499 X-0663 CLER:BATA
a. W-2237 William Andrews
b. William Andrews
c. None

S-10425 640a D:11 X-0340 X-0730 CHAM:WAYN
a. W-6417 Joseph Britton
b. John Evans
c. None

S-10426
S-10427
S-11041 140a D:27 X-0730 X-0750 LOGA:JEFF
a. W-6124 Thomas Hopper
W-5749 David Williams
W-5885 William Mosby, deceased, by Ann W. Chamberlayn
b. Walter Dun
c. M. Bonner, 1827

S-10428. See S-10246 (Source A says S-10267)

S-10429 143a C:506 X-1000 HARD:TAYL LOGA:---*
a. W-5870 Wood Baldwin, heirs of
W-6218 William Yates
b. Walter Dun
c. R. Kennon; M. Bonner, 1827
* Source A does not give township.

S-10430* 100a C:503 X-0340 MADI:FAIR
a. W-5929 Cage Spiller
b. James McAboy**
c. None
* Source A says "not patented."
** So spelled.

S-10431* 200a -- -- WARR:HAMI
a. --
b. Alexander Hamilton
c. None
* Entry in Source A only.

S-10432 687a C:529 X-0840 MADI:STOK
a. W-3614 Thomas May
W-231 John Mills
b. -- Dun & -- Goodin
c. None

S-10434* 166a D:69 X-0060 LOGA:MCAR
a. W-347 Major David Stephenson
b. David Stephenson
c. Hiram B. Strother, 1833
* Source A says "not patented."

S-10435 285a C:507 X-1000 HARD:DUDL LOGA:---*
a. W-194 James Galt, heir to Dr. P. Galt
b. James Galt**
c. A. J. McDowell; George Irwin, 1832
* Source A does not mention Logan County.
** Source A says James Galt, heir. According to schedule bound in Source A at S-10012, the owners of record were the heirs of James Gault (so spelled). Property sold to A. J. McDowell at judgment sale of 8 February 1827. "Lands are all north of Indian Boundary."

S-10436. See S-10270; S-10678

S-10438
S-10689
S-10690 300a C:511 X-1000 HARD:TAYL LOGA:---*
a. W-6217 Thomas Treplett? (Triplett?)
W-6218 William Yates
b. Walter Dun
c. M. Bonner, 1827
* Source A does not give township.

S-10438. See also S-10246

S-10440
S-10597 32a C:457 X-1120 BROW:JACK
a. W-6286 Robert Powell, representatives of
W-6375 John Emmerson
b. Silvanus Bourne
c. None

S-10441
S-10442
S-10596 160a C:457 X-1300 HIGH:WHIT BROW:---*
a. W-6286 Robert Powell, representatives of
W-6375 John Emmerson
b. Silvanus Bourne
c. None
* Source A does not mention Brown County.

S-10454 350a D:84 X-0360 MADI:DEER
a. W-6382 George McCormick, heirs of
b. George McCormick, representatives of
c. S. Watson, 1836

S-10456 1000a C:491 X-1120 BROW:JACK
a. W-6377 Joseph Pugh
b. Joseph Pugh
c. R. McKnight, 1837; S. Ewalt; J. S. Beasley, 1842

S-10457 333a C:491 X-0360 PICK:MONR
a. W-6377 Joseph Pugh
b. Joseph Pugh
c. None

S-10458 800a C:494 X-0390 PICK:MONR
PICK:MUHL
a. W-6247 Edward Garland, heirs of
b. John Garland
c. None

S-10459
S-10370 499a C:513 X-0663 CLIN:CLAR
a. W-154 Captain Beaverley Roy
W-1792 Lieutenant Colonel Edward Carrington
W-2740 Captain James Wright
b. -- Roy, -- Carrington, & -- Wright
c. None

S-10459 109a C:497 X-1173 CLIN:CLAR
a. W-347 Major David Stephenson
b. David Stephenson
c. None

S-10460* 333a -- -- PICK:WAYN
a. --
b. Duncan McArthur
c. None
* Entry in Source A only; says "not patented."

S-10463; S-10464. See S-10246 (Source A says S-10267)

S-10465 60a D:39 X-0870 PIKE:PEBB
a. W-6162 James Whaley
b. A. C. Looker
c. John Devors? (Devore?); A. G. Thurman, 1833; J. R. Anderson; A. Latham, 1837; J. Penniston, 1836; patented to Catherine Hough Looker; J. Dervice? (Devore?)

S-10466. See S-9829

S-10469 143a D:180 X-0340 MADI:DARB
a. W-6417 Joseph Britton
b. John Evans
c. None

S-10470 130a D:149 X-1180 MADI:CANA
a. W-6417 Joseph Britton
b. John Evans
c. None

S-10472 775a C:493 X-1120 BROW:FRAN
X-1300
a. W-6373 John Gist, heirs of
b. Joshua Gist
c. None

S-10473 100a C:493 X-1120 BROW:FRAN
a. W-6373 John Gist, heirs of
b. Joshua Gist
c. None

S-10475 571a D:55 X-1000 HIGH:---*
HARD:DUDL
a. W-6373 John Gist, heirs of
b. David Gist
c. Lyne Starling, 1831
* Source A does not mention Highland County.

S-10476 240a C:498 X-0360 PICK:DARB
a. W-5474 Holman Minnis, representatives of
b. Daniel Brown
c. None

S-10477 45a C:499 X-0360 MADI:UNIO
a. W-5474 Holman Minnis, representatives of
b. Daniel Brown
c. Thomas Jones, 1831

S-10478 523a C:519 X-0360 PICK:DARB
a. W-5474 Holman Minnis, representatives of
W-5475 Benjamin Minnis, representatives of
b. Daniel Brown
c. Mathew Bonner, 1831

S-10479 167a C:493 X-0360 PICK:MONR
a. W-6330 John Sturdivant
b. Cadwallader Wallace
c. None

S-10483 400a D:82 X-0250 HIGH:LIBE
a. W-350 Captain Samuel K. Bradford
b. Samuel K. Bradford
c. None

S-10484 200a E:1 X-1205 HIGH:UNIO
a. W-6052 John Winfree, representatives of
b. John Winfree, representatives of
c. J. Stewart, 1824

S-10488
S-10809 162a C:528 X-1300 HIGH:SALE
a. W-1474 Captain Francis Alices? (Aticez? Allen?)
b. Allen Latham
c. John Davidson, 1828

S-10489 100a D:89 X-1300 BROW:EAGL
HIGH:---*
a. W-6367 Thomas Bates
b. Thomas Bates
c. J. A. Trimble, 1824
* Source A does not give township.

S-10490
S-12120 179a D:124 X-0840 FAYE:UNIO
a. W-6370 Charles Neal
W-6367 Thomas Bates
W-6395 John Harrison
b. Nathaniel Sawyer*
c. None
* Source A says "patented to Allen Latham."

S-10493 225a D:44 X-0460 HIGH:CLAY
a. W-6381 George McCormick, heirs of
b. George McCormick
c. George Smith, 1837

S-10495 250a D:87 X-0663 CLER:BATA
a. W-6382 George McCormick, heirs of
b. George McCormick
c. None

S-10498 100a D:61 X-0130 ADAM:MEIG
a. W-3003 Ambrose Jones
b. Joseph Hill
c. Isaac Thompson; A. Ellison, 1824

S-10500 1002a C:451 X-1000 HARD:TAYL
a. W-735 Captain Alexander Parker, heir to Colonel -- Parker
b. Alexander Parker*
c. None
* Owners of record were the heirs of Alexander Parker. Sold to Lyne Sterling at judgment sale of 8 February 1827 (per schedule bound in Source A at S-10012). "Lands are all north of the Indian Boundary."

S-10501 165a C:451 X-0060 HARD:MCDO
a. W-735 Captain Alexander Parker, heir to Colonel -- Parker
b. Alexander Parker*
c. None
* Owners of record were the heirs of Alexander Parker. Sold to Lyne Sterling at judgment sale of 8 February 1827 (per schedule bound in Source A at S-10012). "Lands are all north of the Indian Boundary."

S-10502 575a C:450 X-0060 LOGA:---* HARD:TAYL
a. W-2257 Captain Chiswell Barrett? (Barrette?)
b. Chiswell Barrett
c. None
* Source A does not mention Logan County.

S-10503 333a D:203 X-0730 LOGA:MCAR HARD:---*
a. W-2257 Captain Chiswell Barrett? (Barrette?)
b. Chiswell Barrett
c. Helen Massie; Lyne Starling, 1831 (Logan County)
* Source A does not give township.

S-10503 130a D:203 X-0730 LOGA:MCAR
a. W-2257 Captain Chiswell Barrett? (Barrette?)
b. Chiswell Barrett
c. None

S-10503* 463a -- -- LOGA:MCAR
a. W-2257 Captain Chiswell Barrett? (Barrette?)
b. Chiswell Barrett
c. None
* Entry in Source A only.

S-10504 200a C:456 X-0841 FAYE:MADI PICK:---*
a. W-30 Captain John Marshall
b. Hubbard Wyatt
c. None
* Source A does not mention Pickaway County.

S-10505 250a C:457 X-0360 FAYE:MADI PICK:PERR
a. W-30 Captain John Marshall
W-31 Francis Coombes
b. Hubbard Wyatt
c. H. Phelps, 1829; Samuel Work; W. Y? Emmett, 1837 (Pickaway County); Andrew Work; David Hays, 1839 (Pickaway County)

S-10506 450a C:456 X-0290 FAYE:MADI
a. W-31 Francis Coombes
W-6272 Billy H. Avery, executor of
b. Hubbard Wyatt
c. Amos Jones; Henry Phelps, 1831

S-10507 300a C:456 X-0360 CHAM:---* MADI:SUMM CLAR:---*
a. W-6267 Billy H. Avery, executor of
W-6272 Billy H. Avery, executor of
b. Hubbard Wyatt
c. John Moore, 1834; J. Leffis, 1842 (Clark County)
* Source A does not mention Champaign or Clark counties.

S-10508 200a D:117 X-0360 MADI:DEER
a. W-6381 George McCormick, heirs of
b. George McCormick, representatives of
c. N. Sawyer, 1826; J. Warner, 1828; J. W. Warner, 1830

S-10510* 80a -- -- ROSS:HUNT
a. --
b. Hubbard Wyatt
c. None
* Entry in Source A only.

S-10512 56a C:513 X-1303 HIGH:WHIT
a. W-6391 James Sanders
b. Samuel Bell
c. None

S-10513 44a C:513 X-1301 HIGH:CLAY
a. W-6391 James Sanders
b. Samuel Bell
c. George Barngrove; John A. Smith, 1846

S-10515 100a C:526 X-0870 ROSS:HUNT
a. W-6368 James Wright
b. Henry Asbury
c. Absalom Chinowith, 1831 (Pike County)

S-10516
S-8163 415a D:76 X-1385 PICK:JACK PICK:DEER
a. W-6417 Joseph Britton
W-6130 Richard M. Owen
b. John Evans
c. -- Brush & -- Gilbert; J. Olds, 1842

S-10517 125a D:77 X-0679 PICK:DEER
a. W-6417 Joseph Britton
b. John Evans
c. None

S-10519 300a C:517 X-0841 FAYE:MADI
a. W-5401 William Sanford, representatives of
b. William Sanford, representatives of
c. H. Phelps, 1829; Joshua Robinson; John Shough, 1832; J. L. Taylor, 1831

S-10520 80a C:519 X-0360 MADI:UNIO
a. W-5944 William Higginbotham
b. Mathew Hobson
c. None

S-10521 400a C:533 X-1000 HARD:MCDO
a. W-6379 Hedgeman Triplett
b. Thomas Marshall
c. None

S-10522 4a D:110 X-1000 SCIO:WASH
a. W-6033 Peter Treplett? (Triplett?)
b. Jeremiah Kendal*
c. None
* Source A spells Kendall.

S-10527 125a C:491 X-1120 PIKE:MIFF
a. W-6375 John Emmerson
b. Cadwallader Wallace
c. None

S-10531
S-10635 1044a D:27 X-1000 MARI:GREE
a. W-5242 John Stokeley, assignee of Abraham Shepherd
W-5245 Robert Means, assignee of Thomas D. Harris, assignee of representatives of John Cobbs, heir to Samuel Cobbs
W-5169 Thomas D. Harris, assignee of Erasmus Gill, administrator of Peter Minor
W-3740? or W-3741? Philip Faint or Thomas Bird
b. -- Means & -- McArthur
c. Samuel Thomas; Benjamin Rine? (Kine?) & David Baughman; P. Lawrence; R. George, 1842; S. & S. Thomas; William Humphreys, 1842; I? (J?) Thomas

S-10532* 200a D:23 X-1315 HARD:DUDL
a. W-6305 John Slaughter
W-5353 John Jones
b. -- Slaughter & -- Jones
c. -- Swearingen & -- Johns**; -- Templeton & -- Elder, 1831 (Logan County); Jones Slater**; Giellen? Johns** & William Swearingen, 1833 (Hardin County)
* Source A says "not patented."
** So spelled.

S-10533 80a C:516 X-0390 PIKE:SUNF
a. W-6423 William Sharp
b. Daniel McCarty Payne
c. None

S-10534* 390a -- X-1000 ----:----
a. --
b. David Williams**
c. None
* Entry in Source A only.
** Sold to Lyne Sterling at judgment sale of 8 February 1827 (per schedule bound in Source A at S-10012). "Lands are all north of Indian Boundary."

S-10535* 150a -- -- ----:----
a. W-5867 Abraham Bowman
W-5169 Thomas D. Harris, assignee of Erasmus Gill, administrator of Peter Minor
b. -- Bowman & -- Means
c. None
* Entry in Source A only.

S-10536 440a D:344 X-1000 HARD:DUDL
a. W-3843 James Coleman
W-4023 William Reynolds
W-3578 Leonard Botts
W-3989 Thomas Fair
W-4015 Benjamin Lockett
b. David Bradford*
c. Lyne Starling, 1831 (Logan County); Duncan McArthur; -- Taylor, -- Turney? -- Cary, & -- Elzey, 1833 (Hardin County)
* Source A says "David Bradford, assignee."

S-10537 400a D:10 X-0929 CHAM:RUSH
a. W-5867 Abraham Bowman
b. Abraham Bowman
c. None

S-10539 96a D:228 X-0841 PICK:PERR ROSS:---*
a. W-5952 Richard Hooper
b. John Evans
c. None
* Source A does not mention Ross County.

S-10540 28a* D:448 X-0360 PICK:MONR
a. W-5952 Richard Hooper
b. John Evans
c. None
* Source A says 24 acres.

S-10541; S-10542. See S-8874; S-9214

S-10543 33a C:355 X-1370 PICK:WAYN ROSS:---*
a. W-5961 Barnabas Arthur
b. John Evans
c. None
* Source A does not mention Ross County.

S-10544; S-10545; S-10546. See S-8322

S-10547. See S-6480

S-10548
S-10910 191a D:149 X-1385 PICK:WAYN
a. W-6417 Joseph Britton
b. John Evans
c. None

S-10550
S-12915 184a D:242 X-0340 PICK:DARB
a. W-6417 Joseph Britton
W-6648 William Christian?
b. John Evans
c. None

S-10551 11a C:463 X-0800 CLER:OHIO
a. W-6394 John Harrison
b. Samuel Forrer? (Farrer?)*
c. None
* Source A spells Forrer.

S-10552 9a D:209 X-1385 PICK:DEER
a. W-4134 Jesse Nicholson
b. Jessup N. Corick? (Conch?)*
c. Samuel Kinnear, 1831
* Source A may spell Couch.

S-10556 75a D:200 X-0800 SCIO:NILE
a. W-6308 Charles Stewart, heirs of
b. Charley Stewart, representatives of
c. Isaiah Clark, 1831 (Clinton County)

S-10556* 400a -- -- CLIN:----
a. --
b. Charles Stewart, representatives of
c. Joseph? (James?) Owen; Isaiah Clark; R. B. Harlan? (Haslam?), 1835; C. B. Harlan? (Haslam?); A. Grantham, 1837
* Entry in Source A only (at top of page before S-10537).

S-10557* 267a -- -- CLIN:----
a. --
b. Charles Stewart, representatives of
c. None
* Entry in Source A only.

S-10559
S-10561 314a E:479 X-0300 PIKE:PEBB BROW:---*
a. W-6308 Charles Stewart, heirs of
b. Allen Latham**
c. Samuel Hannah, 1833; J. S. Barnes, 1835
* Source A does not give township.
** Source A says "representatives of Charles Stewart; patented to Allen Latham."

S-10559* 218a D:201 X-0300 PIKE:----
a. W-6308 Charles Stewart, heirs of
b. Charles Stewart, representatives of
c. None
* This entry not mentioned in Source A. Probably combined with the preceding entry.

S-10561 63a D:201 X-1040 PIKE:PEEP
a. W-6308 Charles Stewart, heirs of
b. Charles Stewart, representatives of
c. None

S-10561* 84a -- -- SCIO:BRUS
a. --
b. Charles Stewart, representatives of
c. None
* Entry in Source A only.

S-10561* 250a -- -- HIGH:----
a. --
b. C(harles) Stewart
c. J. A. Trimble, 1824
* Entry in Source A only (at top of page beginning with S-10537).

S-10561. See also S-10559

S-10562 25a* D:202 X-1040 SCIO:MORG
a. W-6308 Charles Stewart, heirs of
b. Charles Stewart, representatives of
c. None
* Source A says 50 acres.

S-10562 125a D:202 X-1040 SCIO:WASH
a. W-6308 Charles Stewart, heirs of
b. Charles Stewart, representatives of
c. None

S-10562* 250a -- -- HIGH:----
a. --
b. C(harles) Stewart
c. J. A. Trimble, 1824
* Entry in Source A only (at top of page beginning with S-10537).

S-10563 100a D:87 X-0660 CLIN:JEFF BROW:GREE
a. W-6324 John Bennett
b. John Bennett
c. John Hillicost*, 1826; James M. Kirkpatrick; J. Riley, 1838; John Hillegus*; John Burnet*
* So spelled.

S-10565 150a D:117 X-0840 FAYE:WAYN
a. W-6381 George McCormick, heirs of
W-6482 George McCormick, heirs of
b. George McCormick, representatives of
c. None

S-10568 140a D:117 X-1300 HIGH:CLAY
a. W-1474 Captain Francis Alices? (Aticez?, Allen?)
W-6394 John Harrison
b. Allen Latham
c. Isaac Carretson, 1833

S-10569 400a C:520 X-0360 PICK:MONR
a. W-6268 Billy H. Avery, executor of
W-6263 Billy H. Avery, executor of
b. Hubbard Wyatt
c. G. W. Doan, 1827

S-10570 100a C:496 X-0841 FAYE:WAYN
a. W-6389 Elisha Sorrell
b. Allison C. Looker
c. William Cockrill, 1831

S-10571 56a D:453 X-0840 FAYE:WAYN
a. W-5719 William Price
b. Angus L. Langham
c. A. C. Looker; Adam Kidd? (Kidds?), 1829

S-10572* 69a C:526 X-0870 ROSS:--** PIKE:--**
a. W-6255 William Yates, administrator of
W-6254 William Yates, administrator of
b. John Watkins
c. B. Hough; P. N. White, 1826; William P. Cook; A. G. Thurman, 1833; J. R. Anderson; A. Latham, 1837
* Entire entry crossed out in Source A.
** Source A does not mention Ross County and gives no township for Pike County.

S-10575 100a D:241 X-1301 HIGH:SALE
a. W-6383 Reuben Calvert
b. Reuben Calvert, representatives of
c. N. Sawyer, 1824

S-10577 200a D:469 X-1000 HARD:HALE
a. W-3743 John Doland
b. John Doland
c. John Pollard? (Polland?); -- Templeton & -- Elder, 1831 (Logan County)

S-10578 200a D:469 X-1000 HARD:HALE
a. W-3734 Andrew Wolf
b. Andrew Wolf
c. Lyne Starling, 1831 (Logan County)

S-10579 200a D:84 X-0841 FAYE:MADI
a. W-6382 George McCormick, heirs of
b. George McCormick, (represesentatives of)
c. None

S-10580* 120a -- -- ALLE:GOSH
a. --
b. -- Somers, -- Ralph, & -- Taylor
c. James Taylor; James Cunningham, 1836; S. Somers; T. Kennedy, 1840
* Entry in Source A only; there is no Allen County, and Goshen township is in either Champaign or Clermont counties.

S-10581 20a C:455 X-1000 HARD:TAYL LOGA:---*
a. W-1474** Captain Francis Alices? (Aticez? Allen?)
b. Allen Latham
c. R. B. Arnold, 1836
* Source A lists Logan County but does not give township.
** Source A says W-1470.

S-10582* 160a -- -- HIGH:UNIO
a. --
b. C(adwallader) Wallace
c. Abraham Lowman, 1840; D. Sharp; M. Rawlings, 1842 (Fayette County)
* Entry in Source A only.

S-10585 606a D:85 X-1180 MADI:JEFF
a. W-596 Lieutenant John Hackley
b. John Hackley
c. None

S-10585 151a D:85 X-1180 MADI:JEFF
a. W-596 Lieutenant John Hackley
b. John Hackley*
c. None
* Source A says "patented to Allen Latham."

S-10587*
S-12154 80a E:212 X-0179 PICK:----
a. W-459 --**
W-6462 Thomas Hill?
b. Allen Latham
c. None
* This entry not mentioned in Source A.
** Warrantee's name not listed in Source C.

S-10587. See also S-12154

S-10589 250a D:113 X-0360 X-1180 MADI:DEER
a. W-5921 Richard Taylor, heirs of
b. Mary Reddick & Mills Reddick
c. John Negby, 1827; Charles Cissna (Cessna?); J. Scott, 1837; Thomas Jones, 1831

S-10593* 100a -- -- UNIO:LIBE
a. --
b. Charles Neal
c. None
* Entry in Source A only.

S-10594 235a D:72 X-0360 MADI:PLEA
a. W-2274 Doctor Basel Middleton
b. John Campbell
c. -- Worsel & -- Mickle, 1828

S-10596. See S-10441

S-10597. See S-10440

S-10598 60a C:457 X-1300 HIGH:WHIT
a. W-6375 John Emmerson
b. Silvanus Bourne
c. J. Long; J. Roads, 1826

S-10600 533a C:520 X-0841 FAYE:MADI
a. W-6325 Edward Beeson
b. Levi Springer
c. None

S-10601 100a C:505 X-0870 PIKE:PEBB
a. W-6420 Thomas Sorrell, heirs of
b. Thomas Sorrell, heirs of
c. James Sargeant, 1831

S-10602 100a D:198 X-0420 BROW:HUNT ADAM:---*
a. W-6171 Dennis McCarty
b. John Brady
c. None
* Source A does not mention Adams County.

S-10603 300a D:198 X-1300 HIGH:SALE
a. W-6317 Nicholas Oliver
W-6388 Free? Acts?
b. Samuel Smith
c. M. Kirby & J. Kirby; William Scott, 1837; -- Kirby & -- Starling, 1831

S-10604 300a D:198 X-1300 HIGH:CLAY
a. W-6301 Mercer? Beeson
W-6274 David Miller
b. -- Mercer, -- Beeson, & -- Clark, representatives of
c. None

S-10605. See S-10081

S-10606 300a F:243 X-0340 FRAN:PRAI
a. W-4321 George Yates
b. George Yates
c. None

S-10607* 131a -- -- FRAN:PRAI
a. --
b. George Yates
c. None
* Entry in Source A only.

S-10608 120a D:125 X-0500 MADI:SUMM
a. W-6380 James Thatcher? (Hatcher?)
b. Nathaniel Sawyer
c. William Turner, 1836

S-10609
S-10848
S-10894 120a D:11 X-0420 BROW:BYRD
a. W-1754 James Huls
W-6352 Philip Johnson
W-6394 John Harrison
b. Allen Latham
c. None

S-10610
S-10612 53a E:113 X-0130 HIGH:NEWM
a. W-6375 John Emmerson
b. George W. Barriere, heirs of
c. None

S-10611 50a D:458 X-1190 HIGH:UNIO
a. W-6375 John Emmerson
b. George W. Barriere
c. None

S-10612. See S-10610

S-10614. See S-9367

S-10616 20a C:461 X-0340 FRAN:PRAI
a. W-5812 John Goodrich, heirs of
b. James Galloway, Junior
c. None

S-10618 300a C:460 X-0180 GREE:ROSS
a. W-2094 Patrick Thompson
W-2890 William White
b. James Galloway, Junior
c. None

S-10619. See S-9839

S-10620 51a C:461 X-0340 UNIO:JERO
a. W-4601 John Massenburg
b. John Massenburg
c. J. Galloway, 1840

S-10622. See S-6745

S-10623* 100a -- -- UNIO:WASH
a. W-6341 Samuel McCay
b. William Scott, assignee
c. M. S. Butler, 1836
* Entry in Source A only.

S-10624 40a C:520 X-0841* FAYE:UNIO
a. W-5536 George Handy
b. George Handy
c. None
* West branch of.

S-10625 100a C:508 X-0360 FAYE:UNIO MADI:---*
a. W-5101 William Bird, assignee of Philip Courtney
b. Robert Means
c. T. Skeles; John Moore, 1836
* Source A does not give township.

S-10626. See S-9285

S-10627* 40a -- -- FRAN:BROW
a. --
b. Anthony T. Dixon
c. None
* Entry in Source A only.

S-10628* 80a -- -- FRAN:BROW
a. --
b. Anthony T. Dixon, representatives of
c. Thomas Brown; E. Backus, 1838; J. Galloway, Junior; C. Higgins, 1836
* Entry in Source A only.

S-10629 74a D:12 X-0340 CLAR:MADI
a. W-5727 Anthony Dixon, representatives of
b. Anthony T. Dixon, representatives of
c. None

S-10631 410a C:509 X-0991 LOGA:RUSH
a. W-3477 Abraham Shepherd
b. Duncan McArthur
c. John S? (L?) Galloway

S-10632 240a D:38 X-0340 PICK:JACK
a. W-3477 Abraham Shepherd
b. Duncan McArthur
c. A. C. McArthur; J. Olds, 1842

S-10632* 15a -- -- PIKE:CAMP
a. --
b. S. Starr
c. W. White; R. Douglas, 1842
* Entry in Source A only (at top of page beginning with S-10601).

S-10634 140a C:498 X-1000 ROSS:FRAN
a. W-5169 Thomas D. Harris, assignee of Erasmus Gill, administrator of Peter Minor
b. Robert Means
c. None

S-10635. See S-10531

S-10636 120a C:508 X-0340 PICK:JACK
a. W-3477 Abraham Shepherd
b. Duncan McArthur
c. None

S-10637 30a C:508 X-1000 PICK:JACK
a. W-3477 Abraham Shepherd
b. Duncan McArthur
c. A. C. McArthur; J. Olds, 1842

S-10638* 272a -- X-1000 ----:----
a. --
b. David Williams**
c. None
* Notation also in Source A at S-10637.
** Sold to Lyne Sterling at judgment sale of 8 February 1827 (per schedule bound in Source A at S-10012). "Lands are all north of Indian Boundary."

S-10639 450a C:504 X-0663 CLER:STON CLER:JACK
a. W-6378 Hedgeman Triplett
W-6375 John Emmerson
b. Silvanus Bourne
c. None

S-10640 100a E:435 X-0650 ADAM:TIFF
a. W-921 Venet? (Vincent?) Tapp
b. Vincent Tapp
c. None

S-10641 100a F:159 X-0650 ADAM:TIFF
a. W-3138 John Clarke
b. John Brown
c. A. Ellison, 1824

S-10642 50a C:521 X-0130 ADAM:MEIG
a. W-6184 Robert Hanson Harrison, heirs of
b. Andrew Ellison
c. None

S-10643 60a C:522 X-0650 ADAM:TIFF
a. W-6394 John Harrison
b. Andrew Ellison*
c. None
* Source A says Andrew Ellison, Junior.

S-10644 40a C:522 X-0650 ADAM:TIFF
a. W-6394 John Harrison
b. Andrew Ellison
c. None

S-10645* 100a D:84 X-1300 BROW:--**
a. W-6294 David Turner, representatives of
b. Mary Walker***, heir
c. Jacob McFadden, 1834; Caleb O. Parker; J. S. Beasley, 1840
* The entry is crossed out in Source A.
** Source A does not give township.
*** Source A says Mary Walke.

S-10646 100a D:18 X-0663 HIGH:---* CLIN:CLAR
a. W-6371 James Holmes
b. James Holmes
c. None
* Source A does not mention township.

S-10649 320a C:504 X-0360 PICK:DEER
a. W-6020 John Baldwin
b. -- Dawson & -- Beeson*
c. Lyne Starling, 1831
* Source A spells Beason.

S-10652 15a D:394 X-0190 PIKE:CAMP
a. W-6425 George Purcell, heirs of
b. Samuel Starr
c. None

S-10653. See S-12325

S-10654 50a D:397 X-0939 SCIO:BRUS
a. W-6425 George Purcell, heirs of
b. Joseph Mustard
c. None

S-10656. See S-6696

S-10657 26a D:110 X-0270 BROW:PIKE
a. W-2237 William Andrews
b. William Andrews
c. George C. Light; J. Chapman

S-10658 100a D:44 X-0270 BROW:CLAR
a. W-745 Barnabas Mars
b. Peter Casey
c. None

S-10659 451a D:151 X-1000 HARD:ROUN
ALLE:GOSH
a. W-2443 Captain William Pierce
W-617 Captain Alexander Breckenridge
b. -- Pierce & -- Breckenridge
c. James Taylor; Ezekiel Hoover, 1833

S-10663
S-10870
S-10047 2400a D:7 X-1000 HARD:TAYL
a. W-5803 John Remay, representatives of
W-6201 Abraham Davenport
W-6249 Edward Garland, heirs of
W-5981 John Daw? (Daws?)
W-6247 Edward Garland, heirs of
W-5887 Thomas Herbert, representatives of
b. -- Walke, -- Devinport?*, & -- Bourne
c. None
* Source A spells Davenport.

S-10663. See also S-10047

S-10664 1235a C:534 X-1000 HARD:TAYL
a. W-5803 John Remay, representatives of
b. Anthony Walke
c. None

S-10665
S-10666 2000a C:533 X-1000 HARD:HALE
a. W-5803 John Remay, representatives of
b. Anthony Walke
c. None

S-10667 633a C:535 X-1000 MARI:GREE
a. W-6378 Hedgeman Triplett
W-6379 Hedgeman Triplett
W-6392 Richard Bennett
b. Cadwallader Wallace
c. J. N. Williams; A. J? Russell, 1842

S-10668
S-12002 126a D:40 X-1240 ROSS:PAIN
a. W-5825 Richard Foster, heirs of
W-6284 Barnard Clement
W-3879 Charles Forklin? (Focklin?), heirs of
b. -- Wallace & -- Bonner
c. None

S-10672
S-10673 149a C:520 X-0840 MADI:RANG
a. W-5870 Wood Baldwin, heirs of
W-5978 John E. Scott, representatives of
b. -- Ladd*, -- Norvell, & -- Dunlap
c. None
* Source A says: "-- Ladds (plural) & -- Norvell."

S-10675 200a C:536 X-1000 MARI:BOWL
a. W-2808 John Wimbish*
b. John Wimbesh*
c. None
* So spelled.

S-10676 100a C:536 X-1000 MARI:BOWL
a. W-6431 Jacob Gideon
b. Jacob Gideon
c. Newton Messenger, 1834; J. Hockinberry; J. Copeland, 1842

S-10677. See 10270; S-10678

S-10678
S-10270
S-10344
S-10436
S-10677 591a C:500 X-1000 HARD:TAYL
LOGA:---*
a. W-5335 Richard Kennon, representatives of
W-6217 Thomas Treplett? (Triplett?)
W-6218 William Yates
W-6098 Harry Terrell
W-5887 Thomas Herbert, representatives of
b. -- Dun & -- Kennon
c. M. Bonner, 1827
* Source A does not give township.

S-10678. See also S-10270

S-10682 200a D:126 X-0340 MADI:DARB
PICK:---*
a. W-5908 Mahlon Wilson, heirs of
b. Mahlon Wilson
c. P. Douglas, 1829; M. Wilson; James Johnson, 1831; J. Defebaugh**, 1837
* Source A does not mention township.
** So spelled.

S-10683 50a D:112 X-0030 SCIO:BRUS
a. W-6033 Peter Treplett? (Triplett?)
b. William Kendall
c. None

S-10684 16a D:110 X-0030 SCIO:BRUS
a. W-6035 Jacob Moore
b. William Kendall
c. None

S-10687
S-10688 275a C:510 X-1000 HARD:DUDL
LOGA:---*
a. W-6217 Thomas Treplett? (Triplett?)
W-6098 Harry Terrell
W-6064 William Connor
W-6218 William Yates
b. Walter Dun
c. M. Bonner, 1827
* Source A does not give township.

S-10689; S-10690. See S-10438

S-10691
S-19692 170a C:510 X-1000 HARD:HALE
LOGA:---*
a. W-5963 Barnabas Arthur
W-6216 William Holt
W-6217 Thomas Treplett? (Triplett?)
b. Walter Dun
c. M. Bonner, 1827
* Source A does not give township.

S-10695 150a D:414 X-1000 ROSS:FRAN
a. W-5367 Charles Harrison, representatives of
b. Duncan McArthur
c. R. Means; T. J. McArthur, 1824

S-10696
S-10725 90a D:414 X-0860 ROSS:FRAN
a. W-5367 Charles Harrison, representatives of W-4016 William Daniel Moore
b. Duncan McArthur
c. R. Means; T. J. McArthur, 1824

S-10698 450a D:123 X-1180 MADI:DEER MADI:JEFF
a. W-6440 John Stephenson, widow & devisees? of
b. Mary Stephenson
c. Joshua Smith; George Pew, 1833; C. Melvin & J. Melvin; H. Warner, 1836; Thomas M. Farrar; Stephen Moore, 1839

S-10700
S-12134
S-12135
S-12136
S-12137
S-12138 3300a D:88 X:1180 MADI:MONR MADI:CANA MADI:PIKE
a. W-6512 James Davis, deceased
W-6474 William Woolfolk
W-6440 John Stephenson, widow & devisees? of
W-6376 Joseph Pugh
b. -- Sawyer, -- Woolfolk*, -- Stephenson, & -- Pugh
c. Mary Stephenson; James Millikan, 1830; J. B. Andrews; John Moore, 1836; E. Niles, 1837
* Source A spells Wolfolk.

S-10701 150a D:85 X-1160 X-0340 MADI:CANA
a. W-6440 John Stephenson, widow & devisees? of
b. Mary Stephenson
c. N. Sawyer; A. McCologh, 1836; Eli Francis; Thomas Morrison, 1840; J. Stanton; W. T. Davidson, 1841

S-10704
S-10705 2000a C:536 X-1000 UNIO:JACK
a. W-6373 John Gist, heirs of
b. Joshua Gist
c. Lyne Starling

S-10706 554a C:533 X-0710 HARD:HALE MARI:BOWL
a. W-6373 John Gist, heirs of
b. Joshua Gist & States Gist
c. Lyne Starling, 1831 (Logan County)

S-10708 94a D:377 X-0340 UNIO:JERO MADI:---*
a. W-5265 Tuttle Hudson, et al?, administrators of William Hudson
b. William S. Sullivant, Michael S. Sullivant, & James Sullivant
c. L. Starling; L. Sullivant; R. P. Mann, 1833
* Source A does not give township.

S-10709* 100a -- -- FRAN:FRAN
a. --
b. John Knight
c. J--? McLane, 1823
* Entry in Source A only.

S-10710 30a D:26 X-1000 SCIO:UNIO
a. W-5803 John Remay, representatives of
b. Anthony Walke
c. None

S-10711 3000a D:31 X-0840 ROSS:TWIN
a. W-4785 Margaret Starke & Maria Starke, representatives of Richard (Starke)
b. Robert Means
c. William Read, 1824

S-10712 21a D:32 X-0663 CLER:STON
a. W-5989 John Yancey
b. Henry Massie
c. H. P. Hill

S-10713 333a C:517 X-0360 PICK:DARB
a. W-6427 Joseph Scott
b. Joseph Scott
c. Walter Thrall; Thomas Hundley; W. Heath & J. Troutman, 1835; J. Thornton; M. H. Alkyre, 1840

S-10716 200a C:529 X-0663 BROW:PIKE
a. W-4159 James Alexander
b. Andrew Hurst*
c. None
* Source A spells Hunt.

S-10717 100a C:514 X-0270 BROW:CLAR
a. W-6347 Edward Garland, heirs of (or Joseph Terry)*
b. Jacob Maw
c. A. McIlree, 1839; J. Redman, 1841
* Source C lists two warrantees for this warrant number.

S-10718; S-10719. See S-9851; S-9878

S-10721 7a C-530 X-0660 GREE:CAES
a. W-6124 Thomas Hopper
b. Walter Dun
c. None

S-10723 72a D:409 X-0860 ROSS:FRAN
a. W-3989 Thomas Fair
b. Duncan McArthur
c. None

S-10724 70a D:409 X-0860 ROSS:FRAN
a. W-4016 William Daniel Moore
b. Duncan McArthur
c. None

S-10725. See S-10696

S-10726 50a D:409 X-0861 ROSS:FRAN
a. W-4022 William Reynolds
b. Duncan McArthur
c. None

S-10727 123a D:410 X-0600 ROSS:FRAN
a. W-4022 William Reynolds
W-4023 William Reynolds
b. Duncan McArthur
c. None

S-10728 108a D:208 X-1000 ROSS:UNIO
a. W-5997 William Treplett? (Triplett?)
b. A. C. Looker
c. None

S-10730 10a C:526 X-0870 PIKE:PEBB
a. W-5997 William Treplett? (Triplett?)
b. A. C. Looker
c. A. Chinowith, 1826

S-10731 30a C:527 X-0870 PIKE:PEBB
a. W-4851 George Breech
W-3749 Andrew Dunbar
W-5997 William Treplett? (Triplett?)
b. A. C. Looker
c. A. Chinowith, 1826; R. G. Sweezie; J. Penniston, 1830

S-10732 12a D:13 X-0740 CLAR:GREE
GREE:---*
a. W-5812 John Goodrich, heirs of
b. Horace** Lawrence
c. Horatio** Lawrence; John Bacon? 1825
* Source A does not mention Green County.
** So spelled.

S-10734* 300a -- -- HIGH:CLAY
a. --
b. Thomas M. Bayley
c. None
* Entry in Source A only.

S-10735 250a E:415 X-1300 HIGH:CLAY
a. W-5753 John Walker, deceased, heirs of
b. Joseph J. McDowell*
c. None
* Source A says Thomas M. Bayley.

S-10736 126a E:415 X-1303 BROW:WASH
HIGH:WHIT
a. W-5753 John Walker, deceased, heirs of
b. Joseph J. McDowell*
c. None
* Source A says Thomas M. Bayley.

S-10737
S-10738 90a* E:426 X-1060 BROW:--**
X-1300 MADI:SUMM
a. W-5753 John Walker, deceased, heirs of
b. Allen Latham***
c. None
* Source A says 60 acres.
** Source A does not mention Brown County.
*** Source A says Thomas M. Bayley.

S-10738* 40a -- -- ROSS:DEER
a. --
b. Thomas M. Bayley
c. None
* Entry in Source A only.

S-10739 500a C:512 X-0640 HIGH:FAIR
a. W-6321 Gowin? Jeffries
W-6326 John Roberts
W-5997 William Treplett? (Triplett?)
W-3969 George Blakemore, heir to Thomas (Blakemore)
b. -- Chalfant & -- McLane
c. None

S-10740 111a C:513 X-0640 HIGH:FAIR
a. W-6439 Jeremiah Morgan, heirs of
b. Robert Buchannan
c. None

S-10741 160a C:513 X-0640 HIGH:FAIR
a. W-6439 Jeremiah Morgan, heirs of
b. Robert Buchannan
c. None

S-10742 46a C:512 X-0847 HIGH:PAIN
a. W-3836 John Mecham
b. David Dodge
c. None

S-10744 200a C:513 X-1170 CLIN:CLAR
a. W-5751 John Wright
W-5930 Reuben Coghill, heirs of
b. Philip H. Jones
c. None

S-10745 100a D:16 X-1140 PIKE:MIFF
X-0760
a. W-6439 Jeremiah Morgan, heirs of
b. John Barton
c. None

S-10746 25a D:18 X-0220 PIKE:SUNF
a. W-6439 Jeremiah Morgan, heirs of
b. Daniel Morgan
c. None

S-10747
S-10995 130a D:29 X-1140 PIKE:BENT
a. W-6439 Jeremiah Morgan, heirs of
W-6425 George Purcell, heirs of
b. Daniel Morgan
c. None

S-10750 40a D:18 X-1145 PIKE:BENT
a. W-6439 Jeremiah Morgan, heirs of
b. Daniel Morgan
c. None

S-10752 50a D:16 X-0939 ADAM:FRAN
SCIO:---*
a. W-6439 Jeremiah Morgan, heirs of
b. Samuel Carter

c. J. Pyles, 1824
* Source A does not give township.

S-10754* 100a -- -- BROW:--**
a. --
b. Jacob Myres***
c. Aaron F. Sisco; James Baird, 1837; P. L? (S?) Wilson, 1839; R. C. Anderson; Jacob Myers***; William Scott, 1833 (Highland County)
* Entry in Source A only, where crossed out.
** Source A does not give township.
*** So spelled.

S-10755 294a D:28 X-0230 ADAM:WAYN
a. W-6439 Jeremiah Morgan, heirs of
W-6425 George Purcell, heirs of
b. Robert Buchanan*
c. Heirs of Andrew Boyd; Robert Boyd, 1826; A. Boyd; B. Bowman, 1827; Thomas Huston, 1829; B. Bowman, Junior, 1831; J. M? Campbell, 1835; heirs of B. Bowman
* Source A spells Buchannan.

S-10756 68a D:28 X-0381 ADAM:MONR
a. W-6425 George Purcell, heirs of
b. Robert Buchanan*
c. Heirs of Andrew Boyd; Robert Boyd, 1826; A. Boyd; Ben(jamin) Bowman, 1827
* Source A spells Buchannan.

S-10757 12a D:351 X-0800 ADAM:MONR
a. George Purcell, heirs of
b. George Pike*
c. None
* Source A spells Pyke.

S-10758 3a C:527 X-0660 HAMI:ANDE
a. W-6394 John Harrison
b. Samuel Forrer
c. None

S-10759* 5a -- -- HAMI:ANDE
a. --
b. Samuel Forrer
c. None
* Entry in Source A only.

S-10760 41a D:17 X-0424 BROW:BYRD
a. W-6439 Jeremiah Morgan, heirs of
b. Asher Wychoff*
c. None
* Source A spells Wyckoff.

S-10761 8a D:16 X-0424 BROW:BYRD
a. W-6439 Jeremiah Morgan, heirs of
b. John Pilson
c. None

S-10762 38a C:515 X-0420 ADAM:LIBE
a. W-6312 William Pullen? (Patton?)
b. Peter Rankin
c. W. F. Davidson; L? (S?) Cole, 1839

S-10763 62a C:515 X-0423 ADAM:LIBE
a. W-6312 William Pullen? (Patton?)
b. Peter Rankin
c. Heirs of John Gray; James Hood, 1840

S-10764 200a C:514 X-0340 MADI:DARB
a. W-6326 John Roberts
b. Allen Latham
c. None

S-10766 38a C:517 X-1310 ROSS:PAIN
a. W-5072 Isaac Browning
b. Nathaniel Massie
c. None

S-10767* 50a -- -- HIGH:BRUS
a. --
b. James Craig
c. Absalom Lafferty, 1824 (Adams County); S. Porter; R. Douglas, 1842 (Pike County)
* Entry in Source A only.

S-10768. See S-7794

S-10770 120a D:73 X-0360 PICK:MONR
a. W-4245 John Donaghe, executor of John Masser? (Mosser? Moser?)
b. Hugh Donighe*
c. James Cook; Hugh Donaghe
* Source A spells Donahe.

S-10771 20a D:74 X-0340 FRAN:PLEA
a. W-6275 Virgil Poe
b. John Roberts
c. C. Higgins; D. Nelson, 1838; J. Roberts

S-10772 222a C:518 X-0360 PICK:DARB
MADI:DEER
a. W-1203 Captain Beverly Stubblefield
b. Beverly Stubblefield
c. Heirs of John Waddle; John Moore, 1835; heirs of W? (M?) Pritchard; H. White, 1837 (Pickaway County); Jacob Alkyre

S-10773 613a C:519 X-0840 MADI:STOK
X-0660 CLAR:MADI
a. W-2742 Jasper Hughes
b. Thomas Pemberton
c. None

S-10774 107a D:55 X-0663 CLER:JACK
a. W-2126 Abrington Jones
b. Arbridgeton* Jones
c. U.S. Bank; John T. Baush, 1834
* Source A spells Albridgton.

S-10775 60a C:514 X-0040 ADAM:MONR
a. W-6425 George Purcell, heirs of
b. Robert Ellison
c. None

S-10776
S-12715 229a F:22 X-0423 ADAM:LIBE
a. W-6425 George Purcell, heirs of
W-5972 Edward Wells? (Wills?)
b. Robert Ellison
c. None

S-10777 25a D:67 X-1229 ADAM:MONR
a. W-6425 George Purcell, heirs of
b. John Ellison, Junior
c. None

S-10778 25a D:169 X-0381 ADAM:MONR
a. W-6425 George Purcell, heirs of
b. John Ellison, Junior
c. None

S-10780. See S-9901

S-10784 500a D:16 X-1300 BROW:FRAN
a. W-6439 Jeremiah Morgan, heirs of
b. John Lindsay
c. None

S-10785. See S-10187

S-10786 100a D:86 X-1300 HIGH:SALE
a. W-6340 David Anderson
b. David Anderson*
c. None
* Source A says "patented to Allen Latham & David Anderson."

S-10787 150a C:524 X-0870 ROSS:HUNT
PIKE:PEBB
a. W-3548 Henry Bales
b. Henry Boyles*
c. Jacob Loy, 1831
* Source A spells Bayles.

S-10788 120a C:524 X-1180 MADI:DEER
a. W-6202 Robert Ballen? heirs of
W-6064 William Connor
b. Walter Dun
c. None

S-10789
S-10791 418a C:524 X-1180 MADI:DEER
a. W-6202 Robert Ballen?, heirs of
W-6125 Stephen Young
W-6098 Harry Terrell
W-6064 William Connor
W-5349 John Nicholas
W-5749 David Williams
W-6124 Thomas Hopper
W-3548 Henry Bales
W-5765 John Spelfatham? (Spilfatham?)
b. -- Dun, -- Boyles*, & -- Graham
c. None
* Source A spells Bayles.

S-10793 200a D:155 X-0340 UNIO:DARB
MADI:---*
a. W-6428 Vachel Howard
b. David Chapman
c. A. Permenter; J. H. Morton, 1829
* Source A does not give township.

S-10794 300a C:525 X-0360 PICK:DARB
a. W-2275 David Murray
W-6320 George Neal
b. Cadwallader Wallace
c. Abijah Cary; John Holstead, 1832; D. Montgomery*, 1831
* Source A says "supposed."

S-10795 251a C:525 X-0360 PICK:MONR
a. W-6375 John Emmerson
W-6369 Thomas Fitzsimmons
b. Cadwallader Wallace
c. Henry Ely; Richard Seymour, 1831; James Pennywell; Jacob Eagle, 1831; Jacob Slagle, 1837

S-10796. See S-10199

S-10797 130a C:525 X-0840 MADI:STOK
a. W-6313 Obadiah Carter
W-6275 Virgil Poe
b. Mathew Bonner
c. None

S-10798 125a C:531 X-1140 PIKE:MIFF
a. W-6374 John Emmerson
W-6286 Robert Powell, representatives of
b. Mathew Bonner
c. None

S-10801 185a D:35 X-1000 HARD:TAYL
a. W-4992 Thomas Wells? (Wills?), representatives of
W-5647 Stiles Seldon, heir to G. A. Seldon, devisee? of Samuel Seldon
W-4087 William Ashmore, devisee of Charles Gallahue
W-3477 Abraham Shepherd
b. Nathaniel Massie
c. C. Wallace; M. Bonner, 1838; Craud? Wallace, 1840

S-10806. See S-8899

S-10808 88a D:18 X-0540 PICK:PERR
a. W-6387 Charles Green
b. Allen Latham
c. None

S-10809. See S-10448

S-10810 75a C:524 X-0340 UNIO:DARB
a. W-6124 Thomas Hopper
W-6241 William Yates, heirs of
b. Walter Dun
c. None

S-10811 222a C:522 X-0130 ADAM:MEIG
a. W-5781 Joseph Crockett
W-6425 George Purcell, heirs of
b. Andrew Ellison
c. None

S-10812 33a* C:522 X-0650 ADAM:TIFF
a. W-5848 William Mitchell
W-5750 John Pollet
b. Andrew Ellison
c. None
* Source A says 38 acres.

S-10813 75a C:524 X-0423 ADAM:TIFF
a. W-6439 Jeremiah Morgan, heirs of
b. Samuel McKaraham*
c. None
* Source A spells Karahan.

S-10814 116a C:522 X-1190 ADAM:MEIG
a. W-6184 Robert Hanson Harrison, heirs of
W-6425 George Purcell, heirs of
b. Andrew Ellison
c. John Hoobler; Thomas Huston, 1831

S-10815* 42a -- -- PIKE:SUNF
a. --
b. Andrew Ellison
c. Jacob Loy? (Lay?), 1831
* Entry in Source A only.

S-10816 35a C:530 X-0840 ROSS:PAXT
a. W-6217 Thomas Treplett? (Triplett?)
W-5226 Thomas D. Harris, assignee of John Peger? (Peyer?)
b. -- Dun & -- Means
c. None

S-10817* 413a -- X-1000 LOGA:--** HARD:HALE HARD:DUDL
a. --
b. James Gault***, heirs of
c. H. Hendrickson, 1830
* Entry in Source A only.
** Source A does not give township.
*** Source A spells Galt. Sold to Jere(miah?) McLane at judgment sale of 8 February 1827 (per schedule bound in Source A at S-10012). "Lands are all north of Indian Boundary."

S-10818 160a D:23 X-1316 HARD:DUDL LOGA:---*
a. W-194 James Galt, heir to Dr. P. Galt
b. James Galt**
c. None
* Source A does not give township.
** Source A says "heirs of James Gault." Sold to Jere(miah?) McLane at judgment sale of 8 February 1827 (per schedule bound in Source A at S-10012). "Lands are all north of Indian Boundary."

S-10819 50a D:251 X-0800 ADAM:MONR
a. W-6425 George Purcell, heirs of
b. George Miller
c. None

S-10820
S-10999 26a D:30 X-0420 BROW:HUNT
a. W-6439 Jeremiah Morgan, heirs of
b. Daniel Morgan
c. Archibald Leggett, 1826

S-10821 46a D:17 X-0424* BROW:BYRD
a. W-6439 Jeremiah Morgan, heirs of
b. Daniel Morgan
c. Archibald Leggett, 1826
* Branch of.

S-10822 50a D:17 X-1190 SCIO:BRUS
a. W-6439 Jeremiah Morgan, heirs of
b. Daniel Morgan
c. None

S-10824 50a D:29 X-1040* SCIO:BRUS
a. W-6439 Jeremiah Morgan, heirs of
b. Daniel Morgan
c. H. Gunn, 1826
* Northwest fork of.

S-10825 60a D:17 X-0760 ROSS:PAXT
a. W-6439 Jeremiah Morgan, heirs of
b. Daniel Morgan
c. None

S-10826 100a D:17 X-1140 PIKE:BENT
X-0840 ROSS:PAXT
a. W-6439 Jeremiah Morgan, heirs of
b. Daniel Morgan
c. P. Douglas; N. Massie, 1833

S-10828 100a D:17 X-0190 SCIO:BRUS
X-0939 PIKE:---*
a. W-6425 George Purcell, heirs of
b. Daniel Morgan
c. None
* Source A does not give township.

S-10830 40a D:30 X-1049 PIKE:MIFF
a. W-6439 Jeremiah Morgan, heirs of
b. Daniel Morgan
c. None

S-10831 27a D:244 X-0230 ADAM:WAYN
a. W-6439 Jeremiah Morgan, heirs of
b. Daniel Morgan
c. L. Cole, 1842

S-10834
S-10835 100a D:10 X-0360 MADI:UNIO
a. W-5160 John Moore
b. John Moore
c. None

S-10837 800a D:140 X-0991 LOGA:RUSH
a. W-6465 James Higgins
b. James Higgins
c. None

S-10839 667a D:139 X-1000 HARD:HALE
a. W-6466 James Higgins
W-6465 James Higgins
b. James Higgins
c. None

S-10840 50a E:137 X-1138 ADAM:GREE
a. W-6425 George Purcell, heirs of
b. Moses B. Adams
c. None

S-10843 18a D:323 X-0769 ADAM:GREE
a. W-6425 George Purcell, heirs of
b. Alfred Purcell
c. Levi Mattison, 1824

S-10844* 12a -- -- SCIO:NILE
a. --
b. Alfred Purcell
c. Levi Mattison, 1824; R. Hodge, 1825
* Entry in Source A only.

S-10845 12a D:323 X-0769 ADAM:GREE
a. W-6425 George Purcell, heirs of
b. Alfred Purcell
c. Robert Baird, 1826

S-10846 21a D:323 X-0800 ADAM:GREE
a. W-6425 George Purcell, heirs of
b. Alfred Purcell
c. Levi Mattison, 1824

S-10847 40a C:528 X-1000 PICK:JACK
a. W-6356 Henry Dahe? (Dohe?)
W-6352 Philip Johnson
b. Allen Latham
c. None

S-10848. See S-10609

S-10851. See S-10244

S-10853 135a C:530 X-0730 LOGA:MONR
a. W-6240 William Yates, heirs of
W-6241 William Yates, heirs of
W-6098 Harry Terrell
b. Walter Dun
c. M. Bonner, 1827

S-10854
S-12029
S-12082
S-12083
S-12173 618a D:48 X-1000 HARD:DUDL
a. W-6461 William May, heirs of
W-5870 Wood Baldwin, heirs of
W-6124 Thomas Hopper
W-6125 Stephen Young
W-5825 Richard Foster, heirs of
W-6520 William Terrell
b. Walter Dun
c. None

S-10858. See S-10081

S-10859 33a D:284 X-0340 MADI:DARB
a. W-6428 Vachel Howard
b. David Chapman
c. None

S-10860
S-11027 255a D:22 X-1180 MADI:PIKE
a. W-6428 Vachel Howard
W-6489 Robert Wilmott
b. David Chapman*
c. None
* Source A says "patented to Allen Latham."

S-10861 438a C:529 X-0663* BROW:PERR
a. W-6440 John Stephenson, widow & devisees of
b. Mary Stephenson
c. None
* Branch of.

S-10862* 178a -- -- FAYE:--**
a. --
b. Henry Lee
c. None
* Source A notation: "Withdrawn."
** Source A does not give township.

S-10862* 74a -- -- FAYE:--**
a. --
b. Henry Lee
c. None
* Source A notation: "Withdrawn."
** Source A does not give township.

S-10863* 50a -- -- SCIO:NILE
a. --
b. James S? (L?) Leammon**
c. Otis Bean; John Noel, 1832; J. S. Lemerson**; E. Osborn, 1830; J. Seanthing, 1824; J. S. Leamerson**; O. Craine**, 1826; O. Crane**
* Entry in Source A only.
** So spelled.

S-10864 34a D:12 X-1010 GREE:XENI
a. W-6463 Thomas Ousley
b. Robert D. Foresman
c. None

S-10866 6a C:527 X-0660 HAMI:ANDE
a. W-6394 John Harrison
b. Samuel Forrer
c. None

S-10867 50a D:96 X-0230 ADAM:WAYN
a. W-6425 George Purcell, heirs of
b. John Barrett
c. None

S-10868 300a D:85 X-0460 HIGH:WHIT
a. W-6381 George McCormick, heirs of
b. George McCormick
c. John Milton; John Borden, 1838; John E. Stearns; George Smith, 1837; John A. Smith, 1840

S-10869 100a D:84 X-1305 BROW:GREE HIGH:WHIT
a. W-6460 Jesse Poe, heirs of
b. Nathaniel Sawyer*
c. George Smith, 1836
* Source A says "patented to Allen Latham & Nathaniel Sawyer."

S-10870. See S-10047; S-10663

S-10872. See S-9848

S-10873* 67a -- -- HIGH:WHIT
a. --
b. John A. Fulton
c. None
* Entry in Source A only.

S-10880* 250a -- -- UNIO:--**
a. --
b. -- Roberts & -- Latham
c. M. S. Butler, 1836
* Entry in Source A only, where crossed out.
** Source A does not give township.

S-10884 217a D:45 X-1030 HIGH:SALE
a. W-6440 John Stephenson, widow & devisees of
b. Mary Stephenson
c. None

S-10886 50a D:33 X-0663 BROW:PIKE
a. W-6164 Joseph Lemaster
b. George C. Light
c. None

S-10887 150a D:33 X-0800 X-0663 BROW:PIKE
a. W-6164 Joseph Lemaster
b. Joseph Lemaster
c. None

S-10889 40a D:165 X-1190 ADAM:JEFF LOGA:---*
a. W-6439 Jeremiah Morgan, heirs of
b. Joseph? (James?) Freeman
c. Samuel Carter; J. Pyles, 1824
* Source A does not give township.

S-10890* 10a -- -- SCIO:--**
a. --
b. Joseph? (James?) Freeman
c. S. Carter; J. Pyles, 1824
* Entry in Source A only.
** Source A does not give township.

S-10891. See S-8867

S-10892 100a D:8 X-0841 FAYE:MADI
a. W-6014 Benjamin Harrison, representatives of
b. Benjamin Harrison, representatives of
c. None

S-10893* 50a -- -- FAYE:MADI
a. --
b. Allen Latham
c. None
* Entry in Source A only.

S-10894. See S-10609

S-10895 50a D:68 X-0650 ADAM:TIFF
a. W-3984 Arthur Leath, representative of Peter (Leath)
b. Alexander Fowler
c. Thomas Hustin

S-10895. See S-9607

S-10896 42a D:68 X-1140 PIKE:MIFF
a. W-5711 Andrew A. Gilchrist, heir to George (Gilchrist)
b. Andrew Ellison
c. John Deross, 1825

S-10897 26a D:172 X-0040 ADAM:MONR
a. W-5781 Joseph Crockett
b. Andrew Ellison
c. A. Boyd; B. Bowman, 1827; heirs of B. Boman*; W. McColm, 1831; Andrew Boyd; T. Huston, 1833; G. Yocum
* So spelled.

S-10899 3433a D:2 X-1000 HARD:HALE
a. W-6309 John Rudolph*, heirs of
b. John Randolph*, representatives of
c. Lyne Starling, 1831 (Logan County)
* So spelled.

S-10900 1900a D:3 X-1000 HARD:HALE
a. W-6309 John Rudolph*, heirs of
b. John Randolph*, heirs of
c. Lyne Starling, 1831 (Logan County)
* So spelled.

S-10902* -- -- X-1000 ----:----
a. W-5879 Benjamin Taylor
b. J. Hobson & M. Hobson
c. None
* Entry in Source A only.

S-10903 400a D:9 X-0230 ADAM:WAYN
a. W-6385 Charles Pierce, heirs of
b. Edward C. Payne
c. -- Lafferty & -- McDaide, 1825

S-10904
S-12364 200a D:176 X-0360 MADI:UNIO
a. W-6459 John Yarborough
W-6539 William Withers?
b. -- Yarberough* & -- Withers
c. None
* Source A spells Yarborough.

S-10905. See S-5572 (in volume 4, part 1)

S-10907 225a D:9 X-0840 CLAR:HARM
a. W-1880 John Corbett
b. Joseph Watkins
c. None

S-10910. See S-10548

S-10911 40a D:209 X-0360 FAYE:MADI
a. W-6423 William Sharp
b. Daniel McCarty Payne
c. None

S-10912 100a D:8 X-0840 ROSS:PAXT
a. W-6475 William Woolfolk
b. Allen Latham
c. None

S-10913 65a D:9 X-0150 ROSS:PAIN
a. W-6475 William Woolfolk
b. Allen Latham
c. None

S-10914 35a D:9 X-0841 FAYE:MADI
a. W-6475 William Woolfolk
b. Allen Latham
c. None

S-10915 8a D:11 X-0300 PIKE:JACK
X-1360 ROSS:---*
a. W-6475 William Woolfolk
b. Allison C. Looker
c. None
* Source A does not give township.

S-10918 1000a D:6 X-1000 MARI:GREE
a. W-6285 Robert Slaughter
W-6277 Alexander Keeth
W-6327 John Roberts
W-5876 William Treplett? (Triplett?)
b. Walter Dun
c. Daniel Marsh; George H. Busby, 1828; Charles Chard; Alfred Walker, 1837; A. Riser; T. M. Sloan, 1842

S-10919 275a D:7 X-1000 HARD:TAYL
a. W-6286 Robert Powell, representatives of
W-6374 John Emmerson
b. Mathew Bonner
c. None

S-10920 250a D:15 X-0660 CLAR:HARM
a. W-6374 John Emmerson
b. Cadwallader Wallace
c. None

S-10922 90a D:51 X-1120 BROW:PLEA
a. W-5887 Thomas Herbert, representatives of
b. Sylvanus Bourne
c. William Lyons; James Louden? 1826

S-10923. See S-7169 (footnote)

S-10926 60a D:27 X-1180 MADI:SUMM
a. W-4350 Isaac Jenkins, heir
b. Sylvanus Bourne
c. None

S-10927. See S-8965

S-10928 110a D:14 X-1180 MADI:MONR
a. W-5513 Thomas Bowyer, assignee of Martha? Lanier, widow, Barnabas? Rallings & Lucy, his wife, late L. Lanier, children of Thomas? Lanier
W-5514 Thomas Lanier, representatives of
W-5597 Thomas Howell, heir to Robert (Howell), deceased
b. George Clarke
c. None

S-10929 250a D:60 X-1180 MADI:JEFF
a. W-5514 Thomas Lanier, representatives of
b. George Clarke
c. None

S-10930 160a D:14 X-0730 CLAR:PLEA
a. W-5514 Thomas Lanier, representatives of
b. George Clarke
c. None

S-10931 258a D:15 X-0340 MADI:FAIR
a. W-5514 Thomas Lanier, representatives of
W-5420 William Sanford, representatives of
b. George Clarke
c. None

S-10934 200a D:124 X-0360 PICK:DARB
FRAN:PLEA
a. W-6479 Matthew* Cummings
b. Mathew* Cummings
c. None
* So spelled.

S-10937 80a D:11 X-0841 ROSS:CONC
a. W-6475 William Woolfolk
b. Allison C. Looker
c. None

S-10938* 200a D:145 X-0991 UNIO:WASH
a. W-683 John Lipscomb with John Barretts
b. John Lipscomb
c. None
* Source A says "not patented."

S-10938* 200a D:145 X-0991 UNIO:WASH
a. W-682 Richard Davies** with John Barretts
b. Richard Davie**
c. None
* Source A says "not patented."
** So spelled. Source A says Nathaniel Massie.

S-10938* 200a D:145 X-0991 UNIO:WASH
a. W-157 Robert Dugan

b. Robert Dagan**
c. None
* Source A says "not patented."
** Source A spells Dugan.

S-10939 41a D:207 X-0870* PIKE:PEBB
a. W-5740 Elias Langham
W-5997 William Treplett? (Triplett?)
b. A. C. Looker
c. None
* Wolf Fork of.

S-10940 25a D:207 X-0900 ROSS:HUNT
a. W-5740 Elias Langham
b. A. C. Looker
c. None

S-10943 100a D:60 X-1000 HARD:DUDL
a. W-999 Thomas Mitchell
b. Thomas Mitchell
c. None

S-10945 166a D:152 X-0991 UNIO:WASH HARD:---*
a. W-323 Lieutenant Robert Green
b. Robert Green
c. J. Galloway, Junior; Robert Green; M. Collins, 1828; A. Hall, 1836
* Source A does not give township.

S-10948* 267a -- -- HARD:HALE
a. --
b. -- Ladd & -- Norvell
c. None
* Entry in Source A only.

S-10950 50a D:15 X-0300 PIKE:JACK
a. W-5981 John Daw? (Daws?)
b. Sylvanus Bourne
c. None

S-10951 100a D:49 X-0060 LOGA:WASH
a. W-6482 Peter Bowles, heirs of
b. Walter Dun
c. M. Bonner, 1827

S-10952* 100a -- -- UNIO:JACK
a. --
b. Henry Pulten? (Putten?)
c. Adam Woolford, 1831
* Entry in Source A only.

S-10953 64a D:12 X-0360 MADI:SUMM
a. W-5065 Welling Jones, representatives of
W-6463 Thomas Ousley
b. -- Galloway & -- Foresman
c. None

S-10954 40a D:13 X-0180 GREE:SILV
a. W-6357 John Stephen
b. James Galloway, Junior
c. None

S-10955* 400a -- -- MADI:----
a. --
b. -- Galloway & -- Forsythe
c. None
* Entry in Source A only, where crossed out.

S-10956 28a D:12 X-0340 CHAM:UNIO
a. W-1941 Samuel Sandifer
b. Benjamin Cheney
c. None

S-10958 20a D:122 X-0841 ROSS:CONC
a. W-5164 Peter Manifold, assignee of Matthew Irvine
b. John A. Fulton
c. None

S-10960 360a D:50 X-0179 PICK:MONR
a. W-6232 George Hale? (Wale?)
W-6233 George Hale? (Wale?)
W-6533 Nicholas Rickels? (Nickels?)
b. -- Wale & -- Evans
c. None

S-10961 96a D:364 X-1140 PIKE:MIFF
a. W-5019 Ferdinand Oneal (O'Neal)
b. Cadwallader Wallace
c. J. Watts; J. Smith, 1826 (Highland County)

S-10964 400a D:23 X-1000 HARD:DUDL
a. W-6483 Beverly Ferry, heirs of
W-5898 Anselm Bailey
W-6192 Robert Hanson Harrison, heirs of
b. Walter Dun
c. None

S-10965* 72a -- -- HARD:DUDL
a. --
b. Gross Scruggs
c. None
* Entry in Source A only.

S-10966* 400a -- -- ----:----
a. --
b. Walter Dun
c. None
* Entry in Source A only, where crossed out. (Possibly the same as S-10964.)

S-10967 40a D:82 X-0840 ROSS:HUNT
a. W-6475 William Woolfolk*
b. William Wolfolk*
c. P. Douglas, 1830
* So spelled.

S-10968 40a D:82 X-0841 FAYE:MADI
a. W-6475 William Woolfolk*
b. William Wolfolk*
c. None
* So spelled.

S-10969 150a D:38 X-1000 HARD:DUDL
a. W-3477 Abraham Shepherd

b. James R. Hulse, assignee
c. None

S-10971 2667a D:34 X-0991 UNIO:WASH
a. W-6484 George Winchester, heirs of
b. George Winchester, representatives of
c. E. W. H. Reid, 1831

S-10972* 200a D:141 X-1000 HARD:--**
a. W-3733 Hugh Wood
b. Hugh Wood***
c. C. Wallace, 1839
* Entry crossed out in Source A.
** Source A does not give township.
*** Source A says Isham Britton.

S-10972* 100a -- -- HARD:--**
a. --
b. Hugh Wood
c. None
* Entry in Source A only, where crossed out.
** Source A does not give township.

S-10973* 100a D:141 X-1000 HARD:MCDO
a. W-3679 William Eaton
b. William Eaton**
c. William Easton**; -- Templeton & -- Elder, 1831 (Logan County)
* Source A says "not patented."
** So spelled.

S-10973 100a D:141 X-1000 HARD:MCDO
a. W-3666 John Saxton*
b. John Saxon*
c. Lyne Starling, 1831 (Logan County)
* So spelled.

S-10974 100a D:146 X-1000 HARD:MCDO
a. W-3310 John Allen
b. John Allen
c. John T. Scott, 1831

S-10974 133a F:240 X-1000 HARD:MCDO
a. W-2767 Cosby Foster
b. Rebecca Jackson
c. James Hays, 1831 (Logan County)

S-10974* 17a D:240 X-1000 HARD:----
a. W-2676 Cosby Foster
b. John R. Gunn
c. None
* This entry not listed in Source A.

S-10977 100a D:15 X-0991 ADAM:FRAN
a. W-5729 Archibald Elliot*, representatives of
b. Thomas Elliott*
c. James? (Joseph?) Robertson; Abraham Lafferty, 1826; T. Huston, 1834
* So spelled

S-10978 120a D:15 X-0991 ADAM:FRAN
a. W-5729 Archibald Elliot*, representatives of
b. Thomas Elliott*
c. Isaac Straine? & G. Shelley; D. P. Wilkins, 1826; James Lewis; P. Meen; William Richardson, 1838; M. Fellows & R. Fellows; T. Huston
* So spelled.

S-10979 120a D:16 X-1000 ROSS:FRAN
a. W-5729 Archibald Elliot*, representatives of W-6439 Jeremiah Morgan, heirs of
b. -- Elliott* & -- Lindsay
c. None
* So spelled.

S-10981* 100a D:141 X-1000 MARI:BOWL
a. W-4222 John Overstreet
b. John Overstreet
c. Lyne Starling
* Source A says "not patented."

S-10982 700a D:283 X-0340 MADI:CANA
a. W-6489 Robert Wilmott
b. David Chapman
c. None

S-10983 100a D:285 X-0340 MADI:DARB
a. W-6489 Robert Wilmott
b. David Chapman
c. R. Douglas, 1836

S-10984. See S-10081

S-10985 50a D:284 X-0340 MADI:DARB
a. W-6489 Robert Wilmott
b. David Chapman
c. R. Douglas, 1836

S-10986 150a D:285 X-0340 MADI:DARB
a. W-6489 Robert Wilmott
b. David Chapman
c. None

S-10987
S-12170 153a D:69 X-0340 MADI:DARB
UNIO:---*
a. W-6489 Robert Wilmott
b. David Chapman
c. None
* Source A does not mention Union County.

S-10988 10a D:22 X-0660 GREE:XENI
a. W-5988 Benjamin Chappell
b. Walter Dun
c. None

S-10989 30a D:208 X-0300 ROSS:PEB*
a. W-6475 William Woolfolk**
b. William Wolfolk**
c. J. R. Anderson; A. Latham, 1837; James Sargent; A. C. Looker; Van S. Murphy
* This description, given in Source A, may be incorrect.
** So spelled.

S-10990* 30a -- -- PIKE:SUNF
a. --
b. William Wolfolk
c. H. Hampstead? (Hempstead?), 1829
* Entry in Source A only.

S-10991 60a D:25 X-0841 FAYE:WAYN ROSS:CONC
a. W-6475 William Woolfolk*
b. William Wolfolk*
c. None
* So spelled.

S-10992 40a D:39 X-0841 ROSS:DEER
a. W-6475 William Woolfolk
b. A. C. Looker
c. None

S-10993. See S-10084

S-10994 60a D:30 X-1146 PIKE:MIFF
a. W-6425 George Purcell, heirs of
b. Daniel Morgan
c. T. McCoy; George Penniston, Junior, 1826

S-10995. See S-10747

S-10996 49a D:31 X-0840 X-1140 ROSS:PAXT
a. W-6425 George Purcell, heirs of
b. Daniel Morgan
c. Henry Bliss; James A. White, 1834

S-10997 183a D:31 X-0420 BROW:HUNT
a. W-6439 Jeremiah Morgan, heirs of
b. Daniel Morgan
c. None

S-10998 194a D:30 X-0800 ADAM:SPRI
a. W-6439 Jeremiah Morgan, heirs of
b. Daniel Morgan
c. J. Clark, 1836

S-10999. See S-10820

S-11000 260a D:30 X-1140 PIKE:SUNF PIKE:MIFF
a. W-6425 George Purcell, heirs of
b. Daniel Morgan
c. Archibald Liggett, 1826 (Brown County); A. Williamson; W. Satterfield, 1833

S-11001 80a D:31 X-0760 X-1140 PIKE:BENT
a. W-6425 George Purcell, heirs of
b. Daniel Morgan
c. None

S-11003 113a D:52 X-0840 ROSS:HUNT
a. W-6477 Richard Wo(r)sham
W-6360 Richard Bennett
b. -- Kercheval & -- Bennett
c. None

S-11004 75a D:52 X-0179 PICK:MONR
a. W-6360 Richard Bennett
b. Richard Bennett
c. None

S-11005 262a D:52 X-1300 BROW:SCOT
a. W-6477 Richard Wo(r)sham
b. Samuel Kercheval
c. M. Weaver, 1827

S-11007 73a D:22 X-0660 CLAR:MADI
a. W-5885 William Mosby, deceased, by Ann W. Chamberlayn
b. Walter Dun
c. None

S-11008 100a D:21 X-0340 MADI:CANA
a. W-6098 Harry Terrell
W-5885 William Mosby, deceased, by Ann W. Chamberlayn
b. Walter Dun
c. None

S-11011* 64a -- -- MADI:SUMM
a. --
b. George Dawson
c. R. Douglas, 1825
* Entry in Source A only.

S-11012 120a D:22 X-0340 UNIO:---* MADI:DARB
a. W-5988 Benjamin Chappell
W-5885 William Mosby, deceased, by Ann W. Chamberlayn
b. Walter Dun
c. None
* Source A does not mention Union County.

S-11013 79a D:22 X-0659 PICK:WAYN
a. W-5885 William Mosby, deceased, by Ann W. Chamberlayn
b. Walter Dun
c. A. C. McArthur; J. Olds, 1842

S-11014*
S-12104
S-12253 350a -- -- PICK:----
a. --
b. -- McArthur, -- Evans, & -- Withers
c. D. McArthur; Samuel Kinnear; W. Y. Emmitt, 1837
* This entry is crossed out in Source A.

S-11015* 190a -- -- HARD:----
a. --
b. Martin Hawkins
c. None
* Entry in Source A only, where crossed out and "withdrawn."

S-11015 260a D:147 X-0060 HARD:MCDO
LOGA:---*
a. W-5365 Thomas M. Bayly, assignee of Robert Davis, representative of Ishmael Davis
W-5377 Thomas M. Bayly, assignee of Rachel Richards, representative of John Richards
W-5372 Thomas M. Bayly, assignee of Jonathan Bunting, representative of Holloway Bunting
W-5408 Thomas M. Bayly, assignee of Ben(jamin) Phillips, representative of Elijah Phillips
b. James Taylor
c. None
* Source A does not mention Logan County.

S-11016 156a D:148 X-0991 LOGA:RUSH
a. W-5436 Charles Scott
b. Charles Scott
c. James Taylor, 1831

S-11017* 250a -- -- MARI:----
a. --
b. William Croghan
c. W. Cochran; William S. Drake, 1826; James Taylor, 1827; G. H. Busby, 1834; Jesse Taylor, 1838
* Entry in Source A only, where crossed out.

S-11020
S-12019 380a D:108 X-1180 MADI:SUMM
a. W-6467 Prosley* Terrell
W-5902 Ann Garnett? (Garrett?), heir to Benjamin (Garnett? Garrett?)
b. James Galloway, Junior
c. None
* So spelled; no doubt Presley is meant.

S-11023 82a D:250 X-0130 HIGH:BRUS
a. W-6496 Joshua Younger
b. Jacob Kinsley*
c. None
* Source A spells Knisley.

S-11025 133a D:332 X-0840 HIGH:BRUS
X-0130
a. W-6353 Elisha King
b. Elisha King
c. None

S-11026 200a D:20 X-0841 FAYE:PAIN
a. W-6493 James Busby
b. James Busby
c. None

S-11027. See S-10860

S-11028 130a D:21 X-0340 MADI:DARB
a. W-5998 William Triplett? (Treplett?)
W-6218 William Yates
W-5825 Richard Foster, heirs & etc.
W-5885 William Mosby, deceased, by Ann W. Chamberlayn
b. Walter Dun
c. None

S-11029 100a D:388 X-0420 BROW:HUNT
ADAM:---*
a. W-6425 George Purcell, heirs of
b. James Pilson
c. None
* Source A does not mention Adams County.

S-11030 225a E:37 X-1300 HIGH:WHIT
HIGH:CLAY
a. W-5945 William Higginbotham
b. William Robinson
c. John Patterson, heirs; S. Bell, 1828; J. H. Trimble, 1833

S-11031* 300a E:85 X-1180 MADI:SUMM
a. W-6296 Garret Cronk
W-6297 Jeremiah Devor
W-6306 John Pope
b. -- Cronk, -- Dover**, & -- Pope
c. R. Douglas, 1825
* Source A says "not patented."
** Source A spells Devor; Cronk & Pope are crossed out.

S-11032 100a D:25 X-0304 PIKE:PEEP
a. W-6493 James Busby
b. James Busby
c. None

S-11033 200a D:33 X-0329 CLER:MONR
a. W-6351 Levi Hornsby, heirs of
b. George C. Light
c. J. C. Jeffrey; R. Dunham, 1826; S. McLaughlin, 1839

S-11034 100a D:82 X-0870 ROSS:HUNT
X-0300?
a. W-6464 Shadrach Battle
b. Stephen Coram
c. None

S-11035 100a D:333 X-0135* HIGH:BRUS
a. W-1215 Samuel Drury
b. Samuel Drury
c. J. A? Trimble, 1825
* R(attlesnake) Fork of.

S-11036 100a D:109 X-0700 SCIO:MORG
a. W-3819 William Patten? (Patton?)
b. William Philips
c. Heirs of William Philips; William Kendall, 1832

S-11037* 10a -- -- SCIO:NILE
a. --
b. Alfred Purcell
c. David Mitchell, 1827; T. McAtee, Senior; D. Stour, 1841
* Entry in Source A only.

S-11038* 10a -- -- SCIO:NILE
a. --
b. Alfred Purcell
c. D(avid) Mitchell, 1825; heirs of D. Mitchell; J. Waller? (Walles?), 1842
* Entry in Source A only.

S-11039 183a D:63 X-0840 FAYE:PAIN
a. W-937 Colonel John Nevill
b. John McClean
c. None

S-11040 40a D:63 X-0840 FAYE:UNIO
a. W-937 Colonel John Nevill
b. John McClean
c. None

S-11041. See S-10426

S-11043* 200a D:145 X-0991 UNIO:JACK
a. W-2969 Robert C. Bruce
b. Robert C. Bruce
c. -- Parker & -- Bruce; J. S. Gregory, 1831
* Source A says "not patented."

S-11044 200a D:41 X-1120 BROW:FRAN BROW:SCOT BROW:PLEA
a. W-6051 Benjamin Chaney
b. George Brown
c. None

S-11051 90a C:52 X-1007 PIKE:JACK
a. W-4349 Abraham Jenkins, heirs of
W-4350 Isaac Jenkins, heirs of
b. Sylvanus Bourne
c. William Crow*; C. McCollister, 1840; L. Byington, 1842; William Crew*
* So spelled.

S-11052
S-12384 85a D:101 X-0360 MADI:DEER
a. W-6468 Thomas Morton
W-6303 William Naolor? (Nailer? Naylor?)
b. -- Melton & -- Galloway
c. None

S-11055 100a D:29 X-0134 BROW:EAGL ADAM:---*
a. W-6390 Thomas Ashley
b. Thomas Ashley
c. None
* Source A does not give township.

S-11056* 200a -- -- HIGH:SALE
a. --
b. John Wilkins**, Junior
c. John Watkins**, Junior; -- Kirby & -- Starling, 1831
* Entry in Source A only.
** So spelled.

S-11057 100a D:170 X-0130 HIGH:JACK
a. W-6497 James Bolt
b. Job Haigh*
c. None
* Source A may spell Haight.

S-11059 25a D:108 X-0420 BROW:BYRD
a. W-6425 George Purcell, heirs of
b. Daniel Morgan
c. None

S-11060 56a D:108 X-0420 BROW:HUNT
a. W-6425 George Purcell, heirs of
b. Daniel Morgan
c. None

S-11061 50a D:227 X-0840 ROSS:---* PIKE:MIFF
a. W-6425 George Purcell, heirs of
b. Daniel Morgan
c. None
* Source A does not give township.

S-11063 52a D:32 X-0840 FAYE:GREE
a. W-6284 Barnard Clement
b. Mathew Bonner
c. None

S-11064 225a D:32 X-0730 CHAM:SALE
a. W-6281 Meshack Pierson
W-6276 Alexander Adkins
W-6283 John Brownlee
W-6287 Samuel Roundtree, representatives of
W-6284 Barnard Clement
b. Mathew Bonner
c. None

S-11065 166a D:32 X-0730 CHAM:SALE
a. W-6282 John Story
W-6369 Thomas Fitzsimmons
b. Mathew Bonner
c. Adam Rader; William McDonald, 1841

S-11066 50a D:32 X-0620 CHAM:SALE
a. W-4227 James McGovern
b. Mathew Bonner
c. None

S-11067 478a D:34 X-1000 HARD:TAYL
a. W-2024 Captain James Craig?
W-4569 William Carter, Senior
b. -- Craig & -- Carter
c. C. Wallace; M. Bonner, 1838; Craud Wallace, 1840; Lyne Starling, 1831 (Logan County)

S-11068
S-12198 1333a D:191 X-1000 HARD:MCDO
a. W-6490 Robert Wilmott*
b. Robert Wilmet*
c. C. Wallace; Joseph Newell, 1831 (Logan County)
* So spelled.

S-11070 55a D:122 X-0133 HIGH:JACK ADAM:---*
a. W-6425 George Purcell, heirs of
b. John Barrett
c. Willis Lee, 1825
* Source A does not give township.

S-11071 100a D:248 X-0130 HIGH:JACK ADAM:---*

a. W-6425 George Purcell, heirs of
b. John Barrett
c. Isaac Newman; Willis Lee, 1825; John W. Pike; Peter Crager, 1831
* Source A does not give township.

S-11072* 60a -- -- CLER:----
a. --
b. Isaac Pancake
c. W. Shacker, 1825
* Entry in Source A only, where crossed out and "withdrawn."

S-11073 257a D:33 X-1000 HARD:MCDO LOGA:---*
a. W-5594 John B. Johnson
W-5825 Richard Foster, heirs & etc.
b. -- Johnston** & -- Dun
c. John B. Johnson; M. Bonner, 1827
* Source A does not give township.
** Source A spells Johnson.

S-11074 500a D:33 X-1000 HARD:MCDO
a. W-5594 John B. Johnson
b. John B. Johnston*
c. M. Bonner, 1838
* Source A spells Johnson.

S-11076 150a D:67 X-0730 LOGA:JEFF
a. W-64 --*
b. James Herron
c. W. Dun; M. Bonner, 1827
* Warrantee not listed in Source C.

S-11079 500a D:38 X-0730 HARD:DUDL
a. W-6299 James Heard?
b. Mordecai Myres
c. None

S-11080 300a D:48 X-1006* HARD:DUDL
a. W-6299 James Heard?
W-6216 William Holt
W-5825 Richard Foster, heirs & etc.
b. -- Myres & -- Dun
c. M. Bonner, 1827
* Ash Run of.

S-11081 582a D:36 X-1060 BROW:GREE
a. W-1937 Major Francis Taylor
b. Henry Lee
c. Thomas L. Alexander; Samuel Day, 1837

S-11082 291a D:36 X-1060 BROW:GREE
a. W-1937 Major Francis Taylor
b. Henry Lee
c. -- Herbert; Fred Bingaman, 1834; forfeited, 1838

S-11083 291a D:36 X-1060 BROW:GREE
a. W-1937 Major Francis Taylor
b. Henry Lee
c. T. G. Seward; J. M. Trimble, 1837

S-11084 145a D:36 X-1060 BROW:GREE
a. W-1937 Major Francis Taylor
b. Henry Lee
c. None

S-11085 291a D:36 X-1060 BROW:GREE
a. W-1937 Major Francis Taylor
b. Henry Lee
c. None

S-11086 145a D:36 X-1060 BROW:GREE
a. W-1937 Major Francis Taylor
b. Henry Lee
c. None

S-11087 145a D:37 X-1060 BROW:GREE
a. W-1937 Major Francis Taylor
b. Henry Lee
c. None

S-11088 135a D:37 X-1060 BROW:GREE
a. W-1474 Captain Francis Aticez? (Allen?)
W-6387 Charles Green
W-6228 Abraham Jones
b. Allen Latham
c. John Fiscus, Junior; F. Bingaman, 1828; William Baird; W. Hewitt, 1833; M. Smith, 1837; Ansil Collins, 1835

S-11089 72a D:86 X-0540 PICK:PERR
a. W-6440 John Stephenson, widow & devisees of
b. Mary Stephenson*
c. None
* According to Source A, patented to Allen Latham.

S-11096 250a D:86 X-0360 X-0340 MADI:FAIR
a. W-852 John Beck
b. John Beck
c. None

S-11096*
S-12141 750a D:118 X-0360 X-0340 MADI:----
a. W-852 John Beck
b. John Beck
c. None
* This entry does not appear in Source A.

S-11098 75a D:87 X-1064 BROW:GREE
a. W-6228 Abraham Jones
b. Robert C. Jones
c. R. C. Jacobs; R. Jones; Thomas Reynolds, 1831

S-11099
S-13766 233a E:211 X-0991 UNIO:JACK
a. W-6286 Robert Powell, representatives of
W-2370 Thomas Trent
b. Allen Latham
c. Robert Powell; Samuel Jameson, 1831

S-11216 80a* E:248 X-0840 ROSS:PAIN
a. W-8681 --**
b. E. P. Kendrick
c. None
* Source A says 100 acres.
** Source C does not list this warrant number.

S-11217 181a E:236 X-0300 ROSS:HUNT
a. W-348 Captain James Curry
W-6326 John Roberts
W-6516 James Barnley?
b. Allen Latham
c. None

S-11345 800a E:36 X-1060 BROW:GREE
a. W-6308 Charles Stewart, heirs of
b. Allen Latham
c. None

S-11346 1200a E:330 X-0480 UNIO:---*
X-0110
a. W-6402 Allen McLane
W-6403 Allen McLane
W-6404 Allen McLane
W-6415 Allen McLane
W-6400 Allen McLane
b. Allen Latham
c. None
* Source A does not give township.

S-11347 280a E:327 X-0800 SCIO:---*
X-1190
a. W-6658 Wood Jones, heirs of
b. Allen Latham
c. None
* Source A does not give township.

S-11923. See S-7169

S-12000* -- -- X-1000 ----:----
a. W-6280 William Lent
b. Nathaniel Lawqier? (Sawyer?), assignee
c. None
* Entry in Source A only.

S-12001 222a D-53 X-0841 FAYE:PAIN
a. W-937 Colonel John Nevill
b. Mathew Hoonagle*
c. None
* Source A spells Hoofnagle.

S-12002. See S-10668

S-12003 25a D:40 X-1007 SCIO:---*
ADAM:---*
a. W-6369 Thomas Fitzsimmons
b. Mathew Bonner
c. None
* Source A says "not found."

S-12005 25a D:40 X-0840 ROSS:SCIO
a. W-3879 Charles Forklin? (Focklin?), heirs of
b. Mathew Bonner
c. None

S-12006 100a D:40 X-0130 ADAM:FRAN
a. W-5912 Thomas Gordon
b. Thomas Gorden*
c. D. P. Wilkins, 1825; Allen D. Beasley, 1828
* Source A spells Gordon.

S-12007 50a D:355 X-1203 HIGH:UNIO
a. W-3978 Absalom Yancey
b. Samuel Shepherd
c. G. W. Barriere, 1825; J. Hart & B. Thompson, 1833

S-12008 50a D:75 X-0300 PIKE:PEEP
a. W-6304 Michael Naldorffer? (Holdorffer?)
b. Andrew Ellison
c. Mischeck Downing, 1825

S-12009 35a D:111 X-1300 BROW:CLAR
a. W-6478 Richard Worsham
b. Justus F. Randolph
c. None

S-12010 319a D:111 X-0663 BROW:PIKE
a. W-6478 Richard Worsham
b. Justus F. Randolph
c. P. Purdell*, 1838; Daniel Trimbley; P. L. Wilson, 1840
* So spelled.

S-12011 100a D:111 X-0663 BROW:PIKE
a. W-6348 Philip Roth
b. Daniel Trembley
c. None

S-12012 100a D:111 X-0270 BROW:PIKE
a. W-6298 Helebrand Lozier
b. Justus F. Randolph
c. None

S-12013* 100a D:189 X-0840 PICK:PERR
ROSS:PAXT
a. W-1610 Ambrose Barnett
b. Nathaniel Massie
c. None
* Source A says "not patented."

S-12014 200a D:87 X-0340 MADI:DARB
a. W-6509 Joseph Campbell
W-6510 James Campbell
b. Thomas Green
c. A. Latham, 1825; S. N. Kerr, 1835

S-12015* 100a -- -- BROW:PIKE
a. --
b. Samuel D. Rawlins
c. T. L. Hames? (Haines?), 1826; P. L. Wilson, 1841
* Entry in Source A only.

S-12016 50a D:86 X-0340 MADI:DARB
a. W-6507 Casper Myers

b. Stephen Myers
c. S. N. Kerr, 1831

S-12017 200a D:139 X-0991 LOGA:BOAK
a. W-6508 Archibald Gordon
b. Archibald Gordon
c. None

S-12019. See S-11020

S-12020 44a D:102 X-0340 UNIO:PARI
a. W-6463 Thomas Ousley
b. James Galloway
c. None

S-12021
S-12251
S-12287
S-12383 205a D:100 X-1180 MADI:MONR
MADI:PIKE
a. W-6458 Joseph Sames?
W-6433 Thomas Sharp, heirs of
W-6303 William Newton
W-6499 William Schooler
b. -- Galloway & -- Schooler
c. None

S-12022 200a D:102 X-1180 MADI:JEFF
a. W-3617 John Jacobs
b. James Galloway, Junior*
c. None
* Source A says James Galloway.

S-12023 682a D:37 X-1130 FAYE:UNIO
a. W-5600 Lewis Lowry
b. Allen Latham
c. William S? (L?) Cockrell, 1831

S-12024 54a D:39 X-0663 HIGH:UNIO
a. W-3836 John Mecham
b. David Dodge
c. None

S-12025
S-8458 140a D:413 X-0190 PIKE:CAMP
a. W-6425 George Purcell, heirs of
W-5871 Francis M. Boykin & Ann Johnson, heirs of
F(rancis) Boykin
b. Thomas Mountjoy
c. None

S-12026
S-12903 95a D:230 X-1041 SCIO:BRUS
a. W-6439 Jeremiah Morgan, heirs of
W-6425 George Purcell, heirs of
b. Daniel Morgan
c. John Barbee, 1833

S-12027* 25a -- -- PIKE:--**
a. --
b. John Karney
c. E. Hase, 1825
* Entry in Source A only (at top of page beginning S-11082).
** Source A does not give township.

S-12027. See also S-12325

S-12028 175a D:49 X-1000 HARD:DUDL
a. W-5870 Wood Baldwin, heirs of
W-5867 Abraham Bowman
b. -- Dun & -- Bowman
c. None

S-12029. See S-10854

S-12030 222a D:61 X-1000 HARD:DUDL
a. W-937 Colonel John Nevill
b. Joseph Scott
c. None

S-12031 200a D:54 X-0360 MADI:SUMM
a. W-5367 Charles Harrison, representatives of
b. Robert Means
c. R. Douglas, 1825

S-12032 75a D:56 X-1000 HARD:DUDL
LOGA:---*
a. W-5367 Charles Harrison, representatives of
b. Robert Means**
c. William Thompson, 1830
* Source A does not give township.
** Source A says Robert Means, assignee.

S-12033
S-13400 165a D:415 X-1000 HARD:DUDL
a. W-5367 Charles Harrison, representatives of
W-5537 Peter Manifold, assignee of George Handy
b. Duncan McArthur
c. None

S-12034 25a D:49 X-0840 ROSS:BUCK
a. W-3477 Abraham Shepherd
b. Duncan McArthur
c. None

S-12035* 1000a D:38 X-0019 CLIN:LIBE
a. W-456 Captain Lieutenant William F. Gaines
b. William F. Gaines, representatives of
c. -- Latham & -- Leonard; William Hunnicut, 1831
* Source A says "not patented."

S-12036 860a D:39 X-0840 FAYE:WAYN
a. W-2505 Lieutenant Charles Erskine
b. P. A. Erskine & J. M. Erskine
c. None

S-12037 807a D:39 X-0840 FAYE:WAYN
a. W-2505 Lieutenant Charles Erskine
b. P. A. Erskine & J. M. Erskine
c. None

S-12038 1200a D:128 X-1160 MADI:CANA
a. W-6442 Rees Bowen
W-6443 Rees Bowen
W-6444 Rees Bowen
W-6445 Rees Bowen
W-6446 Rees Bowen
W-6447 Rees Bowen
b. Rus* Hill
c. None
* Source A may spell Rees.

S-12039 267a D:86 X-0360 MADI:PLEA
a. W-6454 Rees Bowen
b. Rus* Hill
c. James? Millikan, 1830; Jonathan? Farrar; Samuel N. Kerr, 1841
* Source A may spell Rees.

S-12044* 198a E:51 X-1300 HIGH:--**
a. W-2274 Doctor Basel Middleton
W-2247 Reverend John Hurt
b. -- Campbell & -- Hurt
c. Joseph? Rankin; James M. Trimble, 1833
* Entry marked out in Source A.
** Source A does not give township.

S-12045* 34a -- -- BROW:HUNT
a. --
b. -- Ladds** & -- Norvell
c. None
* Entry in Source A only.
** Plural.

S-12046* 50a -- -- SCIO:WASH
a. --
b. -- Ladds** & -- Norvell
c. Robert Wood, 1827
* Entry in Source A only.
** Plural.

S-12047 667a D:57 X-1000 HARD:DUDL
a. W-6518 John Reynolds, heirs of
b. Samuel Smith*
c. None
* Source A says Samuel Smith, assignee.

S-12051
S-12167 1000a D:49 X-1000 HARD:TAYL
a. W-6519 John Reynolds, heirs of
W-6476 Andrew Garner? (Gasner?)
b. Samuel Smith
c. Gideon Johnson & William Swearingen, 1833

S-12052 100a D:49 X-0060 LOGA:WASH
a. W-6476 Andrew Garner? (Gasner?)
b. Isaac Gardner
c. J. S. Gardner

S-12053 50a D:435 X-1140 PIKE:MIFF
a. W-6245 Newman Landman
W-6494 Francis L. Slaughter
b. Allen Trimble
c. Burgess Elliot, 1831

S-12054
S-12055
S-12209 235a D:203 X-1300 HIGH:CLAY
a. W-5770 Nathaniel Terry
b. Samuel Bell
c. None

S-12056 80a D:122 X-0059 HIGH:WHIT
a. W-5770 Nathaniel Terry
b. Samuel Bell
c. Daniel Daugherty; Morris Call, 1840

S-12057 110a D:90 X-1303 HIGH:WHIT
a. W-5770 Nathaniel Terry
b. Samuel Bell
c. None

S-12058 41a D:207 X-0300 ROSS:FRAN
PIKE:---*
a. W-6374 John Emmerson
b. A. C. Looker
c. Henry Boswell; A. G. Thurman, 1833; John R. Brown, 1836
* Source A does not give township.

S-12063 20a D:182 X-1190 ADAM:JEFF
a. W-5872 Francis M. Boykin & Ann Johnson, heirs to F(rancis) Boykin
b. -- Boyken* & -- Johnson
c. None
* So spelled.

S-12066 109a D:69 X-1000 HARD:DUDL
a. W-5887 Thomas Herbert, representatives of
b. Joshua Poythress
c. None

S-12067
S-12176 465a D:66 X-1180 MADI:DEER
a. W-5885 William Mosby, deceased, by Ann W. Chamberlayn
W-5870 Wood Baldwin, heirs of
W-5825 Richard Foster, heirs, etc.
W-6523 William Terrell, heirs of
W-6521 William Terrell, heirs of
b. Walter Dun
c. None

S-12069* 90a -- -- LOGA:JEFF
LOGA:PERR
a. --
b. Walter Dun
c. None
* Entry in Source A only.

S-12069*
S-12072 335a F:249 X-0300 ROSS:----
PIKE:----
a. W-6217 Thomas Treplett? (Triplett?)
b. Walter Dun, heirs of
c. None
* Entry not listed in Source A.

S-12070
S-12237
S-12245 800a P:65 X-1180 MADI:SUMM
a. W-6523 William Terrell, heirs of
W:6522 William Terrell, heirs of
b. Walter Dun
c. None

S-12071
S-12881 338a P:275 X-0340 MADI:MONR
a. W-6523 William Terrell, heirs of
W-6620 Ransome Colquett
W-6648 William Christian
W-5139 Robert Means, assignee of James Smith
b. Walter Dun
c. None

S-12072* 540a -- -- HARD:MCDO
a. --
b. -- Dun & -- Dawson
c. David Camper; G. Dawson
* Entry in Source A only.

S-12072. See also S-12069

S-12074 100a D:152 X-0300 LOGA:MCAR
a. W-6488 Robert H. Reid
b. John H. Reed*
c. None
* Source A spells Reid.

S-12075 55a D:61 X-0340 UNIO:DARB
a. W-1751 Captain Hughes Woodson
b. Hughes* Woodson
c. None
* Source A spells Hughs.

S-12078* 46a -- -- CLAR:MADI
CLAR:HARM
MADI:--**
a. --
b. William Sanford, representatives of
c. R. Douglass, 1825
* Entry in Source A only.
** Source A does give township.

S-12079 1981a D:46 X-0660 CLIN:MARI
CLER:---*
WARR:SALE
a. W-5858 William Pierce, heirs of
W-5334 Samuel J. Cabell & James Taylor
W-6198 Simon Sommers
W-6109 William Porter
W-617 Captain Alexander Breckenridge
W-5439 William Miller, representatives of
W-1348 Lieutenant David Allen
b. -- Cabell, -- Taylor, -- Pierce, et al**
c. R. R. Bartlett; J. A. Stokes, 1833; E. Harper; J. W. Roads; George Kesling, 1836; E. Whitney; B. Hathaway, 1837; H. R. Sealey***; E. Stowel, 1839; W. Fox; A. Stephens, 1842 (Warren County); H. A. Seely***
* Source A does not give township.
** Source A says -- Cabell, -- Taylor, -- Pierce, -- Somers; -- Porter, -- Breckenridge, -- Miller, & -- Beale
*** So spelled; also initials as shown.

S-12080 41a D:46 X-1080 CLER:STON
a. W-4951 Matthew Griggs
b. Mathew Grigg*
c. L. B. Cleveland, 1824; James McKinney, 1830; C. Whitman; Grist mill; Josiah Osborn, 1837; John Kill, 1831
* So spelled.

S-12081
S-12744 82a D:205 X-0340 UNIO:ALLE
CHAM:RUSH
LOGA:---*
a. W-6216 William Stephens, heirs of
W-6648 William Christian
b. -- Dun & -- Clark
c. G. Clark; M. Bonner, 1827; W. Dun
* Source A does not give township.

S-12083. See also S-10854

S-12084 180a D:325 X-1303 HIGH:WHIT
a. W-5781 Joseph Crockett
b. James Wilson
c. None

S-12084. See also S-10854

S-12086 108a D:61 X-0663 HIGH:DODS
a. W-5812 John Goodrich, heirs of
b. James Galloway
c. None

S-12089* 400a -- -- HARD:DUDL
a. --
b. -- Ladds** & -- Norvell
c. None
* Entry in Source A only.
** Plural.

S-12090 47a D:107 X-1180 MADI:SUMM
a. W-1941 Samuel Sandifer
b. Benjamin Cheney? (Chency?)
c. None

S-12091* 280a -- -- LOGA:MCAR
a. W-3236 Henry Eaton, assignee
W-5812 John Goodrich, heirs of
b. James Galloway, Junior, assignee
c. George Irwin, 1832
* Entry in Source A only.

S-12092
S-12386
S-12387 280a D:101 X-0360 MADI:DEER
a. W-6216 William Stephens, heirs of
W-6303 William Newton
W-1941 Samuel Sandifer
W-6581 John Shanks
b. -- Galloway, -- Chency? (Cheney?), & -- Shanks
c. None

S-12093 444a D:361 X-1000 HARD:TAYL
a. W-5741 William Barret, deceased, representatives of
b. William Barrett, representatives of
c. None

S-12093 526a D:361 X-1000 HARD:TAYL
a. W-5420 John P. Hungerford, assignee of Reuben Briscoe
W-5606 William Aylett & Philip Aylett
W-5710 Charles Snead, heir to Smith (Snead)
b. -- James & -- Clark
c. None

S-12094 133a D:203 X-1000 HARD:PLEA
a. W-4785 Harriet Starke & Maria Starke, representatives of Richard (Starke)
W-5606 William Aylett & Philip Aylett
b. -- Means & -- Clark*
c. None
* Source A says -- Means & -- Clark, assignees.

S-12094 200a D:203 X-1000 HARD:PLEA
a. W-3620 John Stephens
W-963 Anthony Grove
b. Benjamin Hough*
c. None
* Source A says Benjamin Hough, assignee.

S-12095* 78a D:41 X-1000 HARD:TAYL
a. W-64 --**
W-584 Aquilla Norvell
b. -- Bowne & -- Norvell
c. Lyne Starling, 1831 (Logan County)
* Source A says "not patented."
** Page torn in Source C.

S-12096* 150a D:41 X-1000 HARD:TAYL
a. W-584 Aquilla Norvell
b. Aquilla Norvell
c. Lyne Starling, 1831 (Logan County)
* Source A says "not patented."

S-12097 200a D:43 X-1000 HARD:TAYL
a. W-5469 Charles Carter, representatives of
b. William Carter
c. Lyne Starling, 1831 (Logan County)

S-12097 100a D:43 X-1000 HARD:TAYL
a. W-4641 Cornelius Beazley
b. Cornelius Beasley
c. Ralph E. Bunkle, 1831 (Logan County)

S-12097* 100a D:43 X-1000 HARD:TAYL
a. W-4935 Samuel Cole
b. Samuel Cole
c. Lyne Starling, 1831
* Source A says "not patented."

S-12099 400a D:63 X-0730 LOGA:MONR
a. W-6526 Young Wilkerson
b. John Evans
c. None

S-12102
S-12163 150a D:62 X-0215 ADAM:MEIG
a. W-629 Captain Walker Baylor
W-6526 Young Wilkerson
b. -- McArthur & -- Evans
c. John Evans; Daniel P. Wilkins, 1825

S-12103*
S-13528
S-13557 576a -- -- LOGA:PERR
a. --
b. -- McArthur & -- Evans
c. None
* Entry in Source A only.

S-12104
S-12253 310a D:64 X-0810 FRAN:PLEA PICK:---*
a. W-6526 Young Wilkerson
W-6539 William Withers?
b. -- Evans & -- Withers
c. P. Foster; William Y? (J?) Emmit, 1837
* Source A does not give township.

S-12104. See also S-11014

S-12105 1000a D:158 X-0991 UNIO:WASH
a. W-6526* Young Wilkerson
b. Richard Dorsey
c. R. Beard
* Source A says W-6525 (Richard Dorsey, heirs of)

S-12106 40a D:458 X-1000 HARD:MCDO
a. W-6525 Richard Dorsey, heirs of
b. Cadwallader Wallace
c. None

S-12106 210a D:459 X-1000 HARD:MCDO
a. W-6525 Richard Dorsey, heirs of
b. Cadwallader Wallace
c. None

S-12109* 333a -- -- HARD:MCDO
a. --
b. Young Wilkinson**
c. --
* Entry in Source A only.
** So spelled; possibly Wilkerson is meant.

S-12110* 200a -- X-0060 ----:----
a. W-6514 John Clark
b. John Clark
c. None
* Entry in Source A only, where crossed out.

S-12112 467a D:311 X-0991 LOGA:---* UNIO:WASH
a. W-6524 Richard Dorsey, heirs of
b. John Evans
c. None
* Source A does not mention Logan County.

S-12112 1333a E:199 X-0991 UNIO:WASH LOGA:---*
a. W-6530 Nicholas Ricket(t)s
b. Elizabeth R. Worthington, heirs of
c. None
* Source A does not mention Logan County.

S-12113 533a D:329 X-0060 HARD:MCDO
a. W-6524 Richard Dorsey, heirs of
b. John Evans*
c. None
* Source A says John Evans, assignee.

S-12113* 533a -- X-0060 LOGA:MCAR
a. W-6524 Richard Dorsey, heirs of
b. John Evans, assignee
c. None
* Entry in Source A only.

S-12114* 100a -- -- ----:----
a. --
b. Duncan McArthur
c. None
* Entry in Source A only.

S-12115 150a D:56 X-1000 HARD:DUDL
a. W-5344 Robert Means, assignee of John Stockley, assignee of Andrew Waggener
b. Robert Means*
c. None
* Source A says Robert Means, assignee.

S-12116* -- -- X-0060 ----:----
a. W-3204 James King
b. Samuel Walker
c. None
* Entry in Source A only.

S-12116 50a D:421 X-0060 HARD:MCDO
a. W-5344 Robert Means, assignee of John Stockley, assignee of Andrew Waggener
b. Duncan McArthur*
c. None
* Source A says "patented to Allen Latham."

S-12117* 100a** D:87 X-0660 HIGH:-*** CLIN:CLAR
a. W-6528 Christopher Daniel
b. Thomas Green
c. P. West, 1842
* Entry in Source A at top of page beginning with S-12091.
** Source A says 1337 acres.
*** Source A does not give township.

S-12118 200a D:89 X-0360 FAYE:MADI
a. W-1937 Major Francis Taylor
b. Henry Lee*
c. None
* Source A says "patented to Allen Latham."

S-12119 184a D:89 X-0360 MADI:DEER
a. W-1937 Major Francis Taylor
b. Henry Lee
c. M. L. Sullivant, 1831

S-12120. See S-10490

S-12121 150a D:89 X-1300 BROW:PIKE BROW:SCOT
a. W-6356 Henry Duke
W-6352 Philip Johnson
b. -- Duke & -- Johnson
c. William Sellman; John McCann, 1834; Daniel Breck? (Beck?)

S-12122* 300a -- -- PICK:JACK PICK:DEER
a. --
b. -- Cronch, -- Jarvis, & -- Winder
c. R. Cronch et al; Lyne Starling, 1831
* Entry in Source A only.

S-12124 905a D:123 X-0750 UNIO:YORK
a. W-6440 John Stephenson, widow & devisees of
W-6462 Thomas Holt? (Hill?)
b. -- Stephenson & -- Holt
c. None

S-12125 200a D:90 X-1300 HIGH:CLAY
a. W-6381 George McCormick, heirs of
b. George McCormick, representatives of
c. S. Bell, 1826

S-12126 200a D:90 X-0340 X-1160 MADI:CANA
a. W-6465 James Higgins
b. James Higgins
c. None

S-12127 2200a D:129 X-0360 X-0340 MADI:FAIR
a. W-5921 Richard Taylor, heirs of
b. Mary Reddick & Miles Reddick
c. M. Bonner; A. Latham, 1833

S-12128 300a D:90 X-0500 MADI:JEFF
a. W-6382 George McCormick, heirs of
b. George McCormick, representatives of
c. Heirs of George McCormick; John Kious, 1831

S-12129 250a D:119 X-0350 MADI:JEFF
a. W-6381 George McCormick, heirs of
b. George McCormick, representatives of
c. N. Sawyer, 1826; John Warner, 1828

S-12130 250a D:119 X-0350 MADI:JEFF
a. W-6381 George McCormick, heirs of
b. George McCormick, representatives of
c. N. Sawyer, 1826

S-12131
S-12132
S-12133 1034a* D:128 X-1180 MADI:PIKE

a. W-6376 Joseph Pugh
b. Joseph Pugh
c. None
* Source A says 1033 acres.

S-12134. See S-10700

S-12135. See S-10700

S-12136. See S-10700

S-12137. See S-10700

S-12138. See S-10700

S-12139
S-12818 240a E:211 X-1064 BROW:GREE
a. W-852 John Beck
W-6462 Thomas Hill? (Holt?)
b. Allen Latham
c. Thomas Holt; William Scott (Highland County)

S-12140 650a D:118 X-0360 MADI:PLEA
a. W-6381 George McCormick, heirs of
W-6382 George McCormick, heirs of
b. George McCormick, representatives of
c. None

S-12141
S-11096 750a D:118 X-0360 MADI:FAIR
a. W-852 John Beck
b. John Beck
c. None

S-12141. See also S-11096

S-12142
S-12153 1478a D:125 X-0360 MADI:DEER
a. W-6441 John Stephenson, widow & devisees of
b. Mary Stephenson
c. N. Sawyer, 1826

S-12143 1000a D:127 X-0360 MADI:JEFF
a. W-6466 James Higgins
b. James Higgins
c. None

S-12144
S-12145 1005a D:124 X-0360 MADI:SUMM
a. W-6440 John Stephenson, widow & devisees of
b. Mary Stephenson
c. None

S-12146 300a D:123 X-0360 MADI:DEER
a. W-6441 John Stephenson, widow & devisees of
b. Mary Stephenson
c. None

S-12148 150a D:327 X-0340 MADI:JEFF
a. W-6308 Charles Stewart, heirs of
b. Mathew Bonner
c. None

S-12149 80a E:212 X-0340 MADI:JEFF
a. W-6308 Charles Stewart, heirs of
b. Allen Latham
c. None

S-12149* 152a -- -- MADI:----
a. --
b. C. Stewart, representatives of
c. J. H. Cartwright; Samuel Ford, 1842
* Entry in Source A only (at top of page beginning with S-12128).

S-12150 255a D:117 X-1180 MADI:JEFF
a. W-6381 George McCormick, heirs of
b. George McCormick, representatives of
c. N. Sawyer; John Kious, 1831

S-12151* 90a -- -- ----:----
a. --
b. Henry Lee
c. None
* Entry in Source A only, where crossed out.

S-12152 200a D:84 X-1300 BROW:SCOT
a. W-6329 Jesse Crosby, heirs of
b. Jesse Crosby, heirs of
c. Michael Pindall, 1831

S-12153. See S-12142

S-12154
S-10587 80a E:212 X-0179 PICK:MONR
a. W-4592 William Merrick, heir to John (Merrick)
W-6462 Thomas Hill? (Holt?)
b. Allen Latham
c. G. Botkin, 1836; P. N. White, 1838; Thomas Holt; M. L. Sullivant (Madison County)

S-12154. See also S-10587

S-12157* 156a -- -- ----:----
a. --
b. Charles Stewart, representatives of
c. None
* Entry in Source A only, where crossed out.

S-12159* 50a -- -- CLAR:MADI
a. --
b. John Roberts
c. None
* Entry in Source A only.

S-12161 437a D:44 X-1380 BROW:GREE
a. W-1937 Major Francis Taylor
b. Henry Lee
c. Lawrence Fitzhugh; Samuel Ross, 1833

S-12162* 100a -- -- HARD:HALE
a. --
b. John Walker
c. R. B. Truman, 1836; -- McArthur & -- Walker; James Hays, 1831 (Logan County)
* Entry in Source A only.

S-12163. See S-12102

S-12166 600a D:57 X-0340 UNIO:UNIO
a. W-6518 John Reynolds, heirs of
b. Samuel Smith
c. None

S-12167. See S-12051

S-12168 300a D:49 X-0060 LOGA:MCAR
a. W-6519 John Reynolds, heirs of
b. Samuel Smith
c. None

S-12169 200a D:207 X-0340 MADI:DARB UNIO:DARB
a. W-6518 John Reynolds, heirs of
W-6519 John Reynolds, heirs of
b. Samuel Smith
c. John W. Warner, 1831

S-12170. See S-10987

S-12171. See S-10081

S-12171
S-12177
S-12236 425a* D:66 X-1180 MADI:MONR
a. W-6520 William Terrell, heirs of
W-6523 William Terrell, heirs of
W-6522 William Terrell, heirs of
b. Walter Dun
c. None
* Source A says 495 acres.

S-12173. See S-10854

S-12174. See S-9371

S-12176. See S-12067

S-12179 600a D:137 X-1000 HARD:HALE
a. W-6452 Rees Bowen
W-6453 Rees Bowen
W-6455 Rees Bowen
b. Rus* Hill
c. None
* Source A spells Rees.

S-12180 800a D:138 X-1000 HARD:HALE LOGA:---*
a. W-6448 Rees Bowen
W-6449 Rees Bowen
W-6450 Rees Bowen
W-6451 Rees Bowen
b. Rus** Hill
c. William Andrews & Peter Andrews; Levi D. Tharp, 1831
* Source A does not give township.
** Source A spells Rees.

S-12181 300a D:117 X-0060 HARD:---* LOGA:MCAR
a. W-6485 Samuel Johnson
b. William R. Miller**
c. Jacob R. Hall, 1826
* Source A does mention Hardin County.
** Source A says William R. Miller, assignee.

S-12182 178a D:45 X-1130 FAYE:CONC
a. W-6535 Nicholas Ricket(t)s
b. Allen Latham
c. None

S-12183 74a D:45 X-1130 FAYE:CONC
a. W-6535 Nicholas Ricket(t)s
b. Allen Latham
c. Robert Eyre, 1831

S-12184 300a D:398 X-0060 HARD:MCDO
a. W-6502 Lewis Yancey, heirs of
W-6280 William Lent
b. Nathaniel Sawyer & William Lent
c. None

S-12185 281a D:338 X-0061 HARD:MCDO
a. W-6535 Nicholas Ricket(t)s
b. John Evans
c. None

S-12186 12a D:203 X-0130 PIKE:PERR
a. W-5367 Charles Harrison, representatives of
b. Bailey Johnson, representatives of
c. None

S-12187* 252a -- -- LOGA:--**
a. --
b. H. Lee
c. J. R. Hale? (Hall?), 1826
* Entry in Source A only.
** Source A does not give township.

S-12188 509a D:139 X-0991 UNIO:JACK MARI:---*
a. W-5367 Charles Harrison, representatives of
b. Charles Harrison, representatives of
c. None
* Source A does not mention Marion County.

S-12189 100a D:99 X-1000 UNIO:JACK MARI:---*
a. W-6279 Thomas Pasley
b. Thomas Pasley
c. R. Kennedy, 1826
* Source A does not give township.

S-12189 100a D:99 X-1000 UNIO:JACK HARD:---*
a. W-6279 Thomas Pasley
b. Thomas Pasley
c. John Custar, 1837
* Source A does not give township.

S-12190 928a D:98 X-1000 HARD:PLEA
a. W-6375 John Emmerson
W-6374 John Emmerson
W-6286 Robert Powell, representatives of
W-6369 Thomas Fitzsimmons
b. Nathaniel Sawyer
c. J. Weaver, 1842

S-12191 580a D:98 X-1000 HARD:PLEA
a. W-6374 John Emmerson
b. Nathaniel Sawyer*
c. None
* Source A says Nathaniel Sawyer, assignee.

S-12192 1483a D:98 X-1000 MARI:BOWL HARD:HALE
a. W-6379 Hedgman Treplett? (Triplett?)
W-6275 Virgil Poe
W-6281 Meshack Pearson
W-6276 Alexander Adkins
W-6283 John Brownlee
W-6287 Samuel Roundtree, representatives of
W-6282 John Story
W-6284 Barnard Clement
W-6392 Richard Bennett
W-6277 Alexander Keith
W-6278 John Forrester
W-6386 William Poe?, heirs of
W-6286 Robert Powell, representatives of
b. Nathaniel Sawyer*
c. None
* Source A says Nathaniel Sawyer, assignee.

S-12193
S-12194 90a D:73 X-0199 ROSS:TWIN
a. W-4349 Abraham Jenkins, heirs of
W-6029 John Stokes, representatives of
b. -- Bourne & -- Pancake
c. None

S-12195 220a* D:137 X-0841 FAYE:PAIN
a. W-5964 William Poyner
W-5954 Richard Harper
b. William Robison
c. Daniel Rotrick; James Woods, 1828
* Source A says 230 acres.

S-12195 246a D:137 X-0841 FAYE:PAIN
a. W-5403 William Sanford, representatives of
b. William Robison
c. Henry Myres; S. P. Reed, 1830

S-12196 200a D:143 X-1000 MARI:BOWL
a. W-6513 John Clark
b. John Clark
c. J. G. Clark, 1826; A. Smith; Isaac Holderman, 1840

S-12197
S-12244 232a* D:59 X-1000 PIKE:JACK
a. W-937 Colonel John Nevill
W-5887 Thomas Herbert, representatives of
b. -- McCoy & -- Bourne
c. A. McCoy; L. Howard, 1826
* Source A says 230 acres.

S-12198. See S-11068

S-12199 150a D:50 X-0360 PICK:DARB
a. W-6531 Nicholas Ricket(t)s
b. John Evans
c. C. Wallace; E. Cooper, 1830

S-12201. See S-10969

S-12202 50a D:52 X-0360 MADI:RANG
a. W-6531 Nicholas Ricket(t)s
b. John Evans
c. None

S-12203 45a D:51 X-0540 PICK:DEER PICK:PERR
a. W-6532 Nicholas Ricket(t)s
W-6533 Nicholas Ricket(t)s
b. John Evans
c. C. Wallace; J. Irvine, 1829; Eliza Taylor; George Reeder, 1837; W. H. Leffingwell, 1839

S-12204 560a D:53 X-0810 PICK:DARB
a. W-5163 Peter Manifold, representatives of Matthew Irvine
b. George Renick
c. None

S-12205
S-12258 200a D:71 X-1137 FAYE:UNIO FAYE:GREE
a. W-6534 Nicholas Ricket(t)s
W-6539 William Withers?
b. -- Evans & -- Withers
c. William Withers; John L? (S?) Taylor, 1831

S-12206 40a D:51 X-0540 PICK:DEER
a. W-6533 Nicholas Ricket(t)s
W-6534 Nicholas Ricket(t)s
b. John Evans
c. None

S-12207 55a D:50 X-0670 ROSS:PAIN
a. W-6534 Nicholas Ricket(t)s
b. John Evans
c. None

S-12208 75a D:91 X-0469 HIGH:CLAY
a. W-5770 Nathaniel Terry
b. Samuel Bell
c. None

S-12209. See S-12054

S-12212 225a D:60 X-0019A HARD:DUDL
a. W-6521 William Terrell, heirs of
b. Walter Dun
c. None

S-12213 100a D:111 X-1300 BROW:CLAR
a. W-6495 Thomas Armon? or Harmon
b. Jonathan S. Donham
c. None

S-12214 367a D:163 X-0340 UNIO:JERO
a. W-4631 William Ross
W-3196 Samuel Wallace
b. Lucas Sullivant
c. None

S-12215* 64a -- -- UNIO:UNIO
a. --
b. Lucas Sullivant
c. E. W. H. Reed, 1831
* Entry in Source A only.

S-12216* 300a -- -- UNIO:--**
a. --
b. -- Gratton & -- Sullivant
c. None
* Entry in Source A only.
** Source A does not give township.

S-12217* 962a -- -- LOGA:RUSH
a. --
b. Robert Kays**
c. Robert Hays**; Joshua Fulsom, 1833
* Entry in Source A only.
** So spelled.

S-12218* 667a -- -- MADI:JEFF
a. --
b. Robert Kays
c. M. L. Sullivant; R. Bidwell, 1833; R. Douglas, 1836
* Entry in Source A only.

S-12219* 738a -- -- FRAN:BROW FRAN:PRAI
a. --
b. Robert Kays
c. None
* Entry in Source A only.

S-12220 100a D:316 X-1040 ADAM:JEFF
a. W-6184 Robert Hanson Harrison
b. Jonathan Wait
c. None

S-12221 245a D:90 X-0800 ADAM:SPRI
a. W-3962 Miles Cardiff
W-6304 Michael Naldorffer? (Holdorffer?)
W-4094 Philip Main
W-3690? or W-3791? John Hays or Hezekiah Clark
b. John Ellison
c. None

S-12222 70a D:68 X-0135* ADAM:TIFF
a. W-6304 Michael Naldorffer? (Holdorffer?)
b. Jesse Freeland
c. None
* L(ic)k Fork of.

S-12224
S-12225 50a D:252 X-1140 PIKE:PERR
a. W-6500 James Lee
b. Samuel Brown
c. G. Penniston, 1826

S-12226 20a D:251 X-0130 HIGH:BRUS
a. W-6496 Joshua Younger
b. Samuel Allison
c. J. L. Hughes, 1842

S-12227 15a D:453 X-0130 HIGH:BRUS
a. W-6496 Joshua Younger
b. Samuel Allison
c. None

S-12228
S-12229 65a D:195 X-1140 HIGH:BRUS
a. W-6496 Joshua Younger
b. David Kniseley*
c. None
* Source A may spell Kinseley.

S-12230 100a E:39 X-1301 HIGH:SALE
a. W-3978 Absalom Yancey
W-6515 Daniel Barnett
b. George W. Barrere*
c. None
* Source A spells Barriere.

S-12232 100a D:55 X-0660 CLER:GOSH
a. W-6470 William Varm--?
b. -- Wilcox & -- Lytle
c. J. M. Kinney, 1829; Peter Stroup; John Erwin, 1839

S-12233. See S-12325

S-12234
S-12601 281a D:368 X-0190 PIKE:CAMP
a. W-6425 George Purcell, heirs of
W-6503 Allen Walker, devisees of
b. Thomas Mountjoy
c. None

S-12235 200a D:142 X-1000 HARD:MCDO
a. W-6471 John Thompson
b. John Thompson
c. None

S-12235. See also S-9741

S-12236. See S-12171

S-12237. See S-12070

S-12238 185a D:205 X-0340 UNIO:UNIO
a. W-6522 William Terrell, heirs of
b. Walter Dun
c. None

S-12239 70a D:205 X-0340 UNIO:UNIO
a. W-6522 William Terrell, heirs of
b. Walter Dun
c. None

S-12240
S-12877 258a D:274 X-0340 MADI:---*
UNIO:DARB
a. W-6499 William Schooler
W-5139 Robert Means, assignee of James Smith
b. -- Schooler & -- Dun
c. None
* Source A does not mention Madison County.

S-12241* 100a -- -- FAYE:--**
a. --
b. John Evans
c. None
* Entry in Source A only.
** Source A does not give township.

S-12242
S-12262 140a D:65 X-0340 UNIO:ALLE
LOGA:ZANE
a. W-6526 Young Wilkerson
W-6539 William Withers?
b. -- Evans & -- Withers
c. William Withers; Daniel Burnham, 1831

S-12243 30a D:150 X-0340 UNIO:DARB
a. W-6526 Young Wilkerson
b. John Evans
c. J. Calloway, Junior

S-12244. See S-12197

S-12245. See S-12070

S-12246 500a D:142 X-1000 HARD:TAYL
X-0060 LOGA:---*
a. W-1387 Captain Ferdinand Oneal
b. Ferdinand Oneal
c. John Watts; Laquinas? Rawson, 1832
* Source A does not give township.

S-12247 492a D:142 X-1000 HARD:MCDO
a. W-1387 Captain Ferdinand Oneal
b. Ferdinand Oneal
c. Loquina Rawson

S-12248 1000a D:83 X-0660 GREE:SUGA
a. W-6524 Richard Dorsey, heirs of
W-348 Captain James Curry
b. Allen Latham
c. Henry Compton, 1829; N. Guin; Thornton Marshall, 1839

S-12250. See S-10955

S-12251. See S-12021

S-12252 50a D:97 X-0600 ADAM:SPRI
X-0590
a. W-6539 William Withers?
b. William Withers
c. None

S-12253. See S-12104; S-11014

S-12254 80a D:64 X-0840 FAYE:JEFF
a. W-6539 William Withers?
b. William Withers
c. John L. Taylor, 1831

S-12254. See also S-7169

S-12255 35a D:63 X-0360 MADI:PLEA
a. W-6539 William Withers?
b. William Withers
c. None

S-12256 280a D:64 X-0340 LOGA:ZANE
a. W-6539 William Withers?
b. William Withers
c. None

S-12257 123a D:70 X-0840 FAYE:WAYN
a. W-6539 William Withers?
b. William Withers
c. None

S-12258. See S-12205

S-12259. See S-7169 (footnote)

S-12260
S-12480 147a D:135 X-0300 PIKE:PEEP
a. W-6539 William Withers?
b. William Withers
c. C. Wallace; J. Evans; N. Franklin, 1828; Jacob Lay, 1831

S-12261* 1080a -- -- HIGH:--**
a. --
b. William Withers
c. None
* Entry in Source A only, where crossed out.
** Source A does not give township.

S-12262. See S-12242

S-12265
S-12371 260a D:176 X-0340 PICK:SCIO
PICK:DARB

a. W-6539 William Withers?
W-6537 Thomas Parremore
b. -- Withers & -- Mayo
c. C. Wallace; Philip McNamar, 1830

S-12266
S-12372 175a D:366 X-0340 PICK:MUHL
a. W-6538 Thomas Parremore
W-6537 Thomas Parremore
b. Cadwallader Wallace
c. None

S-12267 100a D:74 X-0840 ROSS:PAXT
a. W-6538 Thomas Parremore
b. Peter P. Mayo
c. None

S-12269 130a D:444 X-0340 UNIO:DARB
MADI:DARB
a. W-6547 Thomas Lucas
b. Thomas Lucas
c. None

S-12269 12a D:444 X-0340 UNIO:DARB
MADI:DARB
a. W-6547 Thomas Lucas
b. Thomas Lucas
c. None

S-12270 250a E:27 X-0340 UNIO:---*
X-0350 MADI:CANA
a. W-6547 Thomas Lucas
b. Thomas Lucas
c. N. Sawyer, 1826; A. Latham; J. W. Warner, 1829; W. Perin, 1837
* Source A does not mention Union County.

S-12270 90a D:117 X-0340 MADI:CANA
X-0350
a. W-6547 Thomas Lucas
b. Thomas Lucas
c. None

S-12271 180a D:445 X-0340 MADI:CANA
a. W-6547 Thomas Lucas
b. Thomas Lucas
c. None

S-12272 850a E:24 X-1180 MADI:JEFF
X-0340
a. W-6547 Thomas Lucas
b. Thomas Lucas
c. A. Latham; J. W. Warner, 1829

S-12273 750a E:25 X-1180 MADI:CANA
X-0340
a. W-6547 Thomas Lucas
b. Thomas Lucas
c. A. Latham; J. W. Warner, 1829

S-12274* 120a E:70 X-0340 UNIO:DARB
a. W-6547 Thomas Lucas
b. Thomas Lucas
c. None
* Location may have been in Madison County, Darby Township.

S-12275 1060a E:26 X-0350 MADI:DARB
a. W-6547 Thomas Lucas
b. Thomas Lucas
c. None

S-12276 2667a E:178 X-1000 HARD:ROUN
AUGL:---*
LOGA:STOK
a. W-6549 Valentine Peers?
b. Valentine Peers
c. Robert Courtney; Samuel Scott, 1831; Philip G. Pliley; A. Latham; A. Krouskop & Samuel Walker, 1837
* Source A does not mention Auglaise County.

S-12276 1667a E:225 X-0060 LOGA:---*
AUGL:---*
ALLE:GOSH
a. W-6549 Valentine Peers?
b. Valentine Peers
c. R. Courtney
* Source A mentions Hardin County (no township), but not Logan or Auglaise counties.

S-12277 1000a E:225 X-1000 HARD:ROUN
LOGA:---*
a. W-6550 George Lambert
b. George Lambert
c. A. Latham; Lyne Starling, 1831 (Logan County)
* Source A does not mention Logan County.

S-12277 500a E:226 X-1000 HARD:ROUN
LOGA:---*
a. W-6550 George Lambert
b. George Lambert
c. -- Campbell & -- Helphenstine; Enoch Harvey, 1838
* Source A does not mention Logan County.

S-12278
S-12311 280a E:398 X-0060 HARD:ROUN
LOGA:---*
a. W-6547 Thomas Lucas
b. Thomas Lucas
c. None
* Source A does not mention Logan County.

S-12279 450a E:139 X-0060 HARD:MCDO
LOGA:---*
a. W-6550 George Lambert
b. George Lambert
c. None
* Source A does not mention Logan County.

S-12280 1417a* E:227 X-1000 HARD:HALE
LOGA:--**
a. W-6550 George Lambert
b. Thomas Green***

c. S. G. Strong, 1833
* Source A says 1550 acres.
** Source A does not mention Logan County.
*** Source A says George Lambert.

S-12281 500a D:140 X-1000 UNIO:WASH HARD:HALE
a. W-6550 George Lambert
b. George Lambert
c. None

S-12282 750a D:104 X-0340 UNIO:LIBE
a. W-6525 Richard Dorsey, heirs of
b. Richard Dorsey
c. James Olds

S-12283 1000a D:150 X-0340 LOGA:---* UNIO:LIBE
a. W-6527 Young Wilkerson**
b. Young Wilkinson**
c. None
* Source A does not mention Logan County.
** So spelled.

S-12287. See S-12021

S-12288
S-12382 60a D:101 X-0730 CHAM:UNIO
a. W-6468 Thomas Melton
W-6303 William Newton
b. -- Melton & -- Galloway
c. None

S-12289 1556a D:142 X-0991 UNIO:WASH HARD:---*
a. W-6544 Arthur Treackle, heirs of
b. E. A. P. Scarborough
c. Lyne Starling, 1831
* Source A does not give township.

S-12290
S-12359
S-12738 389a D:177 X-1380 PICK:DEER
a. W-6544 Arthur Treackle, heirs of
b. James J. Teackle? (Treackle?)
c. None

S-12291 778a D:169 X-1000 HARD:TAYL
a. W-6545 Charles Sneed, heirs of
b. Mary E. Wilkins
c. Lyne Starling

S-12291* 778a D:177 X-1000 HARD:----
a. W-6545 Charles Sneed, heirs of
b. Mary E. Wilkins
c. None
* Source A does not list this second entry under S-12291. It is probably a copying error (duplication).

S-12292 778a D:143 X-0060 HARD:MCDO
a. W-6545 Charles Sneed, heirs of
b. Edward S. Sneed
c. Lyne Starling

S-12293 200a D:130 X-0840 ROSS:PAXT
a. W-6545 Charles Sneed, heirs of
b. Sally Winder
c. None

S-12294. See S-12355

S-12296 300a D:138 X-1000 HARD:ROUN
a. W-6545 Charles Sneed, heirs of
b. Sally Winder
c. Lyne Starling, 1831 (Logan County)

S-12304
S-12406 200a D:91 X-0663 CLER:STON CLER:JACK
a. W-6537 Thomas Parremore
b. Peter P. Mayo
c. None

S-12307 200a D:92 X-0420 BROW:HUNT
a. W-6537 Thomas Parremore
b. Peter P. Mayo
c. None

S-12308 1000a D:126 X-0340 UNIO:ALLE
a. W-6558 Mazy or Mary Vance
b. Mary* Vance
c. None
* Source A spells Mazy.

S-12311 220a D:398 X-0060 LOGA:MCAR
a. W-6560 Mazy or Mary Vance
b. Mary* Vance
c. None
* Source A spells Mazy.

S-12311. See also S-12278

S-12314 90a D:151 X-0340 UNIO:PARI
a. W-6539 William Withers?
b. William Withers
c. Jacob Pasthermore? (Parthermore?), 1831

S-12315* 100a -- -- UNIO:--**
a. --
b. Duncan McArthur
c. None
* Entry in Source A only, where crossed out.
** Source A does not give township.

S-12316
S-13676 67a F:220 X-1000 HARD:MCDO
a. W-5021 George Charlton, representatives of
b. Duncan McArthur, heirs of
c. None

S-12319. See S-12325

S-12320 101a D:205 X-0060 LOGA:MCAR
a. W-5824 Elijah Moody
W-6218 William Yates
W-6520 William Terrell, heirs of
b. Walter Dun
c. M. Bonner, 1827

S-12321* 167a** -- -- ----:----
a. --
b. Isaac Tyne
c. S. Hinton, 1828; Peter Andrew; forfeited, 1839
* Entry in Source A only.
** Acreage crossed out.

S-12322 50a D:166 X-0130 ADAM:JEFF
a. W-6537 Thomas Parremore
b. Peter P. Mayo
c. John Sphar; A. Ellison, 1826

S-12323 75a D:413 X-0079 SCIO:MORG
a. W-6537 Thomas Parremore
b. Thomas Mountjoy
c. P. P. Mayo*; L. Howard, 1826; John Berry; P. P. Mayhew*; E. R. Hitchcock, 1830
* So spelled.

S-12324 100a E:108 X-0420 ADAM:TIFF
a. W-6537 Thomas Parremore
b. Thomas Mountjoy
c. None

S-12324. See also S-7512

S-12325
S-12327
S-12319
S-12690
S-12604
S-12700
S-12695
S-12694
S-12599
S-10653
S-12233
S-12027 785a D:396 X-0030 PIKE:CAMP
X-0190 SCIO:MORG
a. W-6537 Thomas Parremore
W-6425 George Purcell, heirs of
W-6588 Allen Walker, deceased, devisees of
W-6504 Allen Walker, deceased, devisees of
W-6503 Allen Walker, deceased, devisees of
W-5871 Francis M. Boykin & Ann Johnson, heirs of F(rancis) Boykin
b. -- Mountjoy & -- Mayo
c. P. P. Mayo; J. Ruckman, 1826; T. Mountjoy; L. Byington, 1842; R. Douglas, 1842

S-12326* 120a -- -- SCIO:UNIO
a. --
b. Peter P. Mayo
c. None
* Entry in Source A only.

S-12328
S-12329 85a D:205 X-0304 PIKE:PEEP
a. W-6499 William Schooler
W-6520 William Terrell, heirs of
b. -- Schooler & -- Dun
c. William Schools*; J. Hinds, 1826
* So spelled.

S-12332
S-12404 425a DS:92 X-1300 BROW:LEWI
BROW:CLAR
a. W-6537 Thomas Parremore
b. Peter P. Mayo
c. Ignatius Mitchell; Samuel Glaze, 1837; James Henry, 1831

S-12333 200a D:92 X-0730 CLAR:PLEA
a. W-6537 Thomas Parremore
b. Peter P. Mayo
c. None

S-12336* 50a -- -- PICK:WAYN
a. --
b. John Evans
c. None
* Entry in Source A only.

S-12337. See S-8322

S-12338 345a D:93 X-1240 ROSS:PAIN
a. W-6537 Thomas Parremore
b. Peter P. Mayo
c. None

S-12339 100a D:93 X-0840 ROSS:PAXT
a. W-6537 Thomas Parremore
b. Peter P. Mayo
c. None

S-12340 75a D:80 X-0660 CLAR:MADI
a. W-6537 Thomas Parremore
b. Peter P. Mayo
c. None

S-12341
S-12373 254a D:94 X-0660 MADI:---*
CLAR:MADI
a. W-6537 Thomas Parremore
b. Peter P. Mayo
c. Enoch Jones; H. Warner, 1837
* Source A does not give township.

S-12342 250a D:107 X-0750 DELA:SCIO
a. W-323 Lieutenant Robert Green
b. Robert Green
c. None

S-12343 250a D:152 X-1000 HARD:HALE
a. W-323 Lieutenant Robert Green
b. Robert Green
c. None

S-12344 78a D:153 X-0080 BROW:HUNT
HARD:---*

a. W-6546 Robert Green, heirs of
b. Robert Green
c. John W. Tibatts, 1826
* Source A does not give township.

S-12345 587a* E:380 X-0663 HIGH:UNIO
a. W-1264 Asa Cauley
W-2239 Ensign Clement Carrington
W-46 Clement Read**, heir to Colonel -- Read**
b. -- Carrington & -- Reid**
c. None
* Source A says 687 acres.
** So spelled; Source A says "patented to Allen Latham."

S-12345* 500a E:335 X-0663 HARD:----
a. W-1264 Asa Cauley
W-46 Clement Read, heir to Colonel -- Read
W-2239 Ensign Clement Carrington
b. Allen Latham
c. None
* Source A does not list this entry (possibly a duplicate of the preceding one).

S-12345* 87a E:335 X-0663 BROW:----
a. W-46 Clement Read, heir to Colonel -- Read
b. Allen Latham
c. None
* Source A does not list this entry.

S-12345* 687a -- -- HIGH:UNIO
a. --
b. James Taylor
c. -- Taylor, -- Carrington, & -- Reed; Samuel Bell, 1831
* Entry in Source A only.

S-12346 75a D:78 X-0360 PICK:DARB
a. W-6498 Martin Mooney
b. John E. Wilson*
c. P. Douglas, 1829
* Source A says John L. Wilson.

S-12347 25a D:78 X-0840 ROSS:TWIN
a. W-6498 Martin Mooney
b. Mathew Bonner
c. None

S-12349 38a D:102 X-0340 UNIO:PARI
a. W-6463 Thomas Ousley
b. James Galloway
c. R? P. Mann, 1831

S-12350
S-13274 230a D:425 X-0060 LOGA:MCAR
a. W-3236 Henry Eaton, assignee
W-2947 John Means
b. James Galloway
c. None

S-12350. See also S-12091

S-12352* 1200a -- -- CLIN:RICH
a. --
b. T. J. McArthur
c. None
* Entry in Source A only.

S-12353* 1200a -- -- GREE:SILV
a. --
b. -- Wallace & -- McArthur
c. C. Wallace; -- Ervin & -- Lee, 1829; Daniel Dean, 1836; T. J. McArthur; John Huffy, 1831
* Entry in Source A only.

S-12354* 1000a -- -- ROSS:CONC
a. --
b. C. Wallace
c. None
* Entry in Source A only.

S-12355 100a D:78 X-0841 FAYE:PAIN
a. W-2377 Doctor John Trezevant
b. Cadwallader Wallace
c. None

S-12355 175a D:79 X-0841 FAYE:PAIN
a. W-2377 Doctor John Trezevant
b. Cadwallader Wallace
c. None

S-12355 175a D:79 X-0841 FAYE:PAIN
a. W-2377 Doctor John Trezevant
b. Cadwallader Wallace
c. None

S-12357. See S-12294

S-12358 578a D:80 X-1380 PICK:DEER
a. W-6545 Charles Sneed, heirs of
b. Sally Winder
c. None

S-12359. See S-12290

S-12360 916a D:144 X-0991 HARD:---* UNIO:WASH
a. W-6544 Arthur Treackle**, heirs of
b. James J. Teackle**
c. M. Bonner, 1831
* Source A does not give township.
** So spelled.

S-12361 25a D:94 X-1230 ROSS:BUCK
a. W-6539 William Withers?
b. William Withers
c. None

S-12362 40a D:95 X-0133 PIKE:PERR
a. W-6539 William Withers?
b. William Withers
c. None

S-12363 50a D:94 X-0130 PIKE:PERR
a. W-6539 William Withers?
b. William Withers
c. C. Wallace; J. Penniston, 1830

S-12364. See S-10904

S-12365 16a E:91 X-0340 LOGA:ZANE
a. W-6526 Young Wilkerson
b. Joseph H. Garwood
c. None

S-12365* 100a -- -- UNIO?:---
a. --
b. John Evans
c. None
* Entry in Source A only, where crossed out.

S-12366 30a D:113 X-0800 BROW:UNIO
a. W-6546 Robert Green, heirs of
b. John Barrett
c. None

S-12368* 250a -- -- ----:----
a. --
b. C. Wallace
c. None
* Entry in Source A only, where crossed out.

S-12369 75a D:94 X-0663 CLER:JACK
a. W-6537 Thomas Parremore
b. Peter P. Mayo
c. None

S-12370 43a D:366 X-1380 PICK:WAYN
a. W-6537 Thomas Parremore
b. Cadwallader Wallace
c. None

S-12371. See S-12265

S-12372. See S-12266

S-12373. See S-12341

S-12376 40a D:208 X-0840 ROSS:HUNT
a. W-6584 John Sidebotham
b. A. C. Looker
c. None

S-12377 30a D:208 X-0300 ROSS:HUNT
a. W-6584 John Sidebotham
b. A. C. Looker
c. None

S-12378 30a D:208 X-0300 ROSS:HUNT
a. W-6584 John Sidebotham
b. A. C. Looker
c. None

S-12379 100a D:397 X-0133 ADAM:FRAN
a. W-6546 Robert Green, heirs of
b. Robert Green
c. None

S-12380 58a D:97 X-0423 BROW:HUNT
a. W-6546 Robert Green, heirs of
b. Robert Payne
c. Heirs of Robert Payne; William Davidson, 1831

S-12381 133a D:111 X-0423 BROW:PIKE
a. W-6346 James Archer?
b. William M. P. Quinn
c. John Palmer, 1826; David P. Quinn, 1831

S-12382. See S-12288

S-12383. See S-12021

S-12384. See S-11052

S-12385 80a D:103 X-1180 MADI:DEER
a. W-6303 William Newton
b. James Galloway
c. None

S-12386. See S-12092

S-12387. See S-12092

S-12388
S-12401 200a D:102 X-0750 UNIO:LIBE
a. W-6581 John Shanks
W-6578 Joshua McQueen
b. -- Shanks & -- McQueen
c. None

S-12391 8a D:172 X-0040 ADAM:TIFF
a. W-6585 John Bryant*
b. Joseph Curry
c. None
* Possibly.

S-12392* 36a -- -- ROSS:TWIN
a. --
b. -- Ladd & -- Norvell
c. None
* Entry in Source A only.

S-12393. See S-12400

S-12394 50a D:107 X-1000 FRAN:PRAI
a. W-5074 James Morgan, representatives of
b. James Curl*
c. W. S. Sullivant; M. L. Sullivant
* Source A spells Curle.

S-12395. See S-12399

S-12396 88a D:161 X-0420 BROW:UNIO
X-0570
a. W-6546 Robert Green, heirs of
b. Robert Payne
c. None

S-12397* 196a D:97 X-0663 HIGH:--**
a. W-348 Captain James Curry
W-6326 John Roberts
W-6516 James Barnley
b. Allen Latham
c. None
* Entry is crossed out in Source A.
** Source A does not give township.

S-12398. See S-5292 (in volume 4, part 1)

S-12399
S-12402
S-12395
S-12427
S-12428 523a D:108 X-0340 UNIO:LIBE
LOGA:ZANE
a. W-712 Doctor William Brown
W-5812 John Goodrich, heirs of
W-6463 Thomas Ousley
W-6499 William Schooler
W-6578 Joshua McQueen
b. -- Galloway, -- Schooler, & -- McQueen
c. J. Galloway, Junior

S-12400
S-12403
S-12393
S-12413 1823a D:100 X-0750 UNIO:LIBE
X-0340
a. W-6573 Andrew Rodgers
W-6578 Joshua McQueen
W-6546 Robert Green, heirs of
W-3711 William Write (Wright)
b. -- Rodgers, -- McQueen, -- Green, -- Payne, & -- Galloway
c. None

S-12401. See S-12388

S-12402. See S-12399

S-12404. See S-12332

S-12406. See S-12304

S-12407 100a E:195 X-1300 BROW:CLAR
a. W-6537 Thomas Parremore
W-6538 Thomas Parremore
b. Cadwallader Wallace
c. D. F. Barney, 1826; P. P. Mayo; John Anderson, Junior, 1832

S-12408 100a D:92 X-0570 CLER:FRAN
a. W-6538 Thomas Parremore
b. Peter P. Mayo
c. None

S-12410 56a D:154 X-0381 ADAM:MONR
a. W-6585 John Bryant*
b. Charles Stephenson
c. None
* Possibly.

S-12411 30a D:248 X-0130 ADAM:MONR
a. W-6585 John Bryant*
b. John W. Pyke
c. None
* Possibly.

S-12412 22a D:96 X-0420 ADAM:LIBE
a. W-6586 Jesse Rose*
b. Henry Asbury
c. Her--? Rapge, 1826; J. Francis, Senior, 1827
* Possibly.

S-12413. See S-12400

S-12414 32a D:251 X-0130 HIGH:BRUS
a. W-6553 Obadiah Terry
b. John Perrill
c. None

S-12415 81a D:154 X-0381* ADAM:MONR
a. W-6585 John Bryant**
b. S. Naylor & D. Naylor
c. None
* West Fork of.
** Possibly.

S-12416 45a D:95 X-0360 MADI:UNIO
a. W-6459 John Yarborough
b. John Yarborough
c. None

S-12419* -- -- X-1000 ----:----
a. W-6545 Charles Sneed, heirs of
b. Edward S. Sneed
c. None
* Entry in Source A only.

S-12420 50a D:134 X-0870 PIKE:PEEP
a. W-5802 George Norvell, deceased
b. Thomas Worthington
c. R. Woods, 1826

S-12423 78a D:96 X-0420 BROW:---*
ADAM:LIBE
a. W-6586 Jesse Rose**
b. Henry Asbury
c. Henry Rape, 1826
* Source A does not give township.
** Possibly.

S-12424
S-12585 65a D:166 X-0130* HIGH:BRUS
a. W-6537 Thomas Parremore
b. Peter P. Mayo
c. None
* Baker's Fork of.

S-12425 35a D:168 X-1190 X-1000 ADAM:MEIG
a. W-6537 Thomas Parremore
b. Peter P. Mayo
c. None

S-12426 100a D:97 X-0490 ADAM:MEIG
a. W-6582 Israel Meadows
b. Samuel McKory? (McKoy?)*
c. None
* Source A spells McCoy.

S-12427. See S-12399

S-12428. See S-12399

S-12429 60a D:204 X-0300 PIKE:JACK
a. W-6499 William Schooler
W-6520 William Terrell, heirs of
b. -- Schooler* & -- Dun
c. William Schools*; James Black, 1826; W. Dun; Edward H. Smith, 1832; A. Organ; James? Penniston, 1841
* So spelled.

S-12430 200a D:99 X-0420 ADAM:LIBE
a. W-6577 Francis Mills
b. Elijah Holliday
c. None

S-12431 50a D:166 X-0134 ADAM:MEIG
a. W-6574 Andrew Rodgers
b. Alexander Hemphill
c. John Linton, 1826

S-12432 50a D:154 X-0600 ADAM:MONR
a. W-6574 Andrew Rodgers
b. William Anderson
c. None

S-12433 50a D:213 X-0423 ADAM:TIFF
a. W-6546 Robert Green, heirs of
b. Robert Payne
c. None

S-12438* 100a -- -- CHAM:UNIO
a. --
b. Fielding Brown
c. None
* Entry in Source A only.

S-12439 200a D:133 X-1140 HIGH:BRUS PIKE:---*
a. William Dix, heirs of
b. -- Dix, -- Watson, et al**
c. S. B. Finley; G. W. Smith, 1838
* Source A does not mention Pike County.
** Source A says -- Dix, -- Watson, -- Bonwell, & -- Sparrow.

S-12440* 400a -- -- ADAM:----
a. --
b. Joseph Carter
c. -- McDaid & -- Wilkins, 1826; J. Hood, 1841
* Entry in Source A only.

S-12441 80a D:474 X-0840 ROSS:TWIN
a. W-6501 Bailey Johnson, heirs of
b. Bailey Johnson, heirs of
c. M. Pardam, 1832

S-12442 50a D:226 X-0700 SCIO:BRUS
a. W-6588 Allen Walker, deceased, devisees of
b. James Rardin
c. Otis Bean; J. Cardin; John Noel, 1833; William Powers; J. P. Noel; W. Powers, 1826; heirs of James Rardin

S-12443 50a D:227 X-1140 PIKE:MIFF
a. W-6588 Allen Walker, deceased, devisees of
b. Daniel Morgan
c. None

S-12444 45a D:246 X-0490 ADAM:SCOT
a. W-6575 William Jackson?, heirs of
b. George Vinsonhaller*
c. None
* Source A spells Vinsonhaler.

S-12445 55a D:246 X-0133 X-0134 ADAM:SCOT
a. W-6575 William Jackson?, heirs of
b. George Vinsonhaller*
c. None
* Source A spells Vinsonhaler.

S-12446 45a D:246 X-0133 ADAM:SCOT HIGH:JACK
a. W-6575 William Jackson?, heirs of
b. George Vinsonhaller*
c. None
* Source A spells Vinsonhaler.

S-12447 35a D:356 X-0133 ADAM:SCOT
a. W-6575 William Jackson?, heirs of
b. George Vinsonhaller*
c. None
* Source A spells Vinsonhaler.

S-12448 20a* D:356 X-0133 ADAM:FRAN
a. W-6575 William Jackson?, heirs of
b. George Vinsonhaller**
c. None
* Source A says 10 acres.
** Source A spells Vinsonhaler.

S-12449 12a D:178 X-0800 ADAM:MONR
a. W-6574 Andrew Rodgers
b. David Bradford
c. None

S-12450 50a D:167 X-0650 ADAM:TIFF
a. W-6588 Allen Walker, deceased, devisees of
b. Andrew Ellison
c. None

S-12452* 250a -- -- --**:----
a. --
b. Mazy Vance
c. None
* Entry in Source A only, where crossed out.
** Source A may read Madison or Union county.

S-12453 100a D:109 X-0700* SCIO:MORG
a. W-6481 William Chambers
b. William Chambers
c. Willis** Chambers; William Kendall, 1826
* Called "Cullock's Creek."
** So spelled.

S-12455 100a D:152 X-0423 ADAM:LIBE
a. W-6574 Andrew Rodgers
b. Thomas J. Rankin*
c. None
* Source A says Thomas T. Rankin.

S-12457* 250a -- -- HARD:--**
a. --
b. James J. Teackle
c. Joseph Newell, 1831 (Logan County)
* Entry in Source A only, where crossed out.
** Source A does not give township.

S-12458 100a D:206 X-0840 ROSS:PAXT
a. W-6571 Elisha Eastes*
b. Elisha Easter*
c. None
* So spelled.

S-12459 60a D:204 X-0300 PIKE:JACK
a. W-6620 Ransome Colquett
b. Walter Dun
c. None

S-12460 75a D:134 X-0841 FAYE:PAIN MADI:RANG
a. W-6537 Thomas Parremore
b. Peter P. Mayo
c. John McLane, 1830; Alexander Douglas, 1838

S-12461 160a D:134 X-0840 ROSS:PAIN
a. W-6537 Thomas Parremore
b. Peter P. Mayo
c. None

S-12462 235a D:135 X-0150 ROSS:PAIN
a. W-6537 Thomas Parremore
b. Peter P. Mayo
c. None

S-12463* 68a E:353 X-0133 HIGH:----
a. W-6553 Obadiah Terry
b. James D. Noland
c. None
* Source A says "not found."

S-12464 24a E:42 X-0790 CLER:GOSH
a. W-6587 William Abner? (Abney?)
b. James Taylor
c. None

S-12465 160a D:481 X-0840 ROSS:TWIN
a. W-6501 Bailey Johnson, heirs of
b. Bailey Johnson, heirs of
c. Robert Stewart, 1827; Jesse Johnson; M. Purdam, 1832

S-12466 27a E:312 X-0130 ADAM:TIFF
a. W-6574 Andrew Rodgers
b. David Smith
c. None

S-12467 28a E:67 X-0809 ADAM:TIFF
a. W-6574 Andrew Rodgers
b. John Baird
c. None

S-12469*
S-14695 142a E:329 X-0663 HIGH:---- BROW:---- CLIN:----
a. W-6325 Edward Beeson
W-1937 Major Francis Taylor
b. Allen Latham
c. None
* Entry not listed in Source A.

S-12469* 252a -- -- ADAM:----
a. --
b. Henry Lee
c. None
* Entry in Source A only, where notation says "withdrawn."

S-12472 1600a E:126 X-0750 UNIO:LIBE
a. W-6559 Mazy or Mary Vance
W-6560 Mazy or Mary Vance
b. Marzey* Vance
c. John N. Sloan; S. G. Strong, 1836; Phebe Ann Mc-Ewen
* Source A spells Mazy.

S-12474 500a E:225 X-0110 X-0750 LOGA:RUSH
a. W-6512 James Davis, deceased
b. Thomas Green
c. S. G. Strong, 1833

S-12475* 67a -- -- HIGH:BRUS
a. --
b. William B. Coalter
c. None
* Entry in Source A only.

S-12476* 100a -- -- HIGH:BRUS
a. --
b. Jordan Anderson
c. None
* Entry in Source A only.

S-12478 20a E:351 X-0130 ADAM:MONR
a. W-6425 George Purcell, heirs of

b. Jonathan Pollard
c. None

S-12479* 13a -- -- ADAM:MONR
a. --
b. John Ellison, Junior
c. None
* Entry in Source A only.

S-12480. See S-12260

S-12482 20a E:133 X-0840 ROSS:TWIN
a. W-6538 Thomas Parremore
b. Peter P. Mayo
c. None

S-12483 128a E:183 X-0660 CLER:WILL
CLER:MIAM
a. W-1936 Captain Reuben Taylor
b. John Watts
c. None

S-12483*
S-10244
S-2754
S-1575
S-1769 118a -- -- CLER:----
a. --
b. -- Watts, -- Wright, -- Starke, & -- Roberts
c. None
* Entry in Source A only, where notation says "not recorded."

S-12484 200a E:162 X-0750 UNIO:LIBE
a. W-6567 Joseph Spencer
b. Joseph Spencer
c. None

S-12485 60a E:162 X-0060 LOGA:LAKE
a. W-6567 Joseph Spencer
b. Joseph Spencer
c. Samuel Donnell, 1831

S-12486 35a E:162 X-1000 FRAN:NORW
a. W-6567 Joseph Spencer
b. Joseph Spencer
c. Hugh McGill; C. Higgins, 1837

S-12487* 50a -- -- CLAR:PLEA
a. --
b. Joseph Spencer
c. None
* Entry in Source A only.

S-12494 8a E:162 X-1180 MADI:---*
UNIO:UNIO
a. W-6567 Joseph Spencer
b. Joseph Spencer
c. None
* Source A does not mention Madison County.

S-12495 451a D:116 X-0800 HAMI:ANDE
CLER:OHIO
a. W-6380 James Thatcher
W-6376 Joseph Pugh
W-6395 John Harrison
W-6381 George McCormick, heirs of
b. T. B. Miller
c. Ebenezer Worley, 1837

S-12503 500a D:334 X-1000 AUGL:---*
HARD:---*
ALLE:GOSH
a. W-6623 David Kirkpatrick
b. Thomas Green**
c. Ezekiel Hoover, 1833
* Source A does not mention Auglaize or Hardin counties.
** Source A says Thomas Green, assignee.

S-12504
S-13320 64a D:458 X-1303 HIGH:SALE
a. W-6678 Richard Stevens
b. George W. Barrire*
c. None
* Source A spells Barriere.

S-12505 100a E:39 X-1301 HIGH:SALE
a. W-6432 Peter McIntosh
b. James L. Davidson
c. John Davidson, 1828

S-12506* 14a -- -- BROW:UNIO
a. --
b. James Pilson
c. Abraham Burgit
* Entry in Source A only.

S-12507 55a E:53 X-0840 ROSS:PAXT
a. W-6176 Edward Shepherd, heirs of
W-6143 Harry Gramsell
b. John Watts
c. None

S-12508 15a D:163 X-0570 CLER:TATE
a. W-6346 James Archer?
b. William Winters
c. None

S-12509 43a F:121 X-0040 ADAM:MONR
a. W-6628 William Spencer, representatives of
b. James Moore
c. None

S-12510 70a D:227 X-0700 SCIO:BRUS
a. W-6588 Allen Walker, deceased, devisees of
b. Daniel Morgan
c. M. Rardin & P. Rardin, 1842

S-12511 54a D:226 X-0130 PIKE:MIFF
X-1140 ADAM:---*
a. W-6588 Allen Walker, deceased, devisees of
b. Daniel Morgan
c. None
* Source A does not mention Adams County.

S-12512 270a D:227 X-1040 ADAM:FRAN
a. W-6588 Allen Walker, deceased, devisees of
b. Daniel Morgan
c. Tennison B. Anderson, 1831

S-12513
S-12851 222a D:229 X-0080 ADAM:SPRI
a. W-33 Dennis Reddy
b. George F. Wilkins
c. None

S-12514 200a D:195 X-0660 HIGH:JACK
a. W-6517 John Thompson
b. John Thompson
c. D. Miller, 1839

S-12520 148a D:179 X-0760 PIKE:BENT
a. W-6501 Bailey Johnson, heirs of
b. Daniel Drais
c. Jacob Darr, 1826; A. Bryan, 1829

S-12522 87a D:153 X-0423 ADAM:LIBE
a. W-6579 Richard Powell
b. Hugh Meharey*
c. Stephen Mitchell; Hempleman Jacob, 1838 (possibly Jacob Hempleman?)
* Source A spells Maharey.

S-12523 21a D:153 X-0423 ADAM:LIBE
a. W-3814 Griffith Matthias
W-6579 Richard Powell
b. Hugh Meharey*
c. None
* Source A spells Maharey.

S-12524 73a D:149 X-0840 ROSS:TWIN
a. W-6563 Richard Johnson
b. Allen Latham
c. None

S-12526* 214a? -- -- ----:----
a. W-6567 Joseph Spencer
b. Joseph Spencer
c. None
* Entry in Source A only.

S-12528 33a D:263 X-0590 ADAM:SPRI
a. W-6628 William Spencer, representatives of
b. Jonathan Parmer
c. None

S-12529 30a D:257 X-0590 ADAM:SPRI
a. W-6628 William Spencer, representatives of
b. James Long
c. None

S-12530
S-13161 90a D:352 X-0590 ADAM:SPRI
a. W-6628 William Spencer, representatives of
W-6626 Archibald Alexander
b. -- Mowry & -- Riggs
c. None

S-12531* 93a D:180 X-0270 CLER:----
a. W-1600 John Green
b. Bezer Latham
c. None
* Entry not listed in Source A.

S-12531*
S-12532 79a D:180 X-0663 CLER:----
X-0270
a. W-1601 William Bigbie
b. Bezer Latham
c. None
* Entry not listed in Source A.

S-12533* 20a D:180 X-0663 CLER:----
a. W-1601 William Bigbie
b. Bezer Latham
c. None
* Entry not listed in Source A.

S-12534 200a E:215 X-1180 MADI:MONR
a. W-1600 John Green
W-1601 William Bigbie
b. James Guy
c. None

S-12535 100a D:172 X-0130 ADAM:TIFF
a. W-6576 James Dugan?
b. Jonathan Walmsley
c. None

S-12536 102a D:434 X-0991 LOGA:RUSH
a. W-6526 Young Wilkerson
W-6539 William Withers?
b. -- Evans & -- Withers
c. John Evans; William Flagg*, 1836; William Clagg*
* So spelled.

S-12538 50a F:202 X-0959 SCIO:UNIO
a. W-6588 Allen Walker, deceased, devisees of
b. Joseph Henry*
c. T. Mountjoy, 1826
* Source A says Thomas Mountjoy.

S-12539 25a D:182 X-1040 ADAM:JEFF
a. W-6628 William Spencer, representatives of
b. Michael Freeman
c. None

S-12541* 80a -- -- ADAM:WINC
a. --
b. Deborah Odill
c. None
* Entry in Source A only.

S-12542 789a D:427 X-0480 UNIO:YORK
a. W-679 Seymour Powel, heir
b. Joseph Miller
c. None

S-12543*
S-14316 170a -- -- HIGH:CONC

a. --
b. George W. Barriere, heirs of
c. G. W. Barriere; A. Malcom, 1835
* Entry in Source A only.

S-12544 100a D:338 X-1303 HIGH:WHIT
a. W-6574 Andrew Rodgers
b. Daniel H. Murphey
c. None

S-12545 200a D:159 X-0360 MADI:SUMM
a. W-6648 William Christian
b. James Galloway
c. None

S-12548 135a E:54 X-0750 ROSS:FRAN
a. W-6651 William Scott, heirs of
b. Cadwallader Wallace
c. None

S-12554 167a D:192 X-1140 HIGH:---* PIKE:MIFF
a. W-6649 William Christian
b. William Christian
c. S. B. Finley; C. McCollister, 1840
* Source A does not give township.

S-12556 25a D:199 X-1300* ADAM:JEFF
a. W-6585 John Bryant**
b. Nathaniel Abbott
c. None
* "W(hite?) Oak Brush Creek."
** Possibly.

S-12566 1324a D:188 X-0670 ROSS:PAIN
a. W-6654 William Langborn, heirs of
b. William Langborn, heirs of
c. Peter Douglas; Isaac Hanks, 1833

S-12567 500a D:190 X-0360 CHAM:GOSH CLAR:---*
a. W-6654 William Langborn, heirs of
b. William Langborn, heirs of
c. William B. Bryard & H. Curle, 1840; W. Lankton; M. Bonner, 1831 (Madison County)
* Source A does not give township.

S-12568 1000a D:191 X-1120 X-1300 BROW:FRAN
a. W-6654 William Langborn, heirs of
b. William Langborn, heirs of
c. John A. Glaze, 1831

S-12569 400a D:189 X-1120 BROW:EAGL
a. W-6654 William Langborn, heirs of
b. William Langborn, heirs of
c. Robert Chalfant; F. J. Philips, 1842

S-12570 1500a D:190 X-0130 HIGH:JACK ADAM:---*
a. W-6654 William Langborn, heirs of
b. William Langborn, heirs of
c. -- Kirby? & -- Sterling, 1831
* Source A does not mention Adams County.

S-12571 1500a D:189 X-0130 HIGH:JACK
a. W-6654 William Langborn, heirs of
b. William Langborn, heirs of
c. -- Kirby? & -- Sterling, 1831

S-12572 150a D:204 X-0300 PIKE:PEEP
a. W-5139 Robert Means, assignee of James Smith
W-5825 Richard Foster, heirs, etc.
W-6520 William Terrell, heirs of
b. Walter Dun
c. None

S-12573 66a D:206 X-1000 ROSS:FRAN
a. W-5139 Robert Means, assignee of James Smith
b. Walter Dun
c. None

S-12574. See S-9503

S-12575 50a D:339 X-1044 ADAM:MEIG
a. W-6628 William Spencer, representatives of
b. Jesse Murphey
c. -- Wilkins & -- McDaid, 1826

S-12576* 200a -- -- ADAM:----
a. --
b. Bezer Latham
c. None
* Entry in Source A only, where crossed out.

S-12577 200a D:210 X-0650 ADAM:WAYN
a. W-6646 Jesse? Poole? (Peck?)
b. Jesse Peck*
c. None
* Source A may spell Park.

S-12578 100a D:166 X-0650 ADAM:TIFF
a. W-6639 Jacob Dooley
b. Jackob* Dooley
c. None
* Source A spells Jacob.

S-12579 75a D:167 X-1040 PIKE:MIFF ADAM:---*
a. W-6439 Jeremiah Morgan, heirs of
b. Andrew Ellison
c. None
* Source A does not mention Adams County.

S-12580 50a D:165 X-0130 ADAM:MEIG
a. W-6644 John Austen?
b. John Austin
c. None

S-12581 50a D:165 X-1043 ADAM:JEFF SCIO:---*
a. W-6439 Jeremiah Morgan, heirs of
b. Andrew Ellison
c. S? (L?) Delong, 1826
* Source A does not give township.

S-12582* 200a D:165 X-0650 ADAM:TIFF
a. W-1209 John Barbee

b. John Barbee
c. None
* Source A says "not patented."

S-12583* 25a -- -- ADAM:MEIG
a. --
b. Andrew Ellison
c. None
* Entry in Source A only.

S-12584 50a D:166 X-0650 ADAM:WAYN
a. W-6644 John Austen?
b. John Austin
c. None

S-12585 142a D:167 X-1040* ADAM:MEIG
a. W-6628 William Spencer, representatives of
b. Andrew Ellison
c. None
* Northwest fork of.

S-12585. See also S-12424

S-12588 50a D:370 X-0130 X-0630 PIKE:PERR
a. W-6500 James Lee
b. John Obriant
c. None

S-12589 70a D:167 X-0800 ADAM:MONR
a. W-6439 Jeremiah Morgan, heirs of
b. Andrew Ellison
c. None

S-12590* 1000a -- -- UNIO:----
a. --
b. Allen McLane
c. None
* Entry in Source A only, where crossed out.

S-12591* 500a -- -- LOGA:PERR
a. --
b. Allen McLane
c. None
* Entry in Source A only.

S-12592* 500a -- -- UNIO:----
a. --
b. Allen McLane
c. None
* Entry in Source A only, where crossed out.

S-12593* 210a -- -- BROW:----
a. --
b. Bezer Latham
c. John McCall, 1831
* Entry in Source A only (at top of page beginning with S-12568).

S-12594 150a D:157 X-0130 ADAM:FRAN
a. W-6549 Valentine Peers?
b. Bezer Latham
c. None

S-12595
S-12596 57a E:212 X-0360 MADI:PLEA
a. W-6549 Valentine Peers?
b. Allen Latham
c. None

S-12597 50a D:426 X-0360 MADI:DEER
a. W-6549 Valentine Peers?
b. Nathaniel Sawyer
c. None

S-12598 134a D:247 X-1044 ADAM:FRAN SCIO:---*
a. W-6628 William Spencer, representatives of
b. John Kees**
c. John Kerr**; J. Clingman, 1826
* Source A does not give township.
** So spelled.

S-12599. See S-12325

S-12600. See S-12701

S-12601. See S-12234

S-12602* 15a -- -- SCIO:MORG
a. --
b. Thomas Mountjoy
c. T. Morgan, 1836
* Entry in Source A only.

S-12603* 54a -- -- SCIO:MORG
a. --
b. Thomas Mountjoy
c. R. Raudy? (Randy?), 1836
* Entry in Source A only (at top of page beginning with S-12568).

S-12604. See S-12325

S-12605 10a D:411 X-0130 SCIO:UNIO
a. W-6503 Allen Walker, devisees of
b. Thomas Mountjoy
c. None

S-12605* 32a -- -- PIKE:---- SCIO:----
a. --
b. Thomas Mountjoy
c. None
* Entry in Source A only; note says "not found."

S-12605 70a D:411 X-1000 SCIO:MORG
a. W-6503 Allen Walker, devisees of
b. Thomas Mountjoy
c. None

S-12605 48a D:411 X-0030 SCIO:MORG
a. W-6503 Allen Walker, devisees of
b. Thomas Mountjoy
c. None

S-12607
S-12691 30a D:482 X-1000 SCIO:MORG
a. W-6503 Allen Walker, devisees of
b. Thomas Mountjoy
c. None

S-12608 120a D:200 X-0420 ADAM:SPRI
a. W-6637 Isaac Farrell
b. Isaac Farrell*
c. None
* Source A spells Terrell.

S-12609 80a D:200 X-0420 BROW:---* ADAM:SPRI
a. W-6637 Isaac Farrell
b. Isaac Farrell**
c. None
* Source A does not mention Brown County.
** Source A spells Terrell.

S-12610. See S-8322

S-12611 11a D:228 X-1380 PICK:WAYN
a. W-6524 Richard Dorsey, heirs of
b. John Evans
c. None

S-12612. See S-8874; S-9214

S-12613 212a D:155 X-0340 CHAM:RUSH
a. W-6567 Joseph Spencer
b. Joseph Spencer
c. None

S-12614* -- -- X-1000 ----:----
a. W-6567 Joseph Spencer
b. Joseph Spencer
c. None
* Entry in Source A only.

S-12615 30a D:163 X-0660 MADI:STOK
a. W-6567 Joseph Spencer
b. Joseph Spencer
c. J. Galloway; S. Herod, 1829

S-12616* 319a -- X-1000 ----:----
a. W-6567 Joseph Spencer
W-6638 Thomas Morris
W-3042 John Collins
b. -- Spencer, -- Morris, & -- Galloway
c. None
* Entry in Source A only.

S-12617 80a D:214 X-0730 CLAR:PLEA
a. W-3042 John Collins
b. James Galloway
c. None

S-12618
S-12786 75a D:238 X-0730 CLAR:HARM CLAR:PLEA
a. W-3042 John Collins
b. James Galloway
c. None

S-12619 16a D:159 X-0730 CLAR:HARM
a. W-3042 John Collins
b. James Galloway
c. None

S-12620 8a D:376 X-0660 CLAR:MADI
a. W-3042 John Collins
b. James Galloway
c. None

S-12621* 100a -- X-1000 ----:----
a. W-6229 Hulsey Carter
b. Hulsey Carter
c. None
* Entry in Source A only.

S-12622
S-12623
S-12624
S-12625
S-12626
S-12627
S-12628
S-12629 712a* E:326 X-0300 PIKE:PEBB
a. W-6554 Littleberry Mosby, heirs of
W-6555 Littleberry Mosby, heirs of
W-6556 Littleberry Mosby, heirs of
W-6557 Littleberry Mosby, heirs of
b. -- Tennison & -- Anderson
c. A. G. Thurman, 1833; J. R. Anderson
* Source A says 4000 acres to Littleberry Mosby; patented to Allen Latham, 617a; James L. Mosby, 256a; J. B. Anderson & John Anderson, 712a

S-12623* 60a E:476 X-0870 PIKE:----
a. W-6554 Littleberry Mosby, heirs of
b. Allen Latham
c. None
* Entry not listed separately in Source A (see S-12622).

S-12624*
S-12625 617a F:40 X-0870 PIKE:----
a. W-6555 Littleberry Mosby, heirs of
b. Allen Latham
c. None
* Entry not listed separately in Source A (see S-12622).

S-12628*
S-12629 148a F:41 X-0870 PIKE:----
a. W-6554 Littleberry Mosby, heirs of
W-6555 Littleberry Mosby, heirs of
W-6556 Littleberry Mosby, heirs of
W-6557 Littleberry Mosby, heirs of
b. Robert Mosly? (Mosby?), representatives of
c. None
* Entry not listed separately in Source A (see S-12622).

S-12628*
S-12629 298a F:41 X-0870 PIKE:----
a. W-6554 Littleberry Mosby, heirs of
W-6555 Littleberry Mosby, heirs of
W-6556 Littleberry Mosby, heirs of
W-6557 Littleberry Mosby, heirs of
b. Robert Mosly? (Mosby?)
c. None
* Entry not listed separately in Source A (see S-12622).

S-12628*
S-12629 260a F:39 X-0870 PIKE:----
a. W-6557 Littleberry Mosby, heirs of
b. Allen Latham
c. None
* Entry not listed separately in Source A (see S-12622).

S-12630* 2000a -- -- PIKE:PEBB
a. --
b. M. Scott
c. A. Latham; George W. Reynold, 1841
* Entry in Source A only (at top of page beginning with S-12609).

S-12630
S-12631
S-12632
S-12633 464a E:138 X-0300 ROSS:FRAN PIKE:---*
a. W-6652 William Scott, heirs of
W-6653 William Scott, heirs of
b. Allen Latham
c. None
* Source A does not mention Pike County.

S-12634
S-12635 180a E:74 X-0300 PIKE:---* ROSS:FRAN
a. W-6645 Alexander Brownlee, heirs of
b. E. P. Kendrick
c. None
* Source A does not mention Pike County.

S-12634
S-12635 320a E:75 X-0300 PIKE:---* ROSS:FRAN
a. W-6645 Alexander Brownlee, heirs of
b. E. P. Kendrick
c. None
* Source A does not mention Pike County.

S-12634
S-12635 500a E:75 X-0300 ROSS:FRAN PIKE:---*
a. W-6645 Alexander Brownlee, heirs of
b. E. P. Kendrick**
c. Heirs of A. Brownlee; A. G. Thurman, 1831; A. Latham; Porter Hines & -- Grimes, 1831
* Source A does not give township.
** May have been patented to Allen Latham "& (S)-15685."

S-12640
S-12641
S-12642
S-12643
S-12644
S-12645 2667a D:216 X-1000 PIKE:PEBB
a. W-6655 Charles Woodson, heirs of
b. Charles Woodson
c. N. Sawyer; Hallam Hempstead, 1829; A. G. Thurman, 1831; heirs of C. Woodson; William Barnes, Junior, 1835; J. Penniston, 1837

S-12641. See also S-15685

S-12646 333a D:336 X-0301 ROSS:HUNT PIKE:PEBB
a. W-6658 Wood Jones, heirs of
b. Wood Jones, heirs of
c. A. G. Thurman, 1831; John Jones, 1836

S-12647 333a D:336 X-0301 PIKE:PEBB ROSS:HUNT
a. W-6658 Wood Jones, heirs of
b. Wood Jones, heirs of
c. None

S-12648 333a D:337 X-0301 PIKE:PEBB ROSS:HUNT
a. W-6658 Wood Jones, heirs of
b. Wood Jones, heirs of
c. -- Droombole, agent for -- Hamlin

S-12649 333a D:336 X-0303 ROSS:HUNT
a. W-6658 Wood Jones, heirs of
b. Wood Jones, heirs of
c. None

S-12652* 232a** -- -- ----:----
a. --
b. William Washington, heirs of
c. None
* Entry in Source A only; says "not found."
** Note says 1333 acres.

S-12654 500a D:232 X-0480 UNIO:CLAI
a. W-6628 William Spencer, representatives of
b. William Murdock
c. None

S-12663* 100a -- -- ----:----
a. --
b. John Holloway**
c. None
* Entry in Source A only; says "not found."
** Note says "patented to Allen Latham."

S-12668*
S-12669 60a F:12 X-0840 ROSS:----
a. W-6647 William Christian
b. Charles M. Hester
c. None
* Entry not listed in Source A.

S-12668*
S-12669 145a F:204** X-0840 ROSS:----
a. W-6647 William Christian
b. John Christian
c. None
* Not listed in Source A.
** Possiby F-214.

S-12668*
S-12669 145a F:204** X-0840 ROSS:----
a. W-6647 William Christian
b. Allen Christian
c. None
* Not listed in Source A.
** Possibly F-214.

S-12668*
S-12669 400a -- -- ROSS:TWIN
a. --
b. William Christian
c. None
* Entry in Source A only.

S-12668*
S-12669 500a -- -- ----:----
a. --
b. William Christian
c. None
* Entry in Source A only, where crossed out.

S-12671*
S-12692
S-12696 250a -- -- ----:----
a. --
b. Thomas Mountjoy
c. None
* Entry in Source A only, where crossed out.

S-12671* 500a -- -- ADAM:----
a. --
b. John Evans
c. None
* Entry in Source A only, where crossed out.

S-12671* 115a -- -- PIKE:----
a. --
b. John Evans
c. None
* Entry in Source A only, where crossed out.

S-12672* 275a -- X-1000 ----:----
a. W-6666 --
b. John Evans, assignee
c. None
* Entry in Source A only.

S-12685 41a D:411 X-0870 PIKE:PEBB
a. W-6504 Allen Walker, devisees of
b. Thomas Mountjoy
c. None

S-12686 50a D:381 X-0030 SCIO:MORG
a. W-6425 George Purcell, heirs of
b. Thomas Mountjoy
c. None

S-12687* 30a -- -- SCIO:MORG
a. --
b. Thomas Mountjoy
c. None
* Entry in Source A only.

S-12688. See S-8575

S-12689* 50a -- -- SCIO:MORG
a. --
b. Thomas Mountjoy
c. None
* Entry in Source A only.

S-12690. See S-12325; S-12701

S-12691 3a E:66 X-1000 SCIO:MORG
a. W-6503 Allen Walker, devisees of
b. Thomas Mountjoy
c. None

S-12691. See also S-12607

S-12692* 35a D:395 X-0870 PIKE:----
a. W-6504 Allen Walker, devisees of
b. Thomas Mountjoy
c. None
* Entry not listed in Source A.

S-12692. See also S-12701

S-12693. See S-12697

S-12694. See S-12325

S-12695. See S-12325

S-12696. See S-12701

S-12697
S-12693
S-12699
S-9851 368a D:395 X-0779 PIKE:PEBB
X-0870
a. W-5871 Francis M. Boykin & Ann Johnson, heirs of F(rancis) Boykin
W-6503 Allen Walker, devisees of
W-6504 Allen Walker, devisees of
b. Thomas Mountjoy
c. R. Douglas, 1842

S-12697. See also S-9851

S-12698. See S-7512

S-12700. See S-12325

S-12701
S-12692
S-12690*
S-12600 250a D:412 X-1140 PIKE:SUNF
a. W-6504 Allen Walker, devisees of
W-6503 Allen Walker, devisees of
b. Thomas Mountjoy
c. None
* Source A says S-12696.

S-12702*
S-12703
S-12704 1000a -- -- PIKE:----
a. --
b. Archibald Alexander
c. Eskridge Hull, 1831; A. G. Thurman, 1833
* Entry in Source A only, where crossed out.

S-12706
S-12707 80a D:180 X-0570 ROSS:HUNT
a. W-6624 David Kirkpatrick
b. David Kirkpatrick
c. None

S-12707 100a D:178 X-0130 ADAM:WAYN ROSS:HUNT
a. W-6624 David Kirkpatrick
b. David Kirkpatrick
c. None

S-12708 80a D:226 X-0130 PIKE:PERR
a. W-6624 David Kirkpatrick
b. David Kirkpatrick*
c. E. H. Smith, 1835; A. Latham; heirs of E. H. Smith; James Moore, 1840
* Source A says Allen Latham.

S-12708 60a D:226 X-0540 PICK:PERR
a. W-6624 David Kirkpatrick
b. David Kirkpatrick*
c. None
* Source A says Allen Latham.

S-12708 140a D:181 X-0340 MADI:DARB
a. W-6624 David Kirkpatrick
b. David Kirkpatrick*
c. None
* Source A says Allen Latham.

S-12708 40a D:181 X-0300 PIKE:JACK
a. W-6624 David Kirkpatrick
b. David Kirkpatrick
c. None

S-12710* 300a -- -- ----:----
a. --
b. Walker Baylor
c. None
* Entry in Source A only; note says "not found."

S-12711* 50a -- -- ----:----
a. --
b. David Allen
c. None
* Entry in Source A only; note says "not found."

S-12712* 250a -- -- SCIO:NILE
a. --
b. Allen McLane
c. L. Bradford, 1831
* Entry in Source A only.

S-12713* 65a -- -- SCIO:WASH
a. --
b. Allen McLane
c. J. Kelly, 1833
* Entry in Source A only.

S-12713* 218a -- -- SCIO:NILE
a. --
b. Allen McLane
c. C. Morrell, 1831
* Entry in Source A onlyly.

S-12715. See S-10776

S-12716 10a D:314 X-1110 ADAM:GREE
a. W-5972 Edward Wells? (Wills?)
b. John Ellison
c. None

S-12717 5a E:267 X-0040 ADAM:MONR
a. W-5972 Edward Wells? (Wills?)
b. David Lovejoy, heirs of*
c. None
* Source A says John Ellison.

S-12718* 37a -- -- ADAM:LIBE
a. --
b. Robert Ellison
c. None
* Entry in Source A only.

S-12718* 20a F:208 X-0423 ADAM:----
a. W-1023 Thomas Shores
W-5972 Edward Wells? (Wills?)
b. Thomas Ellison
c. None
* Entry not listed in Source A.

S-12718*
S-15513 30a F:236 X-0090 ADAM:----
a. W-5972 Edward Wells? (Wills?)
b. Thomas Ellison
c. None
* Entry not listed in Source A.

S-12718*
S-16086 7a F:252 X-0381 ADAM:----
a. W-5972, ex S-537 Edward Wells? (Wills?) or George Forrest
b. Thomas Ellison

c. None
* Entry not listed in Source A.

S-12721 203a D:185 X-0130 HIGH:CONC
a. W-6668 George Backus
b. John Evans
c. None

S-12722 90a D:173 X-0080 ADAM:SPRI
a. W-6668 George Backus
b. John Evans
c. C. Wallace; J. S. Patton, 1833

S-12723 140a D:172 X-0080 BROW:---* ADAM:SPRI
a. W-6668 George Backus
b. John Evans
c. C. Wallace; T. Huston, 1834
* Source A does not mention Brown County.

S-12724 100a D:189 X-1140 PIKE:MIFF
a. W-6668 George Backus
b. John Evans
c. None

S-12726
S-12725 70a D:185 X-0133 HIGH:BRUS PIKE:---*
a. W-6538 Thomas Parremore
b. Peter P. Mayo
c. James Turner, 1831
* Source A does not give township.

S-12727 150a D:187 X-0133 HIGH:---* PIKE:MIFF
a. W-2377 Doctor John Trezevant
b. Cadwallader Wallace
c. None
* Source A does not mention Highland County.

S-12728 110a D:173 X-0133 ADAM:FRAN
a. W-6538 Thomas Parremore
b. Peter P. Mayo
c. None

S-12729 50a D:184 X-0843 FAYE:UNIO FAYE:PAIN
a. W-6538 Thomas Parremore
b. Peter P. Mayo
c. C. Wallace; John McLain, 1831

S-12730
S-12733
S-12734 350a D:186 X-0360 MADI:UNIO
a. W-2377 Doctor John Trezevant
b. Cadwallader Wallace
c. None

S-12730 65a D:174 X-0841 FAYE:PAIN
a. W-2377 Doctor John Trezevant
b. Cadwallader Wallace
c. None

S-12731 35a D:186 X-0800 ADAM:SPRI
a. W-2377 Doctor John Trezevant
b. Cadwallader Wallace
c. None

S-12732 396a D:170 X-1300 BROW:PLEA
a. W-6537 Thomas Parremore
b. Peter P. Mayo
c. None

S-12733. See S-12730

S-12734 350a D:187 X-0130 HIGH:JACK
a. W-2377 Doctor John Trezevant
b. Cadwallader Wallace
c. None

S-12734. See also S-12730

S-12735 200a D:169 X-1000 HARD:TAYL
a. W-3204 James King
b. Samuel Walker
c. None

S-12736 100a D:168 X-1000 HARD:TAYL
a. W-4313 Joseph Henderson & Elizabeth, his wife, late Elizabeth McCommick, representatives of James (McCommick)
b. Nathaniel Massie
c. C. Wallace; M. Bonner, 1838; Craudthon? Wallace, 1840; Lyne Starling, 1831 (Logan County)

S-12738. See S-12290

S-12742 166a D:155 X-0229 LOGA:MCAR
a. W-64 --*
W-3223 Robert Boyd & Thomas Cocke
W-2938 Thomas Glascock
b. -- Herron** & -- Graham
c. W. Dun; M. Bonner, 1827
* Page torn in Source C.
** Source A spells Heron.

S-12743 142a D:155 X-0340 MADI:DEER
a. W-64 --*
W-3223 Robert Boyd & Thomas Cocke
b. -- Herron** & -- Graham
c. None
* Page torn in Source C.
** Source A spells Heron.

S-12744* 170a -- X-1000 ----:----
a. W-6620 Ransome Colquett
W-6668 George Backus
W-6648 William Christian
b. George Clark, assignee
c. None
* Entry in Source A only.

S-12744. See also S-12081

S-12745 100a D:206 X-0340 MADI:DARB
a. W-6670 Henry Gaddis
b. Henry Gaddis
c. M. S? Sullivant, 1831

S-12746 100a D:206 X-0340 MADI:DARB
a. W-6669 John Gaddis
b. John Gaddis
c. Henry Gaddis; M. S? Sullivant, 1831

S-12747 142a D:206 X-0060 HARD:MCDO
a. W-5139 Robert Means, assignee of James Smith
b. Robert Means
c. Jeremiah Stilwell; Moses Bonham, 1840

S-12748 15a D:206 X-0340 UNIO:UNIO
a. W-5139 Robert Means, assignee of James Smith
b. Walter Dun
c. None

S-12752* 50a -- -- HIGH:----
a. --
b. John A. Fulton
c. William Fulton; William Scott, 1833
* Entry in Source A only, where crossed out.

S-12754 52a E:208 X-1060 BROW:PIKE
a. W-6346 James Archer?
b. George C. Light
c. None

S-12755 100a E:207 X-1060 BROW:PIKE
a. W-1952 William Armstead
b. Thomas H. Perkins
c. Michael Zigler, 1829

S-12756* 100a -- -- BROW:PIKE
a. --
b. William Head
c. A. C. Stewart, 1831; H. Wisley**; D. Wisby**, 1842
* Entry in Source A only.
** So spelled.

S-12762 30a D:213 X-0840 ROSS:HUNT
a. W-6563 Richard Johnson
W-5600 Lewis Lowry
b. M. S. Cook
c. None

S-12763 30a D:331 X-0840 ROSS:HUNT
a. W-6828 --*
b. M. S. Cook
c. None
* Warrant number not listed in Source C.

S-12764 12a D:224 X-1380 PICK:WAYN PICK:DEER
a. W-6628 William Spencer, representatives of
W-5600 Lewis Lowry
b. M. S. Cook
c. None

S-12765 183a D:266 X-0840 ROSS:TWIN
a. W-3814 Griffith Matthias
W-6628 William Spencer, representatives of
W-6641 John Cockrell
b. -- Cook & -- Cockrill*
c. None
* So spelled.

S-12766 80a D:212 X-1040 SCIO:BRUS
a. W-6666 James Carson
b. John Evans
c. Ezra Osborn, 1832

S-12767 60a D:212 X-1040 SCIO:BRUS
a. W-6666 James Carson
b. John Evans
c. John Noel, 1832; A. Brewer; D. Pollock, 1836

S-12768 115a D:211 X-0300 PIKE:PEEP
a. W-6666 James Carson
b. John Evans
c. Heirs of Robert Clark; James Hearn, 1836

S-12769 50a D:211 X-0130 ADAM:TIFF ADAM:MEIG
a. W-6641 John Cockrell
b. John Cockrill*
c. None
* So spelled.

S-12770 200a D:211 X-0650 ADAM:TIFF
a. W-6636 James Richards, deceased
b. James Richards
c. None

S-12771 200a D:211 X-0650 ADAM:WAYN
a. W-6636 James Richards, deceased
b. James Richards
c. Henry Asbury; Thomas Huston, 1834

S-12772 600a D:212 X-0650 ADAM:TIFF
a. W-6640 Price Key
W-6643 Reuben Stivers
b. -- Key & -- Stivers
c. None

S-12773 50a D:210 X-0650 ADAM:MEIG
a. W-6641 John Cockrell
b. John Cockrill*
c. None
* So spelled.

S-12774* 102a -- -- PIKE:----
a. --
b. Wood Jones
c. A. G. Thurman, 1833; heirs (of Wood Jones?); J. Stinson, 1831
* Entry in Source A only, where crossed out.

S-12775* 25a -- -- PIKE:----
a. --
b. Wood Jones

c. A. G. Thurman; heirs (of Wood Jones?); E. H. Smith, 1835
* Entry in Source A only.

S-12777
S-12779
S-14582 1354a E:216 X-0870 PIKE:PEBB ROSS:---*
a. W-6512 James Davis, deceased
W-6657 William Washington, heirs of
W-8711 --**
W-8436 --**
b. Allen Latham
c. None
* Source A does not mention Ross County.
** Warrant number not listed in Source C.

S-12778* 667a -- -- PIKE:PEBB
a. --
b. Allen Latham
c. J. R. Anderson
* Entry in Source A only.

S-12779* 2779a -- -- PIKE:----
a. --
b. -- Green & -- Kirkpatrick
c. R. Douglas, 1831
* Entry in Source A only, where crossed out.

S-12779* 2869a -- -- PIKE:----
a. --
b. -- Green & -- Kirkpatrick
c. None
* Entry in Source A only, where crossed out.

S-12779. *See also* S-12777

S-12781 30a D:263 X-1040 ADAM:JEFF SCIO:---*
a. W-6425 George Purcell, heirs of
b. Daniel Shiveley
c. C. Overturf, 1833
* Source A does not give township.

S-12782* 20a -- -- ADAM:JEFF SCIO:--**
a. --
b. Thomas Robb***
c. Thomas Kobb***; Ira? H. Hasenahs? 1833
* Entry in Source A only.
** Source A does not give township.
*** So spelled.

S-12783 50a D:224 X-0423 ADAM:LIBE
a. W-6628 William Spencer, representatives of
b. Jonathan Wormsley*
c. None
* Source A spells Warmsley.

S-12784 50a D:471 X-0420 BROW:HUNT ADAM:---*
a. W-6642 John Fletcher
b. John Bryan
c. None
* Source A does not mention Adams County.

S-12785 20a D:329 X-0420 BROW:UNIO
a. W-6642 John Fletcher
b. Francis Coburn
c. None

S-12786. *See* S-12618

S-12787 35a D:238 X-0660 CLAR:HARM
a. W-3042 John Collins
W-6567 Joseph Spencer
b. -- Galloway & -- Spencer
c. None

S-12789 55a D:224 X-0840 ROSS:TWIN
a. W-6624 David Kirkpatrick
b. David Kirkpatrick
c. None

S-12790 100a D:224 X-0381 ADAM:MONR
a. W-6624 David Kirkpatrick
W-6473 William Woolfolk
W-2297 James Peyton
b. -- Kirkpatrick, -- Woolfolk, & -- Payton*
c. M. S. Cook
* So spelled.

S-12791 30a D:418 X-0840 ROSS:HUNT
a. W-6624 David Kirkpatrick
b. David Kirkpatrick
c. None

S-12792 13a D:228 X-0420 BROW:UNIO
a. W-6524 Richard Dorsey, heirs of
b. John Beasley
c. None

S-12793* 20a -- -- ROSS:SCIO ROSS:UNIO
a. --
b. Joseph Bond
c. None
* Entry in Source A only.

S-12794 36a D:242 X-0360 FAYE:MADI
a. W-6417 Joseph Britton
b. John Evans
c. J. McLene, 1831

S-12795 175a D:235 X-0660 CHAM:SALE
a. W-6666 James Carson
b. John Evans
c. None

S-12796 30a D:238 X-0340 FRAN:PLEA
a. W-6666 James Carson
b. John Evans
c. William Mooberry, 1831

S-12797 85a D:236 X-0730 CLAR:MADI
CLAR:HARM
a. W-6666 James Carson
b. John Evans
c. None

S-12798 25a D:255 X-0360 FAYE:MADI
a. W-6666 James Carson
b. John Evans
c. J. McLane, 1831

S-12799
S-12827
S-12853 200a D:266 X-0840 ROSS:PAXT
PIKE:---*
a. W-6666 James Carson
W-6667 George Backus
b. John Evans
c. Richard Ragen, 1831; William Grimes, 1831; P. Spurck, 1833
* Source A does not give township.

S-12804 1000a D:234 X-0870 ROSS:HUNT
X-0300
X-0840
a. W-6634 Nicholas C. Kinney, assignee
b. Nicholas C. Kinney
c. Samuel McKnight; William Watts, 1830; George Baterin?, 1832

S-12805 1000a D:233 X-0130 ADAM:SCOT
a. W-6633 Nicholas C. Kinney, assignee
b. Nicholas C. Kinney
c. W. McColm, 1831

S-12806 25a D-338 X-0847 HIGH:BRUS
a. W-6393 John McCandless
b. Allen Trimble
c. None

S-12807* 50a -- -- HIGH:----
a. --
b. Allen Trimble
c. None
* Entry in Source A only, where crossed out.

S-12808 150a D:244 X-1000 SCIO:WASH
a. W-32 John --?*
b. William Kendall
c. S. Moss; W. V. Peck, 1842
* Illegible.

S-12809 200a D:245 X-1040 SCIO:UNIO
a. W-32 John --?*
b. William Kendall
c. None
* Illegible.

S-12810 3a* D:245 X-0958 SCIO:UNIO
a. W-32 John --?**
b. William Kendall
c. None
* Source A says 30 acres.
** Illegible.

S-12811 140a D:230 X-1140 PIKE:BENT
a. W-6624 David Kirkpatrick
b. David Kirkpatrick
c. None

S-12812 60a D:230 X-0840 ROSS:PAXT
X-1140
a. W-6624 David Kirkpatrick
b. David Kirkpatrick
c. None

S-12813 47a D:245 X-1000 SCIO:WASH
a. W-32 John --?*
b. William Kendall
c. S? (L?) Moss; W. V. Peck, 1842
* Illegible.

S-12814
S-12873
S-12947 209a D:239 X-0960 ROSS:HUNT
a. W-6624 David Kirkpatrick
W-6667 George Backus
W-6417 Joseph Britton
W-6668 George Backus
b. -- Kirkpatrick, -- Evans, & -- Clark
c. None

S-12815* 40a -- -- PICK:DEER
a. --
b. Allen Latham
c. John Sharp, 1831; Stephen Horsey, 1833
* Entry in Source A only.

S-12816* 15a -- -- PICK:DEER
a. --
b. Allen Latham
c. Jacob Eagle (Engle?), 1831
* Entry in Source A only.

S-12817* 22a -- -- GREE:CAES
a. --
b. Allen Latham
c. None
* Entry in Source A only.

S-12818. See S-12139

S-12819 300a D:239 X-0841 FAYE:WAYN
a. W-852 John Beck
W-6561 Mazy or Mary Vance
b. Allen Latham
c. None

S-12820 100a D:307 X-0841 PICK:PERR
ROSS:DEER
a. W-6561 Mazy or Mary Vance
b. Allen Latham
c. George Newberry, 1831

S-12822
S-12825 200a D:247 X-0841 ADAM:---*
ROSS:DEER
a. W-6667 George Backus

b. John Evans
c. None
* Source A does not mention Adams County.

S-12826 28a D:236 X-0130 ROSS:---* ADAM:JEFF
a. W-6667 George Backus
b. John Evans
c. None
* Source A does not mention Ross County.

S-12827. See S-12799

S-12828
S-12829 300a D:237 X-0840 MADI:---* ROSS:PAIN
a. W-6667 George Backus
b. John Evans
c. None
* Source A does not mention Madison County.

S-12830 40a D:237 X-0840 MADI:UNIO MADI:SUMM
a. W-6667 George Backus
b. John Evans
c. John Kious, 1831

S-12831 30a D:237 X-1260 MADI:UNIO
a. W-6667 George Backus
b. John Evans
c. A. Latham; Stephen Thomas, 1831; A. Corner?, 1832

S-12833 70a D:294 X-1300 HIGH:WHIT
a. W-6667 George Backus
b. John Evans
c. J. Hogsett, 1836

S-12834 317a D:231 X-0663 HIGH:UNIO
a. W-6570 Joseph Spencer
b. Joseph Spencer
c. None

S-12836
S-12955
S-13244 245a D:375 X-0340 FRAN:PRAI
a. W-6568 Joseph Spencer
W-6570 Joseph Spencer
b. Joseph Spencer
c. None

S-12837
S-13245 300a D:376 X-0340 FRAN:PRAI
a. W-4113 Francis McCraw
W-6570 Joseph Spencer
b. -- McCraw & -- Spencer
c. None

S-12840 300a D:429 X-1000 SCIO:UNIO
a. W-6687 Samuel Coulter*
b. John H. Smith
c. Stephen Kendall, 1836
* Possibly.

S-12841 60a D:335 X-0299 SCIO:WASH
a. W-6713 James Jopling, heir to Ralph Jopling
b. William Kendall
c. None

S-12842 40a D:335 X-1000 SCIO:WASH
a. W-6713 James Jopling, heir to Ralph Jopling
b. William Kendall
c. S? (L?) Moss; W. V. Peck, 1842

S-12848* 169a -- -- HIGH:----
a. --
b. David Kirkpatrick
c. None
* Entry in Source A only, where crossed out.

S-12849
S-12855
S-13098 174a D:331 X-1190* ADAM:MEIG ADAM:JEFF
a. W-6666 James Carson
W-6641 John Cockrell
b. M. S. Cook
c. None
* Dry Fork of.

S-12850* 605a -- -- MADI:STOK
a. --
b. John Evans
c. None
* Entry in Source A only.

S-12850* 120a D:275 X-0345 MADI:----
a. W-5139 Robert Means, assignee of James Smith
W-6648 William Christian
b. Walter Dun
c. None
* Entry in Source B only (entered after S-12876).

S-12852 33a D:270 X-0360 MADI:FAIR
a. W-6666 James Carson
b. John Evans
c. John Kious, 1831

S-12853. See S-12799

S-12855. See S-12849

S-12857
S-12858 1400a D:291 X-1060 BROW:PIKE BROW:GREE
a. W-6691 David Hix, heirs of*
b. -- Jordan & -- Thompson
c. G. H. Bohrer, 1832; Vincent Crabb, 1834; Anthony Evans; Burnet Hays, 1837; S? (L?) B. Rose; E. Mannion? 1838; John Keithler; J. S. Beasley, 1840; Ezekiel Wright; J? Ewing; J. Stansbury, 1841; A. Leonard; H. Young, 1841; F. Feike; Z. Kay, 1842; J. Stump; A. McElree, 1842; A. Stevens; H. Barton; T? Adams, 1842; J. Trevitt
* Possibly.

S-12859 100a D:428 X-0959 SCIO:UNIO
a. W-6687 Samuel Coulter*
b. John S. Smith
c. Stephen Kendall, 1836
* Possibly.

S-12861* 12a -- -- ----:----
a. --
b. Henry Warner
c. None
* Entry in Source A only, where crossed out.

S-12870* 307a -- -- PIKE:PEBB ROSS:HUNT
a. --
b. Mary Winston
c. Joseph Carter; Peter Spurck, 1833; S. Sargent, 1835; William Bussard, 1840
* Entry in Source A only.

S-12873. See S-12814

S-12875* 300a -- -- FAYE:----
a. --
b. James Jopling
c. James Bell, 1831
* Entry in Source A only, where crossed out.

S-12876 200a D:422 X-1301 HIGH:SALE
a. W-6707 Mathew Worley, heirs of
b. Mathew Worley, heirs of
c. G. Smith, 1837

S-12877. See S-12240

S-12878. See S-7398

S-12880* 120a D:275 X-0345 MADI:CANA
a. W-5139 Robert Means, assignee of James Smith
W-6648 William Christian
b. Walter Dun
c. None
* Source B erroneously lists as S-12850, but after S-12876.

S-12881. See S-12071

S-12882 30a E:353 X-0345 MADI:CANA
a. W-5139 Robert Means, assignee of James Smith
b. Walter Dun
c. None

S-12883
S-13021 65a D:277 X-0345 MADI:CANA
a. W-5139 Robert Means, assignee of James Smith
b. Walter Dun
c. None

S-12884 100a D:26 X-0040 ADAM:TIFF
a. W-947 Archibald Botts
b. Andrew Ellison
c. None

S-12885 175a D:254 X-1040 SCIO:UNIO
a. W-6561 Mazy or Mary Vance
b. -- Russell & -- Cole
c. None

S-12886 250a D:253 X-1040 SCIO:UNIO
a. W-6561 Mazy or Mary Vance
b. -- Russell & -- Cole
c. None

S-12887 215a D:319 X-1040 ADAM:JEFF
a. W-6561 Mazy or Mary Vance
b. -- Sparks, -- Means, -- Fear, & -- Rodgers
c. None

S-12888 235a D:259 X-0130 ADAM:JEFF
a. W-6561 Mazy or Mary Vance
b. -- Sparks, -- Means, -- Fear, & -- Rodgers
c. None

S-12889 60a D:257 X-0040 ADAM:TIFF
a. W-6561 Mazy or Mary Vance
b. Joseph* L. Finley
c. None
* Source A may read James.

S-12890 40a D:254 X-0230 ADAM:WAYN ADAM:WINC
a. W-6561 Mazy or Mary Vance
b. Israel Donaldson
c. None

S-12891 256a D:259 X-0230 ADAM:WAYN
a. W-3775 John Chenault
W-6524 Richard Dorsey, heirs of
W-6572 Andrew Rodgers
b. -- Thompson & -- Rodgers
c. None

S-12892 30a D:258 X-1040 ADAM:JEFF
a. W-6524 Richard Dorsey, heirs of
b. Solomon Sparks, Junior
c. None

S-12898 50a D:407 X-0760 PIKE:BENT
a. W-6572 Andrew Rodgers
b. Andrew Rodgers
c. A. G. Thurman; -- Scott; C. McCallister? (McCollister?), 1840

S-12899 60a D:407 X-0760 PIKE:BENT
a. W-6572 Andrew Rodgers
b. Andrew Rodgers
c. William Grimes, 1831; -- Scott, -- Cook*, 1836; C. McCallister? (McCollister?)
* Might read Scott Cook (one person).

S-12900 24a D:332 X-0130 ADAM:MEIG
a. W-6641 John Cockrell

b. Andrew Ellison
c. None

S-12902 50a E:59 X-0840 ROSS:PAXT
a. W-6624 David Kirkpatrick
b. David Kirkpatrick
c. John Keenes? (Keener?); George Newman, 1831; John Moss; George Newberry, 1833; John Henn; John Stone, 1835

S-12903. See S-12026

S-12905* 25a -- -- BROW:----
a. --
b. Daniel Morgan
c. John Lindsey, 1831
* Entry in Source A only, where crossed out.

S-12906 30a F:86 X-1301 HIGH:CLAY
a. W-1219 Charles Lyle
b. Charles Lysle*
c. None
* So spelled.

S-12907 70a F:86 X-1301 HIGH:CLAY
a. W-1219 Charles Lyle
b. Charles Lysle*
c. None
* So spelled.

S-12908 25a F:86 X-1301 BROW:PERR
HIGH:SALE
a. W-1213 Samuel Dyer
b. Samuel Dyer
c. None

S-12909 75a F:86 X-0663 BROW:PERR
HIGH:SALE
a. W-1213 Samuel Dyer
b. Samuel Dyer
c. None

S-12911* 200a -- -- ----:----
a. --
b. Thomas Gaines
c. None
* Entry in Source A only, where crossed out.

S-12912* 200a -- -- ----:----
a. --
b. John Means
c. None
* Entry in Source A only, where crossed out.

S-12914 100a E:63 X-1000 PICK:WAYN
a. W-5180 Archibald Lockett, representatives of
b. John Evans
c. None

S-12915. See S-10550

S-12916 340a D:231 X-0360 MADI:SUMM
a. W-6469 Abraham Forsythe
W-6433 Thomas Sharp, heirs of
b. -- Forsythe & -- Galloway
c. None

S-12918 60a D:273 X-0350 MADI:CANA
a. W-5139 Robert Means, assignee of James Smith
b. Walter Dun
c. None

S-12919 400a D:441 X-1301 HIGH:---*
BROW:GREE
a. W-6710 Douglas Irby
W-6711 Douglas Irby
b. Douglas Irby
c. D. G. Devore, 1837; David Crawford; J. S. Beasley, 1839
* Source A does not mention Highland County.

S-12925 100a D:429 X-1190 SCIO:WASH
a. W-6688 Nathaniel Chapman*
b. John H. Smith
c. None
* Possibly.

S-12926 1267a D:290 X-1060 BROW:GREE
a. W-6691 David Hix, heirs of*
b. -- Jordan & -- Thompson
c. Thompson Anderson**; Anderson Thompson**; -- Wisby et al, 1831; Anthony Evans, Junior; J. W. Trimble, 1837; S? (L?) B. Rose, 1836; Joel Wright; David M. Sayers, 1837
* Possibly.
** So shown.

S-12927 40a D:379 X-0340 UNIO:DARB
a. W-6570 Joseph Spencer
b. Joseph Spencer
c. None

S-12928
S-12957 145a D:375 X-0340 FRAN:---*
MADI:FAIR
a. W-6568 Joseph Spencer
W-6570 Joseph Spencer
b. Joseph Spencer
c. None
* Source A does not mention Franklin County.

S-12934
S-10363 300a D:334 X-0663 BROW:STER
a. W-6696 Obadiah Woodson, heirs of
W-154 Captain Beverley Roy
b. Timothy Kirby
c. None

S-12934. See also S-10363

S-12935 50a D:392 X-0663 BROW:STER
a. W-6695 Obadiah Woodson, heirs of
W-6696 Obadiah Woodson, heirs of
b. Timothy Kirby
c. None

S-12937* 100a -- -- ADAM:FRAN
a. --
b. William Johnston
c. None
* Entry in Source A only.

S-12938 76a D:243 X-1044 ADAM:FRAN
a. W-2199 Captain William Johnson
b. William Johnston*
c. Elizabeth Mathews, 1831
* So spelled.

S-12939 18a D:256 X-0810 PICK:DARB
a. W-6624 David Kirkpatrick
b. John Mantle
c. None

S-12940 25a D:313 X-0590 ADAM:SPRI
a. W-345 Captain Arthur Lind
b. -- Ellison & -- Cook
c. None

S-12941 25a D:282 X-1043 SCIO:BRUS
a. W-3445 William Kersey
b. -- Ellison & -- Cook
c. None

S-12943 158a D:273 X-0840 ROSS:HUNT
a. W-6539 William Withers?
W-6538 Thomas Parremore
W-6459 John Yarborough
b. -- Withers, -- Mayo, & -- Tarborough*
c. A. Hunt; B. Malone, 1842
* Source A spells Yarborough.

S-12944 93a D:240 X-0840 ROSS:TWIN
a. W-6560 Mazy or Mary Vance
b. M. S. Cook
c. None

S-12945 17a D:240 X-0840 ROSS:TWIN
a. W-6560 Mazy or Mary Vance
b. M. S. Cook
c. None

S-12946 100a D:238 X-0360 PICK:DARB
a. W-6716 --*
b. Henry Bedinger
c. Samuel Kinnear, 1831
* Warrantee not listed in Source C.

S-12947. See S-12814

S-12948. See S-7398

S-12950 50a D:252 X-0130 HIGH:BRUS
a. W-6486 --*
b. Ezekiel Barnes
c. E. J. McCloud, 1833 (Scioto County)
* Warrantee not listed in Source C.

S-12951 50a D:252 X-0130 HIGH:BRUS
a. W-6486 --*
b. John Pummell
c. John Parmala**; James Cochran, 1833 (Scioto County)
* Warrantee not given in Source C.
** So spelled.

S-12952 120a D-268 X-1301 HIGH:SALE
a. W-6548 Walker Baylor
b. Walker Baylor
c. None

S-12953 45a D:379 X-0660 GREE:ROSS
a. W-6568 Joseph Spencer
b. Joseph Spencer
c. None

S-12954 25a D:376 X-0730 CLAR:PLEA
a. W-6568 Joseph Spencer
b. Joseph Spencer
c. None

S-12955. See S-12836

S-12957. See S-12928

S-12960 500a D:241 X-1380 PICK:WAYN
a. W-6417 Joseph Britton
b. John Evans
c. None

S-12961 100a D:261 X-0800 ADAM:GREE
a. W-6624 David Kirkpatrick
b. John Morrison
c. None

S-12962. See S-8134

S-12963* 90a -- -- SCIO:----
a. --
b. Michael Freeman
c. William Charkey, 1831
* Entry in Source A only, where crossed out.

S-12964 20a D:262 X-0759 ADAM:GREE
a. W-6624 David Kirkpatrick
b. John Russell
c. None

S-12965 21a D:262 X-1110 ADAM:GREE
a. W-6624 David Kirkpatrick
b. John Russell
c. None

S-12966* 66a -- -- ADAM:FRAN
a. --
b. John Crawford
c. None
* Entry in Source A only.

S-12971 25a D:344 X-0130 HIGH:JACK
a. W-6393 John McCandless
b. Allen Trimble
c. None

S-12974. See S-12053

S-12975
S-12976
S-14584 369a E:218 X-0840 ROSS:HUNT ROSS:TWIN PIKE:MIFF
a. W-6624 David Kirkpatrick
W-8687 --*
W-6257 William Yates, administrator of W-6394 John Harrison
b. Allen Latham
c. J. R. Anderson; S? (L?) Byington, 1839; M. Purdam, 1831
* Warrantee not listed in Source C.

S-12977 70a D:250 X-0239 PIKE:SUNF
a. W-6624 David Kirkpatrick
b. Peter Cartwright
c. None

S-12978. See S-12963

S-12979 6a D:249 X-0760 PIKE:BENT
a. W-6624 David Kirkpatrick
b. Allen Latham
c. E. H. Smith, 1835

S-12983
S-13008 145a D:258 X-0040 ADAM:TIFF
a. W-6623 David Kirkpatrick
b. William Kirker
c. None

S-12984 56a D:261 X-0130 ADAM:GREE
a. W-6623 David Kirkpatrick
b. Joseph McKee
c. None

S-12985* 21a -- -- PIKE:----
a. --
b. William Henry
c. None
* Entry in Source A only, where crossed out.

S-12986 76a D:256 X-1000 ROSS:FRAN
a. W-6623 David Kirkpatrick
b. William H. Leffingwell
c. None

S-12987* 4a -- -- PIKE:MIFF
a. --
b. H. S. Saunders
c. None
* Entry in Source A only.

S-12990* 2a -- -- ROSS:HUNT
a. --
b. H. S. Saunders
c. None
* Entry in Source A only.

S-12994* 7a -- -- PIKE:MIFF
a. --
b. H. S. Saunders
c. None
* Entry in Source A only.

S-12997. See S-8134

S-12998. See S-8134

S-12999. See S-8134

S-13001 100a D:255 X-0300 ROSS:HUNT
a. W-6720 William Price
b. Cadwallader Wallace
c. None

S-13002 45a D:254 X-0360 PICK:PERR
a. W-6720 William Price
b. Cadwallader Wallace
c. None

S-13003 27a D:272 X-0870 ROSS:HUNT PIKE:PEBB
a. W-6720 William Price
b. Cadwallader Wallace
c. G. Porter, 1831; D. McDonald, 1833

S-13004 55a D:262 X-0040 ADAM:MONR
a. W-6623 David Kirkpatrick
b. Samuel Thatcher
c. None

S-13005 200a D:253 X-0730 CHAM:WAYN
a. W-4733 Peter Cockrell
b. Allen Latham
c. None

S-13006* 25a -- -- ROSS:----
a. --
b. George Clark
c. None
* Entry in Source A only, where crossed out; "withdrawn."

S-13007. See S-8134

S-13008. See S-12983

S-13009 20a D:258 X-0130 ADAM:MEIG
a. W-6623 David Kirkpatrick
b. Andrew Ellison
c. None

S-13010 18a D:260 X-0130 ADAM:TIFF
a. W-947 Archibald Botts
b. Andrew Ellison
c. None

S-13011. See S-8134

S-13012 6a D:260 X-0420 ADAM:LIBE
a. W-6623 David Kirkpatrick
b. George W. Leedom
c. None

S-13015
S-13023
S-13024
S-13025 300a D:267 X-0840 PIKE:PERR
X-0130
X-1140
a. W-6137 William Shreaves
W-6667 George Backus
b. -- Wallace & -- Evans
c. J. Evans; R. Ragan, 1831; J. Hines, 1832; James Jones, 1838; N. Massie

S-13017 200a D:265 X-0760 PIKE:BENT
ROSS:----*
a. W-6426 Presley Boley
b. John Walls**
c. None
* Source A does not mention Ross County.
** Source A spells Watts.

S-13019* 30a -- -- LOGA:JEFF
LOGA:MONR
a. --
b. James W. Marmon
c. None
* Entry in Source A only.

S-13020 290a D:278 X-0340 MADI:MONR
a. W-5139 Robert Means, assignee of James Smith
W-6668 George Backus
b. Walter Dun
c. None

S-13021. See S-12883

S-13022
S-13038
S-13025 32a D:279 X-0340 MADI:CANA
a. W-5139 Robert Means, assignee of James Smith
W-6668 George Backus
b. Walter Dun
c. None

S-13023. See S-13015

S-13024. See S-13015

S-13025. See S-13015; S-13022

S-13026 100a D:332 X-0133 ADAM:JEFF
a. W-6705 Samuel Dunlop
b. James Barnes*
c. Joshua Van Vettenburg, 1833 (Scioto County)
* Source A may spell Burnes.

S-13027 24a D:266 X-1007 ADAM:JEFF
a. W-6623 David Kirkpatrick
b. John Wyckoff
c. C. Overturf, 1833 (Scioto County)

S-13028 80a D:324 X-0134 ADAM:SCOT
a. W-6548 Walker Baylor
b. Walker Baylor
c. J. McDowell; L? (S?) Cole, 1842

S-13029 14a D:272 X-0840 ROSS:HUNT
a. W-6459 John Yarborough
b. John Yarborough
c. None

S-13032* 50a -- -- ----:----
a. --
b. John Evans
c. None
* Entry in Source A only, where crossed out.

S-13034* 900a -- -- FRAN:----
a. --
b. Thomas Green
c. Thomas Gaines; D. Adams, 1831
* Entry in Source A only, where crossed out.

S-13035* 100a -- -- ----:----
a. --
b. Samuel Drury
c. None
* Entry in Source A only, where crossed out.

S-13035. See also S-13168

S-13036* 300a -- -- BROW:EAGL
a. --
b. Henry Asbury
c. J. Edgington; J. S. Beasley, 1841
* Entry in Source A only.

S-13037* 100a -- -- BROW:----
a. --
b. Thomas Green
c. None
* Entry in Source A only, where crossed out.

S-13038. See S-13022

S-13039* 307a -- -- PIKE:PEBB
ROSS:HUNT
a. --
b. Judith Cimbrew
c. Joseph Carter; A. G. Thurman, 1833; E. H. Smith, 1835; heirs of E. H. Smith; James Moore; William Buzzard, 1840
* Entry in Source A only.

S-13041 130a D:282 X-0979 ADAM:GREE
a. W-6633 Nicholas C. Kinney, assignee
b. John H. Baird, representatives of
c. None

S-13042 50a D:281 X-0800 ADAM:GREE
a. W-6623 David Kirkpatrick
b. Robert Adams
c. None

S-13043* 35a -- -- ADAM:GREE
a. --
b. Joseph Willis
c. None
* Entry in Source A only.

S-13044 20a D:321 X-0130 ADAM:GREE
a. W-6623 David Kirkpatrick
b. John Aldred
c. None

S-13056 135a D:321 X-1007 ADAM:JEFF
a. W-6623 David Kirkpatrick
b. Henry Waite
c. None

S-13057 30a D:313 X-0420 ADAM:LIBE
a. W-6657 William Washington, heirs of
b. Joseph McGrew
c. None

S-13059* 100a -- -- HIGH:----
a. --
b. Joel Hart
c. None
* Entry in Source A only, where crossed out.

S-13060* 50a -- -- ----:----
a. --
b. Joel Hart
c. None
* Entry in Source A only, where crossed out.

S-13061 60a D:288 X-1200 HIGH:UNIO
a. W-6512 James Davis, deceased
b. Abraham Lowman
c. None

S-13062 50a D:423 X-0663 HIGH:UNIO
a. W-6512 James Davis, deceased
b. Joel Hart
c. None

S-13063 10a D:288 X-0660 WARR:WAYN
a. W-6512 James Davis, deceased
b. James Elliot
c. None

S-13064
S-13107 22a D:307 X-0340 PICK:JACK
a. W-6512 James Davis, deceased
b. William N. Forseman*
c. None
* Source A spells Furman.

S-13065* 300a -- -- BROW:GREE
a. --
b. Jeremiah Basham, heirs of
c. G. H. Bohrer, 1832; W. Hunt, 1834
* Entry in Source A only.

S-13066 100a D:293 X-0110 UNIO:LEES
a. W-6661 Cuthbert Harrison
b. Samuel H. Saunders
c. None

S-13067 300a D:292 X-0750 LOGA:JEFF
a. W-6660 Cuthbert Harrison
b. Samuel H. Saunders
c. J. Clark, 1832

S-13068 600a D:293 X-0750 LOGA:BOAK
a. W-6661 Cuthbert Harrison
W-6660 Cuthbert Harrison
b. Samuel H. Saunders
c. B. Stanton, 1836; S. G. Hoge, 1841

S-13069 28a D:312 X-0660 CLAR:MADI
a. W-6568 Joseph Spencer
b. Joseph Spencer
c. None

S-13071 40a D:378 X-0340 FRAN:PRAI
a. W-6568 Joseph Spencer
b. Joseph Spencer
c. None

S-13074 61a D:304 X-1200 HIGH:UNIO
X-0663
a. W-6512 James Davis, deceased
b. Joel Hart
c. None

S-13075 25a D:305 X-0380 HIGH:UNIO
a. W-6512 James Davis, deceased
b. John Bevans
c. None

S-13076 145a D:305 X-1200 HIGH:UNIO
a. W-6512 James Davis, deceased
b. Joel Hart
c. Z. Raines; T. Barry, 1842

S-13078 148a D:294 X-1000 HARD:TAYL
a. W-6652 William Scott, heirs of
b. Samuel H. Saunders
c. John McLain, 1832 (Fayette County); I? Y. Green, 1836 (Fayette County)

S-13079 250a D:295 X-0060 LOGA:---*
HARD:TAYL
a. W-6652 William Scott, heirs of

W-6653 William Scott, heirs of
b. Samuel H. Saunders
c. George Irwin, 1832
* Source A does not give township.

S-13080* 20a -- -- ----:----
a. --
b. Samuel H. Saunders
c. None
* Entry in Source A only, where crossed out.

S-13081 150a D:294 X-0130 ADAM:SCOT
a. W-6651 William Scott, heirs of
b. Samuel H. Saunders
c. None

S-13082* 350a -- -- MADI:UNIO
a. --
b. Samuel H. Saunders
c. None
* Entry in Source A only.

S-13082* 180a E:228 X-0360 MADI:----
a. W-6650 William Scott, heirs of
b. Mathew Bonner
c. None
* Entry not listed in Source A.

S-13083* 125a -- -- ----:----
a. --
b. William Scott, heirs of
c. None
* Entry in Source A only, where crossed out.

S-13084* 125a -- -- ----:----
a. --
b. William Scott, heirs of
c. None
* Entry in Source A only, where crossed out.

S-13085* 250a -- -- ----:----
a. --
b. William Scott, heirs of
c. Heirs of G. Bateman; J. Woodbridge, 1837
* Entry in Source A only, where crossed out.

S-13086 250a D:296 X-0841 FAYE:MADI
a. W-6651 William Scott, heirs of
b. Cadwallader Wallace
c. None

S-13087* 250a -- -- HIGH:----
a. --
b. C. Wallace
c. Henry Bedinger; George Smith, 1836
* Entry in Source A only, where crossed out.

S-13088* 750a -- -- ----:----
a. --
b. Cuthbert Harrison
c. C. Wallace, 1832
* Entry in Source A only, where crossed out.

S-13089 40a D:320 X-0800 ADAM:GREE
a. W-6657 William Washington, heirs of
b. Asa Coan
c. None

S-13090 50a D:312 X-1138 ADAM:GREE
a. W-6657 William Washington, heirs of
b. -- Adams, -- McMahan, & -- Petit
c. None

S-13091 25a D:322 X-0800 ADAM:GREE
a. W-6657 William Washington, heirs of
b. John Morrison
c. None

S-13092 75a D:320 X-0800 ADAM:GREE
a. W-6657 William Washington, heirs of
b. William Murphey
c. None

S-13094
S-13095 130a D:308 X-0840 ROSS:PAIN
a. W-6667 George Backus
b. John Evans
c. M. Purdam, 1832; D. Thompson, 1835

S-13096 30a D:383 X-1140 PIKE:PEBB
a. W-6560 Mazy or Mary Vance
b. M. S. Cook
c. None

S-13097 26a D:332 X-0800 ADAM:MONR
a. W-6641 John Cockrell
b. Andrew Ellison
c. None

S-13098. See S-12849

S-13099
S-14143
S-14146
S-14485 500a E:184 X-0840 ROSS:HUNT
a. W-6560 Mazy or Mary Vance
W-8485 --*
W-8719 --*
b. M. S. Cook
c. None
* Source C does not list this warrant number.

S-13100* 100a -- -- BROW:GREE
a. --
b. Casey Holland, heirs of
c. G. H. Boher (Bohrer), 1832; William Hewitt, 1833; P. L. Wilson, 1840
* Entry in Source A only.

S-13101* 100a -- -- BROW:GREE
a. --
b. Jeremiah Basham, heirs of
c. None
* Entry in Source A only.

S-13102 10a D:315 X-0800 SCIO:NILE
a. W-6657 William Washington, heirs of
b. John Turner
c. None

S-13103 10a D:320 X-0800 ADAM:GREE
a. W-6425 George Purcell, heirs of
b. Simon Smith
c. J. P. Smith, 1841

S-13104 150a D-316 X-1110 ADAM:GREE
a. W-6629 William Spencer, representatives of
b. Asa Coan
c. None

S-13105 57a D:399 X-1200 HIGH:UNIO
CLIN:---*
a. W-6512 James Davis, deceased
b. Joel Hart
c. C. B. Harlan, 1832; Levi Gustin, 1834; R. B. Harlan, 1837
* Source A does not give township.

S-13106 12a D:304 X-1200 HIGH:UNIO
a. W-6512 James Davis, deceased
b. Joel Hart
c. None

S-13107. See S-13064

S-13108 200a D:306 X-0840 ROSS:TWIN
X-0870
a. W-6372 Henry? Stephens, heir to Gabriel (Stephens)
W-6422 Elizabeth Elzey, heir to Conrad Cabbage
b. Joseph Taylor
c. None

S-13109 42a D:368 X-0660 CLAR:MADI
a. W-2274 Doctor Basel Middleton
b. John Campbell
c. None

S-13110 140a D:363 X-1040 ADAM:JEFF
a. W-6629 William Spencer, representatives of
b. Josiah Williams
c. None

S-13111 40a D:317 X-1040 ADAM:JEFF
a. W-6629 William Spencer, representatives of
b. Parker Imitt? (Tmitt?)*
c. None
* Source A spells Truitt.

S-13112 380a D:310 X-0840 MADI:STOK
PICK:---*
a. W-6568 Joseph Spencer
b. Joseph Spencer
c. J. Watts; Seymour G. Renick, 1832
* Source A does not give township.

S-13115 15a F:135 X-0400 FAYE:MADI
a. W-6626 Archibald Alexander
b. Battael Harrison
c. None

S-13116 100a D:310 X-0060 LOGA:MCAR
a. W-6685 John Crutchfield (perhaps)
b. John Huston
c. None

S-13117 87a D:314 X-1220 SCIO:NILE
a. W-6647 William Christian
b. David McCall
c. None

S-13118 63a D:313 X-0800 SCIO:NILE
a. W-6647 William Christian
b. David McCall
c. None

S-13119 140a D:314 X-0800 ADAM:GREE
SCIO:---*
a. W-6647 William Christian
b. David McCall
c. None
* Source A does not mention Scioto County.

S-13120 80a D:320 X-1007 ADAM:JEFF
a. W-6560 Mazy or Mary Vance
b. Andrew Jones
c. None

S-13121 180a D:322 X-1110 ADAM:GREE
a. W-6647 William Christian
W-6560 Mazy or Mary Vance
b. John Puntenney
c. None

S-13122 32a D:313 X-0090 ADAM:JEFF
a. W-6560 Mazy or Mary Vance
b. William Williams
c. None

S-13123 32a D:312 X-1007 ADAM:JEFF
a. W-6560 Mazy or Mary Vance
b. William Parkes*
c. None
* Source A spells Parks.

S-13124* 20a -- -- FAYE:PAIN
a. --
b. Allen Latham
c. None
* Entry in Source A only

S-13125* 250a -- -- ----:----
a. --
b. Allen Latham
c. None
* Entry in Source A only, where crossed out.

S-13126* 171a -- -- ----:----
a. --
b. Allen Latham
c. G. H. Bohrer, 1832
* Entry in Source A only, where crossed out.

S-13128* 20a -- -- CLIN:CLAR
a. --
b. Allen Latham
c. William P. Hunnicut; S. McCune, 1834
* Entry in Source A only.

S-13129* 50a -- -- ADAM:SCOT
a. --
b. William Simmons
c. None
* Entry in Source A only, where crossed out.

S-13130. See S-12887

S-13131 100a D:318 X-0600 ADAM:SPRI
a. W-6512 James Davis, deceased
b. Isaac Foster
c. None

S-13132
S-13210 55a D:349 X-1007 ADAM:JEFF
a. W-6512 James Davis, deceased
W-6561 Mazy or Mary Vance
b. John W. Timmans*
c. None
* Source A spells Timmons.

S-13133 30a D:317 X-0423 ADAM:LIBE
a. W-6512 James Davis, deceased
b. John Kincaid
c. None

S-13134 50a E:141 X-0130 X-1140 PIKE:PERR
a. W-6626 Archibald Alexander
b. Enoch McChord*
c. None
* Source A spells McCord.

S-13135 100a D:344 X-0841 FAYE:MADI
a. W-5400 William Sanford, representatives of
b. William Sanford, representatives of
c. Alexander Douglas, Junior, 1838; I? Y. Green, 1836

S-13136
S-13814 200a E:38 X-1300 HIGH:WHIT
a. W-5942 William Higginbotham
W-5602 Joshua Foster
b. John A. Foster
c. None

S-13137 86a D:438 X-0060 LOGA:MCAR
a. W-6665 James Carson (perhaps)
b. John T. Bayles
c. George Irvin, 1832

S-13138 58a F:123 X-0360 MADI:PLEA
a. W-6665 James Carson (perhaps)
b. A. D. Kendrick*
c. Alexander Comer, 1832
* Source A says John T. Bayles.

S-13139 30a E:215 X-1140 PIKE:MIFF
a. W-6626 Archibald Alexander
b. Allen Latham
c. Daniel Lee, 1832

S-13140 25a D:374 X-1007 SCIO:BRUS ADAM:---*
a. W-6627 Archibald Alexander
b. Isaac Smalley
c. None
* Source A does not mention Adams County.

S-13141 100a D:354 X-0800 ADAM:MONR
a. W-6627 Archibald Alexander
b. Zaphania Wade
c. None

S-13141 110a D:375 X-0800 ADAM:MONR
a. W-6627 Archibald Alexander
b. Zaphania Wade
c. Joseph? (James?) Wade

S-13142 13a F:147 X-0420 BROW:UNIO
a. W-1296 Timothy Peyton
b. Samuel Fitch
c. None

S-13143 9a D:329 X-0420 BROW:UNIO
a. W-1296 Timothy Peyton
b. Isaac Porter
c. None

S-13144 100a D:326 X-0800 HAMI:ANDE
a. W-6363 John Jerrell
b. Joseph B. Humphreys
c. None

S-13145. See S-13168

S-13149 248a D:410 X-0340 CHAM:UNIO
a. W-5537 Peter Manifold, assignee of George Handy
W-6526 Young Wilkerson
b. Duncan McArthur
c. None

S-13150
S-13352 100a D:410 X-0810 MADI:PLEA
a. W-5537 Peter Manifold, assignee of George Handy
W-6526 Young Wilkerson
b. Duncan McArthur
c. None

S-13154* 250a -- -- ----:----
a. --
b. Allen Latham
c. None
* Entry in Source A only, where crossed out; "withdrawn."

S-13155 50a D:353 X-1110 ADAM:GREE
a. W-6512 James Davis, deceased

b. Jonathan Tracy
c. None

S-13156 140a D:352 X-0800 ADAM:MONR
a. W-6625 Archibald Alexander
b. David C. Vance
c. None

S-13160 54a D:351 X-0130 ADAM:TIFF
a. W-6626 Archibald Alexander
b. Richard Thatcher, Junior
c. T. Huston, 1834

S-13161. See S-12530

S-13162
S-13163
S-13164 100a D:326 X-0360 MADI:UNIO
X-0840 CLAR:---*
a. W-6668 George Backus
b. Cad(wallader) Wallace
c. None
* Source A does not mention Clark County.

S-13165*
S-14278 20a E:128 X-1140 PIKE:----
a. Ex-444 No name given
W-6627 Archibald Alexander
b. Cornelius O'Brien
c. None
* Source A does not list this entry.

S-13166* 100a -- -- WARR:HAMI
a. --
b. Thomas Hopkins, representatives of
c. None
* Entry not listed in Source B.

S-13168
S-13171
S-13145
S-13035
S-5266 606a D:347 X-1000 PIKE:CAMP
a. W-6537 Thomas Pairemore?
W-6667 George Backus
W-6668 George Backus
W-5100 David Scott
W-1827 Rawleigh Hawley
b. Cadwallader Wallace
c. None

S-13169 48a D:386 X-0133 ADAM:FRAN
a. W-6512 James Davis, deceased
b. Thomas Shelby
c. None

S-13171. See S-13168

S-13174. See S-2755 (in volume 4, part 1)

S-13174* 200a -- -- PIKE:----
a. --
b. John Miller
c. C. Wallace, 1832
* Entry in Source A only, where crossed out.

S-13175 100a E:38 X-1301 HIGH:SALE
a. W-6590 No name given
b. John* Watson, heirs of
c. None
* Source A says James.

S-13177 100a D:326 X-0134 ADAM:SCOT
a. W-4317 Zenas Macomber
b. Zenas* Macomber
c. T. Huston, 1832
* Source A spells Zenos.

S-13181 300a D:405 X-0061 HARD:MCDO
LOGA:---*
a. W-3667 Julius Rutherford
W-3713 William Dillon, assignee (of?) -- Childress
W-3875 Jacob Whitsell
b. -- Rotherfield*, -- Dillon, & -- Whitsel*
c. Joseph Newell, 1832; -- Rutherford; C. Wallace, 1839
* Source A spells Rutherford Whitsell (one person); does not give township.

S-13182 478a D:327 X-0060 HARD:TAYL
LOGA:---*
a. W-6545 Charles Sneed, heirs of
b. Sally Winder
c. Joseph Newell, 1832; John H. Wear, 1837; James Johnson; -- Campbell & -- Johns, 1838; A. Lambert; George Johns, 1840
* Source A does not give township.

S-13183 13a D:331 X-1190 ADAM:MEIG
X-1040
a. W-4897 George Tucker
W-6512 James Davis, deceased
b. John Calloway
c. None

S-13184 13a D:333 X-1042 ADAM:MEIG
a. W-6512 James Davis, deceased
b. John Calloway
c. None

S-13185
S-13285* 60a D:383 X-0130 PIKE:PERR
a. W-6667 George Backus
W-6560 Mazy or Mary Vance
b. -- Evans & -- Cook
c. J. Evans; Samuel Reed, 1833
* Source A says S-13282.

S-13186 12a D:334 X-0134 ADAM:SCOT
a. W-4897 George Tucker
b. George Vinsonhal(l)er
c. None

S-13187 40a D:351 X-0800 ADAM:MONR
a. W-6623 David Kirkpatrick

b. Nicholas Burwell
c. None

S-13188 9a E:67 X-1150 BROW:HUNT
a. W-1296 Timothy Peyton
b. Jeptha Beasley
c. M. Tomb?, Senior, 1834; J. Beasley, Junior

S-13189. See S-9854

S-13190 30a D:354 X-0423 ADAM:LIBE
a. W-6642 John Cockrell
b. -- Davidson, -- Gray, -- Stevens, et al*
c. None
* Source A says: "-- Davison, -- Franciss, -- Benjamin, -- Gray, -- Rankin, & -- Stevens."

S-13195* 167a -- -- ----:----
a. --
b. C(adwallader) Wallace
c. None
* Entry in Source A only, where crossed out.

S-13196 100a D:391 X-0790 CLER:GOSH
a. W-6695 Obediah Woodson, heirs of
b. Timothy Kirby
c. None

S-13197 94a D:391 X-0663 CLER:---* BROW:STER
a. W-6695 Obediah Woodson, heirs of
b. Timothy Kirby
c. J. S. Beasley, 1840
* Source A does not give township.

S-13198 10a D:339 X-0360 ROSS:DEER
a. W-6127 Stephen Young
b. John A. Fulton
c. None

S-13199 223a D:340 X-0750 LOGA:RUSH
a. W-2898 Thomas Lewen? (Leven?), representatives of
b. William M. Kenton
c. None

S-13200 200a D:340 X-0750 LOGA:RUSH
a. W-4485 John Bridges
b. William M. Kenton
c. None

S-13201* 177a -- -- ----:----
a. W-854 Lieutenant Nicholas Taliaferro
W-3968 Terence Conner
b. Nicholas Taliafer(ro)
c. None
* Entry in Source A only.

S-13202 200a D:340 X-0750 LOGA:RUSH
a. W-3968 Terence Conner
b. Terrence Conner
c. George Irwin, 1832

S-13203* 100a D:340 X-0750 LOGA:RUSH
a. W-5073 Benjamin Dawson
b. Joshua Kenard*
c. Laquinio Rawson, 1832
* Source A says "not patented;" spells Kinard.

S-13204 10a D:341 X-0840 FAYE:PAIN
a. W-6512 James Davis, deceased
b. Thomas C. Rockhill
c. None

S-13205 20a D:345 X-1044 ADAM:MEIG
a. W-6629 William Spencer, representatives of
b. Jarnet* Newman
c. None
* Source A spells Jarret.

S-13206
S-14154 53a E:109 X-0400 FAYE:MADI MADI:RANG
a. W-6667 George Backus
W-8485 --*
b. -- Cook & -- Evans
c. John Evans; -- Conner & -- Bramblet, 1832
* Source C does not list this warrant number.

S-13207 100a D:346 X-0840 ROSS:TWIN
a. W-1827 Rawleigh Hawley
b. Cadwallader Wallace
c. None

S-13210. See S-13132

S-13211 20a D:349 X-0590 ADAM:SPRI
a. W-6561 Mazy or Mary Vance
b. Joseph Riggs
c. None

S-13212 15a D:350 X-0130 ADAM:MEIG
a. W-6561 Mazy or Mary Vance
b. Thomas Thoroman
c. None

S-13213 37a D:353 X-0800 ADAM:SPRI
a. W-5871 Francis M. Boykin & Ann Johnson, heirs of (Francis) Boykin
W-6439 Jeremiah Morgan, heirs of
b. Joseph Darlington
c. None

S-13214 126a D:374 X-0800 ADAM:SPRI
a. W-4992 Thomas Wells? (Wills?), representatives of
W-5946 William Pullen
W-5781 Joseph Crockett
W-237 Lieutenant John Harrison
b. William Bradford
c. None

S-13215* 6a -- -- BROW:HUNT
a. --
b. Jeptha Beasley
c. None
* Entry in Source A only.

S-13216 55a D:356 X-0840 ROSS:TWIN
a. W-6512 James Davis, deceased
b. Hezekiah Pool
c. None

S-13217
S-13218
S-13239 272a D:365 X-0133 HIGH:BRUS
a. W-6085 Thomas Collier?, representatives of
W-1413 Thomas Coverley
b. Cadwallader Wallace
c. None

S-13219* 10a D:362 X-1041 ADAM:----
a. W-6085 Thomas Collier?, representatives of
b. Jonathan Boyd
c. None
* Source A says "not found."

S-13225 140a D:359 X-1170 WARR:SALE
a. W-6512 James Davis, deceased
b. John Shawkaw*
c. Joseph? (James?) Harper; J A. Stokes, 1834
* Source A may spell Shawhan.

S-13226 15a D:360 X-0180 WARR:WAYN CLIN:CHES
a. W-6512 James Davis, deceased
b. Levi Lakens*
c. None
* Source A spells Lukens.

S-13227 23a D:360 X-0409 SCIO:BRUS ADAM:MEIG
a. W-6512 James Davis, deceased
b. Christopher* Newman
c. None
* Source A says Christian.

S-13229 160a D:369 X-1000 HARD:DUDL
a. W-5231 Henry Lee, devisee of Alexander Skinner
W-6567 Joseph Spencer
b. -- Galloway & -- Spencer
c. None

S-13231 639a D:370 X-1000 HARD:DUDL
a. W-5277 Thomas M. Bayly, assignee of Thomas Alen (Allen), representatives of Fr(ancis?)'s (Allen) heirs
W-5278 Thomas M. Bayly, assignee of James Alen (Allen), representatives of James (Allen)
W-5283 (page torn)
b. -- Galloway, -- Morris, & -- Spencer
c. None

S-13232 27a D:361 X-0360 PICK:DEER
a. W-1171 Benjarmin Stubblefield, heir to George Stubblefield
b. Benjamin Stubblefield
c. None

S-13233 30a D:362 X-0840 ROSS:HUNT
a. W-2153 James Bowker?, said to be Thomas Bralley's (Beatty's?) (heir?)
b. Mathew Bonner
c. None

S-13234 100a D:362 X-0730 CLAR:PLEA
a. W-2153 James Bowker?, said to be Thomas Bralley's (Beatty's?)(heir?)
b. Mathew Bonner
c. None

S-13235* 45a D:363 X-0298 ADAM:----
a. W-5934 Robert Thelaball
b. Christian Benner
c. None
* Source A says "not found."

S-13236* 400a -- -- ----:----
a. --
b. Charles Lee
c. None
* Entry in Source A only, where crossed out.

S-13237
S-13441 500a D:442 X-1300 BROW:PIKE
a. W-1413 Thomas Coverley
W-6713 James Jopling, heir of Ralph Jopling
b. Cadwallader Wallace
c. None

S-13239. See S-13217

S-13240. See S-2755 (in volume 4, part 1, footnote 2)

S-13241. See S-9251

S-13242 200a D:369 X-1000 HARD:MCDO
a. W-918 James Flaugherty
b. James Flaugherty
c. Jared S. Dawson, 1837; David Camper

S-13242 200a D:369 X-1000 HARD:MCDO
a. W-1548 Jeremiah Parker
b. Jeremiah Parker
c. -- Flaugherty & -- Parker

S-13243 39a D:372 X-0730 CHAM:GOSH
a. W-6570 Joseph Spencer
b. Joseph Spencer
c. None

S-13244. See S-12836

S-13245. See S-12837

S-13246 40a D:377 X-1300 HIGH:SALE
a. W-5551 John Meanly
W-2154 James Bowker?, said to be Thomas Bralley's? (Beatty's?) (heir?)
b. Mathew Bonner
c. None

S-13247 200a D:371 X-1000 PICK:SCIO
X-0340
a. W-5876 William Triplett? (Treplett?)
W-5878 John Graves
b. Cadwallader Wallace
c. None

S-13248*
S-13279
S-13359
S-13449 693a F:451 X-1000 HARD:----
a. W-6227 Adrian Davenport
W-6423 William Sharp
W-3546 George Lear
W-5026 David Meriwether
W-5980 George Thomas
W-6667 George Backus
W-5697 Joseph Woodson
W-3879 Charles Forklin's? (Focklin's?) heir
W-6720 William Price
W-4087 Walter Ashmore, devisee of Charles Gallahue
W-3477 Abraham Shepherd
W-1921 General Robert Lawson
W-5802 George Norvell, deceased
b. Cadwallader Wallace
c. None
* Entry not listed in Source A.

S-13249*
S-15912 25a F:222 X-0995 SCIO:----
a. W-6647 William Christian
W-9231 --**
b. Joseph Van Mustard
c. None
* Entry not listed in Source A.
** Source C does not list this warrant number.

S-13249* 15a -- -- ADAM:SCOT
a. --
b. George Vinsonhal(l)er
c. None
* Entry in Source A only.

S-13250
S-15264 45a* E:414 X-0995 ADAM:MEIG
a. W-6647 William Christian
W-4096 Ephraim Ralph
b. William Mitchell*
c. None
* Source A says George Vinsonhal(l)er for 25 acres.

S-13253 24a D:377 X-0215 ADAM:MEIG
a. W-5555 Samuel Booker's heirs (perhaps S. Donaldson & David Bradford)
b. Jacob Schults*
c. None
* Source A spells Schultz.

S-13254 7a D:386 X-0040 ADAM:TIFF
a. W-6628 William Spencer, representatives of
b. Gabriel D. Darlington
c. None

S-13255 25a D:391 X-1044 ADAM:FRAN
a. W-6647 William Christian
b. James Cross
c. None

S-13256
S-13257 259a D:378 X-1380 PICK:JACK
a. W-6647 William Christian
b. Allen Latham
c. None

S-13258. See S-6285 (in volume 4, part 1)

S-13269 22a D:378 X-0180 GREE:SILV
a. W-6570 Joseph Spencer
b. Joseph Spencer
c. None

S-13270 73a D:380 X-0840 GREE:SILV
a. W-6570 Joseph Spencer
b. Joseph Spencer
c. None

S-13271 94a D:379 X-0340 UNIO:LIBE
a. W-6570 Joseph Spencer
b. Joseph Spencer
c. None

S-13273 500a E:17 X-1000 HARD:HALE
a. W-6524 Richard Dorsey, heirs of
W-6567 Joseph Spencer
W-6568 Joseph Spencer
W-2947 John Means?
W-2524? Benjamin Sutton?
b. James Galloway
c. None

S-13274. See S-12350

S-13275 51a D:398 X-0840 ROSS:HUNT
a. W-5592 John Hart, representative of John (Hart)
b. John A. Fulton
c. None

S-13276 45a D:381 X-0130 PIKE:PERR
a. W-6629 William Spencer, representatives of
b. Mathew Bonner
c. None

S-13278 25a D:386 X-1041 ADAM:FRAN
a. W-6629 William Spencer, representatives of
b. Peter Wickerham
c. None

S-13279 55a D:456 X-1000 HARD:DUDL
a. W-5510 Thomas Herde?
b. -- Tagert, -- Gray, & -- Taylor
c. None

S-13279. See also S-13248

S-13280
S-14273 45a* E:271 X-1040 ADAM:MEIG
a. W-852 John Beck
W-8395 --**
b. James R. Welty*
c. None
* Source A says Allen Latham for 30 acres.
** Source C does not list this warrant number.

S-13281 10a E:129 X-0340 UNIO:JERO MADI:DARB
a. W-5265 Tuttle Hudson, et al?, administrators of William Hudson
b. David Chapman
c. None

S-13282. See S-13185

S-13283 10a D:386 X-0800 ADAM:MONR
a. W-2156 Simon Baley
b. Joseph Riggs
c. None

S-13284 47a E:162 X-0800 ADAM:SPRI
a. W-323 Lieutenant Robert Green
b. William Strode
c. None

S-13285 20a D:408 X-1000 PICK:SCIO
a. W-6308 Charles Stewart, heirs of
b. Philo N. White
c. None

S-13285. See also S-13185

S-13286 79a D:384 X-0840 ROSS:HUNT
a. W-6653 William Scott, heirs of
b. Allen Latham
c. None

S-13287 40a E:38 X-0840 ROSS:HUNT
a. W-5400 William Sanford, representatives of
b. John A. Fulton
c. None

S-13288 23a* E:217 X-1140 PIKE:PERR
a. W-6653 William Scott, heirs of
b. Allen Latham
c. None
* Source A says 30 acres.

S-13290 150a D:385 X-0010 GREE:SILV
a. W-1849 Major John Belfield
b. James Galloway, Junior
c. None

S-13291 83a D:384 X-0750 UNIO:LIBE
a. W-1849 Major John Belfield
b. James Galloway, Junior
c. None

S-13292 133a D:419 X-0841 FAYE:MADI
a. W-6526 Young Wilkerson
b. Duncan McArthur
c. None

S-13293
S-13300 31a D:387 X-0130 ADAM:MONR
a. W-6628 William Spencer, representatives of
W-1141 Edward Shepherd
b. William Walden
c. None

S-13294 50a D:486 X-0663 CLER:BATA CLER:STON
a. W-6569 --*
b. John Baker
c. None
* No name given; possibly Joseph Spencer.

S-13295 30a D:386 X-0920 SCIO:UNIO
a. W-6194 Robert Hanson Harrison, heirs of
b. Robert Lucas
c. None

S-13296* 20a -- -- ADAM:GREE
a. --
b. Alfred Purcell
c. None
* Entry in Source A only.

S-13297* 21a -- -- SCIO:WASH
a. --
b. Allen Farquher
c. None
* Entry in Source A only.

S-13297* 73a F:163 X-1000 SCIO:----
a. W-167 Captain Thomas Ransdale (Ransdell?)
Ex 546 --**
b. David F. Heaton
c. None
* Entry not listed in Source A.
** No name given in Source C.

S-13298 25a E:248 X-0190 SCIO:MORG
a. W-8682 --*
b. Charles T. Culter**
c. None
* Source C does not list this warrant number.
** Source A spells Cutler.

S-13299* 70a -- -- ----:----
a. --
b. James Galloway, Junior
c. None
* Entry in Source A only, where crossed out.

S-13300. See S-13293

S-13301 28a D:387 X-0040 ADAM:MONR
a. W-3445 William Kersey
W-6628 William Spencer, representatives of
b. William Ellison
c. None

S-13302 70a D:388 X-0130 ADAM:JEFF
a. W-6561 Mazy or Mary Vance
W-6628 William Spencer, representatives of
b. -- Rogers*, -- Means, et al
c. None
* Source A says -- Rodgers, -- Means, -- Voris, & -- Fear

S-13305 100a E:356 X-0380 HIGH:DODS
a. W-6291 --*
b. Stephen Thompson, heirs of
c. None
* Source C does not give name.

S-13306
S-13573
S-13733 325a E:113 X-1301 HIGH:NEWM
a. W-6678 Richard Stevens
W-6574 Andrew Rodgers
W-6515 Daniel Barnett
b. George W. Barriere, heirs of
c. None

S-13307* 73a -- -- HIGH:SALE
a. --
b. G. W. Barriere, heirs of
c. None
* Entry in Source A only

S-13308 20a D:388 X-0360 PICK:PERR
a. W-4892 George Menzies, representatives of
b. Mathew Bonner
c. None

S-13309 13a D:388 X-0360 FAYE:MADI
a. W-4892 George Menzies, representatives of
b. Mathew Bonner
c. None

S-13310 600a E:210 X-0340 FRAN:PLEA
a. W-6512 James Davis, deceased
W-6653 William Scott, heirs of
W-6257 William Yates, administrators of
b. Allen Latham
c. D. Adams; forfeited to State, 1835; James Gates; D. D. Warner, 1839

S-13311 56a E:54 X-0840 ROSS:HUNT
a. W-5400 William Sanford, representatives of
b. John A. Fulton
c. None

S-13313*
S-13322
S-13323 1000a -- -- LOGA:RUSH
a. --
b. Duncan McArthur
c. None
* Entry in Source A only.

S-13314 300a D:419 X-0060 LOGA:RUSH
a. W-2831 John Dupriest, assignee of A. Freeman
W-5470 Robert Means, assignee of Edward Smith
W-6071 George Ryan
b. Duncan McArthur
c. None

S-13315 366a D:419* X-0750 LOGA:PERR LOGA:BOAK
a. W-1628 Stephen Smithers
W-5336 George Handy
b. Duncan McArthur
c. None
* Marginal note: "Lost by 5288."

S-13316
S-13317
S-13410 292a* E:278** X-0750 LOGA:PERR
a. W-1628 Stephen Smithers
W-3477 Abraham Shepherd
W-5169 Thomas D. Harris, assignee of Erasmus Gill
W-5537 Peter Manifold, assignee of George Handy
b. Duncan McArthur
c. None
* Source A says 302 acres.
** Marginal note in Source B: "Lost by 5288."

S-13318 1046a D:389 X-0110 LOGA:RUSH LOGA:BOAK
a. W-854 Lieutenant Nicholas Taliaferro
b. William M. Kenton
c. None

S-13319* 35a E:222 X-0420 BROW:----
a. W-6418 Vachel D. Howard
b. Edward Wallace
c. None
* Entry not listed in Source A.

S-13319* 12a E:222 X-0420 BROW:----
a. W-6418 Vachel D. Howard
b. Cadwallader Wallace
c. None
* Entry not listed in Source A.

S-13319 5a E:12 X-0360 PICK:PERR
a. W-6418 Vachel D. Howard
b. John Evans
c. None

S-13319 30a E:13 X-1000 ROSS:PAXT
a. W-6418 Vachel D. Howard
b. John Evans
c. None

S-13319* 40a -- -- BROW:UNIO
a. --
b. John Evans
c. None
* Entry in Source A only.

S-13319* 125a -- -- BROW:BYRD
a. --
b. John Evans
c. None
* Entry in Source A only.

S-13319* 30a -- -- BROW:HUNT
a. --
b. John Evans
c. None
* Entry in Source A only.

S-13319* 20a -- -- ----:----
a. --
b. John Evans
c. None
* Entry in Source A only, where crossed out.

S-13320* 250a -- -- BROW:HUNT
a. --
b. John Evans
c. None
* Entry in Source A only.

S-13320* 25a E:223 X-0420 BROW:----
a. W-6418 Vachel D. Howard
b. Cadwallader Wallace
c. None
* Entry not listed in Source A.

S-13320 250a E:14 X-0991 MARI:BOWL
a. W-6418 Vachel D. Howard
b. John Evans
c. None

S-13320 160a* E:14 X-0991 MARI:---* UNIO:WASH
a. W-6418 Vachel D. Howard
b. John Evans
c. None
* Source A says 166 acres; does not mention Marion County.

S-13320* 25a E:223 X-0420 BROW:---- ADAM:----
a. W-6418 Vachel D. Howard
b. Cadwallader Wallace
c. None
* Entry not listed in Source A.

S-13320. See also S-12504

S-13322. See S-13313

S-13323. See S-13313

S-13324* 500a -- -- HARD:DUDL
a. --
b. Duncan McArthur
c. None
* Entry in Source A only.

S-13325 370a D:420 X-1000 HARD:DUDL
a. W-6418 Vachel D. Howard
b. Duncan McArthur
c. None

S-13326 330a D:420 X-1000 HARD:MCDO
X-0060 HARD:TAYL
a. W-6418 Vachel D. Howard
W-6417 Joseph Bratton
b. Duncan McArthur
c. None

S-13327 141a D:510 X-0134 ADAM:SCOT
a. W-5948 William Pullen
b. George Vinsonhaller
c. None

S-13328 30a E:180 X-1190 ADAM:MEIG
a. W-5948 William Pullen
b. George Vinsonhaller
c. None

S-13328 46a E:93 X-0215 ADAM:MEIG
a. W-4644 Temple (Thomas?) Elliott
W-5948 William Pullen
b. George Vinsonhaller
c. None

S-13329* 46a -- -- ADAM:JEFF
a. --
b. George Vinsonhaller
c. None
* Entry in Source A only.

S-13330* 13a -- -- ADAM:MEIG
a. --
b. George Vinsonhaller
c. None
* Entry in Source A only.

S-13331 5a D:391 X-1042 ADAM:MEIG
a. W-4644 Temple (Thomas?) Elliott
b. John Calloway
c. None

S-13332 100a D:397 X-0130 ADAM:WAYN
a. W-6649 William Christian
b. Philip Vinsonhaller*
c. None
* Source A spells Vinsonhaler.

S-13333 350a D:390 X-0340 MADI:MONR
a. W-5885 William Mosby, deceased, by Ann W. Chamberlayn
W-5916 Gross Scruggs
W-5470 Robert Means, assignee of Edward Smith
W-6523 William Terrell, heirs of
b. Walter Dun
c. None

S-13334 333a D:397 X-0060 LOGA:MCAR HARD:---*
a. W-6668 George Backus
W-6620 Ransome Colquett
W-6648 William Christian
W-5661 William Pelham
W-5758 illegible
b. Walter Dun
c. None
* Source A does not mention Hardin County.

S-13335
S-13371 55a D:508 X-1000 PICK:WAYN
a. W-6418 Vachel D. Howard
b. John Evans
c. None

S-13335. See also S-13770

S-13336 17a E:93 X-0130 ADAM:MEIG
a. W-5841 Samuel Scroggs
b. Andrew Ellison
c. None

S-13337 100a E:1 X-0130 HIGH:BRUS
a. W-6353 Elisha King
b. Elisha King, representatives of
c. None

S-13338 50a D:392 X-1044 ADAM:FRAN
a. W-6649 William Christian
b. Daniel Hillerbrand*
c. None
* Source A spells Hiltebrand.

S-13339 440a D:393 X-1140 PIKE:SUNF
X-0190
a. W-1 David? Crowley
W-1413 Thomas Coverley
b. -- Ball, -- Dabney, & -- Hoomes
c. John Edwards; J. Moore, 1840; D. Mustard; S? (L?) Blissard, 1842

S-13341. See S-13334

S-13344 90a E:1 X-0130 HIGH:BRUS
a. W-6353 Elisha King
b. Elisha King, representatives of
c. None

S-13345 19a E:215 X-0360 PICK:---*
ROSS:DEER
a. W-6647 William Christian
b. Isaac Fleming
c. None
* Source A does not mention Pickaway County.

S-13347 20a F:173 X-0420 BROW:HUNT
a. W-1296 Timothy Peyton
b. John Neel*
c. John Donaldson; P. L? (S?) Wilson, 1841
* Source A says Jeptha Beasley.

S-13348* 15a -- -- ADAM:MONR
a. --
b. Reuben Cooper
c. None
* Entry in Source A only.

S-13349* 5a -- -- PICK:DEER
a. --
b. Isaac Cook
c. None
* Entry in Source A only.

S-13351
S-13402* 100a D:414 X-0860 ROSS:--**
FRAN:PLEA
a. W-5536 George Handy
W-5537 Peter Manifold, assignee of George Handy
b. Duncan McArthur
c. None
* May read S-13412.
** Source A does not mention Ross County.

S-13352. See S-13150

S-13354 25a D:399 X-1007 ADAM:JEFF
a. W-6628 William Spencer, representatives of
b. John C. Ham
c. None

S-13355 100a D:399 X-0663 BROW:PERR
a. W-6512 James Davis, deceased
b. Joel Hart
c. None

S-13356 80a D:399 X-0663 HIGH:---*
CLIN:CLAR
a. W-6308 Charles Stewart, heirs of
b. James West
c. None
* Source A does not mention Highland County.

S-13357 25a D:436 X-0910?* SCIO:NILE
a. W-6308 Charles Stewart, heirs of
b. James D. Turner
c. None
* "Pond Run of O(hio River?)."

S-13358 36a D:400 X-0840 ROSS:TWIN
a. W-6308 Charles Stewart, heirs of
b. David Brudlove*
c. None
* Source A spells Breedlove.

S-13359. See S-13248

S-13360 600a D:460 X-1000 HARD:MCDO
a. W-6335 John Roberts
W-6314 James Boothe
W-6362 Edward Stevens
W-6537 Thomas Pairemore?
b. Cadwallader Wallace
c. None

S-13361* 682a -- -- CLER:BATA
a. --
b. Allen Latham
c. None
* Entry in Source A only.

S-13362
S-15569* 800a* F:17 X-1000 HARD:TAYL
a. Ex 34 --**
W-8678 --**
b. Cadwallader Wallace
c. None
* Source A says 400 acres; does not mention S-15569.
** Source C does not list these warrant numbers.

S-13363 20a D:403 X-0663 CLER:MONR
CLER:TATE
a. W-5548 Abraham Hite? (Hile?) & James Taylor, assignee of said Hite? (Hile?)
b. James Taylor
c. None

S-13364 109a D:403 X-1083 CLER:STON
a. W-5548 Abraham Hite? (Hile?) & James Taylor, assignee of said Hite? (Hile?)
b. James Taylor
c. None

S-13366 66a D:403 X-0790 CLER:GOSH
a. W-6630 Thomas Clark
W-5254 John Mountjoy
W-5860 Christian Febiger
b. James Taylor
c. None

S-13367 87a D:404 X-0663 CLER:JACK
a. W-5548 Abraham Hite? (Hile?) & James Taylor, assignee of said Hite? (Hile?)
W-6630 Thomas Clark
b. James Taylor
c. None

S-13368 28a D:404 X-0663 CLER:UNIO
a. W-5254 John Mountjoy
b. James Taylor
c. None

S-13369 30a D:404 X-0790 CLER:---*
WARR:HAMI
WARR:SALE
a. W-5254 John Mountjoy
b. James Taylor
c. None
* Source A does not mention Clermont County.

S-13370 80a D:408 X-0847 HIGH:PAIN
a. W-6649 William Christian
b. John C. Howe
c. None

S-13371 10a D:405 X-1380 PICK:DEER
a. W-6666 James Carson
b. John Evans
c. None

S-13371. See also S-13335

S-13372 15a D:406 X-1000 ROSS:SCIO
ROSS:FRAN
a. W-6649 William Christian
b. -- Chandler & -- Kerns
c. None

S-13373 30a D:406 X-1000 ROSS:SCIO
ROSS:FRAN
a. W-6649 William Christian
b. -- Chandler & -- Kerns
c. None

S-13374 35a E:217 X-0290 FAYE:MADI
a. W-6649 William Christian
b. Allen Latham
c. None

S-13375 23a E:215 X-0130 PIKE:PERR
a. W-6649 William Christian
b. Allen Latham
c. None

S-13376 25a E:46 X-0130 PIKE:PERR
a. W-6649 William Christian
b. Allen Latham
c. None

S-13377 1333a D:406 X-0840 FAYE:JEFF
GREE:---*
a. W-209 Colonel Frederick Bland
b. W. H. Dangerfield, R. T. Dangerfield, & M. C. Dangerfield
c. None
* Source A does not mention Green County.

S-13378 1333a D:407 X-0840 GREE:SILV
a. W-209 Colonel Frederick Bland
b. W. H. Dangerfield, R. T. Dangerfield, & M. C. Dangerfield
c. None

S-13380* 56a -- -- FRAN:JACK
PICK:SCIO
a. --
b. William Haywood
c. None
* Entry in Source A only.

S-13381
S-13382 500a E:23 X-1000 ROSS:FRAN
a. W-1000 Brigadier General -- Morgan
b. Allen Latham
c. None

S-13383 100a D:500 X-0130 ADAM:FRAN
a. W-6494 Francis L. Slaughter
b. Cadwallader Wallace
c. James McCullough, 1842

S-13384 72a D:409 X-0423 ADAM:SPRI
a. W-6693 --*
b. John C. Beasley
c. None
* Source C does not give warrantee's name.

S-13385 150a E:209 X-0270 BROW:PIKE
a. W-6693 --*
b. James Redman
c. None
* Source C does not give warrantee's name.

S-13386 7a D:471 X-0080 BROW:HUNT
a. W-1296 Timothy Peyton
b. Benjamin Beasley
c. None

S-13387 239a D:422 X-0663 CLER:JACK
a. W-5477 --*
W-5360 Thomas M. Bayly, assignee of Leven? Bloxom, executor of John Baker, deceased
b. -- Stewart & -- Taylor
c. None
* Name illegible in Source C.

S-13388 53a D:422 X-0663 CLER:JACK
a. W-5360 Thomas M. Bayly, assignee of Leven? Bloxom, executor of John Baker, deceased
b. -- Stewart & -- Taylor
c. None

S-13389 30a D:422 X-0663 CLER:JACK
a. W-5360 Thomas M. Bayly, assignee of Leven? Bloxom, executor of John Baker, deceased
W-5407 Thomas M. Bayly, assignee of Ben(jamin) Philips
b. -- Stewart & -- Taylor
c. None

S-13390 33a D:416 X-0800 SCIO:WASH
a. W-6308 Charles Stewart, heirs of
b. R. Craine & O. Craine
c. None

S-13391 100a D:453 X-0380 HIGH:DODS
a. W-6393 John McCandless
b. Allen Trimble
c. None

S-13392 90a E:10 X-1000 ROSS:PAXT
a. W-6418 Vachel D. Howard
b. John Evans
c. None

S-13393 850a D:417 X-0060 HARD:ROUN LOGA:---*
a. W-6659 William O'Caller? (O'Calles?), heirs of
b. Cadwallader Wallace
c. None
* Source A does not mention Logan County.

S-13394 100a D:417 X-0360 PICK:DARB
a. W-6659 William O'Caller? (O'Calles?), heirs of
b. Cadwallader Wallace
c. None

S-13395 5a D:503 X-1000 PICK:WAYN
a. W-6308 Charles Stewart, heirs of
b. P. N. White
c. None

S-13396* 33a -- -- ADAM:SPRI
a. --
b. Daniel Morgan
c. None
* Entry in Source A only.

S-13397* 75a -- -- HIGH:SALE
a. --
b. Allen Trimble
c. None
* Entry in Source A only.

S-13398* 3a -- -- ROSS:DEER
a. --
b. Thomas J. Timmons
c. None
* Entry in Source A only.

S-13399 138a E:215 X-1039 BROW:WASH
a. W-6326 John Roberts
b. Allen Latham
c. None

S-13400. See S-12033

S-13402. See S-13351

S-13403 170a D:443 X-0060 HARD:ROUN LOGA:---*
a. W-5987 William McCraw
b. Isaac Medley
c. None
* Source A does not mention Logan County.

S-13404 32a D:416 X-0800 SCIO:WASH
a. W-6308 Charles Stewart, heirs of
b. R. Craine & O. Craine
c. None

S-13405 18a D:416 X-0800 SCIO:WASH
a. W-6308 Charles Stewart, heirs of
b. R. Craine & O. Craine
c. None

S-13406 500a D:417 X-1000 HARD:HALE
a. W-6624 David Kirkpatrick
b. Lyne Starling*
c. John Prather; L. Curtis
* Source A spells Sterling.

S-13407 13a D:418 X-0759 ADAM:GREE
a. W-6308 Charles Stewart, heirs of
b. George Collings
c. None

S-13408 221a D:418 X-0800 ADAM:GREE
a. W-6659 William O'Caller? (O'Calles?), heirs of
W-6308 Charles Stewart, heirs of
b. -- McDavid & -- Collings
c. None

S-13409. See S-13315

S-13410. See S-13316

S-13411 16a D:421 X-0360 PICK:MONR
a. W-4892 George Menzies, representatives of
b. Mathew Bonner
c. None

S-13412* 15a -- -- MADI:JEFF
a. --

b. Allen Latham
c. None
* Entry in Source A only.

S-13412. See also S-13351

S-13413 25a D:489 X-0340 MADI:JEFF
a. W-6308 Charles Stewart, heirs of
b. John Mills
c. None

S-13414 14a D:421 X-0420 ADAM:LIBE
a. W-5743 William Green, representatives of
b. Sarah Armstrong
c. None

S-13415 18a F:117 X-0840 ROSS:TWIN
a. W-6308 Charles Stewart, heirs of
b. Aaron Foster
c. None

S-13416 51a D:421 X-0600 ADAM:SPRI
a. W-5743 William Green, representatives of
W-5934 Robert Thelabell
b. George Pence
c. None

S-13421 50a D:423 X-0663 HIGH:UNIO
a. W-6512 James Davis, deceased
b. Joel Hart
c. None

S-13423 50a F:162 X-1300 HIGH:WHIT
a. W-6472 --*
b. E. P. Kendrick**
c. None
* Source C does not list warrantee's name.
** Source A says "Heirs of William Thompson."

S-13424* 12a -- -- MADI:JEFF
a. --
b. Allen Latham
c. None
* Entry in Source A only.

S-13425 20a D:423 X-0663 CLIN:CLAR
HIGH:UNIO
a. W-5978 John E. Scott, representatives of
b. Joel Hart
c. None

S-13426 68a D:423 X-0600 ADAM:SPRI
a. W-5978 John E. Scott, representatives of
b. George Collings
c. None

S-13427 89a D:424 X-0991 UNIO:WASH
a. W-6463 Thomas Ousley
W-5759 Peter Garland, representatives of
b. James Galloway, Junior
c. None

S-13428* 260a -- -- ----:----
a. --
b. -- Galloway & -- Scott
c. None
* Entry in Source A only, where crossed out.

S-13429* 100a -- -- ----:----
a. --
b. Hulsey Carter
c. None
* Entry in Source A only, where crossed out.

S-13431 37a E:231 X-0600 ADAM:SPRI
a. W-1296 Timothy Peyton
b. Jeptha Beasley
c. None

S-13432 350a D:425 X-0750 LOGA:PERR
a. W-5799 James Dillard
W-5743 William Green, representatives of
b. Duncan McArthur
c. None

S-13433 250a D:443 X-1000 HARD:TAYL
LOGA:RUSH
a. W-6713 James Jopling, heir of Ralph Jopling
b. Cadwallader Wallace
c. None

S-13436 300a D:425 X-0663 CLIN:JEFF
a. W-5888 David Wallace, representatives of
b. Allen Latham
c. None

S-13437 20a D:425 X-1110 ADAM:GREE
a. W-4284 Daniel Diskin?
b. Job Denning*
c. None
* Source A spells Dinning.

S-13439* 23a -- -- ROSS:HUNT
a. --
b. John Evans
c. None
* Entry in Source A only.

S-13440*
S-13441 1450a -- -- ALLE:GOSH
ALLE:WAYN
a. --
b. C(adwallader) Wallace
c. None
* Entry in Source A only.

S-13440*
S-16063 200a F:256 X-1360 ROSS:----
PIKE:----
a. W-8683 --**
W-6659 William O'Caller? (O'Calles?), heirs of
b. Cadwallader Wallace
c. None
* Source A does not list this entry.
** Source C does not list this warrant number.

S-13440*
S-13449
S-13526 614a D:444 X-1000 UNIO:----
a. W-4892 George Menzies, representatives of
W-6659 William O'Caller? (O'Calles?), heirs of
b. Cadwallader Wallace
c. None
* Source A does not list this entry.

S-13441* 800a F:255 X-1090 ROSS:----
a. W-6659 William O'Caller? (O'Calles?), heirs of
b. Cadwallader Wallace
c. None
* Source A does not list this entry.

S-13441* 89a F:255 X-1000 HARD:----
a. W-6659 William O'Caller? (O'Calles?), heirs of
b. Cadwallader Wallace
c. None
* Source A does not list this entry.

S-13441* 161a F:256 X-1090 ROSS:----
a. W-6659 William O'Caller? (O'Calles?), heirs of
b. Cadwallader Wallace
c. None
* Source A does not list this entry.

S-13441* 150a F:257 X-1000 ROSS:----
a. W-6659 William O'Caller? (O'Calles?), heirs of
b. Cadwallader Wallace
c. None
* Source A does not list this entry.

S-13441* 146a F:257 X-1090 ROSS:----
a. W-6659 William O'Caller? (O'Calles?), heirs of
b. Cadwallader Wallace
c. None
* Source A does not list this entry.

S-13441* 4a F:258 X-1000 ROSS:----
a. W-6659 William O'Caller? (O'Calles?), heirs of
b. Cadwallader Wallace
c. None
* Source A does not list this entry.

S-13446 150a D:426 X-0991 LOGA:RUSH
a. W-6262 Billy H. Avery
b. Allen Latham
c. None

S-13446 150a D:426 X-0060?* LOGA:RUSH
a. W-6714 James Jopling, heir of Ralph Jopling
b. Allen Latham
c. None
* Entry says only: "Miami River."

S-13446 150a D:426 X-0991 LOGA:RUSH
a. W-6549 Valentine Peers?
W-6262 Billy H. Avery
b. Allen Latham
c. None

S-13446 150a D:426 X-0991 LOGA:RUSH
a. W-6714 James Jopling, heir of Ralph Jopling
b. Allen Latham
c. None

S-13447* 1000a -- -- UNIO:LIBE
a. --
b. Allen Latham
c. None
* Entry in Source A only.

S-13447 455a E-218 X-0750 UNIO:LIBE
a. W-6652 William Scott, heirs of
W-6561 Mazy or Mary Vance
b. Allen Latham
c. None

S-13448* 1600a -- -- UNIO:YORK
a. --
b. Allen Latham
c. None
* Entry in Source A only.

S-13449*
S-13440
S-13526 614a -- -- UNIO:CLAI
a. --
b. C(adwallader) Wallace
c. None
* Entry in Source A only.

S-13449. See also S-13248 & S-13440

S-13450* 40a -- -- MADI:FAIR
a. --
b. Allen Latham
c. None
* Entry in Source A only.

S-13452 10a D:427 X-0840 ROSS:TWIN
a. W-6713 James Jopling, heir to Ralph Jopling
b. -- Kendrick & -- Thurman
c. None

S-13453
S-14069 25a E:88 X-0120 MADI:UNIO
a. W-6713 James Jopling, heir to Ralph Jopling
W-6645 Alexander Brownlee, heirs of
b. William T. Rowe
c. None

S-13454 17a D:427 X-0449 SCIO:WASH
a. W-6308 Charles Stewart, heirs of
b. R. Crane* & O. Crane*
c. None
* Source A spells Craine.

S-13455 107a* E:331 X-1300 BROW:SCOT
a. W-6549 Valentine Peers?
b. Allen Latham
c. None
* Source A says 210 acres.

S-13456 19a D:439 X-1400* SCIO:NILE
a. W-6308 Charles Stewart, heirs of
b. Philo N. White
c. William Lewis; J. Pyles, 1839
* Lamp Black Run.

S-13457 10a D:439 X-1190 SCIO:NILE
a. W-6308 Charles Stewart, heirs of
b. P. N. White
c. S? (L?) Williams; J. Pyles, 1839

S-13458 15a D:439 X-0129 SCIO:WASH
a. W-6308 Charles Stewart, heirs of
b. P. N. White
c. None

S-13459 15a D:428 X-1400* ADAM:GREE
a. W-6713 James Jopling, heir of Ralph Jopling
b. James W. Adams
c. None
* Adam's Run.

S-13460 72a D:428 X-1138 ADAM:GREE
a. W-6713 James Jopling, heir of Ralph Jopling
W-6714 James Jopling, heir of Ralph Jopling
b. George Collings
c. None

S-13461* 75a -- -- PIKE:PERR
a. --
b. Allen Latham
c. None
* Entry in Source A only.

S-13464* 45a -- -- ROSS:FRAN
a. --
b. Joseph Bond
c. None
* Entry in Source A only.

S-13465 18a D:493 -- SCIO:WASH
a. W-6308 Charles Stewart, heirs of
b. R. Crane* & O. Crane*
c. None
* Source A spells Craine.

S-13468 80a D:442 X-1170 CLIN:JEFF
a. W-5888 David Wallace, representatives of
b. Moses Burgess
c. None

S-13469 182a E:204 X-0860 ROSS:FRAN
a. W-5021 George Charlton, representatives of
W-5805 Joseph Hite? (Hile?)
b. Duncan McArthur
c. None

S-13470* 20a -- -- ROSS:FRAN
a. --
b. Joseph Bond
c. None
* Entry in Source A only.

S-13471 140a D:452 X-0800 SCIO:WASH
a. W-860 Lieutenant David Williams
b. Duncan McArthur
c. None

S-13472 20a E:203 X-0860 ROSS:FRAN
a. a. W-4022 William Reynolds
b. Duncan McArthur
c. None

S-13473 10a E:203 X-0860 ROSS:FRAN
a. W-4022 William Reynolds
b. Duncan McArthur
c. None

S-13474 10a E:204 X-0860 ROSS:FRAN
a. W-4022 William Reynolds
b. Duncan McArthur
c. None

S-13475* 40a -- -- ROSS:FRAN
a. --
b. Joseph Bond
c. None
* Entry in Source A only.

S-13476 5a D:434 X-0340 FRAN:PLEA
a. W-6714 James Jopling, heir of Ralph Jopling
b. Thomas Roberts
c. None

S-13477 75a D:429 X-0800 SCIO:NILE
a. W-6723 William Drake
b. Conrad Overturf
c. Joseph Moore, 1839

S-13478 25a D:429 X-0910 SCIO:NILE
a. W-6723 William Drake
b. Conrad Overturf
c. W. Kendall, 1838

S-13479 15a D:430 X-0910 SCIO:NILE
a. W-6723 William Drake
b. Conrad Overturf
c. W. Kendall, 1838

S-13480 35a D:430 X-0910 SCIO:NILE
a. W-6723 William Drake
b. Conrad Overturf
c. W. Kendall, 1838

S-13481 22a D:430 X-0910 SCIO:NILE
a. W-6723 William Drake
b. Conrad Overturf
c. W. Kendall, 1838

S-13482 28a D:430 X-1100 SCIO:WASH
a. W-6723 William Drake
b. Conrad Overturf
c. Levi Moore, 1837

S-13483 31a D:430 X-0800 SCIO:NILE
a. W-6724 William Brown
b. Conrad Overturf
c. W. Kendall, 1838

S-13484 67a D:430 X-0800 SCIO:NILE
a. W-6724 William Brown
b. Conrad Overturf
c. None

S-13485 47a D:431 X-1000 SCIO:WASH
a. W-6713 James Jopling, heir of Ralph Jopling
b. Conrad Overturf
c. S. M. Stilwell; R. Craine, 1838

S-13486 45a D:431 X-1000 SCIO:MORG
a. W-6713 James Jopling, heir of Ralph Jopling
b. Conrad Overturf
c. None

S-13487 20a D:431 X-1190 SCIO:NILE
a. W-6713 James Jopling, heir of Ralph Jopling
b. Conrad Overturf
c. W. Kendall, 1838; J. Piles, 1841

S-13488 21a D:431 X-1000 SCIO:UNIO
a. W:6713 James Jopling, heir of Ralph Jopling
b. Conrad Overturf
c. None

S-13489 100a D:431 X-0800 SCIO:NILE
a. W-6713 James Jopling, heir of Ralph Jopling
b. Conrad Overturf
c. None

S-13490 20a D:432 X-0920 SCIO:UNIO
a. W-6714 James Jopling, heir of Ralph Jopling
b. Conrad Overturf
c. None

S-13491 35a D:432 X-1190 SCIO:NILE
a. W-6714 James Jopling, heir of Ralph Jopling
b. Conrad Overturf
c. W. Kendall, 1838

S-13492 47a D:432 X-0800 SCIO:NILE
a. W-6714 James Jopling, heir of Ralph Jopling
b. Conrad Overturf
c. None

S-13493 12a D:432 X-1240 SCIO:NILE
a. W-6714 James Jopling, heir of Ralph Jopling
b. Conrad Overturf
c. None

S-13494 100a D:432 X-0559 SCIO:UNIO
a. W-6714 James Jopling, heir of Ralph Jopling
b. Conrad Overturf
c. None

S-13495 25a D:432 X-0800 SCIO:NILE
a. W-6714 James Jopling, heir of Ralph Jopling
b. Conrad Overturf
c. W. Kendall, 1838

S-13496 20a D:433 X-1190 SCIO:NILE
a. W-6714 James Jopling, heir of Ralph Jopling
b. Conrad Overturf
c. W. Kendall, 1838

S-13497 74a D:433 X-1400* SCIO:WASH
a. W-6714 James Jopling, heir of Ralph Jopling
b. Conrad Overturf
c. None
* Furt's? Run.

S-13498 100a D:433 X-0390 SCIO:WASH
a. W-6714 James Jopling, heir of Ralph Jopling
b. Leroy Jordan
c. None

S-13499 100a D:433 X-1000 SCIO:WASH
a. W-6714 James Jopling, heir of Ralph Jopling
b. Leroy Jordan
c. None

S-13500 50a D:433 X-1000 SCIO:MORG
a. W-6714 James Jopling, heir of Ralph Jopling
b. Leroy Jordan
c. Charles T. Cutler, 1837

S-13501 417a D:434 X-1000 SCIO:WASH
a. W-6713 James Jopling, heir of Ralph Jopling
W-6714 James Jopling, heir of Ralph Jopling
b. Leroy Jordan
c. None

S-13502 8a D:434 X-0800 SCIO:WASH
a. W-6714 James Jopling, heir of Ralph Jopling
b. Jeremiah Piles
c. None

S-13503 1600a D:441 X-0350 CHAM:RUSH
a. W-1495 John Gratton, heir to J. Gratton
b. Lucas Sullivant, heirs of
c. None

S-13504* 80a -- -- CHAM:RUSH
a. --
b. Lucas Sullivant, heirs of
c. None
* Entry in Source A only.

S-13505* 1000a -- -- UNIO:YORK
a. --
b. David Williams, heirs of
c. None
* Entry in Source A only.

S-13506 500a F:274 X-0110 UNIO:YORK
a. W-860 Lieutenant David Williams

b. David Williams, heirs of
c. None

S-13509 20a E:72 X-0360 MADI:UNIO
a. W-6649 William Christian
b. S. H. Saunders
c. None

S-13513 32a D:451 X-0800 SCIO:WASH
a. W-5536 George Handy
b. Duncan McArthur
c. None

S-13514 50a E:239 X-1000 SCIO:BRUS
a. W-6724 William Brown
b. James Wallis
c. None

S-13515 75a D:437 X-1000 ROSS:FRAN
a. W-6647 William Christian
W-6366 Andrew Chilton
W-6658 Wood Jones, heirs of
b. Allen G. Thurman
c. None

S-13516 270a D:437 X-1400* ROSS:FRAN
a. W-6714 James Jopling, heir of Ralph Jopling
W-6659 William O'Caller? (O'Calles?), heirs of
b. John Foster**
c. None
* Pittinger's Run.
** Entry in Source A says: "John Foster, of Thomas."

S-13517. See S-7749

S-13518 20a F:10 X-1190 SCIO:NILE
a. W-6629 William Spencer, representatives of
b. Allen Latham
c. J. R. Walker

S-13519 25a D:438 X-0910 SCIO:NILE
a. W-6623 David Kirkpatrick
b. Elijah Anderson
c. None

S-13520* 25a -- -- SCIO:NILE
a. --
b. Allen Latham
c. None
* Entry in Source A only.

S-13521 6a D:438 X-1400* SCIO:NILE
a. W-2024 Captain James Craig
b. George Rodes
c. None
* Herbert's Run.

S-13522* 25a -- -- SCIO:NILE
a. --
b. Allen Latham
c. None
* Entry in Source A only.

S-13523 138a D:440 X-0660 CLER:JACK
a. W-5888 David Wallace, representatives of
b. Thomas L. Shields
c. None

S-13524 498a D:440 X-0663 CLER:WAYN
a. W-6659 William O'Caller? (O'Calles?), heirs of
b. Thomas L. Shields
c. None

S-13525 15a D:439 X-0910 SCIO:UNIO
a. W-6308 Charles Stewart, heirs of
b. Aaron Hedges
c. None

S-13526. See S-13440 & S-13449

S-13527 60a E:232 X-0663 CLER:TATE
a. W-6029 John Stokes, representatives of
b. John Collins
c. None

S-13528*
S-13557
S-13553
S-14768 505a E:276 X-0750 LOGA:----
a. W-3414 John Scarborough
W-860 Lieutenant David Williams
W-5536 George Handy
W-6487 James Mill
b. Duncan McArthur, heirs of
c. None
* Entry is incomplete in Source A.

S-13528. See also S-12103

S-13529 90a D:458 X-0750 LOGA:PERR
a. W-6665 James Carson (perhaps)
b. John T. Bayles
c. None

S-13530 6a D:445 -- CLER:BATA
a. W-6714 James Jopling, heir of Ralph Jopling
b. Thomas L. Shields
c. None

S-13531 20a D:445 X-0663 BROW:PERR
BROW:STER
a. W-6714 James Jopling, heir of Ralph Jopling
b. Thomas L. Shields
c. None

S-13532 5a D:445 X-0663 CLER:BATA
a. W-6714 James Jopling, heir of Ralph Jopling
b. Thomas L. Shields
c. W. F. Veith, 1836

S-13533 7a D:445 X-0663 CLER:WILL
a. W-6714 James Jopling, heir of Ralph Jopling
b. John Hill
c. None

S-13534 21a D:446 X-0663 CLER:UNIO
a. W-6714 James Jopling, heir of Ralph Jopling
b. John Hill
c. N. Meguire; J. Walker, 1842

S-13535 11a D:446 X-0663 CLER:JACK
a. W-6714 James Jopling, heir of Ralph Jopling
b. John Hill
c. None

S-13536 11a D:446 X-0663 CLER:BATA
a. W-6714 James Jopling, heir of Ralph Jopling
b. Ezekiel Dimmitt*
c. None
* Source A spells Dimitt.

S-13537 152a D:446 X-1080 CLER:STON
a. W-6714 James Jopling, heir of Ralph Jopling
b. James McKinnie
c. F. Roselett, 1839

S-13538 65a* E:210 X-0600 ADAM:SPRI ADAM:MONR
a. W-1296 Timothy Peyton
b. Jeptha Beasley
c. None
* Source A says 45 acres.

S-13539 57a E:231 X-0420 ADAM:SPRI
a. W-1296 Timothy Peyton
b. Jeptha Beasley
c. None

S-13540 9a F:238 X-0420 BROW:BYRD
a. W-1296 Timothy Peyton
b. Jeptha Beasley
c. None

S-13541 10a F:238 X-0420 BROW:HUNT
a. W-1296 Timothy Peyton
b. Jeptha Beasley
c. None

S-13542 7a F:269 X-0420 BROW:UNIO
a. W-1296 Timothy Peyton
b. Jeptha Beasley
c. None

S-13543 2a E:411 X-0420 BROW:BYRD
a. W-1296 Timothy Peyton
b. Samuel Kerr
c. None

S-13544 35a E:166 X-1300 BROW:CLAR
a. W-1296 Timothy Peyton
b. Jeptha Beasley
c. None

S-13545 45a D:447 X-1000 PICK:WAYN
a. W-6659 William O'Caller? (O'Calles?), heirs of
b. Philo N. White
c. None

S-13546 43a D:447 X-1000 PICK:WAYN
a. W-6659 William O'Caller? (O'Calles?), heirs of
b. Philo N. White
c. None

S-13547 12a D:447 X-1000 PICK:WAYN
a. W-665 Terence McDonald
b. Philo N. White
c. None

S-13548* 667a -- -- ----:----
a. --
b. C(adwallader) Wallace
c. None
* Entry in Source A only, where crossed out.

S-13549* 60a -- -- PIKE:MIFF
a. --
b. Allen Latham
c. None
* Entry in Source A only.

S-13550 150a D:447 X-0215 ADAM:MEIG
a. W-6130 Richard H? Owen
b. Eleazer P. Kendrick
c. None

S-13551* 275a -- -- ----:----
a. --
b. William Robinson
c. None
* Entry in Source A only, where crossed out.

S-13552 70a D:464 X-0663 CLER:BATA CLER:STON
a. W-5355 John Fox, representative of Drury Ragsdale, deceased
b. -- Ewing & -- Moons
c. None

S-13553. See S-13528

S-13555
S-14422
S-14553 400a E:198 X-1300 BROW:SCOT
a. W-6544 Arthur Treackle, heirs of W-4353 John Boze, alias Booze
b. Cadwallader Wallace
c. J. W. Price

S-13556 14a E:209 X-0980 HIGH:BRUS
a. W-6647 William Christian
b. William Head
c. None

S-13557. See S-13528 & S-12103

S-13559 20a D:452 X-1400* SCIO:WASH
a. W-860 Lieutenant David Williams
b. Duncan McArthur
c. None
* Worley's Run.

S-13560 186a D:457 X-0110 LOGA:PERR LOGA:BOAK
a. W-860 Lieutenant David Williams
b. Duncan McArthur
c. None

S-13562* 100a -- -- PIKE:SUNF
a. --
b. C(adwallader) Wallace
c. None
* Entry in Source A only.

S-13563* 14a -- -- MADI:SUMM
a. --
b. Thomas S. Hinde
c. None
* Entry in Source A only.

S-13564 20a F:251 X-1000 ROSS:FRAN
a. W-8994 --*
b. George W. Rennick**
c. None
* Source C does not list this warrant number.
** Source A says G. W. Renick & H. Renick.

S-13565 30a* E:220 X-1140 PIKE:MIFF
a. W-852 John Beck
b. Jonathan West
c. None
* Source A says 35 acres.

S-13566 120a D:460 X-0130 ADAM:---* X-1140 PIKE:MIFF
a. W-6539 William Withers?
b. Cadwallader Wallace
c. None
* Source A does not mention Adams County.

S-13566* 300a -- -- HIGH:DODS
a. --
b. C(adwallader) Wallace
c. None
* Entry in Source A only.

S-13566. See also S-6179 (in volume 4, part 1)

S-13567 80a D:456 X-0360 MADI:UNIO
a. W-6539 William Withers?
b. Cadwallader Wallace
c. None

S-13568 80a D:456 X-0841 FAYE:MADI
a. W-6539 William Withers?
b. Cadwallader Wallace
c. None

S-13569 500a D:456 X-0841 FAYE:MADI
a. W-6539 William Withers?
b. Cadwallader Wallace
c. None

S-13571 117a D:457 X-1300 HIGH:WHIT
a. W-5810 Thomas McKinley, heir to John (McKinley)
W-6129 Harod Gibbs
b. John A. Fulton
c. None

S-13573. See S-13306

S-13574 40a D:458 X-1303 HIGH:SALE
a. W-6574 Andrew Rodgers
b. George W. Barrere*
c. None
* Source A says: "Heirs of George W. Barriere."

S-13575 83a E:111 X-1303 HIGH:WHIT
a. W-628 Captain Walker Baylor
W-629 Captain Walker Baylor
b. George W. Barrere*
c. None
* Source A says: "Heirs of George W. Barriere."

S-13576 60a D:460 X-0660 BROW:PERR
a. W-2753 Lewis Thomas
b. James Taylor*
c. None
* Source A says James Taylor, Junior.

S-13577
S-13727
S-14354* 352a* E:248 X-0660 BROW:---* CLIN:CLAR
a. W-5824 Elijah Moody
W-2744 Anthony Singleton (of?)
W-8678 --**
b. Cadwallader Wallace
c. -- Scott & -- Reed; J. Rovermons?, 1838; R. Reed; Amos T. Sewell, 1840
* Source A says 252 acres; does not mention Brown County or S-14354.
** Source C does not list this warrant number.

S-13577* 367a -- -- ----:----
a. --
b. C(adwallader) Wallace
c. None
* Entry in Source A only, where crossed out.

S-13580 40a D:466 X-1300 HIGH:CLAY
a. W-1413 Thomas Coverley
b. Cadwallader Wallace
c. M. Call, 1840 (McCall?)

S-13580
S-13584 80a D:466 X-1300 HIGH:WHIT
a. W-1413 Thomas Coverley
b. Cadwallader Wallace
c. None

S-13582*
S-13727 400a E:41 X-1300 HIGH:----
a. W-3432 John M. Galt
W-2744 Anthony Singleton, heir (of?)

b. Cadwallader Wallace
c. None
* Source A does not list this entry.

S-13582* 535a -- -- HIGH:----
a. --
b. C(adwallader) Wallace
c. J. A. Trimble, 1840
* Entry in Source A only, possibly crossed out.

S-13582*
S-13727 1100a -- -- HIGH:SALE
a. --
b. C(adwallader) Wallace
c. None
* Entry in Source A only.

S-13583* 100a -- -- HIGH:SALE
a. --
b. C(adwallader) Wallace
c. None
* Entry in Source A only.

S-13583. See also S-6179 (in volume 4, part 1)

S-13584 40a D:466 X-1140 PIKE:SUNF
a. W-1413 Thomas Coverley
b. Cadwallader Wallace
c. None

S-13584 40a D:466 X-1300 HIGH:CLAY
a. W-1413 Thomas Coverley
b. Cadwallader Wallace
c. None

S-13584. See also S-13580

S-13585 6a E:137 X-1000 PICK:WAYN
a. Charles Stewart, heirs of
b. Philip Terwilleger*
c. None
* Source A spells Terwillager.

S-13586 27a D:502 X-1380 PICK:DEER
a. W-6308 Charles Stewart, heirs of
b. Philo N. White
c. None

S-13587 13a E:81 X-0250 HIGH:LIBE
a. W-4284 Daniel Diskin?
b. Daniel Evans
c. None

S-13588 333a D:464 -- HIGH:WHIT
HIGH:CLAY
a. W-6660 Cuthbert Harrison
W-6661 Cuthbert Harrison
b. Cadwallader Wallace
c. None

S-13589 40a E:217 X-1120 PIKE:MIFF
ADAM:---*
a. W-6394 John Harrison
b. Simon Shoemaker
c. None
* Source A does not mention Adams County.

S-13590 100a D:467 X-1300 BROW:---*
HIGH:SALE
HIGH:WHIT
a. W-5879 Benjamin Porter
b. Elias Langham
c. E. T. Langham; Thomas Shockley, 1837
* Source A does not mention Brown County.

S-13590 163a D:467 X-1300 HIGH:SALE
HIGH:WHIT
a. W-5879 Benjamin Porter
b. Cadwallader Wallace
c. None

S-13590 62a* D:464 X-0663 HIGH:CLAY
a. W-5879 Benjamin Porter
b. Cadwallader Wallace
c. None
* Source A says 60 acres.

S-13590
S-14354 375a* E:246 X-0663 HIGH:WHIT
a. W-5879 Benjamin Porter
W-8678 --**
b. Cadwallader Wallace
c. None
* Source A says 175 acres.
** Source C does not list this warrant number.

S-13591 333a D:465 X-1300 HIGH:CLAY
a. W-6660 Cuthbert Harrison
W-6661 Cuthbert Harrison
b. Anna Carwell*
c. None
* Source A spells Harwell.

S-13592 666a F:125 X-0750 UNIO:LEES
X-0110
a. W-6660 Cuthbert Harrison
W-6661 Cuthbert Harrison
b. -- Short & -- Williams
c. W. Wright

S-13593 100a D:468 X-0110 UNIO:LEES
a. W-5052 Jesse Davis
b. Cadwallader Wallace
c. None

S-13593 80a D:468 X-0730 LOGA:JEFF
a. W-5052 Jesse Davis
b. Cadwallader Wallace
c. None

S-13593 25a D:468 X-0991 LOGA:RUSH
a. W-5052 Jesse Davis
b. Cadwallader Wallace
c. None

S-13593 112a D:467 X-1000 HARD:HALE
a. W-5052 Jesse Davis
b. Cadwallader Wallace
c. None

S-13593 150a D:467 X-0991 LOGA:BOAK
a. W-5052 Jesse Davis
b. Cadwallader Wallace
c. None

S-13598 250a D:478 X-1060 BROW:GREE
a. W-5872 William Triplett? (Treplett?)
b. -- Woodbridge, -- Bond, & -- James
c. D. Scott; P. L. Wilson, 1840

S-13606 5a D:469 X-0663 CLER:UNIO
a. W-6560 Mazy or Mary Vance
b. William H. Robinson
c. None

S-13608*
S-13610 667a -- -- MARI:BOWL
a. --
b. Louis McLane
c. None
* Entry in Source A only.

S-13609
S-13610 550a D:470 X-1000 MARI:BOWL
a. W-6399 Allen McLane
W-6398 Allen McLane
W-6400 Allen McLane
b. Lewis McLane
c. None

S-13613* 736a -- ---- ----:----
a. --
b. Thomas L. Shields
c. None
* Entry in Source A only, where crossed out.

S-13614 250a D:483 X-1060 BROW:STER
a. W-285 Captain Lieutenant Ambrose Bohannan
b. Thomas L. Shields
c. P. L. Wilson, 1840

S-13615* 2a -- -- PIKE:SUNF
a. --
b. John Shanks
c. None
* Entry in Source A only.

S-13616* 12a -- -- PIKE:SUNF
a. --
b. Joseph Smith
c. None
* Entry in Source A only.

S-13617 15a D:471 X-0230 ADAM:SCOT
a. W-6548 Walker Baylor
b. Walker Baylor
c. None

S-13618 230a D:472 X-0340 FRAN:PRAI
a. W-5484 Nancy Smith, wife of Michael? Smith, representative of Ravely Gowen
W-5355 John Fox, representative of Drury Ragsdale, deceased
W-6229 Hulsey Carter
b. -- Galloway & -- Carter
c. None

S-13621 50a D:485 X-0340 PICK:MUHL
a. W-6308 Charles Stewart, heirs of
b. Philo N. White
c. J. D. Caldwell; Z. R. Martin, 1842

S-13622 100a D:485 X-1000 ROSS:FRAN
a. W-3809 Richard Baker
b. Charles Davis
c. None

S-13623
S-13663 75a D:493 X-0940 GREE:SILV
a. W-6647 William Christian
W-5799 James Dillard
b. -- Kendrick & -- Warner
c. None

S-13624 10a D:475 X-0130 ADAM:GREE
a. W-5799 James Dillard
b. Sarah Philips
c. None

S-13625 15a D:489 X-0130 ADAM:JEFF
a. W-5799 James Dillard
b. John Scott
c. None

S-13633 60a E:60 X-1173 CLIN:JEFF
a. W-5888 David Wallace, representatives of
W-5799 James Dillard
b. Moses Burgess
c. None

S-13639* 1300a -- -- BROW:PERR
a. --
b. C(adwallader) Wallace
c. D. Scott & R. Reed; J. M. Trimble, 1838
* Entry in Source A only.

S-13639. See also S-8465

S-13640 200a D:476 X-1300 HIGH:WHIT
HIGH:CLAY
a. W-6572 Andrew Rodgers
b. Cad(wallader) Wallace
c. None

S-13641 233a D:475 X-0663 BROW:STER
BROW:PERR
a. W-5052 Jesse Davis
b. Cad(wallader) Wallace
c. D. Scott & R. Reed; E. Hughes, 1838; P. L. Wilson, 1840

S-13642 100a D:477 X-1000 SCIO:WASH
a. W-6456 Edmund Brown
b. Lemuel Moss
c. J. M. Merrell, 1842

S-13643 25a D:477 X-1400* PIKE:MIFF
a. W-6658 Wood Jones, heirs of
b. Samuel H. Saunders
c. None
* Davis Fork.

S-13645 19a D:477 X-0800 CLER:OHIO
a. W-5799 James Dillard
b. -- Brush & -- Hill
c. None

S-13646 69a D:505 -- LOGA:RUSH
a. W-6652 William Scott, heirs of
W-6653 William Scott, heirs of
W-6658 Wood Jones, heirs of
b. Samuel Saunders
c. None

S-13652 30a D:479 X-0840 ROSS:TWIN
a. W-6653 William Scott, heirs of
b. Cad(wallader) Wallace
c. None

S-13661 60a D:490 X-0340 MADI:JEFF MADI:MONR
a. W-5799 James Dillard
b. -- Kendrick & -- Warner
c. None

S-13661 20a D:490 X-0340 MADI:MONR
a. W-5799 James Dillard
b. -- Kendrick & -- Warner
c. None

S-13662 15a D:490 X-0340 MADI:JEFF
a. W-5799 James Dillard
b. -- Kendrick & -- Warner
c. None

S-13663. See S-13623

S-13664 20a D:489 -- CLER:GOSH WARR:SALE
a. W-5254 John Mountjoy
b. James Taylor, Junior
c. None

S-13666 30a D:480 X-0847 HIGH:PAIN
a. W-5799 James Dillard
b. Joseph W. Sparger
c. None

S-13667 45a D:484 X-1230 X-1240 ROSS:TWIN
a. W-5799 James Dillard
b. John McKinzie
c. None

S-13668 5a D:483 X-0130 ADAM:MONR
a. W-5799 James Dillard
b. John Rader
c. None

S-13670 15a D:483 X-0130 ADAM:---* PIKE:PERR
a. W-5799 James Dillard
b. Martin Countraman
c. None
* Source A does not mention Adams County.

S-13671 40a D-481 X-1044 SCIO:BRUS
a. W-5799 James Dillard
b. Isme Freeman
c. None

S-13672 32a D:484 X-0800 SCIO:WASH
a. W-6308 Charles Stewart, heirs of
b. -- Roswell & -- Crane*
c. None
* Source A says R. Craine & O. Craine.

S-13673 50a D:485 X-1190 SCIO:NILE
a. W-6308 Charles Stewart, heirs of
b. Philo N. White
c. None

S-13676* 200a -- -- ----:----
a. --
b. C(adwallader) Wallace
c. None
* Entry in Source A only, where crossed out.

S-13676
S-13770 89a D:508 X-1000 PICK:WAYN
a. W-6414 Allen McLane
b. John Evans
c. None

S-13676. See also S-12316 & S-13770

S-13677 50a D:486 X-0420 ADAM:SPRI ADAM:LIBE
a. W-4409 Michael Rachel? (Rochel?)
b. George Collings
c. None

S-13679
S-13680 59a E:27 X-0940 FAYE:CONC CLIN:RICH
a. W-6572 Andrew Rodgers
b. Allen Trimble
c. None

S-13681 14a D:488 X-1000 PIKE:JACK
a. W-6572 Andrew Rodgers
b. -- Swearingen & -- Barnes
c. None

S-13682 20a D:502 X-1380 PICK:DEER
a. W-6308 Charles Stewart, heirs of
b. Philo N. White
c. None

S-13683 50a D:493 X-0590 X-0600 ADAM:SPRI
a. W-4409 Michael Rachel? (Rochel?)
b. George Collings
c. None

S-13684* 2a -- -- ADAM:SPRI
a. --
b. Massie Beasley
c. None
* Entry in Source A only.

S-13685 22a D:508 X-1380 PICK:DEER
a. W-6418 Vachel D. Howard
b. John Evans
c. None

S-13686 16a D:509 X-1380 PICK:DEER
a. W-6418 Vachel D. Howard
b. John Evans
c. None

S-13687 10a D:509 X-1380 PICK:DEER
a. W-6418 Vachel D. Howard
b. John Evans
c. None

S-13688 8a E:122 X-1380 PICK:DEER
a. W-6418 Vachel D. Howard
b. George Reed
c. None

S-13689 10a D:509 X-1380 PICK:DEER
a. W-6418 Vachel D. Howard
b. John Evans
c. None

S-13690 10a F:85 X-0250 HIGH:LIBE
a. W-6494 Francis L. Slaughter
b. Allen Trimble
c. None

S-13691. See S-8874 & S-9214

S-13692* 50a -- -- PIKE:JACK
a. --
b. John Woodman
c. None
* Entry in Source A only.

S-13693 28a D:488 X-0010 CLIN:LIBE GREE:SILV
a. W-6308 Charles Stewart, heirs of
b. Marshall Jenkins
c. None

S-13694 400a E:205 X-0060 LOGA:MCAR HARD:---*
a. W-4672 Bartholomew Yates, representatives of
b. Walter Dun, Ex(ecutor)*
c. None
* Source A does not mention Hardin County nor Ex-(ecutor).

S-13695 170a D:489 X-0663 BROW:PERR
a. W-4735 Henry Moss
b. William Humber
c. None

S-13696* 1208a -- -- ----:----
a. --
b. James Galloway, Junior
c. None
* Entry in Source A only, where crossed out.

S-13697* 1000a -- -- ----:----
a. --
b. James Galloway, Junior
c. None
* Entry in Source A only, where crossed out.

S-13698 75a D:487 X-0360 MADI:SUMM
a. W-3042 John Collins
W-5123 Francis Lewis, administrator of the estate of William (Lewis)
W-1500 John? Sneade?, heir to William (Sneade?)
W-6567 Joseph Spencer
W-2947 John Means?
b. James Galloway, Junior
c. None

S-13701 50a D:488 -- ADAM:WAYN
a. W-6308 Charles Stewart, heirs of
b. J. Dilinger
c. None

S-13702 52a D:488 X-0136 ADAM:JEFF
a. W-6724 Robert Brown
b. William McFerris
c. None

S-13703 50a D:488 X-0800 SCIO:NILE
a. W-6059 Jeremiah Kendall
b. Jeremiah Kendall
c. None

S-13704 5a D:489 X-0381 ADAM:WAYN
a. W-5799 James Dillard
b. Mathias Yocam
c. None

S-13707* 308a -- -- UNIO:YORK
a. --
b. Caleb Parr**
c. None
* Entry in Source A only.
** Representatives of Martha Ruff? (Huff?) is crossed out.

S-13708* 404a -- -- UNIO:YORK
a. --
b. Martha Ruff, heirs of
c. None
* Entry in Source A only.

S-13709 202a D:491 X-0750 LOGA:RUSH
a. W-3195 John Collins
b. E. P. Kendrick
c. None

S-13710 120a D:491 X-0190 PIKE:CAMP
ROSS:---*
a. W-111 Captain Clough Shelton
b. Cad(wallader) Wallace
c. None
* Source A does not mention Ross County.

S-13711 104a D:492 X-1140 PIKE:SUNF
a. W-111 Captain Clough Shelton
b. Cad(wallader) Wallace
c. John Edwards; James Moore, 1840

S-13713 100a D:492 X-0130 ADAM:JEFF
a. W-1226 Alexander S. Dandridge
b. George Collings
c. None

S-13715 200a D:500 X-0060 LOGA:MCAR
a. W-6514 John Clark
b. John Evans
c. None

S-13717 70a D:494 X-0133 ADAM:MEIG
a. W-5799 James Dillard
W-3195 John Collins
b. William Eakins
c. None

S-13718* 600a -- -- UNIO:PARI
a. --
b. James Galloway, Junior
c. None
* Entry in Source A only.

S-13719 75a D:495 X-1220 ROSS:TWIN
a. W-3195 John Collins
b. -- McKinzie & -- Browning
c. None

S-13720 69a D:495 X-0840 ROSS:TWIN
a. W-5400 William Sanford, representatives of
W-6014 Benjamin Harrison, representatives of
b. John A. Fulton & William Fulton
c. None

S-13722
S-13723 75a D:495 X-0940 FAYE:JEFF
a. W-6425 George Purcell, heirs of
W-5946 William Pullen
b. James Browder
c. None

S-13724 200a D:496 X-1300 BROW:WASH
a. W-5703 Archibald Moon? (Moore?), representatives of
b. John Hill
c. C. Thompson; J. S. Beasley, 1842

S-13725 24a D:511 X-0230 ADAM:WAYN
a. W-3195 John Collins
b. Nathan Plummer
c. None

S-13726 20a D:499 X-0980 HIGH:BRUS
a. W-3195 John Collins
b. -- Wilson & -- Fearneaw? (Fearneau?)
c. None

S-13727 100a D:498 X-0750 LOGA:RUSH
a. W-2744 Anthony Singleton, heir (of?)
b. Cad(wallader) Wallace
c. None

S-13727* 565a -- -- HIGH:----
a. --
b. C(adwallader) Wallace
c. Moses Call, 1840
* Entry in Source A only, where crossed out.

S-13727* 400a -- -- HIGH:SALE
a. --
b. C(adwallader) Wallace
c. -- Scott & -- Reed; J. Rovermons?, 1838
* Entry in Source A only.

S-13727* 100a -- -- HIGH:CONC
a. --
b. C(adwallader) Wallace
c. None
* Entry in Source A only.

S-13727* 500a -- -- CLIN:CLAR
a. --
b. C(adwallader) Wallace
c. Lewis Silver; George Smith, 1839
* Entry in Source A only.

S-13727* 390a -- -- CLIN:CLAR
a. --
b. C(adwallader) Wallace
c. D. Scott & R. Reed; Jacob Ronemans?, 1838; J. Stewart; R. B. Corwine?, 1842
* Entry in Source A only.

S-13727. See also S-6179 (in volume 4, part 1), S-13577, & S-13582

S-13731*
S-13732 35a -- -- CLIN:CLAR
CLIN:JEFF
a. --
b. George W. Barriere
c. None
* Entry in Source A only.

S-13732* 65a -- -- HIGH:CLAY
a. --
b. George W. Barriere
c. None
* Entry in Source A only.

S-13732. See also S-8465

S-13733. See S-13306

S-13735 65a E:5 X-1300 BROW:SCOT
a. W-6098 Harry Terrell
b. John Tweed
c. None

S-13736 28a D:499 X-1400* SCIO:NILE
a. W-6624 David Kirkpatrick
b. John McCall
c. None
* Ohio Twin Creek.

S-13738 40a E:185 X-0840 ROSS:HUNT
a. W-6666 James Carson
b. -- Cook & -- Ellison
c. None

S-13739*
S-13775 100a -- -- ADAM:MONR
a. --
b. N. Massie & H. Massie
c. None
* Entry in Source A only.

S-13740* 2a -- -- BROW:UNIO
a. --
b. William Bayne
c. None
* Entry in Source A only.

S-13741 30a D:500 X-0840 ROSS:TWIN
ROSS:PAXT
a. W-6572 Andrew Rodgers
b. Cad(wallader) Wallace
c. None

S-13742 20a D:500 X-0360 PICK:DEER
a. W-6572 Andrew Rodgers
b. Cad(wallader) Wallace
c. None

S-13748 260a D:502 X-1000 UNIO:WASH
a. W-1963 William Taliaferro, heir to Colonel (William?) Taliaferro
b. Cad(wallader) Wallace
c. None

S-13749 14a D:503 X-0980 HIGH:PAIN
a. W-6624 David Kirkpatrick
b. James Waddel*
c. None
* Source A spells Waddle.

S-13750 40a D:503 X-1240 SCIO:NILE
a. W-6624 David Kirkpatrick
b. Ranson* Hodges
c. None
* Source A spells Ransom.

S-13751 32a D:511 X-0230 ADAM:WAYN
a. W-2319 Captain William Meredith
b. Robert Finley
c. None

S-13752 403a D:502 X-1180 CHAM:---*
LOGA:PERR
a. W-2007 Thomas Adams
W-3195 John Collins
b. Gray Gary
c. None
* Source A does not mention Champaign County.

S-13753* 101a -- -- UNIO:LIBE
a. --
b. William C. Wallace
c. None
* Entry in Source A only.

S-13754* 8a -- -- CLER:BATA
a. --
b. Samuel Brush
c. None
* Entry in Source A only.

S-13755 25a D:503 X-1190 SCIO:NILE
a. W-6308 Charles Stewart, heirs of
b. William Nichols
c. None

S-13756* 30a -- -- ADAM:SPRI
a. --
b. John Bryan
c. None
* Entry in Source A only.

S-13757* 1a -- -- ADAM:TIFF
a. --
b. Joseph Darlington
c. None
* Entry in Source A only.

S-13758 24a D:504 X-0790 CLER:GOSH
CLER:STON
a. W-6624 David Kirkpatrick
W-6649 Valentine Peers?
b. -- Hill & -- Bryan
c. None

S-13759 80a D:504 X-0847 HIGH:BRUS
a. W-6393 John McCandless
W-6549 Valentine Peers?
b. Joseph W. Spargur*
c. None
* Source A spells Sparger.

S-13760* 667a -- -- UNIO:YORK
UNIO:LEES
a. --
b. Samuel H. Saunders
c. None
* Entry in Source A only.

S-13760 100a D:509 X-0750 UNIO:LIBE
a. W-5574 Joseph Dunlap
b. Jacob Lease
c. None

S-13764* 517a* -- -- HARD:PLEA
a. --
b. Walter Dun, Executor
c. None
* Entry in Source A only, where it shows 517 acres crossed out and 401 & 116 acres, as if in two parcels.

S-13765* 469a -- -- ----:----
a. --
b. E. P. Kendrick
c. None
* Entry in Source A only, where crossed out.

S-13766. See S-11099

S-13768 100a D:506 X-1180 CHAM:GOSH
a. W-4126 Thomas Eamines? (Emmins?)
b. James H. Spain
c. None

S-13769 50a E:29 X-0133 HIGH:BRUS
a. W-6494 Francis L. Slaughter
b. Allen Trimble
c. None

S-13770*
S-13676
S-13771
S-13335
S-13772
S-9214
S-13774 736a D:510 X-1060 BROW:----
a. --
b. Thomas L. Shields
c. None
* Entry not listed in Source A.

S-13770. See also S-13676

S-13772. See also S-8874 & S-9214

S-13774* 736a -- -- BROW:STER
a. --
b. Thomas L. Shields
c. None
* Entry in Source A only.

S-13775. See S-13739

S-13776* 50a -- -- ADAM:GREE
a. --
b. George Collings
c. None
* Entry in Source A only.

S-13777 12a D:511 X-0130 HIGH:BRUS
a. W-6549 Valentine Peers?
b. John Perrill
c. None

S-13778 50a D:511 X-0215 ADAM:JEFF
a. W-6549 Valentine Peers?
b. Daniel Wallace
c. None

S-13779 24a D:511 X-0215 ADAM:JEFF
a. W-6549 Valentine Peers?
b. Joseph Freeman
c. None

S-13780 25a D:512 X-1110 ADAM:GREE
a. W-6549 Valentine Peers?
b. John P. Newman
c. None

S-13781 25a D:512 X-0650 ADAM:TIFF
a. W-2319 Captain William Meredith
b. Robert Thompson, Junior*
c. None
* Source A says 140 acres patented to Allen Latham.

S-13782 75a D:512 X-0809 ADAM:TIFF
a. W-4662 Robert Means, assignee of H. Young
W-1089 Benjamin Brooke?
W-2319 Captain William Meredith
b. Martin Kramer
c. None

S-13783 15a E:1 X-0360 PICK:MONR
a. W-6308 Charles Stewart, heirs of
b. Philo N. White
c. None

S-13787 10a E:6 X-0660 WARR:WASH
a. W-6549 Valentine Peers?
b. Jesse Downard
c. None

S-13789 25a E:2 X-1040 ADAM:JEFF
a. W-2319 Captain William Meredith
b. Abraham McCarty
c. None

S-13790* 50a -- -- HIGH:SALE
a. --
b. N. Sawyer
c. None
* Entry in Source A only.

S-13790* 35a -- -- HIGH:SALE
a. --
b. N. Sawyer
c. None
* Entry in Source A only.

S-13791 5a E:282 X-0540 PICK:PERR PICK:DEER
a. W-6418 Vachel D. Howard
b. John Evans
c. None

S-13792 4a E:282 X-0540 PICK:PERR
a. W-6418 Vachel D. Howard
b. John Evans
c. None

S-13797 10a E:4 X-1230 ADAM:GREE SCIO:---*
a. W-6549 Valentine Peers?
b. John McCall
c. None
* Source A does not mention Scioto County.

S-13798 43a E:5 X-1400* SCIO:NILE
a. W-6549 Valentine Peers?
W-3195 John Collins
b. John McCall
c. None
* Lower Dry Run.

S-13799* 16a -- -- ADAM:GREE
a. --
b. Samuel Montgomery
c. None
* Entry in Source A only.

S-13800 40a E:5 X-0130 ADAM:MEIG
a. W-5139 Robert Means, assignee of James Smith
b. James Spurgeon
c. None

S-13801 10a E:3 X-1110 ADAM:GREE
a. W-323 Lieutenant Robert Green
b. George Collings
c. None

S-13802 26a E:3 X-0809 ADAM:JEFF
a. W-323 Lieutenant Robert Green
b. George Collings
c. None

S-13803 50a E:3 -- ADAM:GREE
a. W-323 Lieutenant Robert Green
b. George Collings
c. None

S-13804 25a E:3 X-0809 ADAM:JEFF
a. W-3835 Andrew Barnes
b. George Collings
c. None

S-13805* 10a -- -- ADAM:JEFF
a. --
b. George Collings
c. None
* Entry in Source A only.

S-13808 16a E:7 X-1140 PIKE:MIFF
a. W-5139 Robert Means, assignee of James Smith
b. William Kincaid
c. None

S-13809 20a E:7 X-1140 PIKE:PERR
a. W-5139 Robert Means, assignee of James Smith
b. James Murdock
c. None

S-13810 21a E:7 X-1140 PIKE:PERR
a. W-5139 Robert Means, assignee of James Smith
b. James Murdock
c. None

S-13814. See S-13136

S-13815 50a E:7 X-0133 PIKE:PERR
a. W-5139 Robert Means, assignee of James Smith
b. -- Melson* & -- Jones
c. None
* So spelled.

S-13816 25a E:9 X-0360 MADI:PLEA
a. W-5139 Robert Means, assignee of James Smith
W-3195 John Collins
b. Henry Warner
c. None

S-13817 15a E:9 X-0360 PICK:---* MADI:PLEA
a. W-3195 John Collins
b. Henry Warner
c. None
* Source A does not mention Pickaway County.

S-13818 15a E:8 X-0809 ADAM:GREE
a. W-2319 Captain William Meredith
b. John Beach
c. None

S-13819 50a E:8 X-1138 ADAM:GREE
a. W-3835 Andrew Barnes
b. Oliver Rogers*
c. None
* Source A says O. C. Rodgers.

S-13820 35a E:8 X-0800 ADAM:GREE
a. W-3835 Andrew Barnes
b. Henry England
c. None

S-13821 30a E:8 X-0910 ADAM:GREE
a. W-3835 Andrew Barnes
b. George Collings
c. None

S-13822 10a E:15 X-0910 SCIO:NILE
a. W-6130 Richard H? Owen
b. Philo N. White
c. J. Hutton, 1842

S-13823 10a E:15 X-0910 SCIO:NILE
a. W-6130 Richard H? Owen
b. Philo N. White
c. None

S-13824
S-13825 48a E:15 X-0910 SCIO:NILE
a. W-6130 Richard H? Owen
b. Philo N. White
c. None

S-13827* 25a -- -- ROSS:PAXT
a. --
b. N. Massie & H. Massie
c. None
* Entry in Source A only.

S-13828 8a E:14 X-0360 PICK:MONR
a. W-6130 Richard H? Owen
b. Abraham Birt
c. J. Olds, 1842

S-13829 50a E:14 X-0800 SCIO:WASH
a. W-4128 --*
b. Philo N. White
c. None
* Source C does not give warrantee's name.

S-13835 30a E:22 X-1000 HARD:DUDL
a. W-3618 Thomas Martin
b. James Galloway, Junior
c. None

S-13838 25a* F:83 X-0840 FAYE:CONC CLIN:---*
a. W-8399 --**
b. James M. Trimble
c. None
* Source A says 100 acres; does not mention Clinton County.
** Source C does not list this warrant number.

S-13839 10a E:54 X-1400* SCIO:BRUS
a. W-5139 Robert Means, assignee of James Smith
b. Samuel Smith
c. None
* R(attle) Sna(ke) Fork of S(outh) Brush Cr(eek).

S-13840 10a E:15 X-0660 WARR:WASH
a. W-5139 Robert Means, assignee of James Smith
b. Jesse Downard
c. D. Dill, 1842

S-13841 50a E:18 X-0030 CLER:WASH
a. W-6114 Georrge Greenway
b. E. P. Kendrick
c. None

S-13842 50a E:16 X-1301 HIGH:SALE HIGH:WHIT
a. W-681 Captain Lieutenant? William? Brownlee
b. Allen Latham
c. None

S-13843 200a E:132 X-0800 SCIO:WASH
a. W-6491 --*
b. -- White & -- Force**
c. None
* Source C does not give warrantee's name.
** Source A says: "-- Force, -- White, & -- Craine."

S-13844 60a E:17 X-0381 ADAM:MONR
a. W-323 Lieutenant Robert Green
b. William Robe
c. None

S-13845 50a E:17 X-0809 ADAM:JEFF
a. W-323 Lieutenant Robert Green
b. William Solberry
c. James Hood, 1842

S-13846 63a E:22 X-1300 BROW:CLAR
a. W-1920 Colonel Josiah Parker
b. Jeptha Beasley
c. James Hines

S-13847 15a E:20 -- CLER:FRAN
a. W-2319 Captain William Meredith
b. George Lee*
c. None
* Source A says George S. Lee.

S-13848 45a E:17 X-0840 ROSS:TWIN
a. W-6114 George Greenway
b. Jacob Storms*
c. None
* Source A spells Storm.

S-13849 80a E:21 X-0340 UNIO:LIBE
a. W-6568 Joseph Spencer
b. James Galloway, Junior
c. None

S-13851 30a E:18 X-0809* ADAM:MEIG
a. W-6114 George Greenway
b. John Spurgeon
c. None
* West branch of.

S-13852 56a E:19 X-0040 ADAM:MONR
a. W-323 Lieutenant Robert Green
b. Isaac Foster
c. None

S-13853 20a E:19 X-0423 ADAM:LIBE
a. W-323 Lieutenant Robert Green
b. Abraham Washburn
c. None

S-13854 27a E:19 X-0381 ADAM:MONR
a. W-2319 Captain William Meredith
b. John Penniwith*
c. None
* Source A spells Pennewith.

S-13855 25a E:19 X-1113 ADAM:GREE
a. W-6114 George Greenway
b. John P. Newman
c. None

S-13856 25a E:20 X-1113 ADAM:GREE
a. W-6114 George Greenway
b. William Montgomery
c. None

S-13859* 7a -- -- BROW:EAGL
a. --
b. Jeptha Beasley
c. None
* Entry in Source A only.

S-13860 105a E:21 X-1000 HARD:DUDL
a. W-3618 Thomas Martin
b. James Galloway, Junior
c. None

S-13861 12a E:32 X-0360 MADI:UNIO
a. W-6114 George Greenway
b. Henry Warner
c. None

S-13863 100a E:22 X-1007 ADAM:MEIG
a. W-6114 Geroge Greenway
b. E. P. Kendrick
c. None

S-13864 15a E:260 X-1007 SCIO:BRUS
a. W-6114 George Greenway
b. Christopher Opey*
c. None
* Source A spells Opy.

S-13865 18a E:22 X-0423 ADAM:LIBE BROW:BYRD
a. W-1920 Colonel Josiah Parker
b. Samuel Maharry
c. None

S-13866 14a E:57 X-0130 ADAM:JEFF
a. W-323 Lieutenant Robert Green
b. George Collings
c. None

S-13867 125a E:23 X-0840 ROSS:PAIN
a. W-2876 Robert Young
W-2093 John Carnahan?
b. Gabriel Hayse*
c. None
* Source A spells Hays.

S-13867 175a E:23 X-0840 ROSS:PAIN
a. W-889 John Brent
W-2093 John Carnahan?
b. Gabriel Hayse*
c. None
* Source A spells Hays.

S-13868* 350a -- -- PIKE:PEBB
a. --
b. James M. Smith
c. None
* Entry in Source A only.

S-13869 20a E:29 X-0841 ROSS:CONC
a. W-6114 George Greenway
b. Simeon Mallow
c. None

S-13871* 37a -- -- CHAM:GOSH MADI:SUMM
a. --
b. James Galloway, Junior
c. None
* Entry in Source A only.

S-13872* 800a -- -- CLIN:CLAR BROW:PERR
a. --
b. Allen Latham
c. None
* Entry in Source A only.

S-13873 140a E:25 X-1180 X-0340 MADI:PIKE
a. W-6547 Thomas Lewis? (Lucas?)
b. Thomas Lucas
c. None

S-13874 113a E:25 X-0340 MADI:JEFF MADI:CANA
a. W-6547 Thomas Lewis? (Lucas?)
b. Thomas Lucas
c. None

S-13875 50a E:29 X-0340 PICK:DARB
a. W-6114 George Greenway
b. B. G Leonard
c. None

S-13876 10a E:27 X-0133 HIGH:---* PIKE:PERR
a. W-6114 George Greenway
b. Nathan Maddox
c. None
* Source A does not mention Highland County.

S-13877*
S-13890 160a -- -- CLIN:RICH
a. --
b. Jacob Jamison
c. None
* Entry in Source A only.

S-13878 2a E:325 X-0515 PICK:PERR
a. W-6114 George Greenway
b. Moses Konns*
c. None
* Source A spells Kouns.

S-13880 40a E:28 X-0809 ADAM:JEFF
a. W-1920 Colonel Josiah Parker
b. Jeremiah McClain Stewart
c. None

S-13881 15a E:29 X-0040 ADAM:MONR
a. W-1920 Colonel Josiah Parker
b. John Pulley
c. None

S-13882* 40a -- -- HIGH:DODS BROW:PERR
a. --
b. James M. Trimble
c. None
* Entry in Source A only.

S-13883*
S-14944 100a E:356 X-0340 PICK:----
a. W-6308 Charles Stewart, heirs of
W-5803 John Remay, representatives of
b. Philo N. White
c. None
* Entry not listed in Source A.

S-13884 428a E:28 X-0360 MADI:UNIO
a. W-6658 Wood Jones, heirs of
W-6649 William Christian
b. S. Hide Saunders
c. None

S-13885 10a E:261 X-1400* SCIO:WASH
a. W-6658 Wood Jones, heirs of
b. Sylvester Veach
c. None
* Shafer's Run.

S-13886 200a E:30 -- PIKE:BENT
a. W-6418 Vachel D. Howard
b. John Benner
c. None

S-13887 180a E:30 -- BROW:FRAN
a. W-2744 Anthony Singleton, heir (of?)
W-6418 Vachel D. Howard
b. Cad(wallader) Wallace
c. None

S-13888 130a E:31 -- ROSS:PAIN
a. W-6658 Wood Jones, heirs of
b. Cad(wallader) Wallace
c. None

S-13889 6a E:31 X-0660 CLAR:HARM
a. W-6658 Wood Jones, heirs of
b. Mathew Bonner
c. None

S-13890. See S-13877

S-13895 85a E:29 X-0809 ADAM:MEIG
a. W-8424 --*
b. Joshua Florea
c. None
* Source C does not list this warrant number.

S-13896 20a E:35 X-0940 CLIN:RICH
a. W-6658 Wood Jones, heirs of
b. Wade Loofborough*
c. None
* Source A spells Loofborow.

S-13897 38a E:64 -- FAYE:CONC CLIN:RICH
a. W-6572 Andrew Rodgers
b. Allen Trimble
c. None

S-13898 31a E:31 X-1138 ADAM:GREE
a. W-1226 Alexander S. Dandridge
W-4284 Daniel Diskin?
b. George Collings
c. None

S-13900 47a E:32 X-1400* ADAM:GREE
a. W-1920 Colonel Josiah Parker
W-2319 Captain William Meredith
b. Benjamin Gifford
c. None
* Long Run.

S-13901 14a E:32 X-0133 ADAM:SCOT ADAM:FRAN
a. W-8424 --*
b. Joseph B. Case
c. None
* Source C does not list this warrant number.

S-13902 95a E:32 X-0134 ADAM:SCOT
a. W-8424 --*
b. Andrew Burns, Senior
c. None
* Source C does not list this warrant number.

S-13903 20a E:37 X-0809* HIGH:--** ADAM:SCOT
a. W-8424 --***
b. Andrew Burns, Junior
c. None
* East Fork of.
** Source A does not mention Highland County.
*** Source C does not list this warrant number.

S-13904 15a E:35 X-1340 CLER:FRAN
a. W-617 Captain Alexander Breckenridge
b. Ralph Stires*
c. None
* Source A may spells Stiers.

S-13905 10a E:66 X-0570 CLER:WASH
a. W-617 Captain Alexander Breckenridge
b. Ralph Stires*
c. None
* Source A spells Steers.

S-13906 5a E:32 X-0809 ADAM:MONR
a. W-6658 Wood Jones, heirs of
b. John Rader
c. None

S-13907 50a E:33 X-1007 ADAM:JEFF
a. W-6658 Wood Jones, heirs of
b. E. P. Kendrick
c. None

S-13909 92a E:33 X-0230 ADAM:WAYN
a. W-8424 --*
b. David McCreight
c. None
* Source C does not list this warrant number.

S-13910 15a E:34 X-1190 SCIO:NILE
a. W-6308 Charles Stewart, heirs of
W-4128 --*
b. P. N. White
c. None
* Source C does not give warrantee's name.

S-13911 25a E:34 X-0809 ADAM:MONR
a. W-3835 Andrew Barnes
b. David C. Vance
c. None

S-13912 50a E:34 X-0650 ADAM:WAYN
a. W-8424 --*
b. Thomas Thompson
c. None
* Source C does not list this warrant number.

S-13913 50a E:34 X-0040 ADAM:MONR
a. W-8424 --*
b. John Moore & William Moore
c. None
* Source C does not list this warrant number.

S-13914 15a E:35 X-0134 ADAM:SCOT
a. W-8424 --*
b. John Simmons
c. None
* Source C does not list this warrant number.

S-13915 35a E:36 X-0910 SCIO:UNIO
a. W-6114 George Greenway
W-6658 Wood Jones, heirs of
b. Jeremiah Piles
c. None

S-13916 25a E:69 X-0134 HIGH:---*
ADAM:SCOT
a. W-8424 --**
b. Bazil Shockey
c. None
* Source A does not mention Highland County.
** Source C does not list this warrant number.

S-13917 50a E:65 X-0490 ADAM:SCOT
a. W-8424 --*
b. John A. Smiley
b. None
* Source C does not list this warrant number.

S-13919 40a E:123 X-0130 ADAM:WAYN
a. W-1920 Colonel Josiah Parker
b. Jeptha Beasley
c. None

S-13920 15a E:123 X-0130 ADAM:WAYN
a. W-1920 Colonel Josiah Parker
b. Jeptha Beasley
c. None

S-13921* 5a -- -- BROW:EAGL
a. --
b. Jeptha Beasley
c. None
* Entry in Source A only.

S-13922 9a E:123 X-0130 ADAM:WAYN
a. W-1920 Colonel Josiah Parker
b. Jonathan McNeil
c. None

S-13923 11a E:124 X-0130 ADAM:WAYN
a. W-1296 Timothy Peyton
b. Hester McComis*
c. None
* Source A spells McComas.

S-13924 15a E:37 X-0809 ADAM:SCOT
ADAM:JEFF
ADAM:MONR
a. W-5799 James Dillard
b. E. P. Kendrick
c. None

S-13925 30a E:205 X-0660 WARR:WASH
a. W-2834 --*
b. James Taylor
c. None
* Source C does not give warrantee's name.

S-13927
S-14000 28a E:71 X-0340 PICK:MUHL
X-0360 PICK:JACK
a. W-4128 --*
b. Philo N. White
c. None
* Source C does not give warrantee's name.

S-13928 31a E:73 X-1060 BROW:GREE
a. W-6645 Alexander Brownlee, heirs of

b. Nicholas Smith
c. None

S-13929 100a E:39 X-0133 ADAM:SCOT
a. W-6574 Andrew Rodgers
b. David Gaston
c. None

S-13930* 35a -- -- ADAM:SCOT
a. --
b. William Williamson
c. None
* Entry in Source A only.

S-13931* 200a -- -- HIGH:SALE
a. --
b. Allen Trimble
c. None
* Entry in Source A only.

S-13932 200a E:42 X-0060 HARD:MCDO
a. W-6630 Thomas Clark
b. Thomas Clark
c. None

S-13932 133a E:42 X-0060 HARD:MCDO
a. W-6030 John Stokes, representatives of
W-6587 Jesse Rose or John Bryant (perhaps)
b. James Taylor
c. None

S-13933* 42a -- -- HARD:MCDO
a. --
b. -- Taylor & -- Hubbard
c. None
* Entry in Source A only.

S-13934*
S-7105
S-13937 63a E:43 X-0130 ADAM:----
a. W-8424 --**
b. Joshua Florea
c. None
* Entry not listed in Source A, but see S-13937.
* Source C does not list this warrant number.

S-13934. See also S-7105

S-13935* 20a -- -- ----:----
a. --
b. -- Taylor & -- Sutton
c. None
* Entry in Source A only, where crossed out.

S-13936* 100a -- -- ADAM:SPRI
ADAM:LIBE
a. --
b. Michael Hogg
c. None
* Entry in Source A only.

S-13937* 63a -- -- ADAM:MEIG
a. --
b. Joshua Florea
c. None
* Entry in Source A only; see S-13934, however.

S-13938 204a E:44 X-1000 HARD:TAYL
a. W-6291 --*
W-1963 William Taliaferro, heir to Colonel (William?) Taliaferro
b. Cad(wallader) Wallace
c. None
* Source C does not give warrantee's name.

S-13939* 100a -- -- HARD:HALE
a. --
b. C(adwallader) Wallace
c. None
* Entry in Source A only.

S-13940* 5a -- -- FAYE:UNIO
a. --
b. -- Loofborow & -- Jamison
c. None
* Entry in Source A only.

S-13941* 5a -- -- FAYE:UNIO
a. --
b. Wade Loofborow
c. None
* Entry in Source A only.

S-13942 5a E:45 X-0840 FAYE:UNIO
a. W-4859 Leven Joynes? (Joyner?)
b. Orlando Loofborrow
c. None

S-13943 10a E:46 X-0800 ADAM:GREE
a. W-4859 Leven Joynes? (Joyner?)
b. John Tolan*
c. None
* Source A spells Toland.

S-13944 70a E:45 X-1000 SCIO:WASH
a. W-4991 Thomas Wells? (Wills?), representatives of
b. Ruluff Whitney
c. None

S-13945
S-14044 253a* E:239 X-1300 HIGH:---*
BROW:EAGL
a. W-3818 Peter Johnston
W-369 James Tutt, heir to Charles Tutt
W-5254 John Mountjoy
W-6587 Jesse Rose or John Bryant (perhaps)
W-5450 Beverley Stubblefield
b. -- Taylor, -- Sutton, & -- Lytle
c. None
* Source A says 283 acres; does not mention Highland County.

S-13945* 230a -- -- ----:----
a. --
b. -- Taylor, -- Sutton, & -- Lytle
c. None
* Entry in Source A only, where crossed out.

S-13946 13a F:253 X-1300 HIGH:SALE
a. W-6649 William Christian
b. Allen Latham
c. None

S-13947 50a E:82 X-1300 BROW:EAGL HIGH:---*
a. W-4818 William Hubbard
W-6587 Jesse Rose or John Bryant (perhaps)
b. James Taylor
c. None
* Source A does not mention Highland County.

S-13948 400a E:53 X-1000 ROSS:HUNT
a. W-6457 --*
b. William Pike
c. None
* Source C does not give warrantee's name.

S-13950 258a E:48 X-0660 BROW:STER
a. W-8452 --*
W-8454 --*
b. James Stallings
c. None
* Source C does not list this warrant number.

S-13950 175a E:49 X-1000 HARD:MCDO
a. W-8455 --*
b. James Stallings
c. None
* Source C does not list this warrant number.

S-13950 337a E:50 X-1230 ROSS:CONC ROSS:TWIN
a. W-8454 --*
W-8455 --*
b. James Stallings
c. W. Galbraith; B. Malone, 1842
* Source C does not list this warrant number.

S-13950 425a E:51 X-0663 HIGH:DODS
a. W-8454 --*
b. James Stallings
c. None
* Source C does not list this warrant number.

S-13950 110a E:51 X-1000 FRAN:FRAN FRAN:BROW
a. W-8455 --*
b. James Stallings
c. None
* Source C does not list this warrant number.

S-13951* 1500a -- -- ROSS:HUNT
a. --
b. C(adwallader) Wallace
c. None
* Entry in Source A only.

S-13951* 4000a -- -- ROSS:FRAN
a. --
b. W. Grimes & -- Wallace, representatives of
c. -- Wallace & -- King; C. Wallace, 1839; representative of W. Gugan? (Guqan?); O. H. W. Luckett, 1841
* Entry in Source A only.

S-13952 3a E:52 X-0663 CLER:JACK
a. W-4818 William Hubbard
b. James Taylor
c. None

S-13953
S-13967 370a E:213 X-0300 PIKE:JACK ROSS:FRAN
a. W-6020 John Baldwin
b. Allen Latham
c. None

S-13953* 1390a -- -- ROSS:FRAN
a. --
b. John (Dawson?) & John L. Dawson
c. None
* Entry in Source A only.

S-13955 7a E:61 X-0759 ADAM:GREE
a. W-6645 Alexander Brownlee, heirs of
b. Patrick H. Reynolds
c. None

S-13956 5a E:61 X-0759 ADAM:GREE
a. W-6645 Alexander Brownlee, heirs of
b. Theoph(ilus?) P. Barrett
c. None

S-13957 40a E:61 X-0220 PIKE:SUNF
a. W-6645 Alexander Brownlee, heirs of
b. R. Willborn* & R. Willborn*
c. None
* Source A spells Wilbourne.

S-13958 35a E:57 X-0663 CLER:JACK
a. W-4818 William Hubbard
b. James Taylor
c. None

S-13959 14a E:58 X-1138 ADAM:GREE
a. W-1920 Colonel Josiah Parker
b. R. McMahan
c. None

S-13960 8a E:58 X-0800 ADAM:GREE
a. W-1920 Colonel Josiah Parker
b. Martin Cox
c. None

S-13961 25a E:58 X-0800 ADAM:GREE
a. W-1920 Colonel Josiah Parker
b. Harvey* B. Baird
c. None
* Source A says Henry.

S-13962 23a E:58 X-0650 ADAM:TIFF
a. W-1920 Colonel Josiah Parker
b. John Smith
c. None

S-13963 50a E:59 X-0800 ADAM:GREE
a. W-5762 John Gladding, deceased
b. David W. Murphy
c. None

S-13964 325a E:60 X-0840 ROSS:TWIN
a. W-6250 William Yates, heirs of
W-6251 William Yates, heirs of
W-6252 William Yates, heirs of
W-6256 William Yates, administrator of
b. Cad(wallader) Wallace
c. None

S-13965 250a E:59 X-0840 ROSS:TWIN
a. W-6256 William Yates, administrator of
b. John Woodbridge
c. None

S-13966* 300a -- -- HIGH:DODS BROW:PERR
a. --
b. Allen Latham
c. None
* Entry in Source A only.

S-13967. See S-13953

S-13968* 120a E:335 X-1300 BROW:----
a. W-6020 John Baldwin
b. Allen Latham
c. None
* Entry not listed in Source A.

S-13969*
S-13970 1367a -- -- ALLE:GOSH HARD:ROUN
a. --
b. C(adwallader) Wallace
c. None
* Entry in Source A only.

S-13970* 229a -- -- ----:----
a. --
b. Nathaniel Taylor
c. None
* Entry in Source A only, where crossed out.

S-13971 222a E:198 X-0779 PIKE:PEBB
a. W-6651 William Scott, heirs of
W-6652 William Scott, heirs of
b. Robert Scott & W Wigginton, heirs
c. None

S-13972 17a E:61 X-0809 ADAM:TIFF ADAM:GREE
a. W-1920 Colonel Josiah Parker
b. Thomas Young
c. None

S-13976 22a E:462 X-0010 CLIN:LIBE
a. W-1985 William Bussell
b. James Galloway
c. None

S-13977 20a E:462 X-0360 CHAM:---* UNIO:DARB
a. W-3618 Thomas Martin
b. James Galloway
c. None
* Source A does not mention Champaign County.

S-13983 3a E:76 X-0759 ADAM:GREE
a. W-6645 Alexander Brownlee, heirs of
b. Jessee* Cole
c. None
* Source A spells Jesse.

S-13984 6a E:81 X-0910 SCIO:NILE
a. W-6130 Richard H? Owen
b. P. N. White
c. None

S-13986 15a E:66 X-0360 MADI:UNIO
a. W-6645 Alexander Brownlee, heirs of
b. Henry Warner
c. None

S-13988 40a E:70 X-0060 HARD:MCDO
a. W-5451 John Swan & James Taylor
b. John Swan & James Taylor, representatives of
c. None

S-13988 59a E:70 X-0060 HARD:MCDO
a. W-4818 William Hubbard
W-5440 James Taylor, assignee of Joshua Barbee, legal representative of Thomas Barbee
b. James Taylor
c. None

S-13989 4a E:65 X-0991 LOGA:JEFF LOGA:RUSH
a. W-6198 Simon Sommers
b. James Taylor
c. None

S-13990 18a E:66 X-0980 HIGH:PAIN
a. W-6572 Andrew Rodgers
b. John C. Howe
c. None

S-13991 20a E:67 X-0630 PIKE:MIFF
a. W-6645 Alexander Brownlee, heirs of
b. E. P. Kendrick
c. None

S-13992
S-14024 110a E:86 X-0809 ADAM:TIFF
a. W-224 Captain Benjamin Biggs
W-6645 Alexander Brownlee, heirs of
b. John Baird
c. None

S-13993 10a E:68 X-0980 SCIO:BRUS
a. W-6645 Alexander Brownlee, heirs of
b. Jeremiah Piles
c. None

S-13994 3a E:69 X-1190 SCIO:BRUS
a. W-6645 Alexander Brownlee, heirs of
b. Jeremiah Piles
c. None

S-13995 15a E:69 X-1190 SCIO:NILE
a. W-6645 Alexander Brownlee, heirs of
b. Jeremiah Piles
c. None

S-13996 20a E:69 X-0920 SCIO:UNIO
a. W-6645 Alexander Brownlee, heirs of
b. Jeremiah Piles
c. None

S-13997 25a E:70 X-1400* PIKE:SUNF
a. W-6645 Alexander Brownlee, heirs of
b. Randolph Wilbourne**
c. None
* Grassy Fork.
** Source A says R. & R. Wilborn.

S-13998 35a E:71 X-0220 PIKE:SUNF
a. W-6645 Alexander Brownlee, heirs of
b. James Henry
c. None

S-13999 15a E:71 X-1170 WARR:WASH
a. W:6645 Alexander Brownlee, heirs of
b. Jesse Downard
c. None

S-14000. See S-13927

INDEX BY
COUNTY AND TOWNSHIP

INDEX TO WATERCOURSES

NAME INDEX